Tort:
Cases and Materials

TORT:
CASES AND MATERIALS

by

B. A. HEPPLE, M.A., LL.B.

*of Gray's Inn, Barrister, Fellow of Clare College and
University Lecturer in Law, Cambridge*

and

M. H. MATTHEWS, M.A., LL.B., B.C.L.,

of Gray's Inn, Barrister, Fellow of University College, Oxford.

LONDON
BUTTERWORTHS
1974

ENGLAND: BUTTERWORTH & CO. (PUBLISHERS) LTD.
                 LONDON: 88 Kingsway, WC2B 6AB

AUSTRALIA: BUTTERWORTHS PTY. LTD.
                 SYDNEY: 586 Pacific Highway, Chatswood,
                 NSW 2067
                 Also at Melbourne, Brisbane
                 Adelaide and Perth

CANADA: BUTTERWORTH & CO. (CANADA) LTD.
                 TORONTO: 2265 Midland Avenue, Scarborough
                 M1P 4S1

NEW ZEALAND: BUTTERWORTHS OF NEW ZEALAND LTD.
                 WELLINGTON: 26/28 Waring Taylor Street, 1

SOUTH AFRICA: BUTTERWORTH & CO. (SOUTH AFRICA) (PTY.) LTD.
                 DURBAN: 152–154 Gale Street

U.S.A.   BUTTERWORTH (PUBLISHERS) INC.
                 BOSTON: 19 Cummings Park, Woburn, Mass. 01801

©

B. A. HEPPLE and M. H. MATTHEWS

1974

First Reprint . . . 1976
Second Reprint . . 1977

ISBN—Casebound: 0 406 59480 5
Limp: 0 406 59481 3

Preface

This is a collection of cases, statutes and other materials on the English law of tort, intended for use by those studying for a first degree in law. It has two distinctive features: the arrangement of the subject matter according to an interests classification of the law of tort, and a contextual approach. An attempted justification and explanation of the arrangement will be found in the Introduction which, unlike this Preface, is intended to be read by students. The contextual approach will, we hope, help to satisfy a need which has been widely expressed by teachers and has gained added relevance with the establishment, in late 1972, of the Royal Commission on Civil Liability and Compensation for Personal Injury.

However, in attempting to compile an English-based sourcebook, more in the spirit of Llewellyn than of Langdell, we have had to face some major constraints. These stem from the present methods and content of teaching in British law schools, and the almost complete absence of empirical research on the operation of tort law in this country.

Teaching methods generally relegate source materials to second place after the textbook. This has consequences for law publishing, and our publishers, wisely from the commercial viewpoint, insisted upon limiting the maximum size for this book so as to enable them to keep the price within the range of the average student's limited resources. This means that, although we want to encourage its use for case-method teaching (indeed it originated as a set of materials for teaching of this type at Nottingham University between 1966 and 1968), this sourcebook should be used in conjunction with the standard text-books and periodical literature. (A number of articles and notes are referred to in the text and in Appendix H.) Reasons of space, as well as our determination to avoid writing a mini-textbook, have led us to keep our own comments to a minimum. In addition to the general introduction, most Chapters have a brief introductory explanation of their scope and the notes which follow the extracted source materials are used mainly to illustrate points raised in the materials or to digest other relevant materials.

Another constraint has been in respect of subject-matter. Tort law, by its nature as a residual legal category, is frequently used as a garbage can for other overcrowded law school courses. Topics with little functional connection are simply lumped together. The contents of this sourcebook are something of a compromise between a purely functional study of subjects such as Compensation for Accidents, on the one hand, and the more traditional conceptual classification. The basis of this compromise is our interests classification, and the actual topics covered are we believe representative of those being taught in most law schools under rubrics such as Tort or Common Law. Answers by teachers at 17 law schools to a questionnaire which we circulated in July 1971 (briefly noted in (1972), 12 J.S.P.T.L. (N.S.) 189) indicated that most of the topics in Part I and in Chapters 13 and 15 of Part II and Chapters 18 and 19 of Part III are exclusively taught in Tort courses, while the topics in Chapter 14 (deliberate interference with interests in trade or business), and 16 (defamation with an excursus on privacy), and 17 (malicious abuse of power) usually overlap with or, occasionally, are taught exclusively in other courses such as Labour Law, Business Law and Constitutional and Administrative Law. Our reasons for devoting as much space as we have to these latter topics is partly pragmatic, being based on the present structure of Tort courses, and partly dictated by our interests classification which would be seriously distorted if these topics were excluded. The most glaring omissions are those torts (conversion, detinue, trespass to goods) which relate to misappropriation of property. Apart from reasons of space, our justification for this important gap is that this is a self-contained subject nearly always taught outside conventional Tort courses, in subjects such as Personal Property or Mercantile or Consumer Law.

Perhaps the most important of all the constraints, which has meant that the main focus is still upon the appellate judicial process, is the absence of published research on the operation of tort law. We raise several questions at the end of the first Chapter about the functioning of tort law but we have to confess that these cannot be adequately answered simply by using the insurance materials in Chapter 20 and the statistical information in Appendices A to E. It will be several years yet before we can expect a satisfactory factual basis for discussing such questions in a British context. We could have reproduced some of the considerable amount of American research on these matters, but we have resisted the temptation to abuse comparative legal study in this way. There is also the question of space and of technique: since this book is addressed to law students the insurance materials and statistics which are included are there not as the primary object of study, but in order to make the law intelligible.

Many of our colleagues, through their writings and by discussion with us, have contributed to our own understanding and so to this book, in a general way. Those whose valuable help has been specific are Professor J. C. Smith, who inspired and made possible the use of a first draft of part of these materials in case-method teaching at Nottingham, Professor Glanville Williams, who allowed us access to his annotations and cuttings, Professor Jeffrey O'Connell, who commented on Appendix G, Mr. Anthony D. Woolf, who provided the materials on which Chapter 1 is based and kindly read through a draft of that Chapter, Mr. D. R. Harris who provided some information for Appendices F and H, Mr. A. I. Ogus, who made comments on Chapters 3, 5, 7, 9, 10 and 11, and Mrs. Tanya Parker and Mr. Rex Bretten, whose course materials on the law of defamation formed the foundation for parts of Chapter 16. None of them, however, bears responsibility for our mistakes or misjudgments. A special tribute must be paid to our publishers for the extraordinary care and patience which they have shown these past six years. We have endeavoured to present the law as at 1 May 1974, by including an Addendum which mentions some developments which could not be incorporated in the text.

June, 1974   B.A.H.
                                                              M.H.M.

Table of Contents

PART TWO: TORTS TO NON-PHYSICAL INTERESTS

PART THREE: LOSS DISTRIBUTION

Acknowledgements

The Publishers and Authors wish to thank the following for permission to reprint material from the sources indicated:

American Law Institute: *Restatement (2d) of the Law of Torts*. Copyright 1965. Reprinted with the permission of the American Law Institute.

Professor P. S. Atiyah: *Accidents, Compensation and the Law* and *Vicarious Liability in the Law of Torts*.

Cambridge University Press and contributors: *Cambridge Law Journal*, 1961, p. 31; 1962, pp. 179–80; 1964, p. 8; 1967, p. 66.

Estates Gazette: *Estates Gazette*, 1966, Vol. 197, pp. 877–79.

W. Green & Sons Ltd.: *Scots Law Times*.

Guardian Royal Exchange Assurance Group: Extracts from Liability Policy, Business Interruption Policy and Libel Policy.

The Controller of Her Majesty's Stationery Office: Extracts from official reports Cmnd. 1536, Cmnd. 4812, Cmnd. 5012, Cmnd. 5034 and Law Commission No. 56; Law Commission Working Papers Nos. 47 and 52; Compensation of Victims of Uninsured Drivers: Text of the Agreement dated 22 November 1972 (Motor Insurers' Bureau); and Road Accidents 1970 (extract) and 1971 (extract and Table 1).

Incorporated Council of Law Reporting for England and Wales: *The Law Reports; The Weekly Law Reports*.

Lady Herbert: A. P. Herbert, *The Uncommon Law*.

"Justice" (British Section of the International Commission of Jurists): Report, *Trial of Motor Accident Cases*.

Lloyds Bank Review and Professor D. S. Lees and Neil Doherty: Extract from *Lloyds Bank Review* No. 108 (April 1973), pp. 19–22.

Lloyds of London Press Ltd.: *Lloyds Reports*.

Michigan Law Review Association: *Michigan Law Review*, 1953, Vol. 52, p. 7.

Professor M. A. Millner: *Negligence in Modern Law*.

Modern Law Review Limited and contributors: *Modern Law Review*, 1951, Vol. 14, pp. 505–6; 1954, Vol. 17, p. 102; 1960, Vol. 23, p. 233; 1966, Vol. 29, p. 31; 1970, Vol. 33, p. 391; 1972, Vol. 35, pp. 340–41.

Mr. P. M. North: *Modern Law of Animals*.

Scottish Council of Law Reporting: *Session Cases*.

Stevens & Sons Ltd. and contributors: *Law Quarterly Review*, 1961, Vol. 77, p. 196.

Sweet & Maxwell Ltd. and editors: *Salmond on Torts*; *Winfield and Jolowicz on Tort*; *Clerk and Lindsell on Tort*.

Times Publishing Co. Ltd.: *Times Law Reports*.

West Publishing Co.: *North Eastern Reports*.

Professor Glanville Williams: "Two Cases on False Imprisonment" in *Law Justice and Equity*, Chapter 5, p. 51; and (1951), Current L.P. 137.

Table of Statutes

References in this Table to "*Statutes*" are to Halsbury's Statutes of England (Third Edition) showing the page at which the annotated text of the Act will be found. Page references printed in bold type indicate where the Act is set out in part or in full.

List of Cases

Page references printed in bold type indicate where the facts of the case are set out.

Table of Papers Referred To

REPORTS OF THE LAW COMMISSION

REPORTS OF COMMITTEES

OTHER OFFICIAL PUBLICATIONS

PERIODICAL LITERATURE

[Notes and articles from which there are extracts of
five or more lines]

Table of Abbreviations

Atiyah—*Accidents, Compensation and the Law*, by P. S. Atiyah (London, 1970).

Atiyah, *Vicarious Liability—Vicarious Liability in the Law of Torts*, by P. S. Atiyah (London, 1967).

A.L.J.—*Australian Law Journal*.

Clerk & Lindsell—*Law of Torts*, by J. F. Clerk and W. H. B. Lindsell, 13th Edn. (London, 1969).

C.L.J.—*Cambridge Law Journal*.

Crim. L.R.—*Criminal Law Review*.

Current L.P.—*Current Legal Problems*.

Elliott & Street—*Road Accidents* by D. W. Elliott and Harry Street (Harmondsworth, 1968).

Fleming—*Law of Torts*, by J. G. Fleming, 4th Edn. (London, 1971).

Gatley—*Law and Practice of Libel and Slander*, by J. C. Gatley, 7th Edn. (London, 1971).

Harv. L.R.—*Harvard Law Review*

Heydon—*Economic Torts*, by J. D. Heydon (London, 1973).

I.L.J.—*Industrial Law Journal*.

Ison—*The Forensic Lottery: a Critique of Tort Liability as a System of Personal Injury Compensation*, by Terence G. Ison (London, 1967).

J.S.P.T.L.—*Journal of the Society of Public Teachers of Law*.

L.Q.R.—*Law Quarterly Review*.

M.L.R.—*Modern Law Review*.

Millner—*Negligence in Modern Law*, by M. A. Millner (London, 1967).

North—*Occupiers' Liability*, by P. M. North (London, 1971).

North, *Animals—Modern Law of Animals*, by P. M. North (London, 1972).

Ogus—*Law of Damages*, by A. I. Ogus (London, 1973).

Prosser—*Handbook of the Law of Torts*, by W. L. Prosser, 4th Edn. (St. Paul, Minn., 1971).

Salmond—*Law of Torts*, by Sir John Salmond, 16th Edn., by R. F. V. Heuston (London, 1973).

Smith & Hogan—*Criminal Law*, by J. C. Smith and Brian Hogan, 3rd Edn. (London, 1973).

Street—*Law of Torts*, by Harry Street, 5th Edn. (London, 1972).

Univ. Tor. L.J.—*University of Toronto Law Journal*.

Glanville Williams—*Joint Torts and Contributory Negligence*, by Glanville L. Williams (London, 1950).

Winfield & Jolowicz—*Law of Tort*, by Sir Percy Winfield, 9th Edn. by J. A. Jolowicz (London, 1971).

Introduction

"1 have gathered a posie of other men's flowers and
nothing but the thread that binds them is my own."

—MONTAIGNE

The materials in this book are concerned with the protection against *harm* afforded by the English common law and statutory extensions of the common law to a variety of *interests*. The primary function of the law of tort is to define the circumstances in which a person whose interests are harmed by another may seek *compensation*. Scots law, more accurately than English law, calls this branch of the law reparation. The name given to it by most civil law systems is delict which, like the old Norman French word "tort", simply means a wrong.

Compensation is not the only function of the law of tort. It can sometimes be used as an alternative to the law of contract where a person has relied on a promise (e.g. to do work carefully) or to supplement the law of contract (e.g. where lies induce a person to contract (p. 498)). Torts like detinue (wrongful detention of goods) are useful appendages to the law of restitution which is concerned with preventing unjust enrichment. An award of damages for tort may have an admonitory effect (p. 400); an injunction granted to stop a threatened or continuing tort (e.g. nuisance, p. 378, or inducing breach of contract, p. 453) may act as a specific deterrent. Tort law may also be used as a vehicle for determining rights. Disputed possession of land may be tested through an action for trespass: the misappropriation of chattels is peculiarly dealt with in English law through the tort of conversion, which is primarily concerned with questions of title, although the ultimate remedy is to compensate the owner for his loss. Important questions of civil liberty may be tested by an action for nominal damages (e.g. the right to vote; trespass to the person (p. 25); trespass to land (p. 368); or trespass to goods, such as the seizure of a passport).

These subsidiary functions of the law of tort make it particularly difficult to present a rational or logical classification of the subject. The lawyer in a civil law system does not face exactly this problem, largely because questions of title to property are not dealt with through the law of delict, but by means of the vindicatory action of the owner, that is, as a part of property law. Infringements of the citizen's constitutional rights (rather than liberties) are a part of a relatively distinct body of public law. Even in the uncodified hybrid systems (like Roman–Dutch law and Scots law) there is a body of general principle, traceable to the Roman law of Justinian as received in medieval Europe, which gives the law of delict an inner coherence and unity. This is a quality which the English law of tort still lacks, although several attempts have been made by writers and judges to lay down certain general propositions. Of these attempts, Pollock and Winfield's suggested principle that the infliction of harm is tortious unless justified, and Lord Atkin's famous formulation of the duty of care to

I

one's "neighbours" (p. 59) stand out as landmarks. But these attempts to find a single unifying principle have usually raised more questions than they have resolved, for example, what conduct is "justified", and who is my "neighbour" to whom a duty of care is owed?

The really striking and all-important development has been the emergence of negligence into a distinct tort (p. 59) and its subsequent octopus-like spread into the waters once occupied by older torts such as trespass (p. 25). The creation of new duty-situations in the tort of negligence (p. 56) paradoxically reveals both the flexible, open-ended nature of this tort (e.g. in regard to the duty to control the conduct of others, p. 99) and the difficulties in formulating a general principle of liability or non-liability (e.g. in regard to loss to economic interests, p. 71).

The fact is that common lawyers (and this is as true in other common law jurisdictions as it is in England), like the classical Roman lawyers, are far more interested in finding a practical solution to the immediate case than in dogma. Here too, the growth of negligence has had a liberating effect on the judges. Once a "duty-situation" (i.e. a duty in tort) has been found to exist (e.g. the duty owed by a prison authority to those in the locality in respect of damage done by prisoners negligently allowed to escape, p. 106) that operates as a precedent binding on judges of the lower courts for the decision of future cases. But the question whether there has been a breach of that duty, and the connection between that breach and the resultant damage, are ultimately questions of fact for the court to decide, according to the objective standards of the "reasonable man". Here there are no precedents, only analogies. The skilful use of maxims such as *res ipsa loquitur* (the matter speaks for itself) can enable a judge to require relatively high standards of behaviour (p. 162); alternatively, by an unsympathetic attitude to the plaintiff, he can allow the defendant considerable freedom of action.

The empiricism of the courts, coupled with the piecemeal nature of statutory reform, means that the student of tort is immediately confronted with a confusing and contradictory use of concepts. Here are some examples—

Duty— which may be used to refer to the existence of a tort (created by judicial precedent or statute, pp. 56, 266) or to the standard of behaviour required of the defendant (p. 134) or, in the case of contributory fault, of the plaintiff (p. 292).

Cause— which may refer to the factual chain of events (p. 170) or to a legal policy decision as to the extent of damage for which the wrongdoer should be made to pay (p. 188).

Damage— which may refer to a particular interest (e.g. in property, person etc.) or to the manner in which that interest was harmed (e.g. by fire, by impact etc., p. 188).

Reasonable— an oft-repeated incantation in tort law, used to *limit* (the range *foresight* of potential plaintiffs (p. 120) or the nature of the conduct for which defendants may be made liable (p. 137), or the kind of damage for which defendants may be made to pay (p. 188).

Risk— sometimes used as a shorthand description of the forseeability test (p. 152), and sometimes as the basis for the imposition of strict liability (e.g., the person who collects explosives on his premises *risks* an explosion, p. 338).

These examples could be multiplied. The student should be careful to ask what purpose a word is being made to serve, instead of simply mouthing the judicial formula. An analysis of language in this way is an essential part of the study of law, but it is not sufficient in itself to convey an understanding of what the law is trying to achieve and, more important, what it in fact achieves.

It has been in an attempt to find this deeper understanding that the study of tort law has recently been moving away from the purely conceptual approach, that is from the law's internal logic as expressed in the specialised language of lawyers, towards a study of the law as it actually operates in society. This means that the questions are no longer simply, is there a duty, or is the defendant in breach of duty, or what formula is to be applied to the assessment of damages? Further questions have to be asked by those wishing to understand the aims and future of tort law, such as, what is the effect of granting or denying the plaintiff compensation, as the case may be, what other sources of compensation are available to him, how is this loss absorbed, either by the group to which the plaintiff (e.g. houseowners) or the defendant (e.g. motorists or employers or manufacturers) belongs, or by taxpayers, and how is the spreading of that loss administered (e.g. through private insurance or a form of social security)? It means taking into account the reality of insurance and the various other methods of compensation which exist. This approach has certain consequences for the classification of the law of tort, and this is reflected in the arrangement of this book.

If, as was suggested earlier, the primary function of tort law is compensation for harm, then, following this functional approach, we are bound to ask what are the main interests which may be harmed? A textbook which aims to set out these interests in detail might contain a number of divisions such as (i) interests in personal security; (ii) interests in one's own property (here distinguishing land and chattels); (iii) interests in another's life (e.g. a breadwinner or employee); (iv) interests in another's property (e.g. a car hirer's interest in the car he has hired); (v) interests of a purely economic nature (e.g. loss of production through a strike, competition by a rival trader); (vi) interests in reputation (protected by the torts of libel and slander); (vii) interests in privacy (a nascent interest only partially protected by some existing torts, p. 570). A sourcebook, in the existing state of English law, cannot make these detailed classifications for the simple reason that several of these interests are discussed interchangeably in many of the cases. This is particularly true of interests in persons and property (Lord Atkin's "duty" test clearly applies to both); but there is a fairly sharp dividing line between these and what may be termed "non-physical" interests. The reluctance of the judiciary to find a duty-situation in the case of negligent interference with pure contractual interests (p. 71) cannot be realistically explained in terms of the absence of foresight (p. 76). The question is sometimes confused by calling this "pecuniary" loss (p. 75) and saying that there is no obvious or intrinsic reason why this should be differently treated from other kinds of loss. Of course, all compensation is "pecuniary" in the sense that the harm to the interest affected must be translated into money terms. The real distinction is between the different *interests* which the law seeks to protect, and not between the money terms in which those interests are compensated for harm.

The interests which the law protects are neither static nor rigidly defined. In the feudal period it was interests in land, the predominant economic asset, which were regarded as meriting the greatest degree of protection. They were vindicated through the writ of trespass. So important were the interests in land that very little attention was paid to the quality of the defendant's behaviour. Unless he was not the master of his own volition (p. 375), he was liable for the act of trespass irrespective of his mental state or the consequences. The need to restore law and order after the ruinous Barons' Wars meant that trespass to the person (particularly assault and battery) and trespass to goods, were used as devices to suppress feuding. These wrongs also did not rest on any notion of fault, although, as Winfield showed, liability was never absolute. Reputation was another interest which received early protection, on the basis of strict liability; here the social need was to provide a legal alternative to duelling.

The rise of industrial capitalism, with the consequent proliferation of dangerous machinery, railways, road traffic and polluting activities, brought other interests to the fore. Interests in personal security became important. The interests of entrepreneurs ran counter to those of the people whom their activities hurt: their workers, the consumers of their products, travellers on their railways and so on. A balance was struck by the judges. This worked as follows. First, there was to be no liability without fault. This principle was not established overnight or without exceptions, indeed it was only in 1959 that it was finally established that the plaintiff in a personal injuries case must prove fault (p. 26) and there are still exceptional situations in which liability for personal injuries is strict, such as where a lamp overhanging a highway falls on a passerby (public nuisance, p. 390), dangerous escapes from land (p. 338) and damage by certain classes of animal (p. 357). Secondly, an important class of plaintiffs, that is employees, were denied compensation from their employers when they were injured by the fault of fellow-employees. This doctrine of common employment, invented in 1837 (p. 262), was qualified by statute in 1880 and by-passed by the Workmen's Compensation Acts (p. 267) after 1897, but it remained a part of the law until scrapped by Parliament in 1948. In the changed economic and social climate at the end of the 19th century, the judiciary found ways around the doctrine, for example by creating torts out of industrial safety legislation to which the doctrine did not apply (p. 266) and by expanding the concept of "personal" duties owed by an employer to his employees (p. 264). But the fault principle has risen to its zenith in this century as a limitation on the protection of physical interests, in particular interests in personal security. In the words of Professor Friedmann, "as emphasis shifted from definition by the kind of *interest* injured (as in the older torts) to the kind of *conduct* which engenders liability, negligence was obviously better fitted to become the modern tort action *par excellence*" (*Law in a Changing Society*, 2nd Edn., p. 162).

This emphasis on negligence is reflected in Part I of this sourcebook (Torts to Physical Interests). Although the various forms of Intentional Interference with the Person (Chap. 2, p. 25) remain distinct in theory they are of far less practical importance than the negligence action. Chapters 3 to 7, 9 and the first section of Chapter 10 are concerned with the various aspects of that action. The rest of Chapter 10 contains materials on liability for things, in which there is a mixture of fault and strict liability. Chapter 11 relates to the protection of the possession of land (trespass) and its use and enjoyment (nuisance). The latter has been greatly influenced by the fault principle, as have statutory torts (Chap. 8).

Part II of the sourcebook (Torts to Non-Physical Interests) deals with a collection of torts, one of whose distinctive features is that three parties are usually involved. There is a plaintiff (P) who has suffered damage, a middleman (X) who has been the vehicle through which that loss has been inflicted on P, and a defendant (D) who is alleged to be responsible. The loss arises not from an infringement of personal security or tangible property, but from an interference with P's relations with X. That is why these are sometimes called *relational* interests. Examples are D's interference with P's interest in the life of X by negligently killing X (p. 424) or P's interest in X's services by negligently injuring X (p. 433); D's inducement of X to break his contract with P (p. 453) or intentionally causing loss to P by the use of some "unlawful means" involving X (e.g. threatening X with violence or some other wrong if he does not break off relations with P, p. 474).

The protection of relational interests conjures up a spectre which haunts the law of tort, but one which is not confined to relational interests. This is the prospect of limitless liability to an unlimited range of plaintiffs. When harm is done to physical interests there are natural safeguards—bodies and tangible property are finite—and the fault principle operates to limit the extent of liability and the range of plaintiffs still further. But when harm is done to relational interests the prospects of loss appear to be infinite. Not surprisingly therefore the law has preferred a general principle of non-liability for interference with non-physical interests to a general principle of liability. The presumption which favours freedom of action in the economic sphere is compatible with an economic and political system which is committed to the notion of workable competition. The examples already given are exceptions to the general principle of non-liability. The most striking illustration of the general principle is the refusal of the courts (and not only in England) to extend the tort of negligence to purely economic losses (p. 71) although a plaintiff who suffers some injury to a *physical* asset may add on to his damages any consequential economic losses (e.g. lost profits).

An exception to the general principle was the extension in the 1960's of the tort of negligence to loss caused by negligent statements about financial matters (p. 499). Although it was at one time predicted that this would have a radical effect on the general rule of non-liability, this has not happened; in fact the rules about negligent statements have themselves been restrictively interpreted. One might now say that liability for negligent statements, like the historically earlier tort of deceit (p. 496), serves to keep men to their word. A promise arouses expectations and it is a function of the law of tort, as well as the law of contract, to allow men of business to arrange their affairs on the basis of those expectations. The probity of commercial dealings is also upheld to a limited extent by the tort of malicious falsehood (p. 522). The tort of passing-off (p. 487) deters unfair competition of another kind: the misappropriation of the plaintiff's name or the simulation of his products.

Interests in business and trade are not the only ones with which Part II is concerned. Reputation might, if one preferred, be classed as an aspect of personal security, but it is a relational interest in English law because liability depends on publication to a third party: the plaintiff's esteem in the eyes of others and not his own injured feelings are at stake. The tort of defamation (p. 527) might be considered from another angle as an aspect of English civil liberty, since the essential task of the court (within an over-complex set of technical rules) is to balance reputation against free speech. Liberty, in its constitutional sense, is also underpinned by the protection given by the law of tort to the right to vote, freedom from abuse of legal procedure (p. 576), and abuse of governmental or monopoly power (p. 585).

The rules and concepts through which tort law seeks to balance the plaintiff's interest against the defendant's claim for freedom of action are essentially judge-made in the area of torts to physical interests. Where statutes have intervened it has principally been to reform areas where the case by case development of principles has led to anomalous or socially undesirable results. Examples are the continuation of claims by and against the estates of deceased persons (1934), p. 400, the establishment of a general right of contribution between tortfeasors (1935), p. 651, the replacement of the "all or nothing rule" with a rule of comparative fault where the plaintiff has contributed to his damage (1945), p. 296, the reform of the complex rules about an occupier's duty to those who enter his land with permission (1957), p. 222, the reform of the law relating to liability for damage caused by animals (1971), p. 359, and for defective premises (1972), p. 259.

But legislative intervention has been of overwhelming importance for the so-called "economic torts" (Chap. 14). The relatively short heyday of economic liberalism, which economic historians date from abolition of the Corn Laws in 1846 to the ending of free trade in 1931, was reflected in deliberate Parliamentary abstention from economic regulation. Where the judges appeared to be following a different policy, as in the development of torts of conspiracy and inducing breach of contract in the context of trade disputes, Parliament intervened to protect economic liberties. In the new era of state regulation particularly since World War II, however, the common law of torts to economic interests is being replaced by a statutory law of tort. The intentional infliction of loss in the labour market is now controlled by a number of "unfair industrial practices", justiciable before a special tribunal, the National Industrial Relations Court. Monopolies and restrictive practices in the business market are controlled by complex legislation justiciable before another special body, the Restrictive Practices Court, and by the rules of the European Economic Community. Misappropriation of ideas and other intellectual property is regulated by a specialised body of patents, trade marks and copyright legislation. While the judges have an important function in interpreting these and other statutes, their former unique role as creators of tort law in this sphere is limited, and is now essentially supplementary to the role of statute law. The new specialised bodies of law, while in theory a part of the law of tort, are in practice best studied in the context of subjects such as Labour Law, Monopolies and Restrictive Practices, and Industrial Property.

While the critical point has already been passed for the development of judge-made torts to economic interests, judge-made law in the sphere of torts to physical interests—in particular personal injuries—has reached its crisis point more recently. The theoretical underpinning of the law of tort as it has been developed since the 19th century is that losses are being shifted from plaintiffs to defendants on the basis of fault. The economic and sociological reality is that losses are typically not simply shifted, but are absorbed by being *spread* or *distributed*. Part III of this sourcebook is concerned with some of the legal devices for loss-distribution. The oldest method for ensuring that the person best able to absorb the loss is made to bear it, is itself judge-made. Vicarious liability, while not exempting the person actually inflicting the loss from personal liability, means that his employer or principal is made a joint tortfeasor (p. 593). The statutory rules for contribution between tortfeasors (p. 651) mean that the defendant who pays may be able to recover from other tortfeasors on the basis of comparative fault. But the most significant modern influence towards loss distribution is the practice of liability insurance. When victims of industrial accidents became entitled, under the Workmen's Compensation Act 1897, to claim compensation from employers regardless of fault, employers looked to liability insurance to cover themselves; the cost of premiums was widely spread by employers, being reflected (at least in theory) in the price of products and the wages paid to workers. The risks of tort liability created by the driving of motor vehicles gave another major impetus to liability insurance. When it became clear that this insurance was beneficial not only to potential tortfeasors, but also to their victims, Parliament intervened, first in 1930, to make it compulsory. Employers' liability insurance has been compulsory since 1972. This kind of loss distribution has been described by Professor John Fleming as "vertical" in contrast to the "horizontal" spreading of losses, by making collateral sources of compensation available to the plaintiff. In the United Kingdom, social security benefits (including industrial injuries insurance, supplementary benefits and criminal injuries compensation) are the most important of these collateral sources (p. 693). Social insurance, which has broken away entirely from the theory of tort law, is already a more significant source of compensation for personal injuries than tort law (p. 712). To some extent duplication is avoided by requiring credit to be given for some benefits received (one half only of some social security benefits for five years) when assessing common law damages (p. 413).

In the two-dimensional world of loss-shifting, writers and judges tended to emphasise the admonitory or deterrent functions of the law of tort. In the three-dimensional reality of loss-distribution, the emphasis has come to rest upon the compensatory aims of the law. The conflict between this aim and the working of the fault principle has led to a widespread attack on the whole edifice of the law and practice of personal injury compensation. This phenomenon is not confined to England, nor to countries of the common law tradition, and is prevalent even in those which impose some measure of strict liability in the field of road accidents. Unfortunately, outside the United States, little research has been done on the actual workings of the various compensation systems. (The reading list, p. 728, gives an indication of some of the major Anglo-American writings.)

The practical objections to the present systems are manifold. For example, it is argued that courts are congested (despite some procedural improvements in England since 1969, p. 416); that litigation is a "lottery" because of the uncertainty produced by the vagaries of the fault rules and the difficulties of reconstructing, usually years after the event, the minute details of "negligent" conduct upon which liability is made to turn; that the assessment of damages, and in particular the calculation of lump-sums, means that some plaintiffs get too much (e.g. the young widow who remarries, p. 431) and many get too little or nothing at all; that the insurers and lawyers engaged in the "injury industry" cream off as administrative costs (estimates put these at between 50%–75% of premium income, p. 712), money which could be more efficiently distributed among accident victims; that there are legal gaps in insurance protection although most of these are now covered by an arrangement between the Motor

Insurers' Bureau and the government (p. 679), so far as motor insurance is concerned; and that the excessive concentration on compensation results in little time being devoted to the problems of accident prevention and rehabilitation of accident victims.

The theoretical arguments against the present system of personal injuries compensation proceed on the assumption that these and other practical defects merely reflect fundamental weaknesses. The debate raises legal, economic and political issues. From the legal vantage point, writers such as Professor André Tunc, point out that the tort rules, historically designed to deal with damage caused by fault, that is either intentionally or through a lack of the standard of care of the "reasonable" man, are now indiscriminately applied to human errors—such as a momentary lack of attention or an unfortunate reaction to danger—which are the main causes of traffic and industrial "accidents". The very word "accident"—usually applied to occurrences whether or not fault, in the legal sense, can be established—reveals the fortuitous nature of the facts to which the legal principles have to be applied. According to this view, the historic task now facing law reformers is to separate the moral, or deterrent, function of tort law, based on the fault principle, from the compensatory function, which arises in the case of human errors. Another legal aspect of the debate is the argument about co-ordination of the rules of insurance with those of tort law: to avoid the duplication of compensation; and to rationalise the distribution of losses, for example by replacing the tort-and-liability insurance system with a system of compulsory first party insurance, as has already occurred, to a limited extent, in regard to road accidents, in several American states (p. 723). A more far-reaching reform has been initiated in New Zealand with abolition of tort liability and its replacement by a state accident compensation scheme (p. 715).

The student who works his way through the pages which follow is likely to be left with a sense of unease. This is a period of transition for tort law; indeed, the very right of an important part of the subject to continue to exist is now in question. Whatever survives may itself be reformed and translated into a statutory code. This, then, is one of the those moments in legal and social history when the student has to live through the process of profound change. A most important lesson of tort law, is the one that Shelley wrote of Man: "Naught may endure but mutability."

Torts to Physical Interests

An Action for Damages in Perspective

The purpose of this Chapter is to give the student a bird's-eye view of an action for damages arising from torts to the person, before he begins his detailed study of the technical rules. The consolidated actions which have been used for this purpose suggest a number of fundamental questions about the aims and functions of the law of tort. These questions are raised at the end of the Chapter where they might serve as the basis for a preliminary discussion of issues which will recur throughout this sourcebook. Some reading has been suggested. In order to keep the list within bounds it has been limited to writings on contemporary English law. The student will want to return to these writings at the end of his course and may by then also be equipped to read some of the American and foreign materials, and the proposals to reform tort law which are collected in the select bibliography, p. 728.

1. THE ASBESTOSIS CASES

(a) The Background[1]

Asbestos is a mineral, which is mined in Africa. It is useful because it resists fire and does not burn. It comes to England in the form of a fibre. It is ground down into dust and put into bags. The process is dangerous for the men doing it. If they inhale the dust, it gets into their lungs and damages them. They suffer from a disease called asbestosis, which is a form of pneumoconiosis. It reduces the elasticity of the lungs and makes it difficult to breathe in and out. This affects the oxygen in the blood, which in turn affects the heart. The disease follows an inevitable progression. The capacity for work gets less and less. In time the sufferer cannot walk, but only sit. Finally he expires. Sometimes the end is hastened by his developing a malignant growth, which is more painful but kills more quickly. Blue asbestos is the worst for this. It was worked by the Central Asbestos Co., Ltd. at their premises in Bermondsey.

Ever since 1931 there have been statutory regulations prescribing the precautions which employers should take for the protection of their men.

---

1. This account is based on the judgment of Lord Denning M.R. in *Smith* v. *Central Asbestos Co., Ltd.*, [1971] 3 All E.R. 204, at pp. 207–208, and an article by A. D. Woolf, "Enforcement?: The Asbestosis Case", *Industrial Law Society*, Bulletin No. 8, September 1970, p. 12.

The asbestos dust must be prevented from escaping into the air. This must be done by exhaust draughts. The sacks containing the dust must be impermeable. They must be beaten by machines, not by hand. Every man must be provided with a breathing apparatus, i.e. a mask which excludes the dust, and must use it. Breach of the regulations is a criminal offence. Conviction can lead to only a small fine, but magistrates have power to close down a machine, a process or a whole factory until the law is obeyed. Responsibility for enforcing the regulations rests on the Factory Inspectorate (Department of Employment), one of the seven central government inspectorates concerned with occupational safety and health.

The Central Asbestos Co., Ltd. were "guilty of grave breaches of the regulations."[1] Time after time from 1953 onwards, the district inspectors of factories who visited the premises complained and wrote letters to the company; but nothing much was done. Conditions were lethal. As late as 29 December 1961 the factory inspector wrote:

> "... the failure to comply with the requirements of the Asbestos Industry Regulations and the consequent conditions, which are dangerous to the health of employed persons, are a matter for grave concern."

In 1962 the company closed down one plant and made modifications to others. This improved matters. But still the company broke the regulations. In May 1964 the factory inspector brought four charges against the company to three of which it pleaded guilty and was fined sums of £75, £75 and £20. In 1967, the factory inspector was still complaining of breaches. The company has since closed down its factories.

Nearly all the workers employed at the company's premises between 1953 and 1967 contracted asbestosis. Some of them died as a result and most of the survivors have been restricted to light work or have become unemployable.

Seven of the men commenced legal proceedings for damages against the company in 1967 and 1968. The company was insured against claims of this kind and the insurance companies resisted the claims. The legal obstacles which the men had to surmount before recovering damages appear from the extracts (printed below) of the pleadings, the judgment of Thesiger J., and the subsequent appeals to the Court of Appeal and the House of Lords. The seven actions were consolidated and so were heard together. The pleadings below, however, relate to only one of the actions. The time between the issue of the writ of summons (18 January 1967) and the date of the House of Lords' judgment (28 June 1972) was five years five months.

(b) The issues

In the High Court of Justice   1967 S. No. 355
Queen's Bench Division
(Writ issued the 18th day of January 1967)
between:

Robert Frederick Smith   *Plaintiff*

and

Central Asbestos Company Limited   *Defendants*

---

1. *Per* Lord Denning M.R., [1971] 3 All E.R. 204, at p. 207. Mr. Woolf calls the breaches "flagrant".

AMENDED STATEMENT OF CLAIM

1. From 17th February 1958 until about 5th August 1966 the Plaintiff was employed by the Defendants at their premises at Horney Lane and at 148a Abbey Street, Bermondsey, S.E.1 in Greater London.

2. The Factories Acts 1937 and 1961, and the Asbestos Industry Regulations 1931 applied to the said premises.

3. In the course of his said employment the Plaintiff together with other workmen was regularly engaged in workshops at the said premises in processes incidental to the preparation of asbestos including the following processes:

(1) opening and emptying sacks containing asbestos material;

(2) feeding asbestos material into mill;

(3) attending to, removing and replacing sacks into which asbestos which had passed through the said mills was discharged and flattening such sacks by treading or jumping upon them;

(4) cleaning the said mills and cyclones used for the extraction of dust;

(5) loading and unloading onto and from lorries sacks containing asbestos or asbestos material.

4. The said processes and each of them gave rise to fumes, dust and/or impurities which were liable to be injurious to persons who inhaled the same and which accumulated in the said workshops.

5. In the course of his said employment the Plaintiff inhaled such fumes dust and impurities whereby he contracted the disease of pneumoconiosis and/or the said disease and its effects became aggravated.

6. The Plaintiff so contracted the said disease and/or its effects became so aggravated as a result of the negligence and/or breach of statutory duty of the Defendants.

PARTICULARS OF NEGLIGENCE

(1) The Defendants knew or ought to have known that the said fumes, dust and/or impurities were liable to be injurious to the health of persons who might inhale the same but they nonetheless caused or permitted the Plaintiff to work in their said workshops in circumstances in which, as they knew or ought to have known, such fumes, dust and/or impurities were given off and accumulated therein.

(2) They failed to provide and maintain adequate ventilation in, or adequate exhaust appliances to collect and remove fumes, dust and impurities given off in, the said workshops.

[There followed twelve further particular allegations of negligence.]

PARTICULARS OF BREACH OF STATUTORY DUTY

(1) Effective and suitable provision was not made for securing and maintaining by
· the circulation of fresh air in the said workshops the adequate ventilation thereof or for rendering harmless the said fumes, dust and impurities, contrary to Section 4 of the Factories Acts 1937 and 1961.

(2) All practical measures were not taken to protect the Plaintiff against the inhalation of the said fumes, dust and impurities or to prevent their accumulating in the said workshops and in particular exhaust appliances were not provided and maintained as near as possible to the points of origin of the said fumes, dust and impurities, contrary to Section 47 of the Factories Act 1937 and Section 63 of the Factories Act 1961.

[There followed eight further particular allegations of breaches of statutory duty.]

7. As a result of the matters hereinbefore set out the Plaintiff has suffered physical harm, damage and loss.

PARTICULARS OF PHYSICAL HARM

The Plaintiff suffers and will suffer from pneumoconiosis. He is unfit for work. The prognosis is uncertain. Pain and suffering.

PARTICULARS OF SPECIAL DAMAGE

Particulars will be given after discovery.

AND the Plaintiff claims DAMAGES

[Counsel]

In the High Court of Justice   1967 S. No. 355
Queen's Bench Division
between:

Robert Frederick Smith   *Plaintiff*
and
Central Asbestos Company Limited   *Defendants*

AMENDED DEFENCE

1. Paragraphs 1 and 2 of the *Amended* Statement of Claim are admitted, and it is admitted that from time to time the Plaintiff was engaged in all the processes referred to in paragraph 3 of the *Amended* Statement of Claim.

2. It is admitted that asbestos dust was liable to be injurious to persons who inhaled the same. Save as aforesaid paragraph 4 of the *Amended* Statement of Claim is denied.

3. Paragraph 5 of the *Amended* Statement of Claim is not admitted.

4. The Defendants deny that they were negligent or in breach of statutory duty for the reasons alleged or at all, and the allegation of causation is denied.

5. Further and alternatively, if the Plaintiff contracted the said disease in the course of his employment, this was caused or contributed to by his own negligence and/or breach of statutory duty.

PARTICULARS OF NEGLIGENCE AND/OR BREACH OF STATUTORY DUTY

[Here were set out a number of specific allegations that the Plaintiff had failed to wear a respirator with which he had been provided and which he had been instructed to use. This was said to be contrary to his duties under the Factories Act and the Asbestos Industry Regulations.]

6. The injury, loss and damage alleged is not admitted.

7. Further and alternatively, the Plaintiff's cause of action if any arose more than three years prior to the commencement of proceedings, and is statute barred by reason of the Limitation Act 1939 as amended by the Law Reform (Limitation of Actions, &c.) Act 1954.

[Counsel]

In the High Court of Justice   X1967 S. No. 355
Queen's Bench Division
between:

Robert Frederick Smith   *Plaintiff*
and
Central Asbestos Company Limited   *Defendants*

REPLY

1. Save in so far as the same consists of admissions the Plaintiff joins issue with the Defendants on their Defence.

2. In so far as the Plaintiff's cause of action herein may be proved to have arisen more than three years prior to the commencement of the proceedings and the Defendants rely upon the Limitation Act 1939, as amended by the Law Reform (Limitation of Actions &c.) Act 1954, as affording them a defence thereto the Plaintiff will rely upon the following facts.

3. Until 27th April 1966 it was outside the Plaintiff's knowledge that he was suffering from pneumoconiosis.

4. Until 6th December 1966 it was outside the Plaintiff's knowledge that he had contracted the said disease as a result of the negligence or breach of statutory duty of the Defendants.

5. On 17th January 1967 the Plaintiff was granted leave pursuant to and for the purposes of the Limitation Act 1963.[1]

[Counsel]

(c) The Judgments

The actions instituted by Mr. Smith and the other plaintiffs were consolidated. At the opening of the trial, the defendants admitted breaches of statutory duty, but claimed that all the damage was attributable to breaches of statutory duty and contributory negligence by the plaintiffs. They contended that the compensation awarded to the plaintiffs should be reduced under the provisions of the Law Reform (Contributory Negligence) Act 1945, s. I (I) of which states:

"Where any person suffers damage as the result partly of his own fault and partly of the fault of any other person or persons, a claim in respect of that damage shall not be defeated by reason of the fault of the person suffering the damage, but the damages recoverable in respect thereof shall be reduced to such extent as the court thinks just and equitable having regard to the claimant's share in the responsibility for the damage."

In the case of four of the seven plaintiffs (Messrs Raper, Roof, Sampson and Dodd), the defendants also contended that the claims were barred because the actions were not brought in time. (This defence was withdrawn in the case of Mr. Smith and the other men because they satisfied the requirements of the Limitation Act 1963, p. 19, *post*.) Difficult questions also arose as to the amount of compensation appropriate in all seven cases. The trial lasted ten days.

High Court of Justice
Queen's Bench Division   Royal Courts of Justice
7th & 8th July 1970

Before: Mr. Justice Thesiger

Robert Frederick Smith *v.* Central Asbestos Company Ltd.

(and 6 other actions consolidated)

MR. JUSTICE THESIGER: . . . In this particular set of cases certain curious aspects of human nature with which any jury would be familiar must, I think, be taken into

1. The relevant provisions of this statute are discussed (p. 19, *post*) by Lord Reid.

account both in considering contributory negligence and in assessing damages. One is that many people despite the clearest warnings of the probability of lung cancer nevertheless smoke cigarettes. Another is that many of the younger generation and by no means only the uneducated smoke cannabis or otherwise take drugs despite the clearest warnings of danger.

In order to see what I have observed as to the defendants' breaches of duty I will read the correspondence which illustrates and which was amplified by the clear and reliable evidence of [the district factory inspectors] who were in the witness box before me . . . [His Lordship went through this evidence, and then referred to the evidence for the defendants given by a Mr. French who started with them as a lorry driver, became Charge Hand and then Works Manager] . . . It seemed clear to me that [Mr. French] was not well acquainted with the Asbestos Industry Regulations. It seemed to me that he and Mr. Kimbell and Mr. Wood who gave evidence for the defendants, each tended to leave it to the other to get on with the production of the asbestos as fast as possible. The pay structure was arranged in order to secure this. The admissions of the defendants' witnesses in the witness box seemed to me to corroborate the evidence of the factory inspectors who were of course corroborated by the contemporaneous correspondence. I prefer the evidence of the plaintiffs where it is in conflict with the evidence of the defendants' witnesses.

There is no doubt in my mind on the evidence that the breaches of statutory duty which are, of course, admitted, were numerous, persistent and that the conditions resulting from the breaches were properly described as lethal . . .

[His Lordship then considered whether the plaintiffs' "fault" was a cause of the damage. He found that they had probably worn the respirators provided for particularly dusty work, this being the work in respect of which the Asbestos Industry Regulations specifically provided: "Every person employed at work specified . . . shall wear and make proper use of the breathing apparatus provided . . ." He went on:] Now the fact that I am not satisfied that there was any breach of the absolute statutory duty imposed upon these workmen does not of course mean that they may not have been guilty of contributory negligence; that is to say of carelessness contributing in some degree to causing the asbestosis which they contracted. In considering that matter however I was referred by [counsel] to the judgment of Goddard L.J. (as he then was) in *Hutchinson* v. *London North Eastern Rail Co.*, [1942] 1 K.B. 481, where, at p. 488, Lord Justice Goddard said:

> "It is only too common to find in cases where the plaintiff alleges that a defendant employer has been guilty of a breach of statutory duty, that a plea of contributory negligence has been set up. In such a case I always directed myself to be exceedingly chary of finding contributory negligence where the contributory negligence alleged was the very thing which the statutory duty of the employer was designed to prevent. The real incentive for the observance by employers of their statutory duties under the Railways Acts, Factory Acts, Dock Acts and similar legislation is not their liability to substantial fines, but the possibility of heavy claims for damages. Such legislation would be nugatory if, in every case, employers could disregard the statute, and allege that, although they did not provide a look-out or a guard or a fence, as the case might be, nevertheless the plaintiff could see the danger and therefore, ought to have ceased working, which in many cases might mean dismissal, or to have taken some extra precaution which was not taken."

I would add there, to what Lord Justice Goddard said, that I venture to think that the real sanction for the observance by employers of their statutory duty under such things as the Asbestos Industry Regulations, might well be a communication by the factory inspectors, if they were allowed to do it, to those who are paid by the employers in many cases to insure them against claims, for if the insurers knew what was happening in certain cases they would probably take very effective steps to see that they were not subsequently faced by very substantial claims. It may, however, be contrary to some civil service rule to communicate with the people who are really concerned with seeing that the regulations are obeyed . . .

[His Lordship considered certain other reported cases, and then dealt with the evidence on the issue of contributory negligence] . . . I consider it was unreasonable to expect, or to suppose that men in the circumstances that prevailed in these premises would never remove their respirators . . . Mr. French who unhappily has contracted asbestosis himself, did not appreciate at the relevant time that the breathing in of dust that might be invisible was really very dangerous indeed, even more dangerous than breathing in larger particles which would probably be ejected by blowing the nose or by coughing.

The attitude adopted by the defendants and by Mr. French was really similar to that of cigarette smokers to the risk of lung cancer and by many young people to the smoking of "pot". In any event I do not believe that the defendants, as employers, made it evident to the men that there was real danger in not wearing the respirators when the mill was not running. The position was that for the sake of comfort . . . men would no doubt generally wear their respirators in the same sort of way that one might tie a handkerchief over one's nose and mouth when brushing out a dirty garage or shed on a dry day . . . My conclusion is that it would not be just and equitable to reduce the damages awarded to any of these plaintiffs under the provisions of the Law Reform (Contributory Negligence) Act because (1) I am not satisfied that any Plaintiff was guilty of negligence in connection with the use of respirators, and (2) I am not satisfied that any breach of the written undertaking [provided by each employee that he would wear a respirator] was the cause of or really contributed to the contraction of asbestosis. The sole direct and effective cause was the breach of the statutory regulations by the defendants . . .

[His Lordship then considered the defence raised in the cases of four of the men based on their alleged failure to bring the action within twelve months of the alleged discovery of the decisive facts by the particular plaintiff. He rejected this defence, which was the subject of further consideration by the Court of Appeal and House of Lords, *post*. He then considered the question of the amount of damages to be awarded and came to the following conclusions].

Some cases have a long time with pain and suffering and some loss with considerable loss in the distant future. Some cases have a short time of pain and suffering but total disablement sooner. Each receives a lump sum now. The latter cases cannot set by invested money for the future and there is no time in such cases for many contingencies to materialise. Smith is only 44. He has severe and progressive asbestosis and is severely disabled. He is not likely to work again. Though not a case of immediate death . . . his expectation of life is only six to eight years and all this is in contrast to others. His continuing loss is £1,325 p.a. His special damage is agreed at £2,888. I assess the general damages at £13,500 including within that sum £500 for loss of expectation of life and £7,000 for loss of future earnings.

McCourt is 42. He has moderate asbestosis with moderate disability. The disease though it has progressed slightly in the last two years now appears to be stabilised. He has to take pain-killing tablets now. He is capable of light work if he can find it. His expectation of life is ten to fifteen years, i.e. up to about 55. He will be unable to work at all in the last four years of his life. McCourt, however, raises the question of whether he will get light work. My conclusion is that he will and that the figure of £413 p.a. for loss of earnings is reasonable. His special damage is agreed at £1,257. I assess the general damages in addition to that at £12,850 including in that sum £350 for loss of expectation of life and £6,500 for loss of future earnings.

Drake is 44. He has moderate asbestosis with moderate disability. At present the progression is slight and slow but he has deteriorated since 1967. He has trouble with his breathing at night. His expectation of life is ten to fifteen years, that will take him to 57 or thereabouts. He will not be able to work in the last four years but until then he could do his present job at a continuing loss of only £83 p.a. . . . Special damages are agreed at £379. I assess the general damages at £11,850 with loss of expectation of life at £350 within that and also within that the loss of future earnings at £4,000.

Dodd is 55, and is older than Smith or Drake. He has severe asbestosis, severe disability and a moderate rate of progression. His expectation of life is only six to eight years. He will not be able to work in the last three years. His continuing loss is agreed at £367 p.a. . . . In the case of Dodd the special damages are agreed at £700. I assess the general damages at £13,000 which includes £500 loss of expectation of life and £4,500 for loss of future earnings.

Roof is much the youngest, now 32. He has slight asbestosis with slight disability and mild x-ray abnormality. There has been no progression since 1968. I doubt if he will continue to lose at the rate of £464 p.a. In the absence of complications or relevant illness his expectation of life is 25 years, i.e. to about 57. He will possibly be unable to work in the last four years. He has a life span during which many contingencies may occur including the possibility of cancer which in the case of Smith was one in ten over thirty years. In the case of Roof which is different to the others, the special damages are agreed at £920. I assess the general damages at £3,900 allowing within that sum £200 for loss of expectation of life and £1,700 for loss of future earnings.

[In the case of Raper aged 57 general damages were assessed at £10,800 including £300 for loss of expectation of life: and £4,000 for loss of future earnings; in the case of Sampson, aged 46 general damages were assessed at £11,900, including £400 for loss of expectation of life, and £4,500 for loss of future earnings.]

The defendants appealed from this Judgment, on the ground that the damages awarded against them were excessive, and in the case of four of the plaintiffs, Raper, Dodd, Sampson and Roof, on the additional ground that their claims were statute-barred. All the plaintiffs cross-appealed on the ground that the damages awarded to them were too low.

The Court of Appeal (Lord Denning M.R., Edmund Davies and Stamp L.JJ.) dismissed the appeal and cross-appeals on 26 May 1971 (reported [1971] 3 All E.R. 204). The defendants then appealed to the House of Lords in respect of the case of Dodd only, and restricted themselves to the plea that the action was statute barred.

The relevant facts relating to this plea had been summarised as follows by Lord Denning M.R. ([1971] 3 All E.R. 204, at p. 210):

"Mr. Dodd started work for the defendants in 1952 when he was 36. Nothing was found wrong with him until January 1964. The Pneumoconiosis Panel then notified him that he was suffering from pneumoconiosis and considered that he should not continue to work in the occupation of charge hand fibrizer. They told him that he could claim disablement benefit and gave him the form to fill in. He filled it in and on 17 March 1964 his disablement was assessed at 10 per cent and he was awarded a disablement pension of 11s 6d a week from 15 January 1964. But the pneumoconiosis did not have any adverse effect on him at that time. So he continued to work, drawing his pay from the defendants, and his disability pension from the Ministry. A little later he saw the works manager, Mr. French (who was also receiving disablement benefit for asbestosis). Mr. French told him: 'You cannot have a disablement pension and claim damages from the company as well.' Mr. Dodd accepted what Mr. French told him. He went on working for the defendants and drew his disability pension, but he did not claim damages. In September 1965, however, his doctor told him that he ought to leave the employment of the defendants because 'he didn't think the dust there was doing me any good'. So Mr. Dodd left the defendants and got employment with the Home Office. He still received his disablement benefit which was assessed year after year at 10 per cent, from which he inferred that the asbestosis had got no worse. He did not think of claiming damages. None of his fellow workers had done so. At the end of April 1967, however, he met a Mr. Smith, who had been a fellow workman with him at the defendants. Mr. Smith told him that he was claiming damages against the defendants. Thereupon Mr. Dodd went to see Mr. Smith's solicitor to see if he could make a claim. In consequence, on 6 October 1967, he issued a writ against the defendants."

The House of Lords (*sub nom. Central Asbestos Co., Ltd. v. Dodd,* [1972] 2 All E.R. 1135) affirmed the decision of the Court of Appeal.

LORD REID: "The appellants plead that this action is barred by the Limitation Act 1963. Before coming to examine the terms I must recall the circumstances in which it was passed. Under the previous law time ran from the date when the damage was suffered. In *Cartledge* v. *E. Jopling & Sons, Ltd.*[1] the appellant workmen had contracted pneumoconiosis by inhaling noxious dust before 1950. In this disease, as in asbestosis, the sufferer's lungs may have been damaged many years before any symptoms develop or even many years before any x-ray or other examination can disclose that there is anything wrong. So the men only discovered that they had the disease at various dates from 1955 onwards; and this House was compelled by the terms of the statute to reach the absurd result that a man's claim may be time barred before it is possible for him to know that he has suffered any damage.

Obviously one of the purposes of the 1963 Act was to remedy the defect in the law brought to light in *Cartledge's* case.[1] But that cannot have been the only purpose. That purpose could have been achieved by a short and simple amendment providing that in cases where the existence of damage caused by a wrongful act or omission cannot (or cannot reasonably) be discovered immediately, time shall not begin to run against the injured person until the first date when by reasonable enquiry he could have discovered the damage. The appellants suggest that Parliament only had in mind that case and the case where, although the injured person knows at once that he has suffered some damage, he cannot know until later the true nature or extent of the damage. That case could have been covered by the kind of amendment which I have suggested by making it apply not only where the existence of the damage but also its true character or extent could not reasonably be discovered immediately.

But the 1963 Act goes far farther than that. It provides by s. 1 that the time limit of three years shall not afford a defence in any action for damages for personal injuries caused by negligence, nuisance or breach of duty if the requirements of the section are satisfied. The types of case to which the appellants say the application of the Act is confined form only a minute proportion of such actions of damage for personal injuries. So one must suppose that the Act must be intended to have some more general application to the vast majority of such actions. . . .

This at least is plain. The Act extends the three years' time limit in cases where some fact was for a time after the damage was suffered outside the knowledge of the plaintiff, if that fact was 'material' and 'decisive'. Before a person can reasonably bring an action he (or his advisers) must know or at least believe that he can establish (1) that he has suffered certain injuries; (2) that the defendant (or those for whom he is responsible) has done or failed to do certain acts; (3) that his injuries were caused by those acts or omissions; and (4) that those acts or omissions involved negligence or breach of duty.

In the present case the first three of these were all known to the respondent more than 12 months before this action was brought, but the fourth was not; he only got to know of it some six months before the writ was issued.[2] The question for decision is whether the fact that the appellants' acts involved or amounted to negligence or

---

1. [1963] A.C. 758; [1963] 1 All E.R. 341.
2. [At the time of this case, proceedings had to be instituted within twelve months of acquiring knowledge of the "material" and "decisive" facts. The period is now *three* years after acquiring such knowledge: Law Reform (Miscellaneous Provisions) Act 1971, s. 1.]

breach of duty is or can be a 'material' or 'decisive' fact within the meaning of the Act.

Some clue as to the intention of Parliament can perhaps be got from the way in which the Act deals with the plaintiff's knowledge. His knowledge may be actual or constructive and s. 7 (5) provides that, if he does not have actual knowledge, he does not have constructive knowledge if—

'(b) in so far as that fact was capable of being ascertained by him, he had taken all such action (if any) as it was reasonable for him to have taken before that time for the purpose of ascertaining it; and (c) in so far as there existed, and were known to him, circumstances from which, with appropriate advice, that fact might have been ascertained or inferred, he had taken all such action (if any) as it was reasonable for him to have taken before that time for the purpose of obtaining appropriate advice with respect to those circumstances.'

Section 7 (8) provides:

'In this section "appropriate advice", in relation to any fact or circumstances, means the advice of competent persons qualified, in their respective spheres, to advise on the medical, legal and other aspects of that fact or those circumstances as the case may be.'

In order to avoid constructive knowledge the plaintiff must have taken all such action as it was reasonable *for him* to take to find out. I agree with the view expressed in the Court of Appeal that this test is subjective. We are not concerned with 'the reasonable man'. Less is expected of a stupid or uneducated man than of a man of intelligence and wide experience.

Apart from opinions recently expressed in this House on a very limited class of case in *British Railways Board* v. *Herrington*[1] this is, I think, a novelty in the law of tort. It shews that Parliament had in mind the common knowledge that most people do not have a legal or businesslike turn of mind. Among other things they are reluctant to visit the terra incognita of a solicitor's office. Indeed that reluctance has been recognised as relevant in the present case because it has been held that it was reasonable for this respondent to rest content with the wrong advice given to him by his works manager although it must have been obvious that the works manager had no real competence to give the advice.

Is it then more likely that Parliament, looking as it did to the circumstances of each individual plaintiff, intended that his ignorance of his legal rights should be treated in the same way as his ignorance of any other material fact, or that the intention was to refuse relief where his ignorance concerned his legal rights but to give relief in all other cases. There is much to be said either way but on the whole I think the former more likely. . . ."

[His Lordship then dealt with problems of interpretation and held that the time did not begin to run against Dodd until the date on which he learnt that he had a legal remedy or cause of action against the defendants in respect of his injuries.] Lord Morris of Borth-y-Gest and Lord Pearson concurred in dismissing the appeal.[2] Lord Simon of Glaisdale and Lord Salmon dissented.

2. POINTS FOR DISCUSSION

1. The Plaintiffs

If Mr. Dodd had not had the good fortune to learn that his former colleague, Mr. Smith was claiming damages, he might never have brought his own action

---

1. [1972] A.C. 877; [1972] 1 All E.R. 749.
2. On different grounds: for a full discussion see Anthony D. Woolf, *Law Guardian/Law Society's Gazette*, 28 March 1973, p. 1596.

and so would have lost £13,700 compensation. Even then it was touch-and-go because it was only by a strict interpretation of the wording of the Limitation Act 1963 that the House of Lords decided that ignorance of the law was an excuse enabling him to institute proceedings after the expiry of the three-year limitation period.

This raises three interrelated, but distinct, problems—

(a) who thinks of bringing a tort claim?
(b) who gets legal advice?
(c) who gets legal aid to institute civil proceedings?

These questions are important because the performance of the law of tort as a means for compensating accident victims must be judged by the extent to which it is capable of being used and is used.

Reading:

Atiyah, Chap. 8, pp. 217–230: a general discussion.

Brian Abel-Smith, Michael Zander and Rosalind Brooke, *Legal Problems and the Citizen* (London, 1973): report on the facilities for advice, particularly legal advice, in three London boroughs. The following parts are particularly relevant to accident claims: pp. 135–140, 169–178, 220–221. Among their main conclusions are: that compensation was obtained much more frequently where advice had been taken, and that larger amounts of compensation were obtained by those who took advice. This should be read in the light of their finding that one household in 16 reported a personal injury case which had not been handled by a lawyer; of 181 cases in which the researchers identified a clear need for advice, 77 (42 *per cent*) had taken no advice of any kind.

Steven J. Hartz, "A Road Accident Survey" (1969), 119 New L.J. 492: report of a survey by the writer and D. R. Harris of all road accidents occurring within the City of Oxford during 1965. 16 *per cent* of those who were off work or unable to carry on their ordinary life for six weeks or more took no advice at all.

Pauline Morris, Richard White and Philip Lewis, *Social Needs and Legal Action* (London, 1973): a stimulating disscusion of the underlying assumptions made about the need for legal advice and aid.

2. The Defendants

The Central Asbestos Co., Ltd. was a *corporate* body which was *insured.* These points are relevant to *financial responsibility*: if an aim of tort law is to compensate the victim, how does it ensure that the defendant can pay? In particular, (a) a corporation acts through people, and it was people in a supervisory position who did not appreciate the dangers of breathing fine particles of asbestos and the need to wear respirators. But it was the corporation which was sued. Why? (b) It was the corporation's liability insurance company which defended the proceedings in the corporation's name. The right to do so arose under the terms of the insurance policy between the corporation and the insurer. (A specimen policy—not the one in this case, nor with the same insurer—will be found in Chap 20, *post*.) Since 1 January 1972 such insurance has been compulsory in the case of employers' liability (Chap. 20, p. 676, *post*) and it is also compulsory in respect of road traffic accidents (Chap. 20, p. 670, *post*). What happens in each of the following circumstances: (i) the defendant is made bankrupt (see Third Parties (Rights Against Insurers) Act 1930, p. 678, *post*, and Road Traffic Act 1972, s. 150, p. 673, *post*); and (ii) the defendant fails to insure in breach of his statutory duty to do so (for employers' liability, see Employers' Liability (Compulsory Insurance) Act 1969, s. 5, p. 677, *post*; for road accidents, see *Monk v. Warbey*, [1935] 1 K.B. 75; [1934] All E.R. Rep. 373, p. 674, *post*, and the Motor Insurers' Bureau Agreement, p. 679, *post*)?

It will be noted that the judges in the *Asbestosis* cases made no explicit mention of insurance covering the claims in question. Why not? (See p. 667, *post*.)

Reading (Materials will be found in Chap. 20, p. 667, *post*):

Atiyah, Chap. 9, pp. 231–280: a general discussion.

Elliott and Street, pp. 209–224: very interesting on insurance in relation to road accidents (but note that insurance is now compulsory in respect of liability to passengers, p. 670, *post*).

Ison, pp. 22–25: refers to a number of specific problems, e.g. the need to locate and identify a defendant (but see the Motor Insurers' Bureau agreement on untraced drivers, p. 682, *post*).

3. The cause of action

Consider the statement of claim, defence and reply. What are the differences between the claims in respect of negligence and breach of statutory duty? Would it be correct to describe the former as depending on the proof of fault, and the latter as resting on strict liability?

Note: The distinction between fault and strict liability will feature in many chapters of this sourcebook. In personal injury and death cases, negligence is usually the only possible cause of action; but sometimes, particularly in the employment context, there may be an action for breach of statutory duty (p. 266, *post*); strict liability may also arise in certain torts arising from the use of land (p. 338, *post*) the spread of fire (p. 352) and the keeping of animals (p. 359).

4. The Defences

(a) *Contributory fault*: why did the judge decide that the damages should not be reduced, under the terms of the Law Reform (Contributory Negligence) Act 1945, in these cases? (This subject is considered in detail in Chap. 9, p. 292, *post*.)

(b) *Limitation*: This is a highly technical subject, details of which the student might safely avoid at this stage of his studies, although he should be aware of the main limitation periods and the principal grounds for extending them. (For reference see Anthony D. Woolf, *The Time Barrier in Personal Injury Claims* (London, 1969); and in *Law Guardian/Law Society's Gazette*, 28 March 1973, p. 1596.)

5. Sources of compensation

Each plaintiff appears to have been drawing a state disability pension. They discovered, some just in time, that they could claim tort damages as well.

(1) What are the main sources of compensation for accident victims? Consider in particular (a) social security benefits (Chap. 20, p. 693, *post*); (b) criminal injuries compensation (p. 698), *post*; and (c) "personal" (sometimes called loss or "first party") insurance (specimens, p. 683, *post*).

(2) To what extent is "double compensation" possible? (For the deductions which are made from common law tort damages, see Chap. 12, p. 414, *post*.)

Reading:

Atiyah, Chaps. 12–17, pp. 307–413: a general discussion of personal insurance, criminal injuries, social security including industrial injuries benefits, and other methods of compensation.

Ison, Chap. 3, pp. 31–54: a shorter account of the "rivals to negligence".

D. Lees and N. Doherty, "Compensation for Personal Injury", *Lloyds Bank Review*, April 1973, No. 108, p. 18: the most comprehensive unofficial estimate available of the amount, distribution and administrative costs of the various types of compensation. An extract is reproduced in Appendix E, p. 712, *post*.

6. The damages: aims of the law of tort

(a) It will be noted that in assessing the damages due to each plaintiff, no account was taken of the findings that the breaches of duty were "grave" (Lord Denning M.R.), and "numerous and persistent" (Thesiger J.). Can this be reconciled with Lord Goddard C.J.'s statement (p. 16, *ante*) that "the real incentive for the observance by employers of their statutory duties . . . is not their liability to substantial fines, but the possibility of heavy claims for damages."? What light does this throw on the purposes of an award of damages?

(b) "It is commonly said that the civil action for damages aims at compensation, as opposed to the criminal prosecution which aims at punishment. This, however, does not look below the surface of things. Granted that the immediate object of the tort action is to compensate the plaintiff at the expense of the tortfeasor, why do we wish to do this? Is it to restore the *status quo ante*?—but if so, why do we want to restore the *status quo ante*? And could we not restore this status in some other and better way, for instance by a system of national insurance? Or is it really that we want to deter people from committing torts? Or again, is it that the payment of compensation is regarded as educational, or as a kind of expiation for a wrong?" (Glanville Williams (1951), 4 Current L.P. 137).

Reading:

Glanville Williams, "The Aims of the Law of Tort" (1951), 4 Current L.P. 137–176: the basic article on the aims of the law of tort, although the reader should note that a number of the specific examples are now out of date; essential reading on the deterrent theory.

John G. Fleming, *An Introduction to the Law of Torts* (Oxford, 1967), Chap. 1, pp. 1–23: in discussing the task of tort law draws attention to the loss-spreading function; a useful complement to Glanville Williams' article.

W. G. Friedmann, *Law in a Changing Society* (Harmondsworth, 2nd Edn., 1972), Chap. 5, pp. 161–173: a masterly short account of the effect of changing social conditions on the functions of tort law.

F. H. Lawson, *The Rational Strength of English Law* (London, 1951), pp. 122–135: a stimulating discussion of the characteristics of those torts (e.g. trespass, ejectment, conversion and defamation) which are primarily concerned with responsibility for interference with the rights of others rather than with damage.

A. Tunc, "Tort Law and the Moral Law", [1972A] C.L.J. 247–259: sees the main challenge to modern tort jurists as being to establish the borderline between damage caused by fault and damage caused by "accident". "[W]hen someone has taken a deliberate decision, the moral law demands that he bear the responsibility for what he has done. . . . [W]hen an accident has occurred, the moral law demands as a matter of priority that the victim be indemnified". But Professor C. J. Hamson, [1973] C.L.J. 52, 244, argues that this seriously erodes the ambit of moral obligation in the law of tort.

Reference might also be made to the statistics in Appendices A (p. 705) and B (p. 707), *post*, on trends on road and industrial accidents; and to the estimates of the social cost of road accidents and industrial accidents in Appendices C (p. 709) and D (p. 710), *post*.

2

Intentional Injuries to the Person

This Chapter includes not only the torts traditionally known as assault, battery and false imprisonment, which can be grouped under the heading trespass to the person, but also liability for wrongful interference with the person in situations where an action under any of the first three torts may be inappropriate. Winfield and Jolowicz (at p. 31) define an assault as "an act of the defendant which causes to the plaintiff reasonable apprehension of the infliction of a battery on him by the defendant", and a battery as "the intentional application of force to another person", although they accept that trespass to the person is probably still actionable where the defendant has acted negligently rather than intentionally (see also Street, pp. 13–17, 18 and 21; Salmond, p. 123; cf. *Letang* v. *Cooper*, [1965] 1 Q.B. 232; [1964] 2 All E.R. 929, p. 31, *post*). In relation to this last point, the first section of this Chapter (admittedly "trespassing" to some extent from its title) deals with the inter-relationship of the trespass action and an action in the tort of negligence, and the cases provide a brief glimpse of the history of these two actions.

Whereas an action in the tort of negligence requires proof of damage, trespass to the person is actionable *per se* and, although this difference is not often of great importance, in *John Lewis & Co., Ltd.* v. *Tims*, [1952] 1 All E.R. 1203, at p. 1204, Lord Porter stated (in the context of false imprisonment) that when "the liberty of the subject is at stake questions as to the damage sustained become of little importance." Indeed, the trespass action can be a particularly important weapon in safeguarding the freedom of the individual.

Assault, battery and false imprisonment are torts, but they are also crimes (see Smith and Hogan, *Criminal Law* (3rd Edn. 1973), Chap. 12), and acts giving rise to tortious liability may, therefore, involve criminal liability as well. Criminal cases are used as precedents in determining the scope of these torts, but, since the policy of the law in the two spheres may differ, some caution must be exercised when this is done. Apart from the possibility of the same act giving rise to both civil and criminal liability, a particular factual situation may well involve liability under more than one of the various torts which come within the category of trespass to the person. A battery will usually, but not always, be preceded by an assault, although each can exist independently of the other, and acts amounting to false imprisonment could in addition involve liability for assault or battery. The student should be warned, however, that the word assault is often used loosely to cover both the technical assault and the battery.

In the section on false imprisonment references will occasionally be found to

"Felonies" which at one time were of importance in relation to powers of arrest. However, it will be seen that since the enactment of the Criminal Law Act 1967 (p. 49, *post*) the position has changed. The relevant distinction now, when dealing with powers of arrest without a warrant, is that between arrestable and non-arrestable offences, but, despite this change in the law, many of the requirements of a valid arrest are still to be found in the pre-1967 authorities.

The wrongful interference principle has the potential to develop a wide area of liability which has not yet been fully explored by the courts. Very few cases have been brought to their attention. It is distinct from the trespass action, and consequently does not suffer from the disadvantages of the latter. For example, there does not appear to be any requirement that the harm be a direct consequence of the defendant's act, a limitation which could still cause problems with the trespass action. (See Street, p. 23, for certain cases which, he suggests, are not trespasses, but which may be actionable under this principle: see also *ibid.*, p. 20, note 8.)

1. TRESPASS, INTENTION AND NEGLIGENCE
Fowler v. Lanning
Queen's Bench Division   [1959] 1 All E.R. 290

DIPLOCK J.: ... The writ in this case claims damages for trespass to the person committed by the defendant at Corfe Castle, in the county of Dorset, on 19 November 1957. The statement of claim alleges laconically that at that place and on that date "the defendant shot the plaintiff", and that by reason thereof the plaintiff sustained personal injuries and has suffered loss and damage. By his defence the defendant, in addition to traversing the allegations of fact, raises the objection

"that the statement of claim is bad in law and discloses no cause of action against him on the ground that the plaintiff does not allege that the said shooting was intentional or negligent."

An order has been made that this point of law be disposed of before the trial of the issues of fact in the action. That order is binding on me, and, in disposing of it, I can look no further than the pleadings. I must confess that at first glance at the pleadings I felt some anxiety lest I was being invited to decide a point which has long puzzled the professors (see the article by Professors Goodhart and Winfield (1933), 49 Law Quarterly Review 359; *Pollock on Torts* (15th Edn.), p. 129; *Salmond on Torts* (12th Edn.), p. 311; *Winfield on Tort* (5th Edn.), p. 213), only to learn ultimately that, just as in *M'Alister (or Donoghue)* v. *Stevenson* ([1932] All E.R. Rep. 1), there was in fact no snail in the ginger beer bottle, so in this case there was in fact no pellet in the defendant's gun.

The point of law is not, however, a mere academic one even at the present stage of the action. The alleged injuries were, I am told, sustained at a shooting party; it is not suggested that the shooting was intentional. The practical issue is whether, if the plaintiff was in fact injured by a shot from a gun fired by the defendant, the onus lies on the plaintiff to prove that the defendant was negligent, in which case, under the modern system of pleading, he must so plead and give particulars of negligence (see R.S.C., Ord. 19, r. 4)[1] or whether it lies on the defendant to prove that the plaintiff's injuries were not caused by the defendant's negligence, in which case the plaintiff's statement of claim is sufficient and discloses a cause of action (see R.S.C., Ord. 19, r. 25).[2] The issue is thus a neat one of onus of proof.

... It is fashionable today to regard trespass to the person as representing the historic principle that every man acts at his peril and is liable for all the consequences of his acts;

---

1. [See now R.S.C., Ord. 18, r. 7 (1).]
2. [See now R.S.C., Ord. 18, r. 7 (3).]

negligence as representing the more modern view that a man's freedom of action is subject only to the obligation not to infringe any duty of care which he owes to others (see per Lord Macmillan in *Read* v. *J. Lyons & Co., Ltd.*, [1946] 2 All E.R. 471, at p. 476).

But whether this was true of trespass in medieval times—and I respectfully doubt whether it ever was—the strict principle that every man acts at his peril was not applied in the case of trespass to the person even as long ago as 1617. It is true that in that year, in the much-cited case of *Weaver* v. *Ward* ((1616), Hob. 134), which arose out of a shooting accident during an exercise of trained bands, the Court of King's Bench held that a plea that

> "the defendant casualiter et per infortunium et contra voluntatem suam, in discharging of his piece did hurt and wound the plaintiff"

was demurrable. But it would seem that this was because the plea, which was a special plea, was insufficient, because, although it denied intention, it did not negative negligence on the part of the defendant. It is clear from the report that the court was of opinion that the action of trespass to the person would fail if it should appear that the accident was

> "inevitable, and that the defendant had committed no negligence to give occasion to the hurt."

This phrase is repeated in many of the later cases. Where it appears, however, it must be read in its historical context and not as if it were being used by judges to whom modern concepts of negligence, contributory negligence, and causation were familiar. An examination of the cases up to 1842 in which this or some similar phrase was adopted shows, I think, that the word "inevitable" was superfluous, and that the phrase meant no more than that the accident could not have been avoided by the exercise of reasonable care on the part of the defendant. . . .

Apart from the question of onus of proof, which I must now examine, there does not appear by 1852 to have been any difference between the substantive law applicable whether the action were framed in trespass on the case or trespass to the person. Differences as regards pleading were, of course, in those days, vital, but are not relevant for the purposes of the present case in 1959, except in so far as they throw any light on where the onus of proof lay.

In trespass on the case the onus of proof of the defendant's negligence undoubtedly lay on the plaintiff. Where it lay in trespass is much more difficult to determine. . . .

I do not find the pre-Common Law Procedure Act cases conclusive or, indeed, helpful as to where the onus of proof of the defendant's negligence or absence of negligence lay where the action was founded on trespass to the person and not on trespass on the case. The reported cases turn on points of pleading, a science on which the legal mind was then wonderfully concentrated, and when, in any particular case, that science had achieved its object in arriving at an issue of fact for the jury in an action of trespass to the person, it could only be very rarely that the question of onus of proof was crucial. Since trespass to the person only lay where the injury to the plaintiff was the direct consequence of the personal act of the defendant, proof that the defendant did the act and that the plaintiff was thereby injured would normally be prima facie evidence of the defendant's negligence sufficient also to sustain an action on the case in accordance with the common sense view applied at nisi prius long before Pollock C.B., in *Byrne* v. *Boadle* ((1863), 2 H. & C. 722, at p. 725), translated it into Latin as res ipsa loquitur. At the time the case came before the jury, therefore, there can have been little practical difference between trespass and case, even if in the former the onus of negativing negligence did lie on the defendant while in the latter the onus of proving negligence lay on the plaintiff. But whatever the reason, I can find no trace in the reports that the possibility that the onus of proof might be different in the two classes of cases was a question which ever occurred to the judges of those days, or that their charge to the jury differed according to whether the action were framed in trespass or in case.

The majority of pre-Common Law Procedure Act cases in which the question of unintentional trespass to the person or to goods was discussed were, it is true, cases of collision on the highway either on land or on water. There is, however, no trace that I can find in the judgments that this was a relevant consideration, or that the law as to trespass vi et armis to the person or to goods was different according to whether the injury took place on a highway or not. Prima facie, therefore, one would suppose that the onus of proof lay on the same party to the action in either case. If, therefore, it is conceded—as all agree that it must be at any rate today—that in the case of an in-voluntary trespass to the person on a highway the onus of proving negligence lies on the plaintiff; why should it be otherwise when the involuntary trespass to the person is not committed on a highway? There is, nevertheless, a formidable body of academic opinion—but not, I think, any binding judicial authority—that highway cases have in the last hundred years become an exception to a previously existing general rule that the onus of proof of absence of negligence on the part of a defendant in a case founded on trespass to the person lies on the defendant himself.

As I have already said, I do not think that the cases prior to the Common Law Procedure Act 1852, establish that there ever was such a general rule, nor do I think that the subsequent cases, on analysis, suggest that those judges who were familiar with the procedure before 1852 took the view that there ever had been such a rule. The *dictum* of Blackburn J. in *Fletcher* v. *Rylands* ((1866), L.R. 1 Exch. 265) is generally regarded as the origin of some modern rule special to highways. But what he said (*ibid.*, at p. 286) in a case which, after all, was about the flooding of coal mines, was not limited to accidents on highways or to trespass to the person.

> "Traffic on the highways, whether by land or sea, cannot be conducted without exposing those whose persons or property are near it to some inevitable risk; and that being so, those who go on the highway, or have their property adjacent to it, may well be held to do so subject to their taking upon themselves the risk of injury from that inevitable danger . . ."

So far he is dealing with highway accidents and with trespass to land as well as with trespass to the person. But he goes on:

> "and persons who by the licence of the owner pass near to warehouses where goods are being raised or lowered, certainly do so subject to the inevitable risk of accident. In neither case, therefore, can they recover without proof of want of care or skill occasioning the accident; and it is believed that all the cases in which inevitable accident has been held an excuse for what prima facie was a trespass, can be explained on the same principle, viz., that the circumstances were such as to show that the plaintiff has taken that risk upon himself."

Here is no sudden emergence of a rule peculiar to highways, but a rationalisation of what appeared to Blackburn J. to be well-settled law by explaining it on the basis—of which there is no trace to be found in the cases to which he refers—of the voluntary acceptance of risk by the plaintiff. It is to be noted that he refers specifically to ware-house cases, which are not highway cases, and among the other cases alluded to in which "inevitable accident has been held an excuse for what prima facie was a trespass" must be included *Weaver* v. *Ward* ((1616), Hob. 134), the trained band shooting accident. But what is even more germane to the matter which I have to decide is that that great lawyer, who, having been called to the Bar in 1838 and to the Bench in 1859, must have been very familiar with the practice at nisi prius, appears to have regarded it as a commonplace that in all cases in which inevitable accident is an excuse for what prima facie was a trespass the onus of proving negligence lies on the plaintiff.

Ten [1] years later in *Holmes* v. *Mather* ((1875, L.R. 10 Exch. 261, at p. 268), an equally great common lawyer, Bramwell B., stated the same proposition quite generally:

> "The result of [the cases cited] is this, and it is intelligible enough: if the act that does an injury is an act of direct force vi et armis, trespass is the proper remedy (if

---

1. ["Nine" years later, according to the report in [1959] 1 Q.B. 426, at p. 437.]

there is any remedy) where the act is wrongful, either as being wilful or as being the result of negligence. Where the act is not wrongful for either of these reasons, no action is maintainable, though trespass would be the proper form of action if it were wrongful.". . .

This brings me to *Stanley* v. *Powell* ([1891] 1 Q.B. 86), a case of a shooting accident, not on a highway, in which Denman J. held that trespass to the person would not lie in the absence of negligence by the defendant. The action was originally pleaded in negligence, the onus of proof of which undoubtedly lay on the plaintiff, and the jury had found that there was no negligence—or, I suppose, more accurately, that the plaintiff had not proved any negligence on the part of the defendant. There are phrases in the judgment of Denman J. which can be read as suggesting that his view was that, had the action been framed in trespass to the person, the onus of negativing negligence would have lain on the defendant. But this can hardly have been present to his mind or he would presumably have ordered a new trial. I regard the decision as neutral on the question of onus of proof.

Stanley v. *Powell*, although assailed by some text-book writers, has stood for nearly seventy years. It was approved by all members of the Court of Appeal in *National Coal Board* v. *J. E. Evans & Co. (Cardiff), Ltd. & Maberley Parker, Ltd.* ([1951] 2 All E.R. 310) —an approval which, it may be, was obiter. I have, however, no doubt that the decision in *Stanley* v. *Powell* is good law.

Little assistance is to be obtained from any later cases. Since *Stanley* v. *Powell* and perhaps as a result of that decision, there appears to be no case in the reports where unintentional trespass to the person has been relied on as distinct from negligence, despite the encouragement of the learned authors of the article on Trespass and Negligence in (1933), 49 Law Quarterly Review 359, and the continued appearance in successive editions of *Bullen and Leake's Precedents of Pleadings* of a precedent of a pleading in trespass to the person in which neither intention nor negligence is alleged. No doubt in many cases it is the master who is sued for the act of his servant, and here trespass as opposed to case would never lie; but in the sixty-eight years which have passed since *Stanley* v. *Powell* there must have been many cases where the injury to the plaintiff was the direct consequence of the act of the defendant himself.

I think that what appears to have been the practice of the profession during the present century is sound in law. I can summarise the law as I understand it from my examination of the cases as follows:

(1) Trespass to the person does not lie if the injury to the plaintiff, although the direct consequence of the act of the defendant, was caused unintentionally and without negligence on the defendant's part.

(2) Trespass to the person on the highway does not differ in this respect from trespass to the person committed in any other place.

(3) If it were right to say with Blackburn J. in 1865 [1] that negligence is a necessary ingredient of unintentional trespass only where the circumstances are such as to show that the plaintiff had taken on himself the risk of inevitable injury (i.e. injury which is the result of neither intention nor carelessness on the part of the defendant), the plaintiff must today in this crowded world be considered as taking on himself the risk of inevitable injury from any acts of his neighbour which, in the absence of damage to the plaintiff, would not in themselves be unlawful—of which discharging a gun at a shooting party in 1957 or a trained band exercise in 1617 are obvious examples. For Blackburn J. in the passage I have quoted from *Fletcher* v. *Rylands* ((1866), L.R. 1 Exch., at p. 286) was in truth doing no more than stating the converse of the principle referred to by Lord Macmillan in *Read* v. *J. Lyons & Co., Ltd.* ([1946] 2 All E.R., at p. 476), that a man's freedom of action is subject only to the obligation not to infringe any duty of care which he owes to others.

---

1. See *Fletcher* v. *Rylands* (1866), L.R. 1 Exch. 265.

(4) The onus of proving negligence, where the trespass is not intentional, lies on the plaintiff, whether the action be framed in trespass or in negligence. This has been unquestioned law in highway cases ever since *Holmes* v. *Mather* ((1875), L.R. 10 Exch. 261), and there is no reason in principle, nor any suggestion in the decided authorities, why it should be any different in other cases. It is, indeed, but an illustration of the rule that he who affirms must prove, which lies at the root of our law of evidence.

I am glad to be able to reach this conclusion and to know that the Supreme Court of British Columbia has recently done the same (*Walmsley* v. *Humenick*, [1954] 2 D.L.R. 232) for

> ". . . while admiring the subtlety of the old special pleaders, our courts are primarily concerned to see that rules of law and procedure should serve to secure justice between the parties":

per Viscount Simon L.C. in *United Australia, Ltd.* v. *Barclays Bank, Ltd.* ([1940] 4 All E.R. 20, at p. 32).

If, as I have held, the onus of proof of intention or negligence on the part of the defendant lies on the plaintiff, then, under the modern rules of pleading, he must allege either intention on the part of the defendant, or, if he relies on negligence, he must state the facts which he alleges constitute negligence. Without either of such allegations the bald statement that the defendant shot the plaintiff in unspecified circumstances with an unspecified weapon in my view discloses no cause of action. . . .

Turning next to the alternative of negligent trespass to the person, there is here the bare allegation that on a particular day at a particular place "the defendant shot the plaintiff". In what circumstances, indeed with what weapon, from bow and arrow to atomic warhead, is not stated. So bare an allegation is consistent with the defendant's having exercised reasonable care. It may be—I know not—that, had the circumstances been set out with greater particularity, there would have been disclosed facts which themselves shouted negligence, so that the doctrine of res ipsa loquitur[1] would have applied. In such a form the statement of claim might have disclosed a cause of action even although the word "negligence" itself had not been used, and the plaintiff in that event would have been limited to relying for proof of negligence on the facts which he had alleged. But I have today to deal with the pleading as it stands. As it stands, it neither alleges negligence in terms nor alleges facts which, if true, would of themselves constitute negligence; nor, if counsel for the plaintiff is right, would he be bound at any time before the trial to disclose to the defendant what facts he relies on as constituting negligence.

I do not see how the plaintiff will be harmed by alleging now the facts on which he ultimately intends to rely. On the contrary, for him to do so, will serve to secure justice between the parties. It offends the underlying purpose of the modern system of pleading that a plaintiff, by calling his grievance "trespass to the person" instead of "negligence", should force a defendant to come to trial blindfold; and I am glad to find nothing in the authorities which compels the court in this case to refrain from stripping the bandage from his eyes.

I hold that the statement of claim in its present form discloses no cause of action.

Order accordingly. Leave to make immediate amendments to statement of claim granted; consequential amendments to defence to be made within fourteen days.

Note

At the ultimate trial of the action, the plaintiff failed because he was unable to prove whose shot had caused the injury: see (1959), "*Times*", May 21 and 22, Dworkin (1959), 22 M.L.R. 538. For general comment, see Glanville Williams, [1959] C.L.J. 33.

---

1. [This will be met in Chap. 4, p. 134, *post.*]

Letang v. Cooper

Court of Appeal   [1964] 2 All E.R. 929

LORD DENNING M.R.: On 10 July 1957, Mrs. Letang, the plaintiff, was on holiday in Cornwall. She was staying at a hotel and thought she would sunbathe on a piece of grass where cars were parked. While she was lying there, Mr. Cooper, the defendant, came into the car park driving his Jaguar motor car. He did not see her. The car went over her legs and she was injured. On 2 February 1961, more than three years after the accident, the plaintiff brought this action against the defendant for damages for loss and injury caused by (i) the negligence of the defendant in driving a motor car and (ii) the commission by the defendant of a trespass to the person. The sole question is whether the action is statute barred. The plaintiff admits that the action for negligence is barred after three years, but she claims that the action for trespass to the person is not barred until six years have elapsed. The judge has so held and awarded her £575 damages for trespass to the person.

Under the Limitation Act 1939, the period of limitation was six years in all actions founded "on tort"; but in 1954 Parliament reduced it to three years in actions for damages for personal injuries, provided that the actions come within these words of s. 2 (1) of the Law Reform (Limitation of Actions, &c.) Act 1954:

> ". . . in the case of actions for damages for negligence, nuisance or breach of duty (whether the duty exists by virtue of a contract or of a provision made by or under a statute or independently of any contract or any such provision) where the damages claimed by the plaintiff for the negligence, nuisance or breach of duty consist of or include damages in respect of personal injuries to any person . . ."

The plaintiff says that these words do not cover an action for trespass to the person, and that, therefore, the time bar is not the new period of three years, but the old period of six years.

The argument, as it was developed before us, became a direct invitation to this court to go back to the old forms of action and to decide this case by reference to them. The statute bars *an action on the case*, it is said, after three years, whereas *trespass to the person* is not barred for six years. The argument was supported by reference to text-writers, such as *Salmond on Torts* (13th Edn), p. 790. I must say that if we are, at this distance of time, to revive the distinction between trespass and case, we should get into the most utter confusion. The old common lawyers tied themselves in knots over it, and we should find ourselves doing the same. Let me tell you some of their contortions. Under the old law, whenever one man injured another by the *direct* and immediate application of force, the plaintiff could sue the defendant in *trespass* to the person, without alleging negligence (see *Leame* v. *Bray*),[1] whereas if the injury was only *consequential*, he had to sue in *case*. You will remember the illustration given by Fortescue J. in *Reynolds* v. *Clarke*, in 1725:[2]

> "If a man throws a log into the highway and in that act it hits me, I may maintain trespass because it is an immediate wrong; but if, as it lies there, I tumble over it and receive an injury, I must bring an action upon the case because it is only prejudicial in consequence."

Nowadays, if a man carelessly throws a piece of wood from a house into a roadway, then whether it hits the plaintiff or he tumbles over it the next moment, the action would not be *trespass* or *case*, but simply negligence. Another distinction which the old lawyers drew was this: If the driver of a horse and gig negligently ran down a passer-by, the plaintiff could sue the driver either in *trespass* or in *case* (see *Williams* v. *Holland*, in 1833);[3] but if the driver was a servant, the plaintiff could not sue the master in trespass,

---

1. (1803), 3 East. 593.
2. (1725), 1 Stra. 634, at p. 636.
3. (1833), 10 Bing. 112.

but only in case (see *Sharrod* v. *London and North Western Rail. Co.*, in 1849).[1] In either case today, the action would not be *trespass* or *case*, but only negligence.

If we were to bring back these subtleties into the law of limitation, we should produce the most absurd anomalies; and all the more so when you bear in mind that under the Fatal Accidents Acts the period of limitation is three years from the death. The decision of Elwes J., if correct, would produce these results. It would mean that if a motorist ran down two people, killing one and injuring another, the widow would have to bring her action within three years, but the injured person would have six years. It would mean also that if a lorry driver was in collision at a cross-roads with an owner driver, an injured passenger would have to bring his action against the employer of the lorry driver within three years, but he would have six years in which to sue the owner-driver. Not least of all the absurdities is a case like the present. It would mean that the plaintiff could get out of the three-year limitation by suing in trespass instead of in negligence.

I must decline, therefore, to go back to the old forms of action in order to construe this statute. I know that in the last century Maitland said "the forms of action we have buried but they still rule us from their graves". But we have in this century shaken off their trammels. These forms of action have served their day. They did at one time form a guide to substantive rights; but they do so no longer. Lord Atkin told us what to do about them:

> "When these ghosts of the past stand in the path of justice, clanking their mediaeval chains, the proper course for the judge is to pass through them undeterred",

see *United Australia, Ltd.* v. *Barclays Bank, Ltd.*[2]

The truth is that the distinction between trespass and case is obsolete. We have a different sub-division altogether. Instead of dividing actions for personal injuries into *trespass* (direct damage) or *case* (consequential damage), we divide the causes of action now according as the defendant did the injury intentionally or unintentionally. If one man intentionally applies force directly to another, the plaintiff has a cause of action in assault and battery, or, if you so please to describe it, in trespass to the person. "The least touching of another in anger is a battery." If he does not inflict injury intentionally, but only unintentionally, the plaintiff has no cause of action today in trespass. His only cause of action is in negligence, and then only on proof of want of reasonable care. If the plaintiff cannot prove want of reasonable care, he may have no cause of action at all. Thus, it is not enough nowadays for the plaintiff to plead that "the defendant shot the plaintiff".[3] He must also allege that he did it intentionally or negligently. If intentional, it is the tort of assault and battery. If negligent and causing damage, it is the tort of negligence.

The modern law on this subject was well expounded by my brother Diplock J. in *Fowler* v. *Lanning*[4] with which I fully agree. But I would go this one step further: when the injury is not inflicted intentionally, but negligently, I would say that the only cause of action is negligence and not trespass. If it were trespass, it would be actionable without proof of damage; and that is not the law today.

In my judgment, therefore, the only cause of action in the present case (where the injury was unintentional) is negligence and is barred by reason of the express provision of the statute.

In case I am wrong about this, and the plaintiff has a cause of action for trespass to the person, I must deal with a further argument which was based on the opinion of text-writers, who in turn based themselves on a report of the committee which preceded the legislation. This was a committee over which Lord Tucker presided.[5] They reported in

---

1. (1849), 4 Exch. 580.
2. [1941] A.C. 1, at p. 29; [1940] 4 All E.R. 20, at p. 37.
3. See *Fowler* v. *Lanning*, [1959] 1 Q.B. 426; [1959] 1 All E.R. 290.
4. [1959] 1 Q.B. 426; [1959] 1 All E.R. 290.
5. Cmd. No. 7740.

1949. They recommended that, in actions for damages for personal injuries, the period of limitation should be reduced to two years; but they said:

> "We wish, however, to make it clear that we do not include in that category actions for trespass to the person, false imprisonment, malicious prosecution or defamation of character, but we do include such actions as claims for negligence against doctors."

I think that the text-writers have been in error in being influenced by the recommendations of the committee. It is legitimate to look at the report of such a committee, so as to see what was the mischief at which the Act was directed. You can get the facts and surrounding circumstances from the report, so as to see the background against which the legislation was enacted. This is always a great help in interpreting it. But you cannot look at what the committee recommended, or at least, if you do look at it, you should not be unduly influenced by it. It does not help you much, for the simple reason that Parliament may, and often does, decide to do something different to cure the mischief. You must interpret the words of Parliament as they stand, without too much regard to the recommendations of the committee: see *Assam Railways and Trading Co., Ltd.* v. *I.R. Comrs.*[1] In this very case, Parliament did not reduce the period to two years. It made it three years. It did not make any exception of "trespass to the person" or the rest. It used words of general import; and it is those words which we have to construe, without reference to the recommendations of the committee.

So we come back to construe the words of the statute with reference to the law of this century and not of past centuries. So construed, they are perfectly intelligible. The tort of "negligence" is firmly established. So is the tort of "nuisance". These are given by the legislature as sign-posts. Then these are followed by words of the most comprehensive description:

> "Actions for breach of duty (whether the duty exists by virtue of a contract or of a provision made by or under a statute or independently of any contract or any such provision)."

Those words seem to me to cover not only a breach of a contractual duty, or a statutory duty, but also a breach of any duty under the law of tort. Our whole law of tort today proceeds on the footing that there is a duty owed by every man not to injure his neighbour in a way forbidden by law. Negligence is a breach of such a duty. So is nuisance. So is trespass to the person. So is false imprisonment, malicious prosecution or defamation of character. Professor Winfield indeed defined "tortious liability" by saying that it

> "arises from the breach of a duty primarily fixed by law; this duty is towards persons generally and its breach is redressible by an action for unliquidated damages."

see Winfield on Tort (7th Edn.) p. 5.

In my judgment, therefore, the words "breach of duty" are wide enough to comprehend the cause of action for trespass to the person as well as negligence. In support of this view, I would refer to the decision of this court in *Billings* v. *Reed*,[2] where Lord Greene M.R. gave the phrase "breach of duty" a similar wide construction. I would also refer to the valuable judgment in Australia of Adam J. in *Kruber* v. *Grzesiak*.[3] The Australian Act is in the self-same words as ours; and I would, with gratitude, adopt his interpretation of it.

I come, therefore, to the clear conclusion that the plaintiff's cause of action here is barred by the statute of limitation. Her only cause of action here, in my judgment

---

1. [1935] A.C. 445, at pp. 458, 459; [1934] All E.R. Rep. 646, at pp. 655, 656.
2. [1945] K.B. 11; [1944] 2 All E.R. 415.
3. [1963] V.L.R. 621.

(where the damage was unintentional), was negligence and not trespass to the person. It is therefore barred by the word "negligence" in the statute; but even if it was trespass to the person, it was an action for "breach of duty" and is barred on that ground also.

I would allow the appeal accordingly.

DIPLOCK L.J.: A cause of action is simply a factual situation the existence of which entitles one person to obtain from the court a remedy against another person. Historically the means by which the remedy was obtained varied with the nature of the factual situation and causes of action were divided into categories according to the "form of action" by which the remedy was obtained in the particular kind of factual situation which constituted the cause of action; but that is legal history, not current law. If A., by failing to exercise reasonable care, inflicts direct personal injury on B., those facts constitute a cause of action on the part of B. against A. for damages in respect of such personal injuries. The remedy for this cause of action could, before 1873, have been obtained by alternative forms of action, namely, originally either trespass vi et armis or trespass on the case, later either trespass to the person or negligence. (See Bullen and Leake's *Precedents of Pleadings*, 3rd Edn.) Certain procedural consequences, the importance of which diminished considerably after the Common Law Procedure Act 1852, flowed from the plaintiff's pleader's choice of the form of action used. The Supreme Court of Judicature Act 1873, abolished forms of action. It did not affect causes of action; so it was convenient for lawyers and legislators to continue to use, to describe the various categories of factual situations which entitled one person to obtain from the court a remedy against another, the names of the various "forms of action" by which formerly the remedy appropriate to the particular category of factual situation was obtained. But it is essential to realise that when, since 1873, the name of a form of action is used to identify a cause of action, it is used as a convenient and succinct description of a particular category of factual situation which entitles one person to obtain from the court a remedy against another person. To forget this will indeed encourage the old forms of action to rule us from their graves.

If A., by failing to exercise reasonable care, inflicts direct personal injuries on B., it is permissible today to describe this factual situation indifferently, either as a cause of action in negligence or as a cause of action in trespass, and the action brought to obtain a remedy for this factual situation as an action for negligence or an action for trespass to the person—though I agree with Lord Denning M.R. that today "negligence" is the expression to be preferred. But no procedural consequences flow from the choice of description by the pleader (see *Fowler* v. *Lanning*).[1] They are simply alternative ways of describing the same factual situation.

In the judgment under appeal, Elwes J.[2] has held that the Law Reform (Limitation of Actions, etc.) Act 1954, has, by s. 2 (1) created an important difference in the remedy to which B. is entitled in the factual situation postulated according to whether he chooses to describe it as negligence or as trespass to the person. If he selects the former description, the limitation period is three years; if he selects the latter, the limitation period is six years. The terms of the subsection have already been cited, and I need not repeat them.

The factual situation on which the plaintiff's action was founded is set out in the statement of claim. It was that the defendant, by failing to exercise reasonable care (of which failure particulars were given), drove his motor car over the plaintiff's legs and so inflicted on her direct personal injuries in respect of which the plaintiff claimed damages. That factual situation was the plaintiff's cause of action. It was the cause of action "for" which the plaintiff claimed damages in respect of the personal injuries which she sustained. That cause of action or factual situation falls within the description of the tort of "negligence" and an action founded on it, that is, brought to obtain the remedy to which the existence of that factual situation entitles the plaintiff, falls within

---

1. [1959] 1 Q.B. 426; [1959] 1 All E.R. 290.
2. [1964] 1 All E.R. 669, at p. 673.

the description of an "action for negligence". The description "negligence" was in fact used by the plaintiff's pleader; but this cannot be decisive, for we are concerned not with the description applied by the pleader to the factual situation and the action founded on it, but with the description applied to it by Parliament in the enactment to be construed. It is true that that factual situation also falls within the description of the tort of "trespass to the person". But that, as I have endeavoured to show, does not mean that there are two causes of action. It merely means that there are two apt descriptions of the same cause of action. It does not cease to be the tort of "negligence", because it can also be called by another name. An action founded on it is none the less an "action for negligence" because it can also be called an "action for trespass to the person".

It is not, I think, necessary to consider whether there is today any respect in which a cause of action for unintentional as distinct from intentional "trespass to the person" is not equally aptly described as a cause of action for "negligence". The difference stressed by Elwes J.[1] that actual damage caused by failure to exercise reasonable care forms an essential element in the cause of action for "negligence", but does not in the cause of action in "trespass to the person", is, I think, more apparent than real when the trespass is unintentional; for, since the duty of care, whether in negligence or in unintentional trespass to the person, is to take reasonable care to avoid causing actual damage to one's neighbour, there is no breach of the duty unless actual damage is caused. Actual damage is thus a necessary ingredient in unintentional as distinct from intentional trespass to the person. Whether this be so or not, the subsection which falls to be construed is concerned only with actions in which actual damage in the form of personal injuries has is fact been sustained by the plaintiff. Where this factor is present, every factual situation which falls within the description "trespass to the person" is, where the trespass is unintentional, equally aptly described as negligence.

I am, therefore, of opinion that the facts pleaded in the present action make it an "action for negligence . . . where the damages claimed by the plaintiff for the negligence . . . consist of or include damages in respect of personal injuries to" the plaintiff, within the meaning of the subsection,[2] and that the limitation period was three years.

In this respect I agree with the judgment of Adam J. in the only direct authority on this point, the Victorian case of *Kruber* v. *Grzesiak*.[3] To his lucid reasoning I am much indebted. This is yet another illustration of the assistance to be obtained from the citation of relevant decisions of courts in other parts of the Commonwealth, and I am particularly grateful to counsel for the defendant and those instructing him for drawing our attention to this case. I agree, however, with my brethren and with Adam J. that this action also falls within the words "action . . . for breach of duty (whether the duty exists by virtue of a contract or of a provision made by or under a statute or independently of any contract or any such provision)". I say "also falls", for in the absence of the word "other" before "breach of duty" that expression as explained by the words in parenthesis is itself wide enough to include "negligence" and "nuisance". . . .

[DANCKWERTS L.J. agreed with LORD DENNING M.R.]

Appeal allowed

Questions

1. What do you understand by the "forms of action"?

2. Shepherd threw a lighted squib into a crowded market house where it landed on the stall of Yates, a gingerbread seller. Willis, to prevent injury to himself and Yates' wares, instantly took up the squib and threw it across the market house, where it fell upon the stall of Ryal, who, to save his own goods, in turn picked it up and threw it away. It struck the plaintiff in the face and burst,

---

1. [1964] 1 All E.R., at p. 673.
2. Law Reform (Limitation of Actions, etc.) Act 1954, s. 2 (1).
3. [1963] V.L.R. 621.

putting out one of his eyes. In *Scott* v. *Shepherd* (1773), 2 Wm. Bl. 892, the majority of the Court of King's Bench held that an action of trespass was properly brought against Shepherd. Blackstone J. (dissenting) was of the opinion that Willis and Ryal, being free agents, were not "instruments" in the hands of Shepherd, and so the damage was not sufficiently "direct" for trespass to be maintainable. How would this case be pleaded today?

3. Does an action for trespass lie if the injury, though direct, was caused neither intentionally nor by negligence?

4. D accidentally parked his car on P's foot but refused to remove it when asked several times to do so. He then relented and moved the car. How would you plead this as a civil case, assuming alternatively that (a) P's foot was injured; (b) P suffered only momentary distress but no physical injury? (cf. *Fagan* v. *Metropolitan Police Commissioner*, [1969] 1 Q.B. 439; [1968] 3 All E.R. 442.)

5. Can trespass be committed negligently? (A number of technical distinctions between negligent trespass to the person and the tort of negligence are suggested by F. A. Trinidade, "Some Curiosities of Negligent Trespass to the Person—a Comparative Study" (1971), 20 I.C.L.Q. 706, but these would probably require the English courts to depart from *Fowler* v. *Lanning* and *Letang* v. *Cooper*.)

Note

Those interested in exploring the history of trespass and case will derive pleasure from the research of Professor S. F. C. Milsom, *Historical Foundations of the Common Law* (London, 1969) Chap. 11, and his earlier articles (1958), 74 L.Q.R. 195, 407 and 561; (1965), 81 L.Q.R. 496; [1954] C.L.J. 105. M. J. Prichard, "Trespass, Case and the Rule in *Williams* v. *Holland*", [1964] C.L.J. 234 provides an illuminating account of the line of cases which decided that the action upon the case for negligence overlapped trespass.

2. BATTERY AND ASSAULT

Cole v. Turner

Nisi Prius   (1704), 6 Mod. 149

HOLT C.J.: Upon evidence in trespass for assault and battery, declared,

First, that the least touching of another in anger is a battery.

Secondly, if two or more meet in a narrow passage, and without any violence or design of harm, the one touches the other gently, it will be no battery.

Thirdly, if any of them use violence against the other, to force his way in a rude inordinate manner, it will be a battery; or any struggle about the passage to that degree as may do hurt, will be a battery . . .

Question

What do you think Holt C.J. means by the words "in anger" in his first proposition?

Innes v. Wylie

Nisi Prius   (1844), 1 Car. & Kir. 257

The plaintiff belonged to a Society which purported to expel him, and a policeman, acting under the defendants' orders, stopped the plaintiff from entering a room to attend a dinner of the Society. For reasons which need not be mentioned here, Lord Denman C.J. took the view that the expulsion was invalid, but his summing up to the jury also dealt with the question of assault.

LORD DENMAN C.J.: . . . You will say, whether, on the evidence, you think that the policeman committed an assault on the plaintiff, or was merely passive. If the policeman was entirely passive like a door or a wall put to prevent the plaintiff from entering the room, and simply obstructing the entrance of the plaintiff, no assault has been committed on the plaintiff, and your verdict will be for the defendant. The question is, did the policeman take any active measures to prevent the plaintiff from entering the room, or did he stand in the door-way passive, and not move at all.

Verdict for the plaintiff, damages 40*s*.

[A motion for a new trial was later made, but without success.]

Stephens v. Myers

Nisi Prius   (1830), 4 C. & P. 349

Assault. The declaration stated, that the defendant threatened and attempted to assault the plaintiff. Plea—Not guilty.

It appeared, that the plaintiff was acting as chairman, at a parish meeting, and sat at the head of a table, at which table the defendant also sat, there being about six or seven persons between him and the plaintiff. The defendant having, in the course of some angry discussion, which took place, been very vociferous, and interrupted the proceedings of the meeting, a motion was made, that he should be turned out, which was carried by a very large majority. Upon this, the defendant said, he would rather pull the chairman out of the chair, than be turned out of the room; and immediately advanced with his fist clenched towards the chairman, but was stopt by the churchwarden, who sat next but one to the chairman, at a time when he was not near enough for any blow he might have meditated to have reached the chairman; but the witnesses said, that it seemed to them that he was advancing with an intention to strike the chairman.

Spankie, Serjt., for the defendant, upon this evidence, contended, that no assault had been committed, as there was no power in the defendant, from the situation of the parties, to execute his threat—there was not a present ability—he had not the means of executing his intention at the time he was stopt.

TINDAL C.J. in his summing up, said—It is not every threat, when there is no actual personal violence, that constitutes an assault, there must, in all cases, be the means of carrying the threat into effect. The question I shall leave to you will be, whether the defendant was advancing at the time, in a threatening attitude, to strike the chairman, so that his blow would almost immediately have reached the chairman, if he had not been stopt; then, though he was not near enough at the time to have struck him, yet if he was advancing with that intent, I think it amounts to an assault in law. If he was so advancing, that, within a second or two of time, he would have reached the plaintiff, it seems to me it is an assault in law. If you think he was not advancing to strike the plaintiff, then only can you find your verdict for the defendant; otherwise you must find it for the plaintiff, and give him such damages, as you think the nature of the case requires.

Verdict for the plaintiff—Damages, 1*s*.

Question

Would there have been an assault in this case if the defendant "was not advancing to strike the plaintiff", but the plaintiff reasonably believed that he was?

Note

A particular problem which has arisen in this context is whether it is an assault to point a gun at a person when that gun is unloaded. In *R* v. *St. George* (1840), 9 C. & P. 483, a criminal case, Parke B. stated in the course of argument (at p. 490), that "it is an assault to point a weapon at a person, though not loaded, but so near, that if loaded, it might do injury" (see also p. 493). Whether the *ratio decidendi* of the case covers this point is a matter on which the text books differ—Winfield and Jolowicz, p. 33; Smith and Hogan, *op. cit.*, p. 282, note 13; Street, p. 22. The view of Lord Abinger C.B. in *Blake v. Barnard* (1840), 9 C. & P. 626 is in conflict with that of Parke B. but the *ratio* of this case is also disputed—see Winfield and Jolowicz, p. 33, note 28, and Street, p. 21, note 5.

Tuberville v. Savage

Court of King's Bench   (1699), 1 Mod. 3

Action of *assault, battery* and *wounding.* The evidence to prove a provocation was, that the plaintiff put his hand upon his sword and said, "*If it were not assize-time, I would not take such language from you.*"—The question was, If that were an assault?—The Court agreed that it was not; for the declaration of the plaintiff was, that he would not assault him, the Judges being in town; and *the intention* as well as *the act* makes an assault. Therefore if one strike another upon the hand, or arm, or breast in discourse, it is no assault, there being no *intention* to assault; but if one, intending to assault, strike *at* another and miss him, this is an assault: so if he hold up his hand against another in a threatening manner and say nothing, it is an assault.—In the principal case the plaintiff had judgment.

Question

Would there have been an assault if, as both parties knew, the assizes were ending that day?

Note

As *Tuberville* v. *Savage* shows, words accompanying an act may lead the court to deny that there has been any assault, but there is a conflict of authority on the question whether words alone can amount to an assault. Compare *Meade and Belt's Case* (1823), 1 Lewin 184, where Holroyd J. denied that words were "equivalent to an assault", with *R.* v. *Wilson*, [1955] 1 All E.R. 744, at p. 745: "He called out 'Get out knives', which itself would be an assault..." (*per* Lord Goddard C.J.). Both were criminal cases. See generally Glanville Williams, "Assault and Words", [1957] Crim. L.R. 219.

The Offences Against the Person Act 1861

44. If the magistrates shall dismiss any complaint of assault or battery, they shall make out a certificate to that effect.—If the justices, upon the hearing of any such case of assault or battery upon the merits, where the complaint[1] was preferred by or on behalf of the party aggrieved, under either of the last two preceding sections,[2] shall deem the offence not to be proved, or shall find the assault or battery to have been justified, or so trifling as not to merit any punishment, and shall accordingly dismiss the complaint,[1] they shall forthwith make out a certificate under their hands stating the fact of such dismissal, and shall deliver such certificate to the party against whom the complaint[1] was preferred.

45. Certificate or conviction shall be a bar to any other proceedings.—If any

---

1. [The word should now be read as "information"—Magistrates' Courts Act 1952, s. 42.]
2. [These sections deal with magistrates hearing and determining cases of common assault or battery or cases of aggravated assaults on boys under the age of 14 and females.]

person against whom any such complaint[1] as in either of the last three preceding sections mentioned shall have been preferred by or on the behalf of the party aggrieved shall have obtained such certificate, or, having been convicted, shall have paid the whole amount adjudged to be paid, or shall have suffered the imprisonment or imprisonment with hard labour[2] awarded, in every such case he shall be released from all further or other proceedings, civil or criminal, for the same cause.

Notes

1. The problems of interpretation of these provisions are considered by P. M. North, "Civil and Criminal Proceedings for Assault" (1966), 29 M.L.R. 16 who points out incidentally that the rule which bars later civil proceedings "can easily be evaded by the simple expedient of suing first and making a complaint later". He concludes (at p. 31): "The moral is: sue first. This does not detract from the conclusion that section 45 does appear to be based upon the fallacious assumption that the rules of civil and criminal liability for assault and battery are identical."

2. Under s. 1 of the Criminal Justice Act 1972, where a person is convicted of an offence, the court may "make an order . . . requiring him to pay compensation for any personal injury, loss or damage resulting from that offence or any other offence which is taken into consideration by the court in determining sentence". (Subsection 3, however, forbids the making of such compensation orders for the loss suffered by the dependants of a person as a result of that person's death. It also forbids such orders where injury, loss or damage is "due to an accident arising out of the presence of a motor vehicle on a road", although excepting certain cases of property damage.) Where later civil proceedings are brought, no attention should be paid to an earlier compensation order in assessing the damages but the amount paid under such an order is taken into account in the awarding of such damages (s. 4). Note also, in relation to magistrates' courts, the limits imposed by s. 1 (5). These provisions will be replaced by the Powers of Criminal Courts Act 1973, when that Act comes into force on 1 July 1973.

3. A person who has been intentionally injured may recover compensation from the Criminal Injuries Compensation Board; but note para. 24 of the scheme, p. 701, *post*.

3. FALSE IMPRISONMENT

Herring v. Boyle

Court of Exchequer (1834), 1 Cr. M. & R. 377

The facts of this case appear in the judgment of Bolland B. The plaintiff had been nonsuited at the trial of the action, and a rule which was obtained to set aside the nonsuit and for a new trial was discharged by the Court of Exchequer.

BOLLAND B.: This was an action of trespass for assault and false imprisonment, brought by an infant by his next friend. The facts of the case were these: the plaintiff had been placed by his mother at the school kept by the defendant, and it appeared that she had applied to take him away. The schoolmaster very improperly refused to give him up to his mother, unless she paid an amount which he claimed to be due. The question is, whether it appears upon the Judge's notes that there was any evidence of a

1. [The word should now be read as "information"—Magistrates' Courts Act 1952, s. 42.]
2. [The courts may no longer sentence to imprisonment with hard labour: Criminal Justice Act 1948, s. 1 (2).]

trespass to go to the jury? I am of opinion that there was not, and, consequently, that this rule must be discharged. It has been argued on the part of the plaintiff that the misconduct of the defendant amounted to a false imprisonment. I cannot find any thing upon the notes of the learned Judge which shews that the plaintiff was at all cognizant of any restraint. There are many cases which shew that it is not necessary, to constitute an imprisonment, that the hand should be laid upon the person; but in no case has any conduct been held to amount to an imprisonment in the absence of the party supposed to be imprisoned. An officer may make an arrest without laying his hand on the party arrested; but in the present case, as far as we know, the boy may have been willing to stay; he does not appear to have been cognizant of any restraint, and there was no evidence of any act whatsoever done by the defendant in his presence. I think that we cannot construe the refusal to the mother in the boy's absence, and without his being cognizant of any restraint, to be an imprisonment of him against his will; and therefore I am of opinion that the rule must be discharged.

[ALDERSON B. and GURNEY B., delivered judgments in favour of discharging the rule. PARKE B. and LORD LYNDHURST concurred.]

Meering v. Grahame-White Aviation Co., Ltd.

Court of Appeal   (1920), 122 L.T. 44

The plaintiff, an employee of the defendant company, lived in a bedroom of Rose Cottage, which was occupied by Lamb, another employee of the company. There had been several thefts of materials from the company, and the cottage was searched under a magistrate's warrant by Askew and Burgess (detective officers of the Metropolitan Police), and after the search Lamb was arrested. A sergeant of the works police, Prudence, was told that the plaintiff was wanted for questioning at the company's offices, and he instructed two of the works police to inform the plaintiff of this. The plaintiff, accompanied by these two men, went to the offices and was taken or invited to go to the waiting room. He said that if he was not told what he was there for and why he was wanted, he would go away, but was informed that he was wanted for the purpose of inquiries as things had been stolen and he was wanted to give evidence. Having been told this he stayed. Three members of the works police remained on duty in the neighbourhood of the waiting room until the Metropolitan Police arrived. The plaintiff was later arrested by the Metropolitan Police, and subsequently brought an action for damages for false imprisonment and malicious prosecution. Only the former claim is dealt with here. In his statement of claim the plaintiff alleged imprisonment by the Metropolitan Police, acting at the defendant's instance and under their direction or at their request, but at the trial the question of false imprisonment by the defendants' servants was also raised. The extracts below deal with the question of knowledge of restraint, in relation to the defendants' servants' acts.

DUKE L.J. (dissenting on the question of false imprisonment) . . . Can it be said upon what is affirmatively proved here that there is evidence upon which the jury could act that the plaintiff was so restrained as that he had not his liberty freely to go whither he would? To my mind there is a conclusive fact proved in the case with regard to that matter, which is, that the plaintiff himself does not show the slightest indication of a suspicion that he was restrained of his liberty to go if he had thought fit to go.

. . . cases of false imprisonment and malicious prosecution are not of uncommon occurrence, and the fact of imprisonment is a fact which very often has to be ascertained, and I can only say on my own part that in my opinion there is not in this case, taking the whole of the evidence together, any proof upon which a jury was reasonably warranted in finding that the plaintiff was imprisoned by the defendants in their office.

ATKIN L.J.: . . . it is said that inasmuch as the plaintiff did not know that he was being imprisoned it is not possible that there could be evidence that he was imprisoned. I think that the case is important when that contention is to be dealt with, because it seems to me upon a review of the possibilities of what is meant by imprisonment, that it is perfectly possible for a person to be imprisoned in law without his knowing the fact and appreciating that he is imprisoned. . . .

It appears to me that a person could be imprisoned without his knowing it. I think a person can be imprisoned while he is asleep, while he is in a state of drunkenness, while he is unconscious, and while he is a lunatic. Those are cases where it seems to me that the person might properly complain if he were imprisoned, though the imprisonment began and ceased while he was in that state. Of course, the damages might be diminished and would be affected by the question whether he was conscious of it or not.

So a man might in fact, to my mind, be imprisoned by having the key of a door turned against him so that he is imprisoned in a room in fact although he does not know that the key has been turned. It may be that he is being detained in that room by persons who are anxious to make him believe that he is not in fact being imprisoned, and at the same time his captors outside that room may be boasting to persons that he is imprisoned, and it seems to me that if we were to take this case as an instance supposing it could be proved that Prudence had said while the plaintiff was waiting: "I have got him detained there waiting for the detective to come in and take him to prison"—it appears to me that that would be evidence of imprisonment. It is quite unnecessary to go on to show that in fact the man knew that he was imprisoned.

If a man can be imprisoned by having the key turned upon him without his know-ledge, so he can be imprisoned if, instead of a lock and key or bolts and bars, he is prevented from, in fact, exercising his liberty by guards and warders or policemen. They serve the same purpose. Therefore it appears to me to be a question of fact. It is true that in all cases of imprisonment so far as the law of civil liability is concerned that "stone walls do not a prison make", in the sense that they are not the only form of imprisonment, but any restraint within defined bounds which is a restraint in fact may be an imprisonment.

Under those circumstances, it appears to me that the sole issue in this case is whether there is evidence upon which the jury could find, quite apart from the plaintiff's knowledge of what the real fact was—that he was in fact imprisoned in the sense which I have mentioned, so that his liberty was in fact restrained; so that he was substantially in the same position as if the key had been turned in the door of the waiting-room where he was in fact waiting.

I think that there is evidence. . . .

[WARRINGTON L.J. did not discuss whether a person must be aware of any imprison-ment. He held that there was ample evidence to justify the jury's conclusion that the company's officers had detained the plaintiff, and decided that there had been a false imprisonment.]

Question

A is wandering around in a drunken condition. B locks him up in a small room to sleep it off, but A, who is not aware that he is locked in, lurches into the wall and knocks himself unconscious. B finds him the next morning still unconscious. If A gets to know what has happened, has he any action against B? (See W. L. Prosser, "False Imprisonment: Consciousness of Confinement" (1955), 55 Columbia L.R. 847.)

Note

The American *Restatement of the Law of Torts* (2nd), § 35, requires that the person confined "is conscious of the confinement or is harmed by it", before there can be liability for false imprisonment. (See further § 42.)

Bird v. Jones

Court of Queen's Bench   (1847), 7 Q.B. 742

The following statement of facts is taken from the judgment of Patteson J.: "A part of Hammersmith Bridge which is ordinarily used as a public footway was appropriated for seats to view a regatta on the river, and separated for that purpose from the carriage way by a temporary fence. The plaintiff insisted on passing along the part so appropriated, and attempted to climb over the fence. The defendant, being clerk of the Bridge Company, seized his coat, and tried to pull him back: the plaintiff, however, succeeded in climbing over the fence. The defendant then stationed two policemen to prevent, and they did prevent, the plaintiff from proceeding forwards along the foot-way; but he was told that he might go back into the carriage way, and proceed to the other side of the bridge, if he pleased. The plaintiff would not do so, but remained where he was above half an hour: and then, on the defendant still refusing to suffer him to go forwards along the footway, he endeavoured to force his way, and, in so doing, assaulted the defendant: whereupon he was taken into custody." By virtue of the pleadings in the case, the question arose whether there had been an imprisonment of the plaintiff before he committed the assault. At the trial the Lord Chief Justice told the jury that there had, and a rule nisi for a new trial was obtained on the ground of misdirection:

COLERIDGE J.: . . . And I am of opinion that there was no imprisonment. To call it so appears to me to confound partial obstruction and disturbance with total obstruction and detention. A prison may have its boundary large or narrow, visible and tangible, or, though real, still in the conception only; it may itself be moveable or fixed: but a boundary it must have; and that boundary the party imprisoned must be prevented from passing; he must be prevented from leaving that place, within the ambit of which the party imprisoning would confine him, except by prison-breach. Some confusion seems to me to arise from confounding imprisonment of the body with mere loss of freedom: it is one part of the definition of freedom to be able to go whithersoever one pleases; but imprisonment is something more than the mere loss of this power; it includes the notion of restraint within some limits defined by a will or power exterior to our own.

. . . If, in the course of a night, both ends of a street were walled up, and there was no egress from the house but into the street, I should have no difficulty in saying that the inhabitants were thereby imprisoned; but, if only one end were walled up, and an armed force stationed outside to prevent any scaling of the wall or passage that way, I should feel equally clear that there was no imprisonment. If there were, the street would obviously be the prison; and yet, as obviously, none would be confined to it.

Knowing that my Lord has entertained strongly an opinion directly contrary to this, I am under serious apprehension that I overlook some difficulty in forming my own: but, if it exists, I have not been able to discover it, and am therefore bound to state that, according to my view of the case, the rule should be absolute for a new trial.

PATTESON J.: . . . But imprisonment is, as I apprehend, a total restraint of the liberty of the person, for however short a time, and not a partial obstruction of his will, whatever inconvenience it may bring on him. . . .

LORD DENMAN C.J. (dissenting): . . . I had no idea that any person in these times supposed any particular boundary to be necessary to constitute imprisonment, or that the restraint of a man's person from doing what he desires ceases to be an imprisonment because he may find some means of escape.

It is said that the party here was at liberty to go in another direction. I am not sure that in fact he was, because the same unlawful power which prevented him from taking one course might, in case of acquiescence, have refused him any other. But this liberty to do something else does not appear to me to affect the question of imprisonment. As long as I am prevented from doing what I have a right to do, of what importance is it that I am permitted to do something else? How does the imposition of an unlawful condition shew that I am not restrained? If I am locked in a room, am I not imprisoned because I might effect my escape through a window, or because I might find an exit dangerous or inconvenient to myself, as by wading through water or by taking a route so circuitous that my necessary affairs would suffer by delay?

It appears to me that this is a total deprivation of liberty with reference to the purpose for which he lawfully wished to employ his liberty: and, being effected by force, it is not the mere obstruction of a way, but a restraint of the person. . . .

[WILLIAMS J. also delivered a judgment to the effect that there was no imprisonment on these facts.]

Rule made absolute

Robinson v. Balmain New Ferry Co., Ltd.

Judicial Committee of the Privy Council   [1910] A.C. 295

The plaintiff, who intended to cross a harbour on the defendant company's ferry, paid one penny to enter the company's wharf. Between the wharf and the street there was a barrier with two turnstiles, and a notice board (above the turnstiles and on each side of the barrier) stated that a penny must be paid on entering or leaving the wharf, whether or not the passenger had used the ferry. The practice of the company was to collect fares on one side of the harbour only. The plaintiff, who had gone through the entry turnstile, discovered that there would be a 20 minute wait before the next steamer left, and, wishing to leave the wharf, he approached the exit turnstile. He refused to pay a penny, however, and was prevented from forcing his way out for some time by two of the company's officers. On appeal from a decision of the High Court of Australia by the plaintiff who claimed damages for assault and false imprisonment:

LORD LOREBURN L.C. (delivering the judgment of their Lordships): . . . There was no complaint, at all events there was no question left to the jury by the plaintiff's request, of any excessive violence, and in the circumstances admitted it is clear to their Lordships that there was no false imprisonment at all. The plaintiff was merely called upon to leave the wharf in the way in which he contracted to leave it. There is no law requiring the defendants to make the exit from their premises gratuitous to people who come there upon a definite contract which involves their leaving the wharf by another way; and the defendants were entitled to resist a forcible passage through their turnstile.

The question whether the notice which was affixed to these premises was brought home to the knowledge of the plaintiff is immaterial, because the notice itself is immaterial.

When the plaintiff entered the defendants' premises there was nothing agreed as to the terms on which he might go back, because neither party contemplated his going back. When he desired to do so the defendants were entitled to impose a reasonable condition before allowing him to pass through their turnstile from a place to which he had gone of his own free will. The payment of a penny was a quite fair condition, and if he did not choose to comply with it the defendants were not bound to let him through. He could proceed on the journey he had contracted for. . . .

Their Lordships will humbly advise His Majesty that this appeal should be dismissed with costs.

Question

Why was the notice immaterial?

Herd v. Weardale Steel, Coal and Coke Co., Ltd.

House of Lords   [1915] A.C. 67

The appellant (and his fellow workers) descended the respondent company's mine at 9.30 a.m. and he would have been entitled to be raised to the surface at the end of his shift (about 4 p.m.) by a cage which was used at other times to carry coal. The cage was, in fact, the only way out of the mine. The appellant, whose verbal contract of service provided for 14 days notice on either side, refused to do certain work which he had been told to do on the grounds that it was unsafe, and also that the instruction was in breach of an oral agreement between the men's representative and the colliery manager. At about 11 a.m. he asked to be allowed to use the cage, but this request was refused. The appellant was not allowed to use the cage until approximately 1.30 p.m., although it had been standing at the bottom of the mine shaft since 1.10 p.m. and could have been used to carry him to the surface. He was employed subject to the provisions of the Coal Mines Regulation Acts 1887–1908, certain rules established under the 1887 Act and an agreement between the Durham Coal Owners' Association and the Durham Miners' Association. One of the terms of his contract was that he should be raised from the mine at the end of his shift, and a notice containing the times of raising and lowering, which had been fixed under the 1887 Act and the agreement, was posted at the pit head. In an earlier action the company were awarded 5s. damages for the appellant's breach of contract. The appellant sued for damages for false imprisonment, but Pickford J.'s judgment in his favour was reversed by the Court of Appeal, [1913] 3 K.B. 771. An appeal to the House of Lords was dismissed.

VISCOUNT HALDANE L.C.: My Lords, by the law of this country no man can be restrained of his liberty without authority in law. That is a proposition the maintenance of which is of great importance; but at the same time it is a proposition which must be read in relation to other propositions which are equally important. If a man chooses to go into a dangerous place at the bottom of a quarry or the bottom of a mine, from which by the nature of physical circumstances he cannot escape, it does not follow from the proposition I have enunciated about liberty that he can compel the owner to bring him up out of it. The owner may or may not be under a duty arising from circumstances, on broad grounds the neglect of which may possibly involve him in a criminal charge or a civil liability. It is unnecessary to discuss the conditions and circumstances which might bring about such a result, because they have, in the view I take, nothing to do with false imprisonment.

My Lords, there is another proposition which has to be borne in mind and that is the application of the maxim volenti non fit injuria. If a man gets into an express train and the doors are locked pending its arrival at its destination, he is not entitled, merely because the train has been stopped by signal, to call for the doors to be opened to let him out. He has entered the train on the terms that he is to be conveyed to a certain station without the opportunity of getting out before that, and he must abide by the terms on which he has entered the train. So when a man goes down a mine, from which access to the surface does not exist in the absence of special facilities given on the part of the owner of the mine, he is only entitled to the use of these facilities (subject possibly to the exceptional circumstances to which I have alluded) on the terms on which he has entered. I think it results from what was laid down by the Judicial Committee of the Privy Council in *Robinson* v. *Balmain New Ferry Co.*[1] that that is so. There there was a pier, and by the regulations a penny was to be paid by those who entered and a penny on getting out. The manager of the exit gate refused to allow a man who had gone in, having paid his penny, but having changed his mind about embarking on a steamer, and wishing to return, to come out without paying his penny. It was held that that was not false imprisonment; volenti non fit injuria. The man had gone in upon the pier knowing that those were the terms and conditions as to exit, and it was not

---

1. [1910] A.C. 295.

false imprisonment to hold him to conditions which he had accepted. So, my Lords, it is not false imprisonment to hold a man to the conditions he has accepted when he goes down a mine.

My Lords, I do not wish to be understood as saying that no other question than that of contract comes into this case, for the Coal Mines Regulation Act 1887 lays down a statutory obligation on the owner of mines to provide access to the surface, and it lays down conditions as regards the availability of that access. But the material point is this: that on considering the provisions of that statute I find nothing which entitles a miner to claim to use the winding-up cage at any moment he pleases. It may be that the cage is full of coal; it may be that it is employed in drawing other people up; it may be that it it very inconvenient for other reasons to use it at the moment. It is enough that no right is given by statute which enables the workman to claim to use the cage at any moment he pleases.

Now, my Lords, in the present case what happened was this. The usage of the mine—a usage which I think must be taken to have been notified—was that the workman was to be brought up at the end of his shift. In this case the workman refused to work; it may have been for good reasons or it may have been for bad,—I do not think that question concerns us. He said that the work he had been ordered to do was of a kind that was dangerous, and he threw down his tools and claimed to come up to the surface. The manager, or at any rate the person responsible for the control of the cage, said: "No, you have chosen to come at a time which is not your proper time, and although there is the cage standing empty we will not bring you up in it," and the workman was in consequence under the necessity of remaining at the bottom of the shaft for about twenty minutes. There was no refusal to bring him up at the ordinary time which was in his bargain; but there was a refusal,—and I am quite ready to assume that the motive of it was to punish him, I will assume it for the sake of argument, for having refused to go on with his work—by refusing to bring him up at the moment when he claimed to come. Did that amount to false imprisonment? In my opinion it did not. No statutory right under the Coal Mines Regulation Act 1887 avails him, for the reason which I have already spoken of. Nor had he any right in contract. His right in contract was to come up at the end of his shift. Was he then falsely imprisoned? There were facilities, but they were facilities which, in accordance with the conditions that he had accepted by going down, were not available to him until the end of his shift, at any rate as of right.

My Lords, under these circumstances I find it wholly impossible to come to the conclusion that the principle to which I have alluded, and on which the doctrine of false imprisonment is based, has any application to the case. Volenti non fit injuria. The man chose to go to the bottom of the mine under these conditions,—conditions which he accepted. He had no right to call upon the employers to make use of special machinery put there at their cost, and involving cost in its working, to bring him to the surface just when he pleased. . . .

[LORD SHAW OF DUNFERMLINE and LORD MOULTON delivered speeches in favour of dismissing the appeal.]

Question

1. Does Viscount Haldane's explanation of *Robinson's* case accord with what is stated in that case? (See M. S. Amos (1928), 44 L.Q.R. 464, at pp. 465–466.)

2. Once the miners got to the surface would it have been false imprisonment for the respondent to have stopped them leaving the colliery before the end of their shift by (a) refusing to unlock the gates of the pit yard or (b) locking those gates? (See *Burns* v. *Johnston*, [1916] 2 I.R. 444; affd., [1917] 2 I.R. 137, C.A., cited by Glanville Williams, *Law, Justice and Equity*, Chap. 5, an essay which discusses both *Herd's* case and *Robinson's* case.)

Note

In his essay entitled "Two Cases on False Imprisonment" (*loc. cit.*), Glanville Williams concludes that "*Robinson's* case is of small general interest because it is confined to a situation that is not likely to occur frequently. A condition may be attached to exit, but only when the plaintiff has a choice of two exits, A and B, the condition being attached to A. Further, no condition may be attached when exit B is extremely onerous. . . . Nor does the decision apply when the condition attached to exit A is unreasonable, unless exit B gives practically immediate freedom. If exit B is in an intermediate position, neither being extremely onerous nor giving practically immediate freedom, the reasonableness of the condition attached to exit A becomes relevant; and this is the only case where it is relevant."

Christie v. Leachinsky

House of Lords   [1947] 1 All E.R. 567

The appellants, police officers, had arrested the respondent in Liverpool on a charge of "unlawful possession" of cloth under the Liverpool Corporation Act 1921. There was in fact no power of arrest under that Act in the circumstances of the case, but in this later action for false imprisonment, the officers pleaded that they had reasonably suspected the respondent of having stolen or feloniously received the bale of cloth. However, it did not appear that the respondent was told that this was the ground for his arrest. Subsequently, the charge of "unlawful possession" was withdrawn, but the respondent was further detained and later charged with larceny. At his trial he was acquitted. In the course of considering the first arrest, which was held to be invalid, Viscount Simon stated that, in his view, the following propositions were established:

1. If a policeman arrests without warrant on reasonable suspicion of felony,[1] or of other crime of a sort which does not require a warrant, he must in ordinary circumstances inform the person arrested of the true ground of arrest. He is not entitled to keep the reason to himself or to give a reason which is not the true reason. In other words, a citizen is entitled to know on what charge or on suspicion of what crime he is seized.

2. If the citizen is not so informed, but is nevertheless seized, the policeman, apart from certain exceptions, is liable for false imprisonment.

3. The requirement that the person arrested should be informed of the reason why he is seized naturally does not exist if the circumstances are such that he must know the general nature of the alleged offence for which he is detained.

4. The requirement that he should be so informed does not mean that technical or precise language need be used. The matter is a matter of substance, and turns on the elementary proposition that in this country a person is, *prima facie*, entitled to his freedom and is only required to submit to restraint on his freedom if he knows in substance the reason why it is claimed that this restraint should be imposed.

5. The person arrested cannot complain that he has not been supplied with the above information as and when he should be, if he himself produces the situation which makes it practically impossible to inform him, e.g. by immediate counter-attack or by running away.

There may well be other exceptions to the general rule in addition to those I have indicated, and the above propositions are not intended to constitute a formal or complete code, but to indicate the general principles of our law on a very important matter. These principles equally apply to a private person who arrests on suspicion. If a

---

1. [See p. 25, *ante.*]

policeman who entertained a reasonable suspicion that X had committed a felony[1] were at liberty to arrest him and march him off to a police station without giving any explanation of why he was doing this, the *prima facie* right of personal liberty would be gravely infringed. No one, I think, would approve a situation in which, when the person arrested asked for the reason, the policeman replied: "That has nothing to do with you. Come along with me." Such a situation may be tolerated under other systems of law, as, for instance, in the time of *lettres de cachet* in the eighteenth century in France, or in more recent days when the Gestapo swept people off to confinement under an overriding authority which the executive in this country happily does not in ordinary times possess. This would be quite contrary to our conceptions of individual liberty. . . .

[LORD SIMONDS and LORD DU PARCQ delivered speeches in which they agreed with VISCOUNT SIMON on this point. LORD THANKERTON and LORD MACMILLAN concurred.

John Lewis and Co., Ltd. v. Tims

House of Lords   [1952] 1 All E.R. 1203

Mrs. Tims (the respondent) and her daughter were suspected of stealing calendars from the appellants' store. After they had visited another store, one of the appellants' store detectives asserted that they had stolen the calendars and they were taken back to the appellants' store. They were kept against their will in the chief store detective's office until the chief store detective and a managing director had been summoned and informed of the circumstances of the case. There was some dispute over the length of the detention, but it was not suggested that it was other than was reasonable to inform a director or manager of the details of the case and to get his direction as to whether to prosecute or not. The respondent was later charged at the police station, but the charge was subsequently withdrawn. An appeal from the Court of Appeal, [1951] 1 All E.R. 814, holding that there had been a false imprisonment by the appellants, was allowed by the House of Lords.

LORD PORTER: . . . There remains only the question, therefore, whether the appellants were rightly mulcted in damages for false imprisonment because their servants did not take the respondent immediately before a magistrate, but brought her back to a part of the appellants' premises. It was maintained on her behalf that, though an arrest might originally be justified, yet it became wrongful if the person accused was not taken forthwith before a justice of the peace. The appellants admitted that they could not retain her for an unreasonable time before handing her over to a constable or a jailor, or bringing her before a justice, but contended that their obligation was only to act within a reasonable time and that an immediate and direct journey to the magistrate's court was not required. Of the three courses which the respondents asserted were open to them commitment to prison may today be neglected. The accused would not be received nor would the prison be available. The choice lies between an immediate bringing before a magistrate or, possibly, handing over to a police officer, and the like course taken within a reasonable time. As I have said, if the latter is the true obligation and if the appellants' representatives were justified in bringing back the respondent to the appellants' premises to get the advice of a manager and to obtain, if he thought fit, his authority to prosecute, there is no ground for saying that the time taken was unreasonable. But it is said on behalf of the respondent that it is not enough for the arrester to bring the person whom he has arrested before a justice or the police within a reasonable time: he must be brought before them "immediately" or "forthwith". If not, the arrest is wrongful. . . .

Before I analyse the cases and consider the history and principles which lie behind the problem presented to your Lordships, it is, I think, expedient to set out the grounds on which the appellants justify their action. It is undesirable, they say, that their detectives, who must of necessity be subordinate officials, should be entrusted with the

---

1. [See p. 25, *ante*.]

final decision whether a prosecution should take place or not. Such a decision should only rest with a senior and responsible officer, and after he has heard any explanation which the accused person has to offer. Indeed, it is in the interest of the person arrested that, however conclusive the evidence should appear against him, he should have the opportunity of stating what he has to say and that, in a proper case, he should avoid the publicity of a public trial. The complaint here is not that the appellants acted unreasonably or harshly or detained the respondent for an unnecessarily long time, but only that it is the law and expedient in the interests of the public generally that the supposed criminal should be brought before the court as speedily as possible and afforded the opportunity of applying for, and being granted, bail. . . .

What the common law requires is that, if a man be arrested on suspicion of felony, he should be taken before a tribunal which can deal with his case expeditiously. The question throughout should be: Has the arrester brought the arrested person to a place where his alleged offence can be dealt with as speedily as is reasonably possible? But all the circumstances in the case must be taken into consideration in deciding whether this requirement is complied with. A direct route and a rapid progress are, no doubt, matters for consideration, but they are not the only matters. Those who arrest must be persuaded of the guilt of the accused; they cannot bolster up their assurance or the strength of the case by seeking further evidence and detaining the man arrested meanwhile or taking him to some spot where they can or may find further evidence. But there are advantages in refusing to give private detectives a free hand and leaving the determination of whether to prosecute or not to a superior official. Whether there is evidence that the steps taken were unreasonable or the delay too great is a matter for the judge. Whether, if there be such evidence, the delay was in fact too great is for the jury: see *Cave* v. *Mountain* (1840), 1 Man. & G. 257. In the present case the complaint was, as I have said, not that the detention was too long, but that a direct route from the place of arrest to the magistrate's court had not been taken. In my opinion, that is not the vital question. Rather it is whether, in all the circumstances, the accused person has been brought before a justice of the peace within a reasonable time, it being always remembered that that time should be as short as is reasonably practicable. I would allow the appeal.

[Lord Oaksey and Lord Cohen agreed with Lord Porter's speech. Lord Reid concurred and Lord Morton of Henryton delivered a speech in favour of allowing the appeal.]

Notes

1. The position of the police in this context should be noted. In *Dallison* v. *Caffery*, [1965] 1 Q.B. 348; [1964] 2 All E.R. 610 Lord Denning M.R. with whom Danckwerts L.J. agreed, stated that a constable had greater powers than a private citizen and could take reasonable steps to investigate the matter when he had taken someone into custody—e.g. the holding of identification parades. Cf. *Wright* v. *Court* (1825), 4 B. & C. 596.

2. In *John Lewis & Co., Ltd.* v. *Tims*, it appeared that the mother was deaf. The relevance of her deafness to the arrest was only briefly mentioned by Lord Porter (in a passage which has been omitted), and in fact was more fully discussed by the Court of Appeal, [1951] 2 K.B. 459; [1951] 1 All E.R. 814. The views expressed in *John Lewis & Co., Ltd.* v. *Tims* were recently followed in *Wheatley* v. *Lodge*, [1971] 1 All E.R. 173 in which the court stated (at pp. 178–179) that "if a police officer arrests a deaf person or somebody who cannot speak English, what he has to do is to do what a reasonable person would do in the circumstances". This rule, therefore, constitutes a further exception to the general rule in *Christie* v. *Leachinsky*, [1947] A.C. 573; [1947] 1 All E.R. 567.

The Criminal Law Act 1967

1. Abolition of distinction between felony and misdemeanour.—(1) All distinctions between felony and misdemeanour are hereby abolished.

(2) Subject to the provisions of this Act, on all matters on which a distinction has previously been made between felony and misdemeanour, including mode of trial, the law and practice in relation to all offences cognisable under the law of England and Wales (including piracy) shall be the law and practice applicable at the commencement of this Act in relation to misdemeanour.

2. Arrest without warrant.—(1) The powers of summary arrest conferred by the following subsections shall apply to offences for which the sentence is fixed by law or for which a person (not previously convicted) may under or by virtue of any enactment be sentenced to imprisonment for a term of five years, and to attempts to commit any such offence; and in this Act, including any amendment made by this Act in any other enactment, "arrestable offence" means any such offence or attempt.

(2) Any person may arrest without warrant anyone who is, or whom he, with reasonable cause, suspects to be, in the act of committing an arrestable offence.

(3) Where an arrestable offence has been committed, any person may arrest without warrant anyone who is, or whom he, with reasonable cause, suspects to be, guilty of the offence.

(4) Where a constable, with reasonable cause, suspects that an arrestable offence has been committed, he may arrest without warrant anyone whom he, with reasonable cause, suspects to be guilty of the offence.

(5) A constable may arrest without warrant any person who is, or whom he, with reasonable cause, suspects to be, about to commit an arrestable offence.

(6) For the purpose of arresting a person under any power conferred by this section a constable may enter (if need be, by force) and search any place where that person is or where the constable, with reasonable cause, suspects him to be.

(7) This section shall not affect the operation of any enactment restricting the institution of proceedings for an offence, nor prejudice any power of arrest conferred by law apart from this section.

3. Use of force in making arrest, etc.—(1) A person may use such force as is reasonable in the circumstances in the prevention of crime, or in effecting or assisting in the lawful arrest of offenders or suspected offenders or of persons unlawfully at large.

(2) Subsection (1) above shall replace the rules of the common law on the question when force used for a purpose mentioned in the subsection is justified by that purpose.

Question

Why should the private citizen who arrests a person whom he reasonably believes to have committed an arrestable offence, be liable to an action for false imprisonment if it transpires that no arrestable offence has been committed?

Note

It is clear that a person need not be seized to be arrested, but too much courtesy on the part of the arrester may lead a court to deny that there has been an arrest. For example, in *Alderson v. Booth*, [1969] 2 Q.B. 216; [1969] 2 All E.R. 271 the defendant had been involved in a road accident and was required to take a breath-test, which proved positive. Having informed the defendant of this fact, the police constable said "I shall have to ask you to come to the police station for further tests", and the defendant went with the police constable to the police station where, after another breath-test had proved positive, the defendant gave a sample of blood. The prosecution had to prove that the blood specimen was taken from the defendant after he had been lawfully arrested (s. 3 (I) of the Road Safety Act 1967—see now s. 9 (I) of the Road Traffic Act 1972), and the justices, dismissing the information, did not think that the defendant had been arrested. They took the view that it had not been made clear to the defendant that he was under *compulsion* to go to the police station. The Divisional Court declined to interfere with that finding, and dismissed the appeal. The Court of Appeal has recently stressed that in arrest cases there is no "magic formula", but that it should be made clear to the person in question that he has lost his freedom—*R.* v. *Inwood*, [1973] 2 All E.R. 645. Cf. *Wheatley* v. *Lodge*, [1971] I All E.R. 173; p. 48, *ante*.

4. WRONGFUL INTERFERENCE

Wilkinson v. Downton

Queen's Bench Division   [1895–99] All E.R. Rep. 267

WRIGHT J.: read a judgment in which he referred to the plaintiff's allegations, in the statement of claim, and continued: The defendant, in the execution of what he seems to have regarded as a practical joke, represented to the female plaintiff that he was charged by her husband with a message to her to the effect that the husband had been smashed up in an accident, and was lying at the Elms public-house at Leytonstone with both legs broken, and that she was to go at once in a cab to fetch him home. All this was false. The effect of this statement on the female plaintiff was a violent shock to the nervous system producing vomiting and other more serious and permanent physical consequences, at one time threatening her reason and entailing weeks of suffering and incapacity to her as well as expense to her husband for medical treatment of her. These consequences were not in any way the result of previous ill-health or weakness of constitution, nor was there any evidence of predisposition to nervous shock or of any other idiosyncrasy. In addition to these matters of substance there is a small claim for 1*s*. 10½*d*. for the cost of railway fares of persons sent by the female plaintiff to Leytonstone in obedience to the pretended message. As to this 1*s*. 10½*d*. expended in railway fares on the faith of the defendant's statement, it is clearly within the scope of the decision in *Pasley* v. *Freeman*.[1] It was a misrepresentation intended to be acted on to the damage of the plaintiff.

The real question is as to the £100, the greatest part of which is given as compensation for the female plaintiff's illness and suffering. It was argued for her that she is entitled to recover this as being damage caused by fraud, and, therefore, within the doctrine established by *Pasley* v. *Freeman*[1] and *Langridge* v. *Levy*.[2] I am not sure that this would not be an extension of that doctrine, the real ground of which appears to be that a person who makes a false statement, intending it to be acted on, must make good the damage naturally resulting from its being acted on. Here is no injuria of that kind. I think, however, that the verdict may be supported on another ground. The defendant has, as I assume for the moment, wilfully done an act calculated to cause physical harm to the female plaintiff, i.e., to infringe her legal right to personal safety, and has thereby in fact caused physical harm to her. That proposition, without more, appears to me to state a good cause of action, there being no justification alleged for the act. This wilful

---

1. (1789), 3 Term Rep. 51.
2. (1837), 2 M. & W. 519; affd. (1838), 4 M. & W. 337.

injuria is in law malicious, although no malicious purpose to cause the harm which was caused, nor any motive of spite, is imputed to the defendant.

It remains to consider whether the assumptions involved in the proposition are made out. One question is whether the defendant's act was so plainly calculated to produce some effect of the kind which was produced, that an intention to produce it ought to be imputed to the defendant regard being had to the fact that the effect was produced on a person proved to be in an ordinary state of health and mind. I think that it was. It is difficult to imagine that such a statement, made suddenly and with apparent seriousness, could fail to produce grave effects under the circumstances upon any but an exceptionally indifferent person, and therefore an intention to produce such an effect must be imputed, and it is no answer in law to say that more harm was done than was anticipated, for that is commonly the case with all wrongs. The other question is whether the effect was, to use the ordinary phrase, too remote to be in law regarded as a consequence for which the defendant is answerable. Apart from authority I should give the same answer, and on the same grounds, as to the last question, and say that it was not too remote. Whether, as the majority of the Lords thought in *Lynch* v. *Knight*,[1] the criterion is in asking what would be the natural effect on reasonable persons, or whether, as Lord Wensleydale thought, the possible infirmities of human nature ought to be recognised, it seems to me that the connection between the cause and the effect is sufficiently close and complete.

It is, however, necessary to consider two authorities which are supposed to have laid down that illness through mental shock is a too remote or unnatural consequence of an injuria to entitle the plaintiffs to recover in a case where damage is a necessary part of the cause of action. One is *Victorian Railways Comrs.* v. *Coultas*,[2] where it was held in the Privy Council that illness which was the effect of shock caused by fright was too remote a consequence of a negligent act which caused the fright, there being no physical harm immediately caused. That decision was treated in the Court of Appeal in *Pugh* v. *London, Brighton, and South Coast Rail. Co.*[3] as open to question. It is inconsistent with an earlier decision of the Court of Appeal in Ireland (*Bell* v. *Great Northern Rail. Co. of Ireland*[4]) where the Irish Exchequer Division declined to follow *Victorian Railways Comrs.* v. *Coultas*,[2] and it has been disapproved in the Supreme Court of New York (see *Pollock on Torts* (4th Edn.), p. 47 (n.)). Nor is it altogether in point, for there was not in that case any element of wilful wrong, nor was perhaps the illness so direct and natural a consequence of the defendant's conduct, as in this case.

On these grounds it seems to me that *Victorian Railway Comrs.* v. *Coultas*[2] is not an authority on which this case ought to be decided.

A more serious difficulty is the decision in *Allsop* v. *Allsop*,[5] which was approved in the House of Lords in *Lynch* v. *Knight*.[1] In that case it was held by Pollock C.B., Martin, Bramwell and Wilde BB., that illness caused by a slanderous imputation of unchastity in the case of a married woman did not constitute such special damage as would sustain an action for such a slander. That case, however, appears to have been decided on the grounds that, in all the innumerable actions for slander which had occurred, there were no precedents for alleging illness to be sufficient special damage; and that it would be an evil consequence to treat it as sufficient, because such a rule might lead to an infinity of trumpery or groundless actions. Neither of these reasons is applicable to the present case, nor could such a rule be adopted as of general application without results which it would be difficult or impossible to defend. Suppose that a person is in a precarious and dangerous condition, and another person falsely tells him that his physician has said that he has but a day to live. In such a case, if death ensued from the shock caused by the false statement, I cannot doubt that the case might be one

---

1. (1861), 9 H.L. Cas. 577.
2. (1888), 13 App. Cas. 222.
3. [1896] 2 Q.B. 248.
4. (1890), 26 L.R. Ir. 428.
5. (1860), 5 H. & N. 534.

of criminal homicide; or that, if a serious aggravation of illness ensued, damages might be recovered. I think, however, that it must be admitted that the present case is without precedent. Some English decisions are cited in Mr. Beven's book on *Negligence* as inconsistent with the decision in *Victorian Railways Comrs.* v. *Coultas*,[1] such as *Jones* v. *Boyce*,[2] *Wilkins* v. *Day*,[3] *Harris* v. *Mobbs*.[4] But I think that those cases are to be explained on a different ground, namely, that the damage which immediately resulted from the act of the passenger or the horse was really the result not of that act, but of a fright which rendered that act involuntary, and which, therefore, ought to be regarded as itself the direct and immediate cause of the damage.

In *Smith* v. *Johnson & Co.*,[5] decided in January, 1897, Bruce J., and I held that, where a man was killed in the sight of the plaintiff by the defendant's negligence, and the plaintiff became ill, not from the shock from fear of harm to himself but from the shock of seeing another person killed, this harm was too remote a consequence of the negligence. But that was a very different case from the present one.

Judgment for plaintiffs

Janvier v. Sweeney

Court of Appeal   [1918–19] All E.R. Rep. 1056

This was an appeal by Sweeney, a private detective and Barker, his assistant from a judgment for the plaintiff for £250 entered by Avory J. sitting with a jury.

BANKES L.J: . . . The case for the plaintiff was that she was employed by a lady in whose house she resided, and that, on 16 July 1917, a man called at the house and told her that he was a detective inspector from Scotland Yard representing the military authorities and that she was the woman they wanted as she had been corresponding with a German spy. The plaintiff said that she was extremely frightened, with the result that she suffered from a severe nervous shock, and she attributed a long period of nervous illness to the shock she received from the language used to her on that occasion. If she could establish the truth of that story and satisfy the jury that her illness was the direct result of the shock, she was entitled to maintain this action. At the trial the defendants disputed the plaintiff's story altogether. They said that Barker had never spoken the words alleged, and that, so far from suffering any shock, the plaintiff was a very self-possessed woman with her wits about her all the time during which the defendants were in communication with her, and that she was mainly occupied in attempting to trick these two men whom she suspected of being private inquiry agents. These matters were entirely for the jury. The court cannot interfere with their findings merely because it might think the opposite inference preferable. It is clear that the learned judge would not have arrived at the same conclusion as the jury. The defendants cannot complain of the summing-up. But in spite of that summing-up in favour of the defendants, the jury accepted the plaintiff's story, and their findings as to the words used by Barker is not challenged in this court. We must take it then that Barker went to this house and deliberately threatened the plaintiff in order to induce or compel her to commit a gross breach of the duty[6] she owed to her employer.

It is no longer contended that this was not a wrongful act which would amount to an actionable wrong if damage which the law recognises can be shown to have flowed directly from that act. But counsel for the defendant, Barker, contended that no action would lie for words followed by such damage as the plaintiff alleges here. In order to sustain that contention it would be necessary to overrule *Wilkinson* v. *Downton*.[7] In my opinion, that judgment was right. It has been approved in subsequent cases. It did not

---

1. (1888), 13 App. Cas. 222.
2. (1816), 1 Stark. 493, N.P.
3. (1883), 12 Q.B.D. 110.
4. (1878), 3 Ex. D. 268.
5. Unreported.
6. [I.e. to allow him to see some letters in the possession of a resident in the house.]
7. [1897] 2 Q.B. 57.

create any new rule of law, though it may be said to have extended existing principles over an area wider than that which they had been recognised as covering, because the court there accepted the view that the damage there relied on was not in the circumstances too remote in the eye of the law. . . .

. . . In my view of the present state of the authorities, it is impossible to suggest that *Wilkinson* v. *Downton*[1] is not good law or that it ought to be reversed. So much for the main point. . . .

Duke L.J.: I am anxious not to overlay or weaken the force of the judgment which has just been delivered, with every word of which I agree. My observations will, therefore, be brief. This is a much stronger case than *Wilkinson* v. *Downton*.[1] In that case there was no intention to commit a wrongful act; the defendant merely intended to play a joke upon the plaintiff. In the present case there was an intention to terrify the plaintiff for the purpose of attaining an unlawful object in which both the defendants were jointly concerned. . . .

[A. T. Lawrence J. delivered a judgment in favour of dismissing the appeal.]

Appeal dismissed

Question

A shopkeeper, as a joke, sends out a grossly inflated bill to a customer. Would there be any liability to the customer if (a) he is upset, or (b) he becomes ill as a result of worry over the bill? What if the customer commits suicide as this large bill is the "last straw"?

5. DEFENCES

(a) Consent

Latter v. Braddell

Common Pleas Division   (1881), 50 L.J.Q.B. 166

The plaintiff, a housemaid, was suspected by her mistress of being pregnant. The mistress had called a doctor and the plaintiff submitted reluctantly to the doctor's examination which was accompanied by her sobs and protests. The doctor found that the plaintiff was not pregnant. In an action against the mistress and her husband (Captain and Mrs. Braddell) and the doctor for assault, the trial judge, Lindley J., withdrew the case against Captain and Mrs. Braddell from the jury. The jury returned a verdict for the doctor. A rule was granted for the defendants to show cause why the verdict should not be set aside and a new trial granted. On the question whether the rule should be made absolute:

Lindley J.: . . . The plaintiff's case cannot be put higher than this, namely, that, without consulting her wishes, her mistress ordered her to submit to be examined by a doctor, in order that he might ascertain whether she (the plaintiff) was in the family way, and that she (the plaintiff) complied with that order reluctantly—that is, sobbing and protesting—and because she was told she must, and she did not know what else to do. There was, however, no evidence of any force or violence, nor of any threat of force or violence, nor of any illegal act done or threatened by the mistress beyond what I have stated; nor did the plaintiff in her evidence say that she was in fear of the mistress or of the doctor, or that she was in any way overcome by fear. She said she did not consent to what was done; but the sense in which she used this expression was not explained, and to appreciate it regard must be had to the other facts of the case. The plaintiff had it entirely in her own power physically to comply or not to comply with

1. [1897] 2 Q.B. 57.

her mistress's orders, and there was no evidence whatever to shew that anything improper or illegal was threatened to be done if she had not complied. It was suggested that her mistress ordered the examination with a view to see whether she could dismiss her without paying a month's wages. But there was no evidence of any threat to with-hold wages, nor of any conversation on the subject of wages, until the plaintiff was paid them on leaving. The question, therefore, is reduced to this: Can the plaintiff, having complied with the orders of her mistress, although reluctantly, maintain this action upon the ground that what was done to her by the doctor was against her will, or might properly be so regarded by a jury? I think not. It is said that the jury ought to have been asked whether the plaintiff in effect gave her mistress leave to have her examined, or whether the plaintiff's will or mind went with what she did. But, in my opinion, such questions inadequately express the grounds on which alone the defendants can be held liable. The plaintiff was not a child; she knew perfectly well what she did and what was being done to her by the doctor. She knew the object with which he examined her, and upon the evidence there is no reason whatever for supposing that any examination would have been made or attempted if she had told the doctor she would not allow herself to be examined. Under these circumstances I am of opinion that there was no evidence of want of consent as distinguished from reluctant obedience or submission to her mistress's orders, and that in the absence of all evidence of coercion, as distinguished from an order which the plaintiff could comply with or not as she chose, the action cannot be maintained. . . .

I am of opinion that this rule ought to be discharged.

[LOPES J. delivered a judgment in favour of there being a rule absolute for a new trial.]

Rule discharged

[On appeal (1881), 50 L.J.Q.B. 448, the Court of Appeal affirmed the view of Lindley J. Bramwell L.J. expressed the opinion that the plaintiff did submit to the examination although he conceded that she may well have thought that the defendants had a right to have her examined. He continued: "She may have submitted under an erroneous notion of law, but it was not through fear of violence."]

Question

Would the action have succeeded if the mistress had threatened to spread the story that the plaintiff *was* pregnant around the neighbourhood, if she did not submit to the examination?

(b) Defence of the person or property

Cockcroft v. Smith

Court of Queen's Bench   (1705), 11 Mod. 43

Cockcroft in a scuffle ran his finger towards Smith's eyes, who bit a joint off from the plaintiff's finger.

The question was, whether this was a proper defence for the defendant to justify in an action of *mayhem*?

Holt C.J., said, if a man strike another, who does not immediately after resent it, but takes his opportunity, and then some time after falls upon him and beats him, in this case, *son assault* is no good plea; neither ought a man, in case of a small assault, give a violent or an unsuitable return; but in such case plead what is necessary for a man's defence, and not who struck first; though this, he said, has been the common practice, but this he wished was altered; for hitting a man a little blow with a little stick on the shoulder, is not a reason for him to draw a sword and cut and hew the other, &c.

Criminal Law Act 1967

See Section 3: p. 49, *ante.*

Question

A, who is playing tennis, is mocked by B whereupon A throws his tennis racquet at B, injuring him. Does A have any defence? If not, is B's conduct at all relevant? (See *Lane* v. *Holloway,* [1968] 1 Q.B 379; [1967] 3 All E.R. 129.)

Green v. Goddard

Court of Queen's Bench   (1704), 2 Salk. 641

. . . *Et per Cur.* There is a force *in law,* as in every trespass *quare clausum fregit*: as if one enters into my ground, in that case the owner must request him to depart before he can lay hands on him to turn him out; for every *impositio manuum* is an assault and battery, which cannot be justified upon the account of breaking the close in law, without a request. The other is an *actual force,* as in burglary, as breaking open a door or gate; and in that case it is lawful to oppose force to force; and if one breaks down the gate, or comes into my close *vi & armis,* I need not request him to be gone, but may lay hands on him immediately, for it is but returning violence with violence: so if one comes forcibly and takes away my goods, I may oppose him without any more ado, for there is no time to make a request. . . .

(c) Lawful authority

Leigh v. Gladstone

King's Bench Division   (1909), 26 T.L.R. 139

The plaintiff, a suffragette, claimed damages for assault for the forcible feeding of her in prison and an injunction to restrain its repetition, the defence being that the acts were necessary to save her life and that the force used was the minimum necessary.

LORD ALVERSTONE C.J. (in summing up): . . . It was the duty, both under the rules and apart from the rules, of the officials to preserve the health and lives of the prisoners, who were in the custody of the Crown. If they forcibly fed the plaintiff when it was not necessary, the defendants ought to pay damages. The plaintiff did not complain— and it did her credit—of any undue violence being used towards her. The medical evidence was that at the time she was first fed it had become dangerous to allow her to abstain from food any longer. . . . If Dr. Helby had allowed the plaintiff to fast for a few days longer, and she had died in consequence, what answer could he have made? It was said that the treatment had failed. That had nothing to do with the case, for there was evidence that it had been successfully continued in some cases for 2½ years, and they had heard that two other ladies who were also guilty of this wicked folly— for it was wicked folly to attempt to starve themselves to death—had completed their full sentences although fed by force. If they thought this poor woman had been improperly treated, in the interests of justice they must not hesitate to say so.

The jury, after considering two minutes, returned a verdict for the defendants, and judgment was entered accordingly.

Questions

1. Is this case an example of the defence of necessity?
2. Is it at all relevant that suicide was then (but is not now) a crime?
3. If a political extremist set fire to himself in the street, would there be any defence for (a) a private person who threw water over him or (b) a fireman who did likewise?

Note

See also the note on necessity, p. 378, *post.*

3

The Duty of Care

The tort of negligence has been the subject of varying classifications. It is sometimes said that it involves a duty, a breach of that duty, and damage caused to the plaintiff by that breach. One can delve deeper, as R. W. M. Dias (particularly in [1967] C.L.J. 62 at p. 66) has done, in putting forward the following questions as determining liability:

> "(1) Is the careless infliction, by act or omission, of this kind of harm on this type of plaintiff by this type of defendant recognised by law as remediable? (2) Was the defendant's conduct in the given situation carelesss, i.e. did it fall short of the standard, and come within the scope, set by law? (3) Was it reasonably foreseeable that the defendant's carelessness would have inflicted on this plaintiff the kind of harm of which he complains? (4) Was it the defendant's conduct that caused the plaintiff's damage? If the answers are in the affirmative, the defendant is liable in negligence."

All these questions are covered at one point or another in this sourcebook. Question 1 and that part of Question 3 which is concerned with the foreseeability of the plaintiff are traditionally dealt with under the "Duty of Care" heading and are covered by the materials in this Chapter. Question 2 relates to breach of duty and is covered in Chap. 4; the remaining part of Question 3 and Question 4 relate to causation and remoteness of damage and are covered by materials in Chap. 5.

The point at which to commence a consideration of the duty of care is the broad "neighbour principle" enunciated by Lord Atkin in *M'Alister* (or *Donoghue*) v. *Stevenson*, [1932] A.C. 562 (p. 57, *post*) in which he attempted to rationalise and develop the earlier case law. The principle works fairly well when applied to negligent interference with physical interests. Indeed, in *Home Office* v. *Dorset Yacht Co., Ltd.*, [1970] A.C. 1004; [1970] 2 All E.R. 294 (p. 106, *post*) Lord Reid went so far as to say that "the time has come when we can and should say that it ought to apply unless there is some justification or valid explanation for its exclusion." One attempt to limit the principle has been in the distinction controversially drawn between liability for words and liability for conduct (p. 68, *post*). A more significant distinction has been that between what is variously called "financial" or "pecuniary" or "economic" loss, on the one hand, and physical damage, on the other hand. Since all damage is translated into money terms, it would be simpler if the distinction were seen to be that between interference with non-physical interests, on the one hand, and physical interests, on the other. Although torts of the former kind are the subject of Part II of this sourcebook, it has been considered necessary for an understanding of the limits of the duty concept to include in this Chapter cases which draw the line between the two types of interest (p. 71, *post*). The pragmatic objections to the extension of the "neighbour principle" to the protection of non-physical interests, have not been matched by similar objections in regard to the kinds of conduct—such as omissions (p. 82, *post*) and control of the conduct of others (p. 99, *post*)—which may give rise to a duty of care. Lines have had to be drawn, on pragmatic grounds, around the kinds of plaintiff entitled to a remedy, but here there has been understandable sympathy for classes such as rescuers (p. 123, *post*).

The use of the concept of "duty-situations" has become so deeply entrenched in judicial thinking that the academic controversies about whether it is a necessary element in the tort of negligence now seem somewhat strange (but W. W. Buckland, "The Duty to take Care" (1935), 51 L.Q.R. 637, still repays reading. See also the views expressed more recently by P. S. Atiyah, *Accidents, Compensation and the Law*, Chap. 2). It has been generally recognised that concepts such as "Duty", "Remoteness", "Causation" and "Negligence" (in the sense of breach of duty) are interchangeably used as mechanisms to control judgment; at times the ambiguity inherent in the notion of "foreseeability" has been stretched to provide a sole determinant of liability, but its very ambiguity and the realisation that defendants are not always made responsible for foreseeable harm, have revitalised the other verbal mechanisms. It is not a new suggestion that instead of putting the decisions into pigeon-holes such as "No duty" or "Too remote" or "Unforeseeable" it would be better, as Lord Denning M.R. has recently expressed it (p. 78, *post*) "to consider the particular relationship in hand" and decide whether, "as a matter of policy", the loss should be recoverable. This approach confronts the judiciary with an uncontrolled choice of policy, sometimes in matters which may be more rationally dealt with through the informed processes of the Law Commission and Parliament. But the rapid growth of technology and new situations of danger mean that the judiciary will always have to deal with the unexpected. It is this which gives to the Duty of Care cases a special importance for understanding the judicial process.

1. THE ACTIVITY DUTY

(a) In general

Donoghue (or M'Alister) v. Stevenson

House of Lords   [1932] All E.R. Rep. 1

Appeal from an interlocutor of the Second Division of the Court of Session in Scotland.

On 26 August 1928, the appellant, a shop assistant, drank a bottle of ginger-beer manufactured by the respondent, which a friend had ordered on her behalf from a retailer in a shop at Paisley and given to her. She stated that the shopkeeper, who supplied the ginger-beer, opened the bottle, which she said was sealed with a metal cap and was made of dark opaque glass, and poured some of its contents into a tumbler which contained some ice cream, and that she drank some of the contents of the tumbler, that her friend then lifted the bottle and was pouring the remainder of the contents into the tumbler, when a snail which had been in the bottle floated out in a state of decomposition. As a result, the appellant alleged, she had contracted a serious illness, and she claimed from the respondent damages for negligence. She alleged that the respondent, as the manufacturer of an article intended for consumption and contained in a receptacle which prevented inspection, owed a duty to her as consumer of the article to take care that there was no noxious element in the article, that he neglected such duty, and that he was, consequently, liable for any damage caused by such neglect. The case then came before the Lord Ordinary, who rejected the plea in law of the respondent and allowed the parties a proof of their averments, but on a reclaiming note the Second Division (the Lord Justice Clerk, Lord Ormidale and Lord Anderson; Lord Hunter dissenting) recalled the interlocutor of the Lord Ordinary and dismissed the action. The plaintiff (pursuer) appealed.

LORD ATKIN: The sole question for determination in this case is legal: Do the averments made by the pursuer in her pleading, if true, disclose a cause of action? I need not re-state the particular facts. The question is whether the manufacturer of an article of drink sold by him to a distributor in circumstances which prevent the distributor or the ultimate purchaser or consumer from discovering by inspection any defect is under any legal duty to the ultimate purchaser or consumer to take reasonable care that the article is free from defect likely to cause injury to health. I do not think a more important problem has occupied your Lordships in your judicial capacity, important both because of its bearing on public health and because of the practical test which it applies to the system of law under which it arises. The case has to be determined in accordance with Scots law, but it has been a matter of agreement between the experienced counsel who argued this case, and it appears to be the basis of the judgments of the learned judges of the Court of Session, that for the purposes of determining this problem the law of Scotland and the law of England are the same. I speak with little authority on this point, but my own research, such as it is, satisfies me that the principles of the law of Scotland on such a question as the present are identical with those of English law, and I discuss the issue on that footing. The law of both countries appears to be that in order to support an action for damages for negligence the complainant has to show that he has been injured by the breach of a duty owed to him in the circumstances by the defendant to take reasonable care to avoid such injury. In the present case we are not concerned with the breach of the duty; if a duty exists, that would be a question of fact which is sufficiently averred and for the present purposes must be assumed. We are solely concerned with the question whether as a matter of law in the circumstances alleged the defender owed any duty to the pursuer to take care.

It is remarkable how difficult it is to find in the English authorities statements of general application defining the relations between parties that give rise to the duty. The courts are concerned with the particular relations which come before them in actual litigation, and it is sufficient to say whether the duty exists in those circumstances. The result is that the courts have been engaged upon an elaborate classification of duties as they exist in respect of property, whether real or personal, with further divisions as to ownership, occupation or control, and distinctions based on the particular relations of the one side or the other, whether manufacturer, salesman or landlord, customer, tenant, stranger, and so on. In this way it can be ascertained at any time whether the law recognises a duty, but only where the case can be referred to some particular species which has been examined and classified. And yet the duty which is common to all the cases where liability is established must logically be based upon some element common to the cases where it is found to exist. To exist[1] a complete logical definition of the general principle is probably to go beyond the function of the judge, for, the more general the definition, the more likely it is to omit essentials or introduce non-essentials. The attempt was made by Lord Esher in *Heaven* v *Pender*[2] . . . As framed it was demon-

---

1. [This word does not appear in the Law Reports, [1932] A.C. 562, at p. 580, but is replaced by the word "seek".]
2. (1883), 11 Q.B.D. 503.

strably too wide, though it appears to me, if properly limited, to be capable of affording a valuable practical guide.

At present I content myself with pointing out that in English law there must be and is some general conception of relations giving rise to a duty of care, of which the particular cases found in the books are but instances. The liability for negligence, whether you style it such or treat it as in other systems as a species of "culpa", is no doubt based upon a general public sentiment of moral wrongdoing for which the offender must pay. But acts or omissions which any moral code would censure cannot in a practical world be treated so as to give a right to every person injured by them to demand relief. In this way rules of law arise which limit the range of complainants and the extent of their remedy. The rule that you are to love your neighbour becomes in law: You must not injure your neighbour, and the lawyers' question: Who is my neighbour? receives a restricted reply. You must take reasonable care to avoid acts or omissions which you can reasonably foresee would be likely to injure your neighbour. Who then, in law, is my neighbour? The answer seems to be persons who are so closely and directly affected by my act that I ought reasonably to have them in contemplation as being so affected when I am directing my mind to the acts or omissions which are called in question. This appears to me to be the doctrine of *Heaven* v. *Pender*[1] as laid down by Lord Esher when it is limited by the notion of proximity introduced by Lord Esher himself and A. L. Smith L.J. in *Le Lievre* v. *Gould*.[2] Lord Esher, M.R. says ([1893] 1 Q.B. at p. 497):

> "That case established that, under certain circumstances, one man may owe a duty to another, even though there is no contract between them. If one man is near to another, or is near to the property of another, a duty lies upon him not to do that which may cause a personal injury to that other, or may injure his property."

So A. L. Smith L.J. says ([1893] 1 Q.B. at p. 504):

> "The decision of *Heaven* v. *Pender*[1] was founded upon the principle that a duty to take due care did arise when the person or property of one was in such proximity to the person or property of another that, if due care was not taken damage might be done by the one to the other."

I think that this sufficiently states the truth if proximity be not confined to mere physical proximity, but be used, as I think it was intended, to extend to such close and direct relations that the act complained of directly affects a person whom the person alleged to be bound to take care would know would be directly affected by his careless act. That this is the sense in which nearness or "proximity" was intended by Lord Esher is obvious from his own illustration in *Heaven* v. *Pender*[1] (11 Q.B.D. at p. 510) of the application of his doctrine to the sale of goods.

> "This [i.e., the rule he has just formulated] includes the case of goods, &c., supplied to be used immediately by a particular person or persons, or one of a class of persons, where it would be obvious to the person supplying, if he thought, that the goods would in all probability be used at once by such persons before a reasonable opportunity for discovering any defect which might exist, and where the thing supplied would be of such a nature that a neglect of ordinary care or skill as to its condition or the manner of supplying it would probably cause danger to the person or property of the person for whose use it was supplied, and who was about to use it. It would exclude a case in which the goods are supplied under circumstances in which it would be a chance by whom they would be used, or whether they would be used or not, or whether they would be used before there would probably be means of observing any defect, or where the goods would be of such a nature that a want

---

1. (1883), 11 Q.B.D. 503
2. [1893] 1 Q.B. 491.

of care or skill as to their condition or the manner of supplying them would not probably produce danger of injury to person or property."

I draw particular attention to the fact that Lord Esher emphasises the necessity of goods having to be "used immediately" and "used at once before a reasonable opportunity of inspection". This is obviously to exclude the possibility of goods having their condition altered by lapse of time, and to call attention to the proximate relationship, which may be too remote where inspection even by the person using, certainly by an intermediate person, may reasonably be interposed. With this necessary qualification of proximate relationship, as explained in *Le Lievre and another* v. *Gould*,[1] I think the judgment of Lord Esher expresses the law of England. Without the qualification, I think that the majority of the court in *Heaven* v. *Pender*[2] was justified in thinking that the principle was expressed in too general terms. There will, no doubt, arise cases where it will be difficult to determine whether the contemplated relationship is so close that the duty arises. But in the class of case now before the court I cannot conceive any difficulty to arise. A manufacturer puts up an article of food in a container which he knows will be opened by the actual consumer. There can be no inspection by any purchaser and no reasonable preliminary inspection by the consumer. Negligently in the course of preparation he allows the contents to be mixed with poison. It is said that the law of England and Scotland is that the poisoned consumer has no remedy against the negligent manufacturer. If this were the result of the authorities, I should consider the result a grave defect in the law and so contrary to principle that I should hesitate long before following any decision to that effect which had not the authority of this House. . . . There are other instances than of articles of food and drink where goods are sold intended to be used immediately by the consumer, such as many forms of goods sold for cleaning purposes, when the same liability must exist. The doctrine supported by the decision below would not only deny a remedy to the consumer who was injured by consuming bottled beer or chocolates poisoned by the negligence of the manufacturer, but also to the user of what should be a harmless proprietary medicine, an ointment, a soap, a cleaning fluid or cleaning powder. I confine myself to articles of common household use, where everyone, including the manufacturer, knows that the articles will be used by persons other than the actual ultimate purchaser—namely, by members of his family and his servants, and, in some cases, his guests. I do not think so ill of our jurisprudence as to suppose that its principles are so remote from the ordinary needs of civilised society and the ordinary claims which it makes upon its members as to deny a legal remedy where there is so obviously a social wrong.

It will be found, I think, on examination, that there is no case in which the circumstances have been such as I have just suggested where the liability has been negatived. There are numerous cases where the relations were much more remote where the duty has been held not to exist. There are also dicta in such cases which go further than was necessary for the determination of the particular issues, which have caused the difficulty experienced by the courts below. I venture to say that in the branch of the law which deals with civil wrongs, dependent in England, at any rate, entirely upon the application by judges of general principles also formulated by judges, it is of particular importance to guard against the danger of stating propositions of law in wider terms than is necessary, lest essential factors be omitted in the wider survey and the inherent adaptability of English law be unduly restricted. For this reason it is very necessary, in considering reported cases in the law of torts, that the actual decision alone should carry authority, proper weight, of course, being given to the dicta of the judges. . . .

I do not find it necessary to discuss at length the cases dealing with duties where a thing is dangerous, or, in the narrower category, belongs to a class of things which are

---

1. [1893] 1 Q.B. 491.
2. (1883), 11 Q.B.D. 503.

dangerous in themselves. I regard the distinction as an unnatural one so far as it is used to serve as a logical differentiation by which to distinguish the existence or non-existence of a legal right. In this respect I agree with what was said by Scrutton L.J. in *Hodge & Sons* v. *Anglo-American Oil Co.*[1] (12 Ll. L. Rep. at p. 187), a case which was ultimately decided on a question of fact:

> "Personally, I do not understand the difference between a thing dangerous in itself as poison and a thing not dangerous as a class, but by negligent construction dangerous as a particular thing. The latter, if anything, seems the more dangerous of the two; it is a wolf in sheep's clothing instead of an obvious wolf."

The nature of the thing may very well call for different degrees of care, and the person dealing with it may well contemplate persons as being within the sphere of his duty to take care who would not be sufficiently proximate with less dangerous goods, so that not only the degree of care but the range of persons to whom a duty is owed may be extended. But they all illustrate the general principle. In *Dominion Natural Gas Co., Ltd.* v. *Collins and Perkins*[2] the appellants had installed a gas apparatus and were supplying natural gas on the premises of a railway company. They had installed a regulator to control the pressure and their men negligently made an escape valve discharge into the building instead of into the open air. The railway workmen—the plaintiffs—were injured by an explosion in the premises. The defendants were held liable. Lord Dunedin, in giving the judgment of the Judicial Committee, consisting of himself, Lord Macnaghten, Lord Collins, and Sir Arthur Wilson, after stating that there was no relation of contract between the plaintiffs and the defendants, proceeded ([1909] A.C., at p. 646):

> "There may be, however, in the case of anyone performing an operation, or setting up and installing a machine, a relationship of duty. What that duty is will vary according to the subject-matter of the things involved. It has, however, again and again been held that in the case of articles dangerous in themselves, such as loaded firearms, poisons, explosives, and other things ejusdem generis, there is a peculiar duty to take precaution imposed upon those who send forth or install such articles when it is necessarily the case that other parties will come within their proximity."

This, with respect, exactly sums up the position. The duty may exist independently of contract. Whether it exists or not depends upon the subject-matter involved, but clearly in the class of things enumerated there is a special duty to take precautions. This is the very opposite of creating a special category in which alone the duty exists. I may add, though it obviously would make no difference in the creation of a duty, that the installation of an apparatus to be used for gas perhaps more closely resembles the manufacture of a gun than a dealing with a loaded gun. In both cases the actual work is innocuous; it is only when the gun is loaded or the apparatus charged with gas that the danger arises. . . .

If your Lordships accept the view that the appellant's pleading discloses a relevant cause of action, you will be affirming the proposition that by Scots and English law alike a manufacturer of products which he sells in such a form as to show that he intends them to reach the ultimate consumer in the form in which they left him, with no reasonable possibility of intermediate examination, and with the knowledge that the absence of reasonable care in the preparation or putting up of the products will result in injury to the consumer's life or property, owes a duty to the consumer to take that reasonable care.

It is a proposition that I venture to say no one in Scotland or England who was not a lawyer would for one moment doubt. It will be an advantage to make it clear

---

1. (1922), 12 Ll. L. Rep. 183.
2. [1909] A.C. 640.

that the law in this matter, as in most others, is in accordance with sound common sense. I think that this appeal should be allowed.

LORD THANKERTON: . . . The duties which the appellant accuses the respondent of having neglected may be summarised as follows: (a) that the ginger-beer was manufactured by the respondent or his servants to be sold as an article of drink to members of the public (including the appellant), and that, accordingly, it was his duty to exercise the greatest care in order that snails should not get into the bottles, render the ginger-beer dangerous and harmful, and be sold with the ginger-beer; (b) a duty to provide a system of working his business which would not allow snails to get into the sealed bottles, and, in particular, would not allow the bottles when washed to stand in places to which snails had access; (c) a duty to provide an efficient system of inspection, which would prevent snails from getting into the sealed bottles; and (d) a duty to provide clear bottles, so as to facilitate the said system of inspection.

There can be no doubt, in my opinion, that equally in the law of Scotland and of England it lies upon the party claiming redress in such a case to show that there was some relation of duty between her and the defender which required the defender to exercise due and reasonable care for her safety. It is not at all necessary that there should be any direct contract between them, because the action is not based upon contract but upon negligence; but it is necessary for the pursuer in such an action to show there was a duty owed to her by the defender, because a man cannot be charged with negligence if he has no obligation to exercise diligence: *Kemp and Dougall* v. *Darngavil Coal Co.*,[1] per Lord Kinnear (1909 S.C. at p. 1319); see also *Clelland* v. *Robb*[2] per Lord President Dunedin and Lord Kinnear (1911 S.C. at p. 256). The question in each case is whether the pursuer has established, or, in the stage of the present appeal, has relevantly averred, such facts as involve the existence of such a relation of duty.

We are not dealing here with a case of what is called an article per se dangerous or one which was known by the defender to be dangerous, in which cases a special duty of protection or adequate warning is placed upon the person who uses or distributes it. The present case is that of a manufacturer and a consumer, with whom he has no contractual relation, of an article which the manufacturer did not know to be dangerous, and, unless the consumer can establish a special relationship with the manufacturer, it is clear, in my opinion, that neither the law of Scotland nor the law of England will hold that the manufacturer has any duty towards the consumer to exercise diligence. In such a case the remedy of the consumer, if any, will lie against the intervening party from whom he has procured the article. . . .

The special circumstances, from which the appellant claims that such a relationship of duty should be inferred, may, I think, be stated thus, namely, that the respondent, in placing his manufactured article of drink upon the market, has intentionally so excluded interference with, or examination of, the article by any intermediate handler of the goods between himself and the consumer that he has, of his own accord, brought himself into direct relationship with the consumer, with the result that the consumer is entitled to rely upon the exercise of diligence by the manufacturer to secure that the article shall not be harmful to the consumer. If that contention be sound, the consumer, on her showing that the article has reached her intact, and that she has been injured by the harmful nature of the article owing to the failure of the manufacturer to take reasonable care in its preparation before its enclosure in the sealed vessel, will be entitled to reparation from the manufacturer.

In my opinion, the existence of a legal duty in such circumstances is in conformity with the principles of both the law of Scotland and the law of England. The English cases demonstrate how impossible it is finally to catalogue, amid the ever-varying types of human relationships, those relationships in which a duty to exercise care arises apart from contract, and each of these cases relates to its own set of circumstances, out

---

1. 1909 S.C. 1314.
2. 1911 S.C. 253.

of which it was claimed that the duty had arisen. In none of these cases were the circumstances identical with the present case as regards that which I regard as the essential element in this case, namely, the manufacturer's own action in bringing himself into direct relationship with the party injured. . . .

I am of opinion that the contention of the appellant is sound and that she has relevantly averred a relationship of duty as between the respondent and herself, as also that her averments of the respondent's neglect of that duty are relevant. . . .

LORD MACMILLAN: . . . At your Lordships' Bar counsel for both parties to the present appeal, accepting, as I do also, the view that there is no distinction between the law of Scotland and the law of England in the legal principles applicable to the case, confined their arguments to the English authorities. The appellant endeavoured to establish that according to the law of England the pleadings disclose a good cause of action; the respondent endeavoured to show that on the English decisions the appellant had stated no admissible case. I propose, therefore, to address myself at once to an examination of the relevant English precedents.

I observe in the first place that there is no decision of this House upon the point at issue, for I agree with Lord Hunter that such cases as *Cavalier* v. *Pope*[1] and *Cameron* v. *Young*[2] which decided that

"a stranger to a lease cannot found upon a landlord's failure to fulfil obligations undertaken by him under contract with his lessee,"

are in a different chapter of the law. Nor can it by any means be said that the cases present "an unbroken and consistent current" of authority, for some flow one way and some the other.

It humbly appears to me that the diversity of view which is exhibited in such cases as *George* v. *Skivington*[3] on the one hand, and *Blacker* v. *Lake and Elliot*[4] on the other hand—to take two extreme instances—is explained by the fact that in the discussion of the topic which now engages your Lordships' attention two rival principles of the law find a meeting place where each has contended for supremacy. On the one hand, there is the well-established principle that no one other than a party to a contract can complain of a breach of that contract. On the other hand, there is the equally well-established doctrine that negligence, apart from contract, gives a right of action to the party injured by that negligence—and here I use the term negligence, of course, in its technical legal sense, implying a duty owed and neglected. The fact that there is a contractual relationship between the parties which may give rise to an action for breach of contract does not exclude the co-existence of a right of action founded on negligence as between the same parties independently of the contract though arising out of the relationship in fact brought about by the contract. Of this the best illustration is the right of the injured railway passenger to sue the railway company either for breach of the contract of safe carriage or for negligence in carrying him. And there is no reason why the same set of facts should not give one person a right of action in contract and another person a right of action in tort. . . .

Where, as in cases like the present, so much depends upon the avenue of approach to the question it is very easy to take the wrong turning. If you begin with the sale by the manufacturer to the retail dealer, then the consumer who purchases from the retailer is at once seen to be a stranger to the contract between the retailer and the manufacturer and so disentitled to sue upon it. There is no contractual relation between the manufacturer and the consumer, and thus the plaintiff if he is to succeed is driven to try to bring himself within one or other of the exceptional cases where the strictness of the rule that none but a party to a contract can found on a breach of that contract

---

1. [1906] A.C. 428.
2. [1908] A.C. 176.
3. (1869), L.R. 5 Exch. 1.
4. (1912), 106 L.T. 533.

has been mitigated in the public interest, as it has been in the case of a person who issues a chattel which is inherently dangerous or which he knows to be in a dangerous condition. If, on the other hand, you disregard the fact that the circumstances of the case at one stage include the existence of a contract of sale between the manufacturer and the retailer and approach the question by asking whether there is evidence of carelessness on the part of the manufacturer and whether he owed a duty to be careful in a question with the party who has been injured in consequence of his want of care, the circumstance that the injured party was not a party to the incidental contract of sale becomes irrelevant and his title to sue the manufacturer is unaffected by that circumstance. The appellant in the present instance asks that her case be approached as a case of delict, not as a case of breach of contract. She does not require to invoke the exceptional cases in which a person not a party to a contract has been held to be entitled to complain of some defect in the subject-matter of the contract which has caused him harm. The exceptional case of things dangerous in themselves or known to be in a dangerous condition has been regarded as constituting a peculiar category outside the ordinary law both of contract and of tort. I may observe that it seems to me inaccurate to describe the case of dangerous things as an exception to the principle that no one but a party to a contract can sue on that contract. I rather regard this type of case as a special instance of negligence where the law exacts a degree of diligence so stringent as to amount practically to a guarantee of safety. . . .

. . . Having regard to the inconclusive state of the authorities in the courts below, and to the fact that the important question involved is now before your Lordships for the first time, I think it desirable to consider the matter from the point of view of the principles applicable to this branch of law which are admittedly common to both English and Scottish jurisprudence.

The law takes no cognizance of carelessness in the abstract. It concerns itself with carelessness only where there is a duty to take care and where failure in that duty has caused damage. In such circumstances carelessness assumes the legal quality of negligence and entails the consequences in law of negligence. What then are the circumstances which give rise to this duty to take care? In the daily contacts of social and business life human beings are thrown into or place themselves in an infinite variety of relationships with their fellows, and the law can refer only to the standards of the reasonable man in order to determine whether any particular relationship gives rise to a duty to take care as between those who stand in that relationship to each other. The grounds of action may be as various and manifold as human errancy, and the conception of legal responsibility may develop in adaptation to altering social conditions and standards. The criterion of judgment must adjust and adapt itself to the changing circumstances of life. The categories of negligence are never closed. The cardinal principle of liability is that the party complained of should owe to the party complaining a duty to take care and that the party complaining should be able to prove that he has suffered damage in consequence of a breach of that duty. Where there is room for diversity of view is in determining what circumstances will establish such a relationship between the parties as to give rise on the one side to a duty to take care and on the other side to a right to have care taken.

To descend from these generalities to the circumstances of the present case I do not think that any reasonable man or any twelve reasonable men would hesitate to hold that if the appellant establishes her allegations the respondent has exhibited carelessness in the conduct of his business. For a manufacturer of aerated water to store his empty bottles in a place where snails can get access to them and to fill his bottles without taking any adequate precautions by inspection or otherwise to ensure that they contain no deleterious foreign matter may reasonably be characterised as carelessness without applying too exacting a standard. But, as I have pointed out, it is not enough to prove the respondent to be careless in his process of manufacture. The question is: Does he owe a duty to take care, and to whom does he owe that duty? I have no hesitation in affirming that a person who for gain engages in the business of manufacturing articles of food and drink intended for consumption by members of the public in the form in which he issues them is under a duty to take care in the manufacture of these articles. That duty, in my opinion, he owes to those whom he intends to consume his products. He manufactures his commodities for human consumption; he intends and contemplates that they shall be consumed. By reason of that very fact he places himself in a relationship with all the potential consumers of his commodities, and that relationship, which he assumes and desires for his own ends, imposes upon him a duty to take care to avoid injuring them. He owes them a duty not to convert by his own carelessness an article which he issues to them as wholesome and innocent into an article which is dangerous to life and health.

It is sometimes said that liability can arise only where a reasonable man would have foreseen and could have avoided the consequences of his act or omission. In the present case the respondent, when he manufactured his ginger-beer, had directly in contemplation that it would be consumed by members of the public. Can it be said that he could not be expected as a reasonable man to foresee that if he conducted his process of manufacture carelessly he might injure those whom he expected and desired to consume his ginger-beer? The possibility of injury so arising seems to me in no sense so remote as to excuse him from foreseeing it. Suppose that a baker through carelessness allows a large quantity of arsenic to be mixed with a batch of his bread, with the result that those who subsequently eat it are poisoned, could he be heard to say that he owed no duty to the consumers of his bread to take care that it was free from poison, and that, as he did not know that any poison had got into it, his only liability was for breach of warranty under his contract of sale to those who actually bought the poisoned bread from him? Observe that I have said "through carelessness" and thus excluded the case of a pure accident such as may happen where every care is taken. I cannot believe, and I do not believe, that neither in the law of England nor in the law of Scotland is there redress for such a case. The state of facts I have figured might well give rise to a criminal charge, and the civil consequences of such carelessness can scarcely be less wide than its criminal consequences. Yet the principle of the decision appealed from is that the manufacturer of food products intended by him for human consumption does not owe to the consumers whom he has in view any duty of care, not even the duty to take care that he does not poison them.

The recognition by counsel that the law of Scotland applicable to the case was the same as the law of England implied that there was no special doctrine of Scots law which either the appellant or the respondent could invoke to support her or his case, and your Lordships have thus been relieved of the necessity of a separate consideration of the law of Scotland. For myself I am satisfied that there is no speciality of Scots law involved, and that the case may safely be decided on principles common to both systems. I am happy to think that in their relation to the practical problem of everyday life which this appeal presents the legal systems of the two countries are in no way at variance and that the principles of both alike are sufficiently consonant with justice and common sense to admit of the claim which appellant seeks to establish.

I am anxious to emphasise that the principle of judgment which commends itself to me does not give rise to the sort of objection stated by Parke B., in *Longmeid* v. *Holliday*,[1] where he said (6 Exch. at p. 768):

"But it would be going much too far to say that so much care is required in the ordinary intercourse of life between one individual and another, that if a machine not in its nature dangerous—a carriage for instance—but which might become so by a latent defect entirely unknown, although discoverable by the exercise of ordinary care, should be lent or given by one person, even by the person who manufactured it, to another, the former should be answerable to the latter for a subsequent damage accruing by the use of it."

---

1. (1851), 6 Exch. 761.

I read this passage rather as a note of warning that the standard of care exacted in the dealings of human beings with one another must not be pitched too high than as giving any countenance to the view that negligence may be exhibited with impunity. It must always be a question of circumstances whether the carelessness amounts to negligence and whether the injury is not too remote from the carelessness. I can readily conceive that where a manufacturer has parted with his product and it has passed into other hands it may well be exposed to vicissitudes which may render it defective or noxious and for which the manufacturer could not in any view be held to be to blame. It may be a good general rule to regard responsibility as ceasing when control ceases. So also where between the manufacturer and the user there is interposed a party who has the means and opportunity of examining the manufacturer's product before he re-issues it to the actual user. But where, as in the present case, the article of consumption is so prepared as to be intended to reach the consumer in the condition in which it leaves the manufacturer and the manufacturer takes steps to ensure this by sealing or otherwise closing the container, so that the contents cannot be tampered with, I regard his control as remaining effective until the article reaches the consumer and the container is opened by him. The intervention of any exterior agency is intended to be excluded, and was in fact in the present case excluded. It is doubtful whether in such a case there is any redress against the retailer: *Gordon* v. *M'Hardy*.[1]

The burden of proof must always be upon the injured party to establish that the defect which caused the injury was present in the article when it left the hands of the party whom he sues, that the defect was occasioned by the carelessness of that party, and that the circumstances are such as to cast upon the defender a duty to take care not to injure the pursuer. There is no presumption of negligence in such a case as the present, nor is there any justification for applying the maxim res ipsa loquitur. Negligence must be both averred and proved. The appellant accepts this burden of proof and, in my opinion, she is entitled to have an opportunity of discharging it if she can. I am, accordingly, of opinion that this appeal should be allowed, the judgment of the Second Division of the Court of Session reversed, and the judgment of the Lord Ordinary restored.

[LORD BUCKMASTER and LORD TOMLIN delivered speeches in favour of dismissing the appeal.]

Appeal allowed

Questions

1. It has been said that this case exploded the "privity of contract fallacy". What does this mean?

2. What policy reasons might there have been for the existence of this "fallacy"?

3. What is the *ratio decidendi* of the case? (See R. F. V. Heuston, "*Donoghue* v. *Stevenson* in Retrospect", (1957), 20 M.L.R. 1 at pp. 5–9.)

4. If a person purchases a chattel which causes him injury, what action would you advise him to bring (outside the tort of negligence) and against whom? What advantages might this action have?

Notes

1. Whether a snail was present in the ginger beer bottle was never judicially determined. (See (1955) 71 L.Q.R. 472.)

2. This case has been important in the general development of the tort of

---

1. 1903, 6 F. (Ct. of Sess.) 210.

negligence as well as the more specific area of liability for chattels. This latter point is dealt with in Chap. 10, p. 327, *post.*

3. In *Deyong* v. *Shenburn*, [1946] K.B. 227; [1946] 1 All E.R. 226, Du Parcq L.J. stated ([1946] 1 All E.R. at p. 229):

> "It is not true to say that wherever a man finds himself in such a position that unless he does a certain act another person may suffer, or that if he does something another person will suffer, then it is his duty in the one case to be careful to do the act and in the other case to be careful not to do the act. Any such proposition is much too wide. One has to find that there has been a breach of a duty which the law recognises, and to see what the law recognises one can only look at the decisions of the courts."

In *Langbrook Properties, Ltd.* v. *Surrey C.C.*, [1969] 3 All E.R. 1424, the construction of a motorway meant that an aqueduct had to be diverted and the position of certain water mains had to be changed: this in turn necessitated excavations in land near to that owned by the plaintiffs who were property developers. Water had to be pumped out of the land where the excavations were made, and in this action (which also included a claim in nuisance) the plaintiffs alleged that percolating water under their own land was abstracted by this pumping, causing settlements in the buildings thereon. They further alleged that this was caused by the negligence of the second defendants (the area water authority) and the third and fourth defendants (the contractors engaged to carry out this whole operation). On the trial of a preliminary issue as to whether the plaintiffs had any cause of action, in which the allegations of fact in the statement of claim had to be assumed to be true, the question was answered in the negative. To Plowman J.'s mind, the authorities established that water percolating in undefined channels under a man's land could be abstracted by that person even though this would abstract water percolating through another's land. Plowman J. further stated (at p. 1440) that "since it is not actionable to cause damage by the abstraction of underground water, even where this is done maliciously, it would seem illogical that it should be actionable if it were done carelessly. Where there is no duty not to injure for the sake of inflicting injury, there cannot, in my judgment, be a duty to take care not to inflict the same injury." (The claim in nuisance also failed.)

4. *Smith* v. *Scott*, [1973] Ch. 314; [1972] 3 All E.R. 645, is also an instructive case. The Scott family had been placed in a house by the London Borough of Lewisham. The Scotts' behaviour was found by Pennycuick V-C to have been "altogether intolerable both in respect of physical damage and of noise", and the Smiths, who lived in an adjoining house, moved out. Several points were argued for the plaintiff (Mr. Smith) in this unsuccessful action against the Borough, but it might be noted at this stage that the court held that the Borough owed no duty of care to the neighbours in this situation i.e. in the selection of a tenant. Particular reference was made to Lord Reid's speech in *Home Office* v. *Dorset Yacht Co., Ltd.*, [1970] A.C. 1004, at p. 1026, p. 108, *post,* where he mentioned the "long chapter of the law" governing the use by a landowner of his proprietary rights. Pennycuick V-C declined to alter the law by the introduction of a duty of care, although he acknowledged that the position could well have been different if this had been an area of the law which was being brought to the court's attention for the first time.

(b) Words or conduct

Clayton v. Woodman & Son (Builders), Ltd

Queen's Bench Division   [1961] 3 All E.R. 249

[NOTE:—The position in regard to misstatements leading to financial loss must today be considered in the light of the later decisions in *Hedley Byrne & Co., Ltd.* v. *Heller & Partners, Ltd.*, [1964] A.C. 465; [1963] 2 All E.R. 575, p. 501, *post*, and *Mutual Life and Citizens' Assurance Co., Ltd.* v. *Evatt*, [1971] A.C. 793; [1971] 1 All E.R. 150, p. 511, *post*, but, subject to this modification, the case is still relevant in a consideration of the distinctions between words and acts.]

In the course of the installation of a lift, a chase (groove) was cut in a stone gable on a building, but the gable was not strutted or shored. The judge found that with proper strutting and shoring the chase could have been cut with no real danger of a fall of the gable, but that without such strutting and shoring it was unsafe to do this. He also found that an architect employed by the third defendants (the firm of architects involved in the work) had instructed the plaintiff to cut the chase. The plaintiff, a senior bricklayer, in fact told another man to cut the chase, but some hours later, after the plaintiff had cut a small piece of stone out of the gable, it fell inwards and injured him. He sued his employers (the first defendants), the building owner (the second defendants) and the architect's employers (the third defendants). On the claim against the third defendants:

SALMON J.: . . . I . . . agree that had the third defendants issued instructions direct to the first defendants to cut the chase, and as a result of those instructions being obeyed, the plaintiff had been injured, the third defendants would have been under no liability to him. The first defendants would in such circumstances have been interposed between the instructions and the doing of the work, and the proximity between the plaintiff and the third defendants would not have been sufficiently close to impose any duty of care on them. But the instructions were in fact given direct to the plaintiff. They concerned a subject-matter, i.e., the cutting of the chase, about which, as between the third defendants and the second defendants, the third defendants had a duty to decide, and as between the third defendants and the first defendants, the third defendants had a right to issue instructions. The architect chose to give the instructions direct to the bricklayer, who had no reason to suspect that any danger was involved. The architect certainly knew that these instructions would be promptly obeyed and equally certainly should have realised that in the existing circumstances they would probably lead to the bricklayer's serious injury or death. Having regard to the exceptionally close relationship between the architect and the bricklayer on the particular facts of this case, the law to my mind imposed a duty on the architect to take reasonable care for the safety of the bricklayer. Had he exercised any such care, he would not have issued the instructions. . . . Can anyone doubt that the bricklayer was so closely and directly affected by the instructions that the architect ought to have had him in contemplation as being so affected when the architect was directing his mind to the instructions? . . . Can anyone doubt that the reasonable man would conclude that the particular relation between this architect and this bricklayer gave rise to a duty to take care?

Counsel for the third defendants submitted that the instructions amounted to no more than a statement, and that in law a careless as distinct from a fraudulent statement is not actionable in the absence of a contractual or fiduciary relationship between the parties, for in the absence of such a relationship there is no duty to take care, and in the absence of such a duty there can be no actionable negligence.[1] He

---

1. [But see the Note, *ante*.

relies on the well-known cases of *Derry* v. *Peek*,[1] *Le Lievre* v. *Gould*,[2] and *Candler* v. *Crane, Christmas & Co.*[3]

On the whole I have come to the conclusion that those authorities are not in point, for in my view orders and instructions are different in their nature from mere statements or representations. To make a statement or representation believing that someone will probably act on it is not, in my view, equivalent to issuing orders or instructions which one knows will certainly be obeyed. But even if this distinction be not valid, in my judgment the third defendants were still under a duty of care to the plaintiff. It is to be observed that *M'Alister* (or *Donoghue*) v. *Stevenson*[4] has frequently been applied, but only where the damage complained of was physical, i.e., damage to persons or property; see e.g., *Haseldine* v. *Daw & Son, Ltd.*,[5] *Denny* v. *Supplies & Transport Co., Ltd.*[6] On the other hand, in *Derry* v. *Peek*,[1] *Le Lievre* v. *Gould*[7] and *Candler* v. *Crane, Christmas & Co.*[8] the damage complained of was not physical but financial. May it be that the latter cases can be read as authorities for excluding from the ambit of *Donoghue* v. *Stevenson*[4] only careless misstatements resulting in financial loss, but not those causing physical damage?

It appears from the judgment of Denning L.J. in *Candler* v. *Crane, Christmas & Co.*[9] that it was not seriously disputed by the respondents in that case that a careless statement resulting in physical damage to persons or property is actionable. Asquith L.J., however, appears to take a different view, for he says:[10]

"The inference seems to me to be that Lord Atkin continued to accept the distinction between liability in tort for careless (but non-fraudulent) misstatements and liability in tort for some other forms of carelessness, and that his formula defining 'who is my neighbour' must be read subject to his acceptance of this overriding distinction."

In the same sense are the reference of Asquith L.J.[10] to *George* v. *Skivington*.[11] On the other hand, he does appear to find support for the decision at which he arrives from the fact that the formula in *Donoghue* v. *Stevenson*[4] "has never been applied to injury other than physical".[12] Cohen L.J. expresses no concluded view whether a careless misstatement resulting in physical damage may be actionable, but he does cite[13] apparently with approval, the following passage from the judgment of Wrottesley J. in *Old Gate Estates, Ltd.* v. *Toplis & Harding & Russell*: [14]

"The exceptions laid down by *Donoghue* v. *Stevenson*[4]—the exceptions to the rule that a man is obliged to be careful only to those to whom he owes a duty by contract —are, as I understand the decision in that case, confined to negligence which results in danger to life . . . limb, or . . . health, and, this being no one of those I think that the plaintiffs have no cause of action on the analogy of *Donoghue* v. *Stevenson*."[4]

The inference seems to be that had the case been one of those exceptions, Wrottesley J. would have concluded that there was a cause of action notwithstanding that the claim was based on a careless misstatement.

---

1. (1889), 14 App. Cas. 337.
2. [1893] 1 Q.B. 491.
3. [1951] 2 K.B. 164; [1951] 1 All E.R. 426.
4. [1932] A.C. 462; [1932] All E.R. Rep. 1.
5. [1941] 2 K.B. 343; [1941] 3 All E.R. 156.
6. [1950] 2 K.B. 374.
7. [1893] 1 Q.B. 491
8. [1951] 2 K.B. 164; [1951] 1 All E.R. 426.
9. [1951] 2 K.B. at p. 179; [1951] 1 All E.R. at p. 433.
10. [1951] 2 K.B. at p. 190; [1951] 1 All E.R. at p. 439.
11. (1869), L.R. 5 Exch. 1.
12. [1951] 2 K.B. at p. 189; [1951] 1 All E.R. at p. 439.
13. [1951] 2 K.B. at p. 197; [1951] 1 All E.R. at p. 444.
14. [1939] 3 All E.R. at p. 216.

Although the dicta of Asquith L.J. must carry the greatest weight, I do not consider that the decision in *Candler* v. *Crane, Christmas & Co.*[1] excludes careless statements causing physical damage from the ambit of *Donoghue* v. *Stevenson*.[2] . . .

I reach the conclusion that since neither *Le Lievre* v. *Gould*[3] nor *Candler* v. *Crane, Christmas & Co.*[1] was concerned with a careless statement causing physical damage, they cannot exclude the application of the principle enunciated in *Donoghue* v. *Stevenson*[2] to the particular facts of the present case. . . .

[Judgment was given against the first defendants and the third defendants, but for the second defendants against the plaintiff. The case went to the Court of Appeal, and the judgment against the third defendants was reversed. The full report can be found at [1962] 2 All E.R. 33, but the decision is neatly summarised at [1962] 2 Q.B. 546 as follows: ". . . the Court of Appeal allowed the appeal, holding that the evidence did not justify the judge's finding that the architect had instructed the plaintiff to do anything which he knew to be dangerous, or that he had acted negligently, as he had given no direct order but had merely decided not to vary the contract and made a statement to that effect; that accordingly, responsibility for the accident rested solely on the builders, whose duty it was to ensure that the chase was cut without unnecessary risk to the plaintiff."]

Question

Read the facts of *Dutton* v. *Bognor Regis U.D.C.*, [1972] 1 Q.B. 373; [1972] 1 All E.R. 462 (p. 86, *post*). Did that case concern liability for words or acts?

Hedley Byrne & Co., Ltd. v. Heller & Partners, Ltd.

House of Lords   [1963] 2 All E.R. 575

For the facts and the speeches, see p. 501, *post*. The question in issue in the case was whether there could be liability for statements causing pure financial loss: no physical injury was in fact involved.

LORD REID: . . . Apart altogether from authority I would think that the law must treat negligent words differently from negligent acts. The law ought so far as possible to reflect the standards of the reasonable man, and that is what *M'Alister* (or *Donoghue*) v. *Stevenson*[2] sets out to do. The most obvious difference between negligent words and negligent acts is this. Quite careful people often express definite opinions on social or informal occasions, even when they see that others are likely to be influenced by them; and they often do that without taking that care which they would take if asked for their opinion professionally, or in a business connexion. The appellants agree that there can be no duty of care on such occasions, and we were referred to American and South African authorities where that is recognised, although their law appears to have gone much further than ours has yet done. But it is at least unusual casually to put into circulation negligently-made articles which are dangerous. A man might give a friend a negligently-prepared bottle of home-made wine and his friend's guests might drink it with dire results; but it is by no means clear that those guests would have no action against the negligent manufacturer. Another obvious difference is that a negligently-made article will only cause one accident, and so it is not very difficult to find the necessary degree of proximity or neighbourhood between the negligent manufacturer and the person injured. But words can be broadcast with or without the consent or the foresight of the speaker or writer. It would be one thing to say that the speaker owes a

---

1. [1951] 2 K.B. 164; [1951] 1 All E.R. 426.
2. [1932] A.C. 562; [1932] All E.R. Rep. 1.
3. [1893] 1 Q.B. 491.

duty to a limited class, but it would be going very far to say that he owes a duty to every ultimate "consumer" who acts on those words to his detriment. It would be no use to say that a speaker or writer owes a duty, but can disclaim responsibility if he wants to. He, like the manufacturer, could make it part of a contract that he is not to be liable for his negligence: but that contract would not protect him in a question with a third party at least if the third party was unaware of it.

So it seems to me that there is good sense behind our present law that in general an innocent but negligent misrepresentation gives no cause of action. There must be something more than the mere misstatement. . . .

LORD DEVLIN: . . . A simple distinction between negligence in word and negligence in deed might leave the law defective but at least it would be intelligible. This is not, however, the distinction that is drawn in counsel for the respondents' argument and it is one which would be unworkable. A defendant who is given a car to overhaul and repair if necessary is liable to the injured driver (a) if he overhauls it and repairs it negligently and tells the driver that it is safe when it is not; (b) if he overhauls it and negligently finds it not to be in need of repair and tells the driver that it is safe when it is not; and (c) if he negligently omits to overhaul it at all and tells the driver that it is safe when it is not. It would be absurd in any of these cases to argue that the proximate cause of the driver's injury was not what the defendant did or failed to do but his negligent statement on the faith of which the driver drove the car and for which he could not recover. In this type of case where if there were a contract there would undoubtedly be a duty of service, it is not practicable to distinguish between the inspection or examination, the acts done or omitted to be done, and the advice or information given. . . .

Note

The distinction between words and acts has proved to be important so far as liability for economic loss (i.e. negligent interference with economic interests) is concerned. The cases which follow show that there will generally be no liability for what is loosely termed "financial" loss resulting from another's negligent *act* where that loss is not consequent upon some physical injury to the plaintiff's person or property; but we shall see, in Chap. 15, that if pure "financial" loss is caused by negligent *words* then, provided a "special relationship" exists, there is likely to be liability (p. 501).

(c) Pure economic interests

Weller & Co. *v.* Foot and Mouth Disease Research Institute

Queen's Bench Division   [1965] 3 All E.R. 560

Several questions of law were raised for the court's decision in this case, and the court was asked to assume the following facts: that there was an escape from the defendants' premises of foot and mouth disease virus which infected cattle on neighbouring land, that the plaintiffs were not in occupation of this land, that an order was made closing Guildford and Farnham markets as a result of the outbreak of the disease, and that the plaintiffs, who were cattle auctioneers, suffered a loss of business because of this closure. It was further assumed that this loss was foreseeable and that the escape of the virus was caused by the defendants' negligence for the purpose of discussing the claim in negligence, with which this extract deals.

WIDGERY J.: . . . Counsel for the plaintiffs bases his contention on the well-known speech of Lord Atkin in *M'Alister* (or *Donoghue*) v. *Stevenson*[1] . . . Applying this principle, counsel for the plaintiffs says that, since the defendants should have foreseen the

---

1. [1932] A.C. 562, at p. 580; [1932] All E.R. Rep. 1, at p. 11.

damage to his clients but nevertheless failed to take proper precaution against the escape of the virus, their liability is established. It may be observed that if this argument is sound, the defendants' liability is likely to extend far beyond the loss suffered by the auctioneers, for in an agricultural community the escape of foot and mouth disease virus is a tragedy which can foreseeably affect almost all businesses in that area. The affected beasts must be slaughtered, as must others to whom the disease may conceivably have spread. Other farmers are prohibited from moving their cattle and may be unable to bring them to market at the most profitable time; transport contractors who make their living by the transport of animals are out of work; dairymen may go short of milk, and sellers of cattle feed suffer loss of business. The magnitude of these consequences must not be allowed to deprive the plaintiffs of their rights, but it emphasises the importance of this case.

The difficulty facing counsel for the plaintiffs is that there is a great volume of authority both before and after *M'Alister* (or *Donoghue*) v. *Stevenson*[1] to the effect that a plaintiff suing in negligence for damages suffered as a result of an act or omission of a defendant cannot recover if the act or omission did not directly injure, or at least threaten directly to injure, the plaintiff's person or property but merely caused consequential loss as, for example, by upsetting the plaintiff's business relations with a third party who was the direct victim of the act or omission. The categories of negligence never close, but when the court is asked to recognise a new category, it must proceed with some caution. . . .

[Having quoted extracts from the judgments in *Simpson* v. *Thomson*[2] and *Société Anonyme de Remorquage à Hélice* v. *Bennetts*,[3] he continued:] Then, passing to the cases decided after *M'Alister* (or *Donoghue*) v. *Stevenson*,[1] I take first a decision of the House of Lords in *Morrison Steamship Co., Ltd.* v. *Owners of Cargo lately laden on S.S. Greystoke Castle*.[4] This was a case where two ships had been in collision, one being held one-fourth to blame and the other three-fourths to blame. The latter ship had to put into port for repairs and a general average expenditure was incurred. The cargo owners of that ship, being liable to their ship owners for general average contribution, brought an action against the owners of the colliding ship claiming one-quarter of this contribution, and it was held by a majority (Lord Roche, Lord Porter and Lord Uthwatt, Viscount Simon and Lord Simonds dissenting) that the cargo owners had a direct claim against the owners of the colliding ship. Lord Roche, dealing with this matter, and dealing in particular with the issues which interest me in the present case, said this:[5]

"There remains for consideration the contention on behalf of the appellants that the respondents had no direct right to suit because it was said that: (a) their cargo sustained no material or physical damage and an expense occasioned to them after the collision in connexion with a contract was not actionable; (b) they were really in the same position as underwriters and the doctrine of *Simpson* v. *Thomson*[2] negativing the right of underwriters to any direct cause of action against a wrong-doer, applied to the case of the respondents. As to reason (a) the latter branch of this contention appears to me to be largely a repetition of the argument based on *Mersey Docks and Harbour Board* v. *Marpessa (Owners)*[6] and the supposed remoteness of the expense as a result from the collision. As to the first branch of this contention, I would observe that, in my judgment, if the expense is occasioned by the collision and if it is the expense in whole or in part of the cargo owners—a matter to which I

---

1. [1932] A.C. 562; [1932] All E.R. Rep. 1.
2. (1877), 3 App. Cas. 279.
3. [1911] 1 K.B. 243.
4. [1947] A.C. 265; [1946] 2 All E.R. 696.
5. [1947] A.C., at p. 279; [1946] 2 All E.R., at pp. 699, 700.
6. [1907] A.C. 241; [1904–07] All E.R. Rep. 855.

shall direct your lordships' attention when dealing with contention (b)—if, I say, these things be so, then no authority was cited to support the proposition that whether by land or by sea physical or material damage is necessary to support a cause of action in a case like this. I do not regard the case of *Société Anonyme de Remorquage à Hélice* v. *Bennetts*[1] which was cited, as any such authority. If it was correctly decided, as to which I express no opinion, I think it must depend on a view that one vessel (A) does not owe to the tug which is towing vessel (B) any duty not negligently to collide with (B). On the other hand, if two lorries A and B are meeting one another on the road, I cannot bring myself to doubt that the driver of lorry A owes a duty to both the owner of lorry B and to the owner of goods when carried in lorry B. Those owners are engaged in a common adventure with or by means of lorry B and if lorry A is negligently driven and damages lorry B so severely that, while no damage is done to the goods in it, the goods have to be unloaded for the repair of the lorry and then reloaded or carried forward in some other way and the consequent expense is (by reason of his contract or otherwise) the expense of the goods owner, then in my judgment the goods owner has a direct cause of action to recover such expense. No authority to the contrary was cited and I know of none relating to road transport."

Lord Roche there is, as I understand it, recognising in his illustration concerning two lorries that the driver of one lorry does owe a duty of care towards the owners of the goods carried by the other. Lord Porter, who was also a member of the majority in deciding this case, said[2] in relation to the argument about the remoteness of damage:

"It may, however, be said that this is an answer to the contention that the damage is too remote, but does not deal with the allegation that it does not flow from the tortious act but from the contractual relationship between the ship and its cargo. Counsel for the appellants put this contention in the words: 'Liability or damage arising from a contract with a third party gives no ground for a claim for damages in an action for negligence against a wrongdoer unless the liability or damage arose from physical injury to the plaintiff's person or to property owned by or in the possession of the plaintiff'. For this contention there may be much to be said where the person or thing injured was not engaged, as is cargo when being carried in a ship, on a joint adventure."

Counsel for the defendants in the present case drew my attention to those words and contended, I think rightly, that on the main issue with which I am concerned in this case Lord Porter appears to support the defendants' view although he was in favour of the plaintiff in the particular circumstances of the case which he was deciding. Lord Simonds, in a speech with which Lord Simon concurred, deals with the present issue directly. He said:[3]

"In simple terms, A, the ship, has suffered damage which is recoverable against the wrongdoer. B is bound to contribute to A's loss. Can B recover the amount of his contribution from the wrongdoer? It will be observed that, to simplify the problem, I have ignored a point, which may yet be of significance, that A has included in the expenditure, in respect of which contribution is claimed, items which were agreed to be irrecoverable from the wrongdoer, but, taking the problem in the simple form that I have stated, I do not see how, on the ordinary principles of the law of damages, B can recover from the wrongdoer."

He then went on to deal with *Simpson* v. *Thomson*[4] in some detail, and continued:[5]

"This case [*Simpson* v. *Thomson*[4]] was lightly dismissed by the counsel for the

1. [1911] 1 K.B. 243.
2. [1947] A.C. at p. 296; [1946] 2 All E.R. at p. 710.
3. [1947] A.C. at p. 304; [1946] 2 All E.R. at p. 714.
4. (1877), 3 App. Cas. 279.
5. [1947] A.C. at p. 305; [1946] 2 All E.R. at p. 715.

respondents on the ground that general average contribution had nothing to do with insurance. That did not meet the point. The insurer has no independent claim in respect of a wrong suffered by the assured, though he may be subrogated to his right and sue in his name with all the consequences that ensue from subrogation; and this is so notwithstanding that the wrongdoer might well assume, as in the case of a collision between two motor cars, that not only the owner of the innocent car but also its insurer would suffer loss. The reason why he cannot recover is not because it could not be reasonably foreseen that he, or at least some insurer, would suffer, but because his loss is of a kind which the law does not regard as recoverable. So, too, with general average contribution. The loss arises from the obligation, whether contractual or imposed by the general law, to indemnify another from loss sustained by him. The contributor has no property in, or possession of, the damaged ship. In respect of that damage he has no independent right: in respect of his own loss he can have no action against the wrongdoer. It is irrelevant that the latter might reasonably have foreseen that, if his negligence caused a collision, owners of cargo on the injured ship would probably be called on to make a general average contribution."

The decision in that case no doubt depended to some extent on its special facts, but in my judgment it supports the view that in an action of negligence founded on failure to take care to avoid damage to the property of another, only those whose property is injured, or is at least directly threatened with injury, can recover. . . .

Then, finally, I would like to refer to a decision of the Privy Council in *A.-G. for New South Wales* v. *Perpetual Trustee Co., Ltd.*[1] In that case the Government of New South Wales unsuccessfully claimed damages from a person who had negligently injured a policeman and thus deprived the plaintiffs of the policeman's services. Again, I refer to the case not for its own facts but for the statement of principle which is contained in the opinion of Lord Simonds which was delivered as the opinion of the Board. He said:[2]

"... it is fundamental (as Rich J. pointed out in *Commonwealth* v. *Quince*[3]) that the mere fact that an injury to A prevents a third party from getting from A a benefit which he would otherwise have obtained does not invest the third party with a right of action against the wrongdoer",

and Lord Simonds there referred to *Bennetts'* case[4] again.

As I have said, there are probably a dozen other cases which could be cited to illustrate the application of that principle, but I am invited to consider those cases in the light of the more recent decision of the House of Lords in *Hedley Byrne & Co., Ltd.* v. *Heller & Partners, Ltd.*[5] That was a case in which an action was brought against a bank for having negligently given a reference as to the standing of one of its customers on which reference the plaintiffs were alleged to have acted to their detriment. No contract existed between the plaintiffs and the defendants and the claim was based on negligence at common law, the injury to the plaintiffs being the foreseeable consequence of the defendants' failure to take care. The giving of the reference was not an act which could conceivably do direct injury to the person or property of anyone, and the claim was of a kind sometimes described as an action for negligent words rather than for negligent acts, and of a kind which had not previously been recognised in the absence of a contractual or fiduciary relationship between the parties. It is now submitted that the plaintiffs' ultimate success[6] in the House of Lords in *Hedley Byrne & Co., Ltd.* v. *Heller & Partners, Ltd.*[5] has swept away any existing notion that direct

1. [1955] A.C. 457; [1955] 1 All E.R. 846.
2. [1955] A.C. at p. 484; [1955] 1 All E.R. at p. 854.
3. (1944), 68 C.L.R. 227, at p. 240.
4. [1911] 1 K.B. 243.
5. [1964] A.C. 465; [1963] 2 All E.R. 575.
6. [Note the action in fact failed, see p. 501, *post.*]

injury to the person or property of the plaintiff is necessary to support an action in negligence and that the door is now open for the plaintiffs in the present action to recover the indirect or consequential loss which they have suffered.

I think it important to remember at the outset that in the cases to which I have referred, the act or omission relied on as constituting a breach of the duty to take care was an act or omission which might foreseeably have caused direct injury to the person or property of another. The world of commerce would come to a halt and ordinary life would become intolerable if the law imposed a duty on all persons at all times to restrain from any conduct which might foreseeably cause detriment to another, but where an absence of reasonable care may foreseeably cause direct injury to the person or property of another, a duty to take such care exists. It is against the background of this duty that the judgments to which I have referred must be considered. . . . What then is the explanation of the plaintiff's failure in these earlier cases? Is it that the courts mistakenly thought that "indirect" or "consequential" or "economic" damage, as it has variously been called, should not be accepted as sufficient injury to the plaintiff to support an action in negligence, or is it that in the particular circumstances of the case no duty of care was owed to the plaintiff at all? Economic or consequential damage may be as real to the plaintiff as direct physical injury and Lord Devlin demonstrated the illogicality of a distinction on those lines in *Hedley Byrne's* case where he said:[1]

"That is why the distinction is now said to depend on whether financial loss is caused through physical injury or whether it is caused directly. The interposition of the physical injury is said to make a difference of principle. I can find neither logic nor common sense in this. If irrespective of contract, a doctor negligently advises a patient that he can safely pursue his occupation and he cannot and the patient's health suffers and he loses his livelihood, the patient has a remedy. But if the doctor negligently advises him that he cannot safely pursue his occupation when in fact he can and he loses his livelihood, there is said to be no remedy. Unless, of course, the patient was a private patient and the doctor accepted half a guinea for his trouble: then the patient can recover all. I am bound to say, my lords, that I think this to be nonsense. It is not the sort of nonsense that can arise even in the best system of law out of the need to draw nice distinctions between borderline cases. It arises, if it is the law, simply out of a refusal to make sense. The line is not drawn on any intelligible principle. It just happens to be the line which those who have been driven from the extreme assertion that negligent statements in the absence of contractual or fiduciary duty give no cause of action have in the course of their retreat so far reached."

In my judgment, the plaintiff's failure in these earlier cases was not because this truth to which Lord Devlin refers had escaped the eminent judges who decided those cases, but because the plaintiff was regarded as being outside the scope of the defendant's duty to take care. The duty of care arose only because a lack of care might cause direct injury to the person or property of someone, and the duty was owed only to those whose person or property were foreseeably at risk. The decision in *Hedley Byrne & Co., Ltd.* v. *Heller & Partners, Ltd.*[2] does not depart in any way from the fundamental that there can be no claim for negligence in the absence of a duty of care owed to the plaintiff. It recognises that a duty of care may arise in the giving of advice even though no contract or fiduciary relationship exists between the giver of the advice and the person who may act on it, and having recognised the existence of the duty it goes on to recognise that indirect or economic loss will suffice to support the plaintiff's claim. What the case does not decide is that an ability to foresee indirect or economic loss to another as a result of one's conduct automatically imposes a duty to take care to avoid that loss.

---

1. [1964] A.C. at p. 517; [1963] 2 All E.R. at p. 602.
2. [1964] A.C. 465; [1963] 2 All E.R. 575.

In my judgment, there is nothing in *Hedley Byrne & Co., Ltd.* v. *Heller & Partners, Ltd.*[1] to affect the common law principle that a duty of care which arises from a risk of direct injury to person or property is owed only to those whose person or property may foreseeably be injured by a failure to take care. If the plaintiff can show that the duty was owed to him, he can recover both direct and consequential loss which is reasonably foreseeable, and for myself I see no reason for saying that proof of direct loss is an essential part of his claim. He must, however, show that he was within the scope of the defendant's duty to take care.

In the present case, the defendants' duty to take care to avoid the escape of the virus was due to the foreseeable fact that the virus might infect cattle in the neighbourhood and cause them to die. The duty of care is accordingly owed to the owners of cattle in the neighbourhood, but the plaintiffs are not owners of cattle and have no proprietary interest in anything which might conceivably be damaged by the virus if it escaped. Even if the plaintiffs have a proprietary interest in the premises known as Farnham Market, these premises are not in jeopardy. In my judgment, therefore, the plaintiffs' claim in negligence fails even if the assumptions of fact most favourable to them are made. . . .

Judgment for the defendants

Spartan Steel and Alloys, Ltd. v. Martin & Co. (Contractors), Ltd.

Court of Appeal   [1972] 3 All E.R. 557

LORD DENNING M.R.: The plaintiffs, Spartan Steel & Alloys, Ltd., have a factory in Birmingham where they manufacture stainless steel. The factory obtains its electricity by a direct cable from a power station of the Midlands Electricity Board.

In June 1969 contractors called Martin & Co. (Contractors), Ltd., the defendants, were doing work on a road about a quarter of a mile away. They were going to dig up the road with a big power-driven excavating shovel. They made enquiries about the place of the cables, mains and so forth, under the road. They were given plans showing them. But unfortunately their men did not take reasonable care. The shovel damaged the cable which supplied electricity to the plaintiffs' works. The electricity board shut down the power whilst they mended the cable.

The factory was at that time working continuously for 24 hours all round the clock. The electric power was shut off at 7.40 p.m. on 12 June 1969, and was off for 14½ hours until it was restored at 10.00 a.m. on 13 June 1969. This was all through the night and a couple of hours more. But, as this factory was doing night work, it suffered loss. At the time when the power was shut off, there was an arc furnace in which metal was being melted in order to be converted into ingots. Electric power was needed throughout in order to maintain the temperature and melt the metal. When the power failed, there was a danger that the metal might solidify in the furnace and do damage to the lining of the furnace. So the plaintiffs used oxygen to melt the material and poured it from a tap out of the furnace. But this meant that the melted material was of much less value. The physical damage was assessed at £368. In addition, if that particular melt had been properly completed, the plaintiffs would have made a profit on it of £400. Furthermore, during those 14½ hours, when the power was cut off, the plaintiffs would have been able to put four more melts through the furnace; and, by being unable to do so, they lost a profit of £1,767.

The plaintiffs claim all those sums as damages against the defendants for negligence. No evidence was given at the trial, because the defendants admitted that they had been negligent. The contest was solely on the amount of damages. The defendants take their stand on the recent decision in this court of *S.C.M. (United Kingdom), Ltd.* v.

---

1. [1964] A.C. 465; [1963] 2 All E.R. 575.

W. J. Whittall & Son, Ltd.[1] They admit that they are liable for the £368 physical damages. They did not greatly dispute that they are also liable for the £400 loss of profit on the first melt, because that was truly consequential on the physical damages and thus covered by *S.C.M.* v. *Whittall.*[1] But they deny that they are liable for the £1,767 for the other four melts. They say that was economic loss for which they are not liable. The judge rejected their contention and held them liable for all the loss. The defendants appeal to this court. . . .

At bottom I think the question of recovering economic loss is one of policy. Whenever the courts draw a line to mark out the bounds of *duty*, they do it as a matter of policy so as to limit the responsibility of the defendant. Whenever the courts set bounds to the *damages* recoverable—saying that they are, or are not, too remote— they do it as matter of policy so as to limit the liability of the defendant.

In many of the cases where economic loss has been held not to be recoverable, it has been put on the ground that the defendant was under no *duty* to the plaintiff. Thus where a person is injured in a road accident by the negligence of another, the negligent driver owes a duty to the injured man himself, but he owes no duty to the servant of the injured man: see *Best* v. *Samuel Fox & Co., Ltd.;*[2] nor to the master of the injured man: *I.R. Comrs.* v. *Hambrook;*[3] nor to anyone else who suffers loss because he had a contract with the injured man: see *Simpson & Co.* v. *Thomson;*[4] nor indeed to anyone who only suffers economic loss on account of the accident: see *Kirkham* v. *Boughey.*[5] Likewise, when property is damaged by the negligence of another, the negligent tortfeasor owes a duty to the owner or possessor of the chattel, but not to one who suffers loss only because he had a contract entitling him to use the chattel or giving him a right to receive it at some later date: see *Elliott Steam Tug Co.* v. *Shipping Controller*[6] and *Margarine Union GmbH* v. *Cambay Prince Steamship Co., Ltd.*[7]

In other cases, however, the defendant seems clearly to have been under a duty to the plaintiff, but the economic loss has not been recovered because it is too remote. Take the illustration given by Blackburn J. in *Cattle* v. *Stockton Waterworks Co.*[8] when water escapes from a reservoir and floods a coalmine where many men are working; those who had their tools or clothes destroyed could recover, but those who only lost their wages could not. Similarly, when the defendants' ship negligently sank a ship which was being towed by a tug, the owner of the tug lost his remuneration, but he could not recover it from the negligent ship although the same duty (of navigation with reasonable care) was owed to both tug and tow: see *Société Remorquage à Hélice* v. *Bennetts.*[9] In such cases if the plaintiff or his property had been physically injured, he would have recovered; but, as he only suffered economic loss, he is held not entitled to recover. This is, I should think, because the loss is regarded by the law as too remote: see *King* v. *Phillips.*[10]

On the other hand, in the cases where economic loss by itself has been held to be recoverable, it is plain that there was a duty to the plaintiff and the loss was not too remote. Such as when one ship negligently runs down another ship, and damages it, with the result that the cargo has to be discharged and reloaded. The negligent ship was already under a duty to the cargo-owners; and they can recover the cost of discharging and reloading it, as it is not too remote: see *Morrison Steamship Co., Ltd.* v. *Steamship Greystoke Castle (Owners of Cargo lately laden on).*[11] Likewise, when a banker

---

1. [1971] 1 Q.B. 337; [1970] 3 All E.R. 245.
2. [1952] A.C. 716, at p. 731; [1952] 2 All E.R. 394, at p. 398.
3. [1956] 2 Q.B. 656, at p. 660; [1956] 3 All E.R. 338, at pp. 339, 340.
4. (1877), 3 App. Cas. 279, at p. 289.
5. [1958] 2 Q.B. 338, at p. 341; [1957] 3 All E.R. 153, at p. 155.
6. [1922] 1 K.B. 127, at p. 139.
7. [1969] 1 Q.B. 219, at pp. 251, 252; [1967] 3 All E.R. 775, at p. 794.
8. (1875) L.R. 10 Q.B. 453, at p. 457; [1874–80] All E.R. Rep. 220, at p. 223.
9. [1911] 1 K.B. 243, at p. 248.
10. [1953] 1 Q.B. 429, at pp. 439, 440; [1953] 1 All E.R. 617, at p. 622.
11. [1947] A.C. 265; [1946] 2 All E.R. 696.

negligently gives a reference to one who acts on it, the duty is plain and the damage is not too remote: see *Hedley Byrne & Co., Ltd.* v. *Heller & Partners, Ltd.*[1]

The more I think about these cases, the more difficult I find it to put each into its proper pigeon-hole. Sometimes I say: "There was no duty." In others I say: "The damage was too remote." So much so that I think the time has come to discard those tests which have proved so elusive. It seems to me better to consider the particular relationship in hand, and see whether or not, as a matter of policy, economic loss should be recoverable. Thus in *Weller & Co.* v. *Foot and Mouth Disease Research Institute*[2] it was plain that the loss suffered by the auctioneers was not recoverable, no matter whether it is put on the ground that there was no duty or that the damage was too remote. Again, in *Electrochrome, Ltd.* v. *Welsh Plastics, Ltd.*,[3] it is plain that the economic loss suffered by the plaintiffs' factory (due to the damage to the fire hydrant) was not recoverable, whether because there was no duty or that it was too remote.

So I turn to the relationship in the present case. It is of common occurrence. The parties concerned are the electricity board who are under a statutory duty to maintain supplies of electricity in their district; the inhabitants of the district, including this factory, who are entitled by statute to a continuous supply of electricity for their use; and the contractors who dig up the road. Similar relationships occur with other statutory bodies, such as gas and water undertakings. The cable may be damaged by the negligence of the statutory undertaker, or by the negligence of the contractor, or by accident without any negligence by anyone; and the power may have to be cut off whilst the cable is repaired. Or the power may be cut off owing to a short-circuit in the power house; and so forth. If the cutting off of the supply causes economic loss to the consumers, should it as matter of policy be recoverable? And against whom?

The first consideration is the position of the statutory undertakers. If the board do not keep up the voltage or pressure of electricity, gas or water—or, likewise, if they shut it off for repairs—and thereby cause economic loss to their consumers, they are not liable in damages, not even if the cause of it is due to their own negligence. The only remedy (which is hardly ever pursued) is to prosecute the board before the justices. Such is the result of many cases, starting with a water board: *Atkinson* v. *Newcastle and Gateshead Waterworks Co.*;[4] going on to a gas board: *Clegg, Parkinson & Co.* v. *Earby Gas Co.*;[5] and then to an electricity company: *Stevens* v. *Aldershot Gas, Water and District Lighting Co.*[6] In those cases the courts, looking at the legislative enactments, held that Parliament did not intend to expose the board to liability for damages to the inhabitants en masse: see what Lord Cairns L.C. said[7] and Wills J.[8] No distinction was made between economic loss and physical damage; and taken at their face value the reasoning would mean that the board was not liable for physical damage either. But there is another group of cases which go to show that, if the board, by their negligence in the conduct of their supply, cause direct physical damage to person or property, the cases seem to show that they are liable: see *Milnes* v. *Huddersfield Corpn.*[9] per Lord Blackburn; *Midwood & Co., Ltd.* v. *Manchester Corpn.*;[10] *Heard* v. *Brymbo Steel Co., Ltd.*[11] and *Hartley* v. *Mayoh & Co.*[12] But one thing is clear, the board have never been held liable for economic loss only. If such be the policy of the legislature in regard to electricity boards, it would seem right for the common law to

1. [1964] A.C. 465; [1963] 2 All E.R. 575.
2. [1966] 1 Q.B. 569; [1965] 3 All E.R. 560.
3. [1968] 2 All E.R. 205.
4. (1877), 2 Ex. D. 441; [1874–80] All E.R. Rep. 757.
5. [1896] 1 Q.B. 592.
6. (1932), 102 L.J.K.B. 12.
7. In *Atkinson* v. *Newcastle and Gateshead Waterworks Co.* (1877), 2 Ex. D. at p. 445.
8. In *Clegg, Parkinson & Co.* v. *Earby Gas Co.*, [1896] 1 Q.B. at p. 595.
9. (1886), 11 App. Cas. 511, at p. 530.
10. [1905] 2 K.B. 597.
11. [1947] K.B. 692.
12. [1954] 1 Q.B. 383; [1954] 1 All E.R. 375.

adopt a similar policy in regard to contractors. If the electricity boards are not liable for economic loss due to negligence which results in the cutting off of the supply, nor should a contractor be liable.

The second consideration is the nature of the hazard, namely, the cutting of the supply of electricity. This is a hazard which we all run. It may be due to a short circuit, to a flash of lightning, to a tree falling on the wires, to an accidental cutting of the cable, or even to the negligence of someone or other. And when it does happen, it affects a multitude of persons; not as a rule by way of physical damage to them or their property, but by putting them to inconvenience, and sometimes to economic loss. The supply is usually restored in a few hours, so the economic loss is not very large. Such a hazard is regarded by most people as a thing they must put up with—without seeking compensation from anyone. Some there are who install a stand-by system. Others seek refuge by taking out an insurance policy against breakdown in the supply. But most people are content to take the risk on themselves. When the supply is cut off, they do not go running round to their solicitor. They do not try to find out whether it was anyone's fault. They just put up with it. They try to make up the economic loss by doing more work next day. This is a healthy attitude which the law should encourage.

The third consideration is this. If claims for economic loss were permitted for this particular hazard, there would be no end of claims. Some might be genuine, but many might be inflated, or even false. A machine might not have been in use anyway, but it would be easy to put it down to the cut in supply. It would be well-nigh impossible to check the claims. If there was economic loss on one day, did the applicant do his best to mitigate it by working harder next day? And so forth. Rather than expose claimants to such temptation and defendants to such hard labour—on comparatively small claims—it is better to disallow economic loss altogether, at any rate when it stands alone, independent of any physical damage.

The fourth consideration is that, in such a hazard as this, the risk of economic loss should be suffered by the whole community who suffer the losses—usually many but comparatively small losses—rather than on the one pair of shoulders, that is, on the contractor on whom the total of them, all added together, might be very heavy.

The fifth consideration is that the law provides for deserving cases. If the defendant is guilty of negligence which cuts off the electricity supply and causes actual physical damage to person or property, that physical damage can be recovered: see *Baker* v. *Crow Carrying Co., Ltd.*,[1] referred to by Buckley L.J. in *S.C.M.* v. *Whittall*,[2] and also any economic loss truly consequential on the material damage: see *British Celanese, Ltd.* v. *A. H. Hunt (Capacitors), Ltd.*[3] and *S.C.M.* v. *Whittall*.[4] Such cases will be comparatively few. They will be readily capable of proof and will be easily checked. They should be and are admitted.

These considerations lead me to the conclusion that the plaintiffs should recover for the physical damage to the one melt (£368), and the loss of profit on that melt consequent thereon (£400); but not for the loss of profit on the four melts (£1,767), because that was economic loss independent of the physical damage. I would, therefore, allow the appeal and reduce the damages to £768.

EDMUND DAVIES L.J. (dissenting on the question of the pure financial loss): . . . For my part, I cannot see why the £400 loss of profit here sustained should be recoverable and not the £1,767. It is common ground that both types of loss were equally foreseeable and equally direct consequences of the defendants' admitted negligence, and the only distinction drawn is that the former figure represents the profit lost as a result of the physical damage done to the material in the furnace at the time when the power

---

1. 1 February (1960) (unreported).
2. [1971] 1 Q.B. at p. 356; [1970] 3 All E.R. at p. 261.
3. [1969] 2 All E.R. 1252; [1969] 1 W.L.R. 959.
4. [1971] 1 Q.B. 337; [1970] 3 All E.R. 245.

was cut off. But what has that purely fortuitous fact to do with legal principle? In my judgment, nothing. . . .

Having considered the intrinsic nature of the problem presented in this appeal, and having consulted the relevant authorities, my conclusion . . . is that an action lies in negligence for damages in respect of purely economic loss, provided that it was a reasonably foreseeable and direct consequence of failure in a duty of care. The application of such a rule can undoubtedly give rise to difficulties in certain sets of circumstances, but so can the suggested rule that economic loss may be recovered *provided* it is directly consequential on physical damage. Many alarming situations were conjured up in the course of counsel's arguments before us. In their way, they were reminiscent of those formerly advanced against awarding damages for nervous shock; for example, the risk of fictitious claims and expensive litigation, the difficulty of disproving the alleged cause and effect, and the impossibility of expressing such a claim in financial terms. But I suspect that they . . . would for the most part be resolved either on the ground that no duty of care was owed to the injured party or that the damages sued for were irrecoverable *not* because they were simply financial but because they were too remote. . . .

LAWTON L.J.: This appeal raises neatly a question which has been asked from time to time since Blackburn J. delivered his well-known judgment in *Cattle* v. *Stockton Waterworks Co.*[1] and more frequently since the decision in *Hedley Byrne & Co., Ltd.* v. *Heller & Partners, Ltd.*,[2] namely, whether a plaintiff can recover from a defendant, proved or admitted to have been negligent, foreseeable financial damage which is not consequential on foreseeable physical injury or damage to property. Any doubts there may have been about the recovery of such consequential financial damage were settled by this court in *S.C.M. (United Kingdom), Ltd.* v. *W. J. Whittall & Son, Ltd.*[3] In my judgment the answer to this question is that such financial damage cannot be recovered save when it is the immediate consequence of a breach of duty to safeguard the plaintiff from that kind of loss.

This is not the first time a negligent workman has cut an electric supply cable nor the first claim for damages arising out of such an incident. When in practice at the Bar I myself advised in a number of such cases. Most practitioners acting for insurers under the so-called "public liability" types of policy will have had similar professional experiences; if not with electrical supply, with gas and water mains. Negligent interference with such services is one of the facts of life and can cause a lot of damage, both physical and financial. Water conduits have been with us for centuries; gas mains for nearly a century and a half; electricity supply cables for about three-quarters of a century; but there is not a single case in the English law reports which is an authority for the proposition that mere financial loss resulting from negligent interruption of such services is recoverable. Why?

Many lawyers would be likely to answer that ever since *Cattle* v. *Stockton Waterworks Co.*[1] such damages have been irrecoverable. Edmund Davies L.J. has just stated that he doubts whether Blackburn J. laid down any such rule. Knowing that he had these doubts, I have re-read *Cattle* v. *Stockton Waterworks Co.*[1] The claim was in negligence. The declaration was as follows:[4]

"... that defendants, being a water company, so negligently laid down under a certain turnpike road their pipes for supplying water to a district, and so negligently kept and maintained the pipes in such insufficient repair, and in such imperfect and leaky condition, that, while the plaintiff was lawfully constructing for reward to the plaintiff a tunnel across the turnpike road, and was lawfully using the road for such purpose, the pipes leaked, and large quantities of water flowed into

1. (1875), L.R. 10 Q.B. 453; [1874–80] All E.R. Rep. 220.
2. [1964] A.C. 465; [1963] 2 All E.R. 575.
3. [1971] 1 Q.B. 337; [1970] 3 All E.R. 245.
4. (1875), L.R. 10 Q.B. at p. 453.

the road, and upon the plaintiff's workings, and flooded them, and plaintiff was hindered and delayed in the work, and suffered great loss."

The declaration raised precisely the problem which has to be solved in this case; Blackburn J.'s answer was in these words:[1]

"In the present case there is no pretence for saying that the defendants were malicious or had any intention to injure anyone. They were, at most, guilty of a neglect of duty, which occasioned injury to the property of Knight, but which did not injure any property of the plaintiff. The plaintiff's claim is to recover the damage which he has sustained by his contract with Knight becoming less profitable, or, it may be, a losing contract, in consequence of this injury to Knight's property. We think this does not give him any right of action."

Earlier in his judgment he had said:[2] "No authority in favour of the plaintiff's right to sue was cited, and, as far as our knowledge goes, there was none that could have been cited." There is still no authority directly in point today. Blackburn J.'s judgment has been cited with approval and followed many times; the judgment of Hamilton J. in *Société Anonyme de Remorquage à Hélice* v. *Bennetts*[3] and of Widgery J. in *Weller & Co.* v. *Foot and Mouth Disease Research Institute*[4] are instances. For nearly 100 years now contractors and insurers have negotiated policies and premiums have been calculated on the assumption that Blackburn J.'s judgment is a correct statement of the law; and those affected financially by the acts of negligent contractors have been advised time and time again that mere financial loss is irrecoverable. . . .

The differences which undoubtedly exist between what damage can be recovered in one type of case and what in another cannot be reconciled on any logical basis. I agree with Lord Denning M.R. that such differences have arisen because of the policy of the law. Maybe there should be one policy for all cases; the enunciation of such a policy is not, in my judgment, a task for this court. . . .

In my judgment the rule enunciated in 1875 by Blackburn J. is the correct one to apply in negligence cases.

When this principle is applied to the facts of this case it produces the result referred to by Lord Denning M.R. in his judgment. I too would allow the appeal and reduce the damages to £768.

Appeal allowed

Questions

1. Are the courts doing anything more than drawing an arbitrary line in these cases? If not, is there any better place to draw the line? (For the relevance of insurance considerations, see a note by J. A. Jolowicz on the *Spartan Steel* case, [1973] C.L.J. 20; and see the specimen policy, p. 689, *post*.)

2. Do you agree with Lord Denning M.R. that the "law provides for deserving cases"?

Notes

1. Whatever the illogicality of it, these last two cases show that an important distinction is drawn between physical and purely financial loss. It should be noted that financial loss which is itself consequential on physical damage

---

1. (1875), L.R. 10 Q.B. at p. 458; [1874–80] All E.R. Rep. at p. 224.
2. (1875), L.R. 10 Q.B. at pp. 457, 458; [1874–80] All E.R. Rep. at p. 223.
3. [1911] 1 K.B. 243, at p. 248.
4. [1966] 1 Q.B. 569, at p. 588; [1965] 3 All E.R. 560, at p. 570.

to the plaintiff's person or property is recoverable e.g. the loss of profit on the first melt in the *Spartan Steel* case.

2. For similarities in the development of this area of the law in the United States of America, see Fleming James Jr., "Limitations on Liability for Economic Loss Caused by Negligence: A Pragmatic Appraisal" (1972), 12 J.S.P.T.L. (N.S.) 105, at pp. 107–108. In the Scottish case of *Dynamco, Ltd.* v. *Holland and Hannen and Cubitts (Scotland), Ltd.*, 1972 S.L.T. 38, another "power failure" case, Lord Migdale, with whom the Lord President agreed, expressed the opinion (at pp. 39–40) that the "law of Scotland has for over a hundred years refused to accept that a claim for financial loss which does not arise directly from damage to the claimants' property can give rise to a legal claim for damages founded on negligence. That is the conclusion at which the Lord Ordinary has arrived and I agree with him."

3. Counsel for the plaintiffs in the *Spartan Steel* case argued unsuccessfully that the £1,767 could be recovered as parasitic damages. On this concept, see McGregor, *Damages* (13th Edn.), paras. 164–170

4. *Hedley Byrne & Co., Ltd.* v. *Heller & Partners, Ltd.*, [1964] A.C. 465; [1963] 2 All E.R. 575 which is mentioned in the cases above, is set out in detail, p. 501, *post*, along with other cases concerning liability for financial loss resulting from negligent statements. Those authorities should be compared with the cases in this section. The whole area is a difficult one, and attention might usefully be paid to the following articles—P. S. Atiyah, "Negligence and Economic Loss" (1967), 83 L.Q.R. 248; A. H. Brown, "The Recovery of Economic Loss in Tort" (1972), 2 Auckland U.L.R. 50.

2 THE DUTY OF POSITIVE ACTION

(a) Omissions

East Suffolk Rivers Catchment Board v. Kent

House of Lords   [1940] 4 All E.R. 527

An exceptionally high tide and a gale caused many breaches in the walls which guarded marshlands lying below the normal high tide level. One of the respondents was the occupier, the other being the owner, of fifty acres of land which were flooded from a breach in the wall twenty or thirty feet across. The appellants, acting under a statutory power, had attempted to mend all the breaches in their area. The trial judge's view of their action in repairing the twenty or thirty foot breach is set out in Viscount Simon's speech in this case, in which the respondents sued the appellants for damages:

VISCOUNT SIMON L.C.: . . . In the other cases, on the River Deben, the appellants seem to have been successful, but Hilbery J. has found, and, following the Court of Appeal,[1] I am prepared to accept his finding on the facts, that the methods adopted and the staff employed in trying to repair the damage to the wall with which we are concerned in this case were so inefficient that, whereas the gap could, by the exercise of reasonable skill, have been closed and the flooding arrested in 14 days, this result was not in fact attained till after the lapse of 164 days. In the meantime, of course, the marsh pastures remained covered by salt water, and the respondents continued to suffer the damage which had been initiated by the breach in the wall. For the purpose of

---

1. [*Kent and Porter* v. *East Suffolk Rivers Catchment Board*, [1939] 4 All E.R. 174; on appeal from Hilberry J., [1939] 2 All E.R. 207.]

deciding the difficult and important issue of principle which now arises, details as to the appellants' unsuccessful efforts do not matter, but it is convenient to state that it was only at the third attempt that the gap was successfully filled, and that, in the view of the judge, who had a body of expert evidence before him, the earlier efforts of the appellants, which consisted in attempting to build straight across the gap instead of building a semi-circular bastion out into the saltings and then reconstructing the wall behind this protection, had only the remotest possibility of success, and caused the delay.

The problem of law which now arises for solution is by no means an easy one. Its essential elements are these: (i) The appellant board were under no statutory duty to repair the breach, but they had the power to enter upon the land for the purpose of endeavouring to effect such repair, and they did so enter. (ii) It was the original breach in the wall, caused by the act of nature, which produced the flooding of the respondents' land, and it was the operations of the tide which kept it flooded. The efforts of the appellants were directed to abating this damage. (iii) If the appellants had not shown such want of skill in trying to repair the wall, and if they had been served by an adequate and well-trained staff, the gap in the wall would have been closed much sooner than it was, and the flooding would have been more promptly abated. The question is whether, in the above circumstances, the appellants are liable to the respondents in damages to such amount as would represent the net loss to the respondents due to the delay in abating the flood. The Court of Appeal were divided on this issue. Slesser and Mackinnon L.JJ. thought that the appellants were liable as for breach of duty to do their work with reasonable care and expedition. du Parcq L.J., differed, and held that the appellant board was [p. 183]:

". . . not liable for damage suffered through failure to exercise its powers adequately, or at all, even though the damage might have been averted or lessened by the exercise of reasonable care and skill."

It is not, of course, disputed that, if the appellants, in the course of exercising their statutory powers, had inflicted fresh injury on the respondents through lack of care or skill, they would be liable in damages for the consequences of their negligent act. If, for example, the appellants by their unskilful proceedings had caused a further area of the respondents' land to be flooded, or had prolonged the period of flooding beyond what it would have been if they had never interfered, they would be liable. Apart from two minor matters, however, which it is agreed do not govern the main issue, nothing of this sort happened. The respondents would have gained if the flooding had been stopped sooner. Their complaint against the appellants is that they did not act with sufficient skill to stop it more promptly, but they cannot point to any injury inflicted upon them by the appellant board, unless it be the board's want of success in endeavouring to stop the flooding at an earlier date.

In order that the respondents should succeed in this action, it is necessary that they should establish, not only that the appellants were wanting in care and skill when exercising their statutory powers, but that they inflicted injury and loss upon the respondents by their negligence. . . . In the present case, the damage done by the flooding was not due to the exercise of the appellants' statutory powers at all. It was due to the forces of nature, which the appellants, albeit unskilfully, were endeavouring to counteract. Supposing, for example, that, after the appellants had made their first unsuccessful attempt, they had decided to abandon their efforts altogether, the respondents could have had no legal claim against them for withdrawing, even though the result might have been to leave the respondents' land indefinitely flooded. This shows, I think, how different is the relation between the catchment board and individual owners or occupiers like the respondents and the relation between a contractor employed by the respondents to mend the wall. In the latter case, the respondents would have a remedy in damages if the contractor did not exercise reasonable skill and promptness in discharging his task, and if damage resulted; but in the former case the catchment board has its responsibilities over the whole of its area to consider. It may be that in its judgment it is necessary to use its skilled staff in mending other breaches. It may be that the outlay involved in making a good job of one particular repair is more than its limited finances will permit. . . .

. . . [T]he respondents' claim is ill-founded. They have suffered damage by the flooding of their land during four months or more. They seek to recover compensation from the appellants for all of this loss except the first fortnight. However, the appellants did not cause the loss. It was caused by the operations of nature which the appellants were endeavouring, not very successfully, to counteract. It is admitted that the respondents would have no claim if the appellants had never intervened at all. In my opinion, the respondents equally have no claim when the appellants do intervene, save in respect of such damage as flows from their intervention and as might have been avoided if their intervention had been more skilfully conducted. In my opinion, therefore, the appeal should be allowed.

LORD ATKIN (dissenting): . . . I treat it . . . as established that a public authority, whether doing an act which it is its duty to do or doing an act which it is merely empowered to do, must, in doing the act, do it without negligence, or, as it is put in some of the cases, must not do it carelessly or improperly. Quite apart from a duty owed to a particular individual, which is the question in this case, I suggest that it would be difficult to lay down that a duty upon a public authority to act without negligence or not carelessly or improperly does not include a duty to act with reasonable diligence, by which I mean reasonable despatch. I cannot imagine this House affording its support to a proposition so opposed to public interests where there are so many public bodies exercising statutory powers and employing public money upon them. I myself have been unable to think of any case where a duty to perform a continuous operation with reasonable care—i.e., without negligence—does not involve an obligation to perform it with reasonable despatch. Of course, what is reasonable means reasonable in all the circumstances of the particular case.

I thus come to the crucial point in this case. To whom is such a duty owed, or who can complain of the failure to use reasonable despatch? It must be conceded that instances will occur of the performance of powers where it might be difficult for a member of the public generally to complain of unreasonable delay. For instance, delay in the work of relaying the surface of a highway may not be actionable at the suit of members of the public who are put to expense and inconvenience by having to make a detour. Even in this case I think something might be said for a householder or shopkeeper on the route under repair who is for an unreasonably long time deprived of access to his premises for himself and his customers. However, we have to deal here with relations between the plaintiffs and the board, which I suggest are much closer than the general relations of members of the public to a public authority. The board were engaging themselves in repairing the plaintiffs' wall with the object of preventing the further flooding of the land of the plaintiffs and I think also one other occupier, and they were operating upon the plaintiffs' land. Subject to what I have to say upon the causation of damage, which I wish for the present purpose to assume, they would know that, the longer the work was delayed, the longer would the waters ebb and flow over the land, with the possibility of damage therefrom. I submit that these relations give rise to a duty owed to the plaintiffs to use reasonable care including despatch, in doing the work. Indeed, over and over again the appellants' counsel admitted that, if and so far as their work was conducted with such unreasonable delay as to deprive the plaintiffs of the use of their land, owing to occupation by the board's workmen or materials, there would be a good claim for damage. This admits a duty owed to the plaintiffs in respect of despatch, and this controversy is confined to the extent of the duty and the injury caused by it. It is in respect of this use of the plaintiffs' land that the question as to the power of the plaintiffs to do the work themselves becomes at all relevant. I feel sure that the reference to this in the judgment of Slesser L.J. was misunderstood in the appellants' argument. It is not that the board owed a duty to the plaintiffs, because the plaintiffs could have done the work themselves. I think that the argument is that the board came upon the plaintiffs' land to do work which the plaintiffs could have done themselves, and that that circumstance indicates a relationship which supports a duty owed to the plaintiffs to do the work with reasonable despatch. I do not wish to refer in detail to *M'Alister (or Donoghue)* v. *Stevenson*,[1] but I venture to think that the principles there accepted by the majority of this House give guidance on this part of the case.

I now come to the second part of the case—namely, whether, if there existed any duty owed by the board to the plaintiffs to conduct the work with reasonable despatch, there was any damage caused by the breach. . . . The doubt which has arisen in the present case is as to whether the particular damage relied on by the plaintiffs was caused by the breach. The flood, it is said, broke down the plaintiffs' wall. The flow of water over their land was caused by the flood. The defendants were engaged in preventing similar damage from happening again to the plaintiffs, and nothing they did or omitted to do caused the damage complained of. I venture to think that this does not quite meet the plaintiff's point. I understand them to say: "True [it] is that we cannot complain of the original flooding, and we must put up with the damage which resulted from the ebb and flow of the water over our lands for a certain time—namely, the time which would expire before our wall was repaired, once you had begun to repair it, with reasonable despatch—x days. On the assumption now made, however, you were under a duty to us to use reasonable despatch, and the water ebbed and flowed over our land for a far longer period, $x+y$ days, and we have suffered damage from the presence of water for this $x+y$ period greater than the damage we would have suffered from the x period alone." If the plaintiffs can prove this, it seems inevitable that the extra damage is directly caused by the breach complained of. . . . I suggest, therefore, that, if the plaintiffs could prove the case indicated above, they should succeed. . . .

LORD ROMER: . . . Where a statutory authority is entrusted with a mere power, it cannot be made liable for any damage sustained by a member of the public by reason of a failure to exercise that power. If, in the exercise of their discretion, they embark upon an execution of the power, the only duty they owe to any member of the public is not thereby to add to the damages which he would have suffered had they done nothing. So long as they exercise their discretion honestly, it is for them to determine the method by which, and the time within which, and the time during which, the power shall be exercised, and they cannot be made liable, except to the extent which I have just mentioned, for any damage which would have been avoided had they exercised their discretion in a more reasonable way.

In the present case, the respondents[2] in the exercise of their discretion selected, and for some time persisted in, a method of repairing the breach in the appellant's wall which no reasonable person would have adopted. I am willing to assume that the result of this was that the appellants were damaged by reason that the sea-water entered and remained upon their marshland for a longer period than it would have done had the respondents adopted the best method of effecting the repair. No one, however, can question, or has attempted to question, the respondents' honesty, and, in my opinion, they cannot be made responsible for that damage. . . .

LORD PORTER . . . The appellants acknowledged their liability for any damage directly due to the action which they took. Under a proper plea, they said, an increase in the amount of soil scoured out by the ebbing and flowing of the flood or damage caused by sacks and soil spread over the respondents' land due to the appellants' activities would form a proper head of damage, but no such claim was made. The only loss complained of was that, owing to the negligent delay in repairing the breach, the respondents' land was flooded for a longer period than it should have been.

. . . where, as here, the damage was not caused by any positive act on the part of

---

1. [1932] A.C. 562.
2. [In this paragraph "respondents" should be read as "appellants" and *vice versa*.]

the appellants, but was caused and would have occurred to the like extent if they had taken no steps at all, I cannot see that the loss which the respondents suffered was due to any breach of a duty owed by the appellants. Their duty was to avoid causing damage, not either to prevent future damage due to causes for which they were not responsible or to shorten its incidence. The loss which the respondents suffered was due to the original breach, and the appellants' failure to close it merely allowed the damage to continue during the time which they took in mending the broken bank. For that I do not think them liable, nor can I find any case the decision in which would lead to that result. . . .

. . . I also desire to make it clear that in what I have said I am not dealing with a case in which it was contended that the authority were estopped from alleging that they were under no obligation to do the work efficiently and with reasonable despatch. No evidence was given, nor was there any plea, that the appellants by their action had caused either of the respondents to change his position in reliance upon anything which they had said or done. Such a case must wait for decision until facts are alleged and proved such as would create an estoppel. The sole question in the present case is whether the mere undertaking of a task which the legislature has empowered an authority to do puts them in the same position as if that task had been imposed as a duty upon them. I agree that it does not, and would allow the appeal.

[LORD THANKERTON delivered a speech in favour of allowing the appeal.]

Appeal allowed

Question

Would this case be more properly classified under the heading "Causation"? (See Chap. 5, p. 170, *post*.)

Dutton v. Bognor Regis United Building Co., Ltd.

Court of Appeal   [1972] 1 All E.R. 462

The facts are taken from the judgment of Sachs L.J.:

In 1958 application was made on behalf of one Mr. Holroyd, a builder, who was developing an area known as Gossamer Estate, Bognor Regis, for planning permission to erect a detached house for private occupation on plot 28 of which he owned the freehold. On 23 October 1958 the council notified their approval of the plans deposited in accordance with the byelaws made by them under the Public Health Act 1936. He proceeded with the erection of a house on that plot and can conveniently be referred to as the "building owner". In due course an inspector from the offices of the Bognor Regis Council ("the council") came to inspect the foundations to see whether they complied with the above byelaws; without his approval the building work could not in practice have gone ahead. He in fact gave approval, but his inspection was so negligent that he failed to observe that the land in the centre of the plot was of such a nature that the foundations being laid were gravely inadequate. The building then went ahead and so the defective foundations were covered up and hidden from any normal subsequent inspection.

After its completion the building owner sold the house on plot 28 to a Mr. Clarke for £4,050, conveying the property to him on 21 January 1960. On 19 December 1960 Mr. Clarke contracted with Mrs. Dutton (the plaintiff in this action) to sell her the house for £4,800. It being a new house no surveyor was employed by her to inspect it—but it was in this court common ground that if such a surveyor had been employed he could not have been expected to find out this particular hidden defect.

The plaintiff moved into the house on 11 January 1961; by the autumn certain cracks commenced to appear in consequence of the hidden defect; the house began to subside with lamentable results which she had no financial means to remedy. The 1962 cost of the necessary work of curing the structural defects and of repairs was at trial agreed to be £2,240 (including surveyors' fees). To that sum there was added £500 described as the reduction in the value of the house; from the resulting £2,740 there was deducted £625 recovered from Mr. Holroyd, and judgment was entered for £2,115. The plaintiff recovered nothing towards the rise over eight years in the cost of the work she could not afford, nor any sum for the gross inconvenience she suffered.''

The action against the builder was settled for £625. The authorities prior to this case had indicated that the builder/vendor of defective premises possessed a certain immunity from liability (see p. 258, *post*). This immunity which was relied upon by the council in its case (the *Bottomley* v. *Bannister* point) was rejected by Lord Denning M.R. and Sachs L.J. although the latter confined his comments to the case of hidden defects on the premises. On the claim against the council, who had appealed:

LORD DENNING M.R. . . .

Power or duty

Much discussion took place before us whether the council were under a *duty* to examine the foundations or had only a *power* to do so. The Public Health Acts do not make this clear. The 1936 Act simply says that it is the duty of the local authority to carry the Act into execution (see s. 1 (1)). The 1961 Act says that it is the function of every local authority to enforce building regulations in their district. The word "function" may mean either a power or a duty.

The reason for this discussion was the case of *East Suffolk Rivers Catchment Board* v. *Kent*.[1] The argument was that if the local authority had a mere *power* to examine the foundations, they were not liable for not exercising that power. But, if they were under a *duty* to do so, they would be liable for not doing it. This argument assumes that the functions of a local authority can be divided into two categories, powers and duties. Every function must be put into one or other category. It is either a *power* or a *duty*. This is, however, a mistake. There is a middle term. It is *control*.

In this case the significant thing, to my mind, is that the legislature gives the local authority a great deal of *control* over building work and the way it is done. They make byelaws governing every stage of the work. They require plans to be submitted to them for approval. They appoint surveyors and inspectors to visit the work and see if the byelaws are being complied with. In case of any contravention of the bye-laws, they can compel the owner to remove the offending work and make it comply with the byelaws. They can also take proceedings for a fine.

In my opinion, the control thus entrusted to the local authority is so extensive that it carries with it a duty. It puts on the council the responsibility of exercising that control properly and with reasonable care. The common law has always held that a right of control over the doing of work carries with it a degree of responsibility in respect of the work. . . . So here, I think, the council, having a right of control over the building of a house, have a responsibility in respect of it. They must, I think, take reasonable care to see that the byelaws are complied with. They must appoint building inspectors to examine the work in progress. Those inspectors must be diligent and visit the work as occasion requires. They must carry out their inspection with reasonable care so as to ensure that the byelaws are complied with. . . .

The position of the professional adviser

Counsel for the council then submitted another reason for saying that the inspector owed no duty to a purchaser. He said that an inspector is in the same position as any professional man who, by virtue of his training and experience, is qualified to give advice to others on how they should act. He said that such a professional man owed

---

1. [1941] A.C. 74; [1940] 4 All E.R. 527.

no duty to one who did not employ him but only took the benefit of his work; and that an inspector was in a like position. . . .

Nowadays, since *Hedley Byrne & Co., Ltd.* v. *Heller & Partners, Ltd.*,[1] it is clear that a professional man who gives guidance to others owes a duty of care, not only to the client who employs him, but also to another who he knows is relying on his skill to save him from harm. It is certain that a banker or accountant is under such a duty. And I see no reason why a solicitor is not likewise. The essence of this proposition, however, is the *reliance*. In *Hedley Byrne* v. *Heller*[1] it was stressed by Lord Reid,[2] by Lord Morris of Borth-y-Gest,[3] and by Lord Hodson.[4] The professional man must know that the other is *relying* on his skill and the other must in fact rely on it.

Reliance

Counsel for the council made a strong point here about reliance. He said that, even if the inspector was under a duty of care, he owed that duty only to those who he knew would rely on this advice—and who did rely on it—and not to those who did not. He said that Mrs. Dutton did not rely on the inspector and he owed her, therefore, no duty.

It is at this point that I must draw a distinction between the several categories of professional men. I can well see that in the case of a professional man who gives advice on financial or property matters—such as a banker, a lawyer or an accountant—his duty is only to those who rely on him and suffer financial loss in consequence. But, in the case of a professional man who gives advice on the safety of buildings, or machines, or material, his duty is to all those who may suffer injury in case his advice is bad. In *Candler* v. *Crane, Christmas & Co.*,[5] I put the case of an analyst who negligently certifies to a manufacturer of food that a particular ingredient is harmless, whereas it is in fact poisonous; or the case of an inspector of lifts who negligently reports that a particular lift is safe, whereas it is in fact dangerous. It was accepted that the analyst and the lift inspector would be liable to any person who was injured by consuming the food or using the lift. Since that case the courts have had the instance of an architect or engineer. If he designs a house or a bridge so negligently that it falls down, he is liable to everyone of those who are injured in the fall: see *Clay* v. *A. J. Crump & Sons, Ltd.*[6] None of those injured would have relied on the architect or the engineer. None of them would have known whether an architect or engineer was employed, or not. But beyond doubt, the architect and engineer would be liable. The reason is, not because those injured relied on him, but because he knew, or ought to have known, that such persons might be injured if he did his work badly. . . .

Proximity

Counsel for the council submitted that in any case the duty ought to be limited to those immediately concerned and not to purchaser after purchaser down the line. There is a good deal in this, but I think the reason is because a subsequent purchaser often has the house surveyed. This intermediate inspection, or opportunity of inspection, may break the proximity. It would certainly do so when it ought to disclose the damage. But the foundations of a house are in a class by themselves. Once covered up, they will not be seen again until the damage appears. The inspector must know this or, at any rate, he ought to know it. Applying the test laid down by Lord Atkin in *M'Alister* (or *Donoghue*) v. *Stevenson*,[7] I should have thought that the inspector ought

---

1. [1964] A.C. 465; [1963] 2 All E.R. 575.
2. [1964] A.C. at p. 486; [1963] 2 All E.R. at p. 583.
3. [1964] A.C. at pp. 502–503; [1963] 2 All E.R. at p. 594.
4. [1964] A.C. at p. 514; [1963] 2 All E.R. at p. 601.
5. [1951] 2 K.B. 164, at p. 179; [1951] 1 All E.R. 426, at p. 433.
6. [1964] 1 Q.B. 533; [1963] 3 All E.R. 687.
7. [1932] A.C. 562, at pp. 580–581; [1932] All E.R. Rep. 1, at p. 11.

to have had subsequent purchasers in mind when he was inspecting the foundations—he ought to have realised that, if he was negligent, they might suffer damage.

Economic loss

· Counsel for the council submitted that the liability of the council would, in any case, be limited to those who suffered bodily harm; and did not extend to those who only suffered economic loss. He suggested, therefore, that although the council might be liable if the ceiling fell down and injured a visitor, they would not be liable simply because the house was diminished in value. He referred to the recent case of *S.C.M. (United Kingdom), Ltd.* v. *W. J. Whittall & Son, Ltd.*[1]

I cannot accept this submission. The damage done here was not solely economic loss. It was physical damage to the house. If counsel's submission were right, it would mean that, if the inspector negligently passes the house as properly built and it collapses and injures a person, the council are liable; but, if the owner discovers the defect in time to repair it—and he does repair it—the council are not liable. That is an impossible distinction. They are liable in either case. I would say the same about the manufacturer of an article. If he makes it negligently, with a latent defect (so that it breaks to pieces and injures someone), he is undoubtedly liable. Suppose that the defect is discovered in time to prevent the injury. Surely he is liable for the cost of repair. . . .

Policy

This case is entirely novel. Never before has a claim been made against a council or its surveyor for negligence in passing a house. The case itself can be brought within the words of Lord Atkin in *M'Alister* (or *Donoghue*) v. *Stevenson*;[2] but, it is a question whether we should apply them here. In *Home Office* v. *Dorset Yacht Co., Ltd.*[3] Lord Reid said that the words of Lord Atkin expressed a principle which ought to apply in general "unless there is some justification or valid explanation for its exclusion". So did Lord Pearson.[4] But Lord Diplock spoke differently. He said[5] that it was a guide but not a principle of universal application. It seems to me that it is a question of policy which we, as judges, have to decide. The time has come when, in cases of new import, we should decide them according to the reason of the thing.

In previous times, when faced with a new problem, the judges have not openly asked themselves the question: what is the best policy for the law to adopt? But the question has always been there in the background. It has been concealed behind such questions as: Was the defendant under any duty to the plaintiff? Was the relationship between them sufficiently proximate? Was the injury direct or indirect? Was it foreseeable, or not? Was it too remote? And so forth.

Nowadays we direct ourselves to considerations of policy. In *Rondel* v. *Worsley*[6] we thought that, if advocates were liable to be sued for negligence, they would be hampered in carrying out their duties. In *Home Office* v. *Dorset Yacht Co., Ltd.*[7] we thought that the Home Office ought to pay for damage done by escaping borstal boys, if the staff was negligent, but we confined it to damage done in the immediate vicinity. In *S.C.M. (United Kingdom), Ltd.* v. *W. J. Whittall & Son, Ltd.*[1] some of us thought that economic loss ought not to be put on one pair of shoulders, but spread amongst all the sufferers. . . . In short, we look at the relationship of the parties; and then say, as a matter of policy, on whom the loss should fall. What are the considerations of policy here? I will take them in order.

---

1. [1971] 1 Q.B. 337; [1970] 3 All E.R. 245.
2. [1932] A.C. at p. 580; [1932] All E.R. Rep. at p. 11.
3. [1970] A.C. 1004, at p. 1027; [1970] 2 All E.R. 294, at p. 297.
4. [1970] A.C. at p. 1054; [1970] 2 All E.R. at p. 321.
5. [1970] A.C. at p. 1060; [1970] 2 All E.R. at pp. 325–326.
6. [1969] 1 A.C. 191; [1967] 3 All E.R. 993.
7. [1970] A.C. 1004; [1970] 2 All E.R. 294.

First, Mrs. Dutton has suffered a grievous loss. The house fell down without any fault of hers. She is in no position herself to bear the loss. Who ought in justice to bear it? I should think those who were responsible. Who are they? In the first place, the builder was responsible. It was he who laid the foundations so badly that the house fell down. In the second place, the council's inspector was responsible. It was his job to examine the foundations to see if they would take the load of the house. He failed to do it properly. In the third place, the council should answer for his failure. They were entrusted by Parliament with the task of seeing that houses were properly built. They received public funds for the purpose. The very object was to protect purchasers and occupiers of houses. Yet, they failed to protect them. Their shoulders are broad enough to bear the loss.

Next I ask: is there any reason in point of law why the council should not be held liable? Hitherto many lawyers have thought that a builder (who was also the owner) was not liable. If that were truly the law, I would not have thought it fair to make the council liable when the builder was not liable. But I hold that the builder who builds a house badly is liable, even though he is himself the owner.[1] On this footing, there is nothing unfair in holding the council's surveyor also liable.

Then, I ask: if liability were imposed on the council, would it have an adverse effect on the work? Would it mean that the council would not inspect at all, rather than risk liability for inspecting badly? Would it mean that inspectors would be harassed in their work or be subject to baseless charges? Would it mean that they would be extra cautious, and hold up work unnecessarily? Such considerations have influenced cases in the past (as in *Rondel* v. *Worsley*).[2] But here I see no danger. If liability is imposed on the council, it would tend, I think, to make them do their work better, rather than worse.

Next, I ask: is there any economic reason why liability should not be imposed on the council? In some cases the law has drawn the line to prevent recovery of damages. It sets a limit to damages for economic loss, or for shock, or theft by escaping convicts. The reason is that, if no limit were set, there would be no end to the money payable. But I see no such reason here for limiting damages. In nearly every case the builder will be primarily liable.[1] He will be insured and his insurance company will pay the damages. It will be very rarely that the council will be sued or found liable. If it is, much the greater responsibility will fall on the builder and little on the council.

Finally, I ask myself: if we permit this new action, are we opening the door too much? Will it lead to a flood of cases which the council will not be able to handle, nor the courts? Such considerations have sometimes in the past led the courts to reject novel claims. But I see no need to reject this claim on this ground. The injured person will always have his claim against the builder. He will rarely allege—and still less be able to prove—a case against the council.

All these considerations lead me to the conclusion that the policy of the law should be, and is, that the council should be liable for the negligence of their surveyor in passing work as good when in truth it is bad. I would therefore dismiss this appeal.

SACHS L.J.: . . . The practical effect of the Act[3] and the byelaws taken together was to give the council through its appointed officers all-embracing control over most of the building operation—and in particular control over sanitation and foundation work. Any work that is not complying with a byelaw can be stopped by the council's officers on their ascertaining that non-compliance. Further, if any work has been done which failed to comply with those byelaws the council can require its alteration or removal and in default could itself remedy the defect. The teeth are to be found in the provisions of the Act, such as ss. 65 and 287.

In the result no builder dare go ahead with sanitation or foundation work without

1. See the Note at p. 258, *post*, and the Defective Premises Act 1972, p. 259, *post*.
2. [1969] 1 A.C. 191; [1967] 3 All E.R. 993.
3. Public Health Act 1936.

the approval of the council's surveyor. The latter's control in practice can and often does override that of any site foreman or architect. It is, moreover, an obvious fact that when control is being exercised over work which is subsequently covered up (such as drains and foundations) any fault in the work thus covered will not in the nature of things be discovered on any normal subsequent survey made either on behalf of a purchaser or on behalf of any building society with whose aid the building is being acquired. It is plain that this control was designed to provide a protection against jerry building, similar faults, and their effects—not least to guard against poor drainage, and foundations.

The question whether the Act and the byelaws result in the council having a duty to those who later purchased the dwellings is one as to which a considerable number of points have been raised in the course of the submissions in this court. I have formed the view that in the end the crucial approach is that indicated by Lord Pearson when, in his speech in the *Dorset Yacht* case,[1] he said:

> "It is true that the *Donoghue* v. *Stevenson*[2] principle as stated . . . is a basic and general but not universal principle and does not in law apply to all the situations which are covered by the wide words of the passage. To some extent the decision in this case must be a matter of impression and instinctive judgment as to what is fair and just."

In the course of that approach due regard must, of course, be had, inter alia, to how far-reaching may be the effect of holding that such a duty existed. In essence it is a matter of the policy of the common law. Before coming to this crucial stage, it is as well to dispose of certain points raised on behalf of the council which, if accepted, would result in a decision in their favour without really having to examine the final question as posed by Lord Pearson.[1]

As regards each point in turn any examination of the law will, of course, be concerned with the liability of a defendant for negligence which produces hidden or latent physical defects—that is to say defects not detectable on any normal earlier examination before they become apparent to the plaintiff who brings a claim. That is the type of defect with which this appeal is concerned and I would wish to guard against anything said later in this judgment being interpreted as affecting other defects: *Bottomley* v. *Bannister*.[3]

. . . [I]t was urged on behalf of the council that the present case was one to which the well-known decision in *Geddis* v. *Bann Reservoir Proprietors*[4] as to liability for the negligent exercise of powers did not apply having regard to what was said in the speeches in the *East Suffolk Rivers Catchment Board* case,[5] where the board was held not to be liable for having failed to use in the exercise of its powers reasonable expedition in repairing a breach in a sea wall (which they do not appear themselves to have erected) with the result that the flooding of the plaintiff's land caused by the breach was not abated as promptly as it would have been had such expedition been used.[6] Particular stress was laid on a passage in the speech of Lord Romer where he summarised the principle he considered to be involved in that case. He said:[7]

> "Where a statutory authority is entrusted with a mere power, it cannot be made liable for any damage sustained by a member of the public by reason of a failure to exercise that power."

---

1. [1970] A.C. 1004, at p. 1054; [1970] 2 All E.R. 294, at p. 321.
2. [1932] A.C. at p. 580; [1932] All E.R. Rep. at p. 11.
3. [1932] 1 K.B. 458.
4. (1878), 3 App. Cas. 430.
5. [1941] A.C. 74; [1940] 4 All E.R. 527.
6. [1941] A.C. at p. 84; [1940] 4 All E.R. at p. 530.
7. [1941] A.C. at p. 102; [1940] 4 All E.R. at p. 543.

He proceeded to emphasise that the only duty of the board was not to add to such damage as would have been suffered by the plaintiff had they done nothing.

As a matter of first impression that statement of the law seemed to provide a formidable point in favour of the council. But even on the basis that the instant case is concerned with a "mere power" there is a very relevant distinction between the facts in the *East Suffolk Rivers Catchment Board* case[1] and the facts now under consideration. Where in a case relating to the exercise of powers the issue arises whether on the facts the cause of any damage is non-feasance or whether that cause is a misfeasance, the borderline can be difficult to discern. The *East Suffolk Rivers Catchment Board* case[1] is one in which the failure to proceed with the building work sufficiently quickly was held to be in essence a case of non-feasance—although Lord Atkin's dissenting speech[2] shows how close it came to that borderline. In the present case, on the contrary, the negligence plainly occurred in the course of a positive exercise by the council of its powers. The moment it exercised its power under s. 61 of the 1936 Act to make byelaws it assumed control over all such building operations within its area as were the subject of those byelaws. That assumption of control was a positive act and thereafter in my opinion any negligence in its exercise fell within the ambit of the decision in the *Geddis* case;[3] had the council's surveyor failed to make any inspection at all of the foundations that, of itself, might, according to the circumstances, have constituted negligence. But be that as it may, it is quite plain that the approval of the foundations by the council's surveyor was a positive exercise of its powers of control—in the same way as would be the switching on of a green light by a signalman, to adopt the helpful analogy raised arguendo by Stamp L.J. Insofar as in the present case we are concerned with the exercise of mere powers, we are dealing with a case of misfeasance.

It follows that on that ground there is, in my judgment, nothing in the decision in the *East Suffolk Rivers Catchment Board* case[1] which can afford a defence to the council; accordingly it is not necessary to consider the further point taken by counsel for the plaintiff, based on passages in the speeches of Viscount Simon L.C., Lord Thankerton and Lord Porter[4] respectively (see also the speech of Lord Atkin)[5] that the decision there in substance turned on the question of causation.

Nature of loss

It was strongly contended on behalf of the council that the nature of the loss suffered by the plaintiff was in essence economic and that for economic loss no action would lie in negligence. For my part, however, I would adopt what was said by Salmon L.J. in *Ministry of Housing and Local Government* v. *Sharp*:[6]

> "So far, however, as the law of negligence relating to civil actions is concerned, the existence of a duty to take reasonable care no longer depends on whether it is physical injury or financial loss which can reasonably be foreseen as a result of a failure to take such care."

That appears to me to accord with the views expressed in *Hedley Byrne & Co., Ltd.* v. *Heller & Partners, Ltd.*[7] by Lord Devlin and by Lord Pearce. That proposition must, of course, be taken in conjunction with what Lord Denning M.R. said in *S.C.M. (United Kingdom), Ltd.* v. *W. J. Whittall & Son, Ltd.*,[8] where he adverted to the need to apply

---

1. [1941] A.C. 74; [1940] 4 All E.R. 527.
2. [1941] A.C. at p. 88; [1940] 4 All E.R. at p. 533.
3. (1878), 4 App. Cas. 430.
4. [1941] A.C. at pp. 87, 96, 105; [1940] 4 All E.R. at pp. 533, 539, 545.
5. [1941] A.C. at pp. 92–93; [1940] 4 All E.R. at pp. 536–537.
6. [1970] 2 Q.B. 223, at p. 278; [1970] 1 All E.R. 1009, at p. 1027.
7. [1964] A.C. 465, at pp. 517, 538; [1963] 2 All E.R. 575, at pp. 602–603, 616–617.
8. [1971] 1 Q.B. 337, at p. 344; [1970] 3 All E.R. 245, at p. 250.

common sense to the particular situation being considered so as to avoid too wide an area of liability for damages being recoverable for some act of negligence.

In the instant case there is ample evidence of physical damage having occurred to the property—but it has been argued that this damage is on analysis the equivalent of a diminution of the value of the premises and does not rank for consideration as physical injury. Counsel for the council found himself submitting that if, for instance, the relevant defect had been in the ceiling of a room then if it fell on somebody's head or on to the occupier's chattels and thus caused physical damage then (subject of course to his other points failing) there would be a cause of action in negligence, but not if it fell on to a bare floor and caused no further damage. Apparently in the former case damages would be limited so as to exclude repairs to the ceiling; in the latter case there would be no cause of action at all. That subtle line of argument failed to attract me and would lead to an unhappily odd state of the law.

If physical damage is, contrary to my view, a sine qua non before a cause of action can arise against a builder or a building owner, then it seems to me to have occurred in the present case. But in my judgment to pose the question is it physical damage or economic damage is to adopt a fallacious approach. In this case—and perhaps generally in cases concerned with the exercise of duties and powers by a public authority—the correct test is: what range of damage is the proper exercise of the power designed to prevent? In this way the question whether any particular damage is recoverable is brought back into the area of policy indicated by Lord Denning M.R. in his judgment in the *S.C.M.* case;[1] and appropriate weight can, if necessary, be given to the fact that this case concerns a house and not a chattel. At this stage, it suffices to say that nothing in the nature of the loss sustained by the plaintiff of itself precludes a claim being maintained for that loss. . . .

As to proximity, it was contended that there was not a sufficiently close relationship between the council's negligence and the plaintiff as regards the subject-matter of the claim on two grounds, each being said to be sufficient to sustain the council's contention, although of course they should also be looked at in combination. First, it was argued that as the defects were due to bad work by the building owner, any negligence on the part of the council was in law not sufficiently proximate to enable the plaintiff to claim against it. There is, however, no substance in this point. . . . Nowadays, at any rate, the signalman who has fallen asleep and the engine driver who fails to see the obstacle on the line can both be liable (cf. *Grange Motors (Cymbran), Ltd.* v. *Spencer*);[2] so can an architect, a building contractor and a demolition contractor all concerned with the same site (*Clay* v. *A. J. Crump & Sons, Ltd.*[3]).

Next came the suggestion that because the plaintiff in the present action was not the original purchaser from the building owner but was next in the line of succession in purchasers the relationship between her and the building owner was not sufficiently proximate. That suggestion overlooks the very essence of the *M'Alister* (or *Donoghue*) v. *Stevenson*[4] decision. As regards hidden defects the fact that there have been intermediate purchasers or users is not in point where the defect can only come to light at the stage when the plaintiff is injuriously affected. Here again there is no distinction in this respect between a defect in a house and a defect in a chattel; so that suggestion also has no substance.

Next came the much pressed point that the plaintiff ought to have established affirmatively that she personally or by her agents relied on the inspection by the council when she entered into the contract to acquire the house. It was correctly pointed out that there was no evidence of any such reliance. In aid of this submission were cited passages in the speeches of Lord Reid, Lord Morris of Borth-y-Gest and

1. [1971] 1 Q.B. at p. 344; [1970] 3 All E.R. at p. 250.
2. [1969] 1 All E.R. 340; [1969] 1 W.L.R. 53.
3. [1964] 1 Q.B. 533; [1963] 3 All E.R. 687.
4. [1932] A.C. 562; [1932] All E.R. Rep. 1.

Lord Pearce in the *Hedley Byrne* case,[1] and also a number of passages to be found in judgments of appeal courts in the United States. Clearly there can be categories of cases in which the duty to a plaintiff may depend on whether he has placed reliance on the defendants' conduct, be it conduct by way of acts or by way of words. On the other hand, in the vast majority of cases the question whether a plaintiff actually thought about and relied on the defendants' conduct is quite irrelevant; the point in those cases is not whether he thought about the matter and can so state in evidence but simply whether he is entitled to the benefit of a duty owed by the defendant irrespective of whether at the time he thought about that question. . . .

A duty situation?

Having thus cleared the way of a number of obstacles each submitted in turn to preclude the plaintiff succeeding in her claim, the stage has now been reached for approaching the final question—as between the council and the plaintiff was there "a duty situation", to adopt the apt phrase used by Lord Morris of Borth-y-Gest in the *Dorset Yacht* case?[2] For that purpose I will, as stated earlier in this judgment, respectfully adopt the approach signposted by Lord Pearson[3] in a passage which follows closely the line taken by Lord Morris of Borth-y-Gest. . . .

. . . The Act was passed to protect those who might come to own or occupy the relevant houses against jerry building and similar faults and was intended to benefit such persons. That protection and benefit was the primary purpose of the relevant provisions of the Act; and that is a purpose which falls within the instructions given to the council by the words in s. 1, "it shall be the duty of the following authorities to carry this Act into execution". It follows that as between the council and the owners and occupiers of houses over the building of which it has control there exists at least in respect of hidden defects of the type under consideration a duty situation—unless (per Lord Reid and Lord Pearson in the *Dorset Yacht* case)[4] there are some countervailing factors which should on policy grounds lead to a contrary conclusion.

Early amongst the countervailing points relied on by counsel for the council was the suggestion that those who might suffer damage had a sufficient remedy against the building contractor (assuming that the *Bottomley* v. *Bannister*[5] point was rejected). That seems a poor point for many reasons—for instance the common law does not normally limit the person who suffers damage to a remedy against one of two culpable persons. In the category of case with which we are here concerned it is moreover particularly important that a dual liability should exist. It is commonplace today that a development project involving the building of a group of houses by a site owner is often so arranged that everything is done by a specially formed company which may be dissolved when the project is completed; such an arrangement can have taxation advantages and can also afford financial protection if the project results in a loss. Those for whose benefit the Act was passed both need and should have the benefit of such dual liability as may be available in a state of affairs which could not have come about if the council had done what it ought to do.

Next came the suggestion that to uphold the plaintiff's claim in this case would open the way to a flood of similar claims against councils and—perhaps more importantly—against others who make inspections under statutory powers, such as factory inspectors and those who carry out annual tests on motor vehicles for which no renewal of a licence can be obtained without the aid of a test certificate. This could be a formidable point if established to the degree propounded by counsel for the council. But as regards similar claims under the 1936 Act there must be remembered the very great difficulties that normally beset a plaintiff on whom lies the burden

1. [1964] A.C. at pp. 487, 502, 538; [1963] 2 All E.R. at pp. 583, 594, 617.
2. [1970] A.C. at p. 1038; [1970] 2 All E.R. at p. 307.
3. [1970] A.C. at p. 1054; [1970] 2 All E.R. at p. 321.
4. [1970] A.C. at pp. 1032, 1054; [1970] 2 All E.R. at pp. 302, 321.
5. [1932] 1 K.B. 458.

of proving that a hidden defect resulted from a surveyor's negligence as opposed to, at highest, from an error of judgment. Practical experience points against any flood of such claims.

As regards inspections under other powers—here again it must be kept in mind that the instant case is concerned with negligence against which normal intermediate examination would not generally afford protection. No doubt there will be some claims made as regards the exercise of other statutory powers; but without a close examination of those particular powers and also of the chances of proving negligence in relation to their exercise no reliable forecasts can be made. For my part I do not find myself in that state of fear in which counsel for the council sought to envelop me. Indeed in the end I find nothing in this point to deter me from deciding this appeal in accordance with the justice of the case. . . .

The suggested countervailing points being found to be ineffective, it follows that as between the council and the plaintiff there existed a duty situation even if the former were exercising mere powers. A fortiori, of course, was there such a situation if, as I would hold, the council were under a duty, imposed by the 1936 Act, to exercise control. In either case the plaintiff is entitled to recover damages for the negligence that has been established. . . .

STAMP L.J.: . . . Before examining the law, or approaching the authorities relied on, I find it convenient to deal first with the submission made on behalf of the council that the injury to the plaintiff was not caused by any act or default of the council. It was, so the argument ran, the builder, and not the council, who carelessly built the house on an insecure foundation, and so created the lack of stability of which the plaintiff complains. I cannot accept this submission. As I see it, the situation was essentially this. The council had power, derived from the Act and the byelaws made thereunder, either to give or refuse its approval to the foundations; to show the green light or the red. In error, because they had carelessly done their work, they showed the green. In my judgment he who shows the green light in such circumstances as these causes the consequential injury. . . .

If it be correct that the action of the council caused injury to the plaintiff, the questions which as I see it fall to be determined are, first, did the council owe a common law duty to the plaintiff not to injure the plaintiff by approving the foundations until they had taken proper steps to ensure that they were fairly laid; . . . and secondly, was the injury which the plaintiff suffered an injury for which damages can be recovered?

If some of the remarks in the speech of Lord Atkin in *M'cAlister* (or *Donoghue*) v. *Stevenson*[1] were to be applied without qualification there would, I venture to think, be no difficulty in answering the questions raised. . . . [Having quoted Lord Atkin's broad neighbour principle, he continued:] Persons who might become the purchaser of a house built on an insecure foundation are in my judgment so closely and directly affected by the act of a local authority in passing or refusing to pass the foundations as secure, that the authority ought reasonably to have them in contemplation as being affected when the local authority apply their mind to the question whether they should or should not do so. . . . If, in the instant case, the council ought reasonably to have had one in the position of the plaintiff in contemplation as one who might be injured by what it did, I ask the rhetorical question, why should not the local authority be liable to the plaintiff for the injury which she has suffered?

Of course, the passage in the speech of Lord Atkin,[1] which I have quoted, is not to be read literally and without regard to the context, or, as has been said, it would comprehend careless conduct of any kind through any means, causing damage of any kind, whether physical or not, to anyone who could bring himself within the

---

1. [1932] A.C. 562, at p. 580; [1932] All E.R. Rep. 1, at p. 11.

definition of a neighbour. Lord Atkin was not formulating a complete criterion, as was indicated by Lord Reid in the *Hedley Byrne* case:[1]

"That decision [in *M'cAlister* (or *Donoghue*) v. *Stevenson*][2] may encourage [the courts] to develop existing lines of authority, but it cannot entitle us to disregard them." . . .

In view of the course which the case took in the court below, counsel for the plaintiff felt unable to contend that this is a case where the council had a statutory duty to inspect the foundations and accepted, as I understand it, that the council in doing what it did was exercising a statutory power. If then, as was submitted on behalf of the council, one came to the conclusion that the council as a result of the carelessness of its officer, merely failed to prevent damage which had already happened, it would, so I think, follow, on the authority of the decision of the House of Lords in *East Suffolk Rivers Catchment Board* v. *Kent*,[3] that here there was no liability. The case is authority for saying that where a statutory body in exercise of a statutory power fails through foolish error to remedy a damaging situation which has already occurred, it is no more liable for the failure than if it had not exercised the power at all. To constitute a tort, there must be a duty owed to the plaintiff by the defendant not to cause injury and an act of omission which causes it; and on the facts of the *East Suffolk* case,[3] the House of Lords concluded that the authority there had not caused any injury. On the facts of this case, however, I take the view that but for what the council did so carelessly, the house would, on the balance of probability, never have been built on the unstable foundation, and I would hold that that careless act did cause the injury and that this is not a case which is to be equated with one where the authority, while endeavouring to exercise a power to cure a damaging situation, fails to do so.

Nor, in my judgment, is the *East Suffolk* case[3] an authority for the proposition advanced on behalf of the council that it would be wrong, because it would deter statutory bodies from exercising their functions, to hold that a council which had no duty to exercise a power may be in a worse position if, while endeavouring to exercise it, it does so in a way which causes injury to the plaintiff. So to hold would in my view be to fly in the face of the authorities which were analysed in the *East Suffolk* case[3] and establish that although an authority exercising a power is not liable for injury which would have been suffered had it not exercised the power, it is liable to[4] injury carelessly caused in the exercise. Viscount Simon L.C. in his speech[5] in that case expressed the view that if what was done had caused fresh damage, the authority would have been liable for that damage. None of their Lordships in the *East Suffolk* case[3] dissented from the statement of the law by Lord Parker of Waddington in *Great Central Rail. Co.* v. *Hewlett*:[6]

". . . it is undoubtedly a well-settled principle of law that when statutory powers are conferred they must be exercised with reasonable care, so that if those who exercise them could by reasonable precaution have prevented an injury which has been occasioned, and was likely to be occasioned, by their exercise, damage for negligence may be recovered."

I add only this in relation to the *East Suffolk* case,[3] namely, that regarded as an authority on causation, the facts there were so very different from those in the present case, that I cannot regard it as authority to support the contention that in the instant case, the local authority cannot be regarded as having caused the injury suffered by the plaintiff. There, the event which caused the damage had already happened before the board did that of which complaint is made. Here, as I emphasise again—and this is the basis of

1. [1964] A.C. 465, at p. 482; [1963] 2 All E.R. 575, at p. 580.
2. [1932] A.C. 562; [1932] All E.R. Rep. 1.
3. [1941] A.C. 74; [1940] 4 All E.R. 527.
4. [The word should be "for"—[1972] 1 Q.B. 373, at p. 412.]
5. [1941] A. C. at p. 87; [1940] 4 All E.R. at p. 533.
6. [1916] 2 A.C. 511, at p. 519; [1916–17] All E.R. Rep. 1027, at p. 1029.

my judgment—the house would on the balance of probability never have been built but for the carelessness of the council. . . .

Nor can I equate the facts of the instant case with those in *Hedley Byrne & Co., Ltd.* v. *Heller & Partners, Ltd.*,[1] where liability for a careless misrepresentation was established. There, the liability was held to extend only in favour of one who acted in reliance on the misrepresentation; and since in the instant case the plaintiff did not rely on the council, so here, it is submitted, there is no liability. But the speeches in the *Hedley Byrne* case[1] extended the area of liability and did not restrict it. The speeches there are to be read with regard to the question which fell to be decided, and I cannot accept that any of their Lordships would have regarded their language as exempting from liability C, a man who having taken on himself the task of directing the traffic, carelessly told B that the road was clear, with the result that A was injured in the ensuing collision. The distinction between the *Hedley Byrne* case[1] and this case is that there there could be no damage suffered except by a person who relied on what was done and said by the defendant, and the defendant could only have had in contemplation as someone who might be injured by his carelessness, a person who might rely on his statement. Hence, the insistence in the speeches in the *Hedley Byrne* case[1] on the necessity for reliance by the plaintiff and proximity as a necessary ingredient of the tort. Here, on the other hand, if my approach to the facts be right, injury could be and was suffered by the plaintiff as a result of the council's carelessness, and she was a person so closely and directly affected by the act of the council that they ought reasonably to have had her in contemplation as being so affected. Accordingly, in my judgment it is not necessary for the plaintiff here to establish that the plaintiff relied on the council in order to complete her cause of action. . . .

I now come to consider the submission advanced by counsel for the council to the effect that it would be an extension of the law to hold that the particular injury suffered by the plaintiff is an injury for which damages may be recovered. It is pointed out that in the past a distinction has been drawn between constructing a dangerous article and constructing one which is defective or of inferior quality. I may be liable to one who purchases in the market a bottle of ginger beer which I have carelessly manufactured and which is dangerous and causes injury to person or property; but it is not the law that I am liable to him for the loss he suffers because what is found inside the bottle and for which he has paid money is not ginger beer but water. I do not warrant, except to an immediate purchaser, and then by the contract and not in tort, that the thing I manufacture is reasonably fit for its purpose. The submission is I think a formidable one and in my view raises the most difficult point for decision in this case. Nor can I see any valid distinction between the case of a builder who carelessly builds a house which, although not a source of danger to person or property, nevertheless owing to a concealed defect in its foundations starts to settle and crack and becomes valueless, and the case of a manufacturer who carelessly manufactures an article which, although not a source of danger to a subsequent owner or to his other property, nevertheless owing to a hidden defect quickly disintegrates. To hold that either the builder or the manufacturer was liable, except in contract, would be to open up a new field of liability, the extent of which could not I think be logically controlled, and since it is not in my judgment necessary to do so for the purposes of this case, I do not, more particularly because of the absence of the builder, express an opinion whether the builder has a higher or lower duty than the manufacturer. But the distinction between the case of the manufacturer of a dangerous thing which causes damage and that of a thing which turns out to be defective and valueless lies I think not in the nature of the injury but in the character of the duty. I have a duty not carelessly to put out a dangerous thing which may cause damage to one who may purchase it, but the duty does not extend to putting out carelessly a defective or useless or valueless thing. So again one goes back to consider what was the character of the duty, if any, owed to the plaintiff, and one finds

---

1. [1964] A.C. 465; [1963] 2 All E.R. 575.

on authority that the injury which is one of the essential elements of the tort of negligence is not confined to physical damage to personal property but may embrace economic damage which the plaintiff suffers through buying a worthless thing, as is shown by the *Hedley Byrne* case.[1] So the point that raises the difficulty in this case does not, as I see it, arise from the fact that the injury suffered here was the loss of the value of the house or the cost of putting it right. What causes the difficulty—and it is I think as this point that the court is asked to apply the law of negligence to a new situation— is that whereas the builder had, as I will assume, no duty to the plaintiff not carelessly to build a house with a concealed defect,[2] yet it is sought to impute a not dissimilar duty to the defendant council. At this point I repeat and emphasise the difference between the position of a local authority clothed with the authority of an Act of Parliament to perform the function of making sure that the foundations of a house are secure for the benefit of the subsequent owners of the house and a builder who is concerned to make a profit. So approaching the matter there is in my judgment nothing illogical or anomalous in fixing the former with a duty to which the latter is not subject. The former by under-taking the task is in my judgment undertaking a responsibility at least as high as that which the defendant in the *Hedley Byrne* case[1] would in the opinion of the majority in the House of Lords have undertaken had he not excluded responsibility.

In coming to the conclusion that the situation in the instant case was what Lord Morris of Borth-y-Gest[3] there called "a duty situation", I derive assistance from the conclusion of the majority in the House of Lords in the *Dorset Yacht* case.[4] There the defendant was held liable not on the ground that it had committed a breach of its statutory duty, nor on the ground that in exercise of its statutory powers it had itself done an act which caused the plaintiff damage, but, as here, for a careless failure or omission while exercising its powers to prevent the happening of that which caused the damage.

If I am correct in my view that the council here was, like the careless architect in *Clay* v. *A. J. Crump & Sons, Ltd.*,[5] in control of the situation, in that it had taken on itself to see whether or not the foundations were safe and that but for its carelessness the house would not have been built, I am also assisted to my conclusion that the council is here liable on the authority of that case. I too would dismiss the appeal. . . .

Appeal dismissed

Questions

1. What type of damage did the plaintiff suffer in this case?

2. Do you agree with Lord Denning that, if, contrary to his view, the builder/ vendor could not have been liable, then it would not have been fair to make the council liable? (Compare the judgment of Stamp L.J.)

3. Was the *East Suffolk* case, [1941]; A.C. 740 [1940] 4 All E.R. 527, satisfactorily distinguished in this case?

Note

The American Restatement on Torts (2d) states:

"s. 321. Duty to Act When Prior Conduct is Found to be Dangerous

(1) If the actor does an act, and subsequently realises or should realise that it has created an unreasonable risk of causing physical harm to another, he is under a duty to exercise reasonable care to prevent the risk from taking effect.

---

1. [1964] A.C. 465; [1963] 2 All E.R. 575.
2. [See the Note, p. 258, *post*, and the Defective Premises Act 1972, p. 259, *post*.]
3. In *Home Office* v. *Dorset Yacht Co., Ltd.*, [1970] A.C. at p. 1038; [1970] 2 All E.R. at p. 307.
4. [1970] A.C. 1004; [1970] 2 All E.R. 294.
5. [1964] 1 Q.B. 533; [1963] 3 All E.R. 687.

(2) The rule stated in subsection (1) applies even though at the time of the act the actor has no reason to believe that it will involve such a risk."

Section 321 of the 1st edition (similarly worded, but not covering the case where the prior conduct was tortious) was said by a majority of the judges in *Silva's Fishing Corpn. (Pty.), Ltd.* v. *Maweza*, 1957 (2) S.A. 256 (Appellate Division of the Supreme Court of South Africa) to accord with South African law's approach. It was alleged in that case that the plaintiff's husband (Bishop Maweza Dlamini) was drowned when the defendant corporation's fishing boat, which drifted for approximately nine days after its engine failed, was wrecked: that the husband, although a member of the crew of the boat, was not directly employed by the defendant corporation (only one crew member was) but was paid a proportion of the value of the fish he caught; that the defendant corporation had been told on more than one occasion that the boat was in distress, and that the defendant "negligently failed . . . to take any or any reasonable and/or adequate steps to rescue the said crew . . . when by the exercise of ordinary diligence it could have done so by making use of effective rescue facilities available to it." It was argued for the corporation that, on the alleged facts, it was not liable in law, but this was not accepted by the Appellate Division, although the two judgments delivered in the case were based on different grounds. How would English law decide this question? For a situation in Canadian law where there was held to be a duty to rescue, see *Horsley* v. *Maclaren* (*The Ogopogo*), [1971] 2 Lloyd's Rep. 410, p. 132, *post*.

(b) Duty to control the conduct of others

Gorely v. Codd

Lincoln Summer Assizes　　　　　　　　[1966] 3 All E.R. 891

The following facts were found by the court. The infant plaintiff was struck by an air rifle pellet, which had been shot by the infant defendant. The accident happened in a field in the course of "larking about", and the court did not think that there was any "deliberate aiming with wrong intent" and held that there had been no assault or trespass to the person in this case. The infant defendant's father (the second defendant), who had knowledge of firearms from his infantry experience, had adequately instructed his son in the use of a less powerful air-rifle which the boy had possessed at an earlier date. The boy was told *inter alia* not to use the rifle on the highway, and not to point it at anyone. Shortly after the acquisition of the more powerful rifle on the day before the accident, the father repeated the instructions with a warning to take even more care, and the two defendants practised for approximately three quarters of an hour with the rifle. In addition, it appeared that the infant defendant would have received some instruction in the use of firearms in his school cadet corps. At the time of the accident, the infant plaintiff was fourteen and a half years old and the infant defendant sixteen and a half years old. The infant defendant was retarded in mental development, but this only related to his "book learning". All the parties lived in the country. On the claim for damages for negligence:

NIELD J.: . . . A very long time ago it was said that the law of England, in its care for human life, requires some caution in the person who deals with dangerous weapons (see *Potter* v. *Faulkner*),[1] and Blackburn J. in *Smith* v. *London and South Western Rail. Co.*[2] in 1870 said[3] that if a man fired a gun across a road, where he might reasonably anticipate

---

1. (1861), 1 B. & S. 800.
2. (1870), L.R. 6 C.P. 14; [1861–73] All E.R. Rep. 167.
3. (1870), L.R. 6 C.P., at p. 22.

that persons might be passing, and hit someone, he was guilty of negligence and liable for the injury he had caused, but if he fired in his own wood, where he could reasonably expect that no one would be, he was not liable to anyone whom he shot. This shows that what a person may reasonably anticipate is important in considering whether he has been negligent. Similarly, it is said that there is a duty on the owner of a loaded gun not to entrust it to a person who, by reason of his youth, his ignorance or his lack of intelligence, is not competent to handle it; so there is plainly laid down a high duty of care for two categories of persons.

My attention has been called by counsel in this case to two decisions which are certainly very helpful. The first is *Donaldson* v. *McNiven*,[1] a case which was tried by Pearson J. at Liverpool Assizes.[2] It was a case where a defendant living in a populous district of Liverpool allowed his son, aged thirteen years, to have an air rifle on condition that it was never used outside the house. The learned judge held[3] that an air rifle was not a dangerous thing per se, in the sense that a savage animal or poison or fire was a dangerous thing per se, but that it was potentially dangerous in the sense that it might cause injury if negligently used; and in that case the learned judge reached the conclusion that the defendant, who was the father of the boy who had caused the injury, was not liable and that it was not proved that he had failed in his duty in this matter. The matter went to the Court of Appeal,[4] where the learned judge's view was upheld, it being held that there was no ground for disturbing the finding of fact in the court below, that there was no such lack of supervision by the defendant of his son's activities as would constitute negligence on his part, and therefore the fault was that of the defendant's son and the defendant was not liable for damages.

The other case to which I am referred is the case of *Newton* v. *Edgerley*,[5] which was heard at the Manchester Assizes before Lord Parker C.J. It was a case in which the infant plaintiff received an injury to the right leg when a shot gun, which the defendant's son, aged twelve years, was carrying under his arm, was discharged by the act of a third boy. Lord Parker C.J. held there that the defendant was negligent in that he should either have forbidden the use of the gun at all or else ensured, by giving very careful instructions as to the use of the weapon if others were present, that if the boy succumbed to temptation it would not be to the danger of others. Of the greatest importance, to my mind, is the passage which occurs in Lord Parker C.J.'s judgment after he had referred to the case of *Donaldson* v. *McNiven*,[4] where the lord chief justice said:[6] "But the first thing I would observe is that each case must depend on its exact facts." He therefore made it very clear that, while general guidance can be given, no two cases can possibly be the same, and I have to decide the present case on its own facts. . . .

[Nield J. referred to the Air Guns and Shot Guns, etc. Act 1962,[7] s. 1 (1)–(4), especially s. 1 (3) which prohibited the possession of air weapons in public places[8] by persons under the age of seventeen, except an air gun or air rifle so covered as to be incapable of firing. He then considered the evidence, held the infant defendant liable for his negligence and continued:] Let me consider then the position of the adult defendant to see whether it is the case that he must be held responsible in having failed in his duty of care in this matter. I observe the first allegation made against the adult defendant is that he failed to give his son proper or sufficient instruction in the use of the air rifle: I am satisfied affirmatively that he gave perfectly proper and sufficient

1. [1952] 2 All E.R. 691; [1952] 1 All E.R. 1213.
2. [1952] 1 All E.R. 1213.
3. [1952] 1 All E.R. at p. 1216, letter A.
4. [1952] 2 All E.R. 691.
5. [1959] 3 All E.R. 337.
6. [1959] 3 All E.R. at p. 339, letter H.
7. [It was repealed by the Firearms Act 1968.]
8. [The field where the accident occurred was not a public place.]

instruction. It is next said that he allowed the son to use the air rifle without any such instructions and without any supervision; I have dealt with the instructions and I am of the opinion that it was not necessary, having regard to all the circumstances, that the son should be supervised. . . .

It is also submitted or alleged that the adult defendant failed to point out to his son the dangers involved: I find that he did point them out. Finally, it is said, and this is perhaps a very important aspect of the allegation, that the father allowed the son, who was to his knowledge of sub-normal intelligence and prone to violence, to possess and to use a dangerous weapon, that is to say the air rifle. It is quite clear as a matter of principle that a person who entrusts a firearm to another must be careful to see that he entrusts it to somebody who is competent, and not to someone who is not responsible by reason of mental illness or otherwise may be said to be incompetent. However, in this case, although there is this retardation in book learning in the infant defendant, I am quite satisfied on Mr. Beaney's evidence that that in no way affects his responsibility in other directions and that for the purposes of this case he was a perfectly normal boy. It will not, I hope, be misunderstood when I say that, but I have already recalled Mr. Beaney's evidence about it and it amounts to this, that in activities other than book learning he is in effect as good as anyone else.

Then it is said, rightly, that if you get someone who is prone to violence you must be more careful. [His Lordship considered evidence on the question and concluded that he was not satisfied that the infant defendant was prone to violence. He continued:] Thus I reach the conclusion that the plaintiffs have failed to show any fault in the adult defendant, who, as I say, impressed me as a responsible person and an acceptable witness. He said quite boldly, when he was asked about it, that he would entrust to that boy of sixteen and a half that weapon, having regard to all the circumstances. In those circumstances it must be the case that the plaintiffs fail against the adult defendant. . . .

[Judgment for the adult defendant but for the infant plaintiff against the infant defendant. The infant plaintiff's father was also awarded damages against the infant defendant.]

Questions

1. What authority is there to support the view that there is no assault or trespass to the person if there is no "deliberate aiming with wrong intent"? (See pp. 26–36, *ante*.)

2. Why should not parents be automatically liable for the torts of their children?

Note

On the standard of care required of infants, see p. 149, *post*.

Carmarthenshire County Council *v.* Lewis

House of Lords   [1955] 1 All E.R. 565

A lorry driver was killed when, in swerving to avoid a child (approaching his fourth birthday) who ran on to the road, the lorry struck a lamp post. It was admitted that the lorry driver himself had not been at fault. The child (David Morgan) attended a nursery school which was maintained by the appellants, the local education authority, and which was near to this road. A teacher, Miss Morgan, was about to take this child and a girl (Shinoa Evans) out for a walk, but found that a third child had cut himself, and spent ten minutes looking after that child. During this period, the child who was to be involved in the accident left the classroom. He went across the playground, through the gate, down a lane and one hundred yards along the road in question to the point where the accident occurred. The widow of the driver (the respondent) brought an action alleging that her husband's death was due to the appellants' or their servant's negligence. The Court of Appeal, [1953] 2 All E.R. 1403, dismissed an appeal from the judgment of Devlin J., [1953] 1 All E.R. 1025, who held that the teacher had been negligent, and there was a further appeal to the House of Lords:

LORD GODDARD: . . . The question of general importance that is raised is whether there is a duty on the occupiers of premises adjoining a highway to prevent young children from escaping on to the highway so as to endanger other persons lawfully passing on it. By young children I mean those of such tender years that they may be presumed to be unable to take any care for their own safety, and whom a prudent parent would not allow to go into a street unaccompanied. . . .

The position, then, is that the appellants maintain a nursery and infant school in premises adjoining a highway in a town and are, in my opinion, under a duty to take care that the children neither themselves became involved in or cause a traffic accident. . . .

[Having decided that the teacher had not been negligent, he continued:] But this does not conclude the matter as far as the appellants are concerned. They maintain a nursery school and an infant school on these premises. In the former they accept the care of children from three to five years and in the latter those of five to seven. During the time when this child was in their care, he is found outside the school premises wandering in the street. That, in my opinion, clearly calls for an explanation from the appellants. They have only shown that the child left the room in the temporary absence of the teacher and so got into the playground. In the playground he would have been safe at least from traffic risks. All we know is that the gates must have been open, or so easy to open that a child of three or four could open them. True, the nursery children are put, when out of school, into the play-pen, but infants from five to seven play in the playground. If it is possible for children of that age, when a teacher's back may be turned for a moment, to get out into a busy street, this does seem to indicate some lack of care or of precautions which might reasonably be required. There is no analogy between a school playground and the home in this respect. At any rate, no satisfactory explanation has been given for this child being found in the street at a time when he was in the care of the appellants, and for this reason I would dismiss the appeal.

LORD REID: . . . two questions arise for decision. In the first place, was the escape of the child David into the street attributable to negligence of the appellants or of those for whom they are responsible? If it was, then it appears to me to be obvious that his being there alone might easily lead to an accident, and, if the child had been killed or injured, the appellants would have been liable in damages, for they certainly owed a duty to the child to protect him from injury. But then a second question is raised by the appellants. They say that, although they owed a duty to the child they owed no duty to other users of the highway, and that, even if they were negligent in letting the child escape on to the street, they cannot be held responsible for damage to others caused by the action of the child when there.

On the first question, I am of opinion that the appellants were negligent. However careful the mistresses might be, minor emergencies and distractions were almost certain to occur from time to time so that some child or children would be left alone without supervision for an appreciable time. The actions of a child of this age are unpredictable and I think that it ought to have been anticipated by the appellants, or their responsible officers, that, in such a case, a child might well try to get out on to the street and that, if it did, a traffic accident was far from improbable. It would have been very easy to prevent this, and either to lock the gates or, if that was thought undesirable, to make them sufficiently difficult to open to ensure that they could not be opened by a child so young that it could not be trusted alone on the street. The classroom door was not an obstacle and, no doubt, it was convenient that the children should be able to open this door themselves, but that meant that the way to the street was open unless the outer gate was so fastened or constructed as to be an obstacle to them.

There was much argument whether Miss Morgan was negligent in leaving these children for ten minutes. I do not think that she was negligent in the first instance because she intended to come back very soon: the real question is whether, when she found that she had to be absent to attend to the injured child, she ought to have paid some attention to the two who were waiting for her. She was next door to the class-room while attending to the injured child, and, without delaying her attention to the injured child, she could have called to David and Shinoa to come into the play-pen where they would have been under supervision or, at least, she could have opened the door of the classroom to see that all was well. But, no doubt, her whole attention was concentrated on the injured child, and the question whether her omission to give any attention to the other children amounted to negligence is, I think, a very narrow one. I prefer to base my judgment on the fact that such a situation ought to have been anticipated by the appellants and provided for.

The appellants argued that, even if they were negligent and even if they owed some duty to the deceased lorry driver, the accident which caused his death was not reason-ably foreseeable; his death, if it was a consequence of their negligence, was too remote to involve them in liability for it. I would deal with that argument in this way. Was it foreseeable by an ordinary reasonable and careful person that a child might sometimes be left alone in the nursery school for a short period? I think it was. I see nothing very extraordinary in the circumstances which caused these children to be left alone. Was it, then, foreseeable that such a child might not sit still but might move out of the class-room? If I am right in my view that it is not safe to make assumptions about the behaviour of such young children, again I think it was. Was it then foreseeable that such a child might go into the street, there being no obstacle in its way? I see no ground for assuming that such a child would stay in an empty playground when the gate was not more than twenty yards or so from the classroom. And once the child was in the street anything might happen. It was argued that it might be reasonable to foresee injury to the child but not reasonable to foresee that the child's action would cause injury to others. I can see no force in that. One knows that every day people take risks in order to save others from being run over, and if a child runs into the street the danger to others is almost as great as the danger to the child. . . .

I turn now to the second question which is one of novelty and general importance. If the appellants are right, it means that, no matter how careless the person in charge of a young child may be and no matter how obvious it may be that the child may stray into a busy street and cause an accident, yet that person is under no liability for damage to others caused solely by the action of the child, because his only duty is towards the child under his care. There appears to be no reported case of an action of this kind, and the appellants say that this indicates that no one has hitherto supposed that such an action would lie, for there must have been many instances of the driver of a vehicle suffering damage caused by a young child running in front of it. But in most cases of that kind it would not be worth while to sue the person who was in charge of the child, and, in any event, "the categories of negligence are never closed".

The case most relied on by the appellants was *Hay* (or *Bourhill*) v. *Young*,[1] where it was held that a motor cyclist was under no duty to a woman who was not in any physical danger from his driving and who did not even see the accident in which he was involved, but who suffered shock from hearing the noise of it. Those facts have not the faintest resemblance to the facts of this case, but the appellants say that the reasoning with regard to remoteness assists them. I do not think that it does. Lord Thankerton ([1942] 2 All E.R. at p. 399) said that the cyclist's duty was to drive

"with such reasonable care as will avoid the risk of injury to such persons as he can reasonably foresee might be injured by failure to exercise such reasonable care"

and he referred to "the area of potential danger". Lord Russell of Killowen (*ibid.*, at

---

1. [1943] A.C. 92; [1942] 2 All E.R. 396.

p. 401) cited the well-known passage in the speech of Lord Atkin in *M'Alister* (*or Donoghue*) v. *Stevenson*[1] ([1932] A.C. at p. 580), beginning "Who, then, in law is my neighbour?", as did Lord Porter ([1942] 2 All E.R. at p. 409). Lord Macmillan said (*ibid.*, at p. 403) that a

> "duty is owed to those to whom injury may reasonably and probably be anticipated if the duty is not observed,"

and Lord Wright (*ibid.*, at p. 404) referred to the

> "general concept of reasonable foresight as the criterion of negligence or breach of duty."

If I am right in the view which I have already expressed that injury to other road users was reasonably foreseeable if this child was allowed to escape on to the street, then the reasoning in *Hay* (or *Bourhill*) v. *Young*,[2] is very much against the appellants, and they could only succeed on this argument if there were, in connection with the care of young children, some special feature which would prevent the application of the general principle.

The appellants say that it would be unreasonable to apply that principle here because, if such a duty is held to exist, it will put an impossible burden on harassed mothers who will have to keep a constant watch on their young children. I do not think so. There is no absolute duty, there is only a duty not to be negligent, and a mother is not negligent unless she fails to do something which a prudent or reasonable mother in her position would have been able to do, and would have done. Even a housewife who has young children cannot be in two places at once, and no one would suggest that she must neglect her other duties, or that a young child must always be kept cooped up. But I think that all but the most careless mothers do take many precautions for their children's safety, and the same precautions serve to protect others. I cannot see how any person in charge of a child could be held to have been negligent in a question with a third party injured in a road accident unless he or she had failed to take reasonable and practicable precaution for the safety of the child.

What precautions would have been practicable and what precautions would have been reasonable in any particular case must depend on a great variety of circumstances. But, in this case, it was not impracticable for the appellants to have their gate so made or fastened that a young child could not open it and, in my opinion, that was a proper and reasonable precaution for them to take. . . .

I am, therefore, of opinion that the appeal should be dismissed.

LORD TUCKER: . . . I think that, in principle, there can be no doubt that both courts below were right in holding that persons in charge of tiny children (the child in question was just under four years of age) in premises adjoining a busy highway owe a duty to persons using the highway to take reasonable care to see that such children—being of an age when they cannot have acquired sufficient "road sense" to permit of their being allowed to travel unattended to and from school—shall not, during school hours, escape unattended on to such a highway, it being reasonably foreseeable that an accident involving injury to other road users as well as to the children may well result therefrom.

In the present case, a child named David Morgan, a week or so before his fourth birthday, had been taken to the nursery school managed by the appellants at Ammanford and left there in charge of the school authorities. Between 12.15 and 12.30 p.m. during school hours the child had somehow got out into College Street—a busy thoroughfare—and caused an accident which resulted in the death of the respondent's husband. My Lords, such an occurrence, I think, calls for an explanation from the appellants. Not because the facts and circumstances are exclusively within their

---

1. [1932] A.C. 562.
2. [1943] A.C. 92; [1942] 2 All E.R. 396.

knowledge—a theory to which I do not subscribe—but because it was an event which should not have happened and which prima facie indicates negligence on the part of those in charge of the child, just as much as the presence of a motor car on the foot pavement prima facie points to negligence on the part of the driver. . . .

My Lords, on this issue I agree with my noble and learned friends Lords Oaksey and Goddard, that the evidence disclosed no negligence on the part of Miss Morgan. It is easy after the event to think of several things she might have done which would have avoided the accident which resulted from her absence, but the question is whether her failure to take such action in the circumstances which existed amounted to negligence. For myself, I have no hesitation in holding that Miss Morgan was not shown to have been guilty of any negligence, and that no responsibility for the death of the deceased man attaches to her.

This does not, however, dispose of the case. The explanation put forward by the appellants entirely fails to explain how or why it was possible for this tiny child to escape from the school premises on to the street. The trial judge drew the inference that the child got out through the unlocked side gate opening on to a lane leading into the street. This was the way the child was brought to, and taken from, school, and I think the judge's inference was the most probable one. No explanation was given why the gate was kept unlocked, or in such a condition that it was possible for a child of four to push it open or unlatch it. Nor was any other means of exit suggested as likely, except by going through other portions of the school premises not forming part of the nursery school and out of a gate leading directly on to the street.

My Lords, I think the appellants failed altogether to show that the child's presence in the street was not due to any negligence on their part, or of those for whom they are responsible. . . .

While entirely absolving Miss Morgan from the finding of negligence against her, I am none the less of opinion that the appellants do not thereby escape responsibility, and for these reasons I would dismiss the appeal.

Lord Keith of Avonholm (agreeing that the appeal should be dismissed): . . . I wish to make it clear that I am dealing with the case of a child so young that it cannot safely be allowed on a busy street by itself. With a child of an age to be allowed to find its own way to school, or to traverse the streets alone, different considerations arise. There can normally be no duty to prevent such a child from getting on to a street and, in the case of a traffic accident in which it is involved, the question of responsibility for the accident will be considered in general with reference to the conduct of the child itself and of the other person involved in the accident. There may also be special cases of country children from wayside cottages using a road in full sight of approaching traffic, or tiny tots on some side street obviously used as a children's playground. Such cases will have to be considered on their special circumstances. . . .

[Lord Oaksey delivered a speech in favour of allowing the appeal.]

Appeal dismissed

Notes

1. In the sort of situation involved in the case above, the appellants could have found themselves facing not just a claim by a road user, but also a claim from the child himself, if he had been injured. Indeed Lord Reid in *Carmarthenshire C.C.* v. *Lewis* thought that the appellants would have been liable if the child had suffered damage. By way of example, mention might also be made of *Barnes* v. *Hampshire C.C.*, [1969] 3 All E.R. 746 where a schoolgirl, aged five, was seriously injured when she ran into a lorry on a busy road which was a short distance from her school. The official time for release from the school she attended was 3.30 p.m., but the trial judge found that on this occasion she

was let out of the school at or very shortly after 3.25 p.m., and that, if she had been let out at the official time, her mother would probably have met the child before the latter reached the busy road. The House of Lords held that the respondents, the education authority, were liable to the child.

2. *Barnes* v. *Hampshire C.C.* concerned the liability of an education authority, but the question of parental liability to children has been discussed in a recent Australian case—*Hahn* v. *Conley*, [1972] A.L.R. 247. Having examined the case law, Barwick C.J. thought that one proposition—and in his view it was correct—clearly emerged. At p. 251 he stated this proposition as follows:

". . . if there be a cause of action available to the child, the blood relationship of the defendant to the child will not constitute a bar to the maintenance by the child of the appropriate proceeding to enforce the cause of action. Whilst perhaps there is no clear decision of an appellate court in the United Kingdom, New Zealand or Australia to that effect, I think that the view for which there is most judicial support, and the view which commends itself to me, is that the moral duties of conscientious parenthood do not, as such, provide the child with any cause of action when they are not, or badly, performed or neglected. Further, I think that the predominant judicial view [to be][1] extracted from those cases, and again a view which commends itself to me as correct is that, whilst in particular situations and because of their nature or elements, there will be a duty on the person into whose care the child has been placed and accepted to take reasonable care to protect the child against foreseeable danger, there is no general duty of care in that respect imposed by the law upon a parent simply because of the blood relationship. Also parents like strangers may become liable to the child if the child is led into danger by their actions. . . . In the case of the parent, as in the case of a stranger it seems to me that the duty of care springs out of the particular situation: the extent and nature of the steps which it may be necessary to take to discharge the duty may well be influenced by the fact of parenthood, though parenthood is not itself the source of the duty."

On parental liability, see also *McCallion* v. *Dodd*, [1966] N.Z.L.R. 710; Bromley, *Family Law* (4th Edn.), pp. 308–310; *Rogers* v. *Rawlings*, [1969] Qd.R. 262.

Question

Might there be any justification for not allowing a child to sue its parents? Although this would be out of line with the approach of the courts, is there a case for restricting recovery to those situations where the parent is actually insured, or, so as not to discriminate against a child with less prudent parents, those cases where there is compulsory insurance (e.g. road traffic)?

Home Office v. Dorset Yacht Co., Ltd.

House of Lords   [1970] 2 All E.R. 294

This was an appeal by the Home Office from the order of the Court of Appeal (Lord Denning M.R. and Edmund Davies and Phillimore L.JJ.) dated 10 March 1969 and reported, [1969] 2 All E.R. 564, dismissing the appeal of the Home Office from a judgment of Thesiger J. dated 19 December 1968 who decided a preliminary issue on a point of law in favour of the respondents, the Dorset Yacht Co., Ltd. The facts are set out in the opinion of Lord Reid.

---

1. [These words do not appear in the report of the case at [1972] A.L.R. at p. 251, but are to be found in the report of the case at (1971), 45 A.L.J.R. at p. 635.]

LORD REID: My Lords, on 21 September 1962, a party of borstal trainees were working on Brownsea Island in Poole Harbour under the supervision and control of three borstal officers. During that night seven of them escaped and went aboard a yacht which they found nearby. They set this yacht in motion and collided with the respondents' yacht which was moored in the vicinity. Then they boarded the respondents' yacht. Much damage was done to this yacht by the collision and some by the subsequent conduct of these trainees. The respondents sue the appellant, the Home Office, for the amount of this damage.

The case comes before your Lordships on a preliminary issue whether the Home Office or these borstal officers owed any duty of care to the respondents capable of giving rise to a liability in damages. So it must be assumed that the respondents can prove all that they could prove on the pleadings if the case goes to trial. The question then is whether on that assumption the Home Office would be liable in damages. It is admitted that the Home Office would be vicariously liable if an action would lie against any of these borstal officers.

The facts which I think we must assume are that this party of trainees was in the lawful custody of the governor of the Portland Borstal Institution and was sent by him to Brownsea Island on a training exercise in the custody and under the control of the three officers with instructions to keep them in custody and under control. But in breach of their instructions these officers simply went to bed leaving the trainees to their own devices. If they had obeyed their instructions they could and would have prevented these trainees from escaping. They would therefore be guilty of the disciplinary offences of contributing by carelessness or neglect to the escape of a prisoner and to the occurrence of loss, damage or injury to any person or property. All the escaping trainees had criminal records and five of them had a record of previous escapes from borstal institutions. The three officers knew or ought to have known that these trainees would probably try to escape during the night, would take some vessel to make good their escape and would probably cause damage to it or some other vessel. There were numerous vessels moored in the harbour, and the trainees could readily board one of them. So it was a likely consequence of their neglect of duty that the respondents' yacht would suffer damage.

The case for the Home Office is that under no circumstances can borstal officers owe any duty to any member of the public to take care to prevent trainees under their control or supervision from injuring him or his property. If that is the law then enquiry into the facts of this case would be a waste of time and money because whatever the facts may be the respondents must lose. That case is based on three main arguments. First, it is said that there is virtually no authority for imposing a duty of this kind. Secondly, it is said that no person can be liable for a wrong done by another who is of full age and capacity and who is not the servant or acting on behalf of that person. And thirdly, it is said that public policy (or the policy of the relevant legislation) requires that these officers should be immune from any such liability.

The first would at one time have been a strong argument. About the beginning of this century most eminent lawyers thought that there were a number of separate torts involving negligence each with its own rules, and they were most unwilling to add more. They were of course aware from a number of leading cases that in the past the courts had from time to time recognised new duties and new grounds of action. But the heroic age was over, it was time to cultivate certainty and security in the law; the categories of negligence were virtually closed. The learned Attorney-General invited us to return to those halcyon days, but, attractive though it may be, I cannot accede to his invitation.

In later years there has been a steady trend towards regarding the law of negligence as depending on principle so that, when a new point emerges, one should ask not whether it is covered by authority but whether recognised principles apply to it.

M'Alister (or _Donoghue_) v. _Stevenson_[1] may be regarded as a milestone, and the well-known passage in Lord Atkin's speech[2] should I think be regarded as a statement of principle. It is not to be treated as if it were a statutory definition. It will require qualification in new circumstances. But I think that the time has come when we can and should say that it ought to apply unless there is some justification or valid explanation for its exclusion. For example, causing economic loss is a different matter; for one thing it is often caused by deliberate action. Competition involves traders being entitled to damage their rivals' interests by promoting their own, and there is a long chapter of the law determining in what circumstances owners of land can, and in what circumstances they may not, use their proprietary rights so as to injure their neighbours. But where negligence is involved the tendency has been to apply principles analogous to those stated by Lord Atkin[2] (cf. _Hedley Byrne & Co., Ltd._ v. _Heller & Partners, Ltd._).[3] And when a person has done nothing to put himself in any relationship with another person in distress or with his property mere accidental propinquity does not require him to go to that person's assistance. There may be a moral duty to do so, but it is not practicable to make it a legal duty. And then there are cases, e.g. with regard to landlord and tenant, where the law was settled long ago and neither Parliament nor this House sitting judicially has made any move to alter it. But I can see nothing to prevent our approaching the present case with Lord Atkin's principles[2] in mind.

Even so it is said that the respondents must fail because there is a general principle that no person can be responsible for the acts of another who is not his servant or acting on his behalf. But here the ground of liability is not responsibility for the acts of the escaping trainees; it is liability for damage caused by the carelessness of these officers in the knowledge that their carelessness would probably result in the trainees causing damage of this kind. So the question is really one of remoteness of damage. . . .

[Having quoted passages from the judgments in _The Oropesa_,[4] _Haynes_ v. _Harwood_[5] and _Scott's Trustees_ v. _Moss_,[6] he continued:] These cases show that, where human action forms one of the links between the original wrongdoing of the defendant and the loss suffered by the plaintiff, that action must at least have been something very likely to happen if it is not to be regarded as novus actus interveniens breaking the chain of causation. I do not think that a mere foreseeable possibility is or should be sufficient, for then the intervening human action can more properly be regarded as a new cause than as a consequence of the original wrongdoing. But if the intervening action was likely to happen I do not think it can matter whether that action was innocent or tortious or criminal. Unfortunately tortious or criminal action by a third party is often the "very kind of thing" which is likely to happen as a result of the wrongful or careless act of the defendant. And in the present case, on the facts which we must assume at this stage, I think that the taking of a boat by the escaping trainees and their unskilful navigation leading to damage to another vessel were the very kind of thing that these borstal officers ought to have seen to be likely.

There was an attempt to draw a distinction between loss caused to the plaintiff by failure to control an adult of full capacity and loss caused by failure to control a child or mental defective. As regards causation, no doubt it is easier to infer novus actus interveniens in the case of an adult but that seems to me to be the only distinction. In the present case on the assumed facts there would in my view be no novus actus when the trainees damaged the respondents' property and I would therefore hold that damage to have been caused by the borstal officers' negligence.

If the carelessness of the borstal officers was the cause of the respondents' loss what

---

1. [1932] A.C. 562; [1932] All E.R. Rep. 1.
2. [1932] A.C. at p. 580; [1932] All E.R. Rep. at p. 11.
3. [1964] A.C. 465; [1963] 2 All E.R. 575.
4. [1943] P. 32, at p. 37; [1943] 1 All E.R. 211, at p. 214.
5. [1935] 1 K.B. 146, at p. 156; [1934] All E.R. Rep. 103, at p. 107.
6. (1889), 17 R. (Ct. of Sess.) 32, at pp. 36 and 37.

justification is there for holding that they had no duty to take care? The first argument was that their right and power to control the trainees was purely statutory and that any duty to exercise that right and power was only a statutory duty owed to the Crown. I would agree but there is very good authority for the proposition that, if a person performs a statutory duty carelessly so that he causes damage to a member of the public which would not have happened if he had performed his duty properly, he may be liable. In *Geddis* v. *Proprietors of Bann Reservoir*[1] Lord Blackburn said:

> "For I take it, without citing cases, that it is now thoroughly well established that no action will lie for doing that which the legislature has authorised, if it be done without negligence, although it does occasion damage to anyone; but an action does lie for doing that which the legislature has authorised, if it be done negligently."

The reason for that is, I think, that Parliament deems it to be in the public interest that things otherwise unjustifiable should be done, and that those who do such things with due care should be immune from liability to persons who may suffer thereby. But Parliament cannot reasonably be supposed to have licensed those who do such things to act negligently in disregard of the interests of others so as to cause them needless damage.

Where Parliament confers a discretion the position is not the same. Then there may, and almost certainly will, be errors of judgment in exercising such a discretion and Parliament cannot have intended that members of the public should be entitled to sue in respect of such errors. But there must come a stage when the discretion is exercised so carelessly or unreasonably that there has been no real exercise of the discretion which Parliament has conferred. The person purporting to exercise his discretion has acted in abuse or excess of his power. Parliament cannot be supposed to have granted immunity to persons who do that. The present case does not raise that issue because no discretion was given to these borstal officers. They were given orders which they negligently failed to carry out. But the county court case of *Greenwell* v. *Prison Comrs.*[2] was relied on and I must deal with it. Some 290 trainees were held in custody in an open borstal institution. During the previous year there had been no less than 172 escapes. Two trainees escaped and took and damaged the plaintiff's motor truck; one of these trainees had escaped on three previous occasions from this institution. For three months since his last escape the question of his removal to a more secure institution had been under consideration but no decision had been reached. The learned judge held that the authorities there had been negligent. In my view, this decision could only be upheld if it could be said that the failure of those authorities to deal with the situation was so unreasonable as to show that they had been guilty of a breach of their statutory duty and that this had caused the loss suffered by the plaintiff.

. . . [T]he responsible authorities must weigh on the one hand the public interest of protecting neighbours and their property from the depredations of escaping trainees and on the other hand the public interest of promoting rehabilitation. Obviously there is much room here for differences of opinion and errors of judgment. In my view there can be no liability if the discretion is exercised with due care. There could only be liability if the person entrusted with discretion either unreasonably failed to carry out his duty to consider the matter or reached a conclusion so unreasonable as again to show failure to do his duty. . . .

We were also referred to *Holgate* v. *Lancashire Mental Hospitals Board, Gill and Robertson*[3] where the alleged fault was in releasing a mental patient. For similar reasons I think this decision could only be supported if it could be said that the release was authorised so carelessly that there had been no real exercise of discretion. . . .

It was suggested that a decision against the Home Office would have very far reach-

1. (1878), 3 App. Cas. 430, at pp. 455, 456.
2. (1951), 101 L. Jo. 486.
3. [1937] 4 All E.R. 19.

ing effects; it was indeed suggested in the Court of Appeal[1] that it would make the Home Office liable for the loss occasioned by a burglary committed by a trainee on parole or a prisoner permitted to go out to attend a funeral. But there are two reasons why in the vast majority of cases that would not be so. In the first place it would have to be shown that the decision to allow any such release was so unreasonable that it could not be regarded as a real exercise of discretion by the responsible officer who authorised the release. And secondly it would have to be shown that the commission of the offence was the natural and probable, as distinct from merely a foreseeable, result of the release—that there was no novus actus interveniens. *Greenwell's* case[2] received a good deal of publicity at the time; it was commented on in the Law Quarterly Review.[3] But it has not been followed by a series of claims. I think the fears of the Home Office are unfounded; I cannot believe that negligence or dereliction of duty is widespread among prison or borstal officers.

Finally, I must deal with public policy. It is argued that it would be contrary to public policy to hold the Home Office or its officers liable to a member of the public for this carelessness—or indeed any failure of duty on their part. The basic question is who shall bear the loss caused by that carelessness—the innocent respondents or the Home Office who are vicariously liable for the conduct of their careless officers? I do not think that the argument for the Home Office can be put better than it was put by the Court of Appeals of New York in *Williams* v. *New York State*:[4]

> ". . . public policy also requires that the State be not held liable. To hold otherwise would impose a heavy responsibility upon the State, or dissuade the wardens and principal keepers of our prison system from continued experimentation with 'minimum security' work details—which provide a means for encouraging better-risk prisoners to exercise their senses of responsibility and honor and so prepare themselves for their eventual return to society. Since 1917, the Legislature has expressly provided for out-of-prison work, Correction Law, § 182, and its intention should be respected without fostering the reluctance of prison officials to assign eligible men to minimum security work, lest they thereby give rise to costly claims against the State, or indeed inducing the State itself to terminate this 'salutary procedure' looking towards rehabilitation."

It may be that public servants of the State of New York are so apprehensive, easily dissuaded from doing their duty, and intent on preserving public funds from costly claims, that they could be influenced in this way. But my experience leads me to believe that Her Majesty's servants are made of sterner stuff. So I have no hesitation in rejecting this argument. I can see no good ground in public policy for giving this immunity to a government department. I would dismiss this appeal.

VISCOUNT DILHORNE [(dissenting) having quoted passages from *Deyong* v. *Shenburn*[5] and *Railways Comr.* v. *Quinlan*[6] continued:] . . . In the light of these passages I think that it is clear that the *M'Alister* (or *Donoghue*) v. *Stevenson*[1] principle cannot be regarded as an infallible test of the existence of a duty of care; nor do I think that if that test is satisfied, there arises any presumption of the existence of such a duty. . . .

LORD PEARSON: . . . It may be artificial and unhelpful to consider the question as to the existence of a duty of care in isolation from the elements of breach of duty and damage. The actual damage alleged to have been suffered by the respondents may be an example of a kind or range of potential damage which was foreseeable, and if the act or

---

1. [1969] 2 Q.B. 412; [1969] 2 All E.R. 564.
2. (1951), 101 L. Jo. 486.
3. Vol. 68, p. 18.
4. (1955), 127 N.E. (2d) 545, at p. 550.
5. [1946] K.B. 227, at p. 233; [1946] A All E.R. 226, at p. 229.
6. [1964] A.C. 1054, at pp. 1070 and 1084; [1964] 1 All E.R. 897, at pp. 902, 912.
7. [1932] A.C. 562; [1932] All E.R. Rep. 1.

omission by which the damage was caused is identifiable, it may put one on the trail of a possible duty of care of which the act or omission would be a breach. In short, it may be illuminating to start with the damage and work back through the cause of it to the possible duty which may have been broken. . . .

What would be the nature of the duty of care owed by the Home Office to the respondents if it existed? In my opinion, the Home Office did not owe to the respondents any general duty to keep the borstal boys in detention. If the Home Office had, in the exercise of its discretion, released some of these boys, taking them on shore and putting them on trains or buses with tickets to their homes, there would have been no prospect of damage to the respondents as boatowners and the respondents would not have been concerned and would have had nothing to complain of. Again the boys might have escaped in such a way that no damage could be caused to the respondents as boatowners; for instance, they might have escaped by swimming ashore or by going ashore in a boat belonging to or hired by the borstal authorities or by having their friends bring a rescue boat from outside and carry them off to a refuge in the Isle of Wight or Portsmouth or elsewhere. On the other hand the boys might interfere with the boats from motives of curiosity and desire for amusement without having any intention to escape from borstal detention. The essential feature of this case is not the "escape" (whatever that may have amounted to) but the interference with the boats. The duty of care would be simply a duty to take reasonable care to prevent such interference. The duty would not be broken merely by the Home Office's failure to prevent an escape from borstal detention or from borstal training. Performance of the duty might incidentally involve an element of physical detention, if interference with the boats by some particular boy could not be prevented by any other means. But if some other means—such as supervision, keeping watch, dissuasion or deterrence—would suffice, physical detention would not be required for performance of the duty.

Can such a duty be held to exist on the facts alleged here? On this question there is no judicial authority except the one decision in the Ipswich county court in *Greenwell* v. *Prison Comrs.*[1] In this situation it seems permissible, indeed almost inevitable, that one should revert to the statement of basic principle by Lord Atkin in *M'Alister* (or *Donoghue*) v. *Stevenson*[2] . . . It seems to me that prima facie, in the situation which arose in this case according to the allegations, the respondents as boatowners were in law "neighbours" of the Home Office and so there was a duty of care owing by the Home Office to the respondents. It is true that the *M'Alister* (or *Donoghue*) v. *Stevenson*[2] principle as stated in the passage which has been cited is a basic and general but not universal principle and does not in law apply to all the situations which are covered by the wide words of the passage. To some extent the decision in this case must be a matter of impression and instinctive judgment as to what is fair and just. It seems to me that this case ought to, and does, come within the *M'Alister* (or *Donoghue*) v. *Stevenson*[2] principle unless there is some sufficient reason for not applying the principle to this case. Therefore, one has to consider the suggested reasons for not applying the principle here.

Proximity or remoteness. As there is no evidence, one can only judge from the allegations in the statement of claim. It seems clear that there was sufficient proximity; there was geographical proximity and it was foreseeable that the damage was likely to occur unless some care was taken to prevent it. In other cases a difficult problem may arise as to how widely the "neighbourhood" extends, but no such problem faces the respondents in this case.

Act of third party. In *Weld-Blundell* v. *Stephens*[3] Lord Sumner said:

"In general (apart from special contracts and relations and the maxim Respondeat superior), even though A. is in fault, he is not responsible for injury to C. which B., a stranger to him, deliberately chooses to do."

---

1. (1951), 101 L. Jo. 486.
2. [1932] A.C. 562, at p. 580; [1932] All E.R. Rep. 1, at p. 11.
3. [1920] A.C. 956, at p. 986; [1920] All E.R. Rep. 32, at p. 47.

In *Smith* v. *Leurs*[1] Dixon J. said:

">. . . apart from vicarious responsibility, one man may be responsible to another
for the harm done to the latter by a third person; he may be responsible on the
ground that the act of the third person could not have taken place but for his own
fault or breach of duty. There is more than one description of duty the breach of
which may produce this consequence. For instance, it may be a duty of care in
reference to things involving special danger. It may even be a duty of care with
reference to the control of actions or conduct of the third person. It is, however,
exceptional to find in the law a duty to control another's actions to prevent harm to
strangers. The general rule is that one man is under no duty of controlling another to
prevent his doing damage to a third. There are, however, special relations which are
the source of a duty of this nature. It appears now to be recognised that it is incumbent upon a parent who maintains control over a young child to take reasonable care
so to exercise that control as to avoid conduct on his part exposing the person or
property of others to unreasonable danger. Parental control, where it exists, must
be exercised with due care to prevent the child inflicting intentional damage on
others or causing damage by conduct involving unreasonable risk of injury to
others."

In my opinion, this case falls under the exception and not the rule, because there was a
special relation. The borstal boys were under the control of the Home Office's officers,
and control imports responsibility. The boys' interference with the boats appears to
have been a direct result of the Home Office's officers' failure to exercise proper control
and supervision. Problems may arise in other cases as to the responsibility of the Home
Office's officers for acts done by borstal boys when they have completed their escape
from control and are fully at large and acting independently. No such problem faces the
respondents in this case.

Statutory duty. Not only with respect to the detention of borstal boys but also with
respect to the discipline, supervision and control of them the Home Office's officers
were acting in pursuance of statutory duties. These statutory duties were owed to the
Crown and not to private individuals such as the respondents. The respondents, however, do not base their claim on breach of statutory duty. The existence of statutory
duties does not exclude liability at common law for negligence in the performance of the
statutory duties. . . . Be it assumed that the Home Office's officers were acting in
pursuance of statutory powers (or statutory duties which must include powers) in
bringing the borstal boys to Brownsea Island to work there under the supervision and
control of the Home Office's officers. No complaint could be made of the Home
Office's officers doing that. But in doing that they had a duty to the respondents as
"neighbours" to make proper exercise of the powers of supervision and control for the
purpose of preventing damage to the respondents as "neighbours".

Public policy. It is said, and in the absence of evidence I assume (and perhaps it is
common knowledge and can be judicially noticed) that one method of borstal training,
which is employed in relation to boys who may be able to respond to it, is to give them
a considerable measure of freedom, initiative and independence in order that they may
develop their self-reliance and sense of responsibility. This method, at any rate when it is
intensively applied, must diminish the amount of supervision and control which can be
exercised over the borstal boys by the Home Office's officers, and there is then a risk,
which is not wholly avoidable, that some of the boys will escape and may in the course
of escaping or after escaping do injury to persons or damage to property. There is no
evidence to show whether or not this method was being employed, intensively or at all,
in the present case. But supposing that it was, I am of opinion that it would affect only
the content or standard and not the existence of the duty of care. It may be that when
the method is being intensively employed there is not very much that the Home Office's

---

1. (1945), 70 C.L.R. 256, at pp. 261, 262.

officers can do for the protection of the neighbours and their property. But it does not follow that they have no duty to do anything at all for this purpose. They should exercise such care for the protection of the neighbours and their property as is consistent with the due carrying out of the borstal system of training. The needs of the borstal system, important as they no doubt are, should not be treated as so paramount and all-important as to require or justify complete absence of care for the safety of the neighbours and their property and complete immunity from any liability for anything that the neighbours may suffer.

. . . I would say that the Home Office owed no duty to the respondents with regard to the detention of the borstal boys (except perhaps incidentally as an element in supervision and control) nor with regard to the treatment or employment of them, but the Home Office did owe to the respondents a duty of care, capable of giving rise to a liability in damages, with respect to the manner in which the borstal boys were disciplined, controlled and supervised.

I would dismiss the appeal.

LORD DIPLOCK: . . . The only cause of action relied on is the "negligence" of the officers in failing to prevent the youths from escaping from their custody and control. It is implicit in this averment of "negligence" and must be treated as admitted not only that the officers by taking reasonable care could have prevented the youths from escaping, but also that it was reasonably foreseeable by them that if the youths did escape they would be likely to commit damage of the kind which they did commit, to some craft moored in the vicinity of Brownsea Island.

The specific question of law raised in this appeal may therefore be stated as: is any duty of care to prevent the escape of a borstal trainee from custody owed by the Home Office to persons whose property would be likely to be damaged by the tortious acts of the borstal trainee if he escaped? This is the first time that this specific question has been posed at a higher judicial level than that of a county court. Your Lordships in answering it will be performing a judicial function similar to that performed in *M'Alister* (or *Donoghue*) v. *Stevenson*[1] and more recently in *Hedley Byrne & Co., Ltd.* v *Heller & Partners, Ltd.*,[2] of deciding whether the English law of civil wrongs should be extended to impose legal liability to make reparation for the loss caused to another by conduct of a kind which has not hitherto been recognised by the courts as entailing any such liability.

This function, which judges hesitate to acknowledge as law-making, plays at most a minor role in the decision of the great majority of cases, and little conscious thought has been given to analysing its methodology. Outstanding exceptions are to be found in the speeches of Lord Atkin in *M'Alister* (or *Donoghue*) v. *Stevenson*[1] and of Lord Devlin in *Hedley Byrne & Co., Ltd.* v. *Heller & Partners, Ltd.*[2] It was because the former was the first authoritative attempt at such an analysis that it has had so seminal an effect on the modern development of the law of negligence.

It will be apparent that I agree with Lord Denning M.R.[3] that what we are concerned with in this appeal "is . . . at bottom a matter of public policy which we, as judges, must resolve". He cited in support Lord Pearce's dictum in *Hedley Byrne & Co., Ltd.* v. *Heller & Partners, Ltd.*:[4]

"How wide the sphere of the duty of care in negligence is to be laid depends ultimately on the courts' assessment of the demands of society for protection from the carelessness of others."

The reference in this passage to "the courts" in the plural is significant for—

"As always in English law the first step in such an inquiry is to see how far the authorities have gone, for new categories in the law do not spring into existence overnight;"

---

1. [1932] A.C. 562; [1932] All E.R. Rep. 1.
2. [1964] A.C. 465; [1963] 2 All E.R. 575.
3. [1969] 2 Q.B. at p. 426; [1969] 2 All E.R. at p. 567.
4. [1964] A.C. at p. 536; [1963] 2 All E.R. at p. 615.

per Lord Devlin.[1]

The justification of the courts' role in giving the effect of law to the judges' conception of the public interest in the field of negligence is based on the cumulative experience of the judiciary of the actual consequences of lack of care in particular instances. And the judicial development of the law of negligence rightly proceeds by seeking first to identify the relevant characteristics that are common to the kinds of conduct and relationship between the parties which are involved in the case for decision and the kinds of conduct and relationships which have been held in previous decisions of the courts to give rise to a duty of care.

The method adopted at this stage of the process is analytical and inductive. It starts with an analysis of the characteristics of the conduct and relationship involved in each of the decided cases. But the analyst must know what he is looking for; and this involves his approaching his analysis with some general conception of conduct and relationships which *ought* to give rise to a duty of care. This analysis leads to a proposition which can be stated in the form: "In all the decisions that have been analysed a duty of care has been held to exist wherever the conduct and the relationship possessed each of the characteristics A, B, C, D etc., and has not so far been found to exist when any of these characteristics were absent."

For the second stage, which is deductive and analytical, that proposition is converted to: "In all cases where the conduct and relationship possess each of the characteristics A, B, C, D etc., a duty of care arises." The conduct and relationship involved in the case for decision is then analysed to ascertain whether they possess each of these characteristics. If they do the conclusion follows that a duty of care does arise in the case for decision.

But since ex hypothesi the kind of case which we are now considering offers a choice whether or not to extend the kinds of conduct or relationships which give rise to a duty of care, the conduct or relationship which is involved in it will lack at least one of the characteristics A, B, C, or D etc. And the choice is exercised by making a policy decision whether or not a duty of care ought to exist if the characteristic which is lacking were absent or redefined in terms broad enough to include the case under consideration. The policy decision will be influenced by the same general conception of what ought to give rise to a duty of care as was used in approaching the analysis. The choice to extend is given effect to by redefining the characteristics in more general terms so as to exclude the necessity to conform to limitations imposed by the former definition which are considered to be inessential. The cases which are landmarks in the common law, such as *Lickbarrow* v. *Mason*,[2] *Rylands* v. *Fletcher*,[3] *Indermaur* v. *Dames*,[4] *M'Alister* (or *Donoghue*) v. *Stevenson*,[5] to mention but a few, are instances of cases where the cumulative experience of judges has led to a restatement in wide general terms of characteristics of conduct and relationships which give rise to legal liability.

Inherent in this methodology, however, is a practical limitation which is imposed by the sheer volume of reported cases. The initial selection of previous cases to be analysed will itself eliminate from the analysis those in which the conduct or relationship involved possessed characteristics which are obviously absent in the case for decision. The proposition used in the deductive stage is not a true universal. It needs to be qualified so as to read: "In all cases where the conduct and relationship possess each of the characteristics A, B, C and D etc., *but do not possess any of the characteristics Z, Y or X etc., which were present in the cases eliminated from the analysis*, a duty of care arises." But this qualification, being irrelevant to the decision of the particular case, is generally left unexpressed.

---

1. [1964] A.C. at p. 525; [1963] 2 All E.R. at p. 608.
2. (1787), 2 Term Rep. 63; [1775–1802] All E.R. Rep. 1.
3. (1868) L.R. 3 H.L. 330; [1861–73] All E.R. Rep. 1.
4. (1866), L.R. 1 C.P. 274; [1861–73] All E.R. Rep. 15.
5. [1932] A.C. 562; [1932] All E.R. Rep. 1.

This was the reason for the warning by Lord Atkin in *M'Alister* (or *Donoghue*) v. *Stevenson*[1] itself when he said:

". . . in the branch of the law which deals with civil wrongs, dependent in England at any rate entirely upon the application by judges of general principles also formulated by judges, it is of particular importance to guard against the danger of stating propositions of law in wider terms than is necessary, lest essential factors be omitted in the wider survey and the inherent adaptability of English law be unduly restricted. For this reason it is very necessary in considering reported cases in the law of torts that the actual decision alone should carry authority, proper weight, of course, being given to the dicta of the judges."

The respondents' argument in the present appeal disregards this warning. It seeks to treat as a universal not the specific proposition of law in *M'Alister* (or *Donoghue*) v. *Stevenson*[2] which was about a manufacturer's liability for damage caused by his dangerous products but the well-known aphorism used by Lord Atkin to describe[3] a "general conception of relations giving rise to a duty of care":

"You must take reasonable care to avoid acts or omissions which you can reasonably foresee would be likely to injure your neighbour. Who, then, in law is my neighbour? The answer seems to be—persons who are so closely and directly affected by my act that I ought reasonably to have them in contemplation . . . when I am directing my mind to the acts or omissions which are called in question."

Used as a guide to characteristics which will be found to exist in conduct and relationships which give rise to a legal duty of care this aphorism marks a milestone in the modern development of the law of negligence. But misused as a universal it is manifestly false.

The branch of English law which deals with civil wrongs abounds with instances of acts and, more particularly, of omissions which give rise to no legal liability in the doer or omitter for loss or damage sustained by others as a consequence of the act or omission, however reasonably or probably that loss or damage might have been anticipated. The very parable of the good Samaritan[4] which was evoked by Lord Atkin in *M'Alister* (or *Donoghue*) v. *Stevenson*[2] illustrates, in the conduct of the priest and of the Levite who passed by on the other side, an omission which was likely to have as its reasonable and probable consequence damage to the health of the victim of the thieves, but for which the priest and Levite would have incurred no civil liability in English law. Examples could be multiplied. . . .

In the present appeal . . . the conduct of the Home Office which is called in question differs from the kind of conduct discussed in *M'Alister* (or *Donoghue*) v. *Stevenson*[2] in at least two special characteristics. First, the actual damage sustained by the respondents was the direct consequence of a tortious act done with conscious volition by a third party responsible in law for his own acts and this act was interposed between the act of the Home Office complained of and the sustension of damage by the respondents. Secondly, there are two separate "neighbour relationships" of the Home Office involved, a relationship with the respondents and a relationship with the third party. These are capable of giving rise to conflicting duties of care. This appeal, therefore, also raises the lawyer's question "Am I my brother's keeper"? A question which may also receive a restricted reply.

I start, therefore, with an examination [of] the previous cases in which both or one of these special characteristics are present. In the county court case of *Greenwell* v. *Prison*

---

1. [1932] A.C. at pp. 583, 584; [1932] All E.R. Rep. at p. 13.
2. [1932] A.C. 562; [1932] All E.R. Rep. 1.
3. [1932] A.C. at p. 580; [1932] All E.R. Rep. at p. 11.
4 Luke x, verse 30.

Comrs.[1] both were present as was the characteristic of physical proximity of the plaintiff's property in the relationship between the plaintiff and the defendant. If this decision is right the respondents are entitled to succeed. But the county court judge simply treated the case as governed by Lord Atkin's aphorism in *M'Alister* (or *Donoghue*) v. *Stevenson*[2] and for reasons already stated I do not think that this approach to the problem is adequate.

In two cases, *Ellis* v. *Home Office*[3] and *D'Arcy* v. *Prison Comrs.*,[4] it was assumed, in the absence of argument to the contrary, that the legal custodian of a prisoner detained in a prison owed to the plaintiff, another prisoner confined in the same prison, a duty of care to prevent the first prisoner from assaulting the plaintiff and causing him physical injuries. Unlike the present case, at the time of the tortious act of the prisoner for the consequences of which it was assumed that the custodian was liable the prisoner was in the actual custody of the defendant and the relationship between them gave to the defendant a continuing power of physical control over the acts of the prisoner. The relationship between the defendants and the plaintiffs in these two cases too bore no obvious analogy to that between the respondents and the Home Office in the present case. In each of the cases the defendant in the exercise of a legal right and physical power of custody and control of the plaintiff had required him to be in a position in which the defendant ought reasonably and probably to have foreseen that he was likely to be injured by his fellow prisoner.

In my view, it is the combination of these two characteristics, one of the relationship between the defendant custodian and the person actually committing the wrong to the plaintiff and the other of the relationship between the defendant and the plaintiff which supply the reason for the existence of the duty of care in these two cases—which I conceded as counsel in *Ellis* v. *Home Office*.[3] The latter characteristic would be present also in the relationship between the defendant and any other person admitted to the prison who sustained similar damage from the tortious act of a prisoner, since the Home Office as occupier and manager of the prison has the legal right to control the admission and the movements of a visitor while he is on the prison premises. A similar duty of care would thus be owed to him. But I do not think that, save as a deliberate policy decision, any proposition of law based on the decisions in these two cases would be wide enough to extend to a duty to take reasonable care to prevent the escape of a prisoner from actual physical custody and control owed to a person whose property is situated outside the prison premises and is damaged by the tortious act of the prisoner *after his escape.* . . .

[His Lordship discussed *Holgate* v. *Lancashire Mental Hospitals Board, Gill and Robertson*[5] and *Carmarthenshire C.C.* v. *Lewis*,[6] and continued:] I do not find it useful to refer to the many other cases cited in which the damage to the plaintiff was not caused by an act of conscious volition of a responsible third person whose conduct the defendant had a legal right to control. The result of the survey of previous authorities can be summarised in the words of Dixon J. in *Smith* v. *Leurs*:[7]

> "The general rule is that one man is under no duty of controlling another man to prevent his doing damage to a third. There are, however, special relations which are the source of a duty of this nature."

From the previous decisions of the English courts, in particular those in *Ellis* v. *Home*

---

1. (1951), 101 L. Jo. 486.
2. [1932] A.C. at p. 580; [1932] All E.R. Rep. at p. 11.
3. [1953] 2 Q.B. 135; [1953] 2 All E.R. 149.
4. (1955), *Times*, 15th, 16th, 17th November.
5. [1937] 4 All E.R. 19.
6. [1955] A.C. 549; [1955] 1 All E.R. 565.
7. (1945), 70 C.L.R. at p. 262.

Office[1] and *D'Arcy* v. *Prison Comrs.*,[2] which I accept as correct, it is possible to arrive by induction at an established proposition of law as respects one of those special-relations: viz. A is responsible for damage caused to the person or property of B by the tortious act of C (a person responsible in law for his own acts) where the relationship between A and C has the characteristics: (1) that A has the legal right to detain C in penal custody and to control his acts while in custody; (2) that A is actually exercising his legal right of custody of C at the time of C's tortious act; and (3) that A if he had taken reasonable care in the exercise of his right of custody could have prevented C from doing the tortious act which caused damage to the person or property of B; and where also the relationship between A and B has the characteristics; (4) that at the time of C's tortious act A has the legal right to control the situation of B or his property as respects physical proximity to C; and (5) that A can reasonably foresee that B is likely to sustain damage to his person or property if A does not take reasonable care to prevent C from doing tortious acts of the kind which he did.

On the facts which your Lordships are required to assume for the purposes of the present appeal the relationship between the Home Office, A, and the borstal trainees, C, did possess characteristics (1) and (3) but did not possess characteristic (2); while the relationship between the Home Office, A, and the respondents, B, did possess characteristic (5) but did not possess characteristic (4). What your Lordships have to decide as respects each of the relationships is whether the missing characteristic is essential to the existence of the duty or whether the facts assumed for the purposes of this appeal disclose some other characteristic which if substituted for that which is missing would produce a new proposition of law which *ought* to be true.

As any proposition which relates to the duty of controlling another man to prevent his doing damage to a third deals with a category of civil wrongs of which the English courts have hitherto had little experience it would not be consistent with the methodology of the development of the law by judicial decision that any new proposition should be stated in wider terms than are necessary for the determination of the present appeal. Public policy may call for the immediate recognition of a new sub-category of relations which are the source of a duty of this nature additional to the sub-category described in the established proposition; but further experience of actual cases would be needed before the time became ripe for the coalescence of sub-categories into a broader category of relations giving rise to the duty, such as was effected with respect to the duty of care of a manufacturer of products in *M'Alister* (or *Donoghue*) v. *Stevenson*.[3] Nevertheless, any new sub-category will form part of the English law of civil wrongs and must be consistent with its general principles. . . .

[LORD DIPLOCK went on to distinguish *Geddis* v. *Proprietors of Bann Reservoir*,[4] and to state that the "public law concept of ultra vires has replaced the civil law concept of negligence as the test of the legality, and consequently of the actionability, of acts or omissions of government departments or public authorities done in the exercise of a discretion conferred on them by Parliament as to the means by which they are to achieve a particular public purpose." Having discussed the application of the ultra vires concept to the Borstal system, he continued:] In a civil action which calls in question an act or omission of a subordinate officer of the Home Office on the ground that he has been "negligent" in his custody and control of a borstal trainee who has caused damage to another person the initial inquiry should be whether or not the act or omission was ultra vires for one or other of these reasons. Where the act or omission is done in pursuance of the officer's instructions, the court may have to form its own view as to what is in the interests of borstal trainees, but only to the limited extent of determining whether or not any reasonable person could bona fide come to the conclusion that the trainee causing the damage or other trainees in the same custody could be benefited

1. [1953] 2 Q.B. 135; [1953] 2 All E.R. 149.
2. (1955), *Times*, 15th, 16th, 17th November.
3. [1932] A.C. 562; [1932] All E.R. Rep. 1.
4. (1878), 3 App. Cas. 430.

in any way by the act or omission. This does not involve the court in attempting to substitute, for that of the Home Office, its own assessment of the comparative weight to be given to the benefit to the trainees and the detriment to persons likely to sustain damage. If on the other hand the officer's act or omission is done contrary to his instructions it is not protected by the public law doctrine of intra vires. Its actionability falls to be determined by the civil law principles of negligence, like the acts of the statutory undertakers in *Geddis* v. *Proprietors of Bann Reservoir*.[1]

This, as it seems to me, is the way in which the courts should set about the task of reconciling the public interest in maintaining the freedom of the Home Office to decide on the system of custody and control of borstal trainees which is most likely to conduce to their reformation and the prevention of crime, and the public interest that borstal officers should not be allowed to be completely disregardful of the interests both of the trainees in their charge and of persons likely to be injured by their carelessness, without the law providing redress to those who in fact sustain injury.

Ellis v. *Home Office*[2] and *D'Arcy* v. *Prison Comrs*.[3] are decisions which are consistent with this principle as respects the initial inquiry. In neither of them was it sought to justify the alleged acts or omissions of the prison officers concerned as being done in compliance with instructions given to them by the appropriate authority (at that date the prison commissioners) or as being in the interests of the prisoner whose tortious act caused the damage or of any other inmates of the prison. If the test suggested were applied to acts and omissions alleged in those two cases they would in public law be ultra vires.

If this analogy to the principle of ultra vires in public law is applied as the relevant condition precedent to the liability of a custodian for damage caused by the tortious act of a person (the detainee) over whom he has a statutory right of custody, the characteristic of the relationship between the custodian and the detainee which was present in those two cases, viz. that the custodian was actually exercising his right of custody at the time of the tortious act of the detainee, would not be essential. A cause of action is capable of arising from failure by the custodian to take reasonable care to prevent the detainee from escaping, if his escape was the consequence of an act or omission of the custodian falling outside the limits of the discretion delegated to him under the statute.

The practical effect of this would be that no liability in the Home Office for "negligence" could arise out of the escape from an "open" borstal of a trainee who had been classified for training at a borstal of this type by the appropriate officer to whom the function of classification had been delegated, on the ground that the officer had been negligent in so classifying him or in failing to reclassify him for removal to a "closed" borstal. The decision as to classification would be one which lay within the officer's discretion. The court could not inquire into its propriety as it did in *Greenwell* v. *Prison Comrs*.[4] in order to determine whether he had given what the court considered to be sufficient weight to the interests of persons whose property the trainee would be likely to damage if he should escape. For this reason I think that *Greenwell* v. *Prison Comrs*.[4] was wrongly decided by the county court judge. But to say this does not dispose of the present appeal for the allegations of negligence against the borstal officers are consistent with their having acted outside any discretion delegated to them and having disregarded their instructions as to the precautions they should take to prevent members of the working party of trainees from escaping from Brownsea Island. Whether they had or not could only be determined at the trial of the action. But this is only a condition precedent to the existence of any liability. Even if the acts and omissions of the borstal officer alleged in the particulars of negligence were done in breach of their instructions

1. (1878), 3 App. Cas. 430.
2. [1953] 2 Q.B. 135; [1953] 2 All E.R. 149.
3. (1955), *Times*, 15th, 16th, 17th November.
4. (1951), 101 L. Jo. 486.

and so were ultra vires in public law it does not follow that they were also done in breach of any duty of care owed by the officers to the respondents in civil law.

. . . To give rise to a duty on the part of the custodian owed to a member of the public to take reasonable care to prevent a borstal trainee from escaping from his custody before completion of the trainee's sentence there should be some relationship between the custodian and the person to whom the duty is owed which exposes that person to a particular risk of damage in consequence of that escape which is different in its incidence from the general risk of damage from criminal acts of others which he shares with all members of the public.

What distinguishes a borstal trainee who has escaped from one who has been duly released from custody, is his liability to recapture, and the distinctive added risk which is a reasonably foreseeable consequence of a failure to exercise due care in preventing him from escaping is the likelihood that in order to elude pursuit immediately on the discovery of his absence the escaping trainee may steal or appropriate and damage property which is situated in the vicinity of the place of detention from which he has escaped.

So long as Parliament is content to leave the general risk of damage from criminal acts to lie where it falls without any remedy except against the criminal himself, the courts would be exceeding their limited function in developing the common law to meet changing conditions if they were to recognise a duty of care to prevent criminals escaping from penal custody owed to a wider category of members of the public than those whose property was exposed to an exceptional added risk by the adoption of a custodial system for young offenders which increased the likelihood of their escape unless due care was taken by those responsible for their custody.

I should therefore hold that any duty of a borstal officer to use reasonable care to prevent a borstal trainee from escaping from his custody was owed only to persons whom he could reasonably foresee had property situate in the vicinity of the place of detention of the detainee which the detainee was likely to steal or to appropriate and damage in the course of eluding immediate pursuit and recapture. Whether or not any person fell within this category would depend on the facts of the particular case including the previous criminal and escaping record of the individual trainee concerned and the nature of the place from which he escaped.

So to hold would be a rational extension of the relationship between the custodian and the person sustaining the damage which was accepted in *Ellis* v. *Home Office* [1] and *D'Arcy* v. *Prison Comrs.* [2] as giving rise to a duty of care on the part of the custodian to exercise reasonable care in controlling his detainee. In those two cases the custodian had a legal right to control the physical proximity of the person or property sustaining the damage to the detainee who caused it. The extended relationship substitutes for the right to control the knowledge which the custodian possessed or ought to have possessed that physical proximity in fact existed.

In the present appeal the place from which the trainees escaped was an island from which the only means of escape would presumably be a boat accessible from the shore of the island. There is thus material, fit for consideration at the trial, for holding that the respondents, as the owners of a boat moored off the island, fell within the category of persons to whom a duty of care to prevent the escape of the trainees was owed by the officers responsible for their custody.

If therefore it can be established at the trial of this action: (1) that the borstal officers in failing to take precautions to prevent the trainees from escaping were acting in breach of their instructions and not in bona fide exercise of a discretion delegated to them by the Home Office as to the degree of control to be adopted: and (2) that it was reasonably foreseeable by the officers that if these particular trainees did escape they would be likely to appropriate a boat moored in the vicinity of Brownsea Island for the

---

1. [1953] 2 Q.B. 135; [1953] 2 All E.R. 149.
2. (1955), *Times*, 15th, 16th, 17th November.

purpose of eluding immediate pursuit and to cause damage to it, the borstal officers would be in breach of a duty of care owed to the respondents and the respondents would, in my view, have a cause of action against the Home Office as vicariously liable for the "negligence" of the borstal officers.

I would accordingly dismiss the appeal on the preliminary issue of law and allow the case to go for trial on those issues of fact.

LORD MORRIS [OF BORTH-Y-GEST delivered a speech in favour of dismissing the appeal.]

Appeal dismissed

Questions

1. Would the Home Office have been liable on the facts of this case (see Lord Reid's speech) if an escaping Borstal boy had reached the mainland and (a) immediately burgled a house, (b) attacked and robbed a man in that house, or (c) robbed a bank in Poole harbour a week later?

2. Do you think government departments and public authorities should be treated (a) more leniently than, (b) more harshly than, or (c) in the same way as a private individual?

Notes

1. A practical problem for the plaintiff concerns the obtaining of evidence. When suing government departments in particular, the plaintiff may be faced with a claim for non-production of a document on the basis of what used to be called "Crown Privilege" (see e.g. *Ellis* v. *Home Office*, [1953] 2 Q.B. 135; [1953] 2 All E.R. 149). This type of claim is not, however, restricted to government departments: indeed the very term "Crown Privilege" was the subject of adverse comment in *Rogers* v. *Secretary of State for the Home Department*, [1973] A.C. 388; [1972] 2 All E.R. 1057. This is not the place to discuss this doctrine, but suffice it to say that it has been made less of an obstacle for the plaintiff by the decision in *Conway* v. *Rimmer*, [1968] A.C. 910; [1968] 1 All E.R. 874. Further reference should be made to the standard works on Constitutional or Administrative Law or on the Law of Evidence.

2. For discussion of how French law approaches "Borstal boys" cases, see C. J. Hamson, "Escaping Borstal Boys", [1969] C.L.J. 273 [but note that the *Dorset Yacht* case, which is discussed in the article, had only been before the Court of Appeal at that stage].

3. Compare the *Dorset Yacht* case with *Smith* v. *Scott*, [1973] Ch. 314; [1972] 3 All E.R. 645, noted p. 67, *ante*.

3. THE RANGE OF PLAINTIFFS

(a) Foreseeability of the plaintiff

Hay (or Bourhill) v. Young, p. 208, *post*

Palsgraf v. Long Island Railroad Co.

Court of Appeals of New York   (1928), 162 N.E. 99

Action by Helen Palsgraf against the Long Island Railroad Company. Judgment entered on the verdict of a jury in favor of the plaintiff was affirmed by the Appellate

Division by a divided court (222 App. Div. 166, 225 N.Y.S. 412), and defendant appeals.

CARDOZO C.J.: Plaintiff was standing on a platform of defendant's railroad after buying a ticket to go to Rockaway Beach. A train stopped at the station, bound for another place. Two men ran forward to catch it. One of the men reached the platform of the car without mishap, though the train was already moving. The other man, carrying a package, jumped aboard the car, but seemed unsteady as if about to fall. A guard on the car, who had held the door open, reached forward to help him in, and another guard on the platform pushed him from behind. In this act, the package was dislodged, and fell upon the rails. It was a package of small size, about fifteen inches long, and was covered by a newspaper. In fact it contained fireworks, but there was nothing in its appearance to give notice of its contents. The fireworks when they fell exploded. The shock of the explosion threw down some scales at the other end of the platform many feet away. The scales struck the plaintiff, causing injuries for which she sues.

The conduct of the defendant's guard, if a wrong in its relation to the holder of the package, was not a wrong in its relation to the plaintiff, standing far away. Relatively to her it was not negligence at all. Nothing in the situation gave notice that the falling package had in it the potency of peril to persons thus removed. Negligence is not actionable unless it involves the invasion of a legally protected interest, the violation of a right. "Proof of negligence in the air, so to speak, will not do." Pollock, *Torts* (11th Edn.), p. 455; . . . The plaintiff, as she stood upon the platform of the station, might claim to be protected against intentional invasion of her bodily security. Such invasion is not charged. She might claim to be protected against unintentional invasion by conduct involving in the thought of reasonable men an unreasonable hazard that such invasion would ensue. These, from the point of view of the law, were the bounds of her immunity, with perhaps some rare exceptions, survivals for the most part of ancient forms of liability, where conduct is held to be at the peril of the actor. *Sullivan* v. *Dunham*, 161 N.Y. 290, 55 N.E. 923, 47 L.R.A. 715, 76 Am. St. Rep. 274. If no hazard was apparent to the eye of ordinary vigilance, an act innocent and harmless, at least to outward seeming, with reference to her, did not take to itself the quality of a tort because it happened to be a wrong, though apparently not one involving the risk of bodily insecurity, with reference to some one else. "In every instance, before negligence can be predicated of a given act, back of the act must be sought and found a duty to the individual complaining, the observance of which would have averted or avoided the injury." McSherry C.J. in *West Virginia Central & P.R. Co.* v. *State*, 96 Md. 652, 666, 54 A. 669, 671 (61 L.R.A. 574). . . . "The ideas of negligence and duty are strictly correlative." Bowen L.J. in *Thomas* v. *Quartermaine* (1887), 18 Q.B.D. 685, at p. 694. The plaintiff sues in her own right for a wrong personal to her, and not as the vicarious beneficiary of a breach of duty to another.

A different conclusion will involve us, and swiftly too, in a maze of contradictions. A guard stumbles over a package which has been left upon a platform. It seems to be a bundle of newspapers. It turns out to be a can of dynamite. To the eye of ordinary vigilance, the bundle is abandoned waste, which may be kicked or trod on with impunity. Is a passenger at the other end of the platform protected by the law against the unsuspected hazard concealed beneath the waste? If not, is the result to be any different, so far as the distant passenger is concerned, when the guard stumbles over a valise which a truckman or a porter has left upon the walk? The passenger far away, if the victim of a wrong at all, has a cause of action, not derivative, but original and primary. His claim to be protected against invasion of his bodily security is neither greater nor less because the act resulting in the invasion is a wrong to another far removed. In this case, the rights that are said to have been violated, the interests said to have been invaded, are not even of the same order. The man was not injured in his person nor even put in danger. The purpose of the act, as well as its effect, was to make his person safe. If there was a wrong to him at all, which may very well be doubted it was a wrong to a property interest only, the safety of his package. Out of this wrong to property, which threatened injury to nothing else, there has passed, we are told, to the plaintiff by derivation or succession a right of action for the invasion of an interest of another order, the right to bodily security. The diversity of interests emphasizes the futility of the effort to build the plaintiff's right upon the basis of a wrong to some one else. The gain is one of emphasis, for a like result would follow if the interests were the same. Even then, the orbit of the danger as disclosed to the eye of reasonable vigilance would be the orbit of the duty. One who jostles one's neighbor in a crowd does not invade the rights of others standing at the outer fringe when the unintended contact casts a bomb upon the ground. The wrongdoer as to them is the man who carries the bomb, not the one who explodes it without suspicion of the danger. Life will have to be made over, and human nature transformed, before prevision so extravagant can be accepted as the norm of conduct, the customary standard to which behavior must conform.

The argument for the plaintiff is built upon the shifting meanings of such words as "wrong" and "wrongful", and shares their instability. What the plaintiff must show is "a wrong" to herself; i.e. a violation of her own right, and not merely a wrong to some one else, nor conduct "wrongful" because unsocial, but not "a wrong" to any one. We are told that one who drives at reckless speed through a crowded city street is guilty of a negligent act and therefore of a wrongful one, irrespective of the consequences. Negligent the act is, and wrongful in the sense that it is unsocial, but wrongful and unsocial in relation to other travelers, only because the eye of vigilance perceives the risk of damage. If the same act were to be committed on a speedway or a race course, it would lose its wrongful quality. The risk reasonably to be perceived defines the duty to be obeyed, and risk imports relation; it is risk to another or to others within the range of apprehension. Seavey, "Negligence, Subjective or Objective", 41 H.L. Rv. 6; *Boronkay* v. *Robinson & Carpenter*, 247 N.Y. 365, 160 N.E. 400. This does not mean, of course, that one who launches a destructive force is always relieved of liability, if the force, though known to be destructive, pursues an unexpected path. "It was not necessary that the defendant should have had notice of the particular method in which an accident would occur, if the possibility of an accident was clear to the ordinarily prudent eye." *Munsey* v. *Webb*, 231 U.S. 150, 156, 34 S. Ct. 44, 45 (58 L. Ed. 162); . . . The range of reasonable apprehension is at times a question for the court, and at times, if varying inferences are possible, a question for the jury. Here, by concession, there was nothing in the situation to suggest to the most cautious mind that the parcel wrapped in newspaper would spread wreckage through the station. If the guard had thrown it down knowingly and willfully, he would not have threatened the plaintiff's safety, so far as appearances could warn him. His conduct would not have involved, even then, an unreasonable probability of invasion of her bodily security. Liability can be no greater where the act is inadvertent.

Negligence, like risk, is thus a term of relation. Negligence in the abstract, apart from things related, is surely not a tort, if indeed it is understandable at all. Bowen L.J. in *Thomas* v. *Quartermaine* (1887), 18 Q.B.D. 685, at p. 694. Negligence is not a tort unless it results in the commission of a wrong, and the commission of a wrong imports the violation of a right, in this case, we are told, the right to be protected against interference with one's bodily security. But bodily security is protected, not against all forms of interference or aggression, but only against some. One who seeks redress at law does not make out a cause of action by showing without more that there has been damage to his person. If the harm was not willful, he must show that the act as to him had possibilities of danger so many and apparent as to entitle him to be protected against the doing of it though the harm was unintended. Affront to personality is still the keynote of the wrong. Confirmation of this view will be found in the history and development of the action on the case. Negligence as a basis of civil liability was unknown to mediaeval law. 8 Holdsworth, *History of English Law*, p. 449; Street, *Foundations of Legal Liability*, Vol. 1, pp. 189, 190. For damage to the person, the sole remedy was trespass, and trespass did not lie in the absence of aggression, and that direct and personal. Holdsworth, *op. cit.*, p. 453; Street, *op. cit.*, Vol. 3, pp. 258, 260, Vol. 1, pp. 71, 74. Liability for other damage, as where a servant without orders from the master does or omits something to the damage of another, is a plant of later growth. Holdsworth, *op. cit.* 450, 457; Wigmore, "Responsibility for Tortious Acts", Vol. 3, *Essays in Anglo-American Legal History,* 520, 523, 526, 533. When it emerged out of the legal soil, it was thought of as a variant of trespass, an offshoot of the parent stock. This appears in the form of action, which was known as trespass on the case. Holdsworth, *op. cit.*, p. 449; cf. *Scott* v. *Sheperd,* 2 Wm. Black, 892; Green, *Rationale of Proximate Cause,* p. 19. The victim does not sue derivatively, or by right of subrogation, to vindicate an interest invaded in the person of another. Thus to view his cause of action is to ignore the fundamental difference between tort and crime. Holland, *Jurisprudence* (12th Edn.), p. 328. He sues for breach of a duty owing to himself.

The law of causation, remote or proximate, is thus foreign to the case before us. The question of liability is always anterior to the question of the measure of the consequences that go with liability. If there is no tort to be redressed, there is no occasion to consider what damage might be recovered if there were a finding of a tort. . . .

[POUND, LEHMAN and KELLOGG JJ. concurred. ANDREWS J. delivered a judgment, concurred in by CRANE and O'BRIEN JJ., in favour of dismissing the appeal.]

Judgment of the Appellate Division reversed

Note

In "Palsgraf Revisited" (1953), 52 Michigan L.R. 1 at p. 7, W. L. Prosser, commenting on the opinions of Cardozo C.J. and Andrews J. in the case, writes:

". . . Both of them beg the question shamelessly, stating dogmatic propositions without reason or explanation. If there is or is not a duty to the plaintiff not to injure her in this way, nothing else remains to be said. Both of them assume that there was no relation whatever between the defendant and the plaintiff on which a duty might be founded; both utterly ignore the fact, on which the appellate division laid stress, that Mrs. Palsgraf was a passenger. From the moment that she bought her ticket the defendant did in fact owe her a duty of the highest care, one of the most stringent known to the law. The question was not one of injury to some stranger across the street, but of whether the duty to a passenger extended to the consequences of negligence threatening another passenger—which may very well be a different thing altogether.

There is, furthermore, the question left unanswered by Cardozo: what would have been the result if the explosion had injured the owner of the package, or had damaged his suitcase on a baggage truck? There is also the troublesome matter of the scale. It is difficult to escape the conclusion that anything on a railroad platform so easily knocked over, whether by a paltry explosion of fireworks which damaged nothing else, or by a jostling and panicky crowd, had no business being there; and if there was negligence in having the scale, it was certainly negligence toward the plaintiff herself, who was standing beside it."

He further states (*ibid.*, note 25) that on this last basis "the question becomes one of negligence toward the foreseeable plaintiff, with the foreseeable result brought about by quite unforeseeable means." (See *Hughes* v. *Lord Advocate*, [1963] A.C. 837; [1963] 1 All E.R. 705, p. 201, *post*.)

(b) Rescuers

Baker v. T. E. Hopkins & Son, Ltd.

Court of Appeal   [1959] 3 All E.R. 225

The defendant company was employed to clean out a contaminated well at a farm, and it was decided to use a pump powered by a petrol engine inside the well. This method would lead to a build-up of carbon monoxide in the well, and was very dangerous. Mr. Hopkins, the defendant company's managing director, who had decided on this method, was not aware of its grave dangers, but, some time later on the day when the pumping started, he said to Ward, one of the company's employees engaged on the job: "Don't go down the well tomorrow until the fumes have cleared." Mr. Hopkins paid another visit to the well that evening, and the next morning the two men involved in the job (Ward and Wileman) were forcefully told by him not to go down the well until he arrived. However, Ward did go down, and he was later followed by Wileman who feared that Ward was ill. In response to a call he had received, Dr. Baker arrived at the farm, and was informed of the position. He was also told about the petrol engine, and that the fire brigade had been sent for. Attempts were made to discourage him from going down the well, but, "prompted by the finest instincts of humanity" (*per* Morris L.J.), Dr. Baker, having attached a rope to himself, went down the well, but was overcome by the fumes. Unfortunately, the rope became caught, and he could not be pulled out of the well. All three men in the well died, and actions relating to the deaths of Ward and Dr. Baker were brought against the defendant company. These succeeded before Barry J., although Ward was found to have been contributorily negligent, and his responsibility for the accident was assessed at 10%. The defendant company appealed. Only the claim in respect of Dr. Baker's death is considered in these extracts, although the Court of Appeal dismissed the appeal in relation to each action.

MORRIS L.J.: . . . It will be convenient to deal first with Dr. Baker's case. The claim which was put forward was that there was negligence, for which the defendant company were responsible and that such negligence resulted in the death of Dr. Baker.

The first stage in the proof of the claim involves proof that the defendant company were negligent towards their employees, the second that such negligence caused such employees to be in peril, the third that this could reasonably have been foreseen, and the fourth that it could also have been reasonably foreseen that someone would be likely to seek to rescue them from their peril and might either suffer injury or lose his life. . . .

[Having discussed the evidence and taken the view that the workmen ought to have been warned of the perils that existed, he continued:] It was . . . as a result of the company's negligence (or at least was in part a result of it) that the time came when Ward was in dire peril in the well. The company could and should in my judgment have anticipated that, if as a result of their negligence their men were exposed to great danger in the well, it would be a natural and probable consequence that someone would attempt a rescue. Subject to a consideration of certain further submissions made by the defendant company, it seems to me, therefore, that it is shown that Dr. Baker's death was a result of the company's negligence.

It is submitted, however, that the action of Dr. Baker in descending the well was a novus actus interveniens, and it is further submitted that the defendant company could not reasonably have foreseen the possibility of such a disaster as that which occurred. In my judgment these submissions are wholly unsustainable once it is held that the company were negligent in creating a situation of great danger and further in failing to warn their servants of it or in failing to ensure that their servants would not be exposed to it. There is happily in all men of good will an urge to save those who are in peril. Those who put men in peril can hardly be heard to say that they never thought that rescue might be attempted or be heard to say that the rescue attempt was not caused by the creation of the peril. As Greer L.J. said in *Haynes* v. *Harwood*:[1]

"If what is relied upon as novus actus interveniens is the very kind of thing which is likely to happen if the want of care which is alleged takes place, the principle embodied in the maxim is no defence."

---

1. [1935] 1 K.B. 146, at p. 156; [1934] All E.R. Rep. 103, at p. 107.

Equally unavailing in my judgment is the plea which is expressed in the words volenti non fit injuria. In *Letang* v. *Ottawa Electric Rail. Co.*[1] it was said:

"It is quite a mistake to treat volenti non fit injuria as if it were the legal equipollent of scienti non fit injuria."

Approval was given of the proposition in the judgment of Wills J. in *Osborne* v. *London & North Western Rail. Co.*[2] that:

"If the defendants desire to succeed on the ground that the maxim volenti non fit injuria is applicable, they must obtain a finding of fact that the plaintiff freely and voluntarily, with full knowledge of the nature and extent of the risk he ran, impliedly agreed to incur it."

In *Dann* v. *Hamilton*[3] Asquith J. said:

"Where a dangerous physical condition has been brought about by the negligence of the defendant, and, after it has arisen, the plaintiff, fully appreciating its dangerous character, elects to assume the risk thereof, the maxim has often been held to apply, and to protect the defendant."

If, however, A by negligence places B in peril in such circumstances that it is a foreseeable result that someone will try to rescue B and if C does so try—ought C in any appropriate sense to be described as a "volunteer"? In my judgment the answer is No. I confess that it seems to me to be indeed ungracious of A even to suggest it. C would not have agreed to run the risk that A might be negligent, for C would only play his part after A had been negligent. C's intervention comes at the moment when there is some situation of peril and the cause of or the responsibility for the creation of the peril may be quite unknown to C. If C, actuated by an impulsive desire to save life, acts bravely and promptly and subjugates any timorous over-concern for his own well-being or comfort, I cannot think that it would be either rational or seemly to say that he freely and voluntarily agreed to incur the risks of the situation which had been created by A's negligence.

When Dr. Baker arrived at the well, he proceeded to act as the promptings of humanity directed. He tried to save life. He tried to save the defendant company's servants. He was doubtless trying to do the very thing that the company hoped could be done. But in any event what he did was brought about by and was caused by the negligence of the company. In these circumstances, the company cannot say that he was a volunteer.

It was further said that Dr. Baker himself acted with negligence and that his death was caused or was partly caused thereby. This contention was not advanced harshly or in the language of any carping criticism: it was said that Dr. Baker had been "unreasonably" brave. If a rescuer acts with a wanton disregard of his own safety it might be that in some circumstances it might be held that any injury to him was not the result of the negligence that caused the situation of danger. Such a contention cannot be here asserted. Dr. Baker tied a strong rope round his body and arranged for the rope to be held by those on the surface and arranged to maintain oral communication with them. It must be remembered also that the chances of success of his attempt would diminish moment by moment if he tarried. He in no way acted recklessly or negligently. In my judgment, the learned judge came to a correct conclusion in regard to the claim made by his widow. . . .

WILLMER L.J.: . . . Dr. Baker's case falls to be determined on the basis that Mr. Hopkins' own negligence was at least a substantial cause of the peril in which the two men, Ward and Wileman, found themselves, and which led to their death. The case,

1. [1926] A.C. 725, at p. 730.
2. (1888), 21 Q.B.D. 220, at pp. 223, 224.
3. [1939] 1 K.B. 509, at p. 517; [1939] 1 All E.R. 59, at p. 63.

therefore, raises once more the not unfamiliar problems, much discussed in the so-called "Rescue cases", which arise where A's wrongful act puts B in a situation of peril, and C, a stranger, suffers injury in the course of attempting to rescue B.

It seems to me that in this case, as in any case where a plaintiff is injured in going to the rescue of a third party put in peril by the defendants' wrongdoing, the questions which have to be answered are fourfold. (1) Did the wrongdoer owe any duty to the rescuer in the circumstances of the particular case? (2) If so, did the rescuer's injury result from a breach of that duty, or did his act in going to the rescue amount to a novus actus? (3) Did the rescuer, knowing the danger, voluntarily accept the risk of injury, so as to be defeated by the maxim volenti non fit injuria? (4) Was the rescuer's injury caused or contributed to by his own failure to take reasonable care for his own safety? All these questions are raised by the circumstances of this case, and have been much canvassed in argument before us. I will endeavour to deal with each in turn.

(1) The question whether the wrongdoer owed any duty to the rescuer must be determined, in my judgment, by reference to Lord Atkin's familiar statement of the law in M'Alister (or Donoghue) v. Stevenson[1] when he said:

"You must take reasonable care to avoid acts or omissions which you can reasonably foresee would be likely to injure your neighbour."

In the circumstances of the particular case, is the rescuer in law the "neighbour" of the wrongdoer, in the sense that he is so closely and directly affected by the wrongdoer's act that the latter ought reasonably to have him in contemplation as being so affected? Where the act of the wrongdoer has been such as to be likely to put someone in peril, reasonable foresight will normally contemplate the probability of an attempted rescue, in the course of which the rescuer may receive injury. In the American case of Wagner v. International Rail. Co.,[2] Cardozo J., as it seems to me, foreshadowed in a remarkable way Lord Atkin's statement of principle, and applied it to a typical rescue case. He said:[3]

"Danger invites rescue. The cry of distress is the summons to relief. The law does not ignore these reactions of the mind in tracing conduct to its consequences. It recognises them as normal. It places their effects within the range of the natural and probable. The wrong that imperils life is a wrong to the imperilled victim; it is a wrong also to his rescuer."

Then a little later he went on:[3]

"The risk of rescue, if only it be not wanton, is born of the occasion. The emergency begets the man. The wrongdoer may not have foreseen the coming of a deliverer. He is accountable as if he had."

The judgment of Cardozo J. was referred to with approval by Lord Wright in Hay (or Bourhill) v. Young[4] and Lord Wright went on to say:

"This again shows how the ambit of the persons affected by negligence or misconduct may extend beyond persons who are actually subject to physical impact. There, indeed, may be no one injured in a particular case by actual impact; but still a wrong may be committed to anyone who suffers nervous shock or is injured in an act of rescue."

I should also refer to Lord v. Pacific Steam Navigation Co., Ltd., The Oropesa[5] where Lord

---

1. [1932] A.C. 562, at p. 580; [1932] All E.R. Rep. 1, at p. 11.
2. (1921), 232 N.Y. Rep. 176.
3. (1921), 232 N.Y. Rep. at p. 180.
4. [1943] A.C. 92, at pp. 108, 109; [1942] 2 All E.R. 396, at p. 405.
5. [1943] P. 32, at p. 39; [1943] 1 All E.R. 211, at p. 216.

Wright said, quoting from the speech of Lord Haldane in *Canadian Pacific Rail. Co.* v. *Kelvin Shipping Co., Ltd., The Metagama*:[1]

"Reasonable human conduct is part of the ordinary course of things . . ."

Assuming the rescuer not to have acted unreasonably, therefore, it seems to me that he must normally belong to the class of persons who ought to be within the contemplation of the wrongdoer as being closely and directly affected by the latter's act. In the present case the fact that Dr. Baker was a doctor is of itself significant. Having regard to the nature of the peril created by the wrongful act of Mr. Hopkins, it was only too likely that a doctor would be summoned—as Dr. Baker in fact was—and, if summoned, would attempt to do all he could for the victim, even at the risk of his own safety. In such circumstances I am satisfied that Dr. Baker was one of the class who ought to have been within the contemplation of Mr. Hopkins when he brought about the dangerous situation in this well. I do not think, therefore, that it is open to the defendant company to contend that no duty was owed by Mr. Hopkins to Dr. Baker.

(2) The question whether the act of the rescuer amounts to a novus actus answers itself, in my judgment, as soon as it is determined that it is the kind of act which ought to have been within the contemplation of the wrongdoer, so as to bring the rescuer within the class of persons to whom a duty was owed. . . . In my judgment, it was a natural and probable result of the wrongdoing of Mr. Hopkins that, in the likely event of someone being overcome by the carbon monoxide poisoning, a doctor would be called in, and that such doctor, having regard to the traditions of his profession, would, even at the risk of his own safety, descend the well for the purpose of attempting a rescue. Unless it can be shown, therefore, that Dr. Baker displayed such an unreasonable disregard for his own safety as to amount to negligence on his own part—with which suggestion I will presently deal—I do not think that it can be said that his act constituted a novus actus interveniens.

(3) The next question is whether the plaintiffs in Dr. Baker's case are defeated by the maxim volenti non fit injuria. . . . It seems to me that, when once it is determined that the act of the rescuer was the natural and probable consequence of the defendant's wrongdoing, there is no longer any room for the application of the maxim volenti non fit injuria. It would certainly be a strange result if the law were held to penalise the courage of the rescuer by depriving him of any remedy. Greer L.J. in *Haynes* v. *Harwood*[2] was clearly of the view that the maxim cannot be applied to defeat the plaintiff's claim in a rescue case. He quotes from an article by Professor Goodhart in the *Cambridge Law Journal* (Vol. V., at p. 196) as follows:[3]

"The American rule is that the doctrine of the assumption of risk does not apply where the plaintiff has, under an exigency caused by the defendants' wrongful misconduct, consciously and deliberately faced a risk, even of death, to rescue another from imminent danger of personal injury or death, whether the person endangered is one to whom he owes a duty of protection, as a member of his family, or is a mere stranger to whom he owes no such special duty."

Greer L.J. goes on:[3]

"In my judgment, that passage not only represents the law of the United States but also the law of this country."

It is by no means clear that the other two members of the court were prepared to go so far as Greer L.J. in stating the principle, and they appear to have based their judgments to a great extent on the fact that in the particular case the plaintiff was a police officer. But for my part I am content to accept Greer L.J.'s statement of the law, and to hold

---

1. (1927), 138 L.T. 369, at p. 370.
2. [1935] 1 K.B. at p. 159; [1934] All E.R. Rep. at p. 109.
3. [1935] 1 K.B. at p. 157; [1934] All E.R. Rep. at p. 108.

that the maxim volenti non fit injuria cannot be invoked in this case to defeat the second plaintiffs' claim. In my judgment, the real question to be determined in a case such as the present is, not whether the rescuer voluntarily accepted the risk of injury, but whether his injury was caused or contributed to by any failure on his part to take reasonable care for his own safety. This was the view expressed by Swift J. in *Brandon* v. *Osborne, Garrett & Co.*[1] and I think that it is the right view.

(4) I pass, therefore, to the fourth and last question, which is raised by the defendant company's plea that the death of Dr. Baker was caused or contributed to by his own negligence. The burden of proof with regard to this allegation is on the defendant company, and in order to succeed I think they would have to show that the conduct of Dr. Baker was so foolhardy as to amount to a wholly unreasonable disregard for his own safety. Bearing in mind that danger invites rescue, the court should not be astute to accept criticism of the rescuer's conduct from the wrongdoer who created the danger. Moreover, I think it should be remembered that it is fatally easy to be wise after the event. It is not enough that, when all the evidence has been sifted and all the facts ascertained in the calm and deliberate atmosphere of a court of law, the rescuer's conduct can be shown ex post facto to have been misguided or foolhardy. He is entitled to be judged in the light of the situation as it appeared to him at the time, i.e., in a context of immediate and pressing emergency. Here Dr. Baker was faced with a situation in which two men were in danger of speedy death in the well, unless something were done very quickly. He was a doctor, and he had been specially summoned to help. Any man of courage in his position would have felt impelled to act, even at the risk of his own safety. Time was pressing; immediate action was necessary if the men in danger were to be helped; there was virtually no opportunity for reflection, or for estimating the risks involved in an act of rescue. If Dr. Baker in such circumstances had instinctively gone straight down the well, without stopping to take any precautions at all, it would, I think, have been difficult enough to criticise him; but in point of fact he did take the very wise precaution of securing himself with a rope, whereby those on the surface could pull him up if he himself were overcome. The immediate cause of his death was the sheer mischance of the rope becoming caught on some obstruction, so as to make it impossible for those on the surface to pull him to safety. I do not think that, having regard to the emergency in which he was acting, he is to be blamed for not foreseeing and guarding against the possibility of such a mischance. On the contrary, I entirely agree with the view expressed by the learned judge that the defendant company, whose negligence brought about the danger, must accept the risk of mischances of this kind. In all the circumstances, I find it impossible to accept the contention that Dr. Baker was guilty of any negligence either causing or contributing to his death. . . .

[ORMEROD L.J. delivered a judgment in favour of dismissing both appeals.]

Appeals dismissed

Questions

1. Would the defendant company have been liable if the rope had snapped without fault on anyone's part before Dr. Baker died, and he had fallen and drowned in the well?

2. Could an action have been brought in respect of Dr. Baker's death against the estates of Ward or Wileman?

Note

In relation to this last question see the judgment of Barry J. at first instance —[1958] 3 All E.R. 147—in the above case where he stated (at p. 153):

---

1. [1924] 1 K.B. 548, at pp. 554, 555.

"Although no one owes a duty to anyone else to preserve his own safety, yet if, by his own carelessness a man puts himself into a position of peril of a kind that invites rescue, he would in law be liable for any injury caused to someone whom he ought to have foreseen would attempt to come to his aid."

Mention might also be made of the Australian case of *Chapman* v. *Hearse* (1961), 106 C.L.R. 112. Chapman had been involved in a car accident and was lying unconscious in the road; his own negligent driving had led to this situation. Dr. Cherry, who came on the scene, attended him, but unfortunately Dr. Cherry was hit and killed by a car driven by Hearse, who was found by the trial judge to have been negligent but who claimed contribution from Chapman. The trial judge's decision that Chapman should pay a contribution of 25% of the damages was upheld by the High Court of Australia.

Question

If X goes potholing, and, through his own carelessness, gets stuck, and Y is injured in trying to rescue him, would X be liable if he had left a note saying that no rescue attempts were to be made if he got into any trouble?

Videan v. British Transport Commission

Court of Appeal   [1963] 2 All E.R. 860

The two year old child of a stationmaster, who lived in the station house, had strayed on to the railway line. His father and a porter saw him there but they also saw a trolley, driven by a petrol engine, fast approaching him. The trolley driver was signalled to stop by the stationmaster and the porter. He slowed down a little, but only saw the child at the last moment when he applied the brake as hard as he could. In an endeavour to save his son, the stationmaster jumped on to the line in the path of the trolley. His son was saved, though injured, but the stationmaster was killed. The trolley driver, Souness, was found by the trial judge to have been at fault in not keeping a proper look-out, in travelling too fast and in not applying his brakes hard enough, soon enough. An action was brought by the stationmaster's widow who also sued as the next friend for her infant son who claimed damages for the injuries he had sustained. The Court of Appeal held the child to be a trespasser and, although his claim was dismissed, the discussion in this case of the duty owed to trespassers was controversial (see p. 239, *post*). However, the law on this topic has now been restated by the House of Lords in *British Railways Board* v. *Herrington*, [1972] A.C. 877; [1972] 1 All E.R. 749 (p. 240, *post*), and the extracts here only deal with the claim relating to the station-master's death, which had been dismissed by the trial judge.

LORD DENNING M.R.: . . . I turn now to the widow's claim in respect of the death of her husband. In order to establish it, the widow must prove that Souness owed a duty of care to the stationmaster, that he broke that duty, and that, in consequence of the breach, the stationmaster was killed. Counsel for the defendants says that the widow can prove none of these things. All depends, he says, on the test of foreseeability; and, applying that test, he puts the following dilemma: If Souness could not reasonably be expected to foresee the presence of the child, he could not reasonably be expected to foresee the presence of the father. He could not foresee that a trespasser would be on the line. So how could he be expected to foresee that anyone would be attempting to rescue him? Counsel for the defendants points out that, in all the rescue cases that have hitherto come before the courts, such as *Haynes* v. *G. Harwood & Son*,[1] and *Baker* v. *T. E. Hopkins & Sons, Ltd.*,[2] the conduct of the defendant was a wrong to the victim or

1. [1935] 1 K.B. 146; [1934] All E.R. Rep. 103.
2. [1959] 3 All E.R. 225.

the potential victim. How can he be liable to the rescuer when he is not liable to the rescued?

I cannot accept this view. The right of the rescuer is an independent right, and is not derived from that of the victim. The victim may have been guilty of contributory negligence—or his right may be excluded by contractual stipulation—but still the rescuer can sue. So, also, the victim may, as here, be a trespasser and excluded on that ground, but still the rescuer can sue. Foreseeability is necessary, but not foreseeability of the particular emergency that arose. Suffice it that he ought reasonably to foresee that, if he did not take care, some emergency or other might arise, and that someone or other might be impelled to expose himself to danger in order to effect a rescue. Such is the case here. Souness ought to have anticipated that some emergency or other might arise. His trolley was not like an express train which is heralded by signals and whistles and shouts of "Keep clear". His trolley came silently and swiftly on the unsuspecting quietude of a country station. He should have realised that someone or other might be put in peril if he came too fast or did not keep a proper look-out; and that, if anyone was put in peril, then someone would come to the rescue. As it happened, it was the stationmaster trying to rescue his child; but it would be the same if it had been a passer-by. Whoever comes to the rescue, the law should see that he does not suffer for it. It seems to me that, if a person by his fault creates a situation of peril, he must answer for it to any person who attempts to rescue the person who is in danger. He owes a duty to such a person above all others. The rescuer may act instinctively out of humanity or deliberately out of courage. But whichever it is, so long as it is not wanton interference, if the rescuer is killed or injured in the attempt, he can recover damages from the one whose fault has been the cause of it. . . .

HARMAN L.J.: . . . The father's case seems to have attracted much less attention than the son's. The judge, I think, decided against the father on the ground that he could not be in a better position than his son was, and the burden of counsel for the defendants' argument was similar, namely, that, if the trolley driver had no reason to expect the presence of the infant on the line, still less reason had he to expect to find the father there. I do not think that the two cases stand or fall together like this. These trolleys are not a part of the regular train service which runs (or ought to run) at stated hours and with the arrival of which the employees of the defendants must be taken to be familiar. The trolleys are occasional visitors, with no stated times and no warning of their approach. It is, to my mind, most significant that it is an instruction to trolley drivers that they must approach stations with care. The inference from this is that they must take care that there are no persons on the line, more especially railway servants engaged in maintenance and like duties. One of these servants was the dead stationmaster. He was a person whose presence on the track was well within the contemplation of the driver. He could not be said to be a trespasser. If the infant had suffered nothing and action had been brought on behalf of the father alone, I do not see what answer the defendants could have to a claim for vicarious liability for the negligent act of their servant, the trolley driver. The fact that the father acted rather as a father than as stationmaster seems to me to obscure the issue. The infant might not have been his son but a child of a passenger. It would clearly be within the scope of the stationmaster's employment to take all steps to rescue such a child. It is not necessary that the exact event should be foreseeable. The presence of the stationmaster, one of the defendants' employees, on the track was within the sphere of contemplation. Whether, if the rescuer had been a member of the public, there would have been liability, I leave out of account.

It is, perhaps, rather a different point of view to hold that the emergency justified the father's presence on the line. In the policeman's case, *Haynes* v. *Harwood*,[1] the policeman dashed into the highway to stop the horse which was a menace to children on the highway. It may be said to be different in that such children were lawfully on the high-

---

1. [1935] 1 K.B. 146; [1934] All E.R. Rep. 103.

way and were not trespassers, but the emergency is the like and the rescuer has an independent right. . . .

PEARSON L.J.: . . . I now come to the appeal of the plaintiff widow, who claims damages for the death of her husband caused, as she contends, by the negligence of Souness acting as the servant of the defendants. It is clear from the evidence and the learned judge's findings that Souness, in his approach to the station, was acting negligently in relation to anyone to whom he owed a duty of care, and that the conduct of Souness in this respect caused the accident. The only disputable question is whether Souness owed any relevant duty of care to the deceased. The defendant's argument, evidently accepted by the learned judge, has been that the position of the rescuer could not be any better than the position of the person rescued, and that, as the infant plaintiff's trespass was unforeseeable, so the act of his father in trying to rescue him was unforeseeable, and that, therefore, both the infant plaintiff and his father were outside the zone of reasonable contemplation and the scope of duty. That would no doubt have been a formidable argument if the deceased had been only a father rescuing his son. But the deceased was the stationmaster, having a general responsibility for dealing with any emergency that might arise at the station. It was foreseeable by Souness that, if he drove his trolley carelessly into the station, he might imperil the stationmaster, as the station-master might well have some proper occasion for going on to the track in the performance of his duties. For this purpose, it is not necessary that the particular accident which happened should have been foreseeable. It is enough that it was foreseeable that some situation requiring the stationmaster to go on the line might arise, and, if any such situation did arise, a careless approach to the station by Souness with his vehicle would be dangerous to the stationmaster. On that ground, I hold that Souness's careless approach to the station was a breach of a duty owing by him to the deceased as station-master, and it caused the accident, and that, consequently, the defendants are liable to the widow and her appeal should be allowed. I agree that this court has no ground for interfering with the learned judge's assessment of the widow's damages at £6,348.

Appeal in relation to the stationmaster's death allowed

Notes

1. Two earlier cases on rescuers may usefully be contrasted. In *Cutler* v. *United Dairies (London), Ltd.,* [1933] 2 K.B. 297 the plaintiff saw a horse and cart, used by the defendants to deliver milk, going quickly past his house without a driver. He was worried about the safety of his children, but found them playing safely in the garden at the rear of the house. He also saw the driver of the cart trying to calm the horse down in an adjoining field, and the driver called out "Help, help". The plaintiff went over the hedge and into the field and endeavoured to hold the horse's head. However, the horse reared, the plaintiff was knocked down and he suffered injury. The jury at the trial of the action found the defendants to have been negligent in employing the horse on this job. The horse had, in fact, bolted once, if not twice, before. The Court of Appeal assumed that the jury's finding was correct, but the defendants' appeal was allowed on the grounds that, on the evidence, the jury was not entitled to find that the defendants' negligence was the cause of the plaintiff's damage, and the defence of *volenti non fit injuria* was applicable (on which see p. 311, post).

The *Cutler* case was distinguished in the later decision of *Haynes* v. *Harwood,* [1935] 1 K.B. 146, where an appeal from a judgment in the plaintiff's favour was dismissed. In that case, Bird, the defendants' servant, had left his two-horse van in the street, but the horses ran away when a boy threw a stone at them. When the horses had reached a spot opposite a police station, the plaintiff, a policeman, saw that a woman was in great danger and that some children would also be in serious danger if the horses were not stopped. He got hold of one of the horses, but, although he stopped them both within 15 yards, he was injured when one of the horses fell on him. It was held that there was negligence in leaving the horses unattended in the circumstances of this case (this was a crowded street and children were likely to be present). It was further held that the claim did not fail on causation grounds and that the maxim *volenti non fit injuria* did not provide a defence.

2. In *Chadwick* v. *British Transport Commission*, [1967] 2 All E.R. 945, which is dealt with in Chap. on Nervous Shock (p. 207, *post*), a rescuer suffered nervous shock. His illness was caused by the horror of his experiences in helping at the scene of a serious railway accident at Lewisham, in which ninety people lost their lives. The test of whether a duty was owed to Mr. Chadwick (the rescuer) was stated to be—"What ought the defendants to have foreseen?"—and it was held that a duty was owed to him. The defendants had been negligent towards their passengers, and, in the court's view, injury and danger to the passengers could have been foreseen, as could injury to someone who was trying to rescue them. It was argued by the defendants' counsel that the risk which the rescuer underwent was not quite the same as that undergone by the passengers. In fact, the court did not accept that the risk was different, but, in any event, Waller J. took the view that "once the possibility of rescue occurs, the precise manner of rescue is immaterial".

3. It should also be noted that there may be liability to a plaintiff who intervenes where property rather than life or limb is threatened—see *Hyett* v. *Great Western Rail. Co.*, [1948] 1 K.B. 345; [1947] 2 All E.R. 264.

4. Interesting problems were raised in *Horsley* v. *Maclaren* (*The Ogopogo*), [1971] 2 Lloyd's Rep. 410. Matthews fell by accident from Maclaren's boat (on which he was a guest) into a lake. Maclaren manoeuvered the boat whilst rescue attempts were unsuccessfully made, and, after some minutes, Horsley, another guest, dived into the water in an attempt to rescue Matthews. Matthews' body, in fact, was never found, and Horsley also died. Ritchie J., delivering the majority judgment of the Supreme Court of Canada, held that there was a duty on Maclaren "in his capacity as a host and as the owner and operator of the *Ogopogo*, to do the best he could to effect the rescue of one of his guests who had accidentally fallen overboard". (Laskin J. (with Hall J. concurring) delivered a dissenting judgment, but on this point was prepared to find that Maclaren had a duty to take reasonable care for his guest's safety, and his obligation extended to "rescue from perils of the sea where this is consistent with his duty to see to the safety of his other passengers and with concern for his own safety".) Ritchie J. went on to say (at p. 412) that:

> "In the present case a situation of peril was created when Matthews fell overboard, but it was not created by any fault on the part of Maclaren, and before Maclaren can be found to have been in any way responsible for Horsley's death, it must be found that there was such negligence in his method of rescue as to place Matthews in an apparent position of increased danger subsequent to and distinct from the danger to which he had been initially exposed by his accidental fall. In other words, any duty owing to Horsley must stem from the fact that a new situation of peril was created by Maclaren's negligence which induced Horsley to act as he did."

Ritchie J., however, held that Maclaren had, in fact, not been negligent. In this situation, should there be a requirement of increased danger "distinct from" the initial danger? Should a first rescuer, who was not under an existing duty to rescue, be liable to a second rescuer who only attempts a rescue because of the first rescuer's careless efforts? (For discussion of these and other issues, see E. R. Alexander, "One Rescuer's Obligation to Another: The 'Ogopogo' lands in the Supreme Court of Canada" (1972), XXII Univ. of Toronto L.J. 98.)

(c) The unborn child

Notes

Since legislation is expected shortly on this topic, (1973) Times, August 31, the materials which would otherwise have appeared under this heading have been omitted. Mention might be made, however, of the provisional legislative proposal of the Law Commission in Working Paper No. 47 (*Injuries to Unborn Children*) which (at para. 34) was that:

> ". . . wherever a plaintiff has suffered ante-natal injury caused by the fault of the defendant he should be entitled to recover damages from the defendant and that those damages should not be reduced by any negligence on the part of the mother. Where a plaintiff suffers ante-natal injury caused by his mother's negligence he should be entitled to recover damages from her. A plaintiff's claim for ante-natal injury should not be extinguished or limited by any contract entered into by his mother or by his mother's voluntary assumption of risk."

For comment, in particular from a medical point of view, see Dr. R. G. Edwards, "The Problem of Compensation for Antenatal Injuries", *Nature*, Vol. 426, 9 November 1973.

For further general reading see: P. H. Winfield, "The Unborn Child" (1942), 8 C.L.J. 76; D. A. Gordon, "The Unborn Plaintiff" (1965), 63 Michigan L.R. 579; and E. Veitch, "*Delicta in Uterum*" (1973), 24 N.I.L.Q. 40. Some interesting cases are: *Montreal Tramways* v. *Leveille*, [1933] 4 D.L.R. 337; *Pinchin* v. *Santam Insurance Co., Ltd.*, 1963 (2) S.A. 254; *Duval* v. *Seguin* (1972), 26 D.L.R. (3d) 418; and *Watt* v. *Rama*, [1972] V.R. 353.

4

Breach of Duty

The tort of negligence, as its very name implies, requires fault to be proved against the defendant. If there is a duty of care imposed upon the defendant, the plaintiff must prove *inter alia* that the defendant acted, or omitted to act, negligently. This is sometimes called the "negligence issue" and it is with this issue that the materials in this Chapter are concerned. The courts are not consistent in their terminology however, and not infrequently the word "duty" is used in relation to this issue (e.g. *Haley* v. *London Electricity Board*, [1965] A.C. 778; [1964] 3 All E.R. 185, p. 152, *post*). The student must therefore question the sense in which the judges use this concept. The standard of care which is formulated is that of the "reasonable man", but it is important to realise that he is a fictional character, the reference to whom is a thin disguise for the value judgment which is made by the judge. Although in general the courts will hold negligent anyone who has fallen below this standard (but see the heading "Infants", p. 149, *post*), the amount of care and skill required of the defendant may be greater than that which could be expected of the ordinary man in the street (e.g. where he is a member of a trade or profession or holds himself out as possessing a particular skill, p. 144, *post*). The cases reveal the factors which the courts take into account in deciding whether a person has been negligent. This is essentially a balancing process, but for the plaintiff it is vital that, at the end of the day, the scales are tipped in his favour. Yet this may be a difficult task for the plaintiff. His case may founder for lack of witnesses—the victim of a hit and run driver is the most obvious but not the only example. Thus the practical problem of proving negligence, even though the plaintiff may be assisted in certain cases by the maxim *res ipsa loquitur* or by statute (pp. 161–169, *post*), should not be underestimated.

It has been pointed out that one merit of the present system is that the courts may exercise some influence in raising standards in businesses or professions by deciding that a defendant has still been negligent, although he has adhered to a common practice (p. 160, *post*). In many cases it will be the reaction, not of the defendant, but of his insurers which will be all important (p. 667, *post*; and see Clerk and Lindsell, para. 904).

1. THE REASONABLE MAN

(a) The average standard

Glasgow Corporation *v.* Muir

House of Lords   [1943] 2 All E.R. 44

A church party, desiring accommodation where they could eat their tea, obtained permission for 12*s.* 6*d.* to use the tea room in a mansion house belonging to the appellants. They had to carry their tea urn to the mansion house, and the route to the tea room then lay along a passage way, the width of which narrowed from five feet to three feet three inches. There were some children from another party buying sweets and ices at a counter at the beginning of this passage and, just after McDonald (a church officer) and Taylor, who were carrying the urn, had turned down the passage, the church officer let go of one handle of the urn, and the scalding tea which escaped injured six children. The action brought on their behalf was grounded on the alleged negligence of Mrs. Alexander (the manageress) who had given the permission to use the tea room. The First Division of the Court of Session reversed the dismissal of the action by the Lord Ordinary. On appeal to the House of Lords:

LORD MACMILLAN: My Lords, the degree of care for the safety of others which the law requires human beings to observe in the conduct of their affairs varies according to the circumstances. There is no absolute standard, but it may be said generally that the degree of care required varies directly with the risk involved. Those who engage in operations inherently dangerous must take precautions which are not required of persons engaged in the ordinary routine of daily life. It is no doubt true that in every act which an individual performs there is present a potentiality of injury to others. All things are possible and, indeed, it has become proverbial that the unexpected always happens. But while the precept *alterum non laedere* requires us to abstain from intentionally injuring others, it does not impose liability for every injury which our conduct may occasion. In Scotland, at any rate, it has never been a maxim of the law that a man acts at his peril. Legal liability is limited to those consequences of our acts which a reasonable man of ordinary intelligence and experience so acting would have in contemplation. . . .

The standard of foresight of the reasonable man is in one sense an impersonal test. It eliminates the personal equation and is independent of the idiosyncrasies of the particular person whose conduct is in question. Some persons are by nature unduly timorous and imagine every path beset with lions; others, of more robust temperament, fail to foresee or nonchalantly disregard even the most obvious dangers. The reasonable man is presumed to be free both from over-apprehension and from over-confidence. But there is a sense in which the standard of care of the reasonable man involves in its application a subjective element. It is still left to the judge to decide what in the circumstances of the particular case the reasonable man would have had in contemplation and what accordingly the party sought to be made liable ought to have foreseen. Here there is room for diversity of view, as, indeed, is well illustrated in the present case. What to one judge may seem far-fetched may seem to another both natural and probable.

. . . The question, as I see it, is whether Mrs. Alexander, when she was asked to allow a tea urn to be brought into the premises under her charge, ought to have had in mind that it would require to be carried through a narrow passage in which there were a number of children and that there would be a risk of the contents of the urn being spilt and scalding some of the children. If as a reasonable person she ought to have had these considerations in mind, was it her duty to require that she should be informed of the arrival of the urn and, before allowing it to be carried through the narrow passage, to clear all the children out of it, in case they might be splashed with scalding water?

The urn was an ordinary medium-sized cylindrical vessel of about 15 ins. diameter and about 16 ins. in height, made of light sheet metal with a fitting lid, which was closed. It had a handle at each side. Its capacity was about 9 gallons, but it was only a third or a half full.[1] It was not in itself an inherently dangerous thing and could be carried quite safely and easily by two persons exercising ordinary care. A caterer, called as a witness on behalf of the pursuers, who had large experience of the use of such urns, said that he had never had a mishap with an urn while it was being carried. The urn was in charge of two responsible persons, McDonald, the church officer, and the lad Taylor, who carried it between them. When they entered the passage-way they called out to the children there congregated to keep out of the way and the children drew back to let them pass. Taylor who held the front handle had safely passed the children when, for some unexplained reason, McDnoald loosened hold of the other handle, the urn tilted over and some of its contents were spilt, scalding several of the children who were standing by. The urn was not upset but came to the ground on its base.

In my opinion, Mrs. Alexander had no reason to anticipate that such an event would happen as a consequence of granting permission for a tea urn to be carried through the passage-way where the children were congregated, and consequently there was no duty incumbent on her to take precautions against the occurrence of such an event. I think that she was entitled to assume that the urn would be in charge of responsible persons (as it was) who would have regard for the safety of the children in the passage (as they did have regard) and that the urn would be carried with ordinary care, in which case its transit would occasion no danger to bystanders. The pursuers have left quite unexplained the actual cause of the accident. The immediate cause was not the carrying of the urn through the passage, but McDonald's losing grip of his handle. How he came to do so is entirely a matter of speculation. He may have stumbled or he may have suffered a temporary muscular failure. We do not know and the pursuers have not chosen to enlighten us by calling McDonald as a witness. Yet it is argued that Mrs. Alexander ought to have foreseen the possibility, nay, the reasonable probability of an occurrence the nature of which is unascertained. Suppose that McDonald let go his handle through carelessness. Was Mrs. Alexander bound to foresee this as reasonably probable and to take precautions against the possible consequences? I do not think so. The only ground on which the view of the majority of the judges of the first division can be justified is that Mrs. Alexander ought to have foreseen that some accidental injury might happen to the children in the passage if she allowed an urn containing hot tea to be carried through the passage and ought, therefore, to have cleared out the children entirely during its transit, which Lord Moncrieff describes as "the only effective step". With all respect I think that this would impose upon Mrs. Alexander a degree of care higher than the law exacts. . . . As, in my opinion, no negligence has been established I agree with what I understand to be the view of all your Lordships that the appeal should be allowed and the judgment of the Lord Ordinary restored.

[LORD WRIGHT, LORD CLAUSON, LORD THANKERTON and LORD ROMER delivered speeches in favour of allowing the appeal.]

Appeal allowed

Notes

1. In *Hall* v. *Brooklands Auto-Racing Club*, [1932] All E.R. Rep. 208, at p. 217, Greer L.J. said that the reasonable member of the public "is sometimes described as 'the man in the street', or 'the man in the Clapham omnibus', or, as I recently read in an American author, 'the man who takes the magazines at home, and in the evening pushes the lawn mower in his shirt sleeves'."

---

1. [Lord Thankerton thought it was no more than two-thirds full.]

2. A. P. Herbert in *Uncommon Law* (3rd Edn.) wrote the following passage as part of the judgment of the Master of the Rolls in a fictitious case (at pp. 5–6):

"... it has been urged for the appellant, and my own researches incline me to agree, that in all that mass of authorities which bears upon this branch of the law *there is no single mention of a reasonable woman.* It was ably insisted before us that such an omission, extending over a century and more of judicial pronouncements, must be something more than a coincidence; that among the innumerable tributes to the reasonable man there might be expected at least some passing reference to a reasonable person of the opposite sex; that no such reference is found, for the simple reason that no such being is contemplated by the law; that legally at least there *is* no reasonable woman, and that therefore in this case the learned judge should have directed the jury that, while there was evidence on which they might find that the defendant had not come up to the standard required of a reasonable man, her conduct was only what was to be expected of a woman, as such . . . I find that at Common Law a reasonable woman does not exist."

(b) Foreseeability and the standard of care

Bolton v. Stone

House of Lords   [1951] 1 All E.R. 1078

A cricket club had played cricket on their ground since about 1864. The respondent, Miss Stone, who was standing on the road outside her house, was hit by a cricket ball which had been straight-driven by a batsman playing for a visiting team. She was nearly one hundred yards from where the ball was struck. The ball cleared a fence which was approximately seventy-eight yards from the striker of the ball, the fence being seven feet high and, in fact, the slope of the ground meant that the top of the fence was seventeen feet above the level of the pitch. A witness with a house nearer the ground than that of Miss Stone, said that cricket balls had hit his house or gone into his yard five or six times in the preceding few years. There was other evidence that the hit was an exceptional one, and that—as was accepted by the trial judge (Oliver J.)—it was a rare occurrence for the ball to go over the fence during a match. The respondent sued the committee and members of the club, the appellants here, for damages for negligence and nuisance. Oliver J., [1949] 1 All E.R. 237, dismissed both claims, but the Court of Appeal, [1949] 2 All E.R. 851, held the appellants liable in negligence. On appeal to the House of Lords:

LORD OAKSEY: ... Cricket has been played for about ninety years on the ground in question and no ball has been proved to have struck anyone on the highways near the ground until the respondent was struck, nor has there been any complaint to the appellants. In such circumstances was it the duty of the appellants, who are the committee of the club, to take some special precautions other than those they did take to prevent such an accident as happened? The standard of care in the law of negligence is the standard of an ordinarily careful man, but, in my opinion, an ordinarily careful man does not take precautions against every foreseeable risk. He can, of course, foresee the possibility of many risks, but life would be almost impossible if he were to attempt to take precautions against every risk which he can foresee. He takes precautions against risks which are reasonably likely to happen. Many foreseeable risks are extremely unlikely to happen and cannot be guarded against except by almost complete isolation. The ordinarily prudent owner of a dog does not keep his dog always on a lead on a country highway for fear it may cause injury to a passing motor cyclist, nor does the ordinarily prudent pedestrian avoid the use of the highway for fear of skidding motor cars. It may very well be that after this accident the ordinarily prudent committee man of a similar cricket ground would take some further precaution, but that is not to say that he would have taken a similar precaution before the accident. . . .

LORD REID: My Lords, it was readily foreseeable that an accident such as befell the respondent might possibly occur during one of the appellants' cricket matches. Balls had been driven into the public road from time to time, and it was obvious that if a person happened to be where a ball fell that person would receive injuries which might or might not be serious. On the other hand, it was plain that the chance of that happening was small. The exact number of times a ball has been driven into the road is not known, but it is not proved that this has happened more than about six times in about thirty years. If I assume that it has happened on the average once in three seasons I shall be doing no injustice to the respondent's case. Then there has to be considered the chance of a person being hit by a ball falling in the road. The road appears to be an ordinary side road giving access to a number of private houses, and there is no evidence to suggest that the traffic on this road is other than what one might expect on such a road. On the whole of that part of the road where a ball could fall there would often be nobody and seldom any great number of people. It follows that the chance of a person ever being struck even in a long period of years was very small.

This case, therefore, raises sharply the question what is the nature and extent of the duty of a person who promotes on his land operations which may cause damage to persons on an adjoining highway. Is it that he must not carry out or permit an operation which he knows or ought to know clearly can cause such damage, however improbable that result may be, or is it that he is only bound to take into account the possibility of such damage if such damage is a likely or probable consequence of what he does or permits, or if the risk of damage is such that a reasonable man, careful of the safety of his neighbour, would regard that risk as material? I do not know of any case where this question has had to be decided or even where it has been fully discussed. Of course there are many cases in which somewhat similar questions have arisen, but, generally speaking, if injury to another person from the defendants' acts is reasonably foreseeable the chance that injury will result is substantial and it does not matter in which way the duty is stated. In such cases I do not think that much assistance is to be got from analysing the language which a judge has used. More assistance is to be got from cases where judges have clearly chosen their language with care in setting out a principle, but even so, statements of the law must be read in light of the facts of the particular case. Nevertheless, making all allowances for this, I do find at least a tendency to base duty rather on the likelihood of damage to others than on its foreseeability alone . . . I think that reasonable men do, in fact, take into account the degree of risk and do not act on a bare possibility as they would if the risk were more substantial. . . .

Counsel for the respondent in the present case had to put his case so high as to say that, at least as soon as one ball had been driven into the road in the ordinary course of a match, the appellants could and should have realised that that might happen again, and that, if it did, someone might be injured, and that that was enough to put on the appellants a duty to take steps to prevent such an occurrence. If the true test is foreseeability alone I think that must be so. Once a ball has been driven on to a road without there being anything extraordinary to account for the fact, there is clearly a risk that another will follow and if it does there is clearly a chance, small though it may be, that somebody may be injured. On the theory that it is foreseeability alone that matters it would be irrelevant to consider how often a ball might be expected to land in the road and it would not matter whether the road was the busiest street or the quietest country lane. The only difference between these cases is in the degree of risk. It would take a good deal to make me believe that the law has departed so far from the standards which guide ordinary careful people in ordinary life. In the crowded conditions of modern life even the most careful person cannot avoid creating some risks and accepting others. What a man must not do, and what I think a careful man tries not to do, is to create a risk which is substantial. Of course, there are numerous cases where special circumstances require that a higher standard shall be observed and where that is recognised by the law, but I do not think that this case comes within any such special category.... In my judgment, the test to be applied here is whether the risk of damage to a person on the road was so small that a reasonable man in the position of the appellants, considering the matter from the point of view of safety, would have thought it right to refrain from taking steps to prevent the danger. In considering that matter I think that it would be right to take into account, not only how remote is the chance that a person might be struck, but also how serious the consequences are likely to be if a person is struck, but I do not think that it would be right to take into account the difficulty of remedial measures. If cricket cannot be played on a ground without creating a substantial risk, then it should not be played there at all. I think that this is in substance the test which Oliver J. applied in this case. He considered whether the appellants' ground was large enough to be safe for all practical purposes and held that it was. This is a question, not of law, but of fact and degree. It is not an easy question, and it is one on which opinions may well differ. I can only say that, having given the whole matter repeated and anxious consideration, I find myself unable to decide this question in favour of the respondent. I think, however, that this case is not far from the border-line. If this appeal is allowed, that does not, in my judgment, mean that in every case where cricket has been played on a ground for a number of years without accident or complaint those who organise matches there are safe to go on in reliance on past immunity. I would have reached a different conclusion if I had thought that the risk here had been other than extremely small because I do not think that a reasonable man, considering the matter from the point of view of safety, would or should disregard any risk unless it is extremely small.

This case was also argued as a case of nuisance, but counsel for the respondent admitted that he could not succeed on that ground if the case on negligence failed. I, therefore, find it unnecessary to deal with the question of nuisance and I reserve my opinion as to what constitutes nuisance in cases of this character. In my judgment, the appeal should be allowed.

LORD RADCLIFFE: ... It seems to me that a reasonable man, taking account of the chances against an accident happening, would not have felt himself called on either to abandon the use of the ground for cricket or to increase the height of his surrounding fences. He would have done what the appellants did. In other words, he would have done nothing. ...

I agree with the others of your Lordships that, if the respondent cannot succeed in negligence, she cannot succeed on any other head of claim.

[LORD PORTER and LORD NORMAND delivered speeches in favour of allowing the appeal.]

Appeal allowed

Question

Would the appellants have been liable if Miss Stone had been one of a large procession which, to their knowledge, was assembling in the road outside?

Note

In *Hilder* v. *Associated Portland Cement Manufacturers, Ltd.*, [1961] 3 All E.R. 709, the defendants allowed small boys to play football on some grassland on their premises. The plaintiff's husband was killed when a football came into the road in front of his motorbike, causing him to have an accident and break his skull. An improvised goal was just over fifteen yards from the road, towards which two boys were kicking. Apart from some trees eight feet apart, the only other barrier between the goal and the road was a wall three feet two inches high on the grassland side. The boys had kicked towards this "goal" before and their football had gone over the wall from time to time. The defendants relied on *Bolton* v. *Stone*, but it was held that they had failed to take reasonable care. In Ashworth J.'s opinion, the reasonable man would not have considered that the risk of damage to road users was so small that it could safely be disregarded.

The Wagon Mound (No. 2)
Overseas Tankship (U.K.), Ltd. v. The Miller Steamship Co. Pty., Ltd.

Judicial Committee of the   [1966] 2 All E.R. 709
Privy Council

LORD REID: This is an appeal from a judgment of Walsh J.,[1] dated 10 October 1963, in the Supreme Court of New South Wales (Commercial Causes) by which he awarded to the respondents sums of £80,000 and £1,000 in respect of damage from fire sustained by their vessels, Corrimal and Audrey D, on 1 November 1951. These vessels were then at Sheerlegs Wharf, Morts Bay, in Sydney Harbour undergoing repairs. The appellant was charterer by demise of a vessel, the Wagon Mound, which in the early hours of 30 October 1951, had been taking in bunkering oil from Caltex Wharf not far from Sheerlegs Wharf. By reason of carelessness of the Wagon Mound engineers a large quantity of this oil overflowed from the Wagon Mound on to the surface of the water. Some hours later much of the oil had drifted to and accumulated round Sheerlegs Wharf and the respondents' vessels. About 2 p.m. on 1 November this oil was set alight: the fire spread rapidly and caused extensive damage to the wharf and to the respondents' vessels.

An action was raised against the present appellant by the owners of Sheerlegs Wharf on the ground of negligence. On appeal to the Board it was held that the plaintiffs were not entitled to recover on the ground that it was not foreseeable that such oil on the surface of the water could be set alight (*Overseas Tankship* (*U.K.*), *Ltd.* v. *Morts Dock and Engineering Co., Ltd.*).[2] Their lordships will refer to this case as the *Wagon Mound* (*No. 1*). The issue of nuisance was also raised but their lordships did not deal with it: they remitted this issue to the Supreme Court and their lordships now understand that the matter was not pursued there in that case.

In the present case the respondents sue alternatively in nuisance and in negligence. Walsh J.[1] had found in their favour in nuisance but against them in negligence. Before their lordships the appellant appeals against his decision on nuisance and the respondents appeal against his decision on negligence. Their lordships are indebted to that learned judge for the full and careful survey of the evidence which is set out in his judgment.[3] Few of his findings of fact have been attacked, and their lordships do not find it necessary to set out or deal with the evidence at any length; but it is desirable to give some explanation of how the fire started before setting out the learned judge's findings.

In the course of repairing the respondents' vessels the Morts Dock Co., the owners of Sheerlegs Wharf, were carrying out oxy-acetylene welding and cutting. This work was apt to cause pieces or drops of hot metal to fly off and fall in the sea. So when their manager arrived on the morning of 30 October and saw the thick scum of oil round

---

1. [1963] 1 Lloyd's Rep. 402.
2. [1961] A.C. 388; [1961] 1 All E.R. 404.
3. [1963] 1 Lloyd's Rep. at pp. 406–408.

the Wharf, he was apprehensive of fire danger and he stopped the work while he took advice. He consulted the manager of Caltex Wharf and, after some further consultation, he was assured that he was safe to proceed: so he did so, and the repair work was carried on normally until the fire broke out on 1 November. Oil of this character with a flash point of 170°F. is extremely difficult to ignite in the open; but we now know that that is not impossible. There is no certainty about how this oil was set alight, but the most probable explanation, accepted by Walsh J., is that there was floating in the oil-covered water some object supporting a piece of inflammable material, and that a hot piece of metal fell on it when it burned for a sufficient time to ignite the surrounding oil.

The findings of the learned trial judge are as follows[1]:

"(i) Reasonable people in the position of the officers of the Wagon Mound would regard furnace oil as very difficult to ignite on water.

"(ii) Their personal experience would probably have been that this had very rarely happened.

"(iii) If they had given attention to the risk of fire from the spillage, they would have regarded it as a possibility, but one which could become an actuality only in very exceptional circumstances.

"(iv) They would have considered the chances of the required exceptional circumstances happening whilst the oil remained spread on the harbour waters, as being remote.

"(v) I find that the occurrence of damage to [the respondents'] property as a result of the spillage, was not reasonably foreseeable by those for whose acts [the appellant] would be responsible.

"(vi) I find that the spillage of oil was brought about by the careless conduct of persons for whose acts [the appellant] would be responsible.

"(vii) I find that the spillage of oil was a cause of damage to the property of each of [the respondents].

"(viii) Having regard to those findings, and because of finding (v), I hold that the claim of each of [the respondents] framed in negligence fails." ...

It is now necessary to turn to the respondents' submission that the trial judge was wrong in holding that damage from fire was not reasonably foreseeable. In *Wagon Mound (No. 1)*[2] the finding on which the Board proceeded was that of the trial judge:

". . . [the appellants] did not know and could not reasonably be expected to have known that [the oil] was capable of being set afire when spread on water."

In the present case the evidence led was substantially different from the evidence led in *Wagon Mound (No. 1)*[3] and the findings of Walsh J.,[4] are significantly different. That is not due to there having been any failure by the plaintiffs in *Wagon Mound (No. 1)*[3] in preparing and presenting their case. The plaintiffs there were no doubt embarrassed by a difficulty which does not affect the present plaintiffs. The outbreak of the fire was consequent on the act of the manager of the plaintiffs in *Wagon Mound (No. 1)*[3] in resuming oxy-acetylene welding and cutting while the wharf was surrounded by this oil. So if the plaintiffs in the former case had set out to prove that it was foreseeable by the engineers of the Wagon Mound that this oil could be set alight, they might have had difficulty in parrying the reply that then this must also have been foreseeable by their manager. Then there would have been contributory negligence and at that time contributory negligence was a complete defence in New South Wales.

---

1. [1963] 1 Lloyd's Rep. at p. 426.
2. [1961] A.C. at p. 413; [1961] 1 All E.R. at p. 407.
3. [1961] A.C. 388; [1961] 1 All E.R. 404.
4. [1963] 1 Lloyd's Rep. 402.

The crucial finding of Walsh J.,[1] in this case is in finding (v): that the damage was "not reasonably foreseeable by those for whose acts the defendant would be responsible". That is not a primary finding of fact but an inference from the other findings, and it is clear from the learned judge's judgment that in drawing this inference he was to a large extent influenced by his view of the law. The vital parts of the findings of fact which have already been set out in full are (i) that the officers of the Wagon Mound "would regard furnace oil as very difficult to ignite on water"—not that they would regard this as impossible: (ii) that their experience would probably have been "that this had very rarely happened"—not that they would never have heard of a case where it had happened, and (iii) that they would have regarded it as a "possibility, but one which could become an actuality only in very exceptional circumstances"— not, as in *Wagon Mound* (*No. 1*),[2] that they could not reasonably be expected to have known that this oil was capable of being set afire when spread on water. The question which must now be determined is whether these differences between the findings in the two cases do or do not lead to different results in law.

In *Wagon Mound* (*No. 1*)[2] the Board were not concerned with degrees of foreseeability because the finding was that the fire was not foreseeable at all. So Viscount Simonds[3] had no cause to amplify the statement that the "essential factor in determining liability is whether the damage is of such a kind as the reasonable man should have foreseen". Here the findings show, however, that some risk of fire would have been present to the mind of a reasonable man in the shoes of the ship's chief engineer. So the first question must be what is the precise meaning to be attached in this context to the words "foreseeable" and "reasonably foreseeable".

Before *Bolton* v. *Stone*[4] the cases had fallen into two classes: (i) those where, before the event, the risk of its happening would have been regarded as unreal either because the event would have been thought to be physically impossible or because the possibility of its happening would have been regarded as so fantastic or far-fetched that no reasonable man would have paid any attention to it—"a mere possibility which would never occur to the mind of a reasonable man" (per Lord Dunedin in *Fardon* v. *Harcourt-Rivington*[5])—or (ii) those where there was a real and substantial risk or chance that something like the event which happens might occur and then the reasonable man would have taken the steps necessary to eliminate the risk.

Bolton v. *Stone*[4] posed a new problem. There a member of a visiting team drove a cricket ball out of the ground on to an unfrequented adjacent public road and it struck and severely injured a lady who happened to be standing in the road. That it might happen that a ball would be driven on to this road could not have been said to be a fantastic or far-fetched possibility: according to the evidence it had happened about six times in twenty-eight years. Moreover it could not have been said to be a far-fetched or fantastic possibility that such a ball would strike someone in the road: people did pass along the road from time to time. So it could not have been said that, on any ordinary meaning of the words, the fact that a ball might strike a person in the road was not foreseeable or reasonably foreseeable. It was plainly foreseeable; but the chance of its happening in the foreseeable future was infinitesimal. A mathematician given the data could have worked out that it was only likely to happen once in so many thousand years. The House of Lords held that the risk was so small that in the circumstances a reasonable man would have been justified in disregarding it and taking no steps to eliminate it.

It does not follow that, no matter what the circumstances may be, it is justifiable to neglect a risk of such a small magnitude. A reasonable man would only neglect

---

1. [1963] 1 Lloyd's Rep. at p. 426.
2. [1961] A.C. 388; [1961] 1 All E. R. 404.
3. [1961] A.C. at p. 426; [1961] 1 All E.R. at p. 415.
4. [1951] A.C. 850; [1951] 1 All E.R. 1078.
5. [1932] All E.R. Rep. 81, at p. 83.

such a risk if he had some valid reason for doing so: e.g. that it would involve considerable expense to eliminate the risk. He would weigh the risk against the difficulty of eliminating it. If the activity which caused the injury to Miss Stone had been an unlawful activity there can be little doubt but that *Bolton* v. *Stone*[1] would have been decided differently. In their lordships' judgment *Bolton* v. *Stone*[1] did not alter the general principle that a person must be regarded as negligent if he does not take steps to eliminate a risk which he knows or ought to know is a real risk and not a mere possibility which would never influence the mind of a reasonable man. What that decision did was to recognise and give effect to the qualification that it is justifiable not to take steps to eliminate a real risk if it is small and if the circumstances are such that a reasonable man, careful of the safety of his neighbour, would think it right to neglect it.

In the present case there was no justification whatever for discharging the oil into Sydney Harbour. Not only was it an offence to do so, but also it involved considerable loss financially. If the ship's engineer had thought about the matter there could have been no question of balancing the advantages and disadvantages. From every point of view it was both his duty and his interest to stop the discharge immediately.

It follows that in their lordships' view the only question is whether a reasonable man having the knowledge and experience to be expected of the chief engineer of the Wagon Mound would have known that there was a real risk of the oil on the water catching fire in some way: if it did, serious damage to ships or other property was not only foreseeable but very likely. Their lordships do not dissent from the view of the trial judge that the possibilities of damage[2] "must be significant enough in a practical sense to require a reasonable man to guard against them", but they think that he may have misdirected himself in saying[3]

"there does seem to be a real practical difficulty, assuming that some risk of fire damage was foreseeable, but not a high one, in making a factual judgment as to whether this risk was sufficient to attract liability if damage should occur."

In this difficult chapter of the law decisions are not infrequently taken to apply to circumstances far removed from the facts which give rise to them, and it would seem that here too much reliance has been placed on some observations in *Bolton* v. *Stone*[1] and similar observations in other cases.

In their lordships' view a properly qualified and alert chief engineer would have realised there was a real risk here, and they do not understand Walsh J. to deny that; but he appears to have held that, if a real risk can properly be described as remote, it must then be held to be not reasonably foreseeable. That is a possible interpretation of some of the authorities; but this is still an open question and on principle their lordships cannot accept this view. If a real risk is one which would occur to the mind of a reasonable man in the position of the defendant's servant and which he would not brush aside as far-fetched, and if the criterion is to be what that reasonable man would have done in the circumstances, then surely he would not neglect such a risk if action to eliminate it presented no difficulty, involved no disadvantage and required no expense.

In the present case the evidence shows that the discharge of so much oil on to the water must have taken a considerable time, and a vigilant ship's engineer would have noticed the discharge at an early stage. The findings show that he ought to have known that it is possible to ignite this kind of oil on water, and that the ship's engineer probably ought to have known that this had in fact happened before. The most that can be said to justify inaction is that he would have known that this could only happen in very exceptional circumstances; but that does not mean that a reasonable man would

---

1. [1951] A.C. 850; [1951] 1 All E.R. 1078.
2. [1963] 1 Lloyd's Rep. at p. 411.
3. [1963] 1 Lloyd's Rep. at p. 413.

dismiss such risk from his mind and do nothing when it was so easy to prevent it. If it is clear that the reasonable man would have realised or foreseen and prevented the risk, then it must follow that the appellants are liable in damages. The learned judge found this a difficult case: he said that this matter is[1] "one on which different minds would come to different conclusions". Taking a rather different view of the law from that of the learned judge, their lordships must hold that the respondents are entitled to succeed on this issue. . . .

Appeal and cross-appeal allowed. [The appeal, which related to the question of nuisance, is dealt with p. 386, *post.*]

Question

Would the appellant have been liable if the oil had been discharged from the ship because there was a fire on board?

Notes

1. On the relevance of the difficulty and cost of remedial measures, compare Lord Reid's views in this case with those in *Bolton* v. *Stone*, p. 139, *ante*, and see also *Latimer* v. *A.E.C., Ltd.*, [1953] A.C. 643; [1953] 2 All E.R. 449, p. 157, *post*.

2. *The Wagon Mound (No. 1)*, [1961] A.C. 388; [1961] 1 All E.R. 404, is the leading authority on remoteness of damage in negligence. A given set of facts may give rise to claims in the torts of nuisance and negligence, and nuisance itself can be subdivided into public and private nuisance. (See Chap. 11.) There are important differences between these torts, but, in the sphere of remoteness of damage, *The Wagon Mound (No. 2)* (in a part of the judgment which has been omitted at this stage) establishes that in nuisance, as in the tort of negligence, there must be foreseeability of the kind of damage suffered before the defendant will be held liable for that particular item of damage. (See p. 386, *post* where the Privy Council's judgment on this aspect of the case is set out.) Foreseeability plays a large and varied role in the tort of negligence. Not only is it relevant to breach of duty (which is under consideration at this point) and remoteness of damage (as has just been mentioned), but it is also relevant to the question whether a duty is owed to this particular plaintiff (pp. 120–123, *ante*). It is important that the different uses of the foreseeability doctrine should be appreciated, and discussion of this point can be found in an article by R. W. M. Dias, "Trouble on Oiled Waters: Problems of *The Wagon Mound (No. 2)*", [1967] C.L.J. 62.

(c) Special skill

Notes

1. Although the possession of special skill by the defendant may affect the standard of care required from him, the fact that the defendant claims to have special skill (usually by the carrying on of a profession whose members have that skill) may also be relevant in particular situations to the question whether or not any duty of care is owed in the first place—see *Mutual Life & Citizens' Assurance Co., Ltd.* v. *Evatt*, [1971] A.C. 793; [1971] 1 All E.R. 150, p. 511, *post*.

2. In many cases where a person with special skill is sued, the plaintiff will

---

1. [1963] 1 Lloyd's Rep. at p. 424.

be in a contractual relationship with the defendant and the same act may be potentially a breach of contract and a tort. Often there can be concurrent liability but there is authority for the view that certain classes of persons can be held liable to the other contracting party only in contract. Thus in *Clark* v. *Kirby-Smith*, [1964] Ch. 506; [1964] 2 All E.R. 835 it was decided that the liability of a solicitor to his client for negligence lay only in contract and not in tort. (See also *Bagot* v. *Stevens Scanlan & Co., Ltd.*, [1966] 1 Q.B. 197; [1964] 3 All E.R. 577 for the position of architects.) *Clark* v. *Kirby-Smith* concerned non-physical interests; cf. *Bagot's* case.

Philips v. William Whiteley, Ltd.

King's Bench Division   [1938] 1 All E.R. 566

The plaintiff went to the defendants' jewellery department to arrange for her ears to be pierced to enable her to wear earrings. The defendants did not have any member of their own staff who did this job, but arranged for Mr. Couzens, an employee of another firm, to pierce the ears. Approximately twelve or thirteen days after the piercing she felt pain in her neck. An abscess developed which had to be operated on and the operation left a small scar. It appeared that Mr. Couzens had performed over one thousand ear piercings and nothing of this nature had happened on any other occasion. The plaintiff claimed damages, alleging negligence against Mr. Couzens, the defendants' agent.

GODDARD J.: . . . In this case, the first thing that I have to consider is the standard of care demanded from Mr. Couzens—or, I should say, from Whiteleys, because Whiteleys were the people who undertook to do this piercing. It is not easy in any case to lay down a particular canon or standard by which the care can be judged, but, while it is admitted here, and admitted on all hands, that Mr. Couzens did not use the same precautions of procuring an aseptic condition of his instruments as a doctor or a surgeon would use, I do not think that he could be called upon to use that degree of care. Whiteleys have to see that whoever they employ for the operation uses the standard of care and skill that may be expected from a jeweller, and, of course, if the operation is negligently performed—if, for instance, a wholly unsuitable instrument were used, so that the ear was badly torn, or something of that sort happened—undoubtedly they would be liable. So, too, if they did not take that degree of care to see that the instruments were clean which one would expect a person of the training and the standing of a jeweller to use. To say, however, that a jeweller warrants or undertakes that he will use instruments which have the degree of surgical cleanliness that a surgeon brings about when he is going to perform a serious operation, or indeed any operation, is, I think, putting the matter too high. The doctors all seem to agree in this case that, if a lady went to a surgeon for the piercing of her ears, he would render his instruments sterile. After all, however, aseptic surgery is a thing of very modern growth. As anybody who has read the life of Lord Lister or the history of medicine in the last fifty or sixty years knows, it is not so many years ago that the best surgeon in the land knew nothing about even antiseptic surgery. Then antiseptic surgery was introduced, and that was followed by aseptic surgery. I do not think that a jeweller holds himself out as a surgeon or professes that he is going to conduct the operation of piercing a lady's ears by means of aseptic surgery, about which it is not to be supposed that he knows anything.

If a person wants to ensure that the operation of piercing her ears is going to be carried out with that proportion of skill and so forth that a Fellow of the Royal College of Surgeons would use, she must go to a surgeon. If she goes to a jeweller, she must expect that he will carry it out in the way that one would expect a jeweller to carry it out. One would expect that he would wash his instruments. One would expect that he would take some means of disinfecting his instrument, just in the same way as one knows that the ordinary layman, when he is going to use a needle to prick a blister or prick a little gathering on a finger, generally takes the precaution to put the needle in a flame, as I think Mr. Couzens did. I accept the evidence of Mr. Couzens as to what he says he did on this occasion—how he put his instrument in a flame before he left his shop, and how he washed his hands, and so forth. I think that he did. I see no reason to suppose that he is not telling me the absolute truth when he says what he did, and, as Dr. Pritchard, who holds the very high qualification of a Fellow of the Royal College of Physicians, said, for all practical purposes that is enough. That is to say, for the ordinary every-day matters that would be regarded as enough. It is not a degree of surgical cleanliness, which is a very different thing from ordinary cleanliness. It is not the cleanliness which a doctor would insist upon, because, as I say, Mr. Couzens is not a doctor. He was known not to be a doctor. One does not go to a jeweller to get one's ears attended to if one requires to have a doctor in attendance to do it. If one wants a doctor in attendance, one goes to his consulting room or one has him come to see one. I do not see any ground here for holding that Mr Couzens was negligent in the way in which he performed this operation. It might be better, and I think that it probably would, if he boiled his instrument beforehand at his place, or if he took a spirit lamp with him and boiled his instrument at the time, but in view of the medical evidence, the evidence of Dr. Pritchard, which I accept, I see no ground for holding that Mr. Couzens departed from the standard of care which you would expect that a man of his position and his training, being what he held himself out to be, was required to possess. Therefore, the charge of negligence fails.

Even if I am wrong in that, and even if another court were to take the view that a person who undertakes to pierce an ear is bound, although he holds himself out to be no more than a jeweller, to take all the precautions that a trained surgeon would take, I am quite unable, on the evidence, to find that the abscess from which Mrs. Philips suffered was due to any action of Mr. Couzens. . . .

Judgment for the defendants

Note

The following warning delivered by Denning L.J. in *Roe* v. *Minister of Health*, [1954] 2 Q.B. 66; [1954] 2 All E.R. 131 should be borne in mind. He said (at p. 137):

"It is so easy to be wise after the event and to condemn as negligence that which was only a misadventure. We ought always to be on our guard against it, especially in cases against hospitals and doctors. Medical science has conferred great benefits on mankind, but these benefits are attended by considerable risks. Every surgical operation is attended by risks. We cannot take the benefits without taking the risks. Every advance in technique is also attended by risks. Doctors, like the rest of us, have to learn by experience; and experience often teaches in a hard way. Something goes wrong and shows up a weakness, and then it is put right. . . . We must not look at the 1947 accident with 1954 spectacles."

Nettleship v. Weston

Court of Appeal   [1971] 3 All E.R. 581

The plaintiff agreed to teach the defendant to drive in the defendant's husband's car after he had been correctly told, in response to a remark of his about the insurance position, that he was covered as a passenger by the fully comprehensive insurance if there was an accident. During the third lesson he in fact assisted her by moving the gear lever, applying the hand brake and occasionally helping with the steering. In the course of that lesson, they made a slow left turn after having stopped at a halt sign. However, the defendant did not straighten out the wheel and panicked. Although the plaintiff got hold of the hand brake with one hand and tried to get hold of the steering wheel with the other hand so as to correct it, the car hit a lamp standard. The plaintiff's left knee-cap was broken and he appealed against the dismissal of his claim for damages from the defendant who had been convicted of driving without due care and attention.

MEGAW L.J.: . . . The important question of principle which arises is whether, because of Mr. Nettleship's knowledge that Mrs. Weston was not an experienced driver, the standard of care which was owed to him by her was lower than would otherwise have been the case.

In *Insurance Comr.* v. *Joyce*,[1] Dixon J. stated persuasively the view that there is, or may be, a "particular relation" between the driver of a vehicle and his passenger resulting in a variation of the standard of duty owed by the driver. . . . He summarised the same principle in these words[2]:

> "It appears to me that the circumstances in which the defendant accepts the plaintiff as a passenger and in which the plaintiff accepts the accommodation in the conveyance should determine the measure of duty . . ."

Theoretically, the principle as thus expounded is attractive. But, with very great respect, I venture to think that the theoretical attraction should yield to practical considerations.

As I see it, if this doctrine of varying standards were to be accepted as part of the law on these facts, it could not logically be confined to the duty of care owed by learner-drivers. There is no reason, in logic, why it should not operate in a much wider sphere. The disadvantages of the resulting unpredictability, uncertainty and, indeed, impossibility of arriving at fair and consistent decisions outweigh the advantages. The certainty of a general standard is preferable to the vagaries of a fluctuating standard.

As a first example of what is involved, consider the converse case: the standard of care (including skill) owed not by the driver to the passenger, but by the passenger-instructor to the learner-driver. Surely the same principle of varying standards, if it is a good principle, must be available also to the passenger, if he is sued by the driver for alleged breach of the duty of care in supervising the learner-driver. On this doctrine, the standard of care, or skill, owed by the instructor, vis-à-vis the driver, may vary according to the knowledge which the learner-driver had, at some moment of time, as to the skill and experience of the particular instructor. Indeed, if logic is to prevail, it would not necessarily be the knowledge of the driver which would be the criterion. It would be the expectation which the driver reasonably entertained of the instructor's skill and experience, if that reasonable expectation were greater than the actuality. Thus, if the learner-driver knew that the instructor had never tried his hand previously even at amateur instructing, or if, as may be the present case, the driver knew that the instructor's experience was confined to two cases of amateur instructing some years previously, there would, under this doctrine, surely be a lower standard than if the driver knew or reasonably supposed that the instructor was a professional or that he had had substantial experience in the recent past. But what that standard would be, and how it would or should be assessed, I know not. For one has thus cut oneself adrift from the standard of the competent and experienced instructor, which up to now the law has required without regard to the particular personal skill, experience, physical characteristics or temperament of the individual instructor, and without regard to a third party's knowledge or assessment of those qualities or characteristics.

Again, when one considers the requisite standard of care of the learner-driver, if this doctrine were to apply, would not logic irresistibly demand that there should be something more than a mere, single, conventional, standard applicable to anyone who falls into the category of learner-driver, i.e. of anyone who has not yet qualified for (or perhaps obtained) a full licence? That standard itself would necessarily vary

---

1. (1948), 77 C.L.R. 39, at pp. 56, 60.
2. (1948), 77 C.L.R. at p. 59.

over a wide range, not merely with the actual progress of the learner, but also with the passenger's knowledge of that progress; or, rather, if the passenger has in fact over-estimated the driver's progress, it would vary with the passenger's reasonable assessment of that progress at the relevant time. The relevant time would not necessarily be the moment of the accident.

The question, what is the relevant time? would itself have to be resolved by reference to some principle. The instructor's reasonable assessment of the skill and competence of the driver (and also the driver's assessment of the instructor's skill and competence) might alter drastically between the start of the first lesson and the start of a later lesson, or even in the course of one particular spell of driving. I suppose the principle would have to be that the relevant time is the last moment when the plaintiff (whether instructor or driver) could reasonably have refused to continue as passenger or driver in the light of his then knowledge. That factor in itself would introduce yet another element of difficulty, uncertainty and, I believe, serious anomaly. I for my part, with all respect, do not think that our legal process could successfully or satisfactorily cope with the task of fairly assessing, or applying to the facts of a particular case, such varying standards, depending on such complex and elusive factors, including the assessment by the court, not merely of a particular person's actual skill or experience, but also of another person's knowledge or assessment of that skill or experience at a particular moment of time.

Again, if the principle of varying standards is to be accepted, why should it operate, in the field of driving motor vehicles, only up to the stage of the driver qualifying for a full licence? And why should it be limited to the quality of inexperience? If the passenger knows that his driver suffers from some relevant defect, physical or temperamental, which could reasonably be expected to affect the quality of his driving, why should not the same doctrine of varying standards apply? Dixon J. thought it should apply. Logically there can be no distinction. If the passenger knows that his driver, though holding a full driving licence, is blind in one eye or has the habit of taking corners too fast, and if an accident happens which is attributable wholly or partly to that physical or that temperamental defect, why should not some lower standard apply vis-à-vis the fully informed passenger, if standards are to vary? Why should the doctrine, if it be part of the law, be limited to cases involving the driving of motor cars? Suppose that to the knowledge of the patient a young surgeon, whom the patient has chosen to operate on him, has only just qualified. If the operation goes wrong because of the surgeon's inexperience, is there a defence on the basis that the standard of skill and care was lower than the standard of a competent and experienced surgeon? Does the young, newly-qualified, solicitor owe a lower standard of skill and care, when the client chooses to instruct him with knowledge of his inexperience?

True, these last two examples may fall within the sphere of contract; and a contract may have express terms which deal with the question, or it may have implied terms. But in relationships such as are involved in this case, I see no good reason why a different term should be implied where there is a contract from the term which the law should attach where there is, or may be, no contract. Of course, there may be a difference—not because of any technical distinction between cases which fall within the law of tort and those which fall within the law of contract—but because the very factor or factors which create the contractual relationship may be relevant on the question of the implication of terms. . . .

In my judgment, in cases such as the present it is preferable that there should be a reasonably certain and reasonably ascertainable standard of care, even if on occasion that may appear to work hardly against an inexperienced driver, or his insurers. The standard of care required by the law is the standard of the competent and experienced driver; and this is so, as defining the driver's duty towards a passenger who knows of his inexperience, as much as towards a member of the public outside the car; and as much in civil as in criminal proceedings.

It is not a valid argument against such a principle that it attributes tortious liability to one who may not be morally blameworthy. For tortious liability has in many cases ceased to be based on moral blameworthiness. For example, there is no doubt whatever that if Mrs. Weston had knocked down a pedestrian on the pavement when the accident occurred, she would have been liable to the pedestrian. Yet so far as any moral blame is concerned, no different considerations would apply in respect of the pedestrian from those which apply in respect of Mr. Nettleship. . . .

[LORD DENNING M.R. adopted the view that the standard of care did not vary— it was that of the skilled, experienced and careful driver. For SALMON L.J.'s judgment, see p. 315, *post*.

LORD DENNING M.R. and SALMON L.J. (MEGAW L.J. dissenting on this point) accepted the apportionment of responsibility which had been made by the trial judge and damages were reduced by one-half because of the plaintiff's contributory negligence.]

Appeal allowed

Question

Does the learner driver hold himself out as possessing the skill and experience required by this case in the light of the fact that "L" plates must be displayed on the car? Why do the courts require him to attain the standard of "the competent and experienced driver"?

Notes

1. The judgments in this case also discuss the defence of *volenti non fit injuria*. (See p. 314, *post*.)

2. Even where odd jobs are done around the house, the courts are prepared to demand a certain level of skill from a defendant householder. In *Wells* v. *Cooper*, [1958] 2 Q.B. 265; [1958] 2 All E.R. 527, where the defendant had fixed a handle to a door, it was held that he must keep to the standard of a reasonably competent carpenter.

(d) Infants

McHale v. Watson

Full Court of the High Court of Australia   [1966] A.L.R. 513

This was an appeal from a judgment of Windeyer J., [1965] A.L.R. 788, dismissing the appellant's action.

KITTO J.: The appellant, a girl of nine, was hit in the eye by a piece of steel welding rod, about six inches in length and a quarter of an inch in diameter, which had been sharpened at the end that struck her. According to findings which are not challenged, the spike, as it has been called, was thrown by the respondent, a boy of 12, with the intention of endeavouring to make it stick into a hardwood post at a point at which he aimed, but it glanced off the post and struck the appellant. The respondent, it has been found, had no intention of either hitting the appellant or frightening her. The question whether he is liable in damages for the injury which the appellant sustained depends upon whether by throwing the spike as he did he committed a breach of a duty of care which he owed her.

The respondent was standing a foot or two from the post, and the appellant was at most four or five feet from him and to his left. He knew that the spike was sharp, and, therefore, that it might injure anyone whom its sharpened end should strike. If he had been an adult the question to be decided would have been whether an ordinary person in his situation, exercising reasonable foresight, would have realized that if he should throw the spike at the point on the post at which in fact he aimed there was such a likelihood of its glancing off the post and hitting the appellant that in ordinary prudence he ought not to throw it as he did. The learned trial judge did not express a concluded opinion as to the answer he would have given to this question. Saying that he did not think he was required to disregard altogether the fact that the respondent was at the time only 12 years old, his Honour reached the conclusion that the injury to the appellant "was not the result of a lack of foresight and appreciation of the risk that might reasonably have been expected, or of a want of reasonable care in aiming the dart". I take this to mean that the test to be applied in determining whether the appellant's injury resulted from a breach of duty owed to her by the respondent should be stated not in terms of the reasonable foresight and prudence of an ordinary person, but in terms of the reasonable foresight and prudence of an ordinary boy of 12; and that the respondent should succeed because an ordinary boy of 12 would not have appreciated that any risk to the appellant was involved in what he did. . . .

[Having mentioned the strict liability existing some centuries ago, he continued:] Partly, no doubt, as a development of the idea always recognized that this strict liability should extend only to immediate and not to remote consequences of the act, the law came in time to limit it to acts involving a shortcoming on the part of the defendant: *Holdsworth, op. cit.*,[1] vol. 3, at p. 379. Act of God and inevitable necessity thus came to be admitted as excuses; and, those steps having been taken, liability not unnaturally became further restricted so as not to attach to acts which, though causes of harm, were inherently proper and were for that reason to be considered not so proximate as to entail liability: *Holdsworth, op. cit.*,[1] vol. 8, at pp. 455 *et seq.* But propriety, in the relevant sense, has never been a matter of a morally blameless state of mind: see Pollock's excursus on negligence in *The Law of Torts*, 15th Edn. (1951), at p. 336, and the observations of Lord Denning as to unsoundness of mind in *White* v. *White*, [1950] P. 39 at p. 58; [1949] 2 All E.R. 339. In so far as "proper" is an apt word to use in this connexion it connotes nothing but conformity with an objective standard of care, namely, the care reasonably to be expected in the like circumstances from the normal person exercising reasonable foresight and consideration for the safety of others. Thus a defendant does not escape liability by proving that he is abnormal in some respect which reduces his capacity for foresight or prudence.

The principle is of course applicable to a child. The standard of care being objective, it is no answer for him, any more than it is for an adult, to say that the harm he caused was due to his being abnormally slow-witted, quick-tempered, absent-minded or inexperienced. But it does not follow that he cannot rely in his defence upon a limitation upon the capacity for foresight or prudence, not as being personal to himself, but as being characteristic of humanity at his stage of development and in that sense normal. By doing so he appeals to a standard of ordinariness, to an objective and not a subjective standard. In regard to the things which pertain to foresight and prudence—experience, understanding of causes and effects, balance of judgment, thoughtfulness—it is absurd, indeed it is a misuse of language, to speak of normality in relation to persons of all ages taken together. In those things normality is, for children, something different from what normality is for adults; the very concept of normality is a concept of rising levels until "years of discretion" are attained. The law does not arbitrarily fix upon any particular age for this purpose, and tribunals of fact may well give effect to different views as to the age at which normal adult foresight and prudence are reasonably to be expected in relation to particular sets of circumstances. But up to that stage the normal capacity to exercise those two qualities necessarily means the capacity which is normal for a child of the relevant age; and it seems to me that it would be contrary to the fundamental principle that a person is liable for harm that he causes by falling short of an objective criterion of "propriety" in his conduct—propriety, that is to say, as determined by a comparison with the standard of care reasonably to be expected in

---

1. [*History of English Law.*]

the circumstances from the normal person—to hold that where a child's liability is in question the normal person to be considered is someone other than a child of corresponding age.

Assistance on the subject is not to be found in the shape of specific decision in England or in this country, and judicial opinions in the United States and Canada have varied both in result and in reasoning. It seems to me, however, that strong support for the view I have indicated is provided by decisions on the cognate subject of contributory negligence. It is true that contributory negligence is not a breach of legal duty; it is only a failure to take reasonable care for one's own safety. But I must respectfully disagree with those who think that the deficiencies of foresight and prudence that are normal during childhood are irrelevant in determining what care it is reasonable for a child to take for the safety of others though relevant in determining what care it is reasonable for a child to take for himself. The standard is objective in contributory negligence no less than in negligence, in the sense that an ordinary capacity for care is postulated and is notionally applied to the circumstances of the case in order to determine what a reasonable person would have done or refrained from doing, regardless of the actual capacity for foresight or prudence possessed by the individual plaintiff or defendant. . . .

I am, therefore, of opinion that the learned trial judge did not misdirect himself on the question of law. There remains the question of fact: did the respondent, in throwing the spike as he did, though aware of the proximity of the appellant, do anything which a reasonable boy of his age would not have done in the circumstances—a boy, that is to say, who possessed and exercised such degree of foresight and prudence as is ordinarily to be expected of a boy of 12, holding in his hand a sharpened spike and seeing the post of a tree-guard before him? On the findings which must be accepted, what the respondent did was the unpremeditated, impulsive act of a boy not yet of an age to have an adult's realization of the danger of edged tools or an adult's wariness in the handling of them. It is, I think, a matter for judicial notice that the ordinary boy of 12 suffers from a feeling that a piece of wood and a sharp instrument have a special affinity. To expect a boy of that age to consider before throwing the spike whether the timber was hard or soft, to weigh the chances of being able to make the spike stick in the post, and to foresee that it might glance off and hit the girl, would be, I think, to expect a degree of sense and circumspection which nature ordinarily withholds till life has become less rosy . . .

In my opinion the appeal should be dismissed.

OWEN J.: . . . There is, then, a considerable body of opinion amongst the textbook writers, supported by decisions in Canada and the United States, that where an infant defendant is charged with negligence, his age is a circumstance to be taken into account and the standard by which his conduct is to be measured is not that to be expected of a reasonable adult but that reasonably to be expected of a child of the same age, intelligence and experience. In none of the other textbooks which I have examined does the question appear to have been considered.

. . . I am of opinion that Windeyer J. rightly took into consideration the fact that Barry Watson was only 12 years old and that he did not misdirect himself as to the degree of care reasonably to be expected of a boy of that age.

I would dismiss the appeal.

[McTIERNAN A.C.J. delivered a judgment in favour of dismissing the appeal. MENZIES J. delivered a judgment in favour of allowing the appeal.]

Appeal dismissed

Questions

1. If it is accepted that the child's age is relevant when considering whether he has been negligent, should the child's own intelligence and experience also be taken into account? (See the extract from Owen J.'s judgment, *ante*.)

2. In the light of *Nettleship* v. *Weston*, [1971] 2 Q.B. 691; [1971] 3 All E.R. 581, p. 146, *ante*, what standard of skill and care would be required of a person aged seventeen who is driving a car? Would his age be taken into account?

3. Did the standard expected of a nineteen year old person change after the coming into force of section 1 of the Family Law Reform Act 1969 which reduced the age of majority to 18?

4. Is there also a separate category of old age pensioners? (Compare *Daly* v. *Liverpool Corpn.*, [1939] 2 All E.R. 142.)

5. Are there any other categories of people to whom special consideration should be given? What standard should be expected of those suffering from mental disorders?

Note

There is a surprising dearth of direct English authority on the standard of care expected of infants. It may be, as McTiernan A.C.J. pointed out in *McHale* v. *Watson*, that a child is not in general worth suing (but see Salmond, pp. 442–443). Thus in fact, the plaintiff who has been injured by a child's act will on occasion sue not the child but one of its parents (or the appropriate school authority) alleging negligence in some respect, e.g. in not properly supervising the child's use of a firearm—see *Donaldson* v. *McNiven*, [1952] 2 All E.R. 691 (father found not negligent). In *Gorely* v. *Codd*, [1966] 3 All E.R. 891, p. 99, *ante*, both father and son were sued; on the facts the son was found to have been negligent, but no negligence was proved against the father. Where English courts have dealt with the contributory negligence of infants (p. 307, *post*) they have taken age into consideration, and it would seem likely that they would adopt the same approach if the issue arose directly for decision in a case where an infant was the defendant.

2. APPLICATION OF THE STANDARD OF CARE

(a) The likelihood of the occurrence of injury

Bolton v. Stone, p. 137, *ante*
The Wagon Mound (No. 2), p. 140, *ante*

Haley v. London Electricity Board

House of Lords   [1964] 3 All E.R. 185

The respondents had, under statutory power, made an excavation in the pavement. One of the precautions which they took was to leave, at one end of this excavation, a punner (a heavy weight attached to a long handle). The weighted end was on the pavement and the other end of the handle was lodged two feet high in some railings so the handle was sloping between these two points. The appellant, who often walked along this stretch of the pavement to reach a bus stop, was blind but could avoid ordinary obstacles by the use of his white stick. He used the stick correctly, but missed the punner handle and tripped over it. When he fell, he banged his head on the pavement and as a result became deaf. The Court of Appeal, [1963] 3 All E.R. 1003, dismissed an appeal from the judgment of Marshall J. who had dismissed the appellant's action for damages. On appeal to the House of Lords:

LORD REID: . . . The trial judge held that what the respondents' men did gave adequate warning to ordinary people with good sight, and I am not disposed to disagree with that. . . .

On the other hand, if it was the duty of the respondents to have in mind the needs of blind or infirm pedestrians, I think that what they did was quite insufficient. Indeed the evidence shows that an obstacle attached to a heavy weight and only nine inches above the ground may well escape detection by a blind man's stick and is for him a trap rather than a warning. So the question for your lordships' decision is the nature and extent of the duty owed to pedestrians by persons who carry out operations on a city pavement. The respondents argue that they were only bound to have in mind or to safeguard ordinary able-bodied people and were under no obligation to give particular consideration to the blind or infirm. If that is right, it means that a blind or infirm person who goes out alone goes at his peril. He may meet obstacles which are a danger to him, but not to those with good sight, because no one is under any obligation to remove or protect them; and if such an obstacle causes him injury he must suffer the damage in silence.

I could understand the respondents' contention if it was based on an argument that it was not reasonably foreseeable that a blind person might pass along that pavement on that day; or that, although foreseeable, the chance of a blind man coming there was so small and the difficulty of affording protection to him so great that it would have been in the circumstances unreasonable to afford that protection. Those are well recognised grounds of defence; but in my judgment neither is open to the respondents in this case.

In deciding what is reasonably foreseeable one must have regard to common knowledge. We are all accustomed to meeting blind people walking alone with their white sticks on city pavements. No doubt there are many places open to the public where for one reason or another one would be surprised to see a blind person walking alone, but a city pavement is not one of them; and a residential street cannot be different from any other. The blind people whom we meet must live somewhere, and most of them probably left their homes unaccompanied. It may seem surprising that blind people can avoid ordinary obstacles so well as they do, but we must take account of the facts. There is evidence in this case about the number of blind people in London and it appears from government publications that the proportion in the whole country is near one in five hundred. By no means all are sufficiently skilled or confident to venture out alone, but the number who habitually do so must be very large. I find it quite impossible to say that it is not reasonably foreseeable that a blind person may pass along a particular pavement on a particular day.

No question can arise in this case of any great difficulty in affording adequate protection for the blind. In considering what is adequate protection again one must have regard to common knowledge. One is entitled to expect of a blind person a high degree of skill and care because none but the most foolhardy would venture to go out alone without having that skill and exercising that care. We know that in fact blind people do safely avoid all ordinary obstacles on pavements; there can be no question of padding lamp posts as was suggested in one case.[1] A moment's reflection, however, shows that a low obstacle in an unusual place is a grave danger: on the other hand it is clear from the evidence in this case and also I think from common knowledge that quite a light fence some two feet high is an adequate warning. There would have been no difficulty in providing such a fence here. The evidence is that the Post Office always provide one, and that the respondents have similar fences which are often used. Indeed the evidence suggests that the only reason why there was no fence here was that the accident occurred before the necessary fences had arrived. So, if the respondents are to

---

1. See *M'Kibbin* v. *Glasgow City Corpn.*, 1920 S.C. 590, at p. 598.

succeed, it can only be on the ground that there was no duty to do more than safeguard ordinary able-bodied people.

The respondents rely on the case of *Pritchard* v. *Post Office*[1] a decision of the Court of Appeal not reported in either of the more commonly cited series of reports. The facts are not fully stated, but it would appear that servants of the Post Office had protected a hole where they were working by surrounding it with their usual light fence, but a blind woman stumbled through the fence and was injured. I would think that the decision was clearly right, the sole cause of the accident being the plaintiff's contributory negligence; but the county court judge based his decision on there being no special duty to protect the blind or infirm and that was repeated by the Court of Appeal in dismissing an appeal. I am aware that the current practice is to regard the ratio of a decision as equally authoritative whether the judgment was given ex tempore after inadequate argument or given after full argument and mature consideration. I think that this places a wholly unreasonable burden on the Court of Appeal. The argument before your lordships in this case occupied three days, which was not at all too long in view of the novelty and difficulty of the points involved. *Pritchard's* case[1] was argued and disposed of in one day, and it would be quite unreasonable to prolong the hearing of a small county court appeal which must obviously fail in order to have a full legal argument even assuming that counsel were prepared to deal fully with the general question of law. . . .

I can see no justification for laying down any hard and fast rule limiting the classes of persons for whom those interfering with a pavement must make provision. It is said that it is impossible to tell what precautions will be adequate to protect all kinds of infirm pedestrians or that taking such precautions would be unreasonably difficult or expensive. I think that such fears are exaggerated, and it is worth recollecting that when the courts sought to lay down specific rules as to the duties of occupiers the law became so unsatisfactory that Parliament had to step in and pass the Occupiers Liability Act 1957. It appears to me that the ordinary principles of the common law must apply in streets as well as elsewhere, and that fundamentally they depend on what a reasonable man, careful of his neighbour's safety, would do having the knowledge which a reasonable man in the position of the defendant must be deemed to have. I agree with the statement of law at the end of the speech of Lord Sumner in *Glasgow Corpn.* v. *Taylor*[2]—

> "a measure of care appropriate to the inability or disability of those who are immature or feeble in mind or body is due from others who know of, or ought to anticipate, the presence of such persons within the scope and hazard of their own operations."

I would therefore allow this appeal. The assessment of damages has been deferred and the case must be remitted for such assessment.

LORD MORTON OF HENRYTON: . . . There is no dispute as to the facts, and only two questions arise for decision—first, what is the duty owed by those who engage on operations on the pavement of a highway and, secondly, was that duty discharged in the present case.

My lords, I would answer the first question as follows. It is their duty to take reasonable care not to act in a way likely to endanger other persons who may reasonably be expected to walk along the pavement. That duty is owed to blind persons if the operators foresee or ought to have foreseen that blind persons may walk along the pavement and is in no way different from the duty owed to persons with sight, though the carrying out of the duty may involve extra precautions in the case of blind pedestrians. I think that everyone living in greater London must have seen blind persons

---

1. (1950), 114 J.P. 370.
2. [1922] 1 A.C. 44, at p. 67; [1921] All E.R. Rep. 1, at p. 13.

walking slowly along on the pavement and waving a white stick in front of them, so as to touch any obstruction which may be in their way, and I think that the respondents' workmen ought to have foreseen that a blind person might well come along the pavement in question.

I have not found it easy to answer the second question, but I have come to the conclusion that the workmen failed adequately to discharge the duty which I have stated, though I would accept the finding of the learned trial judge that "what the [respondents] did was adequate to give reasonable and proper warning to normal pedestrians" . . .

I would allow the appeal. Counsel for the respondents submitted that a decision against them would have very far-reaching consequences and would make it necessary for persons working in any public place to take elaborate and extreme precautions to prevent blind persons from suffering injury. My lords, I do not think that the consequences would be so serious as counsel suggests, bearing in mind, first, that there are many places to which one would not reasonably expect a blind person to go unaccompanied and, secondly, that workmen are entitled to assume that such a person will take reasonable care to protect himself, for example by using a stick in order to ascertain if there is anything in his way and by stopping if his stick touches any object.

LORD HODSON: . . . The respondents conceded that those who engage in operations on the highway owe a duty to take reasonable care not to act in a way likely to endanger other road users. At the same time they say that their duty is confined to a duty owing to normal persons. This contention is surely inconsistent with their concession, for other road users include all sorts of people who cannot be described as normal. In view of the large number of blind persons who fall into the category of abnormal and are users of the road it cannot be said that the risk of causing them injury is so small as to be minimal and therefore to be excluded from the realm of foreseeability. Neither can it fairly be said that such extravagant precautions would be required in order to be useful for their purpose that they cannot be reasonably practicable. Bearing in mind that blind persons to be contemplated are those who behave reasonably and proceed on their way mindful of their own infirmity, and using such means as are available to them to avoid running into obstacles, it is unnecessary to provide special protection for them in the case of all obstacles which stand in their way. I have in mind lamp posts, trees, parking meters, pillar boxes and dustbins and things of that kind which one is likely to encounter in or about the highway. . . .

On the facts of this case I am of opinion that the respondents were in breach of the duty of care which they owed to the appellant and that this breach was the cause of his injury.

I would allow the appeal.

[LORD EVERSHED and LORD GUEST delivered speeches in favour of allowing the appeal.]

Appeal allowed

(b) The gravity of the injury which may be suffered
Paris v. Stepney Borough Council

House of Lords   [1951] I All E.R. 42

LORD SIMONDS: My Lords, this is an appeal from an order of the Court of Appeal[1] setting aside a judgment of Lynskey J., in favour of the appellant for £5,250 damages and costs. On 13 May 1942, the appellant entered the service of the respondents as a garage hand in their cleansing department. He was then for all practical purposes blind in his left eye, having suffered serious injury in May 1941, as the result of enemy action, but this fact was not known to the respondents at that time. On or about 19 July 1946, he was medically examined with a view to his becoming a member of

1. [1950] 1 K.B. 320; [1949] 2 All E.R. 843.

the permanent staff and joining the superannuation scheme, and on 22 July 1946, the medical officer reported to a Mr. Boden, the respondents' public cleansing officer, that the appellant was not fit on account of his disablement to join the superannuation scheme. On 16 May 1947, he was given two weeks' notice expiring on 30 May 1947, to terminate his employment. I will assume that at this date the respondents had notice of his physical disability, including the blindness of his left eye. On 28 May 1947, the accident occurred which gave rise to the present action. The appellant was engaged in dismantling the chassis of a gulley cleaner, a type of vehicle generally used by local authorities for the cleansing and flushing of street gulleys. The vehicle had been raised about four and a half feet from the garage floor by means of a ramp. The appellant had to remove a U-bolt holding the springs of an axle, and, to release it, he hit the U-bolt with a steel hammer. As the result of his doing so a piece of metal flew off and entered his right eye with the disastrous consequence that he lost the sight of it altogether. On 8 August 1947, he commenced his action against the respondents claiming damages for their negligence and breach of statutory duty. The respondents put in a defence denying negligence and raising an alternative plea of contributory negligence which has not been pursued. Nor has the appellant pursued his claim for breach of statutory duty. The single question is whether the appellant proved the negligence of the respondents, a question answered in the affirmative by Lynskey J., in the negative by the Court of Appeal.

What, then, was the negligence alleged by the appellant and denied by the respondents? It was that it was the duty of the respondents to supply the appellant with suitable goggles for the protection of his eyes while he was engaged in such work and to require him to use them. . . . I will say at once that I do not dissent from the view that an employer owes a particular duty to each of his employees. His liability in tort arises from his failure to take reasonable care in regard to the particular employee and it is clear that, if so, all the circumstances relevant to that employee must be taken into consideration. I see no valid reason for excluding as irrelevant the gravity of the damage which the employee will suffer if an accident occurs, and with great respect to the judgments of the Court of Appeal I cannot accept the view, neatly summarised by Asquith L.J. ([1949] 2 All E.R. 845), that the greater risk of injury is, but the risk of greater injury is not, a relevant circumstance. I find no authority for such a proposition nor does it appear to me to be founded on any logical principle. . . .

LORD MORTON OF HENRYTON: My Lords, it cannot be doubted that there are occupations in which the possibility of an accident occurring to any workman is extremely remote, while there are other occupations in which there is constant risk of accident to the workmen. Similarly, there are occupations in which, if an accident occurs, it is likely to be of a trivial nature, while there are other occupations in which, if an accident occurs, the result to the workman may well be fatal. Whether one is considering the likelihood of an accident occurring, or the gravity of the consequences if an accident happens, there is in each case a gradually ascending scale between the two extremes which I have already mentioned. In considering generally the precautions which an employer ought to take for the protection of his workmen it must, in my view, be right to take into account both elements, the likelihood of an accident happening and the gravity of the consequences. I take as an example two occupations in which the risk of an accident taking place is exactly equal. If an accident does occur in the one occupation, the consequences to the workman will be comparatively trivial; if an accident occurs in the other occupation the consequences to the workman will be death or mutilation. Can it be said that the precautions which it is the duty of an employer to take for the safety of his workmen are exactly the same in each of these occupations? My Lords, that is not my view. I think that the more serious the damage which will happen if an accident occurs, the more thorough are the precautions which an employer must take. If I am right as to this general principle, I think it follows logically that if A. and B., who are engaged on the same work, run precisely the same risk of an accident happening, but if the results of an accident will be more serious to

A. than to B., precautions which are adequate in the case of B. may not be adequate in the case of A., and it is a duty of the employer to take such additional precautions for the safety of A. as may be reasonable. The duty to take reasonable precautions against injury is one which is owed by the employer to every individual workman.

In the present case it is submitted by counsel for the appellant that, although the appellant ran no greater risk of injury than the other workmen engaged in the maintenance work, he ran a risk of greater injury. Counsel points out that an accident to one eye might transform the appellant into a blind man, and this event in fact happened. A similar accident to one of his comrades would transform that comrade into a one-eyed man, a serious consequence indeed, but not so serious as the results have been to the appellant. My Lords, the Court of Appeal thought that the one-eyed condition of the appellant, known to his employers, was wholly irrelevant in determining the question whether the employer did or did not take reasonable precautions to avoid an accident of this kind. I do not agree. Applying the general principle which I have endeavoured to state, I agree with your Lordships and with Lynskey J., that the condition of the appellant was a relevant fact to be taken into account. . . .

[LORD OAKSEY, LORD MACDERMOTT and LORD NORMAND delivered speeches to a similar effect on this point. However, on the facts of the case, it was only by a majority (LORD SIMONDS and LORD MORTON OF HENRYTON dissenting) that the judgment of LYNSKEY J. on liability was restored.]

Appeal allowed

Note

In *Withers* v. *Perry Chain Co., Ltd.,* [1961] 3 All E.R. 676 the plaintiff had had an attack of dermatitis resulting from a reaction to grease used in her job. When she returned to work, the defendants put her on work which in their opinion was the best available for her in the circumstances, but she suffered further attacks and sued her employers alleging negligence in employing her on work which they ought to have known could cause (or exacerbate) dermatitis. Sellers L.J. stated (at p. 680) that the duty of the defendants "was to take all reasonable care for the plaintiff in the employment in which she was engaged, including, of course, a duty to have regard to the fact that she had had dermatitis previously", but it was held that no breach of duty had been established in the case. Devlin L.J. said (also at p. 680):

"It may be also (on the principle of *Paris* v. *Stepney Borough Council*) that when the susceptibility of an employee to dermatitis is known there is a duty on the employer to take extra or special precautions to protect such an employee. But it is not suggested that there were any extra or special precautions here which could have been taken."

(c) The cost and practicability of measures necessary to overcome the risk

Latimer v. A.E.C., Ltd.

House of Lords   [1953] 2 All E.R. 449

The respondents' large factory was flooded by an unusually heavy rainstorm and the water mixed with an oily liquid usually collected in channels in the floor. This mixture when it drained away left a film making the surface very slippery. Sawdust was then spread on the floor but there was insufficient to cover all the area, even though the respondents had had enough there to meet any situation they could have been expected to foresee. The appellant, who was working in the factory on the night shift, slipped on a part of the floor which had not had sawdust applied to it, and a barrel, which he was putting on to a trolley, rolled on to and injured his ankle. Pilcher J., [1952] 1 All E.R. 443 gave judgment for the appellant against the respondents in negligence, but the Court of Appeal, [1952] 1 All E.R. 1302, reversed this decision. On appeal to the House of Lords:

LORD TUCKER: ... In the present case, the respondents were faced with an unprecedented situation following a phenomenal rain storm. They set forty men to work on cleaning up the factory when the flood subsided and used all the available supply of sawdust, which was approximately three tons. The judge has found that they took every step which could reasonably have been taken to deal with the conditions which prevailed before the night shift came on duty, and he has negatived every specific allegation of negligence as pleaded, but he has held the respondents liable because they did not close down the factory, or the part of the factory where the accident occurred, before the commencement of the night shift. I do not question that such a drastic step may be required on the part of a reasonably prudent employer if the peril to his employees is sufficiently grave, and to this extent it must always be a question of degree, but, in my view, there was no evidence in the present case which could justify a finding of negligence for failure on the part of the respondents to take this step. This question was never canvassed in evidence, nor was sufficient evidence given as to the condition of the factory as a whole to enable a satisfactory conclusion to be reached. The learned judge seems to have accepted the reasoning of counsel for the appellant to the effect that the floor was slippery, that slipperiness is a potential danger, that the respondents must be taken to have been aware of this, that in the circumstances nothing could have been done to remedy the slipperiness, that the respondents allowed work to proceed, that an accident due to slipperiness occurred, and that the respondents are, therefore, liable.

This is not the correct approach. The problem is perfectly simple. The only question was: Has it been proved that the floor was so slippery that, remedial steps not being possible, a reasonably prudent employer would have closed down the factory rather than allow his employees to run the risks involved in continuing work? The learned judge does not seem to me to have posed this question to himself, nor was there sufficient evidence before him to have justified an affirmative answer. The absence of any evidence that anyone in the factory during the afternoon or night shift, other than the appellant, slipped, or experienced any difficulty, or that any complaint was made by or on behalf of the workers, all points to the conclusion that the danger was, in fact, not such as to impose on a reasonable employer the obligation placed on the respondents by the trial judge. I agree that the appeal be dismissed.

[On the question of common law negligence, LORD REID agreed with LORD TUCKER and LORD PORTER, LORD OAKSEY and LORD ASQUITH OF BISHOPSTONE delivered speeches in favour of dismissing the appeal. A claim for breach of statutory duty was rejected.]

Appeal dismissed

(d) The purpose of the defendant's acts

Daborn v. Bath Tramways Motor Co., Ltd. and T. Smithey

Court of Appeal   [1946] 2 All E.R. 333

The plaintiff was driving an ambulance with a left hand drive. A notice on the back of the vehicle stated "Caution—Left hand drive—No signals". The ambulance was shut in at the back, but, by using a mirror on the left hand side, the plaintiff could see vehicles some yards behind her. She gave evidence that she signalled with her left hand that she was going to make a right turn. However, as the ambulance was turning right, it was hit by a bus, and the plaintiff suffered grave injuries when she was thrown out of the ambulance as a result of the collision. In an unsuccessful appeal by the defendants from a decision of Croom-Johnson J. awarding the plaintiff damages, it was argued that the plaintiff had been negligent.

ASQUITH L.J.: . . . In determining whether a party is negligent, the standard of reasonable care is that which is reasonably to be demanded in the circumstances. A relevant circumstance to take into account may be the importance of the end to be served by behaving in this way or in that. As has often been pointed out, if all the trains in this country were restricted to a speed of 5 miles an hour, there would be fewer accidents, but our national life would be intolerably slowed down. The purpose to be served, if sufficiently important, justifies the assumption of abnormal risk. The relevance of this applied to the present case is this: during the war which was, at the material time, in progress, it was necessary for many highly important operations to be carried out by means of motor vehicles with left-hand drives, no others being available. So far as this was the case, it was impossible for the drivers of such cars to give the warning signals which could otherwise be properly demanded of them. Meanwhile, it was essential that the ambulance service should be maintained. It seems to me, in those circumstances, it would be demanding too high and an unreasonable standard of care from the drivers of such cars to say to them: "Either you must give signals which the structure of your vehicle renders impossible or you must not drive at all." It was urged by counsel for the defendants that these alternatives were not exhaustive, since the driver of such a car should, before executing a turn, stop his car, move to the right-hand seat and look backwards to see if another car was attempting to overtake him and then start up again. Counsel for the plaintiff has satisfied me that such a procedure, besides involving possible delay, might be wholly ineffective. I think the plaintiff did all that in the circumstances she could reasonably be required to do if you include in those circumstances, as I think you should: (i) the necessity in time of national emergency of employing all transport resources which were available, and (ii) the inherent limitations and incapacities of this particular form of transport. In considering whether reasonable care has been observed, one must balance the risk against the consequences of not assuming that risk, and in the present instance this calculation seems to me to work out in favour of the plaintiff. I agree . . . that this appeal should be dismissed.

[MORTON and TUCKER L.JJ. delivered judgments in favour of dismissing the appeal.]

Note

Attention might also be paid to *Watt* v. *Hertfordshire C.C.*, [1954] 2 All E.R. 368, where the plaintiff, a fireman, was in a team called out to an emergency. A jack was to be taken out as the call said that a woman was trapped under a heavy vehicle a few hundred yards away. There was a vehicle specially fitted to carry this jack, which weighed two or three hundredweight, but it was out on other service, and so the jack was lifted on to a lorry. However, the driver had to brake suddenly, and the plaintiff was injured when the jack, which stood on four small wheels, moved and caught his leg. It was held that the defendants, his employers, had not been negligent. Saving life and limb, Denning L.J. said, justified a considerable risk being taken. He went on to state that "I quite agree that fire engines, ambulances and doctors' cars should not shoot past the traffic lights when they show a red light. That is because the risk is too great to warrant the incurring of the danger." Would this view still prevail if the driver of a fire engine, seeing a man ahead of him in dire peril from a fire, had looked both ways before crossing the red light, but had collided with a car which had just come round a bend?

(e) Competitions

Wooldridge v. Sumner, p. 322, *post*

(f) Common practice

Morton v. William Dixon, Ltd.

Court of Session   1909 S.C. 807

LORD DUNEDIN: . . . Where the negligence of the employer consists of what I may call a fault of omission, I think it is absolutely necessary that the proof of that fault of omission should be one of two kinds, either—to shew that the thing which he did not do was a thing which was commonly done by other persons in like circumstances, or—to shew that it was a thing which was so obviously wanted that it would be folly in anyone to neglect to provide it. . . .

Notes

1. This passage from Lord Dunedin's judgment has been cited and interpreted in several cases, on which see Salmond, pp. 235–236.

2. What is the position when there are conflicting views as to the proper practice to adopt? In Bolam v. *Friern Hospital Management Committee,* [1957] 2 All E.R. 118, McNair J., directing the jury, told them that a doctor was not negligent if he adopted a practice which a responsible body of skilled medical men accepted as proper, and that this was unaffected by the mere fact that there was a contrary body of opinion.

3. It should be noted, however, that a defendant can be held to have been negligent, even though there is evidence that he acted in accordance with common practice. (See Cavanagh v. Ulster Weaving Co., Ltd., [1960] A.C. 145; [1959] 2 All E.R. 745.) On the other hand, a defendant is not necessarily negligent if he does not adopt a common practice. In Brown v. Rolls Royce, Ltd., [1960] 1 All E.R. 577 among the facts found by the court below (the Court of Session) were that the appellant contracted industrial dermatitis from contact with oil in his work, that, although there were ample washing facilities, barrier cream was not supplied by his employers (on the advice of their medical officer who was not at fault) and that its value in relation to dermatitis was the subject of strong differences of opinion amongst the medical profession. In addition, it had been found that barrier cream was commonly supplied by employers to be doing the sort of work in which the appellant was involved, but that it was not proved that it would stop them, or would probably have stopped him, contracting dermatitis. The House of Lords held that the employers were not at fault in failing to supply barrier cream. Lord Keith of Avonholm said (at p. 581):

> "A common practice in like circumstances not followed by an employer may no doubt be a weighty circumstance to be considered by judge or jury in deciding whether failure to comply with this practice, taken along with all the other material circumstances in the case, yields an inference of negligence on the part of the employers."

However, he added:

> "The ultimate test is lack of reasonable care for the safety of the workman in all the circumstances of the case."

Lord Denning stated (at p. 582):

> "If defenders do not follow the usual precautions, it raises a *prima facie* case
> against them in this sense, that it is evidence from which negligence *may* be inferred,
> but not in the sense that it *must* be inferred unless the contrary is proved. At the
> end of the day, the court has to ask itself whether the defenders were negligent or
> not."

4. Further consideration was given to the effect of a general practice in the
context of employers' liability by Swanwick J. in *Stokes* v. *Guest, Keen and
Nettlefold (Bolts and Nuts), Ltd.,* [1968] 1 W.L.R. 1776. After referring to
several authorities relating to employers' duty to workmen, he deduced the
following principles (at p. 1783):

> ". . . that the overall test is still the conduct of the reasonable and prudent em-
> ployer, taking positive thought for the safety of his workers in the light of what he
> knows or ought to know; where there is a recognised and general practice which
> has been followed for a substantial period in similar circumstances without mishap,
> he is entitled to follow it, unless in the light of common sense or newer knowledge
> it is clearly bad; but, where there is developing knowledge, he must keep reason-
> ably abreast of it and not be too slow to apply it; and where he has in fact greater
> than average knowledge of the risks, he may be thereby obliged to take more than
> the average or standard precautions."

Is the last part of the quotation an encouragement to ignorance?

3. AIDS IN DISCHARGING THE BURDEN OF PROOF

(a) Statute

The Civil Evidence Act 1968

11. Convictions as evidence in civil proceedings. (1) In any civil proceedings
the fact that a person has been convicted of an offence by or before any court in the
United Kingdom or by a court-martial there or elsewhere shall (subject to subsection
(3) below) be admissible in evidence for the purpose of proving, where to do so is
relevant to any issue in those proceedings, that he committed that offence, whether
he was so convicted upon a plea of guilty or otherwise and whether or not he is a
party to the civil proceedings; but no conviction other than a subsisting one shall be
admissible in evidence by virtue of this section.

(2) In any civil proceedings in which by virtue of this section a person is proved
to have been convicted of an offence by or before any court in the United Kingdom or
by a court-martial there or elsewhere—

  (*a*) he shall be taken to have committed that offence unless the contrary is proved;
  and

  (*b*) without prejudice to the reception of any other admissible evidence for the
  purpose of identifying the facts on which the conviction was based, the contents of any document which is admissible as evidence of the conviction, and
  the contents of the information, complaint, indictment or charge-sheet on
  which the person in question was convicted, shall be admissible in evidence
  for that purpose.

(3) Nothing in this section shall prejudice the operation of section 13[1] of this Act
or any other enactment whereby a conviction or a finding of fact in any criminal pro-

---

1. See p. 549, *post*.

ceedings is for the purposes of any other proceedings made conclusive evidence of any fact.

(b) Common law—*res ipsa loquitur*

Scott v. London and St. Katherine Docks Co.

Court of Exchequer Chamber   [1861–73] All E.R. Rep. 246

The plaintiff by his declaration alleged that the defendants were possessed of certain docks, and warehouses therein, that the plaintiff was lawfully therein, that the defendants by their servants were lowering bags of sugar by means of a crane or hoist, and that by the negligence of the defendants' servants a bag of sugar fell upon the plaintiff and injured him. The defendants denied liability. At the trial before Martin B. and a special jury, the plaintiff, who was the only witness called, gave evidence relative to the accident, and stated that he was a Custom House officer of twenty-six years' standing; that on 19 January 1864, the occasion in question, he was at the defendants' docks, and had performed his duty at the East Quay there as superintendent of the weighing of goods; that he was directed by Mr. Lilley, his superior officer, to go from the East Quay to the Spirit Quay, which he proceeded to do, having to pass the warehouses in his way. Not being able to find Lilley, he inquired of a workman where he was, and was told he was in a warehouse, which was pointed out to him, and, in passing from the doorway of one warehouse to the other, he was felled to the ground by the falling upon him of six bags of sugar which were being lowered to the ground from the upper part of the warehouse by means of a crane or jigger hoist. The plaintiff said that he had no warning, and there was no fence or barrier to show persons that the place was dangerous, and nobody called out to him to stop him from going through the door or under the hoist. He also said that instantly before the bags fell he "heard the rattling of a chain overhead." No other evidence being given, the learned judge proposed to nonsuit the plaintiff for want of evidence showing negligence in defendants, but on the plaintiff's resisting that course, with a view to a bill of exceptions, his Lordship directed the jury to find a verdict for the defendants. A rule was subsequently obtained to set that verdict aside, and for a new trial, on the ground that there was evidence of negligence by the defendants' servants, which rule after argument was made absolute by the Court of Exchequer, on the authority of *Byrne* v. *Boadle*[1] (dubitante Pollock C.B., and dissentiente Martin B., on the authority of *Hammack* v. *White*[2]), and against that decision the defendants now appealed.

ERLE C.J.: The majority of the court have come to the following conclusion. There must be reasonable evidence of negligence, but, where the thing is shown to be under the management of the defendant, or his servants, and the accident is such as, in the ordinary course of things, does not happen if those who have the management of the machinery use proper care, it affords reasonable evidence, in the absence of explanation by the defendant, that the accident arose from want of care. We all assent to the principle laid down in the cases cited for the defendants; but the judgment turns upon the construction to be put on the judge's notes. As my brother Mellor and myself read those notes, we cannot find that reasonable evidence in the present case of the want of care which seems apparent to the rest of the court. The judgment of the court below is, therefore, affirmed, and the case must go down to a new trial, when the real effect of the evidence will, in all probability, be more correctly ascertained.

Appeal dismissed

---

1. (1863), 2 H. & C. 722.
2. (1862), 11 C.B.N.S. 588.

Notes

1. It is reported at (1865–6), 13 L.T. (N.S.) 148 at p. 149 that at the second trial there was a verdict for the defendants.

2. In *Barkway* v. *South Wales Transport Co., Ltd.,* [1950] A.C. 185n.; [1950] 1 All E.R. 392, Lord Porter referred to Erle C.J.'s exposition of the doctrine (*ante*) and stated (at pp. 394–395):

> "The doctrine is dependent on the absence of explanation, and, although it is the duty of the defendants, if they desire to protect themselves, to give an adequate explanation of the cause of the accident, yet, if the facts are sufficiently known, the question ceases to be one where the facts speak for themselves, and the solution is to be found by determining whether, on the facts as established, negligence is to be inferred or not."

3. There are conflicting authorities on the effect of *res ipsa loquitur*. The following extracts represent recent expressions of opinion by appellate courts. (For guidance on this topic generally, see Cross, *Evidence* (3rd Edn.), pp. 126–8 and for a discussion of the recent cases, see P. S. Atiyah, "*Res Ipsa Loquitur* in England and Australia", (1972), 35 M.L.R. 337.)

Henderson v. Henry E. Jenkins & Sons

House of Lords   [1969] 3 All E.R. 756

The hydraulic brakes of a lorry suddenly failed whilst it was descending a hill and it collided with two vehicles and killed the appellant's husband. The reason for the failure was a hole in a corroded part of the brake pipe. Although part of the pipe could be seen whilst it remained on the lorry, the part which in fact was badly corroded could not have been inspected without the pipe being removed. The evidence showed that it was unusual for there to be complete and sudden failure of brakes from corrosion. The respondents pleaded that the brake failure resulted "from a latent defect . . . which occurred without any fault on the part of the [respondents and the driver] and the existence of which was not discoverable by the exercise of reasonable care by them." They argued that ordinary practice only required that the visible parts of the pipe be regularly inspected (which they had done), and it was established that neither the Ministry of Transport nor the manufacturers advised that the pipes be removed for inspection. The appellant's action for damages against the respondents and the driver was dismissed by Nield J. She appealed to the Court of Appeal, [1969] 1 All E.R. 401, against the dismissal of the action against the respondents and, after that appeal had been dismissed, she appealed to the House of Lords.

LORD REID, [having earlier referred to the evidence of the respondents' "leading expert" who, in response to a question, had agreed that the pipe "was subjected to some unusual treatment from outside", continued:]

If there were nothing in the evidence to indicate a probability that something unusual must have happened to this lorry to cause the very unusual type of brake failure which the learned trial judge has held in fact occurred here, then undoubtedly the respondents would have proved that they had exercised all proper care in this case. But if the evidence indicates a likelihood that something unusual has occurred to cause a break-down, then I do not see how the owner can say that he has exercised all proper care unless he can prove that he neither knew nor ought to have known of any such occurrence. For if he did know of it he would have been bound to take adequate steps to prevent any resulting break-down. It may well be that it would be sufficient for him to prove that he had a proper system for drivers reporting all unusual occurrences and that none had been reported to him.

. . . It may be that they [the respondents] could have proved that, so far as they knew or could have discovered by reasonable enquiry, nothing unusual ever happened to it which could have led to this corrosion. Or it may be that they did know of something but did not realise the possible danger resulting from it although they ought to have done so. We do not know. They had to prove that in all the circumstances which they knew or ought to have known that they took all proper steps to avoid danger. In my opinion they have failed to do that, and I am therefore of opinion that this appeal should be allowed. Damages have been agreed to be £5,700.

LORD DONOVAN: . . . The plea of "latent defect" made by the respondents had to be made good by them. It was for them to show that they [had] taken all reasonable care, and that despite this, the defect remained hidden.

They proved that the pipe in question was visually inspected in situ once a week; that the brake pedal was on these occasions depressed to check for leaks from the pipe and none seen; that nothing more than such visual inspection of the pipe was required by the Ministry of Transport rules or the maker's advice. On the question of the likelihood of corrosion of the pipe they produced two expert witnesses, the first of whom said there was nothing unusual about it, and the second of whom said it was extremely unusual. The appellant's expert witness had testified without challenge that corrosion occurred quite often. The trial judge did not resolve this discord by any finding of his own. The respondents' second expert witness considered that the pipe had been subjected to some unusual treatment from outside by some chemical agent.

It is obvious that visual inspection of the pipe in situ, however frequent, could not disclose corrosion on the hidden part of it. The question, therefore, suggests itself at once: did not reasonable care require the removal of the pipe at suitable intervals so that the whole of it could be inspected? It is equally obvious that the answer to this question must depend partly on the age of the vehicle, partly on the mileage it had done, and partly on the load it had been carrying. All these things affected the measure of reasonable care which the respondents had to exercise.

The lorry was an Albion lorry, five years old. The speedometer showed that it had done 52,000 miles, but since speedometers begin again at nought once they have registered 100,000 miles, nobody has suggested that reliance could be placed on the reading of 52,000. But no evidence was tendered as to mileage. So that the lorry might have done either 150,000 or 250,000 miles in its five years of life. As to the loads it carried, we know no more than that on the day of the accident it was carrying 9½ tons of concrete pipes.

Yet the kind of load this lorry had been carrying in the past was something which had to be known in order to assess the measure of the duty of reasonable care resting on the respondents. For the corrosion of the pipe was caused by some chemical agent. Had the lorry, therefore, been carrying chemicals of any kind? Or had it operated under conditions where salt (also a corrosive agent) might come in contact with the pipe? Or had it at some time been adapted for carrying cattle and done so? If any of these things were the case then clearly visual inspection of the pipe in situ would not have been enough. It should have been removed at intervals so that the whole of it, and not merely part of it, could be examined.

It was for the respondents to deal with these matters by evidence. They were asserting, and had to prove, that they exercised all reasonable care; but whether they had or not depended on what the facts were in the foregoing respects. Yet on these matters they chose to give no evidence at all. The result was that they failed to establish their defence and should have lost the case.

Nield J., however, decided in their favour. His final conclusion was thus expressed:

"In these circumstances there is no negligence proved against the driver or against the [respondents]."

The real question, however, was whether the respondents had proved that they had exercised all reasonable care; and, I repeat, facts essential to a conclusion on this point had not been put before the court. Furthermore the learned judge said, after stating that the issue was whether the defect would have been discovered by reasonable care according to standards current at the time—

> "In considering that part of the case, the first matter to notice is that it is agreed that visual inspection was all that could reasonably be required of the owners of such a vehicle and I am much impressed by the evidence that to remove these pipes involves considerable danger in the sense that they may kink or fracture, and thus it is plainly the custom in the ordinary course of things not to remove these fluid pipes."

I am unable to discover how and where it was agreed by the appellant that visual inspection in situ was all that could reasonably be required. Neither she nor her advisers could possibly so agree unless they knew among other things what loads the lorry had been in the habit of carrying. And while the pipes might not be removed "in the ordinary course of things" it was for the respondents to prove that this lorry's life had conformed to "the ordinary course of things". But they chose to leave the case in the state where, for all one knew, the lorry might have been carrying carboys of acid about regularly, or had been coming into contact with sea water or salt frequently, or had been engaged in carrying cattle. One of the respondents' expert witnesses, a Mr. Tyndall, who was a vehicle examiner employed by the Ministry of Transport, said:

> "Unless you had some suspicion of anything, I would never suggest that they [i.e. brake pipes] are removed; unless, of course, they had been making trips to a seaside place where they had been near salt water and then, of course, one would definitely request them to be removed."

It was, therefore, incumbent on the respondents, if they were to sustain their plea of latent defect undiscoverable by the exercise of ordinary care, to prove where the vehicle had been and what it had been carrying whilst in their service and in what conditions it had operated. Only then could the standard of reasonable care be ascertained, and their conduct measured against it. . . .

I differ from Nield J. with regret. But the tenor of his judgment suggests that he dealt with this case as though it were the more usual type where the onus of proof lay on the appellant; whereas in fact the burden of proof that they had taken all reasonable care rested on the respondents. For these reasons, which are substantially those given by Sachs L.J. in his dissenting judgment below,[1] I am of the opinion that the appeal should be allowed and the appellant should recover from the respondents the agreed damage of £5,700. . . .

LORD PEARSON: My Lords, in my opinion, the decision in this appeal turns on what is sometimes called "the evidential burden of proof", which is to be distinguished from the formal (or legal or technical) burden of proof. . . . For the purposes of the present case the distinction can be simply stated in this way. In an action for negligence the plaintiff must allege, and has the burden of proving, that the accident was caused by negligence on the part of the defendants. That is the issue throughout the trial, and in giving judgment at the end of the trial the judge has to decide whether he is satisfied on a balance of probabilities that the accident was caused by negligence on the part of the defendants, and if he is not so satisfied the plaintiff's action fails. The formal burden of proof does not shift. But if in the course of the trial there is proved a set of facts which raises a prima facie inference that the accident was caused by negligence on the part of the defendants, the issue will be decided in the plaintiff's favour unless the defendants by their evidence provide some answer which is adequate to displace the prima facie inference. In this situation there is said to be an evidential

---

1. [1969] 1 All E.R. at p. 403; [1969] 2 W.L.R. at p. 149.

burden of proof resting on the defendants. I have some doubts whether it is strictly correct to use the expression "burden of proof" with this meaning, as there is a risk of it being confused with the formal burden of proof, but it is a familiar and convenient usage. . . .

. . . The respondents and the driver were, by this plea [of latent defect], alleging and, therefore, admitting that the accident was caused by a sudden brake failure resulting from corrosion of the brake fluid pipe, and were assuming an evidential burden of proving that the corrosion occurred without any fault on their part and that its existence was not discoverable by the exercise of reasonable care by them.

That was the effect of the pleading of the respondents and the driver, but in any case the physical facts of the case raise a strong prima facie inference that the respondents and the driver[1] were at fault and that their fault was a cause of the accident. . . .

[Having referred to the facts of the case, he continued:] From these facts it seems to me clear, as a prima facie inference, that the accident must have been due to default of the respondents in respect of inspection or maintenance or both. Unless they had a satisfactory answer, sufficient to displace the inference, they should have been held liable.

The respondents' answer was that they had followed a practice of relying solely on visual inspection of the pipes, and that this was a general and proper practice. The learned judge's finding was that "it is plainly the custom in the ordinary course of things not to remove these fluid pipes". This may be a general and proper practice for an ordinary case in which there are no special circumstances increasing the risk. But I think the respondents' answer should not have been accepted without evidence from the respondents sufficiently showing that this was an ordinary case without special circumstances increasing the risk.

. . . The respondents might perhaps have been able to show by evidence that the lorry had not been used in any way, or involved in any incident, that would cause abnormal corrosion or require special inspection or treatment, or at any rate that they neither knew nor ought to have known of any such use or incident. But they did not call any such evidence. Their answer was incomplete. They did not displace the inference, arising from the physical facts of the case, that the accident must have been due to their default in respect of inspection or maintenance or both.

While fully accepting the learned judge's findings of primary fact, I am of opinion that he drew a wrong conclusion in holding that the accident was not caused by negligence of the respondents. I would allow the appeal.

[LORD GUEST and VISCOUNT DILHORNE delivered speeches in favour of dismissing the appeal.]

Appeal allowed

Question

There is no express mention of *res ipsa loquitur* in the speeches in this case. Is it, nevertheless, correctly classified under this heading?

Notes

1. See the discussion of this case by P. S. Atiyah, *loc. cit.* At p. 341, he points out that, in their dissenting speeches, both Lord Guest and Viscount Dilhorne "seem to have accepted that the defendants had the burden of disproving negligence but both held that the defendants had in fact discharged the burden".

2. In *Colvilles, Ltd.* v. *Devine*, [1969] 2 All E.R. 53, Lord Guest expressed the view (at p. 57) that if *res ipsa loquitur* applied, the appellants in that case

---

1. [But note that there was no appeal from the dismissal of the action against the driver.]

were "absolved if they can give a reasonable explanation of the accident and show this explanation was consistent with no lack of care on their part." See also Lord Upjohn, at p. 58; cf. Lord Donovan also at p. 58, and see generally Atiyah, *loc. cit.*, pp. 342–344, especially in relation to Lord Donovan's speech.

Lloyde v. West Midlands Gas Board

Court of Appeal　　　　　　　　　[1971] 2 All E.R. 1240

The plaintiff was injured in what the trial judge found was an explosion of gas and air caused by a failure of the gas apparatus, which was fixed in an outhouse. The learned judge inferred on a balance of probabilities that the failure was more likely to be due to the defendants' failure either to install it properly or to maintain it than to any other cause. He awarded damages to the plaintiff, and, on appeal by the defendants, the plaintiff relied on *res ipsa loquitur*.

DAVIES L.J.: . . . I have come to the conclusion that unfortunately this case is in an unsatisfactory state. The defendants came to meet the case as pleaded. They defeated the main case made against them, i.e. that of constant leaks and failure to heed complaints; but right at the end of the trial they found themselves confronted with what I regard as an entirely different case, that of defective installation or maintenance. Then, in this court, the judgment against them was sought to be supported on the principle of res ipsa loquitur which . . . formed no part of the argument below. In this state of affairs, though I am quite unable to say that counsel for the defendants has satisfied me that there should be judgment for the defendants, I am of opinion that there should be a new trial on the issue of liability. . . .

MEGAW L.J.: I agree that there should be a new trial, for the reasons given by Davies L.J. I agree that it is undesirable in those circumstances to express anything which might be construed as a view on any question of fact which may arise at the new trial; but since the plaintiff in this appeal contends that the judgment should be upheld on the basis of res ipsa loquitur and the defendants contend that res ipsa loquitur has no application and, therefore, that judgment should be entered in their favour, I think it desirable to express my views on those respective contentions of law.

The defendants urge that the doctrine of res ipsa loquitur has no application in a case such as this. The gas apparatus—meter and pipes—was on the plaintiff's premises and could have been damaged either wilfully or accidentally by the plaintiff himself, or by anyone else who might have had access to the shed in which the apparatus was installed. Hence, it is claimed, the inference cannot be drawn, merely because there was a sudden and unheralded large-scale eruption of gas on 5 January 1968, that this was caused by any negligence on the part of the defendants, whether in supplying defective apparatus or in installing it carelessly or in its maintenance. On the hypothesis which the judge found to be established—that is, no evidence of earlier leakages of gas—the apparatus had been in existence carrying out its function perfectly satisfactorily for nine months or more.

The plaintiff, on the other hand, contends that once it is proved that gas apparatus such as this has suddenly collapsed, or in some other way has suddenly produced a large-scale escape of gas, the doctrine of res ipsa loquitur inevitably comes into operation, and nonetheless because the apparatus is on the plaintiff's premises so that interference with it is at least a possibility. The plaintiff says that res ipsa loquitur applies and entitles the plaintiff to succeed, unless the defendants show that, on balance of probability, there was some cause of the collapse inconsistent with their negligence or that they had exercised all reasonable care. Such a cause would include outside interference with the apparatus; but the onus would be on the defendants.

I doubt whether it is right to describe res ipsa loquitur as a "doctrine". I think it is no more than an exotic, though convenient, phrase to describe what is in essence no more than a common sense approach, not limited by technical rules, to the assessment of the effect of evidence in certain circumstances. It means that a plaintiff prima facie establishes negligence where: (i) it is not possible for him to prove precisely what was the relevant act or omission which set in train the events leading to the accident; but (ii) on the evidence as it stands at the relevant time it is more likely than not that the effective cause of the accident was *some* act or omission of the defendant or of someone for whom the defendant is responsible, which act or omission constitutes a failure to take proper care for the plaintiff's safety.

I have used the words "evidence as it stands at the relevant time". I think this can most conveniently be taken as being at the close of the plaintiff's case. On the assumption that a submission of no case is then made, would, the evidence, as it then stands, enable the plaintiff to succeed because, although the precise cause of the accident cannot be established, the proper inference on balance of probability is that that cause, whatever it may have been, involved a failure by the defendant to take due care for the plaintiff's safety? If so, res ipsa loquitur. If not, the plaintiff fails. Of course, if the defendant does not make a submission of no case, the question still falls to be tested by the same criterion, but evidence for the defendant, given thereafter, may rebut the inference. The res, which previously spoke for itself, may be silenced, or its voice may, on the whole of the evidence, become too weak or muted. That the question of res ipsa loquitur has to be tested on an assessment of evidence is, I think, confirmed by a passage in the judgment of Lord Evershed M.R. in *Moore* v. *R. Fox & Sons, Ltd.*[1] He said:

> "It must, as I venture to think, always be a question whether, on proof of the happening of a particular event, it can with truth be said that the thing speaks for itself. The event or 'thing' may, or may not, produce that result. Not every accident has, without more, that effect. If, on a closer analysis of the happening and its circumstances, it does not in truth appear fairly to follow that the proper inference is one of negligence, then the case is not one of res ipsa loquitur at all."

The plaintiff must prove facts which give rise to what may be called the res ipsa loquitur situation. There is no assumption in his favour of such facts. Thus, in the prototype case of res ipsa loquitur, *Byrne* v. *Boadle*,[2] the plaintiff, in the absence of admissions by the defendant, had to prove, not only that the barrel fell on to his head while he was walking along the street, but also that it fell from the window of a warehouse which was in occupation of and use by the defendant. So here. The plaintiff does not achieve the res ipsa loquitur situation, where the apparatus said to have been defective was in his own house and could have been interfered with by persons or events for whom or which the defendant is not responsible, unless he establishes at least the improbability of such interference having caused the relevant defect. Hence, I do not accept the plaintiff's submission that the onus was on the defendants to prove the probability of some relevant interference with the apparatus.

However, the defendants' submission in my view is also wrong. The application of res ipsa loquitur is not necessarily and inevitably excluded merely because there has been the possibility of outside interference with the thing (here the gas apparatus) through which the accident happened. The authorities do not state or indicate any such artificial limitation. Suppose this explosion had occurred within a few hours, or a few days, after the defendants had installed the apparatus. Could it sensibly be suggested that res ipsa loquitur could not be invoked by the plaintiff, once he had proved the facts as to the nature of the explosion, the date of the installation and the absence of third party interference? Here, of course, it is not a question of a few hours or a few days. It is a question of many months; but the principle cannot be different although, of course, the plaintiff may face a much more difficult task evidentially in

---

1. [1956] 1 Q.B. 596, at p. 614; [1956] 1 All E.R. 182, at p. 190.
2. (1863), 2 H. & C. 722.

relation to the possibility of outside interference. But if at the end of the evidence for the plaintiff, taking into account the possibility, whatever it may be, of outside interference, on the evidence and on proper inferences one way or the other from the evidence or absence of evidence with regard thereto, the correct conclusion is that on balance of probability the cause of the accident was some negligent act or omission on the part of the defendants, then res ipsa loquitur applies, and, subject to the effect of any rebutting evidence on behalf of the defendants thereafter, the plaintiff's claim succeeds. . . .

[KARMINSKI L.J. agreed with DAVIES L.J. that there should be a new trial. DAVIES and KARMINSKI L.JJ. did not express their views on *res ipsa loquitur*.]

New trial ordered on the issue of liability

Question

Is the judgment of Megaw L.J. consistent with *Henderson v. Henry E. Jenkins & Sons*?

Note

M. A. Millner in his book *Negligence in Modern Law* expresses the following opinion (at pp. 92–93, footnotes omitted):

"*Res ipsa loquitur* is an immensely important vehicle for importing strict liability into negligence cases. In practice, there are many cases where *res ipsa loquitur* is properly invoked in which the defendant is unable to show affirmatively either that he took all reasonable precautions to avoid injury or that the particular cause of the injury was not associated with negligence on his part. Industrial and traffic accidents, and injuries caused by defective merchandise, are so frequently of this type that the theoretical limitations of the maxim are quite overshadowed by its practical significance. The result is a certain disparity between the theory of fault liability underlying negligence and the actual functioning of the remedy, which could best be resolved by the open recognition of certain spheres of conduct as carrying an "insurance" against risk. Injuries sustained in the sphere of such guaranteed safety would then cease to be governed by negligence considerations, and the incipient tendency of *res ipsa loquitur* towards strict liability would, in a defined class of case, be consummated by appropriate legislation."

5

Causation and Remoteness of Damage

This topic is relevant to all torts, although most of the decided cases are on the tort of negligence. A connection must be shown between the defendant's breach of duty and the damage suffered by the plaintiff. The language used by writers and judges to describe this problem is perplexing. For example, it is said that a defendant is not liable unless he "caused" the damage; on the other hand, it is said that he is not liable for all the damage he has "caused". Adjectives such as "legal", "proximate" or "remote" do little to unravel the mysteries of this topic.

What the courts are involved in are two distinct inquiries. The first is the question of "cause-and-effect". This is sometimes called "factual causation", and is said to depend upon notions of the physical sequence of events. The "but for" test—the defendant's breach of duty is a cause of the damage if that damage would not have occurred *but for* it—is widely applied, but does not solve all problems particularly where there are multiple causes (p. 173, *post*). In truth the courts do not view causation in the same way as a scientist or metaphysician, but in the manner of the "man in the street" (*per* Lord Wright in *Yorkshire Dale Steamship Co., Ltd.* v. *Minister of War Transport (The Coxwold)*, [1942] A.C. 691, at p. 706).

The second inquiry is how far the defendant should be held liable for the consequences of his breach of duty. A single act of negligence, for example, may lead to disastrous consequences; in theory they may be infinite. Some practical and reasonable limitation has to be placed on loss-shifting. In the tort of negligence, the courts have moved towards the formulation that the kind of *harm to* this plaintiff must be foreseeable (*The Wagon Mound* (No. 1), [1961] A.C. 388; [1961] 1 All E.R. 404, p. 192, *post*). The earlier "direct consequences" test (*Re Polemis*, [1921] 3 K.B. 560, p. 188, *post*) still provides an interesting contrast, and, indeed, may not be wholly irreconcilable with the "foreseeability" approach.

1. FACTUAL CAUSATION

Barnett v. Chelsea & Kensington Hospital Management Committee

Queen's Bench Division   [1968] 1 All E.R. 1068

The plaintiff's husband, after drinking some tea, experienced persistent vomiting for a three hour period. Along with two other men who had also drunk the tea and who were in a similar condition, he went to the casualty department of a hospital. A nurse (against whom no complaint was made) contacted Dr. Banerjee by telephone telling him that the three men were complaining of vomiting after drinking tea. The doctor, who was himself tired and unwell, sent a message to them through the nurse to the effect that they should go home to bed and call their own doctors (with the exception of one of the men who had to have an X-ray on account of a separate incident). Some time later, the plaintiff's husband died from arsenical poisoning, and the coroner's verdict was one of murder by a person or persons unknown.

NIELD J. [having found that "the defendants [the Hospital Management Committee] were negligent and in breach of their duty in that they or their servants or agents did not see and did not examine and did not admit and did not treat the deceased", continued:] . . . It remains to consider whether it is shown that the deceased's death was caused by this negligence or whether, as the defendants have said, the deceased must have died in any event. In his concluding submission counsel for the plaintiff submitted that Dr. Banerjee should have examined the deceased, and, had he done so, he would have caused tests to be made which would have indicated the treatment required and that, since the defendants were at fault in these respects, therefore the onus of proof passed to the defendants to show that the appropriate treatment would have failed, and authorities were cited to me. I find myself unable to accept this argument and I am of the view that the onus of proof remains on the plaintiff, and I have in mind (without quoting it) the decision quoted by counsel for the defendants in *Bonnington Castings, Ltd.* v. *Wardlaw*.[1] However, were it otherwise and the onus did pass to the defendants, then I would find that they have discharged it, as I would proceed to show.

There has been put before me a timetable which, I think, is of much importance. The deceased attended at the casualty department at 8.5 or 8.10 a.m. If Dr. Banerjee had got up and dressed and come to see the three men and examined them and decided to admit them, the deceased . . . could not have been in bed in a ward before 11 a.m. I accept Dr. Goulding's evidence that an intravenous drip would not have been set up before 12 noon, and if potassium loss was suspected it could not have been discovered until 12.30. Dr. Lockett, dealing with this, said "If [the deceased] had not been treated until after 12 noon the chances of survival were not good".

Without going in detail into the considerable volume of technical evidence which has been put before me, it seems to me to be the case that when death results from arsenical poisoning it is brought about by two conditions; on the one hand dehydration and on the other disturbance of the enzyme processes. If the principal condition is one of enzyme disturbance—as I am of the view that it was here—then the only method of treatment which is likely to succeed is the use of the specific or antidote which is commonly called B.A.L. Dr. Goulding said this in the course of his evidence:

"The only way to deal with this is to use the specific B.A.L. I see no reasonable prospect of the deceased being given B.A.L. before the time at which he died,"

and at a later point in his evidence:

"I feel that even if fluid loss had been discovered death would have been caused by the enzyme disturbance. Death might have occurred later."

I regard that evidence as very moderate, and that it might be a true assessment of the situation to say that there was no chance of B.A.L. being administered before the death of the deceased.

For these reasons, I find that the plaintiff has failed to establish, on the grounds of probability, that the defendants' negligence caused the death of the deceased.

Judgment for the defendants

---

1. [1956] A.C. 613; [1956] 1 All E.R. 615.

Note

In the sphere of factual causation the "but for" test is often applied (a point made at p. 170, *ante*). *The Empire Jamaica*, [1957] A.C. 386; [1956] 3 All E.R. 144 provides a useful illustration of the application of this test. In that case the respondents admitted that a collision of two ships at sea was due to the fault of their second mate. Their liability could be limited under the Merchant Shipping Act 1894 if the collision had occurred without the respondents' "actual fault or privity". The House of Lords took the view that the respondents had good reason to think that the second mate was fully competent for the job, but one point raised by the appellants was that there had been a breach of a Hong Kong Shipping Ordinance because the second mate was not duly certificated nor had any exemption been obtained. It was held that even if there had been a breach (in that the respondents had shipped the second mate without any exemption having been granted), nevertheless this was not a cause of the collision. If the application for the exemption had been made, it appeared that it would have been granted immediately, or that the respondents would have been told that it was unnecessary. In other words, all the events would still have taken place.

Performance Cars, Ltd. v. Abraham

Court of Appeal   [1961] 3 All E.R. 413

The defendant, whose car had collided with the plaintiffs' Rolls Royce causing damage to its wing and bumper, accepted responsibility for the accident. The damage to the wing necessitated a respray of the lower part of the car. A fortnight before, this same Rolls Royce had been in a collision caused by the fault of another person and the damages awarded in that case included the cost of a respray of the lower part of the car. However, nothing had been recovered under that judgment, and the claim against the defendant in this case also included the cost of a respray. This sum was included in the award of damages made by the county court judge, but an appeal was allowed by the Court of Appeal.

LORD EVERSHED M.R.: . . . The vital fact is that when the defendant hit the plaintiffs' motor car the work of restoration to the latter as the result of the first accident had not yet been done. In these circumstances it has been said by the defendant that he is not liable for the £75 claimed against him, being the cost of respraying the whole of the lower part of the body of the Rolls-Royce.

What is said may be quite simply thus expressed. At the date of the defendant's collision the Rolls-Royce's condition was such that it had then in any case to be resprayed so that the need for so doing did not arise from the defendant's wrongful act. On the other side it is said that here you have two separate tortfeasors and each must be liable for the consequences of his tortious act naturally and properly flowing from the respective wrongs. It is conceded by the plaintiffs that they could not recover the cost of respraying from both wrongdoers, the earlier motorist and the defendant, and they offer accordingly to assign to the defendant the benefit of the earlier judgment, at least so far as it relates to this part of the claim.

The point appears, as I have said, novel and interesting but, with all respect to the county court judge, I have come to the conclusion that the defendant's view is right and that he is entitled to succeed. . . . The fact in the present case is that the defendant struck a motor car already damaged, the damage including the necessity in any case of respraying the whole of the lower part of the body. The case is to my mind rendered less easy because the respraying is something special to the character of this particular and rather luxurious motor car. The principle, as it seems to me, is the same as that applicable to the example stated by Donovan L.J. in the course of the argument. Suppose a man wrongfully damages my motor car by splintering part of the windscreen so that, as the inevitable result, I must have a new windscreen, the cost of which is damage properly flowing from the wrongful act which I have suffered. Then, suppose before my windscreen has in fact been replaced, if you will, while I am driving my motor car to the place where the new windscreen is to be fitted, another wrongdoer strikes my car and splinters another part of my windscreen. If the plaintiffs are right, it must follow that I can claim, if I have not already actually recovered from the first wrongdoer, the cost of replacing the windscreen from the second. The same result would follow, as it seems to me, if the first damage to my windscreen had been my own fault or if, in the present case, the plaintiffs had by their own fault damaged the back of their Rolls-Royce motor car.

I do not multiply examples but I have in the end felt compelled to the conclusion that the necessity for respraying was not the result of the defendant's wrongdoing because that necessity already existed. The Rolls-Royce, when the defendant struck it, was in a condition which already required that it should be resprayed in any event. . . .

In my judgment in the present case the defendant should be taken to have injured a motor car that was already injured in certain respects, that is, in respect of the need for respraying; and the result is that to the extent of that need or injury the damage claimed did not flow from the defendant's wrongdoing. It may no doubt be unfortunate for the plaintiffs that the collisions took place in the order in which they did. Had the first collision been that brought about by the defendant and had they recovered the £75 now in question from him, they could not clearly have recovered the same sum again from the other wrongdoer. It is, however, in my view irrelevant (if unfortunate for the plaintiffs) that the judgment obtained against the other wrongdoer has turned out to be worthless. For the reasons which I have stated I would allow the appeal.

[HARMAN and DONOVAN L.JJ. delivered judgments in favour of allowing the appeal.]

Note

It should be noted that the "but-for" test does not provide a complete answer to all the difficulties provided by factual causation, as the following passage by D. M. A. Strachan in "The Scope and Application of the 'But-For' Causal Test" (1970), 33 M.L.R. 386, at p. 391 reveals (footnotes omitted):

> "The 'but for' test, though attractive and serviceable because of its basic simplicity, is incapable of dealing with all questions of factual causation. In certain situations common sense demands that a person be held responsible for a certain injury although that injury would have occurred without his participation. It is in situations where there are two independent factors, each being sufficient to produce the injury, that the test proves unsatisfactory. Such factors may operate either concurrently or successively. They operate concurrently if two independent fires, both negligently started, converge on a house and demolish it. Short shrift should be given to the contention that the damage is not caused by one, since another set of circumstances existed which would have caused the damage independently. The logical conclusion, if such a contention were to succeed, would be that the house-owner would be left with no redress since neither fire could be said to have caused the loss.

> The problem becomes more convoluted when the independent factors, each of which is sufficient to produce the injury, are successive rather than concurrent."

Baker v. Willoughby

House of Lords   [1969] 3 All E.R. 1528

The appellant, when crossing a road, had been knocked down by the respondent's car and his left leg and ankle were injured, the ankle becoming stiff. Apart from suffering pain, he lost those "amenities of life" which are dependent on the ability to move freely and his earning capacity was reduced. The House of Lords restored the trial judge's apportionment of 75% responsibility on the respondent motorist for the accident. After the accident but before the trial of the action the appellant was involved in several different sorts of employment. One day he was sorting scrap metal when he was shot by one of two men who had unsuccessfully demanded money from him. His left leg was so badly affected by the shot that its amputation was necessary and the substitution of an artificial limb for what had been a stiff leg increased his disability. On the question of the effect on the respondent's liability of the second injury:

LORD REID: . . . The appellant argues that the loss which he suffered from the car accident has not been diminished by his second injury. He still suffers from reduced capacity to earn although these[1] may have been to some extent increased. And he will still suffer these losses for as long as he would have done because it is not said that the second injury curtailed his expectation of life. The respondent on the other hand argues that the second injury removed the very limb from which the earlier disability had stemmed, and that therefore no loss suffered thereafter can be attributed to the respondent's negligence. He says that the second injury submerged or obliterated the effect of the first and that all loss thereafter must be attributed to the second injury. The trial judge[1a] rejected this argument which he said was more ingenious than attractive. But it was accepted by the Court of Appeal.[2]

The respondent's argument was succinctly put to your Lordships by his counsel. He could not run before the second injury; he cannot run now. But the cause is now quite different. The former cause was an injured leg but now he has no leg and the former cause can no longer operate. His counsel was inclined to agree that if the first injury had caused some neurosis or other mental disability, that disability might be regarded as still flowing from the first accident; even if it had been increased by the second accident the respondent might still have to pay for that part which he caused. I agree with that and I think that any distinction between a neurosis and a physical injury depends on a wrong view of what is the proper subject for compensation. A man is not compensated for the physical injury; he is compensated for the loss which he suffers as a result of that injury. His loss is not in having a stiff leg; it is in his inability to lead a full life, his inability to enjoy those amenities which depend on freedom of movement and his inability to earn as much as he used to earn or could have earned if there had been no accident. In this case the second injury did not diminish any of these. So why should it be regarded as having obliterated or superseded them?

If it were the case that in the eye of the law an effect could only have one cause then the respondent might be right. It is always necessary to prove that any loss for which damages can be given was caused by the defendant's negligent act. But it is commonplace that the law regards many events as having two causes; that happens whenever there is contributory negligence, for then the law says that the injury was caused both by the negligence of the defendant and by the negligence of the plaintiff. And generally it does not matter which negligence occurred first in point of time.

I see no reason why the appellant's present disability cannot be regarded as having two causes, and if authority be needed for this I find it in *Harwood* v. *Wyken Colliery Co.*[3] That was a Workmen's Compensation Act 1906 case. But causation cannot be different in tort. There an accident made the man only fit for light work. And then a heart disease supervened and it also caused him only to be fit for light work. The argument for the employer was the same as in the present case. Before the disease supervened the workman's incapacity was caused by the accident. Thereafter it was caused by the disease and the previous accident became irrelevant; he would have been equally incapacitated if the accident had never happened. But Hamilton L.J. said:[4]

---

1. [The other loss referred to is loss of amenities of life.]
1a. [1969] 1 Q.B. 38; [1968] 2 All E.R. 236.
2. [1969] 2 All E.R. 549; [1969] 2 W.L.R. 489.
3. [1913] 2 K.B. 158.
4. [1913] 2 K.B. at p. 169.

". . . he is not disentitled to be paid compensation by reason of the supervention of a disease of the heart. It cannot be said of him that partial incapacity for work has not resulted and is not still resulting from the injury. All that can be said is that such partial incapacity is not still resulting 'solely' from the injury."

The respondent founded on another workmen's compensation case in this House—*Hogan* v. *Bentinck West Hartley Collieries (Owners), Ltd.*[1] There the man had an accident but his condition was aggravated by an ill-judged surgical operation and it was held by the majority in this House that his incapacity must be attributed solely to the operation and not to the accident. But *Harwood's* case[2] was not disapproved by any one. Lord Simonds, one of the majority, quoted[3] with approval from the judgment of du Parcq L.J. in *Rothwell* v. *Caverswall Stone Co., Ltd.*[4]

"If, however, the existing incapacity ought fairly to be attributed to a new cause which has intervened and ought no longer to be attributed to the original injury, it may properly be held to result from the new cause and not from the original injury even though, but for the original injury, there would have been no incapacity."

Then having said that negligent or inefficient treatment by a doctor may amount to a new cause du Parcq L.J. continued:[4]

"In such a case, if the arbitrator is satisfied that the incapacity would have wholly ceased but for the omission, a finding of fact that the existing incapacity results from the new cause, and not from the injury, will be justified."

This part was also quoted by Lord Simonds.[5] I think it clear that du Parcq L.J. meant that one can only attribute the disability to the new cause alone and disregard the accident if it appears that but for the new cause the man would have recovered, for then the injury by accident can no longer be operative as a cause. But this case is no authority for holding that, during the period when the injury by accident would still have incapacitated the man if he had had proper treatment, the ill-judged operation could be regarded as submerging or obliterating the original accident. It therefore does not assist the respondent.

We were referred to a number of shipping cases where the question was who must pay for demurrage or loss of profit when a vessel damaged by two mishaps was in dock to have both sets of damage repaired at the same time. It would seem that much depends on which mishap rendered the vessel unseaworthy or no longer a profit-earning machine. I get no help from these cases because liability for personal injury cannot depend on which mishap renders the man "unseaworthy" or "not a profit-earning machine". If any assistance is to be got, it is I think from *The Haversham Grange*,[6] where neither collision rendered the vessel unseaworthy. The damage from the first collision took longer to repair than the damage from the second and it was held that the vessel responsible for the second collision did not have to contribute towards payment for time lost in repairs. In my view the latter would have had to pay for any time after the repairs from the first damage had been completed because that time could not be claimed from the first wrongdoer. The first wrongdoer must pay for all damage caused by him but no more. The second is not liable for any damage caused by the first wrongdoer but must pay for any additional damage caused by him. That was the ground of decision in *Performance Cars, Ltd.* v. *Abraham*[7]. . . .

1. [1949] 1 All E.R. 588.
2. [1913] 2 K.B. 158.
3. [1949] 1 All E.R. at p. 592.
4. [1944] 2 All E.R. 350, at p. 365.
5. [1949] 1 All E.R. at p. 592.
6. [1905] P. 307.
7. [1962] 1 Q.B. 33; [1961] 3 All E.R. 413.

These cases exemplify the general rule that a wrongdoer must take the plaintiff (or his property) as he finds him; that may be to his advantage or disadvantage. In the present case the robber is not responsible or liable for the damage caused by the respondent; he would only have to pay for additional loss to the appellant by reason of his now having an artificial limb instead of a stiff leg.

It is argued—if a man's death before the trial reduces the damages why do injuries which he has received before the trial not also reduce the damages? I think that it depends on the nature and result of the later injuries. Suppose that but for the first injuries the plaintiff could have looked forward to 20 years of working life and that the injuries inflicted by the defendant reduced his earning capacity. Then but for the later injuries the plaintiff would have recovered for loss of earning capacity during 20 years. And then suppose that later injuries were such that at the date of the trial his expectation of life had been reduced to two years. Then he could not claim for 20 years of loss of earning capacity because in fact he will only suffer loss of earning capacity for two years. Thereafter he will be dead and the defendant could not be required to pay for a loss which it is now clear that the plaintiff will in fact never suffer. But that is not this case; here the appellant will continue to suffer from the disabilities caused by the car accident for as long as he would have done if his leg had never been shot and amputated.

If the later injury suffered before the date of the trial either reduces the disabilities from the injury for which the defendant is liable, or shortens the period during which they will be suffered by the plaintiff then the defendant will have to pay less damages. But if the later injuries merely become a concurrent cause of the disabilities caused by the injury inflicted by the defendant, then in my view they cannot diminish the damages. Suppose that the plaintiff has to spend a month in bed before the trial because of some illness unconnected with the original injury, the defendant cannot say that he does not have to pay anything in respect of that month; during that month the original injuries and the new illness are concurrent causes of his inability to work and that does not reduce the damages.

Finally, I must advert to the pain suffered and to be suffered by the appellant as a result of the car accident. If the result of the amputation was that the appellant suffered no more pain thereafter, then he could not claim for pain after the amputation which he would never suffer. But the facts with regard to this are not clear, the amount awarded for pain subsequent to the date of the amputation was probably only a small part of the £1,600 damages and counsel for the respondent did not make a point of this. So in these circumstances we can neglect this matter. . . .

LORD PEARSON: . . . There is a plausible argument for the respondent on the following lines. The original accident, for which the respondent is liable, inflicted on the appellant a permanently injured left ankle, which caused pain from time to time, diminished his mobility and so reduced his earning capacity, and was likely to lead to severe arthritis. The proper figure of damages for those consequences of the accident, as assessed by the judge before making his apportionment, was £1,600. That was the proper figure for those consequences if they were likely to endure for a normal period and run a normal course. But the supervening event, when the robbers shot the appellant in his left leg, necessitated an amputation of the left leg above the knee. The consequences of the original accident therefore have ceased. He no longer suffers pain in his left ankle, because there no longer is a left ankle. He will never have the arthritis. There is no longer any loss of mobility through stiffness or weakness of the left ankle, because it is no longer there. The injury to the left ankle, resulting from the original accident, is not still operating as one of two concurrent causes both producing discomfort and disability. It is not operating at all nor causing anything. The present state of disablement, with the stump and the artificial leg on the left side, was caused wholly by the supervening event and not at all by the original accident. Thus the consequences of the original accident have been submerged and obliterated by the greater consequences of the supervening event.

That is the argument, and it is formidable. But it must not be allowed to succeed, because it produces manifest injustice. The supervening event has not made the appellant less lame nor less disabled nor less deprived of amenities. It has not shortened the period over which he will be suffering. It has made him more lame, more disabled, more deprived of amenities. He should not have less damages through being worse off than might have been expected.

The nature of the injustice becomes apparent if the supervening event is treated as a tort (as indeed it was) and if one envisages the appellant suing the robbers who shot him. They would be entitled, as the saying is, to "take the plaintiff as they find him". (*Performance Cars, Ltd.* v. *Abraham.*[1]) They have not injured and disabled a previously fit and able-bodied man. They have only made an already lame and disabled man more lame and more disabled. Take, for example, the reduction of earnings. The original accident reduced his earnings from £x per week to £y per week, and the supervening event further reduced them from £y per week to £z per week. If the respondent's argument is correct, there is, as counsel for the appellant has pointed out, a gap. The appellant recovers from the respondent the £x—y not for the whole period of the remainder of his working life, but only for the short period up to the date of the supervening event. The robbers are liable only for the £y—z from the date of the supervening event onwards. In the Court of Appeal[2] an ingenious attempt was made to fill the gap by holding that the damages recoverable from the later tortfeasors (the robbers) would include a novel head of damage, viz., the diminution of the appellant's damages recoverable from the original tortfeasor (the respondent). I doubt whether that would be an admissible head of damage; it looks too remote. In any case it would not help the appellant, if the later tortfeasors could not be found or were indigent and uninsured. These later tortfeasors cannot have been insured in respect of the robbery which they committed.

I think a solution of the theoretical problem can be found in cases such as this by taking a comprehensive and unitary view of the damage caused by the original accident. Itemisation of the damages by dividing them into heads and sub-heads is often convenient, but is not essential. In the end judgment is given for a single lump sum of damages and not for a total of items set out under heads and sub-heads. The original accident caused what may be called a "devaluation" of the plaintiff, in the sense that it produced a general reduction of his capacity to do things, to earn money and to enjoy life. For that devaluation the original tortfeasor should be and remain responsible to the full extent, unless before the assessment of the damages something has happened which either diminishes the devaluation (e.g. if there is an unexpected recovery from some of the adverse effects of the accident) or by shortening the expectation of life diminishes the period over which the plaintiff will suffer from the devaluation. If the supervening event is a tort, the second tortfeasor should be responsible for the additional devaluation caused by him. . . .

[LORD GUEST, VISCOUNT DILHORNE and LORD DONOVAN concurred with LORD REID.]

Appeal allowed

Question

Would the decision in this case have been different if the second "accident", leading to amputation of the limb, had been non-tortious? (See H. McGregor, "Variations on an Enigma: Successive Causes of Personal Injury" (1970), 33 M.L.R. 378, esp. at pp. 382–383.)

Note

It would seem from the facts stated in this case that the plaintiff would not have been in this particular job at the time of the second "accident" if it had not been for the disability suffered in the first accident. If so, then there was a

---

1. [1962] 1 Q.B. 33; [1961] 3 All E.R. 413.
2. [1969] 2 All E.R. 549; [1969] 2 W.L.R. 489.

link between the first accident and the later shooting of the plaintiff i.e. the shooting of the plaintiff would not have happened if the first accident had not taken place. However, the law clearly is not going to attribute responsibility for the effects of the shooting to the defendant in the first accident, and this next section deals with the process of selection among operative factual causes.

2. SELECTION AMONG OPERATIVE FACTUAL CAUSES

Stapley v. Gypsum Mines, Ltd.

House of Lords   [1953] 2 All E.R. 478

LORD ASQUITH OF BISHOPSTONE: . . . Courts of law must accept the fact that the philosophic doctrine of causation and the juridical doctrine of responsibility for the consequences of a negligent act are not congruent. To a philosopher—a term which I use in no disparaging sense, for what is a philosopher but one who, inter alia, reasons severely and with precision?—to a philosopher, the whole legal doctrine of responsibility must seem anomalous. To him, if event C could not occur unless each of two previous events—A and B—had preceded it, it would be unmeaning to say that A was more responsible for the occurrence of C than was B, or that B was more responsible for its occurrence than was A. The whole modern doctrine of contributory negligence,[1] however, proceeds on the contrary assumption. If not, there would be no question of apportionment. But the fission between law and strict logic goes deeper than that. For I am persuaded that it is still part of the law of this country that two causes may both be necessary preconditions of a particular result—damage to X—yet the one may, if the facts justify that conclusion, be treated as the real, substantial, direct or effective cause, and the other dismissed as at best a causa sine qua non and ignored for purposes of legal liability. . . .

Note

See also the passage from the speech of Lord Reid in this case, which is quoted by Upjohn L.J. in *Clay* v. *A. J. Crump & Sons, Ltd.*, [1964] 1 Q.B. 523; [1963] 3 All E.R. 687, p. 185, *opst*, and see p. 299, *post*.

Lord v. Pacific Steam Navigation Co., Ltd., The *Oropesa*

Court of Appeal   [1943] 1 All E.R. 211

The *Oropesa* and the *Manchester Regiment* were in collision at sea in a gale. The *Oropesa* struck the starboard side of the *Manchester Regiment* causing serious damage. The captain of the latter vessel, Captain Raper, decided to send off fifty members of the crew in lifeboats, leaving one lifeboat and twenty four crew members behind. He later took sixteen men with him in this lifeboat to row across to the *Oropesa* to arrange for messages to be sent, and for the *Oropesa* to be ready to render salvage assistance. He intended, thereafter, to return to his ship, but, on the first journey, the lifeboat capsized, and Lord was one of the nine men who were drowned. In the Admiralty Court, the blame was apportioned ⅔ths to the *Manchester Regiment* and ⅓th to the *Oropesa*, and there was no appeal from that judgment. The plaintiffs, Lord's parents, then successfully brought an action against the defendants, the owners of the *Oropesa*, who appealed.

LORD WRIGHT: . . . The main question which has been argued in this case is whether

---

1. [See Chap. 9.]

the death of Lord was a direct consequence of the collision which took place owing to the negligence of the Oropesa in colliding with the other vessel. Lord's representatives and dependants sue on the basis that the owners of the Oropesa owed a duty not only to the owners of the Manchester Regiment, but to the officers and crew and, if you like, the cargo; and that duty was a duty to navigate with care and skill so as not to injure them. Negligent navigation would obviously be a breach of that duty and, therefore, there is no doubt that there was here a breach of duty towards Lord. Then it is said there is no liability at all, because there is no legal connection between the breach of duty and the damage which took the form of the death of Lord. There are invoked certain well-known formulae, such as that the chain of causation was broken, that there was a *novus actus interveniens*. These somewhat august phrases, sanctified as they are by standing authority, only mean that there was not such a direct relationship between the act of negligence and the injury that the one could be treated as flowing directly from the other. Cases have been cited which have shown a very great difference of opinion on what is the true answer in different cases to that question whether the damage was direct or, on the other hand, to use another phrase, was too remote.

Looking at the various cases and the various possibilities of circumstances which may arise in which that question has to be determined, I confess I find it very difficult to formulate any precise and all-embracing rule. I do not think the cases which have been cited succeed in settling that difficulty. It may be said that in the law of negligence you may state general propositions; but when you come to determine whether in any particular case there has been actionable negligence, you really have to deal with that case on its facts. The principles are general, and can only be general. Unless there is real error in the formulation of the principles, the application of the principles to the actual issue is, therefore, a question of fact.

What were the facts here? The facts here, as I take it, were that Capt. Raper was faced with a very difficult proposition in considering what he was to do. Here was his ship in mid-Atlantic, helpless, without any means of propulsion, without any means of working any of its important auxiliary apparatus, a dead lump in the water, with only the saving thought that she might go on floating as long as her bulkheads did not give way. Capt. Raper had great faith in his ship. He thought she was a very strongly built ship and would go on floating. All the same he did realise (and in fact he so admits) that he was in a heavy sea, with a heavy gale blowing, a south-easterly gale, and that he was in a very perilous plight. As counsel for the respondents has pointed out in his argument, the captain of a ship is guilty of a misdemeanour under the Merchant Shipping Act 1894, s. 220, if he refuses or omits to do any lawful act proper and requisite to be done by him for preserving his ship from immediate loss, destruction or serious danger, or for preserving any person belonging to or on board her from immediate danger to life or limb. That applies to the crew as well. So much for the position of the captain. In those circumstances he took this decision—to separate the men who remained on board, while he went himself to share the danger. I do not think there is any doubt that he thought that on the Oropesa he would find valuable help, and certainly valuable advice. I do not really gather that anybody says he was acting unreasonably or improperly in doing that, or in thinking as he did, or, indeed, was doing anything but his duty. That appears to me so obvious that I do not propose to develop it any further.

So far as Lord was concerned, no one can say he acted unreasonably in getting into the boat. All he did was to obey lawful orders. If he had not obeyed the lawful orders of his captain, he would have committed a criminal offence under the Merchant Shipping Act 1894, s. 225 (1) (*b*). If the test is whether what was done was reasonable in the circumstances, I do not think there can be any question in this case that the action of Capt. Raper and the action of Lord were quite reasonable. Whether Capt. Raper took exactly the right course is another matter. He may have been guilty of an error of judgment; but, as I read the authorities—I think I am stating the effect of them correctly—that would not affect the question of whether the action he took and its consequences flowed directly from the negligence of the Oropesa.

. . . Having regard to the actual situation of this vessel and the situation of those on board her, I think that the vessel itself was in the grip of the casualty, or that the hand of the casualty lay heavily upon her; and that the conduct of Capt. Raper and Lord was directly caused by and directly flowed from it. There was an unbroken sequence of cause and effect between their action and the negligence which caused the ship to run into the Manchester Regiment. I think this view is confirmed by looking at the facts. The statement of the principle involves, I think, that the action was really dictated by the exigencies of the position. You cannot sever the conduct of Capt. Raper and that of Lord from the circumstances of being in mid-Atlantic and all the conditions affecting either ship. With that must be joined the duty which they were under in their positions as captain and sixth engineer.

There are some propositions that I think are well established and beyond question in connection with this class of case. One is that human action does not *per se* sever the connected sequence of acts. The mere fact that human action intervenes does not prevent the sufferer from saying that damages for injury due to that human action, as one of the elements·in the sequence, is recoverable from the original wrongdoer.

[Having discussed *The City of Lincoln*[1] and *Summers* v. *Salford Corpn.*,[2] he continued:] In all these cases the question is not whether there was what one may call negligence or not. Negligence involves a breach of duty as between the plaintiff and the defendant. The captain or Lord, or whoever was deciding what to do, were not then owing a duty to anybody except, possibly, a duty to minimise damage so far as they could; but that is not a point which is relevant here. They were acting in an emergency. If they did something which was outside the exigencies of the emergency, whether it was from miscalculation or from error, or, if you like, from mere wilfulness, they would be debarred from saying that there had not intervened a new cause. The question is not whether there was new negligence, but whether there was a new cause. . . . It must always be shown that there is something which I will call ultroneous, something unwarrantable, a new cause coming in disturbing the sequence of events, something that can be described as either unreasonable or extraneous or extrinsic. I doubt very much whether the law can be stated more precisely than that. . . .

. . . I am not prepared to say, and I do not say in this case that the fact that Lord's death was due in the circumstances to his leaving the ship in a boat, and to the unexpected and very unfortunate capsizing of that boat, prevented his death being a direct consequence of the casualty. It was a risk, no doubt; but a boat would not generally capsize in those circumstances; and I cannot think that that prevents it being held that his death was a direct consequence of the casualty. . . .

[Scott and MacKinnon L.JJ. agreed.]

Appeal dismissed

Questions

1. What would have been the position if the lifeboat had sunk because it was not seaworthy?

2. Would the position have been affected if the captain of the *Manchester Regiment* had been going to the *Oropesa* merely to express his grievance about the collision?

Note

In considering causation, reference should also be made to the section on rescuers in Chap. 3, p. 123, *ante*.

1. (1889), 15 P.D. 15.
2. [1943] A.C. 283; [1943] 1 All E.R. 68.

Stansbie v. Troman

Court of Appeal   [1948] 1 All E.R. 599

Tucker L.J.: This is an appeal from a judgment of His Honour Judge Forbes, given at Birmingham. The plaintiff is a painter and decorator and he was engaged to do certain work at the premises of the defendant. In this connection he claimed £79 15s. 0d. for work and labour done. There was no dispute about that, but the defendant counter-claimed from him the sum of £334 15s. 0d. damages for negligence, and this appeal relates to the defendant's counter-claim which succeeded before the learned judge.

One day, while the plaintiff was working at the defendant's house, the defendant went to business, as was his custom, and his wife also went out for some purpose. During the absence of both of them, the plaintiff was left working in the house. He knew he had been left alone in the house and on similar previous occasions he had been reminded by the wife to pull to the front door when he left. The front door had a Yale lock, and, accordingly, unless the catch was pulled back, when the door was shut it was locked, and entry could only be obtained by the use of the key. On this particular occasion the plaintiff had occasion to leave the premises to get some fresh wallpaper. This was not similar to previous occasions when he was leaving the house at the end of his day's work, when he could, no doubt, pull the door to without thought of regaining access to the premises. This time he knew he would have to get into the house again when he returned, and so he pulled back the catch and so left the front door unlocked. He went to some place not very far away where he expected to obtain the wallpaper, but it had to be sent for elsewhere, with the result that he left the house with the front door unlocked for two hours or so. When he got back he found that the front door was open and that in his absence someone had entered and stolen from the downstairs rooms jewellery to the value of over £300. He waited for some time for the return of the defendant and his wife, but they did not get back until late, and he then telephoned and told them what had happened.

The learned judge stated that the first matter he had to investigate was whether or not there was any duty owed by the plaintiff to the defendant; secondly, whether there had been any breach of that duty; and, thirdly, whether the damage had resulted from that breach. . . .

[Tucker L.J. then dealt with the first two questions, finding that there was a duty to take reasonable care in relation to the state of the premises when the plaintiff left them, and agreeing with the county court judge that the defendant had been negligent. He continued:] With regard to the third question as to which the learned judge said he had found considerable difficulty, and in regard to which his views had wavered, *viz.*, whether the damage resulted directly from the negligent act, he said this:

> "It seems clear that the negligence of the plaintiff was not the direct cause of the defendant's loss. The direct cause was the crime of the thief. The plaintiff was no party to the crime, which was a thing that he never intended. On the other hand, the main purpose of the latch is to keep out thieves, so far as the latch will serve. If the latch be fastened back, the house needs watching, and, therefore, the negligence of the plaintiff really consisted in failure to take reasonable care to guard against the very thing that happened. Forcing a door or breaking a window takes time and may attract attention. The plaintiff's negligence increased the problematic risk of a theft, and the risk matured into a certainty."

Counsel for the plaintiff has referred to *Weld-Blundell* v. *Stephens*,[1] and, in particular, to a passage in the speech of Lord Sumner where he said ([1920] A.C. 986; 123 L.T. 601):

> "In general (apart from special contracts and relations and the maxim *respondeat superior*), even though A. is in fault, he is not responsible for injury to C., which B., a

---

1. [1920] A.C. 956; 123 L.T. 593.

stranger to him, deliberately chooses to do. Though A. may have given the occasion for B.'s mischievous activity, B. then becomes a new and independent cause" . . .

I do not think that Lord Sumner would have intended that very general statement to apply to the facts of a case such as the present, where, as the learned judge points out, the very act of negligence itself consisted in the failure to take reasonable care to guard against the very thing that in fact happened. The reason why the plaintiff owed a duty to the defendant to leave the premises in a reasonably secure state was because otherwise thieves or dishonest persons might gain access to the premises, and it seems to me that if, as I think he was, the plaintiff was negligent in leaving the house in this condition, it was a direct result of his negligence that the thief got in through this door which was left unlocked and stole these valuable goods. Except that I would have phrased the nature of the duty somewhat differently from the way in which the learned county court judge put it, I am in entire agreement with the judgment which he delivered in this case, and, in my view, the appeal fails.

[SOMERVELL L.J. and ROXBURGH J. agreed.]

Appeal dismissed

Question

If the thief who had entered had shot someone who caught him stealing the goods, would the plaintiff have been liable to pay damages for these personal injuries?

Notes

1. This case can be compared with *Deyong* v. *Shenburn*, [1946] K.B. 227; [1946] 1 All E.R. 226, where the defendant was a theatrical producer. He employed the plaintiff to play a part in a pantomime, and, on the second day of rehearsals, some of the plaintiff's property was stolen from his dressing room. For some of the material time, no one was looking after the stage door and there was no effective lock on the door of the dressing room, which the plaintiff shared with another person. In an action for damages by the plaintiff, judgment was given for the defendant in the county court. This was upheld by the Court of Appeal. Du Parcq L.J. stated ([1946] 1 All E.R. at p. 229):

"There has never been a decision that a master must, merely because of the relationship which exists between a master and servant, take reasonable care for the safety of his servants' belongings in the sense that he must take steps to insure, so far as he can, that no wicked person shall have an opportunity of stealing the servants' goods. That duty is the duty which is contended for here, and there is not a shred of authority which suggests that any such duty exists or ever has existed."

Thus the cases can be distinguished on the ground that no duty of care existed in *Deyong* v. *Shenburn*. See also *Edwards* v. *West Herts. Group Hospital Management Committee*, [1957] 1 All E.R. 541, and see generally P. M. North, *Occupiers' Liability*, pp. 105–112.

2. It has even been held that the chain of causation was not broken by a suicide—see *Pigney* v. *Pointers Transport Services, Ltd.*, [1957] 2 All E.R. 807, noted, p. 200, *post*.

3. *Philco Radio and Television Corpn. of G.B., Ltd.* v. *J. Spurling, Ltd.*, [1949] 2 All E.R. 882, is a difficult case, in which different views were expressed in the Court of Appeal. Five packing cases containing highly inflammable material were mistakenly delivered to the plaintiffs' premises by an employee of the

defendants. There was no warning relating to the contents, and the defendants did not dispute that they had been negligent. Serious damage was caused by an explosion when a typist approached the cases with a lighted cigarette. The trial judge, [1949] 2 All E.R. 129, thought that "probably all she meant to do was to make a small and innocuous bonfire of some of the material which she probably took to be ordinary packing". It was held by the Court of Appeal that the defendants were liable. Jenkins L.J. took the view that the evidence did not justify the finding about the typist's intentions: if it had, he would have decided the case differently. Singleton L.J. said that the defendants, on whom in his view the onus of proof lay in this matter, had not shown that the typist had intentionally caused a fire: if they had, he would have allowed the defendants' appeal. Tucker L.J., however, stated that, even on the assumption that there was enough evidence to show that she had acted deliberately and not accidentally, there was no evidence to show that she knew the nature of the contents of the cases and the consequences which would follow from setting light to them. There was, in his view, no such conscious act of volition as would enable the defendants to escape liability.

Home Office v. Dorset Yacht Co., Ltd., p. 108, *ante*

Clay v. A. J. Crump & Sons, Ltd.

Court of Appeal   [1963] 3 All E.R. 687

A site was being cleared and excavated to a particular level by demolition contractors in accordance with the defendant architect's plan. In the course of the work it transpired that there was some objection to the proposed demolition of one particular wall. In response to an enquiry made over the telephone by the architect to Mr. Whitehouse, the demolition contractor, as to whether it was safe to leave the wall, Mr. Whitehouse gave the opinion that it was and then looked at the wall and obtained a similar opinion from his foreman. The architect did not make any examination of the wall himself. At a later date, building contractors came on to the site, but the wall, the foundations of which were at this stage easy to inspect because of the excavation of soil at its base, was not seriously inspected by them. The wall collapsed and fell on a hut placed close to the wall, killing two men and injuring the plaintiff, an employee of the building contractors. The plaintiff sued and the trial judge held the building contractors, the demolition contractors and the architect to be in breach of their respective common law duties to the plaintiff and the building contractors and demolition contractors also to be in breach of statutory duty under the appropriate building regulations. He apportioned the blame amongst the defendants. There was an appeal by these three defendants and the extracts from the Court of Appeal's judgment dismissing the appeal, are concerned with the question of the opportunity of intermediate examination.

ORMEROD L.J., [having referred to LORD ATKIN's statement of the narrow "manufacturers' rule" in *M'Alister* (or *Donoghue*) v. *Stevenson*, [1932] A.C. 562, at p. 599, continued:] ... In my judgment, Lord Atkin is not saying ... that for a negligent person to be liable it is essential that there should be no reasonable possibility of intermediate examination. He is dealing there with a particular type of chattel, an article of food or drink made up in such a way that the manufacturers did not expect and indeed did not intend that there should be an examination between the time when the article left their works and the time when it was consumed. This does not affect the view that he expressed earlier in his speech, when he set out the rule whereby a neighbour should be defined in law. In my judgment, and I do not think that this view is contrary to the views expressed in the decided cases, the important question is to decide first whether the plaintiff comes within the class of persons entitled to recover damages if they suffer loss as a result of another person's negligence and then to decide whether in law that loss has indeed been suffered as a result of the negligence or has been suffered, for example, because of the intervening negligence of some other person. It may well be that in the case of manufactured articles made up in such a way that they are not intended to be examined it is simpler to decide whether they come within the class; but it is none the less the duty of the court to inquire into the facts of other cases, and to determine whether the injury suffered is something which can in law be related to the breach of duty of some particular person. There can be no doubt, as I have said already, that the workmen of the builder must have been in the contemplation of the architect when he formulated his plans and made his decisions. I would say that the builders' workmen were within the class of people to whom the architect owed a duty of care. The question to be decided is whether the injury suffered by the plaintiff was caused by the negligence of the architect or by some other person.

. . . The architect chose to rely on the opinion of the demolition contractor. This must have been wrong if the evidence called before the learned judge is anything to go by; and I can see no reason why it should be said that because an architect, instead of making sure for himself, accepts the opinion of another man whose opinion is given either negligently or certainly without sufficient examination, then the architect is free from liability. He has done nothing more, as I see it, than appoint an agent to act for him to give a decision which it was his duty to give himself. In these circumstances I fail to see how it can be said that the injury to the plaintiff was not caused by the negligence of the architect. It was urged that even if the architect and the demolition contractors were each in turn negligent that negligence was not the cause of the injury to the plaintiff as there was negligence on the part of the building contractors, who did not ensure that the premises were reasonably safe before allowing their workmen to go on to them, and in those circumstances were guilty of negligence which was the cause of the accident to the plaintiff. It was urged on the part of the building contractors that they were entitled to rely on the demolition contractors, as having left the premises in a safe condition, and that nothing other than a cursory examination was required of them. That may, of course, be so, but the evidence appears to have been that even a cursory examination would have disclosed the state of the wall and, to an experienced eye, the fact that it was dangerous. It may be that there was negligence in some degree on the part both of the demolition contractors and the builders. If there was such negligence it may be that it was a contributory cause of the accident. It cannot, however, in my judgment absolve the architect from a share in the blame. To hold otherwise would be to hold that an architect, or indeed anyone in a similar position, could behave negligently by delegating to others duties which he was under an obligation to perform, and could escape liability by the plea that the injuries caused were caused by the negligence of that other person and not of himself. I do not accept that as being the true position in law and I am satisfied that it is not the law as laid down by Lord Atkin in *M'Alister* (or *Donoghue*) v. *Stevenson*[1] or by the judgments in any of the other cases to which we have been referred. . . .

UPJOHN L.J.: . . . the architect and demolition contractors rely on the fact that the building contractors had the last opportunity of examination of the safety of the site. The architect and demolition contractors submit that this broke the chain of causation, so that they are not liable because on the facts they did not cause or contribute to the cause of the accident. . . .

The real truth of the matter, as I think, is that causation is almost entirely a question of fact in each particular case. "It is a fallacy to suppose that the last cause is the sole cause", said Lord Denning in *Miller* v. *South of Scotland Electricity Board*.[2] I would like to quote the well-known observations of Lord Reid in *Stapley* v. *Gypsum Mines, Ltd.*:[3]

1. [1932] A.C. 562; [1932] All E.R. Rep. 1.
2. 1958 S.L.T. 229, at p. 238.
3. [1953] A.C. 663, at p. 681; [1953] 2 All E.R. 478, at pp. 485, 486.

"One may find that, as a matter of history, several people have been at fault and that if any one of them had acted properly the accident would not have happened, but that does not mean that the accident must be regarded as having been caused by the faults of all of them. One must discriminate between those faults which must be discarded as being too remote and those which must not. Sometimes it is proper to discard all but one and to regard that one as the sole cause, but in other cases it is proper to regard two or more as having jointly caused the accident. I doubt whether any test can be applied generally."

The facts there were quite different, but these observations are exactly applicable. Judged as a matter of fact: were the acts or omissions of the architect or the demolition contractor so remote that in the field of causation it can properly be said that they did not contribute to the accident?

To that simple question of fact there can, as I think, be only one answer. The principle cause of the accident was . . . the failure of the architect to perform any of the duties cast on him. The second cause (in order of importance) was that of the demolition contractors who relied on an entirely unqualified employee, and the third (least in importance) was the building contractors, who were not entitled to assume that the other two had completely fulfilled their duty. I, therefore, think that the judge rightly assessed the architect, the demolition contractors and the building contractors to be liable in that descending order. I would not disturb his figures of degree of blame . . .

[DAVIES L.J., who agreed with these two judgments, delivered a judgment in favour of dismissing the appeal. The appeal relating to common law liability was dismissed, although the Court of Appeal did not think that there had been any breach of statutory duty.]

Question

Might the decision on the causation point have been different if, to the knowledge of the architect, the building contractors had been contractually bound to the site owner to check the safety of the site before commencing work on it?

Notes

1. Normally the argument is that a new act has broken the chain of causation, but here, in effect, it was that the chain had been broken by the failure of another person to act in a particular way. See p. 82, *ante*, for liability for omissions.

2. The question of intermediate examination arises particularly in the context of liability for chattels, on which see p. 328, *post*.

McKew v. Holland and Hannen and Cubitts (Scotland), Ltd.

Second Division of the Court of   [1969] 3 All E.R. 1621
Session, and the House of Lords

The appellant was slightly injured as a result of the fault of the respondents and one consequence was that for a short time thereafter he occasionally lost control of his left leg. Shortly after sustaining these injuries, the appellant, along with his wife, child and brother-in-law, went to inspect a flat to which access was provided by a steep flight of stairs with no handrail. Having inspected the flat, he was about to go down the stairs with his child, ahead of his wife and brother-in-law. According to his evidence, his left leg gave way, he thrust the child back and, to avoid going down head first, he threw himself and landed mainly on his right leg. His ankle was broken, and the question was whether the appellant could recover for the damage caused by this accident. The claim failed before the Lord Ordinary and the Court of Session. The following passage from the opinion of the Lord Justice-Clerk in the Court of Session received approval in the House of Lords:

THE LORD JUSTICE-CLERK: . . . It may well be that, in the situation in which he [the appellant] thought he was placed and with, apparently, an immediate choice to be made between two evils, the [appellant] was not unreasonable in jumping as he did. In my opinion, however, the chain of causation had already been broken. On his own evidence, his left leg had 'gone away' from him on several occasions before the second accident, both in the street and in his house. Yet, with this knowledge and experience, he set out to descend a flight of stairs without a stick or other support and without the assistance, which was available, of his wife or brother-in-law. I cannot regard this as a reasonable act and it was, in my opinion, an intervening act which broke the chain of causation. But for the first accident and the resulting weakness of the left leg the second accident would, no doubt, not have happened. The latter was indirectly connected with the former, but it was not the result of it, except possibly in some remote and indirect way, and a fortiori it was not the natural and direct or probable result of it, in whatever sense these words be used. . . .

[On appeal to the House of Lords:]

LORD REID: . . . In my view the law is clear. If a man is injured in such a way that his leg may give way at any moment he must act reasonably and carefully. It is quite possible that in spite of all reasonable care his leg may give way in circumstances such that as a result he sustains further injury. Then that second injury was caused by his disability which in turn was caused by the defender's fault. But if the injured man acts unreasonably he cannot hold the defender liable for injury caused by his own unreasonable conduct. His unreasonable conduct is novus actus interveniens. The chain of causation has been broken and what follows must be regarded as caused by his own conduct and not by the defender's fault or the disability caused by it. Or one may say that unreasonable conduct of the pursuer and what follows from it is not the natural and probable result of the original fault of the defender or of the ensuing disability. I do not think that foreseeability comes into this. A defender is not liable for a consequence of a kind which is not foreseeable. But it does not follow that he is liable for every consequence which a reasonable man could foresee. What can be foreseen depends almost entirely on the facts of the case, and it is often easy to foresee unreasonable conduct or some other novus actus interveniens as being quite likely. But that does not mean that the defender must pay for damage caused by the novus actus. It only leads to trouble . . . if one tries to graft on to the concept of foreseeability some rule of law to the effect that a wrongdoer is not bound to foresee something which in fact he could readily foresee as quite likely to happen. For it is not at all unlikely or unforeseeable that an active man who has suffered such a disability will take some quite unreasonable risk. But if he does he cannot hold the defender liable for the consequences.

So in my view the question here is whether the second accident was caused by the appellant doing something unreasonable. It was argued that the wrongdoer must take his victim as he finds him and that that applies not only to a thin skull [1] but also to his intelligence. But I shall not deal with that argument because there is nothing in the evidence to suggest that the appellant is abnormally stupid. This case can be dealt with equally well by asking whether the appellant did something which a moment's reflection would have shown him was an unreasonable thing to do.

He knew that his left leg was liable to give way suddenly and without warning. He knew that this stair was steep and that there was no handrail. He must have realised, if he had given the matter a moment's thought, that he could only safely descend the stair if he either went extremely slowly and carefully so that he could sit down if his

---

1. [See pp. 196–201, *post*.]

leg gave way, or waited for the assistance of his wife and brother-in-law. But he chose to descend in such a way that when his leg gave way he could not stop himself. I agree with what the Lord Justice-Clerk[1] says at the end of his opinion and I think that this is sufficient to require this appeal to be dismissed.

But I think it right to say a word about the argument that the fact that the appellant made to jump when he felt himself falling is conclusive against him. When his leg gave way the appellant was in a very difficult situation. He had to decide what to do in a fraction of a second. He may have come to a wrong decision; he probably did. But if the chain of causation had not been broken before this by his putting himself in a position where he might be confronted with an emergency, I do not think that he would put himself out of court by acting wrongly in the emergency unless his action was so utterly unreasonable that even on the spur of the moment no ordinary man would have been so foolish as to do what he did. In an emergency it is natural to try to do something to save oneself and I do not think that his trying to jump in this emergency was so wrong that it could be said to be . . . more than an error of judgment. But for the reasons already given I would dismiss this appeal.

[LORD HODSON and VISCOUNT DILHORNE concurred with LORD REID. LORD GUEST delivered a speech in favour of dismissing the appeal, and LORD UPJOHN concurred generally.]

Appeal dismissed

Notes

1. *Wieland v. Cyril Lord Carpets, Ltd.*, [1969] 3 All E.R. 1006, is a case dealing with a similar problem, but one in which the court came to a different decision. The first accident was caused by the defendants' negligence. Two days after the accident, the plaintiff, who wore bi-focal spectacles, returned to the hospital where she had originally been taken, and her neck was fitted with a special collar. The position of her neck in the collar "deprived her of her usual ability to adjust herself automatically to the bi-focals". After leaving the hospital, the plaintiff was in a nervous state as a result of her visit to the doctor and her involvement in the accident, and this fact, coupled with the problem which the bi-focal spectacles now presented, meant that the plaintiff was somewhat unsteady. She went to her son's office to ask him to take her home. He accompanied her down the stairs in the office building, but, on nearing the foot of the stairs, the plaintiff fell and injured her ankles. Eveleigh J. held that the fall and consequent injury were caused by the defendants' negligence in the first accident. The plaintiff's skill in descending stairs whilst wearing the bi-focal spectacles had been impaired, resulting in the fall.

2. In the *McKew* case, if it had been decided that the chain of causation had not been broken, then the doctrine of contributory negligence could have been brought into play. This may be important in a situation where there can be a claim either in contract or in tort. In *Sole v. W. J. Hallt, Ltd.*, [1973] Q.B. 574; [1973] 1 All E.R. 1032 the plaintiff was injured when he fell into the well of an unguarded staircase whilst working on a house which was being constructed. He was working under a labour-only contract with the defendant builders and it was not a master/servant situation. Swanwick J. referred to s. 5 (1) of the Occupiers' Liability Act 1957 with its implied contractual term of the common duty of care, and held that in general a plaintiff who came within the scope of this provision could also claim in tort as a visitor under s. 2 (1) of that Act. (See p. 233, *post.*) He clearly took the view that s. 5 (1)

---

1. *Ante.*

gave an action in contract, a point on which writers have disagreed. (See P. M. North, *Occupiers' Liability*, pp. 153–154.) Swanwick J. went on to hold the defendants to have been in breach of the common duty of care, and that there had been contributory negligence on the part of the plaintiff. The breach of the common duty of care lay in not having boards readily available to cover the well: the contributory negligence lay in the fact that the plaintiff took some steps backwards towards the well of the stairs whilst looking up at the ceiling, which he and another workman had been fixing, whereupon he fell into the well. The importance of this finding of contributory negligence was that, if there had only been a contractual claim, the learned judge stated that he would have felt bound by *Quinn* v. *Burch Bros. (Builders)*, *Ltd.*, [1966] 2 Q.B. 370; [1966] 2 All E.R. 283 to hold that the chain of causation had been broken; however in the tort claim under the 1957 Act the damages were merely reduced.

Leaving aside the question whether the "strength" of the chain of causation differs in contract and tort, it may be questioned whether on these facts Swanwick J. was bound to follow that decision and come to that result. In *Quinn* v. *Burch Bros. (Builders)*, *Ltd.*, the plaintiff was an independent sub-contractor, and the defendants, the main contractors on a job, failed, in breach of contract, to provide stepladders within a reasonable time of the plaintiff asking for them. The plaintiff used a trestle as a step ladder, but he did not have anyone standing on and securing its foot, and he was injured when it slipped. It was held by the Court of Appeal that the breach of contract by the defendants merely provided the occasion for the later injury and did not cause it even if the later events were foreseeable by the defendants. The breach of contract in *Sole* v. *W. J. Hallt, Ltd.* would seem to have done more than provide an occasion for the plaintiff to cause the injuries to himself, and *Quinn* v. *Burch Bros. (Builders)*, *Ltd.* was not, it is submitted, an undistinguishable authority. If the chain of causation were held not to have been broken, then the question of the applicability of contributory negligence and the Law Reform (Contributory Negligence) Act 1945 (p. 296, *post*) to a contractual claim would have arisen—see e.g. Glanville Williams, *Joint Torts and Contributory Negligence*, § 59 and § 80; G. H. Treitel, *Law of Contract* (3rd Edn.), pp. 829–832; *Quinn* v. *Burch Bros. (Builders)*, *Ltd.*, [1966] 2 Q.B. 370; [1965] 3 All E.R. 801 (*per* Paull J. at first instance); *Sayers* v. *Harlow U.D.C.*, [1958] 2 All E.R. 342; *Artingstoll* v. *Hewen's Garages, Ltd.*, [1973] R.T.R. 197.

3. FORESEEABILITY OF THE KIND OF DAMAGE

Re Polemis and Furness, Withy & Co., Ltd.

Court of Appeal   [1921] All E.R. Rep. 40

The charterers of a ship carried in it a cargo which included benzine or petrol in cases. Whilst the vessel was being unloaded at Casablanca, a plank fell into the hold, and there was an explosion leading to a fire which destroyed the ship. The owners alleged that negligence on the part of the charterers' servants caused the loss of the ship, and one of the charterers' arguments was that the damage was too remote. The following findings of fact were made by the arbitrators:

"(a) That the ship was lost by fire. (b) That the fire arose from a spark igniting petrol vapour in the hold. (c) That the spark was caused by the falling board coming into contact with some substance in the hold. (d) That the fall of the board was caused by the negligence of the Arabs (other than the winchman) engaged in the work of discharging. (e) That the said Arabs were employed by the charterers or their agents the Cie Transatlantique on behalf of the charterers, and that the said Arabs were the servants of the charterers. (f) That the causing of the spark could not reasonably have been anticipated from the falling of the board, though some damage to the ship might reasonably have been anticipated. (g) There was no evidence before us that the Arabs chosen were known or likely to be negligent. (h) That the damages sustained by the owners through the said accident amount to the sum of £196,165 1s. 11d. . . . ."

SANKEY J. affirmed the award. The charterers appealed.

BANKES L.J.: . . . In the present case the arbitrators have found as a fact that the falling of the plank was due to the negligence of the defendants' servants. The fire appears to me to have been directly caused by the falling of the plank. In these circumstances I consider that it is immaterial that the causing of the spark by the falling of the plank could not have been reasonably anticipated. The charterers' junior counsel sought to draw a distinction between the anticipation of the extent of damage resulting from a negligent act, and the anticipation of the type of damage resulting from such an act. He admitted that it could not lie in the mouth of a person whose negligent act had caused damage to say that he could not reasonably have foreseen the extent of the damage, but he contended that the negligent person was entitled to rely upon the fact that he could not reasonably have anticipated the type of damage which resulted from his negligent act. I do not think that the distinction can be admitted. Given the breach of duty which constitutes the negligence, and given the damage as a direct result of that negligence, the anticipations of the person whose negligent act has produced the damage appear to me to be irrelevant. I consider that the damages claimed are not too remote. . . .

WARRINGTON L.J.: . . . The presence or absence of reasonable anticipation of damage determines the legal quality of the act as negligent or innocent. If it be thus determined to be negligent, then the question whether particular damages are recoverable depends only on the answer to the question whether they are the direct consequence of the act. . . . In the present case it is clear that the act causing the plank to fall was in law a negligent act, because some damage to the ship might reasonably be anticipated. If this is so then the charterers are liable for the actual loss, that being on the findings of the arbitrators the direct result of the falling board: see per Lord Sumner in *Weld-Blundell* v. *Stephens*[1] ([1920] A.C. at p. 983). On the whole, in my opinion, the appeal must be dismissed with costs.

SCRUTTON L.J.: . . . To determine whether an act is negligent, it is relevant to determine whether any reasonable person would foresee that the act would cause damage; if he would not, the act is not negligent. But if the act would or might probably cause damage, the fact that the damage it in fact causes is not the exact kind of damage one would expect is immaterial, so long as the damage is in fact caused sufficiently directly by the negligent act, and not by the operation of independent causes having no connection with the negligent act, except that they could not avoid its results. Once the act is negligent, the fact that its exact operation was not foreseen is immaterial. . . . In the present case it was negligent in discharging cargo to knock down the planks of the temporary staging, for they might easily cause some damage either to workmen, or cargo, or the ship. The fact that they did directly produce an unexpected result, a spark in an atmosphere of petrol vapour which caused a fire, does not relieve the person who was negligent from the damage which his negligent act directly caused. For these

---

1. [1920] A.C. 956.

reasons the experienced arbitrators and the judge appealed from came, in my opinion, to a correct decision, and the appeal must be dismissed with costs.

Appeal dismissed

Note

In "Remoteness of Liability and Legal Policy", [1962] C.L.J. 178, R. W. M. Dias writes (at pp. 179–180, footnotes omitted):

"A convenient point of departure would be to ask, for what is *Polemis* supposed to be an authority? The decision is open to two possible interpretations, a dichotomy which has considerably obscured the discussions centred upon it. One of these, to be called the "wide" principle, is that the defendant is liable for all the damage directly resulting from his careless behaviour, however caused, and even to a plaintiff who was not foreseeably endangered by it. The other, to be called the "narrow" principle, is that so long as the plaintiff was in foreseeable danger, the defendant is liable to him to the full extent of the damage that directly results, though neither the manner of its incidence nor its extent may have been foreseeable. The second of these versions will be accepted here. This is because, in the *first* place, the point of distinction between the two statements, namely, the foresight of damage to the plaintiff, accords with an abundance of authority which would appear to have submerged the alternative view, although occasional support for the latter does bubble forth from beneath the tide. *Secondly*, the "narrow" proposition is warranted by the facts in *Polemis* where some damage to the plaintiff's ship was found to have been reasonably foreseeable as the result of dropping a plank into its hold, but not the fire which unexpectedly developed. *Thirdly*, only on this footing is the case reconcilable with certain subsequent decisions of the House of Lords, in each of which the defendant was held not liable on the ground that no damage to the plaintiff was initially foreseeable. . . ."

The Edison

House of Lords   [1933] All E.R. Rep. 144

The *Edison*, in leaving the port of Patras, came into contact with the *Liesbosch*'s moorings and pulled that vessel, which had no crew on board, out to sea. In the heavy sea, the *Liesbosch* sank, and the respondents admitted liability. The *Liesbosch* was being used by the appellants for dredging operations as part of certain works they had contracted to carry out. There were penalties for delay. The appellants at that time were unable to buy a substitute dredger as their liquid resources were tied up in the contract, and so they hired a dredger, the *Adria*, at a high rate and the work was re-started. In the light of this high rate of hire, the Harbour Board bought the dredger shortly after its arrival, and resold it to the appellants, payment being on an instalment basis. In assessing the damages, the Registrar of the Admiralty Division took the view that in their circumstances the appellants had acted reasonably in hiring the dredger, and that their acts were the natural and direct results of the defendants' (respondents) wrongful act. He allowed the appellants (1) the actual value to them of the *Liesbosch* (2) reasonable expenses while the work was stopped (3) hiring expenses of the *Adria* until bought by the Harbour Board (4) the extra cost of working the *Adria* (5) loss of interest during the period of delay. He awarded the appellants £19,820. Langton J., [1931] P. 230, basically affirmed the Registrar's report, but an appeal was allowed by the Court of Appeal, [1932] P. 52, and the damages were reduced. On further appeal to the House of Lords:

LORD WRIGHT: . . . The substantial issue is what in such a case as the present is the true measure of damage. It is not questioned that when a vessel is lost by collision due to the sole negligence of the wrong-doing vessel the owners of the former vessel are entitled to what is called restitutio in integrum, which means that they should recover such a sum as will replace them so far as can be done by compensation in money, in the same position as if the loss had not been inflicted on them, subject to the rules of law as to remoteness of damage.

The respondents contend that all that is recoverable as damages is the true value to the owners of the lost vessel, as at the time and place of loss. Before considering what is involved in this contention, I think it desirable to examine the claim made by the appellants, which found favour with the registrar and Langton J., and which in effect is that all their circumstances, in particular their want of means, must be taken into account, and hence the damages must be based on their actual loss, provided only that, as the registrar and the judge have found, they acted reasonably in the unfortunate predicament in which they were placed, even though but for their financial embarrassment they could have replaced the *Liesbosch* at a moderate price and with comparatively short delay. In my judgment, the appellants are not entitled to recover damages on this basis. The respondents' tortious act involved the physical loss of the dredger; that loss must somehow be reduced to terms of money. But the appellants' actual loss in so far as it was due to their impecuniosity arose from that impecuniosity as a separate and concurrent cause, extraneous to and distinct in character from the tort; the impecuniosity was not traceable to the respondents' acts, and, in my opinion, was outside the legal purview of the consequences of these acts. The law cannot take account of everything that follows a wrongful act; it regards some subsequent matters as outside the scope of its selection, because "it were infinite to trace the cause of causes," or consequences of consequences. Thus, the loss of a ship by collision due to the other vessel's sole fault may force the shipowner into bankruptcy and that again may involve his family in suffering, loss of education or opportunities in life, but no such loss could be recovered from the wrongdoer. In the varied web of affairs, the law must abstract some consequences as relevant, not perhaps on grounds of pure logic but simply for practical reasons. In the present case, if the appellants' financial embarrassment is to be regarded as a consequence of the respondents' tort, I think it is too remote, but I prefer to regard it as an independent cause, though its operative effect was conditioned by the loss of the dredger. . . . *Polemis and Furness, Withy & Co.*,[1] a case in tort of negligence, was cited as illustrating the wide scope possible in damages for tort. That case, however, was concerned with the immediate physical consequences of the negligent act, and not with the co-operation of an extraneous matter such as the plaintiff's want of means. I think, therefore, that it is not material further to consider that case here. Nor is the appellants' financial disability to be compared with that physical delicacy or weakness which may aggravate the damage in the case of personal injuries, or with the possibility that the injured man in such a case may be either a poor labourer or a highly paid professional man. The former class of circumstances goes to the extent of actual physical damage and the latter consideration goes to interference with profit-earning capacity; whereas the appellants' want of means was, as already stated, extrinsic.

I agree with the conclusion of the Court of Appeal that the registrar and Langton J. proceeded on a wrong basis and that the damages must be assessed as if the appellants had been able to go into the market and buy a dredger to replace the *Liesbosch*. . . . [T]he value of the *Liesbosch* to the appellants, capitalized as at the date of the loss, must be assessed by taking into account: (1.) the market price of a comparable dredger in substitution; (2.) costs of adaptation, transport, insurance, etc., to Patras; (3.) compensation for disturbance and loss in carrying out their contract over the period of delay between the loss of the *Liesbosch* and the time at which the substituted dredger could reasonably have been available for use in Patras, including in that loss such items as overhead charges, expenses of staff and equipment, and so forth, thrown away, but neglecting any special loss due to the appellants' financial position. . . .

[LORD TOMLIN, LORD BUCKMASTER, LORD WARRINGTON OF CLYFFE and LORD

---

1. [1921] 3 K.B. 560.

RUSSELL OF KILLOWEN concurred. The matter was referred back to the Registrar to assess the measure of damages on the principles which had been laid down by the House of Lords.]

Questions

1. How far does this case limit the decision in *Re Polemis*?

2. The tortfeasor takes his victim as he finds him. If he injures a man earning a large salary, this may cost him more in damages than a similar injury to a low wage earner. Thus the varying earning capacity is taken into account by the law. Is there any logical justification for excluding from this doctrine of taking the victim as you find him his want of means, as in the *Edison* case?

3. Read *Martindale* v. *Duncan*, [1973] 2 All E.R. 355, p. 418, *post*. Do you agree with Davies L.J. who regarded that case as "entirely different" from *The Edison*?

Note

In *Malcolm* v. *Broadhurst*, [1970] 3 All E.R. 508, a woman and her husband had been involved in a road accident caused by the defendant's negligent driving. She recovered damages for her injuries and for certain loss of wages in respect of her full time job. However, she had also worked as a part-time secretary for her husband, who had been injured in the accident. For about a year (until February 1968) her own injuries stopped her from working, but from that time onwards she lost this part-time employment purely because, as a result of his injuries, her husband had ceased to be self-employed, rendering the wife's secretarial services unnecessary. Although any other part-time employment was impractical in her circumstances, she was refused damages for her loss of wages after February 1968. Geoffrey Lane J. refused to extend the rule that one takes one's victim as one finds him so as to cover a person's "infirmities of employment", and this unforeseeable loss was irrecoverable.

Overseas Tankship (U.K.), Ltd. v. Morts Dock and Engineering Co., Ltd. The *Wagon Mound*

Judicial Committee of the   [1961] 1 All E.R. 404
Privy Council

The appellants were charterers of the S.S. *Wagon Mound* which was taking on bunkering oil at the Caltex wharf in Sydney harbour. As a result of the appellants servants' carelessness, some of the oil spilt into the bay, spreading over a large part of it, and, in particular, there was a thick concentration of the oil near to the respondents' wharf (the Sheerlegs Wharf). The respondents' workmen had been using electric and oxy-acetylene welding equipment, and, on becoming aware of the situation, their works manager prohibited any welding or burning until further orders. After making further enquiry, he took the view that their operations could be continued with safety, and he gave the appropriate instructions, but in addition ordered all safety precautions to be taken to prevent inflammable material getting into the oil from the wharf. About two days later the oil caught fire because, the trial judge found, molten metal had fallen from the wharf and set fire to some cotton waste or rag floating in the oil on a piece of débris. The wharf also caught fire and was damaged, as was some equipment on the wharf, and the respondents claimed damages. The trial judge found that the appellants "did not know, and could not reasonably be expected to have known, that [the oil] was capable of being set afire when spread on water", [1958] 1 Lloyd's Rep. at p. 582, and also that some damage was caused to the respondents as a direct result of the spilling of the oil, namely the oil congealing on the slipways of their wharf, although no compensation was claimed for this damage. The Full Court of the Supreme Court of New South Wales dismissed an appeal from Kinsella J., who held the appellants liable, and there was a further appeal to the Judicial Committee of the Privy Council.

VISCOUNT SIMONDS: . . . It is inevitable that first consideration should be given to *Re Polemis and Furness, Withy & Co., Ltd.*,[1] which will henceforward be referred to as *Polemis*. For it was avowedly in deference to that decision and to decisions of the Court of Appeal that followed it that the full court was constrained to decide the present case in favour of the respondents. . . .

There can be no doubt that the decision of the Court of Appeal in *Polemis*[1] plainly asserts that, if the defendant is guilty of negligence, he is responsible for all the consequences, whether reasonably foreseeable or not. The generality of the proposition is, perhaps, qualified by the fact that each of the lords justices refers to the outbreak of fire as the direct result of the negligent act. There is thus introduced the conception that the negligent actor is not responsible for consequences which are not "direct", whatever that may mean. . . .

If the line of relevant authority had stopped with *Polemis*,[1] their Lordships might, whatever their own views as to its unreason, have felt some hesitation about overruling it. But it is far otherwise. It is true that, both in England and in many parts of the Commonwealth, that decision has from time to time been followed; but in Scotland it has been rejected with determination. It has never been subject to the express scrutiny of either the House of Lords or the Privy Council, though there have been comments on it in those supreme tribunals. Even in the inferior courts, judges have, sometimes perhaps unwittingly, declared themselves in a sense adverse to its principle. . . .

[Having referred to several authorities decided after *Re Polemis*,[1] he continued:] Enough has been said to show that the authority of *Polemis*[1] has been severely shaken, though lip-service has from time to time been paid to it. In their Lordships' opinion, it should no longer be regarded as good law. It is not probable that many cases will for that reason have a different result, though it is hoped that the law will be thereby simplified, and that, in some cases at least, palpable injustice will be avoided. For it does not seem consonant with current ideas of justice or morality that, for an act of negligence, however slight or venial, which results in some trivial foreseeable damage, the actor should be liable for all consequences, however unforeseeable and however grave, so long as they can be said to be "direct". It is a principle of civil liability, subject only to qualifications which have no present relevance, that a man must be considered to be responsible for the probable consequences of his act. To demand more of him is too harsh a rule, to demand less is to ignore that civilised order requires the observance of a minimum standard of behaviour. This concept, applied to the slowly developing law of negligence, has led to a great variety of expressions which can, as it appears to their Lordships, be harmonised with little difficulty with the single exception of the so-called rule in *Polemis*.[1] For, if it is asked why a man should be responsible for the natural or necessary or probable consequences of his act (or any other similar description of them), the answer is that it is not because they are natural or necessary or probable, but because, since they have this quality, it is judged, by the standard of the reasonable man, that he ought to have foreseen them. Thus it is that, over and over again, it has happened that, in different judgments in the same case and sometimes in a single judgment, liability for a consequence has been imposed on the ground that it was reasonably foreseeable, or alternatively on the ground that it was natural or necessary or probable. The two grounds have been treated as coterminous, and so they largely are. But, where they are not, the question arises to which the wrong answer was given in *Polemis*.[1] For, if some limitation must be imposed on the consequences for which the negligent actor is to be held responsible—and all are agreed that some limitation there

---

1. [1921] 3 K.B. 560; [1921] All E.R. Rep. 40.

must be—why should that test (reasonable foreseeability) be rejected which, since he is judged by what the reasonable man ought to foresee, corresponds with the common conscience of mankind, and a test (the "direct" consequence) be substituted which leads to nowhere but the never ending and insoluble problems of causation. "The lawyer" said Sir Frederick Pollock

> "cannot afford to adventure himself with philosophers in the logical and metaphysical controversies that beset the idea of cause."

Yet this is just what he has most unfortunately done and must continue to do if the rule in *Polemis*[1] is to prevail. A conspicuous example occurs when the actor seeks to escape liability on the ground that the "chain of causation" is broken by a "nova causa" or "novus actus interveniens".

The validity of a rule or principle can sometimes be tested by observing it in operation. Let the rule in *Polemis*[1] be tested in this way. In *The Edison*,[2] the appellants, whose vessel had been fouled by the respondents, claimed damages under various heads. The respondents were admittedly at fault; therefore, said the appellants, invoking the rule in *Polemis*,[1] they were responsible for all damage whether reasonably foreseeable or not. Here was the opportunity to deny the rule or to place it secure on its pedestal. But the House of Lords took neither course; on the contrary, it distinguished *Polemis*[1] on the ground that, in that case, the injuries suffered were the "immediate physical consequences" of the negligent act. It is not easy to understand why a distinction should be drawn between "immediate physical" and other consequences, nor where the line is to be drawn. It was, perhaps, this difficulty which led Denning L.J. in *Roe* v. *Ministry of Health*[3] to say that foreseeability is only disregarded when the negligence is the immediate or *precipitating* cause of the damage. This new word may well have been thought as good a word as another for revealing or disguising the fact that he sought loyally to enforce an unworkable rule. In the same connexion may be mentioned the conclusion to which the full court finally came in the present case. Applying the rule in *Polemis*[1] and holding, therefore, that the unforeseeability of the damage by fire afforded no defence, they went on to consider the remaining question. Was it a "direct" consequence? On this, Manning J. said:

> "Notwithstanding that, if regard is had separately to each individual occurrence in the chain of events that led to this fire, each occurrence was improbable and, in one sense, improbability was heaped upon improbability, I cannot escape from the conclusion that if the ordinary man in the street had been asked, as a matter of common sense, without any detailed analysis of the circumstances, to state the cause of the fire at Morts Dock, he would unhesitatingly have assigned such cause to spillage of oil by the appellants' employees."

Perhaps he would, and probably he would have added "I never should have thought it possible." But, with great respect to the full court, this is surely irrelevant, or, if it is relevant, only serves to show that the *Polemis* rule[1] works in a very strange way. After the event even a fool is wise. Yet it is not the hindsight of a fool, but it is the foresight of the reasonable man which alone can determine responsibility. The *Polemis* rule,[1] by substituting "direct" for "reasonably foreseeable" consequence, leads to a conclusion equally illogical and unjust.

At an early stage in this judgment, their Lordships intimated that they would deal with the proposition which can best be stated by reference to the well-known dictum of Lord Sumner:[4] "This, however, goes to culpability, not to compensation." It is with

---

1. [1921] 3 K.B. 560; [1921] All E.R. Rep. 40.
2. [1933] A.C. 449; [1933] All E.R. Rep. 144.
3. [1954] 2 Q.B. 66, at p. 85; [1954] 2 All E.R. 131, at p. 138.
4. [1920] A.C. 956, at p. 984. [The preceding words are "What a defendant ought to have anticipated as a reasonable man is material when the question is whether or not he was guilty of negligence, that is, of want of due care according to the circumstances."]

the greatest respect to that very learned judge and to those who have echoed his words that their Lordships find themselves bound to state their view that this proposition is fundamentally false.

It is, no doubt, proper when considering tortious liability for negligence to analyse its elements and to say that the plaintiff must prove a duty owed to him by the defendant, a breach of that duty by the defendant, and consequent damage. But there can be no liability until the damage has been done. It is not the act but the consequences on which tortious liability is founded. Just as (as it has been said) there is no such thing as negligence in the air, so there is no such thing as liability in the air. Suppose an action brought by A for damage caused by the carelessness (a neutral word) of B, for example a fire caused by the careless spillage of oil. It may, of course, become relevant to know what duty B owed to A, but the only liability that is in question is the liability for damage by fire. It is vain to isolate the liability from its context and to say that B is or is not liable, and then to ask for what damage he is liable. For his liability is in respect of that damage and no other. If, as admittedly it is, B's liability (culpability) depends on the reasonable foreseeability of the consequent damage, how is that to be determined except by the foreseeability of the damage which in fact happened—the damage in suit? And, if that damage is unforeseeable so as to displace liability at large, how can the liability be restored so as to make compensation payable? But, it is said, a different position arises if B's careless act has been shown to be negligent and has caused some foreseeable damage to A. Their Lordships have already observed that to hold B liable for consequences, however unforeseeable, of a careless act, if, but only if, he is at the same time liable for some other damage, however trivial, appears to be neither logical nor just. This becomes more clear if it is supposed that similar unforeseeable damage is suffered by A and C, but other foreseeable damage, for which B is liable, by A only. A system of law which would hold B liable to A but not to C for the similar damage suffered by each of them could not easily be defended. Fortunately, the attempt is not necessary. For the same fallacy is at the root of the proposition. It is irrelevant to the question whether B is liable for unforeseeable damage that he is liable for foreseeable damage, as irrelevant as would the fact that he had trespassed on Whiteacre be to the question whether he had trespassed on Blackacre. Again, suppose a claim by A for damage by fire by the careless act of B. Of what relevance is it to that claim that he has another claim arising out of the same careless act? It would surely not prejudice his claim if that other claim failed; it cannot assist it if it succeeds. Each of them rests on its own bottom and will fail if it can be established that the damage could not reasonably be foreseen. We have come back to the plain common sense stated by Lord Russell of Killowen in *Hay (or Bourhill)* v. *Young*.[1] As Denning L.J. said in *King* v. *Phillips*[2] "... there can be no doubt since *Hay (or Bourhill)* v. *Young*[1] that the test of *liability for shock* is foreseeability of *injury by shock*." Their Lordships substitute the word "fire" for "shock" and indorse this statement of the law.

Their Lordships conclude this part of the case with some general observations. They have been concerned primarily to displace the proposition that unforeseeability is irrelevant if damage is "direct". In doing so, they have inevitably insisted that the essential factor in determining liability is whether the damage is of such a kind as the reasonable man should have foreseen. This accords with the general view thus stated by Lord Atkin in *M'Alister (or Donoghue)* v. *Stevenson*:[3]

> "The liability for negligence, whether you style it such or treat it as in other systems as a species of 'culpa,' is no doubt based upon a general public sentiment of moral wrongdoing for which the offender must pay."

It is a departure from this sovereign principle if liability is made to depend solely on the damage being the "direct" or "natural" consequence of the precedent act. Who knows

1. [1943] A.C. 92; [1942] 2 All E.R. 396.
2. [1953] 1 Q.B. 429, at p. 441; [1953] 1 All E.R. 617, at p. 623.
3. [1932] A.C. 562, at p. 580; [1932] All E.R. Rep. 1, at p. 11.

or can be assumed to know all the processes of nature? But if it would be wrong that a man should be held liable for damage unpredictable by a reasonable man because it was "direct" or "natural", equally it would be wrong that he should escape liability, however "indirect" the damage, if he foresaw or could reasonably foresee the intervening events which led to its being done; cf. *Woods* v. *Duncan*.[1] Thus foreseeability becomes the effective test. In reasserting this principle, their Lordships conceive that they do not depart from, but follow and develop, the law of negligence as laid down by Alderson B., in *Blyth* v. *Birmingham Waterworks Co.*[2]

It is proper to add that their Lordships have not found it necessary to consider the so-called rule of "strict liability" exemplified in *Rylands* v. *Fletcher*[3] and the cases that have followed or distinguished it. Nothing that they have said is intended to reflect on that rule. . . .

[An alternative claim in nuisance was remitted to the Full Court to be dealt with as may be thought proper.]

Appeal allowed

Questions

1. Is this a "plaintiffs' decision" or a "defendants' decision"?

2. Is *The Edison* affected by this decision?

3. Does the rule that one takes one's victim as one finds him still remain? (See *Smith* v. *Leech Brain & Co., Ltd., post*.)

4. Should the doctrine of *novus actus interveniens* still be relevant after this case? If so, what is its relationship with the test of remoteness? (See M. A. Millner, "Novus Actus Interveniens: The Present Effect Of The Wagon Mound" (1971), 22 N.I.L.Q. 168.)

Notes

1. For further litigation arising out of this incident, but with a different plaintiff, see *The Wagon Mound (No. 2)*, [1967] 1 A.C. 617; [1966] 2 All E.R. 709, p. 140, *ante*, and p. 386, *post*.

2. In terms of precedent, the Judicial Committee of the Privy Council does not bind other English courts. Therefore it is arguable that *Re Polemis* in strict theory should still survive and be a binding precedent for certain courts. However, it is clear that the decision is being treated as effectively overruled by *The Wagon Mound*, whatever the theoretical precedent position. (On the precedent position, see further *Worcester Works Finance, Ltd.* v. *Cooden Engineering Co., Ltd.*, [1972] 1 Q.B. 210; [1971] 3 All E.R. 708.)

4. DEVELOPMENT OF *THE WAGON MOUND* DOCTRINE

(a) The thin skull rule

Smith v. Leech Brain & Co., Ltd.

Queen's Bench Division   [1961] 3 All E.R. 1159

The plaintiff's husband was a labourer and galvaniser employed by the defendants at the Glaucus Iron Works, Poplar. The articles to be galvanised were lowered into a

---

1. [1946] A.C. at p. 442.
2. (1856), 11 Exch. 781; [1843–60] All E.R. Rep. 478.
3. (1868), L.R. 3 H.L. 330; [1861–73] All E.R. Rep. 1.

tank containing molten metallic zinc and flux. The method used depended on the size of the article. All articles were first dipped in hydrochloric acid and the larger articles were then lowered into the tank by means of an overhead crane, from a position behind a sheet of corrugated iron. On 15 August 1950, the plaintiff's husband was operating the overhead crane, using the corrugated iron sheet supplied, when a piece of molten metal or flux struck and burned his lower lip. The burn was treated at the time but he thought nothing of it. Ultimately the place where the burn had been began to ulcerate and get larger. He consulted his general practitioner who sent him to hospital where cancer was diagnosed. Treatment by radium needles enabled the lip to heal and destroy the primary growth. Subsequently, however, secondary growths were observed. Thereafter he had some six or seven operations, and he died of cancer on 14 October 1953.

Lord Parker C.J. found that the defendants were negligent, that there had been no contributory negligence on the part of the plaintiff's husband, and that the burn was the promoting agency, promoting cancer in tissues which already had a pre-malignant condition as a result of his having worked at gas works, where he would have been in contact with tar or tar vapours from 1926 to 1935.

The case is reported only on the question of remoteness of damage.

Lord Parker C.J.: I am confronted with the recent decision of the Privy Council in *Overseas Tankship (U.K.), Ltd.* v. *Morts Dock and Engineering Co., Ltd.*[1] For convenience, that case is always referred to as *The Wagon Mound*. But for *The Wagon Mound*,[1] it seems to me perfectly clear that, assuming negligence proved, assuming that the burn caused in whole or in part the cancer and the death, this plaintiff would be entitled to recover. It is said on the one side by counsel for the defendants, that, although I am not strictly bound by *The Wagon Mound*[1] since it is a Privy Council case, I should treat myself as free, using the arguments to be derived from that case, to say that other cases in the Court of Appeal have been wrongly decided, and, particularly, that *Re Polemis and Furness, Withy & Co., Ltd.*[2] was wrongly decided, and that a further ground for taking that course is to be found in the various criticisms that have from time to time in the past been made by members of the House of Lords in regard to *Re Polemis*.[2] On the other hand, it is said by counsel for the plaintiff that I should hold that *Re Polemis*[2] was rightly decided and, secondly, that, even if that is not so, I must treat myself as completely bound by it. Thirdly, he said that in any event, whatever the true view is in regard to *Re Polemis*,[2] *The Wagon Mound*[1] has no relevance at all to this case.

For my part, I am quite satisfied that the Judicial Committee in *The Wagon Mound*[1] did not have what I may call, loosely, the "thin skull" cases in mind. It has always been the law of this country that a tortfeasor takes his victim as he finds him. It is unnecessary to do more than refer to the short passage in the decision of Kennedy J. in *Dulieu* v. *White & Sons*,[3] where he said:

> "If a man is negligently run over or otherwise negligently injured in his body, it is no answer to the sufferer's claim for damages that he would have suffered less injury, or no injury at all, if he had not had an unusually thin skull or an unusually weak heart."

To the same effect is a passage in *The Arpad*.[4] But quite apart from those two references, as is well known, the work of the courts for years and years has gone on on that basis. There is not a day that goes by where some trial judge does not adopt that principle, that the tortfeasor takes his victim as he finds him. If the Judicial Committee had any intention of making an inroad into that doctrine, I am quite satisfied that they would have said so.

It is true that, if one takes the wording in the advice given by Viscount Simonds in

---

1. [1961] A.C. 388; [1961] 1 All E.R. 404.
2. [1921] 3 K.B. 560; [1921] All E.R. Rep. 40.
3. [1901] 2 K.B. 669, at p. 679.
4. [1934] P. 189, at pp. 202, 203; [1934] All E.R. Rep. 326, at p. 331.

The Wagon Mound[1] and applies it strictly to such a case as this, it could be said that they were dealing with this point. But, as I have said, it is, to my mind, quite impossible to conceive that they were, and, indeed, it has been pointed out that they disclose the distinction between such a case as this and the one which they were considering, when they comment on *Smith* v. *London & South Western Rail. Co.*[2] Lord Simonds, in deal-with that case in *The Wagon Mound*,[1] said this:

> "Three things may be noted about this case: the first, that, for the sweeping proposition laid down, no authority was cited; the second, that the point to which the court directed its mind was not unforeseeable damage of a different kind from that which was foreseen, but more extensive damage of the same kind . . ."

In other words, Lord Simonds is clearly there drawing a distinction between the question whether a man could reasonably anticipate a type of injury, and the question whether a man could reasonably anticipate the extent of injury of the type which could be foreseen. The Judicial Committee were, I think, disagreeing with the decision in *Re Polemis*[3] that a man is no longer liable for the type of damage which he could not reasonably anticipate. The Judicial Committee were not, I think, saying that a man is only liable for the extent of damage which he could anticipate, always assuming the type of injury could have been anticipated. That view is really supported by the way in which cases of this sort have been dealt with in Scotland. Scotland has never, as far as I know, adopted the principle laid down in *Re Polemis*,[3] and yet I am quite satisfied that they have throughout proceeded on the basis that the tortfeasor takes the victim as he finds him.

In those circumstances, it seems to me that this is plainly a case which comes within the old principle. The test is not whether these defendants could reasonably have fore-seen that a burn would cause cancer and that Mr. Smith would die. The question is whether these defendants could reasonably foresee the type of injury which he suffered, namely, the burn. What, in the particular case, is the amount of damage which he suffers as a result of that burn, depends on the characteristics and constitution of the victim. Accordingly, I find that the damages which the plaintiff claims are damages for which these defendants are liable. Before leaving that part of the case, I should say, in case the matter goes further, that I would follow, sitting as a trial judge, the decision in *The Wagon Mound*;[1] or rather, more accurately, I would treat myself, in the light of the arguments in that case, able to follow other decisions of the Court of Appeal, prior to *Re Polemis*,[3] rather than *Re Polemis*[3] itself. As I have said, *Re Polemis*[3] has been criticised by individual members of the House of Lords, although followed by the Court of Appeal in *Thorogood* v. *Van Den Berghs & Jurgens, Ltd.*[4] I should treat myself as at liberty to do that, and, for my part, I would do so the more readily, because I think that it is important that the common law, and the development of the common law, should be homogeneous in the various sections of the Commonwealth. It would be lamentable if a court sitting here had to say that, while the common law in the Commonwealth and Scotland has been developed in a particular way, yet we in this country, and sitting in these courts, are going to proceed in a different way. However, as I have said, that does not strictly arise in this case.

Judgment for the plaintiff

Question

Could Lord Parker C.J. have classified the type of damage here as cancer? If so, what would have been the result of the case?

---

1. [1961] A.C. 388; [1961] 1 All E.R. 404.
2. (1870), L.R. 6 C.P. 14.
3. [1921] 3 K.B. 560; [1921] All E.R. Rep. 40.
4. [1951] 2 K.B. 537; [1951] 1 All E.R. 682.

Notes

1. The relationship of the "thin skull" rule to *The Wagon Mound* doctrine is no easy one. This consideration was in evidence in the South African case of *Alston* v. *Marine and Trade Insurance Co., Ltd.,* 1964 (4) S.A. 112, noted by C. C. Turpin, [1965] C.L.J. 34, where *The Wagon Mound* doctrine was not accepted, Hiemstra J. spoke in the following terms (at p. 115):

> "This question, whether there can be a different criterion for determining culpability and compensation, so *The Wagon Mound* rightly says, 'goes to the root of the matter'. *The Wagon Mound* sweeps away all difference, and here it immediately becomes unconvincing. An accident and some injury can be foreseeable but the form and extent of the damage hardly ever. The escape from this truism is to say that the *type* of damage can be foreseen, namely, fire or bodily injury, and that the extent thereof was not meant to be included in the foreseeability test. . . .
>
> *The Wagon Mound* has laid down a rule of thumb which will in most cases be easy to apply but is neither intellectually satisfying nor always just. It already breaks down upon the 'eggshell skull' cases. Or, differently put, it has to be lovingly accommodated before it will harmonise with the well-established rule 'You must take your victim as you find him'. It is probably unforeseeable that you will run down a millionaire in a slum, but he is nevertheless entitled to his much higher compensation than the pauper. These considerations convince me that the dichotomy between culpability and compensation is not as fundamentally false as *The Wagon Mound* would make out."

2. As *Smith* v. *Leech Brain & Co., Ltd.* shows, the thin skull rule has been accommodated by English courts, however uneasily, with *The Wagon Mound* doctrine. See further *Wieland* v. *Cyril Lord Carpets, Ltd.,* [1969] 3 All E.R. 1006; *Robinson* v. *The Post Office* (1973), *Times,* 26 October and see A. I. Ogus, *The Law of Damages,* pp. 68–70. Given a foreseeable injury, the plaintiff may suffer further unforeseeable damage. As has been shown above, this may occur where the plaintiff's peculiar susceptibility was in existence before the first injury. However, it may also occur, without such pre-existing susceptibility, where the first injury has *created* a new risk or susceptibility—e.g. where the foreseeable injury becomes infected and leads to more serious injury. In a recent New Zealand case, *Stephenson* v. *Waite, Tileman, Ltd.,* [1973] 1 N.Z.L.R. 152, Richmond J. (with Turner P. concurring) discussed this latter point and the relationship of the thin skull cases with *The Wagon Mound.* He said (at p. 165):

> "The decisions in England, Scotland, Ireland and Canada are of importance because in all of them the Courts have limited the test of foreseeability to the initial kind of injury. The consequences, often unforeseeable, of the initial injury have been treated as falling within the field of *extent* of the injury. These decisions fulfil the earlier prophecy of academic writers that the eggshell skull principle would remain part of English law notwithstanding the decision in *The Wagon Mound.* In my opinion this Court should adopt a similar attitude. It may be difficult to decide upon an adequate theoretical reconciliation of the continued existence of this rule and *The Wagon Mound* principle, but for practical purposes it does not matter whether it be regarded as an exception to the general rule or whether the unforeseeable consequences are regarded simply as going to the extent of the injury rather than to the kind of the injury. Whatever explanation be adopted, it must in my opinion also follow . . . that we should accept as part of our law the principle of liability for harmful consequences arising from a new risk created by a foreseeable kind of injury. These two principles must necessarily go hand in hand. In the result, I gratefully adopt Lord Parker's sentence [in *Smith* v. *Leech Brain & Co., Ltd.,* [1962] 2 Q.B. 405,

at p. 415, p. 196, *ante*]. 'What, in the particular case, is the amount of damage which he suffers as a result of that burn, depends on the characteristics and constitution of the victim'. I would however add thereto the words 'and upon the operation of any new risks to which he is exposed as a result thereof' ".

At p. 168, Richmond J. summarised his conclusions as follows:

"1 In cases of damage by physical injury to the person the principles imposing liability for consequences flowing from the pre-existing special susceptibility of the victim and/or from new risk or susceptibility created by the initial injury remain part of our law.

2 In such cases the question of foreseeability should be limited to the initial injury. The tribunal of fact must decide whether that injury is of a kind, type or character which the defendant ought reasonably to have foreseen as a real risk.

3 If the plaintiff establishes that the initial injury was within a reasonably foreseeable kind, type or character of injury, then the necessary link between the ultimate consequences of the initial injury and the negligence of the defendant can be forged simply as one of cause and effect—in other words by establishing an adequate relationship of cause and effect between the initial injury and the ultimate consequence.

If I am correct in the foregoing conclusions then juries will be left to deal with the question of foreseeability in an area which is readily comprehensible and in which the test of the ordinary reasonable man can be applied in an atmosphere of reality. They will not have to decide the ability of the ordinary man to foresee the risks of 'kinds' of harm resulting from a 'sub-compartmentalisation' of secondary consequences of an initial injury. Nor will it be necessary to decide whether a doctor driving a motor car is to be made liable for a greater field of injury than would the ordinary layman in similar circumstances."

3. The case of *Pigney* v. *Pointers Transport Services, Ltd.*, [1957] 2 All E.R. 807, was mentioned at an earlier stage (see p. 182, *ante*). In that case the plaintiff's husband, an employee of the defendants, had been injured in an accident in July 1955, which occurred whilst he was working at the defendants' premises. He suffered an injury to his head due to the defendants' negligence, and, as a result of the accident, experienced an "acute anxiety neurosis with depressive features". He underwent treatment in a mental hospital as a voluntary patient, but some months later in January 1957, whilst suffering from depression caused by the anxiety neurosis, he hanged himself. Pilcher J. held that the injury was the cause of the husband's death. He had earlier quoted part of the judgment of Scrutton L.J. in *Re Polemis*, [1921] 3 K.B. 560 and stated (at p. 810) that "Whilst the death of the deceased was not the kind of damage that one would expect to result from the injury he received, I am satisfied that his death was, to use Scrutton L.J.'s words, 'directly traceable' to the physical injury which he sustained due to the lack of care of the defendants for his safety." In the light of *The Wagon Mound*, it might be thought that the case would be decided differently today. However, in an article—"The Risk Principle" (1961), 77 L.Q.R. 179—Glanville Williams, in referring to this decision, writes (at p. 196):

"The learned judge based his decision on *Re Polemis*, but it can be supported independently of that case. Either the victim's suicide was a normal reaction to his injuries, or it was abnormal. If it was normal, it should be taken as reasonably foreseeable; if it was abnormal, it comes within the thin skull rule as applied to psychic states."

4. On foreseeability and the extent of damage to property, see Clerk & Lindsell, para. 349, and see *Vacwell Engineering Co., Ltd.* v. *B.D.H. Chemicals, Ltd.*, [1971] 1 Q.B. 88, at p. 110. On the relevance of the plaintiff's want of means, see *The Edison*, [1933] A.C. 499, p. 190, *ante*, and on the "infirmities of employment" of a plaintiff, see *Malcolm* v. *Broadhurst*, [1970] 3 All E.R. 508, p. 192, *ante*.

(b) The type or kind of damage

Hughes v. Lord Advocate

House of Lords   [1963] 1 All E.R. 705

Some men employed by the Post Office were working on cables under a road and they reached the cables by means of a ladder in a manhole. There was a tent over the manhole and at the material time there were red warning paraffin lights around the site. Before going for their teabreak, the men took the ladder from the manhole and put it on the ground outside the tent and they pulled some tarpaulin over the entrance to the tent, leaving a gap of about two feet six inches between it and the ground. In their absence, the appellant and another ten year old boy (his uncle) took one of the lamps and the ladder into the tent and went down the manhole. After they had come out of the manhole, the appellant stumbled over the lamp which was knocked into the hole. There was a violent explosion and flames reached a height of thirty feet. The appellant fell into the hole and was badly burnt. On appeal to the House of Lords from the First Division of the Court of Session, 1961 S.C. 310, who, affirming the Lord Ordinary's decision, had held the respondent not liable:

LORD REID: My Lords, I have had an opportunity of reading the speech which my noble and learned friend Lord Guest is about to deliver. I agree with him that this appeal should be allowed and I shall only add some general observations. I am satisfied that the Post Office workmen were in fault in leaving this open manhole unattended and it is clear that if they had done as they ought to have done this accident would not have happened. It cannot be said that they owed no duty to the appellant. But it has been held that the appellant cannot recover damages.

It was argued that the appellant cannot recover because the damage which he suffered was of a kind which was not foreseeable. That was not the ground of judgment of the First Division or of the Lord Ordinary and the facts proved do not, in my judgment, support that argument. The appellant's injuries were mainly caused by burns, and it cannot be said that injuries from burns were unforeseeable. As a warning to traffic the workmen had set lighted red lamps round the tent which covered the manhole, and if boys did enter the dark tent it was very likely that they would take one of these lamps with them. If the lamp fell and broke it was not at all unlikely that the boy would be burned and the burns might well be serious. No doubt it was not to be expected that the injuries would be as serious as those which the appellant in fact sustained. But a defender is liable, although the damage may be a good deal greater in extent than was foreseeable. He can only escape liability if the damage can be regarded as differing in kind from what was foreseeable.

So we have (first) a duty owed by the workmen, (secondly) the fact that if they had done as they ought to have done there would have been no accident, and (thirdly) the fact that the injuries suffered by the appellant, though perhaps different in degree, did not differ in kind from injuries which might have resulted from an accident of a foreseeable nature. The ground on which this case has been decided against the appellant is that the accident was of an unforeseeable type. Of course the pursuer has to prove that the defender's fault caused the accident and there could be a case where the intrusion of a new and unexpected factor could be regarded as the cause of the accident rather than the fault of the defender. But that is not this case. The cause of this accident was a known source of danger, the lamp, but it behaved in an unpredictable way. The explanation of the accident which has been accepted, and which I would not seek to question, is that, when the lamp fell down the manhole and was broken, some paraffin escaped, and enough was vaporized to create an explosive mixture which was detonated by the naked light of the lamp. The experts agree that no one would have expected that to happen: it was so unlikely as to be unforeseeable. The explosion caused the boy to fall into the manhole: whether his injuries were directly caused by the explosion or aggravated by fire which started in the manhole is not at all clear. . . .

. . . This accident was caused by a known source of danger, but caused in a way which could not have been foreseen, and in my judgment that affords no defence. I would therefore allow the appeal.

LORD JENKINS: . . . It is true that the duty of care expected in cases of this sort is confined to reasonably foreseeable dangers, but it does not necessarily follow that liability is escaped because the danger actually materialising is not identical with the danger reasonably foreseen and guarded against. Each case must depend on its own particular facts. For example . . . in the present case the paraffin did the mischief by exploding, not burning, and it is said that, while a paraffin fire (caused, e.g. by the upsetting of the lighted lamp or otherwise allowing its contents to leak out) was a reasonably foreseeable risk so soon as the pursuer got access to the lamp, an explosion was not. To my mind the distinction drawn between burning and explosion is too fine to warrant acceptance. . . .

LORD GUEST: . . . In dismissing the appellant's claim the Lord Ordinary and the majority of the judges of the First Division reached the conclusion that the accident which happened was not reasonably foreseeable. In order to establish a coherent chain of causation it is not necessary that the precise details leading up to the accident should have been reasonably foreseeable: it is sufficient if the accident which occurred is of a type which should have been foreseeable by a reasonably careful person (*Miller* v. *South of Scotland Electricity Board* per Lord Keith of Avonholm;[1] *Harvey* v. *Singer Manufacturing Co., Ltd.* per Lord Patrick[2]); or as Lord Mackintosh,[3] expressed it in *Harvey's* case[4] the precise concatenation of circumstances need not be envisaged. Concentration has been placed in the courts below on the explosion which it was said could not have been foreseen because it was caused in a unique fashion by the paraffin forming into vapour and being ignited by the naked flame of the wick. But this, in my opinion, is to concentrate on what is really a non-essential element in the dangerous situation created by the allurement. The test might better be put thus:—Was the igniting of paraffin outside the lamp by the flame a foreseeable consequence of the breach of duty? In the circumstances there was a combination of potentially dangerous circumstances against which the Post Office had to protect the appellant. If these formed an allurement to children it might have been foreseen that they would play with the lamp, that it might tip over, that it might be broken, and that when broken the paraffin might spill and be ignited by the flame. All these steps in the chain of causation seem to have been accepted by all the judges in the courts below as foreseeable. But because the explosion was the agent which caused the burning and was unforeseeable, therefore the accident, according to them, was not reasonably foreseeable. In my opinion this reasoning is fallacious. An explosion is only one way in which burning can be caused. Burning can also be caused by the contact between liquid paraffin and a naked flame. In the one case paraffin vapour and in the other case liquid paraffin is ignited by fire. I cannot see that these are two different types of accident. They are both burning accidents and in both cases the injuries would be burning injuries. On this view the explosion was an immaterial event

---

1. 1958 S.C. (H.L.) 20, at p. 34.
2. 1960 S.C. 55, at p. 168.
3. 1960 S.C. at p. 172.
4. 1960 S.C. 155.

in the chain of causation. It was simply one way in which burning might be caused by the potentially dangerous paraffin lamp. . . .

I have therefore reached the conclusion that the accident which occurred and which caused burning injuries to the appellant was one which ought reasonably to have been foreseen by the Post Office employees and that they were at fault in failing to provide a protection against the appellant entering the shelter and going down the manhole.

I would allow the appeal.

LORD PEARCE: . . . Did the explosion create an accident and damage of a different type from the misadventure and damage that could be foreseen? In my judgment it did not. The accident was but a variant of the foreseeable. It was, to quote the words of Denning L.J. in *Roe* v. *Ministry of Health* [1] "within the risk created by the negligence." No unforeseeable extraneous, initial occurrence fired the train. . . .

[LORD MORRIS OF BORTH-Y-GEST delivered a speech in favour of allowing the appeal.]

Appeal allowed

Note

1. *Doughty* v. *Turner Manufacturing Co., Ltd.*, [1964] 1 Q.B. 518; [1964] 1 All E.R. 98 has caused problems. Two cauldrons containing molten liquid at 800° centigrade had loose covers made of an asbestos/cement compound. One of the covers, which were between four and six inches above the liquid, was inadvertently knocked, and slid into the cauldron, becoming submerged in the liquid. This was not regarded as dangerous. Less than two minutes later the liquid erupted, and the plaintiff, who had taken a message to a foreman who was near the cauldrons, suffered burns. The eruption was a consequence, it was later discovered, of a chemical change in the cover because of the heat, but, in the light of the knowledge at the time when the plaintiff was injured, the accident was unforeseeable. Counsel for the plaintiff argued that the accident "was merely a variant of foreseeable accidents by splashing". More than one ground can be put forward as to why the plaintiff should fail on the facts of this case—see Clerk and Lindsell, para. 347—but Harman L.J. did state (at p. 529) that the damage in the case "was of an entirely different kind from the foreseeable splash" (see also Lord Pearce, at p. 527). Can Harman L.J.'s view be reconciled with *Hughes* v. *Lord Advocate*?

Tremain v. Pike

Exeter Assizes   [1969] 3 All E.R. 1303

PAYNE J.: The plaintiff in this case, William Tremain, is claiming damages for a disease which he contracted, and which he alleges to be due to the negligence of the defendants. The case is conveniently summarised in the plaintiff's statement of claim in which it is said that, at the material time, he was employed as a herdsman by the defendants, who are farmers, at Bovey Barton Farm at Beer, Seaton, in Devonshire, and that in the course of his employment he used a water trough and a milking parlour, and also washed his hands in the water trough; further, that at times he handled hay on the farm; that in or about March 1967, and before that date, the premises were infested and over-run with rats; that in or about March 1967, or previously, the water in the trough, or alternatively hay handled by the plaintiff, became infected by rats with the germs and organisms of a disease commonly known as Weil's disease; that in or about March 1967, in the course of his employment, through carrying out the operations described, he contracted Weil's disease and suffered injury. The particulars of negligence, which I need not read in full, concentrate on these complaints; that the defendants permitted the farm to become infested and over-run with rats and that they failed to take adequate

---

1. [1954] 2 Q.B. 66, at p. 85; [1954] 2 All E.R. 131, at p. 138.

steps to keep the farm free from rats or to reduce their number. There are further particulars: they say that the defendants failed to keep the buildings on the farm, and in particular the milking parlour, in good repair so as to prevent rats from entering and breeding in the buildings, they failed to take adequate steps to prevent the water trough or the hay from being infected, and in consequence of all those matters the plaintiff contracted this disease. . . .

[Having referred to the fact that he had heard evidence from Dr. Alston, an authority on the disease, he continued:] . . . The defendants do not dispute that in March 1967 the plaintiff became infected with Weil's disease, and they accept that it would be proper for me to find on the balance of probabilities that he contracted the disease in consesequence of his employment on the farm.

Dr. Alston has made a special study of Weil's disease or leptospirosis for the last 35 years. It is now known that the leptospires are present in about 40 to 50 per cent. of the rats in this country, and that the leptospires are passed from the kidney to the urine of the rat, and remain active in the urine for two or three days if they remain in wet or damp conditions. Rats infect each other and so perpetuate the disease. Human beings contract the disease through contact with the rodent urine and contamination of the skin, especially if the skin is cut, eroded or sodden with water. The incidence of the disease in human beings is rare in spite of the prevalence of the leptospires in rats because of the very slight susceptibility of human beings to the disease. The risk is very low indeed. . . .

[His Lordship considered the evidence as to infestation of rats in and around the farm buildings, and continued:] On that evidence I am satisfied that, in March 1967, there was a growing population of rats in and around the farm buildings, the farmyard and their precincts, and that the time had arrived when a prudent and experienced farmer, once the facts had come to his knowledge, would call in the rodent officer or a contractor, and arrange for an intensive attack on the rats. He would, however, take that course with a view to protecting his milk supply, preventing the contamination of foodstuffs, preserving his animal feed and generally improving cleanliness. He would not have in mind the safety of his farm staff in the performance of their work as his servants as there was no reason for him to suppose that they were in any danger in their daily work. Moreover, I am not satisfied that in March 1967 the defendants knew, or ought reasonably to have known: (i) that the rat population had reached the proportions which the evidence before me establishes; or (ii) that any more precautions were required than those which they applied as a matter of routine. . . .

. . . I feel able on the evidence to find that, on the balance of probabilities, the plaintiff became infected on the farm, but any greater precision would not be justified. The employer's duty to his servants is to take reasonable care for their safety, and this safety extends to the safety of the premises and the plant, and to the method and conduct of the work, but is not restricted to those matters. Put in slightly different words, his duty is to take reasonable steps to avoid exposing his servants to a reasonably foreseeable risk of injury.

It follows from the contents of this judgment that, in my opinion, the defendants were not in breach of any duty of care to the plaintiff, nor was his disease attributable to any such breach. If, contrary to my view, it should be held that the defendants were in breach of duty in that they ought to have known of the extent of the infestation in March 1967, and ought to have foreseen that the plaintiff was, or might be, exposed to some general hazard involving personal injury, illness or disease in consequence of the infestation, the defendants, as I think, are still immune from liability on the grounds that Weil's disease was at best a remote possibility which they could not reasonably foresee, and that the damage suffered by the plaintiff was, therefore, unforeseeable and too remote to be recoverable.

I do not accept the contention of counsel for the plaintiff that it is sufficient to show that the plaintiff was exposed generally to the risk of disease because of the possible contamination of animal feed or of milk at the farm, or the possibility of the plaintiff being bitten, itself, in my view, an unlikely event. Weil's disease is not comparable to the other human disabilities which may flow from an infestation of rats. One must not overlook the fact that, if the defendants had to take effective precautions against Weil's disease, it would not be sufficient merely to keep the rat population in check by poisoning, trapping, hunting and so forth. A rat population of varying size would still remain on the farm as it does on all farms. It would be necessary to introduce protective clothing for the hands and arms, some check on cuts and abrasions and a system of washing facilities and hygiene which, in my view, would be out of all proportion in cost and effort to the risk which had to be countered. . . .

The kind of damage suffered here was a disease contracted by contact with rats' urine. This, in my view, was entirely different in kind from the effect of a rat-bite, or food poisoning by the consumption of food or drink contaminated by rats. I do not accept that all illness or infection arising from an infestation of rats should be regarded as of the same kind. One cannot say in this case, as was said by Lord Reid in *Hughes'* case:[1] ". . . if they [the defenders] had done as they ought to have done there would have been no accident . . ."

It may be that it is less satisfactory in this case to ask the question whether the infection is different in kind from other sequelae of rat infestation which might be foreseeable, as that leads to disputation about what is meant by difference in kind, than to ask the direct question whether, on the facts of this case, the leptospirosis was reasonably foreseeable by the defendants. In my opinion, one has only to ask that question and the answer is inescapably "No". . . .

Judgment for the defendants

Notes

1. On remoteness of damage generally see also *Draper* v. *Hodder*, [1972] 2 Q.B. 556; [1972] 2 All E.R. 210, p. 363, *post*.

2. In *Bradford* v. *Robinson Rentals, Ltd.*, [1967] 1 All E.R. 267, the plaintiff, a 57 year old man, was employed by the defendants in Exeter as a radio service engineer, and he travelled to and from his jobs in a van. One day, when there was snow and ice on the roads, he was told to drive a colleague's van to Bedford to change it for a new one, and to drive the new one back. The chance to change vehicles might have been lost if it were not taken up quickly. Both the A.A. and a B.B.C. broadcast advised that only essential journeys should be made. The plaintiff, who was reluctant to make the journey, protested in vain, and he set off the next day. The van's heater at that time was disconnected, and the radiator had to be topped up frequently during the journey. The plaintiff took all reasonable precautions against the cold, but the lack of a heater meant that his breath formed ice on the windscreen so he had to keep a window open. The new van had no heater either, so a window had to be kept open on the return journey as well. The plaintiff suffered permanent injury to his hands and feet through frostbite. Had the plaintiff established that this was a reasonably foreseeable type of injury? Rees J. apparently thought so. He held that the risk of injury from exposure to extreme cold and tiredness was reasonably foreseeable, and that the defendants were liable to the plaintiff. This was so even if the latter was peculiarly susceptible to frostbite, since a tortfeasor takes his victim as he finds him, although there was no evidence of such susceptibility in fact in the case. In *Tremain* v. *Pike* Payne J. thought the distinction between *Smith* v. *Leech Brain & Co., Ltd.*, [1962] 2 Q.B. 405; [1961] 3 All E.R. 1159, p. 196, *ante*, and the *Bradford* case

---

1. [1963] A.C. at p. 845; 1 All E.R. at p. 706;

on the one hand, and the case he was considering on the other hand, to be "crystal clear". He said—[1969] 3 All E.R., at p. 1309—that "the risk of injury from a burn in the first case and from extreme cold in the second was foreseeable, and it was only the degree of injury or the development of the sequelae which was not foreseeable. In this case, the risk of the initial infection of the plaintiff was, in my view, not reasonably foreseeable." For a note discussing *Tremain* v. *Pike* and *Bradford* v. *Robinson Rentals, Ltd.*, see R. W. M. Dias, [1970] C.L.J. 28.

3. For discussion of causation and remoteness of damage raising policy considerations see Atiyah, *Accidents, Compensation and the Law*, Chap. 4; and J. G. Merrills, "Policy and Remoteness", [1973] Ottawa L.R. 18.

6

Nervous Shock

It is important to realise that the nervous shock with which this Chapter is concerned, is a shock which results in some illness being suffered by the plaintiff. Mere mental distress on its own is not compensated (though for an exception see the tort of assault, and for a suggestion of what is in practice another exception to this statement, see P. S. Atiyah, *Accidents, Compensation and the Law*, p. 66). The courts may find themselves concerned with difficult questions of medical causation, and the legal and medical professions have not always seen eye to eye on the problems involved in nervous shock cases. (See J. Harvard, "Reasonable Foresight of Nervous Shock" (1956), 19 M.L.R. 478). Doubts have been cast, for example, on the number of miscarriages *really* caused by emotional shock—(1956), 19 M.L.R. at p. 481.

The cases this century have revealed a general expansion of the area of liability for nervous shock, although it has been and remains a difficult area of the law, in which policy plays a particularly important part in determining the boundaries of liability.

There is support in the authorities for two different theories in this area of the law—the "area of impact" theory and the "area of shock" theory, although the latter is favoured today. Clerk and Lindsell propound these two theories in the following passage (at para. 872):

> "According to the 'impact' theory, as long as it was reasonably foreseeable that the defendant's conduct might have inflicted injury on the plaintiff by actual impact of some sort, he can recover for illness resulting from shock even though he sustained no injury from impact. . . . According to the 'shock' theory, as long as it was reasonably foreseeable that the defendant's conduct would have caused even only shock to an ordinarily strong-nerved person, situated in the position of the plaintiff, then the plaintiff can recover in respect of the shock to him."

The courts usually talk of the problems in nervous shock cases in terms of whether there was any duty owed by the defendant, but occasionally the notion of remoteness of damage has been brought into play. Judges are still a little wary of claims for damages for nervous shock and there are certain rules to be found in the cases which limit the area of liability e.g. that the shock must be occasioned by something perceived personally by the plaintiff (by his or her "own unaided senses"—*Hambrook v. Stokes Bros.*, [1925] 1 K. B. 141): shock as a result of information received after the event is excluded.

1. INTENTIONALLY CAUSED

Wilkinson v. Downton, p. 50, *ante*

Janvier v. Sweeney, p. 52, *ante*

2. NEGLIGENTLY CAUSED

Hay or Bourhill v. Young

House of Lords   [1942] 2 All E.R. 396

LORD THANKERTON: My Lords, the appellant is the pursuer in an action of reparation, in which she claims damages from the respondent, as executor-dative of the late John Young, in respect of injuries alleged to have been sustained by her owing to the fault of John Young on the occasion of a collision between a motor-cycle which the latter was riding and a motor car on 11 October 1938, which resulted in the death of John Young, to whom I will hereafter refer as the cyclist. After a proof, Lord Robertson assoilzied the respondent on the ground that the cyclist had not been guilty of any breach of duty to the appellant, and this decision was affirmed by the Second Division, Lord Justice-Clerk Aitchison dissenting.

The facts as to the occurrence of the collision and its relation to the appellant are comparatively simple. The appellant, who is a fishwife, was a passenger on a tramway car which was proceeding in the direction of Colinton along the Colinton Road, which may be taken as a south-westerly direction, and which stopped at a stopping-place at a short distance before Colinton Road is joined at right angles by Glenlockhart Road from the south-east, that is, on the near side of the tramcar. The appellant alighted and went round the near side and front of the tramcar, in order to lift her fishbasket from the off-side of the driver's platform. Meantime, the cyclist, travelling in the same direction as the tramcar, had come up and, as the appellant was getting her basket, he passed on the near side of the tramcar and, when mostly across the opening of Glenlockhart Road, his cycle collided with a motor car, which had been travelling in the opposite direction, but had turned across the path of the cycle in order to enter Glenlockhart Road. The cyclist, who was held by the Lord Ordinary to have been travelling at an excessive speed, was thrown on to the street and sustained injuries from which he died. There is no doubt that the appellant saw and heard nothing of the cyclist until the sound of the noise created by the impact of the two vehicles reached her senses. At that moment she had her back to the driver's platform and the driver was assisting to get the basket on to her back and the broad leather strap on to her forehead. It may be taken that the distance between the appellant and the point of impact was between 45 and 50 ft. After the cyclist's body had been removed, the appellant approached and saw the blood left on the roadway. The injuries alleged to have been sustained by the appellant are set out in condescendence 4 of the record, as follows:

> Condescendence 4.—As an immediate result of the violent collision and the extreme shock of the occurrence in the circumstances explained, the pursuer wrenched and injured her back and was thrown into a state of terror and sustained a very severe shock to her nervous system. *Explained that the pursuer's terror did not involve any element of reasonable fear of immediate bodily injury to herself.* The pursuer was about eight months pregnant at the time, and gave birth to a child on 18 November 1938, which was still-born owing to the injuries sustained by the pursuer. . . .

It is clear that, in the law of Scotland, the present action can only be based on negligence, and:

It is necessary for the pursuer in such an action to show there was a duty owed to him by the defenders, because a man cannot be charged with negligence if he has no obligation to exercise diligence.

per Lord Kinnear in *Kemp and Dougall* v. *Darngavil Coal Co., Ltd.*[1] at p. 1319. I may further adopt the words of Lord Johnston in the same case, at p. 1327:

> . . . the obligee in such a duty must be a person or of a class definitely ascertained, and so related by the circumstances to the obligor that the obligor is bound, in the exercise of ordinary sense, to regard his interest and his safety. Only the relation must not be too remote, for remoteness must be held as a general limitation of the doctrine.

My Lords, I doubt whether, in view of the infinite variation of circumstances which may exist, it is possible or profitable to lay down any hard and fast principle, beyond the test of remoteness as applied to the particular case. Lord Justice-Clerk Aitchison, who dissented, accepted the test of proximity, although it is a little difficult to follow how he made his conclusion satisfy this test. In the observations I have to make, I shall confine myself to the question of the range of duty of a motor cyclist on the public road towards other passengers on the road. Clearly this duty is to drive the cycle with such reasonable care as will avoid the risk of injury to such persons as he can reasonably foresee might be injured by failure to exercise such reasonable care. It is now settled that such injury includes injury by shock, although no direct physical impact or lesion occurs. If then the test of proximity or remoteness is to be applied, I am of opinion that such a test involves that the injury must be within that which the cyclist ought to have reasonably contemplated as the area of potential danger which would arise as the result of his negligence, and the question in the present case is whether the appellant was within that area. I am clearly of opinion that she was not, for the following reasons.

Although admittedly going at excessive speed, the cyclist had his machine under his control, and this at once distinguishes this case from such cases as those where the motor has been left standing unoccupied and insufficiently braked, and has started off on an uncontrolled career. At the time of the collision with the motor he was well past the tramcar and the appellant was not within the range of his vision, let alone that the tramcar obstructed any view of her. The risk of the bicycle ricochetting and hitting the appellant, or of flying glass hitting her, in her position at the time, was so remote, in my opinion, that the cyclist could not reasonably be held bound to have contemplated it, and I differ from Lord Justice-Clerk Aitchison on this point, but as already stated, the appellant's case is not now based on any fear of such possibilities, but merely on the sound of the collision. There is no suggestion that the volume of the noise of the collision afforded any ground for argument, and I am clearly of opinion that, in this case, the shock resulting to the appellant, situated as she was, was not within the area of potential danger which the cyclist should reasonably have had in view. In my opinion, none of the cases cited presents sufficiently analogous circumstances, such as should control the decision in the present case. . . .

I am, therefore, of opinion that the appellant has failed to establish that, at the time of the collision, the cyclist owed any duty to her, and that the appeal fails. I accordingly move that the appeal should be dismissed, that the judgment appealed from should be affirmed, and that the appellant should pay the respondent's costs of the appeal.

LORD RUSSELL OF KILLOWEN: . . . In considering whether a person owes to another a duty a breach of which will render him liable to that other in damages for negligence, it is material to consider what the defendant ought to have contemplated as a reasonable man. This consideration may play a double role. It is relevant in cases of admitted negligence (where the duty and breach are admitted) to the question of remoteness of damages, i.e. to the question of compensation not to culpability; but it is also rele-

---

1. 1909 S.C. 1314.

vant in testing the existence of a duty as the foundation of the alleged negligence, i.e. to the question of culpability not to that of compensation. . . .

A man is not liable for negligence in the air; the liability only arises:

> . . . where there is a duty to take care and where failure in that duty has caused damage.

(see *per* Lord Macmillan in *M'Alister* (or *Donoghue*) v. *Stevenson*,[1] at p. 618). In my opinion such a duty only arises towards those individuals of whom it may be reasonably anticipated that they will be affected by the act which constituted the alleged breach. Can it be said that John Young could reasonably have anticipated that a person, situated as was the pursuer, would be affected by his proceeding towards Colinton at the speed at which he was travelling. I think not. His road was clear of pedestrians. The pursuer was not within his vision, but was standing behind the solid barrier of the tramcar. His speed in no way endangered her. In these circumstances I am unable to see how he could reasonably anticipate that, if he came into collision with a vehicle coming across the tramcar into Glenlockhart Road, the resultant noise would cause physical injury by shock to a person standing behind the tramcar. In my opinion he owed no duty to the pursuer, and was, therefore, not guilty of any negligence in relation to her. . . .

LORD MACMILLAN: . . . It is no longer necessary to consider whether the infliction of what is called mental shock may constitute an actionable wrong. The crude view that the law should take cognizance only of physical injury resulting from actual impact has been discarded, and it is now well recognised that an action will lie for injury by shock sustained through the medium of the eye or the ear without direct contact. The distinction between mental shock and bodily injury was never a scientific one, for mental shock is presumably in all cases the result of, or at least accompanied by, some physical disturbance in the sufferer's system, and a mental shock may have consequences more serious than those resulting from physical impact. In the case of mental shock, however, there are elements of greater subtlety than in the case of an ordinary physical injury and these elements may give rise to debate as to the precise scope of legal liability.

Your Lordships have here to deal with a common law action founded on negligence. The pursuer's plea is that she has "sustained loss, injury and damage through the fault of the said John Young," and that she is "entitled to reparation therefor out of his estate." She can recover damages only if she can show that in relation to her the late John Young acted negligently. To establish this she must show that he owed her a duty of care which he failed to observe and that, as a result of this failure in duty on his part, she suffered as she did. . . . The duty to take care is the duty to avoid doing or omitting to do anything the doing or omitting to do which may have as its reasonable and probable consequence injury to others and the duty is owed to those to whom injury may reasonably and probably be anticipated if the duty is not observed.

There is no absolute standard of what is reasonable and probable. It must depend on circumstances and must always be a question of degree. In the present instance the late John Young was clearly negligent in a question with the occupants of the motor car with which his cycle collided. He was driving at an excessive speed in a public thoroughfare and he ought to have foreseen that he might consequently collide with any vehicle which he might meet in his course, for such an occurrence may reasonably and probably be expected to ensue from driving at a high speed in a street. But can it be said that he ought further to have foreseen that his excessive speed, involving the possibility of collision with another vehicle, might cause injury by shock to the pursuer? The pursuer was not within his line of vision, for she was on the other side of a tramway car which was standing between him and her when he passed and it was not until he had proceeded some distance beyond her that he collided with the motor car. The

---

1. [1932] A.C. 562.

pursuer did not see the accident and she expressly admits that her "terror did not involve any element of reasonable fear of immediate bodily injury to herself." She was not so placed that there was any reasonable likelihood of her being affected by the deceased's careless driving.

In these circumstances I am of opinion with the majority of the judges of the second division that the late John Young was under no duty to the pursuer to foresee that his negligence in driving at an excessive speed and consequently colliding with a motor car might result in injury to the pursuer, for such a result could not reasonably and probably be anticipated. He was, therefore, not guilty of negligence in a question with the pursuer.

That is sufficient for the disposal of the case and absolves me from considering the question whether injury through mental shock is actionable only when, in the words of Kennedy J., the shock arises from a reasonable fear of immediate personal injury to oneself (*Dulieu* v. *White & Sons*,[1] at p. 682), which was admittedly not the case in the present instance. It also absolves me from considering whether, if the late John Young neglected any duty which he owed to the pursuer, which, in my opinion, he did not, the injury of which she complains was too remote to entitle her to damages. I shall observe only that the view expressed by Kennedy J. has in Scotland the support of a substantial body of authority, although it was not accepted by the Court of Appeal in England in *Hambrook* v. *Stokes Bros.*,[2] notwithstanding a powerful dissent by Sargant L.J. This House has not yet been called upon to pronounce on the question either as a matter of Scots Law or as a matter of English Law, and I reserve my opinion upon it. . . .

LORD WRIGHT: My Lords, that damage by mental shock may give a cause of action is now well-established and is not disputed in this case, but as Phillimore J. pointed out in his admirable judgment in *Dulieu* v. *White & Sons*,[1] the real difficulty in questions of this kind is to decide whether there has been a wrongful act or breach of duty on the part of the defendant *vis-à-vis* the plaintiff. That being the prior question, if it is answered against the plaintiff, the matter is concluded. I shall, therefore, consider that issue in the first place. . . .

This general concept of reasonable foresight as the criterion of negligence or breach of duty (strict or otherwise) may be criticised as too vague; but negligence is a fluid principle, which has to be applied to the most diverse conditions and problems of human life. It is a concrete not an abstract idea. It has to be fitted to the facts of the particular case. Willes J. defined it as absence of care according to the circumstances (*Vaughan* v. *Taff Vale Rail. Co.*,[3] at p. 688). It is also always relative to the individual affected. This raises a serious additional difficulty in the cases where it has to be determined not merely whether the act itself is negligent against someone but whether it is negligent *vis-à-vis* the plaintiff. This is a crucial point in cases of nervous shock. Thus in the present case John Young was certainly negligent in an issue between himself and the owner of the car which he ran into, but it is another question whether he was negligent *vis-à-vis* the appellant.

In such cases terms like "derivative" and "original" and "primary" and "secondary" have been applied to define and distinguish the type of the negligence. If, however, the appellant has a cause of action, it is because of a wrong to herself. She cannot build on a wrong to someone else. Her interest, which was in her own bodily security, was of a different order from the interest of the owner of the car. That this is so is also illustrated by cases such as have been called in the United States "rescue" or "search" cases. This type has been recently examined and explained in the Court of Appeal in *Haynes* v. *Harwood*,[4] where the plaintiff, a police constable, was injured in stopping runaway horses in a crowded street, in which were many children. His act was due to

1. [1901] 2 K.B. 669.
2. [1925] 1 K.B. 141.
3. (1860), 5 H. & N. 679.
4. [1935] 1 K.B. 146.

his mental reaction, whether instinctive or deliberate, to the spectacle of others' peril. The Court of Appeal approved the language used by the trial judge, Finlay J., at p. 247, when he held that to leave the horses unattended was a breach of duty not only to any person injured by being run over (in fact no one was so injured), but to the constable. The words of Finlay J. were:

> "It seems to me that if horses run away it must be quite obviously contemplated that people are likely to be knocked down. It must also, I think, be contemplated that persons will attempt to stop the horses and try to prevent injury to life and limb."

I may also refer to the admirable judgment of Cardozo J. in the New York Court of Appeals in *Wagner* v. *International Rail. Co.*,[1] a "search" case, which is to the same effect. This again shows how the ambit of the persons affected by negligence or misconduct may extend beyond persons who are actually subject to physical impact. There, indeed, may be no one injured in a particular case by actual impact; but still a wrong may be committed to anyone who suffers nervous shock or is injured in an act of rescue. The man who negligently allows a horse to bolt, or a car to run at large down a steep street, or a savage beast to escape is committing a breach of duty towards every person who comes within the range of foreseeable danger, whether by impact or shock; but, if there is no negligence or other default, there can be no liability for either direct impact or for nervous shock. Thus, if, owing to a latent defect or some mischance for which no one is liable, a terrifying collision occurs between vehicles on the road and the occupants are killed or suffer horrible injuries, a bystander who suffers shock, whether through personal fear or merely through horror, would have no action. On somewhat similar principles may be solved the problem of the old lady at Charing Cross, who suffers shock because she narrowly escapes being run over. She cannot claim damages if the driver is driving carefully, whether he hits her or not.

The present case, like many others of this type, may, however, raise the different question whether the appellant's illness was not due to her peculiar susceptibility. She was 8 months gone in pregnancy. Can it be said, apart from everything else, that it was likely that a person of normal nervous strength would have been affected in the circumstances by illness as the appellant, was? Does the criterion or[2] reasonable foresight extend beyond people of ordinary health or susceptibility, or does it take into account the peculiar susceptibilities or infirmities of those affected which the defendant neither knew of nor could reasonably be taken to have foreseen? Must the manner of conduct adapt itself to such special individual peculiarities? If extreme cases are taken, the answer appears to be fairly clear, unless, indeed, there is knowledge of the extraordinary risk. One who suffers from the terrible tendency to bleed on slight contact, which is denoted by the term "a bleeder," cannot complain if he mixes with the crowd and suffers severely, perhaps fatally, from being merely brushed against. There is no actionable wrong done there. A blind or deaf man who crosses the traffic on a busy street cannot complain if he is run over by a careful driver who does not know of and could not be expected to observe and guard against the man's infirmity. These questions go to "culpability, not compensation", as Bankes L.J. said in the *Polemis* case,[3] at p. 571. No doubt it has long ago been stated and often restated that, if the wrong is established, the wrongdoer must take the victim as he finds him. That, however, is only true, as the *Polemis* case[3] shows, on the condition that the wrong has been established or admitted. The question of liability is anterior to the question of the measure of the consequences which go with the liability. . . .

What is now being considered is the question of liability, and this, I think, in a question whether there is a duty owing to members of the public who come within the ambit of the act, must generally depend on a normal standard of susceptibility.

---

1. 232 N.Y. 176.
2. [This word should be "of" not "or"—see [1943] A.C. 92, at p. 109.]
3. [1921] 3 K.B. 560.

This, it may be said, is somewhat vague. That is true; but definition involves limitation, which it is desirable to avoid further than is necessary in a principle of law like negligence, which is widely ranging and is still in the stage of development. It is here, as elsewhere, a question of what the hypothetical reasonable man, viewing the position, I suppose *ex post facto*, would say it was proper to foresee. What danger of particular infirmity that would include must depend on all the circumstances; but generally, I think, a reasonably normal condition, if medical evidence is capable of defining it, would be the standard. The test of the plaintiff's extraordinary susceptibility, if unknown to the defendant, would in effect make the defendant an insurer. The lawyer likes to draw fixed and definite lines and is apt to ask where the thing is to stop. I should reply it should stop where in the particular case the good sense of the jury, or of the judge, decides. . . .

However, when I apply the considerations which I have been discussing to the present appeal, I come to the conclusion that the judgment should be affirmed. The case is peculiar, as indeed, though to a varying extent, all these cases are apt to be. There is no dispute about the facts. Upon these facts, can it be said that a duty is made out, and breach of that duty, so that the damage which is found is recoverable? I think not. The appellant was completely outside the range of the collision. She merely heard a noise, which upset her, without her having any definite idea at all. As she said: "I just got into a pack of nerves and I did not know whether I was going to get it or not." She saw nothing of the actual accident, or indeed any marks of blood until later. I cannot accept that John Young could reasonably have foreseen, or, more correctly, the reasonable hypothetical observer could reasonably have foreseen, the likelihood that anyone placed as the appellant was, could be affected in the manner in which she was. In my opinion John Young was guilty of no breach of duty to the appellant and was not in law responsible for the hurt she sustained. I may add that the issue of duty or no duty is indeed a question for the court, but it depends on the view taken of the facts. In the present case both courts below have taken the view that the appellant has, on the facts of the case, no redress and I agree with their view.

This conclusion disposes of the present case and makes it unnecessary to decide the difficult question which was the subject of lengthy argument and elaborate citation of authorities before your Lordships. I have carefully considered all the authorities cited, and it may well be that some day this House will have to examine the exact meaning and effect of what Kennedy J. said in *Dulieu* v. *White & Sons*,[1] at p. 675. He was, he said, inclined to think that there was at least one limitation.

"The shock, where it operates through the mind, must be a shock which arises from a reasonable fear of immediate personal injury to oneself."

That statement, if meant to lay down a rigid rule of law, has been overruled by the Court of Appeal in *Hambrook* v. *Stokes Bros.*,[2] which now lays down the English law unless it is set aside by this House. As at present advised, I agree with that decision. The *dictum* of Kennedy J., if intended to lay down a rigid limitation, is not, I think, in accordance with principle or with cases like *Wilkinson* v. *Downton*.[3] It finds no support in the judgment of Phillimore J., who implicitly lays down a wider principle. As I may some day have to decide the question in this House, I prefer to express here no final opinion. . . .

LORD PORTER, [referring to *Hambrook* v. *Stokes Brothers*, [2]] . . . It will be observed that . . . all the Lords Justices were careful to point out that the vital problem was the extent of the duty and not the remoteness of damages—a view in which they were

1. [1901] 2 K.B. 669.
2. [1925] 1 K.B. 141.
3. [1897] 2 Q.B. 57.

supported by the opinions of Kennedy and Phillimore JJ. in *Dulieu* v. *White*.[1] With this view I agree, and ask myself whether the defenders in the present case owed any duty to the pursuer.

In the case of a civil action there is no such thing as negligence in the abstract: there must be neglect of the use of care towards a person towards whom the defendant owes the duty of observing care. And I am content to take the statement of Lord Atkin in *M'Alister* (or *Donoghue*) v. *Stevenson*,[2] at p. 580, as indicating the extent of the duty:

> "You must take reasonable care to avoid acts and omissions which you can reasonably foresee would be likely to injure your neighbour. Who, then, in law is my neighbour? The answer seems to be—persons who are so closely and directly affected by my act that I ought reasonably to have them in contemplation as being so affected when I am directing my mind to the acts or omissions which are called in question."

Is the result of this view that all persons in or near the street down which the negligent driver is progressing are potential victims of his negligence? Though from their position it is quite impossible that any injury should happen to them and though they have no relatives or even friends who might be endangered, is a duty of care to them owed and broken because they might have been but were not in a spot exposed to the errant driving of the peccant car? I cannot think so. The duty is not to the world at large. It must be tested by asking with reference to each several complainant was a duty owed to him or her. If no one of them was in such a position that direct physical injury could reasonably be anticipated to them or their relations or friends, normally I think no duty would be owed: and, if in addition no shock was reasonably to be anticipated to them as a result of the defender's negligence, the defender might, indeed, be guilty of actionable negligence to others but not of negligence towards them.

In the present case the defender was never herself in any bodily danger nor reasonably in fear of danger either for herself or others. She was merely a person who as a result of the action was emotionally disturbed and rendered physically ill by that emotional disturbance. The question whether emotional disturbance or shock, which a defender ought reasonably to have anticipated as likely to follow from his reckless driving, can ever form the basis of a claim is not in issue. It is not every emotional disturbance or every shock which should have been foreseen. The driver of a car or vehicle even though careless is entitled to assume that the ordinary frequenter of the streets has sufficient fortitude to endure such incidents as may from time to time be expected to occur in them, including the noise of a collision and the sight of injury to others, and is not to be considered negligent towards one who does not possess the customary phlegm. . . .

In order . . . to establish a duty towards herself, the pursuer must show that the cyclist should reasonably have foreseen emotional injury to her as a result of his negligent driving, and . . . I do not think she has done so. . . .

[Having referred to several authorities from Scotland and one from Ireland he continued:] These cases are at any rate no more favourable to the pursuer's contention than those decided in England. In all three countries no doubt shock occasioned by deliberate action affords a valid ground of claim: see *Wilkinson* v. *Downton*[3] and *Janvier* v. *Sweeney*,[4] and so, I think, does shock occasioned by reasonable apprehension of injury to oneself or others, at any rate if those others are closely connected with the claimant. What is reasonable may give rise to some difference of opinion, but whether illness due to shock which might reasonably have been anticipated as the result of

---

1. [1901] 2 K.B. 669.
2. [1932] A.C. 562.
3. [1897] 2 Q.B. 57.
4. [1919] 2 K.B. 316.

injury to others can or cannot form the basis of a successful claim need not now be considered. No exceptionally loud noise or particularly gruesome sight is alleged or any circumstance suggesting that the cyclist should have anticipated he would cause a shock to the pursuer.

On the ground that there never was any duty owed by the deceased man to the pursuer or breach of such a duty, I should dismiss the appeal. In so deciding, I believe I am following the reasoning and conclusion of the Lord Ordinary as well as those of the majority in the Inner House, with whose opinions I agree.

Appeal dismissed

Question

Which of these speeches support the "area of impact" theory and which the "area of shock" theory? (See A. L. Goodhart, "*Bourhill* v. *Young*" (1944), 8 C.L.J. 265).

Notes

1. In *Hambrook* v. *Stokes Bros.*, [1925] 1 K.B. 141, due to the defendants' servant's negligence a lorry ran away down a steep and narrow street. A mother knew that her children had just gone along that street, although, by the time she saw the lorry, they had passed out of her sight. One of her children was a girl who wore glasses, and bystanders told her that, in fact, a girl wearing glasses had been injured. She suffered nervous shock which it was alleged had led to her death. A majority of the Court of Appeal took the view that there could be recovery for nervous shock caused by fear, not for one's own safety, but for that of one's children (indeed Atkin L.J. would have gone further— see pp. 156–159, but note also his view that, in any case, there was an admission of a breach of duty to the mother in the pleadings). Although this case was approved by Lord Wright in *Hay or Bourhill* v. *Young*, it received a mixed reception from the House of Lords overall. It should be noted that, in any event, the majority in *Hambrook* v. *Stokes Bros.* would deny recovery unless the shock was suffered because of what a parent perceived through his or her own unaided senses, and not because of what others told him or her. (Cf. *Schneider* v. *Eisovitch*, [1960] 2 Q.B. 430; [1960] 1 All E.R. 169, p. 220, *post*.)

2. There is authority since *Hay or Bourhill* v. *Young* allowing a plaintiff to recover damages for shock suffered as a result of fear for the safety of his fellow workmen. In *Dooley* v. *Cammell Laird & Co., Ltd. and Mersey Insulation Co., Ltd.*, [1951] 1 Lloyd's Rep. 271, materials in a sling hoisted by a crane fell into the hold of a ship when an unsound piece of rope broke. The plaintiff, whose fellow workmen were in the hold, was the crane operator, and he recovered damages for shock which he suffered as a result of fear for their safety. (See also *Carlin* v. *Helical Bar, Ltd.* (1970), 9 K.I.R. 154, and *Mount Isa Mines, Ltd.* v. *Pusey*, [1971] A.L.R. 253.)

King v. Phillips

Court of Appeal   [1953] 1 All E.R. 617.

The plaintiff was at an upstairs window of her house, when she heard a scream which she identified as that of her little boy. At a distance of some seventy or eighty yards, she saw the defendant's taxicab backing on to her son's tricycle. She then saw the tricycle under the taxicab but she could not see her son, who had, in fact, suffered only slight injury. The plaintiff ran down into the roadway where she met him running towards her. She claimed damages for nervous shock sustained by virtue of what she had seen and heard but the trial judge (McNair J.) took the view that the mother "was wholly outside the area or range of reasonable anticipation . . ." ([1952] 2 All E.R. 459, at p. 461). Her claim was not allowed. On appeal:

SINGLETON L.J.: . . . Can it be said that the driver (or any driver in the world) could reasonably or probably anticipate that injury, either physical or from shock, would be caused to the mother who was in No. 12 Birstall Road when he caused his taxicab to move backwards a short distance from Greenfield Road without looking to see if anyone was immediately behind? There can surely be only one answer to that question. The driver owed a duty to the boy, but he knew nothing of the mother; she was not on the highway; he could not know that she was at the window, nor was there any reason why he should anticipate that she would see his taxicab at all; he was not intending to go into Birstall Road except for the purpose of turning. I cannot see that the fact that she saw the tricycle under the taxicab enables one to distinguish this case from *Hay* (or *Bourhill*) v. *Young*.[1] . . .

The decision of the House of Lords[2] shows that the test is whether the driver could reasonably have foreseen any damage to the plaintiff. Unless he could, it was said, no duty was owed to her, and, consequently, there was no negligence *vis-à-vis* the plaintiff. I find it difficult to draw a distinction between damage from physical injury and damage from shock; prima facie one would think that, if a driver should reasonably have foreseen either and damage from the one or from the other resulted, the plaintiff would be entitled to succeed. It is, however, unnecessary to consider this somewhat academic point for the purposes of this appeal for, on the finding of McNair J., no reasonable driver (or no hypothetical bystander) would have anticipated damage of any kind to Mrs. King, and that is a finding of fact with which this court ought not to interfere. Moreover, it is in accord with common sense. . . .

. . . In my opinion, the appeal should be dismissed.

DENNING L.J.: . . . I cannot see why the duty of a driver should differ according to the nature of the injury. I should have thought that every driver was under a plain duty which he owed to everyone in the vicinity. He ought to drive with reasonable care. If he drives negligently with the result that a bystander is injured, then his breach of duty is the same, no matter whether the injury is a wound or is emotional shock. Only the damage is different. The bystander may be so close as to be put in fear for himself, or he may be just a little way off and be shocked by fear for the safety of others. In either case he has been injured by the driver's negligence. If you view the duty of care in this way, and yet refuse to allow a bystander to recover for shock, it is not because there was no duty owed to him, nor because it was not caused by the negligence of the driver, but simply because it is too remote to be admitted as a head of damage.

A different result is reached by viewing the driver's duty differently. Instead of saying simply that his duty is to drive with reasonable care, you say that his duty is to avoid injury which he can reasonably foresee, or, rather, to use reasonable care to avoid it. Then you draw a distinction between physical injury and emotional injury, and impose a different duty on him in regard to each kind of injury, with the inevitable result that you are driven to say there are two different torts, one tort when he can foresee physical injury, another tort when he can foresee emotional injury. I do not think that is right. There is one wrong only, the wrong of negligence. I know that damage to person and damage to property are for historical reasons regarded as different torts, but that does not apply to physical injury and emotional injury. Lord Wright clearly treated impact and shock as one cause of action when he said in *Hay* (or *Bourhill*) v. *Young*[1] ([1942] 2 All E.R., at p. 405):

---

1. [1943] A.C. 92; [1942] 2 All E.R. 396.
2. [In *Bourhill* v. *Young* (see note (1)).]

"The man who negligently allows a horse to bolt, or a car to run at large down a steep street, or a savage beast to escape is committing a breach of duty towards every person who comes within the range of foreseeable danger, whether by impact or shock . . ."

The true principle, as I see it, is this. Every driver can and should foresee that, if he drives negligently, he may injure somebody in the vicinity in some way or other, and he must be responsible for all the injuries which he does in fact cause by his negligence to anyone in the vicinity, whether they are wounds or shocks, unless they are too remote in law to be recovered. If he does by his negligence in fact cause injury by shock, then he should be liable for it unless he is exempted on the ground of remoteness. . . . If this principle is correct, the only consequences for which he is excused are those which are too remote. Howsoever that may be, whether the exemption for shock be based on want of duty or on remoteness, there can be no doubt since *Hay* (or *Bourhill*) v. *Young*[1] that the test of liability for shock is foreseeability of injury by shock. But this test is by no means easy to apply. The test is not what the negligent party himself could reasonably have foreseen, for he rarely has time to foresee anything. The test is what a "reasonable hypothetical observer could reasonably have foreseen": see *Hay* (or *Bourhill*) v. *Young*[1] per Lord Wright ([1942] 2 All E.R. 406). But where must this hypothetical observer be situate? In the driver's seat, or in an observation post on high? It is obvious that much must depend on his powers of observation and the scope of his imagination. One judge may credit him with more foresight than another. One judge may think that he should have foreseen the shock. Another may not. In both *Hambrook* v. *Stokes Brothers*[2] and *Chester* v. *Waverley Municipal Corpn.*,[3] the judges were divided in opinion whether the shock to the mother could reasonably have been foreseen. Some cases seem plain enough. A wife or mother who suffers shock on being told of an accident to a loved one cannot recover damages from the negligent party on that account. Nor can a bystander who suffers shock by witnessing an accident from a safe distance: *Smith* v. *Johnson & Co.*,[4] cited in *Wilkinson* v. *Downton*[5]; *Hay* (or *Bourhill*) v. *Young*,[1] per Lord Porter (*ibid.*, 409). But if the bystander is a mother who suffers from shock by hearing or seeing, with her own unaided senses, that her child is in peril, then she may be able to recover from the negligent party, even though she was in no personal danger herself: *Hambrook* v. *Stokes Brothers*.[2] Lord Wright said he agreed with that decision. So do I.

This brings me to the real question: Is the present case covered by *Hambrook* v. *Stokes Brothers*[2] or not? I think we should follow *Hambrook* v. *Stokes Brothers*[2] so far as to hold that there was a duty of care owed by the taxi-driver, not only to the boy, but also to his mother. In that case the negligence took place three hundred yards from the place where the mother was standing. In this case it was only seventy or eighty yards. In that case the mother was not herself in any personal danger. Nor was she here. In that case she suffered shock by fear for the safety of her children from what she saw and heard. So did she here. In that case the mother was in the street, and in this case at the window of the house. I do not think that makes any difference. Nevertheless, I think the shock in this case is too remote to be a head of damage. It seems to me that the slow backing of the taxicab was very different from the terrifying descent of the runaway lorry. The taxi-driver cannot reasonably be expected to have foreseen that his backing would terrify a mother seventy yards away, whereas the lorry driver ought to have foreseen that a runaway lorry might seriously shock the mother of children in the danger area. . . .

[HODSON L.J. delivered a judgment in favour of dismissing the appeal.]

Appeal dismissed

1. [1943] A.C. 92; [1942] 2 All E.R. 396.
2. [1925] 1 K.B. 141.
3. (1939), 62 C.L.R. 1.
4. (1897), unreported.
5. [1897] 2 Q.B. 57, at p. 61.

Question

Can it be said in all cases that "the test of liability for shock is foreseeability of injury by shock" (*per* Denning L.J.)? (See also *The Wagon Mound (No. 1)*, [1961] A.C. 388, at p. 426, and see Winfield & Jolowicz, p. 122.)

Note

Compare *King* v. *Phillips* with *Hinz* v. *Berry*, [1970] 2 Q.B. 40; [1970] 1 All E.R. 1074. In the latter case the plaintiff's husband and some of her children were in a lay-by where they had parked their Dormobile. A car, which had burst a tyre, crashed into them, with the result that the husband was fatally injured and nearly all the children sustained injuries. The plaintiff, who was on the other side of the road, heard the crash, saw what had happened, and ran to help. She suffered a psychiatric illness caused by shock as a result of what she had seen. The Court of Appeal upheld an award of £4,000 for this head of damage, Lord Denning M.R. stating (at p. 1075) that "for these last 25 years, it has been settled that damages can be given for nervous shock caused by the sight of an accident, at any rate to a close relative." How can these cases be distinguished?

Boardman *v.* Sanderson

Court of Appeal   [1964] 1 W.L.R. 1317

An 8 year old boy and his father, the plaintiffs, went with the defendant to a garage to collect the defendant's car; they were going away together on holiday. In backing the car out of the garage, the defendant negligently ran over the infant's foot. On hearing the boy scream, the father, who at the defendant's request was paying the defendant's garage fees at the office, rushed out to the yard and helped to release the boy. The father later suffered symptoms of shock and was awarded £75 in respect of this damage at the trial of the action. An appeal by the defendant was dismissed.

ORMEROD L.J.: . . . Mr. Richardson, on behalf of the defendant submitted that this case must be considered on a similar basis with *Hay (or Bourhill)* v. *Young*,[1] one of the leading cases on this question of injury by shock. In that case the plaintiff, who was a fish wife loading fish from a tramcar into her basket, did not see the accident happen and only saw the results of it when she was moved by the noise to go and see what had happened. In the present case, too, the father did not see the accident but was only moved to see what had happened when he heard the infant scream. Mr Richardson has endeavoured to submit that the line of distinction must be drawn somewhere and that must depend on whether the accident was witnessed by the plaintiff, and that if, in this case, the father did not witness the accident he cannot succeed. There has been no authority produced to the court to bear out that submission and, for my part, I must say I find it difficult to understand why the line should be drawn in that arbitrary fashion. It may be that, in some cases, that is a proper line to draw, as in *Hay (or Bourhill)* v. *Young*,[1] and it may be that, in that case, as in many others, the proposed plaintiff does not come within the area of contemplated danger. On the other hand, clearly the facts in these cases are infinitely variable and it would be difficult, if not impossible, to draw any line of distinction and say in one case the plaintiff should succeed and in another case he should not.

In this particular case it does appear that all the necessary factors are present which should entitle the judge to come to the view that the father should succeed. The defendant knew that the infant was in the yard and that any carelessness in driving on

---

1. [1943] A.C. 92; [1942] 2 All E.R. 396, H.L.

his part might result in injury to the infant as, in fact, it did. He knew that the father was within earshot and he knew also that the father was in such a position that if he heard a scream from the infant he was bound to run out, human nature being what it is, to see what was happening to the infant; and that is, in fact, what happened. In those circumstances it appears to me that the judge was right in coming to the conclusion which he did. . . .

I think I need say no more than that if the facts of this particular case are fitted to the concept of negligence, it is clear that a duty was owed by the defendant not only to the infant but also to the near relatives of the infant who were, as he knew, on the premises, within earshot, and likely to come upon the scene if any injury or ill befell the infant.

In the circumstances, it appears to me to be clear that the father is entitled to succeed . . .

[DEVLIN and DANCKWERTS L.JJ. agreed with ORMEROD L.J.]

Question

Suppose the appellant in *Bourhill* v. *Young* had seen the body of one of her relatives in the car which was involved in the collision with the motor-cycle. If she had then suffered nervous shock, could she have recovered damages?

Chadwick v. British Transport Commission

Queen's Bench Division   [1967] 2 All E.R. 945

The plaintiff was suing as administratrix of her husband's estate: the death of her husband, who had started this action, was unrelated to the events in the case. In December 1957, a serious railway accident occurred at Lewisham. Mr. Chadwick went to help and in fact continued to give assistance during the night. He later suffered a neurosis. Waller J. stated that ". . . although there was clearly an element of personal danger in what Mr. Chadwick was doing, I think that I must deal with this case on the basis that it was the horror of the whole experience which caused his reaction." The judge set out five questions to be answered:

"(i) Are damages recoverable for injury by shock where the injured man's shock is not caused by fear for his own safety or the safety of his children? (ii) Is foreseeability of injury by shock a necessary ingredient? (iii) Did the defendants owe a duty to Mr. Chadwick who was not their servant but had come to their aid? (iv) Would the fact that the risk run by the rescuer was not precisely that run by the passenger deprive the rescuer of his remedy? (v) Was Mr. Chadwick of such extraordinary susceptibility that he ought not to have been in the contemplation of the reasonable man?"

The answers to questions (ii) and (v) are dealt with in the text below; the answers to questions (iii) and (iv) have been mentioned in note 2, p. 132, *ante*.

WALLER J. [having expressed the opinion in relation to question (i) that "provided that the necessary requisites of liability are there, shock, other than fear for oneself or children, causing injury, may be the subject of a claim for damages", continued:]

. . . The second question which I have to consider is: Is foreseeability of injury by shock necessary? The House of Lords in *Hay* (or *Bourhill*) v. *Young*[1] considered a number of matters in deciding whether or not the defendant owed a duty to the plaintiff and in deciding that the plaintiff was outside the area of contemplation, one of the matters considered, particularly by Lord Wright, was the foreseeability of injury by shock. In *King* v. *Phillips*[2] Denning L.J. said in the passage which was later quoted

---

1. [1943] A.C. 92; [1942] 2 All E.R. 396.
2. [1953] 1 Q.B. 429, at p. 441; [1953] 1 All E.R. 617, at p. 623.

with approval by Viscount Simonds in *Overseas Tankship (U.K.), Ltd.* v. *Morts Dock & Engineering Co., Ltd. (The Wagon Mound)*,[1] that

> ". . . there can be no doubt since *Hay (or Bourhill)* v. *Young*[2] that the test for liability for shock is foreseeability of injury by shock."

I therefore must ask myself whether injury by shock was foreseeable in this case. The scene described by Mrs. Taylor was the kind of thing to be expected if trains collided as these did and it was one which could, in my view, properly be called gruesome. In my opinion, if the defendants had asked themselves the hypothetical question: "If we run one train into another at Lewisham in such circumstances that a large number of people are killed, may some persons who are physically unhurt suffer injury from shock?", I think that the answer must have been "Yes". . . .

The fifth question is: Was Mr. Chadwick of such extraordinary susceptibility that he ought not to have been in the contemplation of the reasonable man? . . .

Modern medicine recognises mental illness in a variety of forms. As I mentioned earlier, neurosis of one kind or another is a frequent visitor to the courts in claims for damages for personal injuries. The community is not formed of normal citizens, [but][3] with all those who are less susceptible or more susceptible to stress to be regarded as extraordinary. There is an infinite variety of creatures, all with varying susceptibilities. Mr. Chadwick was a man who had lived a normal busy life in the community with no mental illness for sixteen years. He was, said Dr. Kendall, not likely to relapse under the ordinary stresses of life. Indeed, the evidence showed that during those sixteen years he had on one occasion been attacked by a gang of youths with bicycle chains, without any mental illness or injury resulting. This illness, according to Dr. Kendall, is a sufficiently common accompaniment of catastrophes to be given a name.[4] In my opinion, there was nothing in Mr. Chadwick's personality to put him outside the ambit of contemplation. I have come to the conclusion, therefore, that the defendants were in breach of the duty they owed to Mr. Chadwick and that the illness which he suffered as a result of that breach was one for which he was or, in this case, his personal representative is, entitled to recover. Mrs. Chadwick is therefore entitled to damages against the defendants. . . .

Judgment for the plaintiff

Note

Attention might finally be paid to a rather difficult "nervous shock" case— *Schneider* v. *Eisovitch*, [1960] 2 Q.B. 430; [1960] 1 All E.R. 169 where the plaintiff and her husband were involved in a car accident which had occurred as a result of the defendant's negligence. The plaintiff's husband was killed, and the plaintiff was injured. When she recovered consciousness, she was told of the death of her husband and the shock of this news in addition to the shock occasioned by her physical injuries, had quite serious results. On the question whether there could be compensation for the effects of the shock suffered as a consequence of hearing of her husband's death, Paull J. stated (at p. 175):

> ". . . it seems to me to follow that once a breach of duty is established the difference between seeing and hearing is immaterial. Hearing can be just as direct a consequence as seeing. The fact that owing to unconsciousness in this case a period of time elapsed before the news was heard makes no difference provided the news was a consequence which flowed directly from the breach of duty towards the plaintiff, any more than it makes any difference that an operation takes place after an inter-

---

1. [1961] A.C. 388, at p. 426; [1961] 1 All E.R. 404, at p. 415.
2. [1943] A.C. 92; [1942] 2 All E.R. 396.
3. [This word is omitted in the report of this case at [1967] 1 W.L.R. 912.]
4. [I.e. "catastrophic neurosis".]

val of time. The fact that the defendant by his negligence caused the death of the plaintiff's husband does not give the plaintiff a cause of action for the shock caused to her, but the plaintiff having a cause of action for the negligence of the defendant may add the consequences of shock caused by hearing of her husband's death when estimating the amount recoverable on her cause of action."

Is this passage from Paull J.'s judgment good law today? (See Clerk & Lindsell, para. 872, note 69, and see J. A. Jolowicz, [1960] C.L.J. 156; Fleming, p. 151: *cf.* Salmond, p. 215.)

7

Examples of the Duty of Care

In Chapters 3, 4 and 5 we examined the main elements of the tort of negligence and in Chapter 6 saw the application of the conceptual apparatus of this tort to the particular problem of Nervous Shock. We turn now to consideration of three situations in which judge-made duties or immunities have been modified or replaced by statute. These are (1) the occupier's liability; (2) the non-occupier's liability in respect of premises; and (3) the employer's liability to his employees. In each area, the duty owed is a combination of the common law and statutory interpretation. The duties may also be viewed as examples of different levels at which "duty" may be formulated. The occupier's duty to "visitors" is described as a "common duty of care" by statute (p. 223, post); his duty to trespassers is called a "low duty" (p. 240, post) by the House of Lords. The non-occupier doing work on the premises owes a common duty of care, at common law, to entrants, while the statutory duty to build dwellings properly (Defective Premises Act 1972, s. 1, p. 259, post) appears to be a high one. The employer's duty of care to his employees is the relatively high one to see that care is taken, a formulation originally designed to overcome the doctrine of common employment, but which has survived the statutory repeal of that doctrine (p. 264, post).

1. OCCUPIERS' LIABILITY

(a) To "Visitors"

Note

A consideration of occupiers' liability at common law had to take into account particular categories of entrant on to the premises. The duty of care required of the occupier varied according to whether the lawful entrant was entering under a contract, or as a non-contractual invitee or licensee. The Occupiers' Liability Act 1957, which followed from the Third Report of the Law Reform Committee (Cmd. 9305) 1954, brings the invitee and the licensee together into the category of lawful visitors to whom the occupier owes the common duty of care (s. 1 (2)). Trespassers remain outside the scope of the Act, as s. 1 (b) of this Chapter will show.

Some doubt has arisen as to the scope of the Act. At common law, if the plaintiff was injured by the occupier's activities on the premises (e.g. driving a car) as opposed to their static condition, then liability could be based on a duty of care arising from those activities. The relevance of the category of lawful entrant in which the law placed the plaintiff was confined to the "occupancy duty" rather than the "activity duty". (For these terms, see F. H. Newark, "*Twine* v. *Bean's Express, Ltd.*" (1954), 17 M.L.R. 102, at p. 109.) Writers disagree whether the 1957 Act now governs the "activity duty" as well as the "occupancy duty", but, in any event, Winfield & Jolowicz state (at p. 173) that "there can be little if any practical difference between the duty of care in negligence and the common duty of care as applied to current activities" (but see Salmond, p. 264, note 62). Following from this, it is interesting to note that the Act provides an example of a statutory duty of care in which Parliament has attempted to lay down certain factors for the courts' consideration (see s. 2 (3)–(5)). The student should consider how far these factors would be relevant in the common law tort of negligence.

The common law is relevant in interpreting the Act. Section 1 (2) of the Act specifically states that "the persons who are to be treated as an occupier and as his visitors are the same (subject to sub-s. (4) of this section) as the persons who would at common law be treated as an occupier and as his invitees or licensees". The common law is also of importance when the liability of the non-occupier is considered, and there is a short section on that topic in this Chapter, following on from the consideration of the common duty of care owed by the occupier, and the occupier's duty to the trespasser.

The Occupiers' Liability Act 1957

LIABILITY IN TORT

1. Preliminary.—(1) The rules enacted by the two next following sections shall have effect, in place of the rules of the common law, to regulate the duty which an occupier of premises owes to his visitors in respect of dangers due to the state of the premises or to things done or omitted to be done on them.

(2) The rules so enacted shall regulate the nature of the duty imposed by law in consequence of a person's occupation or control of premises and of any invitation or permission he gives (or is to be treated as giving) to another to enter or use the premises, but they shall not alter the rules of the common law as to the persons on whom a duty is so imposed or to whom it is owed; and accordingly for the purpose of the rules so enacted the persons who are to be treated as an occupier and as his visitors are the same (subject to subsection (4) of this section) as the persons who would at common law be treated as an occupier and as his invitees or licensees.

(3) The rules so enacted in relation to an occupier of premises and his visitors shall also apply, in like manner and to the like extent as the principles applicable at common law to an occupier of premises and his invitees or licensees would apply, to regulate—

- (*a*) the obligations of a person occupying or having control over any fixed or moveable structure, including any vessel, vehicle or aircraft; and
- (*b*) the obligations of a person occupying or having control over any premises or structure in respect of damage to property, including the property of persons who are not themselves his visitors.

(4) A person entering any premises in exercise of rights conferred by virtue of an access agreement or order under the National Parks and Access to the Countryside Act 1949, is not, for the purposes of this Act, a visitor of the occupier of those premises.

2. Extent of occupier's ordinary duty.—(1) An occupier of premises owes the same duty, the "common duty of care", to all his visitors, except in so far as he is free to and does extend, restrict, modify or exclude his duty to any visitor or visitors by agreement or otherwise.

(2) The common duty of care is a duty to take such care as in all the circumstances of the case is reasonable to see that the visitor will be reasonably safe in using the premises for the purposes for which he is invited or permitted by the occupier to be there.

(3) The circumstances relevant for the present purpose include the degree of care, and of want of care, which would ordinarily be looked for in such a visitor, so that (for example) in proper cases—

(*a*) an occupier must be prepared for children to be less careful than adults; and
(*b*) an occupier may expect that a person, in the exercise of his calling, will appreciate and guard against any special risks ordinarily incident to it, so far as the occupier leaves him free to do so.

(4) In determining whether the occupier of premises has discharged the common duty of care to a visitor, regard is to be had to all the circumstances, so that (for example)—

(*a*) where damage is caused to a visitor by a danger of which he had been warned by the occupier, the warning is not to be treated without more as absolving the occupier from liability, unless in all the circumstances it was enough to enable the visitor to be reasonably safe; and
(*b*) where damage is caused to a visitor by a danger due to the faulty execution of any work of construction, maintenance or repair by an independent contractor employed by the occupier, the occupier is not to be treated without more as answerable for the danger if in all the circumstances he had acted reasonably in entrusting the work to an independent contractor and had taken such steps (if any) as he reasonably ought in order to satisfy himself that the contractor was competent and that the work had been properly done.

(5) The common duty of care does not impose on an occupier any obligation to a visitor in respect of risks willingly accepted as his by the visitor (the question whether a risk was so accepted to be decided on the same principles as in other cases in which one person owes a duty of care to another).

(6) For the purposes of this section, persons who enter premises for any purpose in the exercise of a right conferred by law are to be treated as permitted by the occupier to be there for that purpose, whether they in fact have his permission or not.

3. Effect of contract on occupier's liability to third party.—(1) Where an occupier of premises is bound by contract to permit persons who are strangers to the contract to enter or use the premises, the duty of care which he owes to them as his visitors cannot be restricted or excluded by that contract, but (subject to any provision of the contract to the contrary) shall include the duty to perform his obligations under the contract, whether undertaken for their protection or not, in so far as those obligations go beyond the obligations otherwise involved in that duty.

(2) A contract shall not by virtue of this section have the effect, unless it expressly so provides, of making an occupier who has taken all reasonable care answerable to strangers to the contract for dangers due to the faulty execution of any work of construction, maintenance or repair or other like operation by persons other than himself, his servants and persons acting under his direction and control.

(3) In this section "stranger to the contract" means a person not for the time being entitled to the benefit of the contract as a party to it or as the successor by assignment or otherwise of a party to it, and accordingly includes a party to the contract who has ceased to be so entitled.

(4) Where by the terms or conditions governing any tenancy (including a statutory tenancy which does not in law amount to a tenancy) either the landlord or the tenant is bound, though not by contract, to permit persons to enter or use premises of which he

is the occupier, this section shall apply as if the tenancy were a contract between the landlord and the tenant.

(5) This section, in so far as it prevents the common duty of care from being restricted or excluded, applies to contracts entered into and tenancies created before the commencement of this Act, as well as to those entered into or created after its commencement; but, in so far as it enlarges the duty owed by an occupier beyond the common duty of care, it shall have effect only in relation to obligations which are undertaken after that commencement or which are renewed by agreement (whether express or implied) after that commencement. [The Act came into force on 1 January, 1958.]

LIABILITY IN CONTRACT

5. Implied term in contracts.—(1) Where persons enter or use, or bring or send goods to, any premises in exercise of a right conferred by contract with a person occupying or having control of the premises, the duty he owes them in respect of dangers due to the state of the premises or to things done or omitted to be done on them, in so far as the duty depends on a term to be implied in the contract by reason of its conferring that right, shall be the common duty of care.

(2) The foregoing subsection shall apply to fixed and moveable structures as it applies to premises.

(3) This section does not affect the obligations imposed on a person by or by virtue of any contract for the hire of, or for the carriage for reward of persons or goods in, any vehicle, vessel, aircraft or other means of transport, or by or by virtue of any contract of bailment.

(4) This section does not apply to contracts entered into before the commencement of this Act.

GENERAL

6. Application to Crown.—This Act shall bind the Crown, but as regards the Crown's liability in tort shall not bind the Crown further than the Crown is made liable in tort by the Crown Proceedings Act 1947, and that Act and in particular section two of it shall apply in relation to duties under sections two to four of this Act as statutory duties.

Notes

1. Section 4 of the above Act was repealed by s. 6 (4) of the Defective Premises Act 1972, but see now s. 4 of that Act, p. 260, *post*.

2. The Law Commission's provisional proposals in its Working Paper (No. 52), *Liability for Damage or Injury to Trespassers and Related Questions of Occupiers' Liability*, if accepted, will lead to some changes in the Act—see p. 255, *post*; note also that it provisionally proposes the repeal of s. 2 (5) and the abolition of the assumption of risk defence in this area of the law.

3. On the relation of s. 2 (1) and s. 5 (1) of this Act see *Sole* v. *W. J. Hallt, Ltd.*, [1973] Q.B. 574; [1973] 1 All E.R. 1032, p. 187, *ante*. In the light of Swanwick J.'s views concerning the effect of contributory negligence in that case, his decision that the plaintiff could sue in contract or in tort at his option was an important one. What additional advantages or disadvantages might lead a plaintiff to choose one of these actions rather than the other?

(i) Occupation

Wheat v. E. Lacon & Co., Ltd.

House of Lords   [1966] 1 All E.R. 582

Winn J. had dismissed the appellant's action. The majority of Court of Appeal (Harman and Diplock L.JJ.), [1965] 2 All E.R. 700, dismissed her appeal, holding that the respondents had not owed the common duty of care to the appellant's deceased husband. On appeal to the House of Lords:

LORD DENNING: My Lords, the "Golfer's Arms" at Great Yarmouth is owned by the respondents, the brewery company, E. Lacon & Co., Ltd. The ground floor was run as a public house by Mr. Richardson as manager for the respondents. The first floor was used by Mr. and Mrs. Richardson as their private dwelling. In the summer Mrs. Richardson took in guests for her private profit. Mr. and Mrs. Wheat and their family were summer guests of Mrs. Richardson. About 9 p.m. one evening, when it was getting dark, Mr. Wheat fell down the back staircase in the private portion and was killed. Winn J. held that there were two causes: (i) the handrail was too short because it did not stretch to the foot of the stairs; (ii) someone had taken the bulb out of the light at the top of the stairs.

The case raises this point of law: did the respondents owe any duty to Mr. Wheat to see that the handrail was safe to use or to see that the stairs were properly lighted? That depends on whether the respondents were "an occupier" of the private portion of the "Golfer's Arms", and Mr. Wheat was their "visitor" within the Occupiers' Liability Act 1957: for, if so, the respondents owed him the "common duty of care".

In order to determine this question we must have resort to the law before the Occupiers' Liability Act 1957: for it is expressly enacted by s. 1 (2) that the Act of 1957

> "shall not alter the rules of the common law as to the persons on whom a duty is so imposed or to whom it is owed; and accordingly ... the persons who are to be treated as an occupier and as his visitors are the same ... as the persons who would at common law be treated as an occupier and as his invitees or licensees ..."

At the outset, I would say that no guidance is to be obtained from the use of the word "occupier" in other branches of the law: for its meaning varies according to the subject-matter.

In the Occupiers' Liability Act 1957, the word "occupier" is used in the same sense as it was used in the common law cases on occupiers' liability for dangerous premises. It was simply a convenient word to denote a person who had a sufficient degree of control over premises to put him under a duty of care towards those who came lawfully on to the premises. Those persons were divided into two categories, invitees and licensees: and a higher duty was owed to invitees than to licensees; but by the year 1956 the distinction between invitees and licensees had been reduced to vanishing point. The duty of the occupier had become simply a duty to take a reasonable care to see that the premises were reasonably safe for people coming lawfully on to them: and it made no difference whether they were invitees or licensees, see *Slater* v. *Clay Cross Co., Ltd.*[1] The Act of 1957 confirmed the process. It did away, once and for all, with invitees and licensees and classed them all as "visitors"; and it put on the occupier the same duty to all of them, namely, the common duty of care. This duty is simply a particular instance of the general duty of care, which each man owes to his "neighbour". When Sir Baliol Brett M.R. first essayed a definition of this general duty, he used the occupiers' liability as an instance of it (see *Heaven* v. *Pender*):[2] and when Lord Atkin eventually formulated the general duty in acceptable terms, he, too, used occupiers' liability as

---

1. [1956] 2 Q.B. 264, at p. 269; [1956] 2 All E.R. 625, at p. 627.
2. (1883), 11 Q.B.D. 503, at pp. 508, 509; [1881–85] All E.R. Rep. 35, at pp. 39, 40.

an illustration (see *Donoghue* v. *Stevenson*,[1] and particularly his reference[2] to *Grote* v. *Chester & Holyhead Rail. Co.*[3]). Translating this general principle into its particular application to dangerous premises, it becomes simply this: wherever a person has a sufficient degree of control over premises that he ought to realise that any failure on his part to use care may result in injury to a person coming lawfully there, then he is an "occupier" and the person coming lawfully there is his "visitor"; and the "occupier" is under a duty to his "visitor" to use reasonable care. In order to be an "occupier" it is not necessary for a person to have entire control over the premises. He need not have exclusive occupation. Suffice it that he has some degree of control. He may share the control with others. Two or more may be "occupiers". And whenever this happens, each is under a duty to use care towards persons coming lawfully on to the premises, dependent on his degree of control. If each fails in his duty, each is liable to a visitor who is injured in consequence of his failure, but each may have a claim to contribution from the other.

In *Salmond on Torts* (14th Edn., 1965), p. 372, it is said that an "occupier" is "he who has the immediate supervision and control and the power of permitting or prohibiting the entry of other persons". This definition was adopted by Roxburgh J. in *Hartwell* v. *Grayson Rollo and Clover Docks, Ltd.*,[4] and by Diplock L.J. in the present case.[5] There is no doubt that a person who fulfils that test is an "occupier". He is the person who says "come in"; but I think that that test is too narrow by far. There are other people who are "occupiers", even though they do not say "come in". If a person has any degree of control over the state of the premises it is enough. The position is best shown by examining the cases in four groups.

First, where a landlord let premises by demise to a tenant, he was regarded as parting with all control over them. He did not retain any degree of control, even though he had undertaken to repair the structure. Accordingly, he was held to be under no duty to any person coming lawfully on to the premises, save only to the tenant under the agreement to repair. In *Cavalier* v. *Pope*[6] it was argued that the premises were under the control of the landlord because of his agreement to repair: but the House of Lords rejected that argument. That case has now been overruled by s. 4 of the Act of 1957[7] to the extent therein mentioned.

Secondly, where an owner let floors or flats in a building to tenants, but did not demise the common staircase or the roof or some other parts, he was regarded as having retained control of all parts not demised by him. Accordingly, he was held to be under a duty in respect of those retained parts to all persons coming lawfully on to the premises. So he was held liable for a defective staircase in *Miller* v. *Hancock*,[8] for the gutters of the roof in *Hargroves, Aronson & Co.* v. *Hartopp*[9] and for the private balcony in *Sutcliffe* v. *Clients Investment Co.*[10] The extent of the duty was held to be that owed to a licensee, and not to an invitee, see *Fairman* v. *Perpetual Investment Building Society*;[11] *Jacobs* v. *London County Council.*[12] Since the Act of 1957 the distinction between invitees and licensees has been abolished, and the extent of the duty is now simply the common duty of care. But the old cases still apply so as to show that the landlord is responsible for all parts not demised by him, on the ground that he is regarded as being sufficiently in control of them to impose on him a duty of care to all persons coming lawfully on to the premises.

---

1. [1932] A.C. 562, at p. 580; [1932] All E.R. Rep. 1, at p. 11.
2. [1932] A.C. at pp. 586, 587; [1932] All E.R. Rep. at p. 14.
3. (1848), 2 Exch. 251.
4. [1947] K.B. 901, at p. 917.
5. [1965] 2 All E.R. at p. 711, letter E.
6. [1906] A.C. 428.
7. [See note 1, p. 225, *ante*.]
8. [1893] 2 Q.B. 177; [1891–94] All E.R. Rep. 736.
9. [1905] 1 K.B. 472.
10. [1924] 2 K.B. 746.
11. [1923] A.C. 74.
12. [1950] A.C. 361; [1950] 1 All E.R. 737.

Thirdly, where an owner did not let premises to a tenant but only licensed a person to occupy them on terms which did not amount to a demise, the owner still having the right to do repairs, he was regarded as being sufficiently in control of the structure to impose on him a duty towards all persons coming lawfully on to the premises. So he was held liable for a visitor who fell on the defective step to the front door in *Hawkins* v. *Coulsdon and Purley Urban District Council*;[1] and to the occupier's wife for the defective ceiling which fell on her in *Greene* v. *Chelsea Borough Council*.[2] The extent of the duty was that owed to a licensee, but since the Act of 1957 the duty is the common duty of care to see that the structure is reasonably safe.

Fourthly, where an owner employed an independent contractor to do work on premises or a structure, the owner was usually still regarded as sufficiently in control of the place as to be under a duty towards all those who might lawfully come there. In some cases he might fulfil that duty by entrusting the work to the independent contractor: see *Haseldine* v. *Daw & Son, Ltd.*,[3] and s. 2 (4) of the Act of 1957. In other cases he might only be able to fulfil it by exercising proper supervision himself over the contractor's work, using due diligence himself to prevent damage from unusual danger (see *Thomson* v. *Cremin*[4] as explained by Lord Reid in *Davie* v. *New Merton Board Mills, Ltd.*[5]). But in addition to the owner, the courts regarded the independent contractor as himself being sufficiently in control of the place where he worked as to owe a duty of care towards all persons coming lawfully there. He was said to be an "occupier" also (see *Hartwell* v. *Grayson Rollo and Clover Docks, Ltd.*[6]), but this is only a particular instance of his general duty of care (see *A. C. Billings & Sons, Ltd.* v. *Riden*[7] per Lord Reid).

In the light of these cases, I ask myself whether the respondents had a sufficient degree of control over the premises to put them under a duty to a visitor. Obviously they had complete control over the ground floor and were "occupiers" of it. But I think that they had also sufficient control over the private portion. They had not let it out to Mr. Richardson by a demise. They had only granted him a licence to occupy it, having a right themselves to do repairs. That left them with a residuary degree of control which was equivalent to that retained by the Chelsea Corporation in *Greene's* case.[2] They were in my opinion "an occupier" within the Act of 1957. Mr. Richardson, who had a licence to occupy, had also a considerable degree of control. So had Mrs. Richardson, who catered for summer guests. All three of them were, in my opinion, "occupiers" of the private portion of the "Golfer's Arms". There is no difficulty in having more than one occupier at one and the same time, each of whom is under a duty of care to visitors. The Court of Appeal so held in the recent case of *Fisher* v. *C.H.T., Ltd.*[8]

What did the common duty of care demand of each of these occupiers towards their visitors? Each was under a duty to take such care as "in all the circumstances of the case" was reasonable to see that the visitor would be reasonably safe. So far as the respondents were concerned, the circumstances demanded that on the ground floor they should, by their servants, take care not only of the structure of the building, but also the furniture, the state of the floors and lighting, and so forth, at all hours of day or night when the premises were open. In regard to the private portion, however, the circumstances did not demand so much of the respondents. They ought to have seen that the structure was reasonably safe, including the handrail, and that the system of lighting was efficient; but I doubt whether they were bound to see that the lights were properly switched on or the rugs laid safely on the floor. The respondents were entitled to leave those day-to-day matters to Mr. and Mrs. Richardson. They, too, were occupiers. The

---

1. [1954] 1 Q.B. 319; [1954] 1 All E.R. 97.
2. [1954] 2 Q.B. 127; [1954] 2 All E.R. 318.
3. [1941] 2 K.B. 343; [1941] 3 All E.R. 156.
4. (1941), [1953] 2 All E.R. 1185.
5. [1959] A.C. 604, at pp. 642–645; [1959] 1 All E.R. 346, at pp. 365–367.
6. [1947] K.B. 901, at pp. 912, 913.
7. [1958] A.C. 240, at p. 250; [1957] 3 All E.R. 1, at p. 5.
8. [1966] 1 All E.R. 88.

circumstances of the case demanded that Mr. and Mrs. Richardson should take care of those matters in the private portion of the house. And of other matters, too. If they had realised that the handrail was dangerous, they should have reported it to the respondents.

We are not concerned here with Mr. and Mrs. Richardson. The judge has absolved them from any negligence and there is no appeal. We are only concerned with the respondents. They were, in my opinion, occupiers and under a duty of care. In this respect I agree with Sellers L.J.[1] and Winn J., but I come to a different conclusion on the facts. I can see no evidence of any breach of duty by the respondents. So far as the handrail was concerned, the evidence was overwhelming that no-one had any reason before this accident to suppose that it was in the least dangerous. So far as the light was concerned, the proper inference was that it was removed by some stranger shortly before Mr. Wheat went down the staircase. Neither the respondents nor Mr. and Mrs. Richardson could be blamed for the act of a stranger.

I would, therefore, dismiss this appeal.

LORD MORRIS OF BORTH-Y-GEST: . . . Who, then, for this purpose is an occupier? I say "for this purpose" because in other circumstances there may be different identification (e.g. in connexion with rating or in connexion with the franchise). Section 1 (1) of the Act of 1957 speaks of "an occupier of premises". Section 1 (2) refers to "a person's occupation or control of premises": it goes on to refer to "any invitation or permission he gives (or is to be treated as giving) to another to enter or use the premises". This, I think, shows that exclusive occupation is not necessary to constitute a person an occupier. In his speech in *Glasgow Corpn.* v. *Muir*,[2] Lord Wright said[3]:

> "Before dealing with the facts, I may observe that in cases of invitation the duty has most commonly reference to the structural condition of the premises, but it may clearly apply to the use which the occupier (or whoever has control so far as material) of the premises permits a third party to make of the premises."

This illustrates that there may be someone who would ordinarily be regarded as the occupier of premises while at the same time there may be another occupier who has "control so far as material". . . . Questions of fact may arise as to the nature and extent of occupation and control. Thus in *Prenton* v. *General Steam Navigation Co., Ltd.*[4] there was a question whether contractors were sufficiently in occupation of the 'tween decks of a ship for the purposes of their work to owe a duty to an employee of their sub-contractors. It was said by Jenkins L.J., in *Pegler* v. *Craven*,[5] that the conception of "occupation" is not necessarily and in all circumstances confined to the actual personal occupation of the person termed the occupier himself, and that in certain contexts and for certain purposes it extends to vicarious occupation by a caretaker or other servant or by an agent.

[His Lordship referred to the service agreement between the respondents and Mr. Richardson, under which *inter alia* the respondents retained the right of entry for certain purposes, including inspection of the state of repair of the property. He also referred to the arrangements allowing guests and continued:] . . . The general result of the agreement and of the arrangements to which I have referred was that the respondents through their servant were in occupation of the whole premises. Their servant was required to be there. The contemplation, it would appear, was that the respondents would see to the condition of the premises and would effect any necessary repairs. As the residential part would constitute the home of the manager and his family it was a reasonable inference, and it would be mutually assumed, that his privacy in regard to it

---

1. [1965] 2 All E.R. at p. 705, letter B.
2. [1943] A.C. 448; [1943] 2 All E.R. 44.
3. [1943] A.C. at p. 462; [1943] 2 All E.R. at p. 51.
4. (1944), 77 Lloyd L.R. 174.
5. [1952] 2 Q.B. 69, at p. 74; [1952] 1 All E.R. 685, at p. 687.

would be respected. It would be mutually assumed that the respondents could not as of right enter that part save for the defined purpose of viewing its condition and state of repair. There was freedom for the manager or his wife to make contracts with and to receive and entertain visitors for reward.

The conclusion which I reach is that as regards the premises as a whole both the respondents and the manager were occupiers but that by mutual arrangement the respondents would not (subject to certain over-riding consideration) exercise control over some parts. They gave freedom to their manager to live in his home in privacy. They gave him freedom to furnish it as and how he chose. They gave him freedom to receive personal guests and also to receive guests for reward. I think it follows that both the respondents and the Richardsons were "occupiers" vis-à-vis Mr. Wheat and his party. Both the respondents and the Richardsons owed Mr. Wheat and his party a duty. The duty was the common duty of care. The measure and the content of that duty were not, however, necessarily the same in the case of the respondents and in the case of the Richardsons. The duty was to take such care as in all the circumstances of the case was reasonable to see that Mr. Wheat and his party would be reasonably safe in using the premises as guests for reward. The respondents did not know that Mr. Wheat and his party were to arrive but they had given permission to their manager to take guests and the result was that Mr. Wheat and his party were on the premises with the respondents' permission. The "circumstances of the case" would, however, vary as between the respondents and the Richardsons. Thus, if after Mr. Wheat and his party had arrived they had been ascending the main staircase, and, if it had collapsed and caused them injury, a question would have arisen whether either the respondents or the Richardsons or any or all of them had been lacking in their duty. "The circumstances of the case" in such a situation would have, or might have, been quite different so far as the respondents were concerned from what they would have been so far as the Richardsons were concerned. If, to take another possibility, the Wheats had entered a living room of the Richardsons which had been fitted and equipped and furnished by the Richardsons and had suffered some mishap, which arose from the state or condition of the equipment or furnishings, "the circumstances of the case" would have been, or might have been, quite different so far as the Richardsons were concerned from the circumstances so far as the respondents were concerned.

In the illustrations to which I have referred it might be or could be that there would be some failure on the part of the respondents to take care in regard to the staircase and no failure on the part of the Richardsons: so it might be or could be that there would be some failure on the part of the Richardsons in regard to some equipment or furnishing in a living room and no failure on the part of the respondents.

It may, therefore, often be that the extent of the particular control which is exercised within the sphere of joint occupation will become a pointer as to the nature and extent of the duty which reasonably devolves on a particular occupier.

Mr. Wheat decided to use the backstairs. We have no occasion to consider whether, on the assumption that he fell in the way that the learned judge thought he fell, there was any failure to take care on the part of the Richardsons. The learned judge held that there was not. The only question that now arises is whether the respondents failed to take such care as in all the circumstances it was reasonable for them to take to see that paying guests of the Richardsons would be reasonably safe in using the premises. Though the staircase which Mr. Wheat used was the back staircase, and not the main one, I think that the respondents would and should have realised that a visitor might use the back staircase. Did they negligently provide a staircase which it would be unsafe to use? I cannot think that they did. . . .

LORD PEARSON: . . . It seems to me clear that Mr. and Mrs. Richardson had at least some occupational control of the upper part of the premises to which the appeal relates. They lived there. They provided the furniture. They for their own benefit took in paying guests and received them and looked after them. The paying guests would have been their invitees at common law, and were their visitors under the Act of 1957.

Moreover, Mr. and Mrs. Richardson were present and able to see the state of the premises and what was being done or omitted therein. If anything was wrong, they could take steps to rectify it or have it rectified. If there were any danger, they could protect the paying guests by erecting a barrier or giving a warning or otherwise. Mr. and Mrs. Richardson were appropriate persons for bearing and fulfilling the common duty of care. . . . I think that the respondents, however, also had some occupational control of the upper part of the premises. The lower part, the licensed part, was occupied by the respondents through their servant Mr. Richardson and their agent Mrs. Richardson for the purpose of the liquor-selling business of the respondents. The agreement applied to the whole of the premises without distinguishing between the two parts. Mr. Richardson as manager for the respondents was required as well as entitled to occupy the whole of the premises on their behalf. He was required to live in the upper part for the better performance of his duties as manager of the business of the respondents. His right to live there, and the permission to take in paying guests, were perquisites of the employment. The paying guests, though invited by the Richardsons, had the respondents' permission to come and were therefore visitors of the respondents as well as of the Richardsons. The fact that the respondents gave permission for the Richardsons to take in paying guests is important as showing that the respondents had some control over the admission of persons to the upper part of the premises. The respondents did not themselves say "Come in", but they authorised the Richardsons to say "Come in". The respondents had, under cl. 5 of the agreement, an express right to enter the premises for viewing the state of repair, and, as was conceded (correctly in my opinion), an implied right to do the repairs found to be necessary. It is fair to attribute to the respondents some responsibility for the safety of the premises for those who would, in pursuance of the authority given by the respondents, be invited to enter as paying guests the upper part of the premises. In matters relating to the design and condition of the structure they would be in a position to perform the common duty of care.

For these reasons I agree that there was, for the purposes of occupiers' liability, dual occupation of the upper part of the premises; but as there was no proof of negligence on the part of the respondents I would dismiss the appeal.

[VISCOUNT DILHORNE and LORD PEARCE delivered speeches in favour of dismissing the appeal.]

Appeal dismissed

Question

What was the basis for the decision that the respondents were in occupation of the area in question?

Note

1. In *Fisher* v. *C.H.T., Ltd.*, [1966] 2 Q.B. 475; [1966] 1 All E.R. 88, the second defendants managed the restaurant in a club which was run by the first defendants. The second defendants employed the third defendants to carry out some plastering work as part of a redecoration scheme, but their own employee, Boothroyd, was to do the electrical work. Seabrook, a maintenance man employed by the first defendants, knew about the electrical fittings in the premises, was ready to help and took an interest in the work. All the electrical switches for the restaurant had been switched off while the third defendants' men were working on the ceiling, but to test some of his work on the lighting, Boothroyd, not knowing which was the appropriate switch, turned all the switches on. The plaintiff, an employee of the third defendants, received a shock from a wire which was exposed in the ceiling and which was now live. He fell and was injured. At the trial of the action the first, second and third

defendants were held 20%, 60% and 20% responsible respectively, but the second defendants could not pay their share of the damages. This left the first and third defendants liable for the whole amount. The Court of Appeal held that the first defendants, who retained the right to pass through the restaurant and who controlled the entrance to the premises as a whole, were occupiers of the restaurant, despite the fact that they had granted a licence to the second defendants, who were also occupiers. The apportionment of responsibility was altered, however. The first defendants' share was put at 10% and that of the third defendants, the plaintiff's employers, at 30% (25% and 75% of the damages respectively).

(ii) The common duty of care—relevant factors

Sawyer v. H. & G. Simonds, Ltd.

Queen's Bench Division   (1966), 197 Estates Gazette 877

In this case Mr. Kenneth George Sawyer, of 65, Donnington Gardens, Reading, Berks., claimed damages for personal injury caused by the negligence and/or breach of statutory duty of the defendants, H. & G. Simonds, Ltd., brewers, of Reading, as owners and occupiers of the Ship Hotel, Duke Street, Reading.

Giving judgment, VEALE J., said that on 18 June 1960, Mr. Sawyer received an injury when he fell in a bar in the Ship Hotel and damaged his hand in some way on some glass on the floor. It was a very long time ago, and giving evidence in 1966 was a matter of great difficulty in the recollection of anybody. Mr. Sawyer's story was that he had ordered a half of bitter for himself, his first drink of the day, and a half of bitter for an acquaintance. He positioned himself on a bar stool and placed his feet on the bar rail, when the stool slipped on some liquor on the floor and he fell backwards. In putting out his hand to break the fall his hand was cut by broken glass from which the liquor had come.

Even if the accident had occurred in the way the plaintiff described it, he still had to prove that there was negligence under the Occupiers' Liability Act 1957. The duty owed by the defendant to the plaintiff was a "common duty of care" under s. 2 of the Act. This section read: "The common duty of care is a duty to take such care as in all the circumstances of the case is reasonable to see that the visitor will be reasonably safe in using the premises for the purposes for which he is invited or permitted by the occupier to be there." This did not extend to the duty of *insuring* the safety of the visitor. Of course it was dangerous to allow broken glass to lie about anywhere where the public came and went. Of course broken glass should be cleared up as soon as possible. But one could not clear up broken glass unless one knew that broken glass was there to be cleared.

The occupier was therefore under a duty to keep a reasonable look-out for this type of danger. The accident had occurred at a busy time in the lunch hour on a Saturday. It was the duty of the hall porter to come in every 20 minutes to clear empty glasses, and if he had seen broken glass on the floor he would have removed it. "Reasonable care" involved consideration of the nature of the danger, the length of time that the danger was in existence, the steps necessary to remove the danger and the likelihood or otherwise of an injury being caused. The mere fact that this unfortunate accident happened did not connote negligence. There was an adequate system in the hotel for looking out for this kind of danger. The danger of falling from a stool in this way was remote. The barman had no knowledge that glass was on the floor. He (his Lordship) could not find that the defendants were negligent, and he entered judgment for the defendants with costs limited to £85 from the plaintiff, who was legally aided.

Note

Compare this case with *Martin* v. *Middlesbrough Corp.* (1965), 63 L.G.R. 385, where damages were recovered when a schoolgirl slipped and was injured by broken glass. The injury occurred in a school playground and the broken glass was probably part of a milk bottle. The defendants, the local education authority, were held liable, because, in the court's opinion, there should have been better arrangements for disposing of the empty bottles. The standard of care required of the defendants, who owed the common duty of care under the Occupiers' Liability Act 1957, was stated (at p. 386) to be that of "a prudent parent in relation to his own children": see P. M. North, *Occupiers' Liability*, pp. 68–70.

Roles v. Nathan

Court of Appeal   [1963] 2 All E.R. 908

A central heating boiler produced a great deal of smoke when lit, and a boiler engineer advised that the flues should be cleaned. Two chimney sweeps were, therefore, engaged to clean the flues of the boiler, which burnt coke and gave off carbon monoxide gas. The engineer warned the sweeps of the danger presented by the fumes, but his warning was disregarded, and one of the sweeps crawled into one of the flues. The next day, after the fire had gone out, the flues were cleaned by the sweeps. However, when the boiler was relit, the fumes still caused problems. Mr. Collingwood, an expert, was brought in, and, although he warned the sweeps of the dangers of the fumes, it was only with great difficulty that he could get them to leave the room. Their attitude, he said, was that they were experts. He also advised them amongst others, that, before the boiler was relit, the vent holes (an inspection chamber in the horizontal flue and a sweep hole in the vertical flue) should be sealed, and he repeated the warning about the gases. Some time later the boiler was lit by an unknown person (—it was thought it might have been the caretaker who later disappeared). Whilst the fire was burning, the sweeps carried on with and nearly completed their work. Only the sweep hole in the vertical flue remained to be sealed when they told Mr. Corney (the occupier's son-in-law and the man at that time in charge of the rooms where the boiler was situated) that they would finish the job the next day. In fact they came back that evening, but died when they were overcome by the fumes. The widows of the two sweeps sued the occupier of the rooms.

LORD DENNING M.R.: . . . It is quite plain that these men died because they were overcome by fumes of carbon monoxide. It would appear to a layman that the fumes must have come from the sweep-hole, but the judge on the evidence thought that they probably came from the boiler. But I do not think that it matters. The fumes came from the boiler or the sweep-hole or both. The question is whether anyone was at fault. The judge found Mr. Corney guilty of negligence because he "failed to take such care as should have ensured that there was no fire until the sweep-hole had been sealed". He said: ". . . unhappily, he did not tell the caretaker to draw the fire, or at any rate not to stoke it up". On this account he held that Mr. Corney was at fault, and the occupier liable. But he found the two sweeps guilty of contributory negligence, and halved the damages. The judge said:

"That negligence [of the chimney sweeps] consisted in the knowledge that there was gas about, or probably would be, the way they ignored explicit warnings, and showed complete indifference to the danger which was pointed out to them in plain language, and this strange indifference to the fact that the fire was alight, when Mr. Collingwood had said it ought not to be, until the sweep-hole had been sealed."

The occupier now appeals and says that it is not a case of negligence and contributory negligence, but that, on the true application of the Occupiers' Liability Act 1957, the occupier was not liable at all. This is the first time that we have had to consider that Act. It has been very beneficial. It has rid us of those two unpleasant characters, the invitee and the licensee, who haunted the courts for years, and it has replaced them by the attractive figure of a visitor, who has so far given no trouble at all. The Act has now been in force six years, and hardly any case has come before the courts in which its interpretation has had to be considered. The draftsman expressed the hope[1] that the Act would

> "replace a principle of the common law with a new principle of *the common law*: instead of having the judgment of Willes J.[2] construed as if it were a statute, one is to have a statute which can be construed as if it were a judgment of Willis J."

It seems that his hopes are being fulfilled. All the fine distinctions about traps have been thrown aside and replaced by the common duty of care. . . .

[Having cited s. 2 (3) of the 1957 Act, he continued:] That subsection shows that *Christmas* v. *General Cleaning Contractors, Ltd.*[3] is still good law under this new Act. There a window cleaner (who was employed by independent contractors) was sent to clean the windows of a club. One of the windows was defective; it had not been inspected and repaired as it should have been. In consequence, when the window cleaner was cleaning it, it ran down quickly and trapped his hand, thus causing him to fall. It was held that he had no cause of action against the club. If it had been a guest who had his fingers trapped by the defective window, the guest could have recovered damages from the club. But the window cleaner could not do so. The reason is this: The householder is concerned to see that the windows are safe for his guests to open and close, but he is not concerned to see that they are safe for a window cleaner to hold on to. The risk of a defective window is a special risk, but it is ordinarily incident to the calling of a window cleaner, and so he must take care for himself, and not expect the householder to do so. Likewise, in the case of a chimney sweep who comes to sweep the chimneys or to seal up a sweep-hole. The householder can reasonably expect the sweep to take care of himself so far as any dangers from the flues are concerned. These chimney sweeps ought to have known that there might be dangerous fumes about and ought to have taken steps to guard against them. They ought to have known that they should not attempt to seal up the sweep-hole whilst the fire was still alight. They ought to have had the fire withdrawn before they attempted to seal it up, or at any rate they ought not to have stayed in the alcove too long when there might be dangerous fumes about. All this was known to these two sweeps; they were repeatedly warned about it, and it was for them to guard against the danger. It was not for the occupier to do it, even though he was present and heard the warnings. When a householder calls in a specialist to deal with a defective installation on his premises, he can reasonably expect the specialist to appreciate and guard against the dangers arising from the defect. The householder is not bound to watch over him to see that he comes to no harm. I would hold, therefore, that the occupier here was under no duty of care to these sweeps, at any rate in regard to the dangers which caused their deaths. If it had been a different danger, as for instance if the stairs leading to the cellar gave way, the occupier might no doubt be responsible, but not for these dangers which were special risks ordinarily incidental to their calling.

Even if I am wrong about this point, and the occupier was under a duty of care to these chimney sweeps, the question arises whether the duty was discharged by the warning that was given to them. This brings us to s. 2 (4) . . . We all know the reason for this subsection. It was inserted so as to clear up the unsatisfactory state of the law as it had been left by the decision of the House of Lords in *London Graving Dock Co., Ltd.* v. *Horton.*[4] That case was commonly supposed to have decided that, when a person comes

---

1. See *Salmond on Tort* (13th Edn.), at p. 512, p. 513, note 51.
2. In *Indermaur* v. *Dames* (1866), L.R. 1 C.P. 274, at p. 288.
3. [1952] 1 K.B. 141; [1952] 1 All E.R. 39; *affd. sub nom. General Cleaning Contractors, Ltd.* v. *Christmas*, [1953] A.C. 180; [1952] 2 All E.R. 1110.
4. [1951] A.C. 737; [1951] 2 All E.R. 1.

on to premises as an invitee, and is injured by the defective or dangerous condition of the premises (due to the default of the occupier), it is, nevertheless, a complete defence for the occupier to prove that the invitee knew of the danger, or had been warned of it. Supposing, for instance, that there was only one way of getting into and out of premises, and it was by a footbridge over a stream which was rotten and dangerous. According to *Horton's* case,[1] the occupier could escape all liability to any visitor by putting up a notice: "This bridge is dangerous", even though there was no other way by which the visitor could get in or out, and he had no option but to go over the bridge. In such a case, s. 2 (4) (a) makes it clear that the occupier would not[2] be liable. But if there were two footbridges, one of which was rotten, and the other safe a hundred yards away, the occupier could still escape liability, even today, by putting up a notice: "Do not use this footbridge. It is dangerous. There is a safe one further upstream". Such a warning is sufficient because it does enable the visitor to be reasonably safe.

I think that the law would probably have developed on these lines in any case; see *Greene* v. *Chelsea Borough Council*,[3] where I ventured to say:

". . . knowledge or notice of the danger is only a defence when the plaintiff is free to act on that knowledge or notice so as to avoid the danger."

But the subsection has now made it clear. A warning does not absolve the occupier unless it is enough to enable the visitor to be reasonably safe. Apply s. 2 (4) to this case. I am quite clear that the warnings which were given to the sweeps were enough to enable them to be reasonably safe. The sweeps would have been quite safe if they had heeded these warnings. They should not have come back that evening and attempted to seal up the sweep-hole while the fire was still alight. They ought to have waited till next morning, and then they should have seen that the fire was out before they attempted to seal up the sweep-hole. In any case they should not have stayed too long in the sweep-hole. In short, it was entirely their own fault. The judge held that it was contributory negligence. I would go further and say that, under the Act, the occupier has, by the warnings, discharged his duty.

I would, therefore, be in favour of allowing this appeal and entering judgment for the defendants.

[HARMAN L.J. delivered a judgment in favour of allowing the appeal. PEARSON L.J. delivered a judgment in favour of dismissing the appeal, but differing only as to the interpretation of the evidence, and not as to any question of law."]

Appeal allowed

Question

Suppose a plaintiff was injured by a danger of which the normal occupier of premises would not have been aware. If the occupier was in fact aware of this danger, and put up a warning notice, but in the wrong place, could he be liable? (Compare *Woollins* v. *British Celanese, Ltd.* (1966), I K.I.R. 438.)

(iii) Exclusion of liability

White v. Blackmore

Court of Appeal [1972] 3 All E.R. 158

On a Sunday morning, the plaintiff's husband entered as a competitor for some "jalopy" races. Later that day, he returned with his wife (the plaintiff), baby and mother-in-law to the course, and paid the entrance fee for his wife and mother-in-law. As he was a competitor, he entered free. Near to the entrance there was one of several notices headed "Warning to the Public", "Motor Racing is Dangerous". It stated that it was "a condition of admission that all persons having any connection with the promotion and/or organisation and/or conduct of the meeting, including . . . . the drivers . . . . of the vehicles . . . . are absolved from all liabilities arising out of accidents causing damage

---

1. [1951] A.C. 737; [1951] 2 All E.R. 1.
2. [The word should be "nowadays"—[1963] 1 W.L.R. 1117, at p. 1124.]
3. [1954] 2 Q.B. 127, at p. 139; [1954] 2 All E.R. 318, at p. 325.

or personal injury (whether fatal or otherwise) howsoever caused to spectators or ticketholders." In addition, p. 2 of the programme, of which he received three copies when he entered the course with his family, contained a substantially similar clause, although the cover of the programme made no reference to there being any conditions. At one point after a race, the plaintiff's husband went across to join his family who were behind the spectators' rope some way from the track, although he did not cross the rope. After another race had started, a car's wheel became entangled in the safety ropes about ⅓ of a mile away with the result that it pulled up the stakes holding these ropes, and the master stake, which held several ropes, close to where the husband was standing. He was thrown through the air, badly injured and later died. His widow claimed damages from several defendants, two of whom were the chairman of the jalopy club which was holding the races and the racing organiser. Her claim was rejected by the trial judge on the ground that the maxim *volenti non fit injuria* applied. The plaintiff appealed, but her appeal was dismissed.

BUCKLEY L.J.: The learned judge found the defendants, who are sued personally and as representing the members of the Severn Valley Jalopy Club, guilty of negligence as organisers of the jalopy race meeting on account of the way in which the ropes were attached to the post near which the deceased was standing when the accident happened. Counsel for the defendants has submitted that the judge applied too high a standard in arriving at this decision. There was, in my judgment, material before the learned judge on which he could properly arrive at this conclusion, which I think should not be disturbed. The judge went on to hold that the defendants were nevertheless entitled to succeed in their defence on the ground of the doctrine enshrined in the maxim volenti non fit injuria. Strictly, I think that that doctrine is not applicable in the present case, but the somewhat analogous law relating to exclusion of liability.

The doctrine of volenti non fit injuria affords a shield of defence to a party who would otherwise be liable in tort to an opponent who has by his conduct voluntarily encountered a risk which was fully known to him at the time. . . . The learned judge expressed the view that it might not have been at all obvious to the deceased that he was standing in a particularly dangerous place when the accident occurred. Accepting this, I do not think it can be said in the present case that the deceased had full knowledge of the risk which he was running.

In my judgment the case must turn on the effect of the various warnings which the deceased saw or had ample opportunity to see. If these warnings were, or any of them was, sufficient to exclude any duty of care on the part of the organisers of the meeting towards the deceased, the defendants were not guilty of negligence and consequently they do not need the shield of the doctrine of volenti. The learned judge in fact based his decision on these warnings.

I need not repeat the history of the relevant events on the day of the accident. Counsel for the plaintiff has submitted that when the deceased signed on in the morning of that day he entered into a contractual arrangement with the organisers that he should be permitted to come on to the field for the purpose of competing in the races, and that that contract could not be affected by any of the subsequent events of the day. That contract, he says, was not subject to any limitation of liability except possibly one to the effect that competitors taking part in races did so at their own risk. Consequently, counsel submits, the organisers' liability to the deceased when he came on to the field in the afternoon was subject to no relevant limitation. In my judgment, the evidence does not support the suggestion that the parties had any intention of entering into contractual relations when the deceased signed on in the morning. He was thereby indicating to the organisers, as the learned judge thought and as I think, that he proposed to take part in the racing in the afternoon as a competitor and no more. Accordingly I do not feel able to accept this submission of counsel for the plaintiff.

When the deceased returned with his family in the afternoon, the notice[1] . . . was

1. [See the statement of facts, *ante.*]

prominently displayed near the entrance to the ground. The learned judge found as a fact that the deceased saw that notice and appreciated that it was a notice governing the conditions under which people were to be admitted to watch the racing.

No argument was addressed to us based on the Occupiers' Liability Act 1957, s. 2 (4). This, I think, was right. To the extent that the notice at the entrance was a warning of danger, I agree with Lord Denning M.R.[1] that it did not enable a visitor to be reasonably safe, but the notice was more than a warning of a danger: it was designed to subject visitors to a condition that the classes of persons mentioned in it should be exempt from liability arising out of accidents. Section 2 (4) has, it seems to me, no application to this aspect of the notice.

In my opinion, when the deceased came on to the field in the afternoon, he did so as a gratuitous licensee. I have already said that, in my view, no contract was made in the morning. The deceased made no payment for entry in the afternoon. Nothing that occurred in the morning could afford consideration for any contract entered into in the afternoon. In my judgment, no contract between the promoters and the deceased was made in the afternoon. The deceased remained willing to take part in the races and the promoters remained willing to allow him to do so. On the evidence, he was not, in my judgment, either bound or entitled contractually to take part in the races. In this state of affairs he was allowed on to the field free of charge.

I think that when the deceased came on to the field in the afternoon he did so in a dual capacity, as a prospective competitor and as a spectator. He was not intending to take part in all the races run on that afternoon, and I can feel no doubt that part of his object in attending the meeting was to enjoy watching those races in which he was not a competitor as well as to compete in those races in which he proposed to compete. There was considerable discussion in the course of the argument whether this notice was applicable to the deceased. Counsel for the plaintiff contended that, if he was wrong about a contract having been entered into in the morning, at least a licence was then granted to the deceased to enter the field in the afternoon for the purpose of competing in the races and counsel contended that such licence was irrevocable until the deceased had completed the purpose for which it was granted, that is to say, until he had completed those races in which he proposed to take part. For my part I think that no licence was granted to the deceased in the morning beyond an implied licence permitting him to leave his jalopy in the pits coupled with a further implied licence allowing him in due course to remove his jalopy from the field. Whether this be right or not, whatever licence was granted to the deceased by the organisers in the morning was, in my judgment, a gratuitous one. It was not, as was suggested, a licence coupled with an interest. It could consequently be revoked or varied by the organisers at any time subject only to the deceased being given a suitable opportunity to remove his property from the field. In the absence of any express term, a revocable licence can be revoked by whatever notice is reasonable in the circumstances (*Winter Garden Theatre (London), Ltd.* v. *Millennium Productions, Ltd.*).[2] Since, in my view, the deceased had no legal right to insist on taking part in the races, there is no reason to regard any licence granted to him in the morning as irrevocable until he had completed those races in which he proposed to take part. In the circumstances of this case I think any licence granted to the deceased in the morning was revocable summarily subject only to his right to recover his jalopy. If it was revocable, it was to a like extent variable.

What then was the effect of the situation which arose when the deceased returned to the field in the afternoon? It is clear that the occupier of land, who permits someone else to enter on that land as his licensee, can by imposing suitable conditions limit his own liability to the licensee in respect of any risks which may arise while the licensee is on the land (*Ashdown* v. *Samuel Williams & Sons, Ltd.*[3]). The Occupiers' Liability Act

---

1. [His dissenting judgment has been omitted.]
2. [1948] A.C. 173; [1947] 2 All E.R. 331.
3. [1957] 1 Q.B. 409; [1957] 1 All E.R. 35.

1957, which in s. 2 (1) refers to an occupier excluding his duty of care to any visitor "by agreement or otherwise", has not altered the law in this respect. Counsel for the plaintiff concedes that in the present case the notice displayed at the entrance to the ground was sufficient to exclude liability on the part of the organisers of the meeting to all spectators properly so called, but he contends that a distinction is to be drawn between competitors and spectators for this purpose. It is common ground that the deceased was not a ticket-holder within the meaning of the notice, but, in my judgment, he was a spectator. The learned judge so held, and I think that he was right in doing so. The notice was, in my opinion, sufficiently explicit in its application to the deceased. I feel unable to accept the suggestion that the heading "Warning to the Public" should be read in a restrictive sense excluding competitors. Reading the document as a whole, I think there can be no doubt that it was addressed to all persons answering the descriptions of spectators or ticket-holders. The deceased was not even a member of the Severn Valley Jalopy Club. He was, in my opinion, a member of the public. The organisers are, I think, shown to have taken all reasonable steps to draw the condition contained in the notice to the attention of the deceased. The learned judge found that warnings of this character were a common feature at jalopy races with which the deceased would have been familiar. He also found, as I have already said, that the deceased saw this particular notice and appreciated its character. He also found that the deceased saw a number of other notices in identical terms posted about the field and that he appreciated what these notices were intended to effect. I think that he came on to the field in the afternoon on the terms contained in the notice displayed at the entrance to the ground.

The liability of the organisers of the meeting to visitors attending it for the purpose of taking part in some races and watching others was in my opinion limited in two respects. Such a visitor, in my judgment, as a competitor and when engaged in the role of a competitor, accepted all the risks inherent in the sport of jalopy racing. The organisers owed no duty to him to protect him against those risks. . . . As a spectator, such a visitor was, I think, subject to the condition set out in the warning notice. At the time when the accident occurred the deceased was, in my opinion, a spectator. The limitation on the liability of the organisers in these circumstances is to be found in the notice. The condition set out in the notice was that they were to be absolved from all liabilities arising out of accidents causing damage or personal injury howsoever caused. The use of the words "howsoever caused" makes clear that the absolution was intended to be of a general character. The effect of the condition must, in my judgment, amount to the exclusion of liability for accidents arising from the organisers' own negligence. For these reasons I consider that the learned judge was right in dismissing the action. This makes it unnecessary for me to consider the effect of the warning notice which was printed on the inner face of the programme.

I would dismiss this appeal.

[ROSKILL L.J. delivered a judgment in favour of dismissing the appeal. LORD DEN-NING M.R. delivered a judgment in favour of allowing the appeal.]

Question

If the deceased had been killed as a result of being run over by a negligently driven jalopy, would the notice in this case have protected the driver? (See generally North, *op. cit.*, pp. 126–130.)

Notes

1. The question of exclusion of liability arose in an important case decided just before the 1957 Act—*Ashdown v. Samuel Williams & Sons, Ltd.*, [1957] 1 Q.B. 409; [1957] 1 All E.R. 35. The plaintiff's place of work was on property leased by the first defendants to her employers, the second defendants, and to reach her place of employment the plaintiff used a short cut which lay across

land retained by the first defendants. The short cut crossed several railway lines, and the plaintiff, when crossing one of these lines, was injured by a truck, which was being shunted by the first defendants' employees. They were found to have been negligent. A notice erected by first defendants could be seen by people using the short cut, and it stated that those on the property were there at their own risk, and that they should not have any claim against these defendants for any injury they received, however caused. The Court of Appeal held that the plaintiff entered the land as a licensee, and that the terms of the notice were effective to exclude the first defendants' liability. The defendants had "taken all reasonable steps to bring the conditions to her notice" (*per* Parker L.J.): it did not matter that she had only read part of the notice. It was mentioned above that *Ashdown* v. *Samuel Williams & Sons, Ltd.* was a pre-Occupiers' Liability Act decision. In the light of s. 2 (1) of that Act, it is felt to be valid today (a view supported by *White* v. *Blackmore*): indeed Winfield & Jolowicz state (at p. 185) that the law established in *Ashdown's* case "is given statutory force". See also the comments on this decision in *Burnett* v. *British Waterways Board*, [1973] 2 All E.R. 631. For further comment on *Ashdown's* case, see notes by L. C. B. Gower (1956), 20 M.L.R. 532 (dealing with the decision in the court below) and (1957), 20 M.L.R. 181, and see F. J. Odgers, "Occupiers' Liability: A Further Comment", [1957] C.L.J. 39, at pp. 42–54.

2. For the Law Commission's provisional proposals on exclusion of liability in this area see p. 255, *post*.

(b) To Trespassers

Note

The Occupiers' Liability Act 1957 does not regulate the duty which is owed to trespassers. This depends on the common law, which, once a person has been classified as a trespasser, has traditionally excluded him from the ambit of any duty of reasonable care. This is shown by *R. Addie & Sons (Collieries), Ltd.* v. *Dumbreck*, [1929] A.C. 358; [1929] All E.R. Rep. 1, where a wheel forming one part of a haulage system crushed and killed a four year old boy. The wheel which was attractive to children, and which was not sufficiently protected, was situated in a field adjoining the road, and could not be seen from the appellants' pithead from where it was put into operation. There was a hedge between the field and the road, but it contained many gaps. The appellants knew that the area was used as a short cut, and that children played there despite the fact that on occasions they were warned off by the appellants' servants. The appellants had been held liable to the child's father in the Scottish courts, but the House of Lords allowed their appeal. The child was held to be a trespasser, and, in the course of his speech, Lord Hailsham L.C. put forward (at p. 4) the following celebrated proposition:

> "Towards the trespasser the occupier has no duty to take reasonable care for his protection or even to protect him from concealed danger. The trespasser comes on to the premises at his own risk. An occupier is in such a case liable only where the injury is due to some wilful act involving something more than the absence of reasonable care. There must be some act done with the deliberate intention of doing harm to the trespasser, or at least some act done with reckless disregard of the presence of the trespasser."

Whilst it might be said that a burglar deserves no better treatment, it is much more difficult to apply this remark to the case of an "innocent" trespassing child. Nevertheless, the traditional approach asserted that this was the only duty owed to the "innocent" child, once he was classified as a trespasser, and it equated the position of the adult and the child within this category. This was a rigid approach which could operate harshly, and yet if the magic tag "occupier" was absent, then the contractor, who was carrying on activities on the land but who was not an occupier of that land, could be held liable for negligence to a person whom he injured, even though that person was a trespasser *vis-à-vis* the occupier. Thus it is not surprising that ways were sought to mitigate the harshness of the law. This could be achieved if it were decided that the plaintiff had an implied licence and, therefore, was not a trespasser, a decision which could more readily be reached in the case of a child. A more drastic step was taken in *Videan* v. *British Transport Commission*, [1963] 2 Q.B. 650; [1963] 2 All E.R. 860, in which the Court of Appeal made some progress towards the imposition of liability for negligence. Lord Denning M.R. took the view that, where the occupier was conducting activities on his land, a duty of care extended to a trespasser whose presence ought to be foreseen, and Harman L.J. also based the occupier's liability to trespassers for activities he carried out on his land on the foreseeability doctrine (cf. Pearson L.J.). However, it was not long before these views were criticised by the Privy Council in *Railways Commissioner* v. *Quinlan*, [1964] A.C. 1054; [1964] 1 All E.R. 897, which basically reaffirmed the *Addie* rule. Undeterred, the Court of Appeal in *Kingzett* v. *British Railways Board* (1968), 112 Sol. Jo. 625, followed *Videan*, but when it returned to this problem in *Herrington* v. *British Railways Board*, [1971] 2 Q.B. 107; [1971] 1 All E.R. 897, the Court of Appeal (Salmon, Edmund Davies and Cross L.JJ.) took a different line. For reasons which need not be discussed here, the case was decided on the basis of the "reckless disregard" test (see *ante*), although a majority of the court thought that this phrase could encompass very careless conduct. This confused area of case law, of which this brief survey has merely skimmed the surface, has not been pursued further, and is not set out in this Chapter because there was an appeal in the *Herrington* case, and the House of Lords, [1972] A.C. 877; [1972] 1 All E.R. 749, *post*, took the opportunity to restate the duty which is owed to trespassers. (This is a task which, it might be felt, should have been performed by Parliament in 1957.) Unfortunately, their Lordships did not speak with one voice, and, therefore, it has been necessary to set out the five speeches in some detail. The final solution is likely to lie in legislation, as the Law Commission has published a Working Paper on this topic (see p. 255, *post*).

British Railways Board v. Herrington

House of Lords   [1972] 1 All E.R. 749

This was an appeal from the judgment of the Court of Appeal, [1971] 1 All E.R. 897, in which an appeal from the judgment of Cairns J., granting the respondent damages, had been dismissed.

LORD REID: My Lords, on 7 June 1965 the respondent, then a child of six years old, was playing with other children on National Trust property at Mitcham which is open to the public. Immediately adjoining this property the appellants have an electrified railway line a few yards from the boundary. Their boundary is marked by a fence which, if it had been in good repair, would have sufficed to prevent the respondent from reaching the railway line. But it was in very bad repair so that when the respondent strayed away from his playmates he was able to get through or over it. He then went a few yards farther and came in contact with the live electrified rail. Fortunately he was rescued but he had already sustained severe injury. His age was such that he was unable to appreciate the danger of going on to the railway line and probably unable to appreciate that he was doing wrong in getting over the fence.

I have no doubt that if the appellants owed to potential child trespassers any duty of care to take steps for their safety, they were in breach of any such duty. Enquiry soon after the accident showed that this was by no means the only place where their fence was defective and a well trodden track leading to the point where the respondent got on to their property showed that a considerable number of trespassers must have crossed the line at this point to other National Trust property on the other side. The appellants led no evidence at the trial and it cannot be inferred that they knew about these trespassers before the accident. The only evidence of their knowledge was a report produced by them which showed that they knew that a few weeks before the accident some children had been seen on the line at some point not very far away. But in my view the evidence was sufficient to show either that there was no systematic inspection of their fence or that if there was any system it was not operated or enforced. . . .

. . . We are confronted with the position that persistent attempts have been made to confer on child trespassers greater rights and to impose on occupiers greater obligations than are to my mind consistent with the decision of this House in *Addie's* case.[1] I shall not deal with the forthright Australian authorities farther than to say that those attempts are even more persuasive and far reaching than those in this country. So it appears to me that no satisfactory solution can be found without a re-examination of the whole problem and a reconsideration by this House of its decision in *Addie's* case.[1]

Child trespassers have for a very long time presented to the courts an almost insoluble problem. They could only be completely safeguarded in one or other of two ways. Either parents must be required always to control and supervise the movements of their young children, or occupiers of premises where they are likely to trespass must be required to take effective steps to keep them out or else to make their premises safe for them if they come. Neither of these is practicable. The former course was practicable at one time for a limited number of well-to-do parents but that number is now small. The latter, if practicable at all, would in most cases impose on occupiers an impossible financial burden.

Legal principles cannot solve the problem. How far occupiers are to be required by law to take steps to safeguard such children must be a matter of public policy. The law was uncertain when *Addie's* case[1] was decided. That decision was intended to make the law certain. It did so. This House must have taken the view that as a matter of public policy occupiers should have no duty at all to keep out such children or to make their premises safe for them. Their only duty was a humanitarian duty not to act recklessly with regard to children whom they knew to be there.

It may have been arguable 40 years ago that that was good public policy. But for one fact I would think it unarguable today. That is the fact that only 14 years ago Parliament when it had an obvious opportunity to alter that policy failed to do so. . . .

[Having referred to the fact that the Occupiers' Liability Act 1957 had not dealt with liability to trespassers, but that the Occupiers' Liability (Scotland) Act 1960 had, Lord Reid stated that he felt justified in treating this omission in the 1957 Act as due to indecision on Parliament's part over a replacement for *Addie's* case,[1] and continued:] The question, then, is to what extent this House sitting in its judicial capacity can do what Parliament failed to do in 1957. I dislike usurping the functions of Parliament. But it appears to me that we are confronted with the choice of following *Addie*[1] and putting the clock back or drastically modifying the *Addie*[1] rules. It is suggested that

---

1. [1929] A.C. 358; [1929] All E.R. Rep. 1.

such a modification can be achieved by developing the law as laid down in *Addie's* case[1] without actually overruling any part of the decision. I do not think that that is possible. It can properly be said that one is developing the law laid down in a leading case so long but only so long as the "development" does not require us to say that the original case was wrongly decided. But it appears to me that any acceptable "development" of *Addie's* case[1] must mean that *Addie's* case[1] if it arose today would be decided the other way. The case for the pursuer in *Addie's* case[1] was stronger on the facts than the case for the present respondent and I do not think that we could dismiss this appeal without holding or at least necessarily implying that *Addie's* case[1] was wrongly decided.

I do not think that it would be satisfactory merely to follow the scheme of the Scottish Act.[2] That Act provides by s. 2 that the care which an occupier is required to show to a person entering his land (which includes a trespasser) in respect either of its dangerous state or of dangerous activities on it shall be—

"such care as in all the circumstances of the case is reasonable to see that that person will not suffer injury or damage by reason of any such danger."

That may work satisfactorily where actions for damages for failure to exercise such care are generally decided by juries. Juries do not give reasons and so no verdict of a jury can establish a precedent. But in England such actions are decided by judges who must give reasons and whose decisions can be the subject of appeal. No doubt if the matter were left at large in this way a body of case law with regard to the position of trespassers would develop over the years. The matter would in one form or another come before this House before very long and some authoritative guidance would then emerge. But I would not create such a period of uncertainty if that can be avoided, and I think it can be avoided.

The first matter to be determined is the nature of the duty owed by occupiers to trespassers. Here I think we can get good guidance from *Addie's* case.[1] The duty there laid down was a duty not to act recklessly. Recklessness has, in my opinion, a subjective meaning; it implies culpability. An action which would be reckless if done by a man with adequate knowledge, skill or resources might not be reckless if done by a man with less appreciation of or ability to deal with the situation. One would be culpable, the other not. Reckless is a difficult word. I would substitute culpable.

The duty laid down in *Addie's* case[1] was a humanitarian duty. Normally the common law applies an objective test. If a person chooses to assume a relationship with members of the public, say by setting out to drive a car or to erect a building fronting a highway, the law requires him to conduct himself as a reasonable man with adequate skill, knowledge and resources would do. He will not be heard to say that in fact he could not attain that standard. If he cannot attain that standard he ought not to assume the responsibility which that relationship involves. But an occupier does not voluntarily assume a relationship with trespassers. By trespassing they force a "neighbour" relationship on him. When they do so he must act in a humane manner—that is not asking too much of him—but I do not see why he should be required to do more. So it appears to me that an occupier's duty to trespassers must vary according to his knowledge, ability and resources. It has often been said that trespassers must take the land as they find it. I would rather say that they must take the occupier as they find him.

So the question whether an occupier is liable in respect of an accident to a trespasser on his land would depend on whether a conscientious humane man with his knowledge, skill and resources could reasonably have been expected to have done or refrained from doing before the accident something which would have avoided it. If he knew before the accident that there was a substantial probability that trespassers would come, I think that most people would regard as culpable failure to give any thought to their safety. He might often reasonably think, weighing the seriousness of the danger and the

1. [1929] A.C. 358; [1929] All E.R. Rep. 1.
2. I.e. the Occupiers' Liability (Scotland) Act 1960.

degree of likelihood of trespassers coming against the burden he would have to incur in preventing their entry or making his premises safe, or curtailing his own activities on his land, that he could not fairly be expected to do anything. But if he could at small trouble and expense take some effective action again I think that most people would think it inhumane and culpable not to do that. If some such principle is adopted there will no longer be any need to strive to imply a fictitious licence. It would follow that an impecunious occupier with little assistance at hand would often be excused from doing something which a large organisation with ample staff would be expected to do.

It is always easy to be wise after the event and in judging what ought to have been done one would have to put out of one's mind the fact that an accident had occurred and visualise the position of the occupier before it had happened. Quite probably this would not be the only point on his land where trespass was likely. One would have to look at his problem as a whole and ask whether if he had thought about the matter it would have been humane or decent of him to do nothing. That may sound a low standard but in fact I believe that an occupier's failure to take any preventive steps is more often caused by thoughtlessness than by any shirking of his moral responsibility. I think that current conceptions of social duty do require occupiers to give reasonable attention to their responsibilities as occupiers, and I see nothing in legal principles to prevent the law from requiring them to do that.

If I apply that test to the present case I think that the appellants must be held responsible for this accident. They brought on to their land in the live rail a lethal and to a young child a concealed danger. It would have been very easy for them to have and enforce a reasonable system of inspection and repair of their boundary fence. They knew that children were entitled and accustomed to play on the other side of the fence and must have known, had any of their officers given the matter a thought, that a young child might easily cross a defective fence and run into grave danger. Yet they did nothing. I do not think that a large organisation is acting with due regard to humane considerations if its officers do not pay more attention to safety. I would not single out the stationmaster[1] for blame. The trouble appears to have been general slackness in the organisation. For that the appellants are responsible and I think in the circumstances culpable. I would therefore hold them liable to the respondent and dismiss this appeal.

LORD MORRIS OF BORTH-Y-GEST: . . . The facts in the present case differ from those in *Addie's* case.[2] In the present case a question arises whether some duty may be owed to a person before he becomes a trespasser. In that case a question arose whether a duty was owed to someone who was already a trespasser. . . .

. . . Although, generally speaking, an occupier is not obliged to fence his land and although, generally speaking, there is no obligation to prevent somebody from becoming a trespasser—are there some circumstances in which a duty arises to take some action to lessen the risk of peril both in the case of a potential or prospective trespasser and in the case of someone who has become a trespasser? . . .

. . . It is today basic to our legal thinking that every member of a community must have regard to the effect on others of his actions or his inactions. If in all probability the boy in the present case would not have suffered injury had the fence been in ordinary repair instead of being left dilapidated for weeks on end the question might be asked— even so as the boy would be a trespasser the moment he crossed the line of the fence why and for what reason should the appellants owe him any duty at all beyond that of not deliberately harming him thereafter or of acting with reckless disregard of his presence on their land? I would answer for reasons of common sense and common humanity. The nature and extent of any duty owed will call for separate consideration. But there must be some circumstances in which, by reason of them, a duty is owed by an

---

1. [Some weeks before he had been notified of the presence of children on the line in his area. He had asked the police to investigate.]
2. [1929] A.C. 358; [1929] All E.R. Rep. 1.

occupier of land to potential trespassers as well as to actual trespassers of whom he is positively aware. As my noble and learned friend Lord Pearson said in *Videan* v. *British Transport Commission*,[1] it is a heresy to suggest that occupation of land is a ground of exemption from liability; on the contrary (he said) occupation of land is a possible ground of liability and if a duty of care is owed then any person to whom it is owed is a neighbour although the content of the duty will vary according to the circumstances.

If it is asked, why need the appellants give any thought to the question whether a trespasser might come to harm by trespassing on their land? the answer must I think again be that common sense and common intelligence so direct. What has been called ordinary civilised behaviour would so prompt. . . . By taking ordinary thought and exercising "common sense and ordinary intelligence"—even apart from the guidance of common humanity—I think that the appellants would see that in the circumstances of this case there was a likelihood that some child might pass over the broken down fence and get on to the track with its live rail and be in peril of serious injury. Even though the child would be a trespasser ought it not to be their "plain duty" to repair the fence? That would be a relatively simple operation not involving any unreasonable demands of time or labour or expense.

In the classic definition of negligence in 1856 in *Blyth* v. *Birmingham Waterworks Co.*[2] Alderson B. said that negligence was—

"the omission to do something which a reasonable man, guided upon those considerations which ordinarily regulate the conduct of human affairs, would do, or doing something which a prudent and reasonable man would not do."

Ought not the "considerations which ordinarily regulate the conduct of human affairs" under some circumstances (and I would include those of the present case) produce the result that some duty is owed by an occupier of land towards those who if they proceed further may suffer injury at a time when they are trespassing? . . .

I consider that it is abundantly clear that the appellants, if they had taken thought, must have realised that if they allowed the fence to be broken down at the particular place in question there was a considerable risk that a small child would pass through it and might as a result either be killed or come to serious harm. . . .

Could a child such as the boy in the present case be regarded as a "neighbour"? When Lord Atkin posed the question, who then in law is my neighbour? he said[3] that the answer seemed to be—

"persons who are so closely and directly affected by my act that I ought reasonably to have them in contemplation as being so affected when I am directing my mind to the acts or omissions which are called in question."

No one would suggest that every trespasser is a "neighbour" but within these words was not the small boy in the present case a neighbour? When the railway track and its electrified rail were laid and at all times when they were maintained the risks of injury resulting if there was neither warning nor impediment such as a fence would provide would be clear to anyone who gave the matter a moment's thought. Yet when the boy went on to the track he undoubtedly became a trespasser. Does this mean that the strict edict of *Addie's* case[4] prevents any kind of duty from arising towards such a neighbour, especially as Parliament has not legislated in terms which cover trespassers? In my view, while it cannot be said that the appellants owed a common duty of care to the young boy in the present case they did owe to him at least the duty of acting with common humanity towards him. . . . I do not think that the appellants (through their servants) did any act with the deliberate intention of doing harm to the boy; their omission for a long time to repair the fence and their continuing distribution of electric

1. [1963] 2 Q.B. 650, at pp. 677, 678; [1963] 2 All E.R. 860, at p. 873.
2. (1856), 11 Exch. 781, at p. 784; [1843–60] All E.R. Rep. 478, at pp. 479, 480.
3. See *M'Alister* (or *Donoghue*) v. *Stevenson*, [1932] A.C. 562, at p. 580; [1932] All E.R. Rep. 1, at p. 11.
4. [1929] A.C. 358; [1929] All E.R. Rep. 1.

power along their live rail did not, in my view, amount to a "reckless disregard of the presence of a trespasser". If those last quoted words can be said to cover the likely or expected or anticipated presence of a trespasser then the question arises whether the lamentable inaction of the appellants is to be characterised as "reckless". As to this I have doubt. The word "reckless" seems more apposite in reference to positive conduct than to inaction.

The duty that lay on the appellants was a limited one. There was no duty to ensure that no trespasser could enter on the land. And certainly an occupier owes no duty to make his land fit for trespassers to trespass in. Nor need he make surveys of his land in order to decide whether dangers exist of which he is unaware. The general law remains that one who trespasses does so at his peril. But in the present case there were a number of special circumstances: (a) the place where the fence was faulty was near to a public path and public ground; (b) a child might easily pass through the fence; (c) if a child did pass through and go on to the track he would be in grave danger of death or serious bodily harm; (d) a child might not realise the risk involved in touching the live rail or being in a place where a train might pass at speed. Because of these circumstances (all of them well known and obvious) there was, in my view, a duty which, while not amounting to the duty of care which an occupier owes to a visitor, would be a duty to take such steps as common sense or common humanity would dictate; they would be steps calculated to exclude or to warn or otherwise within reasonable and practicable limits to reduce or avert danger.

I would adopt the approach of my noble and learned friend Lord Pearson, in his judgment in the Court of Appeal in *Videan's* case.[1] In agreement with him, I do not think that there is any sound basis of principle for differentiating sharply between liability for the static condition of land and liability for current operations on land. In general, therefore, a trespasser has not only to take the land as he finds it but the current operations on land as he finds them. Yet a potential or actual trespasser may on occasion be a neighbour and, as my noble and learned friend said,[2] the expression "duty to a neighbour" is more appropriately used as an aid to ascertaining whether or not there is a duty of care owing by one person to another rather than as a definition of the content of such a duty. So:[3]

> "If the person concerned does not know of, or have good reason to anticipate, the presence of the trespasser, that person owes to him no duty of care because he is not within the 'zone of reasonable contemplation' and is not a 'neighbour'. If the person concerned knows of, or has good reason to anticipate, the presence of the trespasser, that person owes to the trespasser a duty of care which is substantially less than the duty of care which is owing to a lawful visitor, because the duty to a trespasser is only a duty to treat him with common humanity and not a duty to make the land and operations thereon safe for the trespasser in his trespassing." . . .

For the reasons which I have given I consider that the learned judge was warranted in deciding that the respondent was entitled to recover. My approach involves some departure from some of what was said in *Railways Comr.* v. *Quinlan*.[4] It involves also that, on its facts, the decision in *Addie's* case[5] should in my view have been the other way. The colliery company knew that young children were in the habit of playing on the ground near to the wheel in question and knew that although at times there were warnings, children continued to frequent the place. They knew that children might be or were likely to be there. I consider that with such knowledge they should have taken reasonable care to avoid the risk of a child trespasser being killed or injured by reason

---

1. [1963] 2 Q.B. 650; [1963] 2 All E.R. 860.
2. [1963] 2 Q.B. at p. 678; [1963] 2 All E.R. at p. 874.
3. [1963] 2 Q.B. at p. 680; [1963] 2 All E.R. at p. 875.
4. [1964] A.C. 1054; [1964] 1 All E.R. 897.
5. [1929] A.C. 358; [1929] All E.R. Rep. 1.

of the wheel being suddenly and blindly put to work. It follows that I consider that the case was wrongly decided.

I would dismiss the appeal.

LORD WILBERFORCE: . . . We have not, in England, any general law as to public enterprise liability. As regards fencing, such duty as the appellants have (Railways Clauses Consolidation Act 1845, s. 68, which, it seems protects cattle but not children) dates from 1845 since when, even after electrification, Parliament has not thought it necessary to impose new obligations on railway companies. So if the respondent is to recover, he must rely on our outdated law of fault liability which involves the need to establish a duty of care towards him and a breach of it. At once he is faced by the formidable authority of R. *Addie & Sons (Collieries), Ltd.* v. *Dumbreck*.[1] . . .

We ought now to ask the question directly, what, in relation particularly to infant trespassers, is the duty of care? (see *Railways Comr. (N.S.W.)* v. *Cardy*)[2] for the recognition of some duty of care, even towards trespassers, in certain limited cases, is what the imputation of a licence really means. We may, although here we are getting near the dangerous ground of legislation, be readier than our predecessors to see liability for injuries to individuals placed on society generally, of which the appellants effectively form part. And if we do not go so far as to recognise that special rules ought to be devised for child trespassers (cf. American Restatement),[3] we can at least accept that fresh and more lethal dangers to their safety have appeared, and come nearer to them, and that somewhere more care has to be used to prevent them being hurt. I say "somewhere" because the occupier of adjoining land is not the only, or indeed the first, person in the line of responsibility. Even today parents have some control and responsibility, and if children are on a playground which someone has provided for the purpose, that person has a responsibility to see that it is safe.

Does, then, *Addie*[1] contain an exhaustive definition of an occupier's duties to persons on his land? One does not see why, in principle, this should be so. It could be so if the fact of occupation of land were to be the basis of exemption from any greater liability than the relevant rule prescribes. But this idea has been refuted more than once (see *Railways Comr.* v. *McDermott*).[4] The correct conception is that stated by the Privy Council[5] when through Viscount Radcliffe the Board said that the *Addie*[1] rules were expressive of certain consequences as regards proximity and foreseeability which flow from the given relationship (occupier and invitee—licensee—trespasser). Or, as was put by Barwick C.J.,[6] there is—

"a quantitative element both in the extent of the foreseeability and of the reasonable steps required to fulfil any resultant duty arising from the circumstances in which the injured persons came on the scene."

If this is generally so, it must follow that the law can, particularly, take into account other relevant factors, if they exist, which bear on these matters of foresight and prudence. It does so when in the general case it considers it relevant to know whether the presence of the relevant person was known, "as good as known" (*Railways Comr.* v. *Quinlan*),[7] or "extremely likely" (*Excelsior Wire Rope Co., Ltd.* v. *Callan*),[8] and it seems a necessary step from this to say that particular circumstances may exist in which an increased duty of "foreseeability" may arise.

---

1. [1929] A.C. 358; [1929] All E.R. Rep. 1.
2. (1961), 104 C.L.R. 274.
3. Torts (2nd), s. 339.
4. [1967] 1 A.C. 169, at p. 186; [1966] 2 All E.R. 162, at p. 167.
5. [1964] A.C. 1054, at p. 1072; in *Railways Comr.* v. *Quinlan*, [1964] 1 All E.R. 897, at p. 904.
6. In *Munnings* v. *Hydro-Electric Commission of Tasmania* (1971), 45 A.L.J.R. 378, at p. 382.
7. [1964] A.C. at p. 1076; [1964] 1 All E.R. at p. 906.
8. [1930] A.C. 404, at p. 410; [1930] All E.R. Rep 1, at p. 4.

There are other indications, in the law as it stands, of the relevance of particular factors as modifying the general rules. First there is the doctrine of allurements. It has been criticised, as a device, like imputed licences, for escaping from the *Addie*[1] rules. But it is older than *Addie*[1] and reflects the perfectly sound conception that as particular things are ("foreseeably") likely to be attractive to children, the occupier owes a duty, if they are dangerous, not to put them in the children's way. The classic case is that of the berries in the park (*Glasgow Corpn.* v. *Taylor*).[2] Secondly, there is the law as to fencing. In general an occupier is under no duty to fence his land so as to exclude trespassers, a rule of importance to railway companies and of validity as this House has decided (*Edwards* v. *Railway Executive*).[3] The fact that Parliament has not imposed a duty securely to fence children or others out is a recognition that a compromise must be struck between the desire to save everyone from every danger and the cost to the community of doing so. It means that there are situations where even children will not recover. But the courts have qualified this exemption by reference to particular circumstances as, for example, that persons are known frequently to have access along a track, *Cooke* v. *Midland Great Western Railway of Ireland*[4] and *Lowery* v. *Walker*[5] which, although put on the imputation of a licence, really reflect the fact that some elementary duty is owed. Similarly, there are the cases of pitfalls—where an occupier makes an excavation near a highway (cf. *Prentice* v. *Assets Co., Ltd.*)[6] (the same would surely be true of other hazards, e.g. an electric wire); he is under a duty, even to trespassers, to take some steps to keep them off.

Thirdly, there is the position of contractors carrying out work on land. A number of cases, *Davis* v. *St. Mary's Demolition and Excavation Co., Ltd.*,[7] *Mooney* v. *Lanarkshire C.C.*,[8] *A. C. Billings & Sons, Ltd.* v. *Riden*,[9] which I need not examine in detail (some of them I think put the duty too high), have established their responsibility in principle, through a duty of care, toward trespassers, including infant trespassers. Their liability should not depend solely on whether they were, or were not, themselves occupiers of the land, and it would be absurd if there were one law for contractors doing work and another law if the occupier did the same work himself (cf. *Buckland* v. *Guildford Gas Light and Coke Co.*[10] and *Creed* v. *John McGeoch & Sons, Ltd.*[11]) both perfectly sound decisions in themselves. This is not to say that the contractor's duty is to be imposed or measured regardless of the fact that the victim may have been a trespasser, but it is to say that there may be circumstances in which contractors and occupiers alike may have some (I am not saying the same) responsibility for trespassers' safety, outside the bare *Addie*[1] principle. . . .

These are merely examples to illustrate the proposition that *Addie*[1] is not an all embracing code, but a piece in the larger whole of a man's duty of care to those who may come into his proximity, and may be injured by actions or events occurring on his land. . . .

How does the matter rest? It is often said that the law on this topic is in confusion, but this is to do it less than justice. When one has eliminated from it complexities of fact situation . . . and when once one has discarded fictions, rules can be seen to emerge from the mists with reasonable clarity, but I emphasise no greater clarity than

---

1. [1929] A.C. 358; [1929] All E.R. Rep. 1.
2. [1922] 1 A.C. 44; [1921] All E.R. Rep. 1.
3. [1952] A.C. 737; [1952] 2 All E.R. 430.
4. [1909] A.C. 229; [1908–10] All E.R. Rep. 16.
5. [1911] A.C. 10; [1908–10] All E.R. Rep. 12.
6. (1890), 17 R. 484.
7. [1954] 1 All E.R. 578; [1954] 1 W.L.R. 592.
8. 1954 S.C. 245.
9. [1958] A.C. 240; [1957] 3 All E.R. 1.
10. [1949] 1 K.B. 410; [1948] 2 All E.R. 1086.
11. [1955] 3 All E.R. 123; [1955] 1 W.L.R. 1005.

we ought to expect from the common law, which always leaves a residue to be completed by common sense.

In general, an occupier of land owes no duty to trespassers, or intending trespassers; he is not obliged to make his land safe for their trespassing. If he knows, or "as good as knows" (*Quinlan*)[1] of the actual presence of a trespasser, he is under a duty—as defined in *Addie's* case[2]—not to act with the deliberate intention of doing harm to him or to act with reckless disregard of his presence. I must return to this matter of recklessness, but at present it is enough to say that reckless disregard as used by Lord Hailsham L.C. surely bears its normal meaning in the law—as akin to intentional injury, but instead of intention, not caring whether he does so or not. And this involves knowledge of the trespasser's presence.

I see no reason to discard the alternative test of "extremely likely" (Lord Buckmaster in *Callan*),[3] in relation to the trespasser's presence. Apart from its origin it has received support from Dixon C.J.[4] and Windeyer J.[5] and other judges as well as the Privy Council in *Quinlan*.[6] It excludes necessarily any lower duty of foreseeability in the general case by an occupier of trespassers' presence (see *Quinlan*).[7]

This is the general rule as stated by Lord Hailsham L.C. I think it is still a sound rule and I think that we must support it. The question remains whether, in particular circumstances, a man may be under some duty of a particular kind, other than to abstain from wilful injury, or reckless disregard. A test more specific than that of "foresight of likelihood of trespass" and a definition of duty more limited than that of "the common duty of care" is required.

The dangers of too precise, or exhaustive or codified, a definition are exemplified by *Addie's* case[2] itself. On the other hand, to adopt the expedient of recoiling on the comfortable concept of the reasonable man is hardly good enough. It evades the problem by throwing it into the lap of the judge. We must try at least to set up some boundary marks. I think it is safer to proceed by exclusion, and then to the facts of this case. An occupier is not under any general duty to foresee the possibility or likelihood of trespass on his land, or to carry out an inspection to see whether trespass is occurring or likely. To suppose otherwise would impose impossible burdens. Nor can a trespasser by giving notice to the occupier that he may trespass at a particular place or time, by that fact create a duty towards him.

An occupier is under no general duty to fence his land against trespassers, or even against child trespassers; and in my opinion, in principle, this exclusion is valid whether or not the occupier is carrying on operations on the land or whether some danger exists through a static condition (e.g. a quarry, *Holland* v. *District Committee of Middle Ward of Lanarkshire*).[8] A poisoned pool[9] may give rise to a special duty.

Exceptions may be found (these are only examples) (a) in the case of pitfalls and analogous situations of dangers created near a place where the victim had a right to go, (b) in the case of allurements to children. The principle behind the latter is, in my opinion, not one of imputing a licence, but that of a duty to take reasonable steps not to place in the way of small children potentially hurtful and attractive objects.

In the particular case of railway companies, there is no general duty to erect or maintain fences sufficient to exclude adults or children—the case of *Edwards*[10] is clear on this point and I respectfully think right; the only duty is to mark off the railway

---

1. [1964] A.C. at p. 1070; [1964] 1 All E.R. at p. 903.
2. [1929] A.C. 358; [1929] All E.R. Rep. 1.
3. [1930] A.C. at p. 410; [1930] All E.R. Rep. at p. 4.
4. (1961), 104 C.L.R. at p. 286.
5. (1961), 104 C.L.R. at p. 320.
6. [1964] A.C. 1054; [1964] 1 All E.R. 897.
7. [1964] A.C. at pp. 1072, 1074; [1964] 1 All E.R. at pp. 904, 905.
8. 1909, 2 S.L.T. 7.
9. *United Zinc and Chemical Co.* v. *Britt* (1922), 258 U.S. 268; 42 Sup. Ct. 299.
10. [1952] A.C. 737; [1952] 2 All E.R. 430.

property. If more precautions are needed because of the proximity of a playground they may have to be taken by those in control of the playground fencing in, rather than fencing out.

Then on the positive side I think that we can best serve the development of the law by concentrating on the particular type of case which has engaged the courts, and on which the law has been tested by experience. Just as in the 19th century the introduction of turntables, attractive to children, accessible and dangerous, gave rise to a jurisprudence known by their name, so we must take account of the placing of electrical conductors above or on the ground all over our overcrowded island and see where this leads as regards foresight and care. The ingredients of such duty as may arise must stem from the inevitable proximity to places of access, including highways, from the continuous nature of the danger, from the lethal danger of contact and from the fact that to children the danger may not be apparent. There is no duty to make the place safe, but a duty does arise because of the existence, near to the public, of a dangerous situation. The greater the proximity, the greater the risk, and correspondingly the need of foresight and a duty of care.

What is the nature of this duty of care? Again, it must be remembered that we are concerned with trespassers, and a compromise must be reached between the demands of humanity and the necessity to avoid placing undue burdens on occupiers. What is reasonable depends on the nature and degree of the danger. It also depends on the difficulty and expense of guarding against it. The law, in this context, takes account of the means and resources of the occupier or other person in control—what is reasonable for a railway company may be very unreasonable for a farmer, or (if this is relevant) a small contractor. If a precedent is needed for this concept of relative responsibility I may venture to refer to the Privy Council judgment in *Goldman* v. *Hargrave*,[1] where, in relation to another common law duty, it was said, inter alia:

"... the standard ought to be to require of the occupier what it is reasonable to expect of him in his individual circumstances."

My Lords, in my opinion, if the law is such as I have suggested, the law as stated in *Addie's* case[2] is developed but not denied; not, I venture to think, developed beyond what is permissible and indeed required of this House in its judicial capacity. . . .

Dealing now with the case of the infant respondent. In the Court of Appeal[3] he succeded on a basis of recklessness—that of the stationmaster at the nearest station who some time before had been informed some six weeks earlier that on one occasion children had been seen somewhere on the line. As to this, unless "recklessness' means "gross carelessness' and in my opinion not even then, there is no basis on which the appellants can be liable for this injury. But I agree with Salmon L.J. and not with the majority in the Court of Appeal that recklessness, in this context, has its classical meaning.

In *Quinlan's* case[4] the Privy Council suggested that the way ahead lay through an extended scope of wanton and reckless conduct. This may be enough in some cases, but in others, and in a case such as the present, I prefer a direct acceptance of an appropriate duty of care. The use of "recklessness' or imputed recklessness seems to me too like another fiction of the kind it is better to discard. However, if the approach I have suggested is correct, it will follow that a basis exists here on which, given satisfactory proof, an action in negligence could lie. . . .

. . . I am not prepared, especially in view of the judge's finding,[5] to differ from your Lordships' view that, in relation to the special duty of care incumbent on the appellants in the relevant place, there was a breach of that duty amounting to legal negligence, but

---

1. [1967] A.C. 645, at p. 663; [1966] 2 All E.R. 989, at p. 996.
2. [1929] A.C. 358; [1929] All E.R. Rep. 1.
3. [1971] 2 Q.B. 107; [1971] 1 All E.R. 897.
4. [1964] A.C. 1054; [1964] 1 All E.R. 897.
5. [He held the appellants to have been negligent.]

I am left with the feeling that cases such as these would be more satisfactorily dealt with by a modern system of public enterprise liability devised by Parliament.

I would dismiss the appeal.

LORD PEARSON: My Lords, in relation to an occupier of premises the position of a trespasser must be radically different from that of a lawful visitor. The broad effect of s. 2 of the Occupiers' Liability Act 1957 is that an occupier of premises owes to his lawful visitors, i.e. the persons who come on the premises at his invitation or with his permission, the common duty of care; and that is a duty to take such care as in all the circumstances of the case is reasonable to see that the visitor will be reasonably safe in using the premises for the purposes for which he is invited or permitted to be there. In my opinion, the occupier of premises does not owe any such duty to a trespasser: he does *not* owe to the trespasser a duty to take such care as in all the circumstances of the case is reasonable to see that the trespasser will be reasonably safe in using the premises for the purposes for which he is trespassing. That seems to me to be the fundamental distinction, and it should be fully preserved.

It does not follow that the occupier never owes any duty to the trespasser. If the presence of the trespasser is known to or reasonably to be anticipated by the occupier, then the occupier has a duty to the trespasser, but it is a lower and less onerous duty than the one which the occupier owes to a lawful visitor. Very broadly stated, it is a duty to treat the trespasser with ordinary humanity: *Bird* v. *Holbrook*,[1] *Grand Trunk Rail. Co. of Canada* v. *Barnett*[2] and *Latham* v. *Johnson*.[3] But that is a vague phrase. What is the content of the duty to treat the trespasser with ordinary humanity? The authoritative formulation of the duty, as given in R. *Addie & Sons (Collieries), Ltd.* v. *Dumbreck*,[4] is severely restrictive and is, I think, now inadequate. Subject to the difficulty created by that formulation, I think one can deduce from decided cases that, normally at any rate, the occupier is not at fault, he has done as much as is required of him, if he has taken reasonable steps to deter the trespasser from entering or remaining on the premises, or the part of the premises, in which he will encounter a dangerous situation. In simple language, it is normally sufficient for the occupier to make reasonable endeavours to keep out or chase off the potential or actual intruder who is likely to be or is in a dangerous situation. The erection and maintenance of suitable notice boards or fencing or both, or the giving of suitable oral warning, or a practice of chasing away trespassing children, will usually constitute reasonable endeavours for this purpose ... If the trespasser, in spite of the occupier's reasonable endeavours to deter him, insists on trespassing or continuing his trespass, he must take the condition of the land and the operations on the land as he finds them and cannot normally hold the occupier of the land or anyone but himself responsible for injuries resulting from the trespass, which is his own wrongdoing. But that statement is subject to this proviso: if the occupier knows or as good as knows that some emergency has arisen whereby the trespasser has been placed in a position of imminent peril, ordinary humanity requires further steps to be taken; ...

It seems to me that there is rational justification for the common law attitude towards trespassers, in so far as it has recognised that (a) in relation to an occupier the position of a trespasser is radically different from that of a lawful visitor; (b) the unknown and merely possible trespasser is not a "neighbour" in the sense in which that word "neighbour" was used by Lord Atkin in *M'Alister* (or *Donoghue*) v. *Stevenson*,[5] and the occupier owes to such a trespasser no duty to take precautions for his safety; and (c) if the presence of the trespasser is known to or reasonably to be anticipated by the occupier, then the occupier (i) does not owe to the trespasser the common duty of care

---

1. (1828), 4 Bing. 628, at p. 641.
2. [1911] A.C. 361, at p. 369.
3. [1913] 1 K.B. 398, at p. 411; [1911–13] All E.R. Rep. 117, at pp. 124, 125.
4. [1929] A.C. 358; [1929] All E.R. Rep. 1.
5. [1932] A.C. at p. 580; [1932] All E.R. Rep. at p. 11.

(which is the single statutory substitute for the different duties formerly owing to invitees and licensees); (ii) does not owe to the trespasser a general duty of care; but (iii) does owe to the trespasser a lower and less onerous duty, which has been described as a duty to treat him with ordinary humanity.

So far so good. Insofar as those are the rules of the common law on this subject, they seem to be fully acceptable. The difficulty, however, arises from the narrow formulation of the duty to trespassers in R. *Addie & Sons (Collieries), Ltd.* v. *Dumbreck*.[1] . . . The formulation is too narrow and inadequate in at least three respects.

First, it appears to hold the occupier liable only for positive acts and not in respect of omissions. Suppose that the occupier is running an electrified railway, with an exposed live rail, in the vicinity of a public playground, and that he has not provided any warning notice or fence to deter children from straying on to the railway, and in consequence a child strays on to the live rail and is seriously injured. Surely common sense and justice require that the occupier must be held liable in such a case for his nonfeasance. I doubt, however, whether it was intended to confine liability to positive acts. Perhaps the words "act" and "acting" in *Addie* v. *Dumbreck*[1] can be interpreted as including omissions.

Secondly, the formulation appears to say that the occupier has no duty to do anything for the protection of trespassers until there is a trespasser actually on the land and the occupier knows he is there. But again the case of a child straying on the live rail of an electrified railway shows that there must be a duty on the occupier to take some steps in advance to deter children from trespassing on the railway.

Thirdly, the formulation makes the occupier liable only in respect of deliberate or reckless acts. I think the word "reckless' in the context does not mean grossly negligent but means that there must be a conscious disregard of the consequences—in effect deciding not to bother about the consequences. Thus a subjective, mental element, a sort of mens rea, is required as a condition of liability. Mere negligence would not be enough to create liability, according to this formulation. There would be no duty to take care, but only a duty to abstain from deliberately or recklessly causing injury. That is plainly inadequate. . . .

. . . [I]n more recent times there has been [a] . . . development or attempted development of the law to circumvent the harsh rule in *Addie* v. *Dumbreck*.[1] Distinctions have been made (a) between the liability of the occupier and the liability of other persons who carry out active operations on the land; (b) between the liability of the occupier qua occupier and his liability qua operator himself carrying out active operations on the land. The theory is that, whereas the occupier qua occupier has a large measure of exemption from liability in respect of the static condition of the land, the occupier or any other person carrying out active operations on the land has the full duty of care even towards a trespasser under the "neighbour" principle of *Donoghue* v. *Stevenson*.[2]

I should, however, make it plain that I do not accept the theory. I doubt whether there is any major distinction for the present purpose (i) between the static condition of the land and active operations on the land; (ii) between the occupier and other persons (such as his servants or agents or independent contractors or employees of public authorities) lawfully carrying out operations on the land and having control of the operations and perhaps of the land as well for the time being; (iii) between trespass on land and trespass on installations or railway vehicles. Occupation is associated with control and is a ground of liability, not of exemption from liability. The trespasser's movements are unpredictable and he goes into places where he has no business to be and imposes his unwanted presence; these considerations affect what can reasonably be required not only in the case of the occupier but also in the case of such other persons.

It seems to me that the rule in *Addie* v. *Dumbreck*[1] has been rendered obsolete by changes in physical and social conditions and has become an incumbrance impeding

---

1. [1929] A.C. 358; [1929] All E.R. Rep. 1.
2. [1932] A.C. 562; [1932] All E.R. Rep. 1.

the proper development of the law. With the increase of the population and the larger proportion living in cities and towns and the extensive substitution of blocks of flats for rows of houses with gardens or back yards and quiet streets, there is less playing space for children and so a greater temptation to trespass. There is less supervision of children, so that they are more likely to trespass. Also with the progress of technology there are more and greater dangers for them to encounter by reason of the increased use of, for instance, electricity, gas, fast-moving vehicles, heavy machinery and poisonous chemicals. There is considerably more need than there used to be for occupiers to take reasonable steps with a view to deterring persons, especially children, from trespassing in places that are dangerous for them.

In my opinion the *Addie* v. *Dumbreck*[1] formulation of the duty of occupier to trespasser is plainly inadequate for modern conditions, and its rigid and restrictive character has impeded the proper development of the common law in this field. It has become an anomaly and should be discarded. But in my opinion the duty of occupier to trespasser should remain limited in the ways that I have endeavoured to indicate.

I need not lengthen this already long opinion by describing again the facts of the present case which have been described by my noble and learned friends. The appellants in the circumstances had a duty to take reasonable steps to deter children from straying from the public space on to the electrified railway line. Obviously, reasonable steps for this purpose included proper maintenance of the fence. But the appellants failed to repair the broken down fence even after they had been notified that children had been seen on the line. There was a clear breach of the duty.

I would dismiss the appeal.

LORD DIPLOCK: ... I would then seek to summarise the characteristics of an occupier's duty to trespassers on his land which distinguishes it from the statutory "common duty of care" owed to persons lawfully on his land under the Occupiers' Liability Act 1957, and from the common law duty of care owed by one man to his "neighbour", in the Atkinian sense, where the relationship of occupier and trespasser does not subsist between them. To do so does involve rejecting Lord Hailsham L.C.'s formulation of the duty in *Addie* v. *Dumbreck*[2] as amounting to an exclusive or comprehensive statement of it as it exists today. It takes account, as this House as the final expositor of the common law should always do, of changes in social attitudes and circumstances and gives effect to the general public sentiment of what is "reckless" conduct as it has expanded over the 40 years which have elapsed since the decision in that case.

First, the duty does not arise until the occupier has actual knowledge either of the presence of the trespasser on his land or of facts which make it likely that the trespasser will come on to his land; and has also actual knowledge of facts as to the condition of his land or of activities carried out on it which are likely to cause personal injury to a trespasser who is unaware of the danger. He is under no duty to the trespasser to make any enquiry or inspection to ascertain whether or not such facts do exist. His liability does not arise until he actually knows of them.

Secondly, once the occupier has actual knowledge of such facts, his own failure to appreciate the likelihood of the trespasser's presence or the risk to him involved, does not absolve the occupier from his duty to the trespasser if a reasonable man possessed of the actual knowledge of the occupier would recognise that likelihood and that risk.

Thirdly, the duty when it arises is limited to taking reasonable steps to enable the trespasser to avoid the danger. Where the likely trespasser is a child too young to understand or heed a written or a previous oral warning, this may involve providing reasonable physical obstacles to keep the child away from the danger.

Fourthly, the relevant likelihood to be considered is of the trespasser's presence at the actual time and place of danger to him. The degree of likelihood needed to give

---

1. [1929] A.C. 358; [1929] All E.R. Rep. 1.
2. [1929] A.C. at p. 365; [1929] All E.R. Rep. at p. 4.

rise to the duty cannot, I think, be more closely defined than as being such as would impel a man of ordinary humane feelings to take some steps to mitigate the risk of injury to the trespasser to which the particular danger exposes him. It will thus depend on all the circumstances of the case: the permanent or intermittent character of the danger; the severity of the injuries which it is likely to cause; in the case of children, the attractiveness to them of that which constitutes the dangerous object or condition of the land; the expense involved in giving effective warning of it to the kind of trespasser likely to be injured, in relation to the occupier's resources in money or in labour.

My Lords, on the findings of the trial judge in the instant appeal, I find no difficulty in inferring that through the eyes or ears of one or other of their servants the appellants did know the physical facts that made it likely that little children playing in Bunces Meadow would trespass on their line and that if they did so would run a serious risk of grave if not mortal injury from the electric rail. Breach of the other characteristics of the duty which then arose, is in my view, established. I would, therefore, dismiss this appeal.

It might, however, leave this branch of the common law of England still in confusion if this House did not state categorically the respects in which the test of an occupier's duty to a trespasser differs from that stated by the majority of the Court of Appeal in *Videan* v. *British Transport Commission*[1] and reiterated by the whole court in *Kingzett* v. *British Railways Board*[2] despite the intervening adverse comment by the Privy Council in *Quinlan's* case.[3]

In the instant case the trial judge felt that he was bound to follow the reasoning of *Videan's* case[1] and *Kingzett's* case.[2] The Court of Appeal[4] felt able to decide it without recourse to *Videan's* case,[1] by treating the stationmaster's failure to do anything except to warn the police when children had trespassed on the land two months before, as falling within Lord Hailsham L.C.'s formula in *Addie* v. *Dumbreck*[5] as "an act done with reckless disregard of the presence of a trespasser". This was, I think, unduly censorious of the stationmaster as an individual. It was unnecessary to apportion among their individual servants the blame which lay on the appellants. The reckless act was that of the fictitious person, the appellants themselves, in allowing the deadly current to flow through the live rail when, through one or more of their servants they knew the physical facts which made it likely that a little child would stray from Bunces Meadow and come in contact with the rail.

The test propounded by the majority of the Court of Appeal in *Videan's* case[1] is, in my view, wrong in three respects. (1) It draws an unwarrantable distinction between a "static" condition of the occupier's land and an "activity" which the occupier carries out on it. In respect of activities of the occupier on the land it accords the trespasser the status of "neighbour" vis-à-vis the occupier despite the fact that he has forced this relationship on the occupier against the latter's will and by a wrongful act done to the occupier. (2) It treats the source of the relationship which gives rise to the occupier's duty towards a trespasser in respect of "activities" as mere foreseeability of the trespasser's presence, just as in the case of someone lawfully on his land. This suggests that there is some duty on the occupier to make inspections or enquiries in order to acquaint himself of the likelihood of a trespasser's coming on to his land. There is no such duty. (3) It treats the duty of the occupier to the trespasser in respect of "activities" as identical with his duty to persons lawfully on his land instead of the more restricted duty to take reasonable steps to enable the trespasser to avoid concealed dangers resulting from the existence of facts actually known to the occupier.

In the instant appeal your Lordships are concerned only with the liability of an occupier of land towards a trespasser whose presence on the land is a legal wrong

---

1. [1963] 2 Q.B. 650; [1963] 2 All E.R. 860.
2. (1968), 112 Sol. Jo. 625.
3. [1964] A.C. 1054; [1964] 1 All E.R. 897.
4. [1971] 2 Q.B. 107; [1971] 1 All E.R. 897.
5. [1929] A.C. at p. 365; [1929] All E.R. Rep. at p. 4.

committed by the trespasser on the occupier himself. This is not necessarily the same as the liability of some other person, who carries on an activity on the land with the permission of the occupier, towards a person who, although a trespasser vis-à-vis the occupier, commits no legal wrong on him who carries on the activity. There are three cases at first instance in which it has been held by judges of great eminence that a contractor, who is not the occupier of land, owes to trespassers on the land the ordinary common law duty of care owed by one man to his neighbour. That he is a trespasser vis-à-vis the occupier was treated as relevant only to the foreseeability of his presence. (See *Buckland* v. *Guildford Gas Light and Coke Co.*,[1] *Davis* v. *St. Mary's Demolition & Excavation Co.*[2] and *Creed* v. *John McGeoch & Sons, Ltd.*[3].) In *Videan's* case[4] it was asserted baldly that there was neither rhyme nor reason why the occupier's liability to a trespasser should differ from that of a contractor. There is at least one possible reason in logic and in law. Disapproval of the ratio decidendi of *Videan's* case[4] does not necessarily involve any conflict with the decisions in the three contractors' cases to which I have referred. The instant case is not an appropriate one in which to deal with the liability to a trespasser of persons who are not the occupiers of the land on which the trespass is committed.

Appeal dismissed

Questions

1. Is the concept of "humanity" any more precise than that of reasonable care? (Consider Lord Reid's view, at p. 242, *ante*.)

2. Lord Wilberforce, when stating that the law took account of the particular occupier's resources, referred to *Goldman* v. *Hargrave*, [1967] A.C. 645; [1966] 2 All E.R. 989, p. 393, *post*. Is that case analogous?

3. Is it a sound policy to take into account the knowledge and resources and *per* Lord Reid the ability of the particular occupier?

4. What is the duty owed by the contractor carrying out work on land of which he is not an occupier, if towards a person who is a trespasser vis-à-vis the occupier? Are his resources to be taken into account?

Notes

1. The fact that the Occupiers' Liability Act 1957 had not dealt with liability to trespassers, but that the Occupiers' Liability (Scotland) Act 1960 had, was mentioned, by not only Lord Reid, but also Lord Morris. He pointed out that the English Act had not been amended, but thought that the House of Lords could, without making fundamental changes, "ensure that the tide of development of the common law is not unwarrantably impeded". Does *Herrington's* case represent a fundamental change or not? These statutory sections were also mentioned by Lord Wilberforce, who took the view that the common law could still be developed.

2. Clarification of difficult points in a decision can often be provided by later cases. Unfortunately, little guidance can be obtained from the Court of Appeal's decision in *Pannett* v. *P. McGuinness & Co., Ltd.*, [1972] 2 Q.B. 599; [1972] 3 All E.R. 137, in which the *Herrington* decision was applied. A small boy, whilst trespassing, fell into a fire in a warehouse which had been partly

---

1. [1949] 1 K.B. 410; [1948] 2 All E.R. 1086.
2. [1954] 1 All E.R. 578; [1954] 1 W.L.R. 592.
3. [1955] 3 All E.R. 123; [1955] 1 W.L.R. 1005.
4. [1963] 2 Q.B. 650; [1963] 2 All E.R. 860.

demolished by the defendants, who, it appeared, were occupiers of the land as well as contractors. Edmund Davies L.J. dealt with the case on the basis of occupiers' liability. Lawton L.J.'s brief judgment is ambiguous, referring to the "reasonable contractor", applying *Herrington*, but not specifically mentioning the defendants' occupation of the area in question. Lord Denning M.R. thought that the fact of their occupation was no reason for subjecting the defendants to a lower duty than that imposed upon them as contractors. Nevertheless, he then "applied" the *Herrington* decision, although he made no mention of the relevance of their resources. On this last point, Edmund Davies L.J. applied in particular the test of occupiers' liability to be found in Lord Reid's speech in the *Herrington* case, in which the knowledge, skill and resources of the particular occupier were relevant considerations. Lawton L.J. also took into account the defendants' resources, but it is unclear whether he would have done so if they had not been occupiers. See further *Melvin v. Franklins (Builders), Ltd.* (1973), 71 L.G.R. 142; *Southern Portland Cement, Ltd. v. Cooper*, [1974] 1 All E.R. 87.

3. The law was clearly confused before the House of Lords' decision in *British Railways Board v. Herrington*: it is equally clear that there was still some confusion after that decision, and thus this area of the law was obviously ripe for consideration by the Law Commission. In their Working Paper (No. 52) (*Liability for Damage or Injury to Trespassers and Related Questions of Occupiers' Liability*) the Law Commission provisionally propose (at para. 66) that "new and uniform provisions should be made in relation to all categories of 'non-visitors'" (which include, amongst others, trespassers) and these provisions "may take one or other of two forms:

(a) If it is desired to impose on the occupier an obligation to show reasonable care towards any entrant . . . on his land, leaving the fact that the entrant was, for example, a trespasser to be taken into account in deciding whether the care shown was reasonable in the circumstances, the Occupiers' Liability Act 1957 may be amended to bring all entrants within the common duty of care at present owed only to 'visitors' within the meaning of that Act.

(b) If, on the other hand, it is desired to retain the question of whether there is a duty of care towards a trespasser as a matter of law for the courts, this may be achieved by adding three provisions to the Occupiers' Liability Act 1957 to the effect that—

(i) the mere relationship of occupier and trespasser does not of itself give rise to a duty of care; but

(ii) an occupier owes a duty of care to any trespasser whom, in the light of all the circumstances, he ought as a reasonable man to have in contemplation as likely to be affected by his acts or omissions; and

(iii) the determination of whether there is in the particular case a duty of care owed to a trespasser is a matter of law to be decided by the court.

Of these alternatives, provisionally we prefer the first."

It was further proposed that "in regard to exemption clauses relating to occupiers' liability to all entrants, whether trespassers or not—

(a) There should be no absolute ban on exempting conditions in relation to occupiers' liability to entrants in all circumstances; but

(b) In relation to death or personal injury, there should be an absolute ban on exempting conditions contained in notices and in tickets, passes, programmes and similar documents of admission.

(c) In all other cases, a reasonableness test should be applied to terms purporting to exclude or restrict, or having the effect of excluding or restricting, the occupier's duty of care or any liability for breach thereof.

(d) If the proposal in (b) lacks support or otherwise proves to be unacceptable, a reasonableness test as outlined in (c) should apply to *all* terms purporting to exclude liability."

A final proposal was to abolish the assumption of risk defence in this area.

2. NON-OCCUPIERS' LIABILITY FOR PREMISES

A. C. Billings & Sons, Ltd. *v.* Riden

House of Lords   [1957] 3 All E.R. 1

Mr. and Mrs. Privett lived on the top floor of a house (No. 25) to which access had been provided by a ramp. However, part of the ramp had been removed by the appellant contractors and a foundation of rough stones had been laid for a new path. The only practicable way to get to the front door of No. 25 was through the forecourt of the next house (No. 26), over some muddy ground, and up on to the ramp. There were shrubs along most of the boundary between the houses, and the route had been made possible by the appellants' removal of some railings from alongside the ramp. This route involved passing close to the unfenced sunken basement area of No. 26. Mrs. Privett gave evidence that in fact the workmen advised her that the best way in was on the No. 26 side. A plank was later placed on the muddy ground by Mr. Brown, Mrs. Privett's brother. The respondent, who had been invited into No. 25 by Mrs. Privett had used this route on her advice, but an accident happened when the respondent left at 10 p.m. She had declined an offer from Mrs. Privett's son to go with her and she did not have a torch, but paused for a moment on coming out of the house so that her eyes would get accustomed to the dark. Unfortunately, having stepped down from the ramp to the plank, she fell into the sunken area and was injured. The appellants were held liable by the Court of Appeal, [1956] 3 All E.R. 357, reversing Hallett J., but reducing her damages by 50% for contributory negligence. On appeal to the House of Lords:

LORD REID: . . . In my opinion, the appellants were under a duty to all persons who might be expected lawfully to visit the house, and that duty was the ordinary duty to take such care as in all the circumstances of the case was reasonable to ensure that visitors were not exposed to danger by their actions. It was argued that, even so, that duty was adequately discharged in all cases by giving warning of the danger and that, if a visitor in full knowledge of the danger chose to incur it, she did so at her own risk and the contractor cannot be held liable. I do not agree. There may be many cases in which warning is an adequate discharge of the duty. There may be another safe and reasonably convenient access only a short distance away, or the situation may be such that with knowledge of the danger the visitor can easily and safely avoid it. But there are other cases where that is not so. Let me take the example of a doctor called to an urgent case in a house the only access to which has unnecessarily been made dangerous by a contractor. It cannot be right that he should be entitled to say to the doctor: "Now I have shown you the danger and if you choose to go on you do so at your own risk".

I do not think that there is anything new in what I have just said. The principle was at least adumbrated a century ago in *Clayards* v. *Dethick & Davis* ((1848), 12 Q.B. 439). . . .

[His Lordship discussed that case and one other authority and continued:] The conclusion to be drawn from these cases appears to me to be that there is no magic in giving a warning. If the plaintiff knew the danger, either because he was warned or from his own knowledge and observation, the question is whether the danger was such that, in the circumstances, no sensible man would have incurred it or, in other words, whether the plaintiff's exposing himself to the danger was a want of common or ordinary prudence on his part. If it was not, then the fact that he voluntarily or knowingly incurred the danger does not entitle the defendant to escape from liability.

The only cases brought to our notice which are inconsistent with what I have said are *Malone* v. *Laskey* ([1907] 2 K.B. 141) and *Ball* v. *London County Council* ([1949] 1 All E.R. 1056). In *Malone's* case, a contractor had put up a water tank insecurely and it fell on the caretaker's wife and injured her. *Heaven* v. *Pender* ((1883), 11 Q.B.D. 503) was cited, but not *Clayards* v. *Dethick*. The case, so far as relating to negligence, was decided against the plaintiff on the simple but, in my view, erroneous ground that, as the contractor was not the occupier and there was no contractual relationship between him and the plaintiff, he owed no duty of care to her. In *Ball's* case, *Malone's* case was followed as being binding on the Court of Appeal, and it is to be noted that there were other grounds which might also have been fatal to the plaintiff's case. . . . In my judgment, *Malone's* case ought to be overruled in so far as it dealt with negligence. . . .

[Having found that "it was not unreasonable for her [the respondent] to accept Mrs. Privett's invitation and follow her directions", he continued:] The next question is whether, if she acted reasonably in going in, the fuller knowledge of the route which she gained on the inward journey made it unreasonable for her to try to go out the same way. Now there was some urgency about making the return journey for otherwise she would not get home. Here it is relevant to consider the attitude of the other people in the house when she left, Mrs. Privett, her son, and Mr. and Mrs. Brown. They all knew the route. Mrs. Privett's son offered to accompany the respondent but she said she could manage. It did not occur to any of them that she should not go, or that she should not go alone. I find it very difficult to assume that they were all unreasonable people in letting her go alone, and I think that only a minute proportion of ordinary people, put in the respondent's shoes and faced with the choice of staying the night or taking the route she did, would have chosen to stay the night; but I think that most people would have been more careful than she was. She would certainly have been wiser to take the son's offer, and I agree with the finding that there was contributory negligence on her part in not taking enough care when she left the house, but I cannot find that, in seeking to return by this route, she acted unreasonably or so negligently as to lead to the conclusion that her accident was caused entirely by her own fault.

It is sometimes said that, when a visitor goes on knowing the risk, the test is whether he was free to choose or acted under some constraint. My difficulty about that test is that freedom is a word which has come to have very different meanings to different people. If this test leads to the same answer as the question whether, in all the circumstances, the visitor acted reasonably, well and good; but if not, I think that, in cases like the present, reasonableness is the better test and is more in accordance with principle. The defendant is bound to take reasonable care, but he is entitled to expect that a visitor will behave in a reasonable manner. I leave aside cases where children are concerned.

In my view, the accident was caused partly by the danger of the route and partly by the respondent's own negligence. But the appellants argue that they cannot be held responsible for the danger of the route because they had no right to remove that danger or even to enter the grounds of No. 26 where the danger lay. It is true that they could not remove that danger; their fault lay in making it necessary for visitors to use that route. Their duty was to take reasonable care for the safety of visitors. They interfered with the existing safe access as they had a right to do. But, in my opinion, their duty to visitors required them to mitigate the result of their interference in so far as in all the circumstances it was reasonable that they should do so, and I think that their own defence in this case shows that it would have been reasonable when they left off work to lay down a plank walk over the rough rubble path. But, even if I am wrong in that, I think that they were still at fault. I leave aside the point that they made this route possible by removing the railing at the top of the ramp, because that point was not dealt with at the trial and some explanation might have emerged if it had been; but they should have given warning against use of this route instead of advising its use, and, if they had done so, it is by no means improbable that matters would have developed in such a way that the respondent would never have taken this route. I am, therefore, of opinion that, in so far as the danger of the route contributed to cause the accident, the appellants are liable to the respondent. I see no reason to disagree with the decision of the majority of the Court of Appeal that the appellants and the respondent were equally to blame, and I am, therefore, of opinion that this appeal should be dismissed with costs to the respondent.

LORD KEITH OF AVONHOLM: . . . No case was cited, and I know of none, where a contractor has been held liable for a danger not of his own creation and existing on adjacent property with which he had nothing to do and with which he had no right to interfere. I could go no further than to say that if, in circumstances like the present, a contractor does not provide a reasonably safe approach to the house, he may be liable to a person seeking to enter or leave the house who takes the risk of passing over or on the danger left by the contractor and sustains injury thereby. No case was cited, and I know of none, that would carry the contractor's liability further than this and, in my opinion, the ratio of none of the cases cited can be stretched to cover a peril on adjacent land for which the contractor was in no way responsible.

I think, however, that it is possible to hold that, as a result of operations conducted by the appellants here, the respondent was precipitated from the property of No. 25 into the danger on the adjacent property of No. 26 owing to the dangerous condition of the access to the door of No. 25 created by the appellants, and it is not, I think, a relevant factor that the respondent was intending to trespass on adjacent property. What is material is that the evidence shows that persons were using this route or approach to No. 25, that the appellants' men knew that Mrs. Privett, the caretaker's wife, was using this route and should have contemplated that other persons might use the same route. The appellants had removed the railings alongside the ramp and so made this route possible and they had provided no safe alternative route. I think, therefore, they were liable for the accident that happened.

I would dismiss the appeal.

[VISCOUNT SIMONDS concurred with LORD REID. LORD COHEN and LORD SOMERVELL OF HARROW delivered speeches in favour of dismissing the appeal.]

Appeal dismissed

Question

Would the position of a contractor/non-occupier in a case such as this be any different if he could establish that he was an occupier?

Note

Vendors or lessors of defective premises—it might well be thought that the vendor or lessor of defective premises would be liable to someone injured as a result of his negligence, if not before *M'Alister (or Donoghue) v. Stevenson*, [1932] A.C. 562, then certainly after that decision. However, for a long time the authorities indicated that a vendor or lessor was not liable in negligence for his acts (or failure to act) prior to the sale or letting where persons on the premises were injured after such sale or letting as a result of the premises' defective state. It was thought that this was an area of law which was unaffected by *Donoghue v. Stevenson*. It should be noted that the landlord's immunity was cut down by s. 4 of the Occupiers' Liability Act 1957 (now repealed by the Defective Premises Act 1972, but replaced in wider terms by s. 4 of that Act). It should also be mentioned that in *Dutton v. Bognor Regis U.D.C.*, [1972] 1 Q.B. 373; [1972] 1 All E.R. 462, the facts of which have been given, p. 86, *ante*, Lord Denning M.R. and Sachs L.J. attacked this common law immunity, at least so far as hidden defects were concerned (*per* Sachs L.J.). For fuller discussion of this topic, see Salmond, pp. 295–301.

Before these developments in the Court of Appeal, the Law Commission had given its attention to this area of the law in 1970 (*Civil Liability of Vendors and Lessors of Defective Premises*, Law Com. No. 40) and two years later the Defective Premises Act 1972 was passed. It is because of s. 3 of that Act—see p. 260, *post*, that the common law position was not discussed more fully above. Section 3 will clarify the position, but it does not apparently impose liability for omissions. The crucial words are "where work of construction, repair, maintenance or demolition or any other work is done on or in relation to premises . . ." What if a vendor has merely omitted to repair the floorboards? In this situation the common law position (confused as it is) would still appear to be relevant. (In the case of omissions by landlords the wide terms of s. 4 of the 1972 Act should be noted.)

The Defective Premises Act 1972

1. **Duty to build dwellings properly.**—(1) A person taking on work for or in connection with the provision of a dwelling (whether the dwelling is provided by the erection or by the conversion or enlargement of a building) owes a duty—

   (*a*) if the dwelling is provided to the order of any person, to that person; and
   (*b*) without prejudice to paragraph (*a*) above, to every person who acquires an interest (whether legal or equitable) in the dwelling;

to see that the work which he takes on is done in a workmanlike or, as the case may be, professional manner, with proper materials and so that as regards that work the dwelling will be fit for habitation when completed.

(2) A person who takes on any such work for another on terms that he is to do it in accordance with instructions given by or on behalf of that other shall, to the extent to which he does it properly in accordance with those instructions, be treated for the purposes of this section as discharging the duty imposed on him by subsection (1) above except where he owes a duty to that other to warn him of any defects in the instructions and fails to discharge that duty.

(3) A person shall not be treated for the purposes of subsection (2) above as having given instructions for the doing of work merely because he has agreed to the work being done in a specified manner, with specified materials or to a specified design.

(4) A person who—

   (*a*) in the course of a business which consists of or includes providing or arranging for the provision of dwellings or installations in dwellings; or
   (*b*) in the exercise of a power of making such provision or arrangements conferred by or by virtue of any enactment;

arranges for another to take on work for or in connection with the provision of a dwelling shall be treated for the purposes of this section as included among the persons who have taken on the work.

(5) Any cause of action in respect of a breach of the duty imposed by this section shall be deemed, for the purposes of the Limitation Act 1939, the Law Reform (Limitation of Actions, &c.) Act 1954 and the Limitation Act 1963, to have accrued at the time when the dwelling was completed, but if after that time a person who has done work for or in connection with the provision of the dwelling does further work to rectify the work he has already done, any such cause of action in respect of that further work shall

be deemed for those purposes to have accrued at the time when the further work was finished.

2. Cases excluded from the remedy under section 1.—(1) Where—

(a) in connection with the provision of a dwelling or its first sale or letting for habitation any rights in respect of defects in the state of the dwelling are conferred by an approved scheme to which this section applies on a person having or acquiring an interest in the dwelling; and

(b) it is stated in a document of a type approved for the purposes of this section that the requirements as to design or construction imposed by or under the scheme have, or appear to have, been substantially complied with in relation to the dwelling;

no action shall be brought by any person having or acquiring an interest in the dwelling for breach of the duty imposed by section 1 above in relation to the dwelling.

(2) A scheme to which this section applies—

(a) may consist of any number of documents and any number of agreements or other transactions between any number of persons; but

(b) must confer, by virtue of agreements entered into with persons having or acquiring an interest in the dwellings to which the scheme applies, rights on such persons in respect of defects in the state of the dwellings. . . .

(7) Where an interest in a dwelling is compulsorily acquired—

(a) no action shall be brought by the acquiring authority for breach of the duty imposed by section 1 above in respect of the dwelling; and

(b) if any work for or in connection with the provision of the dwelling was done otherwise than in the course of a business by the person in occupation of the dwelling at the time of the compulsory acquisition, the acquiring authority and not that person shall be treated as the person who took on the work and accordingly as owing that duty.

3. Duty of care with respect to work done on premises not abated by disposal of premises.—(1) Where work of construction, repair, maintenance or demolition or any other work is done on or in relation to premises, any duty of care owed, because of the doing of the work, to persons who might reasonably be expected to be affected by defects in the state of the premises created by the doing of the work shall not be abated by the subsequent disposal of the premises by the person who owed the duty.

(2) This section does not apply—

(a) in the case of premises which are let, where the relevant tenancy of the premises commenced, or the relevant tenancy agreement of the premises was entered into, before the commencement of this Act [1 January, 1974];

(b) in the case of premises disposed of in any other way, when the disposal of the premises was completed, or a contract for their disposal was entered into, before the commencement of this Act; or

(c) in either case, where the relevant transaction disposing of the premises is entered into in pursuance of an enforceable option by which the consideration for the disposal was fixed before the commencement of this Act.

4. Landlord's duty of care in virtue of obligation or right to repair premises demised.—(1) Where premises are let under a tenancy which puts on the landlord an obligation to the tenant for the maintenance or repair of the premises, the landlord owes to all persons who might reasonably be expected to be affected by defects in the state of the premises a duty to take such care as is reasonable in all the circumstances to see that they are reasonably safe from personal injury or from damage to their property caused by a relevant defect.

(2) The said duty is owed if the landlord knows (whether as the result of being notified by the tenant or otherwise) or if he ought in all the circumstances to have known of the relevant defect.

(3) In this section "relevant defect" means a defect in the state of the premises existing at or after the material time and arising from, or continuing because of, an act or omission by the landlord which constitutes or would if he had had notice of the defect, have constituted a failure by him to carry out his obligation to the tenant for the maintenance or repair of the premises; and for the purposes of the foregoing provision "the material time" means—

(*a*) where the tenancy commenced before this Act, the commencement of this Act; and

(*b*) in all other cases, the earliest of the following times, that is to say—

(i) the time when the tenancy commences;

(ii) the time when the tenancy agreement is entered into;

(iii) the time when possession is taken of the premises in contemplation of the letting.

(4) Where premises are let under a tenancy which expressly or impliedly gives the landlord the right to enter the premises to carry out any description of maintenance or repair of the premises, then, as from the time when he first is, or by notice or otherwise can put himself, in a position to exercise the right and so long as he is or can put himself in that position, he shall be treated for the purposes of subsections (1) to (3) above (but for no other purpose) as if he were under an obligation to the tenant for that description of maintenance or repair of the premises; but the landlord shall not owe the tenant any duty by virtue of this subsection in respect of any defect in the state of the premises arising from, or continuing because of, a failure to carry out an obligation expressly imposed on the tenant by the tenancy.

(5) For the purposes of this section obligations imposed or rights given by any enactment in virtue of a tenancy shall be treated as imposed or given by the tenancy.

(6) This section applies to a right of occupation given by contract or any enactment and not amounting to a tenancy as if the right were a tenancy, and "tenancy" and cognate expressions shall be construed accordingly.

5. Application to Crown.—This Act shall bind the Crown, but as regards the Crown's liability in tort shall not bind the Crown further than the Crown is made liable in tort by the Crown Proceedings Act 1947.

6. Supplemental.—(1) In this Act—

"disposal", in relation to premises, includes a letting, and an assignment or surrender of a tenancy, of the premises and the creation by contract of any other right to occupy the premises, and "dispose" shall be construed accordingly;

"personal injury" includes any disease and any impairment of a person's physical or mental condition;

"tenancy" means—

(*a*) a tenancy created either immediately or derivatively out of the freehold, whether by a lease or underlease, by an agreement for a lease or underlease or by a tenancy agreement, but not including a mortgage term or any interest arising in favour of a mortgagor by his attorning tenant to his mortgagee; or

(*b*) a tenancy at will or a tenancy on sufferance; or

(*c*) a tenancy, whether or not constituting a tenancy at common law, created by or in pursuance of any enactment;

and cognate expressions shall be construed accordingly.

(2) Any duty imposed by or enforceable by virtue of any provision of this Act is in addition to any duty a person may owe apart from that provision.

(3) Any term of an agreement which purports to exclude or restrict, or has the effect of excluding or restricting, the operation of any of the provisions of this Act, or any liability arising by virtue of any such provision, shall be void.

(4) Section 4 of the Occupiers' Liability Act 1957 (repairing landlords' duty to visitors to premises) is hereby repealed.

Questions

1. How does s. 1 alter the common law position? Could it cover economic loss? What is the level of the duty which is imposed?

2. Would any of the sections of the Act be of assistance to a trespasser? (See P. M. North, (1973), 36 M.L.R. 628, at p. 636.)

Notes

1. Section 4 of this Act replaces in wider terms s. 4 of the Occupiers' Liability Act 1957.

2. Under s. 2 of the Act, it is for the Secretary of State to approve schemes which he is to do by order exercisable by statutory instrument. Approval has now been given to the scheme operated by the National House-Building Council—see The House-Building Standards (Approved Scheme etc.) Order 1973, S.I. 1973 No. 1843.

3. EMPLOYER'S LIABILITY TO EMPLOYEES

An employee who is injured at work may seek to hold his employer responsible on two possible grounds: (a) the personal breach of a common law or statutory duty by the employer; or (b) the breach of a duty owed by a fellow-employee of the plaintiff, the employer being vicariously liable for the torts of his employees. The second situation is the most usual one in practice, but before the passing of the Law Reform (Personal Injuries) Act 1948, s. 1 (p. 264, *post*) such an action was barred by the doctrine of common employment judicially invented in *Priestley* v. *Fowler* (1837), 3 M. & W. 1 (p. 263, *post*). Although the scope of this defence was partially limited by the Employers' Liability Act 1880, and excluded in the case of breach of *statutory* duties (p. 271, *post*), it caused much injustice. In order to circumvent the doctrine, the courts came to give an extended and artificial meaning to the concept of the *personal* duty owed by an employer. The high point was reached in *Wilsons and Clyde Coal Co., Ltd.* v. *English*, [1938] A.C. 57; [1937] 3 All E.R. 628 (p. 264, *post*). Despite the abolition of the doctrine of common employment in 1948, the concept of personal non-delegable duties persists in this field. In this section the general nature of this relatively high duty may be examined. One of its principal implications is in regard to the employer's responsibility for faults of an independent contractor which cause injury to an employee. That aspect is considered in Chap. 18, p. 639, *post*.

Priestley v. Fowler

Court of Exchequer   [1835–42] All E.R. Rep. 449

The plaintiff was employed by a butcher. He was injured in the course of his employment when the van in which he was being carried was carelessly overloaded by a fellow-servant. A verdict for £100 in his favour was entered. The Court of Exchequer arrested the judgment.

LORD ABINGER C.B. (delivering the judgment of the Court): . . . If the master be liable to the servant in this action, the principle of that liability will be found to carry us to an alarming extent. He who is responsible by his general duty, or by the terms of his contract, for all the consequences of negligence in a matter in which he is the principal, is responsible for the negligence of all his inferior agents. If the owner of the carriage is, therefore, responsible for the sufficiency of his carriage to his servant, he is responsible for the negligence of his coach-builder or his harness-maker or his coachman. The footman, therefore, who rides behind the carriage, may have an action against his master for a defect in the carriage owing to the negligence of the coach-maker or for a defect in the harness arising from the negligence of the harness-maker or for drunkenness, neglect, or want of skill in the coachman; nor is there any reason why the principle should not, if applicable in this class of cases, extend to many others. The master, for example, would be liable to the servant for the negligence of the chambermaid, for putting him into a damp bed; for that of the upholsterer, for sending in a crazy bedstead, whereby he was made to fall down while asleep and injure himself; for the negligence of the cook, in not properly cleaning the copper vessels used in the kitchen; of the butcher, in supplying the family with meat of a quality injurious to the health; of the builder, for a defect in the foundation of the house, whereby it fell and injured both the master and the servant by the ruins.

The inconvenience, not to say the absurdity of these consequences, affords a sufficient argument against the application of this principle to the present case. But, in truth, the mere relation of the master and the servant never can imply an obligation on the part of the master to take more care of the servant than he may reasonably be expected to do of himself. He is, no doubt, bound to provide for the safety of his servant in the course of his employment, to the best of his judgment, information, and belief. The servant is not bound to risk his safety in the service of his master, and may, if he thinks fit, decline any service in which he reasonably apprehends injury to himself: and in most of the cases in which danger may be incurred, if not in all, he is just as likely to be acquainted with the probability and extent of it as the master. In that sort of employment, especially, which is described in the declaration in this case, the plaintiff must have known as well as his master, and probably better, whether the van was sufficient, whether it was overloaded, and whether it was likely to carry him safely. In fact, to allow this sort of action to prevail would be an encouragement to the servant to omit that diligence and caution which he is in duty bound to exercise on the behalf of his master, to protect him against the misconduct or negligence of others who serve him, and which diligence and caution, while they protect the master, are a much better security against any injury the servant may sustain by the negligence of others engaged under the same master, than any recourse against his master for damages could possibly afford.

We are, therefore, of opinion that the judgment ought to be arrested.

Note

The unfortunate Priestley spent some years in the debtors' prison because he could not pay the costs of his unsuccessful action. Munkman, *Employers' Liability at Common Law*, 7th Edn. (London, 1971), p. 6, comments that Lord Abinger, who owned Inverlochy Castle near Ben Nevis, may have been thinking of "his own extensive pre-Victorian household, and the liabilities to which he himself might be subjected", when he delivered this judgment. The philosophy it expresses is the same as that in the then popular "iron law of wages". From the point of view of accident prevention, the decision led to the dilemma which Byles J. saw in *Clarke* v. *Holmes* (1862), 7 H. & N. 937, at p. 949: "If a master's personal knowledge of defects in his machinery be necessary to his liability, the more a master neglects his business and abandons it to others the less will he be liable." An interesting, but little used scheme to aid factory employees was the machinery of penal compensation originating in the Factories Act 1844 and of importance until 1880: see R. L. Howells, "*Priestley* v. *Fowler* and the Factory Acts" (1963), 26 M.L.R. 367.

The Law Reform (Personal Injuries) Act 1948

1. **Common employment.**—(1) It shall not be a defence to an employer who is sued in respect of personal injuries caused by the negligence of a person employed by him, that that person was at the time the injuries were caused in common employment with the person injured.

(2) Accordingly the Employers' Liability Act, 1880, shall cease to have effect, and is hereby repealed.

(3) Any provision contained in a contract of service or apprenticeship, or in an agreement collateral thereto (including a contract or agreement entered into before the commencement of this Act), shall be void in so far as it would have the effect of excluding or limiting any liability of the employer in respect of personal injuries caused to the person employed or apprenticed by the negligence of persons in common employment with him.

Wilsons and Clyde Coal Co., Ltd. v. English

House of Lords   [1937] 3 All E.R. 628

The pursuer claimed damages in respect of personal injuries sustained while employed at the defendant company's Glencraig Colliery, Fife. At the end of a day-shift, as he was proceeding to the pit-bottom, he was crushed when the haulage plant was set in motion. His case was that it was a necessary part of a safe system of working, and recognised mining practice, that during the time when day-shift men were being raised to the surface the haulage plant should be stopped. The defendants claimed that they had effectively discharged their duty of providing a safe system of work by appointing a qualified manager, and they relied upon s. 2 (4) of the Coal Mines Act 1911 which provided that only a qualified manager could control the technical management of the mine. In an appeal against an interlocutor pronounced by a court of seven judges of the Court of Session the House of Lords unanimously rejected this defence, and dismissed the appeal.

LORD WRIGHT: . . . I do not mean that employers warrant the adequacy of plant, or the competence of fellow-employees, or the propriety of the system of work. The obligation is fulfilled by the exercise of due care and skill. But it is not fulfilled by entrusting its fulfilment to employees, even though selected with due care and skill. The obligation is threefold, "the provision of a competent staff of men, adequate material, and a proper system and effective supervision" . . .

The well established, but illogical, doctrine of common employment is certainly one not to be extended, and indeed has never in its long career been pushed so far as the Court of Appeal[1] sought to push it. . . .

I think the whole course of authority consistently recognises a duty which rests on the employer, and which is personal to the employer, to take reasonable care for the safety of his workmen, whether the employer be an individual, a firm, or a company, and whether or not the employer takes any share in the conduct of the operations. The

---

1. [*Inter alia* in *Fanton* v. *Denville*, [1932] 2 K.B. 309.]

obligation is threefold, as I have explained. The obligation to provide and maintain proper plant and appliances is a continuing obligation. It is not, however, broken by a mere misuse of, or failure to use, proper plant and appliances, due to the negligence of a fellow-servant, or a merely temporary failure to keep in order or adjust plant and appliances, or a casual departure from the system of working, if these matters can be regarded as the casual negligence of the managers, foremen, or other employees. It may be difficult, in some cases, to distinguish, on the facts, between the employer's failure to provide and maintain and the fellow-servants' negligence in the respects indicated. . . .

[LORD THANKERTON, LORD MACMILLAN and LORD MAUGHAM delivered speeches in favour of dismissing the appeal. LORD ATKIN agreed with all the speeches.]

Question

In view of the fact that the defendant company was required by statute to delegate the duty to provide a safe system of work, why did the House of Lords describe it as a duty "personal" to the company?

Notes

1. For examples of the employer's threefold duty see Munkman, *Employer's Liability at Common Law* (7th Edn.), Chap. 4. It should be noted that the duty to provide proper plant, equipment and premises, overlaps with the occupier's duty to visitors, and is stringently interpreted: see e.g. *General Cleaning Contractors, Ltd.* v. *Christmas,* [1953] A.C. 180; [1952] 2 All E.R. 1100 (safe system includes an adequate system of instruction and supply of necessary protective equipment); *Wilson* v. *Tyneside Window Cleaning Co.,* [1958] 2 Q.B. 110; [1958] 2 All E.R. 265 (duty extends to premises not in employer's occupation, but less will be required of an employer when the employee is on someone else's premises).

2. For the employee's action for breach of statutory duty see p. 289, *post,* and for the defence of *volenti non fit injuria,* p. 316, *post.* The relevance of the "non-delegable duty" to liability for independent contractors is dealt with, p. 639, *post.*

3. It is compulsory for employers to insure against their liability to employees: Employers' Liability (Compulsory Insurance) Act 1969, p. 676, *post.* Reference should also be made to the Employer's Liability (Defective Equipment) Act 1969, p. 639, *post.*

4. For the relevance of "common practice", see p. 160, *ante.*

8

Statutory Torts

We have so far considered two effects of statutes in relation to legal duties: (a) the removal of anomalies (e.g. the Occupiers' Liability Act 1957, Defective Premises Act 1972, Chap. 7, *ante*, and see too the Animals Act 1971, Employer's Liability (Defective Equipment) Act 1969, Chaps. 10 and 18, *post*); and (b) the negligent exercise of statutory powers as giving rise to liability in certain circumstances in the tort of negligence (*Dorset Yacht Co., Ltd.* v. *Home Office*, [1970] A.C. 1004; [1970] 2 All E.R. 294, Chap. 3, *ante*).

The cases in this Chapter are concerned with a third question. When does a *duty* laid down by statute give rise to civil liability? For this purpose statutes may be classified in three broad categories:

(i) those which *create torts by express words*, either in substitution for common law liability for negligence or other torts (e.g. Nuclear Installations Act 1965, p. 267, *post*) or alongside existing torts (e.g. Mineral Workings (Offshore Installations) Act 1971, p. 269, *post*);

(ii) those which *expressly exclude* civil liability for breach of their provisions (e.g. Medicines Act 1968, *post*);

(iii) those which provide a criminal sanction or some other remedy, but are *silent* on the question of civil liability.

The first two categories give rise to no particular difficulties of statutory interpretation, although compensation for statutory wrongs may sometimes be dealt with by a different tribunal from that which determines liability for common law torts (e.g. "unfair industrial practices" are within the exclusive jurisdiction of the National Industrial Relations Court and, in some cases, the industrial tribunals, but that Court "shall not entertain any proceedings in tort": Industrial Relations Act 1971, s. 136 (*a*), and see Chap. 14).

In dealing with the third category the courts usually pay lip-service to the theory of whether Parliament intended to create civil liability when it laid down the duty. This is a pure fiction because it is only very recently that Parliament has tended to give any thought to this question at all. Even modern statutes, like the Prevention of Oil Pollution Act 1971 (which makes the discharge of oil into navigable waters a criminal offence) are far from explicit. The Law Commission (see Draft Clauses, p. 283, *post*) proposed, in 1969, that there should be a general statute creating a presumption that the breach of a statutory duty is intended to be actionable at the suit of any person who suffers or apprehends damage, unless a contrary intention is expressly stated. But this would apply only to Acts passed after the statutory presumption is enacted and not to the vast body of existing statute law nor to future delegated legislation made under existing statutory powers. So the problems of interpretation will be with us indefinitely.

In reading the cases, the student will discern various principles according to which the courts have purported to determine the presumed intention of Parliament: for example, whether the Act was passed for the benefit of a defined class of persons or a designated individual (liability) or for the public at large (no liability); whether the kind of harm which the plaintiff suffered was the "mischief" which the Act was designed to prevent; and whether the remedy provided by the statute is adequate. None of these is particularly helpful and the results are often contradictory: compare *Groves* v. *Lord Wimborne* (p. 271, *post*) with *Phillips* v. *Britannia Hygienic Laundry Co.* (p. 277, *post*), *Solomons* v. *Gertzenstein* (p. 280, *post*) and *Cutler* v. *Wandsworth Stadium, Ltd.* (p. 279, *post*). In attempting to reconcile these decisions one important historical fact should be kept in mind. In 1837 the courts invented the doctrine of common employment which debarred an employee injured by the negligence of a fellow-employee from recovering damages from their common employer (*Priestly* v. *Fowler* (1837), 3 M. & W. 1). By the end of the century a number of judges realised that this doctrine (although modified by the Employers' Liability Act 1880) was causing much hardship to injured workers; the stream of new factory and mines legislation was being inadequately enforced; and the first Workmen's Compensation Act, passed in 1897, did not provide for full compensation since it was based on the principle of an equal division of the risk of industrial accidents between employer and employee. *Groves* v. *Lord Wimborne* was a response to this situation and enabled the courts to evade the doctrine of common employment. In other fields, such as road accidents, the social reasons for judicial invention have been less compelling. The few exceptions to the general rule that non-industrial statutes do not give rise to civil liability, in the absence of an express provision, may be regarded as anomalies. *Monk* v. *Warbey* (considered in Chap. 20, p. 674, *post*) was based on the premise that victims of road accidents should not only be entitled to compensation but should actually get it; in the light of the Road Traffic Act 1972 (p. 670, *post*) this case is now of little practical importance. Cases such as *Dawson* v. *Bingley U.D.C.* (p. 274, *post*) and *Read* v. *Croydon Corpn.* (p. 275, *post*) are ones in which, quite apart from the statute, a duty situation could be said to exist: compare *Atkinson* v. *Newcastle Waterworks Co.* (p. 273, *post*) where, at common law, no duty of positive action could have been said to arise.

1. EXPRESS CREATION OF NEW TORTS

The Nuclear Installations Act 1965

7. Duty of licensee of licensed site.—(1) Where a nuclear site licence has been granted in respect of any site, it shall be the duty of the licensee to secure that—

    (*a*) no such occurrence involving nuclear matter as is mentioned in subsection (2) of this section causes injury to any person or damage to any property of any person other than the licensee, being injury or damage arising out of or resulting from the radioactive properties, or a combination of those and any toxic, explosive or other hazardous properties, of that nuclear matter; and

(*b*) no ionising radiations emitted during the period of the licensee's responsibility—

(i) from anything caused or suffered by the licensee to be on the site which is not nuclear matter; or

(ii) from any waste discharged (in whatever form) on or from the site,

cause injury to any person or damage to any property of any person other than the licensee.

(2) The occurrences referred to in subsection (1) (*a*) of this section are—

(*a*) any occurrence on the licensed site during the period of the licensee's responsibility, being an occurrence involving nuclear matter;

(*b*) any occurrence elsewhere than on the licensed site involving nuclear matter which is not excepted matter and which at the time of the occurrence—

(i) is in the course of carriage on behalf of the licensee as licensee of that site; or

(ii) is in the course of carriage to that site with the agreement of the licensee from a place outside the relevant territories; and

(iii) in either case, is not on any other relevant site in the United Kingdom;

(*c*) any occurrence elsewhere than on the licensed site involving nuclear matter which is not excepted matter and which—

(i) having been on the licensed site at any time during the period of the licensee's responsibility; or

(ii) having been in the course of carriage on behalf of the licensee as licensee of that site,

has not subsequently been on any relevant site, or in the course of any relevant carriage, or (except in the course of relevant carriage) within the territorial limits of a country which is not a relevant territory.

13. Exclusion, extension or reduction of compensation in certain cases.—

(4) The duty imposed by section 7, 8, 9, 10 or 11 of this Act—

(*a*) shall not impose any liability on the person subject to that duty with respect to injury or damage caused by an occurrence which constitutes a breach of that duty if the occurrence, or the causing thereby of the injury or damage, is attributable to hostile action in the course of any armed conflict, including any armed conflict within the United Kingdom; but

(*b*) shall impose such a liability where the occurrence, or the causing thereby of the injury or damage, is attributable to a natural disaster, notwithstanding that the disaster is of such an exceptional character that it could not reasonably have been foreseen.

Questions

1. Consider the defences in s. 13 (4) of the Act. How does this compare with the defences available in an action for nuisance, negligence or under the *Rylands* v. *Fletcher* rule? (see pp. 352–399, *post*).

2. Section 13 (6) provides that damages may be reduced by reason of the fault of the plaintiff only if he has intentionally caused harm or had reckless disregard for the consequences of his act. Why is this Act more favourable to trespassers both in regard to duty and contributory fault than the common law?

3. "Injury" is defined as personal injury including loss of life (s. 26 (1)). If the presence of emitted radiation keeps campers away from an adjoining holiday camp, does the camp owner have any action under s. 7? Would he be better off at common law? (Common law duties are replaced only insofar as the injury or damage was caused in breach of a duty imposed by the Act: s. 12 (1).)

Notes

1. This statute in effect replaces common law liability (e.g. in respect of nuisance, negligence, and the rule in *Rylands* v. *Fletcher*) arising from the escape of ionising radiations with a new statutory liability. This liability is concentrated on the licensee (a licence for the operation of a nuclear plant on a particular site being required). The new tort was created as part of a carefully worked out scheme between the Government and the insurance companies: see Street & Frame, *The Law Relating to Nuclear Energy* (London, 1965).

2. Another example is the Mineral Workings (Offshore Installations) Act 1971, s. 11, which provides that breach of any provision of the Act, or of regulations made thereunder, shall be actionable so far as it causes personal injury. This Act, like most other safety legislation in England, was passed in response to a particular tragedy, in this case the loss of 13 lives when the Drilling Rig *Sea Gem* collapsed, capsized and sank. A committee of inquiry (Cmnd. 3409) found that there had been several important breaches of the Institute of Petroleum's voluntary Code of Safe Practice (although these failures were not the direct cause of the loss of life). Compliance with this Code had been a condition of the grant of a drilling licence to the owners of the rig. The committee said nothing about the creation of civil liability for breach of statutory duty. It should be noted that (1) civil liability under the Act is co-existent with common law duties; and (2) certain defences available in criminal proceedings (i.e. under s. 9 (3) or regulations made under s. 7 (2) (*b*)) are not available in civil proceedings.

3. Examples of other Acts which expressly create a civil remedy are the Misrepresentation Act 1967, s. 2 (1), p. 498, *post*, the Consumer Protection Act 1961, s. 31; the Resale Prices Act 1964, s. 4 (2); the Restrictive Trade Practices Act 1968, s. 7 (2) (cf. the Trade Descriptions Act 1968 which is silent, although Treitel, (1968), 31 M.L.R. at pp. 665–666 argues that a civil remedy has been impliedly created). These statutes all give a remedy to the victim: compare the Race Relations Act 1968, s. 22, which in effect creates a statutory tort in respect of unlawful racial discrimination (without prejudice to common law liabilities) but provides that only the Race Relations Board may institute proceedings and then only after conciliation proceedings have failed or an assurance has been broken; the Board must account to the victim for damages received.

2. EXPRESS EXCLUSION OF CIVIL REMEDY

The Medicines Act, 1968

133. General provisions as to operation of Act.—(2) Except in so far as this Act otherwise expressly provides, and subject to the provisions of section 33 of the Interpretation Act 1889 (which relates to offences under two or more laws), the provisions of this Act shall not be construed as—

(*a*) conferring a right of action in any civil proceedings (other than proceedings for the recovery of a fine) in respect of any contravention of this Act or of any regulations or order made under this Act, or

(*b*) affecting any restrictions imposed by or under any other enactment, whether contained in a public general Act or in a local or private Act, or

(*c*) derogating from any right of action or other remedy (whether civil or criminal) in proceedings instituted otherwise than under this Act.

Note

The Medicines Act creates various offences in relation to the adulteration of medicinal products and requires compliance with certain standards. But Parliament apparently thought that enforcement could best be left to the criminal law. Do you agree?

Examples of other statutes which expressly exclude a civil remedy for breach of statutory duty are: the Representation of the People Act 1949, s. 50 (2); Radioactive Substances Act 1960, s. 19 (5) (*a*); Water Resources Act 1963, s. 135 (8) (*a*); Fair Trading Act 1973, s. 26 (*a*); Counter-Inflation Act 1973, s. 17 (8).

3. CREATION OF NEW TORTS BY JUDICIAL INTERPRETATION OF STATUTES

The Effect of Penal Legislation in the Law of Tort

Glanville Williams, (1960), 23 M.L.R. 233

> I'm the Parliamentary Draftsman,
> I compose the country's laws,
> And of half the litigation
> I'm undoubtedly the cause.
> —J.P.C., *Poetic Justice* (1947).

It is a favourite charge; and yet (if we may breathe it) others than the draftsman are sometimes accountable for the trouble in interpreting statutes. Good rules of interpretation, consistently applied, could do much to reduce the area of doubt. It is the absence of such rules, or the failure to apply existing rules with sufficient regularity to preserve their character as rules, that has brought about the situation in which it is almost impossible to predict when statutory standards of behaviour will be imported into the law of tort.

The present position of penal legislation in the civil law—and it is only of penal legislation that we are speaking, since a study of other legislation would extend the discussion too much—the position of penal legislation may be oversimplified into two generalisations. When it concerns industrial welfare, such legislation results in absolute liability in tort. In all other cases it is ignored. There are exceptions both ways, but, broadly speaking, that is how the law appears from the current decisions. One may make bold to say that both propositions are the result of a wrong approach to the problem of assimilating statutory rules into the civil law.

Groves v. Lord Wimborne

Court of Appeal   [1895–9] All E.R. Rep 147

A. L. SMITH L.J.—This is an action brought against the occupier of the Dowlais ironworks, founded upon a breach of the defendant's statutory duty to fence certain machinery at the works, by reason of which breach of duty the plaintiff, in the course of his employment there, suffered personal injuries. At the trial of the action Grantham J. gave judgment for the defendant upon the ground that no action would lie for the breach of the statutory duty alleged by the plaintiff.

By the Factory and Workshop Act 1878, certain duties as to fencing machinery are cast upon the occupiers of factories. In imposing these duties that Act has followed the principles of many previous Acts relating to factories and workshops. It is a public Act passed to compel the occupiers of factories to take certain precautions on behalf of their workmen. It is not, as the learned judge at the trial thought it was, in the nature of a private legislative bargain between masters and men, but a legislative enactment in compulsion of the masters. Let us now consider what are the duties imposed by this Act upon occupiers of factories with regard to fencing machinery. Section 5 makes certain provisions "with respect to the fencing of machinery in a factory", and by sub-s. (3) as amended by the Factory and Workshop Act, 1891, s. 6 (2):

"All dangerous parts of the machinery and every part of the mill-gearing shall either be securely fenced or be in such position or of such construction as to be equally safe to every person employed in the factory as it would be if it were securely fenced."

By sub-s. (4):

"All fencing shall be constantly maintained in an efficient state while the parts required to be fenced are in motion."

In the present case it is conceded that the machinery which caused the injury to the plaintiff was not fenced as required by the Act. Proof that there had been a breach of the statutory duty to fence imposed on the defendant, and that the plaintiff had been thereby injured would prima facie establish the plaintiff's cause of action.

Assuming that the matter depended on s. 5 alone, and that ss. 81, 82, and 86 had formed no part of the Act, could it be doubted that a person injured as the plaintiff has been could sue for the damage caused to him by the breach of the statutory duty imposed on the defendant? Clearly not. Therefore, unless it can be found from the whole purview of the Act that the legislature intended that the only remedy for a breach of the duty created by the Act should be the infliction of a fine upon the master, it seems clear to me that upon proof of such a breach of duty and of an injury done to the workman, a cause of action is given to the workman against the master.

That brings me to the question whether the cause of action which would prima facie be given by the Act has been taken away by any of the provisions enacted in the statute. Reliance has been placed upon ss. 81, 82 and 86, and it has been argued that, under these sections, the only remedy provided in a case where a workman has been injured by a breach of a duty imposed upon the master by the Act is an application to a court of summary jurisdiction for the infliction of a fine. In considering this question, I ask myself in whose favour was the Act passed? As was pointed out by Kelly C.B. in *Gorris* v. *Scott*[1] the purposes which the legislature had in view in passing the Act are very material. I feel no doubt that the Act was passed for the benefit of workmen in factories, by compelling the masters to do certain things for their protection. I do

---

1. (1874), 9 L.R. Exch. 125.

not think that ss. 81, 82 and 86 can be interpreted so as to take away from an injured workman the remedy which otherwise he would have under the statute against his master. Not one penny of a fine imposed under these sections need ever go into the pocket of the person injured. It is only when a Secretary of State so determines that any part of the fine is to be applied for the benefit of the injured workman. I cannot think that such an enactment was intended to deprive the workman of his right of action. Moreover, upon what grounds are the magistrates to whom application has been made under these sections to estimate the amount of the fine to be imposed? Suppose that a workman has been killed in consequence of a breach of the master's statutory duty to fence his machinery, should the fine be of the same amount whether the breach of duty was a flagrant one or not? It is contended that the magistrates ought to take into consideration the nature of the injury which the workman has suffered, but I do not feel at all clear that that is what the legislature intended by these sections. I am inclined to think that the object of these provisions is the infliction of punishment on the master who has neglected his duty, and that the fine should be in proportion to his offence. The consideration of these points leads me to the conclusion that it was not the intention of the legislature to take away by means of these sections the right which the workman would otherwise have to be properly compensated for any injury caused to him by his master's neglect of duty.

There is also another ground which I should have mentioned which supports me in arriving at that conclusion. It is this. There is no necessity that the fine inflicted under these sections should be payable by the master, who would presumably be a man of some means. Under ss. 86 and 87 the fine may be imposed upon the actual offender, and it is provided that the master may then obtain exemption from the penalty. The actual offender may be a workman earning weekly wages, and yet it is said that the infliction of a fine on him is to be the only remedy that the injured person is to have. I cannot read this statute in the way in which the defendant seeks to read it. In my opinion, s. 5 gives to a workman a right of action upon the statute, when he has been injured through a breach of the duties created by the statute, and his rights of compensation are not limited by the provisions of the Act with regard to a fine that may be imposed by a court of summary jurisdiction. . . .

[His Lordship then held that the defence of common employment, abolished by the Law Reform (Personal Injuries) Act 1948, was not available in an action for a breach of a statutory duty incumbent on the defendant, and concluded: In my opinion the appeal must be allowed, and judgment entered for the £150 damages assessed by the jury.

RIGBY and VAUGHAN WILLIAMS L.JJ. delivered judgments agreeing that the appeal should be allowed.]

Notes

1. It is not every piece of industrial safety legislation that is so interpreted: e.g. *Biddle* v. *Truvox Engineering Co., Ltd.,* [1952] 1 K.B. 101; [1951] 2 All E.R. 835 in which it was held that a person who sells or lets defective factory machinery contrary to the provisions of s. 17 (3) of the Factories Act 1961 is not civilly liable to a workman injured by reason of the defect. The worker's only remedy is at common law.

2. The modern equivalent of s. 6 (2) of the Factory and Workshop Act 1891, which was under consideration in *Groves* v. *Lord Wimborne*, is s. 14 (1) of the Factories Act 1961. There is no provision in the 1961 Act for applying the fine recovered in criminal proceedings for breach of that section to the benefit of the victim.

Atkinson v. Newcastle Waterworks Co.

Court of Appeal   [1874–8] All E.R. Rep. 757

The plaintiff's premises caught fire and owing to the pressure in the defendant's pipes being insufficient the fire could not be extinguished and the premises were burnt down. The plaintiff brought an action for damages against the defendants alleging that they were in breach of the statutory duty imposed on them by s. 42 of the Waterworks Clauses Act 1847. The section provided:

> "The undertakers shall, at all times, keep charged with water under [sufficient] pressure . . . all their pipes to which fire-plugs shall be fixed, unless prevented by frost, unusual drought or other unavoidable cause or accident, or during necessary repairs, and shall allow all persons at all times to take and use such water for extinguishing fire without making compensation for the same."

The defendants demurred to this count. The Court of Exchequer gave judgment for the plaintiff.

On appeal (six years later) to the Court of Appeal:

LORD CAIRNS L.C.: . . . The statutory duty referred to arises under s. 42 of the Waterworks Clauses Act, 1847. The scheme of these clauses seems to be this: The undertakers apply to Parliament for powers to take land and construct works for the supply of water, and in consideration of the powers which they obtain they come under certain obligations. As to fire-plugs they are under an obligation to fix them at intervals along the streets, and, if requested, to fix them near premises used as manufactories, and to keep them charged up to the prescribed pressure, unless prevented by frost, drought, or other unavoidable cause or accident, and to allow all persons to take and use water for the purpose of extinguishing fire, without making compensation. They are willing to accept the Parliamentary obligation to keep the mains charged. That this creates a statutory duty no one can dispute; but does it give a right of action to any individual who can aver, as the plaintiff does here, that his premises were near the pipes, that a fire broke out, that there was no water to extinguish it, and that his premises were burnt? He does not say that he was not allowed to take the water, but he complains of a failure in the duty to keep the mains charged.

The proposition a priori appears to be somewhat startling that a company supplying a town with water—although they are willing to be put under obligation to keep up the pressure, and to be subject to penalties if they fail to do so—should further be willing to assume, or that Parliament should think it necessary to subject them to liability to individual actions by any householder who could make out a case. In the one case they are merely under liability to penalties if they neglect to perform their duty, in the other case they are practically insurers, so far as water can produce safety from damage by fire. It is necessary to look at the provisions of s. 43. Four cases are there specified, which cover all the duty imposed by the former sections, and for neglect of any one of these duties, there is a penalty of £10. For neglect of two of them, viz. to furnish to the town commissioners a sufficient supply of water for public purposes, and to furnish a supply of water to the owner or occupier, there is a further penalty of 40s. a day, payable to every person who has paid or tendered the rate, for as long as such neglect or refusal continues after notice in writing has been given of the want of supply. It is not material to say, but it is possible that it might be held that neglect or refusal to fix fire-plugs would also subject the company to the 40s. penalty. If so that penalty would be applicable in three cases out of the four. We have to consider why in some cases the penalty should go into the pocket of the individuals injured, and not in others. In the case of the obligation to keep the pipes charged, and allow all persons to use the water for the purpose of extinguishing fires, the provision is for the benefit of the public, and not of any individual specially, and the guarantee for the performance of the obligation is the liability to the public penalty of £10.

Apart from authority, I should be of opinion that the scheme of the Act and its true construction was not to create a duty which should be the subject of an action by any individual who might be injured, not to give a right to an individual to bring an action, but to lay down a series of duties, and provide a guarantee for their performance by s. 43, which imposes penalties in case of neglect or refusal. Where it is convenient that it should be so, the penalty goes into the pocket of the injured party; otherwise they are public penalties, imposed by way of security that all the public duty will be performed. The contrary intention is that we ought to say that where the penalty goes into the pocket of an individual no action will lie, but that otherwise a right of action exists, that in the other cases an individual would have no right of action, but that any one of the public could bring an action if there was no water in the main, and he suffered damage in consequence. I think it is impossible to adopt this view. The scheme must be judged by ss. 42 and 43, taken as a whole. Where we find that in most cases a penalty is imposed which would stop the right of action, it seems to me that the same result would follow in the other case provided for by s. 43. That is my opinion, unless there is some authority to the contrary.

The authority which is said to lead to a different conclusion is *Couch* v. *Steel*.[1] That was a case of some peculiarity. The plaintiff, who was a seaman, and had served on board the defendant's vessel, sued the defendant for not providing a proper supply of medicines for the voyage, which he was bound to do by 7 & 8 Vict., c. 112, s. 18, in consequence of which the plaintiff suffered from illness. In the declaration no claim was made on the Act of Parliament, but it was produced on the argument, and relied on in support of the plaintiff's case. With regard to that case and that Act of Parliament, if the decision were before us for review, I should desire further time for consideration; but that is not the case here, for the Act we have to deal with is widely different from the Act on which that case was decided. I must venture, with the greatest respect for the learned judges who took part in the decision, to express a doubt whether the authorities referred to by Lord Campbell in giving judgment justified the broad expressions which were used. It is not necessary to go through all the authorities which are there referred to, and which will be found collected in 3 E. & B. at p. 411, but it appears to me to be questionable whether they justify the broad general statement that wherever there is a statutory duty imposed, and any person is injured by the non-performance of that duty, an action can be maintained. It must depend on the particular statute, and where it is like a private legislative bargain, into which the undertakers of the works have entered, it differs from the case where a general public duty is imposed. Therefore, I cannot look on *Couch* v. *Steel*[1] as an authority for the decision of the court below in the present case, and no other authority was cited which could govern it.

I have, therefore, come to the conclusion that on the first count of the declaration there is no cause of action, and the demurrer must be allowed.

[COCKBURN C.J. and BRETT L.J. agreed that there should be judgment for defendants.]

Appeal allowed

Question

Why was the fact that the penalty of £10 could not be applied to the benefit of the plaintiff regarded as an argument *against* the imposition of a civil remedy? (cf. *Groves* v. *Lord Wimborne, ante*).

Notes

1. In *Dawson* v. *Bingley U.D.C.*, [1911] 2 K.B. 149; [1911–13] All E.R. Rep. 596 (C.A.), a local authority negligently put up a plate with a misleading direction in that it did not correctly denote the position of a fire-plug, as

---

1. (1854), 3 E. & B. 402.

the authority was required to do under s. 66 of the Public Health Act 1875. The fire-plug became covered in dirt and ashes with the result that a fire-brigade coming to a fire was delayed for 15 or 20 minutes in finding it. The plaintiff's property consequently suffered additional damage in the fire. The local authority was held liable to compensate him. Kennedy L.J. distinguished *Atkinson* v. *Newcastle Waterworks Co.*, *ante*, on the grounds that (1) the defendants there were not a public body but a private company; and (2) the Act in that case imposed remedies in the form of penalties, while the Public Health Act 1875, s. 66, contained no specific remedy for infringement. Is there any other ground for distinction? Is this case an early example of liability for negligent statements? (p. 499, *post*).

2. In *Read* v. *Croydon Corpn.*, [1938] 4 All E.R. 631 (C.A.), the corporation supplied impure drinking water as a result of which the infant plaintiff contracted typhoid. The corporation had negligently failed to take certain precautions during work at the wells which were the source of the water supply. It was held that (1) they were liable for common law negligence; and (2) they were guilty of breach of statutory duty under the Waterworks Clauses Act 1847, s. 35, but that this conferred a right of action upon ratepayers only (and so not the infant plaintiff, but her father who claimed certain special damages he had suffered as a result of her illness). Stable J. said that "in *Atkinson's* case, in the absence of the statute, or of any contractual obligation, there could not have been any common law remedy at the suit of a person whose shop was burnt down because the pressure of water in a particular pipe was insufficient to enable the fire engines to put out the fire." Why? Is this relevant to the existence of an action for breach of statutory duty?

Gorris v. Scott

Court of Exchequer (1874), 9 L.R. Exch. 125

Kelly C.B.: This is an action to recover damages for the loss of a number of sheep which the defendant, a shipowner, had contracted to carry, and which were washed overboard and lost by reason (as we must take it to be truly alleged) of the neglect to comply with a certain order made by the Privy Council, in pursuance of the Contagious Diseases (Animals) Act 1869. The Act was passed merely for sanitary purposes, in order to prevent animals in a state of infectious disease from communicating it to other animals with which they might come in contact. Under the authority of that Act, certain orders were made; amongst others, an order by which any ship bringing sheep or cattle from any foreign port to ports in Great Britain is to have the place occupied by such animals divided into pens of certain dimensions, and the floor of such pens furnished with battens or foot-holds. The object of this order is to prevent animals from being overcrowded, and so brought into a condition in which the disease guarded against would be likely to be developed. This regulation has been neglected, and the question is, whether the loss, which we must assume to have been caused by that neglect, entitles the plaintiffs to maintain an action.

The argument of the defendant is, that the Act has imposed penalties to secure the observance of its provisions, and that, according to the general rule, the remedy prescribed by the statute must be pursued; that although, when penalties are imposed for the violation of a statutory duty a person aggrieved by its violation may sometimes maintain an action for the damage so caused, that must be in cases where the object of the statute is to confer a benefit on individuals, and to protect them against the evil consequences which the statute was designed to prevent, and which have in fact ensued; but that if the object is not to protect individuals against the consequences which have in fact ensued, it is otherwise; that if, therefore, by reason of the precautions in question not having been taken, the plaintiffs had sustained that damage against which it was intended to secure them, an action would lie, but that when the damage is of such a nature as was not contemplated at all by the statute, and as to which it was not intended to confer any benefit on the plaintiffs, they cannot maintain an action founded on the neglect. The principle may be well illustrated by the case put in argument of a breach by a railway company of its duty to erect a gate on a level crossing, and to keep the gate closed except when the crossing is being actually and properly used. The object of the precaution is to prevent injury from being sustained through animals or vehicles being upon the line at unseasonable times; and if by reason of such a breach of duty, either in not erecting the gate, or in not keeping it closed, a person attempts to cross with a carriage at an improper time, and injury ensues to a passenger, no doubt an action would lie against the railway company, because the intention of the legislature was that, by the erection of the gates and by their being kept closed individuals should be protected against accidents of this description. And if we could see that it was the object, or among the objects of this Act, that the owners of sheep and cattle coming from a foreign port should be protected by the means described against the danger of their property being washed overboard, or lost by the perils of the sea, the present action would be within the principle.

But, looking at the Act, it is perfectly clear that its provisions were all enacted with a totally different view; there was no purpose, direct or indirect, to protect against such dangers; but, as is recited in the preamble, the Act is directed against the possibility of sheep or cattle being exposed to disease on their way to this country. The preamble recites that "it is expedient to confer on Her Majesty's most honourable Privy Council power to take such measures as may appear from time to time necessary to prevent the introduction into Great Britain of contagious or infectious diseases among cattle, sheep, or other animals, by prohibiting or regulating the importation of foreign animals," and also to provide against the "spreading" of such diseases in Great Britain. Then follow numerous sections directed entirely to this object. Then comes s. 75, which enacts that "the Privy Council may from time to time make such orders as they think expedient for all or any of the following purposes." What, then, are these purposes? They are "for securing for animals brought by sea to ports in Great Britain a proper supply of food and water during the passage and on landing," "for protecting such animals from unnecessary suffering during the passage and on landing," and so forth; all the purposes enumerated being calculated and directed to the prevention of disease, and none of them having any relation whatever to the danger of loss by the perils of the sea. That being so, if by reason of the default in question the plaintiff's sheep had been overcrowded, or had been caused unnecessary suffering, and so had arrived in this country in a state of disease, I do not say that they might not have maintained this action. But the damage complained of here is something totally apart from the object of the Act of Parliament, and it is in accordance with all the authorities to say that the action is not maintainable.

[PIGGOTT, POLLOCK and AMPHLETT BB. agreed that the declaration disclosed no cause of action, and judgment was given for the defendant.]

Questions

1. Would the plaintiff's action have succeeded had his sheep died from an infectious disease communicated by other animals due to the absence of the required pens?

2. It is sometimes argued that an action upon the statute is an aid to law enforcement, because it encourages the victim to set the law in motion (Morris, (1933), 46 Harv. L.R. 453, at p. 458). Can this rationale be reconciled with the decision in *Gorris* v. *Scott*?

Phillips v. Britannia Hygienic Laundry Co., Ltd.

Court of Appeal   [1923] All E.R. Rep. 127

The Motor Cars (Use and Construction) Order 1904, provided: "the motor car and all fittings thereof shall be in such a condition as not to cause, or to be likely to cause, danger to any person on the motor car or on the highway." The defendants' vehicle was in a defective condition not due to any negligence on their part but because of the negligence of repairers to whom they had sent the vehicle for overhaul. As a result of the defendants using the vehicle on the highway, in this defective condition, there was a collision with a van belonging to the plaintiff. The plaintiff claimed damages on the ground of a breach of the statutory duty imposed by the Use and Construction regulations. A criminal penalty was provided for the breach of any one of those regulations. The Divisional Court held that the action must be dismissed. An appeal to the Court of Appeal was unsuccessful.

BANKES L.J.: . . . We have not here to consider the case of a person injured on the highway. The injury was done to the plaintiff's van, and the plaintiff, as a member of the public, claims a right of action as being a member of a class for whose benefit cl. 6 was enacted. He contends that the public using the highway is the class so favoured. I do not agree. In my view, the public using the highway is not a class; it is the public itself and not a class of the public. I think this clause does not apply to individual members or sections of the public, but to the public generally, and it is included in a batch of regulations for breach of which it cannot have been intended that a person aggrieved should have a civil remedy by way of action in addition to the more appropriate statutory remedy already provided. In my opinion, the plaintiff has failed to show that this case is an exception to the general rule. The appeal, therefore, fails and must be dismissed.

ATKIN L.J.: I am of the same opinion. This is an important and a difficult question. I was much impressed by the argument of counsel for the plaintiff when dealing with these regulations, because there can be little doubt that the scope of the regulations was to promote the safety of the public using the highway. The question is whether they were intended to be enforced only by the special penalty attached to them in the Act. I conceive the rule to be that when a statute imposes a duty of commission or omission upon an individual, the question whether a person aggrieved by a breach of the duty has a right of action depends upon the intention of the statute. Was it intended that a duty should be owed to the individual aggrieved as well as to the State, or is it a public duty only? That depends upon the construction of the statute as a whole, and the circumstances in which it was made and to which it relates. One of the matters to be taken into consideration is this: Does the statute on the face of it contain a reference to a remedy for the breach of it? If so, it would, prima facie, be the only remedy, but that is not conclusive. One must still look to the intention of the legislature to be derived from the words used, and one may come to the conclusion that, although the statute creates a duty and imposes a penalty for the breach of that duty, it may still intend that the duty should be owed to individuals. Instances of this are *Groves* v. *Lord Wimborne*[1] and *Britannic Merthyr Coal Co.* v. *David*.[2] To my mind, and on this point I differ from McCardie J. the question is not to be determined solely by the test whether or not the person aggrieved can fall within some special class of the community, or whether he is some designated individual. It would, I think, be strange if it were so. The duty imposed may be of such paramount importance that it is owed to every member of the public. It would be strange if a less important duty which is owed to a section of the public may be enforced by an action, while a more important duty which is owed to the public at large cannot be so enforced. The right

1. [1898] 2 Q.B. 402.
2. [1910] A.C. 74.

of action does not depend upon whether a statutory enactment or prohibition is proclaimed for the benefit of the public as a whole or for the benefit of a particular class. It may well be enforced by an individual who cannot be otherwise specified than as a member of the public who passed along the highway. Therefore I think McCardie J. is applying too narrow a test when he says ([1923] 1 K.B. at p. 547):

> "In my view, the Motor Car Acts and regulations were not enacted for the benefit of any particular class of folk. They are provisions for the benefit of the whole public, whether pedestrians or vehicle users, whether aliens or British citizens, and whether working or walking or standing upon the highway."

In stating the argument of the defendant in *Gorris* v. *Scott*,[1] Kelly C.B. refers to the obligation imposed upon railway companies by s. 47 of the Railways Clauses Consolidation Act 1845, to erect gates across public carriage roads crossed by the railway on the level and to keep the gates closed except when the crossing is being actually and properly used, under the penalty of 40s. for every default. It has never been doubted that if a member of the public crossing the railway were injured by the railway company's breach of duty, either in not erecting a gate or in not keeping it closed, he would have a right of action. Therefore, the question is whether these regulations, having regard to the circumstances in which they were made and to which they relate, were intended to impose a duty, which is a public duty, or whether they were intended also to impose a duty, enforceable by an individual aggrieved. Upon the whole, I have come to the conclusion that it was not intended to impose a duty enforceable by individuals aggrieved, but only a public duty, the sole remedy for breach of which is the remedy provided by way of a fine. The regulations impose obligations of varying degrees of importance; some of them are more concerned with the maintenance of the highway than with the protection of the public. Yet there is one penalty imposed for the breach of any one of them. Upon the whole, I think the true inference is that the legislature did not permit the Department which had been empowered to make regulations for the use and construction of motor vehicles to impose new duties in favour of individuals and new causes of action for breach of them. That seems to me to be the more reasonable conclusion when it is realised that the obligations of those who bring vehicles upon highways have been already well provided for and regulated by the common law. It is not likely that the legislature intended by these regulations to impose upon the owners of vehicles an absolute obligation to make them roadworthy in all events, even in the absence of negligence. For these reasons I am of opinion that the conclusion arrived at by the Divisional Court was correct, and that the appeal should therefore be dismissed.

[YOUNGER L.J. agreed.]

Notes

1. In general the courts have refused to create civil remedies out of road traffic legislation. In *Tan Chye Choo* v. *Chong Kew Moi*, [1970] 1 All E.R. 266 (P.C.), *Phillips* case was followed in relation to the similar Motor Vehicles (Construction and Use) Rules of Malaysia. In *Coote* v. *Stone*, [1971] 1 All E.R. 657 (C.A.), it was held that there is no civil action for breach of the Various Trunk Roads (Prohibition of Waiting) (Clearways) Order S.I., 1963 No. 1172, which prohibited waiting on a clearway. The only important exception to this general approach is that the House of Lords has held that there is a civil action for breach of the Pedestrian Crossing Places (Traffic) Regulations (*London Passenger Transport Board* v. *Upson*, [1949] A.C. 155; [1949] 1 All E.R. 60). In *Coote* v. *Stone (ante)* Davies L.J. explained this on the ground that those

---

1. (1874), L.R. 9 Exch. 125.

regulations were "designed for the safety of pedestrians". For whose safety were the Motor Vehicle (Use and Construction) Regulations designed?

2. P. S. Atiyah, *Accidents, Compensation and the Law* (London, 1970), p. 165, comments on the *Phillips* case:

> "Perhaps the court was influenced—consciously or unconsciously—by the fact that in 1923 it was still not compulsory to insure against third party liability, and the court may have shrunk from imposing a form of liability without fault on individual motorists who might not have had the resources to meet a judgment for damages. Had this problem arisen after compulsory insurance was introduced in 1930 the result might conceivably have been different. Today it would be impossible for the courts to introduce so substantial a change into the law, though it must not be supposed that strict liability for breach of such statutory duties would be anything like as far reaching as the liability which some would wish to impose on the motorist."

Question

Can Atkin L.J.'s reasoning be reconciled with that of A. L. Smith L.J. in *Groves v. Lord Wimborne* (p. 271, *ante*)?

Cutler v. Wandsworth Stadium, Ltd. (in Liquidation)

House of Lords   [1949] 1 All E.R. 544

The Betting and Lotteries Act 1934, s. 11 (2) provided that, so long as a totalisator is being lawfully operated on a licensed dog-racing track, the occupier "(*a*) shall not . . . exclude any person from the track by reason only that he proposes to carry on bookmaking on the track; and (*b*) shall take such steps as are necessary to secure that . . . there is available for bookmakers space on the track where they can conveniently carry on bookmaking in connection with dog races run on the track on that day; and every person who contravenes, or fails to comply with, any of the provisions of this subsection shall be guilty of an offence." Section 30 provided substantial penalties, on summary conviction and on conviction on indictment, for a breach of, inter alia, section 11.

A bookmaker brought an action against the occupier of a licensed dog-racing track for a breach of his obligation under s. 11 (2). The House of Lords, confirming a decision of the Court of Appeal ([1947] 2 All E.R. 815), held that there was no civil cause of action.

LORD REID [after quoting s. 11 (2)]: . . . For whose benefit was this subsection intended? The appellant's case is that it was primarily, if not solely, for the benefit of bookmakers. I do not think so. I think that it was primarily intended for the protection of those members of the public who might wish to bet on these tracks. Its effect is to prevent the totalisator from having a monopoly and to afford to the public such protection as can be given by making provision for competitive facilities for betting. I am prepared to assume in the appellant's favour that it may also have been an object of the legislature to give some protection to bookmakers (although this is by no means obvious), but it does not follow that to achieve such protection every individual bookmaker must have rights against the occupier of the track which he can enforce by civil action. Broadly speaking, the facilities which the Act requires for bookmakers are similar to the facilities which, in fact, they enjoyed before the Act was passed. I see no reason to infer from the Act, read as a whole, or from the circumstances founded on by the appellant, that the enjoyment of these facilities required or was intended to have any further protection than that afforded by the track occupier's liability to prosecution if he failed to comply with the statutory provisions.

I think, however, that the clearest indication of the intention of the legislature is to be found in the terms of s. 11 (2) itself. I find it extremely difficult to reconcile the nature of the provisions of this subsection with an intention to confer on individual bookmakers rights which each could enforce by civil action. If the legislature had intended to create such rights, I would expect to find them capable of reasonably precise definition, but counsel for the appellant were unable to suggest such definition and I am equally unable to do so. At first sight s. 11 (2) (*a*) might seem to confer on every bookmaker an unqualified right to demand admission, but counsel for the appellant admitted that this cannot be maintained. It cannot have been intended that the occupier must admit as many bookmakers as may present themselves on any occasion, whether there is room for them or not, and, if an unreasonably large number seek admittance, there is nothing in the Act to indicate who is to be admitted and who may be refused. This omission is not surprising if the obligation on the occupier is only a general obligation to admit an adequate number of bookmakers, but it is, in my view, a clear indication that no further obligation was intended to be imposed. If s. 11 (2) (*a*) does not create any civil right in favour of individual bookmakers, I find it difficult to suppose that s. 11 (2) (*b*) creates such a right. The occupier is required to take such steps as are necessary to secure "that there is available for bookmakers space on the track where they can conveniently carry on bookmaking". This cannot mean that space must be provided on every occasion for as many bookmakers as wish to carry on business on that occasion. It cannot mean that, after the allotted space is fully occupied, an individual bookmaker who cannot find room there can demand further space where he can conveniently carry on business. The occupier must provide a space which is adequate in all the circumstances and which is in a convenient situation, but if he does that he has fulfilled his statutory obligation. He is not required by anything in the Act to find a place for each bookmaker who presents himself. If the Act does not give to an individual bookmaker a right to demand a place for himself, I find nothing to suggest that it gives him any other right enforceable by civil action. The sanction of prosecution appears to me to be appropriate and sufficient for the general obligation imposed by the subsection. I, therefore, agree that the appellant has no right to sue in respect of a breach by the respondents of their obligations under s. 11 (2) of the Act and that the appeal should be dismissed.

[LORD SIMONDS, LORD DU PARCQ, LORD NORMAND and LORD MORTON OF HENRYTON agreed that the appeal should be dismissed.]

Questions

1. In *Monk* v. *Warbey*, [1935] I K.B. 75, Greer L.J. (at p. 81) said: "*prima facie* a person who has been injured by breach of a statute has a right to recover damages from the person committing it, unless it can be established by considering the whole of the Act that no such right was intended to be given." Can this still be treated as correct in the light of *Cutler's* case?

2. "On the analogy of the rule for public nuisance, it might be thought that even where the Act was passed for the benefit of the public at large, a plaintiff could sue for breach of statutory duty if he suffered particular damage, over and above that suffered by the rest of the public; and this was formerly held [*Couch* v. *Steel* (1854), 3 E. & B. 402]" (Gl. Williams, (1960), 23 M.L.R. 233, at p. 245). Would it be correct to say that the criterion of particular damage was ignored in *Cutler's* case?

Solomons v. R. Gertzenstein, Ltd.

Court of Appeal   [1954] 2 All E.R. 625

The plaintiff was employed by a furrier who occupied second floor premises in Soho. On 10 November 1950, a fire broke out on the premises and the plaintiff who was on the third floor, being unable to escape by the stairs, climbed out of a window at the back of the premises and was injured. He brought an action for damages. His claim in respect of alleged negligence failed because Lord Goddard C.J. found as a fact that the fire was not caused by the negligence of any of the defendants.

The plaintiff also alleged that there had been a breach of section 133 (2) of the London Building Acts (Amendment) Act 1939, which provided that "all means of escape in case of fire and all safeguards to prevent the spread of fire and any arrangements in connection therewith provided in pursuance of the provisions of . . . this Act or otherwise shall be maintained in good condition and repair and in efficient working order by the owner of the building and no person shall do or permit or suffer to be done anything to impair the efficiency of any such means of escape, safeguards or arrangements." There was a trap door on the third floor leading to the roof but on the date of the fire a ladder with hooks which could be fixed into holes so as to give access to the trap door was not in position but was lying in a passageway on the third floor. Lord Goddard C.J. found that, by reason of the ladder not being in position, there was a breach of section 133 (2) for which the "owner" of the premises was liable in a civil action. An appeal to the Court of Appeal was allowed on the grounds that no breach of the section had been established, and that the defendants were not, in law, the "owners" of the premises. Although unnecessary for the purposes of their decision, different opinions were expressed on the question whether the plaintiff would have had an action for damages had a breach of section 133 (2) by the owner been established.

SOMERVELL L.J.: . . . The provisions, like those in *Atkinson's* case,[1] are, of course, to prevent or lessen damage and injury by fire. I would myself have read Part V of the Act of 1939 and similar provisions as intended to confer powers on the council rather than rights on individuals. This view is, I think, supported by the definition. It is, no doubt, as I have said, reasonable that a rent receiver other than the landlord should be treated as owner for operating the machinery of the Act. I find it impossible to imply an intention that rent receivers should be liable in damages. If one passes from agents to landlords who collect their own rents or owner-occupiers, one is still in a different area quoad this issue from, say, employers of labour or occupiers of factories. If one considers s. 133 (1), the liability would fall on any person who permitted or suffered to be done anything to impair the efficiency of the safeguards. This would be potentially a miscellaneous group, which might include any resident in the premises. The character of the potential defendants supports my prima facie view. I think it is also supported by the fact, to which I have already referred, that there is in certain cases in addition to penalties the further sanction of prohibiting the occupation of the building. Reference was made to the Factories Act 1937, s. 101, dealing with tenement factories as a section under which an "owner" similarly defined would be held liable. The obligations of the Act in that case are primarily placed on the owner, not the occupier. I will assume that an owner would be held liable at common law, but, apart from the difference in subject-matter, there is an express provision, not to be found in the Act which we are considering, that quoad certain obligations the owner is not to be responsible for matters outside his control. I do not think that that section assists the plaintiff. I, therefore, am of opinion that the plaintiff would not have had a cause of action for damages assuming that he had established a breach of s. 133 (2). I, therefore, would allow the appeal.

ROMER L.J.: . . . In these circumstances the question whether the plaintiff could sue for damages if he had established any such breach does not arise for decision. As, however, the point was so elaborately argued, and was decided by the Lord Chief Justice, I agree with my brethren that we should express an opinion on it. It is, of course, clear that the general purpose of the London Building Acts was to promote the welfare and interests of the very considerable section of the English community which lives in London. With this end in view, the Act of 1939 made legislative provision for

---

1. (1877), 2 Ex. D. 441.

such things as the naming and numbering of streets, the construction of buildings, dangerous and neglected structures and so on. There is nothing inconsistent, however, in including in legislation which is generally designed to regulate in various ways the lives of a vast community provision for the safety and protection of individuals; and, in my opinion, it was the object of s. 133 of the Act of 1939 to make provision of this kind. Measures which are taken to prevent the outbreak and spread of fires in a great city are beneficial to the inhabitants of the city as a whole, for they tend to the protection of the lives and property of the general community. Measures that are taken to facilitate the escape of persons who happen to be in a house in which fire breaks out are also in a sense directed to the general welfare, for the death of a few in circumstances of tragedy is, or should be, felt by all. Nevertheless, I cannot but think that the principal purpose of measures such as are found in s. 133 is the protection of individuals rather than the promotion of the interests of the masses. It is a matter of general sorrow to hear of persons who have been trapped in a burning house without any means of escape, but it is death to the victims themselves. I emphasise this point because it appears to me to be of cardinal importance in considering whether a civil suit lies for breach of a statutory duty to see whether on a broad view that duty has been imposed for the general welfare, on the one hand, or in the interests of individuals or of a defined or definable class of the public on the other.

It is, indeed, difficult to reconcile all the decisions which have been reported on this subject, but this criterion does seem in many cases to have been accepted as a guide to Parliament's intention. . . . In all of the above cases, in each of the two categories, considerations other than those as to the public or individual nature of the obligation were also weighed, e.g. whether penalties were imposed for a breach: if so, whether the injured person was given or shared in the penalty; the nature of the obligation and, above all, the general purview and intendment of the Act. No universal rule can be formulated which will answer the question whether in any given case an individual can sue in respect of a breach of statutory duty. In *Cutler's* case[1] Lord Simonds said ([1949] 1 All E.R. 548):

> "The only rule which in all circumstances is valid is that the answer must depend on a consideration of the whole Act and the circumstances, including the pre-existing law, in which it was enacted."

Even, however, if one looks to the whole of the Act of 1939 and to the circumstances which Lord Simonds mentioned, it is difficult, as I think, to hold that no action lies for a breach of s. 133 (2) without disregarding an element which formed an important ground of decision in most of the cases in the first category to which I have referred and the materiality of which was recognised in the cases in both categories; and, in particular, without disregarding the decision and reasoning of this court in *Groves* v. *Lord Wimborne*.[2] Indeed, this case seems in one sense stronger than *Groves* v. *Lord Wimborne*,[2] for in that case the penalties imposed for infringement might be applied to the benefit of the person injured, but there is no similar provision in the Act of 1939. If I am right in the view which I have already expressed that the main object of the subsection, or, as has sometimes been said, its pith and substance, was to provide for the safety of individuals as distinct from promoting the welfare of the general community, I find it difficult to appreciate why an "owner" of a house should be exempt from a liability to which an employer on whom similar or equivalent duties are imposed by the Factories Act 1937, is subject; for the inhabitants of a house are at least as definite a class as are the workers in a factory and I am not sure what logical distinction there is in this regard between a man who employs labour in his factory and one who, for example, employs a staff in a restaurant, or in a block of service flats which he owns. It is true that in the present case we are not concerned with an

---

1. [1949] A.C. 398; [1949] 1 All E.R. 544.
2. [1898] 2 Q.B. 402.

"owner" but with the generality of persons who are prohibited by s. 133 (2) from impairing the efficiency of means of escape. but it is difficult to suppose that offenders under the first part of the subsection are liable to be sued (as I think myself that they are) while those under the later part of the subsection are immune. Moreover, I see no reason why a wrongdoer should not be answerable in damages even though his identity cannot be described or ascertained in advance.

[BIRKETT L.J. agreed that the Act was passed for the benefit of a particular ascertainable class and that those persons had an action for damages for breach of statutory duty.]

Questions

1. Why did Romer L.J. consider that the London Building Acts were "for the protection of individuals [i.e. tenants] rather than the promotion of the interests of the masses"? Compare the approach of Atkin L.J. in the *Phillips* case: "It would be strange if a less important duty, which is owed to a section of the public, may be enforced by an action, while a more important duty owed to the public at large cannot." ([1923] 2 K.B. at pp. 841–842.)

2. Somervell L.J. said that "the character of the defendants supports my *prima facie* view." What does this mean? Is there any relevance, in the Factories Act cases, that liability is usually placed on the "occupier"?

3. Whose approach do you prefer, that of Somervell L.J. or that of Romer L.J.? Whose is more consistent with the decision in *Cutler* v. *Wandsworth Stadium, Ltd.* (p. 279, *ante*)?

Law Commission, "The Interpretation of Statutes"
(Law Com. No. 21, 1969)

Appendix A

DRAFT CLAUSES

Presumption as to enforcement of statutory duty

4. Where any act passed after this Act imposes or authorises the imposition of a duty, whether positive or negative and whether with or without a special remedy for its enforcement it shall be presumed, unless express provision to the contrary is made that a breach of the duty is intended to be actionable (subject to the defences and other incidents applying to actions for breach of statutory duty) at the suit of any person who sustains damage in consequence of the breach.

Notes

1. Roscoe Pound, "Common Law and Legislation", (1908), 21 Harv. L.R. 383, at pp. 406–407, preferred legislation above judicial decision as "the more truly democratic form of law-making". He thought it followed from this that judicial analogies from the social policies expressed in statutes should be encouraged. Will this draft clause, if enacted, help or hinder this kind of judicial legislation?

2. The Law Commission, *The Interpretation of Statutes*, No. 21 (1969), has also proposed that, in ascertaining the meaning of any provision of an Act, the court should be entitled to consider, inter alia, reports of Royal Com-

missions and committees, relevant treaties, command papers and other relevant documents, but not reports of Parliamentary proceedings. The Law Commission's report contains a useful bibliography of material on the interpretation of statutes (pp. 55–56).

London Passenger Transport Board v. Upson

House of Lords   [1949] I All E.R. 60

LORD WRIGHT: . . . I think that the authorities such as *Caswell's* case,[1] *Lewis* v. *Denye*[2] and *Sparks* v. *Edward Ash, Ltd.*[3] show clearly that a claim for damages for breach of a statutory duty intended to protect a person in the position of the particular plaintiff is a specific common law right which is not to be confused in essence with a claim for negligence. The statutory right has its origin in the statute, but the particular remedy of an action for damages is given by the common law in order to make effective for the benefit of the injured plaintiff his right to the performance by the defendant of the defendant's statutory duty. It is an effective sanction. It is not a claim in negligence in the strict or ordinary sense. As I said ([1939] 3 All E.R. 739) in *Caswell's* case:[1]

> "I do not think that an action for breach of a statutory duty such as that in question is completely or accurately described as an action in negligence. It is a common law action based on the purpose of the statute to protect the workman, and belongs to the category often described as that of cases of strict or absolute liability. At the same time it resembles actions in negligence in that the claim is based on a breach of a duty to take care for the safety of the workman."

But, whatever the resemblances, it is essential to keep in mind the fundamental differences of the two classes of claim. Here I shall, perhaps, be guilty of hypercriticism if I were to quarrel with the expression of Asquith L.J. in the Court of Appeal ([1947] 2 All E.R. 516) that the common law duty is enhanced by the duty contained in the regulations. One duty does not, in truth, enhance the other, though the same damage may be caused by action which might equally be characterised as ordinary negligence at common law or as breach of the statutory duty. On the other hand, the damage may be due either to negligence or to breach of the statutory duty. In the present case Asquith L.J., decided, as I understand, in favour of the respondent, not on the ground of negligence, which he did not find, but specifically on the ground of breach of statutory duty. There is, I think, a logical distinction which accords with what I regard as the correct view that the causes of action are different. It follows that the correct pleading would be to allege each cause of action separately so as to avoid the confusion which seems to me to have crept in at certain points of these proceedings. I have desired before I deal specifically with the regulations to make it clear how, in my judgment, they should be approached, and also to make it clear that a claim for their breach may stand or fall independently of a claim for negligence. There is always a danger, if the claim is not sufficiently specific, that the due consideration of the claim for breach of statutory duty may be prejudiced if it is confused with the claim in negligence. . . .

Notes

I. In *Morris* v. *National Coal Board*, [1963] 3 All E.R. 644 (C.A.) it was held that a plaintiff who presents his case exclusively as one of breach of statutory duty cannot on appeal seek to support the decision on grounds that there

---

1. [1940] A.C. 152; [1940] 3 All E.R. 722.
2. [1940] A.C. 921; [1939] 3 All E.R. 299.
3. [1943] 1 K.B. 223; [1943] 1 All E.R. 1.

was common law negligence, even though there is a considerable amount of evidence of breach of a common law duty. Is the result satisfactory in view of the abolition of the forms of action and the fact that the plaintiff is not supposed to plead matters of law? (see *Lewis* v. *Denye*, [1940] A.C. at pp. 924–925).

2. Thayer, "Public Wrongs and Private Action" (1914), 27 Harv. L.R. 317, argued that since the reasonable man does not breach the criminal law, breach of statutory duty automatically establishes common law negligence. This view is popularly held in the U.S.A. (the negligence *per se* doctrine). Can it be supported in England in view of Lord Wright's remarks above? Do you agree with Fricke, "The Juridical Nature of the Action upon the Statute", (1960), 76 L.Q.R. 240, at pp. 241–251, that Thayer's view would (a) lead to "over-punishment" of the defendant, and (b) result in vicarious liability whenever an employee of the defendant was in breach of statutory duty?

4. CAUSATION AND BREACH OF STATUTORY DUTY

Boyle v. Kodak

House of Lords   [1969] 2 All E.R. 439

The appellant was injured when he fell off a ladder while engaged in painting the outside of a large oil storage tank which was some 30 feet high. The upper part had to be painted by a man standing on a ladder the top of which rested on a rail round the roof of the tank. For safety it was necessary to lash the top of the ladder to this rail to prevent it from slipping sideways, and the accident occurred while the appellant was going up the ladder in order to lash it. For some reason, never discovered, the ladder slipped when he was about 20 feet up and he fell with the ladder.

LORD DIPLOCK: My Lords, in this action negligence and contributory negligence were pleaded but as I read the judgment of Chapman J. he found that the ladder from which the appellant fell was so positioned and footed that the risk of its slipping while he was mounting it in order to lash the top of it to the rail of the tank was so small that a reasonable man would not have thought it necessary to expend the time and effort which would have been involved in ascending the staircase to the top of the tank and lashing the ladder before setting foot on it. The judge expressly found that the respondents were not negligent and it is implicit in his judgment that the appellant's conduct did not amount to contributory negligence at common law. All three members of the Court of Appeal agreed with these findings which have not been seriously contested in your Lordships' House.

All that is left in this appeal is the appellant's claim for damages for breach by the respondents of their statutory duty under reg. 29 (4) of the Building (Health, Safety and Welfare) Regulations 1948,[1] which so far as is relevant provides: "Every ladder shall so far as is practicable be securely fixed so that it can move neither from its top nor from its bottom points of rest."

I agree with all your Lordships, with the Court of Appeal and with the trial judge that this regulation applied to the operation on which the appellant was engaged when he fell. I also agree that it was practicable, by lashing the ladder to the rail of the tank before anyone mounted it, to fix the ladder securely so that it could not move from its top points of rest. So the regulation was not complied with. If it had been the top of the ladder would not have slipped and the appellant would not have sustained his

1. S.I. 1948 No. 1145.

physical injuries. So the non-compliance with the regulation was a cause of the appellant's injuries.

The law relating to civil liability for breach of statutory duties imposed by the Factories Act 1961, and its predecessors and by regulations made thereunder is now well settled. It is the creature not of the statutes themselves but of judicial decision by which over the period of 70 years which have passed since *Groves* v. *Lord Wimborne*,[1] a new branch of the law of civil wrongs has been developed. The statutes say nothing about civil remedies for breaches of their provisions. The judgments of the courts say all.

The duty to comply with the requirements of reg. 29 (4) of the Building (Health Safety and Welfare) Regulations 1948, is imposed by reg. 4 on the employer who is undertaking the operation. But it is also imposed on the person, in the instant case the appellant, who performs the act, viz. mounting the ladder, to which the relevant requirement of the regulation relates. We have thus a situation where both appellant and respondents were at fault and the only fault of each was their respective failure to comply with the same requirements of the same regulation.

Although the civil liability of the employer has been engrafted by judicial decision on the criminal liability imposed by Parliament its growth has been separate from the parent stem. It is no good looking to the statute and seeing from it where the criminal liability would lie, for we are concerned only with civil liability. We must look to the cases, and in particular to *Ginty* v. *Belmont Building Supplies, Ltd.*,[2] and those which followed it, by which this branch of the law of civil wrongs is being developed.

The employer's duty to comply with the requirements of the regulation differs from that of his employee. The employer, at any rate when he is a corporation, must needs perform his duty vicariously through his officers, servants, agents or contractors; but he does not thereby rid himself of his duty. He remains vicariously responsible for any failure by any one of them to do whatever was necessary to ensure that the requirements of the regulation were complied with; and among those for whose failure he is prima facie vicariously liable is any employee who is himself under a concurrent statutory duty to comply with those requirements. The employee's duty, on the other hand, is in respect of and is limited to his own acts or omissions. He is not vicariously liable for those of anyone else.

What, then, is the liability of an employer who is sued by an employee plaintiff for damages for personal injuries sustained as a result of a breach of statutory duty by the employer in not complying with the requirements of a regulation when the non-compliance relied on was also a breach of statutory duty by the plaintiff himself?

The plaintiff establishes a prima facie cause of action against his employer by proving the fact of non-compliance with a requirement of the regulation and that he suffered injury as a result. He need prove no more. No burden lies on him to prove what steps should have been taken to avert the non-compliance nor to identify the employees whose acts or defaults contributed to it, for the employer is vicariously responsible for them all. But if the employer can prove that the only act or default of anyone which caused or contributed to the non-compliance was the act or default of the plaintiff himself, he establishes a good defence. For the legal concept of vicarious liability requires three parties: the injured person, a person whose act or default caused the injury and a person vicariously liable for the latter's act or default. To say "You are liable to me for my own wrongdoing" is neither good morals nor good law. But unless the employer can prove this he cannot escape liability. If he proves that it was partly the fault of the employee plaintiff, as ex hypothesi it will be in the postulated case, for the employee's own breach of statutory duty is "fault" within the meaning of s. 1 of the Law Reform (Contributory Negligence) Act 1945, this may reduce the damages recoverable but it will not constitute a defence to the action.

---

1. [1898] 2 Q.B. 402; [1895–99] All E.R. Rep. 147.
2. [1959] 1 All E.R. 414.

Since it is only through other persons that the employer can perform his duty of compliance with the requirements of the regulations it is incumbent on him to ensure that all of those persons understand those requirements and their practical application to the particular work being undertaken and possess the skill and are provided with the plant, equipment and personnel needed to secure compliance. Although in the present case the necessary plant, equipment and personnel was provided for the appellant and he possessed the necessary skill the respondents, who called no evidence, made no attempt to prove that they had taken any steps to ensure that the appellant understood the requirements of reg. 4 of the Building (Health, Safety and Welfare) Regulations 1948, or understood that, in the particular circumstances of the work which he was undertaking, these requirements would not be satisfied unless he lashed the ladder at the top to the rail of the tank before he mounted it.

It has been contended on their behalf that as the appellant was a skilled and experienced craftsman they were entitled to assume that he understood all these things. But however reasonable such assumption might be they would not escape liability unless they proved that the appellant did in fact understand them, although the reasonableness of their assumption if mistaken would be relevant to their share in the responsibility for the damage for the purpose of reducing the damages recoverable under the Law Reform (Contributory Negligence) Act 1945.

On the evidence in the present case, which was that of the appellant himself and of a fellow workman who completed the work after the plaintiff was injured, it appeared that neither was given any instructions about the regulations or was told that the regulations required the top of the ladder to be lashed to the rail of the tank before anyone mounted on it. It also appeared that the appellant, for reasons which are intelligible though unconvincing, believed that the ladder should be lashed while he was mounted on it and not before. So far from establishing that the appellant did know what the requirements of the regulation were and their application to the particular circumstances of the operation on which he was engaged, the evidence discloses that the foreman and the ganger through whom, inter alia, the respondents were purporting to perform their statutory duty and for whose omissions they are vicariously liable, took no steps to give to the appellant instructions on either of these matters which, if carried out, would have prevented the breach of statutory duty. The respondents, in my view, therefore failed to satisfy the onus which lay on them to prove that the only act or default of anyone which caused or contributed to the non-compliance was the act or default of the appellant himself.

In your Lordships' House the respondents relied strongly on a finding of the learned judge that their failure to instruct the appellant to lash the ladder at the top before mounting it did not constitute negligence on their part. For reasons that I have already indicated the fact that a failure to give instructions as to the requirements of the regulations is not negligent does not exonerate an employer from liability for breach of his statutory duty to comply with the requirements of the regulations which he owes to the person whom he has failed to instruct. He is only exonerated if he can show that that person did in fact know the requirements. But in the present case the failure goes further than this. It may well be unnecessary to give a skilled and experienced craftsman instructions how to avoid obvious dangers, and the more obvious the danger the less the need to do so. But in the present case on the findings of the learned judge the risk of the ladder slipping while the appellant was mounting it to lash the top of it was so small that a reasonable man would not have thought it necessary in the interests of his own safety to expend the time and effort and incur the possible loss of bonus which would have been involved in ascending the staircase to the top of the tank and lashing the ladder. The more remote the danger in the particular operation on which the employee is engaged the greater the need to instruct him or to remind him of the application of the regulation to it.

Perhaps because he had already dealt with instructions in connection with the issue of negligence, the cognate question of instructions about the application of the regulations to the task in hand escaped the attention of the judge at the trial when he came to deal with breach of statutory duty. This oversight, in my opinion, led him to err in law in treating it as sufficient to exonerate the respondents from all liability that—

"... he [the appellant] was the one to see that that breach was not carried out ... He had the means of securing the ladder and complying with the Regulations and he did not do so."

In the Court of Appeal, Salmon L.J. in his dissenting judgment was the only one to recognise the vital distinction between the need to instruct a craftsman on how to avoid obvious dangers and the need to instruct him about the application of the regulations in situations where no danger is apparent. On this aspect of the case the majority members of the Court of Appeal, in my view, fell into the same error as the learned trial judge. But they also upheld the judgment on the ground that, even if the appellant had been instructed that he was required by the regulations to lash the ladder at the top before and not after mounting and to ascend to the top of the tank by the staircase to do so, and that he would be committing an offence if he did not, the appellant would nevertheless have disregarded those instructions. Failure to give them, therefore, did not cause or contribute to the breach.

Whether the appellant would or would not have obeyed such instructions is a question of fact. The learned judge made no finding on it. It was never put to the appellant in cross-examination. It was never canvassed in evidence at all. It is, in my view, impermissible for an appellate court to decide this case against the appellant on what is no more than speculation as to a fact which the respondents never sought to prove and with which the appellant was given no opportunity to deal.

I would therefore allow the appeal. Both appellant and respondents were in breach of their statutory duty. This was the only "fault" of each. I find it difficult to apportion their respective shares of the responsibility for the damage. In view of the remoteness of the danger in neither was it a very heinous fault. But however venial the fault of each of them they must share between them the responsibility for the whole of the damage. I would assess the share of each as one-half and reduce the damages recoverable by the appellant accordingly.

I would allow the appeal, declare that the respondents are liable to the appellant for one-half of the damage sustained by him and remit the case for the damages to be assessed.

LORD REID, with whom LORD MORRIS OF BORTH-Y-GEST concurred, and LORD HODSON, delivered speeches in favour of allowing the appeal. LORD UPJOHN concurred.]

Notes

1. The law of causation applies as much to breach of statutory duties as it does to breach of common law duties (see Chap. 5), but it is particularly important where the statute lays down a duty on both the employer and the injured employee, or where the employee is the only person who could carry out the statutory duty. See too, *Cummings* (or *McWilliams*) v. *Sir William Arrol & Co.*, [1962] 1 All E.R. 623 (H.L., Sc): steel erector killed when he fell from a steel tower; had he been wearing a safety belt he would not have been killed; held his widow could not recover reparation in respect of the breach of statutory duty to provide belts because even had he been provided with a belt he would not have worn one.

2. Would the employers have been liable in *Boyle* v. *Kodak* had they been able to show that, even properly instructed, the appellant would have disobeyed? What kind of evidence would be admissible to show "what he would have done in circumstances which never arose"? (*per* Lord Devlin in *McWil-*

liam's case, *ante*). See too, *Ross* v. *Associated Portland Cement Manufacturers, Ltd.*, [1964] 2 All E.R. 452 (H.L.).

3. As regards general defences such as *volenti non fit injuria* and contributory negligence see Chap. 9.

5. THE INTERPRETATION OF INDUSTRIAL SAFETY LEGISLATION: A NOTE

The action for breach of statutory duty, when applied to some industrial legislation, was a neat way around the doctrine of common employment (*Groves* v. *Wimborne*, p. 271, *ante*). Despite the abolition of that doctrine by the Law Reform (Personal Injuries) Act 1948, s. 1, the action has survived. It is not possible in this sourcebook to enter into this complex, capricious and vague area of statutory interpretation of industrial legislation. (A practitioners' book, which also has the merit of being entertainingly written and of use to the student, is John Munkman, *Employers' Liability at Common Law* 7th Edn. (London, 1971).) This Chapter would, however, be incomplete if the student had failed to appreciate that "some of the protection to the workman which at first sight might be thought available turns out on closer scrutiny to be illusory" (*per* Lord Hailsham of St. Marylebone L.C. in *F.E . Callow (Engineers), Ltd.* v. *Johnson*, [1970] 3 All E.R. 639, at p. 641).

Given the existence of a civil right of action, the plaintiff must prove: (1) that he belongs to the class of persons whom the statute is designed to protect; (2) that the defendant was in breach of the duty; and (3) that the breach caused the damage. We have seen (section 4, *ante*) that this third question, the relationship between the breach and the resultant damage, raises questions of fault. The first two questions, particularly the second, may also do so. It all depends upon the precise wording of the statutory duty or, where the meaning is not clear, upon the judicial interpretation of those words.

Unfortunately, industrial safety legislation has grown up in a piecemeal fashion. There are nine main groups of statutes (controlling respectively factories, commercial premises, mining and quarrying, agriculture, explosives, petroleum, nuclear installations, radioactive substances, and alkali etc., works) supported by nearly 500 subordinate statutory instruments, which are added to each year. This mass of statute law comprises—in the words of the Robens Committee on Safety and Health at Work (Cmnd. 5034, 1972)—an "haphazard mass of ill-assorted and intricate detail." The various Acts and instruments show neither internal logic nor consistency with one another. The rate of technological change means that they are often out of date; and they are far from being comprehensive because, according to a Department of Employment estimate, something like 5 million of the 23 million workers in Britain are not subject to any occupational health and safety legislation. Those who are covered will find that some duties are strict (the word "absolute" is a misnomer) while others are based on a requirement of some degree of fault. The random distribution of duties between strict and not-so-strict duties depends upon "the accident of language" (Glanville Williams, (1960), 23 M.L.R. 233, at p. 243—the seminal article). This comment applies, as well, to the coverage of each duty.

An illustration is the situation where a worker is injured while away from his normal workplace, perhaps while visiting a part of his employer's premises where he has no business to be. If the workplace is a shipbuilding site, then, in most cases, the Shipbuilding Regulations expressly exclude any duty to the worker. The same applies to some construction sites to which the Construction (Working Places) Regs. apply. However, the Factories Act 1961, s. 14 (duty to fence dangerous machinery) and the Offices, Shops and Railway Premises Act 1963, s. 16, respectively, have been interpreted (in the absence of express provision) to apply to a worker who is in a part of the premises where he has been forbidden to go: *Uddin* v. *Associated Portland Cement Manufacturers, Ltd.*, [1965] 2 Q.B. 582; [1965] 2 All E.R. 213; *Westwood* v. *Post Office*, [1973] 3 All E.R. 184. One may legitimately ask why the right to compensation of shipbuilding and construction workers should differ from that of factory and office workers, given that all their employers are required by legislation (p. 676, *post*) to insure against their liability?

Some of the judicial interpretations can be explained in terms of a theory of statutory negligence, i.e. an intentional or negligent failure to comply with a statutory duty. An example of this is the interpretation placed by the House of Lords in *Brown* v. *National Coal Board*, [1962] A.C. 574; [1962] 1 All E.R. 81, upon section 48 of the Mines & Quarries Act 1954, which requires the mine manager to take "such steps . . . as may be necessary for keeping the road . . . secure." It was held that "secure" did not mean impregnable. It meant no more than a physical condition which would ordinarily result in safety. In the words of Lord Radcliffe (at p. 86): "It seems plain to me that if a manager's duty is to ask himself from time to time 'What steps are required now to keep the roadway secure?' he can only pose or answer that question in the light of the best obtainable information as to the circumstances, geophysical or otherwise, that he is to deal with and knowledge of skilled and up-to-date engineering science and practice. If he answers the question in those terms and acts accordingly, he cannot, in my view be said to be in breach of his duty, even though there is a state of insecurity or a roof fall." To the objection that this did no more than realise an owner's obligation at common law to avoid negligence, Lord Radcliffe (at p. 88) retorted that "the purpose . . . is to write out in black and white a code of definite specified acts that are to be done and precautions that are to be taken. That is a different and more compulsive method of securing the desired result than to leave particular obligations to be deduced from the general standard of negligence at common law."

Other interpretations have, however, imposed strict duties. An example is the interpretation placed by the House of Lords in *John Summers & Sons, Ltd.* v. *Frost*, [1955] A.C. 740; [1955] 1 All E.R. 870 upon s. 14 (1) of the Factories Act 1961, which requires "every dangerous part of any machinery" to be "securely fenced". A grindstone wheel moving at 1,450 revolutions per minute was held to be "dangerous", although the evidence showed that it would be impossible to provide a guard which would make the machine usable. Glanville Williams comments (*op. cit.*, p. 238): "it is hard to imagine that Parliament really intended when it passed . . . the Factories Act . . . that so common a machine as a grindstone should become unlawful, until such time as the Minister of Labour might bethink himself to make regulations [under section 14 (3)] to legalise it again." On the other hand, in *Close* v. *Steel Co. of Wales*, [1962] A.C. 367; [1962] 2 All E.R. 953 a high speed bit of an electric drill of the kind used in ordinary homes with up to 2,000 revolutions a minute was held not to be "dangerous". The reason given was that no serious injury had ever before been caused when one of these drills broke.

Having interpreted some duties as strict ones, the judges have then re-retreated from the consequences of their own interpretations by resorting to artificial distinctions in order to limit the scope of the particular duty. For example, in regard to section 14 (1) of the Factories Act 1961, it has been held that (a) since it is only *parts* of machinery which have to be fenced there is no obligation to fence a machine if it is dangerous as a *whole* but does not have dangerous parts (*British Railways Board* v. *Liptrot*, [1969] 1 A.C. 136, at p. 159); (b) a part of machinery does not include a workpiece moving under power and held in the machinery by a chuck, nor does it include materials in the machinery (*Eaves* v. *Morris Motors, Ltd.*, [1961] 2 Q.B. 385; [1961] 3 All E.R. 233); (c) the dangers against which fencing is required do not include dangers to be apprehended from the ejection of flying material from the machine even though this is a part of the machine itself (*Close* v. *Steel Co. of Wales, Ltd.*, *ante*); and (d) the worker is not protected if what comes into contact with the dangerous part of a machine is a hand tool operated by the workman as distinct from the worker's body or clothes (*Sparrow* v. *Fairey Aviation Co., Ltd.*, [1964] A.C. 1019; [1962] 3 All E.R. 706). (These and other examples were given by Lord Hailsham in *F.E. Callow (Engineers), Ltd.* v. *Johnson*, [1971] A.C. 335; [1970] 3 All E.R. 639.)

In view of interpretations like these one is bound to ask, with Glanville Williams (*op. cit.*), whether strict liability (which may improve the benefits received by some workers, but in a haphazard fashion) makes any sense in the light of the common law principle of fault and the machinery under the National Insurance (Industrial Injuries) Act 1965 (p. 695, *post*) whereby the injured worker can get state benefits irrespective of his employer's fault. Moreover, we have been told by the Robens Committee (above), paras. 130, 435 and Appendix 7, that the statutory interpretations in actions for breach of statutory duty have had an adverse effect on accident prevention. The Committee suggested a statutory formulation of general principles of industrial safety for the guidance of the courts, an annual review of defects in legislation exposed by case law, and an inquiry into the whole subject of compensation for accidents. The Health and Safety at Work Bill 1974, implementing the main proposals of the Robens Committee, however, keeps the existing actions for damages for breach of industrial safety legislation alive. This legislation is to be gradually replaced by new health and safety regulations; the Bill contains a presumption that breach of a duty imposed by these regulations is to be actionable so far as it causes death or personal injury, unless the regulations provide otherwise. The element of strict liability may, however, disappear because regulations may permit a defendant to show that he used "all due diligence" to prevent a breach.

9

Defences: Contributory Negligence and *volenti non fit injuria*

Although the question of causation has been considered in an earlier Chapter, it also plays an important role in the defence of contributory negligence, which, if successful, serves to reduce the plaintiff's damages. (See e.g. *Stapley* v. *Gypsum Mines, Ltd.*, [1953] A.C. 663; [1953] 2 All E.R. 478, p. 299, *post.*) As the phrase contributory negligence would imply, the plaintiff must not only have been negligent, but his negligence must have contributed to the damage which he has suffered, and in the absence of this causal connection, the plaintiff's damages will not be reduced. On the other hand, in certain situations, the plaintiff's negligence, occuring after the defendant's negligent act, may not only have contributed to some item of damage for which he is claiming compensation, but may be held to have gone so far as to sever the chain of causation between the defendant's act and this damage, with the result that the plaintiff recovers nothing for this particular item. The result here is achieved not by virtue of the defence of contributory negligence, but because there is no sufficient causal connection between the defendant's act and the damage—see *McKew* v. *Holland and Hannen and Cubitts (Scotland), Ltd.*, [1969] 3 All E.R. 1621, p. 185, *ante*; Winfield & Jolowicz, p. 105; M. A. Millner, *"Novus Actus Interveniens: The Present Effect of The Wagon Mound"* (1971), 22 N.I.L.Q. 168, at pp. 176–179.

Whereas the phrase contributory negligence gives some idea of the nature of that defence the maxim *volenti non fit injuria* needs a greater amount of explanation. In the sphere of intentional injuries this defence is to be found under the heading "Consent", p. 53, *post*, and see further Street, p. 74 (cf. contributory negligence, which it would appear does not provide a defence to intentional wrongdoing, at least so far as intended consequences are concerned —Glanville Williams, *Joint Torts and Contributory Negligence* (London, 1951), pp. 197–202 and p. 318, note 3.) In this Chapter the *volenti* maxim is considered as a defence to the unintentional infliction of injuries and, in this context, writers (e.g. Fleming) use the term "voluntary assumption of risk". One difficulty, though perhaps only an academic one, concerns the way in which the *volenti* maxim operates. Salmond (at p. 509) mentions one view—that there has been a breach of duty, which the plaintiff waives—but then states (in a passage which was quoted by John Stephenson J. in *Buckpitt* v. *Oates*, [1968] 1 All E.R. 1145, at p. 1148) that "the better view is that consent here means the agreement of the plaintiff, express or implied, to exempt the defendant from the duty of care which he would otherwise have owed". (See also R. W. M. Dias, "Consent of Parties and *Voluntas Legis*", [1966] C.L.J. 75, esp. at p. 79.)

Contributory negligence and *volenti non fit injuria* are separate defences, but they can both be pleaded as defences in the same action. If the *volenti* defence fails, damages may still be reduced for contributory negligence, and there are important differences between the two defences. These should become apparent from a consideration of the nature of the defences through a study of the materials in this Chapter. The most obvious is that the *volenti* maxim, if successful, provides a complete defence, but a successful plea of contributory negligence leads to a reduction of the damages by the court in accordance with the Law Reform (Contributory Negligence) Act 1945.

The contributory negligence defence must today be considered in the light of the Law Reform (Contributory Negligence) Act 1945. Statute plays a less important role in the *volenti* or assumption of risk doctrine, but it can, of course, intervene so as to negate the defence where it might otherwise apply e.g. s. 148 (3) of the Road Traffic Act 1972. In certain contexts, however, the doctrine has been enshrined in statutory form. Examples are provided by s. 2 (5) of the Occupiers' Liability Act 1957, p. 224, *ante* and by s. 5 (2) of the Animals Act 1971, p. 360, *post*, but see s. 6 (5) of that Act, p. 361, *post*. Finally, comparison should be made with specific cases of exclusion of liability, such as those contemplated by s. 2 (1) of the Occupiers' Liability Act 1957, p. 223 and pp. 235–239, *ante*.

1. CONTRIBUTORY NEGLIGENCE

(a) Before 1945

Note

At common law the rule was that a plaintiff who was contributorily negligent failed in his action (see e.g. *Butterfield* v. *Forrester* (1809), 11 East 60, but see the doctrine of "last opportunity", p. 299, *post*). In contrast to the position at common law the rule which developed in Admiralty was one of equal apportionment of a loss if a collision was caused by the negligence of both vessels, but this was altered by the Maritime Conventions Act 1911. For the history of the Admiralty rule, see Marsden, *The Law of Collisions at Sea* (11th Edn.) esp. Chap. 4; Gl. Williams, *op. cit.*, pp. 341–342.

The Maritime Conventions Act 1911

Rule as to division of loss.—(1) Where, by the fault of two or more vessels, damage or loss is caused to one or more of those vessels, to their cargoes or freight, or to any property on board, the liability to make good the damage or loss shall be in proportion to the degree in which each vessel was in fault:

Provided that—

(a) if, having regard to all the circumstances of the case, it is not possible to establish different degrees of fault, the liability shall be apportioned equally; and

(b) nothing in this section shall operate so as to render any vessel liable for any loss or damage to which her fault has not contributed; and

(c) nothing in this section shall affect the liability of any person under a contract of carriage or any contract, or shall be construed as imposing any liability upon any person from which he is exempted by any contract or by any provision of law, or as affecting the right of any person to limit his liability in the manner provided by law.

Admiralty Commissioners v. *Volute* (Owners), The *Volute*

House of Lords   [1921] All E.R. Rep. 193

There was a collision between the *Volute* (an oil tank ship) and the *Radstock*, one of two destroyers in charge of a convoy of which the *Volute* was a member. The Court of Appeal had held the *Radstock* to be alone to blame. However, there was an appeal, and the House of Lords held on the evidence that the *Volute* had been negligent in not giving a short blast on her whistle on altering her course. They also held the *Radstock* to blame for increasing her speed, shortly before the collision.

VISCOUNT BIRKENHEAD L.C.: . . . The matter, therefore, rests in this way. On the one hand, if the *Volute* had signalled or had postponed her porting unless and until she signalled there would have been no collision. On the other hand, if the *Radstock* had not gone full speed ahead after the position of danger brought about by the action of the *Volute*, there would have been no collision. In all cases of damage by collision on land or sea, there are three ways in which the question of contributory negligence may arise. A. is suing for damage thereby received. He was negligent, but his negligence had brought about a state of things in which there would have been no damage if B. had not been subsequently and severably negligent. A. recovers in full: see, among other cases, *Spaight* v. *Tedcastle*[1] and *The Margaret* (*Cayzer* v. *Carron Co.*).[2] At the other end of the chain, A.'s negligence makes collision so threatening that, though by the appropriate measure B. could avoid it, B. has not really time to think and by mistake takes the wrong measure. B. is not held to be guilty of any negligence and A. wholly fails: *The Bywell Castle*;[3] *Stoomvart Maatschappy Nederland* v. *Peninsula and Oriental Co.*[4] In between these two termini come the cases where the negligence is deemed contributory, and the plaintiff in common law recovers nothing [but now see Law Reform (Contributory Negligence) Act 1945, s. 1 (1)], while in Admiralty damages are divided in some proportion or other. Lord Blackburn, in *The Margaret*,[5] was of opinion that the area of this middle space was the same for Admiralty as for common law, and his opinion may be accepted subject to a possible qualification arising out of the subsequent passing of the Maritime Convention Act 1911. How, then, are its limits to be ascertained? Contributory negligence certainly arises when the negligence is contemporaneous, but are the only cases of contributory negligence cases where the negligence is contemporaneous? Is it to be the rule in all cases if the tribunal can find a period at which A.'s negligence has ceased and after which B.'s negligence has begun that then the negligence of A. is to be disregarded? If such should be the rule it will be found that the cases of contributory negligence would be few. If two roads intersect each other at right angles and there is a large building at the point of intersection, and two people are running or riding or driving at a reckless pace, one down each street, and meet at the corner, it would be easy to say that both were in fault and equally so. If the courses of two motor-cars cross and there is no rule of the road such as that at sea requiring one to give way and the other to keep her course and both hold on both are equally to blame. In *The Margaret*[5] a badly navigated barge came into collision with a schooner which was improperly carrying her anchor over her bows in a dangerous way contrary

---

1. (1881), 6 App. Cas. 217.
2. (1884), 9 App. Cas. 873.
3. (1879), 4 P.D. 219.
4. (1880), 5 App. Cas. 876.
5. (1881), 6 P.D. 76.

to the rule. An impact ensued which would have done no damage but for the fact that the fluke of the anchor knocked a hole in the barge. Sir Robert Phillimore put the whole blame on the badly navigated barge, but the Court of Appeal thought that, though the collision was solely due to her, the damage was due to both, and divided it. But even this class of case was varied by the subsequent decision of Gorell Barnes J. in *The Monte Rosa*,[1] where he distinguished *The Margaret*,[2] saying that the collision there occurred at night and the anchor could not be seen and held the badly navigated vessel alone to blame for the collision because those on board of her might have seen the dangerous position of the anchor.

It is very difficult, except in the cases just mentioned, to think of any cases where there is strictly synchronous negligence. And if that be the rule the application of the doctrine of contributory negligence to collisions, whether on land or sea, would be rare. Still rarer would be cases where the more minute calculations required by the Maritime Conventions Act could find place. . . .

Upon the whole I think that this question of contributory negligence must be dealt with somewhat broadly and upon common-sense principles as a jury would probably deal with it. While, no doubt, where a clear line can be drawn, the subsequent negligence is the only one to look to, there are cases in which the two acts come so closely together, and the second act of negligence is so much mixed up with the state of things brought about by the first act that the party secondly negligent, while not held free from blame under *The Bywell Castle*[3] rule, might, on the other hand, invoke the prior negligence as being part of the cause of the collision so as to make it a case of contribution. The Maritime Conventions Act with its provisions for nice qualifications as to the quantum of blame and the proportions in which contribution is to be made may be taken as to some extent declaratory of the Admiralty rule in this respect.

Your Lordships have now to apply these considerations of law to the facts of the present case. As already stated, if the *Volute* had not neglected to give the appropriate whistle signal when she ported there would have been no collision. On the other hand, if the *Radstock*, in the position of danger brought about by the action of the *Volute* had not gone full speed ahead, there would have been no collision. The case seems to me to resemble somewhat closely that of *The Hero*.[4] In that case, as in this, notwithstanding the negligent navigation of the first ship, the collision could have been avoided if proper action had been taken by the second ship. Indeed, that case is remarkable because the proper order was actually given, but unfortunately countermanded. In that case this House held both vessels to blame, apparently considering the acts of navigation on the two ships as forming parts of one transaction, and the second act of negligence as closely following upon and involved with the first. In the present case there does not seem to be a sufficient separation of time, place or circumstance between the negligent navigation of the *Radstock* and that of the *Volute* to make it right to treat the negligence on board the *Radstock* as the sole cause of the collision. The *Volute*, in the ordinary plain common sense of this business, having contributed to the accident, it would be right for your Lordships to hold both vessels to blame for the collision. Accordingly, I move your Lordships to reverse the order appealed from, and to pronounce the *Volute* partly to blame for the said collision, with the usual consequential directions. . . .

[VISCOUNT CAVE, VISCOUNT FINLAY, LORD SHAW and LORD PHILLIMORE concurred.]

Appeal allowed

Note

In *Marvin Sigurdson* v. *British Columbia Electric Rail. Co., Ltd.*, [1953] A.C. 291, (a post-1945 case) Lord Tucker, delivering judgment in the Privy Council,

1. [1893] P. 23.
2. (1881), 6 P.D. 76.
3. (1879), 4 P.D. 219.
4. [1912] A.C. 300.

referred to certain of the passages quoted above in Viscount Birkenhead's judgment in *The Volute* and (at p. 299) expressed the following opinion:

"This was an Admiralty case, but now that common law courts have to apply the same principles to cases of collisions on land it seems to their Lordships that this language will be found particularly suited to the exposition to a jury of the principles which they have to apply in these cases, and is much to be preferred to attempts to classify acts in relation to one another with reference to time or with regard to the knowledge of one party at a particular moment of the negligence of the other party and his appreciation of the resulting danger, and by such tests to create categories in some of which one party is solely liable and others in which both parties are liable. Time and knowledge may often be decisive factors, but it is for the jury or other tribunal of fact to decide whether in any particular case the existence of one of these factors results or does not result in the ascertainment of that clear line to which Viscount Birkenhead referred—moreover, their Lordships do not read him as intending to lay down that the existence of "subsequent" negligence will alone enable that clear line to be found."

(b) The defence since 1945

The Law Reform (Contributory Negligence) Act 1945

1. Apportionment of liability in case of contributory negligence.—(1) Where any person suffers damage as the result partly of his own fault and partly of the fault of any other person or persons, a claim in respect of that damage shall not be defeated by reason of the fault of the person suffering the damage, but the damages recoverable in respect thereof shall be reduced to such extent as the court thinks just and equitable having regard to the claimant's share in the responsibility for the damage:
Provided that—

(a) this subsection shall not operate to defeat any defence arising under a contract;

(b) where any contract or enactment providing for the limitation of liability is applicable to the claim, the amount of damages recoverable by the claimant by virtue of this subsection shall not exceed the maximum limit so applicable.

(2) Where damages are recoverable by any person by virtue of the foregoing subsection subject to such reduction as is therein mentioned, the court shall find and record the total damages which would have been recoverable if the claimant had not been at fault.

(3) Section six of the Law Reform (Married Women and Tortfeasors) Act, 1935 (which relates to proceedings against, and contribution between, joint and several tortfeasors), shall apply in any case where two or more persons are liable or would, if they had all been sued, be liable by virtue of subsection (1) of this section in respect of the damage suffered by any person.

(4) Where any person dies as the result partly of his own fault and partly of the fault of any other person or persons, and accordingly if an action were brought for the benefit of the estate under the Law Reform (Miscellaneous Provisions) Act, 1934, the damages recoverable would be reduced under subsection (1) of this section, any damages recoverable in an action brought for the benefit of the dependants of that person under the Fatal Accidents Act, 1846 to 1908, shall be reduced to a proportionate extent.

(5) Where, in any case to which subsection (1) of this section applies, one of the persons at fault avoids liability to any other such person or his personal representative by pleading the Limitation Act, 1939, or any other enactment limiting the time within which proceedings may be taken, he shall not be entitled to recover any damages or contributions from that other person or representative by virtue of the said subsection.

(6) Where any case to which subsection (1) of this section applies is tried with a jury, the jury shall determine the total damages which would have been recoverable if the claimant had not been at fault and the extent to which those damages are to be reduced.

3. Saving for Maritime Conventions Act, 1911, and past cases.—(1) This Act shall not apply to any claim to which section one of the Maritime Conventions Act, 1911, applies and that Act shall have effect as if this Act had not been passed. . . .

4. Interpretation.—The following expressions have the meanings hereby respectively assigned to them, that is to say—

"court" means, in relation to any claim, the court or arbitrator by or before whom the claim falls to be determined;

"damage" includes loss of life and personal injury;

"dependant" means any person for whose benefit an action could be brought under the Fatal Accidents Acts, 1846 to 1908;

. . . .

"fault" means negligence, breach of statutory duty or other act or omission which gives rise to a liability in tort or would, apart from this Act, give rise to the defence of contributory negligence.

Note

On the question whether the Act can apply in a contractual action, see the references on p. 188, *ante*.

Nance v. British Columbia Electric Railway Co., Ltd.

Judicial Committee of the   [1951] 2 All E.R. 448
Privy Council

VISCOUNT SIMON: . . . The statement that, when negligence is alleged as the basis of an actionable wrong, a necessary ingredient in the conception is the existence of a duty owed by the defendants to the plaintiff to take due care, is, of course, indubitably correct. But when contributory negligence is set up as a defence, its existence does not depend on any duty owed by the injured party to the party sued and all that is necessary to establish such a defence is to prove to the satisfaction of the jury that the injured party did not in his own interest take reasonable care of himself and contributed, by this want of care, to his own injury. For when contributory negligence is set up as a shield against the obligation to satisfy the whole of the plaintiff's claim, the principle involved is that, where a man is part author of his own injury, he cannot call on the other party to compensate him in full. . . .

Jones v. Livox Quarries, Ltd.

Court of Appeal   [1952] 2 Q.B. 608

The plaintiff, an employee of the defendants, stood contrary to his instructions on the back of a traxcavator, a vehicle which travelled at about two and a half m.p.h. The lunchtime whistle had gone, and the traxcavator was travelling along the route to the canteen. The driver gave evidence that he was not aware of the plaintiff's presence on the vehicle. Having driven the traxcavator round a stationary excavator and made a sharp left turn, the traxcavator was stopped (or nearly stopped) by the driver so that he could change gear. A dumper, travelling behind the traxcavator, collided with the back of that vehicle, injuring the plaintiff. Hallett J. found that the dumper driver had been negligent, but that the plaintiff had been contributorily negligent, and reduced his damages by one-fifth. There was an appeal by the plaintiff, and a cross-appeal by the defendants (the employers of the dumper driver) to the Court of Appeal.

DENNING L.J.: . . . The case of *Davies* v. *Swan Motor Co. (Swansea), Ltd.*[1] has been much discussed before us. It has been said that the three judgments in that case do not proceed on precisely the same lines. That is true, but it is, I suggest, quite understandable, because the court was there feeling its way in difficult country. Since that time, however, the ground has been cleared considerably. It can now be safely asserted that the doctrine of last opportunity[2] is obsolete; and also that contributory negligence does not depend on the existence of a duty. But the troublesome problem of causation still remains to be solved.

Although contributory negligence does not depend on a duty of care, it does depend on foreseeability. Just as actionable negligence requires the foreseeability of harm to others, so contributory negligence requires the foreseeability of harm to oneself. A person is guilty of contributory negligence if he ought reasonably to have foreseen that, if he did not act as a reasonable, prudent man, he might be hurt himself; and in his reckonings he must take into account the possibility of others being careless.

Once negligence is proved, then no matter whether it is actionable negligence or contributory negligence, the person who is guilty of it must bear his proper share of responsibility for the consequences. The consequences do not depend on foreseeability, but on causation. The question in every case is: What faults were there which caused the damage? Was his fault one of them? The necessity of causation is shown by the word "result" in s. 1 (1) of the Act of 1945, and it was accepted by this court in *Davies* v. *Swan Motor Co. (Swansea), Ltd.*[1]

There is no clear guidance to be found in the books about causation. All that can be said is that causes are different from the circumstances in which, or on which, they operate. The line between the two depends on the facts of each case. It is a matter of common sense more than anything else. In the present case, as the argument of Mr. Arthian Davies proceeded, it seemed to me that he sought to make foreseeability the decisive test of causation. He relied on the trial judge's statement that a man who rode on the towbar of the traxcavator "ran the risk of being thrown off and no other risk". That is, I think, equivalent to saying that such a man could reasonably foresee that he might be thrown off the traxcavator, but not that he might be crushed between it and another vehicle.

In my opinion, however, foreseeability is not the decisive test of causation. It is often a relevant factor, but it is not decisive. Even though the plaintiff did not foresee the possibility of being crushed, nevertheless in the ordinary plain common sense of this business the injury suffered by the plaintiff was due in part to the fact that he chose to ride on the towbar to lunch instead of walking down on his feet. If he had been thrown off in the collision, Mr. Arthian Davies admits that his injury would be partly due to his own negligence in riding on the towbar; but he says that, because he was crushed, and not thrown off, his injury is in no way due to it. That is too fine a distinction for me. I cannot believe that that purely fortuitous circumstance can make all the difference to the case. . . .

In order to illustrate this question of causation, I may say that if the plaintiff, whilst he was riding on the towbar, had been hit in the eye by a shot from a negligent sportsman, I should have thought that the plaintiff's negligence would in no way be a cause of his injury. It would only be the circumstance in which the cause operated. It would only be part of the history. But I cannot say that in the present case. The man's negligence here was so much mixed up with his injury that it cannot be dismissed as mere history. His dangerous position on the vehicle was one of the causes of his damage. . . .

The present case is a good illustration of the practical effect of the Act of 1945. In the course of the argument my Lord suggested that before the Act of 1945 he would have regarded this case as one where the plaintiff should recover in full. That would be because the negligence of the dumper driver would then have been regarded as the

---

1. [1949] 2 K.B. 291; [1949] 1 All E.R. 620.
2. [See note 2, p. 299, *post.*]

predominant cause. Now, since the Act, we have regard to all the causes, and one of them undoubtedly was the plaintiff's negligence in riding on the towbar of the traxcavator. His share in the responsibility was not great—the trial judge assessed it at one-fifth—but, nevertheless, it was his share, and he must bear it himself. . . .

It all comes to this: If a man carelessly rides on a vehicle in a dangerous position, and subsequently there is a collision in which his injuries are made worse by reason of his position than they otherwise would have been, then his damage is partly the result of his own fault, and the damages recoverable by him fall to be reduced accordingly.

[SINGLETON and HODSON L.JJ. delivered judgments in favour of dismissing the appeal and cross-appeal.]

Appeal and cross-appeal dismissed

Notes

1. In *Westwood* v. *Post Office*, [1973] 3 All E.R. 184, at p. 193, Lord Kilbrandon quoted the last clause of the second paragraph of Denning L.J.'s judgment above, but doubted its applicability where a court was concerned with a question of statutory liability, as opposed to a common law claim.

2. The effect of the complicated "last opportunity" doctrine (which in Denning L.J.'s opinion is obsolete) is explained by the following passage from Winfield & Jolowicz (p. 107—footnotes omitted):

"The common law rule produced hardship where one of the two negligent parties suffered the greater loss although his negligence was not the major cause of the accident. Accordingly, the courts modified the defence of contributory negligence by the so-called rule of last opportunity. This enabled the plaintiff to recover notwithstanding his own negligence, if upon the occasion of the accident the defendant could have avoided the accident while the plaintiff could not. The authorities were confused, and confusion was made worse confounded by the extension of the rule, in *British Columbia Electric Rail. Co.* v. *Loach*, [1916] 1 A.C. 719, to cases of 'constructive last opportunity'. This meant that if the defendant would have had the last opportunity but for his own negligence, he was in the same position as if he had actually had it, and the plaintiff again recovered in full."

For further reading on this topic, see Gl. Williams, *op. cit.* Chap. 9 and s. 66. Salmond, pp. 524–527 and 538–541; A. L. Goodhart, "The 'Last Opportunity' Rule" (1949), 65 L.Q.R. 237. As Winfield & Jolowicz point out (at p. 113, note 62) the rule at the present time would appear "to have been mercifully forgotten". See further *Rouse* v. *Squires*, [1973] Q.B. 889; [1973] 2 All E.R. 903.

Stapley v. Gypsum Mines, Ltd.

House of Lords   [1953] 2 All E.R. 478

Appeal from an order of the Court of Appeal (Singleton, Birkett and Morris L.JJ.), dated 7 April 1952, and reported, [1952] 1 All E.R. 1092, reversing an order of Sellers J., dated 20 December 1951.

The appellant, the widow of a miner employed in the respondents' gypsum mine, claimed damages against the respondents . . . in respect of the death of her husband which was caused by the fall of the roof of a stope in which he was working. The deceased and a fellow workman had been charged by the respondents with the duty of bringing down the roof so as to make the stope safe to work in, but they had failed to do so, and the deceased had gone to work in the stope. The learned judge found in favour of the appellant on the ground that the respondents were liable for the negligence or breach of statutory duty of the workman who was working with the deceased, but he deducted one half of the award which he would otherwise have made, as he held that the deceased was partly to blame for the accident. On an appeal by the respondents and cross-appeal by the appellant, the Court of Appeal held that the deceased's own negligence and breach of statutory duty, and not that of the respondents, was the substantial cause of the deceased's death, and, accordingly, they allowed the appeal and dismissed the cross-appeal.

LORD REID: My Lords, in the respondents' mines the workings are driven at right angles away from the main haulage way. The actual working place is the stope and the part between it and the haulage way is the twitten. The miners all work in pairs, one being the borer and the other the breaker. There is no sharp demarcation between their work and neither can give orders to the other, though the borer appears to be the senior man. Before the accident Stapley and Dale were working together, Stapley being the breaker. He was a steady workman with long experience, but rather slow. He had for a time been a borer but had reverted to being a breaker. A well recognised danger in the mine is a fall of part of the roof. The roof is not generally shored up as any weakness in it can be detected by tapping it. If it is "drummy", giving a hollow sound, it is unsafe and must be taken down. There are three ways of doing this—with a pick, or with a pinch bar or crow bar, or by firing a shot. Whichever way is adopted, of course, men doing the necessary work must not stand immediately below the dangerous part of the roof. One morning when Stapley and Dale arrived at their stope they tested the roof and found it to be drummy. They saw the foreman, Church, about it and he ordered them to fetch it down. They all knew that that meant that no one was to work under the roof before it had come down. Church did not say which method was to be adopted. Both men were accustomed to this work and the method was properly left to their discretion. They used picks, but after half an hour had made no impression. The work was awkwardly placed as a fault ran across the mouth of the stope, the floor and roof inside being about eighteen inches higher than outside it. Probably they could not use a pinch bar, but they could easily have prepared the place for firing a shot and sent for the shot-firer. Instead, according to Dale whose evidence was accepted, they agreed that the roof was safe enough for them to resume their ordinary work, and did so. There was a quantity of gypsum lying in the stope and if the roof had been safe their first task would have been to get this to the haulage way. To do that, Stapley had to enter the stope and break the gypsum into smaller pieces and Dale had to make preparations in the twitten. So they separated, and when Dale came back half an hour later he found Stapley lying dead in the stope under a large piece of the roof which had fallen on him.

There is no doubt that if these men had obeyed their orders the accident would not have happened. Both acted in breach of orders and in breach of safety regulations, and both ought to have known quite well that it was dangerous for Stapley to enter the stope. The present action against the respondents is chiefly based on Dale's fault having contributed to the accident, and on the respondents being responsible for it, the defence of common employment being no longer available. So it is necessary to consider what would have happened if Dale had done his duty. It was his duty either to try a pinch bar or to start boring holes for the shot-firer, and on the evidence I think that it is highly probable that, if he had insisted on doing that instead of agreeing with Stapley to neglect their orders and the regulations, Stapley would not have stood out against him or tried to resume his ordinary work. Stapley had nothing to gain from his disobedience, and, if he had not found Dale in agreement with him, it appears to me unlikely that he would have persisted. But if he had persisted and thereby prevented Dale from carrying out his orders—because Dale could not have worked at the roof if Stapley had persisted in going below it—then it was Dale's duty to go for the foreman, as he, Dale, could not give orders to Stapley. We do not know how soon the roof fell or how long it would have taken Dale to find and bring the foreman, but it is, at least, quite likely that the foreman would have arrived in time to prevent the accident. If Dale's failure did contribute to the accident, then I do not see on what ground the respondents can escape liability in respect of that failure.

In these circumstances it is necessary to determine what caused the death of Stapley. If it was caused solely by his own fault, then the appellant cannot succeed. But if it was caused partly by his own fault and partly by the fault of Dale, then the appellant can rely on the Law Reform (Contributory Negligence) Act 1945. To determine what caused an accident from the point of view of legal liability is a most difficult task. If there is any valid logical or scientific theory of causation, it is quite irrelevant in this connection. In a court of law, this question must be decided as a properly instructed and reasonable jury would decide it. . . . The question must be determined by applying common sense to the facts of each particular case. One may find that, as a matter of history, several people have been at fault and that if any one of them had acted properly the accident would not have happened, but that does not mean that the accident must be regarded as having been caused by the faults of all of them. One must discriminate between those faults which must be discarded as being too remote and those which must not. Sometimes it is proper to discard all but one and to regard that one as the sole cause, but in other cases it is proper to regard two or more as having jointly caused the accident. I doubt whether any test can be applied generally. It may often be dangerous to apply to this kind of case tests which have been used in traffic accidents by land or sea, but in this case I think it useful to adopt phrases from the speech of Viscount Birkenhead L.C. ([1922] 1 A.C. 129, pp. 144, 145) in *Admiralty Comrs.* v. *S.S. Volute*, and to ask: Was Dale's fault "so much mixed up with the state of things brought about" by Stapley that "in the ordinary plain common sense of this business" it must be regarded as having contributed to the accident? I can only say that I think it was and that there was no "sufficient separation of time, place or circumstance" between them to justify its being excluded. Dale's fault was one of omission rather than commission and it may often be impossible to say that, if a man had done what he omitted to do, the accident would certainly have been prevented. It is enough, in my judgment, if there is a sufficiently high degree of probability that the accident would have been prevented. I have already stated my view of the probabilities in this case and I think that it must lead to the conclusion that Dale's fault ought to be regarded as having contributed to the accident.

Finally, it is necessary to apply the Law Reform (Contributory Negligence) Act 1945. Sellers J. reduced the damages by one half holding both parties equally to blame. Normally one would not disturb such an award, but Sellers J. does not appear to have taken into account the fact that Stapley deliberately and culpably entered the stope. By doing so, it appears to me that he contributed to the accident much more directly than Dale. Section 1 (1) of the Act directs that the damages

". . . shall be reduced to such extent as the court thinks just and equitable having regard to the claimant's share in the responsibility for the damage."

A court must deal broadly with the problem of apportionment, and, in considering what is just and equitable, must have regard to the blameworthiness of each party, but "the claimant's share in the responsibility for the damage" cannot, I think, be assessed without considering the relative importance of his acts in causing the damage apart from his blameworthiness. It may be that in this case Dale was not much less to blame than Stapley, but Stapley's conduct in entering the stope contributed more immediately to the accident than anything that Dale did or failed to do. I agree with your Lordships that in all the circumstances it is proper in this case to reduce the damages by eighty per cent. and to award twenty per cent. of the damages to the appellant. I have not dealt with the question whether, at the time of the accident, the respondents were in breach of reg. 7 (3) of the Metalliferous Mines General Regulations 1938, because, whichever way that question was decided, it would not in this case affect my view as to the amount by which the damages should be reduced.

[LORD TUCKER and LORD OAKSEY delivered speeches in favour of allowing the appeal.

LORD PORTER and LORD ASQUITH OF BISHOPSTONE delivered speeches in favour of dismissing the appeal.]

Appeal allowed

Pasternack v. Poulton

Queen's Bench Division   [1973] 2 All E.R. 74

The plaintiff, who had been at a party, accepted a lift home late at night in the defendant's car. The car was fitted with seat belts, but the plaintiff was not aware of this, and the defendant did not wear his seat belt. On the journey the car hit a lamp-post, and the plaintiff was injured. The defendant's counsel admitted that the defendant had driven negligently, but, in the plaintiff's action for damages, the question of contributory negligence was raised. Evidence was given by Mr. Smith, a statistician, that, in the learned judge's words, "the wearing of seat belts minimised or decreased the risk of injury to some extent irrespective of whether the car was being driven in a built-up area or outside a built-up area".

JUDGE KENNETH JONES Q.C.: . . . The first, and major problem here, arises from the determination whether this plaintiff was guilty of contributory negligence. . . . I must ask the question, was the damage which the plaintiff suffered in this accident caused partly as a result of her own fault, i.e. as a result of her failure to exercise reasonable care for her own safety? It is to be borne in mind that in this case I am called on to deal with a safety device, namely a seat belt, and to consider the plaintiff's failure to use it.

In connection with safety devices, the exercise of reasonable care for one's own safety involves an appreciation or assessment, first of the risk of injury and secondly of the availability and effectiveness of the safety device. As to the risk of injury to the plaintiff here, I am assisted by the decision of the Court of Appeal in *O'Connell* v. *Jackson*.[1] In that case the court was dealing with the driver of a moped driving on a major road in a busy traffic area, and was called on to decide whether or not he ought reasonably to have foreseen the possibility of his being involved in an accident, even though he drove with the greatest care, and the court decided in the circumstances of that case that he ought reasonably to have foreseen the possibility of his being involved in an accident and that he could not rely on other users of the road to exercise reasonable care.

In this case the journey took place at about 1 a.m., at a time when traffic would be expected to be light. It was to lie through the built-up area in or adjacent to the centre of a large city. The journey was to be carried out in this rather old, small car, driven by a fellow student. I can only say that in all the circumstances of this case, in my view the plaintiff ought reasonably to have foreseen the possibility of this car being involved in an accident, either through a want of care on the part of the driver over whom she had no control, or because of some want of care on the part of some other user of the road. I also bear in mind that the extent of the risk of injury has always to be measured in relation to the safety device itself. A seat belt is something which can be easily and quickly put on and worn. Therefore, in my judgment, a reasonable man, in deciding whether or not to use that safety device, would take account of even a comparatively small risk of an accident taking place. In my event I repeat that I have come to the conclusion in this case, that the plaintiff ought, reasonably, to have foreseen the possibility of being involved in an accident and, of course, of suffering injury as a result of such an accident.

I turn to deal with the other assessment which a reasonably prudent passenger must make. First of all, there is the question of the availability to the plaintiff herself of the seat belt. Whether or not that was available to her or provided for her as is alleged in the amended defence must depend on the fitting of the seat belt in the car, on the plaintiff's knowledge of seat belts generally, and of her knowledge or means of knowledge of the

---

1. [1972] 1 Q.B. 270; [1971] 3 All E.R. 129.

existence of the seat belts in this particular car. In this car the seat belt was fitted in an entirely normal position. It was hanging from the post of the car, easily visible in day-light and even if not easily visible at night it needed only the simplest gesture on the part of the passenger, the simplest movement of her hand, to discover whether it was there or not. She knew about seat belts and had often used them herself. I appreciate and I accept that on this particular occasion she did not know that this car was fitted with seat belts and I accept as being wholly in accordance with the probabilities for young people after a party late at night, that she never addressed her mind to the question whether this car had seat belts or not. But in my judgment that is not good enough. She could easily have found out whether the car was fitted with seat belts. If she had done so she would have found the seat belt there available for her use. In my judgment she ought to have known that the seat belt was available.

I turn finally to perhaps the most hotly contested part of this case which deals with the effectiveness of the seat belt as a safety device. The test I can take again from *O'Connell's* case[1] to which I have already referred. In that case the court was dealing with the wearing of a crash helmet and Edmund Davies L.J. set out the test which was applicable in these words:[2]

> "But ought he also to have been mindful of the possibility that were he, riding his moped, involved in an accident, he could well sustain greater hurt if he failed to wear a crash helmet?"

It follows that the test in this case is this: ought the plaintiff to have been mindful of the possibility that, were the car involved in an accident, she could well sustain greater hurt if she failed to wear a seat belt? I observe first of all that, of course, the test must be applied to the plaintiff herself. In *Geier* v. *Kujawa*[3] Brabin J., faced with a very similar problem, held that it had not been shown that the passenger was guilty of contributory negligence because of the peculiar position of the plaintiff herself who was a German girl who had never before seen seat belts and indeed the occasion under review in that case was the first occasion on which she had ever seen a seat belt.

Next, was there a possibility that this plaintiff could well have sustained greater hurt if she failed to wear a seat belt or, put the other way, was there a possibility that she would suffer considerably substantially less hurt if she wore a seat belt? Times change, knowledge of the effectiveness of safety devices increases with the passage of time and in my judgment it is very important that the court should approach this problem, not in any way as an academic exercise, but against the known realities of conditions on our roads today and taking full account of the development and increase with time of the knowledge of the part which seat belts play in reducing injuries or the likelihood of injuries in the course of accidents. I have been referred to *MacDonnell* v. *Kaiser*,[4] where in April 1968 Dubinsky J., sitting in the Nova Scotia Supreme Court, observed that his reading on the subject convinced him that the effectiveness of seat belts was still in the realm of speculation and controversy. Such may have been the position in 1968, but, as Brabin J. observed in *Geier's* case,[3] it is quite clear that factors which might or might not arise in the appropriate cases in respect of the failure to use a seat belt in recent times, that is in 1970, would not be the same as the failure to use seat belts in 1964 which was the date to which he was referring in that case. I am fully prepared to acknowledge that circumstances at the time of this accident in 1971, the factors influencing the advisability of using seat belts might very well be different and were different from what they had been or might have been in 1968 or even earlier in 1964. What then was the position in 1971? First of all, my attention has been directed to the Highway Code itself which was available at the time of this accident, at para. 23, under the part headed "The road user on wheels", there appears this injunction: "Fit seat belts in your car and

---

1. [1972] 1 Q.B. 270; [1971] 3 All E.R. 129.
2. [1972] 1 Q.B. at p. 275; [1971] 3 All E.R. at p. 131.
3. [1970] 1 Lloyd's Rep. 364.
4. (1968), 68 D.L.R. (2d) 104.

see that they are always used, even on short trips." Again the proper approach for a court to the Highway Code, was given in *O'Connell's* case[1] and I need only read from the headnote where it says:[2]

"That the Highway Code was declaratory of sensible practice generally accepted by road users, and to rely upon it in accordance with section 74 of the Road Traffic Act 1960 the defendant did not have to show that the latest edition was available to the plaintiff, or that the plaintiff had actually read it."

So, looked at in that way, the Highway Code at the relevant time declared that the sensible practice, generally accepted by road users, was for the occupants of the car (i.e. by those using the road on wheels) to use seat belts, even on short trips. That was confirmed from his experience by the police officer.[3] As counsel for the defendant pointed out, it was accepted by the plaintiff herself that it was sensible to wear seat belts. I also have the evidence given by Mr. Smith, the statistician, as to the substantial effect in mitigating injury which seat belts have.

On all this evidence I am satisfied, not only that on this occasion the real possibility was that by wearing a seat belt the plaintiff would suffer no, or certainly less, injury if the car were involved in an accident, but also that she, acting reasonably, would have foreseen that possibility. It follows that I find on the facts of this case that this plaintiff was guilty of contributory negligence.

The next matter of which I must be satisfied is that that contributory negligence caused, at least to some extent, the injury which she suffered. It is obvious that in many cases the precise connection between the failure to wear a seat belt and the injuries suffered may be very difficult indeed to determine. It may sometimes happen, as it did in *O'Connell's* case,[1] that the court comes to the conclusion that such a causative connection existed in respect of some of the injuries but not in respect of others. But this is a case where I am driven to the conclusion that this young woman's injuries were caused by her face coming into contact with, either the windscreen or at least with some part of the car which was in front of her and against which she was thrown by her own momentum when the car came into head-on collision with the lamp post.

There remains the question whether the use of the seat belt would have prevented or mitigated those injuries. This is a point which has been argued with great clarity and force by counsel for the plaintiff. I am afraid I cannot accept the arguments which he put forward. In my judgment the application of common sense satisfies me that there was here the clearest connection between her failure to wear a seat belt and the injury which she suffered.

There remains for me to consider the conduct of the defendant himself. . . .

In my judgment the duty to take reasonable care for her safety which he owed to the plaintiff in this case involved not merely a duty to drive and to control the car itself with reasonable care and skill but also involved the taking of some step directed to seeing that the plaintiff wore the seat belt which was fitted to the car. What steps the driver must take must depend on all the facts of the case but in this case, at the very least, the duty of care which the defendant owed to the plaintiff involved either demonstrating the existence of and the need for the use of a safety belt by simply wearing his own, or at least pointing out to the plaintiff the existence of the seat belt and explaining to her in only a very few words that it was there for her to use. He did neither. He did, as he frankly confessed, nothing in relation to the wearing of seat belts either by himself or by his passengers. In my judgment in so conducting himself he was negligent.

I therefore come to deal with the question of apportionment. It is abundantly obvious that by far the greater share of blame for this accident must be borne by the defendant because it was his carelessness in connection with his driving which caused the accident.

---

1. [1972] 1 Q.B. 270; [1971] 3 All E.R. 129.
2. [1972] 1 Q.B. at p. 271.
3. [I.e. the police officer who had given evidence in the case.]

Also, the share of blame which would fall on a plaintiff driving the car and found to blame only in respect of his failure to wear a seat belt would obviously be greater than would be just and appropriate for the plaintiff in this case.

Again, looked at from the point of view of the defendant, his want of care operated not merely in the field of controlling and driving the car, but also in the field of the failure to wear a seat belt, i.e. in the very same field as that in which the plaintiff's want of care alone had effect. I have, therefore, come to the conclusion that as I indicated at an earlier stage of this case, the proportion of blame which should be attributed to the plaintiff here should be very small indeed and I assess it at 5 per cent.

Judgment for the plaintiff, with the damages to be assessed and reduced by 5 per cent.

Question

Suppose a plaintiff who failed to wear a seat belt which was available was badly injured when thrown from a car in a collision caused by the defendant's negligence. What would be the position if it could be shown that the car in which he was travelling caught fire and that he would have been seriously burnt if he had not been thrown from the car?

Notes

1. In *O'Connell* v. *Jackson*, [1972] 1 Q.B. 270; [1971] 3 All E.R. 129, which is referred to in the case above, the Court of Appeal reduced a moped rider's damages by 15% because he did not wear a crash-helmet. If he had done so, his injuries would probably have been less serious. In the course of the judgment, one point was raised which could equally well have applied in *Pasternack* v. *Poulton*—that the failure to wear a crash-helmet [safety belt] did not contribute to the occurrence of the collision, but merely affected the type or severity of the injuries received in the collision. The court pointed out (at p. 130) that in fact "counsel for the plaintiff did not contest that if, as a result of his contributory negligence, a plaintiff suffers greater injury than he would otherwise have sustained, his entitlement to compensation should reflect that fact. In our judgment, counsel for the plaintiff was right in not challenging that proposition". The Court of Appeal laid particular emphasis on the word "damage" in s. 1 (1) of the Law Reform (Contributory Negligence) Act 1945, the word being defined by s. 4 so as to include loss of life and personal injury. For comment on this decision, see notes by J. R. Spencer, [1972A] C.L.J. 27–29, and by Brenda Barrett (1972), 35 M.L.R. 525. It is now compulsory to wear protective headgear whilst riding a motor cycle—The Motor Cycles (Wearing of Helments) Regulations 1973, S.I. 1973 No. 180, made under s. 32 of the Road Traffic Act 1972. See further the Road Traffic Bill 1974, cl. 7.

2. There have been several "seat belt" cases in the Commonwealth in recent years—see the Annual Survey of Commonwealth Law. See generally C. S. Kerse, (1973), 117 Sol. Jo. 45 and 625 and see p. 731, *post.*

3. Reference was made to the Highway Code in *Pasternack* v. *Poulton.* Section 37 (5) of the Road Traffic Act 1972, re-enacting s. 74 (5) of the Road Traffic Act 1960, provides:

> "A failure on the part of a person to observe a provision of the Highway Code shall not of itself render that person liable to criminal proceedings of any kind, but any such failure may in any proceedings (whether civil or criminal . . . .) be relied upon by any party to the proceedings as tending to establish or to negative any liability which is in question in those proceedings."

In *Powell* v. *Phillips*, [1972] 3 All E.R. 864, Stephenson L.J. expressed the view (at p. 868) that a breach of the Code "creates no presumption of negligence calling for an explanation, still less a presumption of negligence making a real contribution to causing an accident or injury. The breach is just one of the circumstances on which one party is entitled to rely in establishing the negligence of the other and its contribution to causing the accident or injury". See also *Kerley* v. *Downes*, [1973] R.T.R. 188; *Parkinson* v. *Parkinson* (Note), [1973] R.T.R. 193.

(c) Emergencies

Jones v. Boyce

Nisi Prius   (1816), 1 Stark. 493

This was an action on the case against the defendant, a coach proprietor, for so negligently conducting the coach, that the plaintiff, an outside passenger, was obliged to jump off the coach, in consequence of which his leg was broken.

It appeared that soon after the coach had set off from an inn, the coupling rein broke, and one of the leaders being ungovernable, whilst the coach was on a descent, the coachman drew the coach to one side of the road, where it came in contact with some piles, one of which it broke, and afterwards the wheel was stopped by a post. Evidence was adduced to shew that the coupling rein was defective, and that the breaking of the rein had rendered it necessary for the coachman to drive to the side of the road in order to stop the career of the horses. Some of the witnesses stated that the wheel was forced against the post with great violence; and one of the witnesses stated, that at that time the plaintiff, who had before been seated on the back part of the coach, was jerked forwards in consequence of the concussion, and that one of the wheels was elevated to the height of eighteen or twenty inches; but whether the plaintiff jumped off, or was jerked off, he could not say. A witness also said, I should have jumped down had I been in his (the plaintiff's) place, as the best means of avoiding the danger. The coach was not overturned, but the plaintiff was immediately afterwards seen lying on the road with his leg broken, the bone having been protruded through the boot.

Upon this evidence, Lord Ellenborough was of opinion, that there was a case to go to the jury, and a considerable mass of evidence was then adduced, tending to shew that there was no necessity for the plaintiff to jump off.

LORD ELLENBOROUGH, in his address to the jury, said,—This case presents two questions for your consideration; first, whether the proprietor of the coach was guilty of any default in omitting to provide the safe and proper means of conveyance, and if you should be of that opinion, the second question for your consideration will be, whether that default was conducive to the injury which the plaintiff has sustained; for if it was not so far conducive as to create such a reasonable degree of alarm and apprehension in the mind of the plaintiff, as rendered it necessary for him to jump down from the coach in order to avoid immediate danger, the action is not maintainable. To enable the plaintiff to sustain the action, it is not necessary that he should have been thrown off the coach; it is sufficient if he was placed by the misconduct of the defendant in such a situation as obliged him to adopt the alternative of a dangerous leap, or to remain at certain peril; if that position was occasioned by the default of the defendant, the action may be supported. On the other hand, if the plaintiff's act resulted from a rash apprehension of danger, which did not exist, and the injury which he sustained is to be attributed to rashness and imprudence, he is not entitled to recover. The question is, whether he was placed in such a situation as to render what he did a prudent precaution, for the purpose of self-preservation.—His Lordship, after recapitulating the facts, and commenting upon them, and particularly on the circumstance of the rein being defective, added:—If the defect in the rein was not the constituent cause of the injury, the plaintiff will not be entitled to your verdict. Therefore it is for your consideration, whether the plaintiff's act was the measure of an unreasonably alarmed mind, or such as a reasonable and prudent mind would have adopted. If I place a man in such a situation that he must adopt a perilous alternative, I am responsible for the consequences; if, therefore, you should be of opinion, that the reins were defective, did this circumstance create a necessity for what he did, and did he use proper caution and prudence in extricating himself from the apparently impending peril. If you are of that opinion, then, since the original fault was in the proprietor, he is liable to the plaintiff for the injury which his misconduct has occasioned. This is the first case of the kind which I recollect to have occurred. A coach proprietor certainly is not to be responsible for the rashness and imprudence of a passenger; it must appear that there existed a reasonable cause for alarm.

The jury found a verdict for the plaintiff. Damages £300.

(d) Infants

Gough v. Thorne

Court of Appeal   [1966] 3 All E.R. 398

LORD DENNING M.R.: On 13 June 1962, a group of children were crossing the New Kings Road, Chelsea, London. They were Malcolm Gough, who was seventeen; his brother John, who was ten; and his sister Elizabeth, the plaintiff, who was 13½. They were coming from the Wandsworth Bridge Road, crossing the New Kings Road, and going to a swimming pool on the other side. They waited on the pavement for some little time to see if it was safe to cross. Then a lorry came up, coming up the Wandsworth Bridge Road and turning left into the New Kings Road. The lorry driver had got pretty well half-way across the road, towards the bollards, and he stopped at about five feet from the bollards. He put his right hand out to warn the traffic which was coming up the road. He saw the children waiting; he beckoned to them to cross; and they did. They had got across just beyond the lorry when a "bubble" car, driven by the defendant, came through the gap between the front of the lorry and the bollard, about five feet, just missed the eldest boy, and struck the young boy of ten, but ran into and seriously injured the plaintiff, Elizabeth, aged 13½. Now, on the plaintiff's behalf, there is a claim against the driver of the "bubble" car for negligence.

The judge has found that the defendant driver was negligent. He said that the "bubble" car was going too fast in the circumstances, and that the driver did not keep a proper look-out because he ought to have seen the lorry driver's signal and he did not see it. He found, therefore, that the defendant, the driver of the "bubble" car, was to blame and negligent. Then there came the question whether the little girl, the plaintiff, was herself guilty of contributory negligence. As to that, the judge found that she was one-third to blame for this accident. I will read what the judge said about it. "Was there contributory negligence?", he asked. He answered:

> "I think that there was. I think that the plaintiff was careless in advancing past the lorry into the open road without pausing to see whether there was any traffic coming from her right. I do not think that her responsibility was very great. After all, the lorry driver had beckoned her on. She might have thought it unlikely that any traffic would try to come through the gap. She might have thought that if there were any traffic coming from that direction, it would wait until the lorry started to move or gave the all clear. She was, after all, only thirteen years old. I assess her degree of responsibility at one-third."

I am afraid that I cannot agree with the judge. A very young child cannot be guilty of contributory negligence. An older child may be; but it depends on the circumstances. A judge should only find a child guilty of contributory negligence if he or she is of such an age as reasonably to be expected to take precautions for his or her own safety: and then he or she is only to be found guilty if blame should be attached to him or her. A child has not the road sense or the experience of his or her elders. He or she is not to be found guilty unless he or she is blameworthy.

In this particular case I have no doubt that there was no blameworthiness to be attributed to the plaintiff at all. Here she was with her elder brother crossing a road. They had been beckoned on by the lorry driver. What more could you expect the child to do than to cross in pursuance of the beckoning? It is said by the judge that she ought to have leant forward and looked to see whether anything was coming. That indeed might be reasonably expected of a grown-up person with a fully developed road sense, but not of a child of $13\frac{1}{2}$.

I am clearly of opinion that the judge was wrong in attributing any contributory negligence to the plaintiff, aged $13\frac{1}{2}$; and I would allow the appeal accordingly.

SALMON L.J.: . . . The question as to whether the plaintiff can be said to have been guilty of contributory negligence depends on whether any ordinary child of $13\frac{1}{2}$ could be expected to have done any more than this child did. I say, "any ordinary child". I do not mean a paragon of prudence; nor do I mean a scatter-brained child; but the ordinary girl of $13\frac{1}{2}$. . . .

[DANCKWERTS L.J. delivered a brief judgment in favour of allowing the appeal, and agreed in particular with LORD DENNING's observations on contributory negligence.]

Appeal allowed

Questions

1. If a young child, who wandered on to the road but who was found not to have been contributorily negligent because of his age, is injured by a negligent motorist, how might the motorist cut down the amount of damages he (or his insurance company) has to pay? (See D. J. Gibson-Watt, (1972), 122 N.L.J. 280 and see pp. 105–106, *ante*.)

2. If a 12 year old plaintiff was found to have a mental age of 15 years, by what standard should the child be judged in deciding whether he has been contributorily negligent?

Notes

1. Compare the position where an infant is the defendant, pp. 149–152, *ante*.

2. The position in tort should not be confused with that in criminal law, where a child below the age of 10 cannot be liable for a crime, whatever mental element that crime might require. (See Smith and Hogan, *Criminal Law* (3rd Edn.) pp. 127–128.)

3. Lord Denning M.R. states in *Gough* v. *Thorne* that a very young child cannot be contributorily negligent. Of course, in the case of extremely young children, it may seem obvious that this is so, but several of the leading textbooks take the view that in fact there is no age below which it can be said, as a matter of law, that a finding of contributory negligence cannot be made against a child— Charlesworth, *Negligence*, para. 1033; Clerk and Lindsell, para. 989; Winfield and Jolowicz, p. 111. This view (as stated in Charlesworth) was accepted in *Speirs* v. *Gorman*, [1966] N.Z.L.R. 897.

(e) Workmen

Caswell *v.* Powell Duffryn Associated Collieries, Ltd., *post*

(f) Apportionment of damages

Stapley *v.* Gypsum Mines, Ltd., p. 299, *ante*

Notes

1. See also *Mullard* v. *Ben Line Steamers, Ltd.,* [1971] 2 All E.R. 424, noted p. 311, *post.* See generally A. I. Ogus, *The Law of Damages,* pp. 103–107; D. Payne, "Reduction of Damages for Contributory Negligence" (1955), 18 M.L.R. 344.

2. For "sub-apportionment", see *The Calliope,* [1970] P. 172; [1970] 1 All E.R. 624.

(g) Application to breach of statutory duty

Caswell *v.* Powell Duffryn Associated Collieries, Ltd.

House of Lords   [1939] 3 All E.R. 722

Arthur Caswell, an employee of the respondents, was killed in their mine, and his mother sued for damages alleging breach of statutory duty (s. 55 of the Coal Mines Act 1911, which related to the fencing of machinery).

LORD ATKIN: . . . Though I have come to the conclusion that in this case the defendants failed to prove negligence on the part of the deceased workman, I feel bound to say something on the topic, which was much discussed in argument, whether contributory negligence is ever a defence to an action based upon a breach of a statutory duty, or, more narrowly, based upon a breach of a statutory duty to protect workmen and others imposed by such Acts as the Factory Acts, Mining Acts, etc. Authority for the proposition that contributory negligence in the ordinary sense is not a defence to such an action is to be found in the judgment of the High Court of Australia in *Bourke* v. *Butterfield and Lewis, Ltd.*[1] The argument is that safety[2] obligations are placed upon employers for the purpose of protecting not only workmen who are careful but also those who are careless: and that the object of the legislature is defeated if the right to sue for injuries caused by the breach of the safety regulations is denied to the careless workman for whose benefit amongst others the legislation was specially enacted. I venture to think that this attractive theory does not give sufficient weight to the true cause of action in such cases. The statute does not in terms create a statutory cause of action. It does not, for instance, make the employer an insurer. The person who is injured, as in all cases where damage is the gist of the action, must show not only a breach of duty but that his hurt was due to the breach. If his damage is due entirely to his own wilful act no cause of action arises as, for instance, if out of bravado he puts his hand into moving machinery or attempts to leap over an unguarded cavity. The injury has not been caused by the defendants' omission but by the plaintiff's own act. The injury may, however, be the result of two causes operating at the same time, a breach of duty by the defendant and the omission on the part of the plaintiff to use the ordinary care for the protection of himself or his property that is used by the ordinary reasonable man in those circumstances. In that case the plaintiff cannot recover because the injury is partly caused by what is imputed to him as his own default.[3] On the other hand, if the plaintiff were negligent, but his negligence was not a cause operating to produce the damage, there would be no defence. I find it impossible to divorce any theory of

---

1. (1927), 38 C.L.R. 354.
2. This word should be "safety"—see, [1940] A.C. at p. 164.
3. [This statement must now be read in the light of the 1945 Act.]

contributory negligence from the concept of causation. It is negligence which "contributes to cause" the injury, a phrase which I take from the opinion of Lord Penzance in *Radley* v. *London and North Western Rail. Co.*[1] And whether you ask whose negligence was responsible for the injury, or from whose negligence did the injury result, or adopt any other phrase you please, you must in the ultimate analysis be asking who "caused" the injury: and you must not be deterred because the word "cause" has in philosophy given rise to embarrassments which in this connection should not affect the judge. . . .

I cannot . . . accept the view that the action for injuries caused by breach of statutory duty differs from an action for injuries caused by any other wrong. I think that the defendant will succeed if he proves that the injury was caused solely or in part by the omission of the plaintiff to take the ordinary care that would be expected of him in the circumstances.[2]

But having come to that conclusion I am of opinion that the care to be expected of the plaintiff in the circumstances will vary with the circumstances; and that a different degree of care may well be expected from a workman in a factory or a mine from that which might be taken by an ordinary man not exposed continually to the noise, strain and manifold risks of factory or mine. I agree with the statement of Lawrence J. in *Flower* v. *Ebbw Vale Steel, Iron and Coal Co., Ltd.*,[3] at p. 140, cited by my noble and learned friend Lord Wright in [1936] A.C., at p. 214:

> "I think, of course, that in considering whether an ordinary prudent workman would have taken more care than the injured man, the tribunal of fact has to take into account all the circumstances of work in a factory and that it is not for every risky thing which a workman in a factory may do in his familiarity with the machinery that a plaintiff ought to be held guilty of contributory negligence."

This seems to me a sensible practical saying, and one which will afford all the protection which is necessary to the workman. . . . I have already said that I see no ground for imputing any negligence to the deceased man in the present case judged by any standard: but in any case judging the question of fact by the standard suggested by Lawrence J. I think that the defence of contributory negligence inevitably failed. . . .

LORD WRIGHT: . . . What is all important is to adapt the standard of what is negligence to the facts, and to give due regard to the actual conditions under which men work in a factory or mine, to the long hours and the fatigue, to the slackening of attention which naturally comes from constant repetition of the same operation, to the noise and confusion in which the man works, to his pre-occupation in what he is actually doing at the cost perhaps of some inattention to his own safety. . . .

LORD PORTER: . . . It is the reasonable man who is to be considered, not the particular individual, and therefore the degree of care will not vary from man to man, but it will, I think, vary from mine to mine and from factory to factory. The skill gained by a worker may enable him to take risks and do acts which in an unskilled man would be negligence, and on the other hand the fatiguing repetition of the same work may make a man incapable of the same care, and therefore not guilty of negligence, in doing or failing to do an act which a man less fatigued would do or leave undone. . . .

[LORD MACMILLAN delivered a speech in which he agreed with LORD ATKIN's exposition of the law. LORD THANKERTON concurred with LORD ATKIN.]

Notes

1. For cases dealing with causation and breach of statutory duty, see pp. 285–289, *ante*.

2. As the case above shows, the defence of contributory negligence is not

---

1. (1876), 1 App. Cas. 754.
2. [This sentence must now, of course, be read in the light of the 1945 Act.]
3. [1934] 2 K.B. 132.

confined to the tort of negligence. For the scope of contributory negligence at common law and of the 1945 Act, see Glanville Williams, *op. cit.* Chaps. 8 and 13.

3. *Mullard* v. *Ben Line Steamers, Ltd.*, [1971] 2 All E.R. 424; was a case in which the plaintiff was engaged on repair work on the hatch covers of a ship. Whilst working in one part of the ship, he had to return to a compartment, where he had been earlier that day, to collect a tool. By this time, a centre compartment through which he had to pass was in complete darkness, and the plaintiff, an experienced fitter, did not ask for a light and did not have a torch with him. In the dark he strayed from the safe part of the centre compartment and was seriously injured when he fell down an open hatch. The defendants were held to have been in breach of regulations 6, 26 and 69 of the Ship-building and Ship-Repairing Regulations 1960, but the Court of Appeal reduced the plaintiff's damages by one-third for his contributory negligence. Sachs L.J. delivered the following warning (at p. 428):

> "What he [the plaintiff] did, however, when stepping from a lighted into a dark compartment, with all the difficulties that can ensue when one goes from one state of light to another, was a momentary error, not to be judged too harshly when balanced against the defendants' flagrant and continuous breach of statutory duty. What happened was indeed exactly of the nature intended to be guarded against by the precautions prescribed by the regulations; and when a defendant's liability stems from such a breach the courts must be careful not to emasculate that regulation by the side-wind of apportionment. Moreover, the more culpable and continuing the breach of the regulation, the higher the percentage of blame that must fall on the defendant."

2. VOLENTI NON FIT INJURIA

Dann v. Hamilton

King's Bench Division   [1939] 1 All E.R. 59

The plaintiff and her mother were driven by Hamilton to see the Coronation decorations, and during the evening Hamilton consumed a certain amount of drink. They met a man named Taunton, and he was given a lift in the car. However, he left the car shortly before it was involved in an accident in which the plaintiff was injured and Hamilton was killed. The action was against his widow who represented his estate. It was found by the learned judge (Asquith J.) that as Taunton left the car a conversation took place along the following lines (although Asquith J. conceded that it was not clear how seriously the words were spoken):—Taunton said to the plaintiff and her mother "You two have more pluck than I have", to which the plaintiff answered "You should be like me. If anything is going to happen, it will happen". The defence relied upon the maxim *volenti non fit injuria*, negligence being admitted at the trial.

Asquith J.: . . . As a matter of strict pleading, it seems that the plea *volenti* is a denial of any duty at all, and, therefore, of any breach of duty, and an admission of negligence cannot strictly be combined with the plea. The plea *volenti* differs in this respect from the plea of contributory negligence, which is not raised in this case: see the observations of Bowen L.J. in *Thomas* v. *Quartermaine*.[1] This technicality, however, is of no consequence in the present case. . . .

. . . [I]t is common ground that the deceased, Hamilton, negligently caused the collision, and the evidence further satisfies me that his driving at the time of the collision

---

1. (1887), 18 Q.B.D. 685.

was that of a man, not only negligent, but negligent through excess of drink. The question is whether, on those facts, the rule or maxim *volenti non fit injuria* applies so as to defeat the plaintiff's claim. It has often been pointed out that the maxim says *volenti*, not *scienti*. A complete knowledge of the danger is in any event necessary, but such knowledge does not necessarily import consent. It is evidence of consent, weak or strong according to circumstances. The question whether the plaintiff was *volens* is one of fact, to be determined on this amongst other evidence: see *Smith* v. *Baker & Sons*,[1] and other authorities.

As to knowledge, I find as a fact that the plaintiff knew at 11.50 p.m., when Taunton was set down, that Hamilton, while far from being dead drunk, was under the influence of drink to such an extent as substantially to increase the chances of a collision arising from his negligence, that with this knowledge she re-entered the car, and that, in so doing, she was not acting under the pressure of any legal or social duty, or through the absence of alternative and practicable forms of transport, since she could have gone home by bus for 2*d*. Is this enough to constitute her *volens* for the purposes of the maxim? Indeed, is it clear that the maxim applies at all to the present case? . . .

The maxim . . . undoubtedly applies in many cases of pure tort, but case law in this field is very scanty. This is not, perhaps, because its application is rare in this field, but because in a large class of cases its applicability is so obvious as not to be brought to the test of litigation. It is manifest, for instance, that the consent of the patient relieves the dentist who extracts a tooth, or the surgeon who extracts an appendix, of liability for assault, to which their action would otherwise amount. In these cases, the certainty of physical injury is consented to. In another class of cases, perhaps more numerous, a man is not courting injury, but wishes to avoid it, but he nevertheless consents to the risk of its occurrence—for example, when he voluntarily engages in a game of cricket, or a boxing-match (with adequately padded gloves), or a fencing bout (with adequately buttoned foils). In such cases, he impliedly consents to the risks ordinarily incident to those sports, and here again, in the absence of consent, the party who sustains injury would be entitled to sue for assault, or otherwise for trespass to the person. . . .

Those are cases of trespass to the person. How stands the matter with regard to the tort of negligence, as we may now venture to call it? Does the maxim apply to negligence at all? . . .

Some text-book writers of authority, notably *Beven on Negligence*, 4th Edn., at p. 790, roundly deny that the maxim applies to cases of negligence at all. This is a hard saying, and must be read, I think, subject to some implied limitation. Where a dangerous physical condition has been brought about by the negligence of the defendant, and, after it has arisen, the plaintiff, fully appreciating its dangerous character, elects to assume the risk thereof, the maxim has often been held to apply, and to protect the defendant. Instances are *Torrance* v. *Ilford U.D.C.*[2] and the more recent *Cutler* v. *United Dairies (London), Ltd.*[3] Where, however, the act of the plaintiff relied on as a consent precedes, and is claimed to license in advance, a possible subsequent act of negligence by the defendant (and this, I think, must be the case Beven had in mind), the case may well be different. Here, *Smith* v. *Baker & Sons*[1] does not help as much as might be expected. In any case, it turned on contract, which is not in question here.

With some qualifications, *Pollock on Torts*, 13th Edn., supports Beven's *dictum*, declaring, at p. 172:

> "The whole law of negligence assumes the principle of *volenti non fit injuria* not to be applicable."

He points out, quoting the observations of Lord Halsbury L.C. in *Smith* v. *Baker & Sons*,[1] that anyone crossing a London street knows that a substantial percentage of drivers are negligent. If a man crosses deliberately, with this knowledge, and is negli-

1. [1891] A.C. 325.
2. (1909), 73 J.P. 225.
3. [1933] 2 K.B. 297.

gently run down, he is certainly not *volens*, and is not, therefore, precluded from a remedy. Sir Frederick Pollock adds, at p. 173:

> "A man is not bound at his peril to fly from a risk from which it is another's duty to protect him, merely because the risk is known."

In *Woodley* v. *Metropolitan District Rail. Co.*,[1] Mellish L.J. carries this illustration a step further. He says, at p. 394:

> "Suppose this case: a man is employed by a contractor for cleansing the street, to scrape a particular street, and for the space of a fortnight he has the opportunity of observing that a particular hansom cabman drives his cab with extremely little regard for the safety of the men who scrape the streets. At the end of a fortnight the man who scrapes the streets is negligently run over by the cabman. An action is brought in the county court, and the cabman says in his defence: 'You know my style of driving, you had seen me drive for a fortnight, I was only driving in my usual style.'"

The judgment of Mellish L.J. in this particular case was a minority judgment, but seems to have been preferred to that of the majority [by] the House of Lords in the later case of *Membery* v. *Great Western Rail. Co.*[2]

Cannot a yet further step be safely taken? I find it difficult to believe, although I know of no authority directly in point, that a person who voluntarily travels as a passenger in a vehicle driven by a driver who is known by the passenger to have driven negligently in the past is *volens* as to future negligent acts of such driver, even though he could have chosen some other form of transport if he had wished. Then, to take the last step, suppose that such a driver is likely to drive negligently on the material occasion, not because he is known to the plaintiff to have driven negligently in the past, but because he is known to the plaintiff to be under the influence of drink. That is the present case. Ought the result to be any different? After much debate, I have come to the conclusion that it should not, and that the plaintiff, by embarking in the car, or re-entering it, with knowledge that through drink the driver had materially reduced his capacity for driving safely, did not impliedly consent to, or absolve the driver from liability for, any subsequent negligence on his part whereby the plaintiff might suffer harm.

There may be cases in which the drunkenness of the driver at the material time is so extreme and so glaring that to accept a lift from him is like engaging in an intrinsically and obviously dangerous occupation, inter-meddling with an unexploded bomb or walking on the edge of an unfenced cliff. It is not necessary to decide whether in such a case the maxim *volenti non fit injuria* would apply, for in the present case I find as a fact that the driver's degree of intoxication fell short of this degree. I therefore conclude that the defence fails, and the claim succeeds. . . .

Judgment for the plaintiff

Notes

1. Whether a passenger is precluded from recovering damages from a driver from whom he has accepted a lift, but who has been drinking, has been discussed in several Commonwealth cases, references to which can be found in D. M. Gordon's article, "Drunken Drivers and Willing Passengers" (1966), 82 L.Q.R. 62. (Consider now s. 148 (3) of the Road Traffic Act 1972, p. 671, *post*.) On a more general point, Gordon's article was cited by Ackner J. in *Bennett* v. *Tugwell*, [1971] 2 Q.B. 267, at p. 273 in support of his opinion that an objective approach is required in deciding whether a plaintiff is *volens*, and that the law

---

1. (1877), 2 Ex. D. 384.
2. (1889), 14 App. Cas. 179.

is concerned with the evidence of consent provided by his words or conduct, not with his innermost thoughts. (See (1966), 82 L.Q.R., at p. 71; see also Millner, p. 100.)

2. In *Slater* v. *Clay Cross Co., Ltd.*, [1956] 2 Q.B. 264; [1956] 2 All E.R. 625, Denning L.J. (at pp. 627–628) referring to *Dann* v. *Hamilton* spoke in the following terms:

> "Asquith J. held that the maxim volenti non fit injuria had no application to the case; and he gave judgment in favour of the injured passenger. I must say that I agree with him. I know that the decision has in some quarters been criticised, but I would point out that Lord Asquith himself wrote a note in the *Law Quarterly Review* for July, 1953, vol. 69 at p. 317, which explains what he decided. He wrote:
>
> > 'The criticisms . . . were to the effect that even if the volenti doctrine did not apply, there was here a cast iron defence on the ground of contributory negligence. I have since had the pleadings and my notes exhumed, and they very clearly confirm my recollection that contributory negligence was not pleaded. Not merely so, but my notes show that I encouraged counsel for the defence to ask for leave to amend by adding this plea, but he would not be drawn: why, I have no idea. As the case has been a good deal canvassed on the opposite assumption, I hope you will not grudge the space for this not unimportant corrigendum.'
>
> In so far as he decided that the doctrine of volenti did not apply, I think the decision was quite correct. In so far as he suggested that the plea of contributory negligence might have been available, I agree with him."

Nettleship *v.* Weston

Court of Appeal   [1971] 3 All E.R. 581

The facts and part of the judgment has been set out, p. 146, *ante*.

LORD DENNING M.R.: . . . This brings me to the defence of volenti non fit injuria. Does it apply to the instructor? In former times this defence was used almost as an alternative defence to contributory negligence. Either defence defeated the action. Now that contributory negligence is not a complete defence, but only a ground for reducing the damages, the defence of volenti non fit injuria has been closely considered, and, in consequence, it has been severely limited. Knowledge of the risk of injury is not enough. Nor is a willingness to take the risk of injury. Nothing will suffice short of an agreement to waive any claim for negligence. The plaintiff must agree, expressly or impliedly, to waive any claim for any injury that may befall him due to the lack of reasonable care by the defendant: or more accurately, due to the failure of the defendant to measure up to the standard of care that the law requires of him. That is shown in England by *Dann* v. *Hamilton*[1] and *Slater* v. *Clay Cross Co., Ltd.*;[2] and in Canada by *Lehnert* v. *Stein*;[3] and in New Zealand by *Morrison* v. *Union Steamship Co. of New Zealand, Ltd.*[4] The doctrine has been so severely curtailed that in the view of Diplock L.J.: ". . . the maxim, in the absence of express contract, has no application to negligence simpliciter where the duty of care is based solely on proximity or 'neighbourship' in the Atkinian sense": see *Wooldridge* v. *Sumner*.[5]

Applying the doctrine in this case, it is clear that Mr. Nettleship did not agree to waive any claim for injury that might befall him. Quite the contrary. He enquired

1. [1939] 1 K.B. 509; [1939] 1 All E.R. 59.
2. [1956] 2 Q.B. 264; [1956] 2 All E.R. 625.
3. (1963), 36 D.L.R. (2d) 159.
4. [1964] N.Z.L.R. 468.
5. [1963] 2 Q.B. 43, at p. 69; [1962] 2 All E.R. 978, at p. 990.

about the insurance policy so as to make sure that he was covered. If and insofar as Mrs. Weston fell short of the standard of care which the law required of her, he has a cause of action. But his claim may be reduced insofar as he was at fault himself—as in letting her take control too soon or in not being quick enough to correct her error.

I do not say that the professional instructor—who agrees to teach for reward—can likewise sue. There may well be implied in the contract an agreement by him to waive any claim for injury.[1] He ought to insure himself, and may do so, for aught I know. But the instructor who is just a friend helping to teach never does insure himself. He should, therefore, be allowed to sue. . . .

SALMON L.J.: . . . In the absence of a special relationship what is reasonable care and skill is measured by the standard of competence usually achieved by the ordinary driver. In my judgment, however, there may be special facts creating a special relationship which displaces this standard or even negatives any duty, although the onus would certainly be on the driver to establish such facts. With minor reservations I respectfully agree with and adopt the reasoning and conclusions of Sir Owen Dixon in his judgment in *Insurance Comr.* v. *Joyce.*[2] I do not however agree that the mere fact that the driver has, to the knowledge of his passenger, lost a limb or an eye or is deaf can affect the duty which he owes the passenger to drive safely. It is well known that many drivers suffering from such disabilities drive with no less skill and competence than the ordinary man. The position, however, is totally different when, to the knowledge of the passenger, the driver is so drunk as to be incapable of driving safely. Quite apart from being negligent, a passenger who accepts a lift in such circumstances clearly cannot expect the driver to drive other than dangerously.

The duty of care springs from relationship. The special relationship which the passenger has created by accepting a lift in the circumstances postulated surely cannot entitle him to expect the driver to discharge a duty of care or skill which ex hypothesi the passenger knows the driver is incapable of discharging. Accordingly in such circumstances, no duty is owed by the driver to the passenger to drive safely, and therefore no question of volenti non fit injuria can arise. The alternative view is that if there is a duty owed to the passenger to drive safely, the passenger by accepting a lift has clearly assumed the risk of the driver failing to discharge that duty. What the passenger has done goes far beyond establishing mere "scienter". If it does not establish "volens", it is perhaps difficult to imagine what can.

Such a case seems to me to be quite different from *Smith* v. *Baker & Sons*[3] and *Slater* v. *Clay Cross Co., Ltd.*[4] Like Sir Owen Dixon, I prefer to rest on the special relationship between the parties displacing the prima facie duty on the driver to drive safely rather than on the ground of volenti non fit injuria. Whichever view is preferable it follows that, in spite of the very great respect I have for any judgment of Lord Asquith, I do not accept that *Dann* v. *Hamilton*[5] was correctly decided. Although Sir Owen Dixon's judgment was delivered in 1948, I cannot think of anything which has happened since which makes it any less convincing now than it was then.

I should like to make it plain that I am not suggesting that whenever a passenger accepts a lift knowing that the driver has had a few drinks, this displaces the prima facie duty ordinarily resting on a driver, let alone that it establishes volenti non fit injuria. . . .

There are no authorities which bear directly on the duty owed by a learner-driver to his instructor. . . . The instructor, in most cases such as the present, knows, however, that the learner has practically no driving experience or skill and that, for the lack of this experience and skill, the learner will almost certainly make mistakes which may well injure the instructor unless he takes adequate steps to correct them. To my mind,

---

1. [See now Road Traffic Act 1972, s. 148 (3), p. 671, *post.*]
2. (1948), 77 C.L.R. 39.
3. [1891] A.C. 325; [1891–94] All E.R. Rep. 69.
4. [1956] 2 Q.B. 264; [1956] 2 All E.R. 625.
5. [1939] 1 K.B. 509; [1939] 1 All E.R. 59.

therefore, the relationship is usually such that the beginner does not owe the instructor a duty to drive with the skill and competence to be expected of an experienced driver. The instructor knows that the learner does not possess such skill and competence. The alternative way of putting the case is that the instructor voluntarily agrees to run the risk of injury resulting from the learner's lack of skill and experience. . . .

. . . I would, but for one factor, agree with the learned judge's decision in favour of the defendant, Mrs. Weston. I have, however, come to the conclusion, not without doubt, that this appeal should be allowed. Mr. Nettleship when he gave evidence was asked:

"*Q* Was there any mention made of what the position would be if you were involved in an accident? *A* I had checked with Mr. and Mrs. Weston regarding insurance, and I was assured that they had fully comprehensive insurance, which covered me as a passenger in the event of an accident."

Mrs. Weston agreed, when she gave evidence, that this assurance had been given before Mr. Nettleship undertook to teach her. In my view this evidence completely disposes of any possible defence of volenti non fit injuria. Moreover, this assurance seems to me to be an integral part of the relationship between the parties. . . .

On the whole, I consider, although with some doubt, that the assurance given to Mr. Nettleship altered the nature of the relationship which would have existed between the parties but for the assurance. The assurance resulted in a relationship under which Mrs. Weston accepted responsibility for any injury which Mr. Nettleship might suffer as a result of any failure on her part to exercise the ordinary driver's standards of reasonable care and skill. . . .

MEGAW L.J. (referring to cases where passengers knew a driver was likely to drive unsafely because of drink or drugs, yet still accepted a lift): . . . There may in such cases sometimes be an element of aiding and abetting a criminal offence; or, if the facts fall short of aiding and abetting, the passenger's mere assent to benefit from the commission of a criminal offence may involve questions of turpis causa. For myself, with great respect, I doubt the correctness on its facts of the decision in *Dann* v. *Hamilton*.[1] But the present case involves no such problem. . . .

[Megaw L.J. was not speaking of the *volenti* maxim here. However he went on to hold the *volenti* maxim inapplicable for, in his view, the facts did not show that the plaintiff had accepted the risk of injury through the defendant's inexperience.]

Notes

1. The majority of the Court of Appeal, pp. 146–149, *ante*, in fact rejected the "doctrine of varying standards" in relation to the standard of care to be found in Salmon L.J.'s judgment.

2. There have been several cases in recent years where the *volenti* defence has been pleaded against passengers in cars in which there were notices stating that passengers travelled at their own risk. (See *Buckpitt* v. *Oates*, [1968] 1 All E.R. 1145; *Bennett* v. *Tugwell*, [1971] 2 Q.B. 267; [1971] 2 All E.R. 248; cf. *Birch* v. *Thomas*, [1972] 1 All E. R. 905; Section 148 (3) of the Road Traffic Act 1972, p. 671, *post*, will now exclude the defence in this situation. The judgments in *Nettleships'* case must be read subject to this section.

Bowater v. The Mayor, Aldermen and Burgesses of the Borough of Rowley Regis

Court of Appeal   [1944] 1 All E.R. 465

The plaintiff was employed by the defendants as a carter, and his job was to take

---

1. [1939] 1 K.B. 509; [1939] 1 All E.R. 59.

away rubbish swept up by the road sweepers. The foreman told him to take out a horse which had tried to run away on more than one occasion when driven by one of the plaintiff's fellow employees. Both the plaintiff and the defendants' foreman were aware of the incidents. The plaintiff expressed his dislike of the proposed course of action, but was told that the borough surveyor had said that he was to take the horse out, and the plaintiff obeyed. About a month later the horse ran away, and the plaintiff was thrown out of the cart and injured. Singleton J. upheld the plea of *volenti non fit injuria*. An appeal to the Court of Appeal was successful and a new trial was ordered on the question of damages.

GODDARD L.J.: . . . The maxim *volenti non fit injuria* is one which in the case of master and servant is to be applied with extreme caution. Indeed, I would say that it can hardly ever be applicable where the act to which the plaintiff is said to be *"volens"* arises out of his ordinary duty, unless the work for which the plaintiff is engaged is one in which danger is necessarily involved. Thus a man in an explosives factory must take the risk of an explosion occurring in spite of the observance and provision of all statutory regulations and safeguards. A horse-breaker must take the risk of being thrown or injured by a restive or unbroken horse; it is an ordinary risk of his employment. But a man whose occupation is not one of a nature inherently dangerous but who is asked or required to undertake a risky operation is in a different position. To rely on this doctrine the master must show that the workman undertook that the risk should be on him. It is not enough that, whether under protest or not, he obeyed an order or complied with a request which he might have declined as one which he was not bound either to obey or to comply with. It must be shown that he agreed that what risk there was should lie on him. I do not mean that it must necessarily be shown that he contracted to take the risk, as that would involve consideration, though a simple case of showing that a workman did take a risk upon himself would be that he was paid extra for so doing, and in some occupations "danger money" is often paid.

This, in my opinion, is the result of *Yarmouth* v. *France*,[1] *Smith* v. *Baker*,[2] and *Monaghan* v. *Rhodes*,[3] and the further citation of authority, in support of what I think is now a well-settled principle, is unnecessary. Though the question in the last resort is one of fact, I find myself unable to agree with Singleton J. on the evidence in this case. I venture to think he approached the case from a wrong angle. A corporation carter or dustman is not like a horse-breaker because he is also a horse-keeper. It is no part of his duty to break or tame the horse which draws the dust cart. Nor is it right to inquire into the mental processes that may lead him to do what he is told or to consider what degree of appreciation of the risk was apparent to him. As Lord Esher M.R. said in *Yarmouth* v. *France*,[1] that would be to say that for the same accident an unintelligent man might recover while a more intelligent one would not. For this maxim or doctrine to apply it must be shown that a servant who is asked or required to use dangerous plant is a volunteer in the fullest sense; that, knowing of the danger, he expressly or impliedly said that he would do the job at his own risk and not at that of his master. The evidence in this case fell far short of that and, in my opinion, the plaintiff was entitled to recover.

The appeal is allowed with costs and the case must go down for a new trial on damages only, unless the parties will agree to this court assessing the damages. . . .

[SCOTT and DU PARCQ L.JJ. delivered judgments in favour of allowing the appeal.]

Notes

1. As this case clearly shows, mere knowledge of the risk by the plaintiff will not *per se* bring him within the scope of the maxim. Indeed, many years earlier, Bowen L.J. had stressed that the maxim was *volenti non fit injuria* and

1. (1887), 19 Q.B.D. 647.
2. [1891] A.C. 325.
3. [1920] 1 K.B. 487.

not *scienti non fit injuria* (*Thomas* v. *Quartermaine* (1887), 18 Q.B.D. 685, at p. 696.)

2. In the employment situation, the workman, who has knowledge of a danger, is unlikely to have true freedom of choice, for this is an area in which economic pressures operate. (See further the comments of Millner, pp. 102–108; cf. the approach in *Latter* v. *Braddell* (1881), 50 L.J.Q.B. 166, p. 53, *ante*, in the sphere of intentional injuries.) The *volenti* maxim has, in fact, been of little importance in master and servant cases since *Smith* v. *Baker & Sons*, [1891] A.C. 325. Compare *Burnett* v. *British Waterways Board*, [1973] 2 All E.R. 631. It would however be a mistake to suppose that the *volenti* defence can never apply in the employment situation, for the next case provides a recent example of its application, though in a rather restricted sphere.

3. Lack of real freedom of choice also exists in the rescuer cases, pp. 123–133, *ante*, where the *volenti* defence has been raised (and see Winfield & Jolowicz, p. 634 for other reasons why the defence will fail in that context.)

Imperial Chemical Industries, Ltd. v. Shatwell

House of Lords   [1964] 2 All E.R. 999

This was an appeal from the Court of Appeal who dismissed an appeal from a judgment of Elwes J. Elwes J. had held the appellants vicariously liable to the respondent for his fellow servant's negligence and breach of statutory duty. He had further held that the *volenti* defence was not open to the appellants in the claim based on breach of statutory duty, but reduced the damages by half because of the respondent's share of the blame for the accident. On appeal to the House of Lords:

LORD REID: My Lords, this case arises out of the accidental explosion of a charge at a quarry belonging to the appellants which caused injuries to the respondent George Shatwell and his brother James, who were both qualified shotfirers. On 8 June 1960, these two men and another shotfirer, Beswick, had bored and filled fifty shot holes and had inserted electric detonators and connected them up in series. Before firing it was necessary to test the circuit for continuity. This should have been done by connecting long wires so that the men could go to a shelter some eighty yards away and test from there. They had not sufficient wire with them and Beswick went off to get more. The testing ought not to have been done until signals had been given, so that other men could take shelter, and these signals were not due to be given for at least another hour. Soon after Beswick had left George said to his brother "Must we test them", meaning shall we test them, and James said "yes". The testing is done by passing a weak current through the circuit in which a small galvanometer is included and if the needle of the instrument moves when a connexion is made the circuit is in order. So George got a galvanometer and James handed two short wires to him. Then George applied the wires to the galvanometer and the needle did not move. This showed that the circuit was defective so the two men went round inspecting the connections. They saw nothing wrong and George said that that meant there was a dud detonator somewhere, and decided to apply the galvanometer to each individual detonator. James handed two other wires to him and George used them to apply the galvanometer to the first detonator. The result was an explosion which injured both men.

This method had been regularly used without mishap until the previous year. Then some research done by the appellants showed that it might be unsafe and in October, 1959, the appellants gave orders that testing must in future be done from a shelter and a lecture was given to all the shotfirers, including the Shatwells, explaining the position.

Then in December, 1959, new statutory regulations[1] were made (S.I. 1959 No. 2259) probably because the Ministry had been informed of the results of the appellants' research. These regulations came into operation in February, 1960, and the Shatwells were aware of them. But some of the shotfirers appear to have gone on in the old way. An instance of this came to the notice of the management in May, 1960, and the management took immediate action and revoked the shotfiring certificate of the disobedient man, and told the other shotfirers about this. George admitted in evidence that he knew all this. He admitted that they would only have had to wait ten minutes until Beswick returned with the long wires. When asked why he did not wait, his only excuse was that he could not be bothered to wait.

George now sues the appellants on the ground that he and his brother were equally to blame for this accident, and that the appellants are vicariously liable for his brother's conduct. He has been awarded £1,500, being half the agreed amount of his loss. There is no question of the appellants having been in breach of the regulation because the duty under the regulation is laid on the shotfirer personally. So counsel for George frankly and rightly admitted that if George had sued James personally instead of suing his employer the issue would have been the same. If this decision is right it means that if two men collaborate in doing what they know is dangerous and is forbidden and as a result both are injured, each has a cause of action against the other.

The appellants have two grounds of defence, first that James's conduct had no causal connexion with the accident the sole cause being George's own fault, and secondly volenti non fit injuria. I am of opinion that they are entitled to succeed on the latter ground, but I must deal shortly with the former ground because it involves the decision of this House in *Stapley* v. *Gypsum Mines, Ltd.*,[2] and I think that there has been some misunderstanding of that case. . . . The only issue before the House was whether the conduct of Dale had contributed to cause the accident, and the House decided by a majority that it had. There was little, if any, difference of opinion as to the principles to be applied; the difference was in their application to the facts of the case. The case gives authoritative guidance on the question of causation, but beyond that it decides nothing. It clearly appears from the argument of counsel[3] that the defence volenti non fit injuria was never taken and nothing about it was said by any of their lordships.

Applying the principles approved in *Stapley's* case[2] I think that James' conduct did have a causal connexion with this accident. It is far from clear that George would have gone on with the test if James had not agreed with him; but, perhaps more important, James did collaborate with him in making the test in a forbidden and unlawful way. His collaboration may not have amounted to much, but it was not negligible. If I had to consider the allocation of fault, I should have difficulty in finding both men equally to blame. If James had been suing in respect of his damage, it would I think be clear that both had contributed to cause the accident, but that the greater part of the fault must be attributed to George. So I do not think that the appellants could succeed entirely on this defence and I turn to consider their second submission.

The defence volenti non fit injuria has had a chequered history. At one time it was very strictly applied. . . . More recently it appears to have been thought in some quarters that, at least as between master and servant, volenti non fit injuria is a dead or dying defence. That, I think, is because in most cases where the defence would now be available it has become usual to base the decision on contributory negligence. Where the plaintiff's own disobedient act is the sole cause of his injury, it does not matter in the result whether one says 100 per cent. contributory negligence or volenti non fit injuria; but it does matter in a case like the present. If we adopt the inaccurate habit of using the word "negligence" to denote a deliberate act done with full knowledge of the risk, it is not surprising that we sometimes get into difficulties. I think that most people

---

1. The Quarries (Explosives) Regulations, 1959.
2. [1953] A.C. 663; [1953] 2 All E.R. 478.
3. See [1953] A.C. at p. 665.

would say, without stopping to think of the reason, that there is a world of difference between two fellow servants collaborating carelessly, so that the acts of both contribute to cause injury to one of them, and two fellow servants combining to disobey an order deliberately, though they know the risk involved. It seems reasonable that the injured man should recover some compensation in the former case, but not in the latter. If the law treats both as merely cases of negligence, it cannot draw a distinction. In my view the law does and should draw a distinction. In the first case only the partial defence of contributory negligence is available. In the second volenti non fit injuria is a complete defence, if the employer is not himself at fault and is only liable vicariously for the acts of the fellow servant. If the plaintiff invited or freely aided and abetted his fellow servant's disobedience, then he was volens in the fullest sense. He cannot complain of the resulting injury either against the fellow servant or against the master on the ground of his vicarious responsibility for his fellow servant's conduct. I need not here consider the common case where the servant's disobedience puts the master in breach of a statutory obligation, and it would be wrong to decide in advance whether that would make any difference. There remain two other arguments for the respondent which I must deal with.

It was argued that in this case it has not been shown that George had a full appreciation of the risk. In my view it must be held that he had. . . .

Finally the respondent argues that there is a general rule that the defence of volenti non fit injuria is not available where there has been a breach of a statutory obligation. It would be odd if that were so. In the present case the prohibition of testing except from a shelter had been imposed by the appellants before the statutory prohibition was made. So it would mean that, if the respondent had deliberately done what he did in full knowledge of the risk the day before the statutory prohibition was made, this defence would have been open to the appellants, but if he had done the same thing the day after the regulation came into operation it would not. . . .

I entirely agree that an employer who is himself at fault in persistently refusing to comply with a statutory rule could not possibly be allowed to escape liability because the injured workman had agreed to waive the breach. If it is still permissible for a workman to make an express agreement with his employer to work under an unsafe system, perhaps in consideration of a higher wage—a matter on which I need express no opinion—then there would be a difference between breach of a statutory obligation by the employer and breach of his common law obligation to exercise due care: it would be possible to contract out of the latter, but not out of the former type of obligation. But all that is very far removed from the present case. . . .

I can find no reason at all why the fact that these two brothers agreed to commit an offence by contravening a statutory prohibition imposed on them as well as agreeing to defy their employer's orders should affect the application of the principle volenti non fit injuria either to an action by one of them against the other or to an action by one against their employer based on his vicarious responsibility for the conduct of the other. I would therefore allow this appeal.

LORD HODSON (referring to the *volenti* defence): . . . The defence was . . . rejected by the Court of Appeal, as well as by the trial judge, because it has long been treated as settled law that the doctrine of volenti non fit injuria affords no defence to a claim based on breach of statutory duty, see *Wheeler* v. *New Merton Board Mills, Ltd.*,[1] a decision of the Court of Appeal following *Baddeley* v. *Earl Granville*.[2] The basis of the latter decision, accepted without enthusiasm by the Court of Appeal in the former case, was, I think, that it was against public policy that as between master and servant the former should escape liability where a servant has accepted a risk by agreement with him in defiance of an obligation enforced by statute. I do not doubt the validity of these decisions, but I do not think that, if public policy is at the root of the problem, there is any reason why

1. [1933] 2 K.B. 669; [1933] All E.R. Rep. 28.
2. (1887), 19 Q.B.D. 423; [1886–90] All E.R. Rep. 374.

the appellants should not avail themselves of the defence. The duty imposed by the regulation was a duty imposed directly on the shotfirers and not directly on the employers. As has already been pointed out, the appellants had done their utmost to see that the regulations were complied with. It is manifestly unjust that each brother who has acted in defiance of orders and of regulations made by the employer should be able to sue the employer and recover damages on the ground that the master is vicariously liable for the wrongful act of the servant committed in the course of his employment. In a situation such as this it seems to me that the pull of public policy is in a direction opposite from that taken in those cases, of which *Stapley* v. *Gypsum Mines, Ltd.*[1] was one, where the statutory duty is imposed directly on the employer.

On this ground I would allow the appeal.

LORD PEARCE: . . . Where Parliament has laid down that certain precautions shall be taken by the master to protect his workmen, a master is not and should not be entitled to neglect those precautions and then rely on an express or implied agreement between himself and the workman that the latter, if injured as a result of the neglect, will bear the loss alone. In *Wheeler* v. *New Merton Board Mills, Ltd.*[2] the Court of Appeal laid down that the defence of volenti non fit injuria was no answer to a claim by a workman against his employer for injury caused through a breach by the employer of a duty imposed on him by statute. They so held (with some reluctance which I do not share) principally because the case of *Baddeley* v. *Earl Granville*[3] had stood for some fifty years. But in those cases the defendants were themselves in breach of statutory duty (as were the defendants in *Stapley's* case).[1] In the present case the defendants themselves were in breach of no statutory duty. The questions of public policy and fairness which reinforced those decisions do not help the plaintiff in the present case but rather tell the other way. In my opinion, the rule which the courts have rightly created disallowing the defence where the employer is in breach of statutory duty should not apply to a case such as the present. The defence should be available where the employer was not himself in breach of statutory duty and was not vicariously in breach of any statutory duty through the neglect of some person who was of superior rank to the plaintiff and whose commands the plaintiff was bound to obey (or who had some special and different duty of care, see, e.g. *National Coal Board* v. *England*,[4] where a miner was injured by the shotfirer firing the charge) and where the plaintiff himself assented to and took part in the breaking of the statutory duty in question. If one does not allow some such exception one is plainly shutting out a defence which, when applied in the right circumstances, is fair and sensible.

So far as concerns common law negligence, the defence of volenti non fit injuria is clearly applicable if there was a genuine full agreement, free from any kind of pressure, to assume the risk of loss. . . .

In the present case it seems clear that as between George and James there was a voluntary assumption of risk. George was clearly acting without any constraint or persuasion; he was in fact inaugurating the enterprise. On the facts it was an implied term (to the benefit of which the employers are vicariously entitled) that George would not sue James for any injury that he might suffer, if an accident occurred. Had an officious bystander raised the possibility, can one doubt that George would have ridiculed it? . . .

[VISCOUNT RADCLIFFE and LORD DONOVAN delivered speeches in favour of allowing the appeal.]

Appeal allowed

---

1. [1953] A.C. 663; [1953] 2 All E.R. 478.
2. [1933] 2 K.B. 669; [1933] All E.R. Rep. 28.
3. (1887), 19 Q.B.D. 423; [1886–90] All E.R. Rep. 374.
4. [1954] A.C. 403; [1954] 1 All E.R. 546.

Questions

1. Would the result of this case have been any different if James, although employed as a shot-firer, had been George's supervisor?

2. Lord Reid did not decide what the position would be in the case "where the servant's disobedience puts the master in breach of a statutory obligation". If this were so, should there be a different result?

3. Could that aspect of public policy which is sometimes termed *ex turpi causa non oritur actio* (see Winfield & Jolowicz, pp. 637–639) also have provided the appellants with a defence here? (Consider *National Coal Board* v. *England*, [1954] A.C. 403; [1954] 1 All E.R. 546.)

Wooldridge v. Sumner

Court of Appeal   [1962] 2 All E.R. 978

The first defendant owned Work of Art, a horse taking part in a competition for heavyweight hunters at the National Horse Show. The horses were required to walk, trot, canter and gallop, and this was a class of competition in which both the horse and its rider, Mr. Holladay, were experienced. There was a line of tubs and benches two feet from the edge of the competition arena, which was surrounded by a cinder running track. The plaintiff, a professional photographer, was standing at the end of one of those benches. The defendant's horse was kept close into the corner of the bandstand end of the arena so as to give the horse the best chance to show off its gallop in the straight. However, having rounded the corner, the horse apparently jumped two of the tubs, knocked over a third, and then moved from the line of tubs on to a course taking it several feet behind the bench at the end of which the plaintiff was standing. The plaintiff, who had become frightened by the horse's approach, tried to pull someone away from the bench, but stepped or fell back and was knocked down by the horse. Barry J. who dismissed the claim against the second defendants (the organisers of the show, who were occupiers of the stadium) found that the horse was being ridden too fast into and out of the corner, so that it was inevitable that it would come into contact with the tubs, and that Mr. Holladay's conduct and control of the horse amounted to negligence for which the first defendant was liable. He also decided that if Mr. Holladay had allowed it, the horse would have gone safely on to the cinder track. However, Barry J. found that Mr. Holladay tried to get the horse back on to the course and so carried along the line of tubs, and that Mr. Holladay knew, or should have known, that the people sitting or standing along the line of benches and tubs were highly likely to be endangered by these efforts. The first defendant appealed:

SELLERS L.J.: ... In all the circumstances, in so far as the judgment found that Mr. Holladay was going "too fast" I would not hold this to be negligence; and in any case its effect had ceased when the horse was straightened up, as it was, some twenty-five yards before the accident, and with regard to the second finding on which the judgment was based, I am unable to find fault in Mr. Holladay amounting to negligence. It was, I think, the horse's course and not his which took them along the line of tubs instead of to the right of that line and for this I do not think that he can be blamed. ...

In my opinion, a competitor or player cannot, at least, in the normal case of competition or game, rely on the maxim volenti non fit injuria in answer to a spectator's claim, for there is no liability unless there is negligence, and the spectator comes to witness skill and with the expectation that it will be exercised. But, provided the competition or game is being performed within the rules and the requirement of the sport and by a person of adequate skill and competence, the spectator does not expect his safety to be regarded by the participant. If the conduct is deliberately intended to injure someone whose presence is known, or is reckless and in disregard of all safety of others so that it is a departure from the standards which might reasonably be expected in anyone pursuing the competition or game, then the performer might well be held liable for any injury his act caused. There would, I think, be a difference, for instance, in assessing blame which is actionable between an injury caused by a tennis ball hit or a racket accidentally thrown in the course of play into the spectators at Wimbledon and a ball hit or a racket thrown into the stands in temper or annoyance when play was not in progress. The relationship of spectator and competitor or player is a special one, as I see it, as the standard of conduct of the participant, as accepted and expected by the spectator, is that which the sport permits or involves. The different relationship involves its own standard of care. There can be no better evidence that Mr. Holladay was riding within the rules than that he won, notwithstanding this unfortunate accident in the course of the event, and I do not think that it can be said that he was riding recklessly and in disregard of all safety or even, on this evidence, without skill. . . .

I would allow the appeal and enter judgment for the first defendant also.

DIPLOCK L.J.: . . . Accepting, then, the primary facts as found by the trial judge but not those inferences which he drew from them and which, on analysis of the evidence, I think are unjustified, one is left with two acts or omissions by Mr. Holladay which were causative factors in the accident. The first was the speed at which he caused Work of Art to negotiate the bend, the second was his omission at some moment before he reached the line of tubs to let the horse run out on to the cinder track. . . .

The matter has to be looked at from the point of view of the reasonable spectator as well as the reasonable participant; not because of the maxim volenti non fit injuria, but because what a reasonable spectator would expect a participant to do without regarding it as blameworthy is as relevant to what is reasonable care as what a reasonable participant would think was blameworthy conduct in himself. The same idea was expressed by Scrutton L.J. in *Hall* v. *Brooklands Auto-Racing Club*:[1]

"What is reasonable care would depend on the perils which might be reasonably expected to occur, *and the extent to which the ordinary spectator might be expected to appreciate and take the risk of such perils.*"

A reasonable spectator attending voluntarily to witness any game or competition knows, and presumably desires, that a reasonable participant will concentrate his attention on winning, and if the game or competition is a fast-moving one will have to exercise his judgment and attempt to exert his skill in what, in the analogous context of contributory negligence, is sometimes called "the agony of the moment". If the participant does so concentrate his attention and consequently does exercise his judgment and attempt to exert his skill in circumstances of this kind which are inherent in the game or competition in which he is taking part, the question whether any mistake he makes amounts to a breach of duty to take reasonable care must take account of those circumstances.

The law of negligence has always recognised that the standard of care which a reasonable man will exercise depends on the conditions under which the decision to avoid the act or omission relied on as negligence has to be taken. The case of the workman engaged on repetitive work in the noise and bustle of the factory is a familiar example. More apposite for present purposes are the collision cases where a decision has to be made on the spur of the moment.

". . . A's negligence makes collision so threatening that, though by the appropriate measure B could avoid it, B has not really time to think and by mistake takes the wrong measure. B is not held to be guilty of any negligence and A wholly fails."

(*Admiralty Comrs.* v. *S.S. Volute*).[2] A fails not because of his own negligence; there

---

1. [1933] 1 K.B. 208, at p. 214; [1932] All E.R. Rep. 205, at p. 213.
2. [1922] 1 A.C. 129, at p. 136; [1921] All E.R. Rep. 193, at p. 197.

never has been any contributory negligence rule in Admiralty. He fails because B has exercised such care as is reasonable in circumstances in which he has not really time to think. No doubt, if he has got into those circumstances as a result of a breach of duty of care which he owes to A, A can succeed on this antecedent negligence; but a participant in a game or competition gets into the circumstances in which he has no time or very little time to think by his decision to take part in the game or competition at all. It cannot be suggested that the participant, at any rate if he has some modicum of skill, is by the mere act of participating in breach of his duty of care to a spectator who is present for the very purpose of watching him do so. If, therefore, in the course of the game or competition at a moment when he really has not time to think, a participant by mistake takes a wrong measure, he is not, in my view, to be held guilty of any negligence.

Furthermore, the duty which he owes is a duty of care, not a duty of skill. Save where a consensual relationship exists between a plaintiff and a defendant by which the defendant impliedly warrants his skill, a man owes no duty to his neighbour to exercise any special skill beyond that which an ordinary reasonable man would acquire before indulging in the activity in which he is engaged at the relevant time. It may well be that a participant in a game or competition would be guilty of negligence to a spectator if he took part in it when he knew or ought to have known that his lack of skill was such that, even if he exerted it to the utmost, he was likely to cause injury to a spectator watching him. No question of this arises in the present case. It was common ground that Mr. Holladay was an exceptionally skilful and experienced horseman.

The practical result of this analysis of the application of the common law of negligence to participant and spectator would, I think, be expressed by the common man in some such terms as these: "A person attending a game or competition takes the risk of any damage caused to him by any act of a participant done in the course of and for the purposes of the game or competition, notwithstanding that such act may involve an error of judgment or a lapse of skill, unless the participant's conduct is such as to evince a reckless disregard of the spectator's safety". The spectator takes the risk because such an act involves no breach of the duty of care owed by the participant to him. He does not take the risk by virtue of the doctrine expressed or obscured by the maxim volenti non fit injuria. The maxim states a principle of estoppel applicable originally to a Roman citizen who consented to being sold as a slave. Although pleaded and argued below, it was only faintly relied on by counsel for the first defendant in this court. In my view, the maxim, in the absence of express contract, has no application to negligence simpliciter where the duty of care is based solely on proximity or "neighbourship" in the Atkinian sense. The maxim in English law pre-supposes a tortious act by the defendant. The consent that is relevant is not consent to the risk of injury but consent to the lack of reasonable care that may produce that risk (see *Kelly* v. *Tarrants, Ltd.*,[1] per Lord MacDermott), and requires on the part of the plaintiff at the time at which he gives his consent full knowledge of the nature and extent of the risk that he ran (*Osborne* v. *London and North Western Rail. Co.*,[2] per Wills J. approved in *Letang* v. *Ottawa Electric Rail. Co.*[3]). In *Dann* v. *Hamilton*,[4] Asquith J. expressed doubts whether the maxim ever could apply to license in advance a subsequent act of negligence, for, if the consent precedes the act of negligence, the plaintiff cannot at that time have full knowledge of the extent as well as the nature of the risk which he will run. Asquith J., however, suggested that the maxim might, nevertheless, be applicable to cases where a dangerous physical condition had been brought about by the negligence of the defendant, and the plaintiff with full knowledge of the existing danger elected to run the risk thereof. With the development of the law of negligence in the last twenty years, a more consistent explanation of this type of case is that the test of liability on the part

1. [1954] N.I. 41, at p. 45.
2. (1888), 21 Q.B.D. 220, at pp. 223, 224.
3. [1926] A.C. 725; [1926] All E.R. Rep. 546.
4. [1939] 1 K.B. 509; [1939] 1 All E.R. 59.

of the person creating the dangerous physical condition is whether it was reasonably foreseeable by him that the defendant would so act in relation to it as to endanger himself. This is the principle which has been applied in the rescue cases (see *Cutler* v. *United Dairies (London), Ltd.*,[1] and contrast *Haynes* v. *Harwood*[2]), and that part of Asquith J.'s judgment in *Dann* v. *Hamilton*[3] dealing with the possible application of the maxim to the law of negligence was not approved by the Court of Appeal in *Ward* v. *T. E. Hopkins & Son, Ltd.*, *Baker* v. *Same*.[4] In the type of case envisaged by Asquith J. if I may adapt the words of Morris L.J. in *Ward* v. *Hopkins*,[5] the plaintiff could not have agreed to run the risk that the defendant might be negligent for the plaintiff would only play his part after the defendant had been negligent.

Since the maxim has, in my view, no application to this or any other case of negligence simpliciter, the fact that the plaintiff, owing to his ignorance of horses, did not fully appreciate the nature and extent of the risk he ran did not impose on Mr. Holladay any higher duty of care towards him than that which he owed to any ordinary reasonable spectator with such knowledge of horses and vigilance for his own safety as might be reasonably expected to be possessed by a person who chooses to watch a heavyweight hunter class in the actual arena where the class is being judged. . . . Beyond saying that the question is one of degree, the learned judge has not expressly stated in his judgment anything which would indicate the considerations which he had in mind in determining that Mr. Holladay was in breach of the duty of care owed by a participant in a competition of this character to a spectator who had chosen to watch the event in the arena in which it was taking place. There is, however, no reference in his judgment to the fact, which is, in my view, of the utmost relevance, that Mr. Holladay's decisions what he should do once the signal for the gallop had been given had to be made in circumstances in which he had no time to exercise an unhurried judgment. It is, I think, clear that, if the trial judge gave any weight to this factor, he did not make proper allowance for it. . . .

[Having stated that, in the circumstances of the case, Mr. Holladay's "conduct in taking the corner too fast could not in my view amount to negligence", he continued:] As regards the second respect in which the learned judge found Mr. Holladay to be negligent, namely, in his attempt to bring back the horse into the arena after it had come into contact with the first shrub . . . I am unable to accept the judge's inference of fact that the course taken by the horse along the line of shrubs was due to Mr. Holladay's attempt to bring it back into the arena instead of letting it run out on to the cinder track. But, even if the judge's inference of fact be accepted, here was a classic case where Mr. Holladay's decision what to do had to be taken in the "agony of the moment" when he had no time to think, and if he took the wrong decision that could not in law amount to negligence. The most that can be said against Mr. Holladay is that, in the course of, and for the purposes of, the competition he was guilty of an error or errors of judgment or a lapse of skill. That is not enough to constitute a breach of the duty of reasonable care which a participant owes to a spectator. In such circumstances, something in the nature of a reckless disregard of the spectator's safety must be proved, and of this there is no suggestion in the evidence.

I, too, would allow this appeal.

[DANCKWERTS L.J. delivered a judgment in favour of allowing the appeal.]

Appeal allowed

Questions

1. Do you think the phrase "reckless disregard of the spectator's safety"

---

1. [1933] 2 K.B. 297; [1933] All E.R. Rep. 594.
2. [1935] 1 K.B. 146; [1934] All E.R. Rep. 103.
3. [1939] 1 K.B. 509; [1939] 1 All E.R. 59.
4. [1959] 3 All E.R. 225.
5. [1959] 3 All E.R. at p. 233.

implies an objective or a subjective standard i.e. must the competitor actually have foreseen the danger to the spectator?

2. If a policeman who was on duty at a sporting event was carelessly injured by a competitor, would the "reckless disregard of safety" test apply?

Notes

1. The criticism to which this decision was subjected by A. L. Goodhart (1962), 78 L.Q.R. 490, was referred to in *Wilks* v. *The Cheltenham Home Guard Motor Cycle and Light Car Club*, [1971] 2 All E.R. 369. Edmund Davies L.J. stated (at p. 374) that he "would with deference adopt the view of Dr. Goodhart (1962), 78 L.Q.R. at p. 496, that the proper test is whether injury to a spectator has been caused 'by an error of judgment that a reasonable competitor, being the reasonable man of the sporting world, would not have made'". Although accepting that spectators expected the competitor to be doing his best to win, his Lordship would still require the competitor to exercise reasonable care *in all the circumstances*. Lord Denning M.R., however, was still prepared to apply the "reckless disregard of safety" test to riders in *races* (cf. pp. 370–371). Phillimore L.J. stressed that the test was one of negligence and that the circumstances might not warrant the application of the tests to be found in *Wooldridge* v. *Sumner*. It is submitted that the test adopted by Edmund Davies L.J. should be followed. It is sufficiently flexible to cater for the special factors which arise in the context of competitions, and, as Dr. Goodhart points out, this test "is more in accord with the general principles on which the law of negligence is based".

2. If a spectator is injured by a competitor in a sporting event, he is not restricted to an action against that person, but may bring an action against the occupier of the place where the event was staged—see *Murray* v. *Harringay Arena, Ltd.*, [1951] 2 K.B. 529; [1951] 2 All E.R. 320; compare *White* v. *Blackmore*, [1972] 2 Q.B. 651; [1972] 3 All E.R. 158, p. 235, *ante*.

3. For a case where a participant in a sporting event (and not a spectator) sued the occupier of the ground, see *Simms* v. *Leigh Rugby Football Club, Ltd.*, [1969] 2 All E.R. 923, referring to s. 2 (5) of the Occupiers' Liability Act 1957— ". . . risks willingly accepted as his by the visitor. . . ." (But see note 2, p. 225, *ante*.)

10

Liability for Damage Caused by Things

Those who keep or put into circulation *things*—such as products, inflammable materials and animals—create special dangers. Not surprisingly, therefore, a study of the materials in this Chapter will reveal attempts to create special rules, going beyond the tort of negligence, to place responsibility for resulting damage on those who create the risk, unless they prove that what happened was the result of an Act of God or of a stranger or was caused by the fault of the injured person. The courts in England in *Phillips* v. *Britannia Hygienic Laundry Co., Ltd.*, [1923] 2 K.B. 832, p. 277, *ante*, missed the opportunity to develop, through statutory interpretation, a principle of strict liability for damage caused by motor vehicles. They have also not yet followed the lead given by courts in the United States in developing a principle of strict enterprise liability for defective products (see W. L. Prosser, *Law of Torts* (4th Edn.), Chap. 17; P. N. Legh-Jones, "Products Liability: Consumer Protection in America", [1969] C.L.J. 54). In the area of liability for chattels, the consumer's protection rests principally in the law of contract and, to some extent, in the criminal law. So far as the law of tort is concerned, the "manufacturer's rule" in *M'Alister* (or *Donoghue*) v. *Stevenson*, [1932] A.C. 562, p. 57, *ante*, has been extended to a wide range of ultimate consumers and has on occasions almost reached the level of strict liability, but the theory of the law still rests firmly upon the tort of negligence. At one time the classification of a chattel as dangerous or non-dangerous was considered important, but today it is clear that this classification affects only the degree of care which will be required of a defendant in a particular situation.

The category of *dangerous* things is, however, still of importance in the area of law dealt with in the second section of this Chapter—the strict liability which exists under the rule in *Rylands* v. *Fletcher* (1868), L.R. 3 H.L. 330, p. 338, *post*. The rule is concerned with the escape of dangerous things from land. However, its sphere of operation at present is rather limited and amongst the difficulties facing the plaintiff is the uncertainty whether damages can be recovered for personal injuries, and whether a non-occupier of land has any title to sue at all. It has been mentioned above, that, on occasions, liability for chattels under *M'Alister* (or *Donoghue*) v. *Stevenson* has come close to strict liability: on the other hand, liability under *Rylands* v. *Fletcher* may virtually become liability for negligence. It will be seen that one requirement of liability under *Rylands* v. *Fletcher* is that there must have been a "non-natural user" of land, and Winfield & Jolowicz suggest (at p. 374) that this concept "is now understood by the courts as being similar to the idea of unreasonable risk in negligence" (see also pp. 389–390; David W. Williams, "Non-Natural Use of Land", [1973] C.L.J. 310, esp. pp. 314–317). Further similarity between liability under *Rylands* v. *Fletcher* and liability in negligence will be discovered when "act of stranger" (a defence to *Rylands* v. *Fletcher* liability) is considered—see *Perry* v. *Kendricks Transport, Ltd.*, [1956] 1 All E.R. 154, p. 349, *post*. Foreseeability of the kind of damage is of course required in negligence (*The Wagon Mound (No. 1)*, [1961] A.C. 388; [1961] 1 All E.R. 404, p. 192, *ante*), but it should be remembered that the Privy Council in *The Wagon Mound (No. 1)* asserted that their judgment was not intended to "reflect on" the rule in *Rylands* v. *Fletcher* which they had not considered. (See generally R. W. M. Dias, "Remoteness of Liability and Legal Policy", [1962] C.L.J. 178, at pp. 193–195.) The rule in *Rylands* v. *Fletcher* was considered by the Law Commission in 1970 (*Civil Liability for Dangerous Things and Activities*, Law Com. No. 32), but, because of the scope of the inquiry which the Law Commission was invited to undertake, that body refrained from making any recommendations to change the law. (See paras. 2, 11 and 18 of the Report.)

The penultimate section of this Chapter deals with liability for fire, which has often been considered to be within the rule in *Rylands* v. *Fletcher*, although liability for fire at common law has its own separate history. Indeed, in a recent case, *H. & N. Emanuel, Ltd.* v. *Greater London Council*, [1971] 2 All E.R. 835, p. 354, *post*, the old common law action for damage by fire received judicial attention. A more modern hazard, nuclear installations, has been subject to special legislation, and liability for such installations should be studied in the light of that legislation, p. 267, *ante*. (For further legislative activity in the sphere of "dangerous things", see the Deposit of Poisonous Waste Act 1972.)

Liability for animals is also the concern of this Chapter, and the recent legislation on this topic (the Animals Act 1971) is set out at p. 359, *post*. Liability for animals can still be based on torts such as negligence, nuisance or *Rylands* v. *Fletcher* (see P. M. North, *The Modern Law of Animals*, Chap. 6), but the 1971 Act contains its own special heads of liability. Nevertheless, it should not be forgotten that liability in negligence is affected by the Act, for s. 8 alters the common law position concerning liability for negligence where animals stray on to a highway; see North, *op. cit.*, pp. 149–161).

1. CHATTELS AND THE LAW OF NEGLIGENCE

(a) In general

M'Alister (or Donoghue) v. Stevenson, p. 57, *ante*

(b) Development of the law

Grant v. Australian Knitting Mills, Ltd.

Judicial Committee of the   [1935] All E.R. Rep. 209
Privy Council

The plaintiff, Dr. Richard Thorold Grant, of Adelaide, South Australia, claimed damages on the ground that he had contracted dermatitis by reason of the improper condition of some underpants bought by him from the defendants, John Martin and Co., Ltd., and manufactured by the defendants, Australian Knitting Mills, Ltd.

The appellant bought the underwear on 3 June 1931. He put on one suit on the morning of 28 June 1931. By the evening of that date he felt itching, but no objective symptoms appeared until the next day, when a redness appeared in front of each ankle over an area of about 2½ in. by 1½ in. His condition got worse, the rash became generalised and very acute, and he was confined to bed for seventeen weeks. In November he became convalescent and went to New Zealand to recuperate. He returned in the following February, but soon had a relapse, and by March his condition was so serious that in April he went into hospital where he remained until July. In April he began this action.

The Supreme Court of South Australia (Murray C.J.) gave judgment against both defendants, against the retailers on the contract of sale, and against the manufacturers in tort, following the decision of the House of Lords in *M'Alister* (or *Donoghue*) v. *Stevenson*,[1] but the decision of the Supreme Court was reversed by the High Court of Australia by a majority. The plaintiff appealed.

LORD WRIGHT: . . . The appellant's claim was that the disease was caused by the presence in the cuffs or ankle ends of the underpants which he purchased and wore, of an irritating chemical, namely, free sulphite, the presence of which was due to negligence in manufacture, and also involved on the part of the respondents, John Martin & Co., Ltd., a breach of the relevant implied conditions under the Sale of Goods Act.

[Having held that the retailers were liable in contract and that there was negligence in the manufacture, he continued:] . . . According to the evidence, the method of manufacture was correct; the danger of excess sulphites being left was recognised and was guarded against; the process was intended to be foolproof. If excess sulphites were left in the garment, that could only be because someone was at fault. The appellant is not required to lay his finger on the exact person in all the chain who was responsible or to specify what he did wrong. Negligence is found as a matter of inference from the existence of the defects taken in connection with all the known circumstances; even if the manufacturers could by apt evidence have rebutted that inference they have not done so.

On this basis, the damage suffered by the appellant was caused in fact (because the interposition of the retailers may for this purpose in the circumstances of the case be disregarded) by the negligent or improper way in which the manufacturers made the garments. But this mere sequence of cause and effect is not enough in law to constitute a cause of action in negligence, which is a complex concept, involving a duty as between the parties to take care, as well as a breach of that duty and resulting damage. It might be said that here was no relationship between the parties at all; the manufacturers, it might be said, parted once and for all with the garments when they sold them to the retailers and were, therefore, not concerned with their future history, except in so far as under their contract with the retailers they might come under some liability; at no time, it might be said, had they any knowledge of the existence of the appellant; the only peg on which it might be sought to support a relationship of duty was the fact that the appellant had actually worn the garments, but he had done so because he had acquired them by a purchase from the retailers, who were at that time the owners of the goods, by a sale which had vested the property in the retailers and divested both property and control from the manufacturers. It was said there could be no legal relationship in the matter save those under the two contracts between the respective parties to those contracts, the one between the manufacturers and the retailers and the other between the retailers and the appellant. These contractual relationships (it might be said) covered the whole field and excluded any question of tort liability; there was no duty other than the contractual duties.

---

1. [1932] A.C. 562.

This argument was based on the contention that the present case fell outside the decision of the House of Lords in *M'Alister* (or *Donoghue*) v. *Stevenson*.[1] Their Lordships, like the judges in the courts in Australia, will follow that decision, and the only question here can be what that authority decides and whether this case comes within its principles. . . .

Their Lordships think that the principle of the decision is summed up in the words of Lord Atkin ([1932] A.C. at p. 599):

> "A manufacturer of products, which he sells in such a form as to show that he intends them to reach the ultimate consumer in the form in which they left him with no reasonable possibility of intermediate examination, and with the knowledge that the absence of reasonable care in the preparation of putting up of the products will result in an injury to the consumer's life or property, owes a duty to the consumer to take that reasonable care."

This statement is in accord with the opinions expressed by Lord Thankerton and Lord Macmillan, who in principle agreed with Lord Atkin.

In order to ascertain whether the principle applies to the present case, it is necessary to define what the decision involves and consider the points of distinction relied upon before their Lordships.

It is clear that the decision treats negligence, where there is a duty to take care, as a specific tort in itself, and not simply as an element in some more complex relationship or in some specialised breach of duty, and still less as having any dependence on contract. All that is necessary as a step to establish the tort of actionable negligence is to define the precise relationship from which the duty to take care is to be deduced. It is, however, essential in English law that the duty should be established; the mere fact that a man is injured by another's act gives in itself no cause of action; if the act is deliberate, the party injured will have no claim in law even though the injury is intentional, so long as the other party is merely exercising a legal right; if the act involves lack of due care, again no case of actionable negligence will arise unless the duty to be careful exists. In *Donoghue's* case,[1] the duty was deduced simply from the facts relied on, namely, that the injured party was one of a class for whose use, in the contemplation and intention of the makers, the article was issued to the world, and the article was used by that party in the state in which it was prepared and issued without it being changed in any way and without there being any warning of, or means of detecting, the hidden danger; there was, it is true, no personal intercourse between the maker and the user; but though the duty is personal, because it is inter partes, it needs no interchange of words, spoken or written, or signs of offer or assent; it is thus different in character from any contractual relationship; no question of consideration between the parties is relevant; for these reasons the use of the word "privity" in this connection is apt to mislead because of the suggestion of some overt relationship like that in contract, and the word "proximity" is open to the same objection; if the term proximity is to be applied at all, it can only be in the sense that the want of care and the injury are in essence directly and intimately connected; though there may be intervening transactions of sale and purchase and intervening handling between these two events, the events are themselves unaffected by what happened between them: proximity can only properly be used to exclude any element of remoteness, or of some interfering complication between the want of care and the injury, and, like "privity" may mislead by introducing alien ideas. Equally also may the word "control" embarrass, though it is conveniently used in the opinions in *Donoghue's* case[1] to emphasise the essential factor that the consumer must use the article exactly as it left the maker, that is in all material features, and use it as it was intended to be used. In that sense the maker may be said to control the thing until it is used. But that again is an artificial use, because, in the natural sense of the word, the makers parted with all control when they sold the article and

---

1. [1932] A.C. 562.

divested themselves of possession and property. An argument used in the present case based on the word "control" will be noticed later.

It is obvious that the principles thus laid down involve a duty based on the simple facts detailed above, a duty quite unaffected by any contracts dealing with the thing, for instance, of sale by maker to retailer, and again by retailer to consumer or to the consumer's friend.

It may be said that the duty is difficult to define, because when the act of negligence in manufacture occurs there was no specific person towards whom the duty could be said to exist: the thing might never be used: it might be destroyed by accident or it might be scrapped, or in many ways fail to come into use in the normal way: in other words, the duty cannot at the time of manufacture be other than potential or contingent, and only can become vested by the fact of actual use by a particular person. But the same theoretical difficulty has been disregarded in cases like *Heaven* v. *Pender*,[1] or in the case of things dangerous per se or known to be dangerous, where third parties have been held entitled to recover on the principles explained in *Dominion Natural Gas Co., Ltd.* v. *Collins and Perkins*.[2] In *Donoghue's* case,[3] the thing was dangerous in fact, though the danger was hidden, and the thing was dangerous only because of want of care in making it; as Lord Atkin points out in *Donoghue's* case[3] ([1932] A.C. at p. 595), the distinction between things inherently dangerous and things only dangerous because of negligent manufacture cannot be regarded as significant for the purpose of the questions here involved.

One further point may be noted. The principle of *Donoghue's* case[3] can only be applied where the defect is hidden and unknown to the consumer, otherwise the directness of cause and effect is absent: the man who consumes or uses a thing which he knows to be noxious cannot complain in respect of whatever mischief follows because it follows from his own conscious volition in choosing to incur the risk or certainty of mischance.

If the foregoing are the essential features of *Donoghue's* case[3] they are also to be found, in their Lordships' judgment, in the present case. The presence of the deleterious chemical in the pants, due to negligence in manufacture, was a hidden and latent defect, just as much as were the remains of the snail in the opaque bottle: it could not be detected by any examination that could reasonably be made. Nothing happened between the making of the garments and their being worn to change their condition. The garments were made by the manufacturers for the purpose of being worn exactly as they were worn in fact by the appellant: it was not contemplated that they should be first washed. It is immaterial that the appellant has a claim in contract against the retailers, because that is a quite independent cause of action, based on different considerations, even though the damage may be the same. Equally irrelevant is any question of liability between the retailers and the manufacturers on the contract of sale between them. The tort liability is independent of any question of contract.

It was argued, but not perhaps very strongly, that *Donoghue's* case[3] was a case of food or drink to be consumed internally, whereas the pants here were to be worn externally. No distinction, however, can be logically drawn for this purpose between a noxious thing taken internally and a noxious thing applied externally: the garments were made to be worn next the skin: indeed Lord Atkin ([1932] A.C. at p. 583) specifically puts as examples of what is covered by the principle he is enunciating things operating externally, such as "an ointment, a soap, a cleaning fluid, or cleaning powder".

Counsel for the respondents, however, sought to distinguish *Donoghue's* case[3] from the present on the ground that in the former the makers of the ginger beer had retained "control" over it in the sense that they had placed it in stoppered and sealed bottles,

---

1. (1883), 11 Q.B.D. 503.
2. [1909] A.C. 640.
3. [1932] A.C. 562.

so that it would not be tampered with until it was opened to be drunk, whereas the garments in question were merely put into paper packets, each containing six sets, which in ordinary course would be taken down by the shopkeeper and opened and the contents handled and disposed of separately so that they would be exposed to the air. He contended that, though there was no reason to think that the garments, when sold to the appellant were in any other condition, least of all as regards sulphur contents, than when sold to the retailers by the manufacturers, still the mere possibility and not the fact of their condition having been changed was sufficient to distinguish *Donoghue's* case[1]: there was no "control" because nothing was done by the manufacturers to exclude the possibility of any tampering while the goods were on their way to the user. Their Lordships do not accept that contention. The decision in *Donoghue's* case[1] did not depend on the bottle being stoppered and sealed; the essential point in this regard was that the article should reach the consumer or user subject to the same defect as it had when it left the manufacturer. That this was true of the garment is in their Lordships' opinion beyond question. At most there might in other cases be a greater difficulty of proof of the fact.

Counsel further contended on behalf of the manufacturers that, if the decision in *Donoghue's* case[1] were extended even a hairsbreadth, no line could be drawn and a manufacturer's liability would be extended indefinitely. He put as an illustration the case of a foundry which had cast a rudder to be fitted on a liner: he assumed that it was fitted and the steamer sailed the seas for some years: but the rudder had a latent defect due to faulty and negligent casting and one day it broke, with the result that the vessel was wrecked, with great loss of life and damage to property. He argued that, if *Donoghue's* case[1] were extended beyond its precise facts, the maker of the rudder would be held liable for damages of an indefinite amount, after an indefinite time and to claimants indeterminate until the event. But it is clear that such a state of things would involve many considerations far removed from the simple facts of this case. So many contingencies must have intervened between the lack of care on the part of the makers and the casualty that it may be that the law would apply, as it does in proper cases, not always according to strict logic, the rule, that cause and effect must not be too remote. In any case the element of directness would obviously be lacking. Lord Atkin deals with that sort of question in *Donoghue's* case[1] ([1932] A.C. at p. 591) where he refers to *Earl* v. *Lubbock*[2]: he quotes the common sense opinion of Mathew L.J.:

> "It is impossible to accept such a wide proposition, and, indeed, it is difficult to see how, if it were the law, trade could be carried on."

In their Lordships' opinion it is enough for them to decide this case on its actual facts. No doubt, many difficult problems will arise before the precise limits of the principle are defined: many qualifying conditions and many complications of fact may in the future come before the Courts for decision. It is enough now to say that their Lordships hold the present case to come within the principle of *Donoghue's* case[1] and they think that the judgment of the Chief Justice was right and should be restored as against both respondents, and that the appeal should be allowed with costs here and in the courts below, and that the appellant's petition for leave to adduce further evidence should be dismissed without costs. They will humbly so advise His Majesty.

Appeal allowed

Evans v. Triplex Safety Glass Co., Ltd.

King's Bench Division   [1936] I All E.R. 283

In 1934, Mr. Evans bought a Vauxhall car which had been fitted by the Vauxhall Motor Co. with a windscreen made of "Triplex Toughened Safety Glass". In July

---

1. [1932] A.C. 562.
2. [1905] 1 K.B. 253.

1935, he was driving the car, with his wife and son as passengers, when the windscreen cracked and disintegrated. Part of the windscreen fell on the boy, part on Mr. Evans and a considerable portion fell on the wife who suffered severe shock. The plaintiffs (Mr. Evans and his wife) brought an action against the manufacturers of the windscreen.

PORTER J.: . . . In this case I do not think that I ought to infer negligence on the part of the defendants. . . . I cannot draw the inference that the cause of the disintegration was the faulty manufacture. It is true that the human element may fail and then the manufacturers would be liable for negligence of their employee, but then that was not proved in this case. The disintegration may have been caused by any accident. There was every opportunity for failure on the part of the human element in fastening the windscreen, and I think that the disintegration was due rather to the fitting of the windscreen than to faulty manufacture having regard to its use on the road and the damage done to a windscreen in the course of user.

It is true that, as Mr. Macaskie[1] points out, in these cases he has not got to eliminate every possible element, but he has got to eliminate every probable element. He has not displaced sufficiently the balance of probabilities in this case. I think that this glass is reasonably safe and possibly more safe than other glasses. One cannot help seeing that in all these cases one has to look with considerable care. One has to consider the question of time. The plaintiff had had the windscreen for about a year. Then there is the possibility of examination. The suppliers of the car had every opportunity to examine the windscreen. I do not propose to lay down any rule of law; it is a question of degree and these elements must be taken into consideration. This article was put into a frame and screwed; one must consider that. As I have said there is the element of time, the opportunity of examination and the opportunity of damage from other causes. One must consider all these factors.

In *M'Alister* (or *Donoghue*) v. *Stevenson*[2] there was a snail in the ginger beer bottle and there was no opportunity of seeing it as you could not see through the glass. In *Grant* v. *Australian Knitting Mills, Ltd.*[3] the article passed on to the purchaser and it is quite clear that a reasonable examination of the garment would not have revealed the presence of the sulphite. That case is different from this. In that case there was found in some of the garments an excess of sulphites and that clearly was the cause of the injury. Here are a number of causes which might have caused disintegration. I do not find any negligence proved against the defendants and I give the defendants judgment with costs.

Kubach v. Hollands

King's Bench Division   [1937] 3 All E.R. 907

A science teacher bought from the second defendants a powder labelled manganese dioxide, but which was in fact a mixture of that chemical and a much larger quantity of antimony sulphide. The second defendants had purchased the powder as manganese dioxide from a third party, but the invoice stated *inter alia* that the goods "must be examined and tested by user before use". The second defendants did not examine or test the powder, nor did they inform the teacher of the need for such examination or test. The use of manganese dioxide in a particular chemical experiment would have been safe but, when this powder was used, there was an explosion and a schoolgirl was injured. The plaintiffs (the schoolgirl and her father) unsuccessfully claimed damages against the first defendant (the proprietress of the school). However, the second defendants, who had notice of the powder's intended use, were held liable for negligence, and they claimed contribution or an indemnity from the third party.

1. Counsel for the plaintiffs.
2. [1932] A.C. 562.
3. [1936] A.C. 85.

LORD HEWART L.C.J.: . . . After hearing and considering the very careful arguments of counsel on both sides, I have come, reluctantly enough, to the conclusion that the third party is entitled to succeed. . . .

[Having quoted Lord Atkin's "manufacturer principle",[1] he continued:] The case which is there contemplated is, I think, in essential respects the opposite of the present case. The manganese dioxide which the third party ought to have supplied here to the second defendants might have been resold for a variety of purposes or in innocuous compounds or mixtures. The use of it for school experiments was only one of the many possible uses, and the third party, unlike the second defendants, had no notice of the intended use. More than that, it was common ground that a very simple test, if it had been carried out, as the third party's invoice prescribed, and as the first defendant was not warned, would immediately have exhibited the fact that antimony sulphide had erroneously been made up and delivered as manganese dioxide. The second defendants had ample and repeated opportunity of intermediate examination, and, if they had taken the simple precaution which the invoice warned them to take, no mischief would have followed . . . The like conclusion is illustrated also in *Grant* v. *Australian Knitting Mills, Ltd.*[2] . . .

Finally, it was attempted, although faintly, to derive some assistance for the second defendants from the provisions of the Law Reform (Married Women and Tortfeasors) Act 1935 . . . In my opinion, there was no joint tort, nor could the plaintiff have sued the third party . . .

Judgment for the third party against the second defendants

Question

What is the relevance of a warning to the question of intermediate examination?

Notes

1. In The *"Diamantis Pateras"*, [1966] 1 Lloyd's Rep. 179, Lawrence J. stated (at p. 188): "A consideration of modern authorities leads me to the conclusion that the opportunity of intermediate examination is a matter which goes now rather to the question of causation than to the issue of whether or not a duty of care is imposed on the defendants."

2. Causation questions may arise where the plaintiff himself had a chance to to inspect the article and has gained some knowledge of its dangerous nature. In *Denny* v. *Supplies and Transport Co., Ltd.*, [1950] 2 K.B. 374, the plaintiff, an employee of certain wharfingers, was injured in the course of unloading timber from a barge. The timber had earlier been loaded from a ship on to the barge by stevedores, who were found by the county court judge to have done the job very badly. The movement of the timber from the ship to the land was "one continuous process". At one time, before the accident occurred, the plaintiff had asked the wharf superintendent for danger money, complaining that the barge had been badly loaded, and was thus unsafe. However, in the Court of Appeal, Evershed M.R. would not assent to the proposition that an experienced man must have realised danger was *imminent*: further, in his Lordship's view, there was "no practical alternative to the course of conduct adopted". It was held that the chain of causation between the stevedores' acts and the plaintiff's injury remained intact, and that the plaintiff was still the

---

1. [1932] A.C. 562, at p. 599.
2. [1936] A.C. 85.

stevedores' "neighbour". The stevedores' appeal from the county court judge's decision awarding the plaintiff £100 was dismissed. (Compare *Farr* v. *Butters Bros. & Co.*, [1932] 2 K.B. 606, and see a note at (1950), 66 L.Q.R. 427.) In considering the "narrow manufacturer's rule" in *M'Alister* (or *Donoghue*) v. *Stevenson*, Street argues (at p. 174) that where the plaintiff is aware that the chattel is defective, no duty is owed. He distinguishes cases which were decided on "grand" principles of negligence, of which *Denny's* case is an example. See generally Street, pp. 170–176: cf. Salmond, pp. 315–316.

Haseldine v. C. A. Daw & Son, Ltd.

Court of Appeal   [1941] 3 All E.R. 156

The day after work had been done on a lift by the second defendants (A. & P. Steven, Ltd.) the lift, which was situated in a block of flats, fell, and the plaintiff, who was using it at the time, was injured. The ram (part of the mechanism of the lift) was worn and scored. The cause of the fall was the fracture of a gland, and the fracture in turn was due to a servant of the second defendants refixing the gland out of true on the worn and scored ram. The contract between the agent of Daw, who owned the flats and the second defendants provided *inter alia* for the adjustment, cleaning and lubrication of the lift mechanism by the latter, and for reports after each periodical visit. On the claim against the second defendants, who had been held liable by Hilbery J., [1941] 1 All E.R. 525, for their workman's failure to exercise reasonable care:

GODDARD L.J.: . . . I now turn to the question of the liability of A. & P. Steven, Ltd., which depends, I think, entirely on whether the principle of *M'Alister* (or *Donoghue*) v. *Stevenson*[1] applies to the case of a repairer as it does to a manufacturer of chattels, when, from the nature of the case, it appears that there is no reasonable opportunity for the examination of the chattel after the repair is complete and before it is used, and when the use by persons other than the person with whom the repairer contracted must be contemplated or expected. The plaintiff contends that it does, and that this view has been taken on more than one occasion by courts of first instance. A. & P. Steven, Ltd., contend that it is the principle of *Earl* v. *Lubbock*[2] which governs this case, and that *M'Alister* (or *Donoghue*) v. *Stevenson*[1] expressly recognises the correctness of that decision. I believe that this is the first time that the question has come before an appellate court, and, accordingly, one must examine with care the principle on which *M'Alister* (or *Donoghue*) v. *Stevenson*[1] depends. It is to be observed that the two noble and learned Lords who formed the minority in that case thought that the decision must necessarily apply to a repairer. I think that one may say that this appears to have been one of the reasons for their dissent. Lord Buckmaster said, at p. 577:

> "The principle contended for must be this: that the manufacturer, *or indeed the repairer* of any article, apart entirely from contract, owes a duty to any person by whom the article is lawfully used to see that it has been carefully constructed."

The italics are mine. Lord Tomlin expressed the same view, at p. 599. Taken alone, the sentence states the proposition too widely, for it omits the all-important qualification that the liability is said to exist only where there is no reasonable opportunity for inspection of the chattel between its leaving the hands of the manufacturer or repairer and its consumption or use. I pause here for a moment to say that I think that it is generally considered that, when Lord Atkin used the expression "reasonable possibility" with relation to inspection, he meant possibility in a commercial sense, and, as I ventured to say in *Paine* v. *Colne Valley Electricity Supply Co., Ltd., and British Insulated Cables, Ltd.*,[3] the word "probability" might perhaps be used instead. One should, I

---

1. [1932] A.C. 562.
2. [1905] 1 K.B. 253.
3. [1938] 4 All E.R. 803.

think, ask oneself the question: "In the circumstances of any particular case, ought the purchaser, or, in the case of repairs, the person for whom the repairs were done, to have made inspection for himself?" Apart from the question whether *Earl* v. *Lubbock*[1] is still good law, the contention of these defendants, as I understand it, is that the true principle underlying *M'Alister* (or *Donoghue*) v. *Stevenson*[2] is that it was to the interest of the manufacturer that his goods should reach the consumer unopened, and that it was his intention that they should, and that this was the reason for privity or proximity or direct relationship, call it what you will, being established between the manufacturer and the ultimate consumer. On the other hand, it is said that the governing factor is the possibility or probability or contemplation that an inspection will take place before the goods are put into use. For my part, I think that the latter proposition is the truth, and for this conclusion I find support in the advice of the Judicial Committee in *Grant* v. *Australian Knitting Mills, Ltd.*[3] The *corpus delicti* in that case was a pair of underpants. Had they been washed before use, no ill effects would have resulted. I cannot see that it matters one iota to a manufacturer whether a purchaser washes them before use or not, from the point of view of his interest in the sale. I can well understand, however, that a canner of food or a manufacturer of mineral water has an interest in his products not being opened by anyone but the consumer, as the product would otherwise be injured. Equally I have no doubt that some rather particular people would have new underclothes washed before using them. However, in *Grant's* case,[3] Lord Wright disposed of the matter in a sentence, at p. 105:

"It was not contemplated that they should be first washed."

If, then, there was any doubt about the governing principle of *M'Alister* (or *Donoghue*) v. *Stevenson*,[2] Lord Wright has dissipated it. The manufacturer was held liable, not because he was interested in his product being used as it left his factory, but because he had no reason to contemplate an examination by the retailer or ultimate buyer before use. . . . On what sound principle, then, can the case of a repairer be distinguished from that of a maker of an article? Of course, the doctrine does not apply to the repair of any article any more than to its manufacture. If I order my tailor to make me a suit, or a watchmaker to repair my watch, no one would suppose that anyone but myself was going to use the suit or watch. If the tailor left a large needle in the lining, and it injured a person to whom at some time I lent the coat, I should think that the latter could not recover against the tailor. The relationship would be altogether too remote, and many of the suggested difficulties of *M'Alister* (or *Donoghue*) v. *Stevenson*[2] disappear if it is realised that the decision was, as I venture to believe, essentially one on the question of remoteness. The case of a lift repairer, however, is very different. A lift in a block of flats is there to be used by the owner and his servants, the tenants and their servants, and all persons resorting thereto on lawful business. Blocks of flats and offices are frequently owned by limited companies, who would be contracting parties with the lift engineers. In such a case, the employer would be the one "person" who could by no possibility use the lift. If the repairers do their work carelessly or fail to report a danger of which, as experts, they ought to be aware, I cannot see why the principle of *M'Alister* (or *Donoghue*) v. *Stevenson*[2] should not apply to them. . . . [Having stated that *Earl* v. *Lubbock*,[1] on which the second defendants relied for the view that the repairer only owed a duty to a contracting party, had not been expressly approved in *M'Alister* (or *Donoghue*) v. *Stevenson*[2] and that the former case "if properly pleaded . . . would be differently decided today" he continued:] . . . It follows that, where the facts show that no intermediate inspection is practicable or is contemplated, a repairer of a chattel stands in no different position from that of a manufacturer, and does owe a duty to a person who, in the ordinary course, may be expected to make use of the thing repaired. . . . To render the . . .

---

1. [1905] 1 K.B. 253.
2. [1932] A.C. 562.
3. [1936] A.C. 85.

repairer liable, there must be (i) a want of care on his part in the performance of the work he was employed to do, and (ii) circumstances which show that the employer will be left in ignorance of the danger which the lack of care has created. Suppose a lift repairer told the owner that a part was worn out, so that, while he could patch it up, he could not leave it in a safe condition. If he were told to do the best he could, and an accident then happened, I cannot conceive that the repairer would be held liable. He has fulfilled his duty by warning the employer, and, if the latter, in spite of that, chooses to allow the lift to be used, the liability rests on him. The accident would be caused, not by the carelessness of the repairer, but by the employer's disregard of the warning given to him. In the present case, Daw is not liable to the plaintiff, because he had a right to rely on the work and reports of the experts he employed, and no examination of their work after completion was contemplated. It would, I venture to think, be a strange and unjust result if the plaintiff, who has been injured directly by the careless performance of the work, is to be left without a remedy. In my opinion, the appeal of A. & P. Steven, Ltd., should be dismissed.

[Scott L.J. delivered a judgment in favour of dismissing the second defendants' appeal. Clauson L.J. delivered a judgment in favour of allowing the second defendants' appeal.]

Appeal of the second defendants dismissed

Note

The case above shows an expansion in the category of defendants, but the class of plaintiffs has also increased and is not restricted to consumers. In *Stennett* v. *Hancock and Peters*, [1939] 2 All E.R. 578, the plaintiff's leg was badly bruised when it was struck by a flange, which had come off one of the wheels of the first defendant's lorry, the plaintiff being on the pavement of the the highway along which the lorry was being driven. In fact, the wheel had earlier been in the possession of the second defendant whose servants had mended a puncture, re-assembled the wheel and on the day of the accident put it back on the lorry. The cause of the accident was found to be the careless re-assembly of the wheel by one of the second defendant's servants. Neither the first defendant himself nor his driver inspected the wheel to see that its re-assembly had been carried out correctly, but the learned judge (Branson J.) relying on the decision in *Phillips* v. *Britannia Hygienic Laundry Co., Ltd.*, [1923] 1 K.B. 539, took the view that the first defendant could assume that the wheel had been properly assembled. The claim against the first defendant failed, but the second defendant (the repairer) was held liable on the principle of *M'Alister* (or *Donoghue*) v. *Stevenson*, [1932] A.C. 562. Each element which according to that decision had been necessary to impose liability on the manufacturer of a product to its ultimate user was, in Branson J.'s opinion, present in this case.

Clay v. A. J. Crump & Sons, Ltd., p. 183, *ante*

(c) The problem of proof

Grant v. Australian Knitting Mills, Ltd., p. 328, *ante*

Mason v. Williams and Williams, Ltd. and Thomas Turton & Sons, Ltd.

Chester Assizes   [1955] 1 All E.R. 808

A piece of metal flew off the head of a cold chisel, which the plaintiff was using, and hit him in the eye: the eye later had to be removed. There was no suggestion that the plaintiff had been at fault in using the chisel, which had been supplied by his employers (the first defendants), and manufactured by the second defendants. The chisel, the head of which was dangerously hard, had only been taken out of the stores a few weeks before the accident. On the claim against the manufacturers:

FINNEMORE J. . . . I appreciate that I am faced with another problem, as was indicated in the case of *M'Alister* (or *Donoghue*) v. *Stevenson*,[1] that res ipsa loquitur does not apply and that the court has to be satisfied, and therefore the plaintiff has got to prove, that there was negligence on the part of the manufacturers. Of course that cannot be proved normally by saying that on such and such a date such and such a workman did this, that or the other. I think that when you have eliminated anything happening in this case at the employers' factory, whither, as is undisputed, this chisel came direct from the manufacturers—and when it came from the manufacturers the head was too hard, and that undue hardness could have been produced only while it was being manufactured by them, and could have been produced by someone there either carelessly or deliberately to make a harder and more durable head—that is really as far as any plaintiff can be expected to take his case. What the plaintiff says here is: "This is your chisel, you made it and I used it as you made it, in the condition in which you made it, in the way you intended me to use it, and you never relied on any intermediate examination; therefore I have discharged the onus of proof by saying that this trouble must have happened through some act in the manufacture of this chisel in your factory, and that was either careless or deliberate, and in either event it was a breach of duty towards me, a person whom you contemplated would use this article which you made, in the way you intended it to be used." He is entitled to succeed against the manufacturers. . . .

Judgment for the plaintiff against the manufacturers

Question

What would the defendants have to do to escape liability in a case of this kind?

Notes

1. This extract should be read along with the statements of Lord MacMillan in *M'Alister* (or *Donoghue*) v. *Stevenson*, [1932] A.C. 562, p. 66, *ante*, and also the views expressed in *Grant* v. *Australian Knitting Mills, Ltd.*, [1936] A.C. 85, p. 328, *ante*.

2. For liability for chattels in the context of the employment situation, see now the Employer's Liability (Defective Equipment) Act 1969, p. 639, *post*.

2. ESCAPE OF DANGEROUS THINGS FROM LAND

Rylands v. Fletcher

Court of Exchequer Chamber   [1861–73] All E.R. Rep. 1
and House of Lords

Appeal from a decision of the Court of Exchequer . . . by the defendants in an action brought against them by the plaintiff for damage done to his mines through the escape of water from a reservoir on the defendants' land.

The plaintiff was a tenant of Lord Wilton. The defendants, who were proprietors of a mill, made upon land of Lord Wilton's, in pursuance of an arrangement made with him for that purpose, a reservoir, employing competent persons to construct the same. It turned out that beneath the site of the reservoir were old shafts running down into

---

1. [1932] A.C. 562.

coal workings long disused which communicated with other old workings situate under the land of one Whitehead. The plaintiff's colliery, called the Red House Colliery, adjoined Whitehead's land, and the plaintiff, soon after he had commenced working the Red House Colliery, made arrangements with Whitehead to get, by means of the Red House pit, the coal lying under Whitehead's land. In pursuance of those arrangements the plaintiff had worked through from the Red House Colliery into the coal lying under Whitehead's land, and so into the old workings situated under Whitehead's land. As a result the workings of the plaintiff's colliery were made to communicate with the old workings under the reservoir. These underground works were effected several years before the defendants commenced making their reservoir, but the fact of their existence was not known to the defendants or any agent of theirs, or any person employed by them, until the reservoir burst, as is hereinafter mentioned. In the course of constructing the reservoir the shafts were perceived, but it was not known or suspected that they had been made for the purpose of getting coal beneath the site of the reservoir. The Special Case stated in the action contained a finding that there was no personal negligence or default on the part of the defendants themselves in relation to the selection of the site or the construction of the reservoir, but reasonable and proper care was not used by the persons employed with reference to the shafts so met with to provide for the sufficiency of the reservoir to bear the pressure which, when filled, it would have to bear. The reservoir in consequence burst downwards into the shafts, and the water found its way into the plaintiff's mine. The majority of the Court of Exchequer held that the non-exercise of sufficient care upon the part of the persons employed to construct the reservoir did not, in the absence of any notice to the defendants of the underground communication, affect the defendants with any liability, there being in the absence of such notice no duty cast upon the defendants to use any particular amount of care in the construction of a reservoir upon their own land. Bramwell B. was of opinion that the question of knowledge was immaterial, and that the defendants were, therefore, liable. The plaintiff appealed to the Court of Exchequer Chamber.

BLACKBURN J. (reading the judgment of the Court): . . . The plaintiff, though free from all blame on his part, must bear the loss, unless he can establish that it was the consequence of some default for which the defendants are responsible.

The question of law, therefore, arises: What is the liability which the law casts upon a person who, like the defendants, lawfully brings on his land something which, though harmless while it remains there, will naturally do mischief if it escape out of his land? It is agreed on all hands that he must take care to keep in that which he has brought on the land, and keep it there in order that it may not escape and damage his neighbour's, but the question arises whether the duty which the law casts upon him under such circumstances is an absolute duty to keep it in at his peril, or is, as the majority of the Court of Exchequer have thought, merely a duty to take all reasonable and prudent precautions in order to keep it in, but no more. If the first be the law, the person who has brought on his land and kept there something dangerous, and failed to keep it in, is responsible for all the natural consequences of its escape. If the second be the limit of his duty, he would not be answerable except on proof of negligence, and consequently would not be answerable for escape arising from any latent defect which ordinary prudence and skill could not detect. Supposing the second to be the correct view of the law, a further question arises subsidiary to the first, namely, whether the defendants are not so far identified with the contractors whom they employed as to be responsible for the consequences of their want of skill in making the reservoir in fact insufficient with reference to the old shafts, of the existence of which they were aware, though they had not ascertained where the shafts went to.

We think that the true rule of law is that the person who, for his own purposes, brings on his land, and collects and keeps there anything likely to do mischief if it escapes, must keep it in at his peril, and, if he does not do so, he is prima facie answerable for all the damage which is the natural consequence of its escape. He can excuse himself by showing that the escape was owing to the plaintiff's default, or, perhaps, that the escape was the consequence of vis major, or the act of God; but, as nothing of this sort exists here, it is unnecessary to inquire what excuse would be sufficient. The general rule, as above stated, seems on principle just. The person whose grass or corn is eaten down by the escaped cattle of his neighbour, or whose mine is flooded by the water from his neighbour's reservoir, or whose cellar is invaded by the filth of his neighbour's privy, or whose habitation is made unhealthy by the fumes and noisome vapours of his neighbour's alkali works, is damnified without any fault of his own; and it seems but reasonable and just that the neighbour who has brought something on his own property which was not naturally there, harmless to others so long as it is confined to his own property, but which he knows will be mischievous if it gets on his neighbour's, should be obliged to make good the damage which ensues if he does not succeed in confining it to his own property. But for his act in bringing it there no mischief could have accrued, and it seems but just that he should at his peril keep it there, so that no mischief may accrue, or answer for the natural and anticipated consequences. On authority this, we think, is established to be the law, whether the thing so brought be beasts or water, or filth or stenches. . . .

The view which we take of the first point renders it unnecessary to consider whether the defendants would or would not be responsible for the want of care and skill in the persons employed by them. We are of opinion that the plaintiff is entitled to recover. . . .

[On appeal by the defendants to the House of Lords:]

LORD CAIRNS L.C.: . . . The principles on which this case must be determined appear to me to be extremely simple. The defendants, treating them as the owners or occupiers of the close on which the reservoir was constructed, might lawfully have used that close for any purpose for which it might, in the ordinary course of the enjoyment of land, be used, and if, in what I may term the natural user of that land, there had been any accumulation of water, either on the surface or underground, and if by the operation of the laws of nature that accumulation of water had passed off into the close occupied by the plaintiff, the plaintiff could not have complained that that result had taken place. If he had desired to guard himself against it, it would have lain on him to have done so by leaving or by interposing some barrier between his close and the close of the defendants in order to have prevented that operation of the laws of nature.

As an illustration of that principle, I may refer to a case which was cited in the argument before your Lordships, *Smith* v. *Kenrick*[1] in the Court of Common Pleas. On the other hand, if the defendants, not stopping at the natural use of their close, had desired to use it for any purpose which I may term a non-natural use, for the purpose of introducing into the close that which, in its natural condition, was not in or upon it—for the purpose of introducing water, either above or below ground, in quantities and in a manner not the result of any work or operation on or under the land, and if in consequence of their doing so, or in consequence of any imperfection in the mode of their doing so, the water came to escape and to pass off into the close of the plaintiff, then it appears to me that that which the defendants were doing they were doing at their own peril; and if in the course of their doing it the evil arose to which I have referred—the evil, namely, of the escape of the water, and its passing away to the close of the plaintiff and injuring the plaintiff—then for the consequence of that, in my opinion, the defendants would be liable. . . .

These simple principles, if they are well founded, as it appears to me they are, really dispose of this case. The same result is arrived at on the principles referred to by Blackburn J. in his judgment in the Court of Exchequer Chamber. . . .

In that opinion, I must say, I entirely concur. Therefore, I have to move your

---

1. (1849), 7 C.B. 515.

Lordships that the judgment of the Court of Exchequer Chamber be affirmed, and that the present appeal be dismissed with costs.

LORD CRANWORTH: I concur with my noble and learned friend in thinking that the rule of law was correctly stated by Blackburn J. in delivering the opinion of the Exchequer Chamber. If a person brings or accumulates on his land anything which, if it should escape, may cause damage to his neighbour, he does so at his peril. If it does escape and cause damage, he is responsible, however careful he may have been, and whatever precautions he may have taken to prevent the damage. In considering whether a defendant is liable to a plaintiff for damage which the plaintiff may have sustained, the question in general is, not whether the defendant has acted with due care and caution, but whether his acts have occasioned the damage. This is all well explained in the old case of *Lambert and Olliot* v. *Bessey*.[1] The doctrine is founded on good sense, for when one person in managing his own affairs causes, however innocently, damage to another, it is obviously only just that he should be the party to suffer. He is bound sic uti suo ut non lædat alienum. This is the principle of law applicable to cases like the present, and I do not discover in the authorities which were cited anything conflicting with it. . . .

. . . The plaintiff had a right to work his coal through the lands of Mr. Whitehead and up to the old workings. If water naturally rising in the defendants' land (we may treat the land as the land of the defendants for the purpose of this case) had by percolation found its way down to the plaintiff's mine through the old workings and so had impeded his operations, that would not have afforded him any ground of complaint. Even if all the old workings had been made by the defendants they would have done no more than they were entitled to do, for, according to the principle acted on in *Smith* v. *Kenrick*,[2] the person working the mine under the close in which the reservoir was made had a right to win and carry away all the coal without leaving any wall or barrier against Whitehead's land. But that is not the real state of the case. The defendants, in order to effect an object of their own, brought on to their land, or on to land which for this purpose may be treated as being theirs, a large accumulated mass of water, and stored it up in a reservoir. The consequence of this was damage to the plaintiff, and for that damage, however skilfully and carefully the accumulation was made, the defendants, according to the principles and authorities to which I have adverted, were certainly responsible. I concur, therefore, with my noble and learned friend in thinking that the judgment below must be affirmed, and that there must be judgment for the defendant in error.

Appeal dismissed

Notes

1. One particular mystery which surrounds this decision is neatly stated in the title of a note by R. F. V. Heuston—"Who was the Third Lord in *Rylands* v. *Fletcher*?" (1970), 86 L.Q.R. 160. See also a note by D. E. C. Yale (1970), 86 L.Q.R. 311, for a further contribution to this question.

2. The need for there to be a non-natural user of land for liability under *Rylands* v. *Fletcher* was apparently introduced in the House of Lords, but, as Viscount Simon pointed out in *Read* v. *J. Lyons and Co., Ltd.*, [1947] A.C. 156, at p. 166, p. 343, *post*, Blackburn J. did at one point refer to a neighbour bringing something on to his land "which was not naturally there". Does this differ from the test of non-natural user? (See generally F. H. Newark, "Non-Natural User and *Rylands* v. *Fletcher*" (1961), 24 M.L.R. 557; David W. Williams, "Non-Natural Use of Land", [1973] C.L.J. 310 and see further note 1, p. 348, *post*.)

---

1. (1680), T. Raym. 421, at p. 467.
2. (1849), 7 C.B. 515.

3. Blackburn J. spoke of "anything likely to do mischief if it escapes", but it should be noted that this may not necessarily be confined to "things". In *A.-G.* v. *Corke,* [1933] Ch. 89, the defendant was held responsible under the *Rylands* v. *Fletcher* principle for the nuisance created by the activities off his land of some of the caravan-dwellers who were licensees on his land. This case should be compared with *Smith* v. *Scott,* [1973] Ch. 314; [1972] 3 All E.R. 645, the facts of which are given at p. 67, *ante.* In that case, Pennycuick V-C. took the view that the rule could not be invoked against a landlord who let premises to undesirable tenants. He continued (at p. 649):

> "The person liable under the rule in *Rylands* v. *Fletcher* (1868), L.R. 3 H.L. 330 is the owner or controller of the dangerous 'thing', and this is normally the occupier and not the owner of the land. . . . A landlord parts with possession of the demised property in favour of his tenant and could not in any sense known to the law be regarded as controlling the tenant on property still occupied by himself. I should respectfully have thought that *A.-G.* v. *Corke,* [1933] Ch. 89 could at least equally well have been decided on the basis that the landowner there was in possession of the property and was himself liable in nuisance for the acts of his licensees: see *White* v. *Jameson* (1874), L.R. 18 Eq. 303."

For an early discussion both of "things" within the rule and of the non-natural user of land, see W. T. S. Stallybrass, "Dangerous Things and the Non-Natural User of Land" (1929), 3 C.L.J. 376.

Read v. J. Lyons & Co., Ltd.

House of Lords   [1946] 2 All E.R. 471

VISCOUNT SIMON L.C.: My Lords, in fulfilment of an agreement dated 26 January 1942, and made between the Ministry of Supply and the respondents, the latter undertook the operation, management and control of the Elstow Ordnance Factory as agents for the Ministry. The respondents carried on in the factory the business of filling shell cases with high explosives. The appellant was an employee of the Ministry, with the duty of inspecting this filling of shell cases, and her work required her (although she would have preferred and had applied for other employment) to be present in the shell filling shop. On 31 August 1942, while the appellant was lawfully in the shell filling shop in discharge of her duty, an explosion occurred which killed a man and injured the appellant and others. No negligence was averred or proved against the respondents. The plea of *volenti non fit injuria,* for whatever it might be worth, has been expressly withdrawn before this House by the Attorney-General on behalf of the respondents, and thus the simple question for decision is whether in these circumstances the respondents are liable, without any proof or inference that they were negligent, to the appellant in damages, which have been assessed at £575 2s. 8d., for her injuries.

Cassels J., who tried the case, considered that it was governed by *Rylands* v. *Fletcher,*[1] and held that the respondents were liable, on the ground that they were carrying on an ultra-hazardous activity and so were under what is called a "strict liability" to take successful care to avoid causing harm to persons whether on or off the premises. The Court of Appeal (Scott, MacKinnon and du Parcq L.JJ.) reversed this decision, Scott L.J., in an elaborately reasoned judgment, holding that a person on the premises had, in the absence of any proof of negligence, no cause of action, and that there must be an escape of the damage-causing thing from the premises and damage caused outside before the doctrine customarily associated with the case of *Rylands* v. *Fletcher*[1] can apply.

I agree that the action fails. . . .

---

1. (1868), L.R. 3 H.L. 330.

Blackburn J., in delivering the judgment of the Court of Exchequer Chamber in *Fletcher* v. *Rylands*[1] (L.R. 1 Exch. 265, at p. 279), laid down the proposition that:

". . . the person who, for his own purposes brings on his lands and collects and keeps there, anything likely to do mischief if it escapes, must keep it in at his peril, and, if he does not do so, is *prima facie* answerable for all the damage which is the natural consequence of its escape."

It has not always been sufficiently observed that in the House of Lords, when the appeal from *Fletcher* v. *Rylands*[1] was dismissed and Blackburn, J.'s pronouncement was expressly approved, Lord Cairns L.C. emphasized another condition which must be satisfied before liability attaches without proof of negligence. This is that the use to which the defendant is putting his land is a "non-natural" use (L.R. 3 H.L. 330, at pp. 338–339). Blackburn J. had made a parenthetic reference to this sort of test when he said (L.R. 1 Exch. 265, at p. 280):

". . . it seems but reasonable and just that the neighbour, who has brought something on his own property, *which was not naturally there*, harmless to others so long as it is confined to his own property, but which he knows to be mischievous if it gets on his neighbour's, should be obliged to make good the damage which ensues if he does not succeed in confining it to his own property."

I confess to finding this test of "non-natural" user (or of bringing on the land what was not "naturally there," which is not the same test) difficult to apply. . . .

The classic judgment of Blackburn J. besides deciding the issue before the court and laying down the principle of duty between neighbouring occupiers of land on which the decision was based, sought to group under a single and wider proposition other instances in which liability is independent of negligence . . . There are instances, no doubt, in our law in which liability for damage may be established apart from proof of negligence, but it appears to me logically unnecessary and historically incorrect to refer to all these instances as deduced from one common principle. The conditions under which such a liability arises are not necessarily the same in each class of case. Lindley L.J. issued a valuable warning in *Green* v. *Chelsea Waterworks Co.*[2] (70 L.T. 547, at p. 549), when he said of *Rylands* v. *Fletcher*[3] that that decision:

". . . is not to be extended beyond the legitimate principle on which the House of Lords decided it. If it were extended as far as strict logic might require, it would be a very oppressive decision."

It seems better, therefore, when a plaintiff relies on *Rylands* v. *Fletcher*[3] to take the conditions declared by this House to be essential for liability in that case and to ascertain whether these conditions exist in the actual case.

Now, the strict liability recognised by this House to exist in *Rylands* v. *Fletcher*[3] is conditioned by two elements which I may call the condition of "escape" from the land of something likely to do mischief if it escapes, and the condition of "non-natural use" of the land. This second condition has in some later cases, which did not reach this House, been otherwise expressed, e.g. as "exceptional" user, when such user is not regarded as "natural" and at the same time is likely to produce mischief if there is an "escape". Dr. Stallybrass, in a learned article in 3 *Cambridge Law Review*, p. 376, has collected the large variety of epithets that have been judicially employed in this connection. The American *Restatement of the Law of Torts*, III, s. 519, speaks of "ultra-hazardous activity", but attaches qualifications which would appear in the present instance to exonerate the respondents. It is not necessary to analyse this second condition on the present occasion, for in the case now before us the first essential condition of "escape" does not seem to me to be present at all. "Escape", for the purpose of applying the proposition in *Rylands* v. *Fletcher*[3] means escape from a place

---

1. (1866), L.R. 1 Exch. 265.
2. (1894), 70 L.T. 547.
3. (1868), L.R. 3 H.L. 330.

which the defendant has occupation of, or control over, to a place which is outside his occupation or control. Blackburn J. several times refers to the defendant's duty as being the duty of "keeping a thing in" at the defendant's peril and by "keeping in" he means, not preventing an explosive substance from exploding, but preventing a thing which may inflict mischief from escaping from the area which the defendant occupies or controls. In two well-known cases the same principle of strict liability for escape was applied to defendants who held a franchise to lay pipes under a highway and to conduct water (or gas) under pressure through them: *Charing Cross West End and City Electric Supply Co.* v. *London Hydraulic Power Co.*[1]; *Northwestern Utilities, Ltd.* v. *London Guarantee and Accident Co., Ltd.*[2] . . .

In these circumstances it becomes unnecessary to consider other objections that have been raised, such as the question whether the doctrine of *Rylands* v. *Fletcher*[3] applies where the claim is for damages for personal injury as distinguished from damages to property. It may be noted, in passing, that Blackburn J. himself when referring to the doctrine of *Rylands* v. *Fletcher*[3] in the later case of *Cattle* v. *Stockton Waterworks*[4] leaves this undealt with. He treats damages under the *Rylands* v. *Fletcher*[3] principle as covering damages to property, such as workmen's clothes or tools, but says nothing about liability for personal injuries.

On the much litigated question of what amounts to "non-natural" use of land, the discussion of which is also unnecessary in the present appeal, I content myself with two further observations. The first is that when it becomes essential for the House to examine this question it will, I think, be found that Lord Moulton's analysis in delivering the judgment of the Privy Council in *Rickards* v. *Lothian*[5] is of the first importance. The other observation is as to the decision of this House in *Rainham Chemical Works, Ltd.* v. *Belvedere Fish Guano Co.*,[6] to which the appellant's counsel in the present case made considerable reference in support of the proposition that manufacturing explosives was a "non-natural" use of land. This was a case of damage to adjoining property. I find in Scrutton L.J.'s judgment (in the court of first instance (123 L.T. 211, at p. 212)) that he understood it to be admitted before him that the person in possession of and responsible for the D.N.P. was liable under the doctrine of *Rylands* v. *Fletcher*[3] for the consequences of its explosions. The point, therefore, was not really open for argument to the contrary before the House of Lords, where Lord Carson begins his opinion by stating that it was not seriously argued, and that the real point to be determined was as to the liability of two directors of the appellant's company. The opinion of Lord Buckmaster which covers many pages, is almost exclusively concerned with establishing the directors' liability, and on the other point his observation ([1921] 2 A.C. 465, at p. 471), merely is that the making of munitions was certainly not the "common and ordinary use of the land" . . . I think it not improper to put on record, with all due regard to the admission and *dicta* in that case, that if the question had hereafter to be decided whether the making of munitions in a factory at the government's request in time of war for the purpose of helping to defeat the enemy is a "non-natural" use of land, adopted by the occupier "for his own purposes", it would not seem to me that the House would be bound by this authority to say that it was. In this appeal the question is immaterial, as I hold that the appellant fails for the reason that there was no "escape" from the respondents' factory. I move that the appeal be dismissed with costs.

LORD MACMILLAN: . . . The action is one of damages for personal injuries. Whatever may have been the law of England in early times I am of opinion that, as the law now stands an allegation of negligence is in general essential to the relevancy of an

1. [1913] 3 K.B. 442.
2. [1936] A.C. 108.
3. (1868), L.R. 3 H.L. 330.
4. (1875), L.R. 10 Q.B. 453.
5. [1913] A.C. 263.
6. [1921] 2 A.C. 465.

action of reparation for personal injuries. The gradual development of the law in the matter of civil liability is discussed and traced with ample learning and lucidity in *Holdsworth's History of English Law*, Vol. 8, pp. 446 *et seq.*, and need not here be rehearsed. Suffice it to say that the process of evolution has been from the principle that every man acts at his peril and is liable for all the consequences of his acts to the principle that a man's freedom of action is subject only to the obligation not to infringe any duty of care which he owes to others. The emphasis formerly was on the injury sustained and the question was whether the case fell within one of the accepted classes of common law actions; the emphasis now is on the conduct of the person whose act has occasioned the injury and the question is whether it can be characterised as negligent. I do not overlook the fact that there is at least one instance in the present law in which the primitive rule survives, namely, in the case of animals *ferae naturae* or animals *mansuetae naturae* which have shown dangerous proclivities.[1]. . . But such an exceptional case as this affords no justification for its extension by analogy.

The appellant in her printed case in this House thus poses the question to be determined:

"Whether the manufacturer of high explosive shells is under strict liability to prevent such shells from exploding and causing harm to persons on the premises where such manufacture is carried on as well as to persons outside such premises."

Two points arise on this statement of the question. In the first place, the expression "strict liability", though borrowed from authority, is ambiguous. If it means the absolute liability of an insurer irrespective of negligence, then the answer, in my opinion, must be in the negative. If it means that an exacting standard of care is incumbent on manufacturers of explosive shells to prevent the occurrence of accidents causing personal injuries I should answer the question in the affirmative, but this will not avail the plaintiff. In the next place, the question as stated would seem to assume that liability would exist in the present case to persons injured outside the defendants' premises without any proof of negligence on the part of the defendants. Indeed, Cassels J. in his judgment ([1944] 2 All E.R. 98, at p. 101) records that:

"It was not denied that if a person outside the premises had been injured in the explosion the defendants would have been liable without proof of negligence."

I do not agree with this view. In my opinion, persons injured by the explosion inside or outside the defendant's premises would alike require to aver and prove negligence to render the defendants liable. . . .

The mainstay of the argument of counsel for the appellant was his invocation of the doctrine of *Rylands* v. *Fletcher*,[2] and especially the passage in the judgment of Blackburn J., so often quoted, approved and followed. Adopting and adapting the language of Blackburn J. he said that the respondents here brought on their lands and collected and kept there things likely to do mischief, but the immediately following words used by that eminent judge did not suit so well, for, according to him the things must be things likely to do mischief if they escape and the duty is to keep them in at peril. In the present case it could not be said that anything had escaped from the defendants' premises or that they had failed in keeping in anything. Counsel was, accordingly, constrained to paraphrase the words of Blackburn J., and read them as if he had said "likely to do mischief if not so controlled as to prevent the possibility of mischief". He invoked, as did Blackburn J., the case of straying cattle as an illustration of such liability. That again, in my opinion, is a special survival with an historical background and affords no analogy to the present case.

The doctrine of *Rylands* v. *Fletcher*,[2] as I understand it, derives from a conception of the mutual duties of adjoining or neighbouring landowners and its congeners are trespass and nuisance. If its foundation is to be found in the injunction *sic utere tuo*

---

1. [See now the Animals Act 1971, p. 359, *post.*]
2. (1868), L.R. 3 H.L. 330.

ut alienum non laedas, then it is manifest that it has nothing to do with personal injuries. The duty is to refrain from injuring not *alium* but *alienum*. The two prerequisites of the doctrine are that there must be the escape of something from one man's close to another man's close and that that which escapes must have been brought on the land from which it escapes in consequence of some non-natural use of that land whatever precisely that may mean. Neither of these features exists in the present case. I have already pointed out that nothing escaped from the defendants' premises, and, were it necessary to decide the point, I should hesitate to hold that in these days and in an industrial community it was a non-natural use of land to build a factory on it and conduct there the manufacture of explosives. I could conceive it being said that to carry on the manufacture of explosives in a crowded urban area was evidence of negligence, but there is no such case here and I offer no opinion on the point.

It is noteworthy in *Rylands* v. *Fletcher*[1] that all the counts in the declaration alleged negligence and that on the same page of the report on which his famous *dictum* is recorded (L.R. 1 Exch. 265, at p. 279), Blackburn J. states that:

> "the plaintiff . . . must bear the loss, unless he can establish that it was the consequence of some default for which the defendants are responsible."

His decision for the plaintiff would thus logically seem to imply that he found some default on the part of the defendants in bringing on their land and failing to confine there an exceptional quantity of water. Notwithstanding the width of some of the pronouncements, particularly on the part of Lord Cranworth, I think that the doctrine of *Rylands* v. *Fletcher*,[1] when studied in its setting, is truly a case on the mutual obligations of the owners or occupiers of neighbouring closes and is entirely inapplicable to the present case, which is quite outside its ambit.

It remains to say a word about the *Rainham Chemical Works* case.[2] There are several features to be noted. Perhaps most important is the fact that the application of the doctrine of *Rylands* v. *Fletcher*[1] was not contested except on the ground that it was not non-natural to use land in war-time for the manufacture of explosives. Lord Carson says ([1921] 2 A.C. 465, at p. 491) that the liability of the defendant company "was not seriously argued." In the next place it was a case of damage to adjoining property. The explosion caused loss of life, but we find nothing in the case about any claim for personal injuries. It is true that Lord Buckmaster states (*ibid.*, at p. 471) (what was not contested, except to the limited extent I have indicated), that the use of the land for the purpose of making munitions was "certainly not the common and ordinary use of the land" and thus brought the case within the doctrine of *Rylands* v. *Fletcher*,[1] but that was a finding of fact rather than of law. In his enunciation of the doctrine he clearly confines it to the case of neighbouring lands. And the case is open to the further observation that the real contest was, not whether there was liability, but who was liable, in particular, whether two directors of the company which was carrying on the manufacture of munitions were in the circumstances liable as well as the company itself. The case clearly affords no precedent for the present plaintiff's claim. . . .

LORD PORTER: My Lords, the point for decision by Your Lordships in this case may be stated in a sentence. It is: Are the occupiers of a munitions factory liable to one of those working in that factory who is injured in the factory itself by an explosion occurring there without any negligence on the part of the occupiers or their servants.

Normally at the present time in an action of tort for personal injuries if there is no negligence there is no liability. To this rule, however, the appellant contends that there are certain exceptions, one of the best known of which is to be found under the principle laid down in *Rylands* v. *Fletcher*.[1] The appellant's counsel relied on that case and naturally put it in the forefront of his argument. To make the rule applicable, it is at least necessary for the person whom it is sought to hold liable to have brought on

---

1. (1868), L.R. 3 H.L. 330.
2. [1921] 2 A.C. 465.

to his premises, or, at any rate, to some place over which he has a measure of control, something which is dangerous in the sense that, if it escapes, it will do damage. Possibly a further requisite is that to bring the thing to the position in which it is found is to make a non-natural use of that place. Such, at any rate, appears to have been the the opinion of Lord Cairns, and this limitation has more than once been repeated and approved: see *Rickards* v. *Lothian*[1] ([1913] A.C. 263, at p. 280, per Lord Moulton). Manifestly, these requirements must give rise to difficulty in applying the rule in individual cases and necessitate at least a decision as to what can be dangerous and what is a non-natural use. Indeed, there is a considerable body of case law dealing with these questions and a series of findings or assumptions as to what is sufficient to establish their existence. Among dangerous objects have been held to be included gas, explosive substances, electricity, oil, fumes, rusty wire, poisonous vegetation, vibrations, a flag-pole, and even dwellers in caravans. Furthermore, in *Musgrove* v. *Pandelis*[2] it was held that a motor-car brought into a garage with full tanks was a dangerous object, a conclusion, which, as Romer L.J. pointed out in *Collingwood* v. *Home and Colonial Stores, Ltd.*[3] ([1936] 3 All E.R. 200, at p. 209) involves the propositions that a motor-car is a dangerous thing to bring into a garage and that the use of one's land for the purpose of erecting a garage and keeping a motor car there is not an ordinary or proper use of the land.

My Lords, if these questions ever come directly before this House it may become necessary to lay down principles for their determination. For the present I need only say that each seems to be a question of fact subject to a ruling of the judge whether the particular object can be dangerous or the particular use can be non-natural, and in deciding this question I think that all the circumstances of the time and place and practice of mankind must be taken into consideration so that what might be regarded as dangerous or non-natural may vary according to those circumstances.

I do not, however, think that it is necessary for Your Lordships to decide these matters now, inasmuch as the defence admits that high explosive shells are dangerous things, and, whatever view may be formed whether the filling of them is or is not a non-natural use of land, the present case can, in my opinion, be determined upon a narrower ground. In all cases which have been decided, it has been held necessary, to establish liability, that there should have been some form of escape from the place in which the dangerous object has been retained by the defendant to some other place not subject to his control. . . .

It was urged on Your Lordships that it would be a strange result to hold the respondents liable if the injured person was just outside their premises but not liable if she was just within them. There is force in the objection, but the liability is itself an extension of the general rule, and, in my view, it is undesirable to extend it further. . . .

I would add that, in considering the matter now in issue before Your Lordships, it is not, in my view, necessary to determine whether injury to the person is one of those matters in respect of which damages can be recovered under the rule. Atkinson J. thought it was: see *Shiffman* v. *Venerable Order of the Hospital of St. John of Jerusalem*[4] and the language of Fletcher Moulton L.J. in *Wing* v. *London General Omnibus Co.*[5] where he says ([1909] 2 K.B. 652, at p. 665):

> "This cause of action is of the type usually described by reference to the well-known case of *Rylands* v. *Fletcher.*[6] For the purpose of to-day it is sufficient to describe this class of actions as arising out of cases where by excessive use of some private right a person has exposed his neighbour's property or person to danger."

---

1. [1913] A.C. 263.
2. [1919] 2 K.B. 43.
3. [1936] 3 All E.R. 200.
4. [1936] 1 All E.R. 557.
5. [1909] 2 K.B. 652.
6. (1868), L.R. 3 H.L. 330.

is to the same effect, and, although the jury found negligence on the part of the defendants in *Miles* v. *Forest Rock Granite Co.* (*Leicestershire*), *Ltd.*,[1] the Court of Appeal
applied the rule in *Rylands* v. *Fletcher*[2] in support of a judgment in favour of the plaintiff for £850 in respect of personal injuries. Undoubtedly, the opinions expressed in
these cases extend the application of the rule and may some day require examination.
For the moment it is sufficient to say that there must be escape from a place over which
a defendant has some measure of control to a place where he has not. In the present
case there was no such escape and I would dismiss the appeal.

LORD SIMONDS: . . . It was urged by counsel for the appellant that a decision against
her when the plaintiff in *Rainham's* case[3] succeeded would show a strange lack of
symmetry in the law. There is some force in the observation, but your Lordships will
not fail to observe that such a decision is in harmony with the development of a strictly
analogous branch of the law, the law of nuisance, in which also negligence is not a
necessary ingredient in the case. For, if a man commits a legal nuisance, it is no answer
to his injured neighbour that he took the utmost care not to commit it. There the
liability is strict, and there only he has a lawful claim who has suffered an invasion of
some proprietary or other interest in land. To confine the rule in *Rylands* v. *Fletcher*[2]
to cases in which there has been an escape from the defendant's land appears to me
consistent and logical. . . .

[LORD UTHWATT delivered a speech in favour of dismissing the appeal.]

Appeal dismissed

Notes

1. Although he found it unnecessary to decide whether there was a non-
natural user of land in *Read* v. *J. Lyons & Co., Ltd.*, Viscount Simon did make
some observations on the problem, and paid tribute to Lord Moulton's
analysis in *Rickards* v. *Lothian*, [1911–13] All E.R. Rep. 71, saying it was "of the
first importance". Lord Moulton, referring to the *Rylands* v. *Fletcher* principle,
stated (at p. 80): "It is not every use to which land is put that brings into play
that principle. It must be some special use bringing with it increased danger
to others and must not merely be the ordinary use of the land or such a use
as is proper for the general benefit of the community."

This passage was quoted by Lawton J. in *British Celanese, Ltd.* v. *A. H. Hunt*
(*Capacitors*), *Ltd.*, [1969] 2 All E.R. 1252. The facts are given on p. 383, *post*,
in detail. The statement of claim alleged *inter alia* that the defendants had
collected strips of metal foil (the "things" which had escaped) on their land
for the purposes of their business (the manufacture of electrical and electronic parts) and that the premises they occupied were on a trading estate.
It was held that to use these premises for manufacturing purposes was an
ordinary use, that neither the manufacturing of these components nor the
storing of the foil was a special use, that no special risks were created by
the mere use of premises to store foil and that the manufacture of the products, in the course of which the foil was used, was beneficial to the community. Thus the plaintiffs did not bring their case within the *Rylands* v.
Fletcher principle. This non-natural user point is a difficult one, and the following words of warning of Windeyer J. in *Benning* v. *Wong*, [1970] A.L.R.
585 should be borne in mind. He said (at pp. 618–619) that some of the
cases on non-natural user of land "seem to me to make a natural or non-

---

1. (1918), 34 T.L.R. 500.
2. (1868), L.R. 3 H.L. 330.
3. [1921] 2 A.C. 465.

natural use of land depend not on any certain objective criteria, but on whether it is a use of such a character that the defendant ought, in the opinion of the court determining the particular case, to take the risk of having a dangerous thing where it was." (See further note 2, p. 341, *ante*, and the articles there referred to.)

2. A point which the speeches in *Read* v. *J. Lyons & Co., Ltd.* touch on, but which was not decided in that case, is whether a plaintiff, relying on the *Rylands* v. *Fletcher* principle, can recover damages for personal injuries. Several authorities would give an affirmative answer to that question, but any consideration of these authorities is further complicated by the question whether the plaintiff under *Rylands* v. *Fletcher* must be an occupier of land. Despite the recent observations by Lawton J. in the *British Celanese* case that the plaintiff under *Rylands* v. *Fletcher* need not be the occupier of adjoining land, or of any land, it cannot be said that the answer to either question is *totally* free from doubt. Although each question can arise independently of the other, both will arise where the court is faced with a claim by a non-occupier for damages for personal injuries. It is, therefore, important for the student to keep the occupier/non-occupier distinction in mind when reading the authorities on compensation for personal injuries under *Rylands* v. *Fletcher*, the references to which may be found in the standard textbooks on tort.

Perry v. Kendricks Transport, Ltd.

Court of Appeal   [1956] 1 All E.R. 154

There was a vehicle park at the south end of the defendants' premises. The defendants objected to people crossing this park, and boys who played there were chased away. In the south-west corner of the park, the defendants kept a motor coach. The petrol tank had been drained and its cap replaced by the defendants who carried out regular inspections of the vehicles in the park. The infant plaintiff gave evidence to the effect that two boys were standing near to the coach. As he approached, they jumped away and there followed an explosion in which the infant plaintiff, who had not reached the defendants' land, was badly burnt. The petrol cap had been removed from the tank, but there was no evidence as to who had done this, and the explosion was found to have been caused by the throwing of a lighted match into the petrol tank by one of the two boys. There was an appeal from the judgment of Lynskey J. who had dismissed the plaintiff's claim for damages.

JENKINS L.J.: . . . So far as the plaintiff's claim is founded on negligence it seems to me that he has wholly failed to make out his case. . . .

As to the alternative contentions that the defendants are liable, even if they were not negligent, on the principle of *Rylands* v. *Fletcher*,[1] I am prepared to accept the view that this motor coach in the condition in which it was on the defendant's land was an object of the class to which the rule in *Rylands* v. *Fletcher*[1] applies, that is to say, that it was, for this purpose, a dangerous thing, because the tank contained inflammable petrol vapour and the defendants were under an obligation under the rule to prevent it, or the dangerous element in it, escaping on to a neighbour's land and doing damage there. It was a dangerous thing for this purpose in that its tank contained inflammable petrol vapour. The fact that it was a thing to which the rule in *Rylands* v. *Fletcher*[1] applied, and the fact that the vapour escaped, was ignited and did damage, cannot, however, conclude the matter against the defendants. It is well settled that an occupant of land cannot be held liable under the rule if the act bringing about the escape was

---

1. (1868), L.R. 3 H.L. 330.

the act of a stranger and not any act or omission of the occupier himself or his servant or agent, or any defect, latent or patent, in the arrangements made for keeping the dangerous thing under control. In this case, it seems to me plain that the escape was caused by the act of a stranger or strangers in the shape of one or both of the two small boys Whittaker and Rawlinson. Counsel for the plaintiff submitted that a child cannot for this purpose be a stranger because ability should not be imputed to a child of doing a conscious and deliberate act when he does such a thing as setting fire to petrol vapour in the tank of a vehicle. Speaking for myself, I see no necessity to confine the exception from the rule in *Rylands* v. *Fletcher*[1] of acts of strangers to acts which proceed from the conscious volition or the deliberate act of the stranger. It seems to me that the relevance of the exception is that the stranger is regarded as a person over whose acts the occupier of the land has no control. Then the real cause of the escape is not the occupier's action in having the dangerous thing on his land, nor is it any failure on his part or on the part of his agents in keeping the dangerous thing on the land, nor is it due to any latent or patent defect in his protective measures. The real cause is none of these things, but the act of the stranger, for whose acts the occupier of the land is in no sense responsible, because he cannot control them. It is interesting in this connection to observe that in *Rickards* v. *Lothian*,[2] Lord Moulton, after referring to the judgment of the Exchequer Chamber in *Nichols* v. *Marsland*,[3] continued ([1913] A.C. at p. 278):

> "To follow the language of the judgment just recited—a defendant cannot in their Lordships' opinion be properly said to have caused or allowed the water to escape if the malicious act of a third person was the real cause of its escaping without any fault on the part of the defendant. It is remarkable that the very point involved in the present case was expressly dealt with by Bramwell B. in delivering the judgment of the Court of Exchequer[4] in the same case. He says: 'What has the defendant done wrong? What right of the plaintiff has she infringed? She has done nothing wrong. She has infringed no right. It is not the defendant who let loose the water and sent it to destroy the bridges. She did indeed store it, and store it in such quantities that if it was let loose it would do as it did, mischief. But suppose a stranger let it loose, would the defendant be liable? If so, then if a mischievous boy bored a hole in a cistern in any London house, and the water did mischief to a neighbour, the occupier of the house would be liable. That cannot be. Then why is the defendant liable if some agent over which she has no control lets the water out? . . . I admit that it is not a question of negligence. A man may use all care to keep the water in . . . but would be liable if through any defect, though latent, the water escaped. . . . But here the act is that of an agent he cannot control'."

There Bramwell B. gives, by way of reductio ad absurdum, the example of a mischievous boy boring a hole in a cistern. He says that if the defendant in *Nichols* v. *Marsland*[3] was liable, then the occupier of a house in which there was a cistern, if a mischievous boy bored a hole in it, would be liable, and adds: "That cannot be". If we are to accept counsel's argument in its full form on this point, then if any mischievous boy chose to come on the defendants' land and chose to set fire to the petrol or the petrol vapour in the tank of a vehicle there, the defendants would be liable. I repeat, with Bramwell B., "that cannot be". It seems to me that this argument must be limited to saying that in the circumstances of a particular case, it may be that children doing some mischievous act whereby the dangerous thing escapes are not strangers. I cannot, however, regard that as aiding a plaintiff in an action such as this, unless it can be shown that in the circumstances of the case the dangerous thing was

---

1. [1868] L.R. 3 H.L. 330.
2. [1913] A.C. 263.
3. (1876), 2 Ex. D. 1.
4. [The judgment of the Court of Exchequer is to be found at (1875), L.R. 10 Ex. 255.]

left by the defendants in such a condition that it was a reasonable and probable consequence of their action, which they ought to have foreseen, that children might meddle with the dangerous thing and cause it to escape. If facts such as those were made out in any particular case, then in my view, the defendants could not claim to rely on the act of the mischievous child as constituting the act of a stranger. It would be an act brought about by the defendants' own negligence in dealing with the dangerous thing, and the foreseeable consequence of a negligent act. If that were made out, however, one reaches the point where the claim based on *Rylands* v. *Fletcher*[1] merges into the claim in negligence: for if such a state of affairs could be made out, then it would no longer be necessary for the plaintiff to rely on *Rylands* v. *Fletcher*[1] at all. He could rely simply on the defendants' negligence. Counsel for the plaintiff is precluded from taking that course here by the circumstance that the learned judge, in my view perfectly rightly, held that there was no negligence on the part of the defendants.

Accordingly, while I feel great sympathy for this unfortunate infant plaintiff, who has sustained very serious injuries through no fault of his own, I have come to the conclusion that no ground has been shown on which this court could properly hold the defendants liable to compensate him for his hurts. . . . [T]his appeal must be dismissed.

PARKER L.J.: I agree and I would only add a word in deference to the argument of counsel for the plaintiff in regard to the rule in *Rylands* v. *Fletcher*.[1] Although the decision in *Musgrove* v. *Pandelis*[2] has been the subject of some criticism (see the speech of Lord Porter in *Read* v. *Lyons & Co., Ltd.*[3]), it is still binding on this court. Accordingly, I feel bound to approach the matter on the basis that the facts here bring the case within the rule in *Rylands* v. *Fletcher*[1]: nor do I think it is open to this court to hold that the rule applies only to damage to adjoining land or to a proprietary interest in land and not to personal injury. It is true that in *Read* v. *Lyons & Co., Ltd.*,[3] Lord Macmillan, Lord Porter and Lord Simonds all doubted whether the rule extended to cover personal injuries, but the final decision in the matter was expressly left over and, as the matter stands at present, I think we are bound to hold that the defendants are liable in this case, quite apart from negligence, unless they can bring themselves within one of the well-known exceptions to the rule.

For a long time there has been an exception to the rule where the defendants can show that the act which brought about the escape was the act of a stranger, meaning thereby someone over whom they had no control. The acts in question here, first, of removing the petrol cap, and, secondly, of inserting a lighted match, are, as it seems to me, prima facie undoubtedly the acts of strangers in that sense. Counsel, however, contends that nevertheless, since at any rate the last of those acts, the insertion of the lighted match, was almost certainly the act of a young child, the exception does not apply, and for this reason, so he says, that in law the act of a young child is not a novus actus interveniens. Speaking for myself, I do not think the matter can be approached in quite that way. In a *Rylands* v. *Fletcher*[1] case the plaintiff need only prove the escape. The onus is then on the defendants to bring themselves within one of the exceptions. Once they prove that the escape was caused by the act of a stranger, whether an adult or a child, they avoid liability, unless the plaintiff can go on to show that the act which caused the escape was an act of the kind which the occupier could reasonably have anticipated and guarded against. In that connection it seems to me that it is not sufficient for the plaintiff to show that the defendants knew that children played in the vehicle park, played on the roof of a motor car or inside a coach. They must show that the defendants reasonably should have anticipated an act of a kind which would cause the escape.

Sorry as one is for the infant plaintiff in this case, it seems to me that he has utterly

---

1. (1868), L.R. 3 H.L. 330.
2. [1919] 2 K.B. 43.
3. [1947] A.C. 156.

failed to show that the defendants should have anticipated any such thing. I agree that this appeal should be dismissed.

[SINGLETON L.J. delivered a judgment in favour of dismissing the appeal.]

Appeal dismissed

Question

If the defence of act of stranger had not been successful in this case and if it is accepted that a non-occupier can recover damages for personal injuries under *Rylands* v. *Fletcher*, could the boy have recovered damages if he had been trespassing on the land where he was standing when he was injured?

Notes

1. Although Jenkins L.J. would not confine the defence of act of stranger to "acts which proceed from the conscious volition or the deliberate act of the stranger," it might be noted that Singleton L.J. stated that the occupier of land was excused from *Rylands* v. *Fletcher* liability where "the damage is caused by the mischievous, deliberate and conscious act of a stranger." See Clerk & Lindsell, para. 1496; cf. Winfield & Jolowicz, p. 381.

2. On the burden of proof, the following statement should be compared with those in *Perry* v. *Kendricks Transport, Ltd.* In *Hanson* v. *Wearmouth Coal Co., Ltd. and Sunderland Gas Co.*, [1939] 3 All E.R. 47, Goddard L.J. stated (at p. 53):

> "A person who brings a dangerous thing on to his land and allows it to escape, thereby causing damage to another, is liable to that other unless he can show that the escape was due to the conscious act of a third party, and without negligence on his own part. Obviously the burden of showing that there was no negligence is on the defendants, and it is not for the plaintiff to prove negligence affirmatively."

See also *A. Prosser & Son, Ltd.* v. *Levy*, [1955] 3 All E.R. 577, at p. 587 *per* Singleton L.J.; *Northwestern Utilities, Ltd.* v. *London Guarantee and Accident Co., Ltd.*, [1936] A.C. 108; cf. Street, p. 254, note 5.

3. FIRE

The Fires Prevention (Metropolis) Act 1774

86. No action to lie against a person where the fire accidentally begins.— And . . . no action, suit or process whatever shall be had, maintained or prosecuted against any person in whose house, chamber, stable, barn or other building, or on whose estate any fire shall . . . accidentally begin, nor shall any recompence be made by such person for any damage suffered thereby, any law, usage or custom to the contrary notwithstanding: . . . provided that no contract or agreement made between landlord and tenant shall be hereby defeated or made void.

Notes

1. Despite the title of this statute, this section is not restricted to the "Metropolis" but applies generally: *Filliter* v. *Phippard* (1847), 11 Q.B. 347. That case also decided that the section does not give any protection where the

fire has been caused by the defendant's negligence, nor where the defendant intentionally lit the fire.

2. Further consideration was given to the 1774 Act in *Musgrove* v. *Pandelis*, [1919] 2 K.B. 43. In that case, a fire occurred in a garage at the back of a house of which the plaintiff was the lessee. The garage had living rooms above. Part of the garage had been let to the defendant, who kept his car there, and on one occasion when his servant started the car, the petrol in the carburettor caught fire. If the servant had turned off the petrol tap straight away the fire would have been rendered harmless, but when he did attempt to do this, the fire, which by then was burning more fiercely, thwarted his efforts. The fire spread, and burnt the car, the garage, the plaintiff's rooms above and some of his furniture. The defendant relied on section 86 of the 1774 Act, and the Court of Appeal resolved two questions relating to its construction. The word "fire" in the Act, was interpreted to mean "the fire which causes the damage". This was held to be the fire, fed by petrol from the tank, which spread and burnt the car, and was to be distinguished from the original fire in the carburettor, which could have burnt itself out if the petrol tap had been turned off. Thus the Act would not protect the defendant since the later fire did not "accidentally begin", but was a result of the servant's negligence. Is this a sensible distinction? It was also held that the Act did not provide a defence in a case, such as the present, where liability for fire could be based on the principle of *Rylands* v. *Fletcher*, a principle which Bankes L.J. thought had existed in the law "long before" that decision. For criticism, see A. I. Ogus, "Vagaries in Liability for the Escape of Fire", [1969] C.L.J. 104, at pp. 113–116.

3. The view that the 1774 Act is inapplicable where the *Rylands* v. *Fletcher* principle is invoked was doubted, but followed by Mackenna J. in *Mason* v. *Levy Auto Parts of England, Ltd.*, [1967] 2 Q.B. 530; [1967] 2 All E.R. 62. Having discussed *Musgrove* v. *Pandelis*, he went on to say (at pp. 69–70):

> "What then is the principle? As Romer L.J. pointed out in *Collingwood* v. *Home and Colonial Stores, Ltd.*, [1936] 3 All E.R. 200, at pp. 208–209, it cannot be exactly that of *Rylands* v. *Fletcher* (1868), L.R. 3 H.L. 330. A defendant is not held liable under *Rylands* v. *Fletcher* unless two conditions are satisfied: (i) that he has brought something on to his land likely to do mischief if it escapes, which has in fact escaped, and (ii) that these things happened in the course of some non-natural user of the land. However, in *Musgrove's* case, [1919] 2 K.B. 43, the car had not escaped from the land, neither had the petrol in its tank. The principle must be, Romer L.J. said, [1936] 3 All E.R. at p. 209, the wider one on which *Rylands* v. *Fletcher* itself was based, *Sic utere tuo ut alienum non laedas*. If, for the rule in *Musgrove's* case to apply, there need be no escape of anything brought on to the defendant's land, what must be proved against him? There is, it seems to me, a choice of two alternatives. The first would require the plaintiff to prove (a) that the defendant had brought something on to his land likely to do mischief if it escaped, (b) that he had done so in the course of a non-natural user of the land, and (c) that the thing had ignited and that the fire had spread. The alternative would be to hold the defendant liable if (a) he brought on to his land things likely to catch fire, and kept them there in such conditions that, if they did ignite, the fire would be likely to spread to the plaintiff's land, (b) he did so in the course of some non-natural use, and (c) the thing ignited and the fire spread.
>
> The second test is, I think, the more reasonable one, since to make the likelihood of damage if the thing escapes a criterion of liability, when the thing has not in fact

escaped but has caught fire, would not be very sensible. I propose, therefore, to apply the second test. . . ."

Honeywill & Stein, Ltd. v. Larkin Bros. (Commercial Photographers), Ltd., p. 637, *post*

Balfour v. Barty-King, p. 636, *post*

Goldman v. Hargrave, p. 393, *post*

H. & N. Emanuel, Ltd. v. Greater London Council

Court of Appeal   [1971] 2 All E.R. 835

The London County Council (L.C.C.—now the Greater London Council (G.L.C.)) managed two prefabricated bungalows for the government, who had put them up on land owned by the Council. In 1962, there was a request by the L.C.C. to the Ministry of Housing for the bungalows to be removed, and their removal was approved by that Ministry: in the meantime, the L.C.C. kept control and their district foreman held the keys. The Ministry of Housing asked the Ministry of Works to remove the bungalows, and the method adopted by the latter Ministry was to sell the bungalows to Mr. King, a contractor. The contract specified that no rubbish was to be burnt on the site, that work was not to be started until the contractor had received written notice of the bungalows' release (which the Ministry of Works issued) and that the local authority, from whom the keys were to be obtained, must be told of the date of the commencement of the dismantling work. After the contractor obtained the written notice of release from the foreman, his men went to the site. However, they lit a bonfire, and sparks set fire to property on the plaintiff's adjoining premises. There was evidence that the burning of rubbish by the contractor was a regular practice, which was known to the Ministry of Works, and it was "reasonable to assume" (*per* Lord Denning M.R.) that the practice and the term in the contract against it were also known by the L.C.C.'s foreman. James J. held both the Council and Mr. King liable and the Council appealed.

LORD DENNING M.R.: . . . After considering the cases, it is my opinion that the occupier of a house or land is liable for the escape of fire which is due to the negligence not only of his servants, but also of his independent contractors and of his guests, and of anyone who is there with his leave or licence. The only circumstances when the occupier is not liable for the negligence is when it is the negligence of a stranger. It was so held in a case in the Year Books 570 years ago. *Beaulieu* v. *Finglam*,[1] which is well translated by Mr. Fifoot in his book on the History and Sources of the Common Law.[2] The occupier is, therefore, liable for the negligence of an independent contractor, such as the man who comes in to repair the pipes and uses a blowlamp: see *Balfour* v. *Barty-King*[3]; and of a guest who negligently drops a lighted match: see *Boulcott Golf Club Inc.* v. *Engelbrecht*.[4] The occupier is liable because he is the occupier and responsible in that capacity for those who come by his leave and licence: see *Sturges* v. *Hackett*.[5]

But the occupier is not liable for the escape of fire which is not due to the negligence of anyone. Sir John Holt himself said in *Tuberville* v. *Stampe*[6] that if a man is properly burning up weeds or stubble and, owing to an unforeseen wind-storm, without negligence, the fire is carried into his neighbour's ground, he is not liable. Again, if a haystack is properly built at a safe distance, and yet bursts into flames by spontaneous

---

1. (1401), Y.B. 2 Hen. 4, fo. 18, pl. 6.
2. 1949, p. 166.
3. [1957] 1 Q.B. 496; [1957] 1 All E.R. 156.
4. [1945] N.Z.L.R. 556.
5. [1963] 3 All E.R. 166; [1962] 1 W.L.R. 1257.
6. (1697), 1 Ld. Raym. 264.

combustion, without negligence, the occupier is not liable. That is to be inferred from *Vaughan* v. *Menlove*.[1] So also if a fire starts without negligence owing to an unknown defect in the electric wiring: *Collingwood* v. *Home and Colonial Stores, Ltd.*[2]; or a spark leaps out of the fireplace without negligence: *Sochacki* v. *Sas*.[3] All those cases are covered, if not by the common law, at any rate by the Fire Prevention (Metropolis) Act 1774, which covers all cases where a fire begins or spreads by accident without negligence. But that Act does not cover a fire which begins or is spread by negligence: see *Filliter* v. *Phippard*,[4] *Musgrove* v. *Pandelis*[5] and *Goldman* v. *Hargrave*.[6]

Nevertheless, as I have said earlier, the occupier is not liable if the outbreak of fire is due to the negligence of a "stranger". But who is a "stranger" for this purpose? In *Beaulieu* v. *Finglam*[7] Markham J. put this case:

"If a man from outside my household against my will sets fire to the thatch of my house or does otherwise per quod my house is burned and also the houses of my neighbours, I shall not be held to answer to them, because this cannot be said to be ill on my part, but against my will."

And in *Tuberville* v. *Stampe*,[8] Sir John Holt C.J. said:

". . . if a stranger set fire to my house, and it burns my neighbour's house, no action will lie against me . . ."

Who then is a stranger? I think a "stranger" is anyone who in lighting a fire or allowing it to escape acts contrary to anything which the occupier could anticipate that he would do: such as the person in *Rickards* v. *Lothian*.[9] Even if it is a man whom you have allowed or invited into your house, nevertheless, if his conduct in lighting a fire is so alien to your invitation that he should qua the fire be regarded as a trespasser, he is a "stranger". Such as the man in Scrutton L.J.'s well-known illustration[10]:

"When you invite a person into your house to use the staircase you do not invite him to slide down the bannisters . . ."

which was quoted by Lord Atkin in *Hillen and Pettigrew* v. *I.C.I. (Alkali), Ltd.*[11]. . .

There has been much discussion about the exact legal basis of liability for fire. The liability of the occupier can be said to be a strict liability in this sense that he is liable for the negligence not only of his servants but also of independent contractors and, indeed, of anyone except a "stranger". By the same token it can be said to be a "vicarious liability", because he is liable for the defaults of others as well as his own. It can also be said to be a liability under the principle of *Rylands* v. *Fletcher*,[12] because fire is undoubtedly a dangerous thing which is likely to do damage if it escapes. But I do not think it necessary to put it into any one of these three categories. It goes back to the time when no such categories were thought of. Suffice it to say that the extent of the liability is now well defined as I have stated it. The occupier is liable for the escape of fire which is due to the negligence of anyone other than a stranger.

Seeing that in this case the contractors were negligent both in lighting the fire in that place and in allowing it to spread, the only question is whether the L.C.C. were "occupiers" of the land and whether the contractors were "strangers" to them. The question of what is an "occupier" was much discussed in *Fisher* v. *C.H.T., Ltd.*[13] and

1. (1837), 3 Bing N.C. 468.
2. [1936] 3 All E.R. 200.
3. [1947] 1 All E.R. 344.
4. (1847), 11 Q.B.D. 347.
5. [1919] 2 K.B. 43.
6. [1966] 2 All E.R. 989.
7. (1401), Y.B., 2 Hen. 4, fo. 18, pl. 6.
8. (1697), 1 Ld. Raym. 264.
9. [1913] A.C. 263.
10. *The Carlgarth*, [1927] P. 93, at p. 110.
11. [1936] A.C. 65, at p. 69; [1935] All E.R. Rep. 555, at p. 558.
12. (1868), L.R. 3 H.L. 330; [1861–73] All E.R. Rep. 1.
13. [1966] 2 Q.B. 475; [1966] 1 All E.R. 88.

Wheat v. *E. Lacon & Co., Ltd.*[1] Those cases show that the word "occupier" has a different meaning according to the subject-matter in which it is employed. There it was the Occupiers' Liability Act 1957. Here it is liability for the escape of fire. Adapting what I said in *Wheat* v. *E. Lacon & Co., Ltd.*,[1] I would say that, for purposes of fire, whenever a person has a sufficient degree of control over premises that he can say, with authority, to anyone who comes there: "Do" or "Do not light a fire", or "Do" or "Do not put that fire out", he as "occupier" must answer for any fire which escapes by negligence from the premises. Applying this test, I am clear that the L.C.C. were occupiers of this site. They were the owners of it. Their foreman had the keys of the prefabs. Anyone who wanted to do anything with them had to get permission from him. On behalf of the L.C.C. he could clearly say to anyone: "You are not to light a fire on the site"; or: "If you do light a fire, it must be well away from the road", or as the case may be. It may be that the Ministry of Housing and the Ministry of Works were also "occupiers" because, as I pointed out in *Wheat* v. *Lacon*,[2] there are often many "occupiers" who have a sufficient degree of control to be responsible. But the position of the Ministry does not arise here.

The question: who is a "stranger"? is more difficult. But I am quite clear that the contractors' men were not strangers. They were present on the site with the leave and with the knowledge of the L.C.C.; true it is that they were prohibited from burning rubbish, but, nevertheless, it was their regular practice to burn it. The L.C.C. ought to have taken better steps to prevent them. Not having done so, they cannot disclaim responsibility for the fire. The L.C.C. could reasonably have anticipated that these men might start a fire; and that is enough, just as in the case in 1401[3] the householder might reasonably have anticipated that his guest might light a candle.

I think the judge was quite right. I would dismiss this appeal.

EDMUND DAVIES L.J.: I agree. There are two main questions involved in this case. First of all, were the L.C.C. in occupation of the site from which the fire spread? And, secondly, how was that fire caused? In other words, was it caused by some one who vis-à-vis the L.C.C. is to be treated as a stranger, as our law understands that term in this context? Counsel for the plaintiffs, Emanuels, has sought to uphold the learned judge's decision in their favour on three grounds. First, that at common law, which he said in this respect still obtains, there was and there is strict liability for the spread of this fire on to Emanuels' land. Secondly, he says that the learned judge was perfectly right in awarding Emanuels judgment on the basis of the principle enunciated in *Rylands* v. *Fletcher*.[4] Thirdly, he says that in any event the L.C.C. ought to be held responsible, contrary to the learned judge's finding, on *two* grounds: (a) that they were guilty of personal negligence in all the circumstances of the case, and (b) that they were also vicariously responsible for the negligence of the second defendant, who is not, so he submitted, to be regarded as a stranger.

The question of who is an occupier has been much canvassed. In *Wheat* v. *E. Lacon & Co., Ltd.*,[1] Lord Denning and Lord Pearson resorted to tests which, when applied to this case, establish that the L.C.C. were in occupation. Lord Pearson used the phrase,[5] "control associated with and arising from presence in and use of or activity in the premises". Having regard to the way in which the L.C.C. came to have an interest in the premises and the history which led up to the Ministry of Works taking steps to have the site cleared ... the occupation of the L.C.C. is clear. Accordingly, we find that the contractor, Mr. King, was required to get a release note from the L.C.C. and to obtain the keys from their foreman. It may be that the Ministry of Works were also in occupation of the site. There is no difficulty about that, for, again, as was held in

1. [1966] A.C. 552; [1966] 1 All E.R. 582.
2. [1966] A.C. at p. 578; [1966] 1 All E.R. at p. 594.
3. *Beaulieu* v. *Finglam* (1401), Y.B. 2 Hen. 4, fo. 18, pl. 6.
4. (1868), L.R. 3 H.L. 330; [1861–73] All E.R. Rep. 1.
5. [1966] A.C. at p. 589; [1966] 1 All E.R. at p. 601.

Wheat v. *E. Lacon & Co., Ltd.*,[1] more than one person can be in occupation. But it would be quite idle to assert that the L.C.C. were not. If trespassers had invaded the site, can it seriously be contended that the L.C.C. would not be entitled to sue them for damages? Indeed, counsel for the G.L.C. conceded that they were in occupation. He contended that so also were the Ministry of Works, but in my judgment that matters not for present purposes.

The second question is, was the contractor, Mr. King, a stranger? Well, he was somebody who was, first of all, there with the knowledge of the L.C.C. Further, he was there in order to discharge a function which the L.C.C. desired to have performed, namely, the clearing of the site; and it is beyond belief that the L.C.C. had no means of controlling his activities. In *Perry* v. *Kendricks Transport, Ltd.*[2] Jenkins L.J. said: ". . . the stranger is regarded as a person over whose acts the occupier of the land has no control." Well, of course, the L.C.C. had control over the activities of the contractor. It is untenable that, assuming knowledge on their part of what he was doing, they could not put a stop to it. So both the question of occupancy and whether the contractor was a stranger, must in my judgment be answered contrary to the defendants.

Counsel for Emanuels, as I have already related, sought to uphold the judgment on three grounds. I do not find it necessary for the purposes of this appeal to consider the question of the strict liability at common law, nor do I propose to go into the validity—for such I believe it to be—of the decision of the learned trial judge that the L.C.C. were in truth and in law liable under *Rylands* v. *Fletcher*.[3] The question which remains is whether they are also liable in negligence. Were they, first of all, personally negligent? I think they were. They initiated the whole process by inviting the Ministry to clear the site. It was a job, having regard to the contiguity of buildings, which required care. Fires lit on land in the close confines of this site could well be a source of danger. Then there is the striking evidence of [a workman] regarding the "standard practice" of lighting fires in clearing such sites as that with which we are concerned. And, although there had been this unqualified assertion with regard to the standard practice, there was no attempt by the L.C.C. to say that the practice was unknown to them or that they could not reasonably be expected to foresee that it would be followed. Mr. Stothard, for the Ministry of Works, told the learned judge of the previous troubles he had had with the contractor over the lighting of fires. In my judgment, in circumstances such as those, the L.C.C., having invited the Ministry of Works to clear the site, could not thereafter wash their hands of the matter and proceed on the assumption that all would be properly done. Some degree of vigilance on their part is required. Were they guilty of personal negligence? It follows from what I have already indicated that in my judgment they were—the personal negligence consisting in failure to exercise any degree of supervision at all.

I am not really concerned as to the exact role which Mr. King, the contractor, occupied. I suspect it was that of a licensee. If it was that of an independent contractor, there is the abundance of authority to which Lord Denning M.R. has referred indicating that there can be in circumstances such as here present vicarious liability in the occupier for his acts. *Balfour* v. *Barty-King*[4] is one illustration of the law applicable to this case; and so also is the Australian decision in *McInnes* v. *Wardle*.[5] In *Erikson* v. *Clifton*[6] McGregor J. said:

"If the employer delegates to an independent contractor work involving the use of fire, a duty arises to exercise control in regard to such action. If the employer fails to exercise such control he is responsible for the negligence of the independent

1. [1966] A.C. 552; [1966] 1 All E.R. 582.
2. [1956] 1 All E.R. 154, at p. 159; [1956] 1 W.L.R. 85, at p. 90.
3. (1868), L.R. 3 H.L. 330; [1861–73] All E.R. Rep. 1.
4. [1957] 1 Q.B. 496; [1957] 1 All E.R. 156.
5. (1932), 45 C.L.R. 548.
6. [1963] N.Z.L.R. 705, at p. 709.

contractor, but this is in truth personal negligence on the part of the employer in failure to exercise control."

There was in my judgment in the present case personal negligence by the L.C.C. in failing to exercise control in the circumstances.

Was the contractor a mere licensee, as has been submitted by counsel for the G.L.C.? Well, that may be the role he occupied. But even so the L.C.C. cannot be absolved from responsibility for his undoubted negligence. Lord Denning M.R. has already referred in this context to the decision in New Zealand in *Boulcott Golf Club Inc.* v. *Engelbrecht,*[1] where the golf club were held liable as occupiers for the consequence of a fire negligently caused by one of the members of the golf club dropping a cigarette. For these reasons, I hold that the L.C.C. were guilty, first of personal negligence, and secondly of vicarious responsibility for the negligence of the second defendant. On that dual ground, as well as on the principle enunciated in *Rylands* v. *Fletcher,*[2] I concur in holding that this appeal should be dismissed.

PHILLIMORE L.J.: The L.C.C. were undoubtedly occupiers of this land. They were sued in that capacity and they did not call any evidence to suggest otherwise. As such they owed a duty to their neighbours which is best described in the old latin maxim: sic utere tuo ut alienum non laedas. As Markham J. put it in *Beaulieu* v. *Finglam*[3]:

> "I shall answer to my neighbour for him who enters my house by my leave or knowledge whether he is guest to me or my servant, if either of them acts in such a way with a candle or other things that my neighbour's house is burned."

Since the Fire Prevention (Metropolis) Act 1774 it is I think necessary to insert the word "negligently" after the word "acts".

. . . Now, it seems to me that if an occupier owes a duty, he cannot, by handing over the performance of the work on his land to somebody else refrain from any sort or kind of supervision, say: "Well, I have delegated my responsibilities to the Ministry." I think the L.C.C. and consequently the G.L.C. are liable for what was in effect the negligence of the Ministry of Works in failing to supervise the activities of the contractor. The Ministry of Works was on the site with leave and licence and indeed at the request of the L.C.C., and the L.C.C. cannot escape liability for their act or omission any more than could the owner of the house in *Beaulieu* v. *Finglam.*[3] Accordingly I would agree that this appeal must be dismissed.

Appeal dismissed

Note

In *H. & N. Emanuel, Ltd.* v. *Greater London Council,* Lord Denning M.R. referred to *Sochacki* v. *Sas,* [1947] I All E.R. 344, where a lodger was held not liable for damage caused by a fire which spread from his room, and which was probably caused by a spark from the fire in the fireplace setting light to the floorboards. It would appear that the lodger had lit the original fire, but he had been negligent. Liability under *Rylands* v. *Fletcher* was denied in particular on the ground that this was an ordinary user of the room. Lord Denning M.R. thought that, whatever the common law position, the case would be covered by the 1774 Act. Although *Filliter* v. *Phippard* (1847), 11 Q.B. 347 appears to exclude from the Act's protection the intentional fire (on which see F. H. Newark, "The Accidental Fires Act (Northern Ireland) 1944" (1944), 6 N.I.L.Q. 134, at pp. 137–140), Lord Denning's view can be supported on the type of analysis adopted in *Musgrove* v. *Pandelis,* [1919] 2 K.B. 43— that the fire with which the Act is concerned started when the floorboards

---

1. [1945] N.Z.L.R. 556.
2. (1868), L.R. 3 H.L. 330; [1861-73] All E.R. Rep 1.
3. (1401), Y.B. 2 Hen. 4, fo. 18, pl. 6.

were set alight, and this fire did "accidentally begin" (cf. *Musgrove* v. *Pandelis*, at p. 51, *per* Duke L.J., but see *Job Edwards, Ltd.* v. *Birmingham Navigations*, [1924] 1 K.B. 341, at p. 361). Salmond (at p. 338) takes the view that the Act almost certainly applies to fires intentionally lit which spread accidentally.

4. ANIMALS

Note

The topic of civil liability for damage caused by animals was the subject of a report in 1953 by a committee with Lord Goddard as its chairman (Cmd. 8746, 1953). More recently it has attracted the Law Commission's attention, and their report in 1967 (*Civil Liability for Animals, No. 13*) contained a draft Bill on this subject. Four years later, the Animals Act 1971 was passed, although it should be noted that it departs in certain respects from the draft Bill. The leading work on the present state of this area of the law is P. M. North, *The Modern Law of Animals*.

The Animals Act 1971

STRICT LIABILITY FOR DAMAGE DONE BY ANIMALS

1. New provisions as to strict liability for damage done by animals.—(1) The provisions of sections 2 to 5 of this Act replace—

- (*a*) the rules of the common law imposing a strict liability in tort for damage done by an animal on the ground that the animal is regarded as ferae naturae or that its vicious or mischievous propensities are known or presumed to be known;
- (*b*) subsections (1) and (2) of section 1 of the Dogs Act 1906 as amended by the Dogs (Amendment) Act 1928 (injury to cattle or poultry); and
- (*c*) the rules of the common law imposing a liability for cattle trespass.

(2) Expressions used in those sections shall be interpreted in accordance with the provisions of section 6 (as well as those of section 11) of this Act.

2. Liability for damage done by dangerous animals.—(1) Where any damage is caused by an animal which belongs to a dangerous species, any person who is a keeper of the animal is liable for the damage, except as otherwise provided by this Act.

(2) Where damage is caused by an animal which does not belong to a dangerous species, a keeper of the animal is liable for the damage, except as otherwise provided by this Act, if—

- (*a*) the damage is of a kind which the animal, unless restrained, was likely to cause or which, if caused by the animal, was likely to be severe; and
- (*b*) the likelihood of the damage or of its being severe was due to characteristics of the animal which are not normally found in animals of the same species or are not normally so found except at particular times or in particular circumstances; and
- (*c*) those characteristics were known to that keeper or were at any time known to a person who at that time had charge of the animal as that keeper's servant or, where that keeper is the head of a household, were known to another keeper of the animal who is a member of that household and under the age of sixteen.

3. Liability for injury done by dogs to livestock.—Where a dog causes damage by killing or injuring livestock, any person who is a keeper of the dog is liable for the damage, except as otherwise provided by this Act.

4. Liability for damage and expenses due to trespassing livestock.—(1) Where livestock belonging to any person strays on to land in the ownership or occupation of another and—

    (*a*) damage is done by the livestock to the land or to any property on it which is in the ownership or possession of the other person; or

    (*b*) any expenses are reasonably incurred by that other person in keeping the livestock while it cannot be restored to the person to whom it belongs or while it is detained in pursuance of section 7 of this Act, or in ascertaining to whom it belongs;

the person to whom the livestock belongs is liable for the damage or expenses, except as otherwise provided by this Act.

(2) For the purposes of this section any livestock belongs to the person in whose possession it is.

5. Exceptions from liability under sections 2 to 4.—(1) A person is not liable under sections 2 to 4 of this Act for any damage which is due wholly to the fault of the person suffering it.

(2) A person is not liable under section 2 of this Act for any damage suffered by a person who has voluntarily accepted the risk thereof.

(3) A person is not liable under section 2 of this Act for any damage caused by an animal kept on any premises or structure to a person trespassing there, if it is proved either—

    (*a*) that the animal was not kept there for the protection of persons or property; or

    (*b*) (if the animal was kept there for the protection of persons or property) that keeping it there for that purpose was not unreasonable.

(4) A person is not liable under section 3 of this Act if the livestock was killed or injured on land on to which it had strayed and either the dog belonged to the occupier or its presence on the land was authorised by the occupier.

(5) A person is not liable under section 4 of this Act where the livestock strayed from a highway and its presence there was a lawful use of the highway.

(6) In determining whether any liability for damage under section 4 of this Act is excluded by subsection (1) of this section the damage shall not be treated as due to the fault of the person suffering it by reason only that he could have prevented it by fencing; but a person is not liable under that section where it is proved that the straying of the livestock on to the land would not have occurred but for a breach by any other person, being a person having an interest in the land, of a duty to fence.

6. Interpretation of certain expressions used in sections 2 to 5.—(1) The following provisions apply to the interpretation of sections 2 to 5 of this Act.

(2) A dangerous species is a species—

    (*a*) which is not commonly domesticated in the British Islands; and

    (*b*) whose fully grown animals normally have such characteristics that they are likely, unless restrained, to cause severe damage or that any damage they may cause is likely to be severe.

(3) Subject to subsection (4) of this section, a person is a keeper of an animal if—

    (*a*) he owns the animal or has it in his possession; or

(*b*) he is the head of a household of which a member under the age of sixteen owns the animal or has it in his possession;

and if at any time an animal ceases to be owned by or to be in the possession of a person, any person who immediately before that time was a keeper thereof by virtue of the preceding provisions of this subsection continues to be a keeper of the animal until another person becomes a keeper thereof by virtue of those provisions.

(4) Where an animal is taken into and kept in possession for the purpose of preventing it from causing damage or of restoring it to its owner, a person is not a keeper of it by virtue only of that possession.

(5) Where a person employed as a servant by a keeper of an animal incurs a risk incidental to his employment he shall not be treated as accepting it voluntarily.

DETENTION AND SALE OF TRESPASSING LIVESTOCK

7. Detention and sale of trespassing livestock.—(1) The right to seize and detain any animal by way of distress damage feasant is hereby abolished.

(2) Where any livestock strays on to any land and is not then under the control of any person the occupier of the land may detain it, subject to subsection (3) of this section, unless ordered to return it by a court.

(3) Where any livestock is detained in pursuance of this section the right to detain it ceases—

(*a*) at the end of a period of forty-eight hours, unless within that period notice of the detention has been given to the officer in charge of a police station and also, if the person detaining the livestock knows to whom it belongs, to that person; or

(*b*) when such amount is tendered to the person detaining the livestock as is sufficient to satisfy any claim he may have under section 4 of this Act in respect of the livestock; or

(*c*) if he has no such claim, when the livestock is claimed by a person entitled to its possession.

(4) Where livestock has been detained in pursuance of this section for a period of not less than fourteen days the person detaining it may sell it at a market or by public auction, unless proceedings are then pending for the return of the livestock or for any claim under section 4 of this Act in respect of it.

(5) Where any livestock is sold in the exercise of the right conferred by this section and the proceeds of the sale, less the costs thereof and any costs incurred in connection with it, exceed the amount of any claim under section 4 of this Act which the vendor had in respect of the livestock, the excess shall be recoverable from him by the person who would be entitled to the possession of the livestock but for the sale.

(6) A person detaining any livestock in pursuance of this section is liable for any damage caused to it by a failure to treat it with reasonable care and supply it with adequate food and water while it is so detained.

(7) References in this section to a claim under section 4 of this Act in respect of any livestock do not include any claim under that section for damage done by or expenses incurred in respect of the livestock before the straying in connection with which it is detained under this section.

ANIMALS STRAYING ON TO HIGHWAY

8. Duty to take care to prevent damage from animals straying on to the highway.—(1) So much of the rules of the common law relating to liability for negligence as excludes or restricts the duty which a person might owe to others to take such care as is reasonable to see that damage is not caused by animals straying on to a highway is hereby abolished.

(2) Where damage is caused by animals straying from unfenced land to a highway a person who placed them on the land shall not be regarded as having committed a breach of the duty to take care by reason only of placing them there if—

(*a*) the land is common land, or is land situated in an area where fencing is not customary, or is a town or village green; and

(*b*) he had a right to place the animals on that land.

PROTECTION OF LIVESTOCK AGAINST DOGS

9. Killing of or injury to dogs worrying livestock.—(1) In any civil proceedings against a person (in this section referred to as the defendant) for killing or causing injury to a dog it shall be a defence to prove—

(*a*) that the defendant acted for the protection of any livestock and was a person entitled to act for the protection of that livestock; and

(*b*) that within forty-eight hours of the killing or injury notice thereof was given by the defendant to the officer in charge of a police station.

(2) For the purposes of this section a person is entitled to act for the protection of any livestock if, and only if—

(*a*) the livestock or the land on which it is belongs to him or to any person under whose express or implied authority he is acting; and

(*b*) the circumstances are not such that liability for killing or causing injury to the livestock would be excluded by section 5 (4) of this Act.

(3) Subject to subsection (4) of this section, a person killing or causing injury to a dog shall be deemed for the purposes of this section to act for the protection of any livestock if, and only if, either—

(*a*) the dog is worrying or is about to worry the livestock and there are no other reasonable means of ending or preventing the worrying; or

(*b*) the dog has been worrying livestock, has not left the vicinity and is not under the control of any person and there are no practicable means of ascertaining to whom it belongs.

(4) For the purposes of this section the condition stated in either of the paragraphs of the preceding subsection shall be deemed to have been satisfied if the defendant believed that it was satisfied and had reasonable ground for that belief.

(5) For the purposes of this section—

(*a*) an animal belongs to any person if he owns it or has it in his possession; and

(*b*) land belongs to any person if he is the occupier thereof.

SUPPLEMENTAL

10. Application of certain enactments to liability under sections 2 to 4.—For the purposes of the Fatal Accidents Acts 1846 to 1959, the Law Reform (Contributory Negligence) Act 1945 and the Limitation Acts 1939 to 1963 any damage for which a person is liable under sections 2 to 4 of this Act shall be treated as due to his fault.

11. General interpretation.—In this Act—

"common land", and "town or village green" have the same meanings as in the Commons Registration Act 1965;

"damage" includes the death of, or injury to, any person (including any disease and any impairment of physical or mental condition);

"fault" has the same meaning as in the Law Reform (Contributory Negligence) Act 1945;

"fencing" includes the construction of any obstacle designed to prevent animals from straying;

"livestock" means cattle, horses, asses, mules, hinnies, sheep, pigs, goats and poultry, and also deer not in the wild state and, in sections 3 and 9, also, while in captivity, pheasants, partridges and grouse;

"poultry" means the domestic varieties of the following, that is to say, fowls, turkeys, geese, ducks, guinea-fowls, pigeons, peacocks and quails; and

"species" includes sub-species and variety.

12. Application to Crown.—(1) This Act binds the Crown, but nothing in this section shall authorise proceedings to be brought against Her Majesty in her private capacity.

(2) Section 38 (3) of the Crown Proceedings Act 1947 (interpretation of references to Her Majesty in her private capacity) shall apply as if this section were contained in that Act.

13. Short title, repeal, commencement and extent.—(1) This Act may be cited as the Animals Act 1971.

(2) The following are hereby repealed, that is to say—

(a) in the Dogs Act 1906, subsection (1) to (3) of sections 1; and

(b) in section 1 (1) of the Dogs (Amendment) Act 1928 the words "in both places where that word occurs".

(3) This Act shall come into operation on 1 October 1971.

(4) This Act does not extend to Scotland or to Northern Ireland.

Draper v. Hodder

Court of Appeal   [1972] 2 All E.R. 210

[*Note*—the judgment in this case refers to the common law *scienter* action. This is explained by North, *op. cit.*, p. 3 as follows—"The keeper of an animal was liable without proof of fault if the animal caused any injury to person or property provided the animal either belonged to the class of wild animals, animals *ferae naturae*, or, if it was a tame animal, *mansuetae naturae*, provided it had a vicious propensity known to the keeper." Section 1 of the Animals Act has abolished the common law *scienter* action but attention should now be paid to s. 2 of the Animals Act 1971 (p. 359, *ante*). The action for negligence in respect of animals exists independently of the Act and is the concern of the extract from this case.]

The infant plaintiff (Gary) was severely injured by a pack of Jack Russell terriers belonging to the defendant who bred dogs and, in particular, that species of terrier. When the boy was found by his mother and one of her friends at the entrance to the yard of the house where he lived (Hyde House), he was surrounded by six or seven of the terriers, and pieces of his clothing were scattered around the yard. The entrance to the yard and the entrance to the defendant's house were fifteen yards apart and both were ungated and it appeared that the defendant's dogs often scavenged among the dustbins in the yard when children were present, but had not caused any trouble. A claim based on *scienter* was rejected by the trial judge. However, on the evidence as a whole, he found that there was a real and foreseeable risk to the inhabitants of Hyde House (and to people on the road between Hyde House and the defendant's property) of injury by the pack of terriers, that "the defendant knew or ought to have known, that two or more of his terriers would be liable to bite human beings if they were allowed to escape from his property and to roam free" and that, in the circumstances, the defendant "was under a duty to take reasonable care to prevent a pack of his terriers from escaping from his land." He found the defendant to be in breach of duty and that the defendant's negligence caused the boy's injuries. An appeal to the Court of Appeal was dismissed.

EDMUND DAVIES L.J.: . . . That liability for negligence can arise from the keeping even of domestic animals with no known vicious propensity is now undoubted, even though what Professor Williams calls "the contagion of scienter" has in not a few of the reported cases resulted in decisions in the defendant's favour, where, had the test of liability in negligence been strictly adhered to, a different conclusion might have been expected. Liability for negligence in respect of the keeping of an animal mansuetae naturae is, in essence, no different from that in respect of the keeping of any other chattel not dangerous per se, although the fact that the former *is* animate and capable of spontaneous action has, of course, an important bearing on more than one facet of negligence such as whether there was any breach of duty at all, and if so whether the damage caused by the animal was such as to render its keeper liable in law.

If I may so put it, as good a starting point as any in this context is *Fardon* v. *Harcourt-Rivington*,[1] where Lord Atkin said:

". . . quite apart from the liability imposed upon the owner of animals or the person having control of them by reason of knowledge of their propensities, there is the ordinary duty of a person to take care either that *his animal or his chattel* is not put to such a use as is likely to injure his neighbour—the ordinary duty to take care in the cases put upon negligence."

From there it is but a short step to *Sycamore* v. *Ley*,[2] decided a few months later and again one arising from damage done by a dog left in a parked car, the defendant once more being absolved from liability. Scrutton and Lawrence L.JJ. dealt with it solely on the "scienter" basis, but Greer L.J.[3] adverted to the case decided earlier that year[4] and, having dealt with "scienter", continued:[5]

"But that is not the end of his liability. He may, in my judgment, be liable for the conduct of a dog which has not been taken out of the category of tame animals if he puts it in such a position and in such circumstances as render it likely that the dog will get excited, will lose its temper, and will cause damage to people lawfully passing along the highway . . . there may be cases in which a defendant may be liable for the bite of a dog even if the dog does not belong to the class of ferocious animals, if it be proved that the dog is put in such a position that a reasonable man would know that it was likely to cause danger and therefore he ought to regard himself as under an obligation to do something by way of precaution."

Although Greer L.J. there spoke twice of a tame animal being "*put* in such a position" that it was likely to cause damage, for my part I do not read his observations as inapplicable to cases where, instead of "putting", a dog-owner *allowed* his dog *to be in* or *to escape to* a place where it might cause damage . . .

For further illustration of the earlier observations as to the basis of liability in negligence being the same whether damage be caused by animals or by other chattels, reference may with advantage be made to *Aldham* v. *United Dairies (London), Ltd*.[6] . . . When *Aldham* v. *United Dairies (London), Ltd*.[6] was decided, the rule as to remoteness of damage was that laid down in *Re Polemis and Furness, Withy & Co., Ltd*.[7]—see per du

1. (1932), 146 L.T. 391, at p. 392; [1932] All E.R. Rep. 81, at p. 83.
2. (1932), 147 L.T. 342; [1932] All E.R. Rep. 97.
3. (1932), 147 L.T. at p. 345; [1932] All E.R. Rep. at p. 102.
4. *Fardon* v. *Harcourt-Rivington* (1932), 146 L.T. 391; [1932] All E.R. Rep. 81 (wrongly named in the report).
5. (1932), 147 L.T. at p. 345; [1932] All E.R. Rep. at pp. 101, 102.
6. [1940] 1 K.B. 507; [1939] 4 All E.R. 522.
7. [1921] 3 K.B. 560; [1921] All E.R. Rep. 40.

Parcq L.J. in *Aldham's* case[1]—whereas the rule we have presently to apply is that the defendant is to be held liable only for such consequences of his negligence as a reasonable man should have foreseen.

. . . The defendant's knowledge of "the nature of the beast" which is basic to "scienter" liability is also directly relevant both to the question of whether he was negligent *at all* and furthermore, if he was, whether he ought reasonably to have foreseen the damage which in fact resulted therefrom. That is not, of course, the same as saying that proof of "scienter" is indispensable in an action for negligence. As Pearson L.J. put it in *Ellis* v. *Johnstone*[2]:

> "For the action of negligence, it is sufficient if the defendant knew, or ought to have known, of the existence of the danger, which does not necessarily arise from a vicious propensity of the animal, although perhaps some special propensity is required."

Ought the defendant in the present case to have known of the risk that danger might befall a human being if a pack of his Jack Russell dogs were free to leave his premises and, having done so, entered the ungated yard of Hyde House a few yards distance along a side road? That he knew of the existence of the three year old plaintiff and his likely presence at the material time in the yard or along the side-road is beyond doubt. It is equally clear that he knew that, in the absence of an effective fence to his property, his dogs were free to roam at will. Furthermore, in my judgment, there must be imputed to him knowledge that they frequently entered Hyde House yard for scavenging purposes. On the other hand, the trial judge's finding clears him of knowledge that any of the seven dogs which escaped on the morning when the accident occurred had ever attempted to attack a human being before, and there is no suggestion that, whatever his own state of knowledge, they had ever done so. What, in these circumstances, should he reasonably have anticipated as a likely result of what must surely be regarded as his failure to keep his dogs within bounds? And is it relevant that these seven Jack Russell dogs (five of them about five months old) were hunt terriers? In *Tallents* v. *Bell and Goddard*,[3] where the defendant was unsuccessfully sued for the damage caused when his dogs broke into rabbit-hutches, Finlay L.J. said[4]:

> "The attempt was made to suggest that these were dogs of a character which would be specially addicted to hunting and, therefore, might be expected to follow and worry animals . . . There seems to be no foundation at all for any distinction between dogs . . . I think it quite plain that if you are going to make out a case in respect of damage done by a dog, you must establish *scienter*."

The basis of the claim advanced in that case (that is, whether or not negligence was alleged) does not emerge from the report, but the passage cited pays no regard to the *number* of dogs involved, and the language employed is more appropriate to the actions of individual dogs than to the activities of dogs in a pack or group.

It is this last-mentioned factor which for my part I regard as of particular importance in the present case, as the expert witnesses clearly did. Mr. Watson, for example, stressed that these terriers are "of a rather excitable breed whose characteristic is *pack* behaviour" and that:

> "If [the defendant] has been breeding dogs for a very large number of years, he must be well aware of the characteristics of terriers of this type. Whatever the *individual* characteristics of one member of the breed, the general characteristics of the breed and and therefore the likely behaviour of any individual must be known to him."

---

1. [1940] 1 K.B. at p. 513; [1939] 4 All E.R. at p. 527.
2. [1963] 2 Q.B. 8, at p. 29; [1963] 1 All E.R. 286, at p. 297.
3. [1944] 2 All E.R. 474.
4. [1944] 2 All E.R. at pp. 475, 476.

Ought the defendant (with many years of practical experience of breeding and training Jack Russell terriers) reasonably to have anticipated that they might dash off and, having done so, were not unlikely to cause physical injury to the infant plaintiff? I have proceeded on the following basis: (a) that the infant plaintiff might well be in the vicinity and was accordingly a person whose welfare should have been borne in mind; and (b) that the proper test in negligence is not whether the particular type of physical harm actually suffered ought reasonably to have been anticipated. but whether broadly speaking it was within the range of likely consequences. For example, were a farm servant negligently to allow a large herd of horses to enter a small field where a school picnic is being held and one of the children was bitten, it would surely be no defence to say that, while it might reasonably be contemplated that one of the children might be trampled on and so maimed, the servant ought not reasonably to have anticipated that the child would be bitten. In this respect, if in no other, in my judgment a distinction needs to be drawn between the "scienter" and the negligence cases, and sometimes this is not done. . . .

I have not overlooked the line of authorities to the effect that the mere possibility of some damage resulting is insufficient to impose liability for negligence. Nevertheless, if injury of a substantial kind ought reasonably to be foreseen as the result of one's negligent act or omission, it is nihil ad rem that what actually follows is not precisely that which one should have foreseen.

Adopting that attitude, I have addressed to myself in the present case this question: ought the defendant reasonably to have foreseen that, by his failure to take any steps to confine his pack of seven dogs within his curtilage, substantial physical harm might well be sustained by the infant plaintiff? The "million to one chance" of harm resulting (to echo the phrase employed by the defendant's expert witness) creates no liability: see *Bolton* v. *Stone*.[1] . . .

[Having posed the question of fact whether in the circumstances known to the defendant, "he was negligent in allowing his dogs to escape and should be held responsible for the consequences," he continued:]

. . . The conclusion I have come to is that the whole body of evidence adduced, . . ., entitled the learned judge to answer it in a manner favourable to the plaintiffs, as he did. The defendant knew that his dogs were young and sprightly, he knew that no less than seven of them were free to go where they willed, and he knew that in a place only some yards down the road to which at least some of his dogs regularly went there was likely to be a very small child. Placing all reasonable reins on his foreseeability, he ought, in my judgment . . . to have realised that risk of real harm to the child was involved. For example, he could well be bowled over by an onward rush of the dogs to the dustbins and thereby, or by their subsequent antics (however innocent), sustain no insubstantial injury to face or body, for which the defendant ought clearly to be made liable. I bear in mind that, in *The Wagon Mound (No. 2)*, *Overseas Tankship (U.K.), Ltd.* v. *Miller Steamship Co. Pty., Ltd.*[2] Lord Reid said:

"It has now been established by the *Wagon Mound (No. 1)*[3] and by *Hughes* v. *Lord Advocate*[4] that . . . damages can only be recovered if the injury complained of was not only caused by the alleged negligence but also was an injury of a class or character foreseeable as a possible result of it."

I also have it in mind that, in the latter of those two cases, Lord Reid had said[5]:

". . . a defender is liable, although the damage may be a good deal greater in extent than was foreseeable. He can only escape liability if the damage can be regarded as differing in kind from what was foreseeable",

1. [1951] A.C. 850; [1951] 1 All E.R. 1078.
2. [1967] 1 A.C. 617, at p. 636; [1966] 2 All E.R. 709, at p. 714.
3. [1961] A.C. 388; [1961] 1 All E.R. 404.
4. [1963] A.C. 837; [1963] 1 All E.R. 705.
5. [1963] A.C. at p. 845; [1963] 1 All E.R. at p. 706.

and I have sought to apply those observations to the known facts of the present case. In the result, to absolve this defendant on the ground that the child was hurt not, for example, by being bowled over and clawed or scratched on the face (possibly with serious consequences to, say, an eye), but by bites all over his body, and that he had no reason to think that his dogs would bite at all would, in my judgment, be to allow "the contagion of scienter" to place unreasonable limits on proceedings brought in negligence. I would therefore be for dismissing this appeal on liability. . . .

[DAVIES and ROSKILL L.JJ. also delivered judgments in favour of dismissing the appeal.]

Interference with Land

It was pointed out in the Introduction (p. I, *ante*) that to a lawyer from a civil law system the arrangement of English law seems faulty because the possession of land is protected in English law through trespass, an action in tort. The law regulating some aspects of the conduct of neighbouring landowners is also dealt with in tort, through the action in respect of nuisance, rather than as a part of the law of property.

It will have been seen (p. 26, *ante*) that fault is now an essential ingredient in trespass to the person, and this is also the position in the case of trespass to goods (*National Coal Board* v. *Evans*, [1951] 2 K.B. 861; [1951] 2 All E.R. 310): whether fault (in the sense of intention or negligence) is essential in an action for trespass to land is less clear. Whatever the position on that point, one common characteristic of all these trespass actions is that they are actionable without proof of damage. Nevertheless, it should be noted that a plaintiff, who has not suffered any damage, risks having a "frivolous action" disapproved of by the awarding of "contemptuous damages", and is likely to have to pay his own costs. (See F. H. Lawson, *The Rational Strength of English Law*, p. 132.) Although actions for trespass are rarely brought, they can be used not simply to settle questions of title to land, but again in common with other trespass actions (in particular false imprisonment) they can be important in the constitutional sphere, protecting the Englishman's castle/home against unlawful intrusions: *Entick* v. *Carrington* (1765), 19 St. Tr. 1029.

The tort of nuisance takes two forms, the one called public nuisance, the other private nuisance, but the same conduct may amount to both. Public nuisance has been said to "cover a multitude of sins, great and small" (*per* Denning L.J. in *Southport Corpn.* v. *Esso Petroleum Co., Ltd.* [1954] 2 Q.B. 182, at p. 196), and a definition will be found in the judgment of Lawton J. in *British Celanese, Ltd.* v. *A. H. Hunt (Capacitors), Ltd.*, [1969] 2 All E.R. 1252, p. 383, *post*. A public nuisance is also a crime, but can give rise to a civil action by an individual only where he suffers some particular damage greater than that suffered by the public. Public nuisances share with private nuisances the element of annoyance or inconvenience; more broadly, private nuisance is described (by Winfield & Jolowicz, p. 326) as "unlawful interference with a person's use or enjoyment of land, or some right over, or in connection with it."

Nuisance differs from trespass in that an action will lie for nuisance, but not trespass, if the damage is merely consequential upon the defendant's act and not "direct"; moreover, nuisance is actionable only on proof of actual damage. Nuisance may overlap with liability under *Rylands* v. *Fletcher* (Chap. 10, *ante*) but the two forms of liability are by no means identical. Some of the differences are clear, but where there is a doubt about one of the rules of liability, then there will be a corresponding doubt about the differences between the actions e.g. in private nuisance the plaintiff must have an interest in land: under *Rylands* v. *Fletcher* it is unclear whether the plaintiff must be in occupation of or have an interest in land. See further W. A. West, "Nuisance or *Rylands* v. *Fletcher*" (1966), 30 Conv. (N.S.) 95.

1. TRESPASS TO LAND

Salmond on Torts (16th Edn., p. 38):

The wrong of trespass to land (trespass *quare clausum fregit*) consists in the act of (1) entering upon land in the possession of the plaintiff, or (2) remaining upon such land, or (3) placing or projecting any material object upon it—in each case without lawful justification.

(a) Special situations

(i) The highway

Hickman v. Maisey

Court of Appeal   [1900] 1 K.B. 752

A. L. SMITH L.J.: This is an application for judgment or a new trial by the defendant in an action for trespass brought by the occupier of certain down land, part of which was used for the purpose of training race-horses. The application is made under the following circumstances. It appears that there is a highway across the plaintiff's land, and the defendant, who was what has been called a "racing tout", had for a considerable period of time been using this highway for the purpose of watching therefrom the trials of race-horses upon the plaintiff's land, and availing himself of the information so obtained by him for the purposes of his business, the effect of which was to depreciate the value of the plaintiff's land as a place for the training and trial of race-horses. The defendant insisting on his right so to use the highway, the plaintiff brought his action for trespass in respect of such use of the highway by the defendant. The defendant justifies the acts complained of on the ground that the locus in quo was a highway, and that he was lawfully using it as such. The question is, therefore, whether the use of the highway in the manner in which the defendant used it was in truth a use of it for the purpose for which a highway is dedicated to the public. The evidence shews that what the defendant did was to walk up and down a short portion of the highway about fifteen yards in length for a period of about an hour and a half with a note-book, watching the horses, and taking notes of their performances. It is contended for the defendant that such a use of the highway is lawful as being a use of it in the ordinary way in which a highway is used, namely, for the purpose of passing and repassing, and therefore not a trespass. Unless what the defendant did comes within the ordinary and reasonable use of a highway as such and is therefore lawful, it is clear that it would be a trespass. Therefore the question is, What is the lawful use of a highway? Many authorities, of which the well-known case of *Dovaston* v. *Payne*[1] is one, shew that prima facie the right of the public is merely to pass and repass along the highway; but I quite agree with what Lord Esher M.R. said in *Harrison* v. *Duke of Rutland*,[2] though I think it is a slight extension of the rule as previously stated, namely,

---

1. 2 H. Bl. 527.
2. [1893] 1 Q.B. 142.

that, though highways are dedicated prima facie for the purpose of passage, "things are done upon them by everybody which are recognised as being rightly done and as constituting a reasonable and usual mode of using a highway as such"; and, "if a person on a highway does not transgress such reasonable and usual mode of using it," he will not be a trespasser; but, if he does "acts other than the reasonable and ordinary user of a highway as such" he will be a trespasser. For instance, if a man, while using a highway for passage, sat down for a time to rest himself by the side of the road, to call that a trespass would be unreasonable. Similarly, to take a case suggested during the argument, if a man took a sketch from the highway, I should say that no reasonable person would treat that as an act of trespass. But I cannot agree with the contention of the defendant's counsel that the acts which this defendant did, not really for the purpose of using the highway as such, but for the purpose of carrying on his business as a racing tout to the detriment of the plaintiff by watching the trials of race-horses on the plaintiff's land, were within such an ordinary and reasonable user of the highway as I have mentioned. It appears to me that in the case of *Harrison* v. *Duke of Rutland*[1] the point which arises in this case was substantially determined, though the user of the highway by the plaintiff in that case was not precisely similar to that in the present case. In that case the plaintiff went upon a highway, the soil of which was vested in the defendant, while a grouse drive was taking place on adjoining land of the defendant, for the purpose of interfering with the drive, which the defendant's keepers prevented him from doing by force. The plaintiff thereupon brought an action for assault against the defendant, and the defendant counter-claimed in trespass. The plaintiff in answer to the counter-claim set up the defence that the locus in quo was a highway. It was clear upon the facts that he was not using the highway for the purpose of passing or re-passing along it, but solely for the purpose of interfering with the defendant's enjoy-ment of his right of shooting over his land, and it was held therefore that the plaintiff's user of the highway was a trespass. I cannot see any real distinction between that case and the present. It is contended that Day J. directed the jury improperly, but I do not think that is so. He told them in effect that the defendant was entitled to use the high-way as a wayfarer, and that it was a question for them whether in what the defendant did he was so using it. I think that his direction was in substance a sufficient direction under the circumstances of the case. I do not agree with the argument of the defen-dant's counsel to the effect that the intention and object of the defendant in going upon the highway cannot be taken into account in determining whether he was using it in a lawful manner. I think that his intention and object were all-important in determining that question. The application must be dismissed.

[COLLINS and ROMER L.JJ. delivered judgments in favour of dismissing the applica-tion.]

Application dismissed

Question

Are any of the following trespasses on the highway?

(i) parking a car overnight
(ii) participating in a procession along the highway, or
(iii) participating in a meeting on the highway.

Notes

1. The soil of the highway is presumed to belong (up to the middle of the highway) to the owner of the land on either side. However, it should be men-tioned that by section 226 of the Highways Act 1959 "every highway main-tainable at the public expense, together with the material and scrapings there-

---

1. [1893] 1 Q.B. 142.

of, shall vest in the authority who are for the time being the highway authority for the highway". For discussion of the interest of the highway authority, see C. A. Cross, *Encyclopedia of Highway Law and Practice*, paras. 1–002–1–004.

2. If a defendant obstructs the highway, he may commit not only a trespass but also a nuisance and may involve himself in a criminal liability under statute. Section 121 of the Highways Act 1959 provides that if "a person, without lawful authority or excuse, in any way wilfully obstructs the free passage along a highway he shall be guilty of an offence. . . ."

(ii) Air space

Kelsen v. Imperial Tobacco Co. (of Great Britain and Ireland), Ltd.

Queen's Bench Division   [1957] 2 All E.R. 343

The defendants fixed an advertising sign on the wall of premises adjoining a tobacconist's shop, of which the plaintiff was the lessee. The sign, which had been fixed there with the consent of the plaintiff's landlord, extended a maximum of eight inches from the wall and protruded into the air space above the tobacconist's shop. The defendants' employees, on the occasions when they wished to repair or maintain the sign, gained access from the tobacconist's shop with the plaintiff's knowledge, After business disputes between the plaintiff and the defendants, the plaintiff gave the defendants formal notice to remove the sign. In this action, in which the plaintiff sought an injunction requiring the removal of the sign by the defendants, McNair J. dealt with the construction of the lease and found "nothing in the lease which displaces the prima facie conclusion which one would otherwise reach that the air space above the demised premises is part of the premises conveyed." He went on to find that "nothing which has happened has deprived the plaintiff of the right which he has in the air space as conveyed to him by the lease".

McNair J.: . . . That leads me to the next and, in some ways, most interesting point of the case, namely, whether an invasion of an air space by a sign of this nature gives rise to an action in trespass or whether the rights, if any, of the owner of the air space are limited to complaining of nuisance; for if his rights are so limited, it is clear on the facts of this case that no nuisance was created, since the presence of this sign in the position which it occupied on the wall of the adjoining premises caused no inconvenience and no interference with the plaintiff's use of his air space. The question of trespass by invasion of the air space has been the subject of considerable controversy. One starts with the decision of Lord Ellenborough in *Pickering* v. *Rudd* ((1815), 4 Camp. 219), where the trespass alleged was that the defendant had broken and entered the plaintiff's close by nailing on the defendant's own house a board which projected several inches from the wall and so far overhung the plaintiff's garden. Lord Ellenborough, in 1815, said (*ibid.*, at p. 220):

"I do not think it is a trespass to interfere with the column of air superincumbent on the close. I once had occasion to rule upon the circuit, that a man who, from the outside of a field, discharged a gun into it, so as that the shot must have struck the soil, was guilty of breaking and entering it. A very learned judge, who went the circuit with me, at first doubted the decision, but I believe he afterwards approved of it, and that it met with the general concurrence of those to whom it was mentioned. But I am by no means prepared to say, that firing across a field in vacuo, no part of the contents touching it, amounts to a clausum fregit. Nay, if this board overhanging the plaintiff's garden be a trespass, it would follow that an aeronaut is liable to an action of trespass quare clausum fregit, at the suit of the occupier of every field over which his balloon passes in the course of his voyage. Whether the action may be maintained cannot depend upon the length of time for which the superincumbent air is invaded. If any damage arises from the object which overhangs the close, the remedy is by an action on the case."

Hawkins, J., followed that decision and took the same view in *Clifton* v. *Viscount Bury* ((1887), 4 T.L.R. 8), where he was dealing with the passage of bullets fired from a musketry range, the bullets passing some seventy-five feet above the surface of the land and not striking the land. He held that that was not trespass, but, if anything, was nuisance.

An early doubt as to the correctness of Lord Ellenborough's statement was expressed by Blackburn, J., in *Kenyon* v. *Hart* ((1865), 6 B. & S. 249, at p. 252), and it seems to me that since that date there has been a consistent line of authority to the contrary. For instance, in *Wandsworth Board of Works* v. *United Telephone Co.* ((1884), 13 Q.B.D. 904), one of the questions at issue was whether a telephone line running across a street constituted a trespass as against the local authority in whom the street was vested. The main contest in the case was as to the extent of the vesting in the local authority, the conclusion being reached that they did not have vested in them the air space above the street beyond what was necessary for its use as a street; but I think that each of the learned lords justices in that case was quite clear in his conclusion that, if the street and the air space above it had been vested in the local authority, the passage of a telephone line through that air space would have constituted a trespass and not a mere nuisance. I need not elaborate my judgment by citing the passages from the three judgments in that case.

In *Gifford* v. *Dent*, [1926] W.N. 336, Romer J. clearly took the view that a sign which was erected on the wall above the ground floor premises, which had been demised to the plaintiff, and projected some four feet eight inches from the wall constituted a trespass over the plaintiff's air space, that air space being the column of air above the basement which projected out under the pavement. Romer J. said ([1926] W.N. at p. 336):

"If he was right in the conclusion to which he had come that the plaintiffs were tenants of the forecourt and were accordingly tenants of the space above the forecourt usque and coelum, it seemed to him that the projection was clearly a trespass upon the property of the plaintiffs."

That decision, I think, has been recognised by the text-book writers, and, in particular, by the late Professor Winfield,[1] as stating the true law. It is not without significance that in the Air Navigation Act, 1920, s. 9 (1), which was replaced by s. 40 (1) of the Civil Aviation Act, 1949, the legislature found it necessary expressly to negative the action of trespass or nuisance arising from the mere fact of an aeroplane passing through the air above the land. It seems to me clearly to indicate that the legislature were not taking the same view of the matter as Lord Ellenborough in *Pickering* v. *Rudd*, (1815), 4 Camp. 219, but were taking the view accepted in the later cases, such as *Wandsworth Board of Works* v. *United Telephone Co.* (1884), 13 Q.B.D. 904, subsequently followed by Romer, J., in *Gifford* v. *Dent*, [1926] W.N. 336. Accordingly, I reach the conclusion that a trespass, and not a mere nuisance, was created by the invasion of the plaintiff's air space by this sign.

There remains for my consideration the final point urged by learned counsel for the defendants that the proper remedy in this case is a remedy in damages and not by way of injunction. In that connexion I was referred to a classic statement by A. L. Smith L.J. in *Shelfer* v. *City of London Electric Lighting Co.* ([1895] 1 Ch. 287), regarding the principles to be applied in deciding whether an injunction should be granted or damages awarded. . . .

[Having quoted from this judgment, MCNAIR J. continued:] I have no doubt at all that in the present case I have a discretion, which I have to exercise judicially, to award

---

1. See *Winfield on Tort* (6th Edn.) (1954), p. 379.

damages in lieu of an injunction, if I see fit. It is true that the injury to the plaintiff's legal rights in this case is small. The sign in his air space does him no harm and does not diminish his enjoyment. I doubt whether it is a case in which one can estimate the damage in terms of money, because the damages, if estimated at all, would have to be stated to be nominal. I do not find, however, that it would be in any way oppressive to the defendants to grant an injunction. It is true that considerable expense, stated to be some £220, was incurred some seven years ago in erecting the sign, but I have no evidence at all whether the defendants have not had good value for that expenditure. I know that Messrs. Gallagher are apparently prepared today to pay £75 a year for a smaller advertisement in a less prominent position. Furthermore, I think it is relevant in this connexion that the defendants throughout the case have been insisting on the right to display this advertisement as a matter of right. I think that that is a circumstance which the court is entitled to take into account in determining whether a small money payment with a declaration of right should be sufficient or whether an injunction should be granted. Cases in which an injunction has not been granted on the ground of hardship have, I believe, been mostly cases in which there has been some accidental invasion of the plaintiff's rights. I was referred by counsel for the plaintiff to *Goodson* v. *Richardson* ((1874), 9 Ch. App. 221), where a strong Court of Appeal held that the mere fact that the invasion of the highway in that case did not cause any serious damage to the owner of the highway did not disentitle him from an injunction. I am further impressed by the fact that, if I refuse to grant an injunction in this case, there is nothing to prevent the defendants from continuing to display the sign, and leaving it to the plaintiff to put forward a subsequent claim for damages in a further action. If I were to decide that an appropriate remedy would be a small money payment of nominal damages, I would be, in effect, saying that, although such implied licence, if any, as the defendants had has been determined, nevertheless, the defendants are entitled to continue to display their sign.

In my judgment, bearing in mind that both parties, in pursuance of what they claimed to be their business interests, have attempted to bring commercial pressure to bear one on the other, this is a proper case in which the court should direct that there should be a mandatory injunction that such portion of the sign as projects over the plaintiff's premises be removed within twenty-eight days.

Judgment for the plaintiff

Note

Trespass in the air space is a case in which the plaintiff may suffer no actual harm, yet this is not a reason against, indeed it may be a reason for, the granting of an injunction. This point was made by Stamp J. in *Woollerton and Wilson, Ltd.* v. *Richard Costain, Ltd.*, [1970] 1 All E.R. 483, a case where the defendants were constructing, for the use of the General Post Office, a building which was to be 300 feet high. In the course of this work, a tower crane was used. This was a "practical necessity" because of the nature of the site, but the jib of the crane would swing (at about 50 feet above roof level) over some property nearby which the plaintiffs owned. No loads were carried over the property. The plaintiffs sought an interlocutory injunction *inter alia* to restrain the defendants from allowing the jib to pass over their property, and it was conceded that there was a trespass. In the exercise of his discretion, in which many factors were taken into account (see pp. 486–487), Stamp J. granted an injunction, but postponed its operation until the end of November 1970, by which time it appeared that the trespass would have ceased. In *Charrington* v. *Simons & Co., Ltd.*, [1971] 2 All E.R. 588; [1971] 1 W.L.R. 598 however, the Court of Appeal reserved its opinion on the correctness of this decision.

The Civil Aviation Act 1949

40. Liability of aircraft in respect of trespass, nuisance and surface damage.— (1) No action shall lie in respect of trespass or in respect of nuisance, by reason only of the flight of an aircraft over any property at a height above the ground, which, having regard to wind, weather and all the circumstances of the case is reasonable, or the ordinary incidents of such flight so long as the provisions of Part II and this Part of this Act and any Order in Council or order made under Part II or this Part of this Act are duly complied with.

(2) Where material loss or damage is caused to any person or property on land or water by, or by a person in, or an article or person falling from, an aircraft while in flight, taking off or landing, then unless the loss or damage was caused or contributed to by the negligence of the person by whom it was suffered, damages in respect of the loss or damage shall be recoverable without proof of negligence or intention or other cause of action, as if the loss or damage had been caused by the wilful act, neglect, or default of the owner of the aircraft:

Provided that where material loss or damage is caused as aforesaid in circumstances in which—

    (*a*) damages are recoverable in respect of the said loss or damage by virtue only of the foregoing provisions of this subsection; and

    (*b*) a legal liability is created in some person other than the owner to pay damages in respect of the said loss or damage;

the owner shall be entitled to be indemnified by that other person against any claim in respect of the said loss or damage.

Note

For a consideration of s. 40, see McNair, *The Law of the Air* (3rd Edn.), Chap. 5. The section now applies to "aircraft belonging to or exclusively employed in the service of Her Majesty, not being military aircraft" (see The Civil Aviation (Crown Aircraft) Order 1970, S.I. 1970 No. 289).

(b) The plaintiff

Graham v. Peat

Court of King's Bench   (1801), 1 East 244

Trespass *quare clausum fregit*. Plea the general issue (and certain special pleas not material to the question). At the trial before Graham B. at the last assizes at Carlisle, the trespass was proved in fact; but it also appeared that the locus in quo was part of the glebe of the rector of the parish of Workington in Cumberland, which had been demised by the rector to the plaintiff, and that the rector had not been resident within the parish for five years last past, and no sufficient excuse was shewn for his absence. Whereupon it was objected that the action could not be maintained, the lease being absolutely void by the Act of the 13 Eliz. c. 20, which enacts, "That no lease of any benefice or ecclesiastical promotion with cure or any part thereof shall endure any longer than while the lessor shall be ordinarily resident and serving the cure of such benefice without absence above fourscore days in any one year; but that every such lease immediately upon such absence shall cease and be void." And thereupon the plaintiff was nonsuited.

A rule was obtained in Michaelmas term last to shew cause why the nonsuit should not be set aside, upon the ground that the action was maintainable against a wrong-doer upon the plaintiff's possession alone, without shewing any title. . . .

LORD KENYON C.J. There is no doubt but that the plaintiff's possession in this case was sufficient to maintain trespass against a wrongdoer; and if he could not have maintained an ejectment upon such a demise, it is because that is a fictitious remedy founded upon title. Any possession is a legal possession against a wrongdoer. Suppose a burglary committed in the dwelling-house of such an one, must it not be laid to be his dwelling-house notwithstanding the defect of his title under that statute.

Per Curiam. Rule absolute

Notes

1. This case shows that the saying that possession is nine tenths of the law is not without truth. (On the concept of possession, see Pollock & Wright, *An Essay on Possession in the Common Law*.) Compare the action of ejectment (or action for recovery of land), on which see Clerk & Lindsell, paras. 1360–1364.

2. A person with possession of property will not always succeed in a trespass action. In *Delaney* v. *T. P. Smith, Ltd.*, [1946] K.B. 393; [1946] 2 All E.R. 23 the plaintiff made an oral agreement with an agent of the defendants for the tenancy of a house which was being repaired. Before the house was ready, the defendants decided that they would sell the house (along with several others), and wrote to the plaintiff to that effect. Some time later the plaintiff obtained a key and took possession of the premises, but nine days later was forcibly ejected by the defendants, from whom he claimed damages for trespass. He alleged that he was the tenant of the house and protected by the provisions of the Rent and Mortgage Interest (Restrictions) Acts 1920–1939, but was faced by an argument from the defendants based on s. 40 of the Law of Property Act 1925—that no note or memorandum existed relating to the alleged tenancy. It was pointed out in the Court of Appeal that in an action for trespass to land, an allegation of possession by a plaintiff would suffice against a wrongdoer, but not against the lawful owner. Against the freeholder here, the plaintiff had to rely on the oral agreement, to which s. 40 provided an answer. (Compare *Lane* v. *Dixon* (1847), 3 C.B. 776.) On the question of who may sue in trespass, see further Winfield & Jolowicz, pp. 308–310; Street, pp. 67–70; Clerk & Lindsell, paras. 1318–1328.

3. The student should also note the doctrine of trespass by relation, which operates where a person had a right to immediate possession but did not enter until a later date. He may sue for trespasses committed between the time when the right arose and the actual entry; he is deemed to have been in possession of the land during that period.

(c) The nature of the defendant's act

Smith v. Stone

Court of King's Bench   (1647), Sty. 65

Smith brought an action of trespasse against Stone pedibus ambulando, the defendant pleads this speciall plea in justification, viz. that he was carried upon the land of the plaintiff by force, and violence of others, and was not there voluntarily, which is the same trespasse, for which the plaintiff brings his action. The plaintiff demurs to this plea: in this case Roll Iustice said, that it is the trespasse of the party that carryed the defendant upon the land, and not the trespasse of the defendant: as he that drives my cattel into another mans land is the trespassor against him, and not I who am owner of the cattell.

Gilbert v. Stone

Court of King's Bench   (1647), Sty. 72

Gilbert brought an action of trespasse quare clausum fregit, and taking of a gelding, against Stone. The defendant pleads that he for fear of his life, and wounding of twelve armed men, who threatened to kill him if he did not the fact, went into the house of the plaintiff, and took the gelding. The plaintiff demurred to this plea; Roll Iustice, This is no plea to justifie the defendant; for I may not do a trespasse to one for fear of threatnings of another, for by this means the party injured shall have no satisfaction, for he cannot have it of the party that threatned. Therefore let the plaintiff have his judgement.

Note

Although these two cases occur in this section on trespass to land, they illustrate a general principle. (See Clerk & Lindsell, para. 44.) Compare p. 378, *post*.

The Limitation Act 1623

5. After judgment for defendant, etc. in trespas quare clausum fregit, upon disclaimer of defendant, etc. plaintiff barred of his action.—And . . . in all accions of trespas quare clausum fregit hereafter to be brought, wherein the defendant or defendantẹ shall disclaime in his or their plea to make any title or claime to the land in which the trespasse is by the declaracion supposed to be done, and the trespas be by negligence, or involuntary, the defendant or defendantẹ shalbe admitted to pleade a disclaymer, and that the trespas was by negligence, or involuntary, and a tender or offer of sufficient amendẹ for such trespase before the accion brought, whereuppon or uppon some of them, the plaintiffe or plaintiffes shalbe enforced to joyne issue; and if the said issue be found for the defendant or defendantẹ, or the plaintiff or plaintiffẹ shalbe nonsuted, the plaintiffe or plaintiffes shalbe clearlie barred from the said accion or accions and all other suite concerning the same.

Basely v. Clarkson

Court of Common Pleas   (1681), 3 Lev. 37

Trespass for breaking his closs called the *balk* and the *hade*, and cutting his grass, and carrying it away. The defendant disclaims any title in the lands of the plaintiff, but says that he hath a *balk* and *hade* adjoining to the balk and hade of the plaintiff, and in mowing his own land he involuntarily and by mistake mowed down some grass growing upon the balk and hade of the plaintiff, intending only to mow the grass upon his own *balk* and *hade*, and carried the *grass &c. quæ est eadem, &c. Et quod ante emanationem brevis* he tendered to the plaintiff 2s. in satisfaction, and that 2s. was a sufficient amends. Upon this the plaintiff demurred, and had judgment; for it appears the fact was voluntary, and his intention and knowledge are not traversable; they cannot be known.

(d) Trespass ab initio

The Six Carpenters' Case

(1610), 8 Co. Rep. 146a

In trespass brought by John Vaux against Thomas Newman, carpenter, and five other carpenters, for breaking his house, and for an assault and battery, 1 Sept. 7 Jac. in London, in the parish of St. Giles *extra* Cripplegate, in the ward of Cripplegate, &c.

and upon the new assignment, the plaintiff assigned the trespass in a house called the Queen's Head. The defendants to all the trespass *præter fractionem domus* pleaded not guilty; and as to the breaking of the house, said, that the said house *præd' tempore quo, &c. et diu antea et postea*, was a common wine tavern, of the said John Vaux, with a common sign at the door of the said house fixed, &c. by force whereof the defendants, *praed' tempore quo, &c.* viz. *hora quarta post meridiem* into the said house, the door thereof being open, did enter, and did there buy and drink a quart of wine, and there paid for the same, &c. The plaintiff, by way of replication, did confess, that the said house was a common tavern, and that they entered into it, and bought and drank a quart of wine, and paid for it: but further said, that one John Ridding, servant of the said John Vaux, at the request of the said defendants, did there then deliver them another quart of wine, and a pennyworth of bread, amounting to 8d. and then they there did drink the said wine, and eat the bread, and upon request did refuse to pay for the same: upon which the defendants did demur in law: and the only point in this case was, if the denying to pay for the wine, or non-payment, which is all one (for every non-payment upon request, is a denying in law) makes the entry into the tavern tortious.

And first, it was resolved when an entry, authority, or licence, is given to any one by the law, and he doth abuse it, he shall be a trespasser *ab initio*: but where an entry, authority, or licence is given by the party, and he abuses it, there he must be punished for his abuse, but shall not be a trespasser *ab initio*. And the reason of this difference is, that in the case of a general authority or licence of law, the law adjudges by the subsequent act, *quo animo*, or to what intent, he entered; for *acta exteriora indicant interiora secreta*. . . . But when the party gives an authority or licence himself to do any thing, he cannot, for any subsequent cause, punish that which is done by his own authority or licence, and therefore the law gives authority to enter into a common inn, or tavern, so to the lord to distrain; to the owner of the ground to distrain damage-feasant; to him in reversion to see if waste be done; to the commoner to enter upon the land to see his cattle, and such like. . . .

But if he who enters into the inn or tavern doth a trespass, as if he carries away any thing; or if the lord who distrains for rent, or the owner for damage-feasant, works or kills the distress; or if he who enters to see waste breaks the house, or stays there all night; or if the commoner cuts down a tree, in these and the like cases, the law adjudges that he entered for that purpose; and because the Act which demonstrates it is a trespass, he shall be a trespasser *ab initio*, as it appears in all the said books. . . .

It was resolved *per totam Curiam*, that not doing, cannot make the party who has authority or licence by the law a trespasser *ab initio*, because not doing is no trespass; and, therefore, if the lessor distrains for his rent, and thereupon the lessee tenders him the rent and arrears, &c. and requires his beasts again, and he will not deliver them, this not doing cannot make him a trespasser *ab initio*. . . .

So in the case at Bar, for not paying for the wine, the defendants shall not be trespassers, for the denying to pay for it is no trespass, and therefore they cannot be trespassers *ab initio*.

Notes

1. This case has been subject to criticism in recent times. In *Chic Fashions (West Wales), Ltd.* v. *Jones*, [1968] 2 Q.B. 299, Lord Denning M.R. stated emphatically (at p. 313) that the case above "was a by-product of the old forms of action. Now that they are buried, it can be interred with their bones." See too the judgment of Diplock L.J. who expressed the following reservation (at p. 317): "What application, if any, the rule applied in the *Six Carpenters' Case* has in the modern law of tort may some day call for re-examination . . ." The doctrine does seem at odds with the idea, which Lord Denning M.R. in

particular has favoured, that the lawfulness of conduct should be judged at the time when it takes place, and not by what happens later.

2. The *Six Carpenters' Case* refers to entry on to land under a licence. This is a topic which is more fully dealt with in books on the law of property, though see *White* v. *Blackmore*, [1972] 2 Q.B. 651; [1972] 3 All E.R. 158, p. 235, *ante*.

(e) Necessity

Note

This defence has already been mentioned in the context of intentional injuries to the person (p. 55, *ante*) but it might also be raised as a defence to trespass to land. However, in *London Borough of Southwark* v. *Williams*, [1971] Ch. 734; [1971] 2 All E.R. 175, a case concerning squatters, the Court of Appeal seemed determined to keep the defence within fairly limited bounds. Lord Denning M.R. stated (at p. 179):

> "If homelessness were once admitted as a defence to trespass, no one's house could be safe. Necessity would open a door which no man could shut. It would not only be those in extreme need who would enter. There would be others who would imagine that they were in need, or would invent a need, so as to gain entry. Each man would say his need was greater than the next man's. The plea would be an excuse for all sorts of wrongdoing. So the courts must, for the sake of law and order, take a firm stand. They must refuse to admit the plea of necessity to the hungry and the homeless; and trust that their distress will be relieved by the charitable and the good."

Edmund Davies L.J. took the view that "all the cases where a plea of necessity has succeeded are cases which deal with an urgent situation of imminent peril", citing *Leigh* v. *Gladstone* (1909), 26 T.L.R. 139, p. 55, *ante*, as an example. Compare the position in cases such as *Cope* v. *Sharpe (No. 2)*, [1912] 1 K.B. 496.

2. NUISANCE

(a) In general

St. Helen's Smelting Co. v. Tipping

House of Lords   (1865), 11 H.L.C. 642

The Lord Chancellor (Lord Westbury) stated the following facts: "Now, in the present case, it appears that the Plaintiff purchased a very valuable estate, which lies within a mile and a half from certain large smelting works. What the occupation of these copper smelting premises was anterior to the year 1860 does not clearly appear. The Plaintiff became the proprietor of an estate of great value in the month of June 1860. In the month of September 1860 very extensive smelting operations began on the property of the present Appellants [defendants] in their works at St. Helen's. Of the effect of the vapours exhaling from those works upon the Plaintiff's property, and the injury done to his trees and shrubs, there is abundance of evidence in the case." The report sets out the direction which was given to the jury by Mellor J.:

The learned Judge told the jury that an actionable injury was one producing sensible discomfort; that every man, unless enjoying rights obtained by prescription or agreement, was bound to use his own property in such a manner as not to injure the property of his neighbours; that there was no prescriptive right in this case; that the law did not regard trifling inconveniences; that everything must be looked at from a reasonable point of view; and therefore, in an action for nuisance to property, arising from noxious vapours, the injury to be actionable must be such as visibly to diminish the value of the property and the comfort and enjoyment of it. That when the jurors came to consider the facts, all the circumstances, including those of time and locality, ought to be taken into consideration; and that with respect to the latter it was clear that in counties where great works had been erected and carried on, persons must not stand on their extreme rights and bring actions in respect of every matter of annoyance, for if so, the business of the whole country would be seriously interfered with.

The Defendants' counsel submitted that the three questions which ought to be left to the jury were, "whether it was a necessary trade, whether the place was a suitable place for such a trade, and whether it was carried on in a reasonable manner." The learned judge did not put the questions in this form, but did ask the jury whether the enjoyment of the Plaintiff's property was sensibly diminished, and the answer was in the affirmative. Whether the business there carried on was an ordinary business for smelting copper, and the answer was, "We consider it an ordinary business, and conducted in a proper manner, in as good a manner as possible." But to the question whether the jurors thought that it was carried on in a proper place, the answer was, "We do not." The verdict was therefore entered for the Plaintiff, and the damages were assessed at £361 18s 4½d. A motion was made for a new trial, on the ground of misdirection, but the rule was refused (4 Best and Sm. 608). Leave was however given to appeal, and the case was carried to the Exchequer Chamber, where the judgment was affirmed, Lord Chief Baron Pollock there observing, "My opinion has not always been that which it is now. Acting upon what has been decided *in this Court*, my brother Mellor's direction is not open to a bill of exception" (4 Best and Sm. 616). This appeal was then brought.

[The direction to the jury was approved by the House of Lords, and by the judges who were summoned. LORD WESTBURY L.C. continued:] ... My Lords, in matters of this description it appears to me that it is a very desirable thing to mark the difference between an action brought for a nuisance upon the ground that the alleged nuisance produces material injury to the property, and an action brought for a nuisance on the ground that the thing alleged to be a nuisance is productive of sensible personal discomfort. With regard to the latter, namely, the personal inconvenience and interference with one's enjoyment, one's quiet, one's personal freedom, anything that discomposes or injuriously affects the senses or the nerves, whether that may or may not be denominated a nuisance, must undoubtedly depend greatly on the circumstances of the place where the thing complained of actually occurs. If a man lives in a town, it is necessary that he should subject himself to the consequences of those operations of trade which may be carried on in his immediate locality, which are actually necessary for trade and commerce, and also for the enjoyment of property, and for the benefit of the inhabitants of the town and of the public at large. If a man lives in a street where there are numerous shops, and a shop is opened next door to him, which is carried on in a fair and reasonable way, he has no ground for complaint, because to himself individually there may arise much discomfort from the trade carried on in that shop. But when an occupation is carried on by one person in the neighbourhood of another, and the result of that trade, or occupation, or business, is a material injury to property, then there unquestionably arises a very different consideration. I think, my Lords, that in a case of that description, the submission which is required from persons living in society to that amount of discomfort which may be necessary for the legitimate and free exercise of the trade of their neighbours, would not apply to circumstances the immediate result of which is sensible injury to the value of the property ...

[Having stated the facts as above, he continued:] My lords, the action has been brought upon that, and the jurors have found the existence of the injury; and the only ground upon which your Lordships are asked to set aside that verdict, and to direct a new trial, is this, that the whole neighbourhood where these copper smelting works were carried on, is a neighbourhood more or less devoted to manufacturing purposes of a similar kind, and therefore it is said, that inasmuch as this copper smelting is carried on in what the Appellant contends is a fit place, it may be carried on with impunity, although the result may be the utter destruction, or the very considerable diminution, of the value of the Plaintiff's property. My Lords, I apprehend that that is not the meaning of the word "suitable", or the meaning of the word "convenient", which has been used as applicable to the subject. The word "suitable" unquestionably cannot carry with it this consequence, that a trade may be carried on in a particular locality, the consequence of which trade may be injury and destruction to the neighbouring property. Of course, my Lords, I except cases where any prescriptive right has been acquired by a lengthened user of the place.

On these grounds, therefore, shortly, without dilating farther upon them . . . I advise your Lordships to affirm the decision of the Court below, and to refuse the new trial, and to dismiss the appeal with costs.

[LORD CRANWORTH delivered a brief speech in which he concurred with the LORD CHANCELLOR. LORD WENSLEYDALE agreed with both their Lordships.]

Judgment of the Exchequer Chamber affirming the judgment of the Court of Queen's Bench affirmed. Appeal dismissed

Question

Would a defendant be liable under *Rylands* v. *Fletcher* if these facts arose today?

Note

1. As the *St. Helen's* case shows, the nuisance action may play some part in the protection of the environment. Attention might also be paid to *Halsey* v. *Esso Petroleum Co., Ltd.*, [1961] 2 All E.R. 145 where the defendants, who operated an oil-distributing depot near to the plaintiff's house, were held liable for: (i) damage caused by acidy smuts escaping from the depot on to laundry hung out to dry (liability in nuisance and under *Rylands* v. *Fletcher*); (ii) damage similarly caused to the plaintiff's motor car on the highway (whether or not there could be a claim in private nuisance, there was liability under *Rylands* v. *Fletcher* and in public nuisance); (iii) nuisance caused by a "nauseating smell" escaping from the depot; (iv) nuisance at night caused by noise from the plant at the depot; (v) nuisance during the night shift caused by noise from tankers arriving at and leaving the depot (liability here was based either on private nuisance or in the alternative on public nuisance by virtue of their use of the highway). The character of the neighbourhood was relevant to the question of nuisance by smell and by noise.

2. Many circumstances may be taken into account in deciding whether there has been a nuisance. It is in this context that malice is relevant, although this statement must be read in the light of *Bradford Corpn.* v. *Pickles*, [1895] A.C. 587. In that case, the defendant's excavations on his land interfered with percolating water under his land, and resulted in the plaintiffs' water supply being diminished and occasionally discoloured. The plaintiffs sought an injunction but were unsuccessful. The defendant had a right to act in this way (see *Chasemore* v. *Richards* (1859), 7 H.L.C. 349), and to the allegation that the defendant was acting maliciously, Lord Halsbury L.C. answered (at p. 594) that "if it was a lawful act, however ill the motive might be, he had a right to do it". In fact, Lord MacNaghten stated that it could be taken that Pickles' objective was to compel the Corporation to purchase his property at a price which suited him, but his Lordship drew attention to the lack of spite and ill-will on Pickles' part. Salmond (at p. 20) suggests that the common law did not

regard his motive as improper. The decision in that case on the irrelevance of motive must be compared with *Hollywood Silver Fox Farm, Ltd.* v. *Emmett*, [1936] 2 K.B. 468; [1936] 1 All E.R. 825. The plaintiff company was engaged in breeding silver foxes. There had been a disagreement between the defendant (an adjoining landowner) and the managing director of the plaintiff company, about a notice on the plaintiff's land, and some months later the defendant sent his son out to the boundary of his land which was closest to the vixens' pens to fire a gun: the shooting was repeated for the next three evenings. The noise affected the vixens and caused the plaintiffs loss, for there was evidence that the number of cubs reared was less than could have been expected. Some vixens did not mate and one ate her cubs. On the defendant's side, there was evidence that his son was shooting there to cut down the number of rabbits, but in fact the learned judge found that the son was sent to shoot there to frighten the vixens. Taking the view that *Bradford Corpn.* v. *Pickles* did not govern the case, and that the defendant's intention was relevant, MacNaghten J. gave judgment for the plaintiff in his action for nuisance. (See also *Christie* v. *Davey*, [1893] 1 Ch. 316). The explanation of *Emmett's* case would appear to lie in the following reasoning. Noise can be an interference with a person's use and enjoyment of land. However, the law of nuisance is concerned with balancing the interests of neighbouring landowners, and to be actionable as nuisance, it appears that there has to be an "unreasonable" use of land by the defendant. Therefore the purpose behind the creation of the "nuisance" becomes a relevant factor, and the presence of malice may mean that a given amount of noise constitutes an actionable nuisance, where, in the absence of malice, it would not do so. As was pointed out in a note on *Emmett's* case, the presence of malice destroys the "qualified privilege to act in a reasonable manner" (1936), 52 L.Q.R. at p. 461, but see (1937) 53, L.Q.R. 1–4. Can *Pickles'* case and *Emmett's* case be reconciled? (See Winfield & Jolowicz, p. 340; Street, p. 223; compare Clerk & Lindsell, para. 30; G. H. L. Fridman, "Malice in the Law of Torts" (1958), 21 M.L.R. 484, at pp. 493–494). In relation to *Pickles'* case, see also *Langbrook Properties, Ltd.* v. *Surrey C.C.*, [1969] 3 All E.R. 1424, noted, p. 67, *ante*, in the context of the negligence claim, where a claim in nuisance also failed. Malice is relevant in the tort of conspiracy but is not in itself a cause of action—see *Allen* v. *Flood*, [1898] A.C. 1, p. 441, *post*.

Bridlington Relay, Ltd. *v.* Yorkshire Electricity Board

Chancery Division   [1965] 1 All E.R. 264

The plaintiffs, who provided a sound and television broadcast relay system in Bridlington, had installed aerials on top of a tower they had built: at a later date, an electricity power line was erected by the defendants in the area. On the evening of 1 June 1964, during a test period when the line was energised, there was some interference on the plaintiffs' television set (apparently only in the case of the B.B.C. transmission from Holme Moss—see [1965] Ch. 436, at p. 442) and they sought an injunction to stop the defendants so operating the line as to interfere with their reception of radio and television broadcasts. Buckley J. found that the interference which had been experienced could be remedied. The defendants had given an assurance to the plaintiffs that they would do their utmost to suppress interference and Buckley J. decided that "it would be wrong for this court in quia timet proceedings to grant relief by way of injunction to compel the defendants to do something which they appear to be willing to do without the imposition of an order of the court". Nevertheless, he went on to consider whether the plaintiffs could claim in nuisance if the power line's tendency to cause interference could not be remedied, or if his view that it may be remediable was irrelevant:

BUCKLEY J.: . . . If interference of the kind experienced by the plaintiffs on 1 June were to recur at all frequently, it is very probable that the plaintiffs' business would be damaged. If such damage were established, and it were shown that it would be likely to continue or recur, would the plaintiffs have a cause of action in nuisance? . . .

I was invited, and am prepared, to take judicial notice of the fact that the reception of television has become a very common feature of domestic life. The evidence has shown that the quality of reception enjoyed in different parts of the country varies widely, mainly for geographical reasons. Where the quality of reception is poor the effect of interference is more serious, for the greater the strength of the wanted signal the less the effect on the screen of interference of any given strength. Where the strength of the wanted signal is low, interference of even quite moderate intensity will degrade the picture. In taking judicial notice of the widespread reception of television in domestic circles, I do so on the footing that in those circles television is enjoyed almost entirely for what I think must be regarded as recreational purposes, notwithstanding that the broadcast programmes include material which may have some educational content, some political content and, it may be, some other content not strictly or exclusively recreational in character. Those programmes, the purposes of which are strictly educational, are not, I presume, intended for domestic consumption or very much looked at in private homes. I mention these matters because, in my judgment, the plaintiffs could not succeed in a claim for damages for nuisance if what I may call an ordinary receiver of television by means of an aerial mounted on his own house could not do so. It is, I think, established by authority that an act which does not, or would not, interfere with the ordinary enjoyment of their property by neighbours in the ordinary modes of using such property cannot constitute a legal nuisance. I quote:

"A man cannot increase the liabilities of his neighbour by applying his own property to special uses, whether for business or pleasure".

(*Eastern and South African Telegraph Co., Ltd.* v. *Cape Town Tramways Cos., Ltd.*[1]).

In *Robinson* v. *Kilvert*, COTTON L.J., stated the principle thus:[2]

"If a person does what in itself is noxious, or which interferes with the ordinary use and enjoyment of a neighbour's property, it is a nuisance. But no case has been cited where the doing something not in itself noxious has been held a nuisance, unless it interferes with the ordinary enjoyment of life, or the ordinary use of property for the purposes of residence or business."

The dissemination of electrical interference is not, in my judgment, "noxious" in the sense in which, I think, the learned lord justice is there using the term. Could such interference as is here in question be held to cause an interference with the ordinary enjoyment of life or the ordinary use of the plaintiffs' property for the purposes of residence or business of such a kind as to amount to an actionable nuisance?

There are, of course, many reported cases in which something adversely affecting the beneficial enjoyment of property has been held to constitute a legal nuisance; but I have been referred to no case in which interference with a purely recreational facility has been held to do so. Considerations of health and physical comfort and well being appear to me to be on a somewhat different level from recreational considerations. I do not wish to be taken as laying down that in no circumstances can something which interferes merely with recreational facilities or activities amount to an actionable

---

1. [1902] A.C. 381, at p. 393.
2. (1889), 41 Ch. D. 88, at p. 94.

nuisance. It may be that in some other case the court may be satisfied that some such interference should be regarded, according to such "plain and sober and simple notions" as Sir J. L. Knight Bruce, V.-C. referred to in a well-known passage in his judgment in *Walter* v. *Selfe*,[1] as detracting from the beneficial use and enjoyment by neighbouring owners of their properties to such an extent as to warrant their protection by the law. For myself, however, I do not think that it can at present be said that the ability to receive television free from occasional, even if recurrent and severe, electrical interference is so important a part of an ordinary householder's enjoyment of his property that such interference should be regarded as a legal nuisance, particularly, perhaps, if such interference affects only one of the available alternative programmes.

Accordingly, I do not think that even if the conditions which existed on the evening of 1 June would have produced the same effect on the screen of a householder using an aerial mounted on his own house at the site of the plaintiffs' mast, this would have constitued an actionable nuisance. . . .

The plaintiffs' complaint is concerned not with interference with domestic amenities; their complaint is that their business will be damaged. But their business is such that to prosper it requires an exceptional degree of immunity from interference. To prosper it must be able to offer its subscribers a better service than they could obtain through aerials of their own. It was not established to my satisfaction that the aerial used by the plaintiffs for receiving B.B.C. transmissions from Holme Moss was proportionately more sensitive to interference than domestic aerials are in the same area, but it was established that the business of the plaintiffs was exceptionally sensitive in the sense which I have just indicated. The use of their aerial for this particular kind of business was, in my judgment, use of a special kind unusually vulnerable to interference, just as the business carried on by the plaintiff in *Robinson* v. *Kilvert*[2] was exceptionally vulnerable to the effects of heat.

For these reasons as well as the other reasons given earlier in this judgment I am of opinion that the plaintiffs cannot succeed in this action. . . .

Action dismissed

Note

Robinson v. *Kilvert* (1889), 41 Ch. D. 88, to which reference is made in the case above, is worthy of further consideration. In that case, the defendants, who had let the ground floor of a warehouse to the plaintiff, started making paper boxes, for which heat and dry air were necessary. The heat passed into the plaintiff's room and dried his stocks of brown paper. Far from gaining any weight (which would happen if this paper was kept at a "proper temperature" in an atmosphere with a normal moisture content) the paper lost weight and became brittle. In fact the paper was sold by weight, and the plaintiff suffered a loss of profit. Ordinary paper would not have been affected by the heat, nor was the heat such as to "incommode" the plaintiff's workers and the action failed. Doing something which was non-noxious was not a nuisance merely because it affected a particularly sensitive trade. What sort of loss did the plaintiff sustain in this case—was it economic or physical loss?

British Celanese, Ltd. *v.* A. H. Hunt (Capacitors), Ltd.

Queen's Bench Division   [1969] 2 All E.R. 1252

This was the trial of a preliminary issue whether the defendants were liable in law for the damage claimed on the alleged facts which were as follows: The defendants,

---

1. (1851), 4 De G. & Sm. 315, at p. 322.
2. (1889), 41 Ch. D. 88.

who made electrical components, occupied a site on the trading estate where the plaintiffs carried on their business. For their business purposes the defendants had collected on their site strips of metal foil, which could be blown about in the wind. An electricity supply sub-station, owned by the local Electricity Board, provided power to both the plaintiffs' and the defendants' factories. The sub-station was 120 yards away from the defendants' premises, and if the foil made contact with more than one of the "bus-bars" which stood in the open air at the sub-station, there could be a "flash-over", which could in turn lead to a power failure. The defendants knew this was likely to to happen, and that damage would be caused to those with premises in the area through interruption of the light and power supply, because, on an earlier occasion, foil had blown into the overhead conductors causing an interruption of supply, and the district engineer of the Electricity Board had written to the defendants and told them what had happened and of the danger of interruption of supplies. Three and a half years after this incident, some foil which was lying about in the open air on or near the defendants' premises, blew away and came into contact with the bus-bars. This led to interruption in the light and power supply at the plaintiffs' factory, and their machinery came to a halt. Certain machines, in which materials had solidified, had to be cleaned: materials and time were wasted and production and profit were lost. The plaintiffs claimed that if they proved these allegations the defendants would be liable under *Rylands* v. *Fletcher*, and in negligence, nuisance and public nuisance. Only the last two heads are dealt with in the extract below, but it should be noted that, in considering the claim under *Rylands* v. *Fletcher*, Lawton J. took the view that the averments "amount to an allegation of damage, including injury to property, flowing directly from the escape of the metal foil from the defendants' premises". When considering remoteness of damage (in the context of the negligence claim), he took the view that there was an "averment that the defendants at the very least ought reasonably to have foreseen that their conduct was likely to cause injury to the plaintiffs' property and that it in fact did so."

LAWTON J.: . . . I turn now to the plaintiffs' contention that the re-amended statement of claim discloses a cause of action both in private and public nuisance. As to private nuisance they say that the defendants' alleged method of storing metal foil resulted, as the defendants knew it would, in an interference with the beneficial enjoyment of their own premises whereby they suffered damage; and as to public nuisance their case is that the nuisance was one which affected a class of persons, namely, those members of the public supplied with electricity from the sub-station, and that as members of that class they suffered special damage.

The defendants made three answers to these contentions: first, that an isolated happening such as the plaintiffs relied on was not enough to found an action in nuisance since this tort can only arise out of a continuing condition: secondly, that if there was a nuisance on the defendants' premises, it did not affect the plaintiffs' premises directly; and thirdly that the re-amended statement of claim did not disclose enough facts to justify a ruling that a class of the public had been injuriously affected by the alleged nuisance.

In my judgment, all three answers are misconceived. Most nuisances do arise from a long continuing condition; and many isolated happenings do not constitute a nuisance. It is, however, clear from the authorities that an isolated happening by itself can create an actionable nuisance. Such an authority is *Midwood & Co., Ltd.* v. *Manchester Corpn.*,[1] where an electric main installed by the defendants fused. This caused an explosion and a fire whereby the plaintiffs' goods were damaged. The Court of Appeal held that the defendants were liable, all the Lords Justices being of the opinion that they had caused a nuisance. The explosion in that case arose out of the condition of the electric main: the "flash-over" in this case was caused by the way in which the defendants stored their metal foil whereby those in the neighbourhood were exposed to the risk of having

---

1. [1905] 2 K.B. 597.

their electric power cut off. I am satisfied that the law is correctly stated in *Winfield on Tort* (8th Edn.) at p. 364:

> "Where the nuisance is the escape of tangible things which damage the plaintiff in the enjoyment of his property, there is no rule that he cannot sue for the first escape."

Anyway, in this case, the alleged happening of 7 December 1964 was not the first escape; there is said to have been one in 1961.

The second of the defendants' answers is a repetition of the argument which was addressed to me on remoteness of damage. I accept that those who are only indirectly affected by a nuisance cannot sue for any damage which they may suffer: but . . . I adjudge that the plaintiffs were directly and foreseeably affected.

Finally, I come to the last of the defendants' answers. Paragraph 6 of the re-amended statement of claim alleges that the defendants knew and foresaw that a "flash-over" caused by pieces of metal foil blowing about was likely to cause an interruption of power—

> ". . . to the premises of members of the public in the said area supplied [with electricity] from the said sub-station including the plaintiffs' said premises . . ."

This averment identifies the class of persons said to have been affected by the nuisance and alleges that the plaintiffs were members of that class. Whether this class was big enough to attract the description "public" to the nuisance must await the evidence at the trial. In *A.-G.* v. *P.Y.A. Quarries, Ltd.*[1] ROMER L.J., after a learned examination of the authorities, summarised the law as follows:

> ". . . any nuisance is 'public' which materially affects the reasonable comfort and convenience of life of a class of Her Majesty's subjects. The sphere of the nuisance may be described generally as 'the neighbourhood'; but the question whether the local community within that sphere comprises a sufficient number of persons to constitute a class of the public is a question of fact in every case."

For the reasons given and to the extent specified, I adjudge that on the facts set out in the re-amended statement of claim the defendants are liable in law for the damage claimed.

Order accordingly

Notes

1. Apart from the claim in nuisance, Lawton J. held that the *Rylands* v. *Fletcher* claim failed, and this point is noted, p. 348. *ante*, but he did not rule out the negligence claim if the allegations could be proved—compare *Spartan Steel and Alloys, Ltd.* v. *Martin & Co. (Contractors), Ltd.* [1973] Q.B. 27; [1972] 3 All E.R. 557, p. 76, *ante*.

2. For discussion of the question whether an isolated escape is actionable, see Winfield & Jolowicz, pp. 337–338. The quotation from Winfield on *Tort* (8th Edn.) in the extract above is not to be found in those terms in the current edition of Winfield & Jolowicz. They do quote (at p. 338) the following statement of Thesiger J. in *S.C.M. (United Kingdom), Ltd.* v. *W. J. Whittall & Son, Ltd.*, [1970] 2 All E.R. 417, at p. 430 that "while there is no doubt that a single isolated escape may cause the damage that entitles a plaintiff to sue for nuisance, yet it must be proved that the nuisance arose from the condition of the defendant's land or premises or property or activities thereon that constituted a nuisance." He denied that one negligent act causing damage to an electric

---

1. [1957] 2 Q.B. 169, at p. 184; [1957] 1 All E.R. 894, at p. 902.

cable was *thereby* a nuisance. An isolated escape is, of course, actionable under the *Rylands* v. *Fletcher* principle, on which see F. H. Newark, "The Boundaries of Nuisance" (1949), 65 L.Q.R. 480, at p. 488.

3. The plaintiffs in the *British Celanese* case argued that they had a cause of action in both public and private nuisance. A common example of public nuisance, which is also a crime, is causing an obstruction on the highway. Public nuisance is only actionable as a tort by a private individual where he suffers some particular damage greater than that suffered by the public. The similarities between the two nuisance actions, however, only go so far— see Street, pp. 213–214; Lord Wright in *Sedleigh-Denfield* v. *O'Callaghan*, [1940] A.C. 880, at p. 905; cf. the observations of Lord Romer in that case at p. 913, and see Lord Porter at p. 918.

(b) Foreseeability, fault and nuisance

The Wagon Mound (No. 2)

Overseas Tankship (U.K.), Ltd. v. The Miller Steamship Co. Pty., Ltd.

Judicial Committee of the Privy Council   [1966] 2 All E.R. 709

The facts are set out, p. 140, *ante.*

LORD REID: . . . Having made these findings Walsh J.[1] went on to consider the case in nuisance. There is no doubt that the carelessness of the appellant's servants in letting this oil overflow did create a public nuisance by polluting the waters of Sydney Harbour. Also there can be no doubt that anyone who suffered special damage from that pollution would have had an action against the appellants; but the special damage sustained by the respondents was caused not by pollution but by fire. So, having held in finding (v) that risk of fire was not reasonably foreseeable, Walsh J. had to consider whether foreseeability has any place in the determination of liability for damage caused by nuisance. He made an extensive survey of the case law and said that the principles which he found there[1]

> "suggest that a plaintiff may set up a case depending on the following steps. The defendant has committed a 'wrongful' act in that it has created a public nuisance by polluting the harbour waters with oil. As a result of the presence of that 'nuisance' (i.e., of the oil) the plaintiff has suffered damage over and above that suffered by others. This gives the plaintiff an action, subject only to proof that there is the requisite relationship between the presence of that nuisance and the injury, so that it can be said that the injury suffered was direct. It matters not that the injury was different in kind from a fouling of the ship by the polluted waters."

Then, coming to the words used by the judges in numerous cases of nuisance, he said that[2]

> ". . . by and large, the judgments are not expressed in terms of the concept of foreseeability. The term used again and again is 'direct'. It is true that other expressions are also used, but one does not find in express terms any testing of the matter by what the defendant might have contemplated or might have foreseen."

---

1. [1963] 1 Lloyd's Rep. 402, at p. 426.
2. [1963] 1 Lloyd's Rep. at p. 432.

And later he added[1]

"I do not find in the case law on nuisance until the time of the [*Wagon Mound (No. 1)*] decision,[2] any authority for the view that liability depends on foreseeability."

Their lordships must now make their own examination of the case law. They find the most striking feature to be the variety of words used: and that is not very surprising because in the great majority of cases the facts were such that it made no difference whether the damage was said to be the direct or the natural or probable or foreseeable result of the nuisance. The word "natural" is found very often, and it is peculiarly ambiguous. It can and often does mean a result which one would naturally expect, i.e., which would not be surprising: or it can mean the result at the end of a chain of causation unbroken by any conscious act, the result produced by so-called natural laws however surprising or even unforeseeable in the particular case. Another word frequently used is "probable". It is used with various shades of meaning. Sometimes it appears to mean more probable than not, sometimes it appears to include events likely but not very likely to occur, sometimes it has a still wider meaning and refers to events the chance of which is anything more than a bare possibility, and sometimes, when used in conjunction with other adjectives, it appears to serve no purpose beyond rounding off a phrase.

Their lordships must first refer to a number of cases on which Walsh J. relied because they require that the damage suffered by the plaintiff must be the direct or immediate result of the nuisance (generally obstruction of a highway), and they make no reference to foreseeability or probability. But that is because they were dealing with quite a different matter from measure of damages.

". . . by the common law of England, a person guilty of a public nuisance might be indicted; but, if injury resulted to a private individual, other and greater than that which was common to all the Queen's subjects, the person injured has his remedy by action"

(per BRETT, J., in *Benjamin* v. *Storr*[3]). So the first step is to decide whether the plaintiff has suffered what may for brevity be called special damage. The authorities on this matter are numerous and exceedingly difficult to reconcile; but one thing is clear. There have been excluded from the category of special damage many cases where the damage suffered by the plaintiff was clearly caused by the nuisance; it was not only foreseeable but probable, and was indeed the inevitable result of the nuisance—the obstruction by the defendant of a highway giving access to the plaintiffs' premises. The words direct and immediate have often been used in determining whether the damage caused by the nuisance is special damage. *Benjamin* v. *Storr*[4] affords a good example. The defendants' vans were constantly standing in the street outside the plaintiff's coffee house. They intercepted the light to his windows so that he had to burn gas nearly all day; they obstructed access by his customers, and the stench from the horses was highly objectionable. The damage caused to the plaintiff by this obstruction of the highway was obvious, but that was not enough. BRETT J. said[3]: "It is not enough for him to show that he suffers the same inconvenience in the use of the highway as other people do . . ." Then he cited two cases[5] in which the plaintiffs, who had clearly suffered damage as a result of obstruction, failed because they were unable to show that they had suffered any injury other and different from that which was common to all the rest of the public. And then he said[6]

---

1. [1963] 1 Lloyd's Rep. at p. 433.
2. [1961] A.C. 388; [1961] 1 All E.R. 404.
3. (1874), L.R. 9 C.P. 400, at p. 406.
4. (1874), L.R. 9 C.P. 400.
5. I.e., *Hubert* v. *Groves* (1794), 1 Esp. 147, and *Winterbottom* v. *Lord Derby* (1867), L.R. 2 Exch. 316.
6. (1874), L.R. 9 C.P. at p. 407.

"Other cases show that the injury to the individual must be direct, and not a mere consequential injury; as where one way is obstructed, but another (though possibly a less convenient one) is left open; in such a case the private and particular injury has been held not to be sufficiently direct to give a cause of action".

But he held that in the case before him there was "a particular, a direct, and a substantial damage".

Such cases have nothing to do with measure of damages: they are dealing with the entirely different question whether the damage caused to the plaintiff by the nuisance was other and different from the damage caused by the nuisance to the rest of the public. When the word direct is used in determining that question, its meaning or connotation appears to be narrower than when it is used in determining whether damage is too remote, so their lordships do not propose to deal further with cases determining what is and what is not special damage. No one denies that the respondents have suffered special damage in this case within the meaning of these authorities. The question is whether they can recover notwithstanding the finding that it was not foreseeable.

Of the large number of cases cited in argument there were few in which there was separate consideration of the proper measure of damages for nuisance. Many of the cases cited deal with the measure of damages for breach of contract, and their lordships will later explain why they do not propose to examine these cases. Moreover a larger number were cases based purely on negligence in which there was no element of nuisance. Their lordships do not intend to examine these cases in detail. It has now been established by the *Wagon Mound* (*No. 1*)[1] and by *Hughes* v. *Lord Advocate*[2] that in such cases damages can only be recovered if the injury complained of not only was caused by the alleged negligence but also was an injury of a class or character foreseeable as a possible result of it. So it would serve no useful purpose in this case to examine the grounds of judgment in earlier cases of negligence. In so far as they are ambiguous they must now be interpreted in light of these two cases: in so far as they exclude foreseeability they must be taken to be disapproved: and in so far as they take account of foreseeability they do no more than amplify the grounds of judgment in these two cases. The respondents can only succeed on this branch of the case by distinguishing nuisance from negligence, either because the authorities indicate that foreseeability is irrelevant in nuisance or because on principle it ought to be held to be irrelevant. . . .

[Having discussed several authorities he continued:] The only case cited where there is an express statement that liability does not depend on foreseeability is *Farrell* v. *John Mowlem & Co., Ltd.*[3] where the defendant had without justification laid a pipe across a pavement and the plaintiff tripped over it and was injured. Devlin J. held this to be a nuisance. He said:[4]

"I think the law still is that any person who actually creates a nuisance is liable for it and for the consequences which flow from it, whether he is negligent or not."

That is quite true, but then he added[4]

"It is no answer to say 'I laid the pipe across the pavement but I did it quite carefully and I did not foresee and perhaps a reasonable man would not have foreseen that anybody would be likely to trip over it'."

That case was before the *Wagon Mound* (*No. 1*)[1] and it may be that Devlin J. thought that the rule was the same in negligence: or it may be that he thought that there was a different rule for nuisance. He cites no authority.

In their lordships' judgment the cases point strongly to there being no difference

---

1. [1961] A.C. 388; [1961] 1 All E.R. 404.
2. [1963] A.C. 837; [1963] 1 All E.R. 705.
3. [1954] 1 Lloyd's Rep. 437.
4. [1954] 1 Lloyd's Rep. at p. 440.

as to the measure of damages between nuisance and negligence, but they are not conclusive. So it is desirable to consider the question of principle.

The appellant's first argument was that damages depend on the same principles throughout the law of tort and contract. This was stated emphatically by Sir Baliol Brett M.R. in *The Notting Hill*[1] and by Lord Esher M.R. in *The Argentino*,[2] and it has often been repeated. But the matter has not been fully investigated recently. There has in recent times been much development of the law of torts, and developments in the law of contract may not have proceded on parallel lines. To give but one example, it is not obvious that the grounds of decision of the House of Lords in *Hughes* v. *Lord Advocate*[3] are consistent with the first rule in *Hadley* v. *Baxendale*[4] as that rule is commonly interpreted. It is unnecessary, however, to pursue this question in this case, and therefore their lordships do not intend to examine cases arising out of breach of contract.

The next argument was that at all events the measure of damages is the same throughout the law of tort; but there are many special features in various kinds of tort, and again their lordships do not find it necessary to make the extensive investigations which would be required before reaching a conclusion on this matter.

Comparing nuisance with negligence the main argument for the respondent was that in negligence foreseeability is an essential element in determining liability, and therefore it is logical that foreseeability should also be an essential element in determining the amount of damages: but negligence is not an essential element in determining liability for nuisance, and therefore it is illogical to bring in foreseeability when determining the amount of damages. It is quite true that negligence is not an essential element in nuisance. Nuisance is a term used to cover a wide variety of tortious acts or omissions, and in many negligence in the narrow sense is not essential. An occupier may incur liability for the emission of noxious fumes or noise, although he has used the utmost care in building and using his premises. The amount of fumes or noise which he can lawfully emit is a question of degree, and he or his advisers may have miscalculated what can be justified. Or he may deliberately obstruct the highway adjoining his premises to a greater degree than is permissible hoping that no one will object. On the other hand the emission of fumes or noise or the obstruction of the adjoining highway may often be the result of pure negligence on his part: there are many cases (e.g., *Dollman* v. *Hillman*)[5] where precisely the same facts will establish liability both in nuisance and in negligence. And although negligence may not be necessary, fault of some kind is almost always necessary and fault generally involves foreseeability, e.g, in cases like *Sedleigh-Denfield* v. *O'Callaghan*[6] the fault is in failing to abate a nuisance of the existence of which the defender is or ought to be aware as likely to cause damage to his neighbour. (Their lordships express no opinion about cases like *Wringe* v. *Cohen*[7] on which neither counsel relied.) The present case is one of creating a danger to persons or property in navigable waters (equivalent to a highway) and there it is admitted that fault is essential—in this case the negligent discharge of the oil.

"But how are we to determine whether a state of affairs in or near a highway is in danger? This depends, I think, on whether injury may reasonably be foreseen. If you take all the cases in the books you will find that if the state of affairs is such that injury may reasonably be anticipated to persons using the highway it is a public nuisance"

---

1. (1884), 9 P.D. 105, at p. 113.
2. (1888), 13 P.D. 191, at p. 197.
3. [1963] A.C. 837; [1963] 1 All E.R. 705.
4. (1854), 9 Exch. 341; [1843–60] All E.R. Rep. 461.
5. [1941] 1 All E.R. 355.
6. [1940] A.C. 880; [1940] 3 All E.R. 349.
7. [1940] 1 K.B. 229; [1939] 4 All E.R. 241.

(per DENNING L.J. in *Morton* v. *Wheeler*).[1] So in the class of nuisance which includes this case foreseeability is an essential element in determining liability.

It could not be right to discriminate between different cases of nuisance so as to make foreseeability a necessary element in determining damages in those cases where it is a necessary element in determining liability, but not in others. So the choice is between it being a necessary element in all cases of nuisance or in none. In their lordships' judgment the similarities between nuisance and other forms of tort to which the *Wagon Mound* (*No. 1*)[2] applies far outweigh any differences, and they must therefore hold that the judgment appealed from is wrong on this branch of the case. It is not sufficient that the injury suffered by the respondents' vessels was the direct result of the nuisance, if that injury was in the relevant sense unforeseeable. . . .

Appeal against the verdict for the respondents on the nuisance claim allowed, but the judgment for the respondents was affirmed, because their cross-appeal against the verdict for the appellants on the negligence claim was allowed

Questions

1. In discussing the relationship of negligence and nuisance, Lord Reid used the term "negligence in the narrow sense". What do you think he meant by this?

2. If one applies the Privy Council's view on the foreseeability of damage (pp. 141–144, *ante*) and the law they laid down relating to nuisance, to the actual nuisance claim in the case, why was the appeal from the verdict in favour of the respondents on the nuisance claim allowed? (See R. J. Buxton (1966), 29 M.L.R. 676, at p. 68 and the answer by L. H. Hoffmann (1967), 83 L.Q.R. 13.)

Notes

1. The use of the term "measure of damages" by Lord Reid in this case should, it is submitted, be read as remoteness of damage, or at least so read for analytical purposes.

2. The Privy Council expressed no opinion on cases such as *Wringe* v. *Cohen*, [1940] 1 K.B. 229; [1939] 4 All E.R. 241. This was understandable for they relate to an area where liability need not be based on fault. In *Wringe* v. *Cohen* the plaintiff's shop stood next to the defendant's premises which he let to a tenant. There was evidence that the wall which formed the gable end of the house above this shop had been in a defective state for three years, and one day it fell, damaging the roof of the shop. In the Court of Appeal it was admitted that there was evidence on which the judge in the court below could find an agreement by the defendant with the tenant that the former would keep the premises in repair, and on which he could hold that the gable end wall had become a nuisance because of the lack of repair. Nevertheless, it was argued that the defendant could only be held liable if he knew or should have known of the want of repair. Atkinson J.'s reply for the Court of Appeal (at p. 243) was that:

". . . if, owing to want of repair, premises upon a highway become dangerous, and, therefore, a nuisance, and a passer-by or adjoining owner suffers damage by their collapse, the occupier, or the owner, if he has undertaken the duty of repair, is answerable, whether or not he knew, or ought to have known, of the danger. The

---

1. (1956), unreported.
2. [1961] A.C. 388; [1961] 1 All E.R. 404.

undertaking to repair gives the owner control of the premises, and a right of access thereto for the purpose of maintaining them in a safe condition. On the other hand, if the nuisance is created, not by want of repair, but, for example, by the act of a trespasser, or by a secret and unobservable operation of nature, such as a subsidence under or near the foundations of the premises, neither an occupier nor an owner responsible for repair is answerable, unless with knowledge or means of knowledge he allows the danger to continue. In such a case, he has in no sense caused the nuisance by any act or breach of duty. I think that every case decided in the English courts is consistent with this view."

The collapse in *Wringe* v. *Cohen*, of course, was not on to the highway, but on to a neighbours' property. If the strict duty can be justified on the grounds of danger to the public on the highway, should it also apply for the benefit of the neighbour? Would the neighbour's action be in public or private nuisance? What, in any case, are premises upon a highway? Does this phrase include a case where the grounds stretch to the highway, and the house is 100 yards away at the end of a private drive but close to the neighbour's house? For comment on *Wringe* v. *Cohen*, see W. Friedmann, "Incidence of Liability in Nuisance" (1943), 59 L.Q.R. 63, at pp. 57–59.

3. In some situations a defendant may be liable in the torts of negligence and nuisance. However, the operation of the concept of negligence in the tort of nuisance, which is discussed by Lord Reid in *The Wagon Mound (No. 2)*, is difficult, and is not made any easier by the existence of the test of unreasonable user of land in nuisance, which has been mentioned, p. 381, *ante*. Reference should also be made to R. W. M. Dias' valuable article, "Trouble on Oiled Waters; Problems of *The Wagon Mound (No. 2)*", [1967] C.L.J. 62. See also *inter alia* Lord Wright in *Sedleigh-Denfield* v. *O'Callaghan*, [1940] A.C. 880, at p. 904; *Goldman* v. *Hargrave*, [1967] I A.C. 645; [1966] 2 All E.R. 989, p. 393, *post*; *Dymond* v. *Pearce*, [1972] I Q.B. 496; [1972] I All E.R. 1142.

(c) Act of trespasser

Sedleigh-Denfield v. O'Callaghan and Others (Trustees for St. Joseph's Society for Foreign Missions)

House of Lords   [1940] 3 All E.R. 349

The appellant (plaintiff) owned land on the north side of which there was a ditch which, it was held, belonged to the respondents (defendants), the owners of adjoining property. A pipe (or culvert) was laid in the ditch by a trespasser, and the workmen involved did not place a grid near the mouth of the pipe so as to intercept any refuse: in fact, they laid it on top of the pipe where it served no useful purpose. When the pipe being laid, Brother Dekker, who was then responsible for cleaning the ditch, saw the work being carried out. Further, the ditch was cleaned out twice a year on behalf of the respondents, by the person in charge of it. After a heavy rainstorm the pipe became blocked with refuse and the appellant's land was flooded. In the House of Lords, Viscount Maugham expressed the view, with which in his opinion all their Lordships agreed, that, before the flooding "the respondents must be taken to have had knowledge of the existence of the unguarded culvert which for nearly 3 years had been the means by which the water coming down the ditch on the respondents' land had flowed away to the sewer in Lawrence Street." Branson J., [1938] 3 All E.R. 321, had dismissed the appellant's action, and that decision had been affirmed by the Court of Appeal, [1939] I All E.R. 725. On further appeal to the House of Lords:

VISCOUNT MAUGHAM: ... The statement that an occupier of land is liable for the continuance of a nuisance created by others, e.g., by trespassers, if he continues or adopts it—which seems to be agreed—throws little light on the matter, unless the words "continues or adopts" are defined. In my opinion, an occupier of land "continues" a nuisance if, with knowledge or presumed knowledge of its existence, he fails to take any reasonable means to bring it to an end, though with ample time to do so. He "adopts" it if he makes any use of the erection, building, bank or artificial contrivance which constitutes the nuisance. In these sentences, I am not attempting exclusive definitions. . . .

My Lords, in the present case, I am of opinion that the respondents both continued and adopted the nuisance. After the lapse of nearly 3 years, they must be taken to have suffered the nuisance to continue, for they neglected to take the very simple step of placing a grid in the proper place, which would have removed the danger to their neighbour's land. They adopted the nuisance, for they continued during all that time to use the artificial contrivance of the conduit for the purpose of getting rid of water from their property without taking the proper means for rendering it safe. For these reasons, I am of opinion that this appeal should be allowed for damages to be assessed . . .

LORD ATKIN: . . . I treat it as established that the entrance to the offending pipe, when it was laid, was on the defendants' land, abutting on the premises occupied by the plaintiff. I agree with the finding of the judge, accepted by the Court of Appeal, that the laying of a 15-ins. pipe with an unprotected orifice was, in the circumstances, the creation of a nuisance, or of that which would be likely to result in a nuisance. It created a state of things from which, when the ditch was flowing in full stream, an obstruction might reasonably be expected in the pipe, from which obstruction flooding of the plaintiff's ground might reasonably be expected to result, though I am not satisfied that, granted this reasonable expectation of obstruction, it would be necessary for the plaintiff to prove that the particular injury was such as reasonably to be expected to result from the obstruction. If the defendants had themselves laid the pipe in the manner described, I have no hesitation in saying that, once the plaintiff had suffered damage from flooding so caused, he would have had a good cause of action against them for nuisance. It is probably strictly correct to say that, as long as the offending condition is confined to the defendants' own land without causing damage, it is not a nuisance, though it may threaten to become a nuisance. Where damage has accrued, however, the nuisance has been caused. I should regard the case on this hypothesis as having the same legal consequences as if the defendants, instead of laying a pipe, had placed an obvious obstruction in the course of the ditch. The question here is what the legal position is if such an obstruction is placed by a trespasser. In the present case, I consider it established that the defendants by their responsible agents had knowledge of the erection of the pipe, of the reasonable expectation that it might be obstructed, of the result of such obstruction, and of its continued existence in the condition complained of since it was first placed in position. Brother Dekker, a member of the community, was in charge of the defendants' farming operations, and obviously represented the defendants in this matter, so far as is relevant. He had doubtless no authority to consent to a trespass, and probably no authority to incur any appreciable expense in remedying it, but the defendants obviously had to rely upon him to report to them what was found on the farm likely to be injurious to them or their neighbours.

In this state of the facts, the legal position is not, I think, difficult to discover. For the purpose of ascertaining whether, as here, the plaintiff can establish a private nuisance, I think that nuisance is sufficiently defined as a wrongful interference with another's enjoyment of his land or premises by the use of land or premises either occupied—or, in some cases, owned—by oneself. The occupier or owner is not an insurer. There must be something more than the mere harm done to the neighbour's property to make the party responsible. Deliberate act or negligence is not an essential ingredient, but some degree of personal responsibility is required, which is connoted in my definition by the word "use". This conception is implicit in all the decisions which impose liability only where the defendant has "caused or continued" the nuisance. We may eliminate, in this case, "caused." What is the meaning of "continued"? In the context in which it is used, "continued" must indicate mere passive continuance. If a man uses on premises something which he finds there, and which itself causes a nuisance by noise, vibration, smell or fumes, he is himself, in continuing to bring into existence the noise, vibration, smell or fumes, causing a nuisance. Continuing in this sense, and causing are the same thing. It seems to me clear that, if a man permits an offensive thing on his premises to continue to offend—that is, if he knows that it is operating offensively, is able to prevent it, and omits to prevent it—he is permitting the nuisance to continue. In other words, he is continuing it. . . .

In the present case . . . there is, as I have said, sufficient proof of the knowledge of the defendants both of the cause and of its probable effect. What is the legal result of the original cause being due to the act of a trespasser? In my opinion, the defendants clearly continued the nuisance, for they come clearly within the terms I have mentioned above. They knew the danger, they were able to prevent it, and they omitted to prevent it. In this respect, at least, there seems to me to be no difference between the case of a public nuisance and that of a private nuisance, and *A.-G.* v. *Tod Heatley*[1] is conclusive to show that, where the occupier has knowledge of a public nuisance, has the means of remedying it, and fails to do so, he may be enjoined from allowing it to continue. I cannot think that the obligation not to "continue" can have a different meaning in "public" and in "private" nuisances. . . . I think, therefore, that, in the present case, the plaintiff established the liability of the defendants to him, and that the appeal should be allowed. The orders of the judge and the Court of Appeal should be set aside and judgment entered for the plaintiff for damages to be assessed. . . .

LORD PORTER: . . . [T]he true view is that the occupier of land is liable for a nuisance existing on his property to the extent that he can reasonably abate it, even though he neither created it nor received any benefit from it. It is enough if he permitted it to continue after he knew, or ought to have known, of its existence. To this extent, but to no greater extent, he must be proved to have adopted the act of the creator of the nuisance. . . .

[LORD WRIGHT and LORD ROMER delivered speeches in favour of allowing the appeal.]

Appeal allowed

Notes

1. The case above is an example where an occupier was held liable in nuisance. Several textbooks take the view, however, that the person who by some positive act creates the nuisance may be liable even though he is not an occupier of the land—but see Street, p. 230, note 1. For the position where an independent contractor creates the nuisance, see p. 632, *post*, and on the liabilities of landlord and tenant, see Salmond, pp. 69–72; Winfield & Jolowicz, pp. 347–352.

2. Compare the *Sedleigh-Denfield* case with *Wringe* v. *Cohen*, [1940] 1 K.B. 229; [1939] 4 All E.R. 241, noted p. 390, *ante*. (See Salmond, p. 68; cf. Street, p. 234.)

(d) Hazards arising accidentally on land

Goldman v. Hargrave

Judicial Committee of the Privy Council   [1966] 2 All E.R. 989

LORD WILBERFORCE: This consolidated appeal from a decision of the High Court of Australia reversing that of the Supreme Court of Western Australia, arises out of a

---

1. [1897] 1 Ch. 560.

bush fire, which developed in the grazing area of Gidgegannup, Western Australia, and did extensive damage to the respondents' properties. The High Court decided that the appellant, on whose property the fire started, was liable for the damage, and this decision the appellant now contests.

The circumstances in which the fire started are concisely stated in the judgments of the High Court, which accepted the findings of the trial judge. There was an electrical storm on Feb. 25, 1961, and a tall redgum tree, about one hundred feet in height, in the centre of the appellant's property, was struck by lightning. This tree was about 250 yards from the western boundary of the appellant's property (in which direction the respondents' properties lie) and rather less from the eastern boundary. The redgum caught fire in a fork eighty-four feet from the ground, and it was evidently impossible to deal with the blaze while the tree was standing. Early in the morning of 26 February, the appellant telephoned the district fire control officer, appointed as such under the Bush Fires Act, 1954–58, and asked for a tree feller to be sent. Pending his arrival the appellant cleared a space round the tree of combustible material and sprayed the surrounding area with water. The tree feller arrived at mid-day on 26 February, at which time the tree was burning fiercely, and it was cut down. The trial judge found, and the High Court accepted the finding, that up to this point the appellant's conduct in relation to the fire was not open to criticism.

The judge also found, however, that if the appellant had taken reasonable care he could, on the Sunday evening (26 February), or at least early on the next morning, have put out the [fire] by using water on it. The appellant indeed claimed that he spent two hours on Monday 27 February, in extinguishing the fire, but his evidence as to this was rejected. The judge referred to evidence which indicated that the appellant's method of extinguishing a fire of this kind was to burn it out. "You burn it out" he was reported as saying "that is the only way I know to put a fire out."

On Tuesday, 28 February, the appellant was away from the property for a substantial part of the day, and it was found that he did not at any time after 27 February take any steps which could be regarded as reasonable to prevent the fire from spreading. On Wednesday, 1 March, there was a change in the weather; the wind, which had previously been light to moderate, freshened to about twenty m.p.h. with stronger gusts. The air temperature rose some 10° to 105°F. The fire revived and spread over the appellant's paddock towards the west and on to the respondents' properties: it was not observed by the appellant until about noon on 1 March, and by then it could not be stopped. The damage to the respondents' properties followed.

It is important at once to deal with an argument, as to the facts, which was advanced by the respondents at the trial. It was sought to contend that although the fire commenced accidentally, the appellant, whether by heaping combustible material on to it, after the tree had been felled, or even by permitting the tree to burn in the way in which it did on the ground, had adopted the fire as his own—as *suus ignis*—and had made use of it for his own purpose or advantage.

Their lordships (in agreement with the High Court) do not accept this view of the facts. The result of the evidence, in their lordships' opinion, is that the appellant both up to 26 February, and thereafter was endeavouring to extinguish the fire: that initially he acted with prudence, but that there came a point, about the evening of 26 February or the morning of 27 February, when, the prudent and reasonable course being to put the fire out by water, he chose to adopt the method of burning it out. That method was, according to the finding of the trial judge, unreasonable, or negligent in the circumstances: it brought a fresh risk into operation, namely the risk of a revival of the fire, under the influence of changing wind and weather, if not carefully watched, and it was from this negligence that the damage arose. That a risk of this character was foreseeable by someone in the appellant's position was not really disputed: in fact danger arising from weather conditions is given official recognition in the Bush Fires Act, 1954–58, which provides for their classification according to the degree of danger arising from them.

This conclusion has an important bearing on the nature of the legal issue which has to be decided. It makes clear that the case is not one where a person has brought a source of danger on to his land, nor one where an occupier has so used his property as to cause a danger to his neighbour. It is one where an occupier faced with a hazard accidentally arising on his land, fails to act with reasonable prudence so as to remove the hazard. The issue is therefore whether in such a case the occupier is guilty of legal negligence, which involves the issue whether he is under a duty of care, and if so, what is the scope of that duty. Their lordships propose to deal with these issues as stated, without attempting to answer the disputable question whether if responsibility is established it should be brought under the heading of nuisance or placed in a separate category. As this Board has recently explained in *The Wagon Mound* (*No. 2*), *Overseas Tankship* (*U.K.*), *Ltd.* v. *The Miller Steamship Co. Pty.*, *Ltd.*,[1] the tort of nuisance, uncertain in its boundary, may comprise a wide variety of situations, in some of which negligence plays no part, in others of which it is decisive. The present case is one where liability, if it exists, rests on negligence and nothing else; whether it falls within or overlaps the boundaries of nuisance is a question of classification which need not here be resolved.

What then is the scope of an occupier's duty, with regard to his neighbour, as to hazards arising on his land? With the possible exception of hazard of fire, to which their lordships will shortly revert, it is only in comparatively recent times that the law has recognised an occupier's duty as one of a more positive character than merely to abstain from creating, or adding to, a source of danger or annoyance. It was for long satisfied with the conception of separate or autonomous proprietors, each of which was entitled to exploit his territory in a "natural" manner and none of whom was obliged to restrain or direct the operations of nature in the interest of avoiding harm to his neighbours.

This approach, or philosophy, found expression in decisions both in England and elsewhere. In *Giles* v. *Walker*[2] a claim that an occupier had a duty to protect his neighbour against the invasion of thistledown was summarily rejected by the Queen's Bench Division. Moreover, in a similar field, it was held in 1908 by the High Court of Australia (*Sparke* v. *Osborne*[3]) that an occupier was not under a duty to prevent a noxious weed, prickly pears, from attacking a neighbour's fence. The case was decided on a demurrer to a pleading in which negligence was not alleged. In relation to fires, there were similar decisions. . . .

[His Lordship discussed several other Commonwealth authorities and continued:] That a person who takes some action (though mistaken) to deal with an accidental fire should not be in a worse position as regards civil liability than one who does nothing is clearly a consideration of importance not to be overlooked when stating a rule as to liability. . . .

A decision which, it can now be seen, marked a turning point in the law was that of *Job Edwards, Ltd.* v. *Birmingham Navigations*.[4] The hazard in that case was a fire which originated in a refuse dump placed on land by the act of a third party. When the fire threatened to invade the neighbouring land, the owners of the latter, by agreement, entered and extinguished the fire at a cost of some £1,000. The issue in the action was whether the owners of the land where the fire was, were liable to bear part of the cost. The Court of Appeal[4] by a majority answered this question negatively, but Scrutton L.J.'s dissenting judgment contained the following passage:[5]

"There is a great deal to be said for the view that if a man finds a dangerous and artificial thing on his land, which he and those for whom he is responsible did

---

1. [1967] 1 A.C. 617; [1966] 2 All E.R. 709.
2. (1890), 24 Q.B.D. 656; [1886–90] All E.R. Rep. 501.
3. (1908), 7 C.L.R. 51.
4. [1924] 1 K.B. 341.
5. [1924] 1 K.B. at pp. 357, 358.

not put there; if he knows that if left alone it will damage other persons; if by reasonable care he can render it harmless, as if by stamping on a fire just beginning from a trespasser's match he can extinguish it; that then if he does nothing, he has 'permitted it to continue', and becomes responsible for it. This would base the liability on negligence, and not on the duty of insuring damage from a dangerous thing under *Rylands* v. *Fletcher*.[1] I appreciate that to get negligence you must have a duty to be careful, but I think on principle that a landowner has a duty to take reasonable care not to allow his land to remain a receptacle for a thing which may, if not rendered harmless, cause damage to his neighbours."

One may note that this passage is dealing with a different set of facts from that involved in the case then under consideration: the one referring to a fire just beginning which can be extinguished by stamping on it, the other concerned with a smouldering dump to extinguish which involves both effort and expense, so that it is quite possible to approve both of the majority decision and of the passage quoted from the dissenting judgment.

This was followed in 1926 by *Noble* v. *Harrison*.[2] The damage there was caused by an overhanging tree with a latent defect and the decision was against liability. The judgment of Rowlatt, J. in the Divisional Court contains this passage:[3]

"... a person is liable for a nuisance constituted by the state of his property (i) if he causes it; (ii) if by neglect of some duty he allows it to arise; and (iii) if, when it has arisen without his own act or default, he omits to remedy it within a reasonable time after he did or ought to have become aware of it."

It will be seen that the learned judge in the third category makes no distinction according to whether the "nuisance" is caused by trespassers or by natural causes, and that he does not enter into any question as to the limits of the effort or expenditure required of the occupier. As a general statement of the law it was cited with apparent approval by Dixon J. in *Torette House Proprietary, Ltd.* v. *Berkman*.[4]

In 1940 the *dictum* of Scrutton L.J.[5] passed into the law of England when it was approved by the House of Lords in *Sedleigh-Denfield* v. *O'Callaghan*.[6] Their lordships need not cite from this case in any detail since it is now familiar law. It establishes the occupier's liability with regard to a hazard created on his land by a trespasser, of which he has knowledge, when he fails to take reasonable steps to remove it. It was clear in that case that the hazard could have been removed by what Viscount Maugham[7] described as the "very simple step" of placing a grid in the proper place. The members of the House approved the passage just cited from Scrutton L.J.'s[5] judgment and Viscount Maugham[8] and Lord Wright[9] also adopted the statement of the law in Salmond's Law of Torts (5th Edn.) (1920), pp. 258–265.

"When a nuisance has been created by the act of a trespasser or otherwise without the act, authority, or permission of the occupier, the occupier is not responsible for that nuisance unless, with knowledge or means of knowledge of its existence, he suffers it to continue without taking reasonably prompt and efficient means for its abatement."

The appellant, inevitably, accepts the development, or statement, of the law which the *Sedleigh-Denfield* case[6] contains—as it was accepted by the High Court of Australia.

---

1. (1868), L.R. 3 H.L. 330; [1861–73] All E.R. Rep. 1.
2. [1926] 2 K.B. 332; [1926] All E.R. Rep. 284.
3. [1926] 2 K.B. at p. 338; [1926] All E.R. Rep. at p. 287;
4. (1940), 62 C.L.R. 637, at p. 652.
5. [1924] 1 K.B. at pp. 357, 358.
6. [1940] A.C. 880; [1940] 3 All E.R. 349.
7. [1940] A.C. at p. 895; [1940] 3 All E.R. at p. 359.
8. [1940] A.C. at p. 893; [1940] 3 All E.R. at p. 358.
9. [1940] A.C. at p. 910; [1940] 3 All E.R. at p. 369.

He seeks to establish, however, a distinction between the type of hazard which was there involved, namely one brought about by human agency such as the act of a trespasser, and one arising from natural causes, or Act of God. In relation to hazards of this kind it was submitted that an occupier is under no duty to remove or to diminish it, and that his liability only commences if and when by interference with it he negligently increases the risk or danger to his neighbour's property.

Their lordships would first observe, with regard to the suggested distinction, that it is well designed to introduce confusion into the law. As regards many hazardous conditions arising on land, it is impossible to determine how they arose—particularly is this the case as regards fires. If they are caused by human agency, the agent, unless detected in flagrante delicto, is hardly likely to confess his fault. And is the occupier, when faced with the initial stages of a fire, to ask himself whether the fire is accidental or man-made before he can decide on his duty? Is the neighbour, whose property is damaged, bound to prove the human origin of the fire? The proposition involves that if he cannot do so, however irresponsibly the occupier has acted, he must fail. The distinction is not only inconvenient, but also it lacks, in their lordships' view, any logical foundation.

Within the class of situations in which the occupier is himself without responsibility for the origin of the fire, one may ask in vain what relevant difference there is between a fire caused by a human agency such as a trespasser and one caused by Act of God or nature. A difference in degree—as to the potency of the agency—one can see but none that is in principle relevant to the occupier's duty to act. It was suggested as a logical basis for the distinction that in the case of a hazard originating in an act of man, an occupier who fails to deal with it can be said to be using his land in a manner detrimental to his neighbour and so to be within the classified field of responsibility in nuisance, whereas this cannot be said when the hazard originates without human action so long at least as the occupier merely abstains. The fallacy of this argument is that, as already explained, the basis of the occupier's liability lies not in the use of his land: in the absence of "adoption" there is no such use: but in the neglect of action in the face of something which may damage his neighbour. To this, the suggested distinction is irrelevant.

On principle therefore, their lordships find in the opinions of the House of Lords in *Sedleigh-Denfield* v. *O'Callaghan*[1] and in the statements of the law by Scrutton L.J.[2] and Salmond,[3] of which they approve, support for the existence of a general duty on occupiers in relation to hazards occurring on their land, whether natural or man-made. The matter does, however, not rest there. First, the principle has been applied to the specific hazards of fire by the more recent decision of the Supreme Court of New Zealand in *Boatswain* v. *Crawford*.[4] . . .

Secondly, it appears that the movement of American decisions has been towards the development of a duty of care on the part of occupiers in relation to hazards arising on their land both generally and of fire. . . .

Thirdly their lordships have considered the modern text books of authority on the law of torts, *Clerk and Lindsell* (12th Edn.) 1961, *Salmond* (13th Edn.) 1961, *Winfield* (7th Edn.) 1963, *Fleming* 1965, as well as a formative article by Dr. A. L. Goodhart in 4 *Cambridge Law Journal* (1932), p. 13. All of these endorse the development, which their lordships find in the decisions, towards a measured duty of care by occupiers to remove or reduce hazards to their neighbours.

So far it has been possible to consider the existence of a duty, in general terms; but the matter cannot be left there without some definition of the scope of his duty. How far does it go? What is the standard of the effort required? What is the position as regards expenditure? It is not enough to say merely that these must be "reasonable"

1. [1940] A.C. 880; [1940] 3 All E.R. 349.
2. [1924] 1 K.B. at pp. 357, 358.
3. Salmond's Law of Torts (5th Edn.) (1920), pp. 258–265.
4. [1943] N.Z.L.R. 109.

since what is reasonable to one man may be very unreasonable, and indeed ruinous, to another: the law must take account of the fact that the occupier on whom the duty is cast, has, ex hypothesi, had this hazard thrust on him through no seeking or fault of his own. His interest, and his resources whether physical or material, may be of a very modest character either in relation to the magnitude of the hazard, or as compared with those of his threatened neighbour. A rule which required of him in such unsought circumstances in his neighbour's interest a physical effort of which he is not capable, or an excessive expenditure of money, would be unenforceable or unjust. One may say in general terms that the existence of a duty must be based on knowledge of the hazard, ability to foresee the consequences of not checking or removing it, and the ability to abate it. Moreover in many cases, as for example in Scrutton, L.J.'s[1] hypothetical case of stamping out a fire, or the present case, where the hazard could have been removed with the little effort and no expenditure, no problem arises; but other cases may not be so simple. In such situations, the standard ought to be to require of the occupier what it is reasonable to expect of him in his individual circumstances. Thus, less must be expected of the infirm than of the able bodied: the owner of a small property where a hazard arises which threatens a neighbour with substantial interests should not have to do so much as one with larger interests of his own at stake and greater resources to protect them: if the small owner does what he can and promptly calls on his neighbour to provide additional resources, he may be held to have done his duty: he should not be liable unless it is clearly proved that he could, and reasonably in his individual circumstance should, have done more. This approach to a difficult matter is in fact that which the courts in their more recent decisions have taken. It is in accordance with the actual decision in the *Job Edwards* case[2] where to remove the hazard would have cost the occupier some £1,000—on this basis the decision itself seems obviously right. It is in accordance with *Pontardawe Rural Council* v. *Moore-Gwyn*[3] where to maintain the rocks in a state of safety would have cost the occupier some £300; and if some of the situations such as those in *Giles* v. *Walker*[4] (thistledown) and *Sparke* v. *Osborne*[5] (prickly-pears) were to recur to-day, it is probable that they would not be decided without a balanced consideration of what could be expected of the particular occupier as compared with the consequences of inaction. That *Giles* v. *Walker*[4] might now be decided differently was indeed suggested by Lord Goddard C.J. giving the judgment of the English Court of Appeal in *Davey* v. *Harrow Corpn.*[6] In the present case it has not been argued that the action necessary to put the fire out on 26 to 27 February was not well within the capacity and resources of the appellant. Their lordships therefore reach the conclusion that the respondents' claim for damages, on the basis of negligence, was fully made out.

[His Lordship then referred to the Fires Prevention (Metropolis) Act 1774, which applied in Western Australia, and, approving *Musgrove* v. *Pandelis*, [1919] 2 K.B. 43, held that the statutory defence failed as the fire which damaged the property of the respondents, was that arising on 1 March as the result of the appellant's negligence.]

Appeal dismissed

Questions

1. How would you resolve the question of classification of liability in this case which the Privy Council declined to do?

2. Is there any other area of the law where the court's approach to the standard of care is similar?

---

1. [1924] 1 K.B. at p. 357.
2. [1924] 1 K.B. 341.
3. [1929] 1 Ch. 656.
4. (1890), 24 Q.B.D. 656; [1886–90] All E.R. Rep. 501.
5. (1908), 7 C.L.R. 51.
6. [1958] 1 Q.B. 60, at p. 72; [1957] 2 All E.R. 305, at p. 310.

Notes

1. The observations on the standard of care in this case should be compared with the cases discussed in the Chapter on Breach of Duty, p. 134, *ante*.

2. For defences to nuisance (especially statutory authority which may also be a defence to liability under *Rylands* v. *Fletcher* ((1868), L.R. 3 H.L. 330), see the standard textbooks on tort.

12

Assessment of Damages

---

1. THE AIMS OF AN AWARD OF DAMAGES

Cassell & Co., Ltd. v. Broome

House of Lords   [1972] 1 All E.R. 801

[For the facts and the assessment of damages in defamation cases see Chap. 16, p. 567, *post.*]

LORD HAILSHAM: . . . Of all the various remedies available at common law, damages are the remedy of most general application at the present day, and they remain the prime remedy in actions for breach of contract and tort. They have been defined as "the pecuniary compensation, obtainable by success in an action, for a wrong which is either a tort or a breach of contract". They must normally be expressed in a single sum to take account of all the factors applicable to each cause of action and must of course be expressed in English currency.[1]

In almost all actions for breach of contract, and in many actions for tort, the principle of restitutio in integrum is an adequate and fairly easy guide to the estimation of damage, because the damage suffered can be estimated by relation to some material loss. It is true that where loss includes a pre-estimate of future losses, or an estimate of past losses which cannot in the nature of things be exactly computed, some subjective element must enter in. But the estimate is in things commensurable with one another, and convertible at least in principle to the English currency in which all sums of damages must ultimately be expressed.

In many torts, however, the subjective element is more difficult. The pain and suffering endured, and the future loss of amenity, in a personal injuries case are not in the nature of things convertible into legal tender. The difficulties arising in the paraplegic cases, or, before *Benham* v. *Gambling*,[2] in estimating the damages for loss of expectation of life in a person who died instantaneously, are only examples of the intrinsically impossible task set judges or juries in such matters. Clearly the £50,000 award upheld in *Morey* v. *Woodfield*[3] could never compensate the victim of such an accident. Nor, so far as I can judge, is there any purely rational test by which a judge can calculate what sum, greater or smaller, is appropriate. What is surprising is not that there is difference of opinion about such matters, but that in most cases professional opinion gravitates so closely to a conventional scale. Nevertheless, in all actions in which damages, purely compensatory in character, are awarded for suffering, from the purely pecuniary point of view the plaintiff may be better off. The principle of

---

1. *Mayne and McGregor on Damages*, 12th Edn., para. 1.
2. [1941] A.C. 157; [1941] 1 All E.R. 7.
3. [1963] 3 All E.R. 533, n.

400

restitutio in integrum, which compels the use of money as its sole instrument for restoring the status quo, necessarily involves a factor larger than any pecuniary loss. . . .

. . . This brings me to the question of terminology. It has been more than once pointed out the language of damages is more than usually confused. For instance, the term "special damage" is used in more than one sense to denominate actual past losses precisely calculated (as in a personal injuries action), or "material damage actually suffered" as in describing the factor necessary to give rise to the cause of action in cases, including cases of slander, actionable only on proof of "special damage". If it is not too deeply embedded in our legal language, I would like to see "special damage" dropped as a term of art in its latter sense and some phrase like "material loss" substituted. But a similar ambiguity occurs in actions of defamation, the expressions "at large", "punitive", "aggravated", "retributory", "vindictive" and "exemplary" having been used in, as I have pointed out, inextricable confusion.

In my view it is desirable to drop the use of the phrase "vindictive" damages altogether, despite its use by the county court judge in *Williams* v. *Settle*.[1] Even when a purely punitive element is involved, vindictiveness is not a good motive for awarding punishment. In awarding "aggravated" damages the natural indignation of the court at the injury inflicted on the plaintiff is a perfectly legitimate motive in making a generous rather than a more moderate award to provide an adequate solatium. But that is because the injury to the plaintiff is actually greater and as the result of the conduct exciting the indignation demands a more generous solatium. Likewise the use of "retributory" is objectionable because it is ambiguous. It can be used to cover both aggravated damages to compensate the plaintiff and punitive or exemplary damages purely to punish the defendant or hold him up as an example.

As between "punitive" or "exemplary", one should, I would suppose, choose one to the exclusion of the other, since it is never wise to use two quite interchangeable terms to denote the same thing. Speaking for myself, I prefer "exemplary", not because "punitive" is necessarily inaccurate, but "exemplary" better expresses the policy of the law as expressed in the cases. It is intended to teach the defendant and others that "tort does not pay" by demonstrating what consequences the law inflicts rather than simply to make the defendant suffer an extra penalty for what he has done, although that does, or course, precisely describe its effect.

The expression "at large" should be used in general to cover all cases where awards of damages may include elements for loss of reputation, injured feelings, bad or good conduct by either party, or punishment, and where in consequence no precise limit can be set in extent. It would be convenient if, as the appellants' counsel did at the hearing, it could be extended to include damages for pain and suffering or loss of amenity. Lord Devlin uses the term in this sense in *Rookes* v. *Barnard*,[2] when he defines the phrase as meaning all cases where "the award is not limited to the pecuniary loss that can be specifically proved". But I suspect that he was there guilty of a neologism. If I am wrong, it is a convenient use and should be repeated.

Finally, it is worth pointing out, although I doubt if a change of terminology is desirable or necessary, that there is danger in hypostatising "compensatory", "punitive", "exemplary" or "aggravated" damages at all. The epithets are all elements or considerations which may, but with the exception of the first need not, be taken into account in assessing a single sum. They are not separate heads to be added mathematically to one another. . . .

LORD REID: . . . Damages for any tort are or ought to be fixed at a sum which will compensate the plaintiff, so far as money can do it, for all the injury which he has suffered. Where the injury is material and has been ascertained it is generally possible to assess damages with some precision. But that is not so where he has been caused mental distress or when his reputation has been attacked—where to use the traditional phrase

1. [1960] 2 All E.R. 806.
2. [1964] A.C. 1129, at p. 1221; [1964] 1 All E.R. 367, at p. 407.

he has been held up to hatred, ridicule or contempt. Not only is it impossible to ascertain how far other people's minds have been affected, it is almost impossible to equate the damage to a sum of money. Any one person trying to fix a sum as compensation will probably find in his mind a wide bracket within which any sum could be regarded by him as not unreasonable—and different people will come to different conclusions. So in the end there will probably be a wide gap between the sum which on an objective view could be regarded as the least and the sum which could be regarded as the most to which the plaintiff is entitled as compensation.

It has long been recognised that in determining what sum within that bracket should be awarded, a jury, or other tribunal, is entitled to have regard to the conduct of the defendant. He may have behaved in a high-handed, malicious, insulting or oppressive manner in committing the tort or he or his counsel may at the trial have aggravated the injury by what they there said. That would justify going to the top of the bracket and awarding as damages the largest sum that could fairly be regarded as compensation.

Frequently in cases before *Rookes* v. *Barnard*[1] when damages were increased in that way but were still within the limit of what could properly be regarded as compensation to the plaintiff, it was said that punitive, vindictive or exemplary damages were being awarded. As a mere matter of language that was true enough. The defendant was being punished or an example was being made of him by making him pay more than he would have had to pay if his conduct had not been outrageous. But the damages although called punitive were still truly compensatory; the plaintiff was not being given more than his due.

On the other hand when we came to examine the old cases we found a number which could not be explained in that way. The sums awarded as damages were more—sometimes much more—than could on any view be justified as compensatory and courts, perhaps without fully realising what they were doing, appeared to have permitted damages to be measured not by what the plaintiff was fairly entitled to receive but by what the defendant ought to be made to pay as punishment for his outrageous conduct. That meant that the plaintiff, by being given more than on any view could be justified as compensation, was being given a pure and undeserved windfall at the expense of the defendant, and that insofar as the defendant was being required to pay more than could possibly be regarded as compensation he was being subjected to pure punishment.

I thought and still think that that is highly anomalous. It is confusing the function of the civil law which is to compensate with the function of the criminal law which is to inflict deterrent and punitive penalties. Some objection has been taken to the use of the word "fine" to denote the amount by which punitive or exemplary damages exceed anything justly due to the plaintiff. In my view the word "fine" is an entirely accurate description of that part of any award which goes beyond anything justly due to the plaintiff and is purely punitive.

Those of us who sat in *Rookes* v. *Barnard*[1] thought that the loose and confused use of words like "punitive" and "exemplary" and the failure to recognise the difference between damages which are compensatory and damages which go beyond that and are purely punitive had led to serious abuses, so we took what we thought was the best course open to us to limit those abuses. Theoretically we might have held that as purely punitive damages had never been sanctioned by any decision of this House (as to which I shall say more later) there was no right under English law to award them. But that would have been going beyond the proper function of this House. There are many well established doctrines of the law which have not been the subject of any decision by this House. We thought we had to recognise that it had become an established custom in certain classes of case to permit awards of damages which could not be justified as compensatory, and that that must remain the law. But we

1. [1964] A.C. 1129; [1964] 1 All E.R. 367.

thought and I still think it well within the province of this House to say that that undesirable anomaly should not be permitted in any class of case where its use was not covered by authority. In order to determine the classes of case in which this anomaly had become established it was of little use to look merely at the words which had been used by the judges because, as I have said, words like "punitive" and "exemplary" were often used with regard to damages which were truly compensatory. We had to take a broad view of the whole circumstances.

I must now deal with those parts of Lord Devlin's speech which have given rise to difficulties. He set out two categories of cases which in our opinion comprised all or virtually all the reported cases in which it was clear that the court had approved of an award of a larger sum of damages than could be justified as compensatory. Critics appear to have thought that he was inventing something new. That was not my understanding. We were confronted with an undesirable anomaly. We could not abolish it. We had to choose between confining it strictly to classes of cases where it was firmly established, although that produced an illogical result, or permitting it to be extended so as to produce a logical result. In my view it is better in such cases to be content with an illogical result than to allow any extension.

It will be seen that I do not agree with Lord Devlin's view that in certain classes of case exemplary damages serve a useful purpose in vindicating the strength of the law. That view did not form an essential step in his argument. Concurrence with the speech of a colleague does not mean acceptance of every word which he has said. If it did there would be far fewer concurrences than there are. So I did not regard disagreement on this side issue as preventing me from giving my concurrence.

I think that the objections to allowing juries to go beyond compensatory damages are overwhelming. To allow pure punishment in this way contravenes almost every principle which has been evolved for the protection of offenders. There is no definition of the offence except that the conduct punished must be oppressive, high-handed, malicious, wanton or its like—terms far too vague to be admitted to any criminal code worthy of the name. There is no limit to the punishment except that it must not be unreasonable. The punishment is not inflicted by a judge who has experience and at least tries not to be influenced by emotion; it is inflicted by a jury without experience of law or punishment and often swayed by considerations which every judge would put out of his mind. And there is no effective appeal against sentence. All that a reviewing court can do is to quash the jury's decision if it thinks the punishment awarded is more than any 12 reasonable men could award. The court cannot substitute its own award. The punishment must then be decided by another jury and if they too award heavy punishment the court is virtually powerless. It is no excuse to say that we need not waste sympathy on people who behave outrageously. Are we wasting sympathy on vicious criminals when we insist on proper legal safeguards for them? The right to give punitive damages in certain cases is so firmly embedded in our law that only Parliament can remove it. But I must say that I am surprised by the enthusiasm of Lord Devlin's critics in supporting this form of palm tree justice.

Lord Devlin's first category is set out in the passage where he said[1]:

> "The first category is oppressive, arbitrary or unconstitutional action by the servants of the government. I should not extend this category—I say this with particular reference to the facts of this case—to oppressive action by private corporations or individuals."

This distinction has been attacked on two grounds: first, that it only includes Crown servants and excludes others like the police who exercise governmental functions but are not Crown servants and, secondly, that it is illogical since both the harm to the plaintiff and the blameworthiness of the defendant may be at least equally great where the offender is a powerful private individual. With regard to the first I think

---

1. [1964] A.C. at p. 1226; [1964] 1 All E.R. at p. 410.

that the context shows that the category was never intended to be limited to Crown servants. The contrast is between "the government" and private individuals. Local government is as much government as national government, and the police and many other persons are exercising governmental functions. It was unnecessary in *Rookes* v. *Barnard*[1] to define the exact limits of the category. I should certainly read it as extending to all those who by common law or statute are exercising functions of a governmental character.

The second criticism is I think misconceived. I freely admit that the distinction is illogical. The real reason for the distinction was, in my view, that the cases showed that it was firmly established with regard to servants of "the government" that damages could be awarded against them beyond any sum justified as compensation, whereas there was no case except one that was overruled where damages had been awarded against a private bully or oppressor to an amount that could not fairly be regarded as compensatory, giving to that word the meaning which I have already discussed. I thought that this House was therefore free to say that no more than that was to be awarded in future.

We are particularly concerned in the present case with the second category. With the benefit of hindsight I think I can say without disrespect to Lord Devlin that it is not happily phrased. But I think the meaning is clear enough. An ill disposed person could not infrequently deliberately commit a tort in contumelious disregard of another's rights in order to obtain an advantage which would outweigh any compensatory damages likely to be obtained by his victim. Such a case is within this category. But then it is said, suppose he commits the tort not for gain but simply out of malice why should he not also be punished. Again I freely admit there is no logical reason. The reason for excluding such a case from the category is simply that firmly established authority required us to accept this category however little we might like it, but did not require us to go farther. If logic is to be preferred to the desirability of cutting down the scope for punitive damages to the greatest extent that will not conflict with established authority then this category must be widened. But as I have already said I would, logic or no logic, refuse to extend the right to inflict exemplary damages to any class of case which is not already clearly covered by authority. On that basis I support this category. . . .

Notes

1. The categories in which Lord Devlin in *Rookes* v. *Barnard*, [1964] 1 All E.R. at p. 410, thought that exemplary damages could serve a useful purpose "in vindicating the strength of the law" were as follows:

> "The first category is oppressive, arbitrary or unconstitutional action by the servants of the government. I should not extend this category—I say this with particular reference to the facts of this case—to oppressive action by private corporations or individuals. Where one man is more powerful than another, it is inevitable that he will try to use his power to gain his ends; and if his power is much greater than the other's, he might perhaps be said to be using it oppressively. If he uses his power illegally, he must of course pay for his illegality in the ordinary way; but he is not to be punished simply because he is the more powerful. In the case of the government it is different, for the servants of the government are also the servants of the people and the use of their power must always be subordinate to their duty of service. It is true that there is something repugnant about a big man bullying a small man and very likely the bullying will be a source of humiliation that makes the case one for aggravated damages, but it is not in my opinion punishable by damages.

1. [1964] A.C. 1129; [1964] 1 All E.R. 367.

Cases in the second category are those in which the defendant's conduct has been calculated by him to make a profit for himself which may well exceed the compensation payable to the plaintiff. I have quoted the dictum of Erle C.J., in *Bell* v. *Midland Rail Co.*,[1] Maule J., in *Williams* v. *Currie*,[2] suggests the same thing; and so does Martin B. in an obiter dictum in *Crouch* v. *Great Northern Rail Co.*[3] It is a factor also that is taken into account in damages for libel; one man should not be allowed to sell another man's reputation for profit. Where a defendant with a cynical disregard for a plaintiff's rights has calculated that the money to be made out of his wrongdoing will probably exceed the damages at risk, it is necessary for the law to show that it cannot be broken with impunity. This category is not confined to moneymaking in the strict sense. It extends to cases in which the defendant is seeking to gain at the expense of the plaintiff some object—perhaps some property which he covets—which either he could not obtain at all or not obtain except at a price greater than he wants to put down. Exemplary damages can properly be awarded whenever it is necessary to teach a wrongdoer that tort does not pay. To these two categories, which are established as part of the common law, there must of course be added any category in which exemplary damages are expressly authorised by statute."

2. Lord Hailsham, [1972] 1 All E.R. 801, at p. 829–830, Lord Diplock (at p. 873) and Lord Kilbrandon (at p. 877) agreed with Lord Reid (*ante*) that the first category should not be limited to servants of the government in the strict sense, but should be extended to others exercising governmental functions.

3. The commonest torts in respect of which exemplary damages have been awarded are trespass to the person or property, false imprisonment, and defamation. Lord Hailsham (at p. 828) and Lord Diplock (at p. 874) expressed the view that Lord Devlin's speech in *Rookes* v. *Barnard* was not to be interpreted as extending the power to award exemplary damages to particular torts where they had not previously been awarded, e.g. deceit and negligence.

4. Only two (Viscount Dilhorne and Lord Wilberforce) of the seven Law Lords who heard *Cassell & Co., Ltd.* v. *Broome* did not think that the principles as to when exemplary damages are appropriate, laid down in *Rookes* v. *Barnard*, were in general correct.

5. Lord Reid's approach to the aims of an award of damages may be compared with that of Lord Wilberforce (at p. 860) who said:

"It cannot lightly be taken for granted, even as a matter of theory, that the purpose of the law of tort is compensation, still less that it ought to be, an issue of large social import, or that there is something inappropriate or illogical or anomalous (a question-begging word) in including a punitive element in civil damages, or, conversely, that the criminal law, rather than the civil law is in these cases the better instrument for conveying social disapproval, or for redressing a wrong to the social fabric; or that damages in any case can be broken down into two separate elements. As a matter of practice English law has not committed itself to either of these theories; it may have been wiser than it knew."

6. Lord Hailsham (at p. 828) suggested that where damages for loss of repu-

---

1. (1861), 10 C.B.N.S. 287, at p. 304.
2. (1845), 1 C.B. 841, at p. 848.
3. (1856), 11 Exch. 742, at p. 759.

tation are concerned, or where a simple outrage to person or property is concerned, *aggravated* damages are appropriate.

7. For general discussion see Ogus, *The Law of Damages* (London, 1973), pp. 27–38; Stone (1972), 46 A.L.J. 311; and, on the earlier law, Street, *Principles of the Law of Damages* (London, 1962), pp. 33–36 and Morris (1931), 44 Harv. L.R. 1173.

2. SPECIAL RULES ON DEATH

The Law Reform (Miscellaneous Provisions) Act 1934

1. Effect of death on certain causes of action.—(1) Subject to the provisions of this section, on the death of any person after the commencement of this Act all causes of action subsisting against or vested in him shall survive against, or, as the case may be, for the benefit of, his estate. Provided that this subsection shall not apply to causes of action for defamation or seduction . . .

(2) Where a cause of action survives as aforesaid for the benefit of the estate of a deceased person, the damages recoverable for the benefit of the estate of that person:—

(*a*) shall not include any exemplary damages;

. . .

(*c*) where the death of that person has been caused by the act or omission which gives rise to the cause of action, shall be calculated without reference to any loss or gain to his estate consequent on his death, except that a sum in respect of funeral expenses may be included.

[(3) *Repealed by the Proceedings Against Estates Act* 1970, s. 1.]

(4) Where damage has been suffered by reason of any act or omission in respect of which a cause of action would have subsisted against any person if that person had not died before or at the same time as the damage was suffered, there shall be deemed, for the purposes of this Act, to have been subsisting against him before his death such cause of action in respect of that act or omission as would have subsisted if he had died after the damage was suffered.

(5) The rights conferred by this Act for the benefit of the estates of deceased persons shall be in addition to and not in derogation of any rights conferred on the dependants of deceased persons by the Fatal Accidents Acts 1846 to 1908, . . . and so much of this Act as relates to causes of action against the estates of deceased persons shall apply in relation to causes of action under the said Acts as it applies in relation to other causes of action not expressly excepted from the operation of subsection (1) of this section.

The Proceedings Against Estates Act 1970

2. Proceedings against estate of deceased.—Rules of court made under section 99 of the Supreme Court of Judicature (Consolidation) Act 1925 or section 102 of the County Courts Act 1959 may make provision—

(*a*) for enabling proceedings to be commenced against the estate of a deceased person (whether by the appointment of a person to represent the estate or otherwise) where no grant of probate or administration has been made;

(*b*) for enabling proceedings purporting to be commenced against a person who has died to be treated as having been commenced against his estate; and

(*c*) for enabling any proceedings commenced or treated as commenced against the estate of a deceased person to be maintained (whether by substitution of parties, amendment or otherwise) against a person appointed to represent the estate or, if a grant of probate or administration is made, against the personal representatives.

Notes

1. The survival of causes of action permitted under the Act of 1934 enables the personal representatives of the deceased to recover such damages as he might have received had he lived. These damages will fall into the estate and pass under his will or on his intestacy. The effect of s. 1 (2) is that any gain to the estate from a life insurance policy or any loss of an annuity or life interest must be disregarded. There is a generous exception for funeral expenses.

2. Quite independently of the survival of the plaintiff's own cause of action under the Act of 1934, the surviving dependants have their own cause of action for the economic loss which they have suffered as a result of the death of their breadwinner. This cause of action was created by the Fatal Accidents Acts 1846–1959 and will be dealt with in Chap. 13. Damages recovered under the Fatal Accidents Acts do not form part of the estate of the deceased, but go directly to his dependants. The provisions of s. 1 (5) of the Act of 1934 (*ante*) emphasise that these are entirely distinct causes of action. However, this does not mean that the dependants can recover the same damages twice over. Damages under the Fatal Accidents Acts are assessed on "the balance of profit and loss" and with "reference to the benefit also accruing from the death to the same individual from |whatever source" (*Davies* v. *Powell Duffryn Associated Collieries, Ltd.*, [1942] A.C. 601; [1942] 1 All E.R. 657). This means that at present, the net amount received from the estate by the dependants after deduction of administration expenses and estate duty must be taken into account in reduction of the damages recoverable under the Fatal Accidents Acts. (The Law Commission has proposed that this be changed, p. 432, *post.*) In an action under the Act of 1934 any possible award under the Fatal Accidents Acts is disregarded. This is because the dependants' separate cause of action cannot affect the damages due to the deceased's estate. In most cases the action under the Fatal Accidents Acts is joined with one under the Act of 1934.

3. In *Andrews* v. *Freeborough*, [1967] 1 Q.B. 1, at p. 26, Winn L.J. commented that the damages awarded under the Act of 1934 "is a somewhat strange form of compensation which is neither received by the person entitled to be compensated nor even awarded to him or her in his or her own right. Money can do little to ease the path of a departed soul". (See too, Salmon L.J. in *Naylor* v. *Yorkshire Electricity Board*, [1967] 1 Q.B. 244, at pp. 257–260, and Lord Devlin in the same case, [1968] A.C. 529, at p. 550.) The significance of this remark must be assessed in the light of the proposals of the Law Commission, *Report on Personal Injury Litigation—Assessment of Damages* (Law Com. No. 56, 1973), *post.*

3. PERSONAL INJURIES

The Law Commission (No. 56) *Report on Personal Injury Litigation—Assessment of Damages* (1973)

Draft Law Reform (Personal Injuries etc.) Bill

Part I

DAMAGES FOR PERSONAL INJURIES

1.—(1) In an action for damages for personal injuries there shall in assessing those damages be taken into account, against any loss of earnings or profits which has accrued or probably will accrue to the injured person from the injuries, only—

(a) anything falling to be so taken into account under section 2 (1) of the Law Reform (Personal Injuries) Act 1948 (which relates to the value of rights accruing to him from the injuries in respect of certain social security benefits); and

(b) in the case of an injured employee, any remuneration or sick pay (however described) which has been or will be paid to him under his contract of employment in respect of any period after the time when he suffered the injuries, except in so far as the employee (or, if he has died, his estate) is under a legal obligation to repay it (including a legal obligation conditional on the recovery of damages for the injuries); and

(c) to such extent as may be appropriate in the circumstances of the particular case, any payment on account made to or for the benefit of the injured person (or if he has died, to his estate) in respect of damages for the injuries.

(2) If in an action for damages for personal injuries it is proved or admitted that the injured person's earning capacity has been reduced as a result of the injuries, he shall not be awarded damages in respect of the loss of earning capacity as such, but the loss of earning capacity shall be taken into account in determining the amount of any damages to be awarded in respect of future loss of earnings or profits.

(3) In this section "employee" means an individual who has entered into or works under (or, where the employment has ceased, worked under) a contract with an employer, whether the contract is for manual labour, clerical work or otherwise, is express or implied, oral or in writing, and whether it is a contract of service or of apprenticeship or a contract personally to perform any work or labour; and related expressions shall be construed accordingly.

(4) For the purposes of this section persons in the service of the Crown shall be treated as employees of the Crown whether or not they would be so treated apart from this subsection.

2.—(1) This section applies to any action for damages for personal injuries in which, it being proved or admitted that the injured person's expectation of life has been reduced by the injuries, damages are claimed in respect of loss of income.

(2) Where an action to which this section applies is brought by or on behalf of the injured person, there shall be recoverable as damages in respect of future loss of income both—

(a) damages in respect of any loss of income that the injuries will probably cause the injured person to suffer during the period from judgment to the time when, in consequence of the injuries, his life will probably end; and

(b) as regards the period after that time for which the injured person would probably have lived but for the injuries ("the lost period"), damages in respect of the amount, if any, by which his probable income (if any) in the lost period would have exceeded his probable expenditure on his own maintenance over that period:

Provided that in determining the amount of any damages recoverable by virtue of paragraph (b) above the court may disregard any of the injured person's probable income in the lost period (and in particular any such probable income from invested capital) to the extent that the court is satisfied that in the circumstances of the particular case it is appropriate to do so in order to avoid over-compensation.

(3) Subsection (2) above shall not prejudice any duty of the court under any enactment or rule of law or arising from any contract to reduce or limit the total damages which, apart from any such duty, would have been recoverable in an action to which this section applies.

3. In an action for damages for personal injuries—

(*a*) no damages shall be recoverable in respect of any loss of expectation of life caused to the injured person by the injuries; but

(*b*) if the injured person's expectation of life has been reduced by the injuies, then, in assessing damages in respect of pain and suffering resulting to him from the injuries, due account shall be taken of any suffering caused or likely to be caused to him by awareness of the fact that his expectation of life has been so reduced.

4.—(1) In an action for damages for personal injuries damages may be awarded in respect of—

(*a*) any reasonable expenses gratuitously incurred by any other person in rendering or causing to be rendered to the injured person any necessary services, as if those expenses had been recoverable by him from the injured person; and

(*b*) the reasonable value of any necessary services gratuitously rendered to the injured person by any other person, as if their reasonable value had been so recoverable by him.

(2) In this section, in relation to an injured person—

(*a*) "services" includes attending, visiting or communicating with the injured person;

(*b*) "necessary services" means services which it was reasonably necessary for the injured person to receive in consequence of the personal injuries suffered by him, having regard to all the circumstances of the case, including the extent to which it is likely that he would have had to obtain the like services at his own expense if he had not received them gratuitously.

5.—(1) In an action for damages for personal injuries damages may, subject to subsection (2) below, be awarded in respect of the reasonable value of any personal services which as a result of the injuries the injured person has been or will or probably will be unable to render to a dependant, being services which the injured person used to render gratuitously to that dependant before suffering the injuries and which but for the injuries he would probably have continued to render gratuitously to him.

(2) Subsection (1) above applies only to personal services of a kind that can ordinarily be obtained by paying a reasonable amount for them (for example services of a kind that might be rendered by a housekeeper, nurse, secretary or domestic servant, whether full-time or part-time, or services involving the provision of transport).

(3) In determining the reasonable value of any services to which subsection (1) above applies regard shall be had to the amount of any expenses incurred before judgment (whether by the injured person or otherwise) in replacing those services, and to the length of the period after judgment for which, but for the injuries, the injured person would probably have continued to render them.

(4) In this section—

"dependant", in relation to an injured person, means any of the persons for whose benefit an action could have been brought under the Fatal Accidents Acts if the injured person had died as a result of his injuries;

"personal services" means services which a person renders personally.

6.—(1) If, in an action for damages for personal injuries in which judgment is given in the High Court, there is proved or admitted to be a chance that at some definite or indefinite time in the future the injured person will, as a result of the act or omission which gives rise to the cause of action, develop some serious disease or suffer some serious deterioration in his physical or mental condition, the following provisions of this section shall have effect in relation to the action.

(2) In the following provisions of this section—

(*a*) "the relevant event" means the event of which there is proved or admitted to be a chance as mentioned in subsection (1) above; and

(*b*) "provisional damages" means damages assessed on the assumption that the relevant event will not occur.

(3) Subject to subsection (5) below, the court on the application of the plaintiff may, if it thinks fit, award the injured person provisional damages in respect of matters falling within any of such one or more of paragraphs 7 to 12 of Schedule 1 to this Act as may be specified in the application.

(4) If the relevant event occurs at any time after an award of provisional damages has been made in respect of any such matters, the court may on the application of the plaintiff award the injured person such additional damages in respect of those matters as are appropriate in all the circumstances:

Provided that if in giving judgment for the provisional damages (with or without any other damages) the court has fixed a period running from the date of that judgment within which any application under this subsection must be made, such an application shall not, without the permission of the court be made after the end of that period.

(5) An award of provisional damages shall not be made under this section unless the defendant or, if judgment has been or is to be given against two or more defendants, at least one of those defendants falls within at least one of the following descriptions, namely—

(*a*) a public authority;

(*b*) a person who is insured in respect of the plaintiff's claim for damages for personal injuries (whether or not the injuries are of the kind mentioned in paragraph (*c*) below);

(*c*) if the injuries are injuries caused by, or arising out of, the use of a motor vehicle on a road, a person whose liability to the plaintiff in respect of the injuries either—

(i) is covered by a security in respect of third-party risks complying with the requirements of Part VI of the Road Traffic Act 1972; or

(ii) would have been required by section 143 of that Act to be covered by a policy of insurance or security in respect of such risks complying with the requirements of the said Part VI but for the fact that a sum had been deposited by him with the Accountant General of the Supreme Court under section 144 of that Act.

In this subsection "motor-vehicle" and "road" have the same meanings as in the Road Traffic Act 1972, and "public authority" includes the Crown.

(6) If in the action there is proved or admitted to be a chance that two or more such events as are mentioned in subsection (1) above will occur, subsections (2) to (5) above shall apply with such modifications as may be necessary to enable the court, on the application of the plaintiff, to award the injured person provisional damages assessed on the assumption that such one or more of those events as may be specified in the application will not occur and to enable the plaintiff, where more than one of those events is so specified, to make separate applications under subsection (4) above in respect of different events so specified (with power for the court to fix different periods under subsection (4) in relation to different events).

(7) The foregoing provisions of this section shall not prejudice any duty of the court under any enactment or rule of law or arising from any contract to reduce or limit the total damages which would have been recoverable apart from any such duty; and where judgment is given for damages consisting of or including provisional damages under this section, or consisting of additional damages under subsection (4) above, any such duty of the court to reduce the damages recoverable shall apply notwithstanding that the damages recoverable on that occasion may not be or are not the only damages recoverable in the action.

7.—(1) This section applies to actions for damages for personal injuries.

(2) Where in an action to which this section applies any of the matters in respect of which damages are claimed fall within a particular paragraph of Schedule 1 to this Act, then, subject to the following provisions of this section, the court shall determine and state separately any amount awarded as damages in respect of matters falling within that paragraph.

(3) Where an action to which section 2 of this Act (as well as this section) applies is brought by or on behalf of the injured person and damages are claimed in respect of matters falling within paragraph 8 or paragraph 9 of Schedule 1 to this Act, then, subject to the following provisions of this section, the court shall, as regards matters falling within the paragraph in question, determine and state separately—

(a) any amount awarded as damages in respect of those matters for the period from judgment to the time when, in consequence of the injuries, the injured person's life will probably end; and

(b) any amount so awarded in respect of those matters for the period after that time for which he would probably have lived but for the injuries,

instead of the single amount which would otherwise have had to be determined and stated as regards those matters under subsection (2) above.

(4) Notwithstanding subsections (2) and (3) above, if in an action to which this section applies a sum is determined by agreement between the parties as the total amount of the damages to be awarded in respect of matters which, apart from this subsection, would have to be the subject of two or more separate determinations under those subsections, it shall not be necessary for the court to determine and state separately the amounts awarded in respect of those matters.

(5) Subject to subsection (7) below, the amount to be awarded in an action to which this section applies in respect of any matters falling within paragraph 12 of Schedule 1 to this Act shall be such amount as the court thinks fair and reasonable for those matters; and in determining the amount to be awarded in respect of matters so falling the court shall not make any reduction by reason only of any amount which the court proposes to award in respect of matters not so falling.

(6) Subject to subsection (7) below, the total amount of damages awarded in an action to which this section applies shall be the sum of the separate amounts (if any) determined in accordance with subsections (2), (3), (4) and (5) above.

(7) The foregoing provisions of this section shall not prejudice any duty of the court under any enactment or rule of law or arising from any contract to reduce or limit the total damages which would have been recoverable apart from any such duty.

(8) Nothing in subsection (2), (3) or (5) above shall be read as precluding the court from itemising with greater or, with the consent of the parties, less particularity than is required by that subsection any damages awarded in an action to which this section applies.

. . .

13.—(1) Where—

(a) in an action under the Fatal Accidents Acts damages are claimed in respect of future pecuniary loss; or

(b) in an action for damages for personal injuries damages are claimed in respect of future pecuniary loss (including future pecuniary loss consisting of the reasonable value of any services to which section 5 (1) of this Act applies, being services that would probably have been rendered after judgment),

then, subject to any relevant rules of court and without prejudice to any power or discretion of the court as to the costs of or incidental to any proceedings, subsection (2) below shall apply in relation to that claim.

(2) For the purpose of establishing the capital value, as at the date of judgment, of

any future pecuniary loss to which the claim relates, or the capital sum which at that date represents the reasonable value of any services to which the claim relates, any party to the action shall be entitled to adduce and rely on any admissible actuarial evidence; and where any such evidence is relied on for that purpose, the court shall have due regard to it in assessing the damages claimed.

(3) The Lord Chancellor may, after consultation with such persons or bodies of persons as appear to him requisite, by order approve for the purposes of this section any actuarial table or set of actuarial tables which in his opinion merit such approval; and any such table or set of such tables that is for the time being so approved shall, as regards any claim in relation to which subsection (2) above applies, be admissible in evidence for the purpose mentioned in that subsection in so far as it is relevant for that purpose.

For the purposes of this subsection any notes or other explanatory material issued in conjunction with any actuarial table or set of actuarial tables shall be treated as part of that table or set.

(4) The power of the Lord Chancellor to make orders under subsection (3) above shall include power to revoke a previous order and shall be exercisable by statutory instrument.

. . .

15.—(1) In this Act—

"action" includes counterclaim;

"action for damages for personal injuries" includes an action for damages for personal injuries arising out of a contract;

"defendant" includes a plaintiff against whom a defendant is counterclaiming;

"the Fatal Accidents Acts" means the Fatal Accidents Acts 1846 to 1959 and Part II of this Act;

"future", in connection with an action for damages, means subsequent to the date of the judgment in the action or, if the action is one in which provisional damages are awarded under section 6 of this Act, subsequent to the date on which judgment is given for those damages;

"pecuniary loss" means loss in money or money's worth, whether by parting with what one has or by not getting what one might get, except that it includes matters for which damages are available under section 4 or 5 of this Act;

"personal injuries" includes any disease and any impairment of a person's physical or mental condition, and "injured" shall be construed accordingly;

"plaintiff" includes a defendant counterclaiming.

(2) References in this Act to any enactment shall, except where the context otherwise requires, be read as references to that enactment as amended by or under any other enactment, including this Act.

16.—(1) Section 1 of the Law Reform (Miscellaneous Provisions) Act 1934 (effect of death on certain causes of action) shall be amended as provided in subsections (2) and (3) below.

(2) In subsection (2) (*a*) (which provides that where by virtue of that section a cause of action survives for the benefit of the estate of a deceased person, the damages recoverable for the benefit of his estate shall not include any exemplary damages) after "exemplary damages" there shall be inserted "or any damages in respect of the reasonable value of any services to which section 5 (1) of the Law Reform (Personal Injuries etc.) Act 1973 applies other than services which would probably have been rendered by that person in the period between the date when the cause of action arose and the date of his death".

(3) After subsection (2) there shall be inserted as subsection (2A)—

"(2A) Where an action for damages for personal injuries to which section 2 of the Law Reform (Personal Injuries etc.) Act 1973 applies is by virtue of subsection

(1) above brought after the death of the injured person for the benefit of his estate, no damages shall be recoverable in respect of loss of income as regards any period after his death."

. . .

SCHEDULE 1

HEADS FOR ITEMISATION OF DAMAGES IN PERSONAL INJURY ACTIONS

Part I

PECUNIARY LOSS BEFORE JUDGMENT

1. Expenses incurred before judgment.
2. Loss of earnings or profits suffered before judgment.
3. Loss of income (other than earnings or profits) suffered before judgment.
4. Matters for which damages are available under section 4 of this Act.
5. The reasonable value of any services to which section 5 (1) of this Act applies, being services which would probably have been rendered before judgment.
6. Pecuniary loss suffered before judgment, not falling within any other paragraph of this Part of this Schedule.

Part II

FUTURE PECUNIARY LOSS

7. Future expenses.
8. Future loss of earnings or profits (including any loss of earning capacity taken into account as provided by section 1 (2) of this Act).
9. Future loss of income (other than earnings or profits).
10. The reasonable value of any services to which secion 5 (1) of this Act applies, being services which would probably have been rendered after judgment.
11. Future pecuniary loss not falling within any other paragraph of this Part of this Schedule.

Part III

NON-PECUNIARY LOSS

12. Pain and suffering, loss of amenities, and any other matters not falling within Part I or Part II of this Schedule.

The Law Reform (Personal Injuries) Act 1948

2.—(1) In an action for damages for personal injuries . . . there shall in assessing those damages be taken into account, against any loss of earnings or profits which has accrued or probably will accrue to the injured person from the injuries, one half of the value of any rights which have accrued or probably will accrue to him therefrom in respect of industrial injury benefit, industrial disablement benefit or sickness benefit or invalidity benefit[1] for five years beginning with the time when the cause of action accrued.

Notes

The Law Commission's proposals for the reform of the present law relating to assessment of damages for personal injuries were made within the context of the existing fault based rules of liability. This means that they were able

---

1. [Inserted by National Insurance Act 1971, Sched. 5, para. 1.]

to make only a partial investigation of the problems of loss distribution which arise when an accident victim is compensated through social security benefits or personal insurance or similar benefits. Nor did they think that the question of "adequacy" of damages could usefully be asked within the context of their inquiries. No doubt these and related matters will be considered by the Royal Commission on Civil Liability and Compensation for Personal Injury. Some relevant materials on these wider questions will be found in Chapter 20 and the appendices to this sourcebook.

The proposals above must be read in the light of the present law which is set out in the standard textbooks on tort and in A. I. Ogus, *The Law of Damages* (London, 1973), pp. 170–230. The following is a brief guide to the major changes which would be made in the present system by the draft clauses.

1. *Clause 1.* This codifies the law as to the extent to which collateral benefits are to be taken into account in assessing damages for loss of earnings or profits (*Parry* v. *Cleaver*, [1970] A.C. 1; [1969] 1 All E.R. 555). Any matters other than those listed would fall to be disregarded (e.g. payments from charitable motives, payments under insurance policies, pensions whether or not discretionary and whether or nor contributory). Sub-s. 1 (*a*) resolves existing doubts about whether social security benefits other than those mentioned in s. 2 of the Law Reform (Personal Injuries) Act 1948, are to be taken into account (compare *Cheeseman* v. *Bowaters United Kingdom Paper Mills, Ltd.*, [1971] 3 All E.R. 513, in which unemployment benefits were taken into account, with *Foxley* v. *Olton*, [1965] 2 Q.B. 306; [1964] 3 All E.R. 248, n., in which supplementary benefits were disregarded, and *Hewson* v. *Downes*, [1970] 1 Q.B. 73; [1969] 3 All E.R. 193, in which a state retirement pension was held to be non-deductible). S. 2 (1) of the 1948 Act (amended by the National Insurance Act 1971, Sched. 5, para. 1 to include invalidity benefit) was the outcome of a compromise between the proposals of a majority of the Monckton Committee on Alternative Remedies (1946) Cmd. 6860, who wanted benefits to be deducted in full from damages, and the views of the trade union members of the Committee who dissented from this proposal. The compromise is strongly criticised by Atiyah, *Accidents, Compensation and the Law*, pp. 438–443; see too the note by J. Unger (1947), 10 M.L.R. 179. Sub-s. (1) (*b*) of the draft Bill restates the present law (summarised in para. 141 of the Law Commission's Report).

2. *Clause 2.* This reverses the existing rule in *Oliver* v. *Ashman*, [1962] 2 Q.B. 210; [1961] 3 All E.R. 323 in which the Court of Appeal held that where the plaintiff's expectation of life is reduced he can only recover damages in respect of his future loss of earnings during the period he is likely to remain alive and that nothing may be awarded in respect of the further period he would probably have lived had it not been for his injury. The injustice of this rule is illustrated by *McCann* v. *Sheppard*, [1973] 2 All E.R. 881 (C.A.), in which after the plaintiff had been awarded damages of £41,252 which included £15,000 for loss of future earnings, and while an appeal by the defendant was pending, the plaintiff died as a result of his injuries (he took an overdose of drugs prescribed to kill his pain). The Court of Appeal varied the original award by reducing the £15,000 for loss of future earnings to £400, being the loss of earnings between judgment and death. As a result, the plaintiff's widow and child were deprived of compensation for their lost dependency.

Had the Law Commission's proposed clause been in force, loss during the "lost period" would have been assessed on the basis of what the plaintiff would have earned less his probable expenditure on his own maintenance over that period. The proposed rule is modelled on the one accepted in the Australian case of *Skelton* v. *Collins* (1966), 39 A.L.J.R. 480. (Other examples of the unsatisfactory results of *Oliver* v. *Ashman* are: *Murray* v. *Shuter, N. and S. Coaches and National Coal Board*, [1972] 1 Lloyd's Rep. 6; and *Smith* v. *Central Asbestos Co., Ltd.*, [1972] 1 Q.B. 244; [1971] 3 All E.R. 204, Chap. 1, p. 17, *ante*).

3. *Clause 3.* Before *Flint* v. *Lovell*, [1935] 1 K.B. 354, it had not occurred to anyone to claim damages for loss of expectation of life. The plaintiff, a septuagenarian, was awarded £4,000 damages, including an unspecified amount for the loss of an "enjoyable, vigorous and happy old age", on the assumption that he would not live for more than a year. Professor O. Kahn-Freund, "Expectation of Happiness" (1941), 7 M.L.R. 81, at p. 102, reveals that the plaintiff was still alive many years afterwards. The same writer points out that "*Flint* v. *Lovell* might have remained a decision of little consequence, had it not been for the survival of the cause of action under the 1934 Act". In *Rose* v. *Ford*, [1937] A.C. 826, the House of Lords extended *Flint* v. *Lovell* to an action brought by the representatives of a 23 year-old girl who died four days after a motor accident. In *Benham* v. *Gambling*, [1941] A.C. 157; [1941] 1 All E.R. 7, the House of Lords said that the award was in effect for "loss of expectation of happiness" and laid down a standard conventional sum of £200, which was increased to £500 in *Yorkshire Electricity Board* v. *Naylor*, [1968] A.C. 529; [1967] 2 All E.R. 1, because of the fall in the value of money since 1941. The Law Commission's proposal will avoid the possibility of decisions like *Burns* v. *Edman*, [1970] 2 Q.B. 541; [1970] 1 All E.R. 886 (noted by D. E. C. Yale, [1971] C.L.J. 17; A. Bissett Johnson (1971), 34 M.L.R. 91) in which Crichton J. halved the award of damages under this head on the ground that the deceased had been an habitual criminal and the "life of a criminal is an unhappy one".

4. *Clause 4.* This broadly reflects the dicta of Paull J. in *Schneider* v. *Eisovitch*, [1960] 2 Q.B. 430, at p. 440, and removes the doubts created by the dicta of Diplock J. in *Gage* v. *King*, [1961] 1 Q.B. 188; [1960] 3 All E.R. 62, who suggested that it was an essential condition that the plaintiff should be under a legal obligation to pay the expenses of the third party. This led to artifices like that in *Haggar* v. *de Placido*, [1972] 2 All E.R. 1029, in which there was a written agreement to reimburse a mother and brother drawn up by a solicitor. The loving spouse or child has to stay home not *ex abundanti cordis* but as a hired drudge, if reimbursement is to be claimed on Diplock J.'s view! Under the draft clause reasonable expenses or the reasonable value of services will be recoverable by the plaintiff (who will be trusted to distribute the damages amongst his benefactors) from the tortfeasor. (See now p. 731, *post*.)

5. *Clause 5.* At present, the *actio per quod servitium amisit* (p. 434, *post*) occasionally ensures that a loss of menial services is compensated. The Law Commission (paras. 158, 159) propose that this action be abolished. This clause is, in part, a replacement for the old action, but here the right to recovery of the loss is placed in the hands of the injured person himself. As in clause 4, this clause does not make the plaintiff legally accountable to those dependants to whom the services were rendered prior to the accident. As to the meaning

of "dependant" under the Fatal Accidents Acts, see p. 425, *post*. (Losses incurred by others on their own account are dealt with in Chap. 13.)

6. *Clause 6.* The present system of awarding damages as a lump sum has many disadvantages, in particular: (a) the uncertainty of medical prognosis (will the plaintiff go blind?); (b) the possibility of mistaken forecasts about future losses of earnings and other future expenses; and (c) in fatal accidents (p. 425, *post*) speculation about contingencies affecting loss of dependency. Although a number of European countries operate a power to award periodic payments (on which see J. G. Fleming, "Damages: Capital or Rent?" (1969), 19 Univ. of Toronto L.J. 295), the Law Commission (paras. 26–30) has rejected a system of periodic payments within the context of the present fault based rules. This clause, however, makes a limited reform by enabling the court to do justice in a case where the plaintiff can prove there is a chance, but no more than a chance, that as a result of his injuries serious consequences may occur in future. A plaintiff who satisfies the stringent conditions (sub-clauses (1), (2) and (3)) against an insured defendant (sub-clause (5)) and obtains a provisional award may come back for additional damages if the "relevant event" does in fact occur. This new power will be in addition to the power given to the courts by Rules of the Supreme Court (Ord. 29, Pt. II, made under s. 20 of the Administration of Justice Act 1969) to make interim awards in order to avoid unnecessary hardship in cases where liability is admitted or established and there is a delay in payment because of a dispute as to the extent of damages.

7. *Clause 7 and Schedule 1.* Prior to the enactment of section 22 of the Administration of Justice Act 1969 (providing for the payment of interest on damages) and the decision of the Court of Appeal in *Jefford* v. *Gee*, [1970] 2 Q.B. 130; [1970] 1 All E.R. 1202 (laying down different rates of interest for special damages and general damages for pain and suffering and loss of amenities), the judges did not usually itemise the amounts awarded under separate heads of damage. This clause will require greater particularity than that which has resulted from *Jefford* v. *Gee*, and implements the Law Commission's proposal that the award for pecuniary loss should be the sum total of the itemised amounts. Itemisation of awards under the Fatal Accidents Acts is provided for in clause 11 (see p. 432, *post*).

8. *Clause 13.* The normal and primary method of assessment of pecuniary loss is by applying a multiplier to the amount of one year's estimated loss of earnings, i.e. the sum which the plaintiff probably would have earned but for the accident. In deciding upon the appropriate multiplier the courts have to make allowance for all uncertainties and possibilities. Even in the case of a young man, it is unusual for the multiplier to be more than 14 or 16 and is often less. This clause is designed to promote the use of actuarial evidence which dicta of the House of Lords in *Taylor* v. *O'Connor*, [1971] A.C. 115; [1970] 1 All E.R. 365, and of the Court of Appeal in *Mitchell* v. *Mulholland* (*No. 2*), [1972] 1 Q.B. 65; [1971] 2 All E.R. 1205, have restricted. (The advantages of such evidence over the traditional method are discussed by J. H. Prevett, "Actuarial Assessment of Damages: the Thalidomide Case" (1972), 35 M.L.R. 140, 257.) The draft clause makes no provision for dealing with the problem of inflation, although the technical committee (clause 13 (3)) may be able to include a factor which allows for inflation in the official actuarial

tables. In the meanwhile, the courts will continue to apply Lord Diplocks' dictum in *Mallet* v. *McMonagle*, [1970] A.C. 166, at pp. 175–176, namely to leave out of account the risk of further inflation, on the one hand, and the high interest rates which reflect the fear of it and capital appreciation of property and equities which are a consequence of it, on the other hand.

9. *Clause 14 and Schedule 2* (which are not reproduced above) amend the Law Reform (Miscellaneous Provisions) Act 1934, s. 3, by the addition of *prima facie* rules for the award of interest on awards of damages in personal injury cases and cases under the Fatal Accidents Acts. These rules improve upon the principles set out in *Jefford* v. *Gee*, [1970] 2 Q.B. 130; [1970] 1 All E.R. 1202.

10. *Clause 15.* It is to be noted that the definition of "pecuniary loss" makes it clear that such loss includes the two new heads of damages proposed in clauses 4 and 5 of the Bill.

11. *Clause 16.* Sub-clause (2) is designed to prevent the defendant paying damages twice over where a tort victim has died but has, in an action brought by him during his lifetime, included a claim under clause 5 for damages in respect of personal services he can no longer render his dependants. Sub-clause (3) deals with the impact of the repeal of the rule in *Oliver* v. *Ashman* by clause 2. This change in the law makes it necessary, when a tort victim dies before obtaining damages for his injuries, to provide against a defendant having to pay damages twice over in respect of the injured person's loss of future income in the "lost period", once to the dependants under the Fatal Accidents Acts and again to the estate of the deceased under s. 1 of the 1934 Act.

12. *Matters on which no change in the law is proposed.* The Law Commission (paras. 31–36) concluded that there should be no changes in the principles of assessment for non-pecuniary loss, and that the courts should not accept any test based upon loss of happiness nor should they, as they do not, take account of the fact that the plaintiff cannot use the damages awarded to him. (On these matters, see A. I. Ogus, "Damages for Lost Amenities: for a Foot, a Feeling or a Function?" (1972), 35 M.L.R. 1, for an analysis of the judgments in *Wise* v. *Kaye*, [1962] 1 Q.B. 638; [1962] 1 All E.R. 257; and *H. West & Son* v. *Shephard*, [1964] A.C. 326; [1963] 3 All E.R. 625.) The idea of a legislative tariff was rejected. The Law Commission (paras. 37–46) was content with the present practice of trial by judge alone (*Ward* v. *James*, [1966] 1 Q.B. 273; [1965] 1 All E.R. 563) and rejected the idea of an increased use of jury trial or the introduction of a special damages tribunal. The Law Commission (paras. 47–52) also accepted as satisfactory the present rule in *British Transport Commission* v. *Gourley*, [1956] A.C. 185; [1955] 3 All E.R. 796, that the plaintiff is entitled to recover compensation only for such lost income as would have remained to him after deduction of tax. This confirms the view of the Law Reform Committee, Seventh Report (1958) Cmnd. 501. The Commission was also in favour of retaining the rule that the plaintiff must deduct from his damages any expenses saved, so long as they are *in pari materia* with his future expenses which are being compensated (*Shearman* v. *Folland*, [1950] 2 K.B. 43; [1950] 1 All E.R. 976).

4. PROPERTY DAMAGE

The Edison, p. 190, *ante*

Martindale v. Duncan

Court of Appeal   [1973] 2 All E.R. 355

By a writ issued on 27 January 1972 the plaintiff, John Peter Martindale, brought an action against the defendant, John Duncan, claiming damages arising out of a motor accident on 27 November 1971 caused by the negligent driving of the defendant. The plaintiff was a private hire operator and used his car, which was damaged in the accident, for the purposes of his business. Particulars of the damages claimed were as follows:

Total net loss of earnings in plaintiff's business during the four weeks immediately following the accident (four weeks at £40 weekly)	£160·00
Cost of hiring another vehicle during the ten weeks immediately following the period referred to above (ten weeks at £22 weekly)	220·00
Cost of repair of the plaintiff's car	241·29
	£621·29

Judgment was given against the defendant in default of appearance and, on an enquiry into damages at the Liverpool District Registry of the High Court, Mr. Registrar Winter assessed damages as follows:

Repair account	£241·29
Hire (after allowing credit of £27 in respect of saving on insurance and servicing of plaintiff's car)	353·00
	£594·29

The defendant appealed against the registrar's order on the grounds (i) that there was evidence that repairs could have been started on the plaintiff's car in the first week of December 1971 but the registrar had nevertheless ordered the defendant to pay to the plaintiff, in addition to the loss of earnings and cost of repairs (which the defendant conceded was due to the plaintiff), a further sum of £220 in respect of the hiring of a motor vehicle for a period of ten weeks after the repairs would have been completed had the plaintiff acted to mitigate his loss by authorising the repairs; (ii) that the registrar had wrongly disregarded the evidence of the plaintiff to the effect that the delay in authorising repairs arose because (a) he had no money to pay for them, and (b) he was "advised" (wrongly) that he could give no authority for repairs "until an inspection had been carried out".

DAVIES L.J.: This is a curious little case. It is an appeal against a decision of the district registrar at Liverpool, Mr. Registrar Winter, given on 22 June 1972, whereby, on an enquiry into damages sustained by the plaintiff, a private hire driver, owing to a car collision which had happened on 27 November 1971, he assessed the damages at the sum of £594·29. So far as concerns the bill for the repairs and the bill of £160 for the loss of profit during the first month or so that the car was off the road, no complaint is made by counsel on behalf of the defendant. What he does complain about, however, is that the registrar allowed as part of the claim a sum of £220, being ten weeks at £22 a week, for the hire of a car during that period, after the first four weeks to which I have referred, when the car was off the road. Counsel complains that the car ought not to have been off the road after the first four weeks; he says that the repairs ought to have been put in hand immediately or much earlier than they were and that the plaintiff thereby has failed properly to mitigate his damage and indeed has increased his damage by not putting the repairs in hand promptly. . . .

. . . In evidence it transpires that what the plaintiff was saying was that he himself was not able to pay the cost of repairs and that is the first reason why they were not put in hand sooner. Secondly, he said—as appears to be the fact—that the Zurich Insurance Co. (for the defendant) did not inspect or authorise the repairs until 26 January 1972; and he also said 'I had to wait for OK from my insurers'. I think that is probably quite a true statement.

With regard to the dates on which the work was done, authorisation having been given on 26 January . . . the evidence was that the repairs were started on 2 February and were completed on 25 February.

Counsel, of course, has referred us to the well-known case of *Owners of Dredger Liesbosch* v. *Owners of Steamship Edison*[1] which is authority for the proposition that impecuniosity is no excuse for not mitigating damage. But I regard this as entirely different from that case. Here was this man who was seeking in the first instance to recover his damages from the Zurich Insurance Co., who were the insurers of the defendant, and, if anything went wrong with that claim, although he obviously would not want to forfeit his "no claims" bonus, the second string to his bow would be to recover the money from his own insurers, whoever they were; and until he had had authorisation for doing the work he could not be at all certain that he would stand in a good position vis-à-vis the insurance company.

Despite the arguments of counsel and despite my uncomfortable feeling that we have not had all the facts fully put before us (I am not blaming learned counsel for that), I think that the argument for the defendant has entirely failed, and I would dismiss the appeal.

[PHILLIMORE L.J. and STAMP L.J. agreed.]

Appeal dismissed

---

1. [1933] A.C. 449; [1933] All E.R. Rep. 144.

PART TWO

Torts to Non-physical Interests

13

Interests in Another's Life or Services

The materials in this Chapter are concerned with the situation in which the plaintiff (P) complains that the defendant (D) has caused him loss by interfering with the well-being of a third person (M, the middleman).

If the interference results in M's death then the common law rule is that P cannot complain in civil court (p. 424, *post*). Like the Romans, the medieval English lawyers took the view that it was impossible to place a value upon the life of a free man. In the emerging industrial society of the 19th century, the rule had the socially inconvenient result of imposing the main burden of supporting the widows and children of victims of machines upon the poor rate, instead of upon the entrepreneurs whose activities had created the new risks. Lord Campbell was able to persuade Parliament, despite the opposition of the railway companies, that there should be a statutory exception for the benefit of certain members of the family, where the death of the breadwinner could be attributed to the fault of the defendant (p. 425, *post*). But non-family plaintiffs must still bear their own losses.

Interference with M, resulting in loss to P, may result in the commission of certain torts.

(1) Where M is a domestic or menial servant of P and has been injured by the wrongful (i.e. negligent or intentional) act of D, and P has thereby been deprived of M's services, P may recover the financial loss which he has suffered (p. 434, *post*).

(2) Where M is the wife of P and has been injured by the wrongful (i.e. negligent or intentional) act of D, and P has thereby been deprived of M's services, P may recover the financial loss which he has suffered (p. 434, *post*). P may also recover a small amount for the loss which he has suffered by being deprived of his wife's society (consortium) (p. 434, *post*).

Although these ancient actions are described as historical anomalies based upon the feudal conception of servants and wives as chattels, they have not yet been abolished despite recommendations to that effect by the Law Reform Committee's Eleventh Report (1963), Cmnd. 2017, and the Law Commission (p. 433, *post*). The problem is to know what should replace them.

As a general rule, apart from these exceptional torts, P has no cause of action against D for *negligent* interference with P's relations with M. So the negligent flooding of M's mine, causing M's workers (P) to lose wages, does not give an action to the workers against D. The traditional approach is that there is no duty-situation (p. 77, *ante*). Cases of *intentional* interference by D with P's relations with M—that is, where D's conduct is *aimed at* P—stand on a different footing. Those cases usually arise in the context of business and labour relations, and will be separately examined in the next Chapter.

1. DEATH AS A CAUSE OF ACTION

Admiralty Commissioners v. Steamship *Amerika* (Owners). *The Amerika*

House of Lords   [1916–17] All E.R. Rep. 177

A submarine sank due to the negligent navigation of respondent's steamship. All but one of the crew were drowned. The Commissioners of Admiralty brought this action to recover the damage they had sustained. This included the capitalised amount of pensions payable by them to relatives of the deceased.

The House of Lords dismissed an appeal from a decision of the Court of Appeal which had disallowed this as an item of damages. Their Lordships held that (1) the payments had been made on compassionate grounds; since a person may not increase his claim for damages by a voluntary act, the payments were not recoverable from the tortfeasor; (2) the rule in *Baker* v. *Bolton* (set out in Lord Sumner's speech, *post*) applied.

LORD SUMNER: This appeal has been brought principally to test the rule in *Baker* v. *Bolton*,[1] that "in a civil court the death of a human being cannot be complained of as an injury", a rule which has long been treated as universally applicable at common law. Some attempt was made to contest it only in its application to the case of master and servant. I will discuss both the narrower and the wider proposition, but it is clear that the action was not brought for the loss to a master of the services of his employee, but for the respondents' bad navigation, which sank the Crown's submarine, and the item of damage now in dispute, namely, pensions and allowances to dependants of seamen who were drowned, was claimed merely as one of the natural consequences of the tort, which consisted in sinking the ship. . . .

Never during the many centuries that have passed since reports of the decisions of English courts first began has the recovery of damages for the death of a human being as a civil injury been recorded. Since Lord Ellenborough's time the contrary has been uniformly decided by the Court of Exchequer and by the Court of Appeal. In addition to the weight of Lord Ellenborough's name (no mean authority even when sitting at nisi prius in spite of Lord Campbell's sneer), the rule has been definitely asserted by Lord Selborne (*Clarke* v. *Carfin Coal Co.*, [1891] A.C. 412, at p. 414), Lord Bowen (*The Vera Cruz* (No. 2) (1884), 9 P.D. 96, at p. 101), and Lord Alverstone and Lord Gorell (*Clark* v. *London General Omnibus Co., Ltd.*[2]). It has been accepted as the rule of the common law by the Supreme Court of the Dominion of Canada (*Re The Garland, Monaghan* v. *Horn*[3]), and the Supreme Court of the United States of America (*The Corsair*[4]). That the rule has also received statutory recognition appears to me to be abundantly plain. I agree that the preamble to s. 1 of the Fatal Accidents Act 1846, should be read as applying to the particular defect in the existing law, which it was passed to remedy, namely, the disadvantageous position of widows and children, and not to the limited rights of masters and employers, though only Bramwell B.'s

---

1. (1808), 1 Camp. 493, *per* Lord Ellenborough.
2. [1906] 2 K.B. 648.
3. (1881), 7 S.C.R. 409.
4. (1892), 145 U.S. 335.

intrepid individualism could dismiss it as a "loose recital in an incorrectly drawn section of a statute, on which the courts had to put a meaning from what it did not rather than what it did say" (*Osborn* (*Osborne*) v. *Gillett* (1873), L.R. 8 Exch. 88, at p. 95). Still I think that the view taken by the legislature in 1846 is clear. . . . It provided a new cause of action and did not merely regulate or enlarge an old one. It excluded Scotland from its operation because a sufficient remedy already existed there, when in England none existed at all. So much seems to me to be indubitable. It did not deal with the case of master and servant as such, presumably because the legislature found nothing in the common law rule in this regard which called for reconsideration . . .

[EARL LOREBURN L.C. and LORD PARKER OF WADDINGTON delivered speeches to the same effect.]

Hansard's Parliamentary Debates, Third Series, House of Lords, 24 April 1846, cols. 967–968

LORD CAMPBELL (moving the second reading of the Death By Accident Compensation Bill [which, when enacted, became popularly known as Lord Campbell's Act, and was given the title the Fatal Accidents Act by the Short Titles Act 1896]) . . . said that he had a great respect for the common law; but still he felt that there could be no doubt that some of its doctrines were not applicable to the present state of society. One of these doctrines was that the life of a man was so valuable that they could not put any estimate upon it in case of a death by accident; and, therefore, if a man had his leg broken, on account of negligence on the part of coach–proprietors or of a railway company, he had his remedy in a court of justice; but if the negligence were still grosser, and if a life were destroyed, there was no remedy whatever. In Scotland, and in foreign countries, the general rule was that where there was a wrong which worked injuriously to another, the law gave compensation . . . He was sorry to perceive that some disposition appeared to exist among hon. and learned gentlemen elsewhere to oppose this measure; but this he could say that his noble and learned Friend the Lord Chief Justice of England had expressed his unqualified approbation of its merits. Some of his learned Friends thought, however, that the law of England was absolute perfection, and that any attempt to infringe it should be resisted. He was told that resistance to this measure, in the other House of Parliament, would be also increased by the influence of the railway companies there, and that the influence was so great that one railway company alone could muster no less than eighty votes . . .

Note

For a critique of the historical reasoning in *The Amerika* see Holdsworth, *History of English Law*, Vol. iii, pp. 231–236 and Appendix viii, pp. 676–677.

The Fatal Accidents Act 1846

[1.] **When death is caused by negligence an action shall be maintainable.—** . . . Whensoever the death of a person shall be caused by wrongful act, neglect, or default, and the act, neglect, or default is such as would (if death had not ensued) have entitled the party injured to maintain an action and recover damages in respect thereof, then and in every such case the person who would have been liable if death had not ensued shall be liable to an action for damages, notwithstanding the death of the person injured, . . .

2. **Action to be for the benefit of certain relations, and brought by executor or administrator of deceased.—** . . . Every such action shall be for the benefit of the wife, husband, parent and child of the person whose death shall have been so caused, and shall be brought by and in the name of the executor or administrator of the person deceased; and in every such action the jury may give such damages as they may think proportioned to the injury resulting from such death to the parties respectively for

whom and for whose benefit such action shall be brought; and the amount so recovered, after deducting the costs not recovered from the defendant, shall be divided amongst the before-mentioned parties in such shares as the jury by their verdict shall find and direct.

3. Action to be commenced within [three years].—Provided always, . . . that not more than one action shall lie for and in respect of the same subject matter of complaint; and that every such action shall be commenced within [three years] after the death of such deceased person.

[*Note*: extensions of time are however possible under the provisions of the Law Reform (Miscellaneous Provisions) Act 1971, s. 2 and Sched. 2.]

4. Plaintiff to deliver particulars.—. . . In every such action the plaintiff on the record shall be required, together with the declaration, to deliver to the defendant or his attorney a full particular of the person or persons for whom and on whose behalf such action shall be brought, and of the nature of the claim in respect of which damages shall be sought to be recovered.

5. Construction of Act.—. . . The following words and expressions are intended to have the meanings hereby assigned to them respectively, so far as such meanings are not excluded by the context or by the nature of the subject matter; that is to say, words denoting the singular number are to be understood to apply also to a plurality of persons or things; and words denoting the masculine gender are to be understood to apply also to persons of the feminine gender; and the word "person" shall apply to bodies politic and corporate; and the word "parent" shall include father and mother, and grandfather and grandmother, . . .; and the word "child" shall include son and daughter, and grandson and granddaughter, . . .

The Fatal Accidents Act 1864

1. Action may be brought by the persons beneficially interested, where no executor, etc.—If and so often as it shall happen at any time or times hereafter, in any of the cases intended and provided for by the said Act, that there shall be no executor or administrator of the person deceased, or that there being such executor or administrator no such action as in the said Act mentioned shall within six calendar months after the death of such deceased person as therein mentioned have been brought by and in the name of his or her executor or administrator, then and in every such case such action may be brought by and in the name or names of all or any of the persons (if more than one) for whose benefit such action would have been, if it had been brought by and in the name of such executor or administrator; and every action so to be brought shall be for the benefit of the same person or persons, and shall be subject to the same regulations and procedure, as nearly as may be, as if it were brought by and in the name of such executor or administrator.

[**2. Payments into court.**—*omitted*]

The Law Reform (Miscellaneous Provisions) Act 1934

2. Amendment of Fatal Accidents Acts 1846 to 1908.—. . .

(3) In an action brought under the Fatal Accidents Acts 1846 to 1908, damages may be awarded in respect of the funeral expenses of the deceased person if such expenses have been incurred by the parties for whose benefit the action is brought. . . .

The Fatal Accidents Act 1959

1. Extension of classes of dependants.—(1) The persons for whose benefit or by whom an action may be brought under the Fatal Accidents Act 1846, shall include any person who is, or is the issue of, a brother, sister, uncle or aunt of the deceased person.

(2) In deducing any relationship for the purposes of the said Act and this Act—

(a) an adopted person shall be treated as the child of the person or persons by whom he was adopted and not as the child of any other person; and, subject thereto,

(b) any relationship by affinity shall be treated as a relationship by consanguinity, any relationship of the half blood as a relationship of the whole blood, and the stepchild of any person as his child; and

(c) an illegitimate person shall be treated as the legitimate child of his mother and reputed father.

(3) In this section "adopted" means adopted in pursuance of an adoption order made under the Adoption Act 1958, or any previous enactment relating to the adoption of children, or any corresponding enactment of the Parliament of Northern Ireland;. . .

2. Exclusion of certain benefits in assessment of damages.—(1) In assessing damages in respect of a person's death in any action under the Fatal Accidents Act 1846, . . . there shall not be taken into account any insurance money, benefit, pension or gratuity which has been or will or may be paid as a result of the death.

(2) In this section—

"benefit" means benefit under the National Insurance Acts 1946 (as amended by any subsequent enactment, whether passed before or after the commencement of this Act), or any corresponding enactment of the Parliament of Northern Ireland and any payment by a friendly society or trade union for the relief or maintenance of a member's dependants;

"insurance money" includes a return of premiums; and

"pension" includes a return of contributions and any payment of a lump sum in respect of a person's employment.

Note

The dependant's claim under the Fatal Accidents Acts is frequently joined with one under the Law Reform (Miscellaneous Provisions) Act 1934 (p. 406, ante). It will be remembered that s. 1 (5) of the 1934 Act states that the rights it provides for the survival of the deceased's cause of action are "in addition to and not in derogation of any rights conferred on the dependants of the deceased person by the Fatal Accidents Acts". But if the damages recovered for the benefit of the estate under the 1934 Act devolve upon the dependants under the deceased's will or on his intestacy, the net amount they receive from the estate must be taken into account in reduction of damages recoverable under the Fatal Accidents Acts. The Law Commission has proposed that this rule should be altered (p. 432, post).

Burns v. Edman

Queen's Bench Division   [1970] 1 All E.R. 886

CRICHTON J.: In the early morning of 22 November 1964, the plaintiff's husband, a man aged 32, a strong and healthy man, was killed in a motor accident. The court here has found as a fact that the defendant in this action was three-quarters to blame for the collision and that the deceased was one-quarter to blame. In these circumstances the plaintiff, now a woman of 32, sues under the Law Reform (Miscellaneous Provisions) Act 1934 on behalf of the deceased's estate and under the Fatal Accidents

Acts 1846–1959 on behalf of herself and the other dependants of the deceased, i.e. his stepson now aged 14, and his children, a girl aged 12 and twin girls aged 10.

It has been found in this case impossible for the plaintiff to establish that the deceased had any capital assets to support his family or that during his lifetime he had any honest employment. The plaintiff, however, said in evidence that the deceased gave her £20 every Friday and paid the rent of the house. Although at death we understand, it is the policy of the Home Office or the prison authorities to destroy the records of criminals, it nevertheless has appeared in evidence in this case that the deceased, in July 1954, was sentenced to three years' imprisonment for robbery with violence at the Central Criminal Court. And that, in May 1962, after his marriage to the plaintiff in December 1958, he was convicted of being an accessory before and after the fact of felony, and at Northampton received a sentence of 21 months' imprisonment.

In these circumstances, it is, in my judgment, a fair inference that such support the deceased afforded his family, and I am far from satisfied that it amounted to regular £20 a week, came from the proceeds of criminal offences. The plaintiff said that the deceased from time to time profited financially from gambling on greyhounds but, in my view, this is wholly uncertain and unproven. The plaintiff further said that she did not know that such money as the deceased gave her came from the proceeds of crime. I have already found as a fact that she did know, or that she did not succeed in establishing that she did not know that such money as the deceased gave her was from the proceeds of crime. So far as the plaintiff is concerned, therefore, in my judgment, she would not be entitled to claim damages because the maxim which has stood the test of time ex turpi causa non oritur actio would apply.

Quite apart from that, however, the court has to consider whether, on the facts as I have found them, the plaintiff and the infant dependants are entitled to damages under the Fatal Accidents Act 1846. Counsel for the plaintiff says that they are so entitled. He puts his case in this way: that being dependants they are prima facie entitled to damages because the death of the deceased was, at any rate in part caused by the negligence of the defendant. Secondly, that the only bar to their recovering damages is that to award damages to them would be contrary to public policy, because the support that they were afforded before the death of the deceased emanated from the proceeds of crime. And thirdly, that under the Fatal Accidents Acts claimants who are suing as innocent parties on their own behalf are not suing as personal representatives of the deceased on behalf of the estate or standing in the shoes of the deceased, as was done in *Beresford* v. *Royal Insurance Co., Ltd.*[1] and *In the Estate of Crippen*,[2] which were both unsuccessful claims. And counsel cited *Pigney* v. *Pointers Transport Services, Ltd.*[3] in support of the proposition that under the Fatal Accidents Acts a widow making her separate claim was entitled to recover damages even though the death of her husband had resulted from his suicide at a time when he was not found to be insane, but it was there held—quite clearly—that the suicide of the deceased was directly attributable to the injuries sustained by him in an accident for which the defendant was responsible. I distinguish that case on that ground from the present case in the sense that, although it is a case undoubtedly in which a widow was entitled to make her own separate case under the Fatal Accidents Acts and is good authority for that proposition, if good authority for it is needed in the light of earlier decisions, it is quite clearly distinguishable from this case in which the support proceeded directly from the proceeds of criminal offences. . . .

Nevertheless, counsel for the plaintiff argued that it was sufficient for the plaintiff to show: first, that the death of the deceased was caused by the negligence of the defendant; and secondly, that from whatever source it did emanate the dependants

---

1. [1938] A.C. 586; [1938] 2 All E.R. 602.
2. [1911] P. 108; [1911–13] All E.R. Rep. 207.
3. [1957] 2 All E.R. 807.

including the plaintiff, had in fact lost the financial support of the deceased through the negligence of the defendant, and he went on to say further that it was good public policy that the dependency should be paid by way of compensation by the defendant as tortfeasor rather than by the taxpayer through the medium of social security. . . .

. . . Counsel for the defendant argues that the injury in the case of each of the dependants really amounts to this on examination: that he or she is saying: "I have been deprived of my share of other people's goods, brought to me by the deceased", and brought from the proceeds of dishonesty—dishonestly obtained, and insofar as that is the injury, it is a mala causa or turpis causa and, says counsel, it is not maintainable under the Fatal Accidents Act 1846. I agree with counsel for the defendant in this argument, and in my judgment neither the plaintiff nor any other dependant is entitled to damages under the Fatal Accidents Act 1846 for that reason.

Now I ought, I think, to deal with another argument put forward by counsel for the plaintiff. He argued in this way: that although at the time of his death such support as the deceased afforded to his family proceeded from criminal offences, yet that might not have been so in the future. He might have reformed and taken up remunerative, honest work and continued to support his family from that source. In the circumstances, I have come to the conclusion that that possibility is, in the circumstances, entirely speculative and unproven to the point of improbability. And *Barnett* v. *Cohen*[1] indicates with clarity that damages under the Fatal Accidents Act 1846 cannot be awarded for such speculative possibilities as the potential support from a child of tender years to its parents in later life. I think that case is comparable to the present case from the point of view of the possibility of reform.

The funeral expenses of £41 are claimed under the Fatal Accidents Acts, and so far as that claim is concerned, in my judgment it succeeds, and under the Fatal Accidents Acts there will be judgment for the plaintiff of £30 15s. being three-quarters of £41. . . .

Question

If Burns had stolen a bottle of ginger beer for consumption by his children and they had been injured by a decomposed snail would their action have been barred by the *ex turpi causa non oritur actio* rule? (This question is suggested by D. E. C. Yale, [1971] C.L.J. 17, who comments that "the children particularly in this case [*Burns* v. *Edman*] seem to be the innocent victims of a Latin maxim"; and see *Smith* v. *Jenkins* (1970), 44 A.L.J. 78.)

Note

Section 1 (4) of the Law Reform (Contributory Negligence) Act 1945 (p. 296, *ante*) has the effect of allowing a reduction of damages if the deceased was contributorily negligent. What if the *dependant* was partly responsible for the breadwinner's death? In *Mulholland* v. *McCrea*, [1961] N.I. 135 the deceased was a passenger in a car driven by her husband. The husband was partly responsible for the accident. He claimed as personal representative under the Fatal Accidents Acts and under the Northern Irish Law Reform (Miscellaneous Provisions) Act 1937 (which corresponds to the English Act of 1934). The Northern Irish Court of Appeal held by a majority that from the amount awarded to the husband as dependant under the Fatal Accidents Acts there should be deducted the benefits accruing from his wife's estate and the resulting sum should be reduced having regard to his share in the responsibility for his wife's death. What would the position have been if the

---

1. [1921] 2 K.B. 461; [1921] All E.R. Rep. 528.

husband had also been suing on behalf of the deceased's children? (See Glanville Williams, *Joint Torts and Contributory Negligence*, pp. 443–444.)

Davies v. Taylor

House of Lords   [1972] 3 All E.R. 836

LORD REID: ... The appellant is the widow of a man who was killed in a road accident owing to the negligence of the respondent. She claims under s. 2 of the Fatal Accidents Act 1846. To succeed she must shew that she has suffered "injury" resulting from her husband's death. Admittedly the injury must be of a financial character. In the ordinary case where the spouses were living together on the husband's earnings what the widow loses is the prospect of future financial support. There can be no question of proving as a fact that she would have received a certain amount of benefit. No one can know what might have happened had he not been killed. But the value of the prospect chance or probability of support can be estimated by taking all significant factors into account. But, perhaps on an application of the de minimis principle, speculative possibilities would be ignored. I think that must apply equally whether the contention is that for some reason or reasons the support might have increased, decreased, or ceased altogether. The court or jury must do its best to evaluate all the chances, large or small, favourable or unfavourable.

The peculiarity in the present case is that the appellant had left her husband some five weeks before his death and there was no immediate prospect of her returning to him. He wanted her to come back but she was unwilling to come. But she says that there was a prospect or chance or probability that she might have returned to him later and it is only in that event that she would have benefited from his survival. To my mind the issue and the sole issue is whether that chance or probability was substantial. If it was it must be evaluated. If it was a mere possibility it must be ignored. Many different words could be and have been used to indicate the dividing line. I can think of none better than "substantial" on the one hand, or "speculative" on the other. It must be left to the good sense of the tribunal to decide on broad lines, without regard to legal niceties, but on a consideration of all the facts in proper perspective.

I am well aware of the fact that in real life chances rarely are or can be estimated on mathematical terms. But for simplicity of argument let me suppose two cases of a widow who had separated from her husband before he was killed. In one case it is estimated that the chance that she would have returned to him is a 60 per cent probability (more likely than not) but in the other the estimate of that chance is a 40 per cent probability (quite likely but less than an even chance). In each case the tribunal would determine what its award would have been if the spouses had been living together when the husband was killed, and then discount it or scale it down to take account of the probability of her not returning to him.

But in the present case the trial judge applied a different test. He held that there was an onus on the appellant to prove that on a balance of probabilities she had an expectation of continued dependency—that it was more probable than not that there would have been a reconciliation. In fairness to him I must note that he understood that this had been agreed by counsel. But we were informed that that was not so and counsel for the respondent very properly did not seek to found on this. I think that the learned judge was misled.

When the question is whether a certain thing is or is not true—whether a certain event did or did not happen—then the court must decide one way or the other. There is no question of chance or probability. Either it did or it did not happen. But the standard of civil proof is a balance of probabilities. If the evidence shews a balance in favour of it having happened then it is proved that it did in fact happen. But here we are not and could not be seeking a decision either that the wife would or that she would not have returned to her husband. You can prove that a past event happened, but you cannot prove that a future event will happen and I do not think that the law is so foolish as to suppose that you can. All that you can do is to evaluate the chance. Sometimes it is virtually 100 per cent, sometimes virtually nil. But often it is somewhere in between. And if it is somewhere in between I do not see much difference between a probability of 51 per cent and a probability of 49 per cent.

"Injury" in the Fatal Accidents Act 1846 does not and could not possibly mean loss of a certainty. It must and can only mean loss of a chance. The chance may be a probability of over 99 per cent but it is still only a chance. So I can see no merit in adopting here the test used for proving whether a fact did or did not happen. There it must be all or nothing.

If the balance of probability were the proper test what is to happen in the two 'cases which I have supposed of a 60 per cent and a 40 per cent probability? The 40 per cent case will get nothing but what about the 60 per cent case? Is it to get a full award on the basis that it has been proved that the wife would have returned to her husband? That would be the logical result. I can see no ground at all for saying that the 40 per cent case fails altogether but the 60 per cent case gets 100 per cent. But it would be almost absurd to say that the 40 per cent case gets nothing while the 60 per cent case award is scaled down to that proportion of what the award would have been if the spouses had been living together. That would be applying two different rules to the two cases. So I reject the balance of probability test in this case.

But I agree with your Lordships that even on the test which I think ought to be applied the appellant has not shewn any significant chance or probability that she suffered any injury financially by her husband's death. So I am of opinion that this appeal must be dismissed.

[LORD MORRIS OF BORTH-Y-GEST, VISCOUNT DILHORNE, LORD SIMON OF GLAISDALE and LORD CROSS OF CHELSEA delivered speeches in favour of dismissing the appeal.]

The Law Reform (Miscellaneous Provisions) Act 1971

4. Assessment of damages for widows.—(1) In assessing damages payable to a widow in respect of the death of her husband in any action under the Fatal Accidents Acts 1846 to 1959 there shall not be taken into account the remarriage of the widow or her prospects of remarriage. . . .

The Law Commission (No. 56) *Report on Personal Injury Litigation—Assessment of Damages* (1973)

Draft Law Reform (Personal Injuries etc.) Bill

Part II

AMENDMENT OF FATAL ACCIDENTS ACTS

8.—(1) The persons for whose benefit or by whom an action may be brought under the Fatal Accidents Acts shall include a former spouse of the deceased person and any person (not being a child of the deceased person) who, in the case of any marriage to which the deceased person was at any time a party, was treated by the deceased person as a child of the family in relation to that marriage.

(2) In subsection (1) above—

"child of the deceased person" includes anyone who is a child of his within the meaning of the Fatal Accidents Act 1846 as amended by section 1 of the Fatal Accidents Act 1959;

"former spouse", in relation to a deceased person, means a person whose marriage with the deceased was during the deceased's lifetime dissolved or annulled (whether by a decree made or deemed to be made under the Matrimonial Causes Act 1973 or otherwise).

9. In assessing damages in respect of a person's death in any action under the Fatal Accidents Acts there shall not be taken into account—

(a) any benefits which have accrued or will or may accrue from the deceased's estate to any of the persons for whose benefit the action is brought; or

(b) as regards any of those persons, the remarriage or prospects of remarriage of the widow or widower of the deceased.

10.—(1) Where an action is brought under the Fatal Accidents Acts for the benefit of the husband or wife of the deceased person (with or without other persons) a sum of £1,000 shall be awarded as damages in respect of his or her personal bereavement.

(2) Where an action in respect of the death of a minor who was never married is brought under the said Acts for the benefit of a parent or both parents of the minor (with or without other persons), a sum of £1,000 shall be awarded as damages in respect of the personal bereavement of that parent or, as the case may be, the parents and, if the action is brought for the benefit of both parents, shall (subject to any deduction falling to be made in respect of costs not recovered from the defendant) be divided equally between them.

(3) For the purposes of subsection (2) above "parent"—

(a) in relation to an adopted person, means the person or one of the persons by whom he was adopted; and

(b) in relation to an illegitimate (and not adopted) person, means his mother.

In this subsection "adopted" has the same meaning as in section 1 of the Fatal Accidents Act 1959.

(4) An action under the said Acts brought for the benefit of a person who dies before judgment is given shall for the purposes of this section be treated as not having been brought for that person's benefit.

(5) The Lord Chancellor may by order made by statutory instrument, subject to annulment in pursuance of a resolution of either House of Parliament, amend this section by increasing or further increasing the sums specified in subsections (1) and (2); but any such order shall apply only as regards actions brought in respect of deaths occurring after the order comes into force.

(6) Nothing in the foregoing provisions of this section shall—

(a) be taken to require any damages to be awarded in the absence of liability on the part of the defendant; or

(b) prejudice any duty of the court under any enactment or rule of law to reduce or limit the total damages which would have been recoverable apart from any such duty; or

(c) be taken to exempt any sum awarded as damages under this section from proportionate reduction in consequence of any reduction or limit affecting the total damages which would have been so recoverable.

11.—(1) In awarding damages in respect of a person's death in any action under the Fatal Accidents Acts the court shall determine and state separately—

(a) any amount awarded as damages in respect of pecuniary loss suffered before judgment;

(b) any amount awarded as damages in respect of future pecuniary loss; and

(c) any amount awarded under section 10 of this Act as damages in respect of personal bereavement.

(2) Subsection (1) above shall not prejudice any duty of the court under any enactment or rule of law to reduce or limit the total damages which would be recoverable apart from any such duty.

(3) Nothing in subsection (1) above shall be read as precluding the court from itemising with greater or, with the consent of the parties, less particularity than is required by that subsection any damages awarded in an action under the Fatal Accidents Acts.

Notes

1. *Clause 8* adds to the classes of persons recognised as dependants under the Fatal Accidents Acts.

2. *Clause 9 (a)* will remove the unfairness to widows whose husbands have saved by buying shares instead of life insurance, the latter being non-deductible under the Fatal Accidents Act 1959, s. 2. *Clause 9 (b)* removes two anomalies under s. 4 of the Law Reform (Miscellaneous Provisions) Act 1971, by making that provision apply to claims made by the children of the deceased and also to a claim made by a widower. The original section was enacted because Parliament agreed with Phillimore J. in *Buckley* v. *John Allen and Ford (Oxford), Ltd.*, [1967] 2 Q.B. 637, at p. 644, that it was distasteful for a judge to have to put a money value upon a widow's chances of remarriage.

3. *Clause 10* will create a statutory exception to the rule (*Blake* v. *Midland Railway* (1852), 18 Q.B. 93) that damages for grief and suffering (*solatium*) are not recoverable under the Fatal Accidents Acts. Under the existing law, an indirect form of *solatium* occurs in the case where the beneficiary under the deceased's will or intestacy was not dependent upon him and so the benefit of the small conventional sum of about £500 for loss of expectation of life comes to the beneficiary. Where the beneficiaries were dependent upon the deceased the £500 is deducted from their damages under the Fatal Accidents Acts. If the Law Commission's proposals for the abolition of claims for loss of expectation of life (Chap. 12, p. 408, *ante*), and for the abolition of various other causes of action (p. 434, *post*) are implemented, dependants would get nothing by way of *solatium* were it not for the proposed clause 10. It is to be noted that the word "bereavement" has been used rather than "mental suffering" because it is intended to comprehend not only psychic damage but also the sort of help, counsel and guidance that is lost by the death of a member of the family (paras. 169, 172). The new claim is subject to the same restrictions as claims under the Fatal Accidents Acts.

4. *Clause 11* makes it necessary to itemise damages in awards under the Fatal Accidents Acts.

2. DOMESTIC AND FAMILY LOSSES

The Law Commission (No. 56) *Report on Personal Injury Litigation—Assessment of Damages* (1973)

Draft Law Reform (Personal Injuries etc.) Bill

12. No person shall be liable in tort under the law of England and Wales—

   (*a*) to a husband on the ground only of his having deprived the husband of the services or society (or both) of his wife;

   (*b*) to a parent (or a person standing in the place of a parent) on the ground only of his having deprived the parent (or other person) of the services of his or her child otherwise than by raping, seducing or enticing that child;

(*c*) to any other person on the ground only of his having deprived that other person of the services of that other person's menial servant;

(*d*) to any other person on the ground only of his having deprived that other person of the services of that other person's female servant by raping or seducing her; or

(*e*) to any other person for enticing or harbouring that other person's servant.

Notes

If implemented this clause will abolish all the remaining actions which, at present, may be brought in respect of domestic or family losses.

1. *Clause 12 (a)* will remove the inequality between the sexes which results from *Best* v. *Samuel Fox & Co., Ltd.*, [1952] A.C. 716; [1952] 2 All E.R. 394, in which it was held that a married woman, whose husband has been injured by a negligent act or omission, has no right of action against that person for the loss or impairment of consortium consequential upon the injury.

2. *Clause 12 (b)* completes the reform begun by s. 5 of the Law Reform (Miscellaneous Provisions) Act 1970 which abolished the old actions for depriving a parent of a child's services by raping, seducing or enticing the child.

3. *Clause 12 (c)* abolished the *actio per quod servitium amisit* (for the history of which see G. H. Jones (1948), 74 L.Q.R. 39) which the Court of Appeal, in *I.R. Comrs.* v. *Hambrook*, [1956] 2 Q.B. 641; [1956] 3 All E.R. 338, confined to actions in respect of the loss of menial servants.

4. *Clauses 12 (d)* and *(e)* abolish the actions for seduction, enticement and harbouring which were left in existence by the Law Reform (Miscellaneous Provisions) Act 1970, s. 5 (which abolished the actions so far as they related to a spouse or child). The right to petition for damages in respect of adultery was abolished by the Law Reform (Miscellaneous Provisions) Act 1970, s. 4.

5. *Consequential changes.* The Law Commission proposes that the words "or seduction" in the Law Reform (Miscellaneous Provisions) Act 1934, s. 1 (1) should be deleted (Draft Bill, Sched. 4). Where others have incurred expense or suffered pecuniary loss on behalf of an accident victim, or where the victim gratuitously rendered services to a Fatal Accidents Acts class of dependant prior to his injury, the victim will, under the Law Commission's draft Bill, be able to recover compensation in respect of these expenses or services, so long as they are reasonable, from the tortfeasor. It will be left to the plaintiff to distribute the amount recovered among these persons (see Chap. 12, p. 409).

14

Deliberate Interference with Interests in Trade or Business

We have seen (Chap. 3, p. 71) that, as a general rule negligently inflicted harm to economic interests is not recoverable in the law of tort. (Apart from the exceptional situations in Chap. 13, p. 423, *ante*, and Chap. 15, p. 499, *post*.) The pragmatic objections to a duty of care do not, however, apply to conduct which is specifically *aimed at* the plaintiff. Indeed, it was at one time suggested (p. 438, *post*) that intentionally inflicted harm is always tortious, unless justified. But this is not the rule of modern English law. Liability is limited to the following circumstances:

(1) Combination to inflict damage on the plaintiff rather than to serve the *bona fide* and legitimate interests of those who combine ("conspiracy to injure", cases in s. 1, p. 436, *post*);

(2) Direct inducement, knowingly, intentionally or recklessly, to breach a contract (s. 2, p. 453, *post*);

(3) An individual act or omission, threat (intimidation), or combination (conspiracy) which threatens to or does make use of unlawful means to interfere with economic interests of the plaintiff (s. 3, p. 474, *post*);

(4) Representations by a trader that the plaintiff is in some way associated with his business, goods or services, where the representation is calculated to deceive (s. 5, p. 487, *post*).

It will be observed that "conspiracy" may be of two kinds, either to injure (no unlawful means being necessary in this case) or to use or threaten unlawful means to cause loss. The tort which is sometimes called "indirect" inducement or procurement of breach of contract (*D. C. Thomson & Co.* v. *Deakin*, [1952] Ch. 646; [1952] 2 All E.R. 361, p. 459, *post*) belongs properly to the third category, although it is usually discussed in the second.

Although an intention to injure the plaintiff (or at least recklessness which is here bracketed with intention, p. 473, *post*) is required in the first three of these categories (and is useful evidence that there was, in fact, deception, in the fourth category), it is probably best to describe them all as instances of deliberate conduct, as distinct from negligent or unintentional conduct. J. A. Jolowicz, "The Law of Tort and Non-Physical Loss" (1972), 12 J.S.P.T.L. (N.S.) 91, at p. 99, describes these torts as fitting into a general category of liability for "premeditated" acts. This categorisation has the advantage of emphasising that it is the limits of the defendant's liberty to act in a manner detrimental to the interests of the plaintiff with which the court is concerned, rather than with the absorption of losses which have occurred. Indeed, it is the injunction to prevent the commission of these torts or their continuance which is usually the most important remedy which the plaintiff seeks. Rarely do these actions go to trial for the determination of liability and the assessment of damages. This introduces problems for an understanding of the legal rules, because the decisions are often simply provisional opinions expressed in *ex parte* applications for injunctions, and without full investigation of the facts.

Although these torts are primarily relevant to the protection of economic interests (and the fourth category, i.e. passing off, appears to be specifically limited to trade or business) there seems to be no reason in principle why the first three should not be extended to other intangible interests such as the alienation of affection. It is particularly interesting to observe how concepts such as "contract", "right" and "property" have been used to delimit the scope of the protected interests; and how ambiguous words such as "malice", "inducement" and "unlawful means" have been used to describe the conduct outlawed in various torts.

The history of these torts is closely connected to industrial conflict. A study of the special immunities which have been granted to persons acting "in contemplation or furtherance of an industrial dispute", and of the statutory "unfair industrial practices" (which are torts in everything but name), belongs to Labour Law, but for the sake of convenience the relevant statutory immunities are printed, without elaboration, in s. 4 of this Chapter.

These torts play an essentially residual role, in labour disputes and in the regulation of competition between traders, to statutory wrongs. They can, however, be independently studied as a fascinating example of the judicial process. By way of general introduction, the student will benefit from reading J. D. Heydon, *Economic Torts* (London, 1973) and K. W. Wedderburn, *The Worker and the Law*, 2nd Edn. (London, 1970), Chaps. 7 and 8.

1. CONSPIRACY

Mogul Steamship Company, Limited v. McGregor, Gow & Co.

Queen's Bench Division	(1888), 21 Q.B.D. 544
Court of Appeal	(1889), 23 Q.B.D. 598
[House of Lords	[1891–4] All E.R. Rep. 263]

The defendants, members of a shipping association, in order to secure a monopoly of the China seas trade for themselves, and with the intention of driving the plaintiffs, an outside shipping company, out of the business, gave a rebate to shippers who dealt exclusively with the association, prohibited any dealings by their agents with the plaintiffs, and cut their charges to a point where they took a loss. The plaintiffs were ruined.

In an action tried before Lord Coleridge C.J., without a jury, the plaintiffs claimed damages for a conspiracy to prevent them from carrying on their trade between London and China, and an injunction against the continuance of the alleged wrongful acts. The action was dismissed; subsequent appeals to the Court of Appeal and the House of Lords were unsuccessful.

LORD COLERIDGE C.J.: . . . It cannot be, nor indeed was it, denied that in order to found this action there must be an element of unlawfulness in the combination on which it is founded, and that this element of unlawfulness must exist alike whether the combination is the subject of an indictment or the subject of an action. But in an indictment it suffices if the combination exists and is unlawful, because it is the combination itself which is mischievous, and which gives the public an interest to interfere by indictment. Nothing need be actually done in furtherance of it. In the *Bridgewater Case*,[1] referred to at the bar, and in which I was counsel, nothing was done in fact; yet a gentleman was convicted because he had entered into an unlawful combination from which almost on the spot he withdrew, and withdrew altogether. No one was harmed, but the public offence was complete. This is in accordance with the express words of Bayley J. in *Rex* v. *de Berenger*.[2] It is otherwise in a civil action: it is the damage which results from the unlawful combination itself with which the civil action is concerned. It is not every combination which is unlawful, and if the combination is lawful, that is to say, is for a lawful end pursued by lawful means, or being unlawful there is no damage from it to the plaintiff, the action will not lie. In these last sentences damage means legal injury; mere loss or disadvantage will not sustain the action.

Once more, to state the proposition somewhat differently with a view to some of the arguments addressed to me, the law may be put thus. If the combination is unlawful, then the parties to it commit a misdemeanour, and are offenders against the State; and if, as the result of such unlawful combination and misdemeanour, a private person receives a private injury, that gives such person a right of private action.

It is, therefore, no doubt necessary to consider the object of the combination as well as the means employed to effect the object, in order to determine the legality or illegality of the combination. And in this case it is clear that if the object were unlawful, or if the object were lawful but the means employed to effect it were unlawful, and if there were a combination either to effect the unlawful object or to use the unlawful means, then the combination was unlawful, then those who formed it were misdemeanants, and a person injured by their misdemeanour has an action in respect of his injury. . . .

. . . I do not doubt the acts done by the defendants here, if done wrongfully and maliciously, or if done in furtherance of a wrongful and malicious combination, would be ground for an action on the case at the suit of one who suffered injury from them. The question comes at last to this, what was the character of these acts, and what was the motive of the defendants in doing them? The defendants are traders with enormous sums of money embarked in their adventures, and naturally and allowably desirous to reap a profit from their trade. They have a right to push their lawful trade by all lawful means. They have a right to endeavour by lawful means to keep their trade in their own hands and by the same means to exclude others from its benefits, if they can. Amongst lawful means is certainly included the inducing by profitable offers customers to deal with them rather than with their rivals. It follows that they may, if they think fit, endeavour to induce customers to deal with them exclusively by giving notice that only to exclusive customers will they give the advantage of their profitable offers. I do not think it matters that the withdrawal of the advantages is out of all proportion to the injury inflicted on those who withdraw them by the customers, who decline to deal exclusively with them, dealing with other traders. It is a bargain which persons in the position of the defendants here had a right to make, and those who are parties to the bargain must take it or leave it as a whole. Of coercion, of bribing, I see no evidence; of inducing, in the sense in which that word is used in the class of cases to which *Lumley* v. *Gye*[3] belongs, I see none either.

One word in passing only on the contention that this combination of the defendants was unlawful because it was in restraint of trade. It seems to me it was no more in restraint of trade, as that phrase is used for the purpose of avoiding contracts, than if

---

1. Unreported.
2. (1814), 3 M. & S. 67, at p. 76.
3. (1853), 2 E. & B. 216.

two tailors in a village agreed to give their customers five per cent. off their bills at Christmas on condition of their customers dealing with them and with them only. Restraint of trade, with deference, has in its legal sense nothing to do with this question.

But it is said that the motive of these acts was to ruin the plaintiffs, and that such a motive, it has been held, will render the combination itself wrongful and malicious, and that if damage has resulted to the plaintiffs an action will lie. I concede that if the premises are established the conclusion follows. It is too late to dispute, if I desired it, as I do not, that a wrongful and malicious combination to ruin a man in his trade may be ground for such an action as this. Was then this combination such? The answer to this question has given me much trouble, and I confess to the weakness of having long doubted and hesitated before I could make up my mind. There can be no doubt that the defendants were determined, if they could, to exclude the plaintiffs from this trade. Strong expressions were drawn from some of them in cross-examination, and the telegrams and letters shewed the importance they attached to the matter, their resolute purpose to exclude the plaintiffs if they could, and to do so without any consideration for the results to the plaintiffs, if they were successfully excluded. This, I think, is made out, and I think no more is made out than this. Is this enough? It must be remembered that all trade is and must be in a sense selfish; trade not being infinite, nay, the trade of a particular place or district being possibly very limited, what one man gains another loses. In the hand to hand war of commerce, as in the conflicts of public life, whether at the bar, in Parliament, in medicine, in engineering, (I give examples only,) men fight on without much thought of others, except a desire to excel or to defeat them. Very lofty minds, like Sir Philip Sidney with his cup of water, will not stoop to take an advantage, if they think another wants it more. Our age, in spite of high authority to the contrary, is not without its Sir Philip Sidneys; but these are counsels of perfection which it would be silly indeed to make the measure of the rough business of the world as pursued by ordinary men of business. The line is in words difficult to draw, but I cannot see that these defendants have in fact passed the line which separates the reasonable and legitimate selfishness of traders from wrong and malice. . . .

[The defendants appealed to the Court of Appeal.]

BOWEN L.J.: We are presented in this case with an apparent conflict or antinomy between two rights that are equally regarded by the law—the right of the plaintiffs to be protected in the legitimate exercise of their trade, and the right of the defendants to carry on their business as seems best to them, provided they commit no wrong to others. . . .

The English law, which in its earlier stages began with but an imperfect line of demarcation between torts and breaches of contract, presents us with no scientific analysis of the degree to which the intent to harm, or, in the language of the civil law, the animus vicino nocendi, may enter into or affect the conception of a personal wrong; see *Chasemore* v. *Richards*.[1] All personal wrong means the infringement of some personal right. "It is essential to an action in tort," say the Privy Council in *Rogers* v. *Dutt*,[2] "that the act complained of should under the circumstances be legally wrongful as regards the party complaining; that is, it must prejudicially affect him in some legal right; merely that it will, however directly, do a man harm in his interests, is not enough." What, then, were the rights of the plaintiffs as traders as against the defendants? The plaintiffs had a right to be protected against certain kind of conduct; and we have to consider what conduct would pass this legal line or boundary. Now, intentionally to do that which is calculated in the ordinary course of events to damage, and which does, in fact, damage another in that other person's property or trade, is actionable if done without just cause or excuse. Such intentional action when done without just cause or excuse is what the law calls a malicious wrong (see *Bromage* v.

---

1. (1859), H.L. Cas. 349, at p. 388.
2. (1860), 13 Moore, P.C. 209.

Prosser;[1] *Capital and Counties Bank* v. *Henty, per* Lord Blackburn[2]). The acts of the defendants which are complained of here were intentional, and were also calculated, no doubt, to do the plaintiffs damage in their trade. But in order to see whether they were wrongful we have still to discuss the question whether they were done without any just cause or excuse. Such just cause or excuse the defendants on their side assert to be found in their own positive right (subject to certain limitations) to carry on their own trade freely in the mode and manner that best suits them, and which they think best calculated to secure their own advantage.

What, then, are the limitations which the law imposes on a trader in the conduct of his business as between himself and other traders? There seem to be no burdens or restrictions in law upon a trader which arise merely from the fact that he is a trader, and which are not equally laid on all other subjects of the Crown. His right to trade freely is a right which the law recognises and encourages, but it is one which places him at no special disadvantage as compared with others. No man, whether trader or not, can, however, justify damaging another in his commercial business by fraud or mis-representation. Intimidation, obstruction, and molestation are forbidden; so is the intentional procurement of a violation of individual rights, contractual or other, assuming always that there is no just cause for it. The intentional driving away of customers by shew of violence: *Tarleton* v. *M'Gawley;*[3] the obstruction of actors on the stage by preconcerted hissing: *Clifford* v. *Brandon;*[4] *Gregory* v. *Brunswick;*[5] the disturbance of wild fowl in decoys by the firing of guns: *Carrington* v. *Taylor,*[6] and *Keeble* v. *Hickerin-gill;*[7] the impeding or threatening servants or workmen: *Garret* v. *Taylor;*[8] the inducing persons under personal contracts to break their contracts: *Bowen* v. *Hall;*[9] *Lumley* v. *Gye;*[10] all are instances of such forbidden acts. But the defendants have been guilty of none of these acts. They have done nothing more against the plaintiffs than pursue to the bitter end a war of competition waged in the interest of their own trade. To the argument that a competition so pursued ceases to have a just cause or excuse when there is ill-will or a personal intention to harm, it is sufficient to reply (as I have already pointed out) that there was here no personal intention to do any other or greater harm to the plaintiffs than such as was necessarily involved in the desire to attract to the defendants' ships the entire tea freights of the ports, a portion of which would other-wise have fallen to the plaintiffs' share. . . .

It is urged, however, on the part of the plaintiffs, that even if the acts complained of would not be wrongful had they been committed by a single individual, they become actionable when they are the result of concerted action among several. In other words, the plaintiffs, it is contended, have been injured by an illegal conspiracy. Of the general proposition, that certain kinds of conduct not criminal in any one individual may become criminal if done by combination among several, there can be no doubt. The distinction is based on sound reason, for a combination may make oppressive or dangerous that which if it proceeded only from a single person would be otherwise, and the very fact of the combination may shew that the object is simply to do harm, and not to exercise one's own just rights. In the application of this undoubted principle it is necessary to be very careful not to press the doctrine of illegal conspiracy beyond that which is necessary for the protection of individuals or of the public; and it may be observed in passing that as a rule it is the damage wrongfully done, and not the conspiracy, that is

---

1. (1825), 4 B. & C. 247.
2. (1882), 7 App. Cas. 741, at p. 772.
3. (1794), Peake, 270.
4. (1809), 2 Camp. 358.
5. (1843), 6 Man. & G. 205.
6. (1809), 11 East 571.
7. (1706), 11 East 574.
8. (1620), Cro. Jac. 567.
9. (1881), 6 Q.B.D. 333.
10. (1853), 2 E. & B. 216.

the gist of actions on the case for conspiracy: see *Skinner* v. *Gunton*;[1] *Hutchins* v. *Hutchins*.[2]. . .

FRY L.J.: . . . We have then to inquire whether mere competition, directed by one man against another, is ever unlawful. It was argued that the plaintiffs have a legal right to carry on their trade, and that to deprive them of that right by any means is a wrong. But the right of the plaintiffs to trade is not an absolute but a qualified right—a right conditioned by the like right in the defendants and all Her Majesty's subjects, and a right therefore to trade subject to competition. Now, I know no limits to the right of competition in the defendants—I mean, no limits in law. I am not speaking of morals or good manners. To draw a line between fair and unfair competition, between what is reasonable and unreasonable, passes the power of the courts. Competition exists when two or more persons seek to possess or to enjoy the same thing: it follows that the success of one must be the failure of another, and no principle of law enables us to interfere with or to moderate that success or that failure so long as it is due to mere competition. I say mere competition, for I do not doubt that it is unlawful and action-able for one man to interfere with another's trade by fraud or misrepresentation, or by molesting his customers, or those who would be his customers, whether by physical obstruction or moral intimidation. The cases of *Garret* v. *Taylor*;[3] *Tarleton* v. *M'Gawley*;[4] *Keeble* v. *Hickeringill*;[5] *Carrington* v. *Taylor*,[6] are all cases of interference by physical acts, driving away either the birds or the customers from the plaintiffs' places of business. Other cases were cited in which one man has persuaded another who is under some contract of service to a third to break that contract to the damage of such third person, and the persuasion has been held actionable. But no case has been or, I believe, can be cited where the only means used by the defendant to injure the plaintiff has been competition pure and simple. I think that if we were now to hold interference by mere competition unlawful, we should be laying down law both novel and at variance with that which modern legislation has shewn to be the present policy of the State. . . .

[LORD ESHER M.R. delivered a dissenting judgment in favour of allowing the appeal. A further appeal to the House of Lords was dismissed. The speeches of their Lordships, of similar effect to those in the courts below, are omitted.]

Notes

1. This is the first case to give direct support to the existence of a *tort* of conspiracy in *two* forms: (1) the "general" form, i.e. to effect an unlawful object by doing acts which are neither criminal nor tortious if done by an individual; and (2) the "narrow" form, i.e. to use "unlawful means". Earlier cases are equivocal because, arguably, the acts done would not have been unlawful if done by an individual, e.g.:

> *Macklin's Case* (1809), 2 Camp. 372 (famous comedian hissed off stage); like *Clifford* v. *Brandon* (1809), 2 Camp. 358 (actors rendered inaudible) this seems to have been a riot i.e. unlawful means were used. In *Gregory* v. *Duke of Brunswick* (1843), 6 Man. & G. 205 (actor hissed off stage) there was no evidence of conspiracy, see Newark (1959), U. Malaya L.J. 111.
> *Garret* v. *Taylor* (1620), Cro. Jac. 567 (threats of violence and vexatious litigation to force workmen not to work for plaintiff); *Keeble* v. *Hickeringill*

---

1. (1669), 1 Wms. Saund. 229.
2. 7 Hill's New York Cases 104; Bigelow's Leading Cases on Torts 207.
3. (1620), Cro. Jac. 567.
4. (1793), Peake 270.
5. (1706), 11 East 574 n.
6. (1809), 11 East 571.

(1706), 11 East 574 n. (intentional disturbance of wildfowl by firing gun); *Tarleton* v. *M'Gawley* (1793), Peake 270 (firing cannon at natives off coast of Africa causing them not to trade with plaintiff).

2. Is it *every* indictable criminal conspiracy that gives a private person who suffers damage a right of *civil* action? Consider, in particular, a conspiracy to effect a public mischief as in *R.* v. *Kamara* (1973), 2 All E.R. 1242; 57 Cr. App. R. 880. The Law Commission, Working Paper No. 50, *Inchoate Offences etc.* (1973), has proposed that the object of criminal conspiracy should be limited, by legislation, to the commission of substantive offences.

3. Does Bowen L.J.'s *dictum* that "intentionally to do that which is calculated in the ordinary course of events to do damage, and which does, in fact damage another in that person's property or trade, is actionable if done without just cause or excuse", represent the modern English law? See *Allen* v. *Flood* (next case).

Allen v. Flood

House of Lords   [1895–9] All E.R. Rep. 52

The plaintiffs, Flood and Taylor, were shipwrights. They were employed to repair the woodwork on the *Sam Weller*. Members of the Boilermakers' Society, who worked with iron, discovered that the plaintiffs had previously repaired ironwork on another ship. Allen, the district secretary of the Boilermakers' Society, told the employers that the boilermakers would not work if the plaintiffs were allowed to do so. As a result the plaintiffs were dismissed that same day. All the men were free to leave their employment at the end of each day and they had no right to re-engagement on the following day.

Kennedy J. ruled that there was no evidence of conspiracy or of intimidation or of coercion or of breach of contract. The jury found that Allen maliciously induced the employers to discharge the plaintiffs from their employment and not to re-engage them. He gave judgment for the plaintiffs for £20 each: [1895] 2 Q.B. 21.

The Court of Appeal affirmed that decision (Lord Esher M.R., Lopes and Rigby L.JJ.): [1895] 2 Q.B. 21. Allen appealed to the House of Lords. The case was argued for four days before Lord Halsbury L.C., Lords Watson, Herschell, Morris, Macnaghten, Davey and Shand. Eight judges were then summoned to attend (Hawkins, Mathew, Cave, North, Wills, Grantham, Lawrance and Wright JJ.) and the case was re-argued before all of them and, in addition, Lord Ashbourne and Lord James of Hereford. The judges were asked the question: "Assuming the evidence given by the [respondent's] witnesses to be correct, was there any evidence of a cause of action fit to be left to the jury?" By a majority of 6–2 the judges answered this in the affirmative. However, the House of Lords allowed the appeal by a majority of 6–3.

LORD WATSON: . . . Although the rule may be otherwise with regard to crimes, the law of England does not, according to my apprehension, take into account motive as constituting an element of civil wrong. Any invasion of the civil rights of another person is in itself a legal wrong, carrying with it liability to repair its necessary and natural consequences, in so far as these are injurious to the person whose right is infringed, whether the motive which prompted it be good, bad, or indifferent. But the existence of a bad motive, in the case of an act which is not in itself illegal, will not convert that act into a civil wrong, for which reparation is due. A wrongful act, done knowingly, and with a view to its injurious consequences, may, in the sense of law, be malicious; but such malice derives its essential character from the circumstance that the act done constitutes a violation of the law. . . . The root of the principle is that, in any legal question, malice depends not upon evil motive which influenced the mind of the actor, but upon the illegal character of the act which he contemplated and committed. In my opinion, it is alike consistent with reason and common sense that when the act done is, apart from the feelings which prompted it, legal, the civil law ought to take no cognisance of its motive. . . .

There are, in my opinion, two grounds only upon which a person who procures the act of another can be made legally responsible for its consequences. In the first place, he will incur liability if he knowingly, and for his own ends, induces that other person to commit an actionable wrong. In the second place, when the act induced is within the right of the immediate actor, and is, therefore, not wrongful in so far as he is concerned, it may yet be to the detriment of a third party, and, in that case, according to the law laid down by the majority in *Lumley* v. *Gye*,[1] the inducer may be held liable if he can be shown to have procured his object by the use of illegal means directed against that third party. . . .

The doctrine laid down by the Court of Appeal in this case and in *Temperton* v. *Russell*,[2] with regard to the efficacy of evil motives in making—to use the words of Lord Esher—"that unlawful which would otherwise be lawful," is stated in wide and comprehensive terms; but the majority of the consulted judges who approve of the doctrine have only dealt with it as applying to cases of interference with a man's trade or employment. Even in that more limited application, it would lead, in some cases, to singular results. One who committed an act not in itself illegal, but attended with consequences detrimental to several other persons, would incur liability to those of them whom it was proved that he intended to injure, and the rest of them would have no remedy. A master who dismissed a servant engaged from day to day, or whose contract of service had expired, and declined to give him further employment because he disliked the man, and desired to punish him, would be liable in an action for tort. And ex pari ratione, a servant would be liable in damages to a master whom he disliked, if he left his situation at the expiry of his engagement and declined to be re-engaged, in the knowledge and with the intent that the master would be put to considerable inconvenience, expense, and loss before he could provide a substitute. . . .

LORD HERSCHELL: . . . It is to be observed, in the first place, that the company in declining to employ the plaintiffs were violating no contract; they were doing nothing wrongful in the eye of the law. The course which they took was dictated by self-interest; they were anxious to avoid the inconvenience to their business which would ensue from a cessation of work on the part of the ironworkers. It was not contended at the Bar that merely to induce them to take this course would constitute a legal wrong, but it was said to do so because the person inducing them acted maliciously. Lord Esher M.R. declined in the present case to define what was meant by "maliciously"; he considered this a question to be determined by a jury. But if acts are, or are not, unlawful and actionable, according as this element of malice be present or absent, I think it essential to determine what is meant by it. I can imagine no greater danger to the community than that a jury should be at liberty to impose the penalty of paying damages for acts which are otherwise lawful because they choose, without any legal definition of the term, to say that they are malicious. No one would know what his rights were. The result would be to put all our actions at the mercy of a particular tribunal whose view of their propriety might differ from our own.

However malice may be defined, if motive be an ingredient of it, my sense of the danger would not be diminished. The danger is, I think, emphasised by the opinions of some of the learned judges. In a case to which I shall refer immediately, Lord Esher M.R. included within his definition of malicious acts persuasion used for the purpose "of benefiting the defendant at the expense of the plaintiff". Wills J. thinks this "going a great deal too far," and that whether the act complained of was malicious depends upon whether the defendant has, in pursuing his own interests, "done so by

---

1. (1853), 2 E. & B. 216; [1843–60] All E.R. Rep. 208.
2. [1893] 1 Q.B. 715; [1891–4] All E.R. Rep. 724.

such means and with such a disregard to his neighbour as no honest and fair-minded man ought to resort to". Here it will be seen that malice is not made dependent on motive. The assumed motive is a legitimate one, the pursuit of one's own interests. The malice depends on the means used and the disregard of one's neighbour, and the test of its existence is whether these are such as no honest and fair-minded man ought to resort to. There is here room for infinite differences of opinion. Some, I daresay, applying this test, would consider that a strike by workmen at a time damaging to the employer or a "lock-out" by an employer at a time of special hardship to the workmen were such means and exhibited such a disregard of his neighbour as an honest and fair-minded man ought not to resort to. Others would be of the contrary opinion. The truth is that this suggested test makes men's responsibility for their actions depend on the fluctuating opinions of the tribunal before whom the case may chance to come as to what a right-minded man ought or ought not to do in pursuing his own interests. Again, Cave J. expressed the view that the action of the appellant might have been justified on the principles of trade competition if it had been confined to the time when the men were doing iron work, but that it "was without just cause or excuse, and consequently malicious", inasmuch as the respondents were not at the time engaged upon iron work. On the other hand, it is evident, from the reasoning of some of the learned judges who think the respondents entitled to succeed, that they would not be prepared to adopt this distinction, and would regard the act as "malicious" in either case. . . .

In *Temperton* v. *Russell*,[1] the further step was taken by the majority of the court—A. L. Smith L.J. reserving his opinion on the point—of asserting that it was immaterial that the act induced was not the breach of a contract, but only the not entering into a contract, provided that the motive of desiring to injure the plaintiff, or to benefit the defendant at the expense of the plaintiff, was present. It seems to have been regarded as only a small step from the one decision to the other, and it was said that there seemed to be no good reason why, if an action lay for maliciously inducing a breach of contract, it should not equally lie for maliciously inducing a person not to enter into a contract. So far from thinking it a small step from the one decision to the other, I think there is a chasm between them. The reason for a distinction between the two cases appears to me to be this: that in the one case the act procured was the violation of a legal right, for which the person doing the act which injured the plaintiff could be sued, as well as the person who procured it, while in the other case, as no legal right was violated by the person who did the act from which the plaintiff suffered, he would not be liable to be sued in respect of the act done, while the person who induced him to do the act would be liable to an action. I think this was an entirely new departure. . . .

It has recently been held in this House in *Bradford Corpn.* v. *Pickles*[2] that acts done by the defendant upon his own land were not actionable when they were within his legal rights, even though his motive were to prejudice his neighbour. The language of the noble and learned Lords was distinct. Lord Halsbury said ([1895] A.C. at p. 594):

> "This is not a case where the state of mind of the person doing the act can affect the right. If it was a lawful act, however ill the motive be, he had a right to do it. If it was an unlawful act, however good the motive might be, he would have no right to do it."

The statement was confined to the class of case then before the House, but I apprehend that what was said is not applicable only to rights of property, but is equally applicable to the exercise by an individual of his other rights. . . .

I think these considerations (subject to a point which I will presently discuss) sufficient to show that the present action cannot be maintained. It is said that the statement that the defendant would call men out, if made, was a threat. It is this aspect of the case which has obviously greatly influenced some of the learned judges. Hawkins J. says that the defendant without excuse or justification

---

1. [1893] 1 Q.B. 715; [1891–4] All E.R. Rep. 724.
2. [1895] A.C. 587.

"wilfully, unlawfully, unjustly, and tyrannically invaded the plaintiffs' right by intimidating and coercing their employers to deprive them of their present and future employment,"

and that the plaintiffs are, therefore, entitled to maintain this action. But "excuse or justification" is only needed where an act is prima facie wrongful. Whether the defendant's act was so is the matter to be determined. To say that the defendant acted "unlawfully", is, with all respect, to beg the question which is whether he did so or not? To describe his acts as unjust and tyrannical proves nothing, for these epithets may be, and are, in popular language constantly applied to acts which are within a man's rights, and unquestionably lawful. In my opinion, these epithets do not advance us a step towards the answer to the question which has to be solved.

The proposition is, therefore, reduced to this, that the appellant invaded the plaintiffs' right by intimidating and coercing their employers. In another passage, in his opinion, the learned judge says that there is no authority for the proposition that to render threats, menaces, intimidation, or coercion available as elements in a cause of action, they must be of such a character as to create fear of personal violence. I quite agree with this. The threat of violence to property is equally a threat in the eye of the law. And many other instances might be given. On the other hand, it is undeniable that the terms "threat", "coercion", and even "intimidation" are often applied in popular language to utterances which are quite lawful and give rise to no liability either civil or criminal. They mean no more than this, that the so-called threat puts pressure, perhaps extreme pressure, on the person to whom it is addressed, to take a particular course. Of this again, numberless instances might be given. Even then, if it can be said without abuse of language that the employers were "intimidated and coerced" by the appellant, even if this be in a certain sense true, it by no means follows that he committed a wrong or is under any legal liability for his act. Everything depends on the nature of the representation or statement by which the pressure was exercised. The law cannot regard the act differently because you choose to call it a threat or coercion instead of an intimation or warning. . . .

The object which the appellant and the iron workers had in view was that they should be freed from the presence of men with whom they disliked working, or to prevent what they deemed an unfair interference with their rights by men who did not belong to their craft doing the work to which they had been trained. Whether we approve or disapprove of such attempted trade restrictions, it was entirely within the right of the iron workers to take any steps, not unlawful, to prevent any of the work which they regarded as legitimately theirs being intrusted to other hands.

Some stress was laid in the court below upon the fact that the plaintiffs were not at the time in question engaged upon iron work, although immediately before that time they had been so employed elsewhere. This, it was said, showed that the motive of the defendant and the iron workers was the "punishment" of the plaintiffs for what they had previously done. I think that the use of the word "punishment" has proved misleading. That word does not necessarily imply that vengeance is being wreaked for an act already done, though no doubt it is sometimes used in that sense. When a court of justice, for example, awards punishment for a breach of the law, the object is not vengeance. The purpose is to deter the person who has broken the law from a repetition of his act, and to deter other persons also from committing similar breaches of the law. In the present case it was admitted that the defendants had no personal spite against the plaintiffs. His object was, at the utmost, to prevent them in the future from doing work which he thought was not within their province, but within that of the iron workers. If he had acted in exactly the same manner as he did at a time when the plaintiffs were engaged upon iron work, his motive would have been precisely the same as it was in the present case, and the result to the plaintiffs would have been in nowise different. I am unable to see, then, that there is any difference either in point of ethics or law between the two cases. The iron workers were no more bound to work with those whose presence was disagreeable to them than the plaintiffs were bound to refuse to work because they found that this was the case. The object which the defendant and those whom he represented had in view throughout was what they believed to be the interest of the class to which they belonged. The step taken was a means to that end. The act which caused the damage to the plaintiffs was that of the iron company in refusing to employ them. The company would not subordinate their own interests to the plaintiffs. It is conceded that they could take this course with impunity. Why, then, should the defendant be liable because he did not subordinate the interests of those he represented to the plaintiffs? Self-interest dictated alike the act of those who caused the damage and the act which is found to have induced them to cause it. . . .

[LORDS MACNAGHTEN, SHAND, DAVEY and JAMES OF HEREFORD delivered speeches in favour of reversing the Court of Appeal's decision and dismissing the action; LORD HALSBURY L.C. and LORDS ASHBOURNE and MORRIS dissented. The appeal was dismissed.]

Notes

1. The principle established in this case has not been followed in America: e.g. *Tuttle* v. *Buck* (1909), 119 N.W. 946 (rival barber shop set up by individual with sole purpose of driving plaintiff out of village, held actionable in tort). See, Morris D. Forkosch (1957), 42 Cornell L.Q. 465; Note (1964), 77 Harv. L.R. 888; W. E. Shipley (1967), 16 A.L.R. (3d) 1191 (a full guide to the U.S. decisions).

2. Do you agree with J. D. Heydon, *Economic Torts* (London, 1973), p. 24, that "a legal system which lacks [a doctrine that malevolent action by one alone is tortious] seems deficient"? If a person has a right to do a lawful act, however ill his motive may be, why is a *conspiracy* tortious if the real purpose is the inflicting of damage as distinct from serving the legitimate purposes of those who combine? Compare, too, the defence of justification as expounded by Lord Denning M.R. in *Morgan* v. *Fry*, [1968] 2 Q.B. 710; [1968] 3 All E.R. 452 and *Cory Lighterage, Ltd.* v. *Transport and General Workers' Union*, [1973] 2 All E.R. 558 (p. 481, *post*).

3. The Race Relations Act 1968, s. 19, allows the Race Relations Board to bring civil proceedings in a specially designated county court for damages and certain other relief in respect of the statutory tort of unlawful racial discrimination. Would this statutory tort have been necessary had *Allen* v. *Flood* been decided in the way favoured by the minority in the House of Lords? (See A. Lester and G. Bindman, *Race and Law* (London, 1972), p. 37, and B. Hepple, *Race, Jobs and the Law in Britain*, 2nd Edn. (London, 1970), p. 234.)

Vegelahn v. Guntner

Supreme Judicial Court of Massachussetts.   (1896), 44 N.E. 1077

HOLMES J. (dissenting): . . . It is plain from the slightest consideration of practical affairs, or the most superficial reading of industrial history, that free competition means combination, and that the organisation of the world, now going on so fast, means an ever-increasing might and scope of combination. It seems to me futile to set our faces against this tendency. Whether beneficial on the whole, as I think it, or detrimental, it is inevitable, unless the fundamental axioms of society, and even the fundamental conditions of life, are to be changed.

One of the eternal conflicts out of which life is made up is that between the effort of every man to get the most he can for his services, and that of society, disguised under the name of capital, to get his services for the least possible return. Combination on the one side is patent and powerful. Combination on the other is the necessary and desirable counterpart, if the battle is to be carried on in a fair and equal way. . . .

Crofter Hand Woven Harris Tweed Co. v. Veitch

House of Lords   [1942] I All E.R. 142

The pursuers marketed cloth woven by crofters on the Isle of Lewis in the Outer Hebrides, using yarn imported from the mainland. Yarn was also produced in spinning mills on the Island and this was woven by the crofters into cloth and sold under the Harris Tweed mark. Most of the spinners in the island mills belonged to the Transport & General Workers' Union. Officials of the union asked for higher wages for mill workers but this was refused on the ground that an increase in costs would prevent the mill owners from competing with the pursuers and other firms on the island, who were importing yarn. To overcome this objection the defenders, officials of the union, instructed their members, who were dockers at Stornaway, the principal port on the island, not to handle yarn consigned to the pursuers or unfinished cloth despatched by them to the mainland. The embargo on the cloth was subsequently lifted. The pursuers sought an interdict (i.e. injunction) to prevent the continuing embargo on the yarn.

The Lord Ordinary recalled the interim interdict, and the Court of Session, Second Division (Lord Mackay dissenting) affirmed the decision: 1940 S.C. 141. An appeal by the pursuers to the House of Lords was dismissed.

LORD WRIGHT: . . . The cause of action set out in the appellants' claim is for a conspiracy to injure, which is a tort. The classical definition of conspiracy is that given by Willes J. in advising the House of Lords in *Mulcahy* v. R.,[1] at p. 317:

"A conspiracy consists not merely in the intention of two or more, but in the agreement of two or more to do an unlawful act, or to do a lawful act by unlawful means."

This must be supplemented by observing that, though the crime is constituted by the agreement, the civil right of action is not complete unless the conspirators do acts in pursuance of their agreement to the damage of the plaintiffs.

The question is, then, what the unlawful acts were with which the respondents were charged, or what the unlawful means were which they employed to do acts otherwise lawful. In other words, what is the legal right of the appellants which is infringed, or what is the legal wrong committed by the respondents? The concept of a civil conspiracy to injure has been in the main developed in the course of the last half-century, particularly since *Mogul S.S. Co.* v. *McGregor, Gow & Co.*[2] Its essential character is described by Lord Macnaghten in *Quinn* v. *Leathem*,[3] at p. 510, basing himself on the words of Lord Watson in *Allen* v. *Flood*,[4] at p. 108:

". . . a conspiracy to injure might give rise to civil liability even though the end were brought about by conduct and acts which by themselves and apart from the element of combination or concerted action could not be regarded as a legal wrong."

In this sense, the conspiracy is the gist of the wrong, though damage is necessary to complete the cause of action. . . . The rule may seem anomalous, so far as it holds that conduct by two may be actionable if it causes damage, whereas the same conduct done by one, causing the same damage, would give no redress. In effect, the plaintiff's right is that he should not be damnified by a conspiracy to injure him, and it is in the fact of the conspiracy that the unlawfulness resides. It is a different matter if the conspiracy is to do acts in themselves wrongful, as to deceive or defraud, to commit violence, or to conduct a strike or lock-out by means of conduct prohibited by the Conspiracy and

1. (1868), L.R. 3 H.L. 306.
2. [1892] A.C. 25.
3. [1901] A.C. 495.
4. [1898] A.C. 1.

Protection of Property Act 1875, or which contravenes the Trade Disputes and Trade Unions Act 1927. A conspiracy to injure, however, is a tort which requires careful definition, in order to hold the balance between the defendant's right to exercise his lawful rights and the plaintiff's right not to be injured by an injurious conspiracy. As I read the authorities, there is a clear and definite distinction which runs through them all between what Lord Dunedin in *Sorrell* v. *Smith*,[1] at p. 730, calls "a conspiracy to injure" and "a set of acts dictated by business interests". I should qualify "business" by adding "or other legitimate interests", using the convenient adjective not very precisely. It may be a difficult task in some cases to apply this distinction. It depends largely on matters of fact, but also on a legal conception of what is meant by "intention to injure". The appellants contend that there was here an intention to injure, even though it is negatived that the respondents were actuated by malice or malevolence. In substance, what the appellants say is that the issue between the millowners and the yarn importers was one between two sets of employers, in which the men were not directly concerned, that the union's action was an unjustifiable and meddlesome interference with the appellants' right to conduct their own businesses as they pleased, and that the union were pushing into matters which did not concern them. The appellants further say, as I understand their case, that this unjustifiable intrusion was due to the union's desire to secure the assistance of the millowners towards the union's object, which was to get 100 *per cent.* membership in the textile workers, and thus there was no common object among the two main parties to the combination. Each set had its own selfish object. In effect, it was said, the union were bribed by the millowners to victimise the appellants in their trade by the promise of help in the matter of the union membership, which was entirely foreign to the question of the importation of yarn. These considerations, it was said, constituted "malice" in law, even if there was no malevolence, and prevented the respondents from justifying the injury which they wilfully did to the appellants' trade, because they could not assert any legitimate interest of their union which was relevant to the action taken. Actual malevolence or spite was, it was said, not essential. There was no genuine intention to promote union interests by the stoppage of importation. The interference with the appellants' trade by stopping import of yarn was wilful and ultroneous action on the part of the union, supported by no relevant union interest. It was malicious or wrongful because it was intentionally and unjustifiably mischievous, even though not malevolent.

Before I refer to the authorities, there are some preliminary observations which I desire to make. I shall avoid the use of what Bowen L.J. in the *Mogul* case[2] described as the "slippery" word "malice" except in quotations. When I want to express spite or ill will, I shall use the word "malevolence". When I want to express merely intentional tortious conduct, I shall use the word "wrongful". As the claim is for a tort, it is necessary to ascertain what constitutes the tort alleged. It cannot be merely that the appellants' right to freedom in conducting their trade has been interfered with. That right is not absolute or unconditional. It is only a particular aspect of the citizen's right to personal freedom, and, like other aspects of that right, is qualified by various legal limitations, either by statute or by common law. Such limitations are inevitable in organised societies, where the rights of individuals may clash. In commercial affairs, each trader's rights are qualified by the right of others to compete. Where the rights of labour are concerned, the rights of the employer are conditioned by the rights of the men to give or withold their services. The right of workmen to strike is an essential element in the principle of collective bargaining. . . .

It is thus clear that employers of workmen, or those who, like the appellants, depend in part on the services of workmen, have in the conduct of their affairs to reckon with this freedom of the men, and to realise that the exercise of the men's rights may involve some limitation on their own freedom in the management of their business. Such

1. [1925] A.C. 700.
2. [1892] A.C. 1.

interference with a person's business, so long as the limitations enforced by law are not contravened, involves no legal wrong against the person. In the present case, the respondents are sued for imposing the "embargo", which corresponds to calling out the men on strike. The dockers were free to obey or not to obey the call to refuse to handle the appellants' goods. In refusing to handle the goods, they did not commit any breach of contract with anyone. They were merely exercising their own rights. However, there might be circumstances which rendered the action wrongful. The men might be called out in breach of their contracts with their employer, and that would be clearly a wrongful act as against the employer, and an interference with his contractual right, for which damages could be claimed, not only as against the contract-breaker, but also against the person who counselled or procured or advised the breach. This is the principle laid down in *Lumley* v. *Gye*[1] which Lord Macnaghten in *Quinn* v. *Leathem*,[2] defined to be that [p. 510]:

"... a violation of legal right committed knowingly is a cause of action and ... it is a violation of legal right to interfere with contractual relations recognised by law if there be no sufficient justification for the interference."

That is something substantially different from a mere interference with a person's qualified right to exercise his free will in conducting his trade. A legal right was violated and needed justification, if it could be justified. This distinction was drawn by the majority of the Lords in *Allen* v. *Flood*,[3] who disapproved of the *dicta* in *Bowen* v. *Hall*[4] and *Temperton* v. *Russell*[5] that every person who persuades another not to enter into a contract with a third person may be sued by that third person, if the object is to benefit himself at the expense of such person. However, in *Allen* v. *Flood*,[3] this House was considering a case of an individual actor, where the element of combination was absent. In that case, it was held, the motive of the defendant is immaterial. Damage done intentionally, and even malevolently, to another thus, it was held, gives no cause of action so long as no legal right of the other is infringed. That I take to be the English rule laid down by this House in *Bradford Corpn.* v. *Pickles*[6] and in *Allen* v. *Flood*,[3] though in *Sorrell* v. *Smith*,[7] at p. 713, Lord Cave L.C. doubts the proposition, and says that in general what is unlawful in two is not lawful in one. This, however, seems to be inconsistent with the express rulings in *Allen* v. *Flood*.[3] Though eminent authorities have protested against the principle, it must, I think, be accepted at present as the law in England. The precise issue does not arise in this case, which is concerned with combination or conspiracy. I need not consider whether any qualification may hereafter be found admissible.

Thus, for the purposes of the present case, we reach the position that, apart from combination, no wrong would have been committed. There was no coercion of the dockers. There were no threats to them. They were legally free to choose the alternative course which they preferred. In *Quinn* v. *Leathem*,[2] a wide meaning was given to words like "threats", "intimidation" or "coercion", especially by Lord Lindley, but that was not the *ratio decidendi* adopted by the House. These words, as pointed out in *Wright on Criminal Conspiracy*, are not terms of art and are consistent with either legality or illegality. They are not correctly used in the circumstances of a case like this. In *Allen* v. *Flood*,[3] *Ware & De Freville, Ltd.* v. *Motor Trade Association*[8] and *Sorrell* v. *Smith*,[7] a more accurate definition was given. I should also refer to the admirable discussion by Peterson J. in *Hodges* v. *Webb*.[9] There is nothing unlawful in giving a

1. (1853), 2 E. & B. 216.
2. [1901] A.C. 495.
3. [1898] A.C. 1.
4. (1881), 6 Q.B.D. 333.
5. [1893] 1 Q.B. 715.
6. [1895] A.C. 587.
7. [1925] A.C. 700.
8. [1921] 3 K.B. 40.
9. [1920] 2 Ch. 70.

warning or intimation that, if the party addressed pursues a certain line of conduct, others may act in a manner which he will not like and which will be prejudicial to his interests, so long as nothing unlawful is threatened or done. In the words of Lord Buckmaster in *Sorrell* v. *Smith*,[1] at p. 747:

> "A threat to do an act which is lawful cannot, in my opinion, create a cause of action whether the act threatened is to be done by many or by one.

No doubt the use of illegal threats or the exercise of unlawful coercion would create by itself a cause of action, but there was nothing of the sort in this case.

The only way in this case in which the appellants can establish a cause of action in tort is by establishing that there was a conspiracy to injure, which would take the case out of the general ruling in *Allen* v. *Flood*[2] and bring it within the exception there reserved by Lord Herschell, at pp. 123, 124:

> "It is certainly a general rule of our law that an act *prima facie* lawful is not unlawful and actionable on account of the motive which dictated it. I put aside the case of conspiracy which is anomalous in more than one respect."

In the same case, Lord Watson made a similar reservation, at p. 108. Lord Macnaghten, at p. 153, said that the decision in *Allen* v. *Flood*[2] could have no bearing on any case which involved the element of oppressive combination. These reservations were acted upon in *Quinn* v. *Leathem*,[3] to which I shall refer later. That the decision in that case turned on conspiracy cannot now be doubted, especially after *Ware & De Freville, Ltd.* v. *Motor Trade Association*[4] and *Sorrell* v. *Smith*.[1]

The distinction between conduct by one man and conduct by two or more may be difficult to justify. Lord Sumner in *Sorrell* v. *Smith*[1] puts the very artificial case of the owner of a large business who gave a small share to a partner and "conspired" with him. For practical purposes, the position there is the same as if he had remained a sole trader. The fact that the sole trader employed servants or agents in the conduct of his business would not, in my opinion, make these others co-conspirators with him. The special rule relating to the effect of a combination has been explained on the ground that it is easier to resist one than two. That may appear to be true if a crude illustration is taken, such as the case of two men attacking another, but even there it would not always be true—for instance, if the one man was very strong and the two were very weak—and the power of a big corporation or trader may be greater than that of a large number of smaller fry in the trade. This explanation of the rule is not very satisfactory. The rule has been explained on grounds of public policy. The common law may have taken the view that there is always the danger that any combination may be oppressive, and may have thought that a general rule against injurious combinations was desirable on broad grounds of policy. Again, any combination to injure involves an element of deliberate concert between individuals to do harm. Whatever the moral or logical or sociological justification, the rule is as well established in English law as I here take to be the rule that motive is immaterial in regard to the lawful act of an individual, a rule which has been strongly criticised by some high legal authorities, who would solve the apparent antinomy by holding that deliberate action causing injury is actionable whether done by one or by several.

A conspiracy to injure involves *ex vi termini* an intention to injure, or, more accurately, a common intention and agreement to injure. Both "intention" and "injure" need definition. The word "injure" is here used in its correct meaning of "wrongful harm", *damnum cum injuria*, not *damnum absque injuria*. That obviously raises the question of when the harm is wrongful. "Intention" is generally determined by reference to overt acts and to the circumstances in which they are done. . . .

. . . On principle, I am of the opinion that malevolence is no more essential to the

---

1. [1925] A.C. 700.
2. [1898] A.C. 1.
3. [1901] A.C. 495.
4. [1921] 3 K.B. 40.

intent to injure, the *mens rea*, than it is to the intent to deceive. On practical grounds, also I prefer that view. To leave to a jury to decide on the basis of an internal mental state, rather than on the facts from which intent is to be inferred, may be to leave the issue in the hands of the jury as clay to mould at their will. After all, the plaintiff has to prove actual damage, which can only result from things done. Mere malevolence does not damage anyone. I cannot see how the pursuit of a legitimate practical object can be vitiated by glee at the adversary's expected discomfiture. Such glee, however deplorable, cannot affect the practical result. I may add that a desire to injure does not necessarily involve malevolence. It may be motivated by wantonness or some object not justifiable.

As to the authorities, the balance, in my opinion, is in favour of the view that malevolence as a mental state is not the test. I accordingly agree with the appellants' contention that they are not concluded by the finding that the respondents were not malevolent. It thus becomes necessary to consider the further arguments on which the appellants base their claim to succeed. I approach the question on the assumption that the appellants have to prove that they have been damnified by tortious action. They do not prove that by showing that they have been harmed by acts done by the respondents in combination, these acts being, apart from any question of combination, otherwise within the respondents' rights. It is not, then, for the respondents to justify these acts. The appellants must establish that they have been damnified by a conspiracy to injure— that is, that there was a wilful and concerted intention to injure without just cause and consequent damage. That was the view accepted by Lord Dunedin and Lord Buck-master in *Sorrell's* case.[1] Lord Sumner proposes the question without deciding it, but the form in which he states it seems to me to suggest the answer. It is not a question of onus of proof. It depends on the cause of action. The plaintiff has to prove the wrong-fulness of the defendant's object. Of course, malevolence may be evidence tending to exclude a legitimate object or to establish a wrongful object. . . .

The respondents had no quarrel with the yarn importers. Their sole object, the courts below have held, was to promote their union's interests by promoting the interest of the industry on which the men's wages depended. On these findings, with which I agree, it could not be said that their combination was without sufficient justification. Nor would this conclusion be vitiated, even though their motives may have been mixed, so long as the real or predominant object, if they had more than one object, was not wrongful. Nor is the objection tenable that the respondent's real or predominant object was to secure the employer's help to get 100 *per cent.* membership of the union among the textile workers. Cases of mixed motives, or, as I should prefer to say, of the presence of more than one object, are not uncommon. If so, it is for the jury or judge of fact to decide which is the predominant object, as it may be assumed the jury did in *Quinn's* case,[2] when they decided on the basis that the object of the combiners was vindictive punishment, and not their own practical advantage. . . .

I may here note that the doctrine of civil conspiracy to injure extends beyond trade competition and labour disputes. *Thompson* v. *British Medical Association* (*N.S.W. Branch*)[3] shows that it may extend to the affairs of a profession, as was expressly stated in that case, at p. 771, in the judgment of the Privy Council. By way of contrast, *Gregory* v. *Duke of Brunswick*[4] may be regarded as a striking illustration of what might be held to constitute a conspiracy to injure. What was alleged was a conspiracy to hiss an actor off the stage in order to ruin him. To what legitimate interests other than those mentioned the general doctrine may extend I do not here seek to define, since beyond question it extends to the present case, whether the object of the action were the prosperity of the industry or the obtaining of 100 *per cent.* membership. The objects or purposes for which combinations may be formed, however, are clearly of great variety. It must be left to the future to decide, on the facts of the particular case, subject to the general

1. [1925] A.C. 700.
2. [1901] A.C. 495.
3. [1924] A.C. 764.
4. (1844), 6 Man. & G. 953.

doctrine, whether any combination is such as to give rise to a claim for a conspiracy to injure.

If, however, the object of securing 100 *per cent.* union membership were operative in inducing the respondents to combine with the employers, it was relied on by the appellants on other grounds as vitiating the combination. It was objected that there could be no combination between the employers and the union, because their respective interests were necessarily opposed. I think that that is a fallacious contention. It is true that employers and workmen are often at variance because the special interest of each side conflicts in the material respect, as, for instance, in questions of wages, conditions of hours of work, exclusion of non-union labour, but, apart from these differences in interest, both employers and workmen have a common interest in the prosperity of their industry, though the interest of one side may be in profits and of the other in wages. Hence a wider and truer view is that there is a community of interest. That view was acted upon in the present case in regard to the essential matter of yarn importation. As to the separate matter of the union membership, while that was something regarded as important by the respondents, it was probably regarded by the employers as a matter of indifference to them. It was, in any case, a side issue in the combination, even from the respondents' point of view. I may add that I do not accept as a general proposition that there must be complete identity of interest between parties to a combination. There must, however, be sufficient identity of object though the advantage to be derived from that same object may not be the same.

The appellants have further contended that the "deal" referred to in the respondent Veitch's letter was a bargain by which the union sold to the employers the dockers' aid in return for the employers' aid in regard to union membership. In other words, the contention was that the respondents or the union were bribed, and were mercenaries, and not interested in the embargo except for the reward, which was in its nature unrelated to the embargo. The facts, however, were not as the contention assumes, so I need not discuss whether a party to a combination whose interest was merely separate and mercenary could ever be held to have a legitimate interest or justification for harm done in pursuance of the combination. I need merely add a few words on the objection that the embargo was the act of the dockers for the benefit, not of themselves, but of the textile workers. It is enough to say that both sections were members of the union, and there was, in my opinion, a sufficient community of interest, even if the matter is regarded from the standpoint of the men, as individuals, and not from the standpoint of the respondents, who were the only parties sued. Their interest, however, was to promote the advantage of the union as a whole. In my opinion, the judgment appealed from should be affirmed and the appeal dismissed.

[VISCOUNT SIMON L.C., VISCOUNT MAUGHAM, LORD THANKERTON and LORD PORTER delivered speeches in favour of dismissing the appeal.]

Notes

1. In *Huntley* v. *Thornton*, [1957] 1 All E.R. 234, the plaintiff had been prevented from obtaining work by a district committee of the Amalgamated Engineering Union because he had failed to participate in an official union strike, and had shown an "arrogant attitude" to the committee at a disciplinary meeting, by describing the committee as a "shower". The Executive Committee of the union refused to countenance his expulsion, but the local boycott continued. Harman J. held that the plaintiff was entitled to damages of £500, and he was granted leave to apply for an injunction in the event of renewed victimisation, because "the district committee had entirely lost sight of what the interests of the union demanded and thought only of their own ruffled dignity . . . It had become a question of the committee's prestige . . " It was also held that they were not entitled to the benefit of the statutory immunity

against tort liability in trade disputes because they had not acted in *furtherance* of such a dispute. Two officials who had helped to implement the boycott were not liable because, being ignorant of the background to the dispute between the plaintiff and the committee, they had acted in what they sincerely believed to be the best interests of the union.

2. In *Scala Ballroom (Wolverhampton), Ltd.* v. *Ratcliffe*, [1958] 3 All E.R. 220 (C.A.) the defendants were officials of the Musicians' Union who had organised a boycott of the plaintiff's ballroom in protest against a colour bar operated there. The plaintiffs were refused an interlocutory injunction on the ground that no cause of action had been made out. The Court of Appeal held that the objects of the combination were legitimate, particularly in the light of an affidavit by one official in which he referred to the "insidious effects" of a colour bar imposed on the audience because "it is impossible for musicians to insulate themselves from their audience". Hodson L.J. said that legitimate interests were not to be confused with those which can be exchanged for cash. Morris L.J. said that so long as the defendants honestly believed a certain policy to be desirable, even though it could not be translated into financial terms, there was no conspiracy to injure.

O. Kahn-Freund (1959), 22 M.L.R. 69 comments: "The line which separates lawful from unlawful action does not run between the markets of commodities or services and the labour market, but between a 'policy of interest' and a 'policy of prestige'." Does the decision mean that a boycott against members of a particular religion would not be tortious? Compare *Sweeney* v. *Coote*, [1907] A.C. 221 (for a fuller exposition of the facts, see [1906] I.R. 51–126) in which an action alleging conspiracy by Protestant parents who withdrew their children from the school of a Catholic schoolmistress, with the alleged purpose of having her dismissed from her post, failed. Earl Halsbury L.C. (at p. 223) said: "If the object [was] . . . to cause her to be dismissed, not upon any ground of personal objection to her, or any spite or ill-will to her, but upon the ground that in the view of the parents . . . it was an undesirable thing for a Roman Catholic to be put into that position, I am of opinion that there would be no ground of action." But in the *Crofters'* case (above) Lord Maugham said: "If the object of the combination is dislike of the religious views or the politics or the race or the colour of the plaintiff or a mere demonstration of power by busybodies . . . there is no authority that [such] a combination . . . would be lawful." (See B. Hepple, *Race, Jobs and the Law in Britain*, 2nd Edn., p. 246; Lester and Bindman, *Race and Law*, p. 53; Heydon, *Economic Torts*, pp. 16–17.)

3. In *Temperton* v. *Russell*, [1893] I Q.B. 715 (C.A.) trade union officials who prevented the formation of a building contract were held liable on the grounds of "malicious" conspiracy to injure. (For another aspect of this case see the note, p. 456, *post*.) In *Midland Cold Storage, Ltd.* v. *Steer*, [1972] 3 All E.R. 941, at p. 953, Megarry J. suggested that the case was correctly decided on that ground. In view of the background to the dispute—the employer's non-compliance with a trade union demand—can the decision stand in the light of the *Crofters'* case?

McKernan v. Fraser

High Court of Australia   (1932), 38 A.L.R. 113

EVATT J.: . . . Take the following illustration:—A, B, C, D, E and F agree to inflict damage on X. A and B agree, because they desire to protect the standards of the professional body to which A, B, C, D, E and F all belong, and have no other object or motive. C and D wish to revenge themselves on X for some personal quarrel, concealing this motive from the other parties to the agreement and from each other. E and F act from mixed motives; they genuinely wish to maintain the professional ideals of their body, but they also have a strong dislike to X and it can truly be said that they are gratifying it when they enter into the agreement.

In such case, the only state of mind which is common to A, B, C, D, E and F is the immediate intention or purpose of inflicting damage upon X. But there are the other facts mentioned. Who is liable for conspiracy to injure? In my opinion A and B, not knowing of the malicious motives animating C and D, or the strong dislike felt to X by E and F, are not liable. C, D, E and F are not the agents of A and B so as to alter the nature and character, the object or motive, of the common agreement.

The example presented by the position of E and F is typical of these group activities. But it is convenient first to examine the question of liability in C and D. Each has agreed with five others, and each is inspired by personal malice. But the fact of the existence of such malice is not made known by either to the other, and it is also unknown to the other parties to the agreement. It is not possible to say that C and D alone are liable for conspiracy to injure, except on the basis that there has been an agreement come to by them alone. But the only agreement entered into, has six parties, not two. The position might be different, if it could be shown that C and D, for the purpose of satisfying their hatred of X, agreed between themselves to procure acts to be done by A, B, E, F, and themselves all in association, for the purpose of causing harm to X. Such agreement would be a separate conspiracy to injure, carried out by using the other persons as instruments for effectuating their own design. In such a case C and D would be liable. But, in the absence of such a separate agreement between them, the uncommunicated existence of an evil motive in each towards X, would not make themselves alone liable to X. . . .

Upon the same footing, E and F would not be liable, because no separate understanding between them is shown. . . .

2. INDUCING BREACH OF CONTRACT

Lumley v. Gye

Court of Queen's Bench   [1843–60] All E.R. Rep. 208

CROMPTON J.: The declaration in this case consisted of three counts. The two first stated a contract between the plaintiff, the proprietor of the Queen's Theatre, and Miss Wagner, for the performance by her for a period of three months at the plaintiff's theatre; and it then stated that the defendant, knowing the premises and with a malicious intention, while the agreement was in full force and before the expiration of the period for which Miss Wagner was engaged, wrongfully and maliciously enticed and procured Miss Wagner to refuse to sing or perform at the theatre and to depart from and abandon her contract with the plaintiff and all service thereunder, whereby Miss Wagner wrongfully, during the full period of the engagement, refused and made default in performing at the theatre. Special damage arising from the breach of Miss Wagner's engagement was then stated. The third count stated that Miss Wagner had been hired and engaged by the plaintiff, then being the owner of the Queen's Theatre, to perform at the theatre for a specified period as the dramatic artiste of the plaintiff for reward to her in that behalf, and had become and was such dramatic artiste for the plaintiff at his theatre for profit to the plaintiff in that behalf, and that the defendant, well knowing the premises and with a malicious intention, while Miss Wagner was such artiste of the plaintiff, wrongfully and maliciously enticed and procured her, so being such artiste of the plaintiff, to depart from and out of the employment of the plaintiff, whereby she wrongfully departed from and out of the service and employ-ment of the plaintiff, and remained and continued absent from such service and employment until the expiration of her said hiring and engagement to the plaintiff by effluxion of time. Special damage arising from the breach of Miss Wagner's engagement was then stated. To this declaration the defendant demurred, and the question for our decision is whether all or any of the counts are good in substance.

The effect of the two first counts is that a person under a binding contract to perform at a theatre is induced by the malicious act of the defendant to refuse to perform and entirely abandon her contract, whereby damage arises to the plaintiff, the proprietor of the theatre. The third count differs in stating expressly that the performer had agreed to perform as the dramatic artiste of the plaintiff, and had become and was the dramatic artiste of the plaintiff for reward to her, and that the defendant maliciously procured her to depart out of the employment of the plaintiff as such dramatic artiste, whereby she did depart out of the employment and service of the plaintiff, whereby damage was suffered by the plaintiff. It was said, in support of the demurrer, that it did not appear in the declaration that the relation of master and servant ever subsisted between the plaintiff and Miss Wagner; that Miss Wagner was not averred, especially in the two first counts, to have entered upon the service of the plaintiff; and that the engagement of a theatrical performer, even if the performer has entered upon the duties, is not of such a nature as to make the performer a servant within the rule of law which gives an action to the master for the wrongful enticing away of his servant. It was laid down broadly, as a general proposition of law, that no action will lie for procuring a person to break a contract, although such procuring is with a malicious intention and causes great and immediate injury. The law as to enticing servants was said to be contrary to the general rule and principle of law, to be anomalous, and probably to have had its origin from the state of society when serfdom existed and to be founded upon, or upon the equity of, the Statute of Labourers. It was said that it would be dangerous to hold that an action was maintainable for persuading a third party to break a contract unless some boundary or limits could be pointed out; that the remedy for enticing away servants was confined to cases where the relation of master and servant, in a strict sense, subsisted between the parties; and that, in all other cases of contract, the only remedy was against the party breaking the contract.

Whatever may have been the origin or foundation of the law as to enticing of servants, and whether it be, as contended by the plaintiff, an instance and branch of a wider rule, or, as contended by the defendant, an anomaly and an exception from the general rule of law on such subjects, it must now be considered clear law that a person who wrongfully and maliciously, or, which is the same thing, with notice, interrupts the relation subsisting between master and servant by procuring the servant to depart from the master's service, or by harbouring and keeping him as servant after he has quitted it and during the time stipulated for as the period of service, whereby the master is injured, commits a wrongful act for which he is responsible at law. I think that the rule applies wherever the wrongful interruption operates to prevent the service during the time for which the parties have contracted that the service shall continue, and I think that the relation of master and servant subsists, sufficiently for the purpose of such action, during the time for which there is in existence a binding contract of hiring and service between the parties. I think that it is a fanciful and technical and unjust distinction to say that the not having actually entered into the service, or that the service is not actually continuing, can make any difference. The wrong and injury are surely the same whether the wrongdoer entices away the gardener, who has hired himself for a year, the night before he is to go to his work, or after he has planted the first cabbage on the first morning of his service. I should be sorry to support a distinction so unjust, and so repugnant to common sense, unless bound to do so by some rule or authority of law plainly showing that such distinction exists. . . .

The objection as to the actual employment not having commenced would not apply in the present case to the third count, which states that Miss Wagner had become the artiste of the plaintiff and that the defendant had induced her to depart from the employment. But it was further said that the engagement, employment, or service, in the present case was not of such a nature as to constitute the relation of master and servant, so as to warrant the application of the usual rule of law giving a remedy in case of enticing away servants. The nature of the injury and of the damage being the same, and the supposed right of action being in strict analogy to the ordinary case of master and servant, I see no reason for confining the case to services or engagements under contracts for services of any particular description; and I think that the remedy, in the absence of any legal reason to the contrary, may well apply to all cases where there is an unlawful and malicious enticing away of any person employed to give his personal labour or service for a given time under the direction of a master or employer who is injured by the wrongful act, more especially when the party is bound to give such personal services exclusively to the master or employer though I by no means say that the service need be exclusive. . . .

In deciding this case on the narrower ground, I wish by no means to be considered as deciding that the larger ground taken by counsel for the plaintiff is not tenable, or as saying that in no case except that of master and servant is an action maintainable for maliciously inducing another to break a contract to the injury of the person with whom such contract has been made. It does not appear to me to be a sound answer to say that the [actionable] act in such cases is the act of the party who breaks the contract, for that reason would apply in the acknowledged case of master and servant. Nor is it an answer to say that there is a remedy against the contractor and that the party relies on the contract, for, besides that reason also applying to the case of master and servant, the action on the contract and the action against the malicious wrongdoer may be for a different matter, and the damages payable for such malicious injury might be calculated on a very different principle from the amount of the debt which might be the only sum recoverable on the contract. Suppose a trader, with a malicious intent to ruin a rival trader, goes to a banker or other party who owes money to his rival, and begs him not to pay the money which he owes him, and by that means ruins or greatly prejudices the party. I am by no means prepared to say that an action could not be maintained, and that damages, beyond the amount of the debt if the injury were great, or much less than such amount if the injury were less serious, might not be recovered. Where two or more parties were concerned in inflicting such injury, an indictment, or a writ of conspiracy at common law, might, perhaps, have been maintainable. Where a writ of conspiracy would lie for an injury inflicted by two, an action on the case in the nature of conspiracy will generally lie, and in such an action on the case the plaintiff is entitled to recover against one defendant without proof of any conspiracy, the malicious injury and not the conspiracy being the gist of the action: see note (4) to *Skinner* v. *Gunton*, 1 Wms. Saund. at p. 230. In this class of cases it must be assumed that it is the malicious act of the defendant, and that malicious act only, which causes the servant or contractor not to perform the work or contract which he would otherwise have done. The servant or contractor may be utterly unable to pay for anything like the amount of the damage sustained entirely from the wrongful act of the defendant, and it would seem unjust, and contrary to the general principles of law, if such a wrongdoer were not responsible for the damage caused by his wrongful and malicious act. . . .

ERLE J.: . . . It is clear that the procurement of the violation of a right is a cause of action in all instances where the violation is an actionable wrong, as in violations of a right to property, whether real or personal, or to personal security. He who procures the wrong is a joint wrongdoer, and may be sued, either alone or jointly with the agent, in the appropriate action for the wrong complained of. Where a right to the performance of a contract has been violated by a breach thereof, the remedy is upon the contract against the contracting party. If he is made to indemnify for such breach, no further recourse is allowed, and, as in case of the procurement of a breach of contract the action is for a wrong and cannot be joined with the action on the contract, and as the act itself is not likely to be of frequent occurrence nor easy of proof, therefore, the action for this wrong, in respect of other contracts than those of hiring, are not numerous, but still they seem to me sufficient to show that the principle has been recognised. . . .

This principle is supported by good reason. He who maliciously procures a damage to another by violation of his right ought to be made to indemnify, and that whether he procures an actionable wrong or a breach of contract. He who procures the non-delivery of goods according to contract may inflict an injury, the same as he who procures the abstraction of goods after delivery, and both ought on the same ground to be made responsible. The remedy on the contract may be inadequate, as where the measures of damages is restricted; or in the case of non-payment of a debt where the damage may be bankruptcy to the creditor who is disappointed, but the measure of damages against the debtor is interest only; or, in the case of the non-delivery of the goods, the disappointment may lead to a heavy forfeiture under a contract to complete a work within a time, but the measure of damages against the vendor of the goods for non-delivery may be only the difference between the contract price and the market value of the goods in question at the time of the breach. In such cases, he who procures the damage maliciously might justly be made responsible beyond the liability of the contractor. . . .

[WIGHTMAN J. delivered a judgment agreeing with CROMPTON J.; COLERIDGE J. dissented.]

Notes

1. *Bowen* v. *Hall* (1881), 6 Q.B.D. 333 (C.A.), was the next case of inducing breach of contract to reach an appellate court. An expert bricklayer had been induced to leave his employer's service by a rival firm. As in *Lumley* v. *Gye*, the relationship of master and servant, in the strict sense, did not exist. The Court of Appeal (Lord Selborne L.C. and Brett L.J.; Lord Coleridge C.J. dissenting) allowed the plaintiff employer an action. The majority took the view that *Lumley* v. *Gye* had been correctly decided on the wide ground stated by Erle J., i.e. the *malicious* violation of contractual rights. However, in *Quinn* v. *Leathem*, [1901] A.C. 495, at p. 510, Lord Macnaghten said: "I think the decision [in *Lumley* v. *Gye*] was right, not on the ground of malicious intention—that was not, I think the gist of the action, but on the ground that a violation of a legal right committed knowingly is a cause of action, and that it is a violation of a legal right to interfere with contractual relations recognised by law if there be no sufficient justification for the interference."

2. In *Temperton* v. *Russell*, [1893] 1 Q.B. 715 (C.A.) three trade unions were in dispute with a firm of builders in Hull. In order to put pressure on the firm the unions sought to interrupt supplies of building materials by requesting the plaintiff to cease making deliveries. When he refused, union officials induced other builders who had entered into contracts with the plaintiff to break their contracts and not to enter into further contracts with him, by threatening them with labour troubles. The plaintiff suffered damage in consequence. The Court of Appeal held that there was an action for inducing breach of *commercial* contracts, and not only contracts for personal services.

South Wales Miners' Federation v. Glamorgan Coal Co., Ltd.

House of Lords   [1904–7] All E.R. Rep. 211

The Miners' Federation had ordered a number of stop-days. Bigham J. held that in doing so the Federation and the members of its executive had been actuated by an honest desire to forward the interests of the men without any prospect of personal gain to themselves and without any intention, malicious or otherwise, to injure the plaintiffs, who were colliery owners. The object had been to restrict output so as to keep up coal prices because, under the sliding scale agreement between the colliery owners and the miners, wages depended upon the selling price of coal. It was not disputed that the federation had induced and procured workmen who were employed by plaintiffs to break their contracts of service, so inflicting loss on the plaintiffs. It was argued, however, that the wrong was justifiable in the circumstances. The Court of Appeal held that it was not, [1903] 2 K.B. 545. An appeal to the House of Lords was dismissed.

LORD MACNAGHTEN: . . . That there may be a justification for that which in itself is an actionable wrong I do not for a moment doubt; and I do not think that it would be difficult to give instances, putting aside altogether cases complicated by the introduction of moral considerations. But what is the alleged justification in the present case? It was said that the council, the executive of the federation, had a duty cast upon them to protect the interests of the members of the union, and that they could not be made legally responsible for the consequences of their action if they acted honestly in good faith and without any sinister or indirect motive. The case was argued with equal candour and ability. But it seems to me that the argument may be disposed of by two simple questions. How was the duty created? What in fact was the alleged duty? The alleged duty was created by the members of the union themselves, who elected or appointed the officials of the union to guide and direct their action; and then it was contended that the body to whom the members of the union have thus committed their individual freedom of action are not responsible for what they do, if they act according to their honest judgment in furtherance of what they consider to be the interest of their constituents. It seems to me that if that plea were admitted there would be an end of all responsibility. It would be idle to sue the workmen, the individual wrongdoers, even if it were practicable to do so. Their counsellors and protectors, the real authors of the mischief, would be safe from legal proceedings. The only other question is, What is the alleged duty set up by the federation? I do not think that it can be better described than it was by counsel for the plaintiffs. It comes to this: it is the duty on all proper occasions, of which the federation or their officials are to be the sole judges, to counsel and procure a breach of duty. . . .

LORD JAMES OF HEREFORD: . . . It yet remains to deal with the words "wrongfully and maliciously" as averred in the statement of claim. As to the word "wrongfully", I think that no difficulty arises. If the breach of the contract of service by the workmen was an unlawful act, any one who induces and procures the workmen, without just cause and excuse, to break such contract also acts unlawfully, and thus the allegation that the act done was wrongfully done is established. But the word "maliciously" has also to be dealt with. The judgment of Bigham J. ([1903] 1 K.B. at p. 133), proceeds on the ground that

> "to support an action for procuring a breach of contract it is essential to prove actual malice."

I cannot concur in this view of the law. The word "maliciously" is often employed in criminal and civil pleadings without proof of actual malice, apart from the commission of the act complained of, being required. If A. utters a slander of B., even if he be a stranger to him, the averment that A. maliciously spoke such words of B. is established by simply proving the uttering of words taken to be false until the contrary be proved. In such an action the word "maliciously" may be treated either as an unnecessary averment or as being proved by inference drawn from the proof of the act being wrongfully committed. . . .

LORD LINDLEY: . . . The constitution of the union may have rendered it the duty of the officials to advise the men what could be legally done to protect their own interests, but a legal duty to do what is illegal and known so to be is a contradiction in terms. A similar argument was urged without success in *Read* v. *Friendly Society of Operative Stonemasons.*[1] Then your Lordships were invited to say that there was a moral or social

---

1. [1902] 2 K.B. 732.

duty on the part of the officials to do what they did, and that, as they acted bona fide in the interests of the men and without any ill-will to the employers, their conduct was justifiable; and your Lordships were asked to treat this case as if it were like a case of libel or slander on a privileged occasion. This contention was not based on authority, and its only merits are its novelty and ingenuity. The analogy is, in my opinion, misleading; and to give effect to this contention would be to legislate and introduce an entirely new law and not to expound the law as it is at present. It would be to render many acts lawful which, as the law stands, are clearly unlawful. I have purposely abstained from using the word "malice". Bearing in mind that malice may or may not be used to denote ill-will, and that in legal language presumptive or implied malice is distinguished from express malice, it conduces to clearness in discussing such cases as these to drop the word "malice" altogether and to substitute for it the meaning which is really intended to be conveyed by it. Its use may be necessary in drawing indictments; but when all that is meant by malice is an intention to commit an unlawful act, and to exclude all spite or ill-feeling, it is better to drop the word and so avoid all misunderstanding. The appeal ought to be dismissed with costs.

[EARL HALSBURY L.C. delivered a speech in favour of dismissing the appeal.]

Brimelow v. Casson

Chancery Division   [1923] All E.R. Rep. 40

The defendants were representatives of five associations formed for the protection of persons engaged in the theatrical profession. They induced the manager of a theatre to break a contract by which he had engaged the plaintiff's theatrical company to perform at the theatre. They had done this because the plaintiff paid chorus girls a wage considerably below the minimum wage approved by the associations with the result that some of the girls were obliged to supplement their wages by resorting to prostitution. In an action by the plaintiff for an injunction and damages:

RUSSELL J.: . . . In these circumstances, have the defendants justification for their acts? That they would have the sympathy and support of decent men and women I can have no doubt. But have they in law justification for those acts? As has been pointed out, no general rule can be laid down as a general guide in such cases, but I confess that, if justification does not exist here, I can hardly conceive the case in which it would be present. These defendants, as it seems to me, owed a duty to their calling and to its members (and I am tempted to add to the public) to take all necessary peaceful steps to terminate the payment of this insufficient wage which in the plaintiff's company had apparently been in fact productive of those results which their past experience had led them to anticipate. "The good sense" of this tribunal leads me to decide that in the circumstances of the present case justification did exist. . . .

Action dismissed

Notes

1. Is *Brimelow v. Casson* consistent with the *South Wales Miners'* case? Does the maxim *ex turpi causa non oritur actio* provide an explanation, as Simonds J. suggested in *Camden Nominees, Ltd. v. Forcey*, [1940] Ch. 352, at p. 366?

2. Why were the combinations of shipping companies in the *Mogul* case (p. 436, *ante*) and of employers and trade union in the *Crofter's* case (p. 446, *ante*) allowed to justify their actions, but not the South Wales Miners' Federation? For general discussion of the defence of justification see J. D. Heydon, "The Defence of Justification in Cases of Intentionally Caused Loss" (1970), 20 Univ. Tor. L.J. 139, at pp. 161–171; and in *Economic Torts*, pp. 32–39. An earlier but still useful discussion of principle is to be found in Charles E. Carpenter (1928), 41 Harv. L.R. 728, at pp. 745 *et seq.*

3. Some examples of the successful invocation of the defence of justification are:

(a) A licensing authority, acting under statutory powers, bans as objectionable a film, so causing a breach of the contract to display it: *Stott v. Gamble,* [1916] 2 K.B. 504.

(b) The promotor of a play (an "angel") induces the dismissal of a bad actress to protect his investment in the success of the play: *Knapp v. Penfield* (1932), 256 N.Y.S. 41; but presumably the *South Wales* case would lead to a different answer for English law?

(c) A trade union induces an employer to break a contract of employment with an individual employer so as to comply with the terms of a prior contract with the union: suggested, *obiter,* by Darling J. in *Read v. Friendly Operative Society of Stonemasons of England,* [1902] 2 K.B. 88, at p. 96; left open by Stirling L.J. on appeal (*ibid.,* p. 742) but denied by Collins M.R. (*ibid.,* p. 737). But the defendant may not induce breach of a contract between the plaintiff and the middleman in retaliation for breach of a prior contract between the plaintiff and defendant: *Smithies v. National Association of Operative Plasterers,* [1909] 1 K.B. 310 (C.A.); *Camden Nominees, Ltd. v. Forcey,* [1940] Ch. 352, at p. 365 (inducing tenants to withhold rents in retaliation for landlord's breach of convenants not justified).

(d) Inducing breach of the employment contract of a broker's man in order to promote reputable financial dealings on the Stock Exchange: *Posluns v. Toronto Stock Exchange and Gardiner* (1964), 46 D.L.R. (2d) 210 (Ont.).

4. The absence of any common law defence of justification in respect of trade union activities resulted in the enactment of a statutory immunity for inducing breach of contract. The Trade Disputes Act 1906, s. 3 (first limb) limited this to contracts of employment (so excluding, for example, "labour-only" contracts: *Emerald Construction Co., Ltd. v. Lowthian,* [1966] 1 All E.R. 1013, p. 473, *post*). The Industrial Relations Act 1971, s. 132 (1), *post,* extends this to the breach of *any* contract provided the act is done "in contemplation or furtherance of an industrial dispute". In New Zealand, in *Pete's Towing Services, Ltd. v. Northern Industrial Union of Workers,* [1970] N.Z.L.R. 32, the common law defence of justification was allowed, where a trade union defendant was found to be putting forward "fair conditions" and the inducement was "not being used as a sword to procure financial betterment but as a shield to avoid involvement in industrial discord" (*per* Speight J., at p. 51). Grunfeld (1971), 34 M.L.R. 181, at p. 185 submits, in the light of this decision, that while the defence of justification is barred in economic disputes (*South Wales Miners' Federation* case, p. 456, *ante*) it is not in labour disputes of "principle" (e.g. about recognition of a union, bona fide compliance with an agreed disputes procedure, or tolerating a breakaway union). See further *Morgan v. Fry,* [1968] 2 Q.B. 710; [1968] 3 All E.R. 452 (defence of justification for tort of intimidation, p. 480, *post*).

D. C. Thomson & Co., Ltd. v. Deakin

Court of Appeal   [1952] 2 All E.R. 361

The plaintiffs, a firm of printers and publishers, maintained a non-union shop. They dismissed a man belonging to a union, whereupon a number of unions organised a boycott. Drivers and loaders employed by Bowaters, who supplied paper to the plaintiffs, expressed reluctance to load or deliver paper to the plaintiffs. Bowaters, not wishing to become involved in the dispute, refrained from ordering any of their employees to do so. The result was that no further supplies were taken to plaintiff's premises. Bowaters wrote to plaintiffs informing them that they had been prevented from performing their contract to supply paper by union action. Plaintiffs issued a writ and sought an inter-locutory injunction to restrain the defendant union officials from procuring any breach of Bowaters' contract with the plaintiffs. Upjohn J. refused to grant an injunction on the ground that there never was any direct action by the defendants with the object of persuading Bowaters to break an existing contract with the plaintiffs. An appeal to the Court of Appeal was dismissed on other grounds.

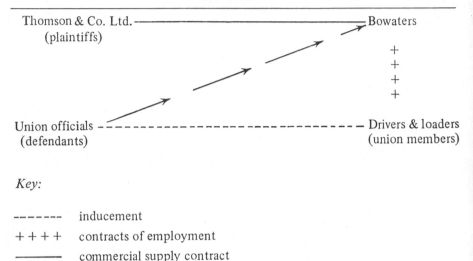

Key:

-------   inducement

+ + + +   contracts of employment

———————   commercial supply contract

→ →   notice of embargo

SIR R. EVERSHED M.R.: . . . It was suggested in the course of argument that the tort must still be properly confined to such direct intervention, i.e., to cases where the intervener or persuader uses by personal intervention persuasion on the mind of one of the parties to the contract so as to procure that party to break it. I am unable to agree that any such limitation is logical, rational or part of our law. In such cases where the intervener (if I may call him such) does so directly act on the mind of a party to the contract as to cause him to break it, the result is, for practical purposes, as though in substance he, the intervener, is breaking the contract, although he is not a party to it. . . .

So far I have considered only the case in which the intervener directly acts himself, either by persuasion or by some wrongful act of his own. What is the situation if he attains the same result, indirectly, by bringing his persuasion or procuration to bear on some third party, commonly a servant of the contracting party, but possibly an in-dependent third person? In my judgment, it is reasonably plain (and the result, as it seems to me, would otherwise be highly illogical and irrational) that, if the act which the third party is persuaded to do is itself an unlawful act or a wrongful act (including in that phrase a breach of contract) and the other elements are present (viz., knowledge and intention to do the damage which is in fact suffered), then the result is the same and the intervener or procurer will be liable for the loss or damage which the injured party sustains. . . .

I have, however, come to the conclusion that the result is otherwise where the persons induced, being third parties, servants or otherwise, are induced to do acts which are in themselves lawful and involve no breach of contract on their part with the contracting party. I think that, if the matter is examined, any other view involves so serious an inroad on the principles of the law that I cannot persuade myself that, from so casual a beginning as would otherwise be the case, that has now to be taken as established as the law. In the course of the reply of counsel for the plaintiffs, I put to him an instance to which I venture to return. It may be useful, since, at any rate, it is quite free from any complication such as may arise from industrial relationships. My instance was of a contract between A and B, whereby A had contracted to sell his house to B at a price beneficial to A. I will assume that it had been disclosed by A to B that there was in fact a public right of way passing close to the property, but that B had been informed, correctly, that the use of such right of way had become so slender that it was of little, if any practical significance. Then let it be supposed that some third party, desiring to cause B to resile from the contract with A and to lose for A the benefit of the contract, persuaded a number of individuals in the neighbourhood to resume the use of the right of way, so that there then passed near the premises a considerable stream of persons, all legitimately using the right of way as such, as a result of which B decided that the amentiites of the premises were so damaged that he was no longer willing to continue. I find it exceedingly difficult to suppose that, the exercise of the right of way by the persons persuaded being lawful, the intervener would be liable according to the principles of the law for having persuaded them to do that lawful thing. The persons using it might or might not themselves have been innocent of any desire to cause damage to A. They might be innocent of any knowledge of the existence of a contract between A and B. If they were so innocent, they themselves would, in my view, clearly not be under any liability, but, if they knew of the existence of a contract and intended to cause its breach, another question might arise (and this is a matter to which I shall have later to return) whether they would in any circumstances be themselves liable. Another instance may be quoted which was taken by Jenkins L.J. earlier in the case. Let it be supposed that A had made a contract to supply certain goods to B and that the intervener, knowing of the contract and intending to deprive B of its benefit, had proceeded to go into the market and buy up all the goods that he could find of that character, so as to render it impossible for A in fact to perform the contract. Again, I think it is impossible to say, according to the principles of our law, that the intervener in such a case was acting tortiously. . . .

I come then to such formulation of the result as seems to me to be correct, but I should first add this. The argument that this tort should be confined to such direct intervention or interference as is illustrated, for example, in *Lumley* v. *Gye*[1] introduces this strange difficulty. A limited liability company, a persona ficta, can only act through agents or servants. If the intervention has to be of so direct a kind, it would obviously create strange problems in the case of a limited liability company. No doubt, if I approach some person in the company who has authority on the company's behalf to make contracts, I may be said to be approaching the company direct. But I think that the illustration of the company emphasises the anomaly which would result if in the case of a limited company a tortious act were only committed if the person approached or induced had a particular office or responsibility (actual or perhaps ostensible) in the company. But dealing, first, with individual contractors, it seems to me that the intervener, assuming in all cases that he knows of the contract and acts with the aim and object of procuring its breach to the damage of B, one of the contracting parties, will be liable not only (i) if he directly intervenes by persuading A to break it, but also (ii) if he intervenes by the commission of some act wrongful in itself so as to prevent A from in fact performing his contract, and also (iii) if he persuades a third party, for example, a servant of A, to do an act in itself wrongful or not legitimate (as committing a breach of a contract of service with A) so as to render, as was intended, impossible A's performance of his contract with B. In the case of a company, the approach to or the persuasion of a managing director, or of some person having like authority, may be regarded as being

---

1. (1853), 2 E. & B. 216.

in all respects equivalent to the direct approach of the individual contractor, as found in *Lumley* v. *Gye*[1] and in the *Glamorgan*[2] case, but, if the approach is made to other servants of the company, the case, in my view, becomes parallel to an approach made, not to the contracting party himself, but to some servant of the contracting party, so that the intervener will only be liable if the act which he procures the servant to do is either a breach of contract towards the servant's master or is otherwise tortious in itself. . . .

[His Lordship continued:] As to the whole of the defendants, it follows, accordingly, from what I have said that, in my judgment, there is not on this motion proved any procuring of any wrongful act by any member of any of the unions concerned. I need only add that on the evidence there was no breach of contract by any workmen, since Bowaters, for reasons which, I doubt not, were prudent, took the line that they would not order any man either to load or to deliver paper for the plaintiffs. They accepted the situation as they found it, and, again I doubt not prudently, made no attempt to contrive to get the paper to the plaintiffs by any other means. It is true, if my analysis is correct, that there was in the case of the first three defendants what might be called a direct approach to Bowaters, but, so far as I understand the evidence, I cannot see that that direct approach amounted to anything more than a statement of the facts as the members of the union understood them to be. In particular, there was a reference to picketing, which was obviously of great significance, and, whether that reference was correct or incorrect, there is no suggestion that it was not made in the bona fide belief of its truth. I appreciate that in these matters there is a difficult question of distinguishing between what might be called persuasion and what might be called advice, meaning by the latter a mere statement of, or drawing of the attention of the party addressed to the state of facts as they were. In *Camden Nominees* v. *Forcey*,[3] it was held that the advice given was of such a character that it was obviously intended to be acted on and so for all practical purposes was equivalent to persuasion. But, if the matter be advice merely (in the ordinary sense of that word), it seems to me that there can be no complaint about it, nor do I think that counsel for the plaintiffs can derive any substantial assistance by saying that Bowaters proved themselves merely chicken-hearted. The ease with which a person may be persuaded is not a relevant consideration in determining whether the persuader was wrongful in what he was doing. That may, as a general proposition, be true, but in this case it seems to me, as I have already more than once indicated, that the evidence on this motion, whatever may emerge when the matter is fully investigated, falls short of any proof of what is required to constitute a cause of action such as would entitle the plaintiffs to an injunction. Put another way, I cannot see that the evidence establishes that there was anything done by Bowaters vis-à-vis the plaintiffs which is fairly attributable to any such pressure, persuasion or procuration on the part of any of these defendants as would in any event cause them to be liable in tort. . . .

[JENKINS and MORRIS L.JJ. delivered judgments in favour of dismissing the appeal.]

J. T. Stratford & Son, Ltd. v. Lindley

House of Lords   [1964] 3 All E.R. 102

The firm of Bowker & King, Ltd. had consistently refused to recognise the Watermen's Union, but had come to an agreement with the Transport & General Workers' Union, to which forty-five of its forty-eight employees belonged. The defendants, officials of the Watermen's Union, decided to put pressure on Jack Stratford, chairman of Bowker & King, Ltd. and also chairman of the plaintiff company. They instructed their members, who were employed by the owners and hirers of barges to refuse to take barges to the plaintiff company for repair or to return barges hired out to customers by that company. This brought plaintiff's trade to a standstill. The plaintiff company, claiming that it was losing £1,000 a week while the embargo continued, brought an

1. (1853), 2 E. & B. 216.
2. [1905] A.C. 239.
3. [1940] Ch. 352; [1940] 2 All E.R. 1.

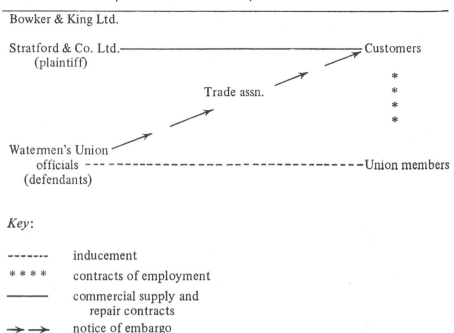

Bowker & King Ltd.

Stratford & Co. Ltd.————————————————→Customers
　　(plaintiff)

　　　　　　　　　　　　　Trade assn.

Watermen's Union
　　officials ----------------------------------Union members
　　(defendants)

Key:

-------	inducement
* * * *	contracts of employment
————	commercial supply and repair contracts
→　→	notice of embargo

action and was granted an interlocutory injunction. This was discharged by the Court of Appeal, [1965] A.C. 269. The plaintiff company's appeal to the House of Lords was allowed.

LORD REID: . . . I do not think that there is any *prima facie* case of conspiracy, because I find nothing in the evidence to indicate that the executive committee or the respondents acted from any motive other than to forward what they believed to be the interests of their union and fundamental trade union principles.

The next question is whether the principle of *Lumley* v. *Gye*[1] has any application. I think that it has. The respondents acted with the intention of preventing barges out on hire from being returned to the appellants, and those barges were in fact immobilised so that they could not be returned. The respondents knew that barges were always returned promptly on the completion of the job for which they had been hired, and it must have been obvious to them that this was done under contracts between the appellants and the barge hirers. It was argued that there was no evidence that they were sufficiently aware of the terms of these contracts to know that their interference would involve breaches of these contracts; but I think that at this stage it is reasonable to infer that they did know that. So I need not consider whether or how far the principle of *Lumley* v. *Gye*[1] covers deliberate and direct interference with the execution of a contract without that causing any breach.

In addition to interfering with existing contracts the respondents' action made it practically impossible for the appellants to do any new business with the barge-hirers. It was not disputed that such interference with business is tortious, if any unlawful means are employed. It was made clear to the barge-hirers that if they ordered their men to handle barges affected by the embargo the men would refuse to obey. If such refusal would have been in breach of the men's contracts of service, then inducing them to break their contracts would be using unlawful means. In the ordinary case of a contract of service, if, before he is engaged, the workman says that he is not prepared to do certain work which is normally done by men in his position and then the

1. (1853), 2 E. & B. 216.

employer simply engages him, I do not think that it would be possible thereafter for the employer to order him to do that work, and, when he refused, to contend that he was in breach of his contract of service. The present case is complicated, however, by the operation of the Dock Workers (Regulation of Employment) Scheme 1947. I shall not attempt to decide the precise effect of that scheme, but broadly the position appears to be that dock workers form a pool and are employed by the Dock Labour Board except when they are allocated to employers. Normally they appear to be engaged by the day. The board shall "be deemed to act as agent for the employer . . ." (Sch. para. 6 (1) (e) (ii)) and the men are bound to "accept any employment in connexion with dock work . . ." (para. 8 (4) (b)). So there appear to be good grounds for saying that a man working under the scheme is not free to make his own contract with his employer, and, even if I assume that members of the respondents' union had made it clear to the board and to the employers that they would refuse to do certain work, it may well be that by accepting the day's work to which he is allocated a man becomes bound to obey all lawful orders, including orders to do the work which he has said that he will refuse to do. That appears to have been the respondents' view. On 8 November 1963, Mr. Lindley wrote to the Dock Labour Board asking that, if any member should be reported for refusing to accept orders contrary to union instructions, the report should be dealt with under procedure laid down in the Ammon Report. The board agreed to that request but I am unable at this stage to determine what was the legal effect of that. Accordingly I am of opinion that the appellants have made a *prima facie* case that the respondents threatened to induce the men of their union to break their contracts and thereby threatened to use unlawful means to interfere with the appellants' business.

I shall not deal separately with the position as to the repairing by the appellants of barges belonging to the Port of London Authority. It may appear at the trial that this is not substantially different from the position as to the barge-hiring. At this stage, however, the facts here seem less clear to me and, as I have already held that there is a *prima facie* case with regard to the hiring of barges, it is unnecessary to reach any decision about this matter. . . .

VISCOUNT RADCLIFFE: . . . What puts the respondents in the wrong in legal analysis is that they have used the procuring of breaches of contract to enforce their policy of attacking Mr. Stratford. I cannot say, when I look at the facts of the case, that this strikes me as a satisfactory or even realistic dividing line between what the law forbids and what the law permits. There is a special point here about the existence of a trade dispute, but that is possibly an accidental specialty; one can see that with a small shift in the facts, which the full trial of the action may itself achieve, there could easily be a trade dispute to be contemplated or furthered. Then there would remain only the hiring contracts: and one sees again how easily a slight difference in the framing of the embargo order might have avoided incitement to breach of contract, while still achieving a virtual cessation of the appellants' business. I cannot see it as a satisfactory state of the law that the dividing line between what is lawful and what is unlawful should run just along this contour. The essence of the matter is that the respondents, conceiving themselves to be acting in the interests of their union, decided to use the power of their control of that union to put the appellants out of business for the time being. When and on what conditions they would be allowed to resume their business was left in the air. In my opinion, the law should treat a resolution of this sort according to its substance, without the comparatively accidental issue whether breaches of contract are looked for and involved; and by its substance it should be either licensed, controlled or forbidden.

LORD PEARCE: . . . The appellants put their case first on the *Lumley* v. *Gye*[1] principle that the respondents have knowingly without lawful justification induced the appellants' customers to break their contracts with the appellants. There were two classes of customer, first, the hirers of appellants' barges, and, secondly, the Port of London

---

1. (1853), 2 E. & B. 216.

Authority who contracted for a sequence of barges to be repaired in the appellants' yard. The hiring contracts were implied from an established course of dealing, and under them the hirers had an obligation to return the barges to the appellants when they had finished with them, whereupon the hiring came to an end. By the respondents' embargo the hirers became unable to return the barges. In consequence, when the barges became empty they were moored to buoys away from the appellants' premises instead of being delivered to the appellants. On the present state of the evidence I do not find any reality in the argument that this was not a breach of contract, that the hiring remained in force until such time as the barges could be returned, and that voluntarily the appellants chose to waive their rights to have the barges returned. The respondents' union maintained their refusal to allow the barges to be returned, and the appellants obviously could not, from a practical point of view, insist on their return; they had to acquiesce in the termination of the hiring without it. That was the situation that the respondents intended to produce. They cannot have envisaged that the contracts of hiring would remain in force while the barges were idle, thus enabling the appellants, whom they wished to injure, to continue collecting the hiring charges to the detriment of the hirers, whom they did not wish to injure. Such a view would not, I think, be reconcilable with the terms of the respondents' letter, in which they announced the embargo to the Association of Master Lightermen, or with their persistence in spite of the letter of the appellants' solicitors of 10 December 1963. On the evidence in its present stage, therefore, it appears that the hirers broke their contracts with the appellants.

Did the respondents have sufficient knowledge of the terms of the hirers' contracts? It is no answer to a claim based on wrongfully inducing a breach of contract, to assert that the respondents did not know with exactitude all the terms of the contract. The relevant question is whether they had sufficient knowledge of the terms to know that they were inducing a breach of contract. At present there is considerable indication that they had the knowledge. Moreover, it seems unlikely that they would be ignorant of the simple commonplace obligation of the hirers under the course of dealing whereby they had a duty to return the barges to the appellants, but this is a point which the evidence at the trial will no doubt illuminate further. Did the respondents induce the breach? Albeit with expressions of regret, the respondents made it clear to the Association of Master Lightermen, which in effect represented the hirers (by letter of 8 November 1963), that the hirers could not return the barges to the appellants. The fact that an inducement to break a contract is couched as an irresistible embargo rather than in terms of seduction does not make it any the less an inducement. The respondents were in effect saying to the hirers: "You shall not carry out your contract with the appellants, and we have taken steps which will make it impossible, though we regret the inconvenience to you." If thereby the hirers were induced to break the contract, the tort is established.

It was argued that the appellants have not shown that the hirers' breach was a necessary consequence, since they might have tried to employ men belonging to other unions. I find that argument quite unreal, since I would think that in practice they were bound to run into great difficulties. Moreover, if the respondents intended to procure the breach, and successfully procured it as a reasonable consequence of their acts and their communications to the hirers through their association and in answer to subsequent inquiries on the telephone, it is not, in my opinion, a defence to say that the hirers could have somehow avoided the breaches. In *Lumley* v. *Gye*[1] it was not necessary for Miss Wagner to break her contract; but the defendant was liable because he successfully persuaded her. *D. C. Thomson & Co., Ltd.* v. *Deakin*[2] was a somewhat different case from the present. In that case:

"There never was any direct action by the defendants or agents on their behalf

---

1. (1853), 2 E. & B. 216.
2. [1952] Ch. 646; [1952] 2 All E.R. 361.

with the object of persuading or causing Bowaters to break their existing contracts with the plaintiffs" (per Upjohn J.).[1]

In a case where the defendant does not communicate any direct pressure or persuasion to the contract-breaker, but merely procures indirectly a situation which causes the breach, I am inclined to agree with the dictum of Jenkins L.J.[2] that it must be shown

"that breach of the contract forming the alleged subject of interference ensued as a necessary consequence of the breaches by the employees concerned of their contracts of employment".

But that is not this case. The facts of this case, therefore, on the evidence in its present stage constitute, in my opinion, an inducement by the respondents to the hirers to break the contracts of hire. As to the contract with the Port of London Authority, the appellants' *prima facie* case is not so strong and I prefer to express no opinion at this stage. . . .

LORD UPJOHN: . . . The form of injunction granted by Marshall J. is not, in my view, entirely appropriate and I would propose an injunction in this form:

"An injunction restraining the respondents and each of them until judgment or further order from doing (whether by themselves or by their servants agents or workmen or any of them or otherwise howsoever) any act which causes or procures a breach or breaches by customers of the appellants of contracts made now or here- after between the appellants and such customers for the hiring of barges of the appellants."

[LORD DONOVAN delivered a speech in which he agreed with LORD PEARCE regarding the hiring contracts.]

Torquay Hotel Co., Ltd. v. Cousins

Court of Appeal   [1969] 1 All E.R. 522

The Torbay Hotel, together with fellow members of the local Hotels Association at Torquay, had refused recognition to the Transport & General Workers' Union, whose local officials P. and L. called a strike and posted pickets outside the Hotel. Newspapers reported statements by C., managing director of the Imperial Hotel (owned by the plaintiff company) that the Hotels Association would "stamp out" the T.G.W.U. Angered by these unconfirmed reports, some of these pickets moved across and picketed the Imperial. P. telephoned Esso, who supplied fuel oil to the Imperial, and warned them that fuel supplies would be stopped. Esso drivers were members of the T.G.W.U. and it was "common knowledge" that they would not cross the picket lines. The Imperial ordered fuel from Alternative Fuels, Ltd. and a delivery was made while the pickets were temporarily absent. A representative of the defendant union telephoned Alternative Fuels, Ltd. and warned that there would be "serious repercussions" if further supplies were made to the Imperial. The plaintiff company's solicitors asked the defendant union for an undertaking that the "blacking" of the Imperial would be withdrawn; they also gave notice of the contract with Esso and summarised its terms. 3,000 gallons were successfully delivered to the Imperial by Esso, but the union did not give the undertaking. Stamp J. granted an interlocutory injunction restraining the defendant union and certain of its officials from causing any supplier of fuel to break his contract to supply fuel oil and from picketing the Imperial to prevent the delivery of fuel oil. On appeal, the Court of Appeal held that an injunction could not be granted against the defendant union because of the provisions of s. 4 of the Trade Disputes Act 1906 (no actions in tort maintainable against trade unions) [now repealed by the Industrial Relations Act 1971], but dismissed the appeals by the individual trade union officials who were also defendants.

---

1. [1952] Ch. at p. 662; [1952] 2 All E.R. at p. 363.
2. [1952] Ch. at p. 697; [1952] 2 All E.R. at pp. 379, 380.

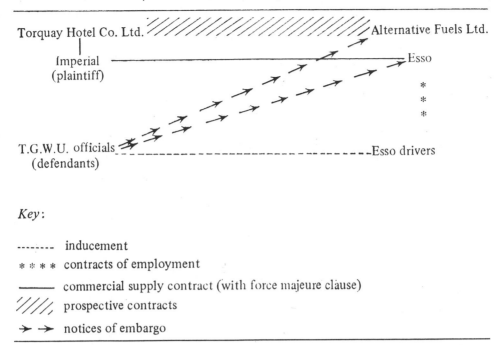

Key:

- - - - - - - inducement

* * * * contracts of employment

————— commercial supply contract (with force majeure clause)

///// prospective contracts

➤ ➤ notices of embargo

LORD DENNING M.R.: . . . The Imperial Hotel had a contract with Esso under which the Imperial Hotel agreed to buy their total requirements of fuel oil from Esso for one year, the quantity being estimated at 120,000 gallons, to be delivered by road tank wagon at a minimum of 3,000 gallons a time. Under that contract there was a *course of dealing* by which the Imperial Hotel used to order 3,000 gallons every week or ten days, and Esso used to deliver it the next day. But there was a *force majeure* or *exception clause* which said that—

"Neither party shall be liable for any failure to fulfil any term of this Agreement if fulfilment is delayed, hindered or prevented by any circumstance whatever which is not within their immediate control, including . . . labour disputes . . ."

It is plain that, if delivery was hindered or prevented by labour disputes, as for instance, because their drivers would not cross the picket line, Esso could rely on that exception clause as a defence to any claim by the Imperial Hotel. They would not be liable in damages. And I am prepared to assume that Esso would not be guilty of a breach of contract. But I do not think that would exempt the defendant union officials from liability, if they unlawfully hindered or prevented Esso from making deliveries. The principle of *Lumley* v. *Gye*[1] extends not only to inducing breach of contract, but also to preventing the performance of it. That can be shown by a simple illustration taken from the books. In *Lumley* v. *Gye*,[1] Miss Wagner, an actress, was engaged by Mr. Lumley to sing at Her Majesty's Theatre. Mr. Gye, who ran Covent Garden, procured her to break her contract with Mr. Lumley by promising to pay her more, see *Lumley* v. *Wagner*.[2] He was held liable to Mr. Lumley for inducing a breach of contract. In *Poussard* v. *Spiers and Pond*,[3] Mme. Poussard was under contract with Messrs. Spiers and Pond to sing in an opera at the Criterion Theatre. She fell sick and was unable to attend rehearsals. Her non-performance, being occasioned by sickness, was not a breach of contract on her part; but it was held to excuse the theatre company from continuing to

1. (1853), 2 E. & B. 216; [1843–60] All E.R. Rep. 208.
2. (1852), 1 De G.M. & G. 604; [1843–60] All E.R. Rep. 368.
3. (1876), 1 Q.B.D. 410.

employ her. Suppose now that an ill-disposed person, knowing of her contract, had given her a potion to make her sick. She would not be guilty of a breach herself. But undoubtedly the person who administered the potion would have done wrong and be liable for the damage suffered by them. So here I think the trade union officials cannot take advantage of the force majeure or exception clause in the Esso contract. If they unlawfully prevented or hindered Esso from making deliveries, as ordered by the Imperial Hotel, they would be liable in damages to the Imperial Hotel, notwithstanding the exception clause. There is another reason too. They could not rely on an excuse of which they themselves had been "the mean" to use Lord Coke's language, see *New Zealand Shipping Co., Ltd.* v. *Société des Ateliers et Chantiers de France*.[1]

The Principles of Law.

The principle of *Lumley* v. *Gye*,[2] is that each of the parties to a contract has a "right to the performance" of it; and it is wrong for another to procure one of the parties to break it or not to perform it. That principle was extended a step further by Lord Macnaghten in *Quinn* v. *Leathem*,[3] so that each of the parties has a right to have his "contractual relations" with the other duly observed. He said:[4]

"... it is a violation of legal right to interfere with contractual relations recognised by law if there be no sufficient justification for the interference."

That statement was adopted and applied by a strong Board of the Privy Council in *Jasperson* v. *Dominion Tobacco Co.*[5] It included Viscount Haldane and Lord Sumner. The time has come when the principle should be further extended to cover "deliberate and direct interference with the execution of a contract without that causing any breach". That was a point left open by Lord Reid in *J. T. Stratford & Son, Ltd.* v. *Lindley*.[6] But the common law would be seriously deficient if it did not condemn such interference. It is this very case. The principle can be subdivided into three elements: First, there must be *interference* in the execution of a contract. The interference is not confined to the procurement of a *breach* of contract. It extends to a case where a third person *prevents* or *hinders* one party from performing his contract, even though it be not a breach. Secondly, the interference must be deliberate. The person must know of the contract or, at any rate, turn a blind eye to it and intend to interfere with it, see *Emerald Construction Co., Ltd.* v. *Lowthian*.[7] Thirdly, the interference must be *direct*. Indirect interference will not do. Thus, a man who "corners the market" in a commodity may well know that it may prevent others from performing their contracts, but he is not liable to an action for so doing. A trade union official, who calls a strike on proper notice, may well know that it will prevent the employers from performing their contracts to deliver goods, but he is not liable in damages for calling it. *Indirect* interference is only unlawful if unlawful means are used. I went too far when I said in *Daily Mirror Newspapers, Ltd.* v. *Gardner*,[8] that there was no difference between direct and indirect interference. On reading once again *D. C. Thomson & Co., Ltd.* v. *Deakin*,[9] with more time, I find there is a difference. Morris L.J. there drew the very distinction between[10] "*direct* persuasion to break a contract" which is unlawful in itself; and "the intentional bringing about of a breach by *indirect* methods involving wrong doing". This distinction must be maintained, else we should take away the right to strike altogether. Nearly every trade union official

---

1. [1919] A.C. 1, at pp. 7, 8.
2. (1853), 2 E. & B. 216; [1843–60] All E.R. Rep. 208.
3. [1901] A.C. 495; [1900–3] All E.R. Rep. 1.
4. [1901] A.C. at p. 510; [1900–3] All E.R. Rep. at p. 9.
5. [1923] A.C. 709.
6. [1965] A.C. 269, at p. 324; [1964] 3 All E.R. 102, at p. 107.
7. [1966] 1 All E.R. 1013; [1966] 1 W.L.R. 691.
8. [1968] 2 Q.B. 762, at p. 781; [1968] 2 All E.R. 163, at p. 168.
9. [1952] Ch. 646; [1952] 2 All E.R. 361.
10. [1952] Ch. at p. 702; [1952] 2 All E.R. at p. 384.

who calls a strike—even on due notice, as in *Morgan* v. *Fry*[1]—knows that it may prevent the employers from performing their contracts. He may be taken even to intend it. Yet no one has supposed hitherto that it was unlawful; and we should not render it unlawful today. A trade union official is only in the wrong when he procures a contracting party *directly* to break his contract, or when he does it indirectly *by unlawful means*. On reconsideration of the *Daily Mirror* case,[2] I think that the defendants there interfered directly by getting the retailers as their agents to approach the wholesalers.

I must say a word about unlawful means, because that brings in another principle. I have always understood that if one person deliberately interferes with the trade or business of another, and does so by unlawful means, that is, by an act which he is not at liberty to commit, then he is acting unlawfully, even though he does not procure or induce any actual breach of contract. If the means are unlawful, that is enough. Thus in *Rookes* v. *Barnard*[3] (as explained by Lord Reid in *J. T. Stratford & Son, Ltd.* v. *Lindley*[4] and also by Lord Upjohn[5]) the respondents interfered with the employment of Rookes—and they did it by unlawful means, namely, by intimidation of his employers —and they were held to be acting unlawfully, even though the employers committed no breach of contract as they gave Rookes proper notice. And in *Stratford* v. *Lindley*,[6] the respondents interfered with the business of Stratford—and they did it by *unlawful means*, namely, by inducing the men to *break their contracts* of employment by refusing to handle the barges—and they were held to be acting unlawfully, even in regard to *new business* which was not the subject of contract. Lord Reid said:[7]

> ". . . the respondents' action made it practically impossible for the appellants to do *any new business* with the barge-hirers. It was not disputed that *such* interference . . . is tortious, if any unlawful means are employed."

So also in the second point in *Daily Mirror Newspapers, Ltd.* v. *Gardner*,[8] the defendants interfered with the business of the Daily Mirror—and they did it by a collective boycott which was held to be *unlawful* under the Restrictive Trade Practices Act 1956—and they were held to be acting unlawfully.

This point about unlawful means is of particular importance when a place is declared "black". At common law it often involves the use of unlawful means. Take the Imperial Hotel. When it was declared "black", it meant that the drivers of the tankers would not take oil to the hotel. The drivers would thus be induced to break their contracts of employment. That would be unlawful at common law. The only case in which "blacking" of such a kind is lawful is when it is done "in contemplation or furtherance of a trade dispute". It is then protected by s. 3 of the Trade Disputes Act 1906, see *D. C. Thomson & Co., Ltd.* v. *Deakin*[9] (per Upjohn J.) for, in that event, the act of inducing a breach of a contract of employment is a lawful act which is not actionable at the suit of anyone, see *Stratford* v. *Lindley*,[10] per Salmon L.J. and *Morgan* v. *Fry*,[11] per myself. Seeing that the act is lawful, it must, I think, be lawful for the trade union officials to tell the employers and their customers about it. And this is so, even though it does mean that those people are compelled to break their commercial contracts. The interference with the commercial contracts is only indirect, and not direct. See what Lord Upjohn said in *Stratford* v. *Lindley*.[12] So, if there had been a "trade

---

1. [1968] 2 Q.B. 710; [1968] 3 All E.R. 452.
2. [1968] 2 Q.B. 762; [1968] 2 All E.R. 163.
3. [1964] A.C. 1129; [1964] 1 All E.R. 367.
4. [1965] A.C. 269, at p. 325; [1964] 3 All E.R. 102, at p. 107.
5. [1965] A.C. at p. 337; [1964] 3 All E.R. at p. 115.
6. [1965] A.C. 269; [1964] 3 All E.R. 102.
7. [1965] A.C. at p. 324; [1964] 3 All E.R. at p. 106.
8. [1968] 2 Q.B. 762; [1968] 2 All E.R. 163.
9. [1952] Ch. at pp. 662, 663.
10. [1965] A.C. at p. 303; [1964] 2 All E.R. 209, at p. 227.
11. [1968] 2 Q.B. at p. 728; [1968] 3 All E.R. at p. 458.
12. [1965] A.C. at p. 337; [1964] 3 All E.R. at p. 115.

dispute" in this case, I think it would have protected the defendant union officials when they informed Esso that the dispute with the Imperial Hotel was an "official dispute" and said that the hotel was "blacked". It would be like the "blacking" of the barges in *Stratford* v. *Lindley*,[1] when we held, in the Court of Appeal, that, on the basis that there was a "trade dispute", the defendants were not liable.

Applying the principle in this case.

Seeing that there was no "trade dispute" this case falls to be determined by the common law. It seems to me that the defendant union officials deliberately and directly interfered with the execution of the contract between the Imperial Hotel and Esso. They must have known that there was a contract between the Imperial Hotel and Esso. Why otherwise did they on that very first Saturday afternoon telephone the bulk plant at Plymouth? They may not have known with exactitude all the terms of the contract. But no more did the defendants in *Stratford* v. *Lindley*.[2] They must also have intended to prevent the performance of the contract. That is plain from the telephone message: "Any supplies of fuel oil will be stopped being made." And the interference was direct. It was as direct as could be—a telephone message from the trade union official to the bulk plant.

Take next the supplies from Alternative Fuels. The first wagon got through. As it happened, there was no need for the Imperial Hotel to order any further supplies from Alternative Fuels. But suppose they had given a further order, it is quite plain that the defendant union officials would have done their best to prevent it being delivered. Their telephone messages show that they intended to prevent supplies being made by all means in their power. By threatening "repercussions" they interfered unlawfully with the performance of any future order which Imperial Hotel might give to Alternative Fuels. And the interference was direct again. It was direct to Alternative Fuels. Such interference was sufficient to warrant the grant of an injunction *quia timet.* . . .

RUSSELL L.J.: . . . The bulk supply contract between Esso Petroleum Co., Ltd., and the Imperial Hotel was such as might be expected for an establishment the size of the latter. It was argued that the exception clause had the effect that Esso could not be in breach of its supply contract if failure to deliver was due to labour disputes. In my view, the exception clause means what it says and no more; it *assumes* a failure to fulfil a term of the contract—i.e. a breach of contract—and excludes liability—i.e. in damages —for that breach in stated circumstances. It is an exception from liability for non-performance rather than an exception from obligation to perform. If, over a considerable period, Esso failed to deliver for one of the stated reasons, it seems to me that the hotel would be entitled to repudiate the contract on the ground of failure by Esso to carry out its terms; otherwise the hotel would be unable to enter into another bulk supply contract until the Esso contract was time expired. . . .

WINN L.J.: . . . The evidence does not establish that in consequence any quantity of fuel which had been ordered was not delivered; no breach of contract by Esso was induced. However, the argument of counsel for the defendants that cl. 10 of the written contract between Esso and the Imperial Hotel for a year's supply would have operated to prevent a failure or failures to deliver ordered instalments of fuel thereunder from being a breach does not seem to me to be sound. As I construe the clause it affords only an immunity against any claim for damages; it could not bar a right to treat the contract as repudiated by continuing breach; despite the clause Esso could well have been held to have committed a breach by non-delivery and Mr. Pedley came close to committing a tort of the *Lumley* v. *Gye*[3] type.

It is not necessary in the instant case to consider to what extent the principle of that case may cover conduct which Lord Reid described in *J. T. Stratford & Son, Ltd.* v.

1. [1965] A.C. 269; [1964] 2 All E.R. 209.
2. [1965] A.C. at p. 332; [1964] 3 All E.R. at p. 112.
3. (1853), 2 E. & B. 216; [1843–60] All E.R. Rep. 208.

Lindley,[1] as "deliberate and direct interference with the execution of a contract without that causing any breach". For my part I think that it can at least be said, with confidence, that where a contract between two persons exists which gives one of them an optional extension of time or an optional mode for his performance of it, or of part of it, but, from the normal course of dealing between them, the other person does not anticipate such postponement, or has come to expect a particular mode of performance, a procuring of the exercise of such an option should, in principle, be held actionable if it produces material damage to the other contracting party.

It was one of counsel for the defendants' main submissions that mere advice, warning or information cannot amount to tortious procurement of breach of contract. Whilst granting arguendi causa that a communication which went no further would, in general, not, in the absence of circumstances giving a particular significance, amount to a threat or intimidation, I am unable to understand why it may not be an inducement. In the ordinary meaning of language it would surely be said that a father who told his daughter that her fiancé had been convicted of indecent exposure, had thereby induced her, with or without justification, by truth or by slander, to break her engagement. A man who writes to his mother-in-law telling her that the central heating in his house has broken down may thereby induce her to cancel an intended visit.

The court is not concerned in this case with any indirect procuring of breach, or non-performance of a contract, or with the adoption of indirect means to produce such a result; it is, therefore, not appropriate to consider whether such a mode of procuring such a result is only actionable, as counsel for the defendants submitted where unlawful means, involving, for example, breaches of contract, or actionable breaches of contract, are involved. . . .

Notes

1. In the *South Wales Miners'* case (p. 456, *ante*) a stop-work order given by union officials (actionable) was distinguished from mere "advice" to stop work which could be disobeyed with impunity (not actionable): [1904–7] All E.R. Rep. at p. 219, *per* Lord Lindley. How does this distinction compare with what was said about (i) the "statement of facts", which included a reference to picketing, by one of the union officials to Bowaters in *Thomson v. Deakin*; (ii) the letter sent by the defendants to the Association in *Stratford v. Lindley* (p. 462, *ante*) that the hirers could not return the barges to the plaintiffs; and (iii) the telephone message to Esso in *Torquay Hotel Co., Ltd. v. Cousins* (p. 466, *ante*) that "any supplies of fuel oil will be stopped being made"? The controversy here is between those who see the gist of the tort of inducement of breach of contract as being the "intention to injure", with the requirement of "inducement" as a "purely verbal device" (e.g. Heydon, *Economic Torts*, p. 26; Guest & Hoffmann (1968), 84 L.Q.R. 310), and those who see a fundamental distinction between *persuading* a person to break a contract *(Lumley v. Gye)*, and *preventing* performance of a contract (*Stratford v. Lindley* insofar as Lords Reid and Upjohn and Viscount Radcliffe relied on the inducement of union members to break contracts of employment) (e.g. Hamson, [1968] C.L.J. 190; Weir, *Casebook on Tort*, 2nd Edn., p. 506; cf. Wedderburn (1968), 31 M.L.R. 440). According to the latter view, if a person is *persuaded* to break a contract all the requirements of the tort of inducing breach of contract (including the existence of a contract) must be proved; on the other hand, if a person is *prevented* from doing something, there is liability only if wrongful means were used. In other words, preventing performance is a species of the wider tort of causing loss by

---

1. [1965] A.C. 269, at p. 324; [1964] 3 All E.R. 102, at p. 106.

unlawful means (p. 474, *post*). How does this distinction between "persuasion" and "prevention" compare with that between "direct" and "indirect" inducement used by Sir R. Evershed M.R. in *Thomson* v. *Deakin*? (p. 459, *ante*). (See Wedderburn (1968), 31 M.L.R. 440.)

In *G.W.K., Ltd.* v. *Dunlop Rubber Co., Ltd.* (1926), 42 T.L.R. 376, 593, B promised C that all B's cars on exhibition at Olympia would be fitted with C's tyres. A, who also manufactured tyres, secretly removed C's tyres and substituted his own. A was held liable. Like the example given by Lord Denning M.R. in the *Torquay* case (an ill-disposed person giving Miss Wagner a potion to make her sick), this would be treated as a case of inducing breach of contract (by "direct" means) by the first school, but as a case of causing loss by unlawful means (irrespective of the existence of a contract) by the second school.

2. The defendant enters into a contract with the middleman knowing that the middleman has already made a prior inconsistent contract with the plaintiff. Is this an actionable *inducement*? (See Lauterpacht, "Contracts to break a contract" (1936), 52 L.Q.R. 494; and *Earl Sefton* v. *Tophams, Ltd.*, [1965] 3 All E.R .1, at p. 9; [1965] Ch. 1140, at p. 1187.) In *H. C. Sleigh, Ltd.* v. *Blight*, [1969] V.R. 931 (Adam J.) the plaintiffs had a contract for the supply of petroleum products to the Blights who ran a service station and who had promised not to cease to carry on their business except on assignment to a purchaser approved by plaintiffs. In breach of this promise Blights contracted to sell their business to the Bishops. Only after this contract was executed did the Bishops become aware of the Blights' promise. The Bishops entered into possession of the service station and refused to enter into a supply agreement with the plaintiffs, preferring to take their supplies elsewhere. Adam J. held that the decision of the Bishops to complete their contract although, by then, they knew that it affected plaintiff's contract with the Blights, was not tortious. Compare *Jones Bros. (Hunstanton), Ltd.* v. *Stevens*, [1955] 1 Q.B. 275; [1954] 3 All E.R. 677 (C.A.): defendant continued to employ an employee of plaintiffs even after discovering existence of plaintiff's contract; this was regarded as tortious but the plaintiff failed because it was not proved that the employee would return to the plaintiffs, i.e. there was no damage. (See, for comment, P. M. North, [1970] A.S.C.L. 518–520.)

3. In *Midland Cold Storage, Ltd.* v. *Steer*, [1972] 3 All E.R. 941, at pp. 952–953, Megarry J. said:

> "As the authorities stand, I am certainly not prepared to hold on motion that, conspiracy or unlawful means apart, there is a tort of wrongfully inducing a person not to enter into a contract. Unless hedged about with many restrictions, such a tort would have an extremely wide ambit that would be likely to work as much injustice as justice."

Note too, the remarks of Lord Herschell in *Allen* v. *Flood* (p. 442, *ante*). An injunction restraining a person from causing or procuring any breach of contract may, however, be applied to contracts which may be made subsequently: see the form of order approved by Lord Upjohn in *Stratford* v. *Lindley* (p. 466, *ante*). Can the remarks of Lord Denning M.R. in the *Torquay* case be explained in this way?

4. In *Heatons Transport (St. Helens), Ltd.* v. *Transport and General Workers Union*, [1972] I.C.R. 308, at p. 355, Buckley L.J. (*obiter*) recognised that a

contract might contain an exemption clause that causing impossibility of its performance might not induce a breach of the contract. How would this differ from the form of *force majeure* clause in the *Torquay* case? (Cf. B. Coote, *Exception Clauses* (London, 1964), pp. 148–149.)

5. In *Earl Sefton v. Tophams, Ltd.*, [1965] Ch. 1140; [1965] 3 All E.R. I (C.A.), Lord Sefton sold Aintree to Tophams subject to a covenant that it would continue to be used for horse racing and agricultural purposes only. Some years later Tophams sold it to a development company called Capital for a housing estate. Assuming that Capital had induced a breach of the contract between Sefton and Tophams, Harman and Russell L.JJ. (Sellers L.J. dissenting on this point) held that, nevertheless, Sefton could not obtain an injunction against Capital because he had failed to show that he personally had suffered any damage. He would lose his private box and the opportunity to act as steward at race meetings, but since he had no right, under the convenant to insist upon racing, these facilities were valueless.

Emerald Construction Co., Ltd. v. Lowthian

Court of Appeal   [1966] I All E.R. 1013

The defendant trade union officers objected to a sub-contract between main building contractors and the plaintiff for the supply only of labour for work on a building site. They demanded that it be terminated and put pressure on the main contractors by industrial action. They did not know, until after the action started, the precise terms of the contract. The plaintiff sought an interlocutory injunction to stop the defendants doing anything to procure termination of the labour only sub-contract. The Court of Appeal held that the injunction should be granted.

LORD DENNING M.R.: . . . This "labour only" sub-contract was disliked intensely by this trade union and its officers; but nevertheless it was a perfectly lawful contract. The parties to it had a right to have their contractual relations preserved inviolate without unlawful interference by others; see per Lord Macnaghten in *Quinn* v. *Leathem*.[1] If the officers of the trade union knowing of the contract deliberately sought to procure a breach of it, they would do wrong; see *Lumley* v. *Gye*.[2] Even if they did not know of the actual terms of the contract, but had the means of knowledge—which they deliberately disregarded—that would be enough. Like the man who turns a blind eye. So here, if the officers deliberately sought to get this contract terminated, heedless of its terms, regardless whether it was terminated by breach or not, they would do wrong. For it is unlawful for a third person to procure a breach of contract knowingly, or recklessly, indifferent whether it is a breach or not. . . .

DIPLOCK L.J.: . . . There are three essential elements in the tort of unlawful procurement of a breach of contract; the act, the intent and the resulting damage. In a *quia timet* action such as this, it is sufficient to prove the act and the intent and the likelihood of damage resulting if the act is successful in procuring a breach of contract. The only issue on this part of the case is one of fact as to the defendants' intent. At all relevant times they knew of the existence of a labour only sub-contract for brickwork between the main contractors and Emerald, but until it was disclosed to them on the interlocutory application to the judge in chambers for an injunction, they did not know its precise terms. They say in somewhat equivocal language that they assumed that it could be lawfully terminated by the main contractors on short notice and that such lawful termination was all that they insisted on. Ignorance of the precise terms of the

---

1. [1901] A.C. at p. 510; [1900–3] All E.R. Rep. at p. 9.
2. (1853), 2 E. & B. 216; [1843–60] All E.R. Rep. 208.

contract is not enough, however, to show absence of intent to procure its breach. The element of intent needed to constitute the tort of unlawful procurement of a breach of contract is in my view sufficiently established if it be proved that the defendants intended the party procured to bring the contract to an end by breach of it if there were no way of bringing it to an end lawfully. A defendant who acts with such intent runs the risk that, if the contract is broken as a result of the party acting in the manner in which he is procured to act by the defendant, the defendant will be liable in damages to the other party to the contract. . . .

[RUSSELL L.J. agreed that the appeal should be allowed.]

Notes

1. The approach of the court in this case to the question of knowledge has been followed in later cases: e.g. the *Torquay* case (p. 466, *ante*); *Daily Mirror Newspapers, Ltd.* v. *Gardner*, [1968] 2 Q.B. 762; [1968] 2 All E.R. 163 (where the evidence of the terms was meagre). In cases of continuing embargo, the defendant can be fixed with knowledge of the terms, even after commencement of the legal proceedings, by being given notice of the contract. See M. Dean (1967), 30 M.L.R. 208, at p. 212.

2. In *White* v. *Riley*, [1921] 1 Ch. 1 (C.A.) it was alleged that members of the Curriers' Union had induced an employer to dismiss an employee belonging to a rival union in breach of his contract of employment. They knew of his contract and that he was entitled to a week's notice to terminate it lawfully. In order to avoid any breach, they offered themselves to find a week's wages for him in lieu of notice. The employer never paid those wages, and so there was a breach. The Court of Appeal held that the defendants were not liable. "What they intended", said Warrington L.J. "was to avoid a breach of contract" (p. 26); alternatively, they had not "caused" the breach (Lord Sterndale M.R. at p. 16).

3. CAUSING LOSS BY UNLAWFUL MEANS

Pratt v. British Medical Association

King's Bench Division   [1918–19] All E.R. Rep. 104

McCARDIE J.: . . . It is necessary, I think, in dealing with actionable conspiracy, to distinguish at once the line of decisions which have established that an action will lie against a man who unlawfully and knowingly procures a person to commit a breach of his contract with another whereby the latter suffers actual pecuniary damage. That such conduct amounts to a well-recognised head of tort was settled in *Lumley* v. *Gye*.[1] This decision is now firmly rooted in our law: see per Lord Macnaghten in *Quinn* v. *Leathem*;[2] and *South Wales Miners' Federation* v. *Glamorgan Coal Co., Ltd.*[3] The latter decision also shows with clearness that malice in the sense of spite or ill-will is not an essential ingredient in such an action. A cause of action may exist under the *Lumley* v. *Gye*[1] principle independently of any question of conspiracy. An individual can commit the tort as effectively as an aggregate of persons. The effect of a conspiracy to commit a wrong within *Lumley* v. *Gye*[1] is only of importance in considering the weight of the acts alleged and the extent of the resultant damage. Persuasion and inducement are more easily effected by many than by one, and the ensuing loss may be the greater. The

1. (1853), 2 E. & B. 216.
2. [1901] A.C. 495, at p. 510.
3. [1905] A.C. 239.

observations I have just made with respect to the procurement of a breach of contract apply (in substance) to any agreement between two or more to commit any other recognised head of tort such as trespass, libel, or assault. If such tort be committed, then all who have aided or counselled, directed or joined in the commission of it are joint tortfeasors: see per Tindal C.J. in *Petrie* v. *Lamont*.[1] The liability of each is, however, independent of the mere circumstance of combination. Such circumstance is, I conceive, only relevant to the question of the agency of one to bind the other by his acts, and to the point that greater damage may result where the wrongdoers are several or many. Conspiracy is not the gist of the matter. . . .

Rookes v. Barnard

House of Lords   [1964] 1 All E.R. 367

The plaintiff was employed by B.O.A.C. as a skilled draughtsman at London airport. He left his union, the Association of Engineering and Shipbuilding Draughtsmen, because of disagreements about its policies. The union had an informal "100 per cent union membership" agreement with B.O.A.C. Barnard and Fistal, two fellow draughtsmen who were local unpaid union officials, and Silverthorne (a district official of the union not employed by B.O.A.C.) conveyed to B.O.A.C. the substance of a resolution passed at a members' meeting that if the plaintiff was not removed from the design office within three days, all labour would be withdrawn. As a result, B.O.A.C. at first suspended and then dismissed the plaintiff with the (long) lawful period of notice. There was a clause in another (formal) collective agreement between B.O.A.C. and the union that there would be no strike or lockout. It was *conceded* by counsel for the defendants that this clause was incorporated into each individual contract of employment with B.O.A.C. The threat by Barnard and Fistal and other employees to withdraw their labour was, in consequence, a threat to break their contracts. The plaintiff sued Barnard, Fistal and Silverthorne for conspiracy. (See diagram, p. 476, *post.*)

At the trial before Sachs J. and a jury, the plaintiff was awarded £7,500 damages, after an instruction that the jury were entitled to award exemplary damages. The Court of Appeal reversed this decision, unanimously taking the view that the tort of intimidation was confined to threats of violence. The House of Lords allowed the plaintiff's appeal on the question of liability (by this stage Silverthorne had died) but held that this was not a suitable case for the award of exemplary damages and sent the case for re-trial on the question of damages (on this aspect of the case see Chap. 12, p. 400, *ante*). The case was later settled for £4,000, plus costs estimated at £30,000; [1965] 3 W.L.R. 1033.

LORD REID: . . . The question in this case is whether it was unlawful for them to use a threat to break their contracts with their employer as a weapon to make him do something which he was legally entitled to do, but which they knew would cause loss to the appellant.

The first contention of the respondents is very far reaching. They say there is no such tort as intimidation. That would mean that, short of committing a crime, an individual could with impunity virtually compel a third person to do something damaging to the plaintiff, which he does not want to do but can lawfully do: the wrongdoer could use every kind of threat to commit violence, libel or any other tort, and the plaintiff would have no remedy. And a combination of individuals could do the same, at least if they acted solely to promote their own interests. It is true that there is no decision of this House which negatives that argument. But there are many speeches in this House and judgments of eminent judges where it is assumed that that is not the law and I have found none where there is any real support for this argument. Most of the relevant authorities have been collected by Pearson L.J.[2] and I see no need to add to

---

1. (1841), Car. & M. 93, at p. 96.
2. [1963] 1 Q.B. at pp. 686–696; [1962] 2 All E.R. at pp. 602–608.

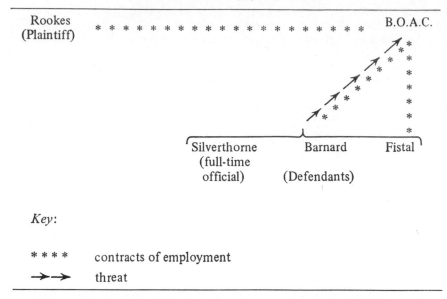

Key:

* * * *   contracts of employment

→→   threat

them. It has often been stated that if people combine to do acts which they know will cause loss to the plaintiff, he can sue if either the object of their conspiracy is unlawful or they use unlawful means to achieve it. In my judgment, to cause such loss by threat to commit a tort against a third person if he does not comply with their demands is to use unlawful means to achieve their object.

. . . I can see no difference in principle between a threat to break a contract and a threat to commit a tort. If a third party could not sue for damage caused to him by the former I can see no reason why he should be entitled to sue for damage caused to him by the latter. A person is no more entitled to sue in respect of loss which he suffers by reason of a tort committed against someone else, than he is entitled to sue in respect of loss which he suffers by reason of breach of a contract to which he is not a party. What he sues for in each case is loss caused to him by the use of an unlawful weapon against him —intimidation of another person by unlawful means. So long as the defendant only threatens to do what he has a legal right to do he is on safe ground. At least if there is no conspiracy he would not be liable to anyone for doing the act, whatever his motive might be, and it would be absurd to make him liable for threatening to do it but not for doing it. But I agree with Lord Herschell (*Allen* v. *Flood*)[1] that there is a chasm between doing what you have a legal right to do and doing what you have no legal right to do, and there seems to me to be the same chasm between threatening to do what you have a legal right to do and threatening to do what you have no legal right to do. It must follow from *Allen* v. *Flood*[2] that to intimidate by threatening to do what you have a legal right to do is to intimidate by lawful means. But I see no good reason for extending that doctrine. Threatening a breach of contract may be a much more coercive weapon than threatening a tort, particularly when the threat is directed against a company or corporation, and, if there is no technical reason requiring a distinction between different kinds of threats, I can see no other ground for making any such distinction. . . .

LORD DEVLIN: . . . My lords, in my opinion there is a tort of intimidation of the nature described in Chap. 18 of *Salmond on the Law of Torts* (13th Edn.), p. 697. The tort can take one of two forms which are set out in Salmond as follows:

1. [1898] A.C. 1, at p. 121; [1895–99] All E.R. Rep. 52, at p. 79.
2. [1898] A.C. 1; [1895–99] All E.R. Rep. 52.

"(1) Intimidation of the plaintiff himself.

"Although there seems to be no authority on the point, it cannot be doubted that it is an actionable wrong intentionally to compel a person, by means of a threat of an illegal act, to do some act whereby loss accrues to him: for example, an action will doubtless lie at the suit of a trader who has been compelled to discontinue his business by means of threats of personal violence made against him by the defendant with the intention.

"(2) Intimidation of other persons to the injury of the plaintiff.

"In certain cases it is an actionable wrong to intimidate other persons with the intent and effect of compelling them to act in a manner or to do acts which they themselves have a legal right to do which cause loss to the plaintiff: for example, the intimidation of the plaintiff's customers whereby they are compelled to withdraw their custom from him, or the intimidation of an employer whereby he is compelled to discharge his servant, the plaintiff. Intimidation of this sort is actionable, as we have said, in certain classes of cases; for it does not follow that, because a plaintiff's customers have a right to cease to deal with him if they please, other persons have a right as against the plaintiff to compel his customers to do so. There are at least two cases in which such intimidation may constitute a cause of action: (i) When the intimidation consists in a threat to do or procure an illegal act; (ii) When the intimidation is the act, not of a single person, but of two or more persons acting together, in pursuance of a common intention."

As your lordships are all of opinion that there is a tort of intimidation and on this point approve the judgments in both courts below. I do not propose to offer any further authorities or reasons in support of my conclusion. I note that no issue on justification was raised at the time and there is no finding of fact on it. Your lordships have not to consider what part, if any, justification plays in the tort of intimidation.

Your lordships are here concerned with the sort of intimidation which Salmond puts into the second category, and with the first of Salmond's two cases. The second case is, so Salmond later observed, "one form of the tort of conspiracy".[1] That form is the *Quinn* v. *Leathem*[2] type, so that it is no use to the appellant here. He relies on "a threat to do or procure an illegal act", namely, a breach of contract. Doubtless it would suit him better if he could rely on the procuring of a breach of contract, for that is a tort; but immunity from that is guaranteed in terms by s. 3. So he complains only of the threat to break the service contracts, and the breach would undoubtedly be an act actionable by B.O.A.C., though it is neither tortious nor criminal. He does not have to contend that in the tort of intimidation, as in the tort of conspiracy, there can be, if the object is injurious, an unlawful threat to use lawful means. I do not think that there can be. The line must be drawn according to the law. It cannot be said that to use a threat of any sort is per se unlawful; and I do not see how, except in relation to the nature of the act threatened, i.e. whether it is lawful or unlawful, one could satisfactorily distinguish between a lawful and an unlawful threat.

This conclusion, while not directly in point, assists me in my approach to the matter to be determined here. It is not, of course, disputed that if the act threatened is a crime, the threat is unlawful. But otherwise is it enough to say that the act threatened is actionable as a breach of contract or must it be actionable as a tort? My lords, I see no good ground for the latter limitation. I find the reasoning on this point of Professor Hamson[3] (which Sellers L.J.[4] sets out in his judgment though he does not himself accept it) very persuasive. The essence of the offence is coercion. It cannot be said that every form of coercion is wrong. A dividing line must be drawn and the natural line runs between what is lawful and unlawful as against the party threatened. If the

---

1. (13th Edn.), p. 699.
2. [1901] A.C. 495; [1900–3] All E.R. Rep. 1.
3. Cambridge Law Journal, November, 1961, p. 189, at pp. 191, 192.
4. [1963] 1 Q.B. at p. 665; [1962] 2 All E.R. at p. 588.

defendant threatens something that that party cannot legally resist, the plaintiff likewise cannot be allowed to resist the consequences; both must put up with the coercion and its results. But if the intermediate party is threatened with an illegal injury, the plaintiff who suffers by the aversion of the act threatened can fairly claim that he is illegally injured.

Accordingly, I reach the conclusion that the respondents' second point fails and on the facts of this case the tort of intimidation was committed. I do not share the difficulties which the lords justices felt about the idea of admitting breach of contract into the tort of intimidation. Out of respect to them I must state what those difficulties are and how in my opinion they can be satisfactorily resolved. I think that in one form or another they all stem from the error that any cause of action by the third party, that is the appellant, must in some way be supplemental to or dependent on a cause of action by B.O.A.C. Thus, it is said to be anomalous that on the facts of this case the appellant should be able to sue the respondents when B.O.A.C. could not. The best way of answering that is to grant that B.O.A.C. would not be able to sue and to assert, as I shall seek to show, that there is nothing anomalous about it. But there was introduced into the argument a suggestion that B.O.A.C. could in fact have sued because although there was no actual breach of contract, one was threatened and therefore there was an anticipatory breach. Against that, it was said that B.O.A.C. could not have sued for an anticipatory breach unless they first elected to rescind, which they never did. I dare say that is right, but I do not think it matters at all whether B.O.A.C. could sue or not. The two causes of action—B.O.A.C.'s and the appellant's—are in law quite independent; and in fact they are virtually alternative because it is difficult to visualise (except in one case) a set of facts on which both could sue.

This last statement is best examined in relation to a threat of physical violence which would unquestionably constitute intimidation. If A threatens B with physical violence unless he harms C, B can either resist or comply. If he resists, B might obtain an injunction against A (as he could also in the case of a threatened breach of contract if the contract were of a kind that permitted that remedy); or if A carries out his threat, B can sue for assault and obtain damages. In neither case can C sue because he has suffered no harm. If B complies with the threat, B cannot sue for damages because ex hypothesi there has been no assault; and he is not likely to obtain an injunction against the execution of a threat which he has already taken other means to avoid. But C will be able to sue because through B's compliance he has been injured. There is no anomaly about this; and if one substitutes "breach of contract" for "physical violence", the position is the same. The only case in which B and C are both likely to sue is if they both sue for the tort of intimidation in a case in which B has harmed himself by also harming C. Then it is said that to give C a cause of action offends against the rule that one man cannot sue on another's contract. I cannot understand this. In no circumstances does C sue on B's contract. The cause of action arises not because B's contract is broken but because it is not broken; it arises because of the action which B has taken to avert a breach.

Then it is asked how it can be that C can sue when there is a threat to break B's contract but cannot sue if it is broken without a threat. This means, it is argued, that if A threatens first, C has a cause of action; but if he strikes without threatening, C has no cause of action. I think that this also is fallacious. What is material to C's cause of action is the threat and B's submission to it. Whether the threat is executed or not is *in law* quite immaterial. *In fact* it is no doubt material because if it is executed (whether it be an assault or a breach of contract) it presumably means that B has not complied with it; and if B has not complied with it, C is not injured; and if C is not injured, he has no cause of action. Thus the reason why C can sue in one case and not in the other is because in one case he is injured and in the other he is not. The suggestion that it might pay A to strike without threatening negatives the hypothesis on which A is supposed to be acting. It must be proved that A's object is to injure C through the instrumentality of B. (That is why in the case of an "innocent" breach of contract, which was remarked on by Sellers L.J.[1] that is, one into which A was forced by circumstances beyond his control, there could never be the basis of an actionable threat.) If A hits B without telling him why, he can hardly hope to achieve his object. Of course A might think it more effective to hit B first and tell him why afterwards. But if then B injures C, it would not be because B had been hit but because he feared that he might be hit again. So if in the present case A.E.S.D. went on strike without threatening, they would not achieve their object unless they made it plain why they were doing so. If they did that and B.O.A.C. then got rid of the appellant, his cause of action would be just the same as if B.O.A.C. had been threatened first, because the cause of the injury to the appellant would have been A.E.S.D.'s threat, express or implied, to continue on strike until the appellant was got rid of.

Finally, it is said that if a threat of breach of contract constitutes intimidation, one party to a contract could be sued for intimidation if he threatened reprisals. Suppose, for example, A has agreed to deliver goods to B in monthly instalments but has not made payment for the first a condition precedent to delivery of the second. If he threatens to withhold the second until payment has been made for the first, is he intimidating B? I doubt it. But the case introduces questions not in issue here—whether a threat in such circumstances would be justifiable and whether it is intimidation to try to force a man into doing what the law, if invoked, would compel him to do. I find therefore nothing to differentiate a threat of a breach of contract from a threat of physical violence or any other illegal threat. The nature of the threat is immaterial, because, as Professor Hamson points out,[2] its nature is irrelevant to the plaintiff's cause of action. All that matters to the plaintiff is that, metaphorically speaking, a club has been used. It does not matter to the plaintiff what the club is made of—whether it is a physical club or an economic club, a tortious club or an otherwise illegal club. If an intermediate party is improperly coerced, it does not matter to the plaintiff how he is coerced.

I think therefore that at common law there is a tort of intimidation and that on the facts of this case each of the respondents has committed it, both individually (since the jury has found that each took an overt and active part) and in combination with others. I must add that I have obtained no assistance from the numerous dicta cited to show what constitutes "unlawful means" in the action of conspiracy. In some of the dicta the language suggests that the means must be criminal or tortious and in others that breach of contract would do; but in no case was the point in issue. Moreover, while a decision on that point might have been most illuminating, it is not the point that I have been considering. I have not been considering what amounts to unlawful means in the tort of conspiracy. I am not saying that a conspiracy to commit a breach of contract amounts to the tort of conspiracy; that point remains to be decided. I am saying that in the tort of intimidation a threat to break a contract would be a threat of an illegal act. It follows from that that a combination to intimidate by means of a threat of a breach of contract would be an unlawful conspiracy; but it does not necessarily follow that a combination to commit a breach of contract simpliciter would be an unlawful conspiracy. . . .

[LORDS EVERSHED, HODSON and PEARCE delivered speeches agreeing that the appeal should be allowed.]

Notes

1. The immediate repercussion of this decision was the enactment of a specific immunity for those committing the tort of intimidation in circumstances similar to *Rookes* v. *Barnard*, by the Trade Disputes Act 1965. The immunity, in slightly extended form, is now contained in the Industrial Relations Act 1971, s. 132, p. 485, *post.*

---

1. [1963] 1 Q.B. at p. 671; [1962] 2 All E.R. at p. 592.
2. Cambridge Law Journal, November, 1961, at pp. 191, 192.

2. Why was Silverthorne, who had no contract to threaten to break, treated as a conspirator? In *Morgan* v. *Fry*, [1968] 2 Q.B. 710; [1968] 3 All E.R. 452, p. 480, *post*, the only reason Lord Denning M.R. could find for Silverthorne not being protected from liability (by the Trade Disputes Act 1906, s. 3) for inducing breach of contract was that he was a conspirator; in the later case Fry was treated as an *inducer* (see p. 480, *post*). See further Wedderburn, *The Worker and the Law*, p. 367.

3. If A breaks his contract with B, this gives no remedy to C who is not a party. Why then, if A merely threatens to break his contract should C have a cause of action? See Hoffmann (1965), 81 L.Q.R. 116, esp. at p. 126; Wedderburn, "Intimidation and the Right to Strike" (1964), 27 M.L.R. 257.

4. Weir, [1964] C.L.J. 225, suggests that the principle which emerges from *Rookes* v. *Barnard* is that "it is tortious intentionally to damage another by means of an act which the actor was not at liberty to commit". From this it follows "that it is a tort intentionally to hurt the plaintiff by breaking your contract with X, just as it is a tort to get X to hurt him by threatening to break your contract with X". The same writer suggests that, if instead of threatening a tort, the defendant actually commits one, there will be recovery irrespective of whether a contract is broken. Similarly where the defendant actually breaks a contract with X in order to hurt the plaintiff, e.g. the chauffeur who refuses to drive a doctor to the bedside of the chauffeur's enemy is liable in tort to the ill man.

Morgan v. Fry

Court of Appeal   [1968] 3 All E.R. 452

The defendant, Fry, a full-time regional organiser of the Transport & General Workers' Union, gave strike notice to the employers of the plaintiff, who with others had formed a breakaway union, on 14 March 1963, that on 1 April 1963, members of the union would be instructed not to work with the plaintiff and other members of the breakaway union, but that T.G.W.U. members were "to carry out their duties as far as possible without the assistance" of the breakaway members. The notice given by the defendant was longer than the one week's notice required to terminate the employment contracts of the union members. The employers terminated plaintiff's employment. The plaintiff brought an action for damages against Fry and others alleging intimidation and conspiracy. Widgery J. gave judgment for the plaintiff, [1967] 2 All E.R. 386. This was reversed by the Court of Appeal.

LORD DENNING M.R.: . . . If *Rookes* v. *Barnard*[1] is carried to its logical conclusion, it applies not only to the threat of a flagrant breach of contract, such as occurred in that case, but also to the threat of any breach of contract—so long as it is of sufficient consequence to induce the other to submit. It applies to the strike notice in this present case if—and this is the point—it was the threat of a breach of contract.

[His Lordship went on to consider the nature of the "strike notice", and held that it was an implied term of each contract that it could be suspended by strike notice of proper length. Since that notice had been given there was no breach of contract in this case.][1]. . . In my opinion, therefore, the defendants here did not use any unlawful means to achieve their aim. They were not guilty of intimidation: because they gave a "strike notice" of proper length. They were not guilty of conspiracy to use unlawful means: because they used none. They were not guilty of conspiracy to injure, because they

---

1. [1964] A.C. 1129; [1964] 1 All E.R. 367.

acted honestly and sincerely in what they believed to be the true interests of their members. That is enough to decide this case. . . .

. . . The courts have not yet been called on to consider what part, if any, justification plays in the tort of intimidation, see *Rookes* v. *Barnard*.[1] So I hesitate to say anything about it; but I must say that if Mr. Hammond and his friends were really trouble-makers who fomented discord in the docks, without lawful cause or excuse, then the defendant Mr. Fry and his colleagues might well be justified in saying the men would not work with them any longer. . . .

RUSSELL L.J.: . . . [I]n spite of the generality of the language of the majority in *Rookes* v. *Barnard*,[2] and encouraged by the attitude of Lord Devlin (as I see it) to a case where the only breach would be a few days missing from due notice of termination, I consider that we are not bound by precedent to hold in the present case that the tort of intimidation has been committed.

What then should we hold? What ought the law to be? There is no doubt that if the workmen in concert had given notice in terms terminating their contracts of employment unless by the expiration of the notice the plaintiff had either rejoined the union or been removed from the lock the result and the effect on the plaintiff would have been exactly the same: the pressure would have been as strong or stronger, and pressure is at the heart of this branch of tort. Further, viewing the question of wrongful or un-lawful conduct as between the employer and the lockmen, while it is perfectly true that abstention from work without determining their contracts is clearly the preferable course for the strikers, it is also the preferable course for the employer, who retains his labour force on his books and has the continued existence of the contracts as the back-ground for negotiation unless and until he wishes to accept a repudiatory breach.

I would not wish in this branch of the law to establish as a proposition applicable to every case that the tort of intimidation is the intended interference with a man's employment by threat of breach of contract with his employer. I would exclude a case such as the present where exactly the same or even greater pressure could be exerted by a threat of concerted due termination of such contract, and where the carrying out of the threatened breach would be preferred by the threatened party to the carrying out of a threatened termination of the contract.

On the more general question of a "right to strike" I would not go so far as to say that a strike notice, provided the length is not less than that required to determine the contracts, cannot involve a breach of those contracts, even when the true view is that it is intended while not determining the contract not to comply with the terms or some of the terms of it during its continuance. . . .

[DAVIES L.J. delivered a judgment in favour of allowing the appeal.]

Cory Lighterage, Ltd. v. Transport and General Workers' Union

Court of Appeal [1973] 2 All E.R. 558

Shute, a lighterman employed by the plaintiffs, asserted the right, granted to him by s. 5 of the Industrial Relations Act 1971, not to belong to a trade union. The crew of his tug refused to work alongside him in view of the traditional practice, accepted by the plaintiffs, of 100 *per cent.* unionism in the Port of London. Lindley, an official of the union, told the plaintiff's manager that if Shute was not withdrawn the tug would not sail nor would any of the rest of the plaintiff's tugs. Shute was sent home on full pay; the plaintiffs were unable to dismiss him because the National Dock Labour Board was not prepared to grant consent to this. The plaintiffs issued a writ against the union

---

1. [1964] A.C. at p. 1206; [1964] 1 All E.R. at p. 398.
2. [1964] A.C. 1129; [1964] 1 All E.R. 367.

and certain officials claiming a declaration that their conduct was unlawful and by notice of motion sought an interim order restraining the union and two officials from instructing any union members employed by plaintiffs to withhold their labour because of the employment of Shute. Brightman J. dismissed the motion on the ground that under s. 132 (1), (2) of the Industrial Relations Act (p. 485, *ante*) the defendants' acts were not actionable in tort since they had been done in contemplation or furtherance of an "industrial dispute" within s. 167 of that Act. The Court of Appeal held that the acts had not been done in contemplation or furtherance of an industrial dispute, because they fell outside the statutory definition. Nevertheless, the Court held that the plaintiffs were not entitled to the interlocutory relief sought. Buckley and Orr L.JJ. so held on the ground that the balance of convenience lay against the grant of an interlocutory injunction because the loss flowing from the alleged torts was wholly financial, precisely quantifiable, modest in amount and within the resources of the union to recoup. Lord Denning M.R. was against the grant of such relief on the grounds set out in the extract from his judgment, below.

LORD DENNING M.R.: . . . If I am right in thinking that there was no industrial dispute, it has important consequences. The union and its officials are not entitled to the immunity given by s. 3 of the Conspiracy and Protection of Property Act 1875. Nor to the immunity given by s. 132 of the 1971 Act (replacing the immunity given by s. 3 of the 1906 Act and s. 1 of the Trade Disputes Act 1965). The union and its officers are exposed to the full effect of the common law as to conspiracy and intimidation. They can be sued in the High Court for those torts and in the High Court only. They cannot be sued in the Industrial Court: see s. 136 (*a*).

At common law conspiracy is a combination of two or more persons to do an unlawful act, or to do a lawful act by unlawful means: see *Mulcahy* v. *R.*[1] and *Crofter Hand Woven Harris Tweed Co., Ltd.* v. *Veitch.*[2] Here it will be said at the trial that the trade union and its officials combined to do an unlawful act, namely, to deter Mr. Shute from exercising his statutory right not to belong to a union; and they combined to do it by unlawful means, namely, by inducing men to break their contract of employment.

At common law intimidation is intentionally to compel a person, by means of a threat of an illegal act, to do some act whereby loss accrues to him or to another: see *Rookes* v. *Barnard.*[3] Here it will be said at the trial that the trade union and its officials threatened the employers that they would do an illegal act, namely, induce the men to break their contracts of employment. By that means they compelled the employers to send Mr. Shute off the tug.

In both conspiracy and intimidation damage is the gist of the action. Here Mr. Shute was damnified. He lost his overtime. The employers were damnified. They had to pay him wages for nothing.

Although those suggestions, and others like them, will be made at the trial, I can well see that a further issue may arise. I raise it because of the views expressed by Lord Donovan and his colleagues in their report.[4] If Mr. Shute's conduct was justifiable—as, for instance, if he conscientiously objected to joining the union, or was dissatisfied with it—then he should, of course, recover compensation for any damage done to him. But, if his conduct was not justifiable as, for instance, if he did it out of malice and with intent to injure—then he should not recover compensation. In such a case, the union and its members may plead that their own conduct—in refusing to work with him—may be justified or excused.

On this footing, the union may well say that Mr. Shute provoked the action of which he now complains. True it is that he has a right not to belong to the union. True it

1. (1868), L.R. 3 H.L. 306, at p. 317.
2. [1942] A.C. 435, at p. 461; [1942] 1 All E.R. 142, at p. 157.
3. [1964] A.C. at p. 1205; [1964] 1 All E.R. at p. 397.
4. Report of the Royal Commission on Trade Unions & Employers' Associations 1965–68, Cmnd. 3623, paras. 563, 564, 567, 614, 615 and 616.

is that he has a right to work. But he abused those rights beyond measure. So far as we know, he joined the union quite willingly. He knew that it was a condition of his employment. He had no possible justification for withholding his dues to the union. All that he did was done maliciously with intent to injure the union and its officers. His own words show it: "I will not rest until I have Mr. Lindley's head on a platter"—"I will do anything in my power to bring this union to its knees"—and so forth.

Suppose that Mr. Shute had himself sued the union and its officers for conspiracy and intimidation, causing him to lose overtime. Would he succeed? He wanted the employers to do what they did. He wanted to be sent off work. He wanted to get full wages for doing no work. And he has made much profit out of it. Would any jury give him a verdict? I doubt it. He may have been a troublemaker just as those in *Morgan* v. *Fry*.[1] . . . So here, Mr. Shute may be said to have brought everything on himself by his own eccentric conduct.

Now, if Mr. Shute could not sue the union and its officials, I doubt whether his employers can. After all, the conspiracy and intimidation was aimed at him, not at the employers. If he cannot sue, how can they? The loss to the employers (in paying wages for nothing) was caused by the conduct of the National Dock Labour Board in refusing to give the employers permission to dismiss Mr. Shute. I would hope that the board would reconsider their decision in this matter. Mr. Shute was threatening to bring dockland to a halt by his own unjustifiable conduct. The employers should not be compelled to employ such a man, or to pay wages to him. . . .

Brekkes, Ltd. v. Cattel

Chancery Division   [1971] 1 All E.R. 1031

The first plaintiff was the parent company of a group engaged in the wholesale fish trade. Through a wholly owned subsidiary, the second plaintiff, it operated a fleet of refrigerated lorries to deliver fish to customers including merchants in the Birmingham fish market. The Birmingham merchants resolved that they would in future only accept fish from vehicles officially nominated by the Hull Fish Merchants Protection Association, Ltd., the second defendants. The first plaintiff was a member of the Hull Association. The haulage contractor nominated by the Hull Association was a rival of the first plaintiff. The first plaintiff resigned from the Association and sought injunctions to restrain the Birmingham merchants (represented by Cattel) and the Hull Association from acting upon the resolution. Pennycuick V-C. was satisfied that there was no reasonable doubt that the resolution constituted a restriction deemed contrary to the public interest by s. 21 of the Restrictive Trade Practices Act 1956. The 1956 Act does not outlaw agreements within its scope. It makes them subject to registration and gives the Registrar the duty of referring them to the Restrictive Practices Court. That Court is given the task, by statute, of deciding whether a restriction is in the public interest. Even if the restriction is declared void, the Act does not state that it is unlawful, but the Court may prevent its enforcement by injunction.

The plaintiffs relied upon the torts of "interference with contracts" and "interference with trade".

PENNYCUICK V-C.: . . . It was put in the alternative that there was interference with contracts made in the ordinary course of business between the first plaintiff and other parties, namely, retailers in Birmingham hotels, institutions and so forth. I do not, however, think that as regards those contracts the resolution goes beyond placing economic difficulties in the way of carrying them out, i.e. the contracts are likely to be less profitable if the first plaintiff has to make deliveries to them only and not to the market. It seems to me that that interference is too indirect to be actionable.

The other ground on which counsel for the plaintiffs relied was interference with

---

1. [1968] 2 Q.B. 710; [1968] 3 All E.R. 452.

the trade of the first plaintiff. At one stage he appeared to be saying—I may have mis-understood him—that interference with trade might be actionable even apart from the use of unlawful means. He cited one or two passages from authorities on this contention, but they did not seem to me to bear out the contention, and I am not persuaded that that tort exists.

It appears from all the textbooks and all the authorities to which I have been able to refer that, so far as now material, the tort of interference with trade involves unlaw-ful means, that is to say, there must be interference by unlawful means with the trade of the plaintiff. The existence of that tort is well established. Counsel in the first place relied on restraint of trade at common law. He contended that the resolution passed by the Birmingham Association represents a restraint of trade at common law. Such a restraint, he said, was unlawful and therefore the resolution represented unlawful means for the purpose of this tort. It was accepted on behalf of the defendants for the purpose of the present motions that the resolution is indeed in restraint of trade at common law. I do not think, however, that on the authorities binding me it would be open to me to say that the mere circumstance of restraint of trade at common law would render this resolution unlawful for the present purpose, i.e. as representing unlawful means. I do not propose to go at length into the authorities on this point. It will be sufficient to mention *Mogul Steamship Co.* v. *McGregor, Gow & Co.*[1]

Towards the end of the hearing on the first day counsel developed another ground, or another aspect of the same ground, which appeared to me much more formidable, namely, that this resolution was unlawful under the provisions of the Restrictive Trade Practices Act 1956, and as such did represent unlawful means for the purpose of the tort of interference with trade by unlawful means. He referred to *Daily Mirror Newspapers, Ltd.* v. *Gardner,*[2] which on the face of it is positive authority for the proposition which he laid down. I will refer in more detail to that case later on. Before doing so I will read one quotation from Clerk and Lindsell on Torts:

> "It has, however, already been remarked in connection with intimidation and unlawful interference, that some uncertainty exists as to the ambit of 'unlawful means' in these torts. The same is true of conspiracy. Thus, while a combination to act in restraint of trade is not tortious, a combination to do damage by means of an arrangement presumed to be contrary to the public interest under the Restrictive Trade Practices Act 1956 is."

That may appear to be a fine distinction, and it is one which may, perhaps, in this or some other case be further elaborated in a higher tribunal, but, as far as I can see, there is no doubt that it exists. . . .

I have reached the conclusion that in this court it is my duty to follow the decision of the Court of Appeal in the *Daily Mirror* case,[2] and I confess that I most gladly do so.

I ought to mention one other contention which was raised by counsel for the second defendant. He pointed to the terms of s. 7 of the Act of 1968 which, so far as now material, provides:

> "If particulars of any agreement . . . are not duly furnished . . . (*b*) it shall be un-lawful for any person party to the agreement who carries on business within the United Kingdom to give effect to, or enforce or purport to enforce, the agreement in respect of any such restrictions."

That provision and the way it is worded, he said, is a clear indication that no illegality is to be implied in the interval between registration and declaration by the Restrictive Practices Court and so the *Daily Mirror* case[2] must be treated as having been, by inference, overruled, in that in 1968 Parliament indicated a different intention. It seems to me that s. 7 goes nowhere near raising an inference of that kind. If Parliament had intended in 1968 to alter the principles laid down in the *Daily Mirror* case[2] it would, I think, certainly have done so in different terms.

---

1. [1892] A.C. 25; [1891–94] All E.R. Rep. 263.
2. [1968] 2 Q.B. 762; [1968] 2 All E.R. 163.

I come back then to the present case. There is to my mind no reasonable doubt that this resolution will in due course be declared void under the Restrictive Trade Practices Act 1956. It follows that it will then represent unlawful means for the purpose of this tort of interference, and it seems to me that, having regard to the decision of the Court of Appeal in the *Daily Mirror* case,[1] I ought in advance of a declaration by the Restrictive Practices Court to act on the footing that this resolution does indeed represent unlawful means. It may well be—and I would certainly welcome it—that in this or some other case a higher tribunal will give further guidance on this difficult matter of law. As far as I am concerned today, I must act on the view which I have expressed. It then becomes a question of what relief should be granted. It is accepted that having reached that decision I ought in this case to make an injunction. The precise terms of the injunction as against the defendants will now require consideration.

Injunction granted

Notes

1. D. M. Kloss (1971), 34 M.L.R. 690 points out the difficulty in determining how far the ordinary courts are entitled to go in deciding that an agreement will not pass the scrutiny of the specialist Restrictive Practices Court. "Presumably, if the High Court judge finds at any stage that he needs to consider technical evidence in order to determine whether to grant an injunction or not, he should refuse the injunction on the grounds that such matters are for the Restrictive Practices Court alone to determine" (at p. 695). The Fair Trading Act 1973, s. 26 (*a*) avoids this kind of difficulty by providing that no civil action shall lie in respect of the breach of an order made under that Act restricting a consumer trade practice. Compare, as well, the provisions in the Industrial Relations Act 1971, s. 131, for avoiding encroachment by the ordinary courts on the jurisdiction of the National Industrial Relations Court and the industrial tribunals in respect of unfair industrial practices. That section gives the High Court a discretion to stay proceedings in tort where the act is one in respect of which proceedings have been brought or could be brought, as unfair industrial practices, in the N.I.R.C. Section 132 (4) imposes an obligatory stay in certain circumstances where there is a combination, and so effectively prevents a breach of the provisions of the Industrial Relations Act being relied upon as "unlawful means" for the purposes of the tort of conspiracy. See generally on s. 131, the judgment of Megarry J. in *Midland Cold Storage, Ltd.* v. *Steer*, [1972] I.C.R. 435; [1972] 3 All E.R. 941.

2. *Acrow (Automation), Ltd.* v. *Rex Chainbelt Inc.*, [1971] 3 All E.R. 1175, affords an example of an *omission* sufficient to constitute an interference by unlawful means (refusal to continue deliveries to which plaintiff had no contractual right unlawful because aiding and abetting breach of an injunction). For comment on this case (in which Lord Denning emphasised the need for *unlawful* means in this tort) see K. W. Wedderburn (1972), 35 M.L.R. 184.

4. INDUSTRIAL DISPUTES: IMMUNITIES

The Industrial Relations Act 1971

132. Acts in contemplation or furtherance of industrial dispute.—(1) An act done by a person in contemplation or furtherance of an industrial dispute shall not be actionable in tort on the ground only—

---

1. [1968] 2 Q.B. 762; [1968] 2 All E.R. 163.

(*a*) that it induces another person to break a contract to which that other person is a party or prevents another person from performing such a contract, or

(*b*) that it consists in his threatening that a contract (whether one to which he is a party or not) will be broken or will be prevented from being performed, or that he will induce another person to break a contract to which that other person is a party or will prevent another person from performing such a contract.

(2) For the avoidance of doubt it is hereby declared that an act done by a person in contemplation or furtherance of an industrial dispute is not actionable in tort on the ground only that it is an interference with the trade, business or employment of another person, or with the right of another person to dispose of his capital or his labour as he wills.

(3) An agreement or combination by two or more persons to do or procure to be done any act in contemplation or furtherance of an industrial dispute shall not be actionable in tort, if the act in question is one which, if done without any such agreement or combination, would not be actionable in tort.

(4) Where in any court proceedings in tort are brought in respect of an agreement or combination by two or more persons to do or procure to be done an act in contemplation or furtherance of an industrial dispute, and subsection (3) of this section does not afford a defence to the proceedings, the court shall nevertheless stay the proceedings if it is satisfied that either of the conditions specified in section 131 (2) of this Act is fulfilled in relation to the act in question.

167 (1) ...

"industrial dispute" ... means a dispute between one or more employers or organisations of employers and one or more workers or organisations of workers, where the dispute relates wholly or mainly to any one or more of the following, that is to say—

(*a*) terms and conditions of employment, or the physical conditions in which any workers are required to work;

(*b*) engagement or non-engagement, or termination or suspension of employment, of one or more workers;

(*c*) allocation of work as between workers or groups of workers;

(*d*) a procedure agreement, or any matter to which in accordance with section 166 of this Act a procedure agreement can relate; ...

Note

A number of acts committed "in contemplation or furtherance of an industrial dispute" constitute unfair industrial practices under the provisions of the Industrial Relations Act. Although these wrongs are distinguished in the Act from "tort", they are, in fact, statutory torts, which are best studied in the context of Labour Law. It should be noted, however, that there appear to be analogies between s. 96 of the Industrial Relations Act (inducing breach of contract by any person except registered organisations) and *Lumley* v. *Gye* (1853), 2 E. & B. 216 (p. 453, *ante*), and between s. 98 (certain secondary boycotts) and *D. C. Thomson & Co., Ltd.* v. *Deakin*, [1952] Ch. 646; [1952] 2 All E.R. 361 (p. 459, *ante*). These unfair industrial practices are to be repealed by the Trade Union and Labour Relations Bill 1974, which also grants immunities in respect of liability in tort for acts "in contemplation or furtherance of a trade dispute".

5. PASSING-OFF AND OTHER FORMS OF UNLAWFUL COMPETITION

J. Bollinger v. Costa Brava Wine Co., Ltd.

Chancery Division   [1959] 3 All E.R. 800

The twelve plaintiffs, all wine producers in the Champagne district of France, objected to and sought an injunction to restrain the use by the defendants of the name "Spanish Champagne" to describe wine produced in Spain or from Spanish grapes.

On a preliminary question of law:

DANCKWERTS J.: ... The well-established action for "passing off" involves the use of a name or get-up which is calculated to cause confusion with the goods of a particular rival trader, and I think that it would be fair to say that the law in this respect has been concerned with unfair competition between traders rather than with the deception of the public which may be caused by the defendant's conduct, for the right of action known as a "passing-off action" is not an action brought by the member of the public who is deceived but by the trader whose trade is likely to suffer from the deception practised on the public but who is not himself deceived at all. ...

The view that the law is interfering to protect rights of property is clearly supported by the observations of Lord Parker in *Spalding and Bros.* v. *A. W. Gamage, Ltd.*[1] (the "Orb" football case):

"There appears to be considerable diversity of opinion as to the nature of the right, the invasion of which is the subject of what are known as passing-off actions. The more general opinion appears to be that the right is a right of property. This view naturally demands an answer to the question—property in what? Some authorities say, property in the mark, name or get-up improperly used by the defendant. Others say, property in the business or goodwill likely to be injured by the misrepresentation. Lord Herschell in *Reddaway & Co.* v. *Banham & Co., Ltd.*,[2] expressly dissents from the former view; and if the right invaded is a right of property at all, there are, I think, strong reasons for preferring the latter view";

and Lord Parker[3] points out that the plaintiff was not the party deceived. The statements of Lord Parker and Lord Herschell are good enough for me; and the same view is supported by the statements of Romer L.J. in *Samuelson* v. *Producers Distributing Co., Ltd.*,[4] and of Goddard L.J. in *Draper* v. *Trist*,[5] where he says:

"In passing-off cases, however, the true basis of the action is that the passing off by the defendant of his goods as the goods of the plaintiff injures the right of property in the plaintiff, that right of property being his right to the goodwill of his business."

The plaintiffs claim that their goodwill in the name or description "Champagne" is injured by the defendants' conduct. Counsel for the defendants did not contest the correctness of the statements in those cases, but pointed out that each of them was a case of interference with the name or description of the goods of a particular trader. The issue still is whether an action lies at the suit of one or more traders who, as well as others, use or are entitled to use the particular name or description. ...

Counsel for the defendants contended that the mere fact that a defendant's conduct is injurious to the plaintiff or even, may be, unlawful does not necessarily give the plaintiff

---

1. (1915), 84 L.J.Ch. 449, at p. 450.
2. [1896] A.C. 199.
3. (1915), 84 L.J.Ch. at p. 450.
4. [1932] 1 Ch. 201, at p. 210; [1931] All E.R. Rep. 74, at p. 81.
5. [1939] 3 All E.R. 513, at p. 526.

a cause of action; and no doubt this is true in certain circumstances. He relied on (amongst other cases) *Patent Agents Institute* v. *Lockwood*.[1] In this case the Institute of Patent Agents and three registered patent agents practising in Glasgow sought to prevent the defender describing himself as a patent agent, and were held not entitled to an injunction. But this case has probably more relevance on the question relating to the Merchandise Marks Acts and is not of assistance on the present point. Another instance of loss being caused without the person so damnified being entitled to a remedy is *Abbott* v. *Sullivan*,[2] to which I was also referred; and there are, of course, the examples of mere extravagance of language, which are recognised as part of everyday life, such as "the puffing" cases, an example of which is *Hubbuck & Sons* v. *Wilkinson, Heywood and Clark*.[3]

The substance of the argument of counsel for the defendants was that, before a person can recover for loss which he suffered from another person's act, it must be shown that his case falls within the class of actionable wrongs. But the law may be thought to have failed if it can offer no remedy for the deliberate act of one person which causes damage to the property of another. There are such cases, of course, but they occur, as a rule, when the claims of freedom of action outweigh the interests of the other persons who suffer from the use which a person makes of his own property. (For example, see *Day* v. *Brownrigg*[4] and *Bradford Corpn.* v. *Pickles*.[5])

There seems to be no reason why such licence should be given to a person, competing in trade, who seeks to attach to his product a name or description with which it has no natural association so as to make use of the reputation and goodwill which has been gained by a product genuinely indicated by the name or description. In my view, it ought not to matter that the persons truly entitled to describe their goods by the name and description are a class producing goods in a certain locality, and not merely one individual. The description is part of their goodwill and a right of property. I do not believe that the law of passing off, which arose to prevent unfair trading, is so limited in scope. . . .

Notes

1. At the subsequent trial of this action, Danckwerts J. granted an injunction to the plaintiffs because a substantial portion of the public were likely to be misled by the description "Spanish Champagne": *J. Bollinger* v. *Costa Brava Wine Co., Ltd. (No. 2)*, [1961] 1 All E.R. 561.

2. In *Serville* v. *Constance*, [1954] 1 All E.R. 662, the welterweight boxing champion of Trinidad unsuccessfully sought an injunction restraining the defendant from representing himself as champion on the ground that the public's lack of knowledge of the plaintiff meant that there could not be any confusion. Can this be reconciled with Danckwerts J.'s reasoning in the "Spanish Champagne" case, above?

3. A publisher advertised for sale certain poems which he falsely represented by advertisement to be the work of Lord Byron. An injunction was granted: *Lord Byron* v. *Johnston* (1816), 2 Mer. 29.

4. Madame Tussaud & Sons, Ltd. was granted an injunction to restrain the registration of a proposed company under the name Louis Tussaud, Ltd., promoted for the purpose of carrying on a similar business to that of the famous waxworks exhibition of Madame Tussaud: *Tussaud* v. *Tussaud* (1890),

---

1. [1894] A.C. 347.
2. [1952] 1 K.B. 189; [1952] 1 All E.R. 226.
3. [1899] 1 Q.B. 86.
4. (1878), 10 Ch.D. 294.
5. [1895] A.C. 587.

44 Ch. D. 678. (Note that under the Companies Act 1948, ss. 17 and 18, a company may, in effect, be prevented from having a registered name similar to that of an existing company; under the Companies Act 1967, s. 46 (1), a name which gives a misleading indication of the company's activities may be prohibited.)

5. The plaintiffs had used the name Corona to describe a particular size of their cigars. The defendants supplied other cigars as Coronas. Plaintiffs were held entitled to an injunction to restrain the defendants from selling cigars other than the plaintiffs' in response to a request for Coronas without first discovering what brand was wanted or making it clear that the brand supplied was not that of the plaintiffs: *Havana Cigar and Tobacco Factories, Ltd.* v. *Oddenino*, [1924] 1 Ch. 179 (C.A.).

6. The plaintiffs sold laundry blue put up in a calico bag with a knobbed wooden stick attached to it. The bag bore no name but had become identified in the mind of the public with the plaintiffs' goods. The defendants exactly imitated the get-up of the plaintiffs' goods except that they attached to the bag a label bearing their name. It was held that the get-up of the defendants was calculated to deceive, the addition of the label not being a sufficient distinction and the general appearance being more than functional. The defendants were restrained by injunction: *William Edge & Sons, Ltd.* v. *William Niccolls & Sons, Ltd.*, [1911] A.C. 693 (H.L.); compare *J. B. Williams & Co.* v. *H. Bronnley & Co., Ltd.* (1909), 26 R.P.C. 765 (C.A.) in which an injunction was refused to prevent the use by the defendant of a normal shape of shaving stick container because the appearance was the result of functional considerations.

The Trade Marks Act 1938

2. No action for infringement of unregistered trade mark.—No person shall be entitled to institute any proceedings to prevent, or to recover damages for, the infringement of an unregistered trade mark, but nothing in this Act shall be deemed to affect rights of action against any person for passing off goods as the goods of another person or the remedies in respect thereof.

Note

If a trade mark is registered under the Act of 1938 in respect of any specification of goods, the registered proprietor has the exclusive right to use of the trade mark in relation to goods within the specification. He may prevent its use by others even in ways that involve no passing-off. The remedies are: (a) an injunction restraining infringement; (b) damages or alternatively an account of profits; and (c) an order for delivery up of the infringing articles or otherwise rendering them innocuous. For detailed discussion see Clerk & Lindsell, Chap. 30; Kerly, *Trade Marks and Trade Names*, 10th Edn. (London, 1972).

Radio Corporation Pty., Ltd. *v.* Henderson

Supreme Court of New South   [1960] N.S.W.R. 279
Wales. Full Court

The Hendersons were a well-known professional ballroom dancing couple. Without their consent the appellant (defendant) manufactured and sold a gramophone record of dance music and marketed it in a cover which had as its background a photograph of the Hendersons dancing, although their names did not appear on the cover. Sugerman

J. granted an injunction to restrain sale or distribution of the cover but refused an inquiry. as to damages. An appeal to the Full Court was dismissed.

EVATT C.J. and MYERS J.: . . . In our opinion, the evidence established a passing off by the appellant and, subject to proof of injury as to which we will have something to say later, the respondents were entitled to relief by way of injunction.

It has been contended, however, that the court has no jurisdiction to grant an injunction unless there is what has been called a common field of activity and in this case, it is said, there is none. The argument is based on a statement by Wynn-Parry J., in *Derek McCulloch* v. *Lewis A. May (Produce Distributors), Ltd.*, [1947] 2 All E.R. 845, at p. 851. "I am satisfied" he said, "that there is discoverable in all those [cases] in which the court has intervened this factor, namely, that there was a common field of activity in which, however remotely, both the plaintiff and the defendant were engaged and that it was the presence of that factor that accounted for the jurisdiction of the court." This principle was accepted by Sugerman J. who found a common field of activity in the capacity of the respondents to place their approval upon a record of ballroom dance music, which, he said, might be regarded as appurtenant or potentially appurtenant to the profession or business of ballroom dancing.

We have some difficulty in accepting the proposition stated in *McCulloch's* case. If deception and damages are proved, it is not easy to see the justification for introducing another factor as a condition of the court's power to intervene. . . .

The remedy in passing off is necessarily only available where the parties are engaged in business, using that expression in its widest sense to include professions and callings. If they are, there does not seem to be any reason why it should also be necessary that there be an area, actual or potential, in which their activities conflict. If it were so, then, subject only to the law of defamation, any businessman might falsely represent that his goods were produced by another provided that other was not engaged, or not reasonably likely to be engaged, in producing similar goods. This does not seem to be a sound general principle.

The present case provides an illustration of the unjust consequences of such a principle. For the purposes of this part of its argument, the appellant concedes that it is falsely representing that the respondents recommend, favour or support its dance music record, but it claims that, because the respondents are not engaged or likely to be engaged in making or selling gramophone records, it is entitled to appropriate their names and reputations for its own commercial advantage and that the court has no power to prevent it doing so. It would be a grave defect in the law if this were so.

In our view, once it is proved that A is falsely representing his goods as the goods of B, or his business to be the same as or connected with the business of B, the wrong of passing off has been established and B is entitled to relief.

While *McCulloch's* case is open to strong criticism, in actual fact the respondents here are in a real sense competing in the special area of providing gramophone records specially adapted to dancing and dancing teaching. Their activities are competitive in a broad sense. If so, *McCulloch's* case provides no obstacle to the plaintiff's success in the suit. . . .

Passing off is a wrong and is actionable at law. In such an action damage is presumed on proof of passing off and, therefore, a nominal sum by way of damages follows as a matter of course. General damages may, however, only be awarded if there is evidence of damage. Instead of proceeding at law a plaintiff may sue in Equity for an injunction, as may be done in respect of other wrongful acts of a different nature. If he sues in Equity, he takes advantage of the equitable principle that the court will interfere by injunction to restrain irreparable injury to property: per Romer L.J. in *Samuelson* v. *Producers Distributing Co., Ltd.*[1] and therefore he must go further than he need at law. He must show irreparable injury, that is that he has suffered injury which cannot be properly compensated by damages, or that he will probably suffer such injury.

---

1. [1932] 1 Ch. 201; [1931] 1 All E.R. Rep. 74, at p. 82.

If a plaintiff in Equity succeeds in having the defendant enjoined, he may also have an account of profits or an inquiry as to damages. Formerly, he could only have had an account, because that was Equity's only remedy, but since Lord Cairns's Act, he may have damages. If he elects to take an inquiry as to damages, he takes a common law remedy and his damages will be ascertained in the same way as they would have been ascertained at law.

With these considerations in mind, we turn to the arguments advanced on behalf of the respondents. First, it was said, it was unnecessary for the respondents to prove damage, because damage is presumed. That is clearly incorrect because the question is whether they have made out a case for an injunction and to do that they must show irreparable injury. We have been strongly pressed with some remarks of the Court of Appeal in *Draper* v. *Trist*, [1939] 3 All E.R. 513, to the effect that, upon proof of passing off, damage is presumed. But in that case the court was dealing with the assessment of damages pursuant to an inquiry, an order for an injunction having been made in the action with the consent of the defendant, and did not deal with the question under discussion here.

That a plaintiff in Equity must prove damage is such a well-established principle that it is almost unnecessary to cite authority for it. We have already referred to the statement of Maugham J. in *British Medical Association* v. *Marsh, supra,*[1] that a plaintiff must prove either positive injury or, in a *quia timet* action, a reasonable probability of injury and will only add to it the remarks of Farwell J. in *British Legion* v. *British Legion Club (Street), Ltd.* (1931), 48 R.P.C. 555. At p. 563, he said: "There must be evidence either of damage already committed, or the circumstances must be such as that the court can properly come to the conclusion that there is a serious risk, a real tangible risk, of damage in the future.". . .

Without the permission of the respondents, and without any other right or justification, the appellant has appropriated the professional reputation of the respondents for its own commercial ends. It claims that a court of Equity has no power to restrain the appellant from falsely representing that the respondents recommend its products, unless the respondents can prove that their professional reputation has thereby been injured, or that in some other way their capacity to earn money by the practice of their profession has thereby been impaired. We do not think that is the law.

It is true that the coercive power of the court cannot be invoked without proof of damage, but the wrongful appropriation of another's professional or business reputation is an injury in itself, no less, in our opinion, than the appropriation of his goods or money. The professional recommendation of the respondents was and still is theirs, to withhold or bestow at will, but the appellant has wrongfully deprived them of their right to do so and of the payment or reward on which, if they had been minded to give their approval to the appellant's record, they could have insisted. In our opinion, it is idle to contend that this wrongful appropriation is not an injury to the respondents. It is as much an injury as if the appellant had paid the respondents for their recommendation and then robbed them of the money. That injury, and the acknowledged intention to continue to inflict it, are ample justification for the injunction which was granted. . . .

[MANNING J. delivered a separate judgment agreeing that the appeal should be dismissed.]

Victoria Park Racing and Recreation Grounds Company, Limited v. Taylor

High Court of Australia   [1937] A.L.R. 597

A broadcasting company described and broadcast without permission, races taking place on the plaintiff's racecourse. They used an observer stationed on a platform erected on Taylor's adjoining land. As a result of the broadcasts, attendances at races dropped and the plaintiffs suffered loss. The High Court of Australia held that no legal

---

1. (1931), 48 R.P.C. 565, at p. 574.

right of the plaintiff's had been infringed and that an injunction had rightly been refused.

DIXON J.: . . . The plaintiff's counsel relied in the first instance upon an action on the case in the nature of nuisance. The premises of the plaintiff are occupied by it for the purpose of a racecourse. They have the natural advantage of not being overlooked by any surrounding heights or raised ground. They have been furnished with all the equipment of a racecourse and so enclosed as to prevent any unauthorised ingress or, unless by some such exceptional devices as the defendants have adopted, any un-authorised view of the spectacle. The plaintiff can thus exclude the public who do not pay and can exclude them not only from presence at, but also from knowledge of, the proceedings upon the course. It is upon the ability to do this that the profitable character of the enterprise ultimately depends. The position of and the improvements to the land thus fit it for a racecourse and give its occupation a particular value. The defendants then proceed by an unusual use of their premises to deprive the plaintiff's land of this value, to strip it of its exclusiveness. By the tower placed where the race will be fully visible and equipped with microphone and line, they enable Angles[1] to see the spectacle and convey its substance by broadcast. The effect is, the plaintiff says, just as if they supplied the plaintiff's customers with elevated vantage points round the course from which they could witness all that otherwise would attract them and induce them to pay the price of admission to the course. The feature in which the plaintiff finds the wrong of nuisance is the impairment or deprivation of the advantages possessed by the plaintiff's land as a racecourse by means of a non-natural and unusual use of the defendants' land.

This treatment of the case will not, I think, hold water. It may be conceded that interferences of a physical nature, as by fumes, smell and noise, are not the only means of committing a private nuisance. But the essence of the wrong is the detraction from the occupier's enjoyment of the natural rights belonging to, or in the case of easements, of the acquired rights annexed to, the occupation of land. The law fixes those rights. Diversion of custom from a business carried on upon the land may be brought about by noise, fumes, obstruction of the frontage or any other interference with the enjoy-ment of recognised rights arising from the occupation of property and, if so, it forms a legitimate head of damage recoverable for the wrong; but it is not the wrong itself. The existence or the use of a microphone upon neighbouring land is, of course, no nuisance. If one, who could not see the spectacle, took upon himself to broadcast a fictitious account of the races he might conceivably render himself liable in a form of action in which his falsehood played a part, but he would commit no nuisance. It is the obtaining a view of the premises which is the foundation of the allegation. But English law is, rightly or wrongly, clear that the natural rights of an occupier do not include freedom from the view and inspection of neighbouring occupiers or of other persons who enable themselves to overlook the premises. An occupier of land is at liberty to exclude his neighbour's view by any physical means he can adopt. But while it is no wrongful act on his part to block the prospect from adjacent land, it is no wrongful act on the part of any person on such land to avail himself of what prospect exists or can be obtained. Not only is it lawful on the part of those occupying premises in the vicinity to overlook the land from any natural vantage point, but artificial erections may be made which destroy the privacy existing under natural conditions. . . .

When this principle is applied to the plaintiff's case it means, I think, that the essential element upon which it depends is lacking. So far as freedom from view or inspection is a natural or acquired physical characteristic of the site, giving it value for the purpose of the business or pursuit which the plaintiff conducts, it is a characteristic which is not a legally protected interest. It is not a natural right for breach of which a legal remedy is given, either by an action in the nature of nuisance or otherwise. The fact is that the substance of the plaintiff's complaint goes to interference, not with its enjoyment of the land, but with the profitable conduct of its business. If English law had followed the

---

1. [An employee of the defendant company.]

course of development that has recently taken place in the United States, the "broad-casting rights" in respect of the races might have been protected as part of the quasi-property created by the enterprise, organisation and labour of the plaintiff in establish-ing and equipping a racecourse and doing all that is necessary to conduct race meetings. But courts of equity have not in British jurisdictions thrown the protection of an injunction around all the intangible elements of value, that is, value in exchange, which may flow from the exercise by an individual of his powers or resources whether in the organisation of a business or undertaking or the use of ingenuity, knowledge, skill or labour. This is sufficiently evidenced by the history of the law of copyright and by the fact that the exclusive right to invention, trade marks, designs, trade name and reputa-tion are dealt with in English law as special heads of protected interests and not under a wide generalisation. . . .

[LATHAM C.J. and McTIERNAN J. delivered judgments in favour of dismissing the appeal. RICH and EVATT JJ. delivered judgments in favour of allowing the appeal.]

International News Service v. Associated Press

United States Supreme Court   248 U.S. 215 (1918)

The Supreme Court enjoined I.N.S., a news agency, from copying and distributing news gathered by its competitor, A.P. The only matter argued before the Supreme Court was whether I.N.S. could be restrained from appropriating news taken, by lawful means, from bulletins issued by A.P. and from using that news gainfully, merely because the news had been originally gathered by A.P. and continued to be of value to some of its members, or because it did not reveal the source from which it was acquired.

HOLMES J.: . . . When an uncopyrighted combination of words is published there is no general right to forbid other people repeating them,—in other words, there is no property in the combination or in the thoughts or facts that the words express. Property, a creation of law, does not arise from value, although exchangeable,—a matter of fact. Many exchangeable values may be destroyed intentionally without compensation. Property depends upon exclusion by law from interference, and a person is not excluded from using any combination of words merely because someone has used it before, even if it took labor and genius to make it. If a given person is to be prohibited from making the use of words that his neighbors are free to make, some other ground must be found. One such ground is vaguely expressed in the phrase "unfair trade". This means that the words are repeated by a competitor in business in such a way as to convey a misrepresentation that materially injures the person who first used them, by appropriat-ing credit of some kind which the first user has earned. The ordinary case is a representation by device, appearance, or other indirection that the defendant's goods come from the plaintiff. But the only reason why it is actionable to make such a representation is that it tends to give the defendant an advantage in his competition with the plaintiff, and that it is thought undesirable that an advantage should be gained in that way. Apart from that, the defendant may use such unpatented devices and un-copyrighted combinations of words as he likes. The ordinary case, I say, is palming off the defendant's product as the plaintiff's; but the same evil may follow from the opposite falsehood,—from saying, whether in words or by implication, that the plaintiff's product is the defendant's; and that, it seems to me, is what has happened here.

Fresh news is got only by enterprise and expense. To produce such news as it is produced by the defendant represents by implication that it has been acquired by the defendant's enterprise and at its expense. When it comes from one of the great news collecting agencies like the Associated Press, the source generally is indicated, plainly importing that credit; and that such a representation is implied may be inferred with some confidence from the unwillingness of the defendant to give the credit and tell the truth. If the plaintiff produces the news at the same time that the defendant does, the defendant's presentation impliedly denies to the plaintiff the credit of collecting the facts and assumes that credit to the defendant. If the plaintiff is later in western cities, it naturally will be supposed to have obtained its information from the defendant. The falsehood is a little more subtle, the injury a little more indirect, than in ordinary cases of unfair trade, but I think that the principle that condemns the one condemns the other. It is a question of how strong an infusion of fraud is necessary to turn a flavor into a poison. The dose seems to be strong enough here to need a remedy from the law. But as, in my view, the only ground of complaint that can be recognised without legislation is the implied misstatement, it can be corrected by stating the truth; and a suitable acknowledgment of the source is all that the plaintiff can require. I think that, within the limits recognised by the decision of the court, the defendant should be enjoined from publishing news obtained from the Associated Press for hours after publication by the plaintiff unless it gives express credit to the Associated Press. A number of hours and the form of the acknowledgment to be settled by the district court.

BRANDEIS J. (dissenting): . . . The general rule of law is, that the noblest of human productions—knowledge, truths ascertained, conceptions and ideas—become, after voluntary communication to others, free as the air to common use. Upon these incorporeal productions the attribute of property is continued after such communication only in certain classes of cases where public policy has seemed to demand it. These exceptions are confined to productions which, in some degree, involve creation, invention, or discovery. But by no means all such are endowed with this attribute of property. The creations which are recognised as property by the common law are literary, dramatic, musical, and other artistic creations; and these have also protection under the copyright statutes. The inventions and discoveries upon which this attribute of property is conferred only by statute are the few comprised within the patent law. There are also many other cases in which courts interfere to prevent curtailment of plaintiff's enjoyment of incorporeal productions; and in which the right to relief is often called a property right, but is such only in a special sense. In those cases, the plaintiff has no absolute right to the protection of his production; he has merely the qualified right to be protected as against the defendant's acts, because of the special relation in which the latter stands or the wrongful method or means employed in acquiring the knowledge or the manner in which it is used. Protection of this character is afforded where the suit is based upon breach of contract or of trust, or upon unfair competition.

The knowledge for which protection is sought in the case at bar is not of a kind upon which the law has heretofore conferred the attributes of property; nor is the manner of its acquisition or use nor the purpose to which it is applied, such as has heretofore been recognised as entitling a plaintiff to relief. . . .

Notes

1. For an illuminating discussion of these and similar cases of unfair competition see W. R. Cornish, "Unfair Competition? A Progress Report" (1972), 12 J.S.P.T.L. (N.S.) 126.

2. Another situation in which damages may be assessed on tort principles is where a person has received information in confidence and takes unfair advantage of it: *Seager* v. *Copydex, Ltd.*, [1967] 2 All E.R. 415; *Seager* v. *Copydex, Ltd. (No. 2)*, [1969] 2 All E.R. 718 (C.A.). It is controversial whether this marks the birth of a new tort: compare the views of P. M. North, "Breach of Confidence: Is there a new Tort?" (1972), 12 J.S.P.T.L. 149, with those of G. H. Jones, "Restitution of Benefits obtained in Breach of Another's Confidence" (1970), 86 L.Q.R. 463.

15

False Statements Affecting Economic Interests

False words or wrong advice may cause loss by interfering with (a) physical interests (i.e. in personal security and property); (b) reputation; and (c) economic interests. In regard to (a), we have seen that foreseeability of physical harm is generally sufficient to establish a duty to act with reasonable care, but that a distinction between negligence in word and negligence in deed is a useful, albeit illogical, device for limiting the description of the duty of care (see in particular the remarks of Lord Reid in *Hedley Byrne & Co., Ltd.* v. *Heller & Partners, Ltd.*, [1964] A.C. 465; [1963] 2 All E.R. 575, Chap. 3, p. 70, *ante*). In protecting (b), reputation, the tort of defamation provides a complex and technical set of rules for balancing the plaintiff's interest against the defendant's interest in free speech; this is separately considered in the next Chapter. It is with (c), the protection of economic interests, that this Chapter is primarily concerned. The rise of financial interests in the 18th century gave birth to the famous case of *Pasley* v. *Freeman* (1789), 3 Term Rep. 51, establishing the tort of deceit: A is liable to B if he knowingly or recklessly, not caring whether it is true or false, makes a false statement to B, with intent that it shall be acted upon by B, who does act upon it and thereby suffers damage. (One might ask how far this tort helped Wright J. in *Wilkinson* v. *Downton*, [1897] 2 Q.B. 57, to extend the action upon the case to cover the intentional infliction of nervous shock by telling lies, Chap. 2, p. 50, *ante*.)

However, until *Hedley Byrne* (p. 501, *post*) in 1964, it was believed that there could be no liability in tort for false statements, honestly but carelessly made, causing loss by interference with economic (as distinct from physical) interests. In that case, their Lordships held that in certain circumstances, where a "special relationship" exists, one person may owe another a duty to exercise reasonable care in giving information or advice. A broad and flexible principle—in which the concept of *reliance* plays a central part—was enunciated, and some attempts were made to define those "special relationships" which attracted a duty of care. The decision of the majority of the Board in the Privy Council case of *Mutual Life and Citizens' Assurance Co., Ltd.* v. *Evatt*, [1971] A.C. 703; [1971] 1 All E.R. 150 (p. 511, *post*), appears to conflict with much of what was said in *Hedley Byrne* and, if followed by the English courts, will restrict the "special relationships" to which the duty extends.

Hedley Byrne may, however, lead to a transformation, or at least modification, of the existing rules covering the situation where A makes a false statement to B concerning C. Apart from defamation (i.e. affecting reputation), it is the tort of malicious (sometimes called injurious) falsehood, to which C must look for a remedy (p. 522, *post*). There is the usual uncertainty about the word "malicious". It is an interesting question whether the apparent extension of the *Hedley Byrne* principle (bearing in mind that *Hedley Byrne* itself was treated as a two-party situation) in *Ministry of Housing and Local Government* v. *Sharp*, [1970] Q.B. 223; [1970] I All E.R. 1009 (p. 519, *post*) will affect the separate tort of malicious falsehood.

1. DECEIT

Derry v. Peek

House of Lords   [1886–90] All E.R. Rep. I

The Plymouth, Devonport and District Tramways Co. Ltd. was authorised by statute to make certain tramways. The enabling Act provided that the tramways might be moved by animal power and, with the Board of Trade's consent, by steam or mechanical power. The defendants, as directors of the company, issued a prospectus containing the following paragraph:

> "One great feature of this undertaking, to which considerable importance should be attached, is, that by the special Act of Parliament obtained, the company has the right to use steam or mechanical motive power, instead of horses, and it is fully expected that by the means of this a considerable saving will result in the working expenses of the line as compared with other tramways worked by horses."

Sir Henry Peek, the plaintiff, relying upon the representations in this paragraph, applied for and obtained shares in the company. The Board of Trade subsequently refused its consent to the use of steam or mechanical power except on certain portions of the tramways. In the result, the company was wound up, and the plaintiff brought an action against the appellants claiming damages for fraudulent misrepresentations by the defendants whereby he was induced to take shares in the company.

Stirling J. dismissed the action. This decision was reversed by the Court of Appeal, which held that negligence was sufficient to support liability. The House of Lords reversed the decision of the Court of Appeal.

LORD HERSCHELL: . . . "This action is one which is commonly called an action of deceit, a mere common law action." This is the description of it given by Cotton L.J. in delivering judgment. I think it important that it should be borne in mind that such an action differs essentially from one brought to obtain rescission of the contract on the ground of misrepresentation of a material fact. The principles which govern the two actions differ widely. Where rescission is claimed it is only necessary to prove that there was misrepresentation. Then, however honestly it may have been made, however free from blame the person who made it, the contract, having been obtained by misrepresentation, cannot stand. In an action of deceit, on the contrary, it is not enough to establish misrepresentation alone; it is conceded on all hands that something more must be proved to cast liability upon the defendant, though it has been a matter of controversy what additional elements are requisite. . . .

To make a statement careless whether it be true or false, and, therefore, without any real belief in its truth, appears to me to be an essentially different thing from making, through want of care, a false statement which is nevertheless honestly believed to be true. And it is surely conceivable that a man may believe that what he states is the fact, though he has been so wanting in care that the court may think that there were no sufficient grounds to warrant his belief.

I shall have to consider hereafter whether the want of reasonable ground for believing the statement made is sufficient to support an action of deceit. I am only concerned for the moment to point out that it does not follow that it is so because there is authority for saying that a statement made recklessly, without caring whether it be true or false, affords sufficient foundation for such an action. . . .

I think there is here some confusion between that which is evidence of fraud, and that which constitutes it. A consideration of the grounds of belief is no doubt an important aid in ascertaining whether the belief was really entertained. A man's mere assertion that he believed the statement he made to be true is not accepted as conclusive proof that he did so. There may be such an absence of reasonable ground for his belief as, in spite of his assertion, to carry conviction to the mind that he had not really the belief which he alleges. If the learned Lord[1] intended to go further, as apparently he did, and to say that, though the belief was really entertained, yet, if there were no reasonable grounds for it, the person making the statement was guilty of fraud in the same way as if he had known what he stated to be false, I say, with all respect, that the previous authorities afford no warrant for the view that an action of deceit would lie under such circumstances. A man who forms his belief carelessly, or is unreasonably credulous, may be blameworthy when he makes a representation on which another is to act, but he is not, in my opinion, fraudulent in the sense in which that word was used in all the cases from *Pasley* v. *Freeman*[2] down to that with which I am now dealing. Even when the expression "fraud in law" has been employed, there has always been present, and regarded as an essential element, that the deception was wilful either because the untrue statement was known to be untrue, or because belief in it was asserted without such belief existing. . . .

I think the authorities establish the following propositions: First, in order to sustain an action of deceit, there must be proof of fraud, and nothing short of that will suffice. Secondly, fraud is proved when it is shown that a false representation has been made (i) knowingly, or (ii) without belief in its truth, or (iii) recklessly, careless whether it be true or false. Although I have treated the second and third as distinct cases, I think the third is but an instance of the second, for one who makes a statement under such circumstances can have no real belief in the truth of what he states. To prevent a false statement being fraudulent, there must, I think, always be an honest belief in its truth. And this probably covers the whole ground, for one who knowingly alleges that which is false has obviously no such belief. Thirdly, if fraud be proved, the motive of the person guilty of it is immaterial. It matters not that there was no intention to cheat or injure the person to whom the statement was made.

I think these propositions embrace all that can be supported by decided cases from the time of *Pasley* v. *Freeman*[3] down to *Addie's Case*[4] in 1867, when the first suggestion is to be found that belief in the truth of what he has stated will not suffice to absolve the defendant if his belief be based on no reasonable grounds.

[His Lordship considered the evidence of the defendants and continued:] I think they were mistaken in supposing that the consent of the Board of Trade would follow as a matter of course because they had obtained their Act. It was absolutely in the discretion of the Board whether such consent should be given. The prospectus was, therefore, inaccurate. But that is not the question. If they believed that the consent of the Board of Trade was practically concluded by the passing of the Act, has the plaintiff made out, which it was for him to do, that they have been guilty of a fraudulent misrepresentation? I think not. I cannot hold it proved as to any one of them that he knowingly made a false statement, or one which he did not believe to be true, or was careless whether what he stated was true or false. In short, I think they honestly believed

---

1. i.e. Lord Chelmsford in *Western Bank of Scotland* v. *Addie* (1867), L.R. 1 Sc. & Div. 145, at p. 162.
2. (1789), 3 Term Rep. 51.
3. (1789), 3 Term. Rep. 51.
4. (1867), L.R. 1 Sc. & Div. 145, H.L.

that what they asserted was true, and I am of opinion that the charge of fraud made against them has not been established. . . . Whenever it is necessary to arrive at a conclusion as to the state of mind of another person, and to determine whether his belief under given circumstances was such as he alleges, we can only do so by applying the standard of conduct which our own experience of the ways of men has enabled us to form, and by asking ourselves whether a reasonable man would be likely under the circumstances so to believe. I have applied this test, with the result that I have a strong conviction that a reasonable man situated as the defendants were, with their knowledge and means of knowledge, might well believe what they state they did believe and consider that the representation made was substantially true. . . .

[LORD HALSBURY L.C., LORD WATSON, LORD BRAMWELL and LORD FITZGERALD delivered speeches agreeing that the appeal should be allowed.]

Note

As a result of this decision the Directors' Liability Act 1890 imposed certain statutory obligations on persons issuing a prospectus. These are now contained in the Companies Act 1948, s. 43 (1). (See L. C. B. Gower, *Principles of Modern Company Law*, 3rd Edn. (London, 1969), pp. 331 *et seq.*)

Question

"Suppose A, by a fraudulent representation of the sobriety of B, who gives no indication of intoxication, but whom A knows to be drunken, authorises and induces a licensed victualler, who has no reason to disbelieve and does honestly believe the truth of the representation, to sell drink to B, and the licensed victualler is convicted and fined." Is there any rule of the common law which would debar B from claiming damages for deceit from A in respect of his loss? (The example is suggested by Kennedy J. in *Burrows* v. *Rhodes*, [1899] 1 Q.B. 816, at p. 831, a case in which a participant in the Jameson Raid into the South African Republic was held entitled to claim damages resulting from his reliance on false statements by Dr. Jameson and Mr. Rhodes that the Raid was lawful.)

The Statute of Frauds Amendment Act 1828

6. Action not maintainable on representations of character, etc., unless they be in writing signed by the party chargeable.—No action shall be brought whereby to charge any person upon or by reason of any representation or assurance made or given concerning or relating to the character, conduct, credit, ability, trade, or dealings of any other person, to the intent or purpose that such other person may obtain credit, money, or goods upon, unless such representation or assurance be made in writing signed by the party to be charged therewith.

Note

This section applies to fraudulent representations only and not to negligent ones: *W. B. Anderson & Sons, Ltd.* v. *Rhodes (Liverpool), Ltd.*, [1967] 2 All E.R. 850. This appears to be the only situation in which there is liability for a negligent act where there would not be liability if it were done intentionally (Clerk & Lindsell, para. 70, note 60).

The Misrepresentation Act 1967

2. Damages for misrepresentation.—(1) Where a person has entered into a contract after a misrepresentation has been made to him by another party thereto and as a result thereof he has suffered loss, then, if the person making the misrepresentation would be liable to damages in respect thereof had the misrepresentation been made fraudulently, that person shall be so liable notwithstanding that the misrepresentation was not made fraudulently, unless he proves that he had reasonable ground to believe and did believe up to the time the contract was made that the facts represented were true.

(2) Where a person has entered into a contract after a misrepresentation has been made to him otherwise than fraudulently, and he would be entitled, by reason of the misrepresentation, to rescind the contract, then, if it is claimed, in any proceedings arising out of the contract, that the contract ought to be or has been rescinded the court or arbitrator may declare the contract subsisting and award damages in lieu of rescission, if of opinion that it would be equitable to do so, having regard to the nature of the misrepresentation and the loss that would be caused by it if the contract were upheld, as well as to the loss that rescission would cause to the other party.

(3) Damages may be awarded against a person under subsection (2) of this section whether or not he is liable to damages under subsection (1) thereof, but where he is so liable any award under the said subsection (2) shall be taken into account in assessing his liability under the said subsection (1).

Note

Section 2 (1) of the Misrepresentation Act 1967 creates a statutory tort which extends the tort of deceit. It enables a party who was induced by the defendant to enter into a contract with him by means of a false representation to recover damages for resulting loss without proving fraud. If the plaintiff proves all the other requirements of the tort of deceit, he will have a good cause of action, unless the defendant proves that he had reasonable grounds to believe that the facts represented were true.

Section 2 (2) gives the court a discretion to award damages in lieu of rescission of the contract to the victim of an innocent misrepresentation. It does not affect the claim for rescission of contract which is usually made in addition to a claim for damages in cases of deceit.

The topic of statements made during negotiations for a contract is dealt with in the books on contract. See in particular, J. C. Smith and J. A. C. Thomas, *A Casebook on Contract*, 5th Edn. (London, 1973), Chap. 7.

Questions

1. Does the word "loss" in s. 2 (1) mean that the new cause of action is limited to cases of pecuniary loss as distinct from damage to physical interests? (See Atiyah & Treitel (1967), 30 M.L.R. 369, 374, who suggest, on the analogy of deceit, that it is not so limited.)

2. Does the word "misrepresentation' 'in s. 2 (1) mean that the new cause of action is restricted to such statements of fact, as distinct from statements of law or opinion, as would, before the passing of the Act, have given rise to a right to rescind the contract? (See Smith & Thomas, *op. cit.*, p. 271, who suggest that this would be the "preferable course".)

2. CARELESS STATEMENTS

Nocton v. Lord Ashburton

House of Lords   [1914–15] All E.R. Rep. 45

The defendant, a solicitor, had an interest in land which he and other owners were attempting to sell to builders for a building development. He persuaded his client, the plaintiff, Lord Ashburton, to advance £65,000 on mortgage loan to the builders, and later induced him to release part of the security from the mortgage. The loan was not repaid and, the security being insufficient to pay the loan, the plaintiff sued the defendant alleging that the defendant in ordering him to surrender part of his security was not acting in good faith but with a view to himself obtaining a first charge on the security released on which he held a first mortgage.

Neville J. held that the plaintiff must fail because he had not established fraud, which was the basis of the action. The Court of Appeal reversed this decision, finding that the defendant had been guilty of fraud. The House of Lords dismissed a further appeal, holding that the solicitor was liable to compensate his client for loss arising from misrepresentation in breach of fiduciary duty.

VISCOUNT HALDANE L.C.: . . . If among the great common lawyers who decided *Derry* v. *Peek*[1] there had been present some versed in the practice of the Court of Chancery it may well be that the decision would not have been different, but that more and explicit attention would have been directed to the wide range of the class of cases in which, on the ground of a fiduciary duty, courts of equity gave a remedy.

It is known that in cases of actual fraud the Courts of Chancery and of common law exercised a concurrent jurisdiction from the earliest times. For some of these cases the greater freedom which, in early days, the Court of Chancery exercised in admitting the testimony of parties to the proceedings made it a more suitable tribunal. Moreover, its remedies were more elastic. Operating in personam as a court of conscience it could order the defendant, not, indeed, in those days, to pay damages as such, but to make restitution, or to compensate the plaintiff by putting him in as good a position pecuniarily as that in which he was before the injury. But in addition to this concurrent jurisdiction, the Court of Chancery exercised an exclusive jurisdiction in cases which, although classified in that court as cases of fraud, yet did not necessarily import the element of dolus malus. The court took it upon itself to prevent a man from acting against the dictates of conscience as defined by the court, and to grant injunctions in anticipation of injury, as well as relief where injury had been done. Common instances of this exclusive jurisdiction are cases arising out of breach of duty by persons standing in a fiduciary relation, such as the solicitor to the client, illustrated by Lord Hardwicke's judgment in *Earl of Chesterfield* v. *Jansen*.[2] I can hardly imagine that those who took part in the decision of *Derry* v. *Peek*[1] imagined that they could be supposed to have cast doubt on the principle of any cases arising under the exclusive jurisdiction of the Court of Chancery. No such case was before the House, which was dealing only with a case of actual fraud as to which the jurisdiction in equity was concurrent. . . .

It must now be taken to be settled that nothing short of proof of a fraudulent intention in the strict sense will suffice for an action of deceit. This is so whether a court of law or a court of equity, in the exercise of concurrent jurisdiction, is dealing with the claim, and in this strict sense it was quite natural that Lord Bramwell and Lord Herschell should say that there was no such thing as legal as distinguished from moral fraud. But when fraud is referred to in the wider sense in which the books are full of the expression, used in Chancery in describing cases which were within its exclusive jurisdiction, it is a mistake to suppose that an actual intention to cheat must always be proved. A man may misconceive the extent of the obligation which a court of equity imposes on him. His fault is that he has violated, however innocently because of his ignorance, an obligation which he must be taken by the court to have known, and his conduct has in that sense always been called fraudulent, even in such a case as a technical fraud on a power. It was thus that the expression "constructive fraud" came into existence. The trustee who purchases the trust estate, the solicitor who makes a bargain with his client which cannot stand, have all for several centuries run the risk of the word "fraudulent" being applied to them. What it really means in this connection is not

---

1. (1889), 14 App. Cas. 337.
2. (1751), 1 Atk. 301.

moral fraud in the ordinary sense, but breach of the sort of obligation which is enforced by a court which from the beginning regarded itself as a court of conscience.

Derry v. *Peek*[1] simply illustrates the principle that honesty in the stricter sense is by our law a duty of universal obligation. This obligation exists independently of contract or of special obligation. If a man intervenes in the affairs of another he must do so honestly, whatever be the character of that intervention. If he does so fraudulently, and through that fraud damage arises, he is liable to make good the damage. A common form of dishonesty is a false representation fraudulently made, and it was laid down that it was fraudulently made if the defendant made it knowing it to be false, or recklessly, neither knowing nor caring whether it was false or true. That is fraud in the strict sense.

The courts had also power to rescind contracts of many kinds obtained by an innocent misrepresentation, so long at least as the contract had not been superseded by being carried into effect. The condition attached to the plaintiff's right was that he should be able and willing to make restitution in integrum. If so, however free the defendant might have been from any intention to deceive, he was not allowed to retain what he had obtained from the plaintiff by a material misstatement on which the latter was entitled to rely as being true. This, like the obligation to be honest, was a principle of general application, which did not depend on any special relationship of the parties or duty arising from it.

But side by side with the enforcement of the duty of universal obligation to be honest and the principle which gave the right to recission, the courts, and especially the Court of Chancery, had to deal with the other cases to which I have referred, cases raising claims of an essentially different character, which have often been mistaken for actions of deceit. Such claims raise the question whether the circumstances and relations of the parties are such as to give rise to duties of particular obligation which have not been fulfilled. Prior to *Derry* v. *Peek*,[1] the distinction between the different classes of case had not been sharply drawn, and there was some confusion between fraud as descriptive of the dishonest mind of a person who knowingly deceives, and fraud as the term was employed by the Court of Chancery and applied to breach of special duty by a person who erred, not necessarily morally but at all events intellectually, from ignorance of a special duty of which the courts would not allow him to say that he was ignorant. Such a special duty may arise from the circumstances and relations of the parties. These may give rise to an implied contract at law or to a fiduciary obligation in equity. If such a duty can be inferred in a particular case of a person issuing a prospectus, as, for instance, in the case of directors issuing to the shareholders of the company which they direct a prospectus inviting the subscription by them of further capital, I do not find in *Derry* v. *Peek*[1] an authority for the suggestion that an action for damages for misrepresentation without an actual intention to deceive may not lie. What was decided there was that from the facts proved in that case no such special duty to be careful in statement could be inferred, and that mere want of care, therefore, gave rise to no cause of action. In other words, it was decided that the directors stood in no fiduciary relation, and, therefore, were under no fiduciary duty to the public to whom they had addressed the invitation to subscribe. I have only to add that the special relationship must, whenever it is alleged, be clearly shown to exist.

[LORD ATKINSON concurred with this speech. LORDS DUNEDIN, SHAW and PARMOOR delivered speeches in favour of dismissing the appeal.]

Hedley Byrne & Co., Ltd. *v.* Heller and Partners, Ltd.

House of Lords   [1963] 2 All E.R. 575

The plaintiffs, a firm of advertising agents, booked advertising time on television channels and space in newspapers, on behalf of a customer, Easipower Ltd., on terms

---

1. (1889), 14 App. Cas. 337.

that they became personally liable. Becoming doubtful of the financial position of Easipower Ltd. they asked their bankers, the National Provincial Bank Ltd., to obtain a report from the defendants, merchant bankers with whom Easipower Ltd. had an account. This was done, in the first place, by telephone conversation in the course of which the defendants said that they believed Easipower "to be respectably constituted and considered good for its normal business engagements" and that "we believe that the company would not undertake any commitments they were unable to fulfil". Three months later, a further inquiry was made by letter as to whether Easipower were "trustworthy ... to the extent of £100,000 per annum advertising contract". The defendants replied in a letter headed: "Confidential. For your private use and without responsibility on the part of this bank or its officials." The letter continued: ". . . Respectably constituted company, considered good for its ordinary business engagements. Your figures are larger than we are accustomed to see." The plaintiffs relied on these statements and as a result they lost sums, calculated as £17,661 18s. 6d., when Easipower went into liquidation. In their statement of claim an allegation of fraud was originally made, but this was abandoned. McNair J. held that the defendants were negligent but that they owed no duty of care to the plaintiffs. The Court of Appeal likewise held that there was no duty of care and it was therefore unnecessary to consider whether the finding of negligence was correct. The House of Lords affirmed the judgment on different grounds.

LORD REID [After considering the distinction between words and deeds, quoted p. 70, *ante*, and considering earlier authorities including a statement by Lord Haldane in *Robinson* v. *Bank of Scotland*, 1916 S.C. (H.L.) 154, at p. 157]: . . . He speaks of other special relationships and I can see no logical stopping place short of all those relationships where it is plain that the party seeking information or advice was trusting the other to exercise such a degree of care as the circumstances required, where it was reasonable for him to do that, and where the other gave the information or advice when he knew or ought to have known that the inquirer was relying on him. I say "ought to have known" because in questions of negligence we now apply the objective standard of what the reasonable man would have done.

A reasonable man, knowing that he was being trusted or that his skill and judgment were being relied on, would, I think, have three courses open to him. He could keep silent or decline to give the information or advice sought: or he could give an answer with a clear qualification that he accepted no responsibility for it or that it was given without that reflection or inquiry which a careful answer would require: or he could simply answer without any such qualification. If he chooses to adopt the last course he must, I think, be held to have accepted some responsibility for his answer being given carefully, or to have accepted a relationship with the inquirer which requires him to exercise such care as the circumstances require. . . .

What the appellants complain of is not negligence in the ordinary sense of carelessness, but rather misjudgment in that Mr. Heller, while honestly seeking to give a fair assessment, in fact made a statement which gave a false and misleading impression of his customer's credit. It appears that bankers now commonly give references with regard to their customers as part of their business. I do not know how far their customers generally permit them to disclose their affairs, but even with permission it cannot always be easy for a banker to reconcile his duty to his customer with his desire to give a fairly balanced reply to an inquiry; and inquirers can hardly expect a full and objective statement of opinion or accurate factual information such as skilled men would be expected to give in reply to other kinds of inquiry. So it seems to me to be unusually difficult to determine just what duty, beyond a duty to be honest, a banker would be held to have undertaken if he gave a reply without an adequate disclaimer of responsibility or other warning. . . .

Here, however, the appellants' bank, who were their agents in making the enquiry, began by saying that "they wanted to know in confidence and without responsibility on our part", i.e. on the part of the respondents. So I cannot see how the appellants can now be entitled to disregard that and maintain that the respondents did incur a responsibility to them.

The appellants founded on a number of cases in contract where very clear words were required to exclude the duty of care which would otherwise have flowed from the contract. To that argument there are, I think, two answers. In the case of a contract it is necessary to exclude liability for negligence, but in this case the question is whether an undertaking to assume a duty to take care can be inferred; and that is a very different matter. Secondly, even in cases of contract general words may be sufficient if there was no other kind of liability to be excluded except liability for negligence: the general rule is that a party is not exempted from liability for negligence "unless[1] adequate words are used"—per Scrutton L.J. in *Rutter* v. *Palmer*.[1] It being admitted that there was here a duty to give an honest reply, I do not see what further liability there could be to exclude except liability for negligence: there being no contract there was no question of warranty.

I am therefore of opinion that it is clear that the respondents never undertook any duty to exercise care in giving their replies. The appellants cannot succeed unless there was such a duty and therefore in my judgment this appeal must be dismissed.

LORD MORRIS OF BORTH-Y-GEST: . . . My lords, it seems to me that if A assumes a responsibility to B to tender him deliberate advice there could be a liability if the advice is negligently given. I say "could be" because the ordinary courtesies and exchanges of life would become impossible if it were sought to attach legal obligation to every kindly and friendly act. But the principle of the matter would not appear to be in doubt. If A employs B (who might, for example, be a professional man such as an accountant or a solicitor or a doctor) for reward to give advice, and if the advice is negligently given, there could be a liability in B to pay damages. The fact that the advice is given in words would not, in my view, prevent liability from arising. Quite apart, however, from employment or contract there may be circumstances in which a duty to exercise care will arise if a service is voluntarily undertaken. A medical man may unexpectedly come across an unconscious man, who is a complete stranger to him, and who is in urgent need of skilled attention: if the medical man, following the fine traditions of his profession, proceeds to treat the unconscious man he must exercise reasonable skill and care in doing so. . . .

. . . It is said, however, that where careless (but not fraudulent) misstatements are in question there can be no liability in the maker of them unless there is either some contractual or fiduciary relationship with a person adversely affected by the making of them or unless through the making of them something is created or circulated or some situation is created which is dangerous to life, limb or property. In logic I can see no essential reason for distinguishing injury which is caused by a reliance on words from injury which is caused by a reliance on the safety of the staging to a ship, or by a reliance on the safety for use of the contents of a bottle of hair wash or a bottle of some consumable liquid. It seems to me, therefore, that if A claims that he has suffered injury or loss as a result of acting upon some missstatement made by B who is not in any contractual or fiduciary relationship with him the inquiry that is first raised is whether B owed any duty to A: if he did the further inquiry is raised as to the nature of the duty. There may be circumstances under which the only duty owed by B to A is the duty of being honest: there may be circumstances under which B owes to A the duty not only of being honest but also a duty of taking reasonable care. The issue in the present case is whether the bank owed any duty to Hedley and if so what the duty was.

Leaving aside cases where there is some contractual or fiduciary relationship there may be many situations in which one person voluntarily or gratuitously undertakes to do something for another person and becomes under a duty to exercise reasonable care. I have given illustrations. Apart from cases where there is some direct dealing, there may be cases where one person issues a document which should be the result of an

---

1. [1922] 2 K.B. 87, at p. 92; cf. [1922] All E.R. Rep. 367, at p. 370.

exercise of the skill and judgment required by him in his calling and where he knows and intends that its accuracy will be relied on by another. . . .

The guidance which Lord Haldane gave in *Nocton* v. *Ashburton*[1] was repeated by him in his speech in *Robinson* v. *National Bank of Scotland*.[2] He clearly pointed out that *Derry* v. *Peek*[3] did not affect (a) the whole doctrine as to fiduciary relationships, (b) the duty of care arising from implied as well as express contracts and (c) the duty of care arising from other special relationships which the courts may find to exist in particular cases.

My lords, I consider that it follows and that it should now be regarded as settled that if someone possessed of a special skill undertakes, quite irrespective of contract, to apply that skill for the assistance of another person who relies on such skill, a duty of care will arise. The fact that the service is to be given by means of, or by the instrumentality of, words can make no difference. Furthermore, if, in a sphere in which a person is so placed that others could reasonably rely on his judgment or his skill or on his ability to make careful inquiry, a person takes it on himself to give information or advice to, or allows his information or advice to be passed on to, another person who, as he knows or should know, will place reliance on it, then a duty of care will arise.

I do not propose to examine the facts of particular situations or the facts of recent decided cases in the light of this analysis, but I proceed to apply it to the facts of the case now under review. As I have stated, I approach the case on the footing that the bank knew that what they said would in fact be passed on to some unnamed person who was a customer of National Provincial Bank, Ltd. The fact that it was said that "they", i.e. National Provincial Bank, Ltd., "wanted to know" does not prevent this conclusion. In these circumstances I think that some duty towards the unnamed person, whoever it was, was owed by the bank. There was a duty of honesty. The great question, however, is whether there was a duty of care. The bank need not have answered the inquiry from National Provincial Bank, Ltd. It appears, however, that it is a matter of banking convenience or courtesy and presumably of mutual business advantage that inquiries as between banks will be answered. The fact that it is most unlikely that the bank would have answered a direct inquiry from Hedleys does not affect the question as to what the bank must have known as to the use that would be made of any answer that they gave but it cannot be left out of account in considering what it was that the bank undertook to do. It does not seem to me that they undertook before answering an inquiry to expend time or trouble "in searching records, studying documents, weighing and comparing the favourable and unfavourable features and producing a well-balanced and well-worded report." (I quote the words of Pearson L.J.[4]) Nor does it seem to me that the inquiring bank (nor therefore their customer) would expect such a process. . . . There was in the present case no contemplation of receiving anything like a formal and detailed report such as might be given by some concern charged with the duty (probably for reward) of making all proper and relevant inquiries concerning the nature, scope and extent of a company's activities and of obtaining and marshalling all available evidence as to its credit, efficiency, standing and business reputation. There is much to be said, therefore, for the view that if a banker gives a reference in the form of a brief expression of opinion in regard to credit-worthiness he does not accept, and there is not expected from him, any higher duty than that of giving an honest answer. I need not, however, seek to deal further with this aspect of the matter, which perhaps cannot be covered by any statement of general application, because in my judgment the bank in the present case, by the words which they employed, effectively disclaimed any assumption of a duty of care. They stated that they only responded to the inquiry on the basis that their reply was without responsibility. If the inquirers chose to receive and act upon the reply they cannot disregard the definite terms upon which it was

1. [1914] A.C. 932; [1914–15] All E.R. Rep. 45.
2. 1916 S.C. (H.L.) 154.
3. (1889), 14 App. Cas. 337.
4. [1962] 1 Q.B. at p. 414; [1961] 3 All E.R. at p. 902, letter E.

given. They cannot accept a reply given with a stipulation and then reject the stipulation. Furthermore, within accepted principles (as illustrated in *Rutter* v. *Palmer*[1]) the words employed were apt to exclude any liability for negligence.

LORD HODSON: . . . It would, I think, be unreasonable to impose an additional burden on persons, such as bankers, who are asked to give references and might, if more than honesty were required, be put to great trouble before all available material had been explored and considered. . . .

I do not think that it is possible to catalogue the special features which must be found to exist before the duty of care will arise in a given case, but since preparing this opinion I have had the opportunity of reading the speech which my noble and learned friend Lord Morris of Borth-y-Gest has now delivered. I agree with him that if in a sphere where a person is so placed that others could reasonably rely on his judgment or his skill or on his ability to make careful inquiry such person takes it on himself to give information or advice to, or allows his information or advice to be passed on to, another person who, as he knows, or should know, will place reliance on it, then a duty of care will arise.

LORD DEVLIN: . . . In my opinion the appellants in their argument tried to press *M'Alister* (or *Donoghue*) v. *Stevenson*[2] too hard. They asked whether the principle of proximity should not apply as well to words as to deeds. I think that it should, but as it is only a general conception it does not yet get them very far. Then they take the specific proposition laid down by *Donoghue* v. *Stevenson*[2] and try to apply it literally to a certificate or a banker's reference. That will not do, for a general conception cannot be applied to pieces of paper in the same way as to articles of commerce, or to writers in the same way as to manufacturers. An inquiry into the possibilities of intermediate examination of a certificate will not be fruitful. The real value of *M'Alister* (or *Donoghue*) v. *Stevenson*[2] to the argument in this case is that it shows how the law can be developed to solve particular problems. Is the relationship between the parties in this case such that it can be brought within a category giving rise to a special duty? As always in English law the first step in such an inquiry is to see how far the authorities have gone, for new categories in the law do not spring into existence overnight.

It would be surprising if the sort of problem that is created by the facts of this case had never until recently arisen in English law. As a problem it is a by-product of the doctrine of consideration. If the respondents had made a nominal charge for the reference, the problem would not exist. If it were possible in English law to construct a contract without consideration, the problem would move at once out of the first and general phase into the particular; and the question would be, not whether on the facts of the case there was a special relationship, but whether on the facts of the case there was a contract.

The respondents in this case cannot deny that they were performing a service. Their sheet anchor is that they were performing it gratuitously and therefore no liability for its performance can arise. My lords, in my opinion this is not the law. A promise given without consideration to perform a service cannot be enforced as a contract by the promisee; but if the service is in fact performed and done negligently, the promisee can recover in an action in tort. This is the foundation of the liability of a gratuitous bailee. In the famous case of *Coggs* v. *Bernard*,[3] where the defendant had charge of brandy belonging to the plaintiff and had spilt a quantity of it, there was a motion in arrest of judgment "for that it was not alleged in the declaration that the defendant was a common porter, nor averred that he had anything for his pains". The declaration was held to be good notwithstanding that there was not any consideration laid. Gould, J. said:[3]

---

1. [1922] 2 K.B. 87; [1922] All E.R. Rep. 367.
2. [1932] A.C. 562; [1932] All E.R. Rep. 1.
3. (1703), 2 Ld. Raym. 909.

"The reason of the action is, the particular trust reposed in the defendant, to which he has concurred by his assumption, and in the executing which he has miscarried by his neglect."

This proposition is not limited to the law of bailment. In *Skelton* v. *London & North Western Rail Co.*[1] Willes J. applied it generally to the law of negligence. He said:[2]

"Actionable negligence must consist in the breach of some duty ... if a person undertakes to perform a voluntary act, he is liable if he performs it improperly, but not if he neglects to perform it. Such is the result of the decision in the case of *Coggs* v. *Bernard.*"[3]

Likewise in *Banbury* v. *Bank of Montreal*,[4] where the bank had advised a customer on his investments, Lord Finlay L.C. said[5]: "He is under no obligation to advise, but if he takes upon himself to do so, he will incur liability if he does so negligently."

The principle has been applied to cases where as a result of the negligence no damage was done to person or to property and the consequential loss was purely financial. In *Wilkinson* v. *Coverdale*[6] the defendant undertook gratuitously to get a fire policy renewed for the plaintiff, but, in doing so, neglected formalities, the omission of which rendered the policy inoperative. It was held that an action would lie. In two similar cases, the defendants succeeded on the ground that negligence was not proved in fact. Both cases were thus decided on the basis that in law an action would lie. In the first of them, *Shiells* v. *Blackburne*,[7] the defendant had, acting voluntarily and without reward, made an entry of the plaintiff's leather as wrought leather instead of dressed leather, with the result that the leather was seized. In *Dartnall* v. *Howard*[8] the defendants purchased an annuity for the plaintiff but on the personal security of two insolvent persons. The court, after verdict, arrested the judgment on the ground that the defendants appeared to be gratuitous agents and that it was not averred that they had acted either with negligence or dishonesty. . . .

De la Bere v. *Pearson, Ltd.*[9] is an example of a case ... decided on the ground that there was a sufficiency of consideration. The defendants advertised in their newspaper that their city editor would answer inquiries from readers of the paper desiring financial advice. The plaintiff asked for the name of a good stockbroker. The editor recommended the name of a person whom he knew to be an outside broker and whom he ought to have known, if he had made proper inquiries, to be an undischarged bankrupt. The plaintiff dealt with him and lost his money. The case being brought in contract, Vaughan Williams L.J. thought[10] that there was sufficient consideration in the fact that the plaintiff consented to the publication of his question in the defendants' paper if the defendants so chose. For Barnes P. the consideration appears to have lain in the plaintiff addressing an inquiry as invited.[11] In the same way when in *Everett* v. *Griffiths*[12] the Court of Appeal was considering the liability of a doctor towards the person he was certifying, Scrutton L.J.[13] said that the submission to treatment would be a good consideration.

My lords, I have cited these instances so as to show that in one way or another the law has ensured that in this type of case a just result has been reached. But I think that

1. (1867), L.R. 2 C.P. 631.
2. (1867), L.R. 2 C.P. at p. 636.
3. (1703), 2 Ld. Raym. 909.
4. [1918] A.C. 626; [1918–19] All E.R. Rep. 1.
5. [1918] A.C. at p. 654.
6. (1793), 1 Esp. 74.
7. (1789), 1 Hy. Bl. 158.
8. (1825), 4 B. & C. 345.
9. [1908] 1 K.B. 280; [1904–7] All E.R. Rep. 755.
10. [1908] 1 K.B. at p. 287; [1904–7] All E.R. Rep. at p. 756.
11. [1908] 1 K.B. at p. 289; [1904–7] All E.R. Rep. at p. 757.
12. [1920] 3 K.B. 163; *affd.* [1921] 1 A.C. 631.
13. [1920] 3 K.B. at p. 191.

today the result can and should be achieved by the application of the law of negligence and that it is unnecessary and undesirable to construct an artificial consideration. I agree with Sir Frederick Pollock's note on the case of *De la Bere* v. *Pearson, Ltd.*,[1] where he wrote in *Pollock on Contract* (13th Edn.) 140 (note 31) that "the cause of action is better regarded as arising from default in the performance of a voluntary undertaking independent of contract".

My lords, it is true that this principle of law has not yet been clearly applied to a case where the service which the defendant undertakes to perform is or includes the obtaining and imparting of information. But I cannot see why it should not be: and if it had not been thought erroneously that *Derry* v. *Peek*[2] negatived any liability for negligent statements, I think that by now it probably would have been. It cannot matter whether the information consists of fact or of opinion or is a mixture of both, nor whether it was obtained as a result of special inquiries or comes direct from facts already in the defendant's possession or from his general store of professional knowledge. One cannot, as I have already endeavoured to show, distinguish in this respect between a duty to inquire and a duty to state.

I think, therefore, that there is ample authority to justify your lordships in saying now that the categories of special relationships, which may give rise to a duty to take care in word as well as in deed, are not limited to contractual relationships or to relationships of fiduciary duty, but include also relationships which in the words of Lord Shaw in *Nocton* v. *Lord Ashburton*[3] are "equivalent to contract" that is, where there is an assumption of responsibility in circumstances in which, but for the absence of consideration, there would be a contract. Where there is an express undertaking, an express warranty as distinct from mere representation, there can be little difficulty. The difficulty arises in discerning those cases in which the undertaking is to be implied. In this respect the absence of consideration is not irrelevant. Payment for information or advice is very good evidence that it is being relied on and that the informer or adviser knows that it is. Where there is no consideration, it will be necessary to exercise greater care in distinguishing between social and professional relationships and between those which are of a contractual character and those which are not. It may often be material to consider whether the adviser is acting purely out of good nature or whether he is getting his reward in some indirect form. The service that a bank performs in giving a reference is not done simply out of a desire to assist commerce. It would discourage the customers of the bank if their deals fell through because the bank had refused to testify to their credit when it was good.

I have had the advantage of reading all the opinions prepared by your lordships and of studying the terms which your lordships have framed by way of definition of the sort of relationship which gives rise to a responsibility towards those who act on information or advice and so creates a duty of care towards them. I do not understand any of your lordships to hold that it is a responsibility imposed by law on certain types of persons or in certain sorts of situations. It is a responsibility that is voluntarily accepted or undertaken either generally where a general relationship, such as that of solicitor and client or banker and customer, is created, or specifically in relation to a particular transaction. In the present case the appellants were not, as in *Woods* v. *Martins Bank, Ltd.*[4] the customers or potential customers of the bank. Responsibility can attach only to the single act, i.e., the giving of the reference, and only if the doing of that act implied a voluntary undertaking to assume responsibility. This is a point of great importance because it is, as I understand it, the foundation for the ground on which in the end the House dismisses the appeal. I do not think it possible to formulate with exactitude all the conditions under which the law will in a specific case imply a voluntary undertaking, any more than it is possible to formulate

---

1. [1908] 1 K.B. 280; [1904-7] All E.R. Rep. 755.
2. (1889), 14 App. Cas. 337.
3. [1914] A.C. at p. 972; [1914-15] All E.R. Rep. at p. 62.
4. [1959] 1 Q.B. 55; [1958] 3 All E.R. 166.

those in which the law will imply a contract. But in so far as your lordships describe the circumstances in which an implication will ordinarily be drawn, I am prepared to adopt any one of your lordships' statements as showing the general rule; and I pay the same respect to the statement by Denning L.J. in his dissenting judgment in *Candler* v. *Crane, Christmas & Co.*[1] about the circumstances in which he says a duty to use care in making a statement exists. . . .

I shall therefore content myself with the proposition that wherever there is a relationship equivalent to contract there is a duty of care. Such a relationship may be either general or particular. Examples of a general relationship are those of solicitor and client and of banker and customer. For the former *Nocton* v. *Lord Ashburton*[2] has long stood as the authority and for the latter there is the decision of Salmon J. in *Woods* v. *Martins Bank, Ltd.*[3] which I respectfully approve. There may well be others yet to be established. Where there is a general relationship of this sort it is unnecessary to do more than prove its existence and the duty follows. Where, as in the present case, what is relied on is a particular relationship created ad hoc, it will be necessary to examine the particular facts to see whether there is an express or implied undertaking of responsibility.

I regard this proposition as an application of the general conception of proximity. Cases may arise in the future in which a new and wider proposition, quite independent of any notion of contract, will be needed. There may, for example, be cases in which a statement is not supplied for the use of any particular person, any more than in *McAlister* (or *Donoghue*) v. *Stevenson*[4] the ginger beer was supplied for consumption by any particular person; and it will then be necessary to return to the general conception of proximity and to see whether there can be evolved from it, or was done in *Donoghue* v. *Stevenson*,[4] a specific proposition to fit the case. When that has to be done, the speeches of your lordships today as well as the judgment of Denning L.J. to which I have referred—and also, I may add the proposition in the "Restatement",[5] and the cases which exemplify it, will afford good guidance as to what ought to be said. I prefer to see what shape such cases take before committing myself to any formulation, for I bear in mind Lord Atkin's warning, which I have quoted, against placing unnecessary restrictions on the adaptability of English law. I have, I hope, made it clear that I take quite literally the dictum of Lord MacMillan, so often quoted from the same case, that[6] "the categories of negligence are never closed". English law is wide enough to embrace any new category or proposition that exemplifies the principle of proximity.

I have another reason for caution. Since the essence of the matter in the present case and in others of the same type is the acceptance of responsibility, I should like to guard against the imposition of restrictive terms notwithstanding that the essential condition is fulfilled. If a defendant says to a plaintiff:—"Let me do this for you, do not waste your money in employing a professional, I will do it for nothing and you can rely on me", I do not think that he could escape liability simply because he belonged to no profession or calling, had no qualifications or special skill and did not hold himself out as having any. The relevance of these factors is to show the unlikelihood of a defendant in such circumstances assuming a legal responsibility and as such they may often be decisive. But they are not theoretically conclusive, and so cannot be the subject of definition. It would be unfortunate if they were. For it would mean that plaintiffs would seek to avoid the rigidity of the definition by bringing the action in contract

---

1. [1951] 2 K.B. 164, at p. 179; [1951] 1 All E.R. 426, at p. 433.
2. [1914] A.C. 932; [1914–15] All E.R. Rep. 45.
3. [1959] 1 Q.B. 55; [1958] 3 All E.R. 166.
4. [1932] A.C. 562; [1932] All E.R. Rep. 1.
5. See 65 CORPUS JURIS SECUNDUM title Negligence, pp. 428, 429, §20, which begins "A false statement negligently made may be the basis of a recovery of damages for injury or loss sustained in consequence of reliance thereon, the American rule, in this respect, being more liberal than the rule in England."•
6. [1932] A.C. at p. 619; [1932] All E.R. Rep. at p. 30.

as in *De la Bere* v. *Pearson, Ltd.*[1] and setting up something that would do for consideration. That to my mind would be an undesirable development in the law and the best way
of avoiding it is to settle the law so that the presence or absence of consideration makes
no difference.

Your lordships' attention was called to a number of cases in courts of first instance
or of appeal which it was said would have been decided differently if the appellant's
main contention was correct. I do not propose to go through them in order to consider
whether on the facts of each it should or should not be upheld. I shall content myself
with saying that in my opinion *Le Lievre* v. *Gould*[2] and all decisions based on its reasoning (in which I specifically include, or otherwise it might be thought that generalia
specialibus non derogant, the decision of Devlin J. in *Heskell* v. *Continental Express,
Ltd.*[3]) can no longer be regarded as authoritative; and when similar facts arise in the
future, the case will have to be judged afresh in the light of the principles which the
House has now laid down.

My lords, I have devoted much time and thought to considering the first reason
given by counsel for the respondents for rejecting the appellants' claim. I have done so,
not only because his reason was based on a ground so fundamental that it called for a
full refutation, but also because it is impossible to find the correct answer on the facts
to the appellants' claim until the relevant criteria ascertaining whether or not there is a
duty to take care have been clearly established. Once that is done their application to the
facts of this case can be done very shortly, for the case then becomes a very simple one.

I am satisfied for the reasons which I have given that a person for whose use a
banker's reference is furnished is not, simply because no consideration has passed, prevented from contending that the banker is responsible to him for what he has said. The
question is whether the appellants can set up a claim equivalent to contract and rely on
an implied undertaking to accept responsibility. Counsel for the respondents' second
point is that in *Robinson* v. *National Bank of Scotland*[4] this House has already laid it down
as a general rule that in the case of a banker furnishing a reference that cannot be done.
I do not agree. The facts in that case have been stated by my noble and learned friend
LORD REID and I need not repeat them. I think it is plain on those facts that the bank
in that case was not furnishing the reference for the use of the pursuer; he was not a person for whose use of the reference they were undertaking any responsibility, and that
quite apart from their general disclaimer. Furthermore, the pursuer never saw the
reference; he was given only what the Lord Justice-Clerk described[5] as "a gloss of it".
This makes the connexion between the pursuer and the defendants far too remote to
constitute a relationship of a contractual character.

On the facts of the present case counsel for the respondents has, under his third head,
argued for the same result. He submits, first, that it ought not to be inferred that the
respondents knew that National Provincial Bank, Ltd. were asking for the reference for
the use of a customer. If the respondents did know that, then counsel submits that they
did not intend that the reference itself should be communicated to the customer; it was
intended only as material upon which the customer's bank could advise the customer
on its own responsibility. I should consider it necessary to examine these contentions
were it not for the general disclaimer of responsibility which appears to me in any event
to be conclusive. I agree entirely with the reasoning and conclusion on this point of
my noble and learned friend LORD REID. A man cannot be said voluntarily to be undertaking a responsibility if at the very moment when he is said to be accepting it he

---

1. [1908] 1 K.B. 280; [1904–7] All E.R. Rep. 755.
2. [1893] 1 Q.B. 491.
3. [1950] 1 All E.R. 1033, at p. 1044.
4. 1916 S.C. (H.L.) 154.
5. 1916 S.C. at p. 58.

declares that in fact he is not. The problem of reconciling words of exemption with the existence of a duty arises only when a party is claiming exemption from a responsibility which he has already undertaken or which he is contracting to undertake. For this reason alone, I would dismiss the appeal.

LORD PEARCE: ... How wide the sphere of the duty of care in negligence is to be laid depends ultimately on the courts' assessment of the demands of society for protection from the carelessness of others. Economic protection has lagged behind protection in physical matters where there is injury to person and property. It may be that the size and the width of the range of possible claims has acted as a deterrent to extension of economic protection. In this sphere the law was developed in the United States in *Glanzer* v. *Shepard*,[1] where a public weigher employed by a vendor was held liable to a purchaser for giving him a certificate which negligently overstated the amount of the goods supplied to him. The defendant was thus engaged on a task in which, as he knew, vendor and purchaser alike depended on his skill and care and the fact that it was the vendor who paid him was merely an accident of commerce. This case was followed and developed in later cases.

In *Ultramares Corpn.* v. *Touche*,[2] however, the court felt the undesirability of exposing defendants to a potential liability "in an indeterminate amount for an indefinite time to an indeterminate class". It decided that auditors were not liable for negligence in the preparation of their accounts (of which they supplied thirty copies although they were not aware of the specific purpose, namely, to obtain financial help) to a plaintiff who lent money on the strength of them. In South Africa, under a different system of law, two cases show a similar advance and subsequent restriction (*Perlman* v. *Zoutendyk*[3] and *Herschel* v. *Mrupe*.[4] ...

If an innocent misrepresentation is made between parties in a fiduciary relationship it may, on that ground, give a right to claim damages for negligence. There is also in my opinion a duty of care created by special relationships which, though not fiduciary, give rise to an assumption that care as well as honesty is demanded.

Was there such a relationship in the present case as to impose on the respondents a duty of care to the appellants as the undisclosed principals for whom National Provincial Bank, Ltd. was making the inquiry? The answer to that question depends on the circumstances of the transaction. If, for instance, they disclosed a casual social approach to the inquiry no such special relationship or duty of care would be assumed (see *Fish* v. *Kelly*).[5] To import such a duty the representation must normally, I think, concern a business or professional transaction whose nature makes clear the gravity of the inquiry and the importance and influence attached to the answer. It is conceded that Salmon J. rightly found a duty of care in *Woods* v. *Martins Bank, Ltd.*[6] but the facts in that case were wholly different from those in the present case. A most important circumstance is the form of the inquiry and of the answer. Both were here plainly stated to be without liability. Counsel for the appellants argues that those words are not sufficiently precise to exclude liability for negligence. Nothing, however, except negligence could, in the facts of this case, create a liability (apart from fraud to which they cannot have been intended to refer and against which the words would be no protection since they would be part of the fraud). I do not, therefore, accept that, even if the parties were already in contractual or other special relationship, the words would give no immunity to a negligent answer. But in any event they clearly prevent a special relationship from arising. They are part of the material from which one deduces whether

1. (1922), 233 N.Y. 236.
2. (1931), 255 N.Y. 170.
3. 1934 C.P.D. 151.
4. 1954 (3) S.A. 464.
5. (1864), 17 C.B.N.S. 194.
6. [1959] 1 Q.B. 55; [1958] 3 All E.R. 166.

a duty of care and a liability for negligence was assumed. If both parties say expressly (in a case where neither is deliberately taking advantage of the other) that there shall be no liability. I do not find it possible to say that a liability was assumed. . . .

Appeal allowed

Mutual Life & Citizens' Assurance Co., Ltd. v. Evatt

Judicial Committee of the Privy Council   [1971] I All E.R. 150

In his pleading, the plaintiff alleged that he was a policy holder in the defendant company and asked them for advice on the financial stability of an associated company of theirs. Knowing that if the advice given were favourable he would invest in it, the defendants carelessly gave him false information, upon which he relied and consequently lost money on an investment in it. The plaintiff did not allege that the defendants carried on the business of supplying information or advice on investments, or that the defendants had claimed to possess any qualification, skill or competence to do so greater than that of the ordinary reasonable man.

The defendants demurred to this pleading on the ground that the facts alleged did not disclose any cause of action known to the law. The demurrer was dismissed by the Court of Appeal of the Supreme Court of New South Wales. On appeal, this judgment was upheld by a majority of the High Court of Australia. A majority of the Board (Lords Diplock, Hodson and Guest) advised Her Majesty that the appeal should be allowed.

LORD DIPLOCK: . . . In *Hedley Byrne*[1] itself and in the previous English cases on negligent statements which were analysed in the speeches, with the notable exceptions of *Fish* v. *Kelly*,[2] *Derry* v. *Peek*[3] and *Low* v. *Bouverie*,[4] the relationship possessed the characteristics (1) that the maker of the statement had made it in the ordinary course of his business or profession and (2) that the subject matter of the statement called for the exercise of some qualification, skill or competence not possessed by the ordinary reasonable man, to which the maker of the statement was known by the recipient to lay claim by reason of his engaging in that business or profession. . . .

The instant appeal is concerned with a statement consisting of "information and advice concerning the financial stability of a certain company . . . and as to the safety of investments therein". In regard to this subject-matter, i.e. financial stability and safety of investment, no distinction need be drawn between "information" and "advice" and it is convenient to use the latter word. Such advice to be reliable (i.e. to be of a quality on which it would be reasonable for the advisee to rely in determining his course of action in a matter which affected his economic interests) calls for the exercise on the part of the advisor of special skill and competence to form a judgment in the subject-matter of the advice, which the advisee does not possess himself. The problem to be solved arises in that field of human activity which calls for the services of a skilled man. The proposition stated in the maxim spondet peritiam artis et imperitia culpae adnumeratur is one of the oldest principles in English law. The duty imposed by law on those who followed a calling which required skill and competence to exercise in their calling such reasonable skill and competence as was appropriate to it, lies at the origin of the action of assumpsit itself. It was first applied to artificers,[5] "for it is the duty of every artificer to exercise his art right and truly as he ought". It was later extended to all other occupations which involve the doing of acts calling for some

---

1. [1964] A.C. 465; [1963] 2 All E.R. 575.
2. (1864), 17 C.B.N.S. 194.
3. (1889), 14 App. Cas. 337; [1886–90] All E.R. Rep. 1.
4. [1891] 3 Ch. 82; [1891–94] All E.R. Rep. 348.
5. Fitzherbert, Natura Brevium (1534), 94D.

special skill or competence not possessed by the ordinary man. The standard of skill and competence was that which is generally possessed to persons who engage in the calling, business or profession of doing acts of that kind for reward. The duty to conform to the standard was attracted by engaging in that particular calling, business or profession because by doing so a man holds himself out as possessing the necessary skill and competence for it. To undertake to do an act requiring special skill and competence for reward was also a sufficient holding out by the obligor to the obligee. But the doing of the act gratuitously by a person who did not engage in the calling, business or profession, did not attract a duty to exercise skill and competence: *Shiells* v. *Blackburne*.[1] See also the references to the relevant cases in the speeches in *Hedley Byrne* of Lord Hodson[2] and Lord Pearce.[3]

Where advice which calls for the exercise of special skill and competence by the advisor is not to be based exclusively on facts communicated to him by the advisee no relevant distinction can be drawn between the ascertaining by the advisor of the facts on which to base his judgment as to the advice to be given, and the forming of that judgment itself. The need for special skill and competence extends to the selection of the particular facts which need to be ascertained in order to form a reliable judgment and to the identification of the sources from which such facts can be obtained.

As in the case of a person who gratuitously does an act which calls for the exercise of some special skill and competence, a duty of care which lies on an advisor must be a duty to conform to an ascertainable standard of skill and competence in relation to the subject-matter of the advice. Otherwise there can be no way of determining whether the advisor was in breach of his duty of care. The problem cannot be solved by saying that the advisor must do his honest best according to the skill and competence which he in fact possesses, for in the law of negligence standards of care are always objective. The passages in the judgment of Sir Herbert Cozens-Hardy M.R. in *Parsons* v. *Barclay & Co., Ltd.*[4] and of Pearson L.J. in the Court of Appeal in *Hedley Byrne*[5] itself, which were quoted with approval in the House of Lords, make it clear that a banker giving a gratuitous reference is not required to do his best by, for instance, making enquiries from outside sources which are available to him, though this would make his reference more reliable. All that he is required to do is to conform to that standard of skill and competence and diligence which is generally shown by persons who carry on the business of providing references of that kind. Equally it is no excuse to him to say that he has done his honest best, if what he does falls below that standard because in fact he lacks the necessary skill and competence to attain to it.

The reason why the law requires him to conform to this standard of skill and competence and diligence is that by carrying on a business which includes the giving of references of this kind he has let it be known to the recipient of the reference that he claims to possess that degree of skill and competence and is willing to apply that degree of diligence to the provision of any reference which he supplies in the course of that business, whether gratuitously so far as the recipient is concerned or not. If he supplies the reference the law requires him to make good his claim. It would not in their Lordships' view be consonant with the principles hitherto accepted in the common law that the duty to comply with that objective standard should be extended to an advisor who, at the time at which his advice is sought, has not let

---

1. (1789) 1 Hy Bl. 158, at p. 162.
2. [1964] A.C. at p. 510; [1963] 2 All E.R. at p. 598.
3. [1964] A.C. at pp. 537, 538; [1963] 2 All E.R. at p. 616.
4. (1910), 103 L.T. 196, at p. 199; [1908–10] All E.R. Rep. 429, at pp. 432, 433.
5. [1962] 1 Q.B. 396, at pp. 414, 415; [1961] 3 All E.R. 891, at p. 902.

it be known to the advisee that he claims to possess the standard of skill and competence and is prepared to exercise diligence which is generally shown by persons who
carry on the business of giving advice of the kind sought. He has given the advisee
no reason to suppose that he is acquainted with the standard or capable of complying
with it, or that he has such appreciation of the nature and magnitude of the loss
which the advisee may sustain by reason of any failure by that advisor to attain that
standard as a reasonable man would require before assuming a liability to answer
for the loss.

But if it would not be just or reasonable to require him to conform to this objective
standard of care which would be incumbent on a person who carried on the business
of giving advice of the kind sought, there is in their Lordships' view no half-way
house between that and the common law duty which each man owes his neighbour
irrespective of his skill, the duty of honesty. No half-way house has been suggested
in the argument in the instant appeal or in any of the decided cases. That the duty
was confined to that of honesty was decided, as their Lordships think rightly, in
Low v. *Bouverie*.[1] . . .

In *Low* v. *Bouverie*[1] it was made plain to the defendant, who was trustee of a settlement, that the information sought from him as to encumbrances on the life interest
of his cestui qui trust was required by the enquirer for the purpose of enabling him
to make a decision on a business transaction and that he would rely on that information. The trustee informed the enquirer of the existence of certain encumbrances
but omitted to mention six prior mortgages whose existence he had forgotten, though
they were recited in the deed by which he had been appointed trustee of the settlement
four years before. The only skill and competence on his part which was called for to
enable him to provide accurate information was the ability to appreciate the need to
look at the deed of appointment. In their Lordships' view the crucial distinction
between this case and those cases which it was held in *Hedley Byrne*[2] gave rise to a duty
of care as well as honesty (i.e. *Cann* v. *Wilson*,[3] *Le Lievre* v. *Gould*,[4] *Candler* v. *Crane,
Christmas & Co.*,[5] *Woods* v. *Martins Bank, Ltd.*[6] and *Hedely Byrne*[2] itself) is that the trustee
in *Low* v. *Bouverie*[1] did not hold himself out to the enquirer as being prepared to supply
in the course of his business information of the kind sought. He had made no claim to
any skill or competence which the law could require him to make good.

The carrying on of a business or profession which involves the giving of advice
of a kind which calls for special skill and competence is the normal way in which a
person lets it be known to the recipient of the advice that he claims to possess that
degree of skill and competence and is willing to exercise that degree of diligence
which is generally possessed and exercised by persons who carry on the business or
profession of giving advice of the kind sought. . . .

While accepting this as the common case giving rise to the duty of care their Lordships would not wish to exclude the case where the advisor, although not carrying
on the business or profession generally, has, at or before the time at which his advice
is sought, let it be known in some other way that he claims to possess skill and competence in the subject-matter of the particular enquiry comparable to those who do
carry on the business or profession of advising on that subject-matter and is prepared
to exercise a comparable skill and competence in giving the advice. Here too, by
parity of reasoning, the law should require him to make good his claim. But the
mere giving of advice with knowledge, as in *Low* v. *Bouverie*[1] that the enquirer intends
to rely on it does not, of itself, in their Lordships' view amount to such a claim. The

---

1. [1891] 3 Ch. 82; [1891–94] All E.R. Rep. 348.
2. [1964] A.C. 465; [1963] 2 All E.R. 575.
3. (1888), 39 Ch. D. 39.
4. [1893] 1 Q.B. 491.
5. [1951] 2 K.B. 164; [1951] 1 All E.R. 426.
6. [1959] 1 Q.B. 55; [1958] 3 All E.R. 166.

converse of this is the case where a person who does carry on a business or profession which involves the giving of advice of the kind sought by the enquirer, does so in circumstances which should let it be known to a reasonable enquirer that he was not prepared to exercise in relation to the particular advice sought that degree of diligence which he would exercise in giving such advice for reward in the course of his business or profession. Casual advice given by a professional man on a social or informal occasion is the typical example, of which *Fish* v. *Kelly*[1] provides an illustration among the decided cases. . . .

. . . The facts alleged if proved at the trial would establish no more than that the company could have provided the respondent with reliable advice if it had chosen to make the enquiries requisite to provide the material necessary to form a reliable judgment and had required its skilled and competent officers, who ex concessu were not employed for that purpose, to divert themselves from their ordinary employment to exercise their skill and competence on the information so obtained. The same could be said of the successful defendant in *Low* v. *Bouverie*.[2] The requisite enquiry which he failed to make, i.e. to inspect his own deed of appointment, indeed, involved no recourse to outside sources. If he did not realise the need to do so or its significance when inspected he could have consulted his solicitor. As respects recourse to outside sources of information the same might be said of any banker giving a reference in the actual course of his business, for, as already pointed out, although by virtue of his carrying on that business the law does impose on him some duty of care, that duty does not extend to making enquiries of outside sources.

In their Lordships' view these additional allegations are insufficient to fill the fatal gap in the declaration that it contains no averment that the company to the knowledge of the respondent carried on the business of giving advice on investments or in some other way had let it be known to him that they claimed to possess the necessary skill and competence to do so and were prepared to exercise the necessary diligence to give reliable advice to him on the subject-matter of his enquiry. In the absence of any allegation to this effect the respondent was not entitled to assume that the company had accepted any other duty towards him than to give an honest answer to his enquiry nor, in the opinion of their Lordships, did the law impose any higher duty on them. This is in agreement with the reasoning of Taylor J. in the High Court of Australia with which the judgment of Owen J. is also consistent.

As with any other important case in the development of the common law, *Hedley Byrne*[3] should not be regarded as intended to lay down the metes and bounds of the new field of negligence of which the gate is now opened. Those will fall to be ascertained step by step as the facts of particular cases which come before the courts make it necessary to determine them. The instant appeal is an example: but their Lordships would emphasise that the missing characteristic of the relationship which they consider to be essential to give rise to a duty of care in a situation of the kind in which the respondent and the company found themselves when he sought their advice, is not necessarily essential in other situations, such as, perhaps, where the advisor has a financial interest in the transaction on which he gives his advice (cf. *W. B. Anderson & Sons, Ltd*. v. *Rhodes (Liverpool), Ltd.*;[4] American Restatement of the Law of Torts).[5] On this, as on any other metes and bounds of the doctrine of *Hedley Byrne*[3] their Lordships are expressing no opinion. The categories of negligence are never closed and their Lordships' opinion in the instant appeal, like all judicial reasoning, must be understood secundum subjectam materiam. . . .

Dissenting judgment by LORD REID and LORD MORRIS OF BORTH-Y-GEST: . . . Much of the argument was directed to establishing that a person giving advice cannot

1. (1864), 17 C.B.N.S. 194.
2. [1891] 3 Ch. 82; [1891–94] All E.R. Rep. 348.
3. [1964] A.C. 465; [1968] 2 All E.R. 575.
4. [1967] 2 All E.R. 850.
5. Third Tentative Redraft.

be under any duty to take care unless he has some special skill, competence, qualification or information with regard to the matter on which his advice is sought. But then how much skill or competence must he have? Even a man with a professional qualification is seldom an expert on all matters dealt with by members of his profession. Must the adviser be an expert or specialist in the matter on which his advice is sought? And when it comes to matters of business or finance where those whose business it is to deal with such matters generally have no recognised formal qualification, how is the sufficiency of the adviser's special skill or competence to be measured? If the adviser is invited in a business context to advise on a certain matter and he chooses to accept that invitation and to give without warning or qualification what appears to be considered advice, is he to be allowed to turn round later and say that he was under no duty to take care because in fact he had no sufficient skill or competence to give the advice?

It must be borne in mind that there is here no question of warranty. If the adviser were to be held liable because his advice was bad then it would be relevant to enquire into his capacity to give the advice. But here and in cases coming within the principles laid down in *Hedley Byrne*[1] the only duty in question is a duty to take reasonable care before giving the advice. We can see no ground for the distinction that a specially skilled man must exercise care but a less skilled man need not do so. We are unable to accept the argument that a duty to take care is the same as a duty to conform to a particular standard of skill. One must assume a reasonable man who has that degree of knowledge and skill which facts known to the enquirer (including statements made by the adviser) entitled him to expect of the adviser, and then enquire whether such a reasonable man could have given the advice which was in fact given if he had exercised reasonable care.

Then it was argued that an adviser ought not to be under any liability to exercise care unless he had, before the advice was sought, in some way held himself out as able and willing to give advice. We can see no virtue in a previous holding out. If the enquirer, knowing that the adviser is in a position to give informed advice, seeks that advice and the adviser agrees to give it, we are unable to see why his duty should be more onerous by reason of the fact that he had previously done the same for others. And again, if the previous conduct of the adviser is relevant, would it be sufficient that, in order to attract new customers or increase the goodwill of existing customers, he had indicated a general willingness to do what he could to help enquirers, or must he have indicated a willingness and ability to deal with the precise kind of matter on which the enquirer seeks his assistance? In our judgment when an enquirer consults a businessman in the course of his business and makes it plain to him that he is seeking considered advice and intends to act on it in a particular way, any reasonable businessman would realise that, if he chooses to give advice without any warning or qualification, he is putting himself under a moral obligation to take some care. It appears to us to be well within the principles established by the *Hedley Byrne*[1] case to regard his action in giving such advice as creating a special relationship between him and the enquirer and to translate his moral obligation into a legal obligation to take such care as is reasonable in the whole circumstances. In *Hedley Byrne*[1] their Lordships were not laying down rules. They were developing a principle which flows, as in all branches of the tort of negligence, from giving legal effect to what ordinary reasonable men habitually do in certain circumstances. Admittedly there is nothing in *Hedley Byrne's* case[1] which governs this case. The principles there indicated must be developed from time to time to cover new cases, and we have attempted to set out what we believe to be a proper development to meet the present case. We are unable to construe the passages from our speeches cited in the judgment of the majority in the way in which they are there construed.[2] In our view they are

---

1. [1964] A.C. 465; [1963] 2 All E.R. 575.
2. [These extracts have been omitted.]

consistent with and support the views which we have already expressed in the present case. We do not think that it would be useful to quote expressions from speeches used without having in mind circumstances'such as we have here . . .

Note

1. What weight is to be attached to the speeches in *Hedley Byrne* on the subject of liability for negligent statements causing "financial" loss? (See Dias, [1963] C.L.J. 221.)

Compare the following statements:

"Whatever may be the weight which might be given to some observations of the learned Lords of Appeal [in *Hedley Byrne*] in fact the action failed simply because the bank had stamped the words 'without responsibility' on their letter. The observations of the Law Lords were *obiter*" (*per* Danckwerts L.J. in *Rondel* v. *W.*, [1966] 3 All E.R. 657, at p. 672).

". . . [T]o treat as *ratio* only that reasoning which is necessary or sufficient to determine the actual result, is surely to overlook that a judge is not a chameleon, flushing with authority when he decides one issue and drained of it when he decides the next" (A. M. Honoré (1965), 8 J.S.P.T.L. (N.S.) 284, at p. 286).

"[T]hose speeches [in *Hedley Byrne*], like all judgments under the common law system, must be understood secundum subjectam materiam" (*per* Lord Diplock in *Mutual Life and Citizens' Assurance Co., Ltd.* v. *Evatt*, [1971] I All E.R. 150, at p. 155).

2. How has the pragmatic objection (liability "in an indeterminate amount for an indefinite time and to an indeterminate class") to recovery for harm to financial interests been met (i) by the speeches in *Hedley Byrne*, and (ii) by the opinion of the majority of the Board in *Mutual Life*? Compare the absence of a duty-situation for negligence in *deed* interfering with financial interests, Chap. 3, p. 71, *ante*.

3. No distinction was drawn by Lord Diplock in *Mutual Life* between "information" and "advice". An example of a misleading prediction giving rise to liability is *Dodds and Dodds* v. *Millman* (1964), 45 D.L.R. (2d) 472 (Brit. Columbia): the defendant, estate agent for the vendor of a block of flats, carelessly prepared misleading estimates of operating costs, so inducing the plaintiff to purchase; the plaintiff was awarded damages. Would a similarly placed plaintiff in England succeed under the Misrepresentation Act 1967, s. 2 (1), p. 498, *ante*?

4. The opinion of the majority of the Board in *Mutual Life* has been criticised, particularly on the ground that it substitutes for "a broad general principle of great flexibility" a series of particular duties imposed on particular classes of defendants according to their status and for particular transactions: see Winfield & Jolowicz, pp. 231–5; cf. Street, p. 206; J. B. F. Rickford (1971), 34 M.L.R. 328; C. S. Phegan, 45 Austr. L.J. 20; K. O. Linogren, 46 Austr. L.J. 176; P. M. North, [1971] A.S.C.L. 491–3. An opposing view is that a limitation on the range of defendants and of transactions makes it easier to decide who should insure: note, e.g., the comment by A. V. Alexander (1972), 12 J.S.P.T.L. (N.S.) 119, at p. 124. that "the position has been reached already when it is not possible for the professions to obtain coverage which, in terms of the total financial indemnity available, fully matches their exposure. In theory at least an insurance broker should have cover equivalent to the largest single risk

which he places and that amount of professional negligence cover is just not available.''

5. The following are examples from decided cases of advisors with *special skills*:

(a) bankers (*Woods* v. *Martin's Bank*, [1959] 1 Q.B. 55; [1958] 3 All E.R. 166, "fiduciary" relationship, described by Lord Hodson in *Hedley Byrne* as a "special" relationship);

(b) accountants, valuers, analysts, surveyors (dissenting judgment of Denning L.J. in *Candler* v. *Crane, Christmas & Co.*, [1951] 2 K.B. 164, at pp. 179–80, approved in *Hedley Byrne* by Lords Hodson, Devlin and Pearce);

(c) insurance brokers (*Osman* v. *J. Ralph Moss, Ltd.*, [1970] 1 Lloyd's Rep. 313), stockbrokers (*Central B.C. Planers* v. *Hocker* (1970), 9 D.L.R. (3d) 689 (Brit. Columbia Sup. Ct.), as a "fiduciary" relationship);

(d) on the application of the test propounded by the majority of the Board in *Mutual Life*, a duty of care will normally be owed by business and professional men such as these if the advice falls within the range of the particular skill. The only class of professional men exempt from liability are barristers who owe no duty of care to their clients in the conduct of litigation; this does not apply to the work done by barristers which is not connected with litigation: *Rondel* v. *Worsley*, [1969] 1 A.C. 191; comment by Roxburgh (1968), 84 L.Q.R. 513; Jolowicz, [1967] C.L.J. 10; [1968] C.L.J. 23. Lord Upjohn, *ibid.*, pp. 293–4, suggests that the immunity operates from the time of the letter before action. Solicitor-advocates are probably also protected when carrying out work in litigation which would have been carried out by counsel had counsel been employed in the case: *per* Lord Reid, *ibid.*, p. 232, and see Lord Pearson, p. 294, Lord Upjohn, pp. 284–5. Advocates in several other countries seem to be able to fulfil their duty to the court and to the administration of justice without this immunity from the actions of disgruntled clients: e.g. *Champion Motor Spares, Ltd.* v. *Phadke* [1969] E.A. 42 (Uganda).

6. In several decisions in common law jurisdictions false information or advice given by government employees has given rise to liability; e.g.

> *Ministry of Housing and Local Government* v. *Sharp*, [1970] 2 Q.B. 223; [1970] 1 All E.R. 1009 (local authority clerk whose work did not require any "special skill" according to Cross L.J.) (p. 519, *post*).
> *Coats Patons (Retail)* v. *Birmingham Corpn.* (1971), 69 L.G.R. 356 (local authority negligently answering questions on conveyancing form)
> *Windsor Motor, Ltd.* v. *District of Powell River* (1969), 4 D.L.R. (3d) 155 (local government officials giving incorrect information as to zoning of premises)
> *Glanzer* v. *Shepard* (1922), 233 N.Y. 236; 135 N.E. 275 (New York: public weigher's certification)

How are these decisions affected by the view of the majority of the Board in *Mutual Life*?

(In some circumstances extra-judicial remedies are available, e.g. a complaint to the Parliamentary Commissioner for Administration: a recent instance will be found in the *Fourth Report of the Commissioner*, Session 1972–73, H.C. 290, Appendix A (incorrect information concerning purchase tax liability).)

7. The majority of the Board in *Mutual Life* recognised that there might be a duty of care where the advisor had *undertaken* to give skilful advice. Why was no *implied* undertaking found in that case? Compare *Hedley Byrne, ante.*

8. The case of *W. B. Anderson & Sons, Ltd.* v. *Rhodes (Liverpool), Ltd.,* [1967] 2 All E.R. 850, was explained by the majority of the Board in *Mutual Life* as one in which "the advisor has a financial interest in the transaction on which he gives his advice". The facts were that the defendants were commission agents on behalf of a company which they negligently certified as creditworthy. Cairns J. held the defendants liable in damages when the company went bankrupt and was unable to pay for potatoes purchased from the wholesaler to whom the representation had been made.

How are the following decisions to be explained or distinguished in the light of *Mutual Life*?

J. Nunes Diamonds, Ltd. v. *Dominion Electric Protection Co.* (1969), 5 D.L.R. (3d) 679; affd., [1971] O.R. 218 (suppliers of burglar alarm system represented that the system had never been circumvented; it was broken into and diamonds were stolen; Addy J. held that had a negligent misrepresentation been made—on the facts none had been—this would have been a "special relationship" giving rise to liability).

Barrett v. *J. R. West, Ltd.,* [1970] N.Z.L.R. 789; noted by L. L. Stevens, [1970] N.Z.L.J. 298 (negligent misrepresentation by defendant estate agents to purchaser that house was on mains drainage when in fact it was on a septic tank. Perry J. held defendants liable despite lack of any special skill or knowledge or profession of such skill).

9. In *Holman Construction, Ltd.* v. *Delta Timber Co., Ltd.,* [1972] N.Z.L.R. 1081 (Sup. Ct.. N.Z.) the plaintiff, a building contractor, asked the defendant, a timber merchant, for his quote for the supply of timber which the plaintiff required in order to submit a tender for a building contract. The plaintiff, intending to accept the defendant's quote, based his own tender thereon, and entered into the building contract. The defendant then discovered a mistake in his calculations and revoked his offer to supply the timber. The plaintiff sued the defendant for damages, being the difference between the price quoted and the next best quote which he was obliged to accept. Henry J. held that the defendant was not liable. The plaintiff had not accepted the defendant's offer at any time before revocation, and the plaintiff could not rely on *Hedley Byrne* as establishing a duty to make a careful estimate. He said (at p. 1083): "Whatever may ultimately be the metes and bounds of *Hedley Byrne* I can see nothing in the cases nor on principle to extend a duty of care to those who express a mere willingness to become bound by contract ... [T]he sole cause of loss, if any, is the plaintiff's failure to exercise his legal right to accept the offer while it was still possible for him to do so."

Compare *Hodgins* v. *Hydro-Electric Commission of the Township of Nepean* (1972), 28 D.L.R. (3d) 174 (Ontario County Ct.) in which the Commission was held liable, on the *Hedley Byrne* principle, for damages suffered by the plaintiff as a result of a carelessly prepared estimate of the cost of heating an addition to plaintiff's home including a swimming pool.

Would either of these cases have been differently decided had the courts applied (a) the "financial interest" test suggested by the majority of the Board in *Mutual Life*? or (b) the concept of a collateral warranty giving rise to liability in contract? (cf. *Willmore* v. *S. E. Electricity Board*, [1957] 2 Lloyd's Rep. 375, in which the main transaction was the supply of electricity under statute, and a collateral contract that the supply would be maintained was defeated because of an absence of intention to create contractual relations; and generally, *Sutton & Shannon on Contracts*, 7th Edn, by A. L. Diamond *et al.* (London, 1970), pp. 129–134, and see *McInerney* v. *Lloyds Bank, Ltd.* [1973] 2 Lloyd's Rep. 389, at p. 401).

10. If the defendant bankers in *Hedley Byrne*, instead of disclaiming responsibility, had simply said, "We have not had time to check our files, but we believe that Easipower is good for its ordinary business engagements," would they have been held liable? For a comparison of the duty of care and the "duty of honesty" see Honoré (1965), 8 J.S.P.T.L. (N.S.) at pp. 290–291, and Stevens (1964), 27 M.L.R. 121, at p. 146. Is there a difference between the "duty of honesty" and the "duty to abstain from deceit"?

11. In *Arenson* v. *Arenson*, [1973] Ch. 346; [1973] 2 All E.R. 235 (C.A.) the plaintiff sold shares to his uncle at a "fair" value to be determined by the company's auditors. The nephew brought these proceedings on the basis that the shares were negligently valued. It was held ((Buckley L.J. and Sir Seymour Karminksi, Lord Denning M.R. dissenting) that *Hedley Byrne* had no effect upon the well-established doctrine that where two parties submitted to a third party some question for arbitrament, that third party was acting in a quasi-judicial capacity and was not liable for anything done in that role if he acted honestly. That doctrine applied here since the parties were seeking an adjudication from the third party: but see note 12, *post*.

12. In *Sutcliffe* v. *Thackrah*, [1974] 1 All E.R. 859 (H.L.), it was held that a firm of architects could be held liable for negligence in issuing certificates which over-stated the amount due by an employer to his building contractor. "A person will only be an arbitrator [entitled to an immunity] if there is a submission to him either of a specific dispute or of present points of difference or of defined differences that may in future arise and if there is agreement that his decision will be binding. The circumstance that an architect in valuing work must act fairly and impartially does not constitute him either an arbitrator or quasi-arbitrator" (*per* Lord Morris of Borth-y-Gest at p. 877).

13. Among the many articles on *Hedley Byrne*, special attention is drawn to: Stevens, "*Hedley Byrne* v. *Heller*: Judicial Creativity and Doctrinal Possibility" (1964), 27 M.L.R. 121; Goodhart, "Liability for Innocent but Negligent Misrepresentations" (1964), 74 Yale L.J. 286; Honoré, *Hedley Byrne & Co., Ltd.* v. *Heller & Partners Ltd.*" (1965), 8 J.S.P.T.L. (N.S.) 284; Weir, "Liability for Syntax", [1963] C.L.J. 216.

Ministry of Housing and Local Government v. Sharp

Court of Appeal   [1970] 1 All E.R. 1009

The Ministry had registered a planning charge in the local land charges registry after the payment of compensation to a Mr. Neale who had been refused permission to develop his land. Any later developer of the land would have to repay this sum to the Ministry before development of the land could take place. Two years' later planning permission was granted, and a prospective purchaser of the land requested an official search in the register of local land charges. The certificate omitted to mention the Ministry's charge, as a result of the carelessness of a clerk employed by the local authority. The Ministry conceded that the purchaser was not liable to repay the sum because the clear certificate was conclusive in his favour. Compensation for the loss was sought from the local registrar of land charges for breach of statutory duty and from the local authority who, it was alleged, were vicariously liable for the clerk's mistake.

Fisher J. dismissed the Ministry's action for damages. The Court of Appeal, by a majority (Salmon and Cross L.JJ., Lord Denning M.R. dissenting) held that the registrar was not under an absolute statutory obligation to issue an accurate certificate and since no negligence on the part of the registrar was alleged, the claim against the registrar failed. However, the Court of Appeal, reversing the judgment of Fisher J. in this respect, held that the clerk was liable to the Ministry and the local authority was vicariously liable for his fault.

LORD DENNING M.R.: . . . I have no doubt that the clerk is liable. He was under a duty at common law to use due care. That was a duty which he owed to any person—incumbrancer or purchaser—who, he knew or ought to have known, might be injured if he made a mistake. The case comes four square within the principles which are stated in *Candler* v. *Crane Christmas & Co.*,[1] and which were approved by the House of Lords in *Hedley Byrne & Co., Ltd.* v. *Heller & Partners, Ltd.*[2]

Counsel for the defendants submitted to us, however, that the correct principle did not go that length. He said that a duty to use due care (where there was no contract) only arose when there was a voluntary assumption of responsibility. I do not agree. He relied particularly on the words of Lord Reid in *Hedley Byrne & Co., Ltd. v. Heller & Partners, Ltd.*[3] and of Lord Devlin.[4] I think that they used those words because of the special circumstances of that case (where the bank disclaimed responsibility). But they did not in any way mean to limit the general principle.

In my opinion the duty to use due care in a statement arises, not from any voluntary assumption of responsibility, but from the fact that the person making it knows, or ought to know, that others, being his neighbours in this regard, would act on the faith of the statement being accurate. That is enough to bring the duty into being. It is owed, of course, to the person to whom the certificate is issued and who he knows is going to act on it, see the judgment of Cardozo J. in *Glanzer* v. *Sheppard*.[5] But it also is owed to any person who he knows or ought to know, will be injuriously affected by a mistake, such as the incumbrancer here. . . .

SALMON L.J.: . . . The present case does not precisely fit into any category of negligence yet considered by the courts. The Ministry has not been misled by any careless statement made to it by the defendants or made by the defendants to someone else who the defendants knew would be likely to pass it on to a third party such as the Ministry, in circumstances in which the third party might reasonably be expected to rely on it, see for example, Denning L.J.'s dissenting judgment in *Candler* v. *Crane, Christmas & Co.*[1] which was adopted and approved by the House of Lords in *Hedley Byrne & Co., Ltd.* v. *Heller & Partners,*[2] *Ltd.* I am not, however, troubled by the fact that the present case is, in many respects, unique. I rely on the celebrated dictum of Lord MacMillan that "The categories of negligence are never closed", *Donoghue* v. *Stevenson*,[6] and the words of Lord Devlin in *Hedley Byrne & Co., Ltd.* v. *Heller & Partners, Ltd.*[2] . . .

---

1. [1951] 2 K.B. 164, at pp. 179–185; [1951] 1 All E.R. 426, at pp. 433–436.
2. [1964] A.C. 465; [1963] 2 All E.R. 575.
3. [1964] A.C. at p. 487; [1963] 2 All E.R. at p. 583.
4. [1964] A.C. at p. 529; [1963] 2 All E.R. at pp. 610, 611.
5. (1922), 23 N.Y. 236.
6. [1932] A.C. at p. 619; [1932] All E.R. Rep. at p. 30.

It has been argued, in the present case, that since the council did not voluntarily make the search or prepare the certificate for their clerk's signature they did not voluntarily assume responsibility for the accuracy of the certificate and, accordingly, owed no duty of care to the Minister. I do not accept that, in all cases, the obligation to take reasonable care necessarily depends on a voluntary assumption of responsibility. Even if it did, I am far from satisfied that the council did not voluntarily assume responsibility in the present case. On the contrary, it seems to me that they certainly chose to undertake the duty of searching the register and preparing the certificate. There was nothing to compel them to discharge this duty through their servant. It obviously suited them better that this somewhat pedestrian task should be performed by one of their comparatively minor servants than by their clerk so that he might be left free to carry out other far more difficult and important functions on their behalf.

I do not think that it matters that the search was made at the request of the purchasers and that the certificate issued to him. It would be absurd if a duty of care were owed to a purchaser but not to an incumbrancer. The rules made under many of the statutes creating local land charges do not apply s. 17 (3); they do, however, apply s. 17 (1) and (2) of the Land Charges Act 1925. If, in such cases, a clear certificate is carelessly given, it will be the purchaser and not the incumbrancer who will suffer. Clearly land may be worth much more unincumbered than if it is subject to a charge. The purchaser who buys on the faith of a clear certificate might suffer very heavy financial loss if the certificate turns out to be incorrect. Such a loss is reasonably to be foreseen as a result of any carelessness in the search of the register or the preparation of the certificate. The proximity between the council and the purchaser is even closer than that between the plaintiff and the defendants in *Candler* v. *Crane Christmas & Co.*[1] The council even receive a fee, although a small one, for the certificate. Clearly a duty to take care must exist in such a case. Our law would be grievously defective if the council did owe a duty of care to the purchaser in the one case but no duty to the incumbrancer in the other. The damage in each case is equally foreseeable. It is in my view irrelevant that in the one case the certificate is issued to the person it injures and in the other case it is not. The purchaser is deceived by the certificate about his legal rights when s. 17 (3) of the Land Charges Act 1925 does not apply whilst the incumbrancer's legal rights are taken away by the certificate when s. 17 (3) does apply. In my view the proximity is as close in one case as in the other and certainly sufficient to impose on the council through their servant a duty to take reasonable care.

[CROSS L.J. delivered a judgment in favour of allowing the appeal.]

Appeal allowed

Notes

1. In *Candler* v. *Crane, Christmas & Co.*, [1951] 2 K.B. 164; [1951] 1 All E.R. 426, at p. 434, Denning L.J. in a dissenting judgment, later approved by Lords Hodson, Devlin and Pearce in *Hedley Byrne & Co., Ltd.* v. *Heller & Partners, Ltd., ante*, said that accountants would be liable to "their employer or client, and also, I think, to any third person to whom they themselves show the accounts, or to whom they know their employer is going to show the accounts so as to induce him to invest money or take some other action on them. I do not think, however, the duty can be extended still further so as to include strangers of whom they have heard nothing and to whom their employer without their knowledge may choose to show their accounts." Denning L.J. also suggested (at p. 435) that the duty extended only to those transactions "for which the accountants knew their accounts were required ... Thus a doctor, who negligently certifies a man to be a lunatic when he is not, is

---

1. [1951] 2 K.B. 164; [1951] 1 All E.R. 426.

liable to him, although there is no contract in the matter, because the doctor knows that his certificate is required for the very purpose of deciding whether the man should be detained or not, but an insurance company's doctor owes no duty to the insured person, becaues he makes his examination only for the purposes of the insurance company . . . Again a scientist or expert (including a marine hydrographer) is not liable to his readers for careless statements in his published works. He publishes his work simply to give information, and not with any particular transaction in mind. When, however, a scientist or an expert makes an investigation and report for the very purpose of a particular transaction, then, in my opinion, he is under a duty of care in respect of that transaction . . ."

2. A solicitor negligently drafts a will (is this "advice" or an "act"?) in terms which make a legacy void for perpetuity. Is he liable in damages to a disappointed beneficiary? In *Biakanja* v. *Irving* (1958), 49 Cal. (2d) 647, and *Lucas* v. *Hamm* (1961), 56 Cal. (2d) 583, noted (1965), 81 L.Q.R. 478, it was held that an action would lie in such circumstances. It has been held in several English cases (e.g. *Cook* v. *Swinfen*, [1967] 1 W.L.R. 457, at p. 461) that a client's only cause of action against his solicitor for professional negligence lies in contract. The better view is that these cases do not mean that a solicitor cannot be liable in the absence of contract: see Poulton (1966), 82 L.Q.R. 346, at pp. 360–363, and see p. 144, *ante*.

3. Winfield & Jolowicz, pp. 242–243, suggest that it was the issue of the certificate and not the purchase of the land which caused the Ministry's loss in the *Sharp* case. But, against this view, it can be argued that if the proposed purchase had fallen through, despite the favourable certificate, no loss would have been suffered by the Ministry. In other words, it was not only the issue of the certificate but also the completion of the purchase which caused the loss.

Question

X, a professional footballer, is transferred from A United F.C. to B City F.C. for a transfer fee of £200,000. He is to receive 5 per cent of the fee. The transfer is conditional upon a satisfactory medical report being obtained from B City F.C.'s doctor. The doctor carelessly states to B City F.C. that X has a disease which may at any time bring his career to an end. As a consequence the transfer falls through. Has X a cause of action against the doctor?

3. MALICIOUS FALSEHOODS

Ratcliffe v. Evans

Court of Appeal   [1891–4] All E.R. Rep. 699

This was an action for damages for publication in a newspaper of a statement that the plaintiff's firm had gone out of business. The plaintiff proved a general loss of business as a result of the publication, but could not prove that he had lost any particular customer or order. The jury found that the words were not libellous in the sense of reflecting on plaintiff's character, but that they were not published bona fide. Mr. Commissioner Bompas Q.C. entered judgment for the plaintiff for £120. The defendant's appeal to the Court of Appeal was dismissed.

BOWEN L.J.: . . . That an action will lie for written or oral falsehoods not actionable per se nor even defamatory, where they are maliciously published, where they are calculated in the ordinary course of things to produce, and where they do produce, actual damage, is established law. Such an action is not one of libel or of slander, but an action on the case for damage wilfully and intentionally done without just occasion or excuse, analogous to an action for slander of title. To support it actual damage must be shown, for it is an action which only lies in respect of such damage as has actually occurred. It was contended before us that in such an action it is not enough to allege and prove general loss of business arising from the publication, since such general loss is general, and not special, damage; and special damage—as has often been said—is the gist of such an action on the case.

Lest we should be led astray in such a matter by mere words, it is desirable to recollect that the term "special damage", which is found for centuries in the books, is not always used with reference to similar subject-matter nor in the same context. At times (both in the law of tort and of contract) it is employed to denote that damage arising out of the special circumstances of the case which, if properly pleaded, may be super-added to the general damage which the law implies in every breach of contract and every infringement of an absolute right: see *Ashby* v. *White*.[1] In all such cases the law presumes that some damage will flow in the ordinary course of things from the mere invasion of the plaintiff's rights, and calls it general damage. Special damage in such a context means the particular damage (beyond the general damage) which results from the particular circumstances of the case and of the plaintiff's claim to be compensated, for which he ought to give warning in his pleadings, in order that there may be no surprise at the trial. But where no actual and positive right (apart from the damage done) has been disturbed, it is the damage done that is the wrong; and the expression "special damage", when used of this damage, denotes the actual and temporal loss which has in fact occurred. Such damage is called variously in old authorities "express loss", "particular damage" (*Cane* v. *Golding*),[2] "damage in fact", special or particular cause of loss" (*Harwood* v. *Lowe*,[3] *Tasburgh* v. *Day*[4]).

The term "special damage" has also been used in actions on the case brought for a public nuisance, such as the obstruction of a river or a highway, to denote that actual and particular loss which the plaintiff must allege and prove that he has sustained (beyond what is sustained by the general public) if his action is to be supported, such particular loss being, as is obvious, the cause of action: see *Iveson* v. *Moore*;[5] *Rose* v. *Groves*.[6] In this judgment we shall endeavour to avoid a term which, intelligible enough in particular contexts, tends when successively employed in more than one context, and with regard to different subject-matter, to encourage confusion in thought. The question to be decided does not depend on words, but is one of substance. . . .

In all actions accordingly on the case where the damage actually done is the gist of the action, the character of the acts themselves which produce the damage and the circumstances under which these acts are done, must regulate the degree of certainty and particularity with which the damage done ought to be stated and proved. As much certainty and particularity must be insisted on, both in pleading and proof of damage, as is reasonable, having regard to the circumstances and to the nature of the acts themselves by which the damage is done. To insist upon less would be to relax old and intelligible principles. To insist upon more would be the vainest pedantry. The rule to be laid down with regard to malicious falsehoods affecting property or trade is only an instance of the doctrines of good sense applicable to all that branch of actions on the case to which the class under discussion belongs. The nature and circumstances

---

1. (1703), 2 Ld. Raym. 938.
2. (1649), Sty. 169.
3. (1628), Palm. 529.
4. (1618), Cro. Jac. 484.
5. (1699), 1 Ld. Raym. 486.
6. (1843), 5 Man. & S. 613.

of the publication of the falsehood may accordingly require the admission of evidence of general loss of business, as the natural and direct result produced, and perhaps intended to be produced.

An instructive illustration, and one by which the present appeal is really covered, is furnished by *Hargrave* v. *Le Breton*,[1] decided a century and a half ago. It was an action of slander of title at an auction. The allegation in the declaration was that divers persons who would have purchased at the auction left the place; but no particular persons were named. The objection that they were not specially mentioned was, as the report tells us ,"easily" answered. The answer given was that in the nature of the transaction it was impossible to specify names; that the injury complained of was in effect that the bidding at the auction had been prevented and stopped; and that everybody had gone away. It had, therefore, become impossible to tell with certainty who would have been bidders or purchasers if the auction had not been rendered abortive. This case shows, what sound judgment itself dictates, that in an action for falsehood producing damage to a man's trade, which in its very nature is intended or reasonably likely to produce, and which in the ordinary course of things does produce, a general loss of business as distinct from the loss of this or that known customer, evidence of such general decline of business is admissible. In *Hargrave* v. *Le Breton*[1] it was a falsehood openly promulgated at an auction. In the case before us to-day it is a falsehood openly disseminated through the press, probably read and possibly acted on by persons of whom the plaintiff never heard. To refuse with reference to such subject-matter to admit such general evidence would be to misunderstand and warp the meaning of old expressions; to depart from and not to follow old rules; and, in addition to all this, would involve an absolute denial of justice and of redress for the very mischief which was intended to be committed.

The Defamation Act 1952

3. Slander of title, &c.—(1) In an action for slander of title, slander of goods or other malicious falsehood, it shall not be necessary to allege or prove special damage—

   (a) if the words upon which the action is founded are calculated to cause pecuniary damage to the plaintiff and are published in writing or other permanent form; or
   (b) if the said words are calculated to cause pecuniary damage to the plaintiff in respect of any office, profession, calling, trade or business held or carried on by him at the time of the publication.

[Section 3 (2) is omitted].

White v. Mellin

House of Lords   [1895] A.C. 154

Defendant sold the plaintiff's "Infants' Food", affixing to plaintiff's wrappers a label stating that defendant's "food for infants and invalids" was far more nutritious and healthful than any other. It has not proved that this statement was untrue or had caused any damage to the plaintiff. Romer J. dismissed an action for an injunction restraining publication and for damages. The Court of Appeal reversed this judgment. The House of Lords restored the judgment of Romer J.

LORD HERSCHELL L.C.: . . . The allegation of a tradesman that his goods are better than his neighbour's very often involves only the consideration whether they possess one or two qualities superior to the other. Of course "better" means better as regards the purpose for which they are intended, and the question of better or worse in many cases depends simply upon one or two or three issues of fact. If an action will not lie because a man says that his goods are better than his neighbour's it seems to me impossible to say that it will lie because he says that they are better in this or that or the

---

1. (1769), 4 Burr. 2422.

other respect. Just consider what a door would be opened if this were permitted. That this sort of puffing advertisement is in use is notorious; and we see rival cures advertised for particular ailments. The Court would then be bound to inquire, in an action brought, whether this ointment or this pill better cured the disease which it was alleged to cure—whether a particular article of food was in this respect or that better than another. Indeed, the courts of law would be turned into a machinery for advertising rival productions by obtaining a judicial determination which of the two was the better. . . .

LORD WATSON: . . . In the first place, I do not think the representation conveyed by the defendant's label is, in any legal sense, a representation of and concerning the infants' food of the plaintiff. It is a highly coloured laudation of Dr. Vance's food and nothing else. It makes no reference to the plaintiff's goods beyond what might be implied in the case of every other kind of food which is recommended and sold as being suitable for consumption by infant children. Nor, in my opinion, is the circumstance that the label was sometimes put upon the plaintiff's wrappers, however distressing it might be to him, sufficient to convert it into a disparagement of the contents of the wrapper. An advertisement in the window of a bootmaker, to the effect that he makes the best boots in the world, may be more offensive to his next neighbour in the same trade than to a bootmaker at a distance; but the disparagement in kind and degree is identical in both cases.

In the second place, assuming that the representation did refer to the plaintiff's food, I am of opinion that his evidence does not prove it to be untrue. At the best, the evidence comes to no more than this, that the plaintiff's food is the more suitable for children under six months old who cannot get their mother's milk; and that Dr. Vance's food is the more suitable for children above that age who are not the victims of indigestion. In these circumstances it appears to me to be difficult to hold that it was not open to either of the parties to say that his was the best food for infants without conveying a false imputation upon the food of the other.

In the third and last place, I am of opinion that, even if the plaintiff had proved that the representation concerned his food and was wilfully false, his evidence discloses no cause of action. There is not in the whole of it an attempt to prove that the plaintiff has suffered in the past or is likely to suffer in the future any damage whatever through the representations of which he complains. . . .

[LORD ASHBOURNE concurred. LORDS MACNAGHTEN and SHAND delivered speeches in favour of allowing the appeal.]

Balden v. Shorter

Chancery Division [1933] All E.R. Rep. 249

A servant of the defendants falsely said of the plaintiff, speaking carelessly but without any intention to injure him, that he was employed by the defendants, whereas he was in fact employed by another firm, Maugham J. dismissed an action for an injunction restraining defendants from making such representations.

MAUGHAM J. [stated, as set out above, the facts, and continued]: If I could properly conclude that the story told in the witness-box by Mr. Bensted was untrue and that he knew that the plaintiff was not employed by the defendants, I should have little difficulty in determining the action in the plaintiff's favour because, if Mr. Bensted said what he did say knowing it to be untrue, I should draw the inference that he did it from a dishonest motive and maliciously. But I cannot come to that conclusion.

The meaning of "malice" in connection with injurious falsehood is dealt with in *Salmond on Torts* (7th Edn., pp. 582–583) in the following passage, which I accept as correct:

"What is meant by malice in this connection? Lord Davey, in the passage already cited [from *Royal Baking Powder Co.* v. *Wright, Crossley & Co.*[1] (18 R.P.C., at p. 99)]

---

1. (1900), 18 R.P.C. 95.

defines it as meaning the absence of just cause or excuse. It is to be observed, however, that this is not one of the recognised meanings of the term malice in other connections. An act done without just cause or excuse is wrongful, but not necessarily malicious; for example, a trespass by mistake on another man's land or the conversion of his chattels under an erroneous claim of right. Notwithstanding Lord Davey's dictum, it is now apparently settled that malice in the law of slander of title and other forms of injurious falsehood means some dishonest or otherwise improper motive. A bona fide assertion of title, however mistaken, if made for the protection of one's own interest or for some other proper purpose, is not malicious."

In *Greers, Ltd.* v. *Pearman and Corder, Ltd.*[1] (1922), 39 R.P.C. at p. 417, Bankes L.J. said that "maliciously" for the purpose which the court was considering meant "with some indirect object", and Scrutton L.J. remarked that the only question in the case was whether there was evidence on which the jury could find that the statements were made maliciously " in the sense of being made with some indirect or dishonest motive".

I think that in the present case the statements were, at the worst, careless statements made without any indirect motive and without any intention of injuring the plaintiff, and I find that Mr. Bensted believed them to be true. The allegation of malice must fail, and on that finding of fact the action must be dismissed. . . .

Question

What are the implications of *Ministry of Housing and Local Government* v. *Sharp, ante,* in respect of the decision in *Balden* v. *Shorter*?

---

1. (1922), 39 R.P.C. 406.

16

Interests in Reputation—
Defamation

The tort of defamation protects interests in reputation. It consists in the *publication* to a third person of matter "containing an untrue imputation against the *reputation* of another" (Gatley on *Libel and Slander*, 7th Edn., para. 3). Since reputation is one's estimation in the eyes of others, the element of publication is essential. Pride, self-respect and dignity may be affronted by a communication to the person defamed: but without publication to a third person there is no hurt to reputation and hence no wrong of defamation. This distinguishes defamation from the Roman law of *injuria*, which, in modified form, exists in most civil law countries, and which protects *dignitas*. It also distinguishes the tort of defamation from criminal libel, for which there may be a prosecution without proof of publication to a third person, provided the words are such as reasonably tend or are calculated to provoke a breach of the peace.

Reputation may include a business reputation; but defamation is distinct from the tort of malicious falsehood considered in Chap. 15, because the latter is committed even if reputation is not besmirched (for a comparison of the torts see Street, p. 360). In order to succeed in an action for defamation the plaintiff must prove: (1) that the statement was defamatory; (2) that it referred to him (p. 532, *post*); (3) that the defendant published it to a third person (p. 546, *post*); and (4) (in a few cases) that damage resulted to him. Damage is presumed to flow from the publication of defamatory matter in permanent form or by broadcast (this is called libel); but if it is in the transitory form (called slander) damage must be proved, unless it falls within certain specified categories (p. 531, *post*).

Since the tort of defamation limits freedom of speech, many safeguards for that freedom have been built into the legal requirements. The first of these is trial by jury. The defendant's right to this *may* be taken away only if the trial requires "any prolonged examination of documents or accounts or any scientific or local investigation which cannot conveniently be made with a jury" (*Rothermere* v. *Times Newspapers, Ltd.*, [1973] 1 All E.R. 1013, C.A., interpreting the Administration of Justice (Miscellaneous Provisions) Act 1933, s. 6 (1)). Secondly, the courts will not allow the issue of a writ in an action for libel to stifle further comment on the matter in issue by treating it as contempt of court (*Thomson* v. *Times Newspapers, Ltd.*, [1969] 3 All E.R.

648, at p. 651, *per* Salmon L.J., and *A.-G.* v. *Times Newspapers, Ltd.,* [1973] 3 All E.R. 54 (H.L.)). Thirdly, the courts will not restrain the threatened publication of a defamatory statement by interlocutory injunction "when the defendant says that he intends to justify it or to make fair comment on a matter of public interest" (*Fraser* v. *Evans,* [1969] 1 All E.R. 8, at p. 10). Finally the defendant may, at the trial, prove any of a number of defences: (1) justification, i.e. truth (p. 549, *post*); (2) fair comment on a matter of public interest (p. 550, *post*); (3) privilege, which may be (a) absolute, or (b) qualified (p. 554, *post*). The plaintiff may defeat the defences of fair comment or qualified privilege by proving "malice", a concept which here includes dishonesty, the introduction of extraneous matter, and ulterior purposes. (The word "malicious" also appears in the plaintiff's allegation that the defendant "maliciously" published the defamatory statement; but there it is mere verbiage.) Apology is no defence at common law, although it may reduce the damages. Section 2 of the Libel Act 1843, as amended by the Libel Act 1845 (p. 567, *post*), introduced a little-used and limited defence of apology and payment of money by way of amends. The conduct of the parties will affect damages: if the plaintiff has a bad reputation his damages may be reduced even down to the "smallest coin in the realm" (p. 570, *post*); if the defendant's conduct has been calculated to make a profit for himself which might well exceed the compensation payable to the plaintiff as damages, then exemplary damages may be awarded (p. 567, *post*).

The publication of untruths is sometimes treated as an invasion of "privacy"; but, as the Younger Committee on Privacy (Cmnd. 5012, 1972) pointed out, the concepts of defamation and privacy need to be kept separate lest the safeguards for freedom of speech built into the defamation action be lost in a wide and vague proposed tort of invasion of privacy (p. 572, *post*). It is worth considering just what "privacy" means, how far the existing law protects this interest, and what could be done in the future (p. 570, *post*).

I. THE DISTINCTION BETWEEN LIBEL AND SLANDER

Monson v. Tussauds, Ltd.

Court of Appeal   [1891–4] All E.R. Rep. 1051

The plaintiff had been tried in Scotland upon a charge of having murdered a young man named Hambrough by shooting him with a gun at a place called Ardlamont. The defence to the charge was that Hambrough was killed by the accidental discharge of his own gun. The jury returned a verdict of "not proven". Shortly after the trial the defendants, who were the proprietors of an exhibition in London, consisting mainly of wax figures of celebrated and notorious personages, placed in their exhibition a portrait model of the plaintiff, bearing his name, with a gun close by described as his gun. The model was displayed in a room containing figures of Napoleon I, a convicted murderer, a suicide, and another person charged in connection with the alleged Ardlamont murder. This room gave access to the Chamber of Horrors. The plaintiff applied for an interim injunction restraining the exhibition of his effigy until the trial of an action for libel. The Court of Appeal (reversing the decision of a Divisional Court) held that an interlocutory injunction ought not to be granted.

LOPES L.J.: . . . Libels are generally in writing or printing, but this is not necessary;

the defamatory matter may be conveyed in some other permanent form. For instance, a statue, a caricature, an effigy, chalk marks on a wall, signs, or pictures may constitute a libel. The plaintiff's case, therefore, is libel, and the application for an interlocutory injunction must be determined upon the principles which are applicable to the granting of injunctions in cases of libel. . . .

The matter of restraining libels on interlocutory motions for injunction was thought of such importance that the question was, in *Bonnard* v. *Perryman*,[1] argued before the full Court of Appeal, and Lord Coleridge, in delivering the considered judgment of the court, said:

"We entirely approve of, and desire to adopt as our own, the language of Lord Esher in *William Coulson & Sons* v. *James Coulson & Co.*[2]:

'To justify the court in granting an interim injunction it must come to a decision upon the question of libel or not. Therefore the jurisdiction was of a delicate nature. It ought only to be exercised in the clearest cases, where any jury would say that the matter complained of was libellous, and where, if the jury did not so find, the court would set aside the verdict as unreasonable.'"

I cannot help thinking that a principle was laid down in that case applicable to all libels without a limitation. . . .

[LORD HALSBURY and DAVEY L.J. delivered speeches in favour of allowing the appeal.]

Youssoupoff v. Metro-Goldwyn-Mayer Pictures, Ltd.

Court of Appeal   (1934), 50 T.L.R. 581

The plaintiff claimed damages for an alleged libel which she said was contained in a sound film entitled *Rasputin, the Mad Monk*, alleging that the defendants had published in the film pictures and words which were understood to mean that she, therein called "Princess Natasha", had been seduced by Rasputin. The jury returned a verdict in favour of the plaintiff and awarded her £25,000 damages. The defendants unsuccessfully appealed to the Court of Appeal.

SLESSER L.J.: This action is one of libel and raises at the outset an interesting and difficult problem which, I believe, to be a novel problem, whether the product of the combined photographic and talking instrument which produces these modern films does, if it throws upon the screen and impresses upon the ear defamatory matter, produce that which can be complained of as libel or as slander.

In my view, this action, as I have said, was properly framed in libel. There can be no doubt that, so far as the photographic part of the exhibition is concerned, that is a permanent matter to be seen by the eye, and is the proper subject of an action for libel, if defamatory. I regard the speech which is synchronized with the photographic reproduction and forms part of one complex, common exhibition as an ancillary circumstance, part of the surroundings explaining that which is to be seen. . . .

[SCRUTTON and GREER L.JJ. delivered speeches in favour of dismissing the appeal.]

Question

Does Slesser L.J.'s reasoning mean that the *vision* constituted the libel? If so, does this imply that a gramophone record or other sound recording would only be a slander?

Note

For the fascinating background to this case see H. Montgomery Hyde, *Sir Patrick Hastings* (London, 1960), pp. 274–283.

---

1. [1891] 2 Ch. 269.
2. (1887), 3 T.L.R. 846.

The Defamation Act 1952

1. Broadcast statements.—For the purposes of the law of libel and slander, the broadcasting of words by means of wireless telegraphy shall be treated as publication in permanent form.

. . .

16. Interpretation.—(1) Any reference in this Act to words shall be construed as including a reference to pictures, visual images, gestures and other methods of signifying meaning.

(2) The provisions of Part III of the Schedule to this Act shall have effect for the purposes of the interpretation of that Schedule.

(3) In this Act "broadcasting by means of wireless telegraphy" means publication for general reception by means of wireless telegraphy within the meaning of the Wireless Telegraphy Act 1949, and "broadcast by means of wireless telegraphy" shall be construed accordingly.

The Theatres Act 1968

4. Amendment of law of defamation.—(1) For the purposes of the law of libel and slander (including the law of criminal libel so far as it relates to the publication of defamatory matter) the publication of words in the course of a performance of a play shall, subject to section 7 of this Act, be treated as publication in permanent form.

(2) The foregoing subsection shall apply for the purposes of section 3 (slander of title, etc.) of the Defamation Act 1952 as it applies for the purposes of the law of libel and slander.

(3) In this section "words" includes pictures, visual images, gestures and other methods of signifying meaning.

. . .

7. Exceptions for performances given in certain circumstances.—(1) Nothing in sections 2 to 4 of this Act shall apply in relation to a performance of a play given on a domestic occasion in a private dwelling.

(2) Nothing in sections 2 to 6 of this Act shall apply in relation to a performance of a play given solely or primarily for one or more of the following purposes, that is to say—

(*a*) rehearsal; or
(*b*) to enable—

> (i) a record or cinematograph film to be made from or by means of the performance; or
> (ii) the performance to be broadcast; or
> (iii) the performance to be transmitted to subscribers to a diffusion service;

but in any proceedings for an offence under section 2, 5 or 6 of this Act alleged to have been committed in respect of a performance of a play or an offence at common law alleged to have been committed in England and Wales by the publication of defamatory matter in the course of a performance of a play, if it is proved that the performance was attended by persons other than persons directly connected with the giving of the performance or the doing in relation thereto of any of the things mentioned in paragraph (*b*) above, the performance shall be taken not to have been given solely or primarily for one or more of the said purposes unless the contrary is shown.

(3) In this section—

> "broadcast" means broadcast by wireless telegraphy (within the meaning of the Wireless Telegraphy Act 1949), whether by way of sound broadcasting or television;
> "cinematograph film" means any print, negative, tape or other article on which a

performance of a play or any part of such a performance is recorded for the purposes of visual reproduction;

"record" means any record or similar contrivance for reproducing sound, including the sound-track of a cinematograph film;

and section 48 (3) of the Copyright Act 1956 (which explains the meaning of references in that Act to the transmission of a work or other subject-matter to subscribers to a diffusion service) shall apply for the purposes of this section as it applies for the purposes of that Act.

Gray v. Jones

King's Bench Division   [1939] 1 All E.R. 798

The plaintiff brought an action for slander, alleging that the defendant had said of him: "You are a convicted person. I will not have you here. You have a conviction." The defendant submitted that the words were not capable of being actionable without proof of special damage. It was held that the words were actionable *per se* and judgment was given for the plaintiff.

ATKINSON J.: . . . The argument for the defendant is that the true view is that the reason why words imputing a crime are actionable is that the plaintiff is put in jeopardy of a criminal prosecution, and, therefore, if the words merely imply that the plaintiff has been guilty of a criminal offence, and has been convicted, and it is a thing of the past, then it is not actionable without proof of special damage, because the plaintiff is not put in jeopardy. That raises the question as to the real basis of the action. What is the real ground upon which a plaintiff may bring an action for such defamation without proof of special damage? Is it because the misconduct alleged is of so serious a character that the law visits it with punishment, and is therefore so likely to cause other people to shun the person defamed, and to exclude him from society, that damage is presumed? Or is the basis the fact that he is put in jeopardy? In my opinion, the former view is the sound one. . . .

Note

1. In *D and L Caterers, Ltd.* v. *Jackson* v. *D'Ajou*, [1945] K.B. 364; [1945] 1 All E.R. 563 the Court of Appeal left open the question whether a company can sue without proof of special damage for a slander imputing an offence punishable, had it been committed by an individual, with imprisonment.

2. *Gray* v. *Jones (ante)* illustrates one of the four categories of slander actionable *per se*. The other three are:

(a) words imputing that the plaintiff is suffering from a contagious or infectious disease: (e.g. *Bloodworth* v. *Gray* (1844), 7 Man. & G. 334: "He has got that damned pox [meaning the French pox otherwise known as venereal disease] from going to that woman on the Derby Road." £50 damages awarded without proof of special damage).

(b) words imputing unchastity or adultery to any woman or girl (Slander of Women Act 1891, *post*); in *Youssoupoff* v. *Metro-Goldwyn-Mayer Pictures, Ltd. (ante)*. Avory J., with whom Scrutton L.J. agreed, said, obiter, that an allegation that a woman had been raped would fall into this category.

(c) words calculated to disparage the plaintiff in any office, profession, calling, trade or business, held or carried on by him at the time of publication (Defamation Act 1952, s. 2, *post*).

3. A committee of the House of Lords in 1843 recommended the abolition of the distinction between libel and slander. The proposal has been acted

upon in New Zealand, some Australian states and Canadian provinces. But the Porter Committee on the Law of Defamation (Cmd. 7536, 1948, para. 38) refused to endorse the recommendation for fear of encouraging litigation over spoken words.

The Slander of Women Act 1891

1. Amendment of law.—Words spoken and published . . . which impute unchastity or adultery to any woman or girl shall not require special damage to render them actionable.

Provided always, that in any action for words spoken and made actionable by this Act, a plaintiff shall not recover more costs than damages, unless the judge shall certify that there was reasonable ground for bringing the action.

The Defamation Act 1952

2. Slander affecting official, professional or business reputation.—In an action for slander in respect of words calculated to disparage the plaintiff in any office, profession, calling, trade or business held or carried on by him at the time of the publication, it shall not be necessary to allege or prove special damage, whether or not the words are spoken of the plaintiff in the way of his office, profession, calling, trade or business.

2. WORDS OR MATTER DEFAMATORY OF THE PLAINTIFF

Sim v. Stretch

House of Lords   [1936] 2 All E.R. 1237

The defendant sent to the plaintiff a telegram concerning a housemaid who had left the plaintiff's employment and was then in the service of the defendant. The relevant part read: "Edith resumed her service with us today. Please send her possessions and the money you borrowed also her wages to Old Barton—Sim." The plaintiff claimed damages for libel alleging that these words were defamatory and further that by them the defendant meant and was understood to mean that the plaintiff was in pecuniary difficulties, that by reason thereof he had borrowed money from his housemaid, that he had failed to pay her wages, and that he was a person to whom no one ought to give any credit. At the trial of the action before Talbot J. and a common jury judgment was given for the plaintiff who was awarded £250 damages. The defendant appealed unsuccessfully to the Court of Appeal, but his appeal to the House of Lords was upheld on the ground that the words were not reasonably capable of a defamatory meaning.

LORD ATKIN: . . . The question, then, is whether the words in their ordinary signification are capable of being defamatory. Judges and textbook writers alike have found difficulty in defining with precision the word "defamatory". The conventional phrase exposing the plaintiff to hatred, ridicule and contempt is probably too narrow. The question is complicated by having to consider the person or class of persons whose reaction to the publication is the test of the wrongful character of the words used. I do not intend to ask your Lordships to lay down a formal definition, but after collating the opinions of many authorities I propose in the present case the test: would the words tend to lower the plaintiff in the estimation of right-thinking members of society generally? Assuming such to be the test of whether words are defamatory or not there is no dispute as to the relative functions of judge and jury, of law and fact. It is well settled that the judge must decide whether the words are capable of a defamatory meaning. That is a question of law: is there evidence of a tort? If they are capable, then the jury is to decide whether they are in fact defamatory. Now, in the present case it is material to notice that there is no evidence that the words were published to anyone who had any knowledge at all of any of the facts that I have narrated above. There is no direct evidence that they were published to anyone who had ever heard of the plaintiff. The post office officials at Maidenhead would not be presumed to know him, and we are left without any information as to the officials at Cookham Dean. The plaintiff and his wife dealt at the shop at which was the sub-post office, but there is no evidence that the shopkeeper was the telegraph clerk; the probability is that he was not. It might, however, be inferred that the publication of the telegram at Cookham Dean was to someone who knew the plaintiff. What would he or she learn by reading the telegram? That Edith Saville had been in the plaintiff's employment; that she had that day entered the defendant's employment; and that the former employer was requested to send on to the new place of employment the servant's possessions together with the money due to her for money borrowed and for wages. How could perusal of that communication tend to lower the plaintiff in the estimation of the right-thinking peruser who knows nothing of the circumstances but what he or she derives from the telegram itself. . . .

[LORD RUSSELL OF KILLOWEN and LORD MACMILLAN concurred in allowing the appeal.]

Byrne v. Deane

Court of Appeal   [1937] 2 All E.R. 204

Automatic gambling machines, known as "diddler" machines, had been kept by the defendants upon golf club premises since 1932 for the use of members of the club. Someone gave information to the police as to the existence of these machines on the club premises which led the police to require the removal of the machines. The day after the machines had been removed someone put upon the wall of the club against which the automatic machines had formerly stood a typewritten paper containing the following lampoon:

> "For many years upon this spot
> You heard the sound of a merry bell
> Those who were rash and those who were not
> Lost and made a spot of cash
> But he who gave the game away
> May he byrnne in hell and rue the day"
> *Diddleramus*

The plaintiff brought an action for libel, alleging that by these words the defendants meant and were understood to mean that the plaintiff had reported to the police the presence of the machines upon the premises, that he was guilty of underhand disloyalty to the defendants and his fellow members of the club, that his conduct was deserving of the gravest censure, that he was a person devoid of all true sporting spirit, and further that he was a person unfit for other members of the club to associate with and should be ostracised by them. Hilbery J. held that the words were defamatory of the plaintiff and awarded 40 shillings damages and costs. On appeal, all members of the Court held that it was not defamatory of a man to say that he has informed the police of a crime. Slesser and Greene L.JJ. held that the words in this case were not defamatory, but Greer L.J. held that they were defamatory because they meant something more than that the police had been informed of a crime, namely that he had been guilty of disloyalty.

SLESSER L.J.: . . . In my view, to allege of a man—and for this purpose it does not matter whether the allegation is true or is not true—that he has reported certain acts, wrongful in law, to the police, cannot possibly be said to be defamatory of him in the minds of the general public. We have to consider in this connection the *arbitrium boni*, the view which would be taken by the ordinary good and worthy subject of the King (to quote the matter which appears in the old declarations), and I have assigned to myself no other criterion than what a good and worthy subject of the King would think of some person of whom it had been said that he had put the law into motion against wrongdoers, in thinking that such a good and worthy subject would not consider such an allegation in itself to be defamatory. That is the view taken by McCardie J. in *Myroft* v. *Sleight*,[1] at p. 884, where he quotes with approval a judgment of the Irish court in *Mawe* v. *Pigott*,[2] at p. 62, where Lawson J. giving the judgment of the court says:

> "[Counsel for the plaintiff], however, argued that amongst certain classes who were either themselves criminal, or who sympathised with crime, it would expose a person to great odium to represent him as an informer or a prosecutor, or otherwise aiding in the detection of crime; that is quite true, but we cannot be called upon to adopt that standard. The very circumstances which will make a person be regarded with disfavour by the criminal classes will raise his character in the estimation of right-thinking men. We can only regard the estimation in which a man is held by society generally. . . ."

. . .

Notes

1. The views of the "ordinary good and worthy subject of the King" are obviously subject to change. At the time of Charles II it was defamatory to call a person a Papist (*Row* v. *Clargis* (1683), T. Raym. 482); during the First World War it was defamatory to describe a firm as German (*Slazengers, Ltd.* v. *Gibbs & Co.* (1916), 33 T.L.R. 35); in 1964 it was thought, by Lord Denning, to be defamatory to call a man with an English name a Czech, if that implied communist sympathies which made him disloyal (*Linklater* v. *Daily Telegraph, Ltd.* (1964), 108 Sol. Jo. 992). But "would it be libellous to write of a lady of fashion that she had been seen on the top of an omnibus?" Even when Pollock C.B. asked this question (in *Clay* v. *Roberts* (1863), 8 L.T. 397, at p. 398) the answer given was in the negative. An imputation of deviationism is not defamatory unless it carries with it an allegation of hypocrisy.

2. In *Youssoupoff* v. *Metro-Goldwyn-Mayer Pictures, Ltd.* (p. 529, *ante*), Scrutton L.J. (at p. 584) preferred the formula that defamation is a statement to a person's *discredit*. Does a statement that a woman has been raped fall within this formula, as the learned judge seemed to believe? Or does it evoke *pity*, which, so far, forms no part of the judicial definition? (See p. 538, *post*.)

3. The test of defamation in *Sim* v. *Stretch* (*ante*) may be compared with the traditional test whether the words bring the plaintiff into "hatred, ridicule or contempt". The question of "ridicule" is clearly one of degree, e.g. in *Emerson* v. *Grimsby Times and Telegraph Co., Ltd.* (1926), 42 T.L.R. 238 (C.A.) a newspaper published an account of the plaintiff's wedding the day before it took place and, as a result, he was subjected to ridicule. The Court of Appeal treated this as simply a feeble joke and not defamatory.

Tolley v. Fry & Sons, Ltd.

House of Lords   [1931] All E.R. Rep. 131

In this action for libel Acton J. and a common jury returned a verdict in favour of the plaintiff and awarded him £1,000 damages. The Court of Appeal by a majority held that the trial judge ought to have withdrawn the case from the jury on the ground

---

1. (1920), 90 L.J.K.B. 883.
2. (1869), I.R. 4 C.L. 54.

that the document complained of as a libel was not reasonably capable of a defamatory meaning and ordered judgment to be entered for the defendants. All the Lords Justices were further of the opinion that in any event there should be a new trial on the ground that the damages were excessive. The plaintiff appealed on the first point. The House of Lords (Lord Blanesburgh dissenting) held that the document was capable of a defamatory meaning, and the new trial would be limited to the assessment of damages. The facts appear from the speech of Lord Hailsham.

LORD HAILSHAM: The plaintiff in this case is a well-known amateur golfer. The defendants are manufacturers of chocolate in various forms. In June 1928, the defendants published in the "Daily Sketch" and "Daily Mail", newspapers enjoying a large circulation in London and the provinces, a caricature of the plaintiff which represented him in golfing costume having just completed a drive, with a packet of the defendants' chocolate protruding from his pocket, in the company of a caddie who is holding up packets of the defendants' chocolate, and below the caricature was a limerick in the following terms:

> "The caddie to Tolley said: 'Oh, Sir!
> Good shot, Sir! That ball, see it go, Sir.
>   My word, how it flies,
>   Like a Cartet of Fry's.
> They're handy, they're good, and priced low, Sir.'"

The caricature and the limerick were surrounded with descriptions of the merits of the defendants' chocolates, and the whole was plainly an advertisement of the defendants' goods.

The plaintiff thereupon brought this action for damages for libel. He did not complain of the caricature or the words as being defamatory in themselves; but the innuendo alleged that the

> "defendants meant and were understood to mean that the plaintiff had agreed or permitted his portrait to be exhibited for the purpose of the advertisement of the defendants' chocolate, that he had done so for gain and reward, that he had prostituted his reputation as an amateur golf player for advertising purposes, that he was seeking notoriety and gain by the means aforesaid, and that he had been guilty of conduct unworthy of his status as an amateur golfer."

. . .

LORD DUNEDIN: The sole question raised by this appeal is whether the case ought to have been withdrawn from the jury by the judge, and judgment entered for the defendants. It has been stated again and again, and is not in dispute, that the question for the judge is whether the writing or publication complained of is capable of a libellous meaning. It is for the jury, if the judge so rules, to say whether it has that meaning.

The most authoritative pronouncement on actions of this sort, because it is a judgment of this House, is to be found in *Capital and Counties Bank* v. *Henty*.[1] Both parties in this case have appealed to it as an authority in their favour. I think the ruling canon in that case is to be found in the judgment of Lord Selborne L.C. That was a case where, as here, the mere words used were not libellous. But Lord Selborne then proceeded to inquire what were the circumstances in which the document was published. In that case he held the circumstances did not and could not lead to any libellous imputation. The circular was directed to Henty's customers alone, and there were quite innocent reasons which would justify the circular. But he pointedly said that if the circumstances had been otherwise, if the circular had been placarded up or published to the world at large the effect might have been quite otherwise. Now, applying this method of reasoning to the present case, I find that the caricature of the plaintiff,

---

1. (1882), 7 App. Cas. 741.

innocent itself as a caricature, is so to speak embedded in an advertisement. It is held out as part of an advertisement so that its presence there gives rise to speculation as to how it got there, or in other words provokes in the mind of the public an inference as to how and why the plaintiff's picture, caricatured as it was, became associated with a commercial advertisement. The inference that is suggested is that the consent was given, either gratuitously or for a consideration, to its appearance. Then it is said, and evidence on that point was given and not cross-examined to, that, if that were so, the status of the plaintiff as an amateur golfer would be called in question. It seems to me that all this is within the province of a jury to determine. The idea of the inference in the circumstances is not so extravagant as to compel a judge to say it was so beside the mark that no jury ought to be allowed to consider it.

I come to this conclusion on a consideration of the advertisement alone, explained with the evidence of the golf players and the golf secretary. There are here two separate propositions: (i) Would the caricature associated with the advertisement admit of a reasonable inference that the plaintiff had assented to be so depicted? That depends on the view taken of the picture, of its surroundings, and of its use. (ii) If that inference were drawn, would it be deleterious to the plaintiff's position as an amateur golfer, and do him harm? That depends on the evidence of the golfers. A great deal of argument was directed to the terms of the letter of 4 June, which has been quoted by his Lordship on the Woolsack. I do not consider that to be material to the question before us. It may well have influenced the jury in coming to the verdict they did, for, to my mind, it shows clearly that the general proposition that amateur status might be called in question by association of an amateur with an advertisement was well before the eyes of the defendants and their advisers. But we are not concerned at present with the justice of the verdict, only with the question of whether there was a case for the jury to consider. I agree with the motion proposed.

[LORD BUCKMASTER and LORD TOMLIN delivered speeches in favour of allowing the appeal; LORD BLANESBURGH delivered a speech in favour of dismissing the appeal.]

Question

Would Tolley have had a cause of action in English law had he been a professional golfer?

Note

This case has been said to be "the nearest the law of defamation ever came to protecting 'privacy' as such" (Report of the Committee on Privacy, Cmnd. 5012, 1972, App. I, para. 5, and see p. 570, *post*). In the United States, on the contrary, a tort of putting a person in a "false light" has been recognised. This makes it actionable to attribute to the plaintiff some opinion or utterance or to include a well-known person, without his consent, in a popularity contest or to use his photograph in a book or article with which he has no connection. (False attribution of authorship—not only of professional authors—is protected in England by the Copyright Act 1956, s. 43; see *Moore v. News of the World*, [1972] 1 Q.B. 441; [1972] 1 All E.R. 915.) In modern Roman–Dutch law the *actio injuriarum* (developed from the Roman law of *iniuria*) has arrived at a similar protection of "privacy" by making the publication, without consent, of non-defamatory matter actionable if it constitutes an aggression upon *dignitas*. So the publication of photographs of a university student, formerly a schoolteacher, describing him as one of the young men in the life of a well-known artiste, was actionable: *Mhlongo v. Bailey*, 1958 (1) S.A. 370 (W); and generally C. F. Amerasinghe, *Aspects of the Actio Iniuriarum in Roman–Dutch Law* (Colombo, 1966), p. 188.

Cassidy v. Daily Mirror Newspapers, Ltd.

Court of Appeal   [1929] All E.R. Rep. 117

The plaintiff, Mrs. Mildred Anna Cassidy, was and was generally known as the lawful wife of one Kettering Edward Cassidy, who was also known as Michael Dennis Corrigan, an owner of race horses and at one time reputed to be a general in the Mexican Army. The plaintiff and her husband did not live together but he occasionally stayed with her at her flat. She brought an action for libel against the defendants alleging that they had printed and published in the Daily Mirror newspaper a photograph of K. E. Cassidy and a woman whose name was not mentioned at the trial, but who was referred to as Miss X, under a heading "Today's gossip. News and views about men, women, and affairs in general." Under the photograph were the words: "Mr. M. Corrigan, the race horse owner and Miss X, whose engagement has been announced." The plaintiff alleged that she had suffered damage through the above publication inasmuch as it was intended, and by several people understood, to mean that K. E. Cassidy was not the plaintiff's husband but was living with her in immoral cohabitation.

McCardie J. held that in the circumstances the publication was capable of conveying a meaning defamatory of the plaintiff. He directed the jury that if the publication conveyed to reasonably minded people who knew the circumstances an aspersion on the moral character of the plaintiff their verdict should be for the plaintiff. The jury returned a verdict for the plaintiff of £500. The defendants appealed. The Court of Appeal (Greer L.J. dissenting) held that the publication was capable of conveying a meaning defamatory of the plaintiff and dismissed the appeal.

SCRUTTON L.J.: . . . In my view, the words published were capable of the meaning: "Corrigan is a single man," and were published to people who knew the plaintiff professed to be married to Corrigan; it was for the jury to say whether those people could reasonably draw the inference that the so-called Mrs. Corrigan was in fact living in immoral cohabitation with Corrigan, and I do not think their finding should be interfered with. . . .

RUSSELL L.J.: . . . Liability for libel does not depend on the intention of the defamer, but on the fact of defamation. If you once reach the conclusion that the published matter in the present case amounts to or involves a statement that Mr. Corrigan is an unmarried man, then, in my opinion, those persons who knew the circumstances might reasonably consider the statement defamatory of the plaintiff. The statement being capable of a meaning defamatory to the plaintiff, it was for the jury, upon the evidence adduced, to decide whether the plaintiff had been libelled or not.

It was said that it would be a great hardship on the defendants if they were made liable in consequence of a statement, innocent on its face and published by them in good faith. The answer to this appeal for sympathy seems to be to point out that, in stating to the world that Mr. Corrigan was an unmarried man—for that construction is the foundation of their liability—they in fact stated that which was false. From a business angle, no doubt, it may pay them not to spend time or money in making inquiries or verifying statements before publication; but if they had not made a false statement they would not now be suffering in damages. They are paying a price for their methods of business. . . .

[GREER L.J. delivered a dissenting judgment.]

Lewis v. Daily Telegraph, Ltd.

House of Lords   [1963] 2 All E.R. 151

The Daily Telegraph newspaper published a paragraph headed "Inquiry on firm by City Police" and the Daily Mail one headed "Fraud Squad probe Firm", the gist of these paragraphs being that the City Fraud Squad was inquiring into the firm's affairs, and identifying the firm and its chairman, Mr. Lewis. In actions for libel by Mr. Lewis and the firm, the defendants admitted that the words were defamatory in their ordinary meaning, but they said that this meaning was that there was a police inquiry on foot and they sought to justify this as true. The plaintiffs, however, contended that the ordinary meaning was that they were guilty of, or suspected by the police of, fraud or dishonesty. The trial judge directed the juries in such a way as to leave it open to them to accept the plaintiffs' contention. From the amounts of damages awarded by them (£25,000 to Mr. Lewis and £75,000 to the firm, in the case of the Daily Telegraph, and, the next day, by a different jury £17,000 and £100,000 respectively, against the Daily Mail) it was clear that the juries must have done this.

On appeal to the House of Lords, a majority (Lord Morris of Borth-y-Gest dissenting) held that the judge's failure to direct the juries whether the words were capable of imputing guilt of fraud as distinct from suspicion was a misdirection sufficient to warrant a new trial.

LORD DEVLIN: . . . If it is said of a man—"I do not believe that he is guilty of fraud but I cannot deny that he has given grounds for suspicion", it seems to me to be wrong to say that in no circumstances can they be justified except by the speaker proving the truth of that which he has expressly said that he did not believe. It must depend on whether the impression conveyed by the speaker is one of frankness or one of insinuation. Equally in my opinion it is wrong to say that, if in truth the person spoken of never gave any cause for suspicion at all, he has no remedy because he was expressly exonerated of fraud. A man's reputation can suffer if it can truly be said of him that although innocent he behaved in a suspicious way; but it will suffer much more if it is said that he is not innocent.

It is not therefore correct to say as a matter of law that a statement of suspicion imputes guilt. It can be said as a matter of practice that it very often does so, because although suspicion of guilt is something different from proof of guilt, it is the broad impression conveyed by the libel that has to be considered and not the meaning of each word under analysis. A man who wants to talk at large about smoke may have to pick his words very carefully, if he wants to exclude the suggestion that there is also a fire; but it can be done. One always gets back to the fundamental question: what is the meaning that the words convey to the ordinary man; a rule cannot be made about that. They can convey a meaning of suspicion short of guilt; but loose talk about suspicion can very easily convey the impression that it is a suspicion that is well founded.

In the libel that the House has to consider there is, however, no mention of suspicion at all. What is said is simply that the plaintiff's affairs are being inquired into. That is defamatory, as is admitted, because a man's reputation may in fact be injured by such a statement even though it is quite consistent with innocence. I daresay that it would not be injured if everybody bore in mind, as they ought to, that no man is guilty until he is proved so, but unfortunately they do not. It can be defamatory without it being necessary to suggest that the words contained a hidden allegation that there were good grounds for inquiry. A statement that a woman has been raped can affect her reputation, although logically it means that she is innocent of any impurity: *Youssoupoff* v. *Metro-Goldwyn-Mayer Pictures, Ltd.*[1] So a statement that a man has been acquitted of a crime with which in fact he was never charged might lower his reputation. Logic is not the test. But a statement that an inquiry is on foot may go further and may positively convey the impression that there are grounds for the inquiry, i.e. that there is something to suspect. Just as a bare statement of suspicion may convey the impression that there are grounds for belief in guilt, so a bare statement of the fact of an inquiry may convey the impression that there are grounds for suspicion. I do not say that in this case it does; but I think that the words in their context and in the circumstances of publication are capable of conveying that impression. But can

---

1. (1934), 50 T.L.R. 581.

they convey an impression of guilt? Let it be supposed, first, that a statement that there is an inquiry conveys an impression of suspicion; and, secondly, that a statement of suspicion conveys an impression of guilt. It does not follow from these two suppositions that a statement that there is an inquiry conveys an impression of guilt. For that, two fences have to be taken instead of one. While, as I have said, I am prepared to accept that the jury could take the first I do not think that in a case like the present, where there is only the bare statement that a police inquiry is being made, it could take the second in the same stride. If the ordinary sensible man was capable of thinking that wherever there was a police inquiry there was guilt, it would be almost impossible to give accurate information about anything: but in my opinion he is not. I agree with the view of the Court of Appeal.

There is on this branch of the case a final point to be considered. It is undoubtedly the law that the judge should not leave the question "libel or no libel" to the jury unless the words are reasonably capable of a defamatory meaning. But if several defamatory meanings are pleaded or suggested, can the judge direct the jury that the words are capable of one meaning but not of another? The point is important here, because the defendants admit that the words are defamatory in one sense but dispute that they are defamatory in the senses pleaded in the statements of claim, and contend that the judge should have so directed the jury. Both counsel for the appellants appear at one time to have argued in the Court of Appeal that the function of the judge was exhausted when he ruled that the words were capable of being defamatory; and that it was not for him to inquire whether they were or were not capable of any particular defamatory meaning. But later they abandoned the point; and, therefore, did not initiate the discussion of it here. Nevertheless there was considerable discussion of it, because some of your lordships at one time felt that it was a point which ought to be considered. In the result I think that all your lordships are now clearly of the opinion that the judge must rule whether the words are capable of bearing each of the defamatory meanings, if there be more than one, put forward by the plaintiff. This supports indirectly my view on the desirability of pleading different meanings. If the plaintiff can get before the jury only those meanings which the judge rules as capable of being defamatory, there is good reason for having the meanings alleged set out precisely as part of the record.

For the reasons that I have given earlier, I agree that there must be a new trial on the ground of misdirection: but I should in any event have considered that there should be a new trial on the issue of damages as they are, in my opinion, ridiculously out of proportion to the injury suffered.

[LORD REID (with whom LORD TUCKER agreed) and LORD HODSON delivered speeches concurring in dismissing the appeal from the Court of Appeal. LORD MORRIS OF BORTH-Y-GEST dissented.]

Morgan v. Odhams Press, Ltd.

House of Lords   [1971] 2 All E.R. 1156

The plaintiff, Johnny Morgan, complained that he was libelled by an article published in the Sun newspaper, which stated: "A girl who is likely to be a key witness in a dog doping scandal went into hiding yesterday after threats were made on her life. Margo Murray left her lodgings in Elsham Road, Shepherd's Bush, accompanied by two men ... Miss Murray ... was kidnapped last week by members of the gang when they heard she had made a statement to the police. She was kept at a house in Finchley but was eventually allowed to leave." No one was named in the article except Miss Murray. The plaintiff, in whose flat Miss Murray had stayed a week before the article was published, relied on extrinsic evidence which he said would entitle an ordinary reader to understand that the article referred to him. At the trial, six witnesses who had seen the plaintiff with Miss Murray a week before the publication gave evidence that

they thought the article referred to the plaintiff. In fact the plaintiff's flat was three
miles from Finchley and Miss Murray had been going about freely with the plaintiff,
although in a distressed condition.

In interlocutory proceedings, the Court of Appeal had refused to strike out particulars of a claim on which the plaintiff relied to show that the article referred to him.
The trial judge held that in view of this refusal to strike out particulars the case was
arguable and should go to the jury. The House of Lords, in this appeal, unanimously
held that the trial judge was wrong in holding that he was bound by the decision of the
Court of Appeal in interlocutory proceedings; the issue whether the plaintiff had a
reasonable cause of action was a matter for the judge to decide at the trial in the light
of the evidence. Nevertheless, by a majority (Lord Guest and Lord Donovan dissenting) the House of Lords held that the judge had been right to allow the case to go to
the jury. The majority (Lord Reid, Lord Morris of Borth-y-Gest and Lord Pearson)
were agreed that the judge had rightly left to the jury the question of fact whether
readers having knowledge of the circumstances would reasonably have understood
that the article referred to the plaintiff. Lord Reid (*post*), Lord Morris of Borth-y-Gest,
Lord Guest and Lord Donovan expressed the view that there was no rule that an
article must contain some "key or pointer" indicating that it referred to the plaintiff.
Lord Pearson, however, thought that in order to be defamatory the article must
contain something which to the mind of the reader with knowledge of the relevant
circumstances contained defamatory imputations and pointed to the plaintiff. On the
facts of this case, however, Lord Pearson held that the article did point to the plaintiff.

The jury had awarded £4,750 damages to the plaintiff. The Court of Appeal had
allowed an appeal by the defendants. The House of Lords reversed the Court of
Appeal's decision.

LORD REID: . . . It must often happen that a defamatory statement published at
large does not identify any particular person and that an ordinary member of the
public who reads it in its context cannot tell who is referred to. But readers with
special knowledge can and do read it as referring to a particular person. A number of
matters are not in dispute in this case. It does not matter whether the publisher intended to refer to the plaintiff or not. It does not even matter whether he knew of the
plaintiff's existence. And it does not matter that he did not know or could not have
known the facts which caused the readers with special knowledge to connect the
statement with the plaintiff. Indeed the damage done to the plaintiff by the publication
may be of a kind which the publisher could not have foreseen. That may be out of
line with the ordinary rule limiting damage for which a tortfeasor is liable, but that
point does not arise in this case.

On the other hand when people come and say that they thought that the plaintiff
was referred to by a statement which does not identify anyone there must be some
protection for a defendant who is thus taken unawares. It is now well settled that the
plaintiff must give sufficient particulars of the special facts on which he or his witnesses rely. But that in itself may not be enough. It may be plain and obvious that no
sensible person could, by reason of knowing these facts, jump to the conclusion that
the defamatory words refer to the plaintiff. Then R.S.C. Ord. 18, r. 19 can be used to
stop the case from going to trial. Otherwise the case goes to trial.

The next protection for the defendant is that at the end of the plaintiff's case the
judge may be called on to rule whether the words complained of are capable of referring to the plaintiff in light of the special facts or knowledge proved in evidence.
The main question in this case is: how is he to make that decision? It is often said
that because a question is for the judge to answer it must be a question of law. I have
more than once stated my view that the meaning of words is not a question of law
in the true sense, even in other departments of the law where a much stricter test of
the meaning of words is adopted than in the law of libel. It is simply a question
which our law reserves for the judge. . . .

. . . Let me test the matter by supposing that the statements in the defendants' article had been somewhat different. Suppose it had said that Margaret Murray had been kidnapped by the doping gang and taken to a house in Cricklewood on a date which corresponded with the date of her arrival at the plaintiff's flat in Cricklewood and suppose that instead of going about with the plaintiff she had felt unwell and had remained in that flat but that her presence there was known to a number of people. There would be no pointer to the plaintiff; there are many thousands of houses in Cricklewood and to regard a reference to a house in an area where, say, 100,000 people reside as a pointer to any one or every one of them would be to reduce this new limitation to an insubstantial formality. But I would think it impossible to say that ordinary sensible people, who knew of the arrival of Margaret Murray at the plaintiff's flat and that she had not gone out, would have been unreasonable in coming to the conclusion that the article meant that the plaintiff was one of, or was in league with, the gang.

Some people may think that the law has gone too far in holding that the publisher of a defamatory statement which identifies no one is liable if knowledge of special facts which the publisher could not know causes sensible people to think that the statement applies to someone the publisher had never heard of. That may be arguable: I express no opinion about it, farther than to say that in deciding the question one would require to have in mind not only the innocent publisher but also the person who wishes to injure the reputation of the plaintiff but tries to avoid liability by disguising his libel so that it conveys nothing to the ordinary reader but causes those with special knowledge to infer that it is aimed at the plaintiff.

If this new limitation is intended to distinguish between an innocent publisher and a publisher who has the plaintiff in mind it fails in its object. It would still leave the publishers of matter ex facie defamatory in its nature liable in at least three cases: where he uses what he thinks is a fancy name (*E. Hulton & Co.* v. *Jones*[1]), where the plaintiff happens to have the same name as the person to whom he intends to refer (*Newstead* v. *London Express Newspaper, Ltd.*[2]) and where he happens to put in something which could be regarded by those with special knowledge as a pointer or peg although he never intended it to point to the plaintiff. I can see no substantial distinction between that case and the case where those with special knowledge are caused to infer that there is a reference to the plaintiff by the narration of facts and circumstances which coupled with that special knowledge do indicate the plaintiff.

The principal authority cited for this novel doctrine is *Astaire* v. *Campling*.[3] That was a very different kind of case. Defamatory statements had been made about Mr. X: no one knew who he was. Then the defendant published something which gave a clue to his identity but he did not in any way adopt the earlier defamatory statements. It was obviously right to hold that he incurred no liability for libels published by others. Sellers L.J. said[4]:

"It may well be that in circumstances where the identity of a plaintiff is not expressly referred to in an article extrinsic evidence may be given to establish identity, but it seems to me a wholly different matter to seek to add to the alleged libel defamatory views expressed and published by somebody else."

Diplock L.J. said[5]:

". . . the statement of fact or expression of opinion relied on as defamatory must be one which can be reasonably said to be contained in the statement in respect of which the action is brought and not merely in some other statement."

I can find nothing in the judgments which throws any light on the question with

---

1. [1910] A.C. 20; [1908–10] All E.R. Rep. 29.
2. [1940] 1 K.B. 377; [1939] 4 All E.R. 319.
3. [1965] 3 All E.R. 666; [1966] 1 W.L.R. 34.
4. [1965] 3 All E.R. at p. 667; [1966] 1 W.L.R. at p. 39.
5. [1965] 3 All E.R. at p. 669; [1966] 1 W.L.R. at p. 41.

which I am now dealing, or which indicates that this question was in the mind of any of the learned judges.

There was no peg or pointer in *Cassidy* v. *Daily Mirror Newspapers, Ltd.*[1] or in *Hough* v. *London Express Newspaper, Ltd.*[2] I see nothing wrong with these decisions. They do, however, show that the court recognises that rather far-fetched inferences may be made by sensible readers. I therefore reject the argument that the plaintiff must fail because the defendants' article contained no pointer or peg for his identification. . . .

One other matter I must mention at this stage. One of the witnesses thought that the article referred to the plaintiff but completely disbelieved it; he thought it was rubbish. It was argued that he must be left out of account because no tort is committed by making a defamatory statement about X to a person who utterly disbelieves it. That is plainly wrong. It is true that X's reputation is not diminished but the person defamed suffers annoyance or worse when he learns that a defamatory statement has been published about him. There may be no clear authority that publishing a defamatory statement is a tort whether it is believed or disbelieved. But very often there is no authority for an obvious proposition: no one has had the hardihood to dispute it. . . .

Note

It was Fox's Libel Act 1792 which made the question of "libel or no libel" essentially one for the jury. Although the Act applied to criminal proceedings only it has been regarded as declaratory of the common law. The judge must, however, be satisfied that there is sufficient evidence to go to the jury, that is the statement must be "reasonably capable" of the meaning alleged. If it is not, it must be withdrawn from the jury.

E. Hulton & Co. v. Jones

House of Lords   [1908–10] All E.R. Rep. 29

The plaintiff, Thomas Artemus Jones Esq., barrister, brought an action for libel against the defendants, the publishers of the Sunday Chronicle newspaper. The libel was said to be contained in an article purporting describing a motor festival at Dieppe. The material parts were as follows: "Upon the terrace marches the world, attracted by the motor races—a world immensely pleased with itself, and minded to draw a wealth of inspiration—and, incidentally, of golden cocktails—from any scheme to speed the passing hour . . . 'whist! there is Artemus Jones with a woman who is not his wife, who must be, you know—the other thing!' whispers a fair neighbour of mine into her bosom friend's ear. Really, is it not surprising how certain of our fellow countrymen behave when they come abroad? Would you suppose by his goings on, that he was a churchwarden at Peckham. No one, indeed, would assume that Jones in the atmosphere of London would take on so austere a job as the duties of a churchwarden. Here, in the atmosphere of Dieppe, on the French side of the Channel, he is the life and soul of a gay little band that haunts the Casino and turns night into day, besides betraying a most unholy delight in the society of female butterflies."

The evidence of the writer of the article and the editor of the paper was that they knew nothing of the plaintiff, and that the article was not intended by them to refer to him, was accepted as true. At the trial, witnesses were called for the plaintiff, who said that they had read the article and thought that it referred to the plaintiff. The jury returned a verdict for the plaintiff with £1,750 damages, and Channell J. gave judgment for the plaintiff. The defendants appealed unsuccessfully to the Court of Appeal, and thence to the House of Lords.

---

1. [1929] 2 K.B. 331; [1929] All E.R. Rep. 117.
2. [1940] 2 K.B. 507; [1940] 3 All E.R. 31.

Lord Shaw: ... In the publication of matter of a libellous character—that is, matter which would be libellous if applying to an actual person—the responsibility is as follows. In the first place, there is responsibility for the words used being taken to signify that which readers would reasonably understand by them; in the second place, there is responsibility also for the names used being taken to signify those whom the readers would reasonably understand by those names; and, in the third place, the same principle is applicable to persons unnamed, but sufficiently indicated by designation or description. I demur to the observation so frequently made in the argument that these principles are novel. Sufficient expression is given to the same principles by Abbott C.J. in *Bourke* v. *Warren*, in which that learned judge said (2 C. & P. 307, at pp. 309, 310):

> "The question for your consideration is, whether you think that the libel designates the plaintiff in such a way as to let those who knew him understand that he was the person meant? It is not necessary that all the world should understand the libel; it is sufficient if those who know the plaintiff can make out that he is the person meant."

I think that it is out of the question to suggest that that means "meant in the mind of the writer" or of the publisher: it must mean "meant by the words employed". ...

[Lord Loreburn L.C. (with whom Lord Atkinson and Lord Gorrell concurred) delivered a speech concurring in affirming the order of the Court of Appeal.]

Note

Salmond, p. 186, n. 50 comments: "There is some evidence that the decision may have been based on the recklessness or even the spite of the defendants ... The plaintiff had been a contributor to the defendants' paper for twelve years and his name was well-known in their office, although not to the actual writer of the article. The managing director admitted in cross-examination that he had read the article in proof and thought at first reading that it referred to the plaintiff ... The point is still important, for if the actual facts of *Hulton* v. *Jones* recurred today, the defendants might be held to have failed to establish reasonable care under s. 4 of the 1952 Act" (see *post*).

Newstead v. London Express Newspaper, Ltd.

Court of Appeal   [1939] 4 All E.R. 319

The Daily Express newspaper published an account of a trial for bigamy and referred to the prisoner as "Harold Newstead, thirty-year old Camberwell man". The account was true as regards a Camberwell barman of that name, but was not true as regards the plaintiff, Harold Newstead, aged about thirty, who assisted his father in a hairdressing business at Camberwell Road, Camberwell. The plaintiff brought an action for damages for libel against the proprietors of the newspaper. Five questions were left to the jury who were unable to agree on the first question: "Would reasonable persons understand the words complained of to refer to the plaintiff?" and they assessed damages at one-farthing. The defendants appealed. The Court of Appeal held that the evidence would have justified an affirmative answer to the first question by the jury; and, assuming the words were capable of a meaning defamatory of the plaintiff, the fact that they were true of another person did not afford a good defence to the defendants.

Sir Wilfred Greene M.R.: ... After giving careful consideration to the matter, I am unable to hold that the fact that defamatory words are true of A makes it as a matter of law impossible for them to be defamatory of B, which was in substance the main argument on behalf of the appellants. At first sight, this looks as though it would lead to great hardship, but the hardships are in practice not so serious as might appear, at any rate in the case of statements which are *ex facie* defamatory. Persons who make statements of this character may not unreasonably be expected, when describing the person of whom they are made, to identify that person so closely as to make it very unlikely that a judge would hold them to be reasonably capable of referring to someone else, or that a jury would hold that they did so refer. This is particularly so in the case of statements which purport to deal with actual facts. If there is a risk of coincidence, it ought, I think, in reason to be borne, not by the innocent party to whom the words are held to refer, but by the party who puts them into circulation. In matters of fiction, there is no doubt more room for hardship. Even in the case of matters of fact it is no doubt possible to construct imaginary facts which would lead to hardship. There may also be hardship if words, not on their faces defamatory, are true of A but are reasonably understood by some as referring to B, and, as applied to B, are defamatory. Such cases, however, must be rare. The law as I understand it is well settled, and can be altered only by legislation. The appeal must be dismissed with costs.

[Du Parcq L.J. delivered a concurring judgment. Mackinnon L.J. thought that the appeal should be allowed by reason of the smallness of the damages which would have been awarded to the plaintiff had the jury returned a verdict in his favour.]

The Defamation Act 1952

4. Unintentional defamation.—(1) A person who has published words alleged to be defamatory of another person may, if he claims that the words were published by him innocently in relation to that other person, make an offer of amends under this section; and in any such case—

    (*a*) if the offer is accepted by the party aggrieved and is duly performed, no proceedings for libel or slander shall be taken or continued by that party against the person making the offer in respect of the publication in question (but without prejudice to any cause of action against any other person jointly responsible for that publication);

    (*b*) if the offer is not accepted by the party aggrieved, then, except as otherwise provided by this section, it shall be a defence, in any proceedings by him for libel or slander against the person making the offer in respect of the publication in question, to prove that the words complained of were published by the defendant innocently in relation to the plaintiff and that the offer was made as soon as practicable after the defendant received notice that they were or might be defamatory of the plaintiff, and has not been withdrawn.

(2) An offer of amends under this section must be expressed to be made for the purposes of a defence under paragraph (*b*) of subsection (1) of this section the facts relied upon by the person making it to show that the words in question were published by him innocently in relation to the party aggrieved; and for the purposes of a defence under paragraph (*b*) of subsection (1) of this section no evidence, other than evidence of facts specified in the affidavit, shall be admissible on behalf of that person to prove that the words were so published.

(3) An offer of amends under this section shall be understood to mean an offer—

    (*a*) in any case, to publish or join in the publication of a suitable correction of the words complained of, and a sufficient apology to the party aggrieved in respect of those words;

    (*b*) where copies of a document or record containing the said words have been distributed by or with the knowledge of the person making the offer, to take such steps as are reasonably practicable on his part for notifying persons to whom copies have been so distributed that the words are alleged to be defamatory of the party aggrieved.

(4) Where an offer of amends under this section is accepted by the party aggrieved—

    (*a*) any question as to the steps to be taken in fulfilment of the offer as so accepted shall in default of agreement between the parties be referred to and determined by the High Court, whose decision thereon shall be final;

    (*b*) the power of the court to make orders as to costs in proceedings by the party aggrieved against the person making the offer in respect of the publication in question, or in proceedings in respect of the offer under paragraph (*a*) of this subsection, shall include power to order the payment by the person making the offer to the party aggrieved of costs on an indemnity basis and any expenses reasonably incurred or to be incurred by that party in consequence of the publication in question;

and if no such proceedings as aforesaid are taken, the High Court may, upon application made by the party aggrieved, make any such order for the payment of such costs and expenses as aforesaid as could be made in such proceedings.

(5) For the purposes of this section words shall be treated as published by one person (in this subsection referred to as the publisher) innocently in relation to another person if and only if the following conditions are satisfied, that is to say—

    (*a*) that the publisher did not intend to publish them of and concerning that other person, and did not know of circumstances by virtue of which they might be understood to refer to him; or

    (*b*) that the words were not defamatory on the face of them, and the publisher did not know of circumstances by virtue of which they might be understood to be defamatory of that other person,

and in either case that the publisher exercised all reasonable care in relation to the publication; and any reference in this subsection to the publisher shall be construed as including a reference to any servant or agent of his who was concerned with the contents of the publication.

(6) Paragraph (*b*) of subsection (1) of this section shall not apply in relation to the publication by any person of words of which he is not the author unless he proves that the words were written by the author without malice.

Report of the Committee on the Law of Defamation, Cmd. 7536 (1948)

30. A considerable body of evidence has been tendered to us dealing with what may conveniently be described as Group Defamation—that is to say, false statements vilifying not identifiable individuals, but groups or classes of persons distinguishable by race, colour, creed or vocation. Under the existing law, such statements cannot form the subject of civil proceedings for libel or slander. If they are made with intent to incite persons to commit any crime, to create a disturbance, to raise discontent or disaffection among His Majesty's subjects, or to promote ill-will and hostility between different classes of such subjects, they may amount to the crime of seditious libel; but prosecutions for seditious libel, save in the most flagrant cases, may easily present the appearance of political prosecutions which the English tradition tends to view with disfavour.

31. The most widespread and deplorable examples of Group Defamation at the date at which we commenced our sittings were directed against the Jews; but complaints were also made to us of unfounded vilification of particular trades. It is, we think, symptomatic of Group Defamation that the subject matter varies with current internal and external political trends. Much as we deplore all provocation to hatred or contempt for bodies or groups of persons with its attendant incitement to violence,

we cannot fail to be impressed by the danger of curtailing free and frank—albeit, hot and hasty—political discussion and criticism. No suggestion has been made to us for altering the existing law which would avoid the prohibition of perfectly proper criticisms of particular groups or classes of persons. The law of seditious libel still exists as an ultimate sanction and we consider that the law as it stands affords as much protection as can safely be given.

32. We do not, therefore, recommend any general change in the existing law to deal with Group Defamation.

Notes

1. Incitement to racial hatred is a criminal offence: Race Relations Act 1965, s. 6. Apart from seditious libels, various other criminal offences may be committed by those who defame groups distinguished by colour, race, ethnic or national origins. But there is no actionable tort in these circumstances: see generally, A. Lester & G. Bindman, *Race and Law* (London, 1972), pp. 355–356.

2. "All lawyers are thieves" (an example given in *Eastwood* v. *Holmes* (1858), 1 F. & F. 347, at p. 349) is group defamation and not actionable. "The reason why a libel published of a large or indeterminate number of persons described by some general name generally fails to be actionable is the difficulty of establishing that the plaintiff was in fact included in the defamatory statement . . ." (*per* Lord Atkin in *Knupffer* v. *London Express Newspaper, Ltd.*, [1944] A.C. 116, at p. 122). Whether or not the plaintiff succeeds will depend upon "the size of the class, the generality of the charge and the extravagance of the accusation" (*ibid.*, *per* Lord Porter at p. 124).

3. Corporate bodies have been allowed to sue in respect of defamation: trading companies (*South Hetton Coal Co.* v. *North Eastern News Association*, [1894] 1 Q.B. 133), trade unions (*Willis* v. *Brooks*, [1947] 1 All E.R. 191) and local authorities (*Bognor Regis U.D.C.* v. *Campion*, [1972] 2 Q.B. 169; [1972] 2 All E.R. 61). There is a strong criticism of the last-mentioned decision by J. A. Weir in [1972A] C.L.J. 238.

3. PUBLICATION

Huth v. Huth

Court of Appeal   [1914–15] All E.R. Rep. 242

The defendant sent a letter to his wife in an unsealed envelope suggesting that they were not married and that their children were illegitimate. The wife could not sue her husband in tort [but see now the Law Reform (Husband and Wife) Act 1962, s. 1]. In order to circumvent this, his children brought this action for libel. To prove publication the family butler was called to give evidence that he had looked at the contents of the envelope before placing it on the breakfast table. The plaintiffs lost their action and an appeal to the Court of Appeal was dismissed.

Lord Reading C.J.: . . . It cannot be contended, and is not contended, as I understand, that if a person, in breach of his duty, opens an envelope and reads a letter, and there is no reason to expect that he would be likely to commit this breach of duty, the fact that he opens the envelope and reads the letter amounts to publication by the person who sends it; but it is argued in this case that, as the document was enclosed in an unsealed and ungummed envelope, it must be assumed that the defendant knew or ought to have known, or might have expected that a servant in the house would open a letter in such an envelope so addressed. It is further said that an envelope unsealed, with a halfpenny stamp on it, is liable always to be opened by the postal authorities and the document is liable to be examined and read, and consequently that it must be taken that there was some evidence of publication to the Post Office.

With regard to the first point, that is the publication to the butler, I am clearly of opinion that there is no evidence of any such publication to the butler upon the point merely whether the fact that the butler opened the letter and read it because he was curious, would make it publication by the defendant. Fortunately, it is no part of a butler's duty to open the letters that come to the house of his master or mistress addressed to the master or mistress; and in this case there is nothing exceptional in it except that his curiosity was excited by reason of the lady being addressed by her maiden name. No one can help a man's curiosity being excited, but it does not justify him in opening a letter, and it could not make the defendant liable for the publication to the butler of the contents of the envelope, because it must of course be borne in mind that, however insulting and offensive the matters may have been which the husband wrote to his wife, they were addressed to the wife and only intended for the wife, and she alone saw them, no action for libel could be brought by her. An action for libel can only be brought if there is publication to some third person. The publication to the butler in this case is not sufficient. . . .

. . . It has been laid down, and I think rightly that the court will take judicial notice of the nature of the document, which is the postcard, and will presume, in the absence of evidence to the contrary, that others besides the person to whom it is addressed will read and have read what is written thereon. In this way the presumption of law based on the authorities arises. If, of course, even in such a case as that, the defendant could establish that the postcard never was read by a single person—if it were possible to establish such a state of things, although it is very difficult to conceive—he would, notwithstanding the presumption, succeed in the action, because he would have proved that there was no publication. But of course he cannot, and does not. The fact that it is practically impossible to prove that anyone did read the postcard is the very reason why the law takes judicial notice of the nature of the document, and says the mere fact that it is written on a postcard which is posted must be taken as some evidence that a third person will read it, or has read it. Now, that is clear law, and is quite beyond dispute. . . .

. . . I cannot think that the court is entitled to presume, merely because the envelope went through the post, that it would be opened. I suppose what is said with regard to these letters is true of every package which is sent through the Post Office. It is true of every parcel which is sent through the Post Office, and in certain circumstances it may be true also of other documents, even though they may be sealed; but that does not justify the presumption to which counsel for the plaintiffs is driven in this case —that is, that such a letter in an envelope which is ungummed is to be treated just as a postcard. I think that that point fails, and that there is therefore no evidence of publication in this case. . . .

SWINFEN EADY L.J.: . . . In my opinion, the question of publication can shortly be disposed of in this way. There was no publication, because there was no evidence that, to the defendant's knowledge, a letter addressed to his wife and enclosed in this envelope, but unsealed and not fastened down, would in the ordinary course be likely to be opened by the butler, or by any other person in the employ of the mistress, or at the mistress's house, before it was delivered to her.

When the cases which were referred to are looked at it will be seen that in each case the defendant, who must be taken to have intended the natural consequences of his own act in the circumstances of the case, must on that footing have intended the publication which in fact took place. . . . [BRAY J. agreed.]

Theaker v. Richardson

Court of Appeal   [1962] 1 All E.R. 229

The defendant wrote a defamatory letter to the plaintiff, a married woman and a fellow-member of the local district council. The letter was placed in a sealed manilla envelope similar to the kind used for distributing election addresses. The envelope was addressed to the plaintiff. The plaintiff's husband, seeing the envelope on the mat, opened it thinking it was an election address. The jury found that it was a natural and probable consequence of the defendant's writing and delivery of the letter that the plaintiff's husband would open and read it. Judgment was given for the plaintiff. The defendant's appeal to the Court of Appeal was dismissed.

PEARSON L.J.: . . . The question arising can be put in this form. The plaintiff's husband, acting carelessly and thoughtlessly but meaning no harm, picked up and opened and began to read the letter. Was his conduct something unusual, out of the ordinary and not reasonably to be anticipated, or was it something which could quite easily and naturally happen in the ordinary course of events? In my judgment that is a fair formulation of the question, and, when so formulated, it is seen to be a question of fact which in a trial with a jury can and should be left to and decided by the jury, who have observed the witnesses giving evidence and have and are expected to use their own common sense and general knowledge of the world and perhaps some particular knowledge (if they have it) of the locality concerned and the ways of its inhabitants. In my judgment, it would not be right to substitute the opinion of this court for the opinion of the jury on such a question arising in the course of a trial with a jury. . . .

[HARMAN L.J. delivered a judgment in favour of dismissing the appeal. ORMEROD L.J., dissenting, delivered a judgment in favour of allowing the appeal.]

Question

A writes a defamatory statement and locks it in his desk. A thief steals it and makes its contents known. Is there publication by A? (The example is given in *Pullman v. Hill*, [1891] 1 Q.B. 524, at p. 527.)

Notes

1. Dictation by the defendant to his secretary is a publication: *Pullman v. Hill*, [1891] 1 Q.B. 524; *Osborn v. Thomas Boulter & Son*, [1930] 2 K.B. 226. Presumably, the dictation is only slander (p. 528, *ante*); when the secretary hands the typewritten letter back to her employer for signature this is not publication: Gatley, p. 113.

2. Although everyone who takes part in publishing a libel is *prima facie* liable (e.g. the editor, printer, publisher and seller of a newspaper) a person who is not the author, printer, or the first or main publisher of a work which contains a libel, e.g. a salesman, librarian or distributor, may raise the defence of innocent dissemination. He must prove—(a) that he did not know that the offending material contained the libel; (b) that he did not know it was of a character likely to contain a libel; and (c) that his absence of knowledge was not due to negligence on his part. In *Vizetelly v. Mudie's Select Library, Ltd.*, [1900] 2 K.B. 170 the defence failed because the defendant circulating library had overlooked a publisher's circular requesting them to return the offending book.

3. Publishers and printers usually protect themselves by an indemnity clause in the contract with the author. The following is a specimen clause:

"The author warrants to the Publishers that the Work will in no way whatever be a violation of any existing copyright and that it will contain nothing of a libellous or scandalous character."

Section 11 of the Defamation Act 1952 provides:

"An agreement for indemnifying any person against civil liability for libel in respect of the publication of any matter shall not be unlawful unless at the time of the publication that person knows that the matter is defamatory, and does not reasonably believe there is a good defence to any action brought upon it."

This section means that an insurance policy against libel damages is valid only in cases of unintentional defamation. A specimen insurance policy provides:

"The insured shall at all times exercise diligence care and restraint in an endeavour to avoid the printed publication of matter which would reasonably be expected to cause offence such as to incur a complaint or legal proceedings which would give rise to a claim under this Policy."

It is usual for the insured to bear some portion of the loss (e.g. the first ten *per cent.*). A usual condition is that the insurer is to have full control of the defence of any claim for indemnity or damages and full discretion in the conduct of any negotiations or settlement proceedings. (These clauses are quoted with kind permission of the Guardian Royal Exchange Assurance Group from their specimen policy.)

4. DEFENCES

(a) Justification

The Defamation Act 1952

5. **Justification.**—In an action for libel or slander in respect of words containing two or more distinct charges against the plaintiff, a defence of justification shall not fail by reason only that the truth of every charge is not proved if the words not proved to be true do not materially injure the plaintiff's reputation having regard to the truth of the remaining charges.

The Civil Evidence Act 1968

13. **Conclusiveness of convictions for purposes of defamation actions.**—(1) In an action for libel or slander in which the question whether a person did or did not commit a criminal offence is relevant to an issue arising in the action, proof that, at the time when that issue falls to be determined, that person stands convicted of that offence shall be conclusive evidence that he committed that offence; and his conviction thereof shall be admissible in evidence accordingly.

(2) In any such action as aforesaid in which by virtue of this section a person is proved to have been convicted of an offence, the contents of any document which is admissible as evidence of the conviction, and the contents of the information, complaint, indictment or charge-sheet on which that person was convicted, shall, without prejudice to the reception of any other admissible evidence for the purpose of identifying the facts on which the conviction was based, be admissible in evidence for the purpose of identifying those facts.

(3) For the purposes of this section a person shall be taken to stand convicted of an

offence if but only if there subsists against him a conviction of that offence by or before a court in the United Kingdom or by a court-martial there or elsewhere. . . .

Question

A writes of B: "B has stolen bicycles from X, Y and Z." B has in fact stolen bicycles from X and Y, but not from Z. In his statement of claim he relies only on A's allegation that he has stolen Z's bicycle. May A plead and prove the thefts from X and Y by way of justification?

Notes

1. The plea that the words published are true "in substance and in fact", must be supported by particulars of the facts relied upon, and evidence at the trial will be strictly limited to those particulars: Gatley, para. 1058 *et seq.* The defendant must justify "the sting of the libel": e.g. in *Alexander v. North Eastern Rail. Co.* (1865), 6 B. & S. 340, the plaintiff brought an action for libel based on the following notice which the defendants had published: "N. E. Railway Company. Caution. J. Alexander was charged before the magistrates at Darlington for riding in a train from Leeds, for which his ticket was not available, and refusing to pay the proper fare. He was convicted in the penalty of £9 1s. 10d., including costs, or three weeks' imprisonment." In fact the plaintiff had been sentenced to fourteen days' imprisonment in default of payment of the fine and costs. The Court of Queen's Bench held that the defence of justification succeeded. It has been said: "It is sufficient if the substance of the libellous statement is justified . . . As much must be justified as meets the sting of the charge, and if anything be contained in a charge which does not add to the sting of it, that need not be justified" (*Edwards v. Bell* (1824), 1 Bing. 402, at p. 409, *per* Burrough J.). The defendant cannot protect himself with a statement like: "There is a rumour that . . .". He must prove that the rumour is true: *Truth (N.Z.), Ltd. v. Holloway*, [1960] 1 W.L.R. 997, at p. 1002 (P.C.).

2. Section 13 of the Civil Evidence Act 1968 (*ante*) was enacted in order to avoid a repetition of cases like *Hinds v. Sparks*, [1964] Crim. L.R. 717 and *Goody v. Odhams Press, Ltd.*, [1967] 1 Q.B. 333; [1966] 3 All E.R. 369, in which defendants seeking to justify their statements were prevented from relying on the criminal convictions in the subsequent actions for libel. See too, Interim Report of the Committee on Defamation, Cmnd. 5571, 1974.

(b) Fair Comment

London Artists, Ltd. v. Littler

Court of Appeal   [1969] 2 All E.R. 193

The four top performers in *The Right Honourable Gentleman* terminated their contracts, through their agents, the plaintiffs. The defendant (Mr. Emile Littler, the impresario) was convinced that there was a plot to stop the play. He wrote a letter to each artiste and distributed the letter to the press. In it he suggested that the plaintiffs, all of them connected with the entertainments industry, had taken part in a plot to end a successful play. In an action for libel, the defendant pleaded justification (this defence was later withdrawn), fair comment on a matter of public interest, namely the fate of the play, and publication on an occasion of qualified privilege. The trial judge held that the plea of privilege failed, as did the plea of fair comment because this was not a matter of public interest. The defendant appealed on the ground that the judge had erred on a question of law when he ruled that the defence of fair comment could not be left to the jury. The Court of Appeal dismissed an appeal.

LORD DENNING M.R.: . . . Three points arise on the defence of fair comment. First, was the comment made on a matter of public interest? The judge ruled that it was not.[1] I cannot agree with him. There is no definition in the books as to what is a matter of public interest. All we are given is a list of examples, coupled with the statement that it is for the judge and not for the jury. I would not myself confine it within narrow limits. Whenever a matter is such as to affect people at large, so that they may be legitimately interested in, or concerned at, what is going on; or what may happen to them or to others; then it is a matter of public interest on which everyone is entitled to make fair comment. A good example is *South Hetton Coal Co., Ltd.* v. *North-Eastern News Association, Ltd.*[2] A colliery company owned most of the cottages in the village. It was held that the sanitary conditions of those cottages—or rather their insanitary condition—was a matter of public interest. Lord Esher M.R. said[3] that it was "a matter of public interest that the conduct of the employers should be criticised". There the public were legitimately *concerned*. Here the public are legitimately *interested*. Many people are interested in what happens in the theatre. The stars welcome publicity. They want to be put at the top of the bill. Producers wish it too. They like the house to be full. The comings and goings of the performers are noticed everywhere. When three top stars and a satellite all give notice to leave at the same time—thus putting a successful play in peril—it is to my mind a matter of public interest on which everyone, press and all, are entitled to comment freely.

The second point is whether the allegation of a "plot" was a fact which the defendant had to prove to be true, or was it only comment? In order to be fair, the commentator must get his basic facts right. The basic facts are those which go to the pith and substance of the matter, see *Cunningham-Howie* v. *F. W. Dimbleby & Sons, Ltd.*[4] They are the facts on which the comments are based or from which the inferences are drawn—as distinct from the comments or inferences themselves. The commentator need not set out in his original article all the basic facts, see *Kemsley* v. *Foot*;[5] but he must get them right and be ready to prove them to be true. He must indeed afterwards in legal proceedings, when asked, give particulars of the basic facts, see *Burton v. Board*;[6] but he need not give particulars of the comments or the inferences to be drawn from those facts. If in his original article he sets out basic facts which are themselves defamatory of the plaintiff, then he must prove them to be true: and this is the case just as much after s. 6 of the Defamation Act 1952, as it was before. It was so held by the New Zealand Court of Appeal in *Truth (N.Z.), Ltd.* v. *Avery*,[7] which was accepted by this court in *Broadway Approvals, Ltd.* v. *Odhams Press, Ltd.*[8] It is indeed the whole difference between a plea of fair comment and a plea of justification. In fair comment, he need only prove the basic facts to be true. In justification he must prove also that the comments and inferences are true also.

So I turn to ask what were the basic facts in this case? In the particulars (as amended by including para. 20A) the defendant set out very many facts which conveyed no clear picture. But, putting them together, it appears that he was relying on three basic facts. First, that the owners wanted to get "The Right Honourable Gentleman" out of Her Majesty's Theatre. Second, that the stars and satellite all gave notice by the same agents at the same time in the same form. Third, that there was a plot between the

1. [1968] 1 All E.R. at p. 1088; [1968] 1 W.L.R. at p. 623.
2. [1894] 1 Q.B. 133.
3. [1894] 1 Q.B. at p. 140.
4. [1951] 1 K.B. at p. 364; [1950] 2 All E.R. at p. 883.
5. [1952] A.C. 345; [1952] 1 All E.R. 501.
6. [1929] 1 K.B. 301; [1928] All E.R. Rep. 659.
7. [1959] N.Z.L.R. 274.
8. [1965] 2 All E.R. 523; [1965] 1 W.L.R. 805.

owners and the stars (through the second plaintiffs, the Grade Organisation, Ltd.) to bring to an end the run of "The Right Honourable Gentleman". The defendant proved the first two basic facts, but did not prove the third. He failed to prove a plot and had to withdraw the allegation. That put him in a quandary on fair comment. He could not prove one of the basic facts. So he turned right about. He then submitted that the allegation of a "plot" was not a fact at all but only a comment. In my view that sub-mission cannot be sustained, and for these reasons: In the first place, the defendant in his pleadings, treated the "plot" as a statement of fact, and I do not think we should look with favour on such a complete turnabout in the middle of the case. In the second place, the defendant in his evidence said it was a statement of fact. He was asked:

"What was said in the letters was deliberately intended by you to be said. That is right, is it not? A.—It was a statement of fact. Q.—What you believed to be a fact? A.—Yes."

In the third place, on a fair reading of the whole letter, I think the allegation of a plot was a statement of fact. The first paragraph runs in guarded language, "it appears"; and the fourth paragraph says "In other words"; but the last paragraph speaks of "the combined effort". Reading the letter as a whole, I have no doubt that it stated *as a fact* that there was a plot between the plaintiffs to bring down a chopper on the head of "The Right Honourable Gentleman".

Counsel for the defendant submitted, however, that the question whether the state-ment was a statement of fact or comment should have been left to the jury. He would be right if it was reasonably capable of being considered as comment. That is clear from many of the cases, finishing with the judgment of the Privy Council in *Jones* v. *Skelton*.[1] But for the three reasons which I have given, I do not think the statement of a "plot" was reasonably capable of being considered as comment. It was a statement of fact which was itself defamatory of the plaintiffs. The defendant, in order to suc-ceed, had to prove it to be true. He failed to do so, and along with it went the defence of fair comment.

In case, however, I am wrong about this and it could be regarded as comment, then I turn to the third point, which is this: Were there any facts on which a fair-minded man might honestly make such a comment? I take it to be settled law that, in order for the defence of fair comment to be left to the jury, there must at least be a sufficient basis of fact to warrant the comment, in this sense, that a fair-minded man might on those facts honestly hold that opinion. There is no need for the defendant to prove that his opinion was correct or one with which the jury agree. He is entitled to the defence of fair comment unless it can be said: "No fair-minded man could honestly hold that opinion." See what Buckley L.J. said in *Peter Walker & Son, Ltd.* v. *Hodgson*.[2]

In this case I am sure that the defendant acted honestly and in good faith. He honestly thought that there was a plot to bring to a stop the run of "The Right Honourable Gentleman". He was himself so convinced of it that he took the extreme step of telling it to the world. But I fear that he went beyond the bounds of a fair-minded man. He jumped too hastily to his conclusion. He ought not to have been so precipitate. He ought to have made enquiries of the artistes. He ought to have made enquiries of his brother, or wait till he had a letter from him. We know that the brother had on 23 June, that very day, written saying "We shall have to continue on the same basis as now". By jumping so quickly to a conclusion the defendant came at odds with the law. He made a public condemnation not only of the artistes themselves but of the plaintiffs, Associated Television, and the agents, London Artists, Mr. Lew Grade and the Grade Organisation. The judge held[3] that in alleging that all those were parties to a plot he was making an imputation without any basis of fact to support it. I think the judge was quite right in so holding and in not leaving it to the jury.

---

1. [1963] 3 All E.R. 952; [1963] 1 W.L.R. 1362.
2. [1909] 1 K.B. 239, at p. 253.
3. [1968] 1 All E.R. at p. 1088; [1968] 1 W.L.R. at p. 624.

In the upshot it comes to this: the fate of "The Right Honourable Gentleman" was a matter of public interest. The defendant was fully entitled to comment on it as long as his comment was fair and honest. He was entitled to give his views to the public through the press. But I think he went beyond the bounds of fair comment. He was carried away by his feelings at the moment. He did not wait long enough to check the facts and to get them right. He had no defence except as to damages; and on that he did well. I would dismiss this appeal.

[EDMUND DAVIES and WIDGERY L.JJ. delivered judgments in favour of dismissing the appeal.]

Notes

1. In *Slim* v. *Daily Telegraph*, [1968] 2 Q.B. 157, at p. 170, Lord Denning M.R. said of fair comment: "We must ever maintain this right intact. It must not be whittled down by legal refinements." Yet, as Diplock L.J. pointed out, in that very case two letters to the *Daily Telegraph* by Mr. John Herbert, neither of which could have taken a literate reader more than 60 seconds to read, became submerged in a legal case in which the pleadings covered 83 pages, the correspondence 300 pages, the evidence 6 days followed by 2 or 3 days' argument, and a judgment of 35 pages, followed by a further three days of minute linguistic analysis in the Court of Appeal. The case of *London Artists, Ltd.* v. *Littler* (*ante*) took 17 days to try, and was followed by five days in the Court of Appeal.

2. In *Sutherland* v. *Stopes*, [1925] A.C. 47 (in which Marie Stopes Ph.D., who worked for birth control, failed in her action for libel against a Roman Catholic doctor who had commented "Charles Bradlaugh was condemned to jail for a less serious crime") there are some *dicta* which suggest that a comment which is expressed in very violent language may be regarded as unfair, although the opinion is honestly held. But *dicta* in *Slim* v. *Daily Telegraph* and *Littler* v. *London Artists, Ltd.* suggest that violence of expression is simply evidence that an opinion is not honestly held.

3. A defence of fair comment can be rebutted by proof of malice: *Thomas* v. *Bradbury, Agnew & Co., Ltd.*, [1906] 2 K.B. 627 (C.A.).

4. A statement may be a comment although no facts, on which that opinion is based, are included, provided the subject-matter is indicated with clarity. In *Kemsley* v. *Foot*, [1952] A.C. 345; [1952] 1 All E.R. 501 an article in *Tribune* by Michael Foot was headed "Lower than Kemsley", and went on to accuse another journalist and the *Evening Standard* of "the foulest piece of journalism perpetrated in this country for many a year". The *Evening Standing* had no connection with Kemsley, the well-known newspaper owner. Kemsley alleged that the article's heading imputed that his name was a byword for false and foul journalism. The House of Lords held that the defendant could plead fair comment because there was sufficient subject-matter on which the comment could be based. Had it been a bare inference it would have been treated as a statement of fact, and the only available defence would have been justification. Here the words implied that Kemsley was dishonest and low, but not as low as the Beaverbrook press. This was enough for the defence of fair comment because the words implied certain conduct and commented on that conduct. The Rules of the Supreme Court (O. 82, r. 3) require the pleader to distinguish comment from the facts upon which the defendant proposes to rely in support of the comment, e.g. "The plaintiff is a crook. He is not fit

to be a company director." Particulars must be given of the allegation that he is a crook.

The Defamation Act 1952

6. Fair comment.—In an action for libel or slander in respect of words consisting partly of allegations of fact and partly of expression of opinion, a defence of fair comment shall not fail by reason only that the truth of every allegation of fact is not proved if the expression of opinion is fair comment having regard to such of the facts alleged or referred to in the words complained of as are proved.

Question

D. writes and publishes the following statement: "P. is an undischarged bankrupt and a drug addict. He is not fit to be a councillor." D. proves the truth of the allegation that P. is a drug addict, but was mistaken about him being an undischarged bankrupt. Does P. have any remedy? What difference would it make if D. had omitted the comment?

(c) Privilege

(i) Absolute privilege

The Parliamentary Papers Act 1840

1. Proceedings, criminal or civil, against persons for publication of papers printed by order of Parliament, to be stayed upon delivery of a certificate and affidavit to the effect that such publication is by order of either House of Parliament.—. . . It shall and may be lawful for any person or persons who now is or are, or hereafter shall be, a defendant or defendants in any civil or criminal proceeding commenced or prosecuted in any manner soever, for or on account or in respect of the publication of any such report, paper, votes, or proceedings by such person or persons, or by his, her, or their servant or servants, by or under the authority of either House of Parliament, to bring before the court in which such proceeding shall have been or shall be so commenced or prosecuted, or before any judge of the same (if one of the superior courts at Westminster), first giving twenty-four hours notice of his intention so to do to the prosecutor or plaintiff in such proceeding, a certificate under the hand of the lord high chancellor of Great Britain, or the lord keeper of the great seal, or of the speaker of the House of Lords, for the time being, or of the clerk of the Parliaments, or of the speaker of the House of Commons, or of the clerk of the same house, stating that the report, paper, votes, or proceedings, as the case may be, in respect whereof such civil or criminal proceeding shall have been commenced or prosecuted, was published by such person or persons, or by his, her, or their servant or servants, by order or under the authority of the House of Lords or of the House of Commons, as the case may be, together with an affidavit verifying such certificate; and such court or judge shall thereupon immediately stay such civil or criminal proceeding; and the same, and every writ or process issued therein, shall be and shall be deemed and taken to be finally put an end to, determined, and superseded by virtue of this Act.

2. Proceedings to be stayed when commenced in respect of a copy of an authenticated report, etc.—. . . In case of any civil or criminal proceeding hereafter to be commenced or prosecuted for or on account or in respect of the publication of any copy of such report, paper, votes, or proceedings, it shall be lawful for the defendant or defendants at any stage of the proceedings to lay before the court or judge such report, paper, votes, or proceedings, and such copy, with an affidavit verifying such report, paper, votes, or proceedings, and the correctness of such copy, and the court or judge shall immediately stay such civil or criminal proceeding; and the same, and every writ or process issued therein, shall be and shall be deemed and taken to be finally put an end to, determined, and superseded by virtue of this Act.

3. In proceedings for printing any extract or abstract of a paper, it may be shewn that such extract was bona fide made.—. . . It shall be lawful in any civil or criminal proceeding to be commenced or prosecuted for printing any extract from or abstract of such report, paper, votes, or proceedings, to give in evidence . . . such report, paper, votes, or proceedings, and to show that such extract or abstract was published bona fide and without malice; and if such shall be the opinion of the jury, a verdict of not guilty shall be entered for the defendant or defendants.

The Defamation Act 1952

9. Extension of certain defences to broadcasting.—(1) Section three of the Parliamentary Papers Act 1840 (which confers protection in respect of proceedings for printing extracts from or abstracts of parliamentary papers) shall have effect as if the reference to printing included a reference to broadcasting by means of wireless telegraphy.

Notes

1. In *Church of Scientology of California v. Johnson-Smith*, [1972] 1 Q.B. 522; [1972] 1 All E.R. 378 the plaintiffs alleged that the defendant, a member of Parliament, had made defamatory remarks concerning them during a television interview. The defendant pleaded fair comment and privilege. In order to defeat these pleas the plaintiffs alleged malice, and, in order to establish this sought to adduce evidence, including extracts from Hansard, of what the defendant had said and done in Parliament. Browne J. held that it was not open to either party to go directly or indirectly into anything said or done in Parliament. Accordingly, although this case arose out of something said outside Parliament, the proceedings in Parliament could not be used to support the allegation of malice and the extracts from Hansard had to be excluded.

2. In *Cook v. Alexander*, [1973] 3 All E.R. 1037, it was held by the Court of Appeal that a reporter writing a sketch of parliamentary proceedings is entitled to select that part of the proceedings which he considers to be of genuine public interest. Provided that the reporting is fair and accurate and not actuated by malice, it is privileged.

Chatterton v. Secretary of State for India

Court of Appeal   [1895–9] All E.R. Rep. 1035

In his statement of claim the plaintiff claimed "damages for libel from the defendant in that he conveyed or caused to be conveyed in writing to the Under-Secretary of State untrue statements affecting the professional reputation of the plaintiff". The statement complained of was made by the Secretary of State for India to the Parliamentary Under-Secretary for India in order to enable him to answer a question asked in the House of Commons. The Master made an order dismissing the action as vexatious. This was affirmed by a judge in chambers, and, subsequently by the Divisional Court. The plaintiff appealed unsuccessfully to the Court of Appeal.

LORD ESHER M.R.: . . . The Queen's Bench Division has held that the action cannot be maintained, on the ground that such an act as that which is the subject of the action cannot be inquired into by a civil court of law. It is beyond the powers of a civil court to hold any inquiry upon the matter. In all the reported cases upon the subject it has been laid down that a judge should stop the case, if such an action came before him for trial, because he would have no jurisdiction even to entertain the question. As the action cannot be maintained at all, I think it would be vexatious to allow it to go on.

What is the reason for the existence of this law? It does not exist for the benefit of the official. All judges have said that the ground of its existence is the injury to the public good which would result if such an inquiry were allowed as would be necessary if the action were maintainable. An inquiry would take away from the public official his freedom of action in a matter concerning the public welfare, because he would have to appear before a jury and be cross-examined as to his conduct. That would be contrary to the interest of the public, and the privilege is, therefore, absolute in regard to the contents of such a document as that upon which this action is founded. I shall not go through the reported cases since they are all to the same effect. The result of them is summed up thus by Mr. Fraser in his book on *Libel and Slander* (1st Edn.), p. 95:

> "For reasons of public policy the same protection would no doubt be given to anything in the nature of an act of State—for example, to every communication relating to State matters made by one Minister to another, or to the Crown."

I adopt that paragraph, which seems to me to be an exact statement of the law. . . .

[KAY and A. L. SMITH L.JJ. delivered judgments concurring in dismissing the appeal.]

Note

Apart from the defence of absolute privilege in these circumstances, the Crown may be able to shield behind the claim of Crown privilege not to disclose certain classes of official documents: *Conway* v. *Rimmer*, [1968] A.C. 910; [1968] 1 All E.R. 874 and discussion in S. A. de Smith, *Constitutional and Administrative Law*, 2nd Edn. (Harmondsworth, 1973), p. 618.

(*ii*) *Qualified privilege*

The Law of Libel Amendment Act 1888

3. Newspaper reports of proceedings in court privileged.—A fair and accurate report in any newspaper of proceedings publicly heard before any court exercising judicial authority shall, if published contemporaneously with such proceedings, be privileged: Provided that nothing in this section shall authorise the publication of any blasphemous or indecent matter.

The Defamation Act 1952

8. Extent of Law of Libel Amendment Act 1888, s. 3.—Section three of the Law of Libel Amendment Act 1888 (which relates to contemporary reports of proceedings before courts exercising judicial authority) shall apply and apply only to courts exercising judicial authority within the United Kingdom.

9. (2) Section seven of this Act and section three of the Law of Libel Amendment Act 1888, as amended by this Act shall apply in relation to reports or matters broadcast by means of wireless telegraphy as part of any programme or service provided by means of a broadcasting station within the United Kingdom, and in relation to any broadcasting by means of wireless telegraphy of any such report or matter, as they apply in relation to reports and matters published in a newspaper and to publication in a newspaper; and subsection (2) of the said section seven shall have effect in relation to any such broadcasting, as if for the words "in the newspaper in which" there were substituted the words "in the manner in which".

(3) In this section "broadcasting station" means any station in respect of which a licence granted by the Postmaster General under the enactments relating to wireless telegraphy is in force, being a licence which (by whatever form of words) authorises the use of the station for the purpose of providing broadcasting services for general reception.

Notes

1. It is not clear whether "privileged" in s. 3 of the Law of Libel Amendment Act 1888 refers to "qualified" or "absolute" privilege, but it is generally understood as the latter: *McCarey* v. *Associated Newspapers, Ltd.*, [1964] 2 All E.R. 335. If the conditions of s. 3 are not satisfied, then the qualified privilege which exists at common law to publish fair and accurate reports of judicial proceedings, becomes relevant.

2. A report is "fair and accurate" even if the reporter selects parts of a trial to report, e.g. counsel's opening speech in a libel case: *Burnett and Hallamshire Fuel, Ltd.* v. *Sheffield Telegraph and Star, Ltd.*, [1960] 2 All E.R. 157.

Webb v. Times Publishing Co., Ltd.

Queen's Bench Division   [1960] 2 All E.R. 789

The Times newspaper published a report of the trial in a Swiss court of a British subject, Brian Donald Hume, charged with criminal offences in Switzerland. Hume told the court that he had recently robbed an English bank and shot a clerk in England, and that in 1950 he had killed one Setty out of jealousy. The report continued: "Asked if he was married and had a child, Hume replied: 'Yes, but it was not mine. The father was Setty.'" Hume had, in 1950, been tried for the murder of Setty but acquitted on that charge, and had subsequently pleaded guilty to being an accessory after the fact to the murder and had served a term of imprisonment for that crime. The plaintiff, who had, in 1950, been the wife of Hume and was the mother of the child referred to, brought an action for libel against the newspaper claiming that the report meant that she had committed adultery. The newspaper by its defence pleaded that the occasion of the publication was privileged in that the words complained of formed part of a fair and accurate report of judicial proceedings publicly heard before a court of competent jurisdiction in Switzerland, published contemporaneously. The case came before Pearson J. for the preliminary determination whether the pleading disclosed a defence in law.

PEARSON J.: [After considering various reasons for the privilege attaching to publication of reports of judicial proceedings] . . . It is at this point that the sum total of the differences between English and foreign judicial proceedings becomes crucial and decisive. As regards English proceedings, it is desirable to have a simple rule, and it is not unreasonable to say that all persons living in England have a real interest in, and are concerned with, anything that happens in any part of the country in the administration of their law in any of their courts. But it would be extravagant to say that the citizens of England have a real interest in, and are concerned with, the adjudication of some trivial and purely personal dispute in some minor court on the other side of the world. In carrying out the balancing operation due regard should be had to the interests of the individuals who may be incidentally defamed in a report of a judicial proceeding. It is one thing to take for the public benefit the risk of incidental defamation in the report of any English judicial proceedings. It would be quite another thing, much more serious, to take the risk of being defamed by the reporting of any judicial proceeding in any court in any part of the world. Moreover, there are special matters which may increase the risk. Subject to certain exceptions, the general rule of English procedure, especially criminal procedure, is that the evidence is confined, so far as possible, to matters relevant to the issues in the case. But there is in some countries a different procedure, under which in criminal trials the accused is questioned about his past life and in particular his previous offences, as is shown by the matters complained of in this case. That procedure extends considerably the risk of incidental defamation of third parties.

Next, there is the possibility that the government of some country might misuse its courts of justice by staging a propaganda trial, in which the prosecutor and witnesses and perhaps even the accused after suitable drilling, would vilify and defame the characters of the internal and external enemies of the government. That involves a large extension of the risk of incidental defamation.

Having regard to the matters that I have mentioned, which have a cumulative effect, and in the absence of any binding authority, I decide that there is no qualified privilege of a general or "blanket" character for fair and accurate reports of foreign judicial proceedings in any courts in any country.

As stated above, counsel for the defendants said that his preliminary contention (that is, that there was qualified privilege of a general or "blanket" character) does not necessarily cover courts in all foreign countries; and it might be limited to courts in Western European countries or limited in some other way to some class of courts which would include the Swiss courts. Counsel for the plaintiff in reply was able to show very convincingly that any geographical limitation was impracticable. It is not necessary to explain that at length. I suggested to counsel for the plaintiff that the privilege might be confined in some way to genuine trials or properly conducted trials, but I was readily convinced by his answer to the effect that it would be impracticable and perhaps not in accordance with international comity for the courts of this country to embark on the task of inquiring into and deciding whether or not some trial in a foreign country was a genuine trial and properly conducted. In my judgment, the defendants' primary contention that there is for fair and accurate reports of foreign judicial proceedings qualified privilege of a general or "blanket" character must be rejected.

That conclusion, however, is not decisive of this case, because the defendants' secondary contention, based on the particular facts of the case, remains to be considered. . . .

Sometimes a report of foreign judicial proceedings will have intrinsic worldwide importance, so that a reasonable man in any civilised country, wishing to be well-informed, will be glad to read it, and would think he ought to read it if he has the time available. Sometimes a report of foreign judicial proceedings will not have such intrinsic world-wide importance, but will have special connection with English affairs, so that it will have a legitimate and proper interest for English readers, and the reasonable man in England will wish to read it or hear about it. For instance, a report of foreign judicial proceedings may throw light on, or be related to or connected with, the administration of justice in England.

That is the present case. The report in "The Times" of 25 September 1959, of the judicial proceedings in the Swiss court is much connected with the administration of justice in England. Not only does it show a British subject being prosecuted in the Swiss court; it purports to show in the proceedings in the Swiss court that he confessed to having committed both the murder of Setty, of which he had been found not guilty in previous English proceedings, and also the serious recent offences in England for which he was wanted by the English police. As the administration of justice in England is a matter of legitimate and proper interest to English newspaper readers, so also is this report, which has so much connection with the administration of justice in England. In general, therefore, this report is privileged. . . .

Judgment for defendants

The Defamation Act 1952

10. **Limitation on privilege at elections.**—A defamatory statement published by or on behalf of a candidate in any election to a local government authority or to Parliament shall not be deemed to be published on a privileged occasion on the ground that it is material to a question in issue in the election, whether or not the person by whom it is published is qualified to vote at the election.

De Buse v. McCarthy

Court of Appeal [1942] 1 All E.R. 19

The defendant, a town clerk, sent out a notice convening a meeting of the borough council to consider, among other matters, a report of a committee of the council regarding the loss of petrol from one of the council's depots. Included in the notice was a long agenda of business, and a complete copy of the report of the committee. The notice was not only affixed on or near the door of the town hall, where the council was to meet, but under instructions from the council and in accordance with long-established practice, copies were also sent to each of the public libraries in the borough, where they were available for perusal by ratepayers and other frequenters of the libraries. In actions brought by four employees of the council, who complained that words in the report of the committee were defamatory of them, one of the defendant's pleas was that the notices sent to the public libraries were privileged. Wrottesley J. ruled that the occasion of the publication was privileged and there was no evidence of malice to be put before the jury, and he directed that judgment be entered for the defendants with costs. The plaintiffs appealed, asking for judgment or a new trial.

LORD GREENE M.R.: . . . The requirements for such a plea can be taken, of course, from many passages in judgments, but they are very conveniently stated in a passage in the opinion of Lord Atkinson in *Adam* v. *Ward*[1] to which du Parcq L.J. referred in the course of the argument. Lord Atkinson said, at p. 334:

> "It was not disputed, in this case on either side, that a privileged occasion is, in reference to qualified privilege, an occasion where the person who makes a communication has an interest or a duty, legal, social, or moral, to make it to the person to whom it is made, and the person to whom it is so made has a corresponding interest or duty to receive it. This reciprocity is essential."

I prefer myself that language which requires the interest or duty to be an interest or duty to make the particular communication in question to language which is sometimes found which refers to an interest in the subject-matter of the communication. The latter phrase appears to me to be vague and to leave uncertain what degree of relevance to a particular subject-matter the communication has to bear. However, adopting the language of Lord Atkinson, we have to consider, in the first instance, what interest or duty the council had to communicate to the ratepayers the report of a committee which the council was proposing to take into its consideration, and which contained not merely statements with regard to the administration of the petrol supply and with regard to the steps which had taken place, but also set out the names of employees who had been accused of complicity in those thefts and made the report and recommendation in relation to them to which I have already referred.

I cannot myself see that it can possibly be said that the council was under any duty to make that communication to the ratepayers. The matter was at that stage, in a sense, *sub judice*, because the committee's report by itself was a thing which could have no practical value unless and until it had been taken into consideration by the council and the council had come to some decision upon it. That decision might have been that the report be adopted, or it might have been that the report be not adopted, or it

1. [1917] A.C. 309.

might have been that the report be referred back to the committee. The appointment of committees of that kind is part of the internal management and administration of a body of this description, and, whatever the duty or the interest of the council might have been after it had dealt with the report and come to some decision upon it, I cannot myself see that at that stage in the operation of the machinery of the borough's administration there was any duty whatsoever to tell the ratepayers how the wheels were going round. There may well have been a duty of the council, or, if not a duty, at any rate an interest in the council, to inform the ratepayers of the result of its own deliberations.

If I am right in thinking that there was no duty to make the communication to the ratepayers at that stage, was there an interest in the council to do so? There, again, I cannot see how it can be said that the council had, at that stage of the inquiries, an interest to communicate to its ratepayers the circumstance that the committee had reported in those terms. It is perfectly true—and, indeed, obvious—that the committee itself had both an interest and a duty to make a report to the council, but there could be no common interest, as far as I can see, between the council and the ratepayers to have what, in the circumstances, was only a preliminary stage in the investigation communicated to the ratepayers in the form in which it was communicated. . . .

I have dealt with the question of the interest or duty of the council, and, looking at the other side of the picture, I cannot myself see what interest or duty the ratepayers had to receive the communication. That ratepayers are interested in the proper administration and safeguarding of their property is, of course, obvious. That they are interested in the way in which their council conducts its business is, of course, obvious, but what I may call the internal working of the administrative machine, and all the details of its domestic deliberations, in a case of this kind, are things in which I should have thought ratepayers are not interested unless and until they emerge in the shape of some practical action or practical resolution. The result, therefore, upon the whole case, is that, in my opinion, contrary to the view taken by the judge, the plea of privilege cannot be made good. . . .

I have dealt with the publication in the public libraries as though it were merely a publication to ratepayers, and, on the basis of its being a legitimate publication to ratepayers, the amended defence was drawn. I did not find it necessary to deal with the argument that, even if, as a communication to ratepayers, privilege had been established for it, nevertheless a communication which laid the whole matter open to those who frequent the public libraries was not justified. I mention this point only because I do not wish it to be thought that I am expressing any opinion one way or the other on that matter. . . .

[GODDARD and DU PARCQ L.JJ. delivered judgments in favour of allowing the appeal and ordering a new trial.]   *Appeal allowed*

Beach v. Freeson

Queen's Bench Division   [1971] 2 All E.R. 854

The plaintiffs, solicitors acting in partnership, alleged that they had been libelled by the defendant, a member of Parliament, in identical letters the defendant had sent to the Law Society and to the Lord Chancellor in which he set out complaints made by one of his constituents, Mr. Gold, concerning the conduct of the plaintiffs. The defendant denied that the letters were defamatory and pleaded that the publication was protected by qualified privilege. The plaintiffs, by their reply, denied the privilege and alleged that in publishing the letters the defendant was actuated by express malice.

GEOFFREY LANE J.: . . . The plaintiffs contend that there was no duty moral, or social, or legal on the defendant to communicate with this body, the Law Society, as he did. Indeed Mr. Norman Beach expressed the somewhat cynical view that any member of Parliament acting in this way on behalf of a constituent was simply vote-catching and no more; that the member of Parliament should confine his activities to the House of Commons and if he did not do so, he acted at his peril. It is only fair to say that counsel for the plaintiffs dissociated himself from his client's view on this point. This may have been the generally held attitude 20 or 30 years ago—I know not. What is quite clear is that this case has to be judged against the background of the conditions prevailing in 1969. There is no doubt at all on the evidence which I have heard that by that time there had been a remarkable increase in the amount of work done by members of Parliament outside the House of Commons on behalf of their constituents. The reasons for this increase are not altogether clear but possibly it is that the private individual feels, increasingly, that he is at the mercy of huge, amorphous and unfeeling organisations who will pay no attention to his feeble cries unless they are amplified by someone in authority. The member of Parliament in those circumstances is the obvious ally to whom to turn. It is short step and, in my judgment, a proper one from there to hold that, in general the member of Parliament has both an interest and a duty to communicate to the appropriate body at the request of a constituent any substantial complaint from the constituent about a professional man in practice at the service of the public. It is a view which I believe would be held by most people who gave it thought and, indeed, according to Mr. Middleton, an officer of the Law Society who gave evidence before me, it is a practice which is adopted by members of Parliament some 40 or so times a year with regard to complaints about solicitors to the Law Society. Therefore, in general, such complaints made by a member of Parliament to the Law Society at the behest of a constituent, acting as the constituent's agent to make the complaint, are made on an occasion of qualified privilege. . . .

The next problem is the publication to the Lord Chancellor. It was faintly suggested by counsel for the defendant that privilege attaches to an occasion where the defendant genuinely, but mistakenly, believes that the recipient of the complaint has a duty or interest in receiving the communication. That suggestion was based on the passage of the judgment of Scrutton L.J. to which I have already made reference, in *Watt* v. *Longsdon*.[1] However, in my judgment, that passage is not an accurate statement of the law. There are a number of judgments to the contrary, the most helpful of which is *Hebditch* v. *MacIlwaine*[2] in which Lord Esher M.R. said:

> "It was argued that, although the board of guardians had no power or duty or interest in the matter, nevertheless the occasion was privileged, because the defendants honestly and reasonably believed that the board had such a duty or power or interest, and were asking them for redress in the matter, which they believed they could give. Assuming that the defendants had such a belief, though I confess I cannot see how there could be any reason in such a belief, the argument in substance seems to come to this: that the belief of the defendants that the occasion was privileged makes it privileged. I cannot accept the proposition so put forward."

Apart from authority it seems contrary to principle that the existence of qualified privilege should depend on the mistaken belief of the defendant. Therefore, the question in issue is shortly this: did the Lord Chancellor have an interest, social or moral, in the complaints levelled against the plaintiffs? If he had, then the defendant would have the corresponding interest, or, possibly duty, to communicate. The defendant himself clearly gave very little thought as to the reason for which he was sending this copy letter to the Lord Chancellor. It was, no doubt, his practice and the practice of very many of his colleagues when making enquiries of, or any complaints about a government department to send, for information, and also as a matter of courtesy, a copy of any letter to the relevant Minister. This, of course, was not such a situation, but that does not necessarily mean that the relevant duty or interest on the part of the Lord Chancellor was missing. There is ample authority for the proposition that in

1. [1930] 1 K.B. 130, at p. 144; [1929] All E.R. Rep. 284, at p. 290.
2. [1894] 2 Q.B. 54, at p. 59; [1891–94] All E.R. Rep. 444, at p. 446.

certain types of case the only relevant interest in the recipient of the communication is the ability to investigate, or to discipline, or to punish the person about whom the complaint is made, e.g. *Dickeson* v. *Hilliard*.[1] There are, however, no rigid or closed categories of interest and the position of the Lord Chancellor is nothing if not unique. . . .

Taking these matters as a whole, the lack of any direct power to discipline or punish does not mean that the Lord Chancellor has no interest in the complaint. It may be that the nature of the interest is difficult to define but he is sufficiently concerned in the proper behaviour of solicitors; in solicitors as potential holders of judicial office; in the expeditious prosecution of litigation and in ensuring that litigants are honestly and conscientiously advised, to give him the necessary interest to protect the communication on occasions such as this with qualified privilege.

Finally, have the plaintiffs proved that the defendant was actuated by express malice? Malice includes any spite or ill-will directed from the defendant at the plaintiffs. It also includes any indirect motive. That is to say, any intention on the part of the defendant to use the occasion, not merely for the purpose for which it is a subject of qualified privilege, but for some extraneous purpose of his own not connected with privilege. That is sufficiently demonstrated in *Nevill* v. *Fine Arts and General Insurance Co., Ltd.*,[2] per Lopes L.J.:

"The effect of the occasion being privileged is to render it incumbent upon the plaintiff to prove malice, that is, to shew some indirect motive not connected with the privilege, so as to take the statement made by the defendant out of the protection afforded by the privileged occasion. This he may do either by extrinsic evidence, by which I mean something outside the statement itself, or by intrinsic evidence, by which I mean something contained in the statement itself."

The plaintiffs here allege a mixture of ill-will and indirect motive. The extraneous purpose which they submit is proved is, in the words of the plaintiffs' counsel "A desire to hot things up for the plaintiffs". . . .

[His Lordship considered the evidence and concluded that the plea of malice was not made out.]

Judgment for the defendant

Horrocks v. Lowe

House of Lords   [1974] I All E.R. 662

The plaintiff, a Conservative Party councillor in Bolton, complained that at a council meeting he was slandered by the defendant, a councillor leading the Labour Party opposition. The trial judge awarded damages of £400 (costs being estimated at £9,000). The judge had decided that the occasion was privileged but that the defendant was guilty of express malice.

The House of Lords confirmed a decision of the Court of Appeal, which had allowed the defendant's appeal.

LORD DIPLOCK . . .

. . . In the instant case Mr. Lowe's speech at the meeting of the Bolton borough council was on matters which were undoubtedly of local concern. With one minor exception the only facts relied on as evidence from which express malice was to be inferred had reference to the contents of the speech itself, the circumstances in which the meeting of the council was held and the material relating to the subject-matter of Mr Lowe's speech which was within his actual knowledge or available to him on enquiry. The one exception was his failure to apologise to Mr. Horrocks when asked to do so two days later. A refusal to apologise is at best but tenuous evidence of malice, for it is consistent with a continuing belief in the truth of what he said. Stirling J. found it to be so in the case of Mr. Lowe.

---

1. (1874), L.R. 9 Exch. 79.
2. [1895] 2 Q.B. 156, at p. 171.

So the judge was left with no other material on which to found an inference of malice except the contents of the speech itself, the circumstances in which it was made and, of course, Mr. Lowe's own evidence in the witness box. Where such is the case the test of malice is very simple. It was laid down by Lord Esher himself, as Brett L.J., in *Clark* v. *Molyneux*.[1] It is: has it been proved that the defendant did not honestly believe that what he said was true, i.e. was he either aware that it was not true or indifferent to its truth or falsity? In *Royal Aquarium & Summer & Winter Garden Society* v. *Parkinson*[2] Lord Esher M.R. applied the self-same test. . . . All Lord Esher M.R. was saying was that such indifference to the truth or falsity of what was stated constituted malice even though it resulted from prejudice with regard to the subject-matter of the statement rather than with regard to the particular person defamed. But however gross, however unreasoning the prejudice it does not destroy the privilege unless it has this result. If what it does is to cause the defendant honestly to believe what a more rational or impractical person would reject or doubt he does not thereby lose the protection of the privilege. . . .

[LORD WILBERFORCE, LORD HODSON and LORD KILBRANDON agreed with LORD DIPLOCK. VISCOUNT DILHORNE delivered a speech in favour of dismissing the appeal.]

Egger v. Viscount Chelmsford

Court of Appeal   [1964] 3 All E.R. 406

The plaintiff was a judge of Alsatian dogs and her name appeared on the list of names kept by the Kennel Club. The secretary of a dog club wrote to the Kennel Club asking that the plaintiff's name might be approved so that she could judge Alsatians at a show A committee of the Kennel Club decided not to approve the plaintiff's appointment as a judge. On their instructions the assistant secretary wrote to the secretary of the dog club saying that the committee were unable to approve the plaintiff's appointment. The plaintiff sued the members of the committee for alleged libel contained in the letter. The letter was found to be defamatory, but the occasion privileged. The jury found that five members of the committee acted with malice, but acquitted the assistant secretary and three members of the committee of malice. Marshall J. held himself bound by the decision in *Smith* v. *Streatfeild*, [1913] 3 K.B. 764, and gave judgment against all the defendants. The four defendants against whom malice was not found by the jury appealed successfully to the Court of Appeal.

LORD DENNING M.R.: . . . I cannot help thinking that the root of all the trouble is the tacit assumption that if one of the persons concerned in a joint publication is a tortfeasor, then all are joint tortfeasors. They must, therefore, stand or fall together. So much so that the defence of one is the defence of all: and the malice of one is the malice of all. I think that this assumption rests on a fallacy. In point of law, no tortfeasors can truly be described solely as *joint* tortfeasors. They are always *several* tortfeasors as well. In any joint tort, the party injured has his choice whom to sue. He can sue all of them together or any one or more of them separately. This has been the law for centuries. It is well stated in Serjeant Williams' celebrated notes to *Saunders' Reports* (1845 Edn.) of *Cabell* v. *Vaughan*:[3]

> "If several persons jointly commit a *tort*, the plaintiff has his election to sue all or any number of the parties; because a *tort* is in its nature the separate act of each individual."

---

1. (1877) 3 Q.B.D. 237.
2. [1892] 1 Q.B. 431, at p. 444; [1891–94] All E.R. Rep 429, at p. 433.
3. (1669), 1 Wms. Saund. 288, at p. 291.

Therein lies the gist of the matter. Even in a joint tort, the tort is the separate act of each individual. Each is severally answerable for it: and, being severally answerable, each is severally entitled to his own defence. If he is himself innocent of malice, he is entitled to be the benefit of it. He is not to be dragged down with the guilty. No one is by our English law to be pronounced a wrongdoer, or be made liable to be made to pay damages for a wrong, unless he himself has done wrong; or his agent or servant has done wrong and he is vicariously responsible for it. Save in the cases where the principle respondeat superior applies, the law does not impute wrongdoing to a man who is in fact innocent.

My conclusion is that *Smith* v. *Streatfeild*[1] was wrongly decided and should be overruled: that the obiter dicta on this point of their lordships in *Adam* v. *Ward*[2] were erroneous: and that the general rule stated by Gatley does not exist. It is a mistake to suppose that, on a joint publication, the malice of one defendant infects his co-defendant. Each defendant is answerable severally, as well as jointly, for the joint publication: and each is entitled to his several defence, whether he be sued jointly or separately from the others. If the plaintiff seeks to rely on malice to aggravate damages, or to rebut a defence of qualified privilege, or to cause a comment, otherwise fair, to become unfair, then he must prove malice against each person whom he charges with it. A defendant is only affected by express malice if he himself was actuated by it: or if his servant or agent concerned in the publication was actuated by malice in the course of his employment. We have come after several years to find that the law is as Lord Porter's Committee recommended that it should be. . . .

[HARMAN L.J. and DAVIES L.J. delivered judgments concurring in allowing the appeal.]

The Defamation Act 1952

7. Qualified privilege of newspapers.—(1) Subject to the provisions of this section, the publication in a newspaper of any such report or other matter as is mentioned in the Schedule to this Act shall be privileged unless the publication is proved to be made with malice.

(2) In an action for libel in respect of the publication of any such report or matter as is mentioned in Part II of the Schedule to this Act, the provisions of this section shall not be a defence if it is proved that the defendant has been requested by the plaintiff to publish in the newspaper in which the original publication was made a reasonable letter or statement by way of explanation or contradiction, and has refused or neglected to do so, or has done so in a manner not adequate or not reasonable having regard to all the circumstances.

(3) Nothing in this section shall be construed as protecting the publication of any matter the publication of which is prohibited by law, or of any matter which is not of public concern and the publication of which is not for the public benefit.

(4) Nothing in this section shall be construed as limiting or abridging any privilege subsisting (otherwise than by virtue of section four of the Law of Libel Amendment Act 1888) immediately before the commencement of this Act.

(5) In this section the expression "newspaper" means any paper containing public news or observations thereon, or consisting wholly or mainly of advertisements, which is printed for sale and is published in the United Kingdom either periodically or in parts or numbers at intervals not exceeding thirty-six days.

---

1. [1913] 3 K.B. 764; [1911–13] All E.R. Rep. 362.
2. [1917] A.C. 309; [1916–17] All E.R. Rep. 157.

SCHEDULE

Sections 7, 16

NEWSPAPER STATEMENTS HAVING QUALIFIED PRIVILEGE

Part I

Statements Privileged Without Explanation or Contradiction

1. A fair and accurate report of any proceedings in public of the legislature of any part of Her Majesty's dominions outside Great Britain.

2. A fair and accurate report of any proceedings in public of an international organisation of which the United Kingdom or Her Majesty's Government in the United Kingdom is a member, or of any international conference to which that government sends a representative.

3. A fair and accurate report of any proceedings in public of an international court.

4. A fair and accurate report of any proceedings before a court exercising jurisdiction throughout any part of Her Majesty's dominions outside the United Kingdom, or of any proceedings before a court-martial held outside the United Kingdom under the Naval Discipline Act, [the Army Act, 1955 or the Air Force Act 1955].

5. A fair and accurate report of any proceedings in public of a body or person appointed to hold a public inquiry by the government or legislature of any part of Her Majesty's dominions outside the United Kingdom.

6. A fair and accurate copy of or extract from any register kept in pursuance of any Act of Parliament which is open to inspection by the public, or of any other document which is required by the law of any part of the United Kingdom to be open to inspection by the public.

7. A notice or advertisement published by or on the authority of any court within the United Kingdom or any judge or officer of such a court.

Part II

Statements Privileged Subject to Explanation or Contradiction

8. A fair and accurate report of the findings or decision of any of the following associations, or of any committee or governing body thereof, that is to say—

(*a*) an association formed in the United Kingdom for the purpose of promoting or encouraging the exercise of or interest in any art, science, religion or learning, and empowered by its constitution to exercise control over or adjudicate upon matters of interest or concern to the association, or the actions or conduct of any persons subject to such control or adjudication;

(*b*) an association formed in the United Kingdom for the purpose of promoting or safeguarding the interests of any trade, business, industry or profession, or of the persons carrying on or engaged in any trade, business, industry or profession, and empowered by its constitution to exercise control over or adjudicate upon matters connected with the trade, business, industry or profession, or the actions or conduct of those persons;

(*c*) an association formed in the United Kingdom for the purpose of promoting or safeguarding the interests of any game, sport or pastime to the playing or exercise of which members of the public are invited or admitted, and empowered by its constitution to exercise control over or adjudicate upon persons connected with or taking part in the game, sport or pastime, being a finding or decision relating to a person who is a member of or is subject by virtue of any contract to the control of the association.

9. A fair and accurate report of the proceedings at any public meeting held in the United Kingdom, that is to say, a meeting bona fide and lawfully held for a lawful purpose and for the furtherance or discussion of any matter of public concern, whether the admission to the meeting is general or restricted.

10. A fair and accurate report of the proceedings at any meeting or sitting in any part of the United Kingdom of—

(*a*) any local authority or committee of a local authority or local authorities;

(*b*) any justice or justices of the peace acting otherwise than as a court exercising judicial authority;

(*c*) any commission, tribunal, committee or person appointed for the purposes of any inquiry by Act of Parliament, by Her Majesty or by a Minister of the Crown;

(*d*) any person appointed by a local authority to hold a local inquiry in pursuance of any Act of Parliament;

(*e*) any other tribunal, board, committee or body constituted by or under, and exercising functions under, an Act of Parliament,

not being a meeting or sitting admission to which is denied to representatives of newspapers and other members of the public.

11. A fair and accurate report of the proceedings at a general meeting of any company or association constituted, registered or certified by or under any Act of Parliament or incorporated by Royal Charter, not being a private company within the meaning of the Companies Act 1948.

12. A copy or fair and accurate report or summary of any notice or other matter issued for the information of the public by or on behalf of any government department, officer of state, local authority or chief officer of police.

Part III

INTERPRETATION

13. In this Schedule the following expressions have the meanings hereby respectively assigned to them, that is to say:—

"Act of Parliament" includes an Act of the Parliament of Northern Ireland, and the reference to the Companies Act 1948, includes a reference to any corresponding enactment of the Parliament of Northern Ireland;

"government department" includes a department of the Government of Northern Ireland;

"international court" means the International Court of Justice and any other judicial or arbitral tribunal deciding matters in dispute between States;

"legislature", in relation to any territory comprised in Her Majesty's dominions which is subject to a central and a local legislature, means either of those legislatures;

"local authority" means any authority or body to which the [Public Bodies (Admission to Meetings) Act 1960,] or the Local Government (Ireland) Act 1902, as amended by any enactment of the Parliament of Northern Ireland, applies;

"part of Her Majesty's dominions" means the whole of any territory within those dominions which is subject to a separate legislature.

14. In relation to the following countries and territories, that is to say, India, the Republic of Ireland, any protectorate; protected state or trust territory within the meaning of the British Nationality Act 1948, any territory administered under the authority of a country mentioned in subsection (3) of section one of that Act, the

Sudan and the New Hebrides, the provisions of this Schedule shall have effect as they have effect in relation to Her Majesty's dominions, and references therein to Her Majesty's dominions shall be construed accordingly.

5. APOLOGY

The Libel Act 1843

[1.] Offer of an apology admissible in evidence in mitigation of damages in action for defamation.—... In any action for defamation it shall be lawful for the defendant (after notice in writing of his intention so to do, duly given to the plaintiff at the time of filing or delivering the plea in such action), to give in evidence, in mitigation of damages, that he made or offered an apology to the plaintiff for such defamation before the commencement of the action, or as soon afterwards as he had an opportunity of doing so, in case the action shall have been commenced before there was an opportunity of making or offering such apology.

2. In an action against a newspaper for libel, the defendant may plead that it was inserted without malice and without negligence, and that he has published or offered to publish an apology.—... In an action for libel contained in any public newspaper or other periodical publication it shall be competent to the defendant to plead that such libel was inserted in such newspaper or other periodical publication without actual malice, and without gross negligence, and that before the commencement of the action, or at the earliest opportunity afterwards, he inserted in such newspaper or other periodical publication a full apology for the said libel, or, if the newspaper or periodical publication in which the said libel appeared should be ordinarily published at intervals exceeding one week, had offered to publish the said apology in any newspaper or periodical publication to be selected by the plaintiff in such action; ... and ... to such plea to such action it shall be competent to the plaintiff to reply generally, denying the whole of such plea.

The Libel Act 1845

2. Defendant not to plead matters allowed by 6 & 7 Vict. c. 96, without payment into court.—... It shall not be competent to any defendant in such action, whether in England of in Ireland, to file any such plea, without at the same time making a payment of money into court by way of amends ..., but every such plea so filed without payment of money into court shall be deemed a nullity, and may be treated as such by the plaintiff in the action.

6. DAMAGES

Cassell & Co., Ltd. v. Broome

House of Lords   [1972] 1 All E.R. 801

The plaintiff, a retired sea captain of unblemished reputation, won an action for libel arising out of the publication of the book "The Destruction of Convoy PQ17" by David Irving. The book contained grave imputations on the conduct of the plaintiff who had been the officer commanding the naval ships escorting the ill-fated convoy PQ17. The jury awarded against the publishers and the author (1) the sum of £1,000 in respect of the publication of 60 proof copies of the book; (2) £14,000 described as "compensatory damages" in respect of the principal or hardback edition of the book, and (3) in respect of the hardback edition a further sum of £25,000 described as "by way of exemplary damages". The defendants appealed against the award of £25,000 exemplary damages, but this was dismissed by the Court of Appeal, [1971] 2 All E.R. 187, which held that (a) the judge's direction on the subject of exemplary damages complied with *Rookes* v. *Barnard*, [1964] A.C. 1129; [1964] 1 All E.R. 367, and (b) in any event, the decision in *Rookes* v. *Barnard* on the question of damages was arrived at *per incuriam* and without argument on the point by counsel. The publishers (but not the author) then appealed against the Court of Appeal's decision, to the House of Lords, which dismissed the appeal. The House of Lords held by a majority (Lord Hailsham of St. Marylebone, Lord Reid, Lord Morris of Borth-y-Gest, Lord Diplock and Lord Kilbrandon; Viscount Dilhorne and Lord Wilberforce dissenting) that *Rookes* v. *Barnard* had correctly formulated the rules governing the award of exemplary damages, and that the principles enunciated in that case were applicable to defamation cases [on this aspect of the case, see the extracts at p. 400, *ante*]. The House held, further (Viscount Dilhorne, Lord Wilberforce and Lord Diplock dissenting) that on the basis of those principles, the jury's award of £25,000 exemplary damages should be upheld.

The material before the jury was that the author knew fully what he was doing and persisted despite repeated warnings that the relevant passages were defamatory of the plaintiff. His original publishers refused to publish the book on the ground that it was a "continuous witch hunt of [the plaintiff]". The defendants then published it despite a warning that it had been rejected by the author's first publishers on the ground that it was libellous. The plaintiff himself warned the publishers that if the book was not modified they must expect an action for libel. Nevertheless the defendants went ahead and published it with a dustjacket which indicated that they were fully aware of the full implications of the passages complained of and were prepared to sell it on the basis of this sensational interpretation of the naval disaster.

LORD HAILSHAM: . . . The final point taken for the appellants was that the award of £25,000 exemplary damages or, as it was equally properly and possibly better put, the total award of £40,000 (which included the exemplary element) was so far excessive of what 12 reasonable men could have awarded that it ought to be set aside and a new trial ordered. I cannot disguise from myself that I found this an extremely difficult point in the case, and have only decided that the verdict should not be disturbed with great hesitation because I am very conscious of the fact that I would certainly have awarded far less myself, and possibly, to use a yardstick which some judges have adopted as a rule of thumb, less than half the £25,000.

A number of factors lead me, however, to the belief that the verdict should not be disturbed. The first, and paramount, consideration in my mind is that the jury is, where either party desires it, the only legal and constitutional tribunal for deciding libel cases, including the award of damages. I do not think the judiciary at any level should substitute itself for a jury, unless the award is so manifestly too large, as were the verdicts in *Lewis* v. *Daily Telegraph, Ltd.*[1] or manifestly too small, as in *English and Scottish Co-op. Properties Mortgage and Investment Society, Ltd.* v. *Odhams Press, Ltd.*[2] that no sensible jury properly directed could have reached the conclusion. I do not think much depends on the exact formula used to describe the test to be applied, whether the traditional language "so large [or small] as that twelve sensible men could not reasonably have given them" (per Lord Esher M.R. in *Praed* v. *Graham*[3]) or that of Palles C.B. in *M'Grath* v. *Bourne*[4] cited by Lord Wright in *Mechanical and General Inventions Co., Ltd. and Lehwess* v. *Austin and Austin Motor Co., Ltd.*,[5] that "no reasonable pro-

---

1. [1964] A.C. 234; [1963] 2 All E.R. 151.
2. [1940] 1 K.B. 440; [1940] 1 All E.R. 1.
3. (1889), 24 Q.B.D. 53, at p. 55.
4. (1876), I.R. 10 C.L. 160, at p. 164.
5. [1935] A.C. 346, at p. 378; [1935] All E.R. Rep. 22, at p. 37.

portion existed between it and the circumstances of the case". The point is that the law makes the jury and not the judiciary the constitutional tribunal, and if Parliament had wished the roles to be reversed in any way, Parliament would have said so at the time of the Administration of Justice (Miscellaneous Provisions) Act 1933, since s. 6 of that Act expressly excepts defamation actions (otherwise than in a limited class of case) from the general change which it then authorised.

In addition to the above cases counsel for Captain Broome cited *Youssoupoff* v. *Metro-Goldwyn-Mayer Pictures, Ltd.,*[1] *Bocock* v. *Enfield Rolling Mills, Ltd.,* [2]*Scott* v. *Musial,*[3] *Morey* v. *Woodfield,*[4] *McCarey* v. *Associated Newspapers, Ltd.*[5] and *Broadway Approvals, Ltd.* v. *Odhams Press, Ltd.*[6] I do not see anything in the above cases which alters the principle involved, nor am I aware of anything in the nature of exemplary damages to alter it in this limited class of case. It may very well be that, on the whole, judges, and the legal profession in general, would be less generous than juries in the award of damages for defamation. But I know of no principle of reason which would entitle judges, whether of appeal or at first instance, to consider that their own sense of the proprieties is more reasonable than that of a jury, or which would entitle them to arrogate to themselves a constitutional status in this matter which Parliament has deliberately withheld from them, for aught we know, on the very ground that juries can be expected to be more generous on such matters than judges. I speak with the greater conviction because my own view is that the legal profession is right to be cautious in such matters and juries are wrong if they can be said to be more generous. But that is not the law and I do not think that judges who hold my view are any more entitled to change the law on this topic than they have been in the past.

Counsel very rightly drew our attention to observations of Lord Devlin in *Rookes* v. *Barnard*[7] when he said:

> "I should not allow the respect which is traditionally paid to an assessment of damages by a jury to prevent me from seeing that the weapon is used with restraint. It may even be that the House may find it necessary to follow the precedent it set for itself in *Benham* v. *Gambling,*[8] and place some arbitrary limit on awards of damages that are made by way of punishment."

I regard *Benham* v. *Gambling*[8] as setting an absolutely necessary but wholly arbitrary rule to solve an absolutely insoluble problem, and I do not think it could readily be extended to exemplary damages for libel simply on the ground that judges do not agree with juries on quantum. I do not think the first sentence in Lord Devlin's observation means more than that the House will use its legitimate powers to interfere with awards by juries with particular regard to the need for preserving liberty, which he was concerned to express, and, if it means that the House was conferring on itself greater powers than it previously possessed, I would have regarded it as an usurpation of the function of the legislature as a whole. We were also referred to the observations of the Court of Appeal in *Ward* v. *James.*[9] If the passage quoted there means more than that court, in exercising its undoubted right to interfere with unreasonable verdicts, will have more regard than heretofore to the general level of damages in cases of a similar nature, and particularly personal injury cases, it may need further consideration.

The second reason which leads me to decline to interfere with the jury's verdict in

---

1. (1934), 50 T.L.R. 581, at pp. 583, 584.
2. [1954] 3 All E.R. 94; [1954] 1 W.L.R. 1303.
3. [1959] 2 Q.B. 429, at p. 436; [1959] 3 All E.R. 193, at p. 194.
4. [1963] 3 All E.R. 533 n.; [1964] 1 W.L.R. 16 n.
5. [1965] 2 Q.B. 86; [1964] 2 All E.R. 947.
6. [1965] 2 All E.R. at pp. 536, 537; [1965] 1 W.L.R. at pp. 818, 820.
7. [1964] A.C. at p. 1227; [1964] 1 All E.R. at p. 411.
8. [1941] A.C. 157; [1941] 1 All E.R. 7.
9. [1966] 1 Q.B. 289, at p. 301; [1965] 1 All E.R. 568, at p. 575.

this case is the peculiar gravity of the facts of this case. I share with Phillimore L.J. the view that the jury must have found that[1]—

> "these were grave libels perpetrated quite deliberately and without regard to their truth by a young man and a firm of publishers interested solely in whether they would gain by the publication of this book. They did not care what distress they caused."

It is true, and I have been constrained to say, that I would have treated this heinous offence against public decency with far less severity than did the jury in this case. But, at the end of the hearing, I found myself as unable to say as were the three eminent judges in the Court of Appeal[2] that no 12 reasonable jurors could have come to a different conclusion from myself. These matters are very highly subjective, and I do not feel myself entitled to substitute my own subjective sense of proportion for that of the constitutional tribunal appointed by law to determine such matters. . . .

Note

At the other end of the scale from exemplary damages for defamation are "contemptuous damages"—the smallest coin in the realm. An example is the action brought by Dr. Dering, an ex-prisoner at Auschwitz who had carried out experimental operations under Nazi pressure, in respect of a passing reference to him in the novel *Exodus* by Leon Uris. The trial of the action against the publisher and author lasted for five weeks, and although the plaintiff's claim succeeded, the jury awarded only a halfpenny damages, marking their disapproval of the plaintiff's action. Such an award can ruin the technically successful plaintiff since no legal aid is available for actions for defamation, and the judge is likely to award costs against the plaintiff. In fact, Dr. Dering died a few months after the trial without having materially contributed to the defence costs which he had been ordered to pay. The result was that the defendants had to bear costs of about £20,000. The publisher's share of these was about £6,000 and it has been revealed that this was "about three or four times more than it would have cost them to make a separate settlement" with the plaintiff: William Kimber in *Wicked, Wicked Libels* (London, 1972), p. 78. Michael Rubinstein (*ibid.*, p. 129) comments: "no uninsured publisher would willingly sustain losses on the scale involved in that action; and the majority of authors who might want to defend a libel claim on principle simply cannot afford to do so."

EXCURSUS: THE PROTECTION OF PRIVACY
Report of the Committee on Privacy, Cmnd. 5012 (1972)

62. We consider first the broadest interpretation of privacy; the state of being let alone. We take this to mean freedom from human interference by any means. Privacy would be an element in it, but there are other elements of equal importance: protection from physical harm and restraint, freedom from direction, and peaceful enjoyment of one's surroundings. The threats to these could take the form of injurious acts by other private persons, of public impositions or of man-made disasters or nuisances, and any one of these might threaten several of the elements which constitute the state of being let alone. A badly maintained factory chimney which falls on your family in your private house causes physical harm and interferes with the peaceful enjoyment of your surroundings; it also invades your privacy, but most people would not spontaneously

---

1. [1971] 2 All E.R. at p. 215; [1971] 2 W.L.R. at p. 887.
2. [1971] 2 All E.R. 187; [1971] 2 W.L.R. 853.

make that the reason for being angry about it. Arbitrary arrest at home interferes with peaceful enjoyment and involves direction; it is also an invasion of privacy, but is unlikely to be condemned primarily on that score.

63. If there were to be a right of privacy under the law it should not, in our opinion, be synonymous with a right to be let alone. An unqualified right of this kind would in any event be an unrealistic concept, incompatible with the concept of society, implying a willingness not to be let entirely alone and a recognition that other people may be interested and consequently concerned about us. If the concept were to be embodied into a right, its adaptation to the dominant pressures of life in society would require so many exceptions that it would lose all coherence and hence any valid meaning. We have concluded therefore that the type of conduct against which legal protection might be afforded on the ground of intrusion on privacy should be confined to injurious or annoying conduct deliberately aimed at a particular person or persons where the invasion of privacy is the principal wrong complained of.

64. The evidence we have received indicates that the main concern about what is termed invasion of privacy involves the treatment of personal information. The "information" which we have been urged to protect is that in which a person should be regarded as having something in the nature of a proprietary interest, either, in most cases, because it relates personally to him or because he has been entrusted with it by the person to whom it relates, as in the case of a doctor, tutor, employer or friend of the family. If the information is passed to another recipient who is also acceptable, then that recipient in turn can be said to be entrusted with it.

65. It is not contended in all the evidence to us that the information concerned need be private, though if the information is also confidential its unauthorised handling is all the more objectionable. The unauthorised handling of information which may well be known or available through approved sources can also constitute a breach of privacy in certain circumstances. The most obvious example is where it is published at large to a far wider audience than would otherwise learn of it: the conduct of the mass information media is the main object of criticism under this heading. Another circumstance is where the information is directly used for commercial gain or other ulterior purpose without authority: use of a name or portrait in an advertisement is the most likely example, which shows how this circumstance may overlap with the first one of media publicity. A third circumstance is where the information is collated with other personal information so that a dossier is compiled on the individual concerned, which tells the compiler more than the isolated pieces could do—on the principle that the whole is greater than the sum of the parts.

66. The unauthorised use, by way of compilation, communication and dissemination, of personal information is not the whole extent of the concern about privacy and information. The means used to extract such information from its private domain may be at least equally offensive. This may involve none of the subsequent stages of handling the information, since it may have as its motive pure inquisitiveness or self-indulgence. A case in point would be the peeping Tom, who normally keeps the "information" very much to himself. Usually, however, those who go to the trouble of prying to get information do so with the object of using it: by passing it on to particular recipients, storing it for future reference or disseminating it. The common factor in all these is intrusion into the domain in which the information has hitherto been kept private.

67. The concept of intrusion implies some geographically private area, and this is commonly conceived of as the home and garden, extending to other forms of accommodation, whether owned or merely occupied, such as a place of business or a hotel room or lodging. But it goes further than that, involving also private, family or domestic activities away from owned or occupied property, which are not meant to be publicly observed though they may occur in what is legally a public place. It is possible that there could be deliberate intrusion without the object of acquiring

information, but to provoke or inhibit a course of action. Ill-disposed neighbours might conduct a campaign of prying to induce people to move house, or otherwise annoy them. The law gives specific protection against this only in the cases of landlords harassing tenants[1] and of the harassment of debtors.[2]

68. Keeping strictly in mind that we are concerned only with injurious or annoying conduct deliberately aimed at a particular person or group of persons, we think it right to give the following activities our particular attention: intrusive gathering and dissemination of information by the publicity media, handling of credit information, unwarrantable intrusion into personal matters at work and in education and medicine, prying by neighbours and landlords, intrusive sales methods, investigations by private detectives, and industrial espionage. We have also given special attention to certain modern technical developments which affect privacy: the technical surveillance devices and computers.

69. It has been suggested to us that there are two other constituents of privacy—freedom from interference with moral and intellectual integrity and freedom from being placed in a false light. These are both constituents of the Nordic Conference concept of the right to be let alone,[3] a concept we have already rejected as a whole in paragraph 63. But they occur elsewhere. As to the first, we received no serious evidence that subliminal influencing, sleep teaching, manipulative selection, group conditioning and other uses of the behavioural sciences to influence people's subconscious minds are a problem in this country or that special legal protection is needed against them.

70. Placing someone in a false light is one of the four torts into which Dean Prosser has analysed the United States law on privacy,[4] which seem to have influenced the Nordic Conference[5] and they in turn the "Justice" Bill.[6] We consider that placing someone in a false light is an aspect of defamation rather than of privacy.[7]

71. We do not support the view of those who argue that the publication of an untruth about a person should be treated by the law as an invasion of privacy rather than under the heading of defamation. In this connection we commend the warning by Professor Harry Kalven about the way in which the "false light" aspect of privacy has been used in the United States to extend the scope for actions of a defamation nature.[8] He says that any extensions of the law of defamation should be made openly as such, but he suggests also that the restrictions on the application of the law of

---

1. Rent Act 1965, section 30.
2. Administration of Justice Act 1970, section 40.
3. Conclusions of the Nordic Conference of International Jurists on the Right of Privacy, Stockholm 1967; . . .
4. "Privacy", Dean William L. Prosser, *California Law Review*, August 1960.
5. Conclusions of the Nordic Conference of International Jurists on the Right of Privacy, Stockholm 1967.
6. "Privacy and the Law", Appendix J, clause 9 (e) and (f).
7. The law on defamation is under consideration by the Committee set up in May 1971 under the Chairmanship of Mr. Justice Faulks "to consider whether, in the light of the Defamation Act 1952, any changes are desirable in the law, practice and procedure relating to actions for defamation".
8. "Privacy in Tort Law—Were Warren and Brandeis Wrong?" *Law and Contemporary Problems*, Chicago University 1966:
    ". . . if the colonization of defamation by privacy does take place, it will only be because by the use of a fiction the courts have turned at last to reform of the law of defamation. It will not be because they have perceived that logically defamation is subsumed in privacy. They will simply be calling false statements by a new name . . . one may wonder if this trend represents even good judicial statesmanship. The technical complexity of the law of defamation, which has shown remarkable stamina in the teeth of centuries of acid criticism, may reflect one useful strategy for a legal system forced against its ultimate better judgment to deal with dignitary harms. . . . In any event, it would be a notable thing if the right of privacy, having, as it were, failed in three-quarters of a century to amount to anything at home, went forth to take over the traditional torts of libel and slander."

defamation may reflect a wise caution about permitting its extension to the mollification of outraged dignity. We were interested in this connection to learn of the development of case law on defamation and "false light" in the decisions of the Federal Court of the Federal Republic of Germany: defamation has lost its identity there as a separate tort and become fused into the broader tort of infringement of the right of personality (Persönlichkeitsrecht).[1] To our mind there could be a real threat to freedom of speech if the safeguards for it that have been built into the law of defamation were to be put in jeopardy by the process of subsuming defamation into a wider tort which is implied by the doctrine of "false light".[2] We believe that the concepts of defamation and of intrusion into privacy should be kept distinct from one another. . . .

83.[3] There is no legal right to privacy as such in the law of England and Wales. There is no recorded case in Scotland to establish that the right is recognised as the basis of an action at law, though there is at least one case which suggests the opposite. However, civil law in Scotland rests more on the notion of generalised rights than in England, so that if a Scottish court held that an invasion of privacy was extreme, it might grant a remedy even though a remedy had never been granted before. Leaving this remote possibility on one side, the protection that the law in Great Britain gives is scattered throughout civil and criminal law, both common and statute. Some of these laws—e.g. that dealing with trespass to land—protect privacy incidentally to protecting something else. Others—e.g. defamation—protect something closely akin to, but not co-extensive with, personal privacy, in this case personal reputation. Some are concerned primarily with privacy in the form of keeping information confidential or in the form of controlling the right to use it, as in the laws on breach of confidence, contract and copyright. Most of the criminal provisions in the statute law are aimed at specific offences in which protection of privacy does not appear to have been a consideration with those who made them: e.g. the Wireless Telegraphy Acts; while in some it was a consideration, if not the main one: e.g. the Rent Act 1965.

84. We look first at the civil law. Here the laws on libel and slander, injurious falsehood[4] and passing off (appropriation of a person's business or professional reputation at his expense) taken together give a fairly comprehensive protection against falsehoods or false implications that are damaging to a person's business or reputation. However, they do not go so far as United States law in giving protection against being put in a false light, which, as we have explained (paragraph 70), we consider to be an aspect of defamation rather than of privacy.

85. The laws of trespass to land and nuisance provide a right of action for invasion of privacy, if the victim is the legal occupier whose property is physically interfered with. But in the absence of actual damage the remedy is an empty one, unless he can obtain exemplary damages (which take into account the heinousness of the defendant's conduct and are now only awarded in a limited number of circumstances); or aggravated damages (which take into account the circumstances in which the wrong was committed, in so far as they have added to the injury or damage done to the plaintiff)—such damages are not given for a single trespass in Scotland; or an injunction (to prevent repetition of the wrong). Otherwise these remedies are no real help. In England and Wales trespass to goods and trespass to the person might give some protection in rather limited circumstances; they are not a cause of action in Scotland.

86. The civil law relating to conspiracy is unlikely to give much protection in fact, because of the difficulty of showing that actual damage results from invasions of privacy; in any event it is doubtful whether the absence of a legitimate motive of self-

1. Oral evidence of Professor Dr. Hein Kötz, 6 January 1972.
2. See also the Report of the Porter Committee on the Law of Defamation, 1948, Cmnd. 7536, paragraphs 24–26.
3. Appendix I to the Report contains a detailed study of the present law.
4. There is no tort of injurious falsehood in Scotland. However, in Scotland there is convicium, which is a form of verbal injury actionable in certain circumstances even if its basis is true.

interest which that tort requires would be easily proved in many cases involving invasions of privacy. An action for the tort of wilfully doing an act calculated to cause harm to the plaintiff is also unlikely to succeed in a privacy case because it is improbable that it could be shown that the harm was calculated. It should be pointed out that, even if such torts could be developed by case law to protect privacy, this development has not up to now taken place, and we are called upon to report on the need for legislation at the present time, not to speculate on the possibilities of the development of case law in the future.

87. The laws on breach of contract, copyright and confidence are effective to protect the privacy of things committed to paper or of oral communications, where the confidence or ownership is specified (as in contract and copyright) or reasonably well implied (as in confidence and, in some circumstances, contract). The law on breach of confidence offers the most effective protection of privacy in the whole of our existing law, civil and criminal. It affords a means of protection for all specific and reasonably implied confidences, except where the disclosure of the information given in confidence is shown by the discloser to be in the public interest.[1] We think that the extent of its potential effectiveness is not widely recognised and that it should be. We make recommendations, later in this report, as to how this might be done (Chapter 21).

88. We turn now to the criminal law. Here the English common law offences of libel and nuisance mostly involve some action which could, by its outrageous nature, inconvenience or otherwise involve the public rather than just annoy the individual victim. The same is true of the Scottish common law crime of breach of the peace, although its scope has been extended in recent years so that it might be useful to deal with a rather wider class of invasions of privacy. The power of English courts to bind a person over to keep the peace and be of good behaviour can be a useful preventive measure, but no more, against persistent eavesdroppers and peeping Toms. The common law offence of conspiracy involves the agreement of two or more persons to commit a criminal offence or an act of cheating falling short of a criminal offence, certain civil wrongs, or a public mischief or outrageous immoral act; some uncertainty surrounds these latter categories.

89. There are several criminal provisions of the statute law which deal with types of intrusion into the home and private life, besides those offences committed only by persons acting in an official capacity, which we do not include in this brief survey. It is a crime to send offensive telephone messages; to open another's mail with intent to injure the addressee (though this would probably not apply where the motive was mere inquisitiveness); to send obscene or indecent matter through the post; to send by any means books depicting or describing human sexual techniques (but it may be open to question if this applies to advertisements for the books unless they themselves depict or describe human sexual techniques); to harass tenants, but not lodgers, to make them quit; and to harass debtors (but not in Scotland). All of these give protection in rather limited situations, incidental to attempts to control abuses other than invasion of privacy.

90. There are statute law offences which give incidental protection also to invasion of privacy by "bugging" and industrial spying. Use of any wireless telegraphy transmitting apparatus without a licence is prohibited; the use of wireless telegraphy receiving apparatus for the interception of non-public messages is an offence; and the import and manufacture of wireless telegraphy apparatus specified by Order (there is one such in force) is prohibited. It is an offence for an employee corruptly to sell his employer's information in certain, and possibly any, circumstances, or to procure such an offence. The "theft" of information is not an offence unless it is taken in some physical

---

1. Lord Denning M.R., *Hubbard* v. *Vosper*, [1972] 2 Q.B. 84; [1972] 1 All E.R. 1023.

form, e.g. on paper. Thus, save where the offence of theft or breaking and entering[1] can be proved, the only application of the criminal law to the commonest form of industrial espionage—that is by a purely human agency—is the one rather restricted provision against corruption. Where technical means are employed there are only the sanctions against "bugging" without the use of wires, where the problems of detection are exceptionally severe.

91. Finally the law gives some protection to privacy in court proceedings ... notably in committal proceedings, proceedings in juvenile courts and in regard to certain aspects of domestic proceedings.

Notes

1. The Committee on Privacy (under the chairmanship of the Rt. Hon. Kenneth Younger) recommended the creation of a new criminal offence of surreptitious surveillance by means of a technical device (paras. 560–564) and that there should be a new tort of unlawful surveillance by device for which damages could be awarded or injunctions granted (para. 565). It was also proposed that there should be a new tort of disclosure or other use of information unlawfully acquired (para. 632, and see p. 494, *ante*), and that the law relating to breach of confidence should be referred to the Law Commission with a view to clarification and statement in legislative form (para. 630). But with two dissentients, the Committee were against the introduction of a general right of privacy (paras. 634–650), despite the existence of such a right in some other common law jurisdictions, e.g. the British Columbia Privacy Act 1968, which includes not only eavesdropping and surveillance but any interference which violates that degree of privacy which is reasonable in the circumstances, subject to a number of specific defences. For a comment on the Report of the Committee, see Gerald Dworkin (1973), 36 M.L.R. 399.

2. Extra-legal protection of privacy may, to some extent be obtained through the activities of bodies such as the Press Council, the B.B.C.'s Programme Complaints Commission and the Independent Broadcasting Authority's Complaints Review Board. The Younger Committee made several minor proposals for improving the work of these bodies (paras. 190–193, 245–249). The Younger Committee approved the practice of the Press Council of requiring the complainant in appropriate cases to surrender his right to sue the newspaper after the adjudication by the Council (paras. 153–155). For a description of the Press Council's work see H. Phillip Levy, *The Press Council* (London, 1967).

3. There is an enormous literature on the subject of privacy. A few particularly useful works are: Alan F. Westin, *Privacy and Freedom* (London, 1970); "Justice", *Privacy and the Law* (London, 1970); Samuel D. Warren and Louis Brandeis, "The Right to Privacy" (1890), 4 Harv. L.R. 193 (the classic starting point of modern conceptions); P. H. Winfield, "Privacy" (1931), 47 L.Q.R. 23; Harry Kalven Jr., "Privacy in tort law—were Warren and Brandeis wrong?" (1966), 31 Law and Contemporary Problems 326; G. D. S. Taylor, "Privacy and the Public" (1971), 34 M.L.R. 288; and Appendix I to the Younger Committee's Report.

---

1. If a dwelling house were involved, which is unlikely, the offences of burglary or housebreaking might be committed.

17

Malicious Abuse of Power

The concept of abuse of discretionary powers belongs properly to administrative law (for a clear discussion see S. A. de Smith, *Constitutional and Administrative Law*, 2nd Edn., p. 589). The circumstances in which the courts will require powers to be exercised in good faith and to promote the purposes of a particular statute are no concern of tort law. But there are some situations in which the defendant inflicts loss on the plaintiff by means of the misuse of the power of the state. If he maliciously and without reasonable and probable cause sets the law in motion against the plaintiff on a criminal charge, and the prosecution ends in the plaintiff's favour, the plaintiff may bring a civil action for damages (*post*). The damage suffered by the plaintiff may be of any one of the three kinds mentioned by Holt C.J. in *Savill* v. *Roberts* (1698), 12 Mod. 208: "First, damage to his fame if the matter whereof he be accused be scandalous. Secondly, to his person whereby he is imprisoned. Thirdly, to his property whereby he is put to charges and expenses." There may, additionally have been some seizure of property or entry upon land.

Another way in which loss may be inflicted is through the abuse of process, although in the case of civil process it appears to be necessary to prove some actual damage, and there can be no action for damages arising out of what is said or done in the course of judicial proceedings (p. 583, *post*). A final example of the misuse of power to inflict loss given in this Chapter is a doubtful one, for which, at present, there exists only indirect authority in English law: this is the infliction of loss by the deliberate abuse of statutory power, or by the usurpation of a power which the public authority knows it does not possess (p. 585, *post*).

1. MALICIOUS PROSECUTION

Austin v. Dowling

Court of Common Pleas   (1870), L.R. 5 C.P. 534

The defendant's wife gave the plaintiff into the custody of a constable on an unfounded charge of felony, namely breaking into the defendant's house, in which he was a tenant, in order to repossess himself of his own property. At the police station the inspector on duty disclaimed all responsibility in respect of the charge unless the defendant signed the charge, which he did. The particulars of demand annexed to the plaint-note in the county court in this action were as follows: "The plaintiff sues the defendant for that the defendant on Monday 13 September 1869 assaulted the plaintiff and unlawfully and wrongfully and without reasonable and probable cause gave him into the custody of a policeman upon a false and unfounded charge of felony . . . and caused him to be conveyed to a police station and then and there to be imprisoned for a long space of time, to wit, 18 hours, whereby the plaintiff has been much damaged; and the plaintiff claims £50." The plaintiff expressly waived any right or cause of action for malicious prosecution. The judge non-suited the plaintiff upon the ground that the evidence supported a case of malicious prosecution and therefore he had no jurisdiction. [This limitation on the jurisdiction of county courts no longer exists: County Courts Act 1959, s. 39.] He held that it was not possible to sever the cause of action for false imprisonment from that for malicious prosecution. On appeal:

WILLES J.: . . . The judge of the county-court, . . . was right in holding that there was evidence in support of a case of false imprisonment. How long did that state of false imprisonment last? So long, of course, as the plaintiff remained in the custody of a ministerial officer of the law, whose duty it was to detain him until he could be brought before a judicial officer. Until he was so brought before the judicial officer, there was no malicious prosecution. The distinction between false imprisonment and malicious prosecution is well illustrated by the case where, parties being before a magistrate, one makes a charge against another, whereupon the magistrate orders the person charged to be taken into custody and detained until the matter can be investigated. The party making the charge is not liable to an action for false imprisonment, because he does not set a ministerial officer in motion, but a judicial officer. The opinion and judgment of a judicial officer are interposed between the charge and the imprisonment. There is, therefore, at once a line drawn between the end of the imprisonment by the ministerial officer and the commencement of the proceedings before the judicial officer. It is fallacious to inquire whether or not the one is severable from the other, until you find some inseparable connection between them. It may very well happen in the superior courts, which have jurisdiction over both descriptions of action, where the plaintiff, having been at once taken before a magistrate, may be content to bring his action for false imprisonment only. In such a case,—which must be within the memory of all of us,—the judge would tell the jury to give damages for the false imprisonment only, and not for what came under the cognizance of the magistrate. What did the judge do here? He ruled that, although there was evidence in support of a case of false imprisonment, yet that he ought not, having regard to the particulars of demand, and as the jury had heard all the evidence, and as the imprisonment before and the imprisonment after the charge-sheet was signed were substantially parts of the same continuous transaction, to sever the evidence which supported a case of false imprisonment, from the evidence which supported a case of malicious prosecution. The former part of the ruling is quite right: the latter part is wrong in two particulars: in the first place, the judge seems to have thought that there was an inception of the malicious prosecution at the time the charge-sheet was signed; and, in the second place, that the false imprisonment merged in that. But, for the reasons already assigned, it was false imprisonment all through, so long as the matter remained in the hands of the ministerial officer. If it were a ground of nonsuit that, either for want of care on the part of the judge, or the absence of objection on the part of counsel, evidence is let in of a matter which is beyond the jurisdiction of the county-court judge, the number of nonsuits would be greatly increased. The proper course in such a case is to warn the jury to exclude such evidence from their minds in considering the question of damages. There having been no contingent assessment of damages here, all we can do is to set aside the nonsuit and direct a new trial, with costs.

[KEATING and MONTAGU SMITH JJ. agreed.]

Judgment accordingly

Note

Although the distinction between false imprisonment (p. 39, *ante*) and malicious prosecution is no longer of importance for jurisdictional purposes, the separate requirements of the two torts emerge from the above case. False imprisonment is a form of trespass to the person: the restraint on liberty must be *directly* imposed. In malicious prosecution (an action upon the case) there is interposed the exercise of an independent discretion. There is also an important difference in the burden of proof. In false imprisonment the arrester must show that the arrest was lawful. In malicious prosecution the plaintiff must prove that (1) the defendant instituted a prosecution (2) which ended in the plaintiff's favour (3) and which was instituted without reasonable and probable cause, and (4) was malicious. For a discussion of the differences, see Salmond, p. 164; Winfield & Jolowicz, p. 43; Street, p. 391.

Basebé v. Matthews

Court of Common Pleas   (1867), L.R. 2 C.P. 684

The declaration alleged malicious prosecution the plaintiff having been convicted "there being no appeal from the said conviction". The defendant demurred.

MONTAGU SMITH J.: . . . in such an action, it is essential to shew that the proceeding alleged to be instituted maliciously and without probable cause has terminated in favour of the plaintiff, if from its nature it be capable of such termination. The reason seems to be, that if in the proceeding complained of the decision was against the plaintiff, and was still unreversed, it would not be consistent with the principles of which law is administered for another court, not being a court of appeal, to hold that the decision was come to without reasonable and probable cause. The only ground upon which Mr. Wood has attempted to distinguish this case from the current of authorities is, that here the plaintiff had no opportunity of appealing against the conviction. If we yielded to his argument, we should be constituting ourselves a court of appeal in a matter in which the legislature has thought fit to declare that there shall be no appeal. It was intended that the decision of the magistrate in a case of this sort should be final. It cannot be impeached in an action.

[BYLES and KEATING JJ. were of the same opinion.]

Judgment for the defendants

Notes

1. In *Everett* v. *Ribbands*, [1952] 2 Q.B. 198; [1952] 1 All E.R. 823 (C.A.), it was held that there could be no action for malicious prosecution where the plaintiff had been ordered by a magistrate to enter into a recognisance to keep the peace and be of good behaviour for 12 months, or in default to undergo a month's imprisonment. This was because, since the passing of the Summary Jurisdiction Act 1879, s. 25 (now the Magistrates' Courts Act 1952, s. 91) both parties and their witnesses are heard in such proceedings which could end in plaintiff's favour. These had not.

2. It is debatable whether the stay of proceedings by the Attorney-General (*nolle prosequi*) amounts to a favourable termination of the prosecution. The answer must depend upon whether the accused is open to fresh indictment on the same charge: *Goddard* v. *Smith* (1704), 1 Salk. 21 suggests that he is.

Glinski v. McIver

House of Lords   [1962] 1 All E.R. 696

The plaintiff sued the defendant, a detective-sergeant in the C.I.D., for false imprisonment and malicious prosecution. He had been tried and acquitted on a charge of conspiracy to defraud brought by the defendant. He also alleged that some months earlier the defendant had wrongfully arrested and imprisoned him and put him up for identification. On this issue he recoverd £100 damages and its only relevance was the bearing, if any, it had on the further claim for malicious prosecution. This claim was in respect of the charge of conspiracy to defraud. At the trial of this action, Cassels J. put two questions to the jury: (1) Has it been proved that the defendant in starting the prosecution of the plaintiff for conspiracy to defraud was actuated by malice, that is, any motive or motives other than a desire to bring the plaintiff to justice. If yes, what damages? On this the jury answered: "Yes. £2,500 damages." (2) Did the defendant honestly believe on 29 September 1955, that the defendant was guilty of the offence of conspiracy to defraud. To this the jury answered "No." The Court of Appeal unanimously allowed an appeal from the judgment for the plaintiff. A further appeal to the House of Lords was unsuccessful, it being held that the second question should not have been left to the jury, because there was no evidence upon which there could be founded a finding, that the defendant did not honestly believe in his case; and if the jury's answer to that question were disregarded, the correct conclusion was that there had been reasonable and probable cause for the prosecution.

VISCOUNT SIMONDS: . . . It appears to me that, just as the prosecutor is justified in acting on information about facts given him by reliable witnesses, so he may accept advice on the law given him by a competent lawyer. That is the course that a reasonable man would take and, if so, the so-called objective test is satisfied. Applying this principle to the case of a police officer who lays an information and prefers a charge and at every step acts on competent advice, particularly perhaps if it is the advice of the legal department of Scotland Yard, I should find it difficult to say that that officer acted without reasonable and probable cause. I assume throughout that he has put all the relevant facts known to him before his advisers.

I must refer to one more matter before I return to the facts. A question is sometimes raised whether the prosecutor has acted with too great haste or zeal and failed to ascertain by inquiries that he might have made facts that would have altered his opinion on the guilt of the accused. On this matter it is not possible to generalise but I would accept as a guiding principle what Lord Atkin said in *Herniman* v. *Smith*,[1] that it is the duty of a prosecutor not to find out whether there is a possible defence but whether there is a reasonable and probable cause for prosecution. Nor can the risk be ignored that in the case of more complicated crimes, and particularly perhaps of conspiracies, inquiries may put one or more of the criminals on the alert. . . .

LORD DEVLIN: My Lords, it is a commonplace that in order to succeed in an action for malicious prosecution the plaintiff must prove both that the defendant was actuated by malice and that he had no reasonable and probable cause for prosecuting. The chief matter which the House has had to consider in this appeal is what is the relevance to either of these elements of a lack on the part of the defendant of an honest belief in the guilt of the plaintiff and in what circumstances a question on this point should be left to the jury. In the present case the second question left to them was:

"Did the defendant honestly believe on Sept. 29, 1955, that the plaintiff was guilty of the offence of conspiracy to defraud?"

It is best to begin by considering more closely what is meant by malice, honest belief in guilt, and reasonable and probable cause, in their application to the facts of this case.

Malice, it is agreed, covers not only spite and ill-will but also any motive other than a desire to bring a criminal to justice. It is agreed also that there was some evidence that when on 29 September 1955, the defendant charged the plaintiff with conspiracy to defraud, he did so not in order to bring him to justice for that offence but with an irrelevant and improper motive. The motive suggested was a desire either to punish the plaintiff for having a week before given evidence, which the police then believed to

1. [1938] A.C. 305, at p. 319; [1938] 1 All E.R. 1, at p. 10.

be perjured, for the defence in R. v. *Comer*[1] or in the hope of obtaining an admission from him that he was guilty of the perjury for which they subsequently prosecuted him unsuccessfully. In answer to the first question addressed to them, the jury found that there was malice in this sense. It has been submitted that this verdict was perverse. I see no reason for thinking that and I am therefore satisfied that the plaintiff has proved the first of the two matters he has to prove in order to succeed. Admittedly it was relevant to the first question for the jury to consider, among other factors, whether the defendant believed in the plaintiff's guilt on the charge of fraud. If that were the only relevance of belief in guilt, it was, in my opinion, neither necessary nor desirable to address a specific question to the jury on it. It would not, however, follow from the finding of malice that the jury were satisfied that the defendant did not believe in the plaintiff's guilt; he could have believed in guilt and still have been actuated by improper motives in launching the prosecution. Was, then, the question of belief relevant to the element of reasonable and probable cause? If so, was it right in the circumstances of this case to leave that question to the jury?

This makes it necessary to consider just what is meant by reasonable and probable cause. It means that there must be cause (that is, sufficient grounds; I shall hereafter in my speech not always repeat the adjectives "reasonable" and "probable") for thinking that the plaintiff was probably guilty of the crime imputed; *Hicks* v. *Faulkner*.[2] This does not mean that the prosecutor has to believe in the probability of conviction; *Dawson* v. *Vansandau*.[3] The prosecutor has not got to test the full strength of the defence; he is concerned only with the question of whether there is a case fit to be tried. As Dixon J. put it, the prosecutor must believe that

> "the probability of the accused's guilt is such that upon general grounds of justice a charge against him is warranted";

Commonwealth Life Assurance Society v. *Brock*.[4] Perhaps the best language in which to leave the question to the jury is that adopted by Cave J. in *Abrath* v. *North Eastern Rail Co.*:[5] ". . . did [the defendants] honestly believe in the case which they laid before the magistrates?"

I venture to think that there is a danger that a jury may be misled by a question in the form left to them in the present case in which the word "guilty" is used without any qualification. The defendant at the trial is usually pressed, as he was in the present case, to declare that he no longer believes that the plaintiff was guilty. Where, as here, the defence was not called on at the criminal trial and the only new factor for the defendant to weigh is the trial judge's ruling that there was no case to go to the jury or no case on which it would be safe for them to convict, the jury in the civil case may ask themselves whether that would be enough to cause an honest man to change his belief. They may not appreciate unless they are carefully directed in the summing-up that there is a substantial difference between a case that warrants the making of a charge and one that survives the test of cross-examination with sufficient strength left in it to require consideration by a jury which is concerned only with guilt beyond reasonable doubt. . . .

Six points are settled about the question of reasonable and probable cause. First, the question is a double one: did the prosecutor actually believe and did he reasonably believe that he had cause for prosecuting? Secondly, provided that the defendant has made sufficient inquiry, the facts on the basis of which the question has to be answered are those, and only those, known to the defendant at the material time. Thirdly, though a question of fact, it is one that in the end has to be determined by the judge and so is to be treated in the same way as if it were a question of law. Fourthly, if in the

---

1. (1955), *Times*, September 24.
2. (1881), 8 Q.B.D. 167, at p. 173.
3. (1863), 11 W.R. 516.
4. (1935), 53 C.L.R. 343, at p. 382.
5. (1883), 11 Q.B.D. 247, at p. 443.

course of the judge's inquiry he finds that it is necessary to resolve some disputed question of incidental fact, that question is a jury question. But, fifthly, like any other jury question, it is to be left to the jury only if there is some evidence put forward by the party on whom the onus lies; and that, in the case of malicious prosecution, means the plaintiff, since it is he who has to show want of cause. Sixthly, a question whether the defendant in fact believed that there was cause for prosecution is, if in dispute and if there is some evidence to support a conclusion that he did not, a question to be left to the jury.

These matters being settled, counsel for the defendant bases on two grounds his submission that the second question, the one about honest belief in guilt, ought not to have been asked and that the answer to it can be disregarded as irrelevant. The first ground involves a further analysis of what is meant by the question—Did the prosecutor believe that he had cause for prosecution? Counsel submits that that means—Did he believe in the facts on which the prosecution was based? If, he submits, the prosecutor believed in the truth of the information or evidence he had obtained, there is no need for him to form any opinion on the strength of it nor to determine whether it is sufficient to sustain a prosecution; his personal opinion, as counsel puts it, on such points is irrelevant. If this submission is correct, it means that the second question was not in a form designed to obtain the relevant answer; and the appropriate form of relief for that would ordinarily be an order for a new trial. But since it is not suggested in the present case that the defendant had any reason to doubt the truth of the information he had obtained, there is here no need for a new trial, for counsel for the defendant will have established that there was no ground for putting any question at all. . . .

In *Herniman* v. *Smith*[1] the plaintiff was a timber merchant and the defendant, a builder, was one of his customers. The plaintiff employed a carrier called Rickard to carry timber which he had imported from the docks to the sites where the defendant required it. The defendant, having discovered that some of the plaintiff's delivery notes were being faked so as to represent larger quantities than were in fact being delivered, prosecuted the plaintiff and Rickard for conspiracy to defraud; they were both convicted but their conviction was quashed in the Court of Criminal Appeal and thereupon the plaintiff sued for malicious prosecution. The material which the defendant had when he initiated the prosecution is summarised by Lord Atkin.[2] First, he had statements from two employees of Rickard who said that they had been told by Rickard to put extra timber over and above that delivered to the customer on the bill; they agreed to do so and were therefore parties to the dishonesty they alleged. Secondly, a comparison between the quantities shown on the dock passes and those shown on the delivery notes established that the latter had been faked, and some of the alterations were shown to be in Rickard's handwriting. Thirdly, the plaintiff delivered invoices based on the fraudulent quantities and so obtained larger payments than were due to him. These facts show that the case bears some general similarity to the present one. There was, as Lord Atkin said, no doubt that a fraud had been practised and the real question was whether the plaintiff Herniman was a party to it. So here it is conceded that there was a fraudulent conspiracy and the whole question is whether the plaintiff Glinski was a participator in it. If in *Herniman* v. *Smith*[1] one tries to separate the primary facts from the others, the only primary facts are the documents, which are undisputed and the statements of the two employees; the extent to which credit was to be given to them, since both men were accomplices, is a matter of opinion. But there was no evidence that directly implicated Herniman and the real question was whether the inference could rightly be drawn that he knew what was going on. Lord Atkin, with whose opinion all the other members of the House agreed, held,[3] applying the de-

---

1. [1938] A.C. 305; [1938] 1 All E.R. 1.
2. [1938] A.C. at p. 318; [1938] 1 All E.R. at p. 9.
3. [1938] A.C. at pp. 317, 318; [1938] 1 All E.R. at pp. 9, 10.

finition of reasonable and probable cause given by Hawkins J. in *Hicks* v. *Faulkner*,[1] that the facts ascertained by Smith

"... would induce a conviction, founded on reasonable grounds, of a state of circumstances which would reasonably lead any ordinarily prudent and cautious man placed in Smith's position to the conclusion that Herniman was probably guilty of the crime imputed."

Lord Atkin's commentary on this definition[2] has been thought by some to be lacking in clarity, but I do not find it so. He says that the question of absence of cause is for the judge, but that the jury are to find for him the relevant facts, when they are disputed, so that he can draw his conclusion. Among the relevant facts that he puts first as one that may be in dispute is whether the defendant honestly believed in the guilt of the accused; other facts are whether the statements which he said were made to him were in fact made, and so on. This language and the language of Hawkins J. whose definition he approved, satisfies me that Lord Atkin was clearly distinguishing between the prosecutor's belief in probable guilt and his belief in the facts on which he acted. It is said that this part of Lord Atkin's speech is obiter. As to that, the first question left to the jury was whether it had been proved that the defendant commenced and proceeded with the prosecution without any honest belief that the plaintiff was guilty of fraud. If counsel for the defendant's argument is right, the proper question on this topic ought to have been:—"Has it been proved that the defendant had no honest belief that the statements made by the two employees were true? There was no other fact in the case that could be disputable. So far from dealing with the matter summarily in this way, Lord Atkin deals at length in the manner I have set out with the question of belief in guilt and finally holds[3] that there was no evidence to go to the jury in support of want of belief. His speech embodies the considered opinion of this House on the whole question; and whether or not it is technically obiter, your Lordships are not now likely to depart from it unless fully convinced that it is wrong.

The examination of these three authorities brings me close to the second reason I have stated for the rejection of counsel for the defendant's main submission. It is true that the exact question your Lordships have to decide was not raised in *Herniman* v. *Smith*:[4] the main point argued seems to have been that the defendant did not take reasonable care to inform himself of the full facts. Nor was the exact point determined in any earlier case. But the conclusion on this point which I find to be implicit in Lord Atkin's speech, is, in my opinion, fully supported by the trend of authority from the earliest times. It must be remembered that the question is not whether there was in the abstract reasonable and probable cause but whether the defendant had such cause. That is how it should be framed. If it were framed in the other way, the test would be purely objective and the defendant's belief in anything immaterial; but it is common ground that the defendant must believe in something. There must therefore be both actual belief and reasonable belief. I can find nothing in any statement of principle throughout the cases to indicate that the area to be covered by the former is smaller than the area to be covered by the latter. No doubt dicta can be found which are consistent with counsel for the defendant's submission, though there are very many more which are not; but the whole current of authority is to my mind against the notion that actual belief is not co-extensive with reasonable belief and that, although the reasonable man as personified by the judge has to draw the appropriate inferences and reach the appropriate conclusions, the actual believer need not. . . .

From this disposition of the legal arguments there emerge two questions of fact to be determined by the judge on which the result of this case turns. First, has the plaintiff shown that objectively there was no reasonable and probable cause for the prosecution?

---

1. (1881), 8 Q.B.D. 167, at p. 171.
2. [1938] A.C. at p. 316; [1938] 1 All E.R. at p. 8.
3. [1938] A.C. at p. 320; [1938] 1 All E.R. at p. 11.
4. [1938[A.C. 305; [1938] 1 All E.R. 1.

Secondly, was there some extraneous evidence, fit to go to the jury, tending to show that the defendant disbelieved in his case? In my judgment both these questions should be answered in the negative and so the appeal fails.

[LORD REID concurred in dismissing the appeal. LORD RADCLIFFE and LORD DENNING delivered speeches in favour of dismissing the appeal.]

Notes

1. Malicious bankruptcy proceedings and malicious proceedings to wind up a company are actionable: *Quartz Hill Gold Mining Co.* v. *Eyre* (1883), 11 Q.B.D. 674. Although there is no reported decision in favour of a cause of action in respect of the malicious institution of *any* civil proceeding, Winfield & Jolowicz, pp. 497–98, make out a case for such a right, at least where the person was maliciously sued for some scandalous tort like deceit. Vexatious civil litigants may be curbed under the Supreme Court of Judicature (Consolidation) Act 1925, s. 51, as amended.

2. The action for malicious prosecution is one upon the case and so damage —of one of the three kinds mentioned by Holt C.J. in *Savill* v. *Roberts* (1698), 12 Mod. 208 (referred to in the introduction to this Chapter, p. 576, *ante*)— must be proved. In *Berry* v. *British Transport Commission*, [1962] 1 Q.B. 306; [1961] 3 All E.R. 65 (C.A.) it was made clear that the plaintiff may recover the actual cost of the defence of the unsuccessful criminal proceedings less any amount awarded as costs by the criminal court.

2. OTHER ABUSE OF LEGAL PROCESS

Roy v. Prior

House of Lords   [1970] 2 All E.R. 729

The defendant, whose client had been charged with a criminal offence, issued a witness summons requiring the plaintiff to attend as a witness at the trial. The plaintiff failed to attend, and after the defendant had stated on oath that the plaintiff was avoiding service of the summons, the plaintiff was arrested on a warrant issued by the trial judge. The plaintiff brought an action for malicious arrest alleging that the defendant had not taken the necessary or sufficient steps to inform the plaintiff of the issue of the summons or to serve it upon him, and that the defendant had maliciously and without reasonable and probable cause instructed counsel to apply for a warrant of arrest and had caused and procured the issue of a warrant by falsely stating an oath that the plaintiff was evading service. The Master refused to strike out the statement of claim and dismiss the action; Mackenna J. dismissed an appeal, but his decision was reversed by the Court of Appeal. The House of Lords allowed a further appeal.

LORD MORRIS OF BORTH-Y-GEST: . . . It is well settled that no action will lie against a witness for words spoken in giving evidence in a court even if the evidence is falsely and maliciously given (see *Dawkins* v. *Lord Rokeby*[1] and *Watson* v. *McEwan*).[2] If a witness gives false evidence he may be prosecuted if the crime of perjury has been committed but a civil action for damages in respect of the words spoken will not lie (see the judgment of Lord Goddard C.J. in *Hargreaves* v. *Bretherton*).[3] Nor is this rule to be circumvented by alleging a conspiracy between witnesses to make false statements (see *Marrinan* v. *Vibart*).[4]

---

1. (1875), L.R. 7 H.L. 744.
2. [1905] A.C. 480; [1904–07] All E.R. Rep. 1.
3. [1959] 1 Q.B. 45; [1958] 3 All E.R. 122.
4. [1963] 1 Q.B. 234; [1962] 1 All E.R. 869.

This, however, does not involve that an action which is not brought in respect of evidence given in court but is brought in respect of an alleged abuse of process of court must be defeated if one step in the course of the abuse of the process of the court involved or necessitated the giving of evidence. It must often happen that a defendant who is sued for damages for malicious prosecution will have given evidence in the criminal prosecution of which the plaintiff complains. The essence of the complaint in such a case is that criminal proceedings have been instituted not only without reasonable and probable cause but also maliciously. So also in actions based on alleged abuses of the process of the court it will often have happened that the court will have been induced to act by reason of some false evidence given by someone. In such cases the actions are not brought on or in respect of any evidence given but in respect of malicious abuse of process (see *Elsee* v. *Smith*).[1] . . .

That the courts have distinguished between actions brought in respect of malicious process and those brought in respect of evidence given in proceedings was illustrated by *Revis* v. *Smith*.[2] The Court of Chancery ordered the sale of a testator's real estate and the plaintiff, an auctioneer, was proposed to the court as a fit and proper person to be appointed by the court to sell the property. The defendant swore and filed an affidavit which seriously reflected on the plaintiff and which contained many defamatory statements. As a result the court did not appoint the plaintiff. He sued the defendant for damages. It was held that the action did not lie. In the judgments a distinction was drawn between the claim then made and cases in which the process of the courts had been abused maliciously and without reasonable or probable cause. Jervis C.J. held that no action for defamation would lie against the defendant.

In *Melia* v. *Neate*[3] there was a claim for damages for having maliciously and without reasonable or probable cause procured an order of a judge for the arrest of the plaintiff for an alleged debt. The action was brought against three persons: one was a builder, another was his attorney and the other was the attorney's clerk. A contract for the erection of a church had been entered into between the plaintiff and the builder. The builder claimed that a sum for extras was due; the architect told the builder that no sum was due. The attorney on behalf of the builder then issued a writ against the plaintiff claiming that a sum was due; the writ was served by the clerk. There followed an application to a judge in chambers to arrest the plaintiff on the ground that he was about to leave England. The application was supported by an affidavit jointly made by the builder and the clerk. As a result the plaintiff was arrested. In the action which he later brought it was said that there was no justification for certain statements in the affidavit. These were fully considered and examined. The jury were directed that to sustain the action it was necessary to prove that the defendants had caused the arrest maliciously and without reasonable and probable cause. There was no suggestion that any immunity from liability could result from the fact that the arrest had been the result of the affidavit. . . .

A point was taken in the present case that in paras 6 and 11 of the statement of claim are the words "at the trial". It was contended that the defendant gave evidence on matters relevant to the defence of Mr Advani and that the defendant was therefore entitled to the immunity from action to which a witness is entitled. This, however, raises questions which can only be determined when the facts are ascertained. The only issue now arising is whether the claim of the plaintiff must at this stage be dismissed. Different considerations would apply if the claim was one for damages in respect of evidence given by a witness. The present claim is not such a claim. The gist and essence of the claim is that process was instituted as a result of which the court was induced to order the arrest of the plaintiff. It is alleged that this was done maliciously and without reasonable cause and that the giving of evidence was merely a step in bringing about the alleged abuse of process.

---

1. (1822), 2 Chit. 304.
2. (1856), 18 C.B. 126.
3. (1863), F. & F. 757.

In my view the learned judge came to the correct conclusion in refusing to dismiss the action.

[Viscount Dilhorne, Lord Wilberforce, Lord Diplock and Lord Reid concurred in allowing the appeal.]

Notes

1. In *Hargreaves* v. *Bretherton*, [1958] 1 Q.B. 45; [1958] 3 All E.R. 122, Lord Goddard C.J. held that an action for damages will not lie at the suit of a person who alleges that he has been damnified by false evidence given against him in criminal proceedings. What is the distinction between this rule and the rule in *Roy* v. *Prior*? (See Street, p. 397.)

2. In *Marrinan* v. *Vibart*, [1963] 1 Q.B. 528; [1962] 3 All E.R. 380 (C.A.), a disbarred barrister brought an action for damages for conspiracy against two police officers alleging that they had conspired together to make false statements defamatory of him as a barrister in a report to the Director of Public Prosecutions, in evidence given by them at a trial at the Central Criminal Court, and in testimony given by them at an inquiry before the Benchers of Lincoln's Inn. Salmon J. held that the statement of claim disclosed no cause of action. The Court of Appeal, dismissing an appeal, held that the rule of public policy which protected witnesses from civil action was not confined to defamation actions (p. 557, *ante*) but applied whatever cause of action was sought to be based upon what was said and done in judicial proceedings. (See too, the advocate's immunity from liability for negligence: *Rondel* v. *Worsley*, [1969] 1 A.C. 191; [1967] 3 All E.R. 993, p. 517, *ante*). Protection from liability in tort extends not only to judicial bodies strictly so called, but also to others having discretion or authority to adjudicate, such as licensing justices, the General Medical Council, arbitrators, and all parties, advocates and witnesses before them (see *Halsbury's Laws of England*, 4th Edn., vol. 1, paras. 206–214). Domestic tribunals are not usually liable for damage caused by their acts, in the absence of malice (e.g. *Abbot* v. *Sullivan*, [1952] 1 K.B. 189; [1952] 1 All E.R. 226, but see *Breen* v. *Amalgamated Engineering Union*, [1971] 2 Q.B. 175, at p. 194, *per* Lord Denning M.R., who suggested that damages may be awarded for wrongful deprivation of office by a trade union committee).

3. ABUSE OF GOVERNMENTAL POWER

Asoka Kumar David v. M. A. M. M. Abdul Cader

Judicial Committee of the Privy Council   [1963] 3 All E.R. 579

The plaintiff was the proprietor of a cinema in Ceylon. He had been refused a cinema licence by the local authority of which the defendant was chairman. He alleged that the defendant had wrongfully and maliciously refused and neglected to issue him with a licence, and claimed Rs. 35,000 as damages and a further sum for continuing damage. The action was dismissed on a preliminary question of law by the District Court of Puttalam, and an appeal was dismissed, on different grounds, by the Supreme Court of Ceylon. An appeal to the Judicial Committee of the Privy Council was allowed.

Viscount Radcliffe: ... The judgment of the Supreme Court (De Silva and Tambiah, JJ.), proceeded on different lines. It did not express any view as to the validity of the point that had succeeded with the trial judge, but accepted the proposition that a plaintiff could not maintain any right of action for damages in respect of a refusal or failure to grant a licence of the kind involved in this case, even though the licensing authority had acted maliciously in withholding the licence. In the opinion of the court no right of the plaintiff could be said to have been infringed in such circumstances and his proper and only remedy was to apply for the issue of the prerogative writ of mandamus to ensure that his application was duly heard and determined. The court's decision was expressly based on the English authority, *Davis* v. *Bromley Corpn.*,[1] a case the facts of which were very similar to those pleaded in the present proceedings.

Before their lordships the appellant challenged both judgments delivered in Ceylon as unsupportable in law. It is convenient to say at once that in their opinion the point on which the district judge dismissed the action is misconceived. Under the Urban Councils Ordinance[2] the chairman is himself, as the pleadings have recognised, the local authority in connection with the granting of licences for cinema performances. The granting or withholding of such licences is his personal responsibility, and his acts are not those of the council, which is a corporation, nor is he a corporation for the purpose of these duties. It follows that, if the law does recognise a right of action against him in any circumstances arising out of a breach of those duties, whether or not a breach accompanied by bad faith or malice, the only way in which he can be sued is as an individual person, and there is no relevant distinction in his status as a party between his official capacity and his personal capacity. In their lordships' opinion the appellant's action cannot be treated as defective on such a ground.

The argument accepted by the Supreme Court raises a different issue. The judgment adopts the view that for an action in delict to succeed and afford a right to damages there must have been an infringement of an antecedent legal right of the person injured. The appellant, it appeared to the court, had no such right, since under the governing statute he was not entitled to exhibit cinematographs in his building without the licence of the local authority, and it had been left to the discretion of the chairman of the local council to decide whether to grant or to withhold the necessary licence. If they were to regard this as a proposition equally valid for the English law of tort as for the Roman-Dutch law of delict (and the Supreme Court judgment relies exclusively on the authority of decisions in the English courts) their lordships would have great difficulty in upholding it in so general a form. It does not appear to them that a right to damages is excluded by the mere circumstance that the appellant could not lawfully operate his cinema without a licence. Plainly the law forbade his doing so. But the question to be determined is not what rights he had without a licence, but rather what rights were created between these two parties by the relationship under which one wished to operate a cinema and had applied for a licence to do so and the other had the statutory responsibility for deciding how to deal with that application. Whatever the limits of the range of the latter's discretion in carrying out that responsibility, a separate question which would need careful consideration if the action came to be tried, the appellant has at any rate pleaded that he had done everything required to qualify him for the grant of a licence and that he was entitled to have one issued. Given that relationship and the assumption of that state of facts, it seems to their lordships impossible to say that the respondent did not owe some duty to the appellant with regard to the execution of his statutory power; and if, as pleaded, he had been malicious in refusing or neglecting to grant the licence, it is equally impossible to say without investigation of the facts that there cannot have been a breach of duty giving rise to a claim for damages.

The Supreme Court's opinion was based on the decision of the English Court of Appeal in *Davis* v. *Bromley Corpn.*,[1] a decision which they presumably regarded as satisfactorily illustrative of the principles of the Roman-Dutch law of delict. The facts indeed of the *Davis* case[1] were closely similar to those pleaded here. There, too, a licence or statutory approval had been sought from and refused by a local authority,

---

1. [1908] 1 K.B. 170.
2. Cap. 255 (Legislative Enactments of Ceylon (revised 1956), Vol. 9, p. 190).

and the applicant issued a writ alleging that the authority had not acted bona fide in rejecting his plans but from motives of spite and claiming a declaration that he was entitled to carry out his proposed works and damages for the refusal. The judgment of the court, which is shortly expressed, is to the effect that no action would lie in these circumstances; that the possible indirect motives attributed to the defendants could not render the exercise of their statutory discretion the more susceptible to judicial review than it would be otherwise; and that the plaintiff's only remedy, if the defendants had really made no true or bona fide exercise of their authority, was to apply for a mandamus to have his application properly heard and determined.

Davis's case[1] was decided in the year 1907. Since then the English courts have had to give much consideration to the general question of the rights of the individual dependent on the exercise of statutory powers by a public authority, and the decision of that case would now have to be seen in the context of a very great number of later decisions that have dealt with the question at more length and with more elaboration. In their lordships' opinion it would not be correct today to treat it as establishing any wide general principle in this field: certainly it would not be correct to treat it as sufficient to found the proposition, as asserted here, that an applicant for a statutory licence can in no circumstances have a right to damages if there has been a malicious misuse of the statutory power to grant the licence. Much must turn in such cases on what may prove to be the facts of the alleged misuse and in what the malice is found to consist. The presence of spite or ill-will may be insufficient in itself to render actionable a decision which has been based on unexceptionable grounds of consideration and has not been vitiated by the badness of the motive. But a "malicious" misuse of authority, such as is pleaded by the appellant in his plaint, may cover a set of circumstances which go beyond the mere presence of ill-will, and in their lordships' view it is only after the facts of malice relied on by a plaintiff have been properly ascertained that it is possible to say in a case of this sort whether or not there has been any actionable breach of duty.

These reasons have forced their lordships to conclude that this action is not appropriately disposed of by argument on the two preliminary issues by which it has so far been judged. The position, as they see it, is this. It has been dismissed in the district court on a ground which is not maintainable in law. It has been dismissed in the Supreme Court in reliance on a general principle derived from certain English authorities which their lordships regard as too widely stated to afford a satisfactory conclusion of the pleadings as they stand. The issue remains what it has been from the beginning, a question of liability dependent directly on the Roman-Dutch law of delict and only indirectly and by way of analogy and illustration on the English law of torts. Such consultation as their lordships have thought it wise to make of the institutional writers on Roman-Dutch Law, Voet, Lee and Wille, has not led them to think that the conceptions of that law would regard as necessarily inadmissible a right of compensation to a plaintiff for a malicious invasion of his statutory "rights" to have his claim to a licence subjected to bona fide determination by a public authority. In view of the order that they propose to advise and the fact that this aspect of the parties' rights and liabilities under the Roman-Dutch law has not been accorded any express treatment in the judgments of the courts in Ceylon, their lordships think that it would be inappropriate for them to say anything more about the merits in law of this appeal than that they could not dismiss it with any confidence that the appellant's case, as pleaded, has as yet received the full consideration that is required for a final determination of the case.

In their opinion, for the reasons stated above, this action is not one that can justly be disposed of on preliminary issues argued in advance of the hearing of evidence. . . .

Appeal allowed

Notes

1. In an illuminating note on this case A. W. Bradley, [1964] C.L.J. 4, at p. 8,

---

1. [1908] 1 K.B. 170.

suggests that malice and bad faith on the part of a public authority may lead to liability in the following situations:

"(a) where an act, e.g. entry on another's land, would constitute a tort but for statutory authority, the presence of malice may deprive the intruder of protection, for Parliament intends statutory powers to be exercised in good faith;

(b) where defamatory words are uttered on an occasion of official duties normally protected by qualified privilege, proof of express malice within the law of defamation will negate the defence;

(c) where there is a statutory duty to act, and failure to act has injured the plaintiff, there may be liability in damages, depending on the interpretation of the statute in question. In general, where there is the remedy of damages failure to act creates liability and motivation is irrelevant. Proof of malice might, as in *David* v. *Abdul Cader*, help to show that a duty has not been performed. But would proof of malice affect a situation, e.g. *Cutler* v. *Wandsworth Stadium, Ltd.*, [1949] A.C. 398; [1949] 1 All E.R. 544 where, apart from malice there is no remedy in damages? [see p. 279, *ante*, for this case]. In one situation where an individual has a statutory right which depends on the co-operation of an official, malicious refusal to co-operate may lead to a remedy in damages. In *Ashby* v. *White* (1703), 2 Ld. Raym. 938, the plaintiff expressly alleged fraud and malice; although doubts exist as to the accuracy of the reporting, and as to Sir John Holt's view on this point, the opinion approved by the House of Lords is apparently that it was the fraud and the malice that entitled the party to the action [for deprivation of the right to vote] (see Smith's *Leading Cases* (13th Edn.), vol. 1, p. 293 *et seq.* and cases there cited);

(d) where a public official knowingly makes a false statement intending to induce a public body to exercise its statutory powers to the detriment of the plaintiff, there may possibly be an action on the case akin to that for injurious falsehood (J. S. Hall, (1957), 21 Conv. (N.S.) 455);

(e) where several public officials for malicious objects collectively procure a public authority to exercise its powers to the injury of the plaintiff, the possibility of liability for conspiracy should not be ruled out; [p. 436, *ante*, for conspiracy].

This does not exhaust all the situations in which an individual might reasonably wish to sue for malicious exercise of statutory powers . . ."

2. In *Beaudesert Shire Council* v. *Smith* (1966), 120 C.L.R. 145; [1966] A.L.R. 1175 (Aust. H.C.) a local authority in Queensland had unlawfully taken gravel from a river resulting in the destruction of a natural water hole and interfering with the flow of the river so that the plaintiff, a riparian owner, could no longer use his pumping installation, situated on the river, to obtain water for irrigation purposes. It was held that he was entitled to claim damages from the local authority, in respect of the loss suffered through failure of his crops and the expense of restoring the water supply, in an action upon the case. It was said that "independently of trespass, negligence or nuisance, but by an action for damages upon the case, a person who suffers harm or loss, as the inevitable consequence of the unlawful, intentional and positive acts of another is entitled to recover damages from that other." This is clearly wrong, as Dworkin and Harari, "Raising the Ghost of the Action Upon the Case" (1966), 40 A.L.J. 296, 347, point out. The council's act was intentional only in the sense that they intended to take gravel. But there is nothing in the case to suggest that they knew that what they were doing was unlawful, nor that their conduct was aimed at the plaintiff. (See further, p. 474, *ante*.)

3. The abuse of private monopoly power is generally not tortious, but it may be possible to obtain a declaration that a particular practice is unlawful

as in restraint of trade: e.g. *Nagle* v. *Feilden*, [1966] 2 Q.B. 633; [1966] 1 All E.R. 689 (C.A.) (declaration but not damages in respect of alleged arbitrary and unreasonable sex discrimination by stewards of Jockey Club in exercise of discretion). There is no general wrong of refusing to contract, see p. 435, *ante*.

Loss Distribution

18

Vicarious Liability

The individual defendant in a tort action is not infrequently a man of straw. The typical modern way of ensuring that the plaintiff actually receives the compensation to which he is entitled is through the device of compulsory insurance (Chap. 20). But there is also an older legal mechanism which enables the plaintiff to fix responsibility upon someone other than the impecunious actor. This is the principle of vicarious liability. The actor and the person to whom responsibility is imputed are jointly liable to the plaintiff. The person who actually pays may be able to recover that payment from the actor (see Chap. 19); but so far as his liability to the plaintiff is concerned this appears as a form of strict liability, imposed regardless of personal fault. The justification for this principle is controversial (e.g. p. 609, *post*). The most widely accepted theory is that the person with the power of control and direction over the actor is usually the best-fitted to absorb the loss: this is likely to be an enterprise which can pass on the costs of insurance or self-insurance to consumers of its products in the form of higher prices, to shareholders in the form of reduced dividends, and to employees in the form of smaller wage increases. If all those who committed torts were adequately insured there would be no need for a doctrine of vicarious liability. So goes the theory. But in reading the cases which follow the student will be unable to test its validity because the courts refuse to investigate the facts of insurance or the economics of loss distribution. *Morgans* v. *Launchbury*, [1973] A.C. 127; [1972] 2 All E.R. 606 (p. 606, *post*) is the clearest example of conscious judicial avoidance of policy-making in this area.

The most important factor delimiting the scope of vicarious liability is not any theoretical principle, but simply judicial precedent. As a matter of law, the defendant (D) will be made vicariously liable to the plaintiff (P) in respect of the acts of another person (X) only if P shows that—

(1) X has committed a *wrongful act* which has caused P damage;

(2) Some *special relationship recognised by law* exists between D and X, for example a contract of employment, or the delegation of the task of driving a motor vehicle for the owner's purposes;

(3) some *connection* exists between the act of X and his special relationship with D—in the traditional formula the act must be in "the course of X's employment" or, what amounts to much the same thing, in "the scope of X's authority".

Each of these points raises its own difficulties. In regard to the first, must X's act constitute a *tort*? Or is the real basis of this form of liability the attribution of X's *act* to D so as to make it D's tort? This point is usually only raised when it is sought to attribute X's knowledge to D (as in *Armstrong* v. *Strain*, [1952] I K.B. 232; [1952] I All E.R. 139, p. 613, *post*) or to allow D to limit his liability by an express prohibition on certain conduct by X (like giving lifts to hitch-hikers in *Twine* v. *Bean's Express* (1946), 175 L.T. 131, p. 622, *post*).

The second point raises problems of definition. There is only one special relationship which, as a general rule, gives rise to vicarious liability. This is the one between employer and employee ("master" and "servant" in the older terminology). It is therefore necessary to consider the various tests by which the existence of a contract of employment (i.e. of service) as distinct from a contract with an independent contractor (i.e. for services) is to be determined, p. 595, *post*). The many borderline cases which arise, particularly in the context of the growing practice of "self-employment" in construction and other industries, indicates the artificiality of the general rule. Another special relationship which may sometimes, but does not always, give rise to vicarious liability is that between "principal" or "agent". These terms have a special connotation in the law of contract; in the law of tort they are simply a form of shorthand descriptive of circumstances in which vicarious liability has been imposed. The materials in the second section of this chapter relate to four such circumstances (p. 606, *post*).

The third point is a question of mixed law and fact. Factual issues such as "Did D authorise X to drive his car" are sometimes closely connected with legal issues such as whether particular acts should be regarded as a custom or should be implied as terms in a contract (e.g. *Heatons Transport (St. Helens), Ltd.* v. *Transport and General Workers Union*, [1972] 3 All E.R. 101). In dealing with this question precedent must be treated with extreme caution, because the cases are so often simply concerned with applying a general test to particular facts. (It should be noted that none of the old Workmen's Compensation Act cases dealing with the phrase "arising out of and in the scope of employment" have been included in this section. This is because that phrase is narrower than the common law "course of employment", e.g. in regard to express prohibitions; and because those cases are concerned with the question whether the injured workman can recover compensation, not with the employer's liability to strangers *outside* the enterprise in respect of the acts of workmen.)

Consideration of the question of liability for independent contractors has been left to sections 4 and 5 (pp. 632, 639, *post*) since this raises the most controversial conceptual problems. The instances of such liability are rare. Do they rest upon the breach of some personal "non-delegable" duty by the employer? Or is the notion of "non-delegable" duties simply a "logical fraud" (in the words of Glanville Williams, [1956] C.L.J. 180) disguising vicarious liability? Historically, the adoption of the concept of "non-delegable" duties enabled the courts to avoid the hardships to employees caused by the doctrine of common employment: see *Wilsons and Clyde Coal Co., Ltd.* v. *English*, [1938] A.C. 57; [1937] 3 All E.R. 628, Chap. 7, p. 264, *ante*. But the continued use of this terminology, despite the statutory abolition of the doctrine of common employment has led to curious results in regard to the employer's liability to his own employees in respect of the acts of an independent contractor

(p. 640, *post*) which have only partially been remedied by the Employer's Liability (Defective Equipment) Act 1969 (p. 639, *post*).

The Chapter concludes with a brief view of some of the problems of distinguishing "personal" and "vicarious" liability in the context of corporations and associations. The plaintiff may have been injured through a failure of team-work in which case the corporation is sometimes treated as "personally" liable; in reality this may simply be another way of saying that one or more employees of the corporation have been negligent. In practice the distinction does not often matter. But in the controversial subject of liability for the acts of officers of associations such as trade unions, everything depends upon drawing a line between personal and vicarious liability (p. 644, *post*).

1. LIABILITY FOR EMPLOYEES

Mersey Docks & Harbour Board v. Coggins & Griffiths, Ltd.

House of Lords   [1946] 2 All E.R. 345

The Board (the appellants) hired out to the respondents, who were master stevedores, the use of a mobile crane together with its driver, Newall, for the purpose of loading a ship. Through his negligent handling of the crane, Newall injured a stevedore called MacFarlane. The question in issue was whether Newall was to be regarded as the employee of the Board or of the respondents, when he set the crane in motion. An agreement between the Board and the respondents said that he was to be the respondent's employee, but the Board continued to pay his wages and had the power to dismiss him. The respondents had the power to tell him *what* to do, i.e. where to station the crane, whether to lift or lower the load etc., but had no power to direct *how* he should work the crane. The manipulation of the controls was a matter for Newall himself.

The Court of Appeal held that he was acting as employee of the Board, who were, accordingly, vicariously liable for his tortious act. On appeal:

VISCOUNT SIMON: . . . It is not disputed that the burden of proof rests upon the general or permanent employer—in this case the board—to shift the *prima facie* responsibility for the negligence of servants engaged and paid by such employer so that this burden in a particular case may come to rest on the hirer who for the time being has the advantage of the service rendered. And, in my opinion, this burden is a heavy one and can only be discharged in quite exceptional circumstances.

It is not easy to find a precise formula by which to determine what these circumstances must be. In the century-old case of *Quarman* v. *Burnett*,[1] which has always been treated as a guiding authority, the defendants owned a carriage, but habitually hired from a jobmaster horses to draw it. The jobmaster also supplied a regular driver who wore a livery provided by the defendants. It was decided that the defendants were not liable for the results of the driver's negligence in handling the horses. The ground of the decision was that the defendants had no control over the way in which the horses were driven, though they could direct the driver where and when to drive. The test suggested by Bowen L.J. in *Donovan* v. *Laing, Wharton and Down Construction Syndicate*,[2] when he said ([1893] 1 Q.B. 629, at p. 634): "by the employer is meant the person who has a right at the moment to control the doing of the act" can be understood in this sense, and in this sense I would accept it: *i.e.*, "to control the doing of the act" would mean "to control the way in which the act involving negligence was done."

1. (1840), 6 M. & W. 499.
2. [1893] 1 Q.B. 629.

I find it somewhat difficult, however, to fit the facts in *Donovan's* case[1] into this proposition, and if that decision is upheld, it must be on the basis found in the words of Lord Esher M.R., when he said (*ibid.*, at p. 632):

> "The man was bound to work the crane according to the orders and under the entire and absolute control of [the hirers]."

But, as the House of Lords insisted in *M'Cartan* v. *Belfast Harbour Comrs.*,[2] the value of an earlier authority lies, not in the view which a particular court took of particular facts, but in the proposition of law involved in the decision. In *M'Cartan's* case[2] Lord Dunedin referred to, and expressly approved, the judgment of Lord Trayner in *Cairns* v. *Clyde Navigation Trustees*,[3] which, on facts closely resembling the present, held that the trustees, as general employers, were in law liable for the negligent driving of a crane which they had let out with its driver for discharging a ship. Notwithstanding the *dictum* of Bowen L.J. in *Donovan's* case,[1] the principle of the carriage cases and the crane cases appears to me to be the same: I would especially refer to what Lord Dunedin said ([1911] 2 I.R. 143, at p. 151) in *M'Cartan's* case.[3]

The Court of Appeal in this case, following its own decision in *Nicholas* v. *F. J. Sparkes & Son*[4] applied a test it had formulated, where a vehicle is lent with its driver to a hirer, by propounding the question ([1945] 1 All E.R. 605, at p. 608):

> "In the doing of the negligent act was the workman exercising the discretion given him by his general employer, or was he obeying or discharging a specific order of the party for whom upon his employer's direction, he was using the vehicle . . .? "

I would prefer to make the test turn on where the authority lies to direct, or to delegate to, the workman, the manner in which the vehicle is driven. It is this authority which determines who is the workman's *superior*. In the ordinary case, the general employers exercise this authority by delegating to their workman discretion in method of driving, and so the Court of Appeal correctly points out ([1945] 1 All E.R. 605, at p. 608), that in this case the driver Newall:

> ". . . in the doing of the negligent act, was exercising his own discretion as driver —a discretion which had been vested in him by his regular employers when he was sent out with the vehicle —and he made a mistake with which the hirers had nothing to do."

If, however, the hirers intervene to give directions as to how to drive which they have no authority to give, and the driver *pro hac vice* complies with them, with the result that a third party is negligently damaged, the hirers may be liable as joint tort-feasors.

I move that the appeal be dismissed with costs.

LORD PORTER: . . . Many factors have a bearing on the result. Who is paymaster, who can dismiss, how long the alternative service lasts, what machinery is employed— all these questions have to be kept in mind. The expressions used in any individual case must always be considered in regard to the subject matter under discussion, but among the many tests suggested I think that the most satisfactory by which to ascertain who is the employer at any particular time is to ask who is entitled to tell the employee the way in which he is to do the work upon which he is engaged. If someone other than his general employer is authorised to do this, he will, as a rule, be the person liable for the employee's negligence. But it is not enough that the task to be performed should be under his control, he must also control the method of performing it. It is true that in most cases no orders as to how a job should be done are given or required. The man is left to do his own work in his own way, but the ultimate question is not what specific

---

1. [1893] 1 Q.B. 629.
2. [1911] 2 I.R. 143.
3. (1898), 25 R. (Ct. of Sess.) 1021.
4. [1945] K.B. 309, n.

orders, or whether any specific orders, were given, but who is entitled to give the orders as to how the work should be done. Where a man driving a mechanical device, such as a crane, is sent to perform a task, it is easier to infer that the general employer continues to control the method of performance since it is his crane and the driver remains responsible to him for its safe keeping. In the present case, if the appellants' contention were to prevail, the crane driver would change his employer each time he embarked on the discharge of a fresh ship. Indeed, he might change it from day to day, without any say as to who his master should be and with all the concomitant disadvantages of uncertainty as to who should be responsible for his insurance in respect of health unemployment and accident.

I cannot think that such a conclusion is to be drawn from the facts established. I should dismiss the appeal.

LORD SIMONDS [read by Lord Uthwatt]: . . . It is not disputed that at the time when the respondents entered into a contract with the appellants under which the latter were to supply the former with the service of a crane and craneman, Newall was the servant of the appellants. He was engaged and paid and liable to be dismissed by them. So also, when the contract had been performed, he was their servant. If, then, in the performance of that contract he committed a tortious act, injuring McFarlane by his negligence, they can only escape from liability if they can show that *pro hac vice* the relation of master and servant had been temporarily constituted between the respondents and Newall and temporarily abrogated between themselves and him. This they can do only by proving, in the words of Lord Esher M.R., in *Donovan's* case[1] that entire and absolute control over the workman had passed to the respondents. In the cited case the court held upon the facts that the burden of proof had been discharged and I do not question the decision. But it appears to me that the test can only be satisfied if the temporary employer (if to use the word "employer" is not to beg the question) can direct not only what the workman is to do but also how he is to do it.

In the case before your Lordships, the negligence of the workman lay, not in the performance of any act which the respondents could and did direct and for which, because they procured it, they would be responsible, but in the manner in which that act was performed, a matter in which they could give no direction and for which they can have no responsibility.

The doctrine of the vicarious responsibility of the *superior*, whatever its origin, is to-day justified by social necessity, but, if the question is where that responsibility should lie, the answer should surely point to that master in whose act some degree of fault, though remote, may be found. Here the fault, if any, lay with the appellants who, though they were not present to dictate how directions given by another should be carried out, yet had vested in their servant a discretion in the manner of carrying out such directions. If an accident then occurred through his negligence, that was because they had chosen him for the task, and they cannot escape liability by saying that they were careful in their choice. Suppose that the negligence of the craneman had resulted in direct damage to the respondents, I do not see how the appellants could escape liability. For the obligation to supply a crane and a man to work it is an obligation to supply a crane which is not defective and a man who is competent to work it. It would be a strange twist of the law if, the negligence resulting in damage not to the respondents but to a third party, the liability shifted from the appellants to the respondents.

LORD UTHWATT: . . . It may be an express term of the bargain between the general employer and the hirer that the workman is to be the servant of the hirer or is to be subject in all respects to his authority. That, in my opinion, does not of itself determine the workman's position. The workman's assent, express or implied, to such a term would, I think, conclude the point one way, and his dissent conclude it the other way.

---

1. [1893] 1 Q.B. 629.

In cases where the point cannot be disposed of in this fashion, the nature of the activities proper to be demanded of the workman by the hirer and the relation of those activities to the activities of the hirer's own workmen are of outstanding importance in determining whether the hirer has in any reasonable sense authority to control the manner of execution of the workman's task. For instance, the position under the hirer of a craftsman entrusted for the hirer's purposes with the management of a machine belonging to his general employer, that machine demanding for its proper operation the exercise of technical skill and judgment, differs essentially from the position under the hirer of an agricultural labourer hired out for a period of weeks for general work. In the case of the craftsman the inference of fact may be drawn that he was not the servant of the hirer even though the bargain provided that he should be; and in the case of the agricultural labourer the inference of fact may be that he became the servant of the hirer, though the bargain provided that he should not be. The realities of the matter have to be determined. The terms of the bargain may colour the transaction; they do not necessarily determine its real character. . . .

Applying the general principles which I have stated to this case, the particular question to be determined is whether or not Coggins & Griffiths (Liverpool), Ltd. had authority to give directions as to the manner in which the crane was to be operated. To my mind it is clear they were not intended to have, and did not have, any such authority. The manner in which the crane was to be operated was and remained exclusively the workman's affair as the servant of the dock board. The workman, in saying in his evidence: "I take no orders from anybody," pithily asserted what was involved in the hiring out of the crane committed to his charge by the dock board and, so far as the company was concerned, gave an accurate legal picture of his relations to the company. The company's part was to supply him with work: he would do that work but he was going to do it for the dock board as their servant in his own way.

With respect to the authorities, I find myself in complete agreement with the observations made by the noble and learned Lord on the Woolsack, and I desire to refer to one matter only. The test suggested on *Nicholas'* case was as follows ([1945] K.B. 309 n., at pp. 311, 312):

> "One test in cases of a vehicle . . . lent with its service to a hirer, is this question: In the doing of the negligent act was the workman exercising the discretion given him by the general employer or was he obeying . . . a specific order of the party for whom upon his employer's direction he was using the vehicle . . . ?"

The test is not, I think, correct and, to my mind, the second question contained in the test leads to confusion. The proper test is whether or not the hirer had authority to control the manner of execution of the act in question. Given the existence of that authority, its exercise or non-exercise on the occasion of the doing of the act is irrelevant. The hirer is liable for the wrongful act of the workman, whether he gave any specific order or not. Where there is no such authority vested in the hirer, he may, by reason of the giving of a specific order, be responsible for harm resulting from the negligent execution of that order. But it is not every order given by the hirer that will result in liability attaching to him. The nature and terms of the order have to be considered. For instance, an order given to unload cargo from a particular hold in the ship would not—assuming that to be a proper operation—subject the hirer to liability for damage resulting from any negligent driving of the crane in carrying out the order. And lastly, where liability does attach to the hirer by reason of a specific order, that liability arises by the reason that in the particular matter he was a joint tortfeasor with the workman. The general relation arising out of the contract of hiring is in no way involved.

I would dismiss the appeal.

[LORD MACMILLAN delivered a speech agreeing that the appeal should be dismissed.]

Appeal dismissed

Question

If the driver (Newall) had been lifting a fragile load too jerkily would the respondents (the hirers) have been entitled to control *how* he wielded the crane? Does Lord Simonds' verbal antithesis between *what* the driver was to do and *how* he was to do it afford any help? (See Grunfeld (1947), 10 M.L.R. 203, at p. 207.)

Servants and Independent Contractors

O. Kahn-Freund (1951), 14 M.L.R. 504, at pp. 505–506

... The traditional test was that a person working for another was regarded as a servant if he was "subject to the command of the master as to the manner in which he shall do his work",[1] but if the so-called "master" was only in a position to determine the "what" and not the "how" of the services, the substance of the obligation but not the manner of its performance, then the person doing the work was said to be not a servant but an independent contractor, and his contract one for work and labour and not of employment. This distinction was based upon the social conditions of an earlier age: it assumed that the employer of labour was able to direct and instruct the labourer as to the technical methods he should use in performing his work. In a mainly agricultural society and even in the earlier stages of the Industrial Revolution the master could be expected to be superior to the servant in the knowledge, skill and experience which had to be brought to bear upon the choice and handling of the tools. The control test was well suited to govern relationships like those between a farmer and an agricultural labourer (prior to agricultural mechanisation), a craftsman and a journeyman, a householder and a domestic servant, and even a factory owner and an unskilled "hand". It reflects a state of society in which the ownership of the means of production coincided with the possession of technical knowledge and skill and in which that knowledge and skill was largely acquired by being handed down from one generation to the next by oral tradition and not by being systematically imparted in institutions of learning from universities down to technical schools. The control test postulates a combination of managerial and technical functions in the person of the employer, i.e. what to modern eyes appears as an imperfect division of labour. The technical and economic developments of all industrial societies have nullified these assumptions. The rule respondeat superior (and, one may add, the whole body of principles governing the contract of employment) "applies even though the work which the servant is employed to do is of a skilful or technical character, as to the method of performing which the employer himself is ignorant".[2] To say of the captain of a ship, the pilot of an aeroplane, the driver of a railway engine, of a motor vehicle, or of a crane,[3] that the employer "controls" the performance of his work is unrealistic and almost grotesque. But one need not think of situations in which the employee is physically removed from his employer's premises: a skilled engineer or toolmaker, draftsman or accountant may as often as not have been engaged just because he possesses that technical knowledge which the employer lacks. If in such a case the employee relied on the employer's instructions "how to do his work" he would be breaking his contract and possibly be liable to summary dismissal for having misrepresented his skill. No wonder that the Courts found it increasingly difficult to cope with the cases before them by using a

---

1. *Per* Bramwell L.J. in *Yewens v. Noakes* (1880), 6 Q.B.D. 530.
2. *Per* MacKinnon L.J. in *Gold v. Essex County Council*, [1942] 2 All E.R. at p. 244.
3. See *Mersey Docks and Harbour Board v. Coggins and Griffiths Liverpool, Ltd.*, [1947] A.C. 1; [1946] 2 All E.R. 345. In this case the House of Lords was compelled to give a new meaning to the "control" test, see *per* Lord Simon, [1946] 2 All E.R. at p. 348; *per* Lord Porter, at p. 351; *per* Lord Simonds, at p. 352; *per* Lord Uthwatt, at p. 353. See C. Grunfeld's Note in (1947), 10 M.L.R. 203.

legal rule which, as legal rules so often do, had survived the social conditions from which it had been an abstraction. The judgments in *Mersey Docks and Harbour Board* v. *Coggins & Griffiths*,[1] show plainly enough that the control test had to be transformed if it was to remain a working rule and to be more than a mere verbal incantation. . . .

Cassidy v. Ministry of Health

Court of Appeal   [1951] I All E.R. 574

The plaintiff lost the use of his left hand and had severe pain and suffering as a result of negligent treatment following an operation on his hand. The evidence showed a prima facie case of negligence on the part of persons in whose care the plaintiff was, although it was not clear whether this was to be imputed to Dr Fahrni, the full time assistant medical officer, or to the house surgeon, or to one of the nurses. The Court of Appeal held that the hospital authority was liable.

SOMERVELL L.J.: . . . The question whether the defendants are so responsible depends in the first instance on examination of the decision of this court in *Gold* v. *Essex County Council*.[2] To appreciate the problem it is necessary to go back to *Hillyer* v. *St. Bartholomew's Hospital (Governors)*.[3] That case is fully analysed and considered in *Gold's* case,[2] and it is unnecessary to repeat in any detail all that is there set out. In his judgment in *Hillyer's* case[3] Kennedy L.J. expressed the view ([1909] 2 K.B. 829) that a hospital, though responsible for the exercise of due care in selecting its professional staff, whether surgeons, doctors or nurses, was not responsible if they or any of them acted negligently in matters of professional care or skill. The other reasoned judgment, that of Farwell L.J. was based on narrower grounds. The Court of Appeal in *Gold* v. *Essex County Council*,[2] after considering that case and other authorities, and certain *dicta* in the House of Lords, decided that the statement of Kennedy L.J. so far as it related to nurses or those in the position of nurses, should not be followed. The question of doctors on the staff did not directly arise in *Gold's* case.[2]

The evidence as to Dr. Fahrni's position in the present case is that he was an assistant medical officer, that he received a sum in lieu of residential emoluments, which indicates that, if there had been accommodation, or, perhaps, if he had been a bachelor, he would have lived in, and that he was employed whole time. His engagement was subject to the standing orders of the council, but these are not before us. Dr. Ronaldson was a house surgeon working under Dr. Fahrni. The first question is whether the principles as laid down in *Gold's* case[2] cover them. In considering this, it is important to bear in mind that nurses are qualified professional persons. It is also important to remember, and MacKinnon L.J. emphasised this (*ibid.*, 244), that the principle of *respondeat superior* is not ousted by the fact that a "servant" has to do work of a skilful or technical character, for which the servant has special qualifications. He instanced the certified captain who navigates a ship. On the facts as I have stated them, I would have said that both Dr. Fahrni and Dr. Ronaldson had contracts of service. They were employed like the nurses as part of the permanent staff of the hospital. Lord Greene M.R. in *Gold's* case,[2] in considering (*ibid.*, 242) what a patient is entitled to expect when he knocks at the door of the hospital, comes to the conclusion that he is entitled to expect nursing, and, therefore, the hospital is liable if a nurse is negligent. It seems to me the

---

1. Lord Simon's formula (at p. 348) comes very near to what one may call the "subordination" or "organisation" test. Where does the authority lie to direct, or to delegate to the workman the manner in which he should do the work? Who delegates the discretion the workman exercises? Here subordination to the employer's managerial power is made the criterion, and this, it is submitted, is the only possible way of dealing with the matter in the conditions of modern industry.
2. [1942] 2 K.B. 293; [1942] 2 All E.R. 237.
3. [1909] 2 K.B. 820.

same must apply in the case of the permanent medical staff. A familiar example is an out-patient's ward. One may suppose a doctor and a sister dealing with the patients. It seems to me the patient is as much entitled to expect medical treatment as nursing from those who are the servants of the hospital. I agree that, if he is treated by someone who is a visiting or consulting surgeon or physician, he is being treated by someone who is not a servant of the hospital. He is in much the same position as a private patient who has arranged to be operated on by "X". . . .

SINGLETON L.J.: . . . In *Hillyer* v. *St. Bartholomew's Hospital Governors*[1] the plaintiff's arm was burned when he was on an operating table. The examination was conducted by a consulting surgeon attached to the hospital, and it was admitted that the relationship of master and servant did not exist between the defendants and the consulting surgeon. Farwell L.J. assumed that the nurses and carriers were servants of the defendants for general purposes, but added ([1909] 2 K.B. 826):

"... as soon as the door of the theatre or operating room has closed on them for the purposes of an operation . . . they cease to be under the orders of the defendants, and are at the disposal and under the sole orders of the operating surgeon until the whole operation has been completely finished; the surgeon is for the time being supreme, and the defendants cannot interfere with or gainsay his orders." . . .

I do not think that the words of Farwell L.J. to which I have referred, can be applied to the facts of this case. The plaintiff was in the care of the hospital authorities. Those responsible for the post-operational treatment were all full-time employees of the corporation and it seems to me that it is not necessary for the plaintiff to establish precisely which individual employee was negligent. . . .

DENNING L.J.: If a man goes to a doctor because he is ill, no one doubts that the doctor must exercise reasonable care and skill in his treatment of him, and that is so whether the doctor is paid for his services or not. If, however, the doctor is unable to treat the man himself and sends him to hospital, are not the hospital authorities then under a duty of care in their treatment of him? I think they are. Clearly, if he is a paying patient, paying them directly for their treatment of him, they must take reasonable care of him, and why should it make any difference if he does not pay them directly, but only indirectly through the rates which he pays to the local authority or through insurance contributions which he makes in order to get the treatment? I see no difference at all. Even if he is so poor that he can pay nothing, and the hospital treats him out of charity, still the hospital authorities are under a duty to take reasonable care of him just as the doctor is who treats him without asking a fee. In my opinion, authorities who run a hospital, be they local authorities, government boards, or any other corporation, are in law under the self-same duty as the humblest doctor. Whenever they accept a patient for treatment, they must use reasonable care and skill to cure him of his ailment. The hospital authorities cannot, of course, do it by themselves. They have no ears to listen through the stethoscope, and no hands to hold the knife. They must do it by the staff which they employ, and, if their staff are negligent in giving the treatment, they are just as liable for that negligence as is anyone else who employs others to do his duties for him. What possible difference in law, I ask, can there be between hospital authorities who accept a patient for treatment and railway or shipping authorities who accept a passenger for carriage? None whatever. Once they undertake the task, they come under a duty to use care in the doing of it, and that is so whether they do it for reward or not. It is no answer for them to say that their staff are professional men and women who do not tolerate any interference by their lay masters in the way they do their work. . . . The reason why the employers are liable in such cases is not because they can control the way in which the work is done—they often have not sufficient knowledge to do so—but because they employ the staff and have chosen them for the task and have in their hands the ultimate sanction for good conduct—the power of dismissal. . . .

---

1. [1909] 2 K.B. 820.

... I decline to enter into the question whether any of the surgeons were employed only under a contract for services, as distinct from a contract of service. The evidence is meagre enough in all conscience on that point, but the liability of the hospital authorities should not, and does not, depend on nice considerations of that sort. The plaintiff knew nothing of the terms on which they employed their staff. All he knew was that he was treated in the hospital by people whom the hospital authorities appointed, and the hospital authorities must be answerable for the way in which he was treated. ...

Notes

1. In *Roe* v. *Ministry of Health*, [1954] 2 Q.B. 66; [1954] 2 All E.R. 131, a hospital authority was held liable for the negligence of an anaesthetist who provided a regular service for the hospital but was also engaged in private practice. Somervell L.J. (at p. 79) regarded him as part of the permanent staff; Morris L.J. (at p. 91) said that he was part of the "organisation" of the hospital, and left open the question whether the hospital was under a personal non-delegable duty; Denning L.J. (at p. 82) adhered to what he had said in *Cassidy's* case (*ante*).

2. "The question may arise whether a hospital authority can be held liable for the negligence of someone who, on any principle, must be treated as an independent contractor and not as a servant, e.g. a surgeon not normally employed by the hospital at all, but engaged to perform a particular operation. If the relationship between the patient and the hospital were contractual, there is little doubt that there would be such liability, for on ordinary contractual principles, it could be said that the hospital is itself under a duty to see that due care is taken in treating the patients, either by its servants or by any other person to whom it entrusts the task of treating him ... If then, this would be the position were the duty a contractual one, is there any reason why it should not also be so where the duty is not contractual, as of course is the case with all National Health Service Hospitals?" (Atiyah, *Vicarious Liability in the Law of Torts* (London, 1967), p. 369). What answer to this question do the above cases suggest? (See too, *Macdonald* v. *Glasgow Western Hospitals Board of Management*, 1954 S.C. 453, where the Court of Session (I.H.) approached the question through a construction of the Act of Parliament establishing the N.H.S.).

Ready-Mixed Concrete (South-East), Ltd. v. Minister of Pensions and National Insurance

Queen's Bench Division   [1968] 1 All E.R. 433

These were three appeals, by way of cases stated, from determinations by the Minister whether each of three owner-drivers were employed under a contract of service for purposes of the National Insurance Act 1965, s. 1 (2). Only those who are so employed pay "Class One" contributions and, in turn, are entitled to certain types of social security benefit. Although not concerned with the imposition of vicarious liability, the case highlights the problems involved in applying traditional tests for identifying a contract of service in a modern "self-employment" situation.

A company in the Ready-Mixed Group organised a scheme for the delivery of ready-mixed concrete to its customers through so-called "owner-drivers" whom it hoped to give "an incentive to work for a higher return without abusing the vehicle in a way which often happens if an employee is given a bonus scheme related to the use of his employer's vehicle". The contract with each owner-driver contained many provisions suggestive of a high degree of control by the company: he was to buy the vehicle on hire-purchase from a finance company within the Group, but he was not to make alterations to, charge or sell the vehicle without the employing company's permission; on termination of his engagement the company had the option to purchase the vehicle from him; he was to make the vehicle available to the company at all times of the day and night, was to comply with all rules and regulations of the company, and was "to carry out all reasonable orders from any competent servant of the company as if he were an employee of the company", and he was not to engage in any other haulage business.

MACKENNA J.: . . . I must now consider what is meant by a contract of service. A contract of service exists if the following three conditions are fulfilled: (i) The servant agrees that in consideration of a wage or other remuneration he will provide his own work and skill in the performance of some service for his master. (ii) He agrees, expressly or impliedly, that in the performance of that service he will be subject to the other's control in a sufficient degree to make that other master. (iii) The other provisions of the contract are consistent with its being a contract of service. . . .

The third and negative condition is for my purpose the important one, and I shall try with the help of five examples to explain what I mean by provisions inconsistent with the nature of a contract of service.

(i) A contract obliges one party to build for the other, providing at his own expense the necessary plant and materials. This is not a contract of service, even though the builder may be obliged to use his own labour only and to accept a high degree of control: it is a building contract. It is not a contract to serve another for a wage, but a contract to produce a thing (or a result) for a price.

(ii) A contract obliges one party to carry another's goods, providing at his own expense everything needed for performance. This is not a contract of service, even though the carrier may be obliged to drive the vehicle himself and to accept the other's control over his performance: it is a contract of carriage.

(iii) A contract obliges a labourer to work for a builder, providing some simple tools, and to accept the builder's control. Notwithstanding the obligation to provide the tools, the contract is one of service. That obligation is not inconsistent with the nature of a contract of service. It is not a sufficiently important matter to affect the substance of the contract.

(iv) A contract obliges one party to work for the other, accepting his control, and to provide his own transport. This is still a contract of service. The obligation to provide his own transport does not affect the substance. Transport in this example is incidental to the main purpose of the contract. Transport in the second example was the essential part of the performance.

(v) The same instrument provides that one party shall work for the other subject to the other's control, and also that he shall sell him his land. The first part of the instrument is no less a contract of service because the second part imposes obligations of a different kind (*Amalgamated Engineering Union* v. *Minister of Pensions and National Insurance*).[1]

I can put the point which I am making in other words. An obligation to do work subject to the other party's control is a necessary, though not always a sufficient, condition of a contract of service. If the provisions of the contract as a whole are inconsistent with its being a contract of service, it will be some other kind of contract, and the person doing the work will not be a servant. The judge's task is to classify the contract (a task like that of distinguishing a contract of sale from one of work and labour). He may, in performing it, take into account other matters besides control. . . .

. . . The opinion of Lord Wright in *Montreal Locomotive Works, Ltd.* v. *Montreal and*

---

1. [1963] 1 All E.R. 864, at pp. 869, 870.

A.-G. for Canada,[1] forgotten by at least one of the counsel who argued the case, and discovered by Mr. Atiyah, must be mentioned here. . . .

. . . Mr. Atiyah cites . . . the following passage from Lord Wright's opinion:[2]

"In earlier cases a single test, such as the presence or absence of control, was often relied on to determine whether the case was one of master and servant, mostly in order to decide issues of tortious liability on the part of the master or superior. In the more complex conditions of modern industry, more complicated tests have often to be applied. It has been suggested that a fourfold test would in some cases be more appropriate, a complex involving (1) control; (2) ownership of the tools; (3) chance of profit; (4) risk of loss. Control in itself is not always conclusive. Thus the master of a chartered vessel is generally the employee of the shipowner though the charterer can direct the employment of the vessel. Again the law often limits the employer's right to interfere with the employee's conduct, as also do trade union regulations. In many cases the question can only be settled by examining the whole of the various elements which constitute the relationship between the parties. In this way it is in some cases possible to decide the issue by raising as the crucial question whose business is it, or in other words by asking whether the party is carrying on the business, in the sense of carrying it on for himself or on his own behalf and not merely for a superior."

. . . If a man's activities have the character of a business, and if the question is whether he is carrying on that business for himself or for another, it must be relevant to consider which of the two owns the assets ("the ownership of the tools") and which bears the financial risk ("the chance of profit", "the risk of loss"). He who owns the assets and bears the risk is unlikely to be acting as an agent or a servant. If the man performing the service must provide the means of performance at his own expense and accept payment by results, he will own the assets, bear the risk, and be to that extent unlike a servant. I should add that there is nothing in the Canadian case to support the view that the ownership of the assets is relevant only to the question of control. Lord Wright treats his three other tests as having a value independent of control in determining the nature of the contract. . . .

There is, . . . the dictum of Denning L.J. in *Bank voor Handel en Scheepvaart N.V.* v. *Slatford*,[3] repeated in his Hamlyn Lectures:

"In this connexion I would observe the test of being a servant does not rest nowadays on submission to orders. It depends on whether the person is part and parcel of the organisation."

This raises more questions than I know how to answer. What is meant by being "part and parcel of an organisation"? Are all persons who answer this description servants? If only some are servants, what distinguishes them from the others if it is not their submission to orders? Though I cannot answer these questions I can at least invoke the dictum to support my opinion that control is not everything. . . .

It is now time to state my conclusion, which is that the rights conferred and the duties imposed by the contract between Mr. Latimer and the company are not such as to make it one of service. It is a contract of carriage.

I have shown earlier that Mr. Latimer must make the vehicle available throughout the contract period. He must maintain it (and also the mixing unit) in working order, repairing and replacing worn parts when necessary. He must hire a competent driver to take his place if he should be for any reason unable to drive at any time when the company requires the services of the vehicle. He must do whatever is needed to make the vehicle (with a driver) available throughout the contract period. He must do all this, at his own expense, being paid a rate per mile for the quantity which he delivers.

---

1. [1947] 1 D.L.R. 161.
2. [1947] 1 D.L.R. at p. 169.
3. [1953] 1 Q.B. 248, at p. 290; [1952] 2 All E.R. 956, at p. 971.

These are obligations more consistent, I think, with a contract of carriage than with one of service. The ownership of the assets, the chance of profit and the risk of loss in the business of carriage are his and not the company's.

If (as I assume) it must be shown that he has freedom enough in the performance of those obligations to qualify as an independent contractor, I would say that he has enough. He is free to decide whether he will maintain the vehicle by his own labour or that of another, and, if he decides to use another's, he is free to choose whom he will employ and on what terms. He is free to use another's services to drive the vehicle when he is away because of sickness or holidays, or indeed at any other time when he has not been directed to drive himself. He is free again in his choice of a competent driver to take his place at these times, and whoever he appoints will be his servant and not the company's. He is free to choose where he will buy his fuel or any other of his requirements, subject to the company's control in the case of major repairs. This is enough. It is true that the company are given special powers to ensure that he runs his business efficiently, keeps proper accounts and pays his bills. I find nothing in these or any other provisions of the contract inconsistent with the company's contention that he is running a business of his own. A man does not cease to run a business on his own account because he agrees to run it efficiently or to accept another's superintendence.

. . .

Judgments accordingly

Questions

1. What would the result have been in the *Ready-Mixed* case had the Judge asked "Is this contract inconsistent with its being a contract for services?"

2. It has been suggested that the arrangement between the company and the "owner-drivers" was no more than "an elaborate incentive scheme" (by G. de N. Clark (1968), 31 M.L.R. 450). Does this alter the character of the relationship into one of service?

3. Under the contract with each owner-driver the company had to insure each vehicle in the owner-driver's name and charge the premiums to him, but monies received by the owner-driver under the insurance policy had to be used to repair and replace vehicles. Assume that due to the negligent driving of an owner-driver the vehicle was damaged and a third party was injured. How would the accident costs be absorbed? What difference would it make if the owner-driver was classified as an employee of the company? (For compulsory road traffic and employer's liability insurance provisions, see p. 670, post.)

The Police Act 1964

48. Liability for wrongful acts of constables.—(1) The chief officer of police for any police area shall be liable in respect of torts committed by constables under his direction and control in the performance or purported performance of their functions in like manner as a master is liable in respect of torts committed by his servants in the course of their employment, and accordingly shall in respect of any such tort be treated for all purposes as a joint tortfeasor.

(2) There shall be paid out of the police fund—

    (*a*) any damages or costs awarded against the chief officer of police in any proceedings brought against him by virtue of this section and any costs incurred by him in any such proceedings so far as not recovered by him in the proceedings; and

    (*b*) any sum required in connection with the settlement of any claim made against the chief officer of police by virtue of this section, if the settlement is approved by the police authority.

(3) Any proceedings in respect of a claim made by virtue of this section shall be brought against the chief officer of police for the time being or, in the case of a vacancy in that office, against the person for the time being performing the functions of the chief officer of police; and references in the foregoing provisions of this section to the chief officer of police shall be construed accordingly.

(4) A police authority may, in such cases and to such extent as they think fit, pay any damages or costs awarded against a member of the police force maintained by them, or any constable for the time being required to serve with that force by virtue of section 14 of this Act, or any special constable appointed for their area, in proceedings for a tort committed by him, any costs incurred and not recovered by him in any such proceedings, and any sum required in connection with the settlement of any claim that has or might have given rise to such proceedings; and any sum required for making a payment under this subsection shall be paid out of the police fund.

Notes

1. At common law a police officer is not a servant of the police authority: *Fisher v. Oldham Corpn.*, [1930] 2 K.B. 364; *Lewis v. Cattle*, [1938] 2 K.B. 454; [1938] 2 All E.R. 368; Geoffrey Marshall, *Police and Government* (London, 1965) comments on s. 48 of the 1964 Act: "the individual constable's 'responsibility to the law' for the exercise of his common law powers presumably remains compatible with this arrangement and means as much or as little as it did before the Act."

2. A servant of the Crown is not responsible for the torts of those in the same employment as himself: e.g. the First Lord of the Admiralty is not responsible for false imprisonment by his subordinates, *Fraser v. Balfour* (1918), 87 L.J.K.B. 1116 (H.L.). At common law the Crown itself enjoyed immunity from proceedings in tort, but the Crown Proceedings Act 1947 subjects the Crown to civil liability as if it were a private person of full age and capacity in respect of torts committed by its servants or agents. (See generally *Halsbury's Laws of England*, 4th Edn., vol. 1, paras. 191–194.) The Post Office cannot be made liable in tort: Post Office Act 1969, s. 29 (1). A public officer may, of course, be liable for his own torts, and exemplary damages may be available against such an officer for arbitrary and unconstitutional action (p. 403, *ante*).

2. LIABILITY FOR DELEGATED TASKS

(a) Driving a motor vehicle

Morgans v. Launchbury

House of Lords   [1972] 2 All E.R. 606

LORD WILBERFORCE: My Lords, this appeal arises out of a motor car accident in which the three respondents were injured. They were passengers in a Jaguar saloon which was registered in the name of the appellant; she was not using the car at the time. The other persons in it were the appellant's husband and a friend of his, Mr. D. J. Cawfield, who was driving: both were killed. It is not disputed that the accident was caused by the negligence of Mr. Cawfield. At first instance, the appellant was sued both in her personal capacity and as administratrix for her deceased husband; judgment was given against her in both capacities on the ground that both she personally and her husband, were vicariously liable for Mr. Cawfield's negligence. It is only in her personal capacity that she brings the present appeal and the question involved is therefore whether as owner of the car, and in the circumstances in which it came to be used and driven, she can be held vicariously liable for the negligence of the driver.

Some further facts require to be stated. Before their marriage the appellant and her husband each had their own car, but after they had been married about a year they decided to sell one, and the one sold was the husband's. The Jaguar was, in the appellant's words, regarded as "our car". It was freely used by either husband and wife; the husband normally used it every day to drive to and from his place of work seven miles from his home.

On the day of the accident, the husband had driven in the car to work. In the evening he telephoned to the appellant to say that he would not be returning home for his evening meal and that he was going out with friends. He visited a number of public houses and had drinks. At some stage he realised that he was unable to drive safely and he asked Mr. Cawfield to drive and gave Mr. Cawfield the keys. Mr. Cawfield drove the husband to other public houses. After the last one had been visited Mr. Cawfield offered the three respondents, one of whom was a friend of his, a lift in the car; and, soon after, the husband got into the back of the car and fell asleep: he was certainly and heavily intoxicated. Mr. Cawfield then drove off, not in the direction of the husband's home, but in the opposite direction, suggesting a meal before he finally drove the passengers home. Soon after, with Mr. Cawfield driving at 90 m.p.h., the car collided with an omnibus.

There was some important evidence as to the circumstances in which the appellant's husband may have asked Mr. Cawfield to drive. According to the appellant's evidence, her husband often liked to stay out and visit public houses. In her words, "We had an understanding, he had always told me he would never drive if he thought there was any reason he should not drive" and "it was an understanding, he told me, 'You need not worry, I would not drive unless I was fit to drive'." Some further questions were put to her and the judge felt entitled to find—

> "that he promised her he never would drive himself if he had taken more drink than he felt he should have, but would do one of two things, either get a friend to drive him, or ring her up and she would come and fetch him."

We must accept the tenor of this finding but it was to be understood in the context of discussion between husband and wife. It is unlikely that it was so crystal clear as it appears from the finding to have been. One other fact: there was no question of the appellant knowing that Mr. Cawfield drove or might drive the car that evening, and he was to her merely an acquaintance.

It is on these facts that liability for the injuries sustained by the respondents must be considered. Who could they sue? In the first place, there was the estate of Mr. Cawfield as the negligent driver; in the second, the estate of the husband who requested Mr. Cawfield to drive, this resting on the normal principle of the law of agency. But the respondents seek to go further and to place vicarious liability on the appellant. As to this, apart from the special circumstances of the "understanding" there would seem, on accepted principle, to be insuperable difficulties in their way. The car cannot by any fair process of analysis be considered to have been used for the appellant's purposes at the time of the accident. During the whole of the evening's progress it was as clearly used for the husband's purposes as any car should be; and if there was any doubt about this the separation from any possible purpose of the appellant's at the time of the accident can only be intensified by the fact that Mr. Cawfield, the husband's agent, was taking the car away from the appellant's (and the husband's) home for some fresh purpose. It seems clear enough that this was the purpose of Mr. Cawfield but even if one attributes this to her husband, I am unable to formulate an argument for attributing it to the wife.

It is said, against this, that there are authorities which warrant a wider and vaguer test of vicarious liability for the negligence of another; a test of "interest or concern".

Skilled counsel for the respondents at the trial was indeed able to put the word "concerned" and "interest" into the wife's mouth and it was on these words that he mainly rested his case.

On the general law, no authority was cited to us which would test vicarious liability on so vague a test, but it was said that special principles applied to motor cars. I should be surprised if this were so, and I should wish to be convinced of the reason for a special rule. But in fact there is no authority for it. The decisions will be examined by others of your Lordships and I do not find it necessary to make my own review. For I regard it as clear that in order to fix vicarious liability on the owner of a car in such a case as the present, it must be shown that the driver was using it for the owner's purposes, under delegation of a task or duty. The substitution for this clear conception of a vague test based on "interest" or "concern" has nothing in reason or authority to commend it. Every man who gives permission for the use of his chattel may be said to have an interest or concern in its being carefully used, and, in most cases if it is a car, to have an interest or concern in the safety of the driver, but it has never been held that mere permission is enough to establish vicarious liability. And the appearance of the words in certain judgments (*Ormrod* v. *Crosville Motor Services, Ltd.*[1] per Devlin J. and per Denning L.J.[2]) in a negative context (no interest or concern, therefore no agency) is no warrant whatever for transferring them into a positive test. I accept entirely that "agency" in contexts such as these is merely a concept, the meaning and purpose of which is to say "is vicariously liable" and that either expression reflects a judgment of value—respondeat superior is the law saying that the owner ought to pay. It is this imperative which the common law has endeavoured to work out through the cases. The owner ought to pay, it says, because he has authorised the act, or requested it, or because the actor is carrying out a task or duty delegated, or because he is in control of the actor's conduct. He ought not to pay (on accepted rules) if he has no control over the actor, has not authorised or requested the act, or if the actor is acting wholly for his own purposes. These rules have stood the test of time remarkably well. They provide, if there is nothing more, a complete answer to the respondents' claim against the appellant.

I must now consider the special circumstances on which the judge relied—the understanding between the appellant and her husband. What does it amount to? In my opinion, it is nothing more than the kind of assurance that any responsible citizen would give to his friends, any child would give to his parent, any responsible husband would give to his wife: that he intends to do what is his legal and moral duty; not to drive if in doubt as to his sobriety. The evidence is that this assurance originated from the husband and no doubt it was welcomed by the wife. But it falls far short of any authority by the wife to drive on her behalf or of any delegation by her of the task of driving. If the husband was, as he clearly was, using the car for his own purposes, I am unable to understand how his undertaking to delegate his right to drive to another can turn the driver into the wife's agent in any sense of the word. The husband remains the user, the purposes remain his. So if one applies accepted principles of the law, the case is clear; I only wish to add that I agree with the judgment of Megaw L.J. in the Court of Appeal[3] both on the law and the facts.

This is not the end of the case. The respondents submitted that we should depart from accepted principle and introduce a new rule, or set of rules, applicable to the use of motor vehicles, which would make the appellant liable as owner. Lord Denning M.R. in the Court of Appeal[4] formulated one such rule, based on the conception of a matrimonial car, a car used in common by husband and wife for the daily purposes of both. All purposes, or at least the great majority of purposes, he would say are matrimonial purposes: shopping, going to work, transporting children, all are purposes of

---

1. [1953] 1 All E.R. 711; [1953] 1 W.L.R. 409.
2. [1953] 2 All E.R. 753; [1953] 1 W.L.R. 1120.
3. *Morgans* v. *Launchbury*, [1971] 2 Q.B. 245, at p. 261; [1971] 1 All E.R. 642, at p. 652.
4. [1971] 2 Q.B. at p. 256; [1971] All E.R. at p. 648.

the owner, the car was bought and owned for them to be carried out. And, consequently (this is the critical step) the owner is ipso jure liable whatever the other spouse is using the car for, unless, it seems, although the scope of the exception is not defined, the latter is "on a frolic of his own". Indeed Lord Denning M.R.[1] seems to be willing to go even further and to hold the owner liable on the basis merely of permission to drive, actual or assumed.

My Lords, I have no doubt that the multiplication of motor cars on our roads, their increasing speed, the severity of the injuries they may cause, the rise in accidents involving innocent persons, give rise to problems of increasing social difficulty with which the law finds it difficult to keep abreast. And I am willing to assume (although I think that more evidence is needed than this one case) that traditional concepts of vicarious liability, founded on agency as developed in relation to less dangerous vehicles, may be proving inadequate. I think, too, although counsel for the appellant argued eloquently to the contrary, that some adaptation of the common law rules to meet these new problems of degree is capable of being made by judges. I do not have to depend on my own judgment for this for it can be seen that in the United States, so long ago as 1913, the judges in the state of Washington developed, without legislative aid, a new doctrine of the family car (*Birch* v. *Abercrombie*)[2] and some other states have, with variations, followed the same road (see Prosser on Torts).[3] Other states have resorted to statute. To be similarly creative, even 70 years later, has its attraction. But I have come to the clear conclusion that we cannot in this House embark on the suggested innovation. I endeavour to state some reasons.

1. Assuming that the desideratum is to fix liability in cases of negligent driving on the owner of the car (an assumption which may be disputable), there are at least three different systems which may be adopted: (a) that apparently advocated by Lord Denning M.R.[1] of a "matrimonial" car, the theory being that all purposes for which it is used by either spouse are or presumed to be matrimonial purposes; (b) that adopted in some American states of a "family" car, the theory being that any user by any member of the family is the owner's "business" (see Prosser);[3] (c) that any owner (including hire-purchaser) who permits another to use his motor vehicle on the highway should be liable by the fact of permission. This principle has been adopted *by statute* in certain Australian states (e.g. the Motor Vehicles Insurance Acts 1936–45 (Queensland), s. 3 (2)). Yet another possibility would be to impose liability on the owner in all cases regardless of whether he had given permission or not. My Lords, I do not know on what principle your Lordships acting judicially can prefer one of these systems to the others or on what basis any one can be formulated with sufficient precision or its exceptions defined. The choice is one of social policy; there are arguments for and against each of them. If any one is preferable on purely logical grounds, to me it is the third, for I am unable to state with any precision a rational (as opposed to a policy) preference for drawing a line at either of the alternative points, the spouses or the family. But apart from the unsupported statement by Lord Denning M.R. in the present case I know of no judicial pronouncement in favour of the third; indeed the cases, amongst them the judgments of Edmund Davies and Megaw L.JJ. below,[4] contain statements to the contrary, i.e. that mere permission is not in law a sufficient basis of liability. I do not doubt that this is the existing law nor the validity of the Australian position that to base liability on permission would be a matter for legislation.

2. Whatever may have been the situation in 1913 in the youth of the motor car, it is very different now, when millions of people of all ages drive for a vast variety of purposes and when there is in existence a complicated legislative structure as to in-

---

1. [1971] 2 Q.B., at p. 256; [1971] 1 All E.R. at p. 648.
2. (1913), 74 Wash. 486, 133 P 1020.
3. (3rd Edn., 1964), pp. 494 *et seq*.
4. [1971] 2 Q.B. 245; [1971] 1 All E.R. 642.

surance—who must take it out, what risks it must cover, who has the right to sue for the sum assured. Liability and insurance are so intermixed that judicially to alter the basis of liability without adequate knowledge (which we have not the means to obtain) as to the impact this might make on the insurance system would be dangerous, and, in my opinion, irresponsible.

3. To declare as from the date of the decision in this House that a new and greatly more extensive principle of liability was to be applied in substitution for well-known and certain rules might inflict great hardships on a number of people, and at least would greatly affect their assumed legal rights. We cannot, without yet further innovation, change the law prospectively only; and in any event this accident occurred in 1964, so any change if it were to be relevant to this case would have to date back until then. Such is the number of accidents now occurring, and the time which elapses before the damages are settled, that any decision in this case would affect, at the least, cases over the last eight years, the parties to which could justly expect to look to the established law to guide them, and whose insurances were arranged on the basis of established law.

My Lords, we may be grateful to Lord Denning M.R. for turning our thoughts in a new direction, a direction perceived, if not with unity of vision, by courts beyond the seas so long ago; but I must invite your Lordships to state that his judgment does not state the law. Any new direction, and it may be one of many alternatives, must be set by Parliament.

I would allow the appeal and dismiss the action.

LORD PEARSON: . . . It seems to me that these innovations, whether or not they may be desirable, are not suitable to be introduced by judicial decision. They raise difficult questions of policy, as well as involving the introduction of new legal principles rather than extension of some principle already recognised and operating. The questions of policy need consideration by the government and Parliament, using the resources at their command for making wide enquiries and gathering evidence and opinions as to the practical effects of the proposed innovations. Apart from the transitional difficulty of current policies of insurance being rendered insufficient by judicial changes in the law, there is the danger of injustice to owners who for one reason or another are not adequately covered by insurance or perhaps not effectively insured at all (e.g. if they have forgotten to renew their policies or have taken out policies which are believed by them to be valid but are in fact invalid, or have taken their policies from an insolvent insurance company). Moreover, lack of insurance cover would in some cases defeat the object of the proposed innovation, because uninsured or insufficiently insured owners would often be unable to pay damages, awarded against them in favour of injured plaintiffs. Any extension of car owners' liability ought to be accompanied by an extension of effective insurance cover. How would that be brought about? And how would it be paid for? Would the owner of the car be required to take out a policy for the benefit of any person who may drive a car? Would there be an exception for some kinds of unlawful driving? A substantial increase in premiums for motor insurance would be likely to result and to have an inflationary effect on costs and prices. It seems to me that if the proposed innovations are desirable, they should be introduced not by judicial decision but by legislation after suitable investigation and full consideration of the questions of policy involved.

I would allow the appeal.

[VISCOUNT DILHORNE, LORD CROSS OF CHELSEA AND LORD SALMON delivered speeches in favour of allowing the appeal.]

Appeal allowed

Questions

1. Megaw L.J. in his dissenting judgment in the Court of Appeal in this case, ([1971] 1 All E.R. 642), approved by Lord Wilberforce, said: "We do not have to decide what the position might have been if the accident had happened in

the course of a normal journey to or from work." What would the position have been?

2. A, a car owner, asks B, a passenger, to close the door of the car. B does so negligently, slamming the door on C's fingers. Is A liable in damages to C?

3. Mr. Morgans was not the registered owner of the car. Why was he vicariously liable for Cawfield's negligence? (See *Nottingham* v. *Aldridge*, [1971] 2 Q.B. 739; [1971] 2 All E.R. 751.)

4. Lord Denning M.R., in the Court of Appeal in this case ([1971] 1 All E.R. 642, at p. 647) said: "The words 'principal' and 'agent' are not used here in the connotation which they have in the law of contract (which is one thing), or the connotation which they have in the business community (which is another thing). They are used as a shorthand to denote the circumstances in which vicarious liability is imposed." Why is there no general principle in the law of tort that a "principal" is liable for the acts of his "agent"? (Note the remarks in the joint opinion of the House of Lords in *Heatons Transport (St. Helens), Ltd.* v. *Transport and General Workers Union*, [1972] 3 All E.R. 101, p. 645, *post*; and Atiyah, *Vicarious Liability in the Law of Torts* (London, 1967), Chap. 9.)

5. The Road Traffic Act 1972, ss. 143, 145 (p. 670, *post*) makes it a criminal offence for the owner to permit any other person to use it on the road unless there is in force a policy of insurance against risks of bodily injury or death to third parties. J. A. Jolowicz, [1972A] C.L.J. 209, at p. 210 asks: "Does it not follow that the owner, and thus his insurer, ought to be made civilly liable for the negligence of all permitted drivers?" How would such a change in the law affect (a) the insured owner and (b) the uninsured owner? Was Mrs. Morgans liable to be sued for breach of the statutory duty to insure? (See Chap. 20, p. 674, *post*.)

6. Would the same result be reached today in each of the following cases decided before the decision of the House of Lords in *Morgans* v. *Launchbury*, [1973] A.C. 127; [1972] 2 All E.R. 606.

    (a) A was negotiating the sale of his car to Mrs. C. He took her for a trial run allowing B, her son, to drive. A sat next to B. As a result of B's negligent driving, P was injured. A was liable because he had not abandoned his "right of control": *Samson* v. *Aitchison*, [1912] A.C. 844 (P.C.).

    (b) D drove E's car with E's consent. After setting down E, D took the car home and negligently parked it on a steep gradient without properly applying the hand brake. P was injured as a result. E was liable because he had the "right of control" even though he was not present: *Parker* v. *Miller* (1926), 42 T.L.R. 408.

    (c) G borrowed his father's (F) car to take home two girl-friends. F was not liable for G's negligent driving. Two reasons were suggested: (a) such liability depends not on ownership but on the delegation of a task or duty; (b) the father had no "social or moral duty" to convey the girls home: *Hewitt* v. *Bonvin*, [1940] 1 K.B. 188.

    (d) H took his car to J's garage for repairs. One of J's mechanics took H to the station in H's car. H was not responsible for the mechanic's negligent driving because H had lost the "right of control" by bailing the car to J: *Chowdhary* v. *Gillot*, [1947] 2 All E.R. 541.

(e) M asked O to drive M's Austin Healey from Liverpool to Monte Carlo. O collided with a bus due in part to his own negligence and, in part, to the negligence of the bus driver. O's wife was injured and she sued the bus driver's employer, who, in turn, brought the owner of the car, M, into the proceedings. At this time (which was prior to the enactment of the Law Reform (Husband and Wife) Act 1962) they could not bring in O's husband because spouses could not sue one another in tort. But if M were held responsible for O's driving, his insurance policy would cover his liability. M was held to be vicariously liable because the car was being used on M's business and for M's purposes: *Ormrod* v. *Crossville Motor Services Co., Ltd.*, [1953] 2 All E.R. 753.

(f) Q let R (his son) use the family car at night provided that Q's chauffeur drove. Q was liable for the chauffeur's negligent driving while on R's business, since he had asked the chauffeur to drive: *Carberry* v. *Davies*, [1968] 2 All E.R. 817; cf. *Rambarran* v. *Gurrucharran*, [1970] 1 All E.R. 749.

(b) Transactions with Third Parties

Udell v. Atherton

Court of Exchequer   (1861), 7 H. & N. 172

The plaintiff bought a log of mahogany from the defendant's agent (who was not their servant) having been induced to do so by certain fraudulent statements made by the agent. The plaintiff paid the defendants the price so obtained, which was twice the real value of the log. In an action for damages for deceit, the question in issue was whether, once the plaintiff had accepted the log, he could claim such damages. The Court of Exchequer was equally divided on this question. Wilde B. and Pollock C.B. found for the plaintiff, and Bramwell and Martin BB. for the defendants.

WILDE B.: I am of opinion that the rule ought to be absolute to enter the verdict for the plaintiff; and I have the authority of the Lord Chief Baron for saying that he agrees with the judgment. . . . It is said that a man who is himself innocent cannot be sued for a deceit in which he took no part, and this whether the deceit was by his agent or a stranger. To this, as a general proposition, I agree. All deceits and frauds practised by persons who stand in the relation of agents, general or particular, do not fall upon their principals. For, unless the fraud itself falls within the actual or the implied authority of the agent, it is not necessarily the fraud of the principal.

On this principle it was that the Court of Common Pleas, in *Grant* v. *Norway* (1851), 10 C.B. 665, held a shipowner not responsible for the fraud of the captain in signing bills of lading without any goods on board; and so, in the case of *Coleman* v. *Riches* (1839), 16 C.B. 104, a wharfinger was held not liable for a false receipt, which his agent had given, representing that goods had been received at the wharf which had not so been received. In neither of these cases did the principal authorise or in any way adopt or obtain the benefit of the fraudulent act. But does this principle apply to fraud committed in the making of contracts which the principal has adopted and of which he has claimed and obtained the benefit?

The contract is made by the agent for the principal, but when made, if authorised or adopted, it becomes in law the contract of the principal. Can the principal treat the contract as his, and repudiate the fraud upon which it was built as the agent's? In the making of the actual contract, when the agent speaks he does so with the voice of the principal, for it is the principal's contract he is making.

In the representations which immediately preceded the contract, is the agent speaking only for himself? If so, on what principle is it that the principal could not sue upon a contract in itself valid, but preceded and brought about by fraudulent representations of the agent? And yet this is the plain law.

This brings me to another difficulty. For it would surely be an anomalous state of things, that the innocent principal could not recover upon his contract because fraudulently obtained by his agent, but that, if before discovery the contract be performed, he may ever after keep the benefit of it. Can the buyer's right, upon any sound principle, be made to depend on the extent to which the transaction has been completed? If the fraud had been discovered before the log was cut, could not the buyer have rescinded the contract? If so, why may he not recover now, when the state of things is unaltered by any laches or default of his.

A distinction has indeed been made in equity between contracts performed and unperformed. The latter are sometimes set aside for mistake or surprise, while the former are not. But no such distinction has ever been made in favour of fraud. Fraud in all Courts and at all stages of the transaction, has, I believe, been held to vitiate all to which it attaches. . . .

The defendant has adopted the sale made by his agent and received the price. He has, by the fraudulent statements of the agent, obtained rather more than twice what he could have obtained by an honest sale. It is not the case of any matter collateral, as a warranty may be. It is not the case of a representation made out of and beyond the particular business then transacting by the agent on the principal's behalf. It is the representations made in the very dealing itself, in the conversation that resulted in the contract, that are in question.

The defendant claims the right of separating the contract from that which induced it, of holding the price and ignoring the false statements which largely enhanced it. In my opinion, justice, the common reason of mankind, and every sound rule of law are opposed to his doing so. Whatever his previous authority to the agent, whatever his own innocence, he must, as it seems to me, adopt the whole contract, including the statements and representations which induced it, or repudiate the contract altogether.

There are, no doubt, many frauds committed by agents which would not bind their principals. But I hold that the statements of the agent which are involved in the contract as its foundation or inducement are in law the statements of the principal. . . .

Notes

1. In *Lloyd* v. *Grace, Smith & Co.*, [1912] A.C. 716, the House of Lords approved Wilde B.'s statement, without expressly overruling the judgments of Bramwell and Martin BB. There is little doubt that Wilde B.'s judgment represents the modern law. Note that it is no longer necessary, in cases of fraud, to show that the fraud was for the employer's benefit (*Lloyd* v. *Grace, Smith & Co.*).

2. In *Armstrong* v. *Strain*, [1952] 1 K.B. 232; [1952] 1 All E.R. 139. the issue arose whether a principal can be held responsible for the misrepresentation of an agent where the agent making the statement honestly believed it to be true, but the principal knew it to be false but had not authorised the making of the statement. The Court of Appeal held that in the absence of actual fraud on the part of the principal, he was not liable for fraudulent misrepresentation. The traditional justification for this (see too *Cornfoote* v. *Fowke* (1840), 6 M. & W. 358) is that one cannot add two innocent states of mind to make a fraudulent state of mind. This, in turn, rests on the theory that vicarious liability is imposed on one person for the tort of another (e.g. Salmond, p. 463). Another view, that propounded by Glanville Williams (1956), 72 L.Q.R. 522, is that the

law attributes the *act* of the employee to his employer. It is the employer's duty which is broken. If this, the "master's tort" theory were applied to the facts of *Armstrong* v. *Strain* the principal would be liable for the composite fraud. (See too, p. 622, *post.*)

(c) Joint enterprises

Brooke v. Bool

King's Bench Division   [1928] All E.R. Rep. 155

The plaintiff was the tenant of certain premises and she requested her landlord, the defendant, to search for a suspected gas leak in her basement. The defendant procured the help of a third party, Morris, who applied a naked light to the pipe they were examining, with the result that there was an explosion damaging the plaintiff's property. The county court judge gave judgment for the defendant. An appeal against this judgment was allowed.

SALTER J.: ... In my opinion there are three grounds on which it was competent in law for the learned judge to find that the defendant was responsible for what was obviously a grossly reckless act on the part of Morris—namely, holding a naked light near to a place where he suspected an escape of gas. First, I think that there was evidence of agency. The defendant desired to examine this pipe, and examined it himself so far as he could in a most reckless and dangerous way with a naked light. He then desired to examine the upper part of it. Now the defendant was an old man of nearly eighty years of age, and he had in his company a much younger man. I think that there was ample evidence that the defendant impliedly invited and instructed Morris to get up on to the counter and complete the examination, when it was not convenient for him to continue it himself, and that Morris did what he did on the instructions of the defendant. The maxim *Qui facit per alium facit per se* applies, and on that first ground I think that there was evidence on which the judge could have found the defendant responsible.

Secondly, he could have been held responsible on the score of the control which he exercised over the proceedings. It is necessary to bear in mind the difference between the position of the defendant and that of Morris. The defendant was on the premises lawfully, at the request of the plaintiff, whereas Morris was a trespasser, unless the defendant had a right to invite him there to help. There was ample evidence on which the judge could find that the invitation by the plaintiff to the defendant to keep a watch over the premises extended to the right to bring in someone to help him on an occasion of that kind. In my opinion, Morris was there by the permission and invitation of the defendant, since otherwise he would have been a trespasser, and the defendant was in control of the enterprise. ...

Thirdly, I think that there was here a joint enterprise on the part of the defendant and Morris, and that the act which was the immediate cause of the explosion was their joint act done in pursuance of a concerted enterprise. ...

... Here the defendant and Morris went into the room, obviously proceeding by tacit agreement to examine this pipe and both employing the same negligent means. I think that what Morris did negligently was done by him in concert with the defendant and in pursuance of their common enterprise. In [a] passage to which I wish to refer, Scrutton, L.J. says:[1]

"I am of opinion that the definition in *Clerk and Lindsell on Torts* (7th Edn.) 59, is much nearer the correct view: 'Persons are said to be joint tortfeasors when their respective shares in the commission of the tort are done in furtherance of a common design ... but mere similarity of design on the part of independent actors, causing

1. *The Koursk*, [1924] P. 140, at p. 156.

independent damage, is not enough: there must be concerted action to a common end.'"

That appears to me precisely to describe this case, and on that third ground also I think that the county court judge was fully entitled in law to find for the plaintiffs . . .

TALBOT J.: I am of the same opinion, and I do not differ from the judgment just delivered or from any part of it. There is, I think, another principle on which the liability of the defendant can be satisfactorily based. . . .

In my opinion, the defendant having undertaken this examination was under a duty to take reasonable care to avoid damage resulting from it to the shop and its contents; and, if so, he could not escape liability for the consequences of failure to discharge this duty by getting (as he did) someone to make the examination, or part of it, for him, whether that person was an agent or a servant or a contractor or a mere voluntary helper. . . . The principle is that if a man does work on or near another's property which involves danger to that property unless proper care is taken, he is liable to the owner of the property for damage resulting to it from the failure to take proper care, and is equally liable, if, instead of doing the work himself, he procures another, whether agent, servant or otherwise, to do it for him. . . .

It appears to me, therefore, that the defendant is liable to the plaintiff for damage caused to her property by the negligence of Morris, who, by the defendant's authority, continued the examination of the premises which the defendant had undertaken and begun. It is, I think, a reasonable inference from the evidence that the defendant thought that Morris would use lighted matches just as he himself had been doing, but it is quite immaterial. It was the defendant's duty to take care that the dangerous operation which he had undertaken was done safely; and he is as much liable for the carelessness of Morris in doing part of the work as he would have been if he had done it himself in the same way.

Appeal allowed

Notes

1. The only other English case in which liability was imposed on the ground of joint enterprise is *Scarsbrook* v. *Mason*, [1961] 3 All E.R. 767, in which Glyn-Jones J. held that a passenger who had agreed to contribute 4s. towards the cost of petrol for a pleasure trip by car to Southend, was liable for the driver's negligence. He said: "They knew they were joining a party, all equally concerned in the trip to Southend, and that one member of the party was going to drive on behalf of the others, so that the party could get to Southend. The members of that party are jointly and severally liable for the manner in which that motor car was driven." Atiyah, *Vicarious Liability in the Law of Torts*, p. 124, suggests that "being a road traffic case [*Scarsbrook* v. *Mason*] may well have been influenced by special policy considerations." What are these policy considerations? How have they been affected by *Morgans* v. *Launchbury* (*ante*)? Atiyah, *loc. cit.*, discusses the American cases in which the tendency is to require something more than a mere common purpose in the journey.

2. What do you understand by Salter J.'s use of the word "agency"? Cf. p. 611, note 4, *ante*.

3. As regard Talbot J.'s alternative reason for holding the defendant liable, see p. 636, *post*.

4. In *R.* v. *Salmon* (1880), 6 Q.B.D. 79 (C.C.R.), a criminal case, several persons shot at a target in a negligent manner so that a stranger was killed. It was held that there was no need to show who fired the fatal shot. They were all principals in manslaughter. Do you agree with Gl. Williams (1953), 31 Can.

B.R. 315, at p. 316 that "had the marksmen been sued in tort they could well have been held joint tortfeasors"? Cf. *Cook* v. *Lewis*, [1951] S.C.R. 830; criticised by T. Brian Hogan (1961), 24 M.L.R. 331.

(d) Partners

The Partnership Act 1890

10. **Liability of the firm for wrongs.**—Where, by any wrongful act or omission of any partner acting in the ordinary course of the business of the firm, or with the authority of his co-partners, loss or injury is caused to any person not being a partner in the firm, or any penalty is incurred, the firm is liable therefor to the same extent as the partner so acting or omitting to act.

11. **Misapplication of money or property received for or in custody of the firm.** In the following cases; namely—

(*a*) Where one partner acting within the scope of his apparent authority receives the money or property of a third person and misapplies it; and

(*b*) Where a firm in the course of its business receives money or property of a third person, and the money or property so received is misapplied by one or more of the partners while it is in the custody of the firm;

the firm is liable to make good the loss.

12. **Liability for wrongs joint and several.**—Every partner is liable jointly with his co-partners and also severally for everything for which the firm while he is a partner therein becomes liable under either of the two last preceding sections.

3. THE COURSE OF EMPLOYMENT

Salmond on Torts (16th Edn., p. 474)

It is clear that the master is responsible for acts actually authorised by him: for liability would exist in this case, even if the relation between the parties was merely one of agency, and not one of service at all. But a master, as opposed to an employer of an independent contractor, is liable even for acts which he has not authorised, provided that they are so connected with acts which he has authorised that they may rightly be regarded as modes—although improper modes—of doing them . . . On the other hand if the unauthorised and wrongful act of the servant is not so connected with the authorised act as to be a mode of doing it, but is an independent act, the master is not responsible; for in such a case the servant is not acting in the course of his employment, but has gone outside of it.

Whatman v. Pearson

Court of Common Pleas   (1868), L.R. 3 C.P. 422

A contractor's men were allowed an hour for dinner but were not permitted to go home to dine or to leave their horses and carts unattended. One of the men went home about a quarter of a mile out of the direct line of his work to his dinner and left his horse unattended in the street before his door. The horse ran away and damaged the plaintiff's railings.

Byles J. reserved leave to the defendant to move to enter a non-suit on the ground that there was no evidence that the driver was acting in the scope of his employment. The Court of Common Pleas held that it was properly left to the jury to decide this question and that they were justified in finding that he was within the scope of his employment.

BYLES. J.: . . . When the defendant's servant left the horse at his own door without any person in charge of it, he was clearly acting within the general scope of his authority to conduct the horse and cart during the day. . . .

[BOVILL C.J., KEATING and MONTAGU SMITH JJ. delivered judgments in favour of refusing the rule.]

Rule refused

Storey v. Ashton

Court of Queen's Bench   (1869), L.R. 4 Q.B. 476

The defendant, a wine merchant, sent his carman and clerk with horse and cart to deliver wine. On their return, about a quarter of a mile from the defendant's offices, the carman was induced by the clerk, it being after business hours, to drive in another direction to visit the clerk's brother-in-law. While driving in that direction the plaintiff was run down due to the carman's negligent driving.

A verdict was directed for the defendant with leave to move to enter judgment for the plaintiff if the Court should be of opinion, on the evidence, that the defendant was responsible for the negligence of his servant. A rule having been obtained accordingly, the defendant showed cause. *Whatman* v. *Pearson* (*ante*) was referred to in argument in support of the rule, but is not discussed in the judgments.

COCKBURN C.J.: I am of opinion that the rule must be discharged. I think the judgments of Maule and Cresswell JJ. in *Mitchell* v. *Crassweller*[1] express the true view of the law, and the view which we ought to abide by; and that we cannot adopt the view of Erskine J. in *Sleath* v. *Wilson*,[2] that it is because the master has intrusted the servant with the control of the horse and cart that the master is responsible. The true rule is that the master is only responsible so long as the servant can be said to be doing the act, in the doing of which he is guilty of negligence, in the course of his employment as servant. I am very far from saying, if the servant when going on his master's business took a somewhat longer road, that owing to this deviation he would cease to be in the employment of the master, so as to divest the latter of all liability; in such cases, it is a question of degree as to how far the deviation could be considered a separate journey. Such a consideration is not applicable to the present case, because here the carman started on an entirely new and independent journey which had nothing at all to do with his employment. It is true that in *Mitchell* v. *Crassweller*[1] the servant had got nearly if not quite home, while, in the present case, the carman was a quarter of a mile from home; but still he started on what may be considered a new journey entirely for his own business, as distinct from that of his master; and it would be going a great deal too far to say that under such circumstances the master was liable.

[MELLOR and LUSH JJ. delivered judgments in favour of discharging the rule.]

Rule discharged

Notes

1. Compare the definition of the "act" found to be authorised in each of the above cases: in *Whatman* v. *Pearson* (1868), L.R. 3 C.P. 422 it was the "care and management of the vehicle"; in *Storey* v. *Ashton* (1869), L.R. 4 Q.B. 476 it was to drive the vehicle on a specific journey. In *Feldman* (*Pty.*), *Ltd.* v. *Mall*, 1945 A.D. 733, the Appellate Division of the Supreme Court of South Africa, rejecting *Storey* v. *Ashton*, said (*per* Tindall J.A. at p. 757) that a servant entrusted with the driving of a vehicle has a twofold duty: "to drive it for the [purposes authorised] and to keep control of it for his employer and return it to his employers' garage".

---

1. (1853), 13 C.B. 237.
2. (1839), 9 C. & P. 607, at p. 612.

2. In *Ruddiman & Co.* v. *Smith* (1889), 60 L.T. 708, the defendants were lessees of premises, occupying the upper floors themselves and sub-letting the ground floor and basement to the plaintiffs. An employee of the defendants left off work at seven o'clock in the evening and a few minutes afterwards went to the lavatory on the second floor to wash his hands before leaving. He went home without turning off the tap. The overflow of water broke through the floor on to the plaintiff's premises and damaged their goods. It was held by the Divisional Court that the employee's negligent act was an incident to the ordinary duties of his employment, and it was not less an incident that it was done when the day's work was over. Would the defendants have been liable had their employee negligently collided with another employee while going up the stairs after knocking-off? Was it material that the employee's negligence related to the employer's premises which, as an employee, he was under an implied obligation to his employer to protect?

3. In *Harvey* v. *R. G. O'Dell, Ltd.*, [1958] 2 Q.B. 78; [1958] 1 All E.R. 657, McNair J. held that it was "fairly incidental" to their work for employees to get a meal during working hours, so a journey for this purpose was held to be impliedly authorised. In *Hilton* v. *Burton (Rhodes), Ltd.*, [1961] 1 All E.R. 74, however, Diplock J. held that it was not within the course of their employment for a group of workmen to travel seven or eight miles from their work site for tea, immediately after finishing their lunch in a public-house. Does this mean (a) that a tea break immediately after lunch is not impliedly authorised, or (b) that, in the second case, the workmen had, in effect, finished off their work for the day? (See too, *Crook* v. *Derbyshire Stone, Ltd.*, [1956] 2 All E.R. 447.)

4. In *Kay* v. *I.T.W., Ltd.*, [1968] 1 Q.B. 140; [1967] 3 All E.R. 22, the issue was whether an employee instructed to drive a fork-lift truck had implied authority to remove obstacles in his path and, if so, what kind of obstacle. The Court of Appeal held that the removal of a five-ton diesel lorry was within the course of his employment. Although agreeing with this result, Danckwerts L.J. was led to say (at p. 27): "[i]t would be a good deal safer to keep lions or other wild animals in a park than to engage in business involving the employment of labour. In fact the position comes close to that in *Rylands* v. *Fletcher* (1868), L.R. 3 H.L. 330."

Century Insurance Co., Ltd. v. Northern Ireland Road Transport Board

House of Lords   [1942] 1 All E.R. 491

The respondent's employee, Davison, was delivering petrol from a tanker into the storage tank of a Belfast garage proprietor. While the petrol was flowing into the tank, Davison lighted a cigarette and threw away the lighted match causing a conflagration in which the tanker, a motor vehicle belonging to the garage proprietor, and several houses in the street were damaged. The appellants had insured the respondents against liability to third parties and, in answer to the claims based on this policy, one of their contentions was that the tanker driver's negligence was not done in the course of his employment so as to make the respondents liable.

The Court of Appeal of Northern Ireland held that the respondents were liable for the driver's negligence and were entitled to claim under the policy. The appellants appealed to the House of Lords. The appeal was dismissed.

LORD WRIGHT: ... The act of a workman in lighting his pipe or cigarette is an act done for his own comfort and convenience and at least, generally speaking, not for his employer's benefit. That last condition, however, is no longer essential to fix liability on the employer (*Lloyd* v. *Grace, Smith & Co.*).[1] Nor is such an act *prima facie* negligent. It is in itself both innocent and harmless. The negligence is to be found by considering the time when and the circumstances in which the match is struck and thrown down. The duty of the workman to his employer is so to conduct himself in doing his work as not negligently to cause damage either to the employer himself or his property or to third persons or their property, and thus to impose the same liability on the employer as if he had been doing the work himself and committed the negligent act. This may seem too obvious as a matter of common sense to require either argument or authority. I think that what plausibility the contrary argument might seem to possess results from treating the act of lighting the cigarette in abstraction from the circumstances as a separate act. This was the line taken by the majority judgment in *Williams* v. *Jones*,[2] from which Mellor and Blackburn JJ. as I think, rightly dissented. ...

[VISCOUNT SIMON L.C., with whom LORD ROMER concurred, delivered a speech in favour of dismissing the appeal. LORD PORTER concurred.]

Williams v. Jones

Court of Exchequer Chamber   (1865), 3 H. & C. 602

Defendant's employee negligently dropped a wood shaving, with which he had been lighting his pipe, causing a fire in the plaintiff's shed. A majority of the Court of Exchequer Chamber (Keating J., Erle C.J. and Smith J.) held that the defendants were not liable. Blackburn and Mellor JJ. dissented. Their judgments were approved by the House of Lords in *Century Insurance Co., Ltd.* v. *Northern Ireland Road Transport Board* (*ante*).

BLACKBURN J. (dissenting): ... Now the general rule of law is clear, that where the relation of master and servant exists between one directing a thing to be done and those employed to do it, the master is considered in law to do it himself, and as a consequence that the master is responsible, not only for the consequences of the thing which he directed to be done, but also for the consequences of any negligence of his servants in the course of the employment, though the master was no party to such negligence and even did his best to prevent it; as in the ordinary case where a master, selecting a coachman believed to be sober, sends him out with orders to drive quietly, and the coachman gets drunk and drives furiously. In such a case it may seem hard that the master should be responsible, yet he no doubt is if he be his master within the definition stated by Parke B. in *Quarman* v. *Burnett* ((1840), M. & W. 499, at p. 509), that the person is liable "who stood in the relation of master to the wrongdoer—he who had selected him as his servant, from the knowledge of or belief in his skill and care, and who could remove him for misconduct, and whose orders he was bound to receive and obey." But the master is not liable for any negligence or tort of the servant which is not in the course of the employment, for such negligence or tort cannot be considered as in any way the act of the master.

In the present case the difficulty is to apply these rules to the facts. It is said that Davies, the servant, was not employed by his master to smoke or to light his pipe, and that is no doubt true; but the act of lighting a pipe was in itself a harmless act; it only became negligent and a breach of duty towards the plaintiff because it was done when using his shed and working there amongst inflammable materials. Had the action been brought against Davies himself, it could not have been maintained for merely lighting his pipe, but that under the circumstances would have been evidence that he failed to take reasonable care when using the plaintiff's shed and working there, which

---

1. [1912] A.C. 716.
2. (1865), 3 H. & C. 602.

would have been the true ground of action. The action would have lain against Davies personally for negligence in doing that very thing which he was employed by the defendant to do as his servant and not otherwise. It seems to me, therefore, that it was negligence in the course of his employment, such as to be in law the negligence of his master, the defendant. The point is not one admitting of being elucidated by argument or by decided cases: in truth the whole case depends upon whether this is a correct statement of the effect of the facts . . .

Limpus v. London General Omnibus Co.

Court of Exchequer Chamber   (1862), 1 H. & C. 526

Bus drivers employed by the defendant company were expressly prohibited from racing with or obstructing the omnibuses of a rival bus company. In disregard of this instruction, and in order to obtain custom for his employer, one of the defendant's drivers raced with a rival's bus, causing considerable damage to the plaintiff.

MARTIN B. directed the jury "that, when the relation of master and servant existed, the master was responsible for the reckless and improper conduct of their servant in the course of the service; and that if the jury believed that the real truth of the matter was that the defendants' driver, being dissatisfied and irritated with the plaintiff's driver, whether justly or unjustly, by reason of what had occurred and in that state of mind acted recklessly, wantonly, and improperly, but in the course of his service and employment, and in doing that which he believed to be for the interest of the defendants, then the defendants were responsible for the act of their servant; that if the act of the defendants' driver, in driving as he did across the road to obstruct the plaintiff's omnibus, although a reckless driving on his part, was nevertheless an act done by him in the course of his service, and to do that which he thought best to suit the interest of his employers and so to interfere with the trade and business of the other omnibus, the defendants were responsible: that the liability of the master depended upon the acts and conduct of the servant in the course of the service and employment; and the instructions given to the defendants' driver, and read in evidence to the jury, were immaterial if the defendants' driver did not pursue them: but that if the true character of the act of the defendants' servant was, that it was an act of his own, and in order to effect a purpose of his own, the defendants were not responsible."

Defendant's counsel excepted to this ruling. The jury gave a verdict for the plaintiff. On error from the Court of Exchequer a majority of the Exchequer Chamber (CROMPTON, WILLES, BYLES and BLACKBURN JJ., WIGHTMAN J. dissenting) upheld MARTIN B.'s direction to the jury.

WILLES J. said—I am of opinion that the judgment of the Court below ought to be affirmed. The direction of my brother Martin was in accordance with principle and sanctioned by authority. It is well known that there is virtually no remedy against the driver of an omnibus, and therefore it is necessary that, for injury resulting from an act done by him in the course of his master's service, the master should be responsible; for there ought to be a remedy against some person capable of paying damages to those injured by improper driving. This was treated by my brother Martin as a case of improper driving, not a case where the servant did anything inconsistent with the discharge of his duty to his master, and out of the course of his employment. The defendants' omnibus was driven before the omnibus of the plaintiff, in order to obstruct it. It may be said that it was no part of the duty of the defendants' servant to obstruct the plaintiff's omnibus, and moreover the servant had distinct instructions not to obstruct any omnibus whatever. In my opinion those instructions are immaterial. If disobeyed, the law casts upon the master a liability for the act of his servant in the course of his employment; and the law is not so futile as to allow a master, by giving secret instructions to his servant, to discharge himself from liability. Therefore, I consider it immaterial that the defendants directed their servant not to do the act.

Suppose a master told his servant not to break the law, would that exempt the master from responsibility for an unlawful act done by his servant in the course of his employment? . . .

BYLES J. said,—I am also of opinion that the direction of my brother Martin was correct. He used the words "in the course of his service and employment", which, as my brother Willes has pointed out, are justified by the decisions. The direction amounts to this, that if a servant acts in the prosecution of his master's business for the benefit of his master, and not for the benefit of himself, the master is liable, although the act may in one sense be wilful on the part of the servant.

It is said that what was done was contrary to the master's instructions; but that might be said in ninety-nine out of a hundred cases in which actions are brought for reckless driving. It is also said that the act was illegal. So, in almost every action for negligent driving, an illegal act is imputed to the servant. If we were to hold this direction wrong, in almost every case a driver would come forward and exaggerate his own misconduct, so that the master would be absolved. Looking at what is a reasonable direction, as well as at what has been already decided, I think this summing up perfectly correct.

BLACKBURN J. said,—I am also of opinion that the direction of the learned Judge was sufficiently correct to afford the jury a guide in the particular case, which is all that is required. It is admitted that a master is responsible for the illegal act of his servant, even if wilful, provided it was within the scope of the servant's employment, and in the execution of the service for which he was engaged. That the learned Judge told the jury, and perfectly accurately, but that alone would not be enough to guide them in coming to a correct conclusion. It was necessary that the jury should understand the principles which they must apply in order to ascertain whether the act was done in the course of the servant's employment. It is upon that part of the summing up that Mr. Mellish has mainly pointed his argument, saying that it gave the jury a wrong guide.

Now, we must look at what the particular employment was, in order to see what was understood by the jury. The defendants' servant was the driver of an omnibus, and as such it was his duty, not only to conduct it from one terminus to another, but to use it for the purpose of picking up traffic during the course of the journey. He drove across another omnibus, under circumstances from which the jury might have thought that it was done for the purpose of reeking his spite against the driver of that omnibus. The learned Judge, having to tell the jury what was the test by which they were to determine whether the act was done in the course of the service or not, used language in which he tells them, perfectly rightly, that if the act was done in the course of the service the defendants were responsible; and he goes on to say, "that if the jury believed that the real truth of the matter was that the defendants' driver, being dissatisfied and irritated with the plaintiff's driver, whether justly or unjustly, by reason of what had occurred, and in that state of mind acted recklessly, wantonly, and improperly, but in the course of his service and employment, and in doing that which he believed to be for the interest of the defendants, then the defendants were responsible for the act of their servant." No doubt what Mr. Mellish said is correct: it is not universally true that every act done for the interest of the master is done in the course of the employment. A footman might think it for the interest of his master to drive the coach, but no one could say that it was within the scope of the footman's employment, and that the master would be liable for damage resulting from the wilful act of the footman in taking charge of the horses. But, in this case, I think the direction given to the jury was a sufficient guide to enable them to say whether the particular act was done in the course of the employment. The learned Judge goes on to say the instructions given to the defendants' servant were immaterial if he did not pursue them (upon which all are agreed); and at the end of his direction he points out that, if the jury were of opinion "that the true character of the act of the defendants' servant was that it was an act of

his own and in order to effect a purpose of his own, the defendants were not responsible." That meets the case which I have already alluded to. If the jury should come to
the conclusion that he did the act, not to further his master's interest or in the course of
his employment, but from private spite, and with the object of injuring his enemy,
the defendants were not responsible. That removes all objection, and meets the suggestion that the jury may have been misled by the previous part of the summing up. . . .

Notes

1. Despite instructions not to do so a bus driver permitted an unauthorised
person to take control of the wheel. This was held to be within the course of
his employment: *Ilkiw v. Samuels*, [1963] 2 All E.R. 879. "The driver of the
vehicle . . . was employed not only to drive but also to be in charge of the
vehicle in all circumstances during such time as he was on duty" (Willmer
L.J. at p. 885). "The express prohibition was . . . a prohibition on the mode in
which he was to do that which he was employed to do, a prohibition dealing
with conduct within the sphere of employment" (Diplock L.J. at p. 889).

2. Despite an instruction not to drive cars out of a parking garage, an
attendant moved a vehicle on to the highway in order to make room for other
vehicles. His employer was held liable for his negligent driving: *L.C.C. v.
Cattermoles (Garages), Ltd.*, [1953] 2 All E.R. 582.

Twine v. Bean's Express, Limited

King's Bench Division   [1946] 1 All E.R. 202

UTHWATT J.: Under an arrangement between Bean's Express Ltd., and the Post
Office Savings Bank, Bean's provided for use by the bank a commercial van and a
driver—Harrison—on terms under which the driver of the van remained the servant
of Bean's, it being part of the bargain between Bean's and the bank that Bean's accepted
no responsibility for injury suffered by persons riding in the van who were not in the
employment of Bean's. The standing instructions to Bean's drivers, which had been
duly brought to the attention of Harrison, provided that no persons (with certain
exceptions not applicable in this case) were allowed to travel on the company's commercial vehicles. On April 6, 1944, Twine, a mail porter employed by the bank, who
had occasion in the course of his duties to go from the bank's headquarters at Hammersmith to a branch office in Kensington, took a lift back from the branch office in the
van which was duly engaged on an authorised journey. Twine did so with the assent
of the driver, but Twine was not authorised by the bank to travel on the van. He had,
in fact, drawn 3d. to cover his bus fare to the branch and back. Twine had travelled on
the van on several prior occasions. There was, at all material times, on the dashboard of
the van a notice:

No unauthorised person is allowed on this vehicle. By order. Bean's Express, Ltd.

On the roof of the van, above the driver's seat, was another notice stating that drivers
had instructions not to allow unauthorised travellers on the van, and that in no event
would Bean's be responsible for damage happening to them. The driver, had, on the
occasion of a former ride in the van by Twine, told him, in substance, that he travelled
at his own risk. He probably put his point more crisply. His description to the court
was that he was not going to take any blame home with him. Unfortunately, owing to
the negligent driving of the driver, an accident occurred resulting in Twine's death.

Those are the facts as I find them. The plaintiff is the widow and legal personal
representative of Twine and brings the action against Bean's, claiming damages for
the benefit of herself and her two infant children under the Fatal Accidents Acts 1846
to 1908, and damages for the benefit of Twine's estate under the Law Reform (Mis-

cellaneous Provisions) Act, 1934. The argument for the plaintiff was put on the following lines. It was said that the driver was negligent and owed to Twine a duty to take care, that the accident happened while the driver was engaged on a duly authorised job in the course of his employment, and that the acts of the driver were done in the course of his employment, notwithstanding the unauthorised presence in the van of the passenger: the employer, therefore, was liable.

The complete accuracy of the second limb of the first proposition may well be questioned in light of the driver's warning to the passenger and the surrounding circumstances, but the defendants were content to fight the case on the lines that the question to be decided was not whether the driver owed a duty to the passenger to take care, but whether the employers owed that duty. In this, I think, the defendants are right. The law attributes to the employer the acts of a servant done in the course of his employment and fastens upon him responsibility for those acts. In determining the duty of the employer and the duty of the servant on any occasion, all the circumstances have to be considered. In the general run of cases, the duty of both is the same; but that is a coincidence, not a rule of law. The general question in an action against the employer, such as the present, is technically: "Did the employer in the circumstances which affected him owe a duty?"—for the law does not attribute to the employer the liability which attaches to the servant. To accord with my view of the law, the first proposition, to be relevant, should be stated thus: "The driver was negligent and the employers owed to Twine a duty (in this case to be performed by the driver) to take care."

On the facts as I have stated them, it was outside the scope of the driver's employment for him to bring within the class of persons to whom a duty to take care was owed by the employer, a man to whom, contrary to his instructions, he gave a lift on a commercial van. On this basis, Twine, *vis-à-vis* Bean's, remained simply a trespasser on the van, who came there in particular circumstances, and the question is whether Bean's, in the circumstances in which Twine was a passenger, owed to him any duty to take care as to the proper driving of the van. In my opinion, they did not. . . .

It is unnecessary for me to consider whether or not the effect of the notices and the driver's warning operated, as a matter of bargain, to deprive the passenger of any right of action against the employers. On the pleadings this point was not open to the defendants, and, indeed, was not argued by them.

There will, therefore, be judgment for the defendants.

[An appeal was dismissed by the Court of Appeal: (1946), 175 L.T. 131.]

Notes

1. In *Conway* v. *George Wimpey & Co., Ltd.*, [1951] 2 K.B. 266; [1951] 1 All E.R. 363, Asquith L.J. treated *Twine's* case as having a double *ratio decidendi*: (a) that the deceased was a trespasser; (b) that the giving of the lift was outside the scope of the driver's employment. (For comment see, Atiyah, *Vicarious Liability in the Law of Torts*, p. 29; Weir, *Casebook on Tort* (2nd Edn.), p. 206.)

2. Professor F. H. Newark, "Twine v. Bean's Express Ltd." (1954), 17 M.L.R. 102, rejects both the "no duty to a trespasser" and the "scope of employment" explanations. His conclusions are:

"1. The general principle enunciated in *Twine's* case, that in master and servant cases where the plaintiff sues in negligence it is the duty of the master which has to be considered, is erroneous and is inconsistent with the essential nature of vicarious liability.

2. In so far as the plaintiff in *Twine's* case failed because Twine was a trespasser on the vehicle, the decision is wrong because the fact that Twine was a trespasser would be material only in a claim based on the unsafe condition of the vehicle.

3. In so far as the plaintiff in *Twine's* case failed because the servant acted outside the scope of his employment in giving Twine a lift, the decision is wrong because Twine was not injured by this act, but by the subsequent negligent driving of the servant.

4. Any claim against the master by an unauthorised passenger whom the servant has permitted aboard the vehicle is barred by the fact that the master can take advantage of the implied term in the contract between servant and passenger that the master is to be exempt from liability for negligence (*Sed quaere*)."

The fourth point could not be argued in respect of facts which arose after 1 December 1972: s. 148 (3) of the Road Traffic Act 1972 prevents such exclusion of legal liability to a passenger either through contract or by operation of the defence of *volenti non fit injuria* (p. 671, post).

3. In *Young* v. *Edward Box & Co., Ltd.*, [1951] 1 T.L.R. 789 (C.A.), Denning L.J. expressed the view that the liability of the owner of a vehicle whose driver gives an unauthorised lift "does not depend upon whether the passenger was a trespasser or not; it depends upon whether the driver was acting in the course of his employment in giving the man a lift." So it would usually not be in the course of employment to give a hitch-hiker a lift, but it would be to give a fellow-servant a lift, even though the giving of such lifts had not been authorised.

Poland v. John Parr and Sons

Court of Appeal   [1926] All E.R. Rep. 177

Hall, a carter employed by the defendants, honestly and reasonably believed that the plaintiff, a boy aged twelve years, was pilfering or about to pilfer sugar from a bag on the defendant's wagon. He hit him on the back of the neck, causing him to fall under one of the wheels of the wagon, which injured his foot. In an action for damages judgment was entered against the defendants in the Liverpool Court of Passage. The defendants appealed.

SCRUTTON L.J.: . . . In order to make a master liable for the act of a person alleged to be his servant, the act must be one of a class of acts which the person was authorised or employed to do. If the act complained of is one of that class, the master is liable, although the act is done negligently, or, in some cases, even if it is done with excessive violence. But the excess may be so great as to take the act in question out of the class of acts which the person is employed or authorised to do. Whether it is so or not is a question of degree. It has been argued that a master cannot be liable if the act of his servant is illegal or excessive. In my opinion, *Dyer* v. *Munday*[1] negatives the proposition that a master cannot be liable if the act of his servant is illegal. In that case, Lord Esher M.R. put the question whether the act complained of was or was not for the master's benefit. That may be one test, but where excessive violence is charged, another question must be considered—namely, whether the excess is such as to take the act complained of out of the class of authorised acts. It was also argued that a master could not authorise an act which he could not lawfully do himself. But in many cases masters have been held responsible for acts of their servants which, if done by themselves, would have been illegal. . . .

ATKIN L.J.: . . . Any servant is, as a general rule, authorised to do acts which are for the protection of his master's property. I say "authorised", for although there are acts which the servant is bound to do, and for which, therefore, his master is responsible, it does not follow that the servant must be bound to do an act in order to make his master responsible for it. For example, a servant may be authorised to stop a runaway

---

1. [1895] 1 Q.B. 742.

horse, but it would be hard to say that every servant was bound to do this, or that a servant commits a breach of his duty if he refrains from doing so, or if he refrains from extinguishing a fire. Some men may have the necessary courage to encounter such dangers, others may shrink from facing them. It cannot be said that all are bound to face such dangers. Thus there is a class of acts which, in an emergency, a servant, though not bound, is authorised to do. And then the question is not whether the act of the servant was for the master's benefit, but whether it is an act of this class. I agree that, where the servant does more than the emergency requires, the excess may be so great as to take the act out of the class. For example, if Mr. Hall had fired a shot at the boy, the act might have been in the interests of his masters, but that is not the test. The question is whether the act is one of the class of acts which the servant is authorised to do in an emergency.

In the present case, Mr. Hall was doing an act of this class—namely, protecting his masters' property, which was or which he reasonably and honestly thought was being pillaged. His mode of doing the act is not, in my opinion, such as to take the act out of the class. He was, therefore, doing an authorised act for which the defendants are responsible. The appeal must be allowed and judgment must be entered for the plaintiff.

[BANKES L.J. delivered a judgment agreeing that the appeal should be allowed.]

Appeal allowed

Warren v. Henley's, Ltd.

King's Bench Division   [1948] 2 All E.R. 935

Beaumont, employed by the defendants as a petrol pump attendant, erroneously accused the plaintiff, in violent language, of having tried to drive away without paying for petrol which had been put into the tank of his car. The plaintiff paid his bill, called the police and told the pump attendant that he would be reported to his employers. The attendant then assaulted and injured the plaintiff, who brought this action for damages against the defendants who were held not liable.

HILBERY J.: . . . Is there any evidence here on which a jury could find that this assault, committed in the circumstances which I have just given, was so connected with the acts which the servant was expressly or impliedly authorised to do as to be a mode of doing those acts? It seems to me the answer must be "No". Of course, as in *Dyer* v. *Munday*,[1] if a manager, who, in the course of the very duties in the business goes to recover furniture, so conducts himself in recovering the furniture that he commits an assault, that is a tortious mode of doing the class of act which he is authorised to do. . . . Clearly, there is no evidence here that this act belonged to the class of acts that Beaumont was authorised to do. In extension of what Scrutton L.J., has said, I have also examined the matter in the light of that statement of the law which I have already read from Salmond on Torts, so as to ask whether, although it was not of the class of acts which Beaumont was authorised to do, it was so connected with that class of acts as to be a mode of doing some act within that class. It seems to me that it was an act entirely of personal vengeance. He was personally inflicting punishment, and intentionally inflicting punishment, on the plaintiff because the plaintiff proposed to take a step which might affect Beaumont in his own personal affairs. It had no connection whatever with the discharge of any duty for the defendants. The act of assault by Beaumont was done by him in relation to a personal matter affecting his personal interests, and there is no evidence that it was otherwise. . . .

Morris v. C. W. Martin & Sons, Ltd.

Court of Appeal   [1965] 2 All E.R. 725

The plaintiff sent her mink stole to Mr. Beder, a furrier, for cleaning. With her consent, he sent it to the defendants, one of the biggest cleaners in the country, who knew

1. [1895] 1 Q.B. 742.

that it belonged to an unspecified customer of Mr. Beder. The current trade conditions were that "goods belonging to customers" on the defendant's premises were held at the customer's risk and the defendants would "not be responsible for loss or damage however caused". Whilst the fur was with the defendants, it was stolen by one of their employees, named Morrissey.

The plaintiff brought an action for damages for loss of the fur against the defendants. The trial judge found that the defendants were not negligent in employing Morrissey, that they had taken all proper steps to safeguard the fur while on their premises and that the act of Morrissey was not done in the scope of his employment. He gave judgment for the defendants. An appeal by the plaintiff was allowed by the Court of Appeal.

LORD DENNING M.R.: . . . The law on this subject has developed greatly over the years. During the nineteenth century it was accepted law that a master was liable for the dishonesty or fraud of his servant if it was done in the course of his employment *and* for his master's benefit. Dishonesty or fraud by the servant for his *own* benefit took the case out of the course of his employment. The judges took this simple view: No servant who turns thief and steals is acting in the course of his employment. He is acting outside it altogether. But in 1912 the law was revolutionised by the case of *Lloyd* v. *Grace, Smith & Co.*,[1] where it was held that a master was liable for the dishonesty or fraud of his servant if it was done within the course of his employment, no matter whether it was done for the benefit of the master or for the benefit of the servant. Nevertheless there still remains the question: What is meant by the phrase "in the course of his employment"? When can it be said that the dishonesty or fraud of a servant, done for his *own* benefit, is in the course of his employment?

On this question the cases are baffling. In particular those cases, much discussed before us, where a bailee's servant dishonestly drives a vehicle for his own benefit. These stretch from *The Coupé Co.* v. *Maddick*[2] to the present day. Let me take an illustration well fitted for a moot. Suppose the owner of a car takes it to a garage to be repaired. It is repaired by a garage hand who is then told to drive it back to the owner. But instead, he takes it out on a "frolic of his own" (to use the nineteenth century phrase) or on a "joy-ride" (to come into the twentieth century). He takes it out, let us say, on a drunken escapade or on a thieving expedition. Nay more, for it is all the same, let us suppose the garage-hand steals the car himself and drives off at speed. He runs into a motor-cyclist. Both the car and the motor-cycle are damaged. Both owners sue the garage proprietor for the negligence of his servant. The motor-cyclist clearly cannot recover against the garage proprietor for the simple reason that at the time of the accident the servant was not acting in the course of his employment; see *Storey* v. *Ashton*.[3] You might think also that the owner of the car could not recover, and for the self-same reason, namely, that the servant was *not* acting in the course of his employment. Before 1912 the courts would undoubtedly have so held; see *Sanderson* v. *Collins*,[4] *Cheshire* v. *Bailey*,[5] as explained by Lord Shaw of Dunfermline in *Lloyd* v. *Grace, Smith & Co.*[6] itself. But since 1912 it seems fairly clear that the owner of the damaged car could recover from the garage proprietor; see *Central Motors (Glasgow), Ltd.* v. *Cessnock Garage & Motor Co.*,[7] on the ground that, although the garage-hand was using the car for his own private purposes, "he should be regarded as still acting in the course of his employment" (see *Aitchison* v. *Page Motors, Ltd.*):[8] and even if he stole the car on the journey, it was a conversion "in the course of the employment" (see *United Africa Co., Ltd.* v. *Saka Owoade* (1954)).[9] I ask myself, how can this be? How can the servant

1. [1912] A.C. 716; [1911–13] All E.R. Rep. 51.
2. [1891] 2 Q.B. 413; [1891–94] All E.R. Rep. 914.
3. (1869), L.R. 4 Q.B. 476.
4. [1904] 1 K.B. 628; [1904–7] All E.R. Rep. 561.
5. [1905] 1 K.B. 237; [1904–7] All E.R. Rep. 882.
6. [1912] A.C. at p. 741; [1911–13] All E.R. Rep. at p. 62.
7. 1925 S.C. 796.
8. [1935] All E.R. Rep. 594, at pp. 596–598.
9. [1955] A.C. 130, at p. 144; [1957] 3 All E.R. 216, at p. 247.

on one and the same journey, be acting both within and without the course of his employment? Within qua the car owner. Without qua the motor-cyclist. It is time we got rid of this confusion. And the only way to do it, so far as I can see, is by reference to the duty laid by the law on the master. The duty of the garage proprietor to the owner of the car is very different from his duty to the motor-cyclist. He owes to the owner of the car the duty of a bailee for reward, whereas he owes no such duty to the motor-cyclist on the road. He does not even owe him a duty to use care not to injure him.

If you go through the cases on this difficult subject, you will find that in the ultimate analysis, they depend on the nature of the duty owed by the master towards the person whose goods have been lost or damaged. If the master is under a duty to use due care to keep goods safely and protect them from theft and depredation, he cannot get rid of his responsibility by delegating his duty to another. If he entrusts that duty to his servant, he is answerable for the way in which the servant conducts himself therein. No matter whether the servant be negligent, fraudulent, or dishonest, the master is liable. But not when he is under no such duty. The cases show this:

(i) *Gratuitous bailment.* Suppose I visit a friend's house and leave my coat with his servant in the hall, so that my friend becomes a gratuitous bailee of it (see *Ultzen* v. *Nicols*).[1] On my departure, I find that my coat has gone. The servant who was entrusted with it has stolen it without my friend's fault. He has converted it, it may be said, in the course of his employment. Nevertheless my friend is not liable for the loss, because he was not under any duty to prevent it being stolen, but only to keep it as his own. "So far is the law from being unreasonable" said Sir John Holt C.J. "as to charge a man for doing such a friendly act for his friend"; see *Coggs* v. *Bernard*,[2] and *Giblin* v. *McMullen*,[3] where it was assumed, rightly or wrongly, that the bank was a gratuitous bailee.

(ii) *Occupier's liability for visitor's belongings.* Suppose an actor leaves his belongings in his dressing room. The porter negligently leaves the stage door unattended. A thief slips in and steals the actor's belongings. The porter was negligent in the course of his employment. Nevertheless the occupiers of the theatre are not liable for the loss, for the simple reason that they were under no duty to protect the actor's belongings from theft; see *Deyong* v. *Shenburn*[4] and *Edwards* v. *West Herts. Group Hospital Management Committee*.[5]

(iii) *Bailment for reward.* Once a man has taken charge of goods as a bailee for reward, it is his duty to take reasonable care to keep them safe; and he cannot escape that duty by delegating it to his servant. If the goods are lost or damaged, whilst they are in his possession, he is liable unless he can show—and the burden is on him to show—that the loss or damage occurred without any neglect or default or misconduct of himself or of any of the servants to whom he delegated his duty. This is clearly established by *Reeve* v. *Palmer*,[6] *Coldman* v. *Hill*,[7] and *Building and Civil Engineering Holidays Scheme Management, Ltd.* v. *Post Office*.[8] There is an old case at nisi prius apparently to the contrary. It is *Finucane* v. *Small*[9] where Lord Kenyon is reported to have said that the bailor must prove that the loss was caused by the negligence of the bailee. That was clearly wrong. The bailee, to excuse himself, must show that the loss was without any fault on his part or on the part of his servants. If he shows that he took due care to employ trustworthy servants, and that he and his servants exercised all diligence, and

---

1. [1894] 1 Q.B. 92; [1891–94] All E.R. Rep. 1202.
2. (1703), 2 Ld. Raym. 909, at p. 914.
3. (1868), L.R. 2 P.C. 317.
4. [1946] K.B. 227; [1946] 1 All E.R. 226.
5. [1957] 1 All E.R. 541.
6. (1858), 5 C.B.N.S. 84.
7. [1919] 1 K.B. 443; [1918–19] All E.R. Rep. 434.
8. [1965] 1 All E.R. 163, at p. 167.
9. (1795), 1 Esp. 315, at p. 318.

yet the goods were stolen, he will be excused; but not otherwise. Take a case where a cleaner hands a fur to one of his servants for cleaning, and it is stolen. If the master can prove that thieves came in from outside and stole it without the fault of any of his servants, the master is not liable. But if it appears that the servant to whom he entrusted it was negligent in leaving the door unlocked, or collaborated with the thieves, or stole the fur himself, then the master is liable; see *Southcote's Case*,[1] *United Africa Co., Ltd.* v. *Saka Owoade* (1954),[2] and *R.* v. *Levy*.[3]

(iv) *Contract to take care to protect the goods.* Although there may be no bailment, nevertheless circumstances often arise in which a person is under a contractual duty to take care to protect goods from theft or depredation; see, for instance, *Stansbie* v. *Troman*.[4] The most familiar case is the keeper of a boarding-house or a private hotel. He is under an implied contract to take reasonable care for the safety of property brought into the house by a guest. If his own servants are negligent and leave the place open so that thieves get in and steal, he is liable; see *Dansey* v. *Richardson*,[5] and *Scarborough* v. *Cosgrove*.[6] So also if they are fraudulent and collaborate with the thieves. Again when a job-master lets out a brougham and coachman, he undertakes impliedly that the coachman will take care to protect the goods in the brougham. If they are stolen owing to the coachman's negligence, the job-master is liable. So also if the coachman steals them himself.

(v) *Apparent authority of servant.* In *Lloyd* v. *Grace, Smith & Co.*,[7] a solicitor's clerk, acting within the *apparent* scope of his authority from his principals, accepted Mrs. Lloyd's deeds so as to sell her cottages on her behalf and to call in a mortgage. When he accepted her instructions, he intended to misappropriate the deeds for his own benefit, and he did so. His principals were held liable. The essence of that case, as stressed in all the speeches (and specially in the judgment of Scrutton J.)[8] was that the clerk was acting within his *apparent* authority in receiving the deeds and thus his principals had them in their charge. (And this was afterwards stressed by Sir Wilfrid Greene M.R. in *Uxbridge Permanent Building Society* v. *Pickard*[9].) In consequence of this *apparent* authority, the firm of solicitors were clearly under a *duty* to deal honestly and faithfully with Mrs. Lloyd's property: and they could not escape that duty by delegating it to their agent. They were responsible for the way he conducted himself therein, even though he did it dishonestly for his own benefit.

(vi) *Where there is only opportunity to defraud.* There are many cases in the books where a servant takes the opportunity afforded by his service to steal or defraud another for his own benefit. It has always been held that the master is not on that account liable to the person who has been defrauded; see *Ruben and Landenburg* v. *Great Fingall Consolidated*.[10] If a window cleaner steals a valuable article from my flat whilst he is working there, I cannot claim against his employer unless he was negligent in employing him; see *De Parrell* v. *Walker*.[11] In order for the master to be liable there must be some circumstance imposing a duty on the master; see *Coleman* v. *Riches*[12] by Williams J.

From all these instances we may deduce the general proposition that when a principal has in his charge the goods or belongings of another in such circumstances that he is under a duty to take all reasonable precautions to protect them from theft or depreda-

---

1. (1601), 4 Co. Rep. 83b.
2. [1955] A.C. 130; [1957] 3 All E.R. 216.
3. (1961), 26 D.L.R. 760.
4. [1948] 2 K.B. 48; [1948] 1 All E.R. 599.
5. (1854), 3 E. & B. 144.
6. [1905] 2 K.B. 805; [1904–7] All E.R. Rep. 48.
7. [1912] A.C. 716; [1911–13] All E.R. Rep. 51.
8. Quoted by Lord Macnaghten, [1912] A.C. at p. 730; [1911–13] All E.R. Rep. at p. 56.
9. [1939] 2 K.B. 248; [1939] 2 All E.R. 344.
10. [1906] A.C. 439; [1904–7] All E.R. Rep. 460.
11. (1932), 49 T.L.R. 37.
12. (1855), 16 C.B. 104, at p. 121.

tion, then if he entrusts that duty to a servant or agent, he is answerable for the manner in which that servant or agent carries out his duty. If the servant or agent is careless so that they are stolen by a stranger, the master is liable. So also if the servant or agent himself steals them or makes away with them. It follows that I do not think that *Cheshire* v. *Bailey*[1] can be supported. The job-master was clearly under a duty to take all reasonable precautions to protect the goods from being stolen, either as a bailee for reward or under the contract. He entrusted that duty to the coachman and must be answerable for the way in which the coachman carried out that duty; and it is all the same whether he did it negligently or fraudulently and whether he did it for his master's benefit or his own benefit. The decision cannot survive *Lloyd* v. *Grace, Smith & Co.*[2] and should be overruled.

So far I have been dealing with the cases where the owner himself has entrusted the goods to the defendant. But here it was not the owner, the plaintiff, who entrusted the fur to the cleaners. She handed it to Mr. Beder, who was a bailee for reward. He in turn, with her authority, handed it to the cleaners who were sub-bailees for reward. Mr. Beder could clearly himself sue the cleaners for loss of the fur and recover the whole value (see *The Winkfield*),[3] unless the cleaners were protected by some exempting conditions. But can the plaintiff sue the cleaners direct for the misappropriation by their servant? And if she does, can she ignore the exempting conditions? . . .

. . . See the history of the matter fully discussed in *Holmes on the Common Law*, pp. 164–180. But now an action does lie by the owner direct against the wrongdoer if he has the right to immediate possession; see *Kahler* v. *Midland Bank, Ltd.*[4] Even if he has no right to immediate possession, he can sue for any permanent injury to, or loss of, the goods by a wrongful act of the defendant; see *Mears* v. *London and South Western Ry. Co.*[5] But what is a wrongful act as between the owner and the sub-bailee? What is the duty of the sub-bailee to the owner? Is the sub-bailee liable for misappropriation by his servant? There is very little authority on this point. *Pollock* and *Wright on Possession* say this (at p. 169):

> "If the bailee of a thing sub-bails it by authority . . . and there is no direct privity of contract between the third person and the owner *it would seem that both the owner and the first bailee have concurrently the rights of a bailor against the third person according to the nature of the sub-bailment.*"

By which I take it that if the sub-bailment is for reward, the sub-bailee owes to the owner all the duties of a bailee for reward: and the owner can sue the sub-bailee direct for loss of or damage to the goods; and the sub-bailee (unless he is protected by any exempting conditions) is liable unless he can prove that the loss or damage occurred without his fault or that of his servants. So the plaintiff can sue the defendants direct for the loss of the goods by the misappropriation by their servant, and the cleaners are liable unless they are protected by the exempting conditions. . . .

[His Lordship went on to find that the exempting conditions did not protect the defendants since, as a matter of construction, the word "customer" meant the furrier and not the plaintiff.]

DIPLOCK L.J.: . . . If the bailee in the present case had been a natural person and had converted the plaintiff's fur by stealing it himself, no one would have argued that he was not liable to her for its loss; but the defendant bailees are a corporate person. They could not perform their duties to the plaintiff to take reasonable care of the fur and not to convert it otherwise than vicariously by natural persons acting as their servants

---

1. [1905] 1 K.B. 237; [1904–7] All E.R. Rep. 882.
2. [1912] A.C. 716; [1911-13] All E.R. Rep. 51.
3. [1902] P. 42; [1900–03] All E.R. Rep. 346.
4. [1950] A.C. 24, at pp. 33, 56; [1949] 2 All E.R. 621, at pp. 627, 628, 641.
5. (1862), 11 C.B.N.S. 850.

or agents. It was one of their servants, to whom they had entrusted the care and custody of the fur for the purpose of doing work on it, who converted it by stealing it. Why should they not be vicariously liable for this breach of their duty by the vicar whom they had chosen to perform it? Sir John Holt, I think, would have answered that they were liable "for seeing that someone must be the loser by this deceit it is more reason that he who employs and puts a trust and confidence in the deceiver should be the loser than a stranger" (*Hern* v. *Nichols*).[1]

The learned county court judge felt that he was precluded from applying this old, robust and moral principle in the present case by the decision of the Court of Appeal in *Cheshire* v. *Bailey*[2] and of the Earl of Reading C.J. in *Mintz* v. *Silverton*.[3] I agree that if the rationes decidendi of the judgments in *Cheshire* v. *Bailey*[2] are still good law today, I cannot find any relevant distinction between its facts and those of the present case which would justify our allowing this appeal; but I do not think that that decision is still good law. I confess that I should be sorry to think that it was so, for I can see no justification in reason or in morals for a rule of law which makes a bailee of goods for reward liable to the bailor for their loss if, as in *Abraham* v. *Bullock*[4] his servant to whom they are entrusted carelessly enables someone else to steal the goods, but protects the bailee from liability if that servant steals it himself. The greater the fault of the servant the less the liability of the master. . . .

I do not think that *Cheshire* v. *Bailey*[2] can be reconciled with *Lloyd* v. *Grace, Smith & Co*.[5] The master put his coachman in his place not only to drive the brougham but also to take care of the plaintiff's goods during the plaintiff's temporary absence. While the goods were in his custody, the servant converted them. The master should have been held liable for his servant's act—at any rate, if the action had been pleaded in conversion. It is true that the House of Lords in *Lloyd* v. *Grace, Smith & Co*.[5] did not expressly overrule *Cheshire* v. *Bailey*[2] although that case was cited to them. Lord Shaw of Dunfermline alone mentions it and distinguishes it[2] on the ground that the servant's conduct was beyond the scope of his employment. With great respect I do not think that this distinction can withstand analysis. As a result, however of Lord Shaw's observation the doubt whether *Cheshire* v. *Bailey*[2] is still good authority on the vicarious liability of a master for his servant's dishonest acts has remained to vex our law and to provide law teachers with a suitable subject for students' essays until the present day. As recently as 1955 the Privy Council in *United Africa Co., Ltd.* v. *Saka Owoade*,[6] although they reached a decision in conflict with *Cheshire* v. *Bailey*,[2] declined to express a view whether it had been overruled by *Lloyd* v. *Grace, Smith & .Co*.[5] or could be distinguished from it. In the present case, we, I think are compelled to make up our minds about this. For my part I find it impossible to reconcile the decision in *Cheshire* v. *Bailey*[2] with the principles laid down in *Lloyd* v. *Grace, Smith & Co*.[5] I think that decision is no longer good law and is not binding on us. In so holding I am reassured by the reflection that this branch of the common law in England will be the same as it has been held to be in Ontario by the Supreme Court of Canada (see *R.* v. *Levy*[7]) and as it has been held to be in Nigeria by the Privy Council (*United Africa Co., Ltd.* v. *Saka Owoade*).[6] It is better that the common law in different common law countries should converge rather than grow apart.

If the principle laid down in *Lloyd* v. *Grace, Smith & Co*.[5] is applied to the facts of the present case, the defendants cannot in my view escape liability for the conversion of the plaintiff's fur by their servant Morrissey. They accepted the fur as bailees for reward in order to clean it. They put Morrissey as their agent in their place to clean the fur and to take charge of it while doing so. The manner in which he conducted himself in doing that work was to convert it. What he was doing, albeit dishonestly, he was

---

1. (1701), 1 Salk. 289.
2. [1905] 1 K.B. 237; [1904–07] All E.R. Rep. 882.
3. (1920), 36 T.L.R. 399.   4. (1902), 86 L.T. 796.
5. [1912] A.C. 716; [1911–13] All E.R. Rep. 51.
6. [1955] A.C. 130; (1954), [1957] 3 All E.R. 216.
7. (1961), 26 D.L.R. 760.

doing in the scope or course of his employment in the technical sense of that infelicitous but time-honoured phrase. The defendants as his masters are responsible for his tortious act.

I should add that we are not concerned here with gratuitous bailment. That is a relationship in which the bailee's duties of care in his custody of the goods are different from those of a bailee for reward. It may be that his duties being passive rather than active, the concept of vicarious performance of them is less apposite. However this may be, I express no views as to the circumstances in which he would be liable for conversion of the goods by his servant. Nor are we concerned with what would have been the liability of the defendants if the fur had been stolen by another servant of theirs who was not employed by them to clean the fur to have the care or custody of it. The mere fact that his employment by the defendants gave him the opportunity to steal it would not suffice. The crucial distinction between *Lloyd* v. *Grace, Smith & Co.*[1] and *Ruben and Ladenburg* v. *Great Fingall Consolidated*[2] is that in the latter case the dishonest servant was neither actually or ostensibly employed to warrant the genuineness of certificates for shares in the company which employed him. His fraudulent conduct was facilitated by the access which he had to the company's seal and documents in the course of his employment for another purpose: but the fraud itself which was the only tort giving rise to a civil liability to the plaintiffs was not committed in the course of doing that class of acts which the company had put the servant in his place to do.

I base my decision in this case on the ground that the fur was stolen by the very servant whom the defendants as bailees for reward had employed to take care of it and to clean it.

I agree that the appeal should be allowed.

SALMON L.J.: ... I accordingly agree with my lords that the appeal should be allowed. I am anxious, however, to make it plain that the conclusion which I have reached depends on Morrissey being the servant through whom the defendants chose to discharge their duty to take reasonable care of the plaintiff's fur. The words of Willes J, in *Barwick's* case[3] are entirely applicable to these facts. The defendants

"put [their] agent [Morrissey] in [the defendants'] place as to such a class of acts, and ... must be answerable for the manner in which the agent conducts himself in doing the business which is the business of the master."

A bailee for reward is not answerable for a theft by any of his servants, but only for a theft by such of them as are deputed by him to discharge some part of his duty of taking reasonable care. A theft by any servant who is not employed to do anything in relation to the goods bailed is entirely outside the scope of his employment and cannot make the master liable. So in this case, if someone employed by the defendants in another depot had broken in and stolen the fur, the defendants would not have been liable. Similarly in my view if a clerk employed in the same depot had seized the opportunity of entering the room where the fur was kept and had stolen it, the defendants would not have been liable. The mere fact that the master, by employing a rogue, gives him the opportunity to steal or defraud does not make the master liable for his depredations. *Ruben and Ladenburg* v. *Great Fingall Consolidated.*[2] It might be otherwise if the master knew or ought to have known that his servant was dishonest, because then the master could be liable in negligence for employing him. ...

---

1. [1912] A.C. 716; [1911–13] All E.R. Rep. 51.
2. [1906] A.C. 439; [1904–07] All E.R. Rep. 460.
3. (1867), L.R. 2 Exch. at p. 266; [1861–73] All E.R. Rep. at p. 198.

4. LIABILITY FOR INDEPENDENT CONTRACTORS

Salsbury v. Woodland

Court of Appeal   [1969] 3 All E.R. 863

The first defendant, an occupier of property adjoining a highway, engaged the second defendant, an experienced and apparently competent tree-feller, as an independent contractor, to fell a large tree in his front garden. If competently felled, there was no risk of injury, but the second defendant did the work so negligently that the tree fouled telephone wires which ran from a telegraph pole on the far side of the highway, bringing them down so that they lay across the highway. The plaintiff, a bystander, attempted to remove the wires from the roadway and while attempting to do so was injured when he took action to avoid an oncoming car as it struck the wires. Judgment for damages was obtained against the second defendant in default of defence. At the trial, judgment was also given against the first defendant, who successfully appealed to the Court of Appeal.

WIDGERY L.J.: . . . So far as the first defendant is concerned, he personally committed no negligent act, and it is not challenged that in selecting the second defendant as the means of having this tree felled he selected a person who was apparently competent and fit to do it. The whole basis of the case against the first defendant is that the second defendant was negligent and that the first defendant is responsible for that negligence. Counsel for the first defendant, was prepared to challenge the judge's finding of negligence on the part of the second defendant, and was prepared to challenge the difficult questions of causation which arose in the course of that issue, but, the court having concluded that the first defendant's appeal succeeded on a different ground, I need not go into those matters now. The basis of the decision of this court (which has already been indicated to the parties) on the liability of the first defendant is simply that the first defendant was not responsible for the negligence of the second defendant even if the second defendant was negligent; and it is to that matter only that I need now direct myself.

It is, of course, trite law that an employer who employs an independent contractor is not vicariously responsible for the negligence of that contractor. He is not able to control the way in which the independent contractor does the work and the vicarious obligation of a master for the negligence of his servant does not arise under the relationship of employer and independent contractor. I think it is entirely accepted that those cases—and there are some—in which an employer has been held liable for injury done by the negligence of an independent contractor are in truth cases where the employer owes a direct duty to the person injured, a duty which he cannot delegate to the contractor on his behalf. The whole question in this case is whether, in the circumstances which I have briefly outlined, the first defendant is to be judged by the general rule, which would result in no liability, or whether he comes within one of the somewhat special exceptions—cases in which a direct duty to see that care is taken rests on the employer throughout the operation.

This is clear from authority . . .

. . . In truth, according to the authorities there are a number of well-determined classes of case in which this direct and primary duty on an employer to see that care is taken exists. Two such classes are directly relevant for consideration in this case. The first class concerns what have sometimes been described as "extra hazardous acts"— acts commissioned by an employer which are so hazardous in their character that the law has thought it proper to impose this direct obligation on the employer to see that care is taken. An example of such a case is *Honeywill and Stein, Ltd.* v. *Larkin Bros.*

(*London's Commercial Photographers*), *Ltd.*[1] Other cases which one finds in the books are cases where the activity commissioned by the employer is the keeping of dangerous things, within the rule in *Rylands* v. *Fletcher*,[2] and where liability is not dependent on negligence at all.

I do not propose to add to the wealth of authority on this topic by attempting further to define the meaning of "extra hazardous acts"; but I am confident that the act commissioned in the present case cannot come within that category. The act commissioned in the present case, if done with ordinary elementary caution by skilled men, presented no hazard to anyone at all.

The second class of case which is relevant for consideration of the present dispute concerns dangers created in a highway. There are a number of cases on this branch of the law, a good example of which is *Holliday* v. *National Telephone Co.*[3] These, on analysis, will all be found to be cases where work was being done in a highway and was work of a character which would have been a nuisance unless authorised by statute. It will be found in all these cases that the statutory powers under which the employer commissioned the work were statutory powers which left on the employer a duty to see that due care was taken in the carrying out of the work, for the protection of those who passed on the highway. In accordance with principle, an employer subject to such a direct and personal duty cannot excuse himself if things go wrong merely because the direct cause of the injury was the act of the independent contractor.

This again is not a case in that class. It is not a case in that class because in the instant case no question of doing work in the highway, which might amount to a nuisance if due care was not taken, arises. In my judgment, the present case is clearly outside the well-defined limit of the second class to which I have referred. Counsel for the plaintiff accordingly invited us to say that there is a third class into which the instant case precisely falls and he suggested that the third class comprised those cases where an employer commissions work to be done *near* a highway in circumstances in which, if due care is not taken, injury to passers-by on the highway may be caused. If that be a third class of case to which the principle of liability of the employer applies, no doubt the present facts would come within the description. The question is, is there such a third class?

Reliance is placed primarily on three authorities. The first is *Holliday's* case,[3] to which I have already referred. *Holliday's* case[3] was a case of work being done in a highway by undertakers laying telephone wires. The injury was caused by the negligent act of a servant of the independent contractor who was soldering joints in the telephone wires. The cause of the injury was the immersion of a defective blow-lamp in a pot of solder, and the pot of solder was physically on the highway—according to the report, on the footpath. The Earl of Halsbury L.C. holding the employers responsible for that negligence, in my view, on a simple application of the cases applicable to highway nuisance to which I have already referred, put his opinions in these words:[4]

> "Therefore, works were being executed in proximity to a highway, in which in the ordinary course of things an explosion might take place."

Counsel for the plaintiff draws our attention to the phrase "in proximity to a highway" and submits that that supports his contention on this point. I am not impressed by this argument, because the source of danger in *Holliday's* case[3] was itself on the highway and also because I do not think it follows (although one need not decide the point today) that in the true highway cases to which I have referred the actual source of injury must arise on the highway itself. Counsel for the plaintiff said that in *Holliday's* case[3] it would have been ridiculous if there had been liability because the pot of solder was on the highway but no liability if it was two feet off the highway. That is an obser-

---

1. [1934] 1 K.B. 191; [1933] All E.R. Rep. 77.
2. (1868), L.R. 3 H.L. 330; [1861–73] All E.R. Rep. 1.
3. [1899] 2 Q.B. 392; [1895–99] All E.R. Rep. 359.
4. [1899] 2 Q.B. at p. 399; [1895–99] All E.R. Rep. at p. 361.

vation with which I entirely symphathise; but I can find nothing in Lord Halsbury's use of the word "proximity" to justify the view that there is therefore a special class of case on the lines submitted by counsel.

The second case relied on is *Tarry* v. *Ashton*,[1] where a building adjoining the highway had attached to it a heavy lamp which was suspended over the footway and which was liable to be a source of injury to passers-by if allowed to fall into disrepair. It fell into disrepair, and injury was caused. The defendant sought to excuse himself by saying that he had employed a competent independent contractor to put the lamp into good repair and that the cause of the injury was the fault of the independent contractor. Counsel for the plaintiff argues that that case illustrates the special sympathy with which the law regards passers-by on the highway. He says this demonstrates that the law has always been inclined to give special protection to persons in that category and so supports his argument that any action adjacent to the highway may be subject to special rights. But in my judgment that is not so. *Tarry* v. *Ashton*[1] seems to me to be a perfectly ordinary and straightforward example of a case where the employer was under a positive and continuing duty to see that the lamp was kept in repair. That duty was imposed on him before the contractor came and after the contractor had gone; and on the principle that such a duty cannot be delegated the responsibility of the employer in that case seems to me to be fully demonstrated. I cannot find that it produces on a side-wind, as it were, anything in support of counsel for the plaintiff's contention.

The last case to which I will refer on this point is *Walsh* v. *Holst & Co., Ltd.*,[2] a decision of this court. In that case the occupier of premises adjoining the highway was carrying out works of reconstruction which involved knocking out large areas of the front wall. He employed for this purpose a contractor, and the contractor employed a sub-contractor. It was obvious to all, no doubt, that such an operation was liable to cause injury to passers-by by falling bricks unless special precautions against that eventuality were taken. Indeed very considerable precautions were so taken. However, on a day when the only workman employed was an employee of the sub-contractor one brick escaped the protective net, fell in the street and injured a passer-by. The passer-by-plaintiff brought his action against the occupier, the contractor, and the sub-contractor, relying on the doctrine of res ipsa loquitur. In my judgment, the only thing that was really decided by that case was that on those facts the precautions which had been taken against such an injury rebutted the presumption of negligence which might otherwise have arisen under the doctrine of res ipsa loquitur. No attempt appears to have been made in argument to distinguish the liability of the occupier as compared with that of the contractor or sub-contractor, and it certainly was not material to the decision; ...

... Accordingly, in my judgment, there is no third class of cases of the kind put forward by counsel for the plaintiff; and it was for those reasons that I concurred in the court's decision, already announced, that the appeal of the first defendant should be allowed and the judgment against him set aside.

SACHS L.J.: ... I would add an observation that ... I derived no assistance at all from any distinction between "collateral and casual" negligence and other negligence. Such a distinction provides too many difficulties for me to accept without question, unless it simply means that one must ascertain exactly what was the occupier's duty and then treat any act that is not part of that duty as giving rise to no liability on his part. How, in *Walsh* v. *Holst & Co., Ltd.*[2] could one distinguish between a falling half-brick and a falling cold chisel?

Again, I would observe that counsel for the plaintiff, in his attempt to bring the instant case into what might be called a special and new category, was constrained to urge that an occupier would be liable if an independent contractor, engaged to fell a

---

1. (1876), 1 Q.B.D. 314; [1874–80] All E.R. Rep. 738.
2. [1958] 3 All E.R. 33; [1958] 1 W.L.R. 800.

tree 100 yards or so away from a highway and remove it from the occupier's property, chose, out of a large number of different routes to an exit gate, the only one that lay close to a highway and then allowed the tree to roll into the road. That seems to me to indicate what unnecessarily absurd results would follow from assenting to the proposition urged on behalf of the plaintiff. . . .

[HARMAN L.J. delivered a judgment in favour of allowing the first defendant's appeal.]

Note

As regards an occupier's liability for the acts of independent contractors see the Occupiers' Liability Act 1957, s. 2 (4), p. 224, *ante*; and for the liability of highway authorities see the Highways (Miscellaneous Provisions) Act 1961, s. 1 (3).

Matania v. National Provincial Bank, Ltd.

Court of Appeal   [1936] 2 All E.R. 633

The defendant Bank demised the second and third floors of certain premises to the plaintiff with a covenant for quiet enjoyment. Without the plaintiff's consent the second defendants, who proposed to occupy the first floor of the building, instructed contractors to carry out extensive alterations. No proper precautions being taken, the plaintiff suffered damage by reason of the dust and noise from the operations. The Court of Appeal, allowing an appeal, held the second defendants liable in damages for nuisance although they had employed an independent contractor to do the work.

SLESSER L.J.: . . . Now there remains one other matter, and an important one, which Mr. Morris has argued before us with great force and with which I have to deal. There is no doubt in this case that Messrs. Adamson are independent contractors, and being independent contractors, save for exceptional circumstances, in the ordinary way those employing them would not be liable for their wrongful acts in negligence or in nuisance. . . . Here, of course, we are not concerned with danger such as might found an action for negligence. We are here concerned with annoyance such as may found an action for nuisance, but the principles in my opinion are the same as regards the liability of a person who employs an independent contractor, that is to say, that if the act done is one which in its very nature involves a special danger of nuisance being complained of, then it is one which falls within the exception for which the employer of the contractor will be responsible if there is a failure to take the necessary precautions that the nuisance shall not arise. Now, what are the facts of the present case? They are these. It is really not in dispute that as regards the place where this work was to be done this noise and this dust were inevitable. That is the evidence of both the plaintiff and the defendants, and it is the conclusion of the learned judge. The only question which I see is whether in that state where the production of noise and dust is inevitable, sufficient precautions were taken to prevent that noise and dust affecting Mr. Matania. In every case, whether it be a case of ordinary employment of a contractor or whether it be a case of a hazardous operation, the problem must arise whether a precaution would or would not prevent the result of an operation. To say that a precaution will prevent the result of an operation does not by itself take the case outside the rule that a person may be responsible, where the act is a hazardous one, for the acts of his contractor. Where the act is hazardous, to presume that every hazardous act would result in the danger or the nuisance would be to say that the act was inevitable in its consequences, regardless of any question of precaution or not, but that is not the right way of looking at it. In the case to which I referred, the case of *Honeywill and Stein, Ltd. v. Larkin Bros., Ltd.*[1] it was not inevitable that the fire, which was brought into the theatre, would necessarily under proper precautions set the theatre on fire, but it was a hazardous operation to bring the fire into the theatre. So it was hazardous as

---

1. [1934] 1 K.B. 191; [1933] All E.R. Rep. 77.

regards the possible nuisance to Mr. Matania to bring the noise and dust immediately below his apartment. What is said is with sufficient and proper precaution the result of that hazardous operation could have been avoided without detriment to him. I am of opinion that this was a hazardous operation within the meaning of the exceptions stated in *Honeywill & Stein, Ltd.* v. *Larkin Bros., Ltd.* that the principle which is there dealing with a case of negligence applies equally to the tort of nuisance, and that, therefore, this being a case of this kind, I think that the Elevenist Syndicate are responsible for the fact that neither they nor the contractors, Messrs. Adamson, took those reasonable precautions which could have been taken to prevent this injury to the plaintiff.

I say nothing about the action in so far as it is framed in trespass. There are difficulties in stating an action in trespass and in nuisance except alternatively. The text book writers seems to differ in their opinions on this point. Sir John Salmond in his book seems to think that the actions are alternative. Sir Frederick Pollock is of the contrary opinion. I think there would be difficulties apart from those, in succeeding in trespass in this case. I think the dust and the noise which were allowed to come upon the premises of Mr. Matania were the result probably of an act indirect and not direct on the part of the contractor, and so probably would found an action in case rather than an action in trespass, but in so far as I have come to the conclusion that the Elevenist Syndicate are liable in nuisance to Mr. Matania, I do not think it necessary to deal with the question of trespass at all. . . .

[ROMER L.J. and FINLAY J. delivered judgments concurring in allowing the appeal.]

Balfour v. Barty-King

Court of Appeal   [1957] I All E.R. 156

The defendants' water-pipes were frozen. Mrs. Barty-King asked two men at work on a nearby site to help unfreeze the pipes. Instead of using a heated brick to do this, they applied a blow-lamp to a pipe in the loft of the Barty-King's house. This was highly dangerous because the pipes were lagged with felt and it was draughty. The lagging caught fire and the fire spread to the plaintiff's adjoining premises causing extensive damage. Havers J. gave judgment against the defendants, who appealed. The appeal was dismissed.

LORD GODDARD C.J. read the judgment of the Court (which included MORRIS L.J. and VAISEY J.): . . . The question which this court has to consider is whether HAVERS J. was right in holding that for the spread of the fire from their premises to those of the plaintiff the defendants are responsible, although the fire was caused by the negligence of independent contractors brought on to the defendants' premises to do the work which I have described. On this matter there seems to be no direct authority . . .

. . . Although there is a difference of opinion among eminent text writers whether at common law the liability was absolute or depended on negligence, at the present day it can safely be said that a person in whose house a fire is caused by negligence is liable if it spreads to that of his neighbour, and this is true whether the negligence is his own or that of his servant or his guest, but he is not liable if the fire is caused by a stranger.

Who then is a stranger? Clearly a trespasser would be in that category, but, if a man is liable for the negligent act of his guest, it is, indeed, difficult to see why he is not liable for the act of a contractor whom he has invited to his house to do work on it, and who does the work in a negligent manner. We do not get much assistance from *Black* v. *Christchurch Finance Co.* ([1894] A.C. 48), although Sir William Holdsworth cites that case in support of his opinion that there is liability for the acts of a contractor in this respect. In that case the fire was certainly the fire of the defendants, for the contractor had been employed by them to make a fire to burn the scrub and saplings on the land, and in carrying out the work the contractor did a negligent act and one which was in breach of a stipulation in the contract. He started the fire in unfavourable weather. The lighting of the fire was not a casual, or, as it is sometimes put, a collateral act of negligence; it was the very thing that he was employed to do, and Lord Shand's judgment is really mainly concerned with whether, as the contractor had disregarded a special term in the contract, the employers were liable.

The argument of counsel for the defendants was that in the present case it was not the defendants' fire, as the contractor was not employed to light a fire or to use a blow-lamp or any other form of fire. That, however, is answered by the fact that the use of a blow-lamp is an ordinary way of freeing frozen pipes. The negligence was in using the lamp in proximity to inflammable material. Counsel also relied on the dictum of Lord Watson in *Dalton* v. *Angus* ((1881), 6 App. Cas. 740, at p. 831), where he said:

"When an employer contracts for the performance of work, which properly conducted can occasion no risk to his neighbour's house which he is under obligation to support, he is not liable for damage arising from the negligence of the contractor."

This observation, no doubt, states the general rule with regard to liability, or the lack of it, for the negligence of an independent contractor; but the noble and learned Lord was not dealing with the case of the escape of a dangerous thing from land to which it has been brought or on which it has been created. We do not think that it is necessary to consider the doctrine of *Rylands* v. *Fletcher* ((1868), L.R. 3 H.L. 330) as a separate head of liability. No doubt the doctrine of that case applies to fire, and is subject to the exception of the damage being caused by a stranger.

In *Perry* v. *Kendricks Transport, Ltd.* ([1956] 1 All E.R. 154, at p. 161), Parker L.J. referred to a stranger as a person over whom the defendant had no control. From one point of view it may be said that the test of an independent contractor is that he is left to carry out the work in his own way, but that is not the sense, I think, in which the lord justice was using the word "control". The defendants here had control over the contractor in that they chose him, they invited him to their premises to do work, and he could have been ordered to leave at any moment. It was left to the men who were sent how to do the work, and in our opinion the defendants are liable to the plaintiff for this lamentable occurrence, the more lamentable in that the persons ultimately responsible are insolvent. The appeal must be dismissed with costs.

Honeywill & Stein, Ltd. v. Larkin Bros. (London's Commercial Photographers), Ltd.

Court of Appeal   [1933] All E.R. Rep. 77

A cinema company engaged the plaintiffs to do acoustics work in their cinema. The plaintiffs, with the cinema company's permission, employed the defendants, an independent firm of photographers to take photographs of the interior of the cinema. At the time, the taking of flashlight photographs was "inevitably attended with danger" because it involved the ignition in a metal tray or holder, held above the lens, of an ounce or more of magnesium powder, which on being ignited flared up and caused intense heat. As a result of the negligence of the operator in lighting the magnesium at a distance of less than four feet from the curtains, the curtains caught fire and were damaged to the extent of £261. 4s. 3d. The plaintiffs paid these damages to the cinema company and now sought an indemnity from the photographers (the defendants in this action) who contended that since they were independent contractors the plaintiffs were not responsible for their actions and so should not have reimbursed the cinema company. The trial judge found for the defendants. The plaintiffs successfully appealed to the Court of Appeal.

SLESSER L.J. read the following judgment of the court—. . . It is well established as a general rule of English law that an employer is not liable for the acts of his independent contractor in the same way as he is for the acts of his servants or agents, even though these acts are done in carrying out work for his benefit under the contract. The determination whether the actual wrongdoer is a servant or agent, on the one hand, or an independent contractor, on the other, depends on whether or not the employer not only determines what is to be done, but retains the control of the actual performance, in which case the doer is a servant or agent, but, if the employer, while prescribing the work to be done, leaves the manner of doing it to the control of the doer, the latter is an independent contractor. . . .

It is clear that the ultimate employer is not responsible for the acts of an independent contractor merely because what is to be done will involve danger to others if negligently done. The incidence of this liability is limited to certain defined classes, and for the purpose of this case it is only necessary to consider that part of this rule of liability which has reference to extra hazardous acts, that is, acts which, in their very nature involve in the eyes of the law special danger to others. . . .

. . . To take a photograph in the cinema with a flashlight was, on the evidence stated above, a dangerous operation in its intrinsic nature, involving the creation of fire and explosion on another person's premises, that is, in the cinema, the property of the cinema company. The plaintiffs, in procuring this work to be performed by their contractors, the defendants, assumed an obligation to the cinema company which was, as we think, absolute, but which was at least an obligation to use reasonable precautions to see that no damage resulted to the cinema company from those dangerous operations. That obligation they could not delegate by employing the defendants as independent contractors, but they were liable in this regard for the defendants' acts. For the damage actually caused the plaintiffs were, accordingly, liable in law to the cinema company, and are entitled to claim and recover from the defendants damages for their breach of contract or negligence in performing their contract to take photographs.

The learned judge has found for the defendants because he has held (founding himself on the words of Lord Watson in *Dallon* v. *Angus*)[1] that the work to be done by the defendants for the plaintiffs,

> "was not necessarily attended with risk. It was work which, as a general rule, would seem to be of quite a harmless nature."

But, with respect, he is ignoring the special rules which apply to extra hazardous or dangerous operations. Even of these it may be predicated that, if carefully and skilfully performed, no harm will follow. As instances of such operations may be given those of removing support from adjoining houses, doing dangerous work on the highway, or creating fire or explosion. Hence it may be said in one sense that such operations are not necessarily attended with risk. But the rule of liability for independent contractors attaches to those operations, because they are inherently dangerous, and hence are done at the principal employer's peril.

For these reasons, we are of opinion that the appeal must be allowed, the judgment set aside and judgment entered for the appellants for the amount of the damage.

Notes

1. "Even if one goes so far as to say that the use of flashlight powder is 'dangerous' it is hyperbolical to describe it as 'extra-hazardous'. If this is 'extra-hazardous' we are left with no language to describe really dangerous conduct": Glanville Williams, [1956] C.L.J. at p. 186. What do you understand by "extra-hazardous"?

2. The cinema company was probably insured in this case, and the photographers may not have been insured. Which of these two potential defendants was best equipped to absorb the loss? Glanville Williams, "Liability for Independent Contractors", [1956] C.L.J., at pp. 193–198, argues that "it may be questioned whether the social evil of the occasional insolvent tortfeasant contractor is of sufficient gravity to justify the imposition of vicarious liability".

---

1. (1881), 6 App. Cas. 740.

3. How would this case have been argued if the plaintiffs' *contract* with the cinema company had permitted them to take photographs (or have photographs taken), i.e. if they had not simply been *licensees* for the purpose of taking photographs?

4. In *Read v. J. Lyons & Co., Ltd.*, [1947] A.C. 156; [1946] 2 All E.R. 471 (p. 342, *ante*), the House of Lords refused to establish a general tort of liability for "extra-hazardous" activities. Atiyah, *Vicarious Liability in the Law of Torts*, p. 373, argues that *Honeywill's* case is the "first cousin" of the rejected doctrine and should suffer the same fate.

5. Consider the liability of the following:

(a) a solicitor for the negligence of counsel in non-litigious work (cf. *Rondel v. Worsley*, [1969] 1 A.C. 191; [1967] 3 All E.R. 993, p. 517, *ante*).

(b) a carrier for the negligence of an independent contractor (see *Riverstone Meat Pty., Ltd. v. Lancashire Shipping Co., Ltd.*, [1961] A.C. 807; [1961] 1 All E.R. 495 (H.L.)).

(c) a bailee for reward who entrusts the care of goods to an independent contractor (*Morris v. C. W. Martin & Sons*, p. 625, *ante*; on gratuitous bailees, Atiyah, *op. cit.*, p. 367).

5. EMPLOYER'S LIABILITY TO EMPLOYEES

The Employer's Liability (Defective Equipment) Act 1969

1. Extension of employer's liability for defective equipment.—(1) Where after the commencement of this Act—

(*a*) an employee suffers personal injury in the course of his employment in consequence of a defect in equipment provided by his employer for the purposes of the employer's business; and

(*b*) the defect is attributable wholly or partly to the fault of a third party (whether identified or not),

the injury shall be deemed to be also attributable to negligence on the part of the employer (whether or not he is liable in respect of the injury apart from this subsection), but without prejudice to the law relating to contributory negligence and to any remedy by way of contribution or in contract or otherwise which is available to the employer in respect of the injury.

(2) In so far as any agreement purports to exclude or limit any liability of an employer arising under subsection (1) of this section, the agreement shall be void.

(3) In this section—

"business" includes the activities carried on by any public body;

"employee" means a person who is employed by another person under a contract of service or apprenticeship and is so employed for the purposes of a business carried on by that other person, and "employer" shall be construed accordingly;

"equipment" includes any plant and machinery, vehicle, aircraft and clothing;

"fault" means negligence, breach of statutory duty or other act or omission which gives rise to liability in tort in England and Wales or which is wrongful and gives rise to liability in damages in Scotland;

"personal injury" includes loss of life, any impairment of a person's physical or mental condition and any disease.

(4) This section binds the Crown, and persons in the service of the Crown shall accordingly be treated for the purposes of this section as employees of the Crown if they would not be so treated apart from this subsection.

Note

The purpose of this statute was to overcome the effects of the decision in *Davie* v. *New Merton Board Mills, Ltd.*, [1959] A.C. 604; [1959] 1 All E.R. 346 (H.L.). In that case the plaintiff employee was blinded when a particle of metal chipped off the tool with which he was working. The employer had purchased the tool from reputable suppliers who, in turn, had bought it from reputable manufacturers. There had been negligence in the course of manufacture which had caused the tool to become excessively hard, but outwardly the tool was in good condition. The manufacturers were liable under the *M'Alister* (or *Donoghue*) v. *Stevenson* rule (p. 328, *ante*). Most people believed that in such circumstances the employer would be liable too, because in *Wilsons and Clyde Coal Co., Ltd.* v. *English*, [1938] A.C. 57; [1937] 3 All E.R. 628 (p. 264, *ante*) the House of Lords had held that the employer's three-fold duty (to provide (i) competent staff, (ii) proper plant, premises and material, and (iii) a safe system of work) was *personal* and *non delegable*. It was thought to follow from this that an employer cannot delegate to an "independent contractor" his duty to provide proper tools. However in *Davie's* case the House of Lords held that an employer who buys a tool from a reputable supplier or manufacturer does not "delegate" his duty: he "discharges" it. This restriction on the "non-delegation" doctrine was criticised on legal and social grounds. C. J. Hamson, [1959] C.L.J. 157, showed that the result was due to the way in which the House of Lords classified the duty as *tortious* rather than *contractual*. Lord Wright had favoured the contractual approach in *Wilsons and Clyde Coal Co., Ltd.* v. *English* (p. 264, *ante*) and had this been followed in *Davie* the standard of care would have amounted to a warranty that the tool was safe (as it would have been had the employer *hired* or *sold* the tool to the employee). The practical effect of the decision was to leave the injured employee without compensation where the negligent manufacturer or supplier could not be identified or was bankrupt. The Employer's Liability (Defective Equipment) Act does not, however, entirely remedy the situation: see B. A. Hepple, [1970] C.L.J. 25.

(Another Act passed around the same time to ensure that employees actually receive their compensation is the Employers' Liability (Compulsory Insurance) Act 1969: see p. 676, *post*.)

Questions

1. Would it be correct to say that the Act of 1969 simply restores the law as laid down in *Wilsons and Clyde Coal Co., Ltd.* v. *English* (p. 264, *ante*)?

2. A self-employed window cleaner is supplied with a defective ladder by a householder as a result of which the window-cleaner is injured. (a) Whom should he sue? (b) Who is likely to be insured against such risks?

3. A refuse removal worker is injured by an object placed in a dustbin by a householder and which unexpectedly explodes. Does he have any claim against (a) his employer, (b) the householder? (See *Pattendon* v. *Beney* (1934), 50 T.L.R. 204.)

4. A travelling salesman (who cannot later be traced) sells a weed exterminator to X, but fails to pass on the information that the substance must not be used unless gloves are worn to protect the skin. X gives the weed exterminator to his gardener who suffers severe skin burns. Advise the gardener.

Sumner v. William Henderson & Sons, Ltd.

Queen's Bench Division   [1963] 1 All E.R. 408

In an action begun by writ issued on 27 July 1960, the plaintiff Isaac Sumner claimed damages under the Fatal Accidents Acts 1846 to 1959, in respect of the death of his wife, Louise Sumner, which was alleged to have been caused by the negligence or breach of duty of the defendants, their servants or agents. The defendants denied negligence and breach of duty. The parties stated certain questions of law in a special case for the opinion of the court, as follows. On 22 June 1960, the defendants were owners and occupiers of a department store in which a fire broke out. On that day the plaintiff's wife was employed by the defendants and died as a result of asphyxiation by smoke from the fire when she was in the course of her employment by the defendants as a restaurant supervisor, on the fourth floor of the store. In the amended statement of claim the plaintiff alleged (a) that the fire originated in a fault in an electrical cable running between the third and fourth floors of the defendants' store and (b) that a cause of his wife's death was the fact that parts of the store were so constructed or installed as to cause a fire to spread with great rapidity. The defendants by their amended defence alleged, (i) that the cable was manufactured by another company, manufacturers of such equipment, and was installed by electrical contractors in accordance with a specification prepared by consultant electrical engineers and under their supervision, and that all these companies or firms were reputable, competent and skilled contractors, who were fully capable of carrying out the work that they did, which was work calling for the exercise of specialised knowledge, skill and experience not possessed by the defendants or their servants. The defendants further alleged, (ii) that the relevant parts of the defendants' store were constructed or installed by building and engineering contractors, their servants or agents; that the parts of the store were constructed or installed in accordance with plans and specifications prepared by architects and under their supervision; that the building contractors, their servants, or agents, and the architects, were competent and properly skilled contractors and architects, who were fully capable of carrying out the work which they did, and of advising the defendants thereon, and that the work called for the exercise of specialised knowledge, skill and experience not possessed by the defendants or their servants. The court was asked for the purposes of the special case to assume the truth of each of the allegations of the plaintiff and the defendants set out as (a), (b) and (i) and (ii) previously in this report.

By para. 10 of the special case the questions for the opinion of the court were stated as being whether, on the facts and assumptions hereinbefore set out, the defendants were liable to the plaintiff in any of the following events, which are here briefly summarised—if the death of the plaintiff's wife was caused or contributed to either (a) by negligence of the manufacturers of the cable; or (b) by negligence of the electrical contractors in installing, inspecting or testing the electrical cable; or (c) by negligence on the part of the consultant electrical engineers in preparing the specification for the installation of the cable or supervising its installation or in inspecting or testing the cable; or (d) by negligence of the building contractors, their servants or agents, in constructing or installing the parts of the store which were assumed to have been so constructed as to have caused the fire to spread with great rapidity; or (e) by negligence of the architects, either in preparing plans and specifications for the construction and installation of the relevant parts of the store or in supervising the construction or installation thereof.

PHILLIMORE J.: . . . The short point which I have to determine is whether the defendants, in the circumstances which I have to assume, remain liable to their servant, the deceased, for the negligence of the manufacturers of the cable or for the negligence of one or other of the firms or companies employed to do the work, such negligence having either caused or promoted a fire which resulted in the deceased's death. I was told by learned counsel that, although the claim had been laid in tort, an amendment was under consideration, and I was asked to deal with the matter on the footing that liability, if any, arises either in contract or in tort.

Counsel for the plaintiff contends that, with the possible exception of the manufacturers of the cable, the defendants as employers are liable for the negligence, if any, of the other firms and companies which did or supervised the doing of the work. He contends that the defendants owed their employee, the deceased, a duty to take reasonable care to provide safe premises; that this was a personal or inalienable duty so that, if they chose to delegate its performance to someone else, whether a servant, agent, or independent contractor, they remained liable to their employee for any negligence in its performance.

Counsel on behalf of the defendants does not seek to deny that an employer owes a certain duty to his employee, the nature of which is personal and inalienable, or that, if he delegates the performance of that duty to an independent contractor, he remains liable to his employee for any negligence in its performance. He contends that the duty is more limited than that contended for by the plaintiff. He put it as follows. First, in regard to anything necessary to the carrying on or establishing of his operations, the master owes a personal duty of care for the safety of a servant so that, if he delegates performance to an independent contractor, he remains personally liable for negligence by that contractor. Secondly, in regard to anything which is not necessary for the carrying on or establishing of his operations, any duty that he may owe is not a personal duty, so that, if it is something which he is not qualified to do, he can delegate the work to a competent independent contractor, for whose negligence the employer will not be liable to his employee.

The phrase "the carrying on or establishing of his operations" was explained by counsel for the defendants, as referring to the essential nature of the employer's business. Thus, a butcher would have a personal and inalienable duty to take reasonable care to provide a safe system of butchery, proper appliances such as choppers and a chopping block, and safe premises to the extent of a floor for his shop which was both sound and not unduly slippery. In regard to the structure of the premises, however, as not being sufficiently connected with his trade and a matter outside his personal competence, he could appoint a competent contractor, and would thereafter be free of liability if, for example, negligence on the part of the contractor resulted in the collapse of the roof, with consequent injury to the butcher's employees. As I understand it, counsel for the defendants agreed that, if the employer was a company owning many shops and having its own repairs department, the company might remain liable for injury to those engaged in butchery as a result of negligence by the employees of the repairs department when engaged in repairing the structure of the premises, since repairs in that event would form part of the employer's operations. I confess that I find the argument of counsel for the defendants quite unacceptable. The anomalies to which it would give rise are obvious, and I cannot think that the liability of the employer depends on so artificial a basis. . . .

In *Davie* v. *New Merton Board Mills, Ltd.*,[1] the House of Lords held that the employers, being under a duty to take reasonable care to provide a reasonably safe tool—in that case a chisel—had discharged that duty by buying one from a reputable supplier, who, in turn, had procured it from a reputable manufacturer. The employers had no means of discovering the latent defect which in fact existed in the chisel. The ratio of this decision is, I think, that on the facts the employers could not be said to have delegated

---

1. [1959] A.C. 604; [1959] 1 All E.R. 346.

their duty to the manufacturers, to whose negligence the latent defect was presumably due. Delegation must always be a question dependent on the facts of the individual case, and it would seem impossible to say of an employer who merely went into a shop to buy a standard tool that he was delegating his responsibility for his employee's safety either to the supplier, who had merely bought it as a standard tool from the manufacturer, or, still less, that he was delegating it to the manufacturer, with whom he entered into no contract and who had manufacturered it months, or even years, before. There were observations in the opinions both of Viscount Simonds and of Lord Reid which, taken in isolation, might be thought to impair the principle that the employer remains responsible when he delegates his duty to an independent contractor. On the other hand, there are passages, notably in Lord Simon's opinion[1] and in Lord Reid's opinion[2] which show that this was not intended. Indeed, if any doubt remained, it is disposed of by the opinions expressed by their Lordships in *Riverstone Meat Co. Pty., Ltd.* v. *Lancashire Shipping Co., Ltd.*[3] . . .

It is not clear from the Case as drafted what were the circumstances in which the cable was obtained from the manufacturers, and I accordingly invited counsel to agree a further statement to cover this point. Counsel accordingly agreed the following addendum to the special case:

"Messrs. Sloan and Lloyd Barnes [the electrical engineers] ordered from [the manufacturers] a cable capable of carrying a given load of electric current and in giving such order they contemplated that the cable would be delivered from stock or, perhaps though unusually, it would be manufactured against the order."

On this somewhat meagre statement of the facts, I find it impossible to hold that the defendants, acting through their agents, the electrical engineers, were delegating their duty to the manufacturers. They were simply ordering a length of a certain type of cable, just as in *Davie's* case,[4] they ordered a certain tool. . . .

In contrast, it seems to me that, in employing the electrical contractors to install the cable and the electrical engineers to order it and to supervise its testing and installation, the defendants were delegating any duty they owed. Likewise, in regard to the reconstruction of the premises, if the defendants were under any duty to their employees, they were clearly delegating it to the architects and to the contractors. . . .

I would accordingly answer the specific questions raised in the case as follows: para. 10 (1), "No"; para. 10 (b), (c), (d) and (e), "Yes". In regard to para. 11, I direct as I am invited to do, that the plaintiff may not adduce at the trial evidence which is solely directed to showing that negligence on the part of the manufacturers of the electrical cable caused or contributed to the death of the plaintiff's wife.

Questions

1. What difference would it have made if the plaintiff's wife had not been an "employee", but a self-employed labour-only sub-contractor? (See *Sole* v. *W. J. Hallt, Ltd.*, [1973] Q.B. 574; [1973] 1 All E.R. 1032, p. 187, *ante*.)

2. Is an employer liable to his employee for an injury caused by the negligent driving of a lorry by a driver employed by a trade supplier to deliver goods to the employer?

3. What difference (if any) does it make if the employer's liability is classified as contractual rather than tortious? (See *Sole* v. *W. J. Hallt, Ltd.*, *ante*; *Davie* v.

---

1. [1959] A.C. at pp. 621, 623; [1959] 1 All E.R. at pp. 351, 354.
2. [1959] A.C. at pp. 642, 646; [1959] 1 All E.R. at pp. 365, 367, 368.
3. [1961] A.C. 807; [1961] 1 All E.R. 495.
4. [1959] 1 All E.R. 346; [1959] A.C. 604.

New Merton Board Mills, Ltd., [1959] A.C. 604; [1959] 1 All E.R. 346; J. A. Jolowicz, [1973] C.L.J. 209.)

4. Would the Employer's Liability (Defective Equipment) Act 1969 (p. 639, *ante*) make the manufacturer liable to the plaintiff, had these facts been stated after that Act came into operation?

6. CORPORATIONS AND ASSOCIATIONS

Lennard's Carrying Co., Ltd. v. Asiatic Petroleum Co., Ltd.

House of Lords   [1914–15] All E.R. Rep. 280

Section 502 of the Merchant Shipping Act 1894 provides that the owner of a British sea-going ship is not liable to make good to any extent whatever "any loss or damage happening without his actual fault or privity" where any goods are lost or damaged by reason of fire on board the ship.

Lennard was the active director of a ship-owning company. One of the company's ships was in an unseaworthy state and as a result the ship became stranded in a gale and the cargo belonging to the respondents was destroyed by fire.

VISCOUNT HALDANE L.C.: . . . Did what happened take place without the actual fault or privity of the owners of the ship who were the appellants? A corporation is an abstraction. It has no mind of its own any more than it has a body of its own; its active and directing will must consequently be sought in the person of somebody who for some purposes may be called an agent, but who is really the directing mind and will of the corporation, the very ego and centre of the personality of the corporation. That person may be under the direction of the shareholders in general meeting; that person may be the board of directors itself, or it may be, and in some companies it is so, that that person has an authority co-ordinate with the board of directors given to him under the articles of association, and is appointed by the general meeting of the company, and can only be removed by the general meeting of the company. Whatever is not known about Mr. Lennard's position, this is known for certain, Mr. Lennard took the active part in the management of this ship on behalf of the owners, and Mr. Lennard as I have said, was registered as the person designated for this purpose in the ship's register. Mr. Lennard, therefore, was the natural person to come on behalf of the owners and give full evidence not only about the events of which I have spoken, and which related to the seaworthiness of the ship, but about his own position and as to whether or not he was the life and soul of the company. For if Mr. Lennard was the directing mind of the company, then his action, unless a corporation is not to be liable at all, have been an action which was the action of the company itself within the meaning of s. 502. It has not been contended at the Bar, and it could not have been successfully contended, that s. 502 is so worded as to exempt a corporation altogether which happened to be the owner of a ship, merely because it happened to be a corporation. It must be upon the true construction of that section in such a case as the present one that the fault or privity is the fault of somebody who is not merely a servant or agent for whom the company is liable upon the footing respondeat superior, but somebody for whom the company is liable because his action is the very action of the company itself. . . .

[LORDS DUNEDIN, ATKINSON, PARKER OF WADDINGTON and PARMOOR concurred.]

Questions

1. If some officers of a company are "the directing mind and will of the corporation" is there any need for a doctrine of vicarious responsibility for

the acts of corporations? (See Atiyah, *Vicarious Liability in the Law of Torts*, pp. 381–83; Gower, *Modern Company Law*, 3rd Edn., pp. 144 *et seq.*)

2. Consider *Carmarthenshire County Council* v. *Lewis*, [1955] A.C. 549; [1955] 1 All E.R. 565 (p. 101, *ante*). The Court of Appeal treated the Council as vicariously liable for the teacher's negligence in allowing the boy to escape on to the highway, while the House of Lords treated the Council as "personally" negligent in allowing such an easy method of escape. Which approach is preferable? Note, as well, the cases on hospital authorities (p. 600, *ante*).

Heatons Transport (St. Helens), Ltd. v. Transport and General Workers' Union

House of Lords   [1972] 3 All E.R. 101

The question in issue was whether the Transport and General Workers' Union, an unregistered organisation of workers (a quasi-corporation in law since proceedings could be brought by or against the organisation in its own name although not a corporate body), was responsible for certain statutory "unfair industrial practices" contrary to the provisions of the Industrial Relations Act 1971, committed by its shop stewards at Liverpool and Hull docks. The House of Lords (overruling a unanimous Court of Appeal) held that the Union was responsible. The actual decision turns on its peculiar facts, and, in the joint opinion of their Lordships, was expressly stated to be confined to liability for unfair industrial practices; the "closely connected subject" of liability for tortious acts was said to be outside the scope of the decision. The remarks of their Lordships set out below, however, do raise a question of general principle about the liability of associations.

LORD WILBERFORCE delivered the joint opinion of their Lordships. . . . In the Court of Appeal Lord Denning M.R. and Roskill L.J. in considering the scope of the shop stewards' authority placed considerable reliance on the fact that the shop stewards were agents rather than servants. But we think that is not an important factor in this case. No new development is involved in the law relating to the responsibility of a master .or principal for the act of a servant or agent. In each case the test to be applied is the same: was the servant or agent acting on behalf of, and within the scope of the authority conferred by, the master or principal? (*Hewitt* v. *Bonvin*;[1] *Morgans* v. *Launchbury*.[2]) Usually a servant, as compared with an agent, has a wider authority because his employment is more permanent and he has a larger range of duties and he may have to exercise discretion in dealing with a series of situations as they arise. The agent in an ordinary case is engaged to perform a particular task on a particular occasion and has authority to do whatever is required for that purpose but has no general authority. That is the explanation of the reasoning in the case of the *Wigan Election Petition Case*[3] and in *Lucas* v. *Mason*.[4] In the former case Martin B. was stating and applying "the ordinary rule with regard to principal and agent: that the principal is only responsible for that which he authorises the agent to do". In the latter case Pollock B. said:[5]

"In the present case there was no relation of master and servant, or of principal and general agent, or agent for such cases as might occur in the absence of the principal, but a particular direction as to a particular matter . . . In the case of master and servant, the character and duties attaching to the employment are known and defined beforehand, the servant who is to perform them is selected accordingly. In the present case no such relationship existed in the first instance, nor did it arise

1. [1940] 1 K.B. 188.
2. [1973] A.C. 127; [1972] 2 All E.R. 606.
3. (1869), 21 L.T. 122.
4. (1875), L.R. 10 Exch. 251.
5. (1875), L.R. 10 Exch. at pp. 253, 254.

during the transaction . . . There is no such pre-existing relationship as exists in the case of master and servant, and there is, we think, no ground for extending by implication an express authority limited in its terms."

Those two cases do not show that for the purpose of determining the responsibility of the master for acts of a servant and that of the principal for the acts of an agent different tests are to be applied. They only show that application of the same test may produce different results.

But there are cases in which an agent who is not a servant does have authority of considerable generality. He may be elected or appointed to some office or post for a substantial period and he may have to perform acts of several classes on behalf of the principal and he may have to exercise a discretion in dealing with a series of situations as they arise. The position of such an agent and the scope of his authority are very similar to those of a servant . . .

Notes

1. The Court of Appeal's approach in this case had been a two-stage inquiry: (1) did the shop stewards fall within any established category of persons for whose acts there could be vicarious responsibility? (2) were the acts authorised so as to make the union responsible? Since the stewards were not employees of the Union the complaint failed at the first stage. Can the approach in *Heatons* be reconciled with that in *Morgans* v. *Launchbury*? (p. 606, *ante*). For general comment, see Bob Hepple, "Union Responsibility for Shop Stewards" (1972), 1 I.L.J. 197.

2. "Authority" must emanate from the members as set out in the rules in the case of unincorporated members' clubs: *Flemyng* v. *Hector* (1836), 2 M. & W. 172; *Re St. James Club* (1852), 2 De G.M. & G. 383. In the case of trade unions the House of Lords, in *Heatons* found that authority to take industrial action had not come "from the top" but from "the bottom", i.e. the membership of the union as a whole by custom. In *Howitt Transport, Ltd.* v. *Transport and General Workers' Union*, [1973] 1 C.R. 1, the National Industrial Relations Court held that a "group of members" could authorise action in this way. This is probably an erroneous "exception" to the general rules of vicarious responsibility: see K. W. Wedderburn (1973), 36 M.L.R. 226 and Bob Hepple (1973), 2 I.L.J. 102. But it has been followed in *General Aviation Services (U.K.), Ltd.* v. *Transport and General Workers' Union*, [1974] I.C.R. 35, at pp. 49–51 (N.I.R.C.). The Trade Union and Labour Relations Bill 1974 proposes to restore, in amended form, the immunity of trade unions in respect of tort actions which existed before the Industrial Relations Act 1971 came into force. The problems raised in this section will still arise in regard to other associations, and to tortious acts of trade unions resulting in personal injury or relating to property use or occupation etc. by trade unions.

19

Joint Liability

The problems with which the materials in this Chapter are concerned arise where the *same* damage is attributable to the conduct of two or more tortfeasors. If they have all participated in the same act leading to that damage they are called *joint* tortfeasors. The main examples of joint tortfeasors are (a) the person who authorises or instigates the commission of a tort and the person who carries out his instructions; (b) those who participate in a joint enterprise (p. 614, *ante*); and (c) employer and employee where the employer is vicariously liable for the torts of his employee (p. 595, *ante*). If, on the other hand, there are several *independent* acts all leading to the same damage, then they are called *several concurrent* tortfeasors. An example would be an accident in which two cars collide due to the negligent driving of each driver causing injury to a pedestrian. The drivers are *severally* liable, and they cannot be described as *joint* tortfeasors. (For an illustration from maritime law see *The Koursk*, [1924] P. 140.)

The distinction between joint tortfeasors and several concurrent tortfeasors is of little practical significance, except in one situation. This is that the release of one joint tortfeasor from his liability discharges all others liable with him, while the release of one of two or more several concurrent tortfeasors will not have this effect (*Cutler* v. *McPhail*, [1962] 2 Q.B. 292; [1962] 2 All E.R. 474, p. 648, *post*). This is an anachronism and the courts have mitigated the strict rules in two ways: (a) by deciding that a mere promise not to sue does not amount to a release; and (b) by allowing the plaintiff, when releasing one joint tortfeasor, to make an express reservation of rights against the other joint tortfeasors. Indeed, this reservation may even be implied: *Gardiner* v. *Moore*, [1969] 1 Q.B. 55; [1966] 1 All E.R. 365.

In all other respects joint tortfeasors and several concurrent tortfeasors are alike. Each tortfeasor is liable in full for the whole of the damage caused to the plaintiff. Satisfaction by any one tortfeasor usually discharges the liability of the others to the plaintiff. Although two or more tortfeasors may be joined as co-defendants in the action, only one sum can be awarded as damages and that sum must, accordingly, be the *lowest* sum for which any of the individual defendants can be held liable (*Cassell & Co., Ltd.* v. *Broome*, [1972] A.C. 1027; [1972] 1 All E.R. 801, p. 650, *post*). If a judgment is obtained against one tortfeasor this is not a bar to later proceedings against the others (Law Reform (Married Women and Tortfeasors) Act 1935, s. 6 (1) (*a*), p. 651, *post*) but the plaintiff may not take advantage of a higher verdict in a later action (*ibid.*, s. 6 (1) (*b*), p. 651, *post*),

There is a right of contribution between tortfeasors and it is with this right that the Chapter is principally concerned. The Law Reform (Married Women and Tortfeasors) Act 1935 (p. 651, *post*) abolishes the common law rule (*Merryweather* v. *Nixan* (1799), 8 Term Rep. 186) which denied this right. But the Act is so obscurely worded that an Australian judge has been led to call it "a piece of law reform which seems itself urgently to call for some reform": (1955), 92 C.L.R. 200, at p. 211. Apart from the statute there is, according to the House of Lords in *Lister* v. *Romford Ice and Cold Storage Co., Ltd.*, [1957] A.C. 555; [1957] 1 All E.R. 125, p. 660, *post*, an implied term in the contract of employment which allows an employer to recover an indemnity from the employee for whose torts he is vicariously liable. The exact scope of this implied term, particularly where insurance by the employer is compulsory (either as vehicle owner or as employer), is a matter for debate (p. 663, *post*). In practice this right of indemnity is of importance only where the employer's insurers choose to exercise their rights of subrogation and sue the employee in the employer's name, a rare occurrence because of a self-denying ordinance (p. 665, *post*).

1. EFFECT OF RELEASE OF JOINT TORTFEASOR

Cutler v. McPhail

Queen's Bench Division   [1962] 2 All E.R. 474

SALMON J.: The points raised on release are extremely interesting and by no means easy. The principle is quite plain, that, if there is a release of one joint tortfeasor, the cause of action against all the tortfeasors is extinguished; on the other hand, if there is merely an agreement not to sue one of several joint tortfeasors, the cause of action does not die and the other tortfeasors can properly be sued. What I have to decide here in respect of the publication in "The Villager", is whether there has been a release of the plaintiffs' cause of action against the defendant. In the *Price* v. *Barker*[1] line of cases, the court has had to consider a release by deed, where, in the body of the document, there is an express release followed by words purporting to retain the right to sue other joint tortfeasors—an express reservation of right. In such cases, it is clear from the authorities that there is no magic in the use of the word "release" in the deed. The deed has to be looked at as a whole, and, if it appears from the deed, looked at as a whole, that, although the parties have used the word "release", the deed is not intended to operate as a release but is merely an agreement or a promise not to sue, then it is merely a promise not to sue and not a release. But in the class of case to which I have referred, the decision, when it has been in favour of the view that the deed did not operate as a release, has always proceeded on the basis that the express reservation of rights in the document showed that it was not intended to operate as a release.

Here, one has to consider a release by accord and satisfaction, and the release with which I am particularly concerned is the release of the Pinner Association officers. They are the persons responsible for the publication in "The Villager", and they settled their case with the plaintiffs on the basis that they paid £250 damages and costs, and published an apology. As far as they are concerned, the matter starts with the letter

---

1. (1855), 4 E. & B. 760.

written by the plaintiffs' solicitor to Messrs. Wyld, Collins and Crosse, appearing for the Pinner Association and its officers. I need not read the whole of the letter, but the vital paragraph reads:

"Upon the apologies being published and the sum mentioned paid over, then my client will, of course, release from any further liability in respect of the publication complained of, all officers and members of the committee including, of course, the editor of 'The Villager'."

Presumably that letter means what it says. One can guess what the probability is; no doubt, when the letter was written the plaintiffs hoped to go on with their action against the present defendant. But I cannot see that stated anywhere in the letter, and, when I look at the rest of the correspondence following that letter, between the plaintiffs' solicitor and the solicitors for the Pinner Association officers, I still cannot find anything to indicate that, when the plaintiffs' solicitor used the word "release" in his letter of 19 February 1959, he did not mean precisely what he said; nor is there any evidence before me from which I can come to the conclusion that a contrary intention was ever expressed by the plaintiffs to the Pinner Association officers.

Counsel for the plaintiffs has sought to rely on a letter which was written by the plaintiffs' solicitor to the solicitors for the printers and publishers, the Pinner Press, Ltd.; that letter also uses these words:

"Upon the publication of the apologies by your clients and payment by them of my costs, they will of course be released from all further liability in the matter",

and adds:

"As a matter of interest, it has not proved possible to effect a settlement of the matter with [the defendant] and I have instructed counsel to settle writ and statement of claim."

It is suggested that those last words amount to an express reservation of rights and an intimation that this letter was intended only as an agreement not to sue. In my judgment, the letter does not contain an express reservation of rights; it is at least as consistent with the view that the solicitor writing the letter intended to release without fully appreciating the legal consequences of a release, as it is with any other suggested interpretation. But, as far as the release to the Pinner Association officers is concerned, there are no such additional words in the relevant letter and, as I have already indicated, I have looked, and looked in vain, to find anything which expresses an intention, or from which an intention could properly be deduced, negativing what the letter of February 19 says in the plainest terms.

It may be that the law relating to release might be re-considered with advantage; the difference between a release and an agreement not to sue is highly technical but very real in its effect, but, whilst the law remains as it is, I feel bound to hold in this case that there has been a release of the Pinner Association officers, and that that release in law extinguishes the claim in respect of the separate tort alleged to have been committed by the defendant in causing his letter to be published in "The Villager"....

Note

In *Gardiner v. Moore*, [1969] 1 Q.B. 55; [1966] 1 All E.R. 365, Thesiger J. held that there was no material difference between an express and an implied covenant not to sue. Being satisfied, on the facts, that there had been no intention to release the author of a libel when a claim against the newspaper proprietors and printers was settled, he held that the author had not been discharged from liability.

2. A SINGLE AWARD
Cassell & Co., Ltd. v. Broome

House of Lords   [1972] I All E.R. 801

[For the facts and other material aspects of the case see Chap. 12, p. 400, *ante*, and Chap. 16, p. 567, *ante*].

LORD HAILSHAM . . . Less meritorious, in my view, was the second criticism of the direction put before us. This was in effect that the judge did not correctly direct the jury as to the principles on which a joint award of exemplary damages can be made against two or more defendants guilty of the joint publication of a libel in respect of which their relevant guilt may be different, and their means of different amplitude. . . . I think the effect of the law is . . . that awards of punitive damages in respect of joint publications should reflect only the lowest figure for which any of them can be held liable. This seems to me to flow inexorably both from the principle that only one sum may be awarded in a single proceeding for a joint tort, and from the authorities which were cited to us by counsel for the appellants in detail in the course of his argument. . . . I think that the inescapable conclusion to be drawn from these authorities is that only one sum can be awarded by way of exemplary damages where the plaintiff elects to sue more than one defendant in the same action in respect of the same publication, and that this sum must represent the highest *common* factor, that as the *lowest* sum for which any of the defendants can be held liable on this score. Although we were concerned with exemplary damages, I would think that the same principle applies generally and in particular to aggravated damages, and that dicta or apparent dicta to the contrary can be disregarded. As counsel conceded, however, plaintiffs who wish to differentiate between the defendants can do so in various ways, for example, by electing to sue the more guilty only, by commencing separate proceedings against each and then consolidating, or, in the case of a book or newspaper article, by suing separately in the same proceedings for the publication of the manuscript to the publisher by the author. Defendants, of course, have their ordinary contractual or statutory remedies for contribution or indemnity so far as they may be applicable to the facts of a particular case. But these may be inapplicable to exemplary damages. . . .

LORD REID: . . . Unless we are to abandon all pretence of justice, means must be found to prevent more being recovered by way of punitive damages from the least guilty then he ought to pay. We cannot rely on his being able to recover some contribution from the other. Suppose printer, author and publisher of a libel are all sued. The printer will probably be guiltless of any outrageous conduct but the others may deserve punishment beyond compensatory damages. If there has to be one judgment against all three then it would be very wrong to allow any element of punitive damages at all to be included because very likely the printer would have to pay the whole and the others might not be worth suing for a contribution. The only logical way to deal with the matter would be first to have a judgment against all the defendants for the compensatory damages and then to have a separate judgment against each of the defendants for such additional sum as he should pay as punitive damages. I would agree that that is impracticable. The fact that it is impracticable to do full justice appears to me to afford another illustration of how anomalous and indefensible is the whole doctrine of punitive damages. But as I have said before we must accept it and make the best we can of it.

So, in my opinion, the jury should be directed that, when they come to consider what if any addition is to be made to the compensatory damages by way of punitive damages, they must consider each defendant separately. If any one of the defendants does not deserve punishment or if the compensatory damages are in themselves sufficient punishment for any one of the defendants, then they must not make any addition to the compensatory damages. If each of the defendants deserves more punishment than is involved in payment of the compensatory damages then they must determine which deserves the least punishment and only add to the compensatory damages such additional sum as that defendant ought to pay by way of punishment. I do not pretend that that achieves full justice but it is the best we can do without separate awards against each defendant. . . .

3. CONTRIBUTION BETWEEN TORTFEASORS

(a) By Statute

The Law Reform (Married Women and Tortfeasors) Act 1935

6. Proceedings against, and contribution between, joint and several tortfeasors.—(1) Where damage is suffered by any person as a result of a tort (whether a crime or not)—

(a) judgment recovered against any tortfeasor liable in respect of that damage shall not be a bar to an action against any other person who would, if sued, have been liable as a joint tortfeasor in respect of the same damage;

(b) if more than one action is brought in respect of that damage by or on behalf of the person by whom it was suffered, or for the benefit of the estate, or of the [dependants] of that person, against tortfeasors liable in respect of the damage (whether as joint tortfeasors or otherwise) the sums recoverable under the judgments given in those actions by way of damages shall not in the aggregate exceed the amount of the damages awarded by the judgment first given; and in any of those actions, other than that in which judgment is first given, the plaintiff shall not be entitled to costs unless the court is of opinion that there was reasonable ground for bringing the action;

(c) any tortfeasor liable in respect of that damage may recover contribution from any other tortfeasor who is, or would if sued have been, liable in respect of the same damage, whether as a joint tortfeasor or otherwise, so, however, that no person shall be entitled to recover contribution under this section from any person entitled to be indemnified by him in respect of the liability in respect of which the contribution is sought.

(2) In any proceedings for contribution under this section the amount of the contribution recoverable from any person shall be such as may be found by the court to be just and equitable having regard to the extent of that person's responsibility for the damage; and the court shall have power to exempt any person from liability to make contribution, or to direct that the contribution to be recovered from any person shall amount to a complete indemnity.

(3) For the purposes of this section—

[(a) the expression "dependants" means the person for whose benefit actions may be brought under the Fatal Accidents Acts 1846 to 1959; and]

(b) the reference in this section to "the judgment first given" shall, in a case where that judgment is reversed on appeal, be construed as a reference to the judgment first given which is not so reversed and, in a case where a judgment is varied on appeal, be construed as a reference to that judgment as so varied.

(4) Nothing in this section shall—

(a) apply with respect to any tort committed before the commencement of this Part of this Act; or

(b) affect any criminal proceedings against any person in respect of any wrongful act; or

(c) render enforceable any agreement for indemnity which would not have been enforceable if this section had not been passed.

George Wimpey & Co., Ltd. v. B.O.A.C.

House of Lords   [1954] 3 All E.R. 661

John Littlewood, an aircraft cleaner employed by B.O.A.C. (the respondents), was injured in a collision between a vehicle driven by an employee of Wimpeys (the appellants) and another vehicle driven by a B.O.A.C. employee. Littlewood brought an action for damages against Wimpeys who, in turn, issued a third party notice addressed to B.O.A.C. claiming contribution or indemnity under s. 6 (1) (c) of the Act of 1935. Littlewood then obtained leave to join B.O.A.C. as co-defendants. His action and the third party proceedings were heard together by Parker J. who held (a) that Littlewood was entitled to judgment against Wimpeys on the grounds of the negligence of their employee; (b) that B.O.A.C. were entitled to judgment against Littlewood because his claim was barred by s. 21 of the Limitation Act 1939 [this section imposed a special time limit in claims against "public authorities" and was later repealed by the Law Reform (Limitation of Actions, &c.) Act 1954]; (c) that Wimpeys were two-thirds to blame and B.O.A.C. one-third to blame for the collision which caused the injuries; and (d) that in the third party proceedings, B.O.A.C. were entitled to judgment against Wimpeys on the ground that the latter's claim for contribution did not come within s. 6 (1) (c) of the Act of 1935. Wimpeys appealed from that part of the judgment which is stated under (d) above, and their appeal was dismissed by the Court of Appeal (Singleton and Morris L.JJ., Denning L.J. dissenting). Wimpeys appealed further to the House of Lords. The appeal was dismissed by a majority of 3:2.

VISCOUNT SIMONDS: . . . The question of construction, as I see it, is whether s. 6 (1) (c) can, according to its natural meaning, be so interpreted as to admit a claim for contribution by one tortfeasor against another when that other has been sued by the injured person and held not liable. I agree with Parker J. and Singleton and Morris L.JJ. in thinking that it cannot. It appears to me that the first matter for consideration is what is the meaning of the word "liable" where it is secondly used in s. 6 (1) (c), and I think it is plain beyond argument that it means held liable in judgment. No other meaning can reasonably be attributed to it in the context "would if sued have been", for these words make a suit the condition of liability. I do not, therefore, think it necessary to discuss what the paragraph might mean, if, as has been suggested, the word "liable" bore some other significance, the precise legal content of which I do not find it easy to define, such as "responsible at law". If the word "liable", where secondly used in para. (c), bears the meaning which I have ascribed to it, I should be reluctant to give it any other meaning where it is first used in the same paragraph, nor do I think it unreasonable that the right of contribution between tortfeasors should be limited to the case where he who seeks contribution has himself been sued to judgment. In the view which I take it is immaterial whether the word, where first used, has the same meaning or another: if it were necessary for me to decide it, I should say it had the same meaning.

The question then can be simply stated. Contribution is recoverable from one who in an actual suit by the injured man had been held liable by judgment: it is recoverable from one who, if sued, would in that hypothetical suit have been held liable. Is it also recoverable from one who has been actually sued by the injured man and held not liable? It happens in the case under appeal that the reason why the party from whom contribution was claimed was held not liable was because the Limitation Act was successfully pleaded; but this is irrelevant to the issue. The same question would arise if the claimant tortfeasor alleged that the defence, though it succeeded on the merits, was successful only because the case had been inadequately presented, or even because the judge or jury had taken a wrong view of it. It appears to me that a construction leading to such a result should only be accepted if the language fairly admits of no other meaning. But, so far from this being the case, in my opinion the subsection plainly contemplates two classes only of persons from whom contribution can be claimed, viz., those who have been sued and those who have not been sued but would, if sued, be held liable. If the intention had been to include a third class of persons who, having been already sued and found not liable, might yet in hypothetical proceedings be sued a second time and then found liable (an extravagant intention, as it appears to me, to impute to the legislature) I should have expected to find it expressed in clear and appropriate language. Not only is it not so expressed, but, on the contrary, I find in the words actually used the clear indication that the class of persons who "if sued would have been liable" does not include persons who, having been sued, have been held not liable. As Morris L.J. aptly put it ([1953] 2 All E.R. at p. 926) the words "if sued" postulate the case of someone who has not been sued.

For these reasons, I am in favour of dismissing this appeal and I do not find it necessary to discuss a question of great difficulty, viz., at what date is the hypothetical suit, in which the "other tortfeasor . . . would if sued have been liable", to be presumed to have been commenced, and I will say no more than that, having read and considered the opinion of my noble and learned friend, Lord Reid, I should on this part of the case accept his conclusion, though I find myself reluctantly differing from him on the first and vital question. . . .

LORD PORTER (dissenting): . . . To me, the wording naturally refers to persons who were implicated in the tort. B.O.A.C. were implicated and, therefore, would have been liable if sued. Any additional words are, I think, unnecessary, but if I had to make any implication it would be to add the words "as a result of the commission of the tort" to the words "would have been liable if sued".

I prefer to interpret s. 6 (1) (*c*) as it stands. It stipulates nothing as to time, but, to my mind, B.O.A.C. in terms come within the category of those who would have been liable if sued, and, unless some qualification is placed on those words, Wimpeys can recover the contribution they ask. In my view, the two types of person referred to are simply those who have been sued or those who would have been liable, if sued, and I see no reason for making the classes mutually exclusive. I think that I should qualify this opinion in one respect. If contribution is to be obtained, the tortfeasor who has not been sued and never could be sued by the plaintiff is not liable to contribute to the party held liable, e.g. the husband sues some wrong-doer in respect of a wrong for which his wife was partly responsible. In that case no contribution is recoverable because the wife would never, if sued, be liable.

I have reached my opinion as to the true construction of s. 6 (1) (*c*) of the Act on its wording alone without adding to or subtracting from its phraseology, but if there is thought to be any ambiguity, then, in my view, that ambiguity should be resolved in favour of Wimpeys. . . .

LORD REID: . . . Section 6 (1) (*c*) appears to be intended to be generally applicable to cases in which one tortfeasor seeks to recover contribution

"from any other tortfeasor who is, or would if sued have been, liable in respect of the same damage."

I agree with your Lordships that the word "liable" in this context must necessarily mean held liable by judgment, and, so reading the word, s. 6 (1) (*c*) in my judgment first requires an answer to the question whether that other tortfeasor has already been held liable in respect of that damage. If he has, and if the other conditions of the section are satisfied, then the Act gives a right to contribution. But if he has not, a second question must be asked: Would that other tortfeasor, if sued, have been held liable in respect of that damage? I do not think that it is disputed that this must mean if sued by the person who suffered the damage. But still there are many cases where that question, as it stands, cannot be answered yes or no. A person may be held liable if sued at one time but not if sued at another time: for example, a person who would have been held liable if sued at an earlier date may at a later date have a good defence under the Limitation Act or because he has had his liability discharged by the grant to him of a release. If s. 6 (1) (c) is to be capable of application to such cases the words "if sued" must have a temporal connotation. The words "would . . . have been liable" show that the hypothetical action must be supposed to have been brought at some time between the date when the damage was suffered and the date when the claim for contribution is determined, but, as I have said, that is often not sufficiently definite to enable the question to be answered. No matter what may be the true construction of the rest of the subsection, this difficulty remains, and if s. 6 (1) (c) is to be operative generally something beyond the bare words of the enactment must at this point be read into it. There are at least four possibilities. The meaning may be "would if sued immediately after the damage was suffered have been held liable," or it may be "if sued when the tortfeasor claiming contribution was sued," or it may be "if sued when the claim for contribution was made," or it may be enough that there was at least some time between these dates when the action would have succeeded.

I can illustrate the practical difference between these interpretations by taking the facts of the present case but supposing that Littlewood had never added the respondents, B.O.A.C., as defendants. If it had been realised that B.O.A.C. were protected by s. 21 (1) of the Limitation Act, 1939, they never would have been added as defendants. The action by Littlewood against the appellants, Wimpeys, and Wimpeys' claim against B.O.A.C. for contribution would have been tried together and, as B.O.A.C. had never been sued by Littlewood, it would, on any interpretation of s. 6 (1) (c) of the Act of 1935, have been necessary to ask the question, would B.O.A.C. if sued by Littlewood have been held liable to Littlewood, and it would have been impossible to answer that question in that form. If B.O.A.C. had been sued by Littlewood before 28 July 1950, they would have been held liable, but if sued after that date they would have been held not liable. The Act of 1935 must, if possible, be construed so as to make it applicable to that case and it can only be made to apply by holding that in their context the words "if sued" mean if sued at some particular date or during some particular period.

Let me assume for the moment that the first of the four possible meanings which I have mentioned is held on a construction of the subsection as a whole to be the true meaning. The question then would be: Would B.O.A.C. if sued by Littlewood immediately after the accident have been held liable to him? The answer would be, Yes, and Wimpeys would be entitled to contribution. Now let me take the facts of the present case. B.O.A.C. were sued by Littlewood, but not until a defence under the Limitation Act was available to them, and they were held not liable. So the first question—Have they been held liable?—must still be answered no. The second question must then be asked, and it must still be the same as before—Would B.O.A.C. if sued immediately after the accident have been held liable?—and the answer must still be yes. "If sued" must still have the same meaning; its meaning depends on the construction of the subsection and cannot alter with the facts of the particular case. The argument against this view is, as I understand it, that the words "would if sued have been liable" imply that that tortfeasor has not, in fact, been sued at any time. I would agree if the words "if sued" did not refer to any particular time. But if they must be construed as referring to a particular time, then, in my view, all that can be implied from them is that that tortfeasor was not, in fact, sued at that time. If the time to which "if sued" refers were immediately after the accident, then the fact that B.O.A.C. were sued unsuccessfully at the wrong time would not alter the fact that, if sued at the right time, they would have been held liable.

If, however, the true meaning of "if sued" is if sued at the time when the tortfeasor claiming contribution was being sued, then Wimpeys, the appellants in this case, must fail and they must equally have failed if Littlewood had never sued B.O.A.C. at all. In neither case could there be an affirmative answer to either of the questions posed by s. 6 (1) (*c*), because on that construction the second question would be: Would B.O.A.C. if sued when Wimpeys were sued have been held liable?

It is, therefore, in my judgment, necessary for the decision of this case to determine as a matter of construction to what period the words "if sued" refer, and that can only be determined by considering the subsection as a whole. I begin by considering the terms of s. 6 (1) (*a*). It is true that this only deals with joint tortfeasors and, therefore, has no application to the present case, but it may be important because in structure and phraseology it closely resembles sub-s. (1) (*c*). It provides:

"(1) Where damage is suffered by any person as a result of a tort (whether a crime or not)—(*a*) judgment recovered against any tortfeasor liable in respect of that damage shall not be a bar to an action against any other person who would, if sued, have been liable as a joint tortfeasor in respect of the same damage;"

Before 1935, if judgment was recovered against one joint tortfeasor that judgment was a bar to any action against another joint tortfeasor even although no sum had been or could be recovered under that judgment. This provision removes that bar.

There are two points in sub-s. (1) (*a*) which should, I think, be noted. In the first place the word "liable" occurs twice, and in each case it is clear that it must mean held liable. And, secondly, in the phrase "who would, if sued, have been liable as a joint tortfeasor", it appears to me that "if sued" most probably means if he had been sued together with the tortfeasor first mentioned, because a person cannot properly be said to be held liable "as a joint tortfeasor" if he is sued alone. If that is right, not only must the words "if sued" here have a temporal connotation, but they must refer to the time when the other tortfeasor was sued. But that conclusion depends on an assumption that the language of the provision is used accurately, and looking to the defective drafting of other parts of the subsection it would, I think, be unsafe to rely on any inference from the form of drafting of sub-s. (1) (*a*). With regard to sub-s. (1) (*b*), I need only observe that the word "liable" is there used in a context where it cannot possibly mean held liable. The context is

"if more than one action is brought . . . against tortfeasors liable in respect of the damage",

and "liable" there can only mean against whom there is a cause of action. So on any construction of the sub-section the word "liable" must be held to have quite different meanings in different places in the subsection. I am not prepared in this case to base my decision on any inference from similarities of expression in either sub-s. (1) (*a*) or sub-s. (1) (*b*).

Next I would consider the mischief against which sub-s. (1) (*c*) is directed. Before 1935, if separate torts by two different tortfeasors contributed to cause the same damage, the plaintiff could, and, I think, commonly did, sue and get judgment against both tortfeasors in the same action. He could then proceed to recover the damages from whichever one he chose and the tortfeasor who had been made to pay had no right to require the other to contribute. Plainly that was thought by Parliament to be unjust and that case is undoubtedly covered by the first alternative in sub-s. (1) (*c*)—

"any tortfeasor liable . . . may recover contribution from any other tortfeasor who is . . . liable in respect of the same damage . . ."

But a plaintiff might, and sometimes did, choose to sue only one when he might have sued and succeeded against both, and the second alternative—

"any tortfeasor liable . . . may recover contribution from any other tortfeasor who . . . would if sued have been, liable in respect of the same damage . . ."

is, I think, designed to cover that case. The second tortfeasor is put in no worse position than he would have been in if the plaintiff had taken the ordinary course of suing both.

But in cases like the present the position is very different. By virtue of statutory protection, when a year had elapsed without the plaintiff, Littlewood, raising any action, the respondents, B.O.A.C., had a complete defence against him and, before 1935, would have been free of all liability. If the appellants' argument is right, in effect Parliament in 1935 partially withdrew that statutory protection and B.O.A.C., although not sued within the year, would now be liable to make a payment in respect of the damage caused by their negligence. It is true that they are not liable to the plaintiff directly, but Wimpeys, the appellants, could only recover from B.O.A.C. because the negligence of B.O.A.C. caused damage to Littlewood. If it had been intended to modify in this way the statutory protection afforded by an earlier Act, I would have expected at least some indication of such an intention in s. 6. But I can find none. The words of sub-s. (1) (c) are amply satisfied if "if sued" is held to mean if sued at the time when action was being taken against the other tortfeasor. I have said that for other reasons "if sued" must have a temporal connotation, and, if that be so, then it seems to me that, if one merely looks at the context, that is, at least, as likely a connotation as any other.

Counsel for the appellants first argued that "if sued" should be held to mean "if sued immediately after the accident", but ultimately, and I think wisely, preferred the meaning "if sued at some time or if sued at the time most favourable to the plaintiff". That argument can be supported on two grounds. If one looks at the matter from the point of view of the tortfeasor claiming contribution, it can be said that, if the statute prevents him from being prejudiced by the whim of the plaintiff in choosing to make him pay when both have been held liable or in choosing to sue him alone when both could have been sued successfully, then it would be reasonable that it should also prevent him from being prejudiced by the plaintiff choosing to delay bringing his action until a time when the other tortfeasor has a statutory defence. The second argument in favour of the appellants' contention arises in this way: a tortfeasor, instead of waiting to be sued, may admit liability and pay damages, and it is said that the statute should be so construed as to entitle him to the same contribution from a second tortfeasor as he would have been entitled to if the plaintiff had sued him and obtained judgment. If that is right, then the words "if sued" cannot mean if sued together with the first tortfeasor and, it is said, must, therefore, have the meaning for which the appellants contend. But sub-s. (1) (c) could mean that a tortfeasor can recover contribution from another tortfeasor if the latter would, if sued by the plaintiff at the time when the former tortfeasor claims contribution, have been held liable; and that would avoid this difficulty. It is not necessary in the present case to decide whether this or "if sued when the tortfeasor claiming contribution was sued" is the true meaning. On either meaning this appeal would fail and this question may arise for decision in some future case.

I think that there is much force in the appellants' arguments and without the aid of more general considerations I would find the case narrow and difficult. But, viewing the case as a whole, there is one matter which confirms me in my opinion. I think that it is clear that the draftsman of s. 6 failed to notice that cases like the present might occur and failed to make any express provision for them. This is, therefore, an example of the not uncommon situation where language not calculated to deal with an unforeseen case must, nevertheless, be so interpreted as to apply to it. In such cases it is, I think, right to hold that, if the arguments are fairly evenly balanced, that interpretation should be chosen which involves the least alteration of the existing law. If the appellants are right, the effect of s. 21 of the Limitation Act 1939, would be considerably modified but that is not so if the respondents are right. I am, accordingly, of opinion that the appeal should be dismissed.

LORD KEITH OF AVONHOLM (dissenting): . . . I reach the result that "liable" where first found in sub-s. (1) (*c*) does not mean "found liable". If so, the words "would if sued have been liable" cannot be read as "would if sued have been found liable in the same action in which the tortfeasor seeking contribution was found liable". The date to be attached to the words "if sued" is thus thrown completely loose and, in my opinion, the words should be referred to a time at which the words will be given efficacy in all cases, a time at which the question of liability for the damage can be sole issue to the exclusion of all special defences. I would only add that the word "liability" where found in the section seems to me to strengthen the view which I take of the meaning of "liable" at the outset of sub-s. (1) (*c*), as do also the reasons given by Denning L.J. in the Court of Appeal.

As it is conceded that the cause of action in an action for contribution does not arise earlier in this case than the date when judgment was given against the appellants, it follows that the action for contribution from the respondents is in time. It may seem a strange result that the action by the injured man against the respondents failed for being out of time and that the action for contribution against them is in time. But no question of policy in this matter can, in my opinion, be appealed to as an aid to arriving at the proper construction of the statute. The apparent anomaly results from the cause of action in the two cases being ascribed to a different point of time. It is to be observed, further, that the construction of the statute contended for by the respondents would put it in the power of the injured party, whether by accident or design, to determine in many cases whether contribution could be got or not. I would allow the appeal.

[LORD TUCKER delivered a speech in effect agreeing with VISCOUNT SIMONDS.]

Question

Does this case decide that where a tortfeasor has been sued and held not liable, no claim for contribution can be made from him? Suppose X is injured by A, a servant of B, a "fly-by-night" employer. Suppose further that X sues A and obtains judgment against him just before the end of the limitation period (which is the same for A and B), but, because A cannot satisfy the whole judgment, X later sues B who has now been traced. If this action against B fails because the limitation period has now expired, could A thereafter claim contribution from B (assuming B to have been to some extent at fault)?

Notes

1. In *Hart* v. *Hall and Pickles, Ltd.*, [1969] 1 Q.B. 405; [1968] 3 All E.R. 291, the Court of Appeal held that *Wimpey's* case (*ante*) is authoritative only in the situation where the tortfeasor from whom contribution is sought has been sued to judgment and held not liable. So where the action against one tortfeasor has been dismissed for want of prosecution by the plaintiff, that tortfeasor is not exempted from contribution by any other tortfeasor. The party claiming the contribution must, of course, show that the other tortfeasor "would . . . if sued . . . have been liable".

2. In *Harvey* v. *O'Dell, Ltd.*, [1958] 2 Q.B. 78; [1958] 1 All E.R. 657, McNair J. disregarded the conflicting opinions expressed in *Wimpeys* case regarding the effect of the words "if sued" and held that they did not have any temporal connotation: they meant "if sued at any time". (For the facts and other aspects of this case see p. 665, *post*.)

McNair J. was not, of course, dealing with a case where the person from whom contribution was claimed, had been sued and held not liable.

Stott v. West Yorkshire Road Car Co., Ltd.
(Home Bakeries, Ltd. and Another, Third Parties)

Court of Appeal   [1971] 3 All E.R. 534

The plaintiff was a motor-cyclist who had been injured by the negligent driving by the second defendant of a bus owned by his employers the first defendants. The defendants joined as third parties to the action the owners and driver of a van which had been parked on a bend on the road where the accident occurred. The defendants reached a settlement with the plaintiff in the sum of £10,000, which the plaintiff acknowledged was made "without any admission of liability by them or either of them". The defendants then sought contribution from the third parties, who denied all liability for the accident. The registrar held that the defendants could proceed with the claim but on appeal the judge held that having made a settlement in which they had not been "held liable" nor "admitted liability" they had lost the right to contribution under s. 6 (1) (*c*) of the Act of 1935. The defendants successfully appealed.

LORD DENNING M.R.: . . . The judge has held that a tortfeasor can only claim contribution when he has been *held liable* for the damage or has *admitted* liability for it. If the tortfeasor has not admitted liability (as in this case) the judge held that he cannot claim contribution. The judge was influenced by the wording of s. 4 (2) (*a*) and (*b*) of the Limitation Act 1963. Those paragraphs provide for the time within which a tortfeasor must claim contribution: (a) where the tortfeasor is "held liable"; (b) where the tortfeasor "admits liability". The judge thought that those subsections showed that a tortfeasor had only a right of contribution if he had been "held liable" or "admitted liability".

I do not myself think that the later Act of 1963 should be allowed to cut down the substantive right given by the 1935 Act. Our task is to find out the meaning of the word "liable" where it is used in s. 6 (1) (*c*) of the 1935 Act. We had to consider it in *Littlewood* v. *George Wimpey & Co., Ltd., British Overseas Airways Corpn. (second defendants and third parties).*[1] My own view at that time[2] was that "liable" does not mean "held liable by judgment"; it means "responsible in law" for the damage. But in the House of Lords[3] Viscount Simonds thought that "liable" meant held liable by judgment. His reason was because the word "liable" in the place where it is secondly used in para. (*c*), clearly means "held liable in judgment"; and he thought that it ought to have the same meaning in the place where it was first used in that paragraph. But the other members of the House did not go with him on that point. Lord Keith of Avonholm said[4] in terms that he agreed with me.

Since that case, we have some guidance from Parliament itself. The Limitation Act 1963 shows that "liable" is not confined to "held liable by judgment". It extends at any rate to "admits liability". That shows that Viscount Simonds's view cannot prevail. Relieved of his view, I come back to the view which I expressed in 1953. I am of opinion that the word "liable" does mean "responsible in law". It follows that a tortfeasor is entitled to recover contribution from another tortfeasor (i) when he has been held liable in judgment; (ii) when he has admitted liability; and (iii) when he has settled the action by agreeing to make payment to the injured person, although, in making the settlement, he has not admitted liability. But, of course, when the tortfeasor settles an action, he cannot claim contribution from the other tortfeasor unless he proves that he himself was "liable". He must prove, therefore, that, if the claim had been fought out, he would have been held responsible in law and liable to pay in whole or in part for the damage. At that subsequent stage, therefore, he must admit liability

---

1. [1953] 2 Q.B. 501; [1953] 2 All E.R. 915.
2. See [1953] 2 Q.B. at pp. 515–518; [1953] 2 All E.R. at pp. 921–923.
3. See *George Wimpey & Co., Ltd.* v. *British Overseas Airways Corpn.*, [1955] A.C. 169, at p. 178; [1954] 3 All E.R. 661, at p. 664.
4. See [1955] A.C. at p. 196; [1954] 3 All E.R. at p. 676.

because otherwise he does not bring himself within the section. In this particular case, therefore, the bus company will have to say to the van owners: "We settled the action because we were liable in part, and we are ready to prove it. And now we claim contribution." On proof that they were responsible in law in part for the injury to the plaintiff, they can claim contribution.

In support of this view, I would quote from one of the first commentators on this Act, Professor Glanville Williams.[1] He wrote:

"... considerations of policy are overwhelmingly in favour of allowing a tortfeasor to settle out of court and then claim contribution, rather than go to the trouble of defending an action merely to qualify for the right to contribution." ...

SALMON L.J.: ... It is the commonest thing in the world for defendants to settle accident cases before even a writ is issued. It would be most unfortunate if the court construed this Act in such a way as to make it necessary for a defendant to go to the expense of insisting on having an action brought and judgment entered against him before he could recover contribution from any joint tortfeasor. I cannot believe that Parliament in passing this Act intended to produce such an unfortunate result; and, since it clearly used the word "liable" in different senses in the same subsection, I would prefer to give the word "liable" as first used in s. 6 (1) (*c*) the same meaning as the word "liable" as used in s. 6 (1) (*b*) rather than the meaning which the House of Lords decided it bore when secondly used in s. 6 (1) (*c*). In my respectful view, the construction that I favour is consistent with common sense and avoids totally unnecessary legal costs, and, as far as I can see has nothing against it except an obiter dictum of Lord Simonds which commands the very greatest respect, but which I do not think ought to outweigh the powerful reasons for construing the word "liable" as first used in s. 6 (1) (*c*) in the way in which Lord Denning M.R. has construed it and I myself would construe it.

[MEGAW L.J. delivered a judgment in favour of allowing the appeal.]

Question

Why should the defendants want to settle "without admission of liability", if they subsequently need to prove that they *were* liable to the plaintiff in order to succeed in their claim for contribution? (See *Corry & Co., Ltd.* v. *Clarke*, [1967] N.I. 62 (C.A., Northern Ireland), not referred to in *Stott's* case, above, in which the tortfeasor from whom contribution was claimed was allowed to argue that the claimant tortfeasor, who had submitted to judgment for the plaintiff, was not liable to the plaintiff at all.)

Notes

1. *Basis of Apportionment:* From *Randolph* v. *Tuck*, [1962] 1 Q.B. 176, at p. 182, it can be seen that "responsibility" in s. 6 (2) of the Act of 1935 refers to (i) who is to *blame* (moral culpability) and (ii) who *caused* the accident (causation). For the difference between blameworthiness and causation see Lord Pearce in *The Miraflores and the Abadesa*, [1967] 1 A.C. 826, at p. 845.

2. *Limitation:* The Limitation Act 1963, s. 4 (1) provides that the right to claim contribution becomes statute-barred after the end of the period of two years from the date when that right accrued. The relevant date is the date of judgment against the first tortfeasor, or, where he admits liability, the date on which he agrees the amount to be paid: s. 4 (2). The Act is silent as to the case in which the first tortfeasor pays without admission of liability, but in *Stott* v. *West Yorkshire Road Car Co., Ltd.*, [1972] 3 All E.R. 534, at pp. 537

1. Joint Torts and Contributory Negligence, 1951, p. 97.

and 541 it was suggested that in such a case time would run from the date on which the amount to be paid by the defendant was agreed between him and the plaintiff.

(b) Under the Contract of Employment

Lister v. Romford Ice & Cold Storage Co., Ltd.

House of Lords   [1957] I All E.R. 125

The appellant, Lister, was employed as a lorry driver by the respondents. He negligently ran down his mate (his father) while backing his lorry in a yard. The father recovered damages against the respondents on grounds of their vicarious liability. The respondents' insurers, acting in their name by virtue of a term in the contract of insurance, brought an action against the appellant for damages for breach of an implied term in his contract of employment that he would exercise reasonable care and skill in his driving. The appellant pleaded that it was an implied term that he was entitled to the benefit of any insurance which his employer either had effected or as a reasonable and prudent person should have effected and consequently the respondents could not claim an indemnity or contribution from him.

The Court of Appeal, Denning L.J. dissenting, held that the respondents' action succeeded both under the Act of 1935 and because of the appellant's breach of the implied term. In the House of Lords this judgment was affirmed on the point of the implied term by 3:2 (the dissentients being Lord Radcliffe and Lord Somervell of Harrow). Although all five of their Lordships held that there was an implied term to use reasonable care, the dissentients took the view that the employee was protected by an implied term that the employer will not seek an indemnity where it is understood that the employer will take out a third-party liability policy. The majority (Viscount Simonds, Lord Morton of Henryton and Lord Tucker) said that such a term could not be implied.

Viscount Simonds: . . . It is, in my opinion, clear that it was an implied term of the contract that the appellant would perform his duties with proper care. The proposition of law stated by Willes J. in *Harmer* v. *Cornelius* ((1858), 5 C.B.N.S. 236, at p. 246) has never been questioned:

"When a skilled labourer, artisan, or artist is employed, there is on his part an implied warranty that he is of skill reasonably competent to the task he undertakes,— Spondes peritiam artis. Thus, if an apothecary, a watchmaker, or an attorney be employed for reward, they each impliedly undertake to possess and exercise reasonable skill in their several arts . . . An express promise or express representation in the particular case is not necessary."

I see no ground for excluding from, and every ground for including in, this category a servant who is employed to drive a lorry which, driven without care, may become an engine of destruction and involve his master in very grave liability. Nor can I see any valid reason for saying that a distinction is to be made between possessing skill and exercising it. No such distinction is made in the cited case; on the contrary, "possess" and "exercise" are there conjoined. Of what advantage to the employer is his servant's undertaking that he possesses skill unless he undertakes also to use it? I have spoken of using skill rather than using care, for "skill" is the word used in the cited case, but this embraces care. For even in so-called unskilled operations an exercise of care is necessary to the proper performance of duty.

I have already said that it does not appear to me to make any difference to the determination of any substantive issue in this case whether the respondents' cause of action lay in tort or breach of contract. But, in deference to Denning L.J. I think it right to say that I concur in what I understand to be the unanimous opinion of your Lordships that the servant owes a contractual duty of care to his master, and that the breach of that duty founds an action for damages for breach of contract, and that this (apart from any defence) is such a case. It is trite law that a single act of negligence may give rise to a claim either in tort or for breach of a term express or implied in a contract. Of this, the negligence of a servant in performance of his duty is a clear example.

I conclude, then, the first stage of the argument by saying that the appellant was under a contractual obligation of care in the performance of his duty, that he committed a breach of it, that the respondents thereby suffered damage and they are entitled to recover that damage from him, unless it is shown either that the damage is too remote or that there is some other intervening factor which precludes the recovery. . . .

My Lords, undoubtedly there are formidable obstacles in the path of the appellant, and they were formidably presented by counsel for the respondents. First, it is urged that it must be irrelevant to the right of the master to sue his servant for breach of duty that the master is insured against its consequences. As a general proposition it has not, I think, been questioned for nearly two hundred years that, in determining the rights inter se of A and B, the fact that one or other of them is insured is to be disregarded: see, e.g. *Mason* v. *Sainsbury* ((1782), 3 Doug. K.B. 61). This general proposition, no doubt, applies if A is a master and B his man; but its application to a case or class of case must yield to an express or implied term to the contrary, and, as the question is whether that term should be implied, I am not constrained by an assertion of the general proposition to deny the possible exception. Yet I cannot wholly ignore a principle so widely applicable as that a man insures at his own expense for his own benefit and does not thereby suffer any derogation of his rights against another man.

Next—and here I recur to a difficulty already indicated—if it has become part of the common law of England that, as between the employer and driver of a motor vehicle, it is the duty of the former to look after the whole matter of insurance (an expression which I have used compendiously to describe the plea as finally submitted), must not that duty be more precisely defined? It may be answered that in other relationships duties are imposed by law which can only be stated in general terms. Partners owe a duty of faithfulness to each other; what that duty involves in any particular case can only be determined in the light of all its circumstances. Other examples in other branches of the law may occur to your Lordships where a general duty is presented and its scope falls to be determined partly by the general custom of the country which is the basis of the law and partly, perhaps, by equitable considerations; but even so, the determination must rest on evidence of the custom or on such broad equitable considerations as have from early times guided a court of equity.

In the area in which this appeal is brought, there is no evidence to guide your Lordships. The single fact that, since the Road Traffic Act 1930, came into force, a measure of insurance against third-party risk is compulsory affords no ground for an assumption that an employer will take out a policy which covers more than the Act requires, for instance, a risk of injury to third parties not on the road but in private premises. There is, in fact, no assumption that can legitimately be made what policy will be taken out and what its terms and qualifications may be. I am unable to satisfy myself that, with such a background, there can be implied in the relationship of employer and driver any such terms as I have indicated. And though, as I have said, I feel the force of the argument as presented by Denning L.J., I must point out that, at least in his view, the indemnity of the driver was conditional on a policy which covered the risk having in fact been taken out. It may be that this was because his mind was directed to a case where such a policy was taken out, and that he would have gone on to say that there was a further implication that the employer would take out a policy whether required by law to do so or not. But here we are in the realm of speculation. Is it certain that, if the imaginary driver had said to his employer: "Of course you will indemnify me against any damage that I may do however gross my negligence may be", the employer would have said: "Yes, of course!". For myself, I cannot answer confidently that he would have said so or ought to have said so. It may well be that, if such a discussion had taken place, it might have ended in some agreement between them or in the driver not entering the service of that employer. That I do not know. But I do not know that I am ever driven further from an assured certainty what is the term which the law imports into the contract of service between the employer and the driver of a motor vehicle.

Another argument was, at this stage, adduced which appeared to me to have some weight. For just as it was urged that a term could not be implied unless it could be defined with precision, so its existence was denied if it could not be shown when it came to birth. Here, it was said, was a duty alleged to arise out of the relation of master and servant in this special sphere of employment which was imposed by the common law. When, then, did it first arise? Not, surely, when the first country squire exchanged his carriage and horses for a motor car or the first haulage contractor bought a motor lorry. Was it when the practice of insurance against third-party risk became so common that it was to be expected of the reasonable man, or was it only when the Act of 1930 made compulsory and, therefore, universal what had previously been reasonable and usual?

Then, again, the familiar argument was heard asking where the line is to be drawn. The driver of a motor car is not the only man in charge of an engine which, if carelessly used, may endanger and injure third parties. The man in charge of a crane was given as an example. If he, by his negligence, injures a third party who then makes his employer vicariously liable, is he entitled to assume that his employer has covered himself by insurance and will indemnify him, however gross and reprehensible his negligence? And does this depend on the extent to which insurance against third-party risks prevails and is known to prevail in any particular form of employment? Does it depend on the fact that there are fewer cranes than cars and that the master is less likely to drive a crane than a car? . . .

LORD MORTON OF HENRYTON: . . . If any such term is to be implied in this case, it must surely be implied in all cases where an employee is employed to drive any kind of vehicle which might cause damage to third parties. And the implied term cannot be limited to cases where the vehicle is being driven on a public highway, for the accident in the present case occurred in a yard. Surely it must logically extend to cases such as a crane driver in factory premises, and many other cases come to mind which cannot logically be distinguished from the present case. Such an obligation might have been imposed on the employer by statute, and it is, perhaps, of some significance that the legislature did not take this course when the law was so strikingly altered by the Road Traffic Act 1930. It cannot be said, in my view, that the implication of either of these terms is necessary in order to give "to the transaction such efficacy as both parties must have intended that . . . it should have". (*The Moorcock* (1889), 14 P.D. 64, at p. 68, per Bowen L.J.)

Turning now to another branch of the argument for the appellant, I cannot see that any events which have occurred in modern times, such as the passing of the Road Traffic Act, 1930, could justify your Lordships in holding it to be the law today that one or other of the implied terms now under discussion forms part of every contract whereby a man is employed to drive a vehicle. No provision of the Act of 1930 suggests to me that the terms to be implied in such a contract immediately after the Act became law should differ in any respect from the terms to be implied immediately before the Act became law. This matter is fully dealt with in the opinion about to be delivered by my noble and learned friend, Lord Tucker, which I have read, and I need only say that I entirely agree with his views on it.

Counsel for the appellant finally suggested that some such term ought to be implied because, in its absence, the employee was placed in a most unfortunate position. It is, however, your Lordships' task to decide what the law is, not what it ought to be. In saying this, I am far from suggesting that either of the terms now under discussion ought to be implied. . . .

LORD TUCKER: . . . It is said that the passing of the Road Traffic Act 1930, has created the new situation which gives rise to the necessity for these implied terms. It is common knowledge that, for many years before 1930, the great majority of prudent motor car owners protected themselves by insurance. Section 35 and s. 26 of the Act were passed not for the protection of the bank balances of car owners, or the life savings of their employees, but simply and solely to ensure that persons injured by the negligent driving of motor cars who established their claims in court might not be deprived of compensation by reason of the defendant's inability to satisfy their judgments. Again, it is said that the passing of the Act has admittedly resulted in the introduction of one implied term, viz. that the servant shall not be required to drive a motor vehicle the user of which has not been covered by insurance as required by the Act. This is merely the application of an existing term to the situation created by the Act. It has always been an implied term that the master will indemnify the servant from liability arising out of an unlawful enterprise on which he has been required to embark without knowing that it was unlawful. When the Road Traffic Act 1930 required the user to be covered by insurance, a journey which would previously have been lawful became unlawful in the absence of the required cover. My Lords, I cannot accept the view that the impact of this Act on the previously existing obligation of the master is in any way comparable to the implied terms which it is now sought to introduce into the contract of service. . . .

[LORD RADCLIFFE and LORD SOMERVELL OF HARROW delivered speeches in favour of allowing the appeal.]

Notes

1. In *Gregory* v. *Ford*, [1951] 1 All E.R. 121, Byrne J. held that it was an implied term of the contract of employment that the employer would not require the employee to do an unlawful act and, consequently, the employer had a contractual duty to the employee to comply with the compulsory insurance provisions of the Road Traffic Act in respect of vehicles the employee was required to drive. The validity of this decision was accepted by both sides in *Lister*'s case (note, however, Lord Morton of Henryton's remarks, *ante*). Gl. Williams, "Vicarious Liability and the Master's Indemnity" (1957), 20 M.L.R. 220, at p. 226, argues that *Gregory* v. *Ford* cannot demonstrably be founded on the wording of the Road Traffic Act. The present Road Traffic Act 1972 (p. 670, *post*) requires the person who uses or causes or permits a motor vehicle to be used on a road to be covered against third party risks. The Act, like its predecessors, does not require the employer to take out a policy which covers the personal liability of his employee. If this is so, how can the Act be said to create an implied contractual duty to insure the employee?

2. In one exceptional case the employee does have a right to indemnity. This is where a road traffic policy is taken out under the provisions of the Road Traffic Act 1972 (p. 670, *post*). In *Lister*'s case the insurance was not compulsory (the accident did not occur on a "road") and, in any event, the insurance company which claimed by subrogation was not the company which issued the road traffic policy, but another company which had issued an employer's liability policy. Since 1 January 1972, employers' liability insurance has been compulsory (p. 676, *post*) but the Employers' Liability (Compulsory Insurance) Act 1969 contains no statutory right of indemnity for an employee analogous to that contained in the Road Traffic Act. Since the Employers' Liability (Compulsory Insurance) Act requires the employer to cover *his* liability to employees and not the personal liability of employees to fellow-employees or others, it does not seem that the Act creates an implied contractual duty to insure the employee (cf. *Gregory* v. *Ford*, *ante*).

Jones v. Manchester Corporation

Court of Appeal   [1952] 2 All E.R. 125

In an action for damages by the widow of a patient who died under negligent hospital treatment, the hospital board claimed an indemnity from Dr. Wilkes, an inexperienced physician who had administered the fatal anaesthetic under the instructions of Dr. Sejrup, a house surgeon.

SINGLETON L.J.: . . . The employer cannot have a right of indemnity if he himself has contributed to the damage or if he bears some part of the responsibility therefor, and the same reasoning applies if some other and senior employee's negligence has contributed to the damage. On the facts of this case I feel bound to reject the claim of the hospital board to an indemnity against Dr. Wilkes. I mentioned in the course of the argument the desirability of pleadings and of discovery if a question such as this was to be raised. Without this it is not easy to determine the true terms of the contract between the parties. All that we know is that Dr. Wilkes was appointed a house surgeon at the hospital a short time after she had been qualified, and after an interview. There is no evidence to show that she was ever instructed, or advised, at the hospital as to the use of drugs. . . .

DENNING L.J.: . . . The hospital authorities cannot come down on every negligent member of the staff for a full indemnity. Such a course could only be justified if the hospital authorities could be regarded as innocent parties who have been made vicariously liable without any fault in them. But the law does not regard them as innocent. It says that they are themselves under a duty of care and skill, and, if that duty is not fulfilled, it regards them as tortfeasors and makes them liable as such, no matter whether the negligence be their personal negligence or the negligence of their staff.

In all these cases the important thing to remember is that when a master employs a servant to do something for him, he is responsible for the servant's conduct as if it were his own. If the servant commits a tort in the course of his employment, then the master is a tortfeasor as well as the servant. The master is never treated as an innocent party. This is well seen by taking a simple case where two cars are damaged in a collision by the fault of both drivers. One is driven by a servant, the other by an owner-driver. The owner-driver can obviously only recover a proportion of the damage to his own car from the owner of the other one, and likewise the owner of the chauffeur-driven car can only recover a proportion of the damage to his car. He cannot recover the whole damage from the owner-driver. He cannot claim as if he was an innocent person damaged by the negligence of the two drivers. He can only claim upon the footing that he himself is a tortfeasor and that the damage is partly the result of his own fault within the Law Reform (Contributory Negligence) Act 1945. Now suppose that a third person was injured in the collision, so that the owners of both cars are liable in tort to the injured person for his full damages. The owner of the chauffeur-driven car obviously cannot recover a full indemnity from his servant or from the owner-driver. He cannot claim as if he were an innocent person who has suffered damage as the result of the negligence of the two drivers. He can only claim as a tortfeasor for contribution under the Act of 1935.

My conclusion, therefore, is that the hospital authorities in this case were themselves tortfeasors who have no right to indemnity or contribution from any member of their staff except in so far as the court thinks it just and equitable having regard to the extent of that person's responsibility for the damage. In considering what is just and equitable, I think the court can have regard to extenuating circumstances which would not be available as against the injured person. Errors due to inexperience or lack of supervision are no defence as against the injured person, but they are available to reduce the amount of contribution which the hospital authorities can demand. It would be in the highest degree unjust that hospital authorities, by getting inexperienced doctors to perform their duties for them, without adequate supervision, should be able to throw all the responsibility on to those doctors as if they were fully experienced practitioners. Applying this principle to the present case, I find it very difficult to place much blame on Dr. Wilkes. . . .

[HODSON L.J. delivered a dissenting judgment.]

Harvey v. R. G. O'Dell, Ltd. (Galway, Third Party)

Queen's Bench Division   [1958] 1 All E.R. 657

Galway was employed by first defendants as a storekeeper. On their instructions he went from London to Hurley to do some repair work, taking the plaintiff, a fellow employee with him as a passenger in his motor cycle combination. While on a journey from fetching some tools and materials, there was an accident partly due to Galway's negligence in which he was killed and the plaintiff was injured. In an action by the plaintiff against the defendants as Galway's employers, the defendants served a third party notice on Galway's administratrix claiming a contribution against his estate under s. 6 (1) (c) of the Act of 1935 or alternatively for breach of an implied term in Galway's contract of service that he would indemnify them for any liability arising out of his negligence. McNair J. held that, as joint tortfeasors, the defendant employers were entitled to a 100 per cent contribution from Galway's estate. He also considered the alleged implied term.

McNAIR J.: . . . Mr. Galway was engaged and employed by the first defendants as a storekeeper; as a concession to the first defendants he from time to time used his own motor cycle on their business and was so using it at the time of the accident. I find it difficult to see on what grounds of justice and reason I should hold that, by making his motor cycle combination available for his employers' business on a particular occasion, he should be held in law to have impliedly agreed to indemnify them if he committed a casual act of negligence. Suppose in a time of labour disturbance in the docks master stevedores, as sometimes happens, induce their office staff to man the cranes or to do stevedoring; if a third party is injured through the negligence of such staff, no doubt the master stevedore would be vicariously liable, as, indeed, they might be primarily liable, on the basis that they had employed unskilled persons. But it would surely be contrary to all reason and justice to hold that the willing office staff, by abandoning their ledgers and undertaking manual tasks, had impliedly agreed to indemnify their employers against liability arising from their negligence in performing work which they were not employed to do.

I should, therefore, dismiss the claim of the first defendants against the third party, in so far as it rests on an allegation of breach of the contract of employment. . . .

Question

Did McNair J. pose the right question? Should it have been "Did Galway agree to exercise reasonable care about his employer's business?" (See J. A. Jolowicz (1959), 22 M.L.R. 71, 189.)

Notes

1. The student who relied simply on the law reports for an understanding of the contribution arrangements between employers and their employees would be seriously misled. *Lister's* case produced an uproar if for no other reason than that "the friendliest relation between the employer and his staff can now be disrupted, and the employee impoverished, by the action of an insurance company, which finds itself in the happy position of having received premiums for a risk that it does not have to bear." (Gl. Williams (1957),

20 M.L.R. 220, at p. 221.) An inter-departmental committee was set up to investigate the position and suggested that trade unions might, by collective bargaining, seek insurance cover for their members. This does not seem to have happened on any significant scale and, in any event, has now been overtaken by the Employers' Liability (Compulsory Insurance) Act 1969 (p. 676 *post*). Moreover, a so-called "gentlemen's agreement" among the majority of insurers not to enforce their subrogation rights against employees except in cases of collusion or wilful misconduct, had, according to the inter-departmental committee, prevented any "practical problem" arising out of *Lister's* case. Mr. (later Lord) Gardiner commented: "It is not clear that the Committee realised that the 'gentlemen's agreement' leaves it open to the insurers to say to a trade union, 'If you go on with this action on behalf of your insured member, and we choose with the consent of the assured to claim over against the foreman whose negligence is alleged to have caused the injury, the foreman who is also one of your members, may have to sell up his home'" ((1959), 22 M.L.R. 652). The "agreement" was later extended to cover all members of the British Insurance Association, all Lloyds underwriters concerned with this class of business and nearly all other insurance companies. Hospital Boards do, however, through private settlements with doctors who are members of a Defence Society, settle between themselves the shares of responsibility for the payment of damages in medical negligence cases. They do not do so in open court, so as not to weaken their common front against the injured plaintiff.

2. In *Morris* v. *Ford Motor Co. Ltd.*, [1973] Q.B. 792; [1973] 2 All E.R. 1084, the Court of Appeal sought to limit the application of *Lister's* case. C. was engaged by F. to perform cleaning services at F.'s factory. M., an employee of C., was injured due to the negligent driving of a fork-lift truck by R., one of F.'s employees. F.'s insurers paid M'.s damages and then, in F.'s name, recovered the full amount from C., in terms of a clause in the contract for cleaning services which obliged C. to indemnify F. against all losses. C. then claimed an indemnity from R., the negligent employee of F. The Court of Appeal acknowledged that C., as indemnitor, was entitled to every right of action of the person indemnified. However, Lord Denning M.R. and James L.J. (Stamp L.J. dissenting) held that, in an industrial setting, subrogation was unacceptable and unrealistic and so there was an implied term that this right was excluded. Lord Denning M.R. also held that subrogation was an equitable right, and it was not just or equitable to compel F. to lend its name to proceedings against R. because this might lead to a strike and, anyway, C. had been imprudent in failing to heed advice to insure. Leave was granted to appeal to the House of Lords which, hopefully, might take the opportunity to depart from its own previous decision in *Lister's* case.

20

Insurance

"As a general proposition it has not, I think, been questioned for nearly two hundred years that in determining the rights inter se of A and B, the fact that one of them is insured is to be disregarded": *per* Viscount Simonds in *Lister v. Romford Ice and Cold Storage Co., Ltd.*, [1957] 1 All E.R. 125, at p. 133.

"Liability and insurance are so intermixed that judicially to alter the basis of liability without adequate knowledge (which we do not have the means to obtain) as to the impact this might make upon the insurance system would be dangerous and, in my opinion, irresponsible": *per* Lord Wilberforce in *Morgans v. Launchbury*, [1972] 2 All E.R. 606, at p. 611.

These observations reveal a fundamental judicial dilemma implicit in many of the cases collected together in this sourcebook. The common law method of determining liability rests upon the notion of *loss shifting*: either the plaintiff or the defendant or sometimes both, must individually bear the loss. The predominant mechanism is fault. At the same time, the fact of insurance makes it possible for losses to be *distributed*. Some large enterprises are able to operate as self-insurers and absorb the cost of paying compensation from their own resources. Most organisations and individuals, however, have recourse to insurance. This spreads the risk among those engaged in the same kind of activity—such as manufacturers, motorists or employers—and paying premiums against similar risks. Once this loss distributing function of the law of tort is acknowledged many of the old arguments in favour of the fault principle have to be modified: in particular the imposition of liability on the defendant will not be a crushing economic burden. Occasionally (e.g. the views of Lord Denning M.R.[1] in cases of economic loss, p. 79, *ante*) the courts have denied the existence of a duty of care on the ground that the defendant is not a suitable loss distributor; or (as in *Ackworth v. Kempe* (1778), 1 Doug. K.B. 40 and *Lloyd v. Grace, Smith & Co.*, [1912] A.C. 716) have allowed recovery against an employer for his employee's wrongdoing on the ground that he could protect himself by fidelity insurance. However, these are exceptional cases. The observations in *Morgans v. Launchbury*, [1973] A.C. 127; [1972] 2 All E.R. 606 (p. 606, *ante*) indicate that English judges are not willing to innovate any general principle of risk distribution, i.e. the imposition of liability upon those parties best placed to act as a conduit of distribution. Any major change in the basis of liability from fault to risk must be sought from Parliament, not the courts. (A reading list on such proposals will be found at p. 728, *post*.)

---

1. [Note, as well, his outspoken remarks in *White v. Blackmore*, [1972] 3 All E.R. 158, at p. 166.]

This does not mean that the student can afford to ignore the facts of insurance. The materials gathered together in this Chapter have been relevant in other Chapters. It has been suggested that the legal rules have been "invisibly" affected by the existence of insurance: examples are the development of the manufacturer's duty (p. 328, *ante*), the raising of the standard of care required from learner drivers (p. 146, *ante*), the conversion from "fault" to "negligence without fault" through the *res ipsa loquitur* doctrine (p. 162, *ante*), and the imposition of strict liability for dangerous escapes (p. 338, *ante*). Legislative policy has also been affected by the insurance situation: examples are the abolition of the rule against actions between husband and wife (Law Reform (Husband and Wife) Act 1962), the removal of the protection afforded to highway authorities (Highways (Miscellaneous Provisions) Act 1961, s. 1 (3)), and the imposition of strict liability for nuclear incidents upon site licensees (Nuclear Installations Act 1965, p. 267, *ante*).

By far the most important reason for understanding the insurance background is that it enables one to examine how far tort law is coping with the social and economic problem of allocating accident losses. Those who criticise the legal rules often do so because they are seen to be deficient in the performance of this function. The materials in this Chapter begin, in s. 1, with the attempts made by Parliament to remedy one obvious injustice, that created by the defendant who is unable to pay. The Road Traffic Act 1972 re-enacts, with later amendments, provisions first enacted in 1930 to compel insurance in respect of death or bodily injury arising from the use of a motor vehicle on a road. The Employers' Liability (Compulsory Insurance) Act 1969, which has been in operation since 1 January 1972, adopts a similar policy in regard to an employer's liability to his employees. Parliament has also assisted the victims of bankrupt tortfeasors by means of the Third Parties (Rights against Insurers) Act 1930 (p. 678, *post*) and the Road Traffic Act 1972, s. 150 (p. 673, *post*).

The courts attempted to create a remedy against the uninsured motorist in *Monk* v. *Warbey*, [1935] 1 K.B. 75 (p. 674, *post*). But this obviously unsatisfactory device has now almost been supplanted by a fascinating instance of "private legislation": the agreements between the insurance industry and the government which, ignoring the formal legal rules, promise compensation to the victims of uninsured and untraced motorists. Like the "gentlemen's agreement" not to rely on *Lister* v. *Romford Ice and Cold Storage Co., Ltd.*, [1957] A.C. 555; [1957] 1 All E.R. 125 (p. 665, *ante*), these agreements remind the student of law that "black letter" legal rules sometimes bear little relation to social reality. The agreements are printed in the second section of this Chapter. There are no corresponding institutions to protect the victims of uninsured or "fly-by-night" employers.

The third section contains examples of policies offered by a particular insurance company. Insurance is a matter of contract between insurer and insured. The policy may be one of *liability* insurance (e.g. products, employers' or "public" liability) by which the insurer agrees, in consideration of a premium, to cover specified types of legal liability which the insured may incur. Or it may be one of *loss* (sometimes called "first-party" or "personal accident") insurance (e.g. on the life of the insured, or his home or business) by which the insurer agrees, in consideration of a premium, to indemnify the insured in respect of particular losses. Or it may be a combination of liability and loss insurance (e.g. a comprehensive motor insurance policy). A particular risk may be covered by both types of insurance (e.g. the owner of a damaged motor vehicle may claim under his own *loss* insurance policy or make a tort claim against the negligent motorist whose insurer will pay under the latter's *liability* policy). The student of tort is not concerned with the many problems of contract interpretation which may arise under policies such as these. His questions ought primarily to be functional ones such as: (1) what limits are there on the various types of liability insurance? (2) what is the effect of the law of contributory negligence on liability insurance? (3) what risks are covered by loss insurance that are not covered by liability insurance? (4) what is the nature and likely effect of no-claims discount clauses? (5) what are the advantages of loss (first-party) insurance in comparison with liability insurance? These and related questions can best be answered by reading the policies in conjunction with P. S. Atiyah, *Accidents, Compensation and the Law*, Chaps. 10 and 12.

The institution of insurance has an important effect on the conduct of litigation, in particular because of the insurer's right of subrogation (p. 692, *post*) and his right to full control over the conduct of legal proceedings in the insured's name (the latter being a contractual condition, e.g. p. 668, *post*). This gives the insured the advantage of expert assistance; but by the same token it means that the uninsured party may find himself without similar assistance. These questions are raised in s. 4. Unfortunately the dearth of empirical research in England makes it impossible to provide materials which tell us what actually happens in practice.

The final section of this Chapter concerns a different kind of loss distribution, that which arises from the fact that tort actions and liability and loss insurance are not the sole sources of compensation. The main burden of compensating the injured and bereaved is borne by the developed system of social insurance in the United Kingdom. (An account of the relative proportions and amount of the various types of compensation will be found in Appendix E, p. 712, *post*.) From the standpoint of the tort lawyer these collateral sources of compensation are important in at least two respects:

(1) what effect do they have on the assessment of damages? (A question dealt with in Chap. 12, p. 413, *ante*.)

(2) what advantages (if any) does the social security system have over (i) tort actions and liability insurance, and (ii) loss (first-party) private insurance, as a method of compensating accident victims?

The materials chosen for this second purpose have had to be strictly limited for reasons of space. There is a brief guide to the main kinds of benefit available to the accident victim, and this is followed by a comparison of the benefits available for industrial and non-industrial accidents. The policy of the social security system in favouring the former may be compared with the policy of the tort system (p. 413, *ante*). The two major schemes are those relating to industrial injuries and criminal injuries. The first rests upon statute, the second upon the royal prerogative, but the bodies administering both are kept within their legal powers by the Divisional Court. The schemes may be compared with each other, and with the tort system. Particular attention might be paid to: (a) the coverage of each system (e.g. "accidents"); (b) the relevance of fault in each system; (c) the problems of causation (e.g. "arising out of employment"); (d) the effect of the claimant's misconduct; (e) the form and amount of compensation; (f) the administration of each system (a note of relevant costs will be found in Appendix E, p. 712, *post*). The materials should be read together with the works referred to in the further reading list, p. 728, *post*, and compared with the schemes now operating in other countries (Appendices F, p. 715 and G, p. 723, *post*).

1. COMPULSORY INSURANCE PROVISIONS
The Road Traffic Act 1972

PART VI
THIRD-PARTY LIABILITIES

Compulsory insurance or security against third-party risks

143. Users of motor vehicles to be insured or secured against third-party risks.—(1) Subject to the provisions of this Part of this Act, it shall not be lawful for a person to use, or to cause or permit any other person to use, a motor vehicle on a road unless there is in force in relation to the use of the vehicle by that person or that other person, as the case may be, such a policy of insurance or such a security in respect of third-party risks as complies with the requirements of this Part of this Act; and if a person acts in contravention of this section he shall be guilty of an offence.

(2) A person charged with using a motor vehicle in contravention of this section shall not be convicted if he proves that the vehicle did not belong to him and was not in his possession under a contract of hiring or of loan, that he was using the vehicle in the course of his employment and that he neither knew nor had reason to believe that there was not in force in relation to the vehicle such a policy of insurance or security as is mentioned in subsection (1) above.

(3) This part of this Act shall not apply to invalid carriages.

144. Exceptions from requirement of third-party insurance or security.— (1) Section 143 of this Act shall not apply to a vehicle owned by a person who has deposited and keeps deposited with the Accountant General of the Supreme Court the sum of £15,000, at a time when the vehicle is being driven under the owner's control.

[Sub-s. (2) provides that s. 143 shall not apply to specified local and police authorities.]

145. Requirements in respect of policies of insurance.—(1) In order to comply with the requirements of this Part of this Act, a policy of insurance must satisfy the following conditions.

(2) The policy must be issued by an authorised insurer, that is to say, a person or body of persons carrying on motor vehicle insurance business in Great Britain.

(3) Subject to subsection (4) below, the policy—

   (a) must insure such person, persons or classes of persons as may be specified in the policy in respect of any liability of which may be incurred by him or them in respect of the death of or bodily injury to any person caused by, or arising out of, the use of the vehicle on a road; and

   (b) must also insure him or them in respect of any liability which may be incurred by him or them under the provisions of this Part of this Act relating to payment for emergency treatment.

(4) The policy shall not, by virtue of subsection (3) (a) above, be required to cover—

   (a) liability in respect of the death, arising out of and in the course of his employment, of a person in the employment of a person insured by the policy or of bodily injury sustained by such a person arising out of and in the course of his employment; or

   (b) any contractual liability.

148. Avoidance of certain exceptions to policies or securities and of certain agreements, etc., as to risks required to be covered thereby.—(1) Where a certificate of insurance or certificate of security has been delivered under section 147 of this Act to the person by whom a policy has been effected or to whom a security has been given, so much of the policy or security as purports to restrict, as the case may be, the insurance of the persons insured by the policy or the operation of the security by reference to any of the following matters, that is to say,—

(*a*) the age or physical or mental condition of persons driving the vehicle, or

(*b*) the condition of the vehicle, or

(*c*) the number of persons that the vehicle carries, or

(*d*) the weight or physical characteristics of the goods that the vehicle carries, or

(*e*) the times at which or the areas within which the vehicle is used, or

(*f*) the horsepower or cylinder capacity or value of the vehicle, or

(*g*) the carrying on the vehicle of any particular apparatus, or

(*h*) the carrying on the vehicle of any particular means of identification other than any means of identification required to be carried by or under the Vehicles (Excise) Act 1971,

shall, as respect such liabilities as are required to be covered by a policy under section 145 of this Act, be of no effect:

Provided that nothing in this subsection shall require an insurer or the giver of a security to pay any sum in respect of the liability of any person otherwise than in or towards the discharge of that liability, and any sum paid by an insurer or the giver of a security in or towards the discharge of any liability of any person which is covered by the policy or security by virtue only of this subsection shall be recoverable by the insurer or giver of the security from that person.

(2) A condition in a policy or security issued or given for the purposes of this Part of this Act providing that no liability shall arise under the policy or security, or that any liability so arising shall cease, in the event of some specified thing being done or omitted to be done after the happening of the event giving rise to a claim under the policy or security, shall be of no effect in connection with such liabilities as are required to be covered by a policy under section 145 of this Act:

Provided that nothing in this subsection shall be taken to render void any provision in a policy or security requiring the person insured or secured to pay to the insurer or the giver of the security any sums which the latter may have become liable to pay under the policy or security and which have been applied to the satisfaction of the claims of third parties.

(3) Where a person uses a motor vehicle in circumstances such that under section 143 of this Act there is required to be in force in relation to his use of it such a policy of insurance or security as is mentioned in subsection (1) of that section, then, if any other person is carried in or upon the vehicle while the user is so using it, any antecedent agreement or understanding between them (whether intended to be legally binding or not) shall be of no effect so far as it purports or might be held—

(*a*) to negative or restrict any such liability of the user in respect of persons carried in or upon the vehicle as is required by section 145 of this Act to be covered by a policy of insurance; or

(*b*) to impose any conditions with respect to the enforcement of any such liability of the user;

and the fact that a person so carried has willingly accepted as his the risk of negligence on the part of the user shall not be treated as negativing any such liability of the user.

For the purposes of this subsection references to a person being carried in or upon a vehicle include references to a person entering or getting on to, or alighting from, the vehicle, and the reference to an antecedent agreement is to one made at any time before the liability arose.

(4) Notwithstanding anything in any enactment, a person issuing a policy of insurance under section 145 of this Act shall be liable to indemnify the persons or classes of persons specified in the policy in respect of any liability which the policy purports to cover in the case of those persons or classes of persons.

149. Duty of insurers or persons giving security to satisfy judgment against persons insured or secured against third-party risks.—(1) If, after a certificate of insurance or certificate of security has been delivered under section 147 of this Act to the person by whom a policy has been effected or to whom a security has been given, judgment in respect of any such liability as is required to be covered by a policy of insurance under section 145 of this Act (being a liability covered by the terms of the policy or security to which the certificate relates) is obtained against any person who is insured by the policy or whose liability is covered by the security, as the case may be, then, notwithstanding that the insurer may be entitled to avoid or cancel, or may have avoided or cancelled, the policy or security, he shall, subject to the provisions of this section, pay to the persons entitled to the benefit of the judgment any sum payable thereunder in respect of the liability, including any amount payable in respect of costs and any sum payable in respect of interest on that sum by virtue of any enactment relating to interest on judgments.

(2) No sum shall be payable by an insurer under the foregoing provisions of this section—

(a) in respect of any judgment, unless before or within seven days after the commencement of the proceedings in which the judgment was given, the insurer had notice of the bringing of the proceedings; or

(b) in respect of any judgment, so long as execution thereon is stayed pending an appeal; or

(c) in connection with any liability, if before the happening of the event which was the cause of the death or bodily injury giving rise to the liability, the policy or security was cancelled by mutual consent or by virtue of any provision contained therein, and either—

(i) before the happening of the said event the certificate was surrendered to the insurer, or the person to whom the certificate was made a statutory declaration stating that the certificate had been lost or destroyed, or

(ii) after the happening of the said event, but before the expiration of a period of fourteen days from the taking effect of the cancellation of the policy or security, the certificate was surrendered to the insurer, or the person to whom it was delivered made such a statutory declaration as aforesaid; or

(iii) either before or after the happening of the said event, but within the said period of fourteen days, the insurer has commenced proceedings under this Act in respect of the failure to surrender the certificate.

(3) No sum shall be payable by an insurer under the foregoing provisions of this section if, in an action commenced before, or within three months after, the commencement of the proceedings in which the judgment was given, he has obtained a declaration that, apart from any provision contained in the policy or security, he is entitled to avoid it on the ground that it was obtained by the non-disclosure of a material fact, or by a representation of fact which was false in some material particular, or, if he has avoided the policy or security on that ground, that he was entitled so to do apart from any provision contained in it:

Provided that an insurer who has obtained such a declaration as aforesaid in an action shall not thereby become entitled to the benefit of this subsection as respects any judgment obtained in proceedings commenced before the commencement of that action unless before, or within seven days after, the commencement of that action he has given notice thereof to the person who is the plaintiff in the said proceedings specifying the non-disclosure or false representation on which he proposes to rely; and a person to whom notice of such an action is so given shall be entitled, if he thinks fit, to be made a party thereto.

(4) If the amount which an insurer becomes liable under this section to pay in respect of a liability of a person who is insured by a policy or whose liability is covered by a security exceeds the amount for which he would, apart from the provisions of this section, be liable under the policy or security in respect of that liability, he shall be entitled to recover the excess from that person.

(5) In this section—

    (*a*) "insurer" includes a person giving a security;

    (*b*) "material" means of such a nature as to influence the judgment of a prudent insurer in determining whether he will take the risk and, if so, at what premium and on what conditions; and

    (*c*) "liability covered by the terms of the policy or security" means a liability which is covered by the policy or security or which would be so covered but for the fact that the insurer is entitled to avoid or cancel, or has avoided or cancelled, the policy or security.

(6) (*Applies to Scotland.*)

150. Bankruptcy, etc., of insured or secured persons not to affect claims by third parties.—(1) Where, after a certificate of insurance or certificate of security has been delivered under section 147 of this Act to the person by whom a policy has been effected or to whom a security has been given, any of the following events happens, that is to say,—

    (*a*) the person by whom the policy was effected or to whom the security was given becomes bankrupt or makes a composition or arrangement with his creditors,

    (*b*) the said person dies, and an order is made under section 130 of the Bankruptcy Act 1914 for the administration of his estate according to the law of bankruptcy,

    (*c*) if the said person is a company, a winding-up order is made with respect to the company or a resolution for a voluntary winding up is passed with respect thereto, or a receiver or manager of the company's business or undertaking is duly appointed or possession is taken, by or on behalf of the holders of any debentures secured by a floating charge, of any property comprised in or subject to the charge,

the happening of that event shall, notwithstanding anything in the Third Parties (Rights Against Insurers) Act 1930,[1] not affect any such liability of the said person as is required to be covered by a policy of insurance under section 145 of this Act, but nothing in this subsection shall affect any rights conferred by that Act on the person to whom the liability was incurred, being rights so conferred against the person by whom the policy was issued or the security was given.

Notes

1. The duty to insure rests upon the person who "uses" or "causes or permits any other person to use" the vehicle. A person may breach this duty even though he does not know that there is no policy of insurance in force for the permitted use: *Houston* v. *Buchanan*, 1940 S.C. (H.L.) 17, and generally, Glanville Williams, *Criminal Law: The General Part*, 2nd Edn., para. 60. The

---

1. [See p. 678, *post*, for this Act.]

penalty for failure to insure is imprisonment for up to three months or a £50 fine or both. The offender's driving licence must be endorsed and he may be disqualified from driving: Road Traffic Act 1972, Sched. 4. There may also be a civil action for breach of statutory duty: see, *post*.

2. It is the *use* of the vehicle which must be covered by insurance and not the personal or vicarious liability of the owner. So a situation may arise in which the owner is responsible in law (limited in *Morgans* v. *Launchbury*, [1972] A.C. 127; [1972] 2 All E.R. 606 (H.L.), p. 606, *ante*, to the delegation of driving for the owner's purposes) but the use is not insured. This can happen because, by contract with the insurer, the owner may stipulate that the insurance covers the use of the vehicle only when used by himself or particular named drivers. If he nevertheless permits someone other than those named to use the vehicle he commits a criminal offence and may be liable in damages for breach of statutory duty. This is cumbersome and of little value to the person who suffers loss by virtue of the owner's failure to insure because, *ex hypothesi*, the owner will be uninsured in such cases and probably without funds to pay. Some other countries arrange matters more sensibly by attaching the insurance to the *vehicle* and not its *user* by particular drivers.

3. Since 1 December 1972, it has been compulsory to insure against liability to passengers (Motor Vehicles (Passenger Insurance) Act 1971, s. 1 (1) replaced by s. 145 of the Road Traffic Act 1972, *ante*). Under s. 148 (3) the user cannot restrict his liability, either through contract or by operation of the defence of *volenti non fit injuria*, by a notice on the dashboard saying "Passengers ride at their own risk and on the condition that no claim shall be made against the driver or owner". Before this section came into force such notices were sometimes held to be effective to bar the injured passenger's claim: e.g. *Birch* v. *Thomas*, [1972] 1 All E.R. 905 (C.A.); comment by O. H. Parsons (1972), 123 N.L.J. 348; and p. 316, *ante*.

4. Section 148 (4) overcomes the inconvenient "privity of contract" rule by enabling any person covered by the policy to sue upon the contract of insurance: *Tattersall* v. *Drysdale*, [1935] 2 K.B. 174 (decided under provisions of the 1930 Road Traffic Act corresponding to s. 148 (4) of the 1972 Act). But the person covered must take the policy as he finds it and must comply with all conditions: *Austin* v. *Zurich Accident and Liability Insurance Co.*, [1945] K.B. 250; [1945] 1 All E.R. 316.

5. Liability to employees will not be covered by a road traffic policy (s. 145 (4) *ante*), but by an employer's liability policy (p. 674, *post*).

Monk *v.* Warbey and Others

Court of Appeal   [1934] All E.R. Rep. 373

GREER L.J.: This appeal raises one question of considerable public importance, and though I might in other respects have been content with saying that I have read Charles J.'s very careful judgment and that I agree with every word of it, having regard to the fact that other cases may be affected by our judgment, I think it necessary to add some few words.

The facts can be stated quite shortly. Warbey, the defendant to the action in the court below and the appellant in this court, was the owner of a motor car which he had insured under a Lloyd's policy in which the liability was described under the head of "Liability to the public" as "liability at law for compensation for death or bodily injury caused by the use of the car". The question whether or not the events which happened in this case were within the terms of the policy has not been presented for argument either in the court below or in this court. It was conceded by the parties when this came before the court that the policy did not cover the events that happened, and the action which was brought by the plaintiff was an action on the ground that there had been a breach of the statutory duty imposed by s. 35 of the Road Traffic Act 1930, and the damages which he sought to recover were alleged to be the result of that breach of the statute.

In his clear-cut argument counsel for the defendant takes three points. First, he submits to this court that the learned judge was wrong in deciding that a breach of s. 35 was available for the benefit of the plaintiff, who alleged that he had been injured by the negligent driving of the motor car by the servant of an uninsured person, and his contention is—and the matter is capable of considerable argument—that, having regard to the fact that a very serious penalty is imposed by the statute for the breach of s. 35, it cannot be concluded that that section was intended to create any right on the part of a member of the public who was injured by reason of the breach. Numbers of cases have been cited. In my judgment, this is a stronger case in favour of the plaintiff than *Groves* v. *Lord Wimborne*[1] and the cases which relate to breaches of statutory duties towards minors, such as *Britannic Merthyr Coal Co., Ltd.* v. *David.*[2]

The Road Traffic Act 1930, was passed in these circumstances. It had become apparent that people who were injured by the negligence of drivers of motor cars on the roads were in a parlous situation if they happened to be injured by somebody who was unable to pay damages for the injuries which they had suffered, and, accordingly, two Acts were passed. One was for the purpose of enabling persons who were so injured to recover, in the case of the bankruptcy of the insured person, the money which would be payable to him by the insurance company—that is the Third Party (Rights against Insurers) Act 1930. It was thought right by Parliament that in such a case the insurers' money should not go to the general creditors of the bankrupt, but should be available for the purpose of compensating the injured person, and it was provided that in the case of bankruptcy proceedings being taken against a defendant who could not pay the amount of the damage, but was insured, then in the course of the bankruptcy the person injured could make the insurance company liable for the damage caused to him although he was not a party to the contract of insurance. But that did not meet the whole difficulty because the owners of motor cars sometimes lent their motor cars to uninsured persons, and if the person causing the injury was an uninsured person then the remedy provided by that Act to which I have just referred was unavailable for the injured person. Provision, therefore, was made in the Road Traffic Act 1930, for the protection of third persons against the risks arising out of the negligent driving of a motor vehicle by an uninsured person to whom an insured owner had lent his car and, in connection with such protection, to amend the Assurance Companies Act 1909. How could Parliament make provision for the protection of third parties against such risks if it did not enable an injured third person to recover for a breach of s. 35 of the Road Traffic Act 1930? That section is to be found in Part II of the Act, which is headed "Provision against third party risks arising out of the use of motor vehicles". It would be a very poor protection of the person injured by the negligence of an uninsured person to whom a car had been lent by an insured person if the person injured had no civil remedy for a breach of the section. . . .

The power to prosecute for a penalty is no protection whatever to the injured person except in the sense that it affords a strong incentive for people not to break the pro-

---

1. [1898] 2 Q.B. 402.
2. [1910] A.C. 74.

visions of the statute. But the power to prosecute is a poor consolation to the man who has been damaged by reason of a breach of the provisions of s. 35. . . .

[MAUGHAM AND ROCHE L.JJ. delivered judgments in favour of dismissing the appeal.]

Appeal dismissed

Notes

1. In *Martin* v. *Dean*, [1971] 2 Q.B. 208; [1971] 3 All E.R. 279, John Stephenson J. held that it is not necessary for the plaintiff in an action of the *Monk* v. *Warbey* type to show that the uninsured driver will not pay at all. The plaintiff may claim damages in the same action against the driver alleging negligence and against the vehicle owner alleging breach of the statutory duty to insure. Judgment will be given against the owner if the evidence shows that the driver is a man of limited means, unable to satisfy the judgment against him promptly.

2. We have seen that breach of the Motor Vehicles (Use and Construction) Regulations, which prescribe in detail the mode of construction of motor vehicles, has been held not to give a private remedy to the person injured (Chap. 8, p. 277, *ante*). Is there any justification for allowing an action in tort in the *Monk* v. *Warbey* situation, when it is not allowed in other cases of breach of road safety legislation? Do you agree with Glanville Williams (1960), 23 M.L.R. at p. 259, that *Monk* v. *Warbey* is an "improper type of judicial invention"? Note that it imposes liability without fault upon a defendant who is, *ex hypothesi*, uninsured.

3. The plaintiff nowadays will give notice of the bringing of proceedings against an uninsured driver, within seven days after the commencement of the proceedings, to the Motor Insurers' Bureau. (See agreement between Secretary of State for the Environment and the M.I.B., p. 679, *post*.) Although the M.I.B. may require the plaintiff to take all reasonable steps to "obtain judgment against all the persons liable" (*ibid*., para. 5 (c)), any unsatisfied judgment will be paid by the M.I.B. The practical importance of *Monk* v. *Warbey* therefore seems to be limited to those situations in which there is a relatively wealthy owner who has permitted his vehicle to be used without compulsory insurance cover. But in law the existence of the M.I.B. agreements does not affect the action for breach of statutory duty: *Corfield* v. *Groves*, [1950] I All E.R. 488.

The Employers' Liability (Compulsory Insurance) Act 1969

An Act to require employers to insure against their liability for personal injury to their employees, and for purposes connected with the matter aforesaid

1. **Insurance against liability for employees.**—(1) Except as otherwise provided by this Act, every employer carrying on any business in Great Britain shall insure, and maintain insurance, under one or more approved policies with an authorised insurer or insurers against liability for bodily injury or disease sustained by his employees, and arising out of and in the course of their employment in Great Britain in that business, but except in so far as regulations otherwise provide not including injury or disease suffered or contracted outside Great Britain.

(2) Regulations may provide that the amount for which an employer is required by this Act to insure and maintain insurance shall, either generally or in such cases or classes of case as may be prescribed by the regulations, be limited in such manner as may be so prescribed.

(3) For the purposes of this Act—

(a) "approved policy" means a policy of insurance not subject to any conditions or exceptions prohibited for those purposes by regulations;

(b) "authorised insurer" means a person or body of persons lawfully carrying on in Great Britain insurance business of any class relevant for the purposes of Part II of the Companies Act 1967 and issuing the policy or policies in the course thereof;

(c) "business" includes a trade or profession, and includes any activity carried on by a body of persons, whether corporate or unincorporate;

(d) except as otherwise provided by regulations, an employer not having a place of business in Great Britain shall be deemed not to carry on business there.

2. Employees to be covered.—(1) For the purposes of this Act the term "employee" means an individual who has entered into or works under a contract of service or apprenticeship with an employer whether by way of manual labour, clerical work or otherwise, whether such contract is expressed or implied, oral or in writing.

(2) This Act shall not require an employer to insure—

(a) in respect of an employee of whom the employer is the husband, wife, father, mother, grandfather, grandmother, step-father, step-mother, son, daughter, grandson, granddaughter, stepson, step-daughter, brother, sister, half-brother or half-sister; or

(b) except as otherwise provided by regulations, in respect of employees not ordinarily resident in Great Britain.

3. Employers exempted from insurance.—(1) This Act shall not require any insurance to be effected by—

(a) any such authority as is mentioned in subsection (2) below; or

(b) any body corporate established by or under any enactment for the carrying on of any industry or part of an industry, or of any undertaking, under national ownership or control; or

(c) in relation to any such cases as may be specified in the regulations, any employer exempted by regulations.

(2) The authorities referred to in subsection (1) (a) above are the Common Council of the City of London, the Greater London Council, the council of a London borough, the council of a county, [. . .] or county district in England or Wales, a county, town or district in Scotland, any joint board or joint committee in England and Wales or joint committee in Scotland which is so constituted as to include among its members representatives of any such council, and any police authority.

. . .

5. Penalty for failure to insure.—An employer who on any day is not insured in accordance with this Act when required to be so shall be guilty of an offence and shall be liable on summary conviction to a fine not exceeding two hundred pounds; and where an offence under this section committed by a corporation has been committed with the consent or connivance of, or facilitated by any neglect on the part of, any director, manager, secretary or other officer of the corporation, he, as well as the corporation shall be deemed to be guilty of that offence and shall be liable to be proceeded against and punished accordingly.

. . .

The Employers' Liability (Compulsory Insurance) General Regulations 1971, S.I. 1971 No. 1117

The Secretary of State, in exercise of his powers under sections 1 (2) and (3) (a), 2 (2), 4 (1) and (2) and 6 of the Employers' Liability (Compulsory Insurance) Act

1969 (hereinafter referred to as "the Act") and of all other powers enabling him in that behalf, hereby makes the following Regulations . . .

Prohibition of certain conditions in policies of insurance.—2.—(1) Any condition in a policy of insurance issued or renewed in accordance with the requirements of the Act after the coming into operation of this Regulation which provides (in whatever terms) that no liability (either generally or in respect of a particular claim) shall arise under the policy, or that any such liability so arising shall cease—

(*a*) in the event of some specified thing being done or omitted to be done after the happening of the event giving rise to a claim under the policy;

(*b*) unless the policy holder takes reasonable care to protect his employees against the risk of bodily injury or disease in the course of their employment;

(*c*) unless the policy holder complies with the requirements of any enactment for the protection of employees against the risk of bodily injury or disease in the course of their employment; and

(*d*) unless the policy holder keeps specified records or provides the insurer with or makes available to him information therefrom,

is hereby prohibited for the purposes of the Act.

(2) Nothing in this Regulation shall be taken as prejudicing any provision in a policy requiring the policy holder to pay to the insurer any sums which the latter may have become liable to pay under the policy and which have been applied to the satisfaction of claims in respect of employees or any costs and expenses incurred in relation to such claims.

Limit of amount of compulsory insurance.—3. The amount for which an employer is required by the Act to insure and maintain insurance shall be two million pounds in respect of claims relating to any one or more of his employees arising out of any one occurrence.

. . .

Notes

1. It will be observed that the employee is not given a statutory right, analogous to that given to the road traffic victim by s. 148 (4) of the Road Traffic Act 1972, to sue upon the contract of insurance. What is the significance of Employers' Liability (Compulsory Insurance) Regulation 2 (2), *ante*? (See Employers' Liability policy, p. 686, *post*.)

2. There is no Employers' Liability Insurers' Bureau comparable to the Motor Insurers' Bureau (p. 679, *post*). For a general comment on the Act, see R. C. Simpson (1972), 35 M.L.R. 63; R. A. Hasson (1974), 3 I.L.J. 79.

The Third Parties (Rights Against Insurers) Act 1930

1. Rights of third parties against insurers on bankruptcy, etc., of the insured.—(1) Where under any contract of insurance a person (hereinafter referred to as the insured) is insured against liabilities to third parties which he may incur, then—

(*a*) in the event of the insured becoming bankrupt or making a composition or arrangement with his creditors; or

(*b*) in the case of the insured being a company, in the event of a winding-up order being made, or a resolution for a voluntary winding-up being passed, with respect to the company, or of a receiver or manager of the company's business or undertaking being duly appointed, or of possession being taken, by or on behalf of the holders of any debentures secured by a floating charge, of any property comprised in or subject to the charge;

if, either before or after that event, any such liability as aforesaid is incurred by the insured, his rights against the insurer under the contract in respect of the liability shall, notwithstanding anything in any Act or rule of law to the contrary, be transferred to and vest in the third party to whom the liability was so incurred.

(2) Where an order is made under section one hundred and thirty of the Bankruptcy Act, 1914, for the administration of the estate of a deceased debtor according to the law of bankruptcy, then, if any debt provable in bankruptcy is owing by the deceased in respect of a liability against which he was insured under a contract of insurance as being a liability to a third party, the deceased debtor's rights against the insurer under the contract in respect of that liability shall, notwithstanding anything in the said Act, be transferred to and vest in the person to whom the debt is owing.

. . .

(4) Upon a transfer under subsection (1) or subsection (2) of this section, the insurer shall, subject to the provisions of section three of this Act, be under the same liability to the third party as he would have been under to the insured, but—

(*a*) if the liability of the insurer to the insured exceeds the liability of the insured to the third party, nothing in this Act shall affect the rights of the insured against the insurer in respect of the excess; and

(*b*) if the liability of the insurer to the insured is less than the liability of the insured to the third party, nothing in this Act shall affect the rights of the third party against the insured in respect of the balance.

. . .

3. Settlement between insurers and insured persons.—Where the insured has become bankrupt or where in the case of the insured being a company, a winding-up order has been made or a resolution for a voluntary winding-up has been passed, with respect to the company, no agreement made between the insurer and the insured after liability has been incurred to a third party and after the commencement of the bankruptcy or winding-up, as the case may be, nor any waiver, assignment, or other disposition made by, or payment made to the insured after the commencement aforesaid shall be effective to defeat or affect the rights transferred to the third party under this Act, but those rights shall be the same as if no such agreement, waiver, assignment, disposition or payment had been made.

. . .

5. Short title.—This Act may be cited as the Third Parties (Rights against Insurers) Act, 1930.

Note

This Act does not prevent the insurer from avoiding the policy, e.g. on grounds of material non-disclosure by the insured: *McCormick* v. *National Motor and Accident Insurance Union, Ltd.* (1934), 49 Ll.L. Rep. 361.

2. MOTOR INSURERS' BUREAU

Compensation of Victims of Uninsured Drivers: Text of an Agreement Dated 22 November 1972 Between the Secretary of State for the Environment and the Motor Insurers' Bureau

In accordance with the Agreement made on 31 December 1945 between the Minister of War Transport and insurers transacting compulsory motor vehicle insurance business in Great Britain (published by the Stationery Office under the title "Motor Vehicle

Insurance Fund") a corporation called the "Motor Insurers' Bureau" entered into an agreement on 17 June 1946 with the Minister of Transport to give effect from 1 July 1946 to the principle recommended in July 1937 by the Departmental Committee under Sir Felix Cassel, (Cmd 5528), to secure compensation to third party victims of road accidents in cases where, notwithstanding the provisions of the Road Traffic Acts relating to compulsory insurance, the victim is deprived of compensation by the absence of insurance, or of effective insurance. That Agreement was replaced by an Agreement which operated in respect of accidents occurring on or after 1 March 1971. The Agreement of 1971 has now been replaced by a new Agreement which operates in respect of accidents occurring on or after 1 December 1972.

The text of the new Agreement is as follows—

> MEMORANDUM OF AGREEMENT made the 22nd day of November 1972 between the Secretary of State for the Environment and the Motor Insurers' Bureau, whose registered office is at Aldermary House, Queen Street, London, EC4N 1TR (hereinafter referred to as "M.I.B.") SUPPLEMENTAL to an Agreement (hereinafter called "the Principal Agreement") made the 31st Day of December 1945 between the Minister of War Transport and the insurers transacting compulsory motor vehicle insurance business in Great Britain by or on behalf of whom the said Agreement was signed in pursuance of paragraph 1 of which M.I.B. was incorporated.
>
> IT IS HEREBY AGREED AS FOLLOWS—

Definitions

1. In this Agreement—

   "contract of insurance" means a policy of insurance or a security;
   "insurer" includes the giver of a security;
   "relevant liability" means a liability in respect of which a policy of insurance must insure a person in order to comply with Part VI of the Road Traffic Act 1972.

Satisfaction of Claims by M.I.B.

2. If judgment in respect of any relevant liability is obtained against any person or persons in any Court in Great Britain whether or not such a person or persons be in fact covered by a contract of insurance and any such judgment is not satisfied in full within seven days from the date upon which the person or persons in whose favour the judgment was given became entitled to enforce it then M.I.B. will, subject to the provisions of Clauses 4, 5 and 6 hereof, pay or satisfy or cause to be paid or satisfied to or to the satisfaction of the person or persons in whose favour the judgment was given any sum payable or remaining payable thereunder in respect of the relevant liability including any sum awarded by the Court in respect of interest on that sum and any taxed costs or any costs awarded by the Court without taxation (or such proportion thereof as is attributable to the relevant liability) whatever may be the cause of the failure of the judgment debtor to satisfy the judgment.

Period of Agreement

3. This Agreement shall be determinable by the Secretary of State at any time or by M.I.B. on twelve months' notice without prejudice to the continued operation of the Agreement in respect of accidents occurring before the date of termination.

Recoveries

4. Nothing in this Agreement shall prevent insurers from providing by conditions in their contracts of insurance that all sums paid by them or by M.I.B. by virtue of the Principal Agreement or this Agreement in or towards the discharge of the liability of their assured shall be recoverable by them or by M.I.B. from the assured or from any other person.

Conditions Precedent to M.I.B.'s Liability

5. (1) M.I.B. shall not incur any liability under Clause 2 of this Agreement unless—

(a) notice of the bringing of the proceedings is given before or within seven days after the commencement of the proceedings—

(i) to M.I.B. in the case of proceedings in respect of a relevant liability which is either not covered by a contract of insurance or covered by a contract of insurance with an insurer whose identity cannot be ascertained, or

(ii) to the insurer in the case of proceedings in respect of a relevant liability which is covered by a contract of insurance with an insurer whose identity can be ascertained;

(b) such information relating to the proceedings as M.I.B. may reasonably require is supplied to M.I.B. by the person bringing the proceedings;

(c) if so required by M.I.B. and subject to full indemnity from M.I.B. as to costs the person bringing the proceedings has taken all reasonable steps to obtain judgment against all the persons liable in respect of the injury or death of the third party and, in the event of such a person being a servant or agent, against his principal;

(d) the judgment referred to in Clause 2 of this Agreement and any judgment referred to in paragraph (c) of this Clause which has been obtained (whether or not either judgment includes an amount in respect of a liability other than a relevant liability) and any order for costs are assigned to M.I.B. or their nominee.

(2) In the event of any dispute as to the reasonableness of a requirement by M.I.B. for the supply of information or that any particular step should be taken to obtain judgment against other persons it may be referred to the Secretary of State whose decision shall be final.

(3) Where a judgment which includes an amount in respect of a liability other than a relevant liability has been assigned to M.I.B. or their nominee in pursuance of paragraph (1) (d) of this Clause M.I.B. shall apportion any monies received in pursuance of the judgment according to the proportion which the damages in respect of the relevant liability bear to the damages in respect of the other liabilities and shall account to the person in whose favour the judgment was given in respect of such monies received properly apportionable to the other liabilities. Where an order for costs in respect of such a judgment has been so assigned monies received pursuant to the order shall be dealt with in the same manner.

Exemptions

6. (1) M.I.B. shall not incur any liability under Clause 2 of this Agreement in a case where—

(a) the claim arises out of the use of a vehicle owned by or in the possession of the Crown, except where any other person has undertaken responsibility for the existence of a contract of insurance under Part VI of the Road Traffic Act 1972 (whether or not the person or persons liable be in fact covered by a contract of insurance) or where the liability is in fact covered by a contract of insurance;

(b) the claim arises out of the use of a vehicle the use of which is not required to be covered by a contract of insurance by virtue of section 144 of the Road Traffic Act 1972, unless the use is in fact covered by such a contract;

(c) at the time of the accident the person suffering death or bodily injury in respect of which the claim is made was allowing himself to be carried in a vehicle and—

(i) knew or had reason to believe that the vehicle had been taken without the consent of the owner or other lawful authority except in a case where—

(A) he believed or had reason to believe that he had lawful authority to be carried or that he would have had the owner's consent if the owner had known of his being carried and the circumstances of his carriage; or

(B) he had learned of the circumstances of the taking of the vehicle since the commencement of the journey and it would be unreasonable to expect him to have alighted from the vehicle; or

(ii) being the owner of or being a person using the vehicle, he was using or causing or permitting the vehicle to be used without there being in force in relation to such use a contract of insurance as would comply with Part VI of the Road Traffic Act 1972, knowing or having reason to believe that no such contract was in force.

(2) The exemption specified in sub-paragraph (1) (*c*) of this Clause shall apply only in a case where the judgment in respect of which the claim against M.I.B. is made was obtained in respect of a relevant liability incurred by the owner or a person using the vehicle in which the person who suffered death or bodily injury was being carried.

(3) For the purposes of these exemptions—

(*a*) a vehicle which has been unlawfully removed from the possession of the Crown shall be taken to continue in that possession whilst it is kept so removed;

(*b*) references to a person being carried in a vehicle include references to his being carried in or upon or entering or getting on to or alighting from the vehicle;

(*c*) "owner" in relation to a vehicle which is the subject of a hiring agreement or a hire-purchase agreement, means the person in possession of the vehicle under that agreement.

Agents

7. Nothing in this Agreement shall prevent M.I.B. performing their obligations under this Agreement by Agents.

Operation

8. This Agreement shall come into operation on the first day of December 1972 in relation to accidents occurring on or after that date. The Agreement made on 1 February 1971 between the Secretary of State and M.I.B. shall cease and determine except in relation to claims arising out of accidents occurring before the first day of December 1972.

Notes

1. There is a separate agreement, also dated 22 November 1972, between the Secretary of State and the M.I.B. to secure compensation for third party victims of road accidents when the driver responsible for the accident cannot be traced. This replaces an earlier agreement and applies to accidents occurring on or after 1 December 1972. The M.I.B. is not required, by this Agreement, to include in the payment awarded to the victim any amount in respect of damages for loss of expectation of life or for pain and suffering which the applicant might have had a right to claim under the Law Reform (Miscellaneous Provisions) Act 1934 (see p. 406, *ante*) nor to make any payment in respect of loss of earnings where the victim has received his wages or salary "in full or in part" from his employer, whether or not he has undertaken to reimburse his employer (cf. p. 434, *ante*): clause 4. There is a right of appeal to an arbitrator against the decision of the M.I.B.: clause 11.

2. These agreements are contracts between the Secretary of State for the Environment and the M.I.B.; there is no privity of contract with third party victims of uninsured or untraced drivers. However, the M.I.B. has said it will never take the point (see the remarks of Viscount Dilhorne in *Albert* v. *Motor*

Insurers' Bureau, [1972] A.C. 301, at p. 320, and Lord Denning M.R. in *Hardy* v. *Motor Insurers' Bureau*, [1964] 2 Q.B. 745, at p. 757; and the Court of Appeal has not been willing to take the point of its own accord: *Coward* v. *Motor Insurers' Bureau*, [1963] 1 Q.B. 259, at p. 265. The Bureau is entitled to be added as a defendant in an action by a third party victim against an uninsured driver (*Gurtner* v. *Circuit*, [1968] 2 Q.B. 587; [1968] 1 All E.R. 328) but not if he is the victim of an untraced driver (*White* v. *London Transport Executive*, [1971] 2 Q.B. 721; [1971] 3 All E.R. 1).

3. The M.I.B. is bound to pay even though the driver intentionally causes the injury: *Hardy* v. *Motor Insurers' Bureau*, [1964] 2 All E.R. 742. Diplock L.J. said in this case, at p. 752:

> The liability of the assured, and thus the rights of the third party against the insurers, can only arise out of some wrongful (tortious) act of the assured. I can see no reason in public policy for drawing a distinction between one kind of wrongful act, of which a third party is the innocent victim, and another kind of wrongful act; between wrongful acts which are crimes on the part of the perpetrator and wrongful acts which are not crimes, or between wrongful acts which are crimes of carelessness and wrongful acts which are intentional crimes. It seems to me to be slightly unrealistic to suggest that a person who is not deterred by the risk of a possible sentence of life imprisonment from using a vehicle with intent to commit grievous bodily harm would be deterred by the fear that his civil liability to his victim would not be discharged by his insurers. I do not, myself, feel that, by dismissing this appeal, we shall add significantly to the statistics of crime.

4. The M.I.B. is bound to pay only if the vehicle is on a "road" at the time of the accident: *Randall* v. *Motor Insurers' Bureau*, [1969] 1 All E.R. 21 (part of lorry on private ground but greater part on public road, held use on road caused injury).

3. INSURANCE DOCUMENTS

There are considerable variations in the type and form of policies available from different companies. Those below are reproduced by kind permission of the Guardian Royal Exchange Assurance Group. Since most students have access to a private motor car insurance policy and a home insurance policy, we have, for reasons of space, limited our selection to two types of policy: liability insurance and business interruption.

Liability Insurance Policy

The Insured by a proposal (including supplementary information) which shall be the basis of and incorporated in this contract having applied to the Guardian Royal Exchange Assurance Limited (The Company) for this insurance and having paid or agreed to pay the Premium

The Company will provide insurance as described in the following pages in respect of the Sections indicated in the Schedule

Section A—Public Liability

The Company will subject to the terms of and endorsements to this Section and the conditions of this Policy indemnify the Insured against all sums which the Insured becomes legally liable to pay as damages in respect of

(1) bodily injury (including death or disease) to any person

(2) loss of or damage to property

happening within the Geographical Limits during the Period of Insurance in connection with the Business

The Company will also pay Legal Costs and Solicitor's Fees

LIMIT OF INDEMNITY

The liability of the Company for all damages payable arising out of one occurrence or series of occurrences consequent on one original cause shall not exceed the Limit of Indemnity

DEFINITIONS

1. *Legal Costs*

The term "Legal Costs" shall mean legal costs and expenses recoverable by any claimant and all costs and expenses incurred with the written consent of the Company

2. *Solicitor's Fees*

The term "Solicitor's Fees" shall mean the solicitor's fees incurred with the written consent of the Company for representation of the Insured at

(*a*) any coroners' inquest or fatal inquiry arising from any death

(*b*) proceedings in any Court of Summary Jurisdiction arising out of any alleged breach of a statutory duty resulting in bodily injury or loss of or damage to property

which may be the subject of a claim under this insurance

3. *Geographical Limits*

(*a*) Great Britain Northern Ireland the Channel Islands and the Isle of Man

(*b*) Elsewhere in the world in connection with commercial visits by directors or non-manual staff normally resident in and travelling from the territories mentioned in (*a*)

EXCEPTIONS TO SECTION A

1. The Company will not indemnify the Insured against liability arising from

(*a*) bodily injury sustained by an Employee and arising out of and in the course of his employment or engagement by the Insured

(*b*) loss of or damage to property belonging to or in the custody or control of the Insured or any servant of the Insured other than personal effects (including vehicles) belonging to directors visitors or Employees

(*c*) (i) libel or slander

(ii) infringement of plans copyright patent trade name trade mark or registered design

(*d*) bodily injury loss or damage

(i) deliberately caused by or on the instructions of the Insured or an Employee whilst engaged in supervisory duties unless caused by the wilful misconduct of such Employee

(ii) arising from any goods whether or not described in the Schedule (after they have ceased to be in the custody or under the control of the Insured) sold supplied repaired altered treated or installed other than food or drink for consumption on the Insured's premises

(*e*) the non-performance non-completion or delay in completion of any contract or agreement or the payment of penalty sums fines or liquidated damages

(*f*) the ownership possession or use of any aircraft hovercraft oil drilling platform, or rig or watercraft (except manually propelled watercraft) (*g*) the ownership possession or use of

  (i) any mechanically propelled vehicle used solely for agricultural or forestry purposes

  (ii) any other mechanically propelled vehicle except the use within the Insured's premises of a vehicle which is not licensed for road use and which does not require a Certificate of Motor Insurance

  Unless an indemnity is granted by another insurance this exception shall not apply to the loading or unloading of any mechanically propelled vehicle

2. The Company will not indemnify the Insured in respect of

  (*a*) any legal liability of whatsoever nature directly or indirectly caused by or contributed to by or arising from

   (i) ionising radiations or contamination by radioactivity from any nuclear fuel or from any nuclear waste from the combustion of nuclear fuel

   (ii) the radioactive toxic explosive or other hazardous properties of any explosive nuclear assembly or nuclear component thereof

  (*b*) any consequence whether direct or indirect of war invasion act of foreign enemy hostilities (whether war be declared or not) civil war rebellion revolution insurrection or military or usurped power

Section B—Products Liability

The Company will subject to the terms of and endorsements to this Section and the conditions of this Policy indemnify the Insured against all sums which the Insured becomes legally liable to pay as damages in respect of

(1) bodily injury (including death or disease) to any person
(2) loss of or damage to property

happening anywhere in the world during the Period of Insurance and caused by the Goods sold supplied repaired altered treated or installed from or in Great Britain Northern Ireland the Channel Islands and the Isle of Man in connection with the Business

The Company will also pay Legal Costs and Solicitor's Fees

Limit of Indemnity

The liability of the Company for all damages in respect of all bodily injury loss or damage happening in any one Period of Insurance shall not in the aggregate exceed the Limit of Indemnity

Definitions

1. *Legal Costs*

The term "Legal Costs" shall mean legal costs and expenses recoverable by any claimant and all costs and expenses incurred with the written consent of the Company

2. *Solicitor's Fees*

The term "Solicitor's Fees" shall mean the solicitor's fees incurred with the written consent of the Company for representation of the Insured at

  (*a*) any coroners' inquest or fatal inquiry arising from any death
  (*b*) proceedings in any Court of Summary Jurisdiction arising out of any alleged breach of a statutory duty resulting in bodily injury or loss of or damage to property

which may be the subject of a claim under this insurance

3. *Replacement Costs*

The term "Replacement Costs" shall mean the cost of repair alteration or replacement of the Goods and the term shall include the cost of demolition breaking out dismantling delivery rebuilding supply and installation of the Goods and any other property (unless physically damaged by the Goods) essential to such repair alteration or replacement

EXCEPTIONS TO SECTION B

1. The Company will not indemnify the Insured against liability arising from

   (*a*) bodily injury sustained by an Employee and arising out of and in the course of his employment or engagement by the Insured

   (*b*) loss of or damage to property belonging to or in the custody or control of the Insured

   (*c*) (i) libel or slander

   　　(ii) infringement of plans copyright patent trade name trade mark or registered design

   (*d*) any action for damages brought in the Courts of Law of any territory outside Great Britain Northern Ireland the Channel Islands and the Isle of Man in which the Insured has a branch or is represented by a party domiciled in such territory or by a party holding the Insured's Power of Attorney

   (*e*) bodily injury loss or damage arising directly or indirectly from

   　　(i) Goods sold supplied repaired altered treated or installed by the Insured on terms less favourable to the Insured than the ordinary process of law governing their sale supply repair alteration treatment or installation

   　　(ii) Goods obtained by the Insured on terms which prevent the Insured exercising his rights of recovery under the ordinary process of law against his supplier or any other party

   　　(iii) the design plan formula or specification of the Goods

   　　(iv) instruction advice or information on the characteristics use storage or application of the Goods

2. The Company will not indemnify the Insured against liability

   (*a*) in respect of loss of or damage to the Goods

   (*b*) for the Replacement Costs of the Goods (see Definition 3 ...)

   (*c*) to make any refund of the payment received for the Goods

3. The Company will not indemnify the Insured in respect of

   (*a*) any legal liability of whatsoever nature directly or indirectly caused by or contributed to by or arising from

   　　(i) ionising radiations or contamination by radioactivity from any nuclear fuel or from any nuclear waste from the combustion of nuclear fuel

   　　(ii) the radioactive toxic explosive or other hazardous properties of any explosive nuclear assembly or nuclear component thereof

   (*b*) any consequence whether direct or indirect of war invasion act of foreign enemy hostilities (whether war be declared or not) civil war rebellion revolution insurrection or military or usurped power

SECTION C—EMPLOYERS' LIABILITY

The Company will subject to the terms of and endorsements to this Section and the conditions of this Policy indemnify the Insured against all sums which the Insured becomes legally liable to pay as damages in respect of bodily injury (including death or disease) sustained by an Employee arising out of and in the course of his employment or engagement by the Insured in the Business and caused within the Geographical Limits during the Period of Insurance

The Company will also pay Legal Costs and Solicitor's Fees

Definitions

1. *Legal Costs*

The term "Legal Costs" shall mean legal costs and expenses recoverable by any claimant and all costs and expenses incurred with the written consent of the Company

2. *Solicitor's Fees*

The term "Solicitor's Fees" shall mean the solicitor's fees incurred with the written consent of the Company for representation of the Insured at

   (*a*) any coroners' inquest or fatal inquiry arising from any death
   (*b*) proceedings in any Court of Summary Jurisdiction arising out of any alleged breach of a statutory duty resulting in bodily injury or loss of or damage to property

which may be the subject of a claim under this insurance

3. *Geographical Limits*

   (*a*) Great Britain Northern Ireland the Channel Islands and the Isle of Man
   (*b*) Elsewhere in the world provided the action for damages is brought in the Courts of Law of the territories mentioned in Geographical Limit (*a*)

AVOIDANCE OF CERTAIN TERMS AND RIGHTS OF RECOVERY ENDORSEMENT

(Applicable to Employers' Liability sections and insured event 3 of Section 6 of Tradepak policies)

The indemnity granted by this insurance is deemed to be in accordance with the provisions of any law relating to the compulsory insurance of liability to employees in Great Britain (and Northern Ireland and the Isle of Man or the Channel Islands in so far as this endorsement applies to these territories).

But the Insured shall repay to the Company all sums paid by the Company which the Company would not have been liable to pay but for the provisions of such law.

General Definitions

1. *Business*

The term "Business" shall include

   (*a*) the provision and management of canteen social sports and welfare organisations for the benefit of Employees
   (*b*) first aid fire and ambulance services
   (*c*) private work carried out by any Employee for the Insured or any director partner or senior official of the Insured

2. *Employee*

The term "Employee" shall include

   (*a*) any person under a contract of service or apprenticeship with
      (i) the Insured
      (ii) any other party and who is borrowed by or hired to the Insured
   (*b*) any labour master or person supplied by him
   (*c*) any person supplied by a labour only subcontractor
   (*d*) any self-employed person working for the Insured
   (*e*) any person supplied to the Insured under a contract or agreement the terms of which deem such person to be in the employment of the Insured for the duration of such contract or agreement

3. *Insured*

The term "Insured" shall include

   (*a*) any party for whom the Insured is carrying out a contract away from the Insured's own premises but only to the extent required by such contract and in respect of Section C—Employers' Liability—only in so far as concerns bodily injury sustained by an Employee of the Insured

(*b*) at the request of the Insured

    (i) any director partner or Employee of the Insured in respect of liability for which the Insured would have been entitled to claim under this insurance if the claim had been made against the Insured

    (ii) any officer or member of the Insured's canteen social sports or welfare organisations first aid fire or ambulance services

in his respective capacity as such

(*c*) in the event of the death of the Insured any personal representative of the Insured in respect of liability incurred by the Insured

CONDITIONS

Interpretation

1. Any word or expression to which a specific meaning has been attached in any part of this Policy or Schedule shall bear such meaning wherever it may appear

Precautions

2. The Insured shall take and cause to be taken all reasonable precautions to

(*a*) prevent bodily injury and loss and damage to property and the sale or supply of goods which are defective in any way

(*b*) comply with all statutory obligations and regulations imposed by any authority

Alterations

3. The Insured shall give immediate notice to the Company of any alteration which materially affects the risk

Claims

4. (*a*) The Insured shall give written notice to the Company of any bodily injury loss or damage or claim or proceeding immediately the same shall have come to the knowledge of the Insured or his representative

(*b*) The Insured shall not admit liability for or negotiate the settlement of any claim without the written consent of the Company which shall be entitled to conduct in the name of the Insured the defence or settlement of any claim or to prosecute for its own benefit any claim for indemnity or damages or otherwise and shall have full discretion in the conduct of any proceedings and in the settlement of any claim and the Insured shall give all such information and assistance as the Company may require

(*c*) If under Section A—Public Liability—the Company is required to indemnify more than one party named in Definition 3 (Insured) the liability of the Company shall not exceed in all the Limit of Indemnity

(*d*) In connection with any one claim or number of claims other than in respect of claims under Section C—Employers' Liability—occurring in any one Period of Insurance the Company may at any time pay to the Insured the amount of the Limit of Indemnity (after deduction of any sum or sums already paid as compensation) or any less amount for which such claim or claims can be settled and thereafter the Company shall be under no further liability under this Policy in connection with such claim or claims except for Legal Costs incurred prior to the date of such payment

Cancellation

5. The Company may cancel any Section by sending thirty days' notice by registered letter to the Insured at his last known address and shall return to the Insured the Premium less the pro rata portion thereof for the period the Section has been in force subject to adjustment under Condition 6

Adjustment

6. If any part of the Premium is calculated on estimates the Insured shall within one month from the expiry of each Period of Insurance furnish such details as the Company may require and the premium for such period shall be adjusted subject to any Minimum Premium

Other Insurances

7. If an Indemnity is or would but for the existence of this insurance be granted by any other insurance the Company shall not provide indemnity except in respect of any excess beyond the amount which is or would but for the existence of this insurance be payable

Observance

8. The liability of the Company shall be conditional on the observance by the Insured of the terms provisions conditions and endorsements of this Policy

Business Interruption Insurance Policy

IN CONSIDERATION of the Insured named in the Schedule hereto paying to the Company named in the said Schedule the First Premium mentioned in the said Schedule

The Company agrees (subject to the Conditions contained herein or endorsed or otherwise expressed hereon which conditions shall so far as the nature of them respectively will permit be deemed to be conditions precedent to the right of the Insured to recover hereunder) that if after payment of the premium any building or other property or any part thereof used by the Insured at the Premises for the purpose of the Business be destroyed or damaged by

(1) Fire (whether resulting from explosion or otherwise) not occasioned by or happening through

(*a*) its own spontaneous fermentation or heating or its undergoing any process involving the application of heat,

(*b*) earthquake, subterranean fire, riot, civil commotion, war, invasion, act of foreign enemy, hostilities (whether war be declared or not), civil war, rebellion, revolution, insurrection or military or usurped power,

(2) Lightning,

(3) Explosion, not occasioned by or happening through any of the perils specified in 1 (*b*) above,

(*a*) of boilers used for domestic purposes only,

(*b*) of any other boilers or economisers on the premises,

(*c*) in a building not being part of any gas works, of gas used for domestic purposes or used for lighting or heating the building,

(destruction or damage so caused being hereinafter termed Damage) at any time before 4 o'clock in the afternoon of the last day of the period of insurance or of any subsequent period in respect of which the Insured shall have paid and the Company shall have accepted the premium required for the renewal of this Policy and the business carried on by the Insured at the premises be in consequence thereof interrupted or interfered with

Then the Company will pay to the Insured in respect of each item in the Schedule hereto the amount of loss resulting from such interruption or interference in accordance with the provisions therein contained

Provided that at the time of the happening of the damage there shall be in force an insurance covering the interest of the Insured in the property at the premises against such damage and that payment shall have been made or liability admitted therefor under such insurance

And that the liability of the Company shall in no case exceed in respect of each item the sum expressed in the said Schedule to be insured thereon nor in the whole the total sum insured hereby or such other sum or sums as may hereafter be substituted therefor by memorandum signed by or on behalf of the Company.

CONDITIONS

1. *Misdescription*

This Policy shall be voidable in the event of misrepresentation misdescription or non-disclosure in any material particular.

2. *Alterations in interest or in risk*

This Policy shall be avoided if:—

      (*a*) the business be wound up or carried on by a liquidator or receiver or permanently discontinued

or   (*b*) the Insured's interest cease otherwise than by death

or   (*c*) any alteration be made either in the business or in the premises or property therein whereby the risk of damage is increased,

at any time after the commencement of this insurance, unless its continuance be admitted by memorandum signed by or on behalf of the Company.

3. *Exclusions*

This Policy does not cover:—

      (*a*) loss resulting from damage occasioned by or happening through explosion (whether the explosion be occasioned by fire or otherwise) except as stated on the face of this Policy

      (*b*) loss resulting from damage occasioned by or happening through or occasioning—

            loss or destruction of or damage to any property whatsoever or any loss or expense whatsoever resulting or arising therefrom or any consequential loss directly or indirectly caused by or contributed to by or arising from—

        (i) ionising radiations or contamination by radioactivity from any nuclear fuel or from any nuclear waste from the combustion of nuclear fuel

       (ii) the radioactive, toxic, explosive or other hazardous properties of any explosive nuclear assembly or nuclear component thereof.

4. *Claims*

On the happening of any damage in consequence of which a claim is or may be made under this Policy, the Insured shall forthwith give notice thereof in writing to the Company and shall with due diligence do and concur in doing and permit to be done all things which may be reasonably practicable to minimise or check any interruption of or interference with the business or to avoid or diminish the loss, and in the event of a claim being made under this Policy shall, not later than thirty days after the expiry of the indemnity period or within such further time as the Company may in writing allow, at his own expense deliver to the Company in writing a statement setting forth particulars of his claim, together with details of all other insurances covering the damage or any part of it or consequential loss of any kind resulting therefrom. The Insured shall at his own expense also produce and furnish to the Company such books of account and other business books, vouchers, invoices, balance sheets and other documents, proofs, information, explanation and other evidence as may reasonably be required by the Company for the purpose of investigating or verifying the claim together with (if demanded) a statutory declaration of the truth of the claim and of any matters connected therewith. No claim under this Policy shall be payable unless the terms of this condition have been complied with and in the event of non-compliance therewith in any respect, any payment on account of the claim already made shall be repaid to the Company forthwith.

5. *Fraud*

If the claim be in any respect fraudulent or if any fraudulent means or devices be used by the Insured or anyone acting on his behalf to obtain any benefit under this Policy or if any damage be occasioned by the wilful act or with the connivance of the Insured, all benefit under this Policy shall be forfeited.

6. *Contribution*

If at the time of any damage resulting in a loss under this Policy there be any other insurance effected by or on behalf of the Insured covering such loss or any part of it, the liability of the Company hereunder shall be limited to its rateable proportion of such loss.

7. *Subrogation*

Any claimant under this Policy shall at the request and at the expense of the Company do and concur in doing and permit to be done all such acts and things as may be necessary or reasonably required by the Company for the purpose of enforcing any rights and remedies, or of obtaining relief or indemnity from other parties to which the Company shall be or would become entitled or subrogated upon its paying for or making good any loss under this Policy, whether such acts and things shall be or become necessary or required before or after his indemnification by the Company.

8. *Arbitration*

If any difference shall arise as to the amount to be paid under this Policy (liability being otherwise admitted) such difference shall be referred to an Arbitrator to be appointed by the parties in accordance with the Statutory provisions in that behalf for the time being in force. Where any difference is by this Condition to be referred to arbitration the making of an Award shall be a condition precedent to any right of action against the Company.

9. *Interpretation*

This Policy and the Schedule annexed (which forms an integral part of this Policy) shall be read together as one contract and words and expressions to which specific meanings have been attached in any part of this Policy or of the Schedule shall bear such specific meanings wherever they may appear.

[The specification attached to and forming part of the policy is omitted. This limits the sum insured in respect of (1) Loss on gross profit, and (2) on professional accountant's charges for producing particulars of loss.]

MEMORANDUM

In consideration of the payment of an additional premium the word Damage where used in the Policy/Section is extended to include destruction or damage (by Fire or otherwise) caused by:—

1. Aircraft and other aerial devices or articles dropped therefrom, excluding destruction or damage occasioned by pressure waves caused by aircraft and other aerial devices travelling at sonic or supersonic speeds.

2. Explosion provided that the extension granted under this heading shall exclude:—

   (*a*) loss resulting from destruction or damage by Explosion (other than destruction or damage by Fire resulting from Explosion) occasioned by the bursting of any vessel, machine or apparatus (not being a boiler or economiser on the premises) in which internal pressure is due to steam only and belonging to or under the control of the Insured.

   (*b*) loss sustained in consequence of the Insured being deprived of the use of any vessel, machine or apparatus (not being a boiler or economiser on the premises) or its contents as a result of the explosion thereof.

3. Riot, Civil Commotion, Strikers, Locked-Out Workers or persons taking part in Labour Disturbances or malicious persons acting on behalf of or in connection with any political organisation, excluding:—

Destruction or damage resulting from cessation of work, or from confiscation or requisition by order of the Government or any Public Authority.

4. Earthquake.

5. Storm or Tempest, excluding:—

(a) destruction or damage by:—

(i) the escape of water from the normal confines of any natural or artificial water course (other than water tanks, apparatus or pipes) or lake, reservoir, canal or dam

(ii) inundation from the sea

whether resulting from Storm or Tempest or otherwise.

(b) destruction or damage by Frost, Subsidence or Landslip.

6. Flood, excluding destruction or damage by Frost, Subsidence or Landslip.

7. Bursting or Overflowing of Water Tanks, Apparatus or Pipes.

8. Impact by any Road Vehicle, Horses or Cattle not belonging to or under the control of the Insured or any member of the Insured's family residing with him or any employee of the Insured.

PROVIDED ALWAYS that the insurance under this memorandum shall be subject to the following Special Conditions and that all the Conditions of the Policy/Section (except in so far as they may be hereby expressly varied) shall apply as if they had been incorporated herein.

SPECIAL CONDITIONS

1. The liability of the Company shall in no case under this memorandum and the Policy/Section exceed the sum insured by the Policy/Section.

2. For the purpose of this insurance pressure waves caused by aircraft and other aerial devices travelling at sonic or supersonic speeds shall not be deemed explosion.

3. This insurance does not cover loss resulting from destruction or damage directly or indirectly occasioned by or happening through or in consequence of War, Invasion, Act of Foreign Enemy, Hostilities (whether War be declared or not), Civil War, Rebellion, Revolution, Insurrection or Military or Usurped Power or Water accidentally discharged or leaking from a Sprinkler Installation.

4. This insurance does not cover loss resulting from damage occasioned by or happening through or occasioning:—

loss or destruction of or damage to any property whatsoever or any loss or expense whatsoever resulting or arising therefrom or any consequential loss directly or indirectly caused by or contributed to by or arising from:—

(i) ionising radiations or contamination by radioactivity from any nuclear fuel or from any nuclear waste from the combustion of nuclear fuel

(ii) the radioactive, toxic, explosive or other hazardous properties of any explosive nuclear assembly or nuclear component thereof.

5. On the happening of any destruction or damage from the perils covered under Item 3 of this memorandum, full details of such destruction or damage shall be furnished to the Company within seven days.

4. THE CONDUCT OF LITIGATION

Justice Report, *Trial of Motor Accident Cases* (London, 1966)

... There are no statistics from which it is possible to deduce with any degree of certainty in how many cases the injured persons, or the relatives of those killed, were obliged to resort to litigation in order to enforce their right. It is however within our knowledge that a very large proportion of the claims are settled by negotiation and without resort to litigation. Insurance of persons driving motor-vehicles against third party liabilities is (with certain exceptions which for the present purpose are immaterial) compulsory, so that negotiations are conducted, at all events on one side, by experts. It is open to insurance companies to settle through their agents direct with injured persons. We recommend that settlements negotiated between an expert on the one hand and a layman on the other should be open to review at the instance of the layman, and to being set aside if shown to be unfair in all the circumstances. It would be necessary to impose a time limit of, say, one year from the date of the settlement, beyond which an application for review could not be made. There is no danger of such a rule giving rise to a substantial increase in litigation. The majority of insurance companies are reputable concerns who do not seek in negotiation to take unjust advantage of their greater knowledge of the law and practice to obtain oppressive settlements. But insurance is a highly competitive business, and it is within the knowledge of some of us that there are insurers who, given the chance to do so, do extract such settlements. It would be in the interests of justice, and, indeed, of the reputable insurers, whose premiums are geared to fair settlements, if their competitors, some of whom under-cut their premiums, were encouraged by law to act fairly in the negotiation of settlements. . . .

. . . A great many cases are settled by negotiation. Experienced insurance claims managers tell us that upwards of 75 *per cent.* of all claims are settled, without the issue of proceedings, by negotiation. But much must depend upon the policy of the particular insurance company. Some are, at all events in the earlier stages, somewhat aggressive and disinclined to negotiate until they smell a whiff of powder. Until the plaintiff finds the money or obtains legal aid or obtains assistance from his trade union with authority to start proceedings, such companies tend, even if it is no more than bluff, to maintain a firm repudiation. After the issue of proceedings it becomes easier to negotiate with them. We note the foregoing in a report upon legal procedure, since negotiation before proceedings forms an essential part of the procedure for settling disputes.

Note

See *Lister* v. *Romford Ice and Cold Storage Co., Ltd.,* [1957] A.C. 555; [1957] I All E.R. 125 (p. 660, *ante*) and *Morris* v. *Ford Motor Co., Ltd.,* [1973] Q.B. 792; [1973] 2 All E.R. 1084 (p. 666, *ante*).

5. SOCIAL INSURANCE

Guide to Social Security Benefits

The following are the main benefits payable on injury or death—

Sickness benefit: This is payable to those who have paid contributions as employed persons (class I contributors) or as self-employed persons (class 2) for a minimum period and who show that they are incapable of work by reason of some specific disease or bodily or mental disablement. After 168 days this is normally replaced for an indefinite period by invalidity benefit, and there may also be an invalidity allowance. An attendance allowance is payable to a person so severely handicapped that he has for six months or more required frequent attention throughout the day and prolonged or repeated attention throughout the night, or required continual supervision in order to avoid substantial danger to himself or others.

Industrial injury benefit: This is payable for a maximum period of six months to those incapable of work as a result of an injury arising out of and in the course of employment or a prescribed disease. (This is not payable to those suffering from pneumoconiosis or byssinosis; special schemes cover these.)

Industrial injury disablement benefit: Long-term benefit for disablement due to industrial injury or disease is payable. This normally follows a period in which injury benefit has been paid. The basic benefit may be a pension or a lump sum, dependent upon the medical assessment or the degree of disablement. There are prescribed degrees of disablement, e.g. loss of a hand or foot, 100%; absolute deafness, 100%; amputation of both feet resulting in end-bearing stumps, 90%; loss of one eye, without complications, the other being normal, 40%; guillotine amputation of tip of middle finger without loss of bone, 4%. (The full list will be found in the National Insurance (Industrial Injuries) Benefit Regulations 1964, S.I. 1964 No. 504, Sched. 2.) Assessment of the degree of disablement takes no account of the claimant's occupation or any loss of earnings, but allowances can be added to meet the circumstances (e.g. special hardship allowance where claimant unable to follow regular occupation or one of equivalent standard; constant attendance allowance for 100% disablement cases; exceptionally severe disablement allowance; hardship treatment allowance, during hospitalisation; unemployability supplement). Sickness and invalidity benefit or a retirement pension, where appropriate, may be payable in addition to disablement benefit.

Widow's benefit: Widow's allowance is payable for the first 26 weeks of widowhood. Thereafter payment depends upon individual responsibilities and age. A guardian's allowance may be payable for orphans and a child's special allowance to a divorced woman where the child's father dies. There is a fixed death grant in all cases of £30. The widow of a man who dies from an industrial accident receives a pension (reduced after the first 26 weeks).

Earnings-related benefits: These are payable in addition to flat-rate sickness, invalidity, injury and widow's benefits for up to six months. The claimant receives one-third of so much of his earnings as lie between £10 and £30 per week and 15 *per cent* of so much as lies between £30 and £42 (for the year 1974: the upper limit is going up each year). The total of all benefits cannot exceed 85 *per cent* of gross earnings, although the flat-rate element cannot be reduced. (See, Mesher (1974), 3 I.L.J. 118.)

Comparison of benefits: industrial and non-industrial accidents

The amounts stated are maxima payable from 22 July 1974. An asterisk indicates that there are contribution requirements. A cross (×) means that the benefit is taxable.

Industrial accidents	*£ per week*
Injury benefit	
flat rate (married couple)	16·65
earnings-related supplement * (see, *ante*)	
two dependent children	4·50
Disablement benefit	
pension (100 *per cent* disabled)	16·40
or gratuity (£1,090 lump sum)	
constant attendance allowance	13·20
special hardship allowance	6·56
exceptionally severe disablement allowance	6·60

	£ per week
unemployability supplement	10·00
two dependent children	4·50
persons over 80	2·05
Industrial death benefit (×)	
death grant * (£30)	
industrial widow's pension (initial)	14·00
industrial widow's supplementary allowance * (see, *ante*)	
two dependent children	4·50

Non-industrial accidents
Sickness benefit

flat rate * (married couple)	13·90
earnings-related supplement * (see, *ante*)	
two dependent children	4·50

Invalidity benefit

pension * (married couple)	16·00
allowance *	2·05
two dependent children *	4·50
attendance allowance *	8·00

Death benefit (×)

death grant * (£30)	
widow's allowance *	14·00
widow's supplementary allowance * (see, *ante*)	
widowed mother's allowance *	10·00
widow's pension *	10·00
two dependent children	4·50
guardian's allowance *	4·90
child's special allowance	4·90

Supplementary benefits may be payable in both industrial and non-industrial accidents where requirements exceed resources.

The National Insurance (Industrial Injuries) Act 1965

5. General right to and description of benefit.—(1) Subject to the provisions of this Act, where an insured person suffers personal injury caused after 4th July 1948 by accident arising out of and in the course of his employment, being insurable employment, then—

    (a) industrial injury benefit (in this Act referred to as "injury benefit") shall be payable to the insured person if during such period as is hereinafter provided he is, as the result of the injury, incapable of work;

    (b) industrial disablement benefit (in this Act referred to as "disablement benefit") by way of disablement gratuity or disablement pension shall be payable to the insured person if he suffers, as the result of the injury, from such loss of physical or mental faculty as is hereinafter provided;

    (c) industrial death benefit (in this Act referred to as "death benefit") shall be payable to such persons as are hereinafter provided if the insured person dies as a result of the injury. . . .

6. General presumption as to accidents.—For the purposes of this Act, an accident arising in the course of an insured person's employment shall be deemed, in the absence of evidence to the contrary, also to have arisen out of that employment.

7. Accidents håppening while acting in breach of regulations, etc.—An accident shall be deemed to arise out of and in the course of an insured person's employment, notwithstanding that he is at the time of the accident acting in contravention of any statutory or other regulations applicable to his employment, or of any orders given by or on behalf of his employer, or that he is acting without instructions from his employer, if—

> (*a*) the accident would have been deemed so to have arisen had the act not been done in contravention as aforesaid or without instructions from his employer, as the case may be; and
>
> (*b*) the act is done for the purposes of and in connection with the employer's trade or business.

8. Accidents happening while travelling in employer's transport.—(1) An accident happening while an insured person is, with the express or implied permission of his employer, travelling as a passenger by any vehicle to or from his place of work shall, notwithstanding that he is under no obligation to his employer to travel by that vehicle, be deemed to arise out of and in the course of his employment if—

> (*a*) the accident would have been deemed so to have arisen had he been under such an obligation; and
>
> (*b*) at the time of the accident, the vehicle—
>
>> (i) is being operated by or on behalf of his employer or some other person by whom it is provided in pursuance òf arrangements made with his employer; and
>>
>> (ii) is not being operated in the ordinary course of a public transport service.

(2) In this section references to a vehicle include references to a ship, vessel or aircraft.

9. Accidents happening while meeting emergency.—An accident happening to an insured person in or about any premises at which he is for the time being employed for the purposes of his employer's trade or business shall be deemed to arise out of and in the course of his employment if it happens while he is taking steps, on an actual or supposed emergency at those premises, to rescue, succour or protect persons who are, or are thought to be or possibly to be, injured or imperilled, or to avert or minimise serious damage to property.

10. Accidents caused by other persons' misconduct, etc.—An accident happening after 19th December 1961 shall be treated for the purposes of this Act, where it would not apart from this section be so treated, as arising out of a person's employment if—

> (*a*) the accident arises in the course of the employment; and
>
> (*b*) the accident either is caused by another person's misconduct, skylarking or negligence, or by steps taken in consequence of any such misconduct, skylarking or negligence, or by the behaviour or presence of an animal (including a bird, fish or insect), or is caused by or consists in the insured person being struck by any object or by lightning; and
>
> (*c*) the insured person did not directly or indirectly induce or contribute to the happening of the accident by his conduct outside the employment or by any act not incidental to the employment.

Notes

1. The National Insurance (Industrial Injuries) Act 1965 amends and consolidates the social security system advocated by Beveridge (Cmd. 6404), paras. 77–107, and first enacted in the National Insurance (Industrial Injuries) Act 1946.

Employer and employee and the Exchequer contribute to the scheme. Three types of question may arise for adjudication under this system: (a) "special" questions, e.g. whether a person is in "insurable employment"; these are determined by a Minister who may refer questions of law by way of case stated to a single judge of the Queen's Bench Division; (b) "disablement questions", e.g. whether an accident has resulted in loss of faculty, degree of disablement etc.; these are determined by medical authorities—a medical board with an appeal to a medical appeal tribunal and a further appeal on questions of law to the National Insurance Commissioner; (c) all other questions, e.g. rights to benefit, disqualifications etc., are determined by insurance officers with an appeal to a local tribunal and a further appeal to the National Insurance Commissioner whose decision is "final". In exceptional cases an application may be made for an order of certiorari to bring up and quash the Commissioner's decision on grounds of an error of law on the face of the record: e.g. *R.* v. *Industrial Injuries Commissioner, ex parte Amalgamated Engineering Union*, [1966] 2 Q.B. 31; [1966] I All E.R. 96.

2. The claimant must establish that there was an "accident", i.e. "an un-looked for mishap or an untoward event which is not expected or designed" by the person injured: Commissioner's decision C.I. 18/49.[1] A "process" is distinguished from an "accident": *Roberts* v. *Dorothea Slate Quarries, Ltd.*, [1948] 2 All E.R. 201. So where death is caused by prolonged exposure to chemical substances this is not an "accident": R (I) 7/66; but a hernia caused by the repeated operation of a stiff lever could be ascribed to a series of specific and ascertainable incidents and so was caused by "accident": R (I) 77/51. The longer the period over which the injury developed the more likely it is to be treated as an "injury by process" rather than an "injury by accident": R (I) 4/62.

3. A person who contracts a disease caused by his work may claim benefits only if (a) the disease was caused by an "accident" (by a strained interpretation of this word several thousand cases a year of "athlete's foot" and hernia are so classified!); *or* (b) it is a *prescribed* disease (e.g. lead poisoning) caused by the nature of the claimant's work in a prescribed occupation (e.g. one involving the use of lead). The diseases and occupations corresponding to them are prescribed by statutory instrument. Section 56 (5) of the National Insurance (Industrial Injuries) Act 1965 provides that if at the time of an "accident" the disease is a prescribed one it cannot be regarded as having been caused by "accident". So non-infective dermatitis (a skin infection slightly different from "athlete's foot") being a prescribed disease cannot be regarded as an injury by accident.

4. The phrase "arising out of and in the course of employment" gives rise to many problems. Here are some illustrations.

(a) An apprentice was injured by a piece of machinery during a lunch-hour trade union meeting held in the workshop with the employer's per-mission. Held, this was an incident of the employment and he was entitled to benefit: R (I) 63/51.

---

1. [The Commissioner's decisions are selectively reported and published by H.M.S.O. The prefix C was used before 1950; the prefix I indicates that the decision relates to industrial injuries.]

(b) A civil servant was injured when locking-up government offices after a trade union meeting held outside working hours. Held, this was outside the course of employment: R (I) 46/59.

(c) A sales representative was injured while returning home after entertaining a business associate. Held, this was in the course of employment: R (I) 38/53.

(d) A civil servant decided to make an official visit to the home of a colleague whose premises were just off his homeward route. He was injured while crossing the road to get there. Held, this was outside the course of employment: R (I) 39/53.

(e) A factory worker was injured while having a permitted smoke when a skylarking fellow-employee slammed a door on his hand. Held, applying s. 10 of the Act, that this was in the course of employment: R (I) 3/67.

(f) A repairer was injured when he joined the wires from a firing battery to a detonator with the implied authority of a shot-firer. This was no part of his well-understood duties and contrary to the Coal Mines (Explosives) Order 1956 which provides that such work is to be done only by the shot-firer. Held, the shot-firer's authority did not widen the scope of the claimant's employment and s. 7 of the Act was of no benefit to him: R (I) 12/61.

5. The fact that the claimant has received common law damages makes no difference to his claim for benefit. The effect of the entitlement to benefit on his claim for damages at common law is dealt with in the Law Reform (Personal Injuries) Act 1948, s. 2 (1) (p. 413, *ante*).

Criminal Injuries Compensation Scheme

The Scheme for compensating victims of crimes of violence was announced in both Houses of Parliament on 24th June 1964, and in its original form came into operation on 1st August 1964.

The Scheme has since been modified in a number of respects. The revised Scheme which came into operation on 21st May 1969, is set out below.

Administration

1. The Compensation Scheme will be administered by the Criminal Injuries Compensation Board, appointments to which will be made by the Home Secretary and the Secretary of State for Scotland, after consultation with the Lord Chancellor. The Chairman will be a person of wide legal experience, and the other members, of whom there are at present eight, will also be legally qualified. The Board will be assisted by appropriate staff.

2. The Board will be provided with money through a Grant-in-Aid out of which payments will be made to applicants for compensation where the Board are satisfied, in accordance with the principles set out below, that compensation is justified. Their net expenditure will fall on the Votes of the Home Office and the Scottish Home and Health Department.

3. The Board will be based on London but may establish offices outside London if the need arises. They will hold hearings in London, Edinburgh, Cardiff and elsewhere as necessary.

4. The Board will be entirely responsible for deciding what compensation should be paid in individual cases and their decisions will not be subject to appeal or to Ministerial

review. The general working of the Scheme will, however, be kept under review by the Government, and the Board will submit annually to the Home Secretary and the Secretary of State for Scotland a full report on the operation of the Scheme, together with their accounts. The report and accounts will be open to debate in Parliament. In addition the Board may at any time publish such information about the Scheme and their decisions in individual cases as may assist intending applicants for compensation.

Scope of the Scheme

5. The Board will entertain applications for *ex gratia* payment of compensation in any case where the applicant or, in the case of an application by a spouse or dependant (see paragraph 12 below), the deceased, sustained in Great Britain, or on a British vessel, aircraft or hovercraft, on or after 1st August 1964 personal injury directly attributable to a crime of violence (including arson and poisoning) or to an arrest or attempted arrest of an offender or suspected offender or to the prevention or attempted prevention of an offence or to the giving of help to any constable who is engaged in arresting or attempting to arrest an offender or suspected offender or preventing or attempting to prevent an offence. In considering for the purpose of this paragraph whether any act is a criminal act, any immunity at law of an offender, attributable to his youth or insanity or other condition, will be left out of account.

6. Compensation will not be payable unless the Board is satisfied—

   (a) that the injury was one for which compensation of not less than £50 would be awarded; and

   (b) that the circumstances of the injury have been the subject of criminal proceedings, or were reported to the police without delay; and

   (c) that the applicant has given the Board all reasonable assistance, particularly in relation to any medical reports that they may require.

Provided that the Board at their discretion may waive the requirement in (b) above.

7. Where the victim who suffered injuries and the offender who inflicted them were living together at the time as members of the same family no compensation will be payable. For the purposes of this paragraph where a man and woman were living together as man and wife they will be treated as if they were married to one another.

8. Traffic offences will be excluded from the scheme, except where there has been a deliberate attempt to run the victim down.

9. The Board will scrutinise with particular care all applications in respect of sexual offences or other offences arising out of a sexual relationship, in order to determine whether there was any responsibility, either because of provocation or otherwise, on the part of the victim (see paragraph 17 below), and they will especially have regard to any delay that has occurred in submitting the application. The Board will consider applications for compensation arising out of rape and sexual assaults, both in respect of pain, suffering and shock and in respect of loss of earnings due to pregnancy resulting from rape and, where the victim is ineligible for a maternity grant under the National Health Scheme, in respect of the expenses of childbirth. Compensation will not be payable for the maintenance of any child born as a result of a sexual offence.

Basis of Compensation

10. Subject to what is said in the following paragraphs, compensation will be assessed on the basis of common law damages and will take the form of a lump sum payment, rather than a periodical pension. More than one payment may, however, sometimes be made—for example, where only a provisional medical assessment can be given in the first instance.

11. Where the victim is alive the amount of compensation will be limited as follows—

   (a) the rate of loss of earnings (and, where appropriate, of earning capacity) to be taken into account will not exceed twice the average of industrial earnings[1] at the time that the injury was sustained;

(b) there will be no element comparable to exemplary or punitive damages.

12. Where the victim has died in consequence of the injury no compensation will be payable for the benefit of his estate, but the Board will be able to entertain claims from his spouse and dependants. For this purpose, compensation will be payable to any person entitled to claim under the Fatal Accidents Acts 1846 to 1959 or, in Scotland, under the appropriate Scottish law. Subject to what is said in the following paragraphs the amount of compensation will be governed by the same principles as under those provisions; the total income of the deceased, earned and unearned, to be taken into account being subject to the limit specified in paragraph 11 (a) above. Where the victim's funeral expenses are paid by any person for whose benefit an action may be brought under the Fatal Accidents Acts or the appropriate Scottish law, whether or not there is any financial dependency, the Board may pay that person a reasonable sum in respect of funeral expenses less any death grant payable under the National Insurance Scheme. For this purpose paragraph 6 (a) above shall not apply.

13. Where the victim has died otherwise than in consequence of the injury, the Board may make an award in respect of loss of wages, expenses and liabilities incurred before death as a result of the injury where, in their opinion, hardship to dependants would otherwise result, whether or not application for compensation in respect of the injury has been made before the death.

14. Compensation will be reduced by the value of any entitlement to social security benefits payable by the Department of Health and Social Security (and of payments made under Treasury authority by analogy with the National Insurance (Industrial Injuries) Act) which accrues as a result of the injury or death to the benefit of the person to whom the award is made.

15. If in the opinion of the Board an applicant may be eligible for any social security benefits or payments mentioned in paragraph 14 the Board may refuse to make an award until the applicant has taken such steps as the Board consider reasonable to claim these benefits or payments.

16. Where the victim is alive the Board will determine on the basis of the common law whether, and to what extent, compensation should be reduced by any pension accruing as a result of the injury. Where the victim has died in consequence of the injury, and any pension is payable for the benefit of the person to whom the award is made as a result of the death of the victim which would not have been payable, or would not have been so large, if his injury had not been sustained while on duty or in the performance of a duty connected with his employment, the compensation will be reduced by four-fifths of the value of that pension or, as the case may be, by four-fifths of the increase of the value attributable to the injuries having been sustained in that way. For the purposes of this paragraph, "pension" means any pension payable in pursuance of pension rights connected with the victim's employment, and includes any gratuity of that kind.

17. The Board will reduce the amount of compensation or reject the application altogether if, having regard to the conduct of the victim, including his conduct before and after the events giving rise to the claim, and to his character and way of life it is inappropriate that he should be granted a full award or any award at all.

18. The Board will have discretion to make special arrangements for the administration of any money awarded as compensation.

---

1. Average Weekly earnings for men (21 years and over) as published in the Employment and Productivity Gazette.

Procedure for determining applications

19. Every application will be made to the Board in writing as soon as possible after the event on a form obtainable from the Board's office.

20. Applications will be sifted initially by the Board's staff, who will seek further information as to the relevant circumstances and, where necessary, medical advice.

21. The initial decision whether the application should be allowed (and, if so, what amount of compensation should be offered) or should be rejected will normally be taken by one member of the Board, whose decision will be communicated to the applicant; if the applicant is not satisfied with that decision, whether because no compensation is offered or because he considers the amount offered to be inadequate, he will be entitled to a hearing before three other members of the Board, excluding the one who made the initial decision. It will, however, also be open to the single member, where he considers that he cannot reach a just and proper decision, himself to refer the application to three other members of the Board for a hearing.

22. At the hearing, it will be for the applicant to make out his case; he and a member of the Board's staff will be able to call, examine and cross-examine witnesses. The Board will reach their decision solely in the light of the evidence brought out at the hearing, and all the information before them will be available to the applicant. While it will be open to the applicant to bring a friend or legal adviser to assist him in putting his case, the Board will not pay the costs of legal representation. They will, however, have discretion to pay the expenses of witnesses.

23. Procedure at a hearing will be as informal as is consistent with a proper determination of the application, and the hearing will be in private.

24. It is not intended that a person who has pursued a claim for damages for personal injuries should obtain compensation from the Board in respect of those injuries in addition to obtaining satisfaction from that claim; and compensation will be reduced by any sum which the victim has received in pursuance of an order for compensation by a criminal court in respect of his injuries. Furthermore, a person who is compensated by the Board will be required to undertake to repay them from any damages, settlement or compensation he may subsequently obtain in respect of his injuries.

Notes

1. The Criminal Injuries Compensation Board publishes Annual Reports. The Ninth Report (Cmnd. 5468) reveals that in 1972–73 £3,457,519 was paid in compensation. 81.2 *per cent* of awards were for less than £400. 0.9 *per cent* were £5,000 or over. It is to be noted that compensation is assessed on the same basis as common law damages (paras. 10–18) and is to be reduced by any amount awarded in other civil or criminal proceedings (para. 24). On the working of the Scheme see Alec Samuels, [1973] Crim. L.R. 418. For the power of criminal courts to make compensation orders against the criminal, see Chap. 2, p. 39, *ante*.

2. The Reports of the Board contain many examples. These are some of them.

(a) A man in a public house, having drunk too much, persisted in making derogatory remarks about the wife of another customer despite warnings to desist. He was struck in the face with a glass. His compensation was reduced by 50 *per cent*. (Seventh Report, p. 11).

(b) A professional housebreaker who in the early hours of the morning was peppered by the shot of the householder fired in the general direction of the housebreaker's retreating figure was denied any award, on the ground that those engaged in criminal activities should not be rewarded (Sixth Report, p. 6).

(c) Awards have been made to applicants injured by airgun pellets, the Board having accepted that the guns must have been fired in circumstances amounting to crimes of violence although the persons responsible were never found (Seventh Report, p. 8).

(d) A man who woke up in his own home one morning with a fractured skull, having spent the previous evening drinking in a public house and being unable to remember leaving the public house or what had happened thereafter, was refused an award (Seventh Report, p. 12).

3. Victims of traffic offences may be able to recover from the M.I.B. (p. 679, *ante*).

APPENDICES

APPENDIX A
Trends in Road Accidents

Population, road motor vehicles, traffic, accidents and casualties: 1934–1971

	Population¹ (Millions)	Road motor vehicles² with licences current (Millions)	Index of vehicle mileage³ 1949=100		Accidents (Thousands)	Casualties from road accidents⁵ (Thousands)			
			Motor traffic	All traffic⁴		Killed	Seriously injured	Slightly injured	Total
1934	45·4	2·4	..	..	205	7·3	232		239
1935	45·6	2·6	..	..	196	6·5	222		228
1936	45·8	2·7	..	..	199	6·6	228		234
1937	46·0	2·9	..	..	196	6·6	52	174	233
1938	46·2	3·1	100	106	196	6·6	51	176	233
1939	46·5	3·1	..	..	..	8·3	..	..	..
1940	46·9	2·3	..	..	..	8·6	..	..	..
1941	46·9	2·4	..	..	..	9·2	..	..	..
1942	47·1	1·8	..	..	..	6·9	36	105	148
1943	47·4	1·4	..	..	..	5·8	31	86	123
1944	47·7	1·5	..	..	..	6·4	33	91	131
1945	47·8	2·4	..	..	..	5·3	33	101	138
1946	47·9	3·0	..	..	..	5·1	37	121	163
1947	48·2	3·3	..	..	..	4·9	36	126	166
1948	48·7	3·5	..	..	..	4·5	33	116	153
1949	49·0	3·8	100	100	147	4·8	43	129	177
1950	49·2	4·1	114	104	167	5·0	49	148	201
1951	48·9	4·3	127	114	178	5·3	52	159	216
1952	49·1	4·6	131	119	172	4·7	50	153	208
1953	49·2	5·0	139	122	186	5·1	57	165	227
1954	49·4	5·4	150	126	196	5·0	57	176	238
1955	49·6	6·0	165	136	217	5·5	62	200	268
1956	49·8	6·5	174	138	216	5·4	61	201	268
1957	50·0	7·0	173	137	219	5·5	64	205	274
1958	50·3	7·5	200	153	237	6·0	69	225	300
1959	50·5	8·2	224	168	261	6·5	81	246	333
1960	50·9	8·9	242	177	272	7·0	84	256	348
1961	51·4	9·5	263	190	270	6·9	85	258	350
1962	51·9	10·0	276	196	264	6·7	84	251	342
1963	52·2	10·9	293	206	272	6·9	88	261	356
1964	52·6	11·8	328	229	292	7·8	95	282	385
1965	53·0	12·4	350	242	299	8·0	98	292	399
1966	53·2⁷	12·8	372	255	292	8·0	100	285	392
1967	53·5⁷	13·5	391	267	277	7·3	94	269	370
1968	53·8⁷	13·9	410	279	264	6·8	89	254	349
1969	54·0⁷	14·2	421	285	262	7·4	91	255	353
1970	54·2⁷	14·5	444	301	267	7·5	93	262	363
1971	54·0⁶	15·0	474	321	259	7·7	91	253	352

1. From 1946 to 1950 population figures include British Forces abroad but exclude allied forces in Great Britain.
2. Excludes agricultural tractors.
3. Estimated from regular traffic census.
4. Pedal cycle and motor traffic.
5. The reporting of injuries was suspended during the early part of the war and it is probable that from 1942 to 1945 the reporting of slight injuries was incomplete.
6. Provisional figure.
7. Revised figures.

This table gives series of figures covering road accidents during the period 1934–1971, together with corresponding figures of population, licensed vehicles and index numbers of vehicle mileage. There was a steady upward trend in all these statistics from the end of the Second World War until 1965. Since then both accidents and casualties have declined.

Accidents and casualties in the years 1935–1938 were lower than in 1934. This reduction was due, at least in part, to the Road Traffic Act 1934, which *inter alia* provided for the introduction of driving tests, the 30 m.p.h. speed limit and pedestrian crossings. There was a further reduction in 1952 after the introduction of the "zebra" striping on crossings. The reductions in 1967 and 1968 may be largely attributed to the introduction of breath tests in the Road Safety Act 1967.

[*Source: Road Accidents in 1971* (H.M.S.O.).]

APPENDIX B

All Accidents at Work in Great Britain 1961–1970

Fatal and non-fatal accidents to employees as reported to various agencies

	1961	1962	1963	1964	1965	1966	1967	1968	1969	1970
1. Factories	161,655	157,600	168,106	217,950	239,158	241,051	247,058	254,454	266,857	255,907
2. Docks and Warehouses	7,506	7,220	7,815	10,207	10,178	9,952	10,483	11,407	10,963	8,865
3. Construction	23,356	25,338	28,348	40,491	44,381	45,607	46,475	46,569	44,570	39,823
Total Factories Act (Lines 1–3)	192,517	190,158	204,269	268,648	293,717	296,610	304,016	312,430	322,390	304,595
4. Mines and Quarries[1]	191,208	201,389	206,234	201,364	209,935	188,909	169,763	144,046	121,402	93,983
5. Agriculture[2]	12,846	13,553	14,548	13,276	11,839	10,680	10,069	8,722	8,783	7,366
6. Offices, Shops and Railway Premises	18,000[3]	18,000[3]	18,000[3]	18,000[3]	17,225	18,533	19,903	19,075	19,018	16,871
7. Railways	14,233	12,139	11,846	11,064	9,838	8,236	8,003	6,912	7,335	7,625
8. Road Transport	16,200	16,400[3]	16,600	18,700	22,700	22,900	25,300	26,700	25,300	33,800
9. Civil Aviation[4]	30	27	25	17	22	35	28	14	6	15
10. Seamen[5]	8,817[3]	8,783[3]	8,805[3]	9,090	8,672	8,769	8,361	8,177	8,421	8,491
Total (Lines 1–10)	453,851	460,449	480,327	540,159	573,948	554,672	545,443	526,076	513,655	472,746

1. Excluding coal mines not operated by the National Coal Board. (The National Coal Board employs about 99% of the total labour force engaged in coal mines.)
2. Employees only, i.e. accidents to farmers, their families and children are not included.
3. Actual figures for these years are not available. Estimates have been included to allow completion of totals.
4. Accidents in Great Britain and overseas to crews of aircraft on the British Register.
5. Merchant seamen and fishermen.

General Notes:

1. In general, the table relates to accidents causing absence from work for more than three days. It does not provide a complete picture of all such accidents. Variable proportions of reportable accidents are not reported, and in addition some five-six million workpeople (approximately 20% of the workforce) do not fall within scope of any occupational safety and health legislation. Accidents to them, unless occurring whilst temporarily employed on premises covered by legislation, would not be legally notifiable to the main safety and health inspectorates, although in some cases information is collected by other agencies.

2. The figures do not include cases of prescribed diseases under the National Insurance (Industrial Injuries) Act 1965; Department of Health and Social Security statistics of new spells of certified incapacity due to prescribed diseases are as follows:—

1961—27,934	1963—23,185	1965—25,235	1967—22,980	1969—23,655
1962—26,076	1964—24,221	1966—23,695	1968—22,841	1970—22,420

[*Source:* Report of the Committee on Safety and Health at Work (Cmnd. 5034) 1972, Table 2, p. 162.]

1. In addition to those injured at work on the railways, must be added some 5,625 passengers and 275 other persons injured in railway accidents in 1970 (Department of the Environment, *Railway Accidents 1970*, App. II, p. 88).

2. In 1971 there were 729,000 claims for industrial injury benefit and 165,000 for disablement benefit (Department of Health and Social Security, *Annual Report* (1971), Cmnd. 5019, p. 112).

APPENDIX C

Cost of Road Accidents

The cost of the 267,000 road accidents in 1970 was immeasurable in terms of pain, grief and suffering. But quite apart from the personal tragedies involved these accidents represent a quantifiable loss to the community in economic terms. In 1969 a new basis for calculating economic costs was used to illustrate the heavy losses to the community through lost output, the cost of medical treatment, time of police and courts and damage to property. It was estimated that the average economic cost of a fatal accident was £12,000, the average serious injury accident cost £700, the average slight injury £220 and the average accident involving only damaged vehicles and property £90. These same costs in 1970 stood at £13,000, £700, £230 and £100 respectively. On this basis it has been calculated that the total economic cost of accidents in 1970 was:

	1970 (£m)	1969 (£m)
Medical treatment, ambulance and funeral costs	17	15
Police and administration costs	28	26
Damage to vehicles and other property	198	183
Lost output	103	96
	346	320

Thus on average road accidents result in an economic loss of approaching £1 million a day on top of the personal suffering caused by the daily toll of more than 20 killed, 250 seriously injured and 700 slightly injured. These figures provide the facts behind a problem which must be the concern not only of the Government and safety organisations but also of all road users.

... Taking into account the lost output of casualties, the cost of medical treatment, the time of police and courts and damage to property, together with an allowance for the more subjective elements of suffering and grief, it is estimated that the average cost of a fatal accident in 1971 was £21,000. A serious injury accident cost £1,600, a slight injury accident £300, and the more numerous "damage-only" accident £120. On this basis it is estimated that the total cost of accidents in 1971 was £492 million.

[Source: Road Accidents in 1970 (H.M.S.O.); Road Accidents in 1971 (H.M.S.O.).

APPENDIX D

Cost of Industrial Accidents

The national resource costs of occupational diseases and accidents were estimated by staff of the Research and Planning Division of the Department of Employment for the Committee on Safety and Health at Work, and published as Appendix 9 to the Report of that Committee (Cmnd. 5034) 1972. The two main sources on which they relied were data of the Department of Health and Social Security (D.H.S.S.) and data of H.M. Factory Inspectorate (H.M.F.I.). Separate estimates were made based on each of these sources: the main estimate was based on the more comprehensive D.H.S.S. data, but for some purposes H.M.F.I. data may be more useful. Both estimates refer to 1969, the latest year for which detailed figures were available.

Main summary of resource costs using D.H.S.S. data
Resource costs of industrial accidents and prescribed industrial diseases in 1969

	£m (conservative estimate)	£m (best estimate)
(a) Fatalities	20·2	20·2
(b) Industrial accidents		
—lost output	84·5	84·5
—medical and hospital costs	8·1	12·4
(c) Damage and administration costs	25·2	42·1
(d) Prescribed diseases	3·5	3·7
(e) Long-term incapacity	8·1	8·1
(f) Non-reportable accidents	37·9	37·9
TOTAL	187·5	208·9
Average resource costs were:	£	£
Fatalities (per person)	13,701	13,701
Industrial accidents and diseases (per spell of incapacity)	149	175

Average resource costs were calculated for industrial accidents by taking the total costs of items (b), (c) and (e) in the above table and dividing them by the total number of accident spells of incapacity. Because spells of incapacity are not exactly equivalent to persons experiencing accidents, the average cost per person is slightly higher than that shown per spell. Resource costs as calculated above amounted to 0·54% of G.N.P. in 1969.

Subjective costs. Accidents give rise to subjective or "warm blooded" costs as well as resource costs. Following Dawson, the subjective costs reflecting personal suffering and bereavement were calculated as:

	£m (conservative estimate)	£m (best estimate)
Fatalities	9·59	9·59
Serious injury	21·04	42·08
Slight injury	79·96	75·75
Total subjective costs	110·59	127·42

When subjective and resource costs are added together, the total costs of accidents and industrial diseases in 1969 amounted to 0·87% of G.N.P.

Summary of resource costs using H.M.F.I. data. Our calculations are best viewed as a range of figures, the acceptability of which will depend to a large extent on the acceptability of the assumptions used—generally the assumptions are conservative ones.

	Assuming damage cost per accident of:	
	£30	£50
(a) Fatalities	£8,277,043	£8,277,043
(b) Industrial accidents (output lost, damage and hospital costs)	£48,283,881	£54,731,681
(c) Under-reporting	£17,390,152	£19,774,952
(d) Non-reportable accidents	£14,507,550	£14,507,550
TOTAL	£88,458,626	£97,291,226

Average resource costs of reported accidents:

	Assumption of damage cost:	
	£30	£50
(a) Fatalities	£12,784	£12,804
(b) Industrial accidents	£150	£170

Subjective costs. These are an estimate of the intangible value of life and good health free from accident or disease. (A more detailed explanation of subjective costs follows in the Annex.) We have applied the figures used by the Road Research Laboratory of £5,000 for a fatality, £500 for a serious injury and £10 for a slight injury. The figures are necessarily arbitrary but do give some indication of a cost which should not be excluded from the calculation. Applying these figures to accidents reported under the Factories Act gives a total of £31,052,130, or £36,626,000 if the estimate of non-reported accidents is included.

[*Source:* Report of the Committee on Safety and Health at Work (Cmnd. 5034) 1972, App. 9, pp. 198–200.]

APPENDIX E

Amount, Distribution and Administrative Costs of Compensation

By Dennis Lees and Neil Doherty

Turning now to compensation paid in various ways, the data in Charts I and 2 have been extracted or estimated from a variety of official and other sources. The accuracy of the figures thus varies. They are intended only to show the general orders of magnitude. So far as possible, payments refer to 1970.

Chart 1 Compensation: All Accidents

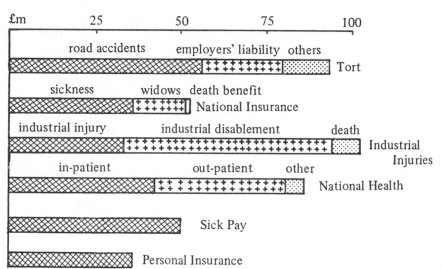

We estimate that, in 1970, a total of over £400 millions was paid out in compensation or support for personal injury, of which the state handled as much as all the others put together. Although tort, the classic remedy of recovering damages under common law, still accounts for a large amount of compensation, it now plays only a supporting role. It will also be seen that personal insurance, particularly for non-fatal injury cases, is relatively unimportant, although life assurance is a rapidly growing form of protection.

712

However, when total compensation is classified by type of accident, a very different pattern emerges, as is shown in Chart 2. For road accidents, the bulk of compensation is administered under the tort system (58 per cent), with social security, national health and personal insurance each accounting for about 13 per cent. For industrial injuries, however, the state is dominant, accounting for 76 per cent of the estimated benefits (social security 62 per cent and national health 14 per cent), with tort and sick pay accounting for about 12 per cent each. Certain small variations in the pattern of compensation can be explained by differences in the severity of road and industrial accidents. For example, the higher ratio of deaths in road accidents together with the wider spread of life insurance over personal accident insurance, explains the

Chart 2   Compensation: Categories of Accidents

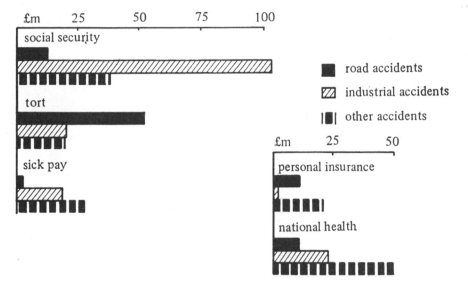

fact that personal insurance accounts for a significant proportion of total road accident compensation, but for a very small proportion of industrial accident compensation. Similarly, the greater proportion of lingering, but not particularly serious, injuries occurring through industrial accidents provides a partial explanation for the greater importance of sick pay for industrial injuries.

The aggregation of compensation in the charts does not show its distribution amongst victims. One of the few surveys of accident compensation conducted in this country suggests that about half of road accident victims and a tenth of industrial accident victims make any recovery in tort. In fact, the 50 per cent figure for road accident victims may be too high, since another pilot survey, concentrating on serious casualties only, produced a figure of 42 per cent.[1] Since recovery from collateral sources will have only a limited effect in reducing a tort claim, the implication is that compensation is concentrated

---

1. See T. G. Ison, *The Forensic Lottery*, London 1967, Appendix G and also D. R. Harris and S. Hartz, *Report of a Pilot Survey of the Financial Consequences of Personal Injuries suffered in Road Accidents in the City of Oxford during* 1965, unpublished, Oxford 1968.

on a minority of people, albeit substantial in number, injured in accidents. Furthermore, it is well known that many payments, particularly the larger ones, are made only after considerable delay.

Perhaps the most startling contrast between the various methods of compensation lies in their administrative and other costs ("transfer costs" for short). Our estimates are shown in Table 2. Estimation here is particularly difficult and involves, among other things, problems of comparing like with like. For example, under the tort system, highly-skilled and expensive resources of the legal and insurance systems are used to provide unique assessment of liability and damages for each individual case. Sickness benefit, at the other extreme, operates on standard scales of benefit and liability is no more complex an issue than checking on contributions. But, even within the social security system, industrial injuries benefit requires individual decision as to whether a given accident occurs "out of and in the course of employment", though in only a very small number of cases is this anything but a

Table 2. Ratio of Administrative Costs to Compensation

	%
Tort	74
Social security*	7
Industrial injury and disablement*	15
Life assurance	15
Personal accident insurance	55
Sick pay	5

* Includes estimate of costs of collection met by employers.

routine issue, and disputes are infrequent. The higher cost of the industrial injuries scheme over other social security benefits largely reflects the costs of providing expert medical testimony as to the degree of disability. We should perhaps mention that, where there has been uncertainty in estimation, we have consciously tried to control the direction of error in a way which will *reduce* the contrast between the high-cost systems (tort and personal accident insurance) and the low-cost systems (social security, life assurance, sick pay). For example, we are fairly confident that the transfer costs of life insurance are overestimated and, though there is little information on the cost of sick pay schemes, we have tried to work on the basis of the highest feasible amount. In spite of this, the contrast is still marked.

The particular feature which emerges is the extremely high transfer costs associated with the tort system. Although only a tiny proportion of tort cases actually reaches the court, the whole operation of tort is supported by liability insurance, which itself accounts for about two-thirds of the cost of administering this system. Similarly, with personal accident insurance: although the cost of settling claims is much lower and does not usually bring into play expensive legal resources, there are still the high costs associated with underwriting expenses, agency commission and other selling costs.

[*Extract from:* Dennis Lees and Neil Doherty, "Compensation for Personal Injury", *Lloyds Bank Review*, April 1973, No. 108, pp. 18–32.]

APPENDIX F

The New Zealand Accident Compensation Act, No. 43 of 1972

This Act has been described as "the most ambitious reform of tort law in the common law world".[1] It makes provision for the compensation[2] of:

    (i) *earners* who suffer personal injury by accident regardless of place, time or cause;

    (ii) *all persons* who, in New Zealand, suffer personal injury by a *motor vehicle* accident;

    (iii) certain *dependants* of those earners and motor vehicle accident victims where *death* results from the injury.

The common law action for damages in respect of injury or death is abolished for those who have cover under the Act.[3] The Act did not originally cover non-earners injured or killed in an accident, unless they were victims of a motor accident. (Amending legislation has since introduced a supplementary scheme for non-earners.[4])

The Act is 185 pages long and sets out a scheme of great complexity, a major source of prolix drafting being the distinction between "earners" and "non-earners". The summary below does not purport to be comprehensive, but simply focuses attention on the main features of this novel and important legislation.

1. Administration

Part I of the Act establishes the Accident Compensation Commission (A.C.C.) which is to consist of three members, the Chairman being a barrister

---

1. Geoffrey W. Palmer, "Compensation For Personal Injury: A Requiem for the Common Law in New Zealand" (1973), 21 *Amer. Jo. Comp. Law* 1. The Editors of the Journal describe the Act as "an unparalleled event in our cultural history, the first casualty among the core legal institutions of the civilised world" (*ibid.*).
2. S. 4 also sets out promotion of safety and rehabilitation among the purposes of the Act.
3. S. 5. The only (very limited) survival of the Fault principle is that a person who wilfully inflicts injuries on himself has no claim, but even then dependants may be compensated if in special need (s. 137).
4. The revised scheme came into operation on 1 April 1974. It has not been possible to take account of the amendments in this Appendix, but see p. 732, *post*.

or solicitor of not less than seven years' practice.[1] Members are to be appointed for three years but are eligible for reappointment;[2] they may be removed for disability, bankruptcy, neglect of duty or misconduct proved to the satisfaction of the Governor-General.[3]

The A.C.C. has overall responsibility for administering the Act:[4] in some cases it makes decisions itself, but in others, particularly in regard to the raising of levies to finance the scheme and the ceiling of compensation,[5] it makes recommendations to the Minister of Labour. In the exercise of its functions and powers the A.C.C. must give effect to the policy of the Government "as communicated to it from time to time in writing by the Minister".[6] A copy of every such communication must be laid before Parliament.[7]

A compromise was reached with the private insurance companies, by permitting the A.C.C. to appoint insurance companies, as well as other bodies, to act as its agents;[8] in particular it may delegate collection of levies and the handling and payment of claims to these bodies.[9]

2. Accident Prevention and Rehabilitation

Part II of the Act makes it "a matter of prime importance" for the A.C.C. to promote safety[10] and "to promote a well co-ordinated and vigorous programme for the medical and vocational rehabilitation of persons who become incapacitated as a result of personal injury by accident".[11] There are detailed provisions as to the manner in which these functions are to be discharged, including the establishment of a safety division[12] and a rehabilitation and medical division.[13]

3. Earners' Scheme

Part III provides for the establishment of an earners' scheme, under which cover may be either (a) continuous cover or (b) work accident cover.[14]

(a) *Continuous cover*

This entitles an earner to rehabilitation assistance and compensation in respect of personal injury, "if the accident occurs at any time while the cover continues, whether or not the accident arises out of and in the course of his employment".[15] To be eligible for this cover the earner must have been ordinarily resident in New Zealand lawfully for a period of, or for periods in the aggregate amounting to twelve months.[16] He must also be either self-employed (as defined)[17] or an employee (as defined).[18] But a series of complex provisions

1. S. 6. Alternatively, one member must be so qualified.
2. S. 7.
3. S. 8. But staff are deemed not to be employed by the Crown, s. 24.
4. Ss. 15, 16, 17, 18, 19.
5. S. 15.
6. S. 20.
7. S. 20 (2).
8. S. 25.
9. S. 29.
10. S. 43.
11. S. 48.
12. S. 45.
13. S. 51.
14. S. 55.
15. S. 56 (a).
16. S. 57 (1).
17. There is a lengthy definition—s. 2 (1).
18. *Ibid.*

exclude those who work casually or whose earnings are below a prescribed minimum.[1] Cover under the earners' scheme extends to New Zealand seamen and airmen where the accident happens outside New Zealand,[2] subject to detailed qualifications, and to certain New Zealand residents temporarily overseas for business purposes.[3]

(b) *Work accident cover*

This entitles an earner who is not eligible for continuous cover (e.g. because he is a casual employee or does not fulfil the residential requirements) to rehabilitation assistance and compensation "in respect of the personal injury, if the accident arises out of and in the course of his employment".[4]

The workers' compensation legislation, which the Act of 1972 replaces, had provided compensation for certain occupational diseases. The Act continues this coverage; but the disease must be "due to the nature of any employment in which the earner was employed" within a prescribed period (usually two years).[5] Compensation is to be granted for industrial deafness contracted within two years of being exposed to a noise hazard at work.[6]

4. Motor Vehicle Accident Scheme

Part IV provides that all persons "shall have cover under the motor vehicle accident scheme in respect of personal injury by a motor vehicle accident in New Zealand and death resulting therefrom", if the vehicle was registered and licensed or required to be registered and licensed.[7] Cover also extends to accidents involving motor vehicles of visitors to New Zealand,[8] towed registered and unregistered vehicles,[9] agricultural trailers[10] and invalid carriages.[11]

5. Provisions related to both schemes on earnings

Part V contains detailed provisions for calculating earnings for the purpose of both schemes.[12] These provisions were essential because the compensation payable is earnings-related. Relevant earnings for the assessment of compensation are subject to a maximum of $200 N.Z. per week (£100). This ceiling may be raised by order-in-council.

6. Compensation

Part VI sets out the rules on compensation payable under both the earners' and motor vehicle accident schemes.

(a) *Medical and related benefits*

These include payment for conveyance to hospital or a medical practi-

---

1. Ss. 57 (1) (*a*), (*b*), (*c*); 57 (2), (3).
2. S. 61.
3. S. 60.
4. S. 56 (*b*).
5. S. 67.
6. S. 68.
7. S. 92.
8. S. 93.
9. S. 94.
10. S. 95.
11. S. 96.
12. Ss. 103–106.

tioner;[1] damage to teeth, artificial limbs or aids, clothing or spectacles being worn at the time of the accident.[2] Where medical treatment is not paid for by the state, there is provision for payment to be made by the A.C.C.[3]

(b) *Compensation in respect of incapacity*

Where the accident arose "out of and in the course of the employment" the employer must pay the employee a full week's wages.[4] In all other cases the injured person must himself bear the first week's loss of earnings.[5] Where an employer fails to pay any amount he is required to pay, the A.C.C. may pay the amount and recover it from the employer.[6]

After the first week the A.C.C. must pay earnings-related compensation "at the rate of 80 *per cent* of the amount of his loss of earning capacity due to the injury for the time being".[7] Earning capacity is determined "by deducting the amount that he is capable of earning directly from his personal exertions during the period from the amount of his relevant earnings for a like period".[8] The person must be "endeavouring to work reasonably to the extent of his capacity".[9] Decisions by the A.C.C. relating to assessments of earnings must be notified to the claimant who has a right to ask for a review.[10]

Where a person does not completely recover from his incapacity, as soon as the A.C.C. considers that his "medical condition is stabilized and all practicable steps have been taken towards his retraining and rehabilitation" the A.C.C. must make a written assessment of the nature and extent of his permanent incapacity, and the amount to be paid to him thereafter, being 80 *per cent.* of his permanent loss of earning capacity.[11] The percentage may be raised by order-in-council[12] (designed to take account of changes in living costs). After the date of assessment the earnings-related compensation cannot be reduced by reason of any reduction in earning capacity, but the A.C.C. may make a further assessment if the person's condition has deteriorated since the last assessment.[13]

The upper-age limit for the payment of earnings-related compensation generally is 65,[14] the age at which age benefit and superannuation becomes payable under the social security system.

Payments in respect of earnings-related compensation and for loss of potential earning capacity are to be made at such intervals not exceeding one

1. Ss. 107, 108, 109.
2. S. 110.
3. S. 111.
4. S. 112.
5. S. 112.
6. S. 112.
7. S. 113 (1) (*a*). This means that the maximum payable is 80 *per cent* of $200 N.Z. per week.
8. S. 113 (2).
9. S. 113 (3).
10. S. 113 (8) & (9).
11. S. 114.
12. S. 114 (4).
13. S. 114 (5). There are special provisions for compensation in the case of subsequent accidents to the same person (s. 115), and for increased compensation (up to 90 *per cent* of weekly earnings) for a full-time earner whose earnings are below a prescribed limit (s. 116). The earnings-related compensation of permanently incapacited earners under 21, must reflect what their adult earnings would have been (s. 117).
14. S. 128. A series of later dates applies if the accident happens after the age of 60.

month as the A.C.C. thinks fit.[1] The A.C.C. may "in very exceptional circumstances" commute periodic payments into a lump sum payment, and commutation will not normally be made if the effect will be that the person concerned will need support out of money appropriated by Parliament.[2] The A.C.C. may reduce, postpone or cancel earnings-related compensation where the person is in a hospital or penal institution.[3]

In addition to earnings-related compensation, the Act provides for compensation for certain *non-economic* losses.

(i) *Related to permanent loss or impairment of bodily function* (including loss of any part of the body): a lump sum up to $5,000 N.Z. The assessment of impairment must be made in accordance with the second schedule to the Act which sets out the percentage of $5,000 payable for specified impairments (e.g. 80 *per cent* for total loss of an arm, 17 *per cent* for deafness in one ear etc.).[4] Where the impairment is not covered by the schedule the A.C.C. must determine the appropriate percentage.[5] Reassessment is possible in the event of further loss or impairment.[6]

(ii) *Other non-economic loss:* a lump sum up to $7,500 N.Z. (payable not later than two years after the date of the accident) as the A.C.C. thinks fit in respect of "the loss suffered by the person of amenities or capacity for enjoying life, including loss from disfigurement" and "pain and mental suffering, including nervous shock and neurosis".[7] The loss, pain or suffering must be of sufficient degree to justify payment, "having regard to its nature, intensity, duration, and any other relevant circumstances",[8] and in assessing compensation regard must also be had to the injured person's knowledge and awareness of his injury or loss.[9] No such payment may be made after the death of the injured person.[10] Certain "enhancement factors", such as the special seriousness of the loss of a paired organ (e.g. kidney or lung) may be specified by order-in-council,[11] and there may be included in the lump sum payment an additional amount on account of the "enhancement factor".[12]

In "special circumstances" the lump sum payable under these two heads of loss or impairment of bodily function and other non-economic loss may be increased, but in no case may the lump sum in aggregate exceed $12,500.

The Act also permits compensation for pecuniary loss not related to earnings, such as any "quantifiable loss of service" sustained by a member of the person's household as a result of the accident,[13] the

---

1. S. 151 (3).
2. S. 133.
3. S. 129.
4. S. 119 (1) & (2).
5. S. 119 (3) & (4).
6. S. 119 (6).
7. S. 120.
8. S. 120 (1), first proviso.
9. S. 120 (7).
10. S. 120 (9).
11. S. 120 (2).
12. S. 120 (3).
13. S. 121.

cost of constant personal attendance required by that person,[1] and funeral expenses.[2] But damage to property, the loss of opportunity to make a profit and loss arising from inability to perform a business contract, are specifically excluded.[3]

(c) *Compensation in the event of death*

Earnings-related compensation is payable to the dependants of a person who dies as a result of personal injury by accident,[4] provided the deceased was covered by the Act as an earner.[5]

If the dependency was total, a widow or widower is entitled to one-half of the earnings-related compensation that would have been payable to the deceased had he survived and suffered total loss of earning capacity,[6] If the dependency was partial such lesser amount as the A.C.C. thinks proper is payable.[7] Each minor totally dependent child is entitled to one-sixth of the earnings-related compensation that would have been payable to the deceased,[8] or to one-third if both parents are dead.[9] The rate of compensation for dependants other than widows, widowers and children is discretionary.[10] If the total payable to all dependants exceeds what the deceased himself would have received had he survived and been totally incapacitated, the A.C.C. must, within that maximum, fix the shares which each is to receive having regard to their relative needs and "all other relevant considerations".

In addition to earnings-related compensation, lump sum payments are payable to dependants who survive the deceased by 48 hours. A totally dependent widow or widower receives $1,000; and each totally dependent child $500 but the total payable to all children cannot exceed $1,500.[11] Upon remarriage a widow or widower receives a lump sum, in lieu of any further earnings-related compensation, equivalent to two years' earnings-related compensation.[12]

7. Procedure and Appeals

Part VII of the Act contains provision for reporting accidents, making claims and appeals. Claims must be made within 12 months after the date of the accident causing injury or within 12 months after the date of death.[13] Decisions on compensation are made by the A.C.C. or one of its agents.[14] The A.C.C. may be asked to review a decision,[15] and from decisions of the A.C.C. or a hearing officer there is an appeal to the Accident Compensation Appeal

---

1. *Ibid.*
2. S. 122.
3. S. 121 (1).
4. S. 123.
5. S. 123 (8). No earnings-related compensation is payable to the dependants of a non-earner but they may claim lump sums, expenses, and loss of support from the termination of a pension or annuity.
6. S. 123 (1) (*a*) (i).
7. S. 123 (1) (*a*) (ii).
8. S. 123 (1) (*b*).
9. S. 123 (3). Lesser amounts are payable in case of partial dependency.
10. S. 123 (1) (*c*).
11. S. 124. Lesser sums are payable in case of partial dependency.
12. S. 125, if the dependant is under 63.
13. S. 149.
14. S. 151.
15. S. 153.

Authority,[1] who is a barrister or solicitor of not less than seven years' practice.[2] A person may, with leave, appeal to the Administrative Division of the Supreme Court against a decision of the Authority,[3] provided the question is one which "by reason of its general or public importance or for any other reason ought to be submitted to the Supreme Court for decision".[4] An appeal, with leave, lies against a decision of the Administrative Division to the Court of Appeal on a question of law only.[5]

8. Finance

The Act creates two main funds from which compensation is to be paid: an Earners' Compensation Fund and a Motor Vehicle Accident Compensation Fund.[6] There is also an Active Service Compensation Fund in respect of accidents in the armed forces, and a General Fund to which most administrative expenses are charged and the income of which is largely derived rateably from the other Funds.[7]

The Motor Vehicle Fund receives money from two sources:

(a) levies charged on every licensed and registered motor vehicle (the amount payable being an adaptation of premiums payable under the former third party liability system, e.g. $11.35 on private motor cars, $7.90 on motor cycles),[8]

(b) an annual flat rate levy of $2 on every driver's licence.[9] There is power to prescribe different levies for different classes of drivers[10] and to impose penalty rates on drivers with bad records.[11]

The Earners' Fund, pays compensation due to earners including that payable in respect of motor vehicle accidents arising out of and in the course of employment. This Fund receives money from levies on employers in respect of earnings of employees and levies on the self-employed.[12] Levies are payable at rates prescribed by order-in-council,[13] and by notice in writing the A.C.C. may impose a penalty rate of levy on any employer or self-employed person whose accident record "is significantly worse than that normally set by others of the same class".[14] The A.C.C. may also set a rebated rate of levy where an accident rate is "significantly better than that normally set by others of the same class".[15] The levies must be within limits specified in Part I of the First Schedule (between 0.25 per $100 and $5 per $100[16]), subject to a maximum amount (at present $10,400) of earnings on which levies are payable.[17]

---

1. S. 162.
2. S. 155. An assessor may be appointed if the appeal involves matters of a professional, technical or specialised nature: s. 160.
3. S. 168.
4. S. 168 (2).
5. S. 169.
6. S. 31.
7. S. 32 (3).
8. First Schedule, Pt. II.
9. First Schedule, Pt. III.
10. S. 100.
11. S. 100 (d).
12. S. 71.
13. S. 72.
14. S. 73 (1) (a). This may not exceed the normal rate for that class by more than 100 *per cent.*
15. S. 73 (1) (a).
16. First Schedule, Pt. I.
17. S. 74.

It has been estimated that the annual gross costs of the scheme will be $50.1 million with a 12.5 *per cent* margin of error on either side.[1] The most serious criticism of the scheme is that accident costs have not been properly allocated to the appropriate risk-creating activities, e.g. employers are levied and may probably even be penalised for injuries suffered by employees away from the job say, during a rugby match or as a result of consuming a snail in a ginger-beer bottle.[2]

9. Accident Compensation and Social Security

The accident compensation system has been kept separate from New Zealand's extensive social welfare system. Major differences between the two systems are that (i) accident compensation is financed by levies on earnings, motor vehicles and drivers, while social welfare is financed out of general taxation, and (ii) accident compensation is earnings-related while social welfare is not. A Royal Commission on Social Welfare[3] justified the latter distinction by saying that the aim of accident scheme is to maintain the living standard enjoyed by the accident victim, while the welfare system aims at ensuring an adequate living standard for all. But the Commission conceded that no logical distinction could be made between incapacity due to accidents and to disease. Accordingly the Commission recommended earnings-related compensation for limited periods during incapacity caused by illnesses. But it rejected any general earnings-related scheme on the ground that the extra cost ($320 million) would be unacceptable to the New Zealand public. It seems likely that, through amending legislation, the welfare scheme may be influenced by the accident scheme and that victims of disease may eventually be compensated on a similar basis to victims of accidents.

Further Reading

The Act was preceded by a number of official reports—
Report of Committee on Absolute Liability (1963).
Report of Royal Commission of Inquiry, Compensation for Personal Injury in New Zealand (December 1967).
Government of New Zealand, Personal Injury—A Commentary on the Report of the Royal Commission of Inquiry into Compensation for Personal Injury in New Zealand (Presented to the House of Representatives by Leave, October 1969).
G. F. Gair et al., Report of Select Committee on Compensation for Personal Injury in New Zealand (House of Representatives, November 1970).

All previous comment is now overtaken by the Act of 1972, on which Geoffrey W. Palmer's (note 1, *ante*) is the leading article.

---

1. Geoffrey W. Palmer (1971), 23 *Amer. Jo. Comp. Law* at p. 26 (an estimate by government officials on 1970–71 figures).
2. *Ibid.*, pp. 29–30.
3. Report of Royal Commission of Inquiry, Social Security in New Zealand (March 1972).

APPENDIX G

No-Fault Insurance Laws in Canada and the U.S.A.

The deficiencies of the tort-and-liability insurance system as a means of compensating accident victims have generated many proposals for reform in North America.[1]

The earliest legislative development was in 1946 in the Canadian province of Saskatchewan. The Automobile Accident Insurance Act[2] established a publicly-owned corporation to operate a system of insurance against loss resulting from bodily injuries sustained through automobile accidents. Modest lump-sum death benefits, weekly indemnities, supplementary allowances for medical, hospital and funeral expenses, and small lump sum payments for impairment of bodily function are payable to everyone domiciled in Saskatchewan who sustains injuries in this way, regardless of fault, leading to the name "no-fault" benefits.[3] Premiums are collected from everyone who buys an operator's licence, and everyone who purchases an owner's licence, with somewhat higher premiums for those with traffic offence records. The most striking feature of the Saskatchewan plan is that, while providing basic compensation for the traffic victim, it leaves the law of tort intact with only a subtraction of no-fault benefits from any tort payment. Tort rights survive, then, but are important only in cases of more serious injuries.

For twenty-five years the Saskatchewan model was not followed elsewhere in Canada. Then, with effect from 1 January 1969, Ontario introduced a voluntary no-fault insurance scheme for automobile accidents.[4] This became mandatory from 1 January 1972[5]. It provides more substantial benefits than the Saskatchewan scheme, and unlike that scheme, it is operated by private insurance companies. Another privately-run scheme has been introduced in British Columbia, with effect from 1 January 1970.[6] In Manitoba[7] a publicly-run

1. For a select reading list see Appendix H, p. 728, *post.*
2. Now Rev. Stat. Sask. c. 409 (1965). The basis of the Act of 1946 was the study of a special committee. Report on the Study of Compensation for Victims of Automobile Accidents, Saskatchewan 8 (1947).
3. The only exceptions to no-fault are where the injured person is under the influence of alcohol, driving without a licence or riding outside the vehicle; *ibid.*, s. 32.
4. Insurance Amendment Act, Stat. Ont. c. 71 (1966).
5. Insurance Amendment Act 1971, Stat. Ont. 1971.
6. Insurance Act, Stat. B.C. 1969 and reg. 267/69 1969 pursuant thereto. The Report of the British Columbia Royal Commission on Automobile Insurance (1968) had recommended the abolition of the tort claim: see Ison (1969), 47 Can. B.R. 304; Atiyah (1969), 32 M.L.R. 547.
7. Automobile Insurance Act, Stat. Man. 1970.

scheme, similar to that in Saskatchewan, has been in operation since 1 November 1971. The amounts of benefits provided vary from scheme to scheme. The common feature of these legislative reforms is that they have introduced compulsory no-fault insurance, while retaining the right to sue in tort.[1]

In the United States, the "no-fault" insurance concept came into vogue in the 1960s. Of the many suggested reforms, the most significant were those put forward by Professors Keeton and O'Connell.[2] The principles underlying their proposals were:

(1) the development of a new form of compulsory automobile insurance (called basic protection insurance) to compensate all persons injured in automobile accidents without regard to fault for all types of out-of-pocket personal injury losses up to $10,000 per person; and

(2) the enactment of legislation granting to those covered by basic protection an exemption from tort liability to some extent. The tort exemption would be total where damages for pain and suffering would not exceed $5,000 and other tort damage would not exceed the $10,000 basic protection coverage. In all other cases, tort liability would be reduced by approximately these amounts. In other words, tort actions would be retained for cases of severe injury.

A modified version of the Keeton–O'Connell plan was adopted by the Massachusetts legislature in 1970,[3] after an abortive attempt in 1967 to enact such legislation. This became operative on 1 January 1971. Since then several other states have enacted versions of no fault insurance, and it seems likely that within the next decade such schemes will become almost universal in the states, and may be implemented at the federal level.

The no-fault schemes in the United States of America have certain common features:

(1) The criterion for determining whether compensation is paid is whether the claimant has suffered loss of a kind described in the statute. An implication of this insurance principle is that fault is not relevant to determining entitlement to compensation, but it may be relevant to determining premium rates.

(2) There is "first-party" insurance. Claims are made by the injured person against his own insurance company and not, as under liability insurance, against the third party (the other motorist).

(3) Benefits are paid periodically rather than in a lump sum. There are special rules under each scheme for determining the amount of compensation but usually the reimbursement is only for out-of-pocket loss, with a statutory maximum on the compulsory benefits payable to each person.

(4) The coverage (differently worded in each scheme) is limited to certain

---

1. For a general review see Allen M. Linden, "Automobile Insurance—Canadian Style" (1972), 21 Catholic Univ. L.R. 369–385.

2. Keeton and O'Connell, *Basic Protection for the Traffic Victim—A Blueprint for Reforming Automobile Insurance* (1965).

3. Personal Injury Protection Act, Mass. Gen. Laws Ann., Chap. 90 (Supp. 1972). By subsequent legislation, no-fault automobile property damage insurance was added with effect from 1 January 1972. Mass. Gen. Laws Ann., Chap. 90, s. 340 (Supp. 1972). Act of 3 November 1971, Chap. 978, Act of 15 November 1971, Chap. 1079.

victims of automobile accidents. Workmen's Compensation Acts in the United States of America provide basic coverage to victims of industrial accidents.

There are, however, a great many differences between each of the schemes. Some of the main features of the Massachusetts statute[1] are summarised below. In this state the purchase of no-fault coverage is a pre-requisite to registering an automobile.[2]

1. Coverage

The claimant must have been injured "while in or upon, or while entering into or alighting from, or being struck as a pedestrian by" the *insured's* automobile.[3] This means that occupants of another no-fault insured vehicle must look to the no-fault policy of the automobile in which they were occupants. This is the "first-party" principle. But the limited coverage does mean that some victims are denied no-fault benefits, e.g. occupants of out-of-state (hence uninsured) vehicles,[4] and those on bicycles and horses, and pedestrians who are not "struck" by the insured's automobile. To some extent these deficiencies are remedied by an "assigned claims plan" under which Massachusetts residents may claim for injuries arising out of "the ownership, operation, maintenance or use of a motor vehicle . . . in any case where no personal injury protection benefits are otherwise available" and while the vehicle is on public ways.

The Massachusetts Act does not provide extra-territorial benefits for injuries suffered in out-of-state accidents.

2. The relevance of fault

The Keeton–O'Connell plan[5] envisaged that the insured would not be able to recover where he had acted intentionally to injure himself or someone else. But the Massachusetts statute has three additional barriers to recovery of benefits; i.e. where the claimant's injuries result from (a) his operation of an automobile under the influence of alcohol or narcotic drugs; (b) his commission of a felony; (c) operating the automobile without the consent of the owner (claimant passengers must also have been authorised).

3. The compensation

The compulsory no-fault bodily injury coverage must provide for (a) payment of medical and funeral expenses; and (b) lost income (based on average weekly income for the year preceding the accident and limited to 75 *per cent* of the earnings).[6] The maximum combined compulsory benefits payable to any

---

1. Mass. Gen. Laws Ann., Chap. 90.
2. In some states, e.g. Oregon, there is no compulsion to purchase motor insurance; only if it is purchased is no-fault coverage required. In South Dakota no-fault coverage is an optional extra. In those and some other states, as in Canada, there is no tort exemption but only a deduction of no-fault benefits from any tort recovery. See p. 726, s. 4, *post*.
3. *Ibid.*, 3 34A (Supp. 1972).
4. Unless the injured person is himself a Massachusetts no-fault insured or a member of his household, in which case he can claim under his own policy: *ibid.*
5. P. 724, note 2, *ante*.
6. The effect of this method of calculation is that a person who was unemployed during the year, or whose earnings would have gone up but for the accident, will be undercompensated.

one claimant is $2,000.[1] There is no limitation upon the number of people
entitled to benefits from any one occurrence, i.e. upon the aggregate amount
of benefits.

"Double-compensation" is to some extent ruled out by providing that
persons entitled to workmen's compensation may not receive no-fault benefits. Nor may a person who is in receipt of benefits under a "wage continuation plan" obtain double compensation by additional recovery under no-fault
insurance.[2] But there is no further limitation on compensation from collateral
sources.

4. Tort exemption

Section 4 of the Massachusetts personal injury protection statute[3] exempts
the owner, registrant, operator or occupant of an automobile having no-fault
coverage from liability in tort to the extent that the injured person is entitled
to no-fault benefits himself. The effect of this appears to be that the amount of
no-fault benefits must be deducted from the tort special damages.[4] However, the insurer paying no-fault benefits to an injured person has a statutory
right of recovery from the liability insurer of the tort-exempt wrongdoer.
These claims between insurers are to be settled by agreement or arbitration,
the obligation to pay depending on the fault of the insured driver.

Section 5 limits the right of the victim of an automobile accident to recover tort general damages. Damages "for pain and suffering, including mental
suffering associated with such injury" may be recovered only if the "reasonable and necessary" medical expenses exceed $500 or the injury causes death,
consists in whole or part of loss of a body member, or permanent or serious
disfigurement, or as loss of sight or hearing, or a fracture.[5] This limitation
on tort damages is confined to those plaintiffs who have no-fault coverage.[6]

The no-fault property damage statute exempts Massachusetts owners and
operators from liability to each other resulting from vehicle damage, and gives
vehicle owners several options by which first-party protection may be
secured.

5. The operation of the Massachusetts Act[7]

It had been forecast, before the Massachusetts law became operative, that
there would be a 30 *per cent* increase in the number of claims under no-fault,
and that the reduction in legal expenses and general damages under no-fault

---

1. Later statutes have gone much further; e.g. New York—$50,000; Delaware $10,000;
   Florida and Connecticut $5,000.
2. This is subject to an exception where the wage-continuation plan benefits have been
   exhausted as a result of an earlier automobile accident injury.
3. P. 724, note 3, *ante*.
4. *Pinnick* v. *Cleary* in which the Supreme Judicial Court of Massachusetts appears to have
   read the statute in this way.
5. The Keeton–O'Connell plan envisaged no recovery for the first $5,000 of pain and
   suffering. A study by O'Connell and Simon, *Payment for Pain and Suffering: Who Wants
   What When and Why?* (1972) discovered that few traffic victims understood or expected
   payment for pain and suffering and that compensation under this head made no significant
   psychological difference to the victim. (Also printed in (1972) Univ. Illinois Law Forum 1.)
6. The Supreme Court of Illinois struck down as unconstitutional a no-fault law which
   deprived plaintiffs who were *not* entitled to no-fault benefits of their tort general damages.
7. For a detailed account see Calvin H. Brainard, "The Impact of No-Fault Underwriting
   results on Massachusetts Insurers" (1973), 44 Mississippi L.J. 174. The results summarised here are derived from this article and from R. Keeton (1973), 121 Univ. Penn.
   L. Rev. 590, at p. 593, note 11.

would lead to a 36 *per cent* reduction in the average cost of claims. It followed that a 15 *per cent* overall reduction in costs could be expected and accordingly at the beginning of the new scheme (1 January 1971) compulsory no-fault coverage premiums were fixed at 15 *per cent* below the 1970 tort-and-liability insurance premium rates.

The overall cost-reduction surpassed all expectations. Losses incurred by insurers in respect of private passenger automobile compulsory cover fell by 51 *per cent* between 1970 and 1971. This led to a decree by the Massachusetts Insurance Department ordering a premium refund to motorists. Taken together with the original 15 *per cent* reduction, this resulted in an overall 38 *per cent* reduction in compulsory coverage premium rates.

The sources for these gains for motorists and insurers were, however, unexpected. Instead of the 30 *per cent* increase in the number of claims there was a 42 *per cent reduction*; instead of a 36 *per cent* reduction in average claims cost, the reduction was only 20 *per cent*.

APPENDIX H

The Future of Accident Law: A Select Bibliography

The literature on the reform of accident law is vast, expanding and international. The following is a highly selective list.

Great Britain

P. S. Atiyah, *Accidents, Compensation and the Law* (London, 1970).

D. W. Elliott and H. Street, *Road Accidents* (Harmondsworth, 1968).

D. R. Harris, "Analysis of the British Auto Accident Compensation System" in *Comparative Studies in Automobile Accident Compensation* (Washington D.C., United States Department of Transportation, 1970), pp. 65–113.

——, "Compensation for Accidents" (1958), 102 Sol. Jo. 729–731.

S. J. Hartz, "A Road Accident Survey" (1969), 112 New L.J. 492–494.

T. Ison, *The Forensic Lottery* (London, 1967).

J. A. Jolowicz, "Liability for Accidents", [1968] C.L.J. 50–63.

Justice (British Section of the International Commission of Jurists), *Trial of Motor Accident Cases* (ed. Kimber) (London, 1966).

Lord Parker, "Compensation for Accidents on the Road" (1965), 18 Current L.P. 1–12.

D. Payne, "Compensating the Accident Victim" (1960), 13 Current L.P. 85–111.

S. J. Stoljar, "Accidents, Costs and Legal Responsibility" (1973), 36 M.L.R. 233–244.

John L. Williams, *Accidents and Ill-Health at Work* (London, 1960).

General Comparative Works

Jan Hellner, "Tort liability and liability insurance" (1962), 6 Scandinavian Studies in Law 129–162.

R. E. Keeton and J. O'Connell, *Basic Protection for the Accident Victim. A Blueprint for Reforming Automobile Insurance* (Boston, Toronto, 1965).

A. Suzman, "Motor Vehicle Accidents. Proposals for a system of collective responsibility irrespective of fault" (1955), 72 South African L.J. 374.

A. Szakats, *Compensation for Road Accidents. A Study of the Question of Absolute Liability and Social Insurance* (Wellington, 1968).

Andre Tunc, "Traffic Accident Compensation: Law and Proposals", Chap. 14 of the *International Encyclopedia of Comparative Law*, vol. XI (Torts)

(Tubingen, Hague, Paris, New York, 1972) [contains an extensive bibliography].

————, *La sécurité routière. Esquisse d'une loi sur les accidents de la circulation* (Paris 1966).

————, "Traffic accident compensation in France. The present law and a controversial proposal" (1966), 79 Harvard L.R. 1409–1433.

United States Department of Transportation, Automobile and Insurance Studies, including *Comparative Studies in Automobile Accident Compensation* (Washington D.C., 1970) [the most exhaustive study of the fault system].

United States

J. N. Benedict, "New York adopts No Fault: a summary and analysis" (1973), 37 Albany L.R. 662–725 [contains extensive U.S. bibliography].

G. Calabresi, *The Costs of Accidents. A Legal and Economic Analysis* (New Haven and London, 1970).

R. E. Keeton, "The Case for No Fault Insurance" (1973), 44 Mississippi L.J. 1–14 [this issue contains other articles on the implementation of no fault].

R. E. Keeton and J. O'Connell, *After Cars Crash. The Need for Legal and Insurance Reform* (Homewood Ill., 1967).

A. M. Linden, "A Symposium on No Fault Automobile Insurance—Perspectives on the Problems and the Plans" (1972), Catholic University L.R. 369–385 [includes Canadian survey].

J. O'Connell and R. J. Simon, *Payment for Pain and Suffering: Who Wants What When and Why?* (California, 1972), also in Univ. of Illinois Law Forum (1972) 1.

Evidence to Royal Commission on Civil Liability and Compensation for Personal Injury.

Justice, *No Fault on the Roads* (London, 1974).

J. O'Connell, "No fault Insurance for Great Britain" (1973), 2 I.L.J. 187.

ADDENDUM

Recent Developments

The following are some of the more important cases and comments published while this sourcebook was in the press, down to 1 May 1974:

tion of others. J. A. Jolowicz, [1974] C.L.J. 40, at p. 42, points out that this solution is more satisfactory than that proposed in clause 4 of the Law Commission's draft Bill, because that clause applies only to *services*, and so would not have covered the infant plaintiff's claim in respect of special boots bought for him by his father or mother. *Donnelly* v. *Joyce* was followed in *Davies* v. *Tenby Corporation, The Times*, 10 April 1974.

416   *Coenen* v. *Payne, The Times*, 5 April 1974 (C.A.) lays down guidelines as to when the issues of liability and damages will be ordered to be separately tried. *Allen* v. *Distillers Company (Biochemicals), Ltd.*, [1974] 2 W.L.R 481, deals with the postponement of an infant's entitlement to damages.

419   In *Payton* v *Brooks, The Times*, 5 February 1974 (C.A.) it was suggested that when a motor vehicle is damaged in an accident the owner can recover not only the cost of repairs but also the amount, if any, by which the value of the repaired vehicle has diminished by reason of the fact that it was involved in an accident. *Smyth* v. *Glasgow Corporation*, 1974 S.L.T. (Sh. Ct.) 17, is an illustration (from Scotland) of taking your victim as you find him: the owner of an expensive foreign car was held to be entitled to hire replacement cars for so long as was necessary to restore his car to its pre-accident condition.

433   Under the present law, savings set aside from the deceased husband's income should be regarded as income partly for the husband's benefit and taken into account when assessing damages due to the widow under the Fatal Accidents Acts: *Gavin* v. *Wilmot Breeden*, [1973] 3 All E.R. 935 (C.A.).

635   In *Bluett* v. *King Core Demolition Services* (1973), 223 E.G. 503 demolition contractors who delegated their duties to another contractor who was negligent, were held personally liable.

673   In *Newbury* v. *Davis, The Times*, 29 January 1974 (D.C.), it was held that "permission" to drive a vehicle on the express condition that the borrower first insured against third party risks did not amount to a "permission".

682   *Persson* v. *London County Buses*, [1974] 1 All E.R. 1251 (C.A.) shows that the plaintiff may be limited to an appeal to the arbitrator, and unable to bring an action against the M.I.B. alleging a breach of the agreement relating to untraced drivers on the basis of a fact which the agreement reserves for the decision of the M.I.B.

715   The Accident Compensation Amendment (No. 2) Act 1973 (N.Z.) establishes a Supplementary Scheme, financed by ordinary taxation, to cover non-earners injured in accidents not involving motor vehicles. See D. R. Harris (1974), 37 M.L.R. (forthcoming).

Index

Printed in Great Britain by offset lithography by
Billing & Sons Ltd, Guildford, London and Worcester